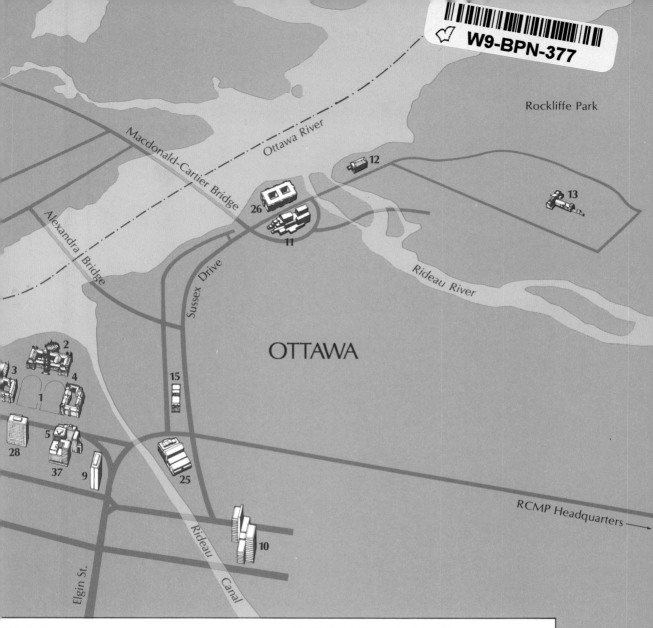

Rockliffe Park

Ottawa River

Macdonald-Cartier Bridge

Alexandra Bridge

Sussex Drive

Rideau River

26

12

13

11

OTTAWA

15

28

3

2

1

4

5

37

9

25

RCMP Headquarters →

Rideau

10

Elgin St.

Canal

14. Justice
15. Revenue Canada
16. Consumer and Corporate Affairs
17. Supply and Services
18. Employment and Immigration
19. Labour
20. Fisheries and Oceans
21. Regional Industrial Expansion, Tourism, Multiculturalism, Wheat Board, Science and Technology, Small Business, Auditor General
22. Health and Welfare
23. Statistics Canada
24. Energy, Mines and Resources
25. Conference Centre

26. National Research Council
27. Transport Canada
28. National Press Club
29. Veterans' Affairs
30. Bank of Canada
31. Environment Canada
32. Indian and Northern Affairs
33. Secretary of State, Youth
34. Fitness and Amateur Sport
35. Solicitor General
36. Agriculture
37. Federal-Provincial Relations Office (FPRO)
38. Public Works

POLITICS
IN CANADA

*Culture, Institutions, Behaviour
and Public Policy*

POLITICS
IN CANADA

Culture, Institutions, Behaviour and Public Policy

Robert J. Jackson, *Carleton University*
Doreen Jackson
Nicolas Baxter-Moore, *Brock University*

Prentice-Hall Canada Inc., Scarborough, Ontario

Canadian Cataloguing in Publication Data

Jackson, Robert J., 1936-
 Politics in Canada

Includes index.
ISBN 0-13-684317-4

1. Canada – Politics and government. I. Jackson,
Doreen, 1939-   II. Baxter-Moore, Nicolas J.,
1949-   III. Title.

JL65.J32 1986   320.971   C85-099158-7

Prentice-Hall Inc., Englewood Cliffs, *New Jersey*
Prentice-Hall International, Inc., *London*
Prentice-Hall of Australia, Pty., Ltd., *Sydney*
Prentice-Hall of India Pvt., Ltd., *New Delhi*
Prentice-Hall of Japan Inc., *Tokyo*
Prentice-Hall of Southeast Asia (Pte.) Ltd., *Singapore*
Editora Prentice-Hall do Brasil Ltda., *Rio de Janeiro*
Prentice-Hall Hispanoamericana, S.A., *Mexico*
Whitehall Books Ltd., Wellington, *New Zealand*

ISBN: 0-13-684317-4

Production Editors: Olga Domján, Sharyn Rosart
Manufacturing Buyer: Sheldon Fischer
Cover Photo: J. Ferguson/Miller Services
Composition: Alphatext
Printed and bound in Canada by T.H. Best Printing Company Limited

1 2 3 4 5 THB 90 89 88 87 86

Contents

PART II CULTURE

PART III INSTITUTIONS

PART IV POLITICAL BEHAVIOUR

PART V PUBLIC POLICY

Preface

As its title suggests, this book stresses the importance of *politics* in the study of Canadian government. As a general treatment of Canadian federal politics, useful for both introductory and more advanced courses, it avoids the rigidity imposed by the adoption of a single approach or framework for the study of politics, yet goes beyond the mere description of governmental institutions and processes. Its orientation could perhaps best be described as comprehensive, drawing upon a wide variety of concepts and middle range theories about Canadian politics. Each chapter is therefore organized around one or two central concepts, which are discussed in comparative terms before being applied to the Canadian context.

Politics in Canada is organized into five major parts. The first is introductory; the remainder correspond to the four elements incorporated in the title: culture, institutions, behaviour and public policy.

PART I, the Introduction, consists of two chapters. Chapter 1 establishes Canada's place in the world, discusses elements of its physical and international environment, introduces some key concepts in the study of politics (including various approaches, power, state, nation and democracy) and offers a rationale for the organization of the book. Chapter 2 provides the necessary historical and contextual background through an examination of the origins and development of the Canadian nation-state and a discussion of the expansion of the role of the state in Canadian society.

The two chapters comprising PART II build on the foundation established in the Introduction. Chapter 3 examines the key components of Canadian political culture, stressing the importance to the Canadian political community of overarching commonly-shared values, which help to avert potential conflicts arising out of the existence of regional and ethnic sub-cultures; Chapter 4, on the transmission of political values, focuses particularly on the educational system, mass media and government as agents of political socialization.

Arguing in part that political institutions represent "congealed tastes" which reflect both the structure and the values of society, PART III presents five chapters dealing in turn with the Constitution, federalism, the inner circle (Cabinet and Central Agencies), bureaucracy and Parliament. PART IV demonstrates how both culture and institutions structure individual and collective behaviour in the political process. Its three chapters respectively discuss elections and electoral behaviour, political parties and interest groups.

Lastly, in PART V, culture, institutions and behaviour are linked together as determinants and components of Canadian public policy and the policy-making process. The first of the two chapters in this Part deals with domestic public policy (including approaches to the study of public policy, policy instruments, three case studies and a discussion of current policy problems in an age of restraint), and the second with Canadian foreign and defence policy (including Canadian-American relations, national security policies, peace-keeping and disarmament issues).

Politics in Canada represents a fresh contribution to the general literature on Canadian politics. This claim is based upon a number of key features.

1. *Focus on the political:* In place of the system or institutional focus or socio-economic determinism of some previous texts, this book emphasizes the importance of *politics* to an understanding of how the federal governmental process works.

2. *Focus on the four key concepts:* Instead of adopting only one approach, the text takes an objective and detached perspective on the relations among culture, institutions, behaviour and public policy.

3. *Focus on the contemporary:* The book avoids overly long discussions of history and the legal system. It concentrates on the present, offering the latest information on the Constitution, Cabinet, federalism, the role of women, interest groups, and the most recent elections and party leaders. The data are based on the 1981 Census.

4. *Focus on the positive:* Avoiding the cynicism which pervades some accounts of Canadian politics, this book explores both the positive and negative aspects of the Canadian political process. While finding many reforms desirable, the authors are optimistic about the ability of the Canadian political process to meet its major challenges – the survival of Canada as a nation-state and the transcending of regional and cultural cleavages.

5. *Focus on style:* The text is simply written with little academic jargon, and the political science terms are clearly defined.

6. *Focus on the global:* This book discusses Canada in a comparative context and examines the relationships between domestic, foreign and defence policy.

In preparing this volume the authors were aided by a large number of students, professionals and friends. Both undergraduate and graduate students from Brock, Carleton, Queen's and McGill Universities have added to our knowledge and appreciation of Canadian politics. Among the most influential were Dan Butler, Abbie Dann, Carl Hodge, Michael Kelly, Gloria Kunka, Michael Laslovich, Maureen Mancuso and Tom Mitchell. As well, the enthusiasm of a decade of Parliamentary Interns for the House of Commons has been a constant source of inspiration.

In the academic community, we have been blessed with the friendship and help of some of Canada's most knowledgeable scholars, among them Michael Atkinson, Scott Bennett, Barbara Carroll, Terry Carroll, Jean-Pierre Gaboury, Jack Grove, Ken Hart, Kal Holsti, Bill Hull, Ken Kernaghan, Peyton Lyon, Roman March, Bill Matheson, Henry Mayo, John Meisel, Kim Nossal, Randy Olling, K.Z. Paltiel, Donald Rowat, David Siegel, Richard Simeon, Michael Stein, and Hugh

Thorburn. This category also includes the five reviewers who diligently ferreted out errors of omission and commission in the preliminary manuscripts. We gratefully acknowledge the insight and detailed knowledge that Donald Blake, Fred Engelmann, Susan McCorquodale, Robert Williams and Nelson Wiseman brought to their work.

Carleton University certainly has some of the finest secretaries in Canada. Betty Weiss lived with this project for years and Lynn Ralph and Joy Inglis completed the final manuscript with diligence and care. Nick Baxter-Moore would also like to acknowledge the invaluable work done by his secretary Cheryl Chalmers at Queen's. And finally, to Mary Mainella, Robert J. Jackson's personal secretary, go our thanks and congratulations on a task brilliantly done. This book could not have been completed without her loyalty and skill.

Most importantly, we owe gratitude to Prentice-Hall's staff, including Cliff Newman, Olga Domján, Sharyn Rosart, Clare Rundall and Marta Tomins whose encouragement and patient prodding has lasted several years. Their understanding of the practical aspects of an academic's duties has been intelligent and thoughtful.

Special thanks are due to the Canadian Studies Directorate of the Department of the Secretary of State for granting the manuscript a Canadian Studies Writing Award. The generous financial assistance it provided was deeply appreciated.

Finally, no book such as *Politics in Canada* could be written without the authors putting emotional burdens on those closest to them. Our supportive parents, Biddy, Dorothy, Velma and Ken have been denied our attention for too long. And in our immediate families Heather and Nicole have sustained us with their delightful good humour while we toiled over the countless contradictions in such a huge undertaking. We dedicate this volume to them. In return they have offered to take responsibility for all errors of a scholarly nature.

Robert J. Jackson,
Doreen Jackson and
Nicolas Baxter-Moore

Ottawa, January 1986

Part 1
Introduction

CanaPress Photo Service

chapter 1

The Canadian Heritage
A Comparative Perspective

"We, Your Majesty's loyal subjects, the House of Commons of Canada in Parliament assembled, respectfully approach Your Majesty, requesting that you may graciously be pleased to cause to be laid before the Parliament of the United Kingdom a measure containing the recitals and clauses hereinafter set forth: . . ."[1]

ON DECEMBER 2, 1981, 114 years after Confederation, the Canadian House of Commons approved the text of the constitutional resolution for presentation to the Queen. It was the final and crucial action by the House in requesting patriation of the Constitution. The last restricting bonds with Britain were about to be severed; total independence was within reach. This event, the culmination of many years of bargaining and compromise, was an historical landmark in Canadian constitutional history.

Yet it was already evident that this was only one more milestone, albeit an important one, in the constitutional evolution of this huge and disparate country. Constitutional reform had merely begun. "History is thus made, in a peculiarly Canadian way," observed *The Globe and Mail* at the time, "with a decision that is wholly acceptable to nobody but which will have the consent of nine of the ten provinces and of Parliament."[2]

The exciting and often exasperatingly difficult tangle of politics and compromise which was involved in patriating the Constitution typifies politics and policy-making in Canada. The final months of the constitutional debate were peppered with fiery oratory, nationalistic fervour, backroom bargaining and par-

---

[1]From the text of the Constitution resolution approved by the House of Commons for presentation to the Queen. *House of Commons Debates*, vol. XII (Dec. 2, 1981), p. 13632.

[2]*The Globe and Mail*, Thursday, December 3, 1981.

ochial bickering as federal, provincial, regional and ethnic interests were expounded and defended in an attempt to define what Canada ought to be. Even seasoned observers despaired that so many conflicting interests could ever be reconciled in the interest of the whole community.

In the end, of course, the compromise reached between nine of the provinces and the federal government excluded and isolated Québec. While the Canadian government prepared to request the Queen and the British government to patriate the Constitution, Québec Premier René Lévesque left Ottawa with tears in his eyes to inform his constituents that they had been deserted; Canada, he said, had separated from Québec. But the politics continued. Within days Québec had appealed to the courts to confirm or deny its right to a constitutional veto, a right symbolic of French Canada's role as a founding nation.

While Québec sought (and eventually lost) satisfaction in the courts, the patriation procedure continued. Four months after the Canadian government's request for patriation was formally delivered to Her Majesty in London it received the approval of both houses of Parliament in Great Britain. The new Constitution, complete with a Charter of Rights and amending formula, was returned to Canada amidst great pomp and ceremony and proclaimed the law of the land on April 17, 1982.

Even as the last vestiges of a colonial past were being erased, Canada ranked proudly among the world's nation-states. A brief profile of the country – its political base, people and socio-economic status – reads impressively.

Since Confederation Canada has enjoyed a stable, liberal democratic government; it is one of the very few countries in the world never to have experienced a civil war or a military coup. This stability has been achieved despite the many factors that complicate political decision-making in this country. Its size alone is a great barrier to progress. Canada has several thousand square kilometres *more* area to administer than all of Europe combined. A Canadian driving from St. John's, Newfoundland to Victoria, British Columbia covers the same distance as a Spaniard from Madrid traversing at least ten countries, travelling almost to Mongolia. Québec, homeland of the French Canadian nation, is roughly equal in size to the entire European Community.

This enormous land mass houses only 25 million people, less than one-half of one percent of the world's population. Yet Canada has a population problem – not in the traditional sense of over-populated countries afflicted by high birth rates, but in a demographic sense. Four-fifths of the territory has never been settled permanently. The result is great regional imbalances in population, from congested urban centres to uninhabited wastelands. Certain areas are progressively being depopulated, while there is an undesirable rate of growth in others. Large tracts of land are being devoured by greedy cities. Today, in this country which was originally settled by farmers, most of the population lives in urban areas which occupy only one percent of the land. Only one-eighth of the territory is suitable for agriculture; settlement has therefore been confined to a long thin line along the southern border, linked by the world's longest national highway.

To these problematic demographic factors must be added the unique ethnic composition of the population. Besides the two founding French and English nations, at least 70 other ethnic groups make their homes here. The French Canadian nation is centred in Québec but is in no sense limited to that province. Large pockets of French-speaking Canadians are ensconced in Manitoba, New Brunswick and Ontario. Of the Native people, more than half reside in the Prairies and British Columbia. The many other ethnic groups scattered across the country add a multicultural dimension which has been the source of much division but also much pride for Canadians.

Canada is a land of extremes, in terms not only of territory and population but also of landscape and climate. Fertile rain forests, arctic barrens, mountains and plains – the variety is as large as the country itself. Most Canadians endure harsh winters, but even here there is great diversity. For example, the area near Kitimat holds the record for highest average snowfall at 1071 cm. a year, but there is almost no snow at all in Victoria. At Eureka on Ellesmere Island it snows all year round, yet at the other extreme towns like Midale in Saskatchewan hold record summer temperatures of 37°C.

Even with these disparities, Canada is one of the rich élite among the world's nations. Canadians enjoy clean, abundant water, great resource wealth, a plentiful food supply, modern industries, safe cities, and good health care and educational facilities. These attributes add up to one of the highest material standards of living in the world.

Of the seven major industrial countries that met in Britain for the 1984 Economic Summit, Canada ranked fourth in terms of *per capita* Gross National Product (GNP), behind the Federal Republic of Germany, France and the United States. Trade accounts for a very significant proportion of the Canadian GNP. As one of the world's top ten trading nations, Canada is among the very few countries in the world with a greater volume of exports than imports. A high percentage of these exports consists of natural resources: fish, lumber and energy.

Yet even within the economy problems exist. Over two-thirds of all Canadian exports go to the United States, a convenience which costs dearly in terms of dependence on American markets. Both lumber and fish stocks are dwindling, and will not be as lucrative in the years ahead; many other resources are not renewable. In the energy field, native supplies of oil, gas, coal and electricity, many as yet untapped, have allowed Canadians to become energy gluttons, consumers of more energy per capita than any other nation. By 1980, each Canadian was consuming nine tonnes of oil annually. Better planning and management of these resources and development of a broader industrial base are fundamental political challenges.

ISSUES IN CANADIAN SOCIETY

It has become a cliché to say that nation-building in a land of such magnitude and climatic extremes is difficult. However, it is true that these aspects of the country impose additional burdens on political leaders. First is the simple necessity of commuting between Ottawa and outlying constituencies. Then, in addition to the task of determining and administering to the needs and interests of provinces far removed from Ottawa, there is the crucial need to discourage the feelings of isolation and alienation that inevitably develop in regions remote from the capital.

One political scientist has commented that "asking a person to say what government is about is like asking for a description of an inkblot. Its form is ambiguous, signifying different things to different people."[3] However, it is clearly the task of the federal government to create within the diversity of Canada some uniform conditions and standards for all its citizens. The processes of sharing the wealth and resources of the country and assuring certain minimal national standards in areas such as health, communications and education are primary functions of governing in Canada. Unfortunately, there is no consensus about the degree to which it is desirable for governments to be directly involved in the lives of citizens by directing the economy of the country or providing social services, let alone agreement about how these things should be accomplished.

Since 1867 the Canadian government has developed into an institution respected throughout the globe as well as within its own borders. Its significance derives from its size, resources, economic power and moral persuasion in many parts of the world. Among other world links, Canada is a member of the Commonwealth and the North Atlantic Treaty Organization (NATO), contributes to the United Nations peace-keeping forces in various parts of the world and has taken a leading position in developing a dialogue between countries of the North and South in order to ameliorate the conditions of the world's poor. Internally, the government is paramount in making laws and regulations for its citizens. The unceasing battle to control the offices and activities of this mammoth institution should be understood by every inquiring and intelligent Canadian.

The constant evolution of governmental structure and priorities necessitates the unceasing re-evaluation of the policies and direction of government and even of the institution itself. In many areas there is room for reform and improvement. It has, for example, been suggested that one test of a good government is how well it provides for the most vulnerable of its citizens: the young, the aged, the sick and the handicapped. The Canadian government does subsidize a great range of social services whose primary intent is sharing the resources of the country more equally. However, despite these efforts, in 1983 nearly 4 million Canadians, or about 17 percent of the population, were officially poor, living below the poverty line as determined yearly by Statistics Canada. The very high GNP disguises the fact that the nation's wealth is very unevenly distributed among Canadians.

Within Canada, the political struggle is focused on institutions, behaviour and policies. The result is an agenda for the resolution of conflict over the very basics of life. Before the turn of the century many fundamental questions need to be addressed. Will the country achieve economic stability or go bankrupt? Will the distribution of wealth, education and power remain heavily influenced by membership in privileged groups, or will the government continue to attempt

---

[3]Richard Rose, *What is Governing? Purpose and Policy in Washington* (Englewood Cliffs, New Jersey: Prentice-Hall, 1978), p. 2.

their redistribution among individuals and regions? Will women receive their rightful place in Canadian society? Will Canadians of Indian and Inuit origin and new immigrants be successfully harmonized into Canadian society?

In the broader context of Canada in the world, there are even more unknowns in the years ahead. A report commissioned by the Canadian government predicts that, as basic resources become scarce in the world, pressures upon Canada to provide them will increase.[4] For instance, in times of famine, Canada may well find itself in the unenviable position of having to decide who eats and who does not. The government will have to husband resources and ensure that the exploitation of natural wealth will be dictated not by short-term gains or political expediency, but by longer-range national and global interests. It will become increasingly important for Canada to turn outward, pursuing foreign trade and playing a role in the resolution of global issues. *Ad hoc* decision-making should give way to greater government investment in research and development and planning for the future.

The supreme test of any polity is whether it has the capacity to establish acceptable and enduring solutions from a multiplicity of conflicting demands. The crucial challenge to the present Canadian political system concerns its ability to manage the policy conflicts discussed above, and others equally critical.

This book is based on the premise that Canadians need to agree on one major issue – how these choices will be made. In a vast country like Canada with two official languages, a multitude of vibrant cultures and an unequal distribution of economic wealth, realists cannot expect agreement on fundamental philosophies about people and their community. What can be expected is a fair, open process of democracy, responsive to the public will; and consensus about how this process ought to work.

POLITICS AND POLITICAL SCIENCE

Politics is as old as human history. It is a fascinating form of behaviour, concerning as it does disputes and decisions about human ideals and interests. Defined by the layman as manipulation or the struggle for advantage, it is omnipresent: in the relations between husband and wife, parent and child, employer and employee – in short, in all societal relations. Political scientists do not study all social relations; they are concerned primarily with organized dispute and its collective resolution.

Two definitions of politics contend in the literature. The most widespread of them, put forth by David Easton, one of the foremost experts of systems analysis, is general and abstract. He defined politics as "the authoritative allocation of values".[5] The second, a more restricted definition, was conceived by Harold

---

[4]G.O. Barnes, P.H. Freeman and C.A. Ulinski, *Global 2000: Implications for Canada* (Toronto: Pergamon Press, 1981).

[5]David Easton, *A Framework for Political Analysis* (Englewood Cliffs, N.J.: Prentice-Hall, 1965), pp. 50-56.

Lasswell, who pointed out that politics always concerns "who gets what, when and how".[6] In the present volume, we delimit the subject by proferring a definition of politics that combines the insights of both Easton and Lasswell: **Politics** embraces all activity which impinges upon the making of binding decisions about who gets what, when and how.

Since valued possessions such as wealth and status are invariably scarce and unevenly distributed, disagreement can be expected to arise among people as they attempt to satisfy their seemingly endless wants. Such general dispute gives rise to the organized conflict pervading society, whether in the election of the president of the Royal Canadian Legion, in the struggle over policy towards South Africa within the United Church or in the election of the Canadian Prime Minister.

To reduce this endless conflict over power, mechanisms have evolved which enforce decisions for all members of society. We refer to these mechanisms as government. Politics and governing are both about organized dispute over power, but are often artificially demarcated: politics is concerned with influencing the governors, while governing consists of the actions of public officials in making decisions. Much of the dynamic character of politics comes from the pervasive conflict between the rulers and the ruled.

Government is thus the organization of people for the resolution of dispute and conflict. Even the most primitive societies have some means of settling problems. In modern societies, government not only provides law and order but also regulates many aspects of private and public affairs. It is one of the most complex and important of institutions.

While anthropologists and sociologists study the rules that regulate all forms of behaviour, political scientists concentrate on describing and analyzing the institutions and behaviour of the political governance of nation-states. Insofar as social processes influence or are influenced by politics or governance, they are also part of the study of political science.

The concept of *power* is central to the study of politics. Power has been part of the vocabulary of politics since the time of Machiavelli, yet it remains the most perplexing issue within the discipline of political science. Even the fundamental question of whether it can be possessed like gold or is simply the result of social relationships remains unanswered.[7] But where would our understanding of politics be without the notion that some individuals hold power over others? Substitution of words such as "influence", "coercion", "compulsion", "control", and "persuasion" for "power" only compounds the difficulties. The problem stems essentially from the impossibility of ascertaining whether power is absolute

---

[6]Harold Lasswell, *Politics: Who Gets What, When and How* (New York: McGraw-Hill, 1936).

[7]For a discussion of the complex methodological issues see R.A. Dahl, "Power," *International Encyclopedia of the Social Sciences* (New York: Macmillan, 1968), vol. 12, pp. 405-15; R.A. Dahl, *Modern Political Analysis*, 2nd ed. (Englewood Cliffs, N.J.: Prentice-Hall, 1970), pp. 14-34; and H.D. Lasswell and A. Kaplan, *Power and Society: A Framework for Political Inquiry* (New Haven: Yale University Press, 1950).

or relative. Any person's ability to influence other individuals to act in a certain way often relies more upon bargaining than on the application of naked force.

Approaches within Political Science

Each generation brings to the study of politics its own interests, values and methodologies. It usually carries over ideas from other disciplines such as history, law, philosophy, sociology, economics or anthropology. In this sense, the study of politics includes multiple approaches and is in reality a multi-disciplinary subject.

The inconsistencies caused by this diversity in the tools for obtaining political understanding are reduced by the accepted principle that scientists should be self-consciously analytical and comparative and should avoid basing generalizations on casual observation. Whether the research is based on experiments, statistics or configurative case studies, it is disciplined by the desire to be explicit in the rules employed to describe and analyze politics.

Some scholars believe that the only way to study politics is to employ a general theory of the polity in an effort to obtain scientific, law-like, generalizations about politics. Such general theories purport to identify all the critical structures and processes of society, to explain all the inter-relationships and then to predict a wide variety of outcomes.[8] A leading example is the essentially legal/formal description of Canadian politics proposed by MacGregor Dawson and some of his students in the immediate post-Second World War period.[9] Critics of Dawson's

Reprinted with permission (Bas. – Tachydromos, Greece/Rothco).

---

[8]For an intelligent overview criticism see Joseph LaPalombara, *Politics Within Nations* (Englewood Cliffs, N.J.: Prentice-Hall, 1974), Chapters 1, 2.

[9]R. MacGregor Dawson's celebrated *Government of Canada* (Toronto: University of Toronto Press) was first published in 1947.

style of analysis founded their arguments on the position that he and much of his generation eschewed the study of informal politics while blindly concentrating on formal institutions.

Other general theories of politics have been applied to Canada, the best-known among them, *systems analysis*. It has been used as an introduction to many textbooks since about 1965. [10] While it was rarely employed in a methodical fashion, it usually served as a short-hand introduction to the study of politics. The essence of this general theory is that the politics of a country can be depicted by the interaction between the societal environment and an abstract political system which processes its demands and supports into outputs, producing an overall stability or homeostasis.[11]

A related general theory is *functionalism*. In essence, functionalism specifies the activities of a viable political system and explains how they help to maintain stability. If the polity does not perform these functions, it ceases to exist.[12] Though influencing writing about politics, it has never found a place as a theory to explain the Canadian polity.

The essential problem with systems analysis, as well as other general theories such as functionalism and *Marxism*,[13] is that they are at such a high level of abstraction that they are remote from empirical research. They describe the polity in such general terms that they neither generate testable propositions nor aid our understanding of concrete political phenomena or problems. Moveover, the general theories have also failed in their fundamental task of identifying all the critical structures and processes of the political system and explaining the relations amongst them.

In Canada, no single general theory of politics has ever been totally accepted. The various theories have been used as heuristic devices in the sense that they helped authors and students collect and analyze fragments of political reality. By the mid-1980s no single theory or approach was being taken as uniquely valid; few, if any, scholars accept the notion that one approach can exhaust all that is to be known about Canadian politics.

Even if no single theory or approach is or should be pre-eminent in the study of Canadian politics, students ought to be aware of the underlying principles governing the basic arguments in the field. Gabriel Almond and Stephen Genco point out that two analogies summarize the core of the debate on the sta-

---

[10]For the latest version see Richard Van Loon and Michael Whittington, *The Canadian Political System*, 3rd ed. (Toronto: McGraw-Hill Ryerson, 1981).

[11]Easton, *op. cit., passim.*

[12]See Gabriel Almond and G. Bingham Powell, *Comparative Politics: A Developmental Approach* (Boston: Little, Brown, 1966).

[13]For modern marxism see Barrington Moore, Jr., *Social Origins of Dictatorship and Democracy: Lord and Peasant in the Making of the Modern World* (Boston: Beacon Press, 1966) and Ralph Miliband, *The State in Capitalist Society* (London: Weidenfield and Nicholson, 1969); for an application to the Canadian context, see Leo V. Panitch, ed. *The Canadian State* (Toronto: University of Toronto Press, 1977).

tus of theory in political science. According to these authors, the discipline is divided over whether the analogy underlying our profession should liken it to the shifting formlessness of clouds, or to the precise causation involved in a machine such as a watch. They conclude that "the current quandary in political science can, to a large extent, be explained by the fact that, by themselves, clock-model assumptions are inappropriate for dealing with the substance of political phenomena."[14] What this argument suggests, then, is that there is no adequate theory about politics which must not perforce include transient and fleeting phenomena. Politics is not totally predictable; its study has not uncovered a world of cause and effect. Almond and Genco's article contends that political reality has distinctive properties which make it unamenable to the forms of explanation used in the natural sciences. Thus, the science of politics should not be seen as a set of methods with a predetermined theory, but as a "commitment to explore and attempt to understand a given segment of empirical reality". Such an argument calls for an eclectic approach to Canadian politics and to comparative government.

Entirely eschewing approaches or theories in the discipline is not much help either. What political scientists call "hyperfactualism" or "barefooted empiricism" may simply lead to the collection of facts without purpose. Collecting parts of reality without any reference to hunches and ideas from theories is as misleading as the wholesale adoption of a single theory of the polity. We need guides to the facts to be examined.

In this volume we adopt a variety of analytic and institutional approaches, what Joseph LaPalombara has called "partial" theories.[15] Our information and conclusions are based on the best available research, but not on the basis that knowledge is obtained uniquely by scientific methods. To adopt a purely scientific approach would be tantamount to declaring that the only knowledge we can have about torture comes from conducting experiments in this field.

If no general theory underlies the framework of this book, what segments of politics have been selected for examination? The choice of the analytical dimensions to be studied is always difficult, but the subject must somehow be delimited. In this volume we analyze Canadian culture, institutions, behaviour and public policy. These four dimensions all impinge on the competing ideas, interests, issues and people that make up the polity. They direct us toward those aspects of the political process which can be observed, compared and evaluated; they are the primary segments of a society concerned with politics and power.

The formal institutions of government are the most visible elements of the political process. Such structures as constitutions, parliaments, bureaucracies and executives are well known to students of Canadian politics and government. And formal institutions do explain much about politics. The way they are struc-

---

[14]Gabriel A. Almond and Stephen J. Genco, "Clouds, Clocks and the Study of Politics," *World Politics*, vol. 29, no. 4 (July 1977), p. 505.

[15]Joseph La Palombara, "Macro-theories and Micro-applications in Comparative Politics: A Widening Chasm," *Comparative Politics*, vol. 1, no. 1, (October 1968) pp. 52-78.

tured affects political actors, bureaucrats and citizens – as well as who gets what, when and how.

Whereas traditional Canadian political science focuses on studies of institutions, contemporary political culture and socialization studies tend to emphasize the study of values and beliefs. The assumption of the latter studies is that political outcomes are determined by amalgamations of individual preferences. Certainly the values of members of society influence social and political decisions. However, institutions also affect social outcomes. Institutions, therefore, can be thought of as "congealed tastes", or conventions about values that are condensed into institutions which make rules for society.[16]

It is extremely difficult to assess the relative significance of institutions and values for the development of government policy. Probably both are necessary. If institutions are constant or stable, we ought to be able to predict outcomes from tastes. If tastes are constant, we ought to be able to predict outcomes from institutions. In turbulent times, institutions, and often values as well, are in constant evolution. "One fundamental and unsolved problem of social science is to penetrate the illusion and to learn to take both values and institutions into account."[17]

The distinction between individual behaviour and institutions is also blurred. If, in calling institutions "structures", we are referring to a process of change so slow as to be negligible for the purposes of investigation,[18] then institutions are stable configurations which change only over long periods, and so are merely the organized collective behaviour of individuals. The collectivity may be more than the sum of its parts, but there is no doubt that its parts are individuals behaving in some routine manner. The study of behaviour and institutions is therefore intertwined at the logical as well as the empirical level of analysis.

Public policy is a more recent jargon-concept in political science. Usually, policy is defined by its ability to set the parameters of future decisions by developing a long-term perspective in an issue area. Policy-making is the activity of arriving at these fundamental conclusions. But policies are themselves the result of the interaction of culture, institutions and behaviour. Moreover, the policies feed back into the politics of a country, helping to determine political culture, to structure institutions and to limit political behaviour.[19]

Thus, culture, institutions, behaviour and public policy all interact to form the Canadian variety of politics. There are two basic approaches to the study of these four components. In the *synchronic* approach, a comparison is made be-

---

[16]William H. Riker, "Implications from the Disequilibrium of Majority Rule for the Study of Institutions," *APSR*, vol. 74, no. 2 (June, 1980), pp. 432-446.

[17]*Ibid.*, p. 432.

[18]See Karl W. Deutsch, "The Crisis of the State," *Government and Opposition*, vol. 16, no. 3 (Summer, 1981), pp. 331-343.

[19]For an introduction to this literature see Peter Aucoin, "Public-Policy Theory and Analysis" in G. Bruce Doern and Peter Aucoin, eds., *Public Policy in Canada* (Toronto: Macmillan, 1979), pp. 1-26 and Anthony King, "Ideas, Institutions and the Policies of Governments: A Comparative Analysis," *British Journal of Political Science*, vol. 3, no. 4 (October 1973), p. 423.

tween these four dimensions in Canada and in other nation-states. In the *diachronic* approach, they are examined over historical time. Both approaches are important. Dynamic (over time) and static views of the four dimensions are also useful in formulating generalizations about the Canadian polity.

In this volume we shall search for significant regularities, similarities and differences in Canadian culture, institutions, behaviour and policies. The approach used is eclectic, seeking evidence through both dynamic and comparative avenues. Too many volumes on Canada have been parochial and cynical about Canada and its future. Canada's system of government is best understood and appreciated when it is compared, even briefly, with those of other countries. The democratic equilibrium is fostered by a comprehensive interplay of culture, institutions, behaviour and policy. Understanding this phenomenon requires sensitivity to the political and administrative environment within which government has to operate, as well as an appreciation of both the cohesive and the disruptive forces of our history and society.

POLITICS AND NATION-STATES

A useful starting point in placing Canada within a comparative context is to consider it as a "nation-state". As one of the 159 nation-states currently recognized by the United Nations, Canada may thus be compared synchronically with a multitude of other more or less similar political entities. Furthermore, a consideration of the origins and development of the Canadian nation-state provides a basis for diachronic comparison and an historical setting for contemporary Canadian politics.

Since the rise of absolutism in the 16th and 17th centuries, when sovereigns in certain parts of Europe began the process of integrating feudal fiefdoms, petty principalities and conquered territories into unified kingdoms, the nation-state has emerged as the dominant form of political organization. Of course, other types of political systems have existed, and continue to do so. Empires have come and gone. Considerable decision-making power may be wielded at sub-national levels of government, especially in federal systems; and the number of international actors, such as the United Nations Organization or the European Community, has grown. Nation-states, too, are born and disappear over time. For example, the Baltic states of Estonia, Latvia and Lithuania, which were recognized as independent countries after the First World War, are all now parts of the Soviet Union. But the general tendency has been for the number of nation-states to grow almost yearly. Of the 159 members of the United Nations, well over half have become independent since 1945.

The State

The term "nation-state" represents a conceptual marriage between the cultural principle of *nation* and the territorial and governmental principles inherent in the idea of the *state*. The **state** is usually defined as a form of political organization in which governmental institutions are capable of maintaining order and implementing rules or laws (through coercion if necessary) over a given population and within a given territory.[20] Hence, a state is normally admitted to the United Nations when it has satisfied the members of this international body that, like themselves, it wields state power and is capable of maintaining order within its territorial boundaries – that is, when it is considered to be *sovereign*. It should be noted, however, that some states recognized as sovereign are not members of the UN – for example, North and South Korea, Switzerland, or the European mini-states of Liechtenstein, San Marino and the Vatican.

While many practical problems circumscribe the concept of **sovereignty,** a state is usually recognizable by its internal and external powers: its ability to tax its citizens or its ability to conduct external relations. Or, as Joseph LaPalombara puts it, "As applied to *internal* matters, national sovereignty means that supreme and final authority rests in the national government as opposed to all other private and governmental organizations that may compose the nation-state itself."[21] External sovereignty, on the other hand, represents the recognition by the international community of the right of a people or government to run their own affairs, free from interference by other states or governments.

A nation-state is also characterized by the subjective feeling its citizens have about it. While some states do exist without widespread public identification with their institutions, this is not usually the case, especially in developed democracies such as Canada. Normally the people strongly identify with their state. When citizens accept that a government ought, or has the right, to make decisions for them, political scientists refer to the system as *legitimate.*[22]

Legitimacy in this sense is closely linked to the concept of **authority**, which we may define as the legitimate right to exercise power. According to the famous German sociologist, Max Weber, authority (and hence legitimacy) may be said to stem from three main sources. *Traditional* authority, which arises from custom and history, is most frequently gained through inheritance and thus has been enjoyed by royal dynasties throughout the ages. *Charismatic* authority is derived from popular admiration of the personal "heroic" qualities of the individual in whom it is vested – whether prophet, warlord or orator. Lastly, *rational-legal* or *bureaucratic* authority, the most common form in western societies, is vested not in individuals *per se* but in the offices they hold and the mechanisms which placed them there.[23] Thus, the authority of the Canadian Prime Minister (though he may be charismatic to some!) is derived primarily from the fact that he is leader of a government placed in power by the routine and legitimate process of popular elec-

---

[20]The usual point of departure for such formulations is Max Weber's famous definition of the state as a human community that "successfully upholds a claim to the monopoly of the legitimate use of physical force in the enforcement of its order . . . within a given territorial area." Max Weber, *The Theory of Social and Economic Organization*, edited and translated by A.M. Henderson and Talcott Parsons (New York: Oxford University Press, 1947), p. 154.

[21]Joseph LaPalombara, *Politics Within Nations*, p. 36.

[22]Jean Blondel, *Comparing Political Systems* (New York: Praeger, 1974) p. 49.

[23]Weber, *op. cit.*, Chapter 3.

tion. As soon as one leader ceases to be Prime Minister, the authority currently vested in him will pass to the new incumbent of the office. In Canada and many other modern societies, therefore, legitimacy and authority tend to be vested not in individuals but in the political institutions and offices of the state.

The concept of legitimacy may be applied not only to regimes and governments but also to their individual acts. Thus, a legitimate government may do some things which are perceived to be illegitimate. Legitimacy in this sense should not be confused with **legality** – while the former denotes the degree of subjective authority vested in the government by public opinion, the latter relates to the constitutional or legal propriety of undertaking certain activities. Some events may therefore be legal (that is, within the letter of the law) without being considered legitimate. The Canadian government's use of the War Measures Act to suppress civil liberties during the 1970 Québec crisis was legal, but many French Canadians and some in English Canada did not think it was legitimate: they did not believe that the federal government ought to have exercised such powers. Or, to cite a more recent example, a majority of the Supreme Court of Canada concluded in 1981 that, while Prime Minister Trudeau's attempt to patriate the Constitution unilaterally was strictly legal, it was not legitimate because it flouted the convention that provincial assent must be obtained. Conversely certain events can be viewed as legitimate without being legal. Some Canadians, for example, supported the action of the RCMP in burning a barn to prevent a "subversive" meeting, but the action was not legal; in fact, it was a criminal offence.

The ability of a state and its political institutions to govern a given population and territory rests on the twin foundations of sovereignty and legitimacy. In the resolution of conflict, a government requires the consent necessary to authoritatively allocate values and resources. All states attempt to maintain political order and viability, to resolve societal conflicts without tearing the country apart, to defend the territory against external enemies and to maintain essential services such as food and water supply, transport, health facilities and educational institutions. The manner in which these and other policy-making activities are performed, while a balance is maintained between power on the one hand and legitimacy and support on the other, is at the core of the study of politics and government.

The Nation

The identification of citizens with their state, and therefore its legitimacy, may be enhanced by the perception that the state and its institutions serve to represent the interests of the population as a whole – in other words, the interests of the *nation*.

In popular usage, and as the title of the United Nations Organization suggests, "nation" is often taken to refer to all people living within a certain territory and under a single government. In this sense, however, the meaning of nation becomes indistinguishable from that of the citizenry of a state. Alternatively, a nation is sometimes identified with respect to certain objective criteria, such as the possession of a common language, racial or physical characteristics, ancestry or cultural heritage. But this usage fails to explain why peoples who share such characteristics, for example, Argentinians and Chileans, continue to think of themselves as constituting separate nations.

The key to understanding the concept of nation is that, "like any other form of social identity . . .", national identity (and its associated concept ethnic identity) is ". . . essentially subjective, a sense of social belonging and ultimate loyalty."[24] While objective criteria such as language or race may play a part in reinforcing these identities, the essence of a nation is that it is a collectivity of people united by a shared sense of loyalty and a common feeling of belonging together. Thus, immigrants to Canada from Eastern Europe or Lebanon may feel themselves to be just as Canadian, as much a part of the Canadian nation, as those who were born in Canada. On the other hand, while some French Canadians are first and foremost "Canadien", others, who share the same language and cultural heritage, consider themselves "Québécois" and demand the independence of their nation from the Canadian state.

National identity is therefore a sense of belonging to a particular community, often (but not necessarily) reinforced by a common language, culture, customs, heritage, or the shared experience of living under the same government. At the same time, national identity consists of a sense of distinctiveness from other peoples who may or may not share certain of these characteristics. This dual subjective aspect of the nation is clearly expressed in one satirical definition of a nation as "a society united by a common error as to its origins and a common aversion to its neighbours."[25]

Not all collectivities which consider themselves culturally or linguistically distinct necessarily constitute separate nations. When individuals and minorities do share cultures distinct from those of other groups, social scientists label them "ethnic groups" or "ethnic minorities". **Ethnicity**, like national identity, is primarily a subjective phenomenon, although it is usually reinforced by the presence of objective traits such as a different language or dialect, different customs and cultural heritage and often distinct racial or physical characteristics. In many societies, such as the United States or much of Canada, ethnic groups may live side by side and consider themselves, though culturally distinct, to constitute one nation. In others, however, certain ethnic groups may think of themselves as nations in their own right. In the latter case, as in Québec, they may mobilize and pursue political action in order to gain independence. The boundary between ethnic group and nation is therefore rather tenuous, but it is possible to relate the two if, as in this volume, we define a **nation** as a politically conscious and mobilized ethnic group (usually with a clear sense of territory) which possesses, or aspires to, self-government or independent statehood.

The concepts of "nation" and "ethnicity" are important to the study of politics because, despite the widespread lip-service paid to the principles of national self-determination or national sovereignty, only rarely do territorial and ethnic

---

[24]George De Vos and Lola Romanucci-Ross, *Ethnic Identity: Cultural Continuities and Change* (Palo Alto, California: Mayfield Publishing Co., 1975), p. 3.

[25]Julian Huxley and Alfred Court Haddon, *We Europeans: A Survey of 'Racial' Problems* (London: Jonathan Cape, 1935), p. 16.

boundaries coincide. For example, the existence of different languages is generally taken as one indication of ethnic pluralism. At the same time, in only about half of the world's states do more than 75 percent of the population speak the same language. Few states in the world consist, as does Japan, of a single ethnic group. Some states, such as the Soviet Union, Canada or the United Kingdom, contain aspiring nations within them. On the other hand, there are nations which are governed by more than one state – for example, Germans in both the Federal Republic and the Democratic Republic ("West" and "East" Germany respectively) or Palestinians in a number of Middle Eastern States. The politicization of demands for the reunification of multi-state nations, as in Germany or Ireland, or for the division of multi-national states into more ethnically homogeneous self-governing communities, as in Cyprus, results in highly emotional and frequently violent conflict and causes serious problems of accommodation for political authorities. Attempting to account for these strains and find solutions for them has become a major concern for politicians and political scientists alike.

Nationalism and Regionalism

A generation ago, "nation-building" was a dominant theme in political science, especially among those studying the political development of new states in the Third World, many of which faced the task of integrating disparate and fragmented societies into cohesive political units. The prevailing view was that the ongoing processes of economic development, modernization, urbanization and industrialization would serve to reduce territorial and cultural tensions, just as they had already apparently enhanced the integration of western advanced industrial societies.[26] In the last decade, however, many western states have been subjected to pressures of a nationalist or regional nature, which had previously been dismissed as threats only to "new" nations.

Nationalism has manifested itself in many forms over the centuries since the nation-state emerged as a major form of socio-political organization. It has been used as a justification for economic expansionism, protectionism and imperialism; as an ideology espousing the supremacy of a particular nation or people (as in German National Socialism); as a quest for emancipation from colonial rule; or as an integrative process in multi-racial or tribal societies of the Third World after independence.[27] In most cases, these forms of nationalism were devoted to integrating the members of an existing or future nation-state. But, as it is found in a number of western societies today, nationalism is a potentially divi-

---

[26]A critique of these forecasts is found in Arend Lijphart, "Political Theories and the Explanation of Ethnic Conflict in the Western World: Falsified Predictions and Plausible Postdictions", in M.J. Esman, ed., *Ethnic Conflict in the Western World* (Ithaca, N.Y.: Cornell University Press, 1977), pp. 46-64. For a discussion of the fundamental issues in this field, see Robert J. Jackson and Michael Stein, *Issues in Comparative Politics* (New York: St. Martins Press, 1971).

[27]On the types of nationalism see Anthony D. Smith, *Nationalism in the Twentieth Century* (Oxford: Martin Robertson, 1979). On Québec see Robert J. Jackson and Abina Dann, "Quebec Foreign Policy? Canada and Ethno-Regionalism," in Werner J. Feld and Werner Link, eds., *The New Nationalism* (New York: Pergamon, 1979), pp. 89-105.

sive force. In several cases, territorially concentrated ethnic minorities, previously assumed to be loyal subjects of a larger nation-state, have been aroused to search for increased self-determination and even total independence.

Ethnic minorities have not been totally assimilated or acculturated by the forces of modernization in most advanced industrial societies. Indeed, since the Second World War, they have become increasingly visible and vocal. However, not all examples of organized ethnic interest should be labelled as nationalism. Many ethnic demands, such as those of Italian or Ukrainian minorities in Canada, involve no challenge to the integrity of the existing state and may be quite easily accommodated within its confines. Examples are demands for minority-language education or ethnically-oriented television programs. Nationalism should rather be viewed as that part of the continuum of ethnic activity in which demands move from those which may be accommodated within the existing nation-state structure to those for political (and usually economic and cultural) autonomy, or even for total separation from the larger state.[28] Thus, in this volume **nationalism** is defined in its contemporary sense as the collective action of a politically conscious ethnic group (or nation) in pursuit of increased territorial autonomy or sovereignty.

Examples of contemporary nationalist movements (often labelled "ethno-nationalist" or "neo-nationalist") may be found in many advanced industrial societies: the Scots and Welsh in the United Kingdom; Basques and Catalans in Spain; Bretons and Corsicans in France; Flemings and Walloons in Belgium; and, of course, the Québécois in Canada.[29] In each case, the ethnic minorities have apparently reduced any previous commitment they may have had to the larger nation-state and have acted collectively to develop political parties, nationalist and cultural organizations and sometimes even terrorist groupings, in order to pursue fundamental changes in the territorial boundaries and sovereignty of the state.

In the above-named countries and elsewhere, territorial tensions have also been manifested by movements espousing regionalist demands and protests, even where a separate ethnic or national identity has been absent. In contrast to nationalist demands, which seek to alter existing political structures, **regionalist** territorial tensions are "those brought about by certain groups that . . . demand a change in the political, economic and cultural relations between regions and central powers *within* the existing state."[30] Regionalist discontent is most often articulated in economic terms, especially by representatives of poorer, peripheral regions within a country, which demand a share of the affluence enjoyed by the

---

[28]See James Lightbody, "A Note on the Theory of Nationalism as a Function of Ethnic Demands," *Canadian Journal of Political Science*, vol. 2, no. 3 (September 1969), pp. 327-337.

[29]For case studies of a number of ethnic and nationalist movements, see, amongst others, Esman, ed., *op. cit.*; Charles Foster, ed., *Nations Without a State: Ethnic Minorities in Western Europe* (New York: Praeger, 1980); Raymond Hall, ed., *Ethnic Autonomy – Comparative Dynamics* (New York: Pergamon Press, 1979); Jeffrey Ross *et al.*, eds., *The Mobilization of Collective Identity* (Lanham, Maryland: University Press of America, 1980).

[30]Riccardo Petrella, "Nationalist and Regionalist Movements in Western Europe," in Foster, ed., *op. cit.*, p. 10 (emphasis added).

rest of their society. However, it can also find expression in political terms, particularly, as in the case of Western Canada, in *"nouveau-riche"* regions which object to the central government's power to impose constraints which prevent them from "cashing in" on their new-found prosperity.

In the short term, because regionalism does not directly challenge territorial sovereignty, it appears to present less of a threat to the existing nation-state structure than does nationalism. In the long term, however, persistent neglect of regionalist demands by central authorities may result in a serious loss of legitimacy for the state in certain parts of the country. Moreover, it may also reinforce or provide the basis for the development of a distinct ethnic or national identity which seeks separation from the state. At the very least, regionalist protests add to the flow of demands which must be considered by policy-makers. Because most political parties, including government parties, have regional concentrations of support, regionalism has become an important dimension of political life in many countries, especially Canada.

The Development of the Nation-State

Territorial strains manifested in nationalism and regionalism are one aspect of what some writers have referred to as a "crisis" of the contemporary nation-state.[31] The modern state originally emerged in Western Europe in the time before the industrial revolution as a strategic and economic unit. As John Herz has aptly put it, the territorial state provided a "hard shell" towards the external environment. Strategically, the hard shell of the state "rendered it to some extent secure from foreign penetration, and thus made it an ultimate unit of protection for those within its boundaries."[32] At the same time, the state became the major locus of economic activity and the guarantor of economic autonomy. In many countries, the state institutions themselves played an active role in promoting economic development, providing transportation networks and other forms of industrial infrastructure, if not actually developing certain industries under state ownership. Less directly, almost all states provided a hard shell for their domestic markets through the imposition of tariffs, quotas and other protective measures and through the management of external trade relations.

With the emergence of the concept of national self-determination, the hard, hollow shell of the territorial state was given some substance. The idea that the state should govern on behalf of all the people, instead of a privileged minority, was first realized by the French Revolution of 1789. With the spread of the principles and institutions of popular sovereignty, often in the form of liberal democracy, the strategic and economic unit also became the primary focus of cul-

---

[31]For example, Karl W. Deutsch, "The Crisis of the State," *op. cit.*; John H. Herz, *The Nation-State and the Crisis of World Politics* (New York: David McKay Co., 1976), esp. Chapter 3; Gordon Smith, "The Crisis of the West European State," in D.M. Cameron, ed., *Regionalism and Supranationalism: Challenges and Alternatives to the Nation-State in Canada and Europe* (Montréal: Institute for Research on Public Policy, 1981), pp. 21-36.

[32]Herz, *op. cit.*, p. 101.

tural and political loyalties. The marriage of state and nation resulted in the emergence of the nation-state.

Today, the hard shell of the nation-state has been rendered somewhat less resistant by changes in the world economy and by the development of new instruments of warfare. As strategic units, most western nation-states are no longer able to defend their citizens against realistic external threats. They are forced to rely instead on the protective cloak offered by the United States and NATO. The economic autonomy of nation-states has been challenged by the increasing interdependence of national economies, the growing importance of international finance capital and multi-national corporations, dependence upon energy supplies and raw materials imported from more assertive Third World countries and the need for economic markets greater than those encompassed by traditional state boundaries. In some cases, these factors have led to the development of new economic and political institutions on a transnational level, perhaps best exemplified by the growth of the European Community. More generally, and especially in Canada, the result has been dependence on foreign capital investment, especially from the United States. Overall, it has become increasingly difficult for nation-states to control the internal dynamics of their own economies.

It is in this context that one author refers to the economic and strategic "inadequacy" of the contemporary nation-state.[33] The nation-state is no longer able to maintain its hard shell towards the outside world. The implied danger for the nation-state and its authorities is that, if this inadequacy is widely perceived by the general public, the legitimacy and loyalty owed to the state will be undermined. Herein may also be found one factor behind the nationalist demands of ethnic minorities: many of the original economic and strategic advantages of remaining within the larger nation-state no longer exist.[34]

Until the 20th century, the role of the state was by and large restricted to the maintenance of law and order, the administration of justice, the defence of the realm and the conduct of diplomacy. In order to maintain or enhance their legitimacy or popular support, nation-states have assumed many new tasks. In particular, state authorities have increasingly taken on service functions – such as education, health care, housing, pensions and unemployment insurance – to provide for the welfare of their citizens. This growth of the "welfare state" has been accompanied by a more interventionist role for the state in the economy. Many governments have intervened directly with budgetary policies or through state ownership of particular industries, for example, air and rail transport, telecommunications, energy development, public utilities. Others have played less overt economic roles, for example, through regulation of the private sector (environmental regulations, health and safety standards) or with tariff policies designed to protect domestic industries or markets.

---

[33]Gordon Smith, *op. cit.*

[34]On this and other potential lines of explanation for nationalist movements in western industrial societies, see Nick Baxter-Moore, "The Causes of Nationalist Movements in Developed Democracies," in D.C. Rowat, ed., *The Referendum and Separation Elsewhere: Implications for Quebec* (Ottawa: Carleton University, 1978), pp. 49-76.

The influence of the state in the daily lives of its citizens is therefore immense. As the scope of government activity has enlarged, the machinery of government has grown more complex and decision-making has become more centralized and bureaucratized. The increased number of state functions, and the personnel to carry them out, must be paid for. The average share of the GNP consumed by the public sector in western societies has risen from five to ten percent in the late 19th century to between 35 and 50 percent today. In countries with large and well-developed welfare state programs, such as Sweden or the Netherlands, total government expenditures actually exceed half the national income. Consequently, as every wage-earner knows, a large proportion of most citizens' income disappears into the hands of the government, either directly in the form of income tax and pension contributions or indirectly through sales tax and customs duties.

This growth of the state in the 20th century underlies a third dimension of the perceived crisis of the contemporary nation-state. In addition to being strategically and economically inadequate, as outlined above, some political scientists and politicians allege that the institutions of government are in danger of becoming *overloaded*.[35] The "overload" thesis consists of two complementary aspects: first, that the state has taken on more functions than it can perform and/or afford; and second, that the policy-making process has become too complex and cumbersome to respond effectively to the expectations of the citizens. Particularly in liberal democracies, the state faces a loss of public support and legitimacy if it cannot cope with the demands of its citizens. Thus, the resurgence of nationalism and regionalism may be attributable in part to a reaction against the centralization of economic and political decision-making. More generally, in a number of western societies there has also been a backlash against "big government" and high levels of government expenditure and taxation.

Though under fire, the nation-state remains the pre-eminent political actor in both the domestic and the international arenas. International organizations, such as the European Community, NATO and particularly the United Nations, remain the creatures of the nation-states which comprise them. Debates regarding nationalism, regionalism and political decentralization are carried to the nation-state capital. Indeed, nationalist movements perpetuate the logic of the nation-state by demanding secession from the larger state in order to form another, smaller one. Major questions of economic policy, welfare provision and the size of government are the vital stuff of "national" politics. In fact, as the state assumes more responsibilities, the scope of national politics grows ever wider. Although the nation-state, by and large, may not be quite as sovereign as it once was – even questions of sovereignty or foreign ownership of the economy have become national political issues – its institutions, policy-making processes,

---

[35]See, for example, Michel J. Crozier, Samuel P. Huntington and Joji Watanuki, *The Crisis of Democracy* (New York: New York University Press, 1975); Richard Rose and B. Guy Peters, *Can Government Go Bankrupt?* (New York: Basic Books, 1978); Richard Rose, ed., *Challenge to Governance: Studies in Overloaded Polities* (Beverly Hills: Sage Publications, 1980).

functions and powers remain at the heart of the study of politics. Thus, an examination of the origins and development of the Canadian nation-state is an essential precursor to the more detailed analysis of politics in Canada. Before turning to this examination in Chapter 2, we shall first discuss the type of nation-state which Canada has adopted.

THE BASIC PREMISES OF DEMOCRACY IN CANADA

Nation-states vary greatly in their governmental forms, politics and policies. Canada is a democracy, and its governmental form is that of a constitutional monarchy with a federal basis. Many principles and structures inherent in this description will be fleshed out throughout this volume. Though these concepts are often fuzzy and debate over their meaning is to be expected, they are extremely important in the daily lives of Canadians.

The type of political system enjoyed by a nation-state is usually encapsulated in the kind and limits of power exercised within it. Aesop's fable of the frogs and their search for the right leadership in their pond comes readily to mind. It seems that the frogs longed for a king, so they appealed to the god Zeus to send them one. He sent them King Log. When the log lolled about without exercising any authority the frogs demanded another king. Zeus sent King Stork, who immediately gobbled them up.

Aesop's fable illustrates the principle that in political systems there is a continuum between total freedom and the government's use of persuasion or coercion. In the real world, an element of power – and so coercion – is always present or implied. The poet Yeats expressed the idea that violence is always available to the nation-state when he wrote in "The Great Day":

'That Canada is a strange country, they change governments without firing a shot.'

"Hurrah for revolution and more cannon-shot!
A beggar upon horseback lashes a beggar on foot.
Hurrah for revolution and cannon come again!
The beggars have changed places, but the lash goes on."[36]

Nation-states differ remarkably in their openness and types of participation. Certain features of each polity are unique, yet the essentials of political systems are similar because all perform the same basic functions. A question, then, at the heart of the study of comparative politics has been whether political systems tend to fall into distinguishable categories or classes.

The search for understanding on this subject usually begins with Aristotle's analysis of the Greek city-states in the 4th century before Christ. This Greek philosopher, the godfather of comparative politics, clearly set out the fundamental rules for scientific investigation and developed the first significant classification of types of political systems.

Aristotle's classical division of polities was based on his knowledge of the 158 Greek city-states. While he lived in Athens, with its principle of equal access of citizens to government positions, he studied the constitutions and governments of other city-states to determine the causes of political instability and change. He employed two criteria to classify these states: the number of people who participated in governing; and whether they ruled in their own or the general interest. A six-fold classification resulted. Aristotle found that only two categories – *aristrocracy* and *polity* – were reasonably stable, and concluded that stability depended on active participation, or at least some degree of representation, of all social classes or citizens.

This classification of rule by the one, the few, or the many (with its resultant spectrum running from tyrannical rule through to democracy) has become part of western thought. While considerably simplifying reality, the classification helped introduce some order into the immense variety of political flora. It has gradually become clear, however, that there is no right or wrong classification, and that comparison requires agreement on at least principles and definitions.

In the contemporary world the governors are never in total control, so a classification which forces either/or distinctions can only be a starting point. The

TABLE 1.1   The Aristotelian Classification

Number of Rulers	Rule in the General Interest	Self-interested Rule
One	Monarchy	Tyranny
Few	Aristocracy	Oligarchy
Many	Polity	Democracy or Ochlocracy

[36]Quoted in Michael Curtis, *Comparative Government and Politics* (New York: Harper & Row, 1968), p. 43.

next step is to examine political systems on a spectrum. The most standard continua are those between democratic and authoritarian governments, and traditional and modern societies. In both cases the difficulty lies in determining the degree to which a state is democratic or modern. This task of measuring the degree of forms of government is very difficult. In this volume, we shall follow the following basic definitions: a **democratic** system conciliates competing political interests; an **autocratic** system imposes one divergent interest on all others.[37] Thus, in this book the form of government is determined by its method of reconciling political diversity and conflict. In autocratic regimes, representative institutions are absent or are facades.

Democracy is an ambiguous concept. The word comes from two Greek roots – *demos*, meaning the people, and *kratos*, meaning authority. As we have seen, in ancient Greek culture democracy meant government by the many. In some Greek city-states all citizens participated in making and implementing laws. Save for rare exceptions (an example is some Swiss communes), such systems no longer exist. Instead, most democracies, Canada among them, consist of a system of elected representatives who make laws for the land.

For Aristotle, "democracy" was characterized by the "poor" ruling in their own favour. When we characterize Canada as a democracy we tend to place it in the "rule in the general interest" category under which, to some extent, the people govern themselves. Unfortunately, today practically all nation-states describe themselves as "democratic" in some fashion. Even the harsh puppet regime of East Germany refers to itself as the "German Democratic Republic". The British writer Bernard Crick played lightly but brilliantly with this problem. For him, "democracy" is perhaps the most promiscuous word in the world of public affairs: "She is everybody's mistress and yet somehow retains her magic even when her lover sees that her favours are being, in his light, illicitly shared by many another. Indeed, even amid our pain at being denied her exclusive fidelity, we are proud of her adaptability to all sorts of circumstances."[38]

Yet, if a democracy is defined as a nation-state in which opposition parties have a reasonable chance of winning office, then fewer than one-quarter of the member states of the U.N. would be called democratic. Only about two dozen contemporary nation-states change their governments without recourse to revolution, coups d'état or other violent forms of change, and Canada is one of them. The fact is that democracy in the sense just cited is not widespread in the developing world.

The pure model of democracy envisages popular assemblies as in the Athenian sense. Readers may like to recall that, at that time, elections to high office were caried out by lottery because the Athenians believed that if choices between individuals were made then the richer, or better connected, candidates would win. In the modern day few observers expect democracy to be rule by the people as a whole. The closest to this goal is representative democracy, in which the peo-

---

[37]In many classifications a third basic form is added. See Bernard Crick, *Basic Forms of Government: A Sketch and A Model* (London: Macmillan, 1973) for a definition and discussion of "totalitarianism" following a reasonably similar definition.

[38]Bernard Crick, *In Defence of Politics* (London: Penguin, 1964), p. 56.

ple choose those who are to make and administer the laws. In principle, all citizens should have equal access to and influence on government policy-making through participation in fair and competitive elections. In this book we define **representative democracy** as that political system in which the governors who make decisions with the force of law obtain their authority directly or indirectly as a result of free elections in which the bulk of the population may participate.

Thus, democracy in Canada is not equivalent to rule by the people as a whole. Our form of government is, properly speaking, a representative democracy, in which those elected to high office are invested with the legitimacy of power to make decisions having the force of law. The system provides a method of electing and monitoring these representatives. It also allows regular and institutionalized opportunities for changing those responsible for governing the political system.[39] Moreover, the elected representatives do not mirror the views of the people or the various regions they represent. It they did so, formulating coherent policy might well be impossible.

Representative democracy requires complex structures, but its basic attributes may be fairly easily outlined. Its essential characteristic is reconciling the need for political order with a degree of influence for competing political interests. Associated with this basic feature are the values of liberty and equality. The primary premise is that representative democracy is the best means or technique of governing a complex society. It is a political means and not necessarily an end in itself. However, representative democracy is generally thought to be accompanied by other political values which are embedded in the notion of reconciling diverse interests through the majority principle: freedom of press and opinion, contested elections, competing political parties, civil rights, rule of law, limited terms of office and constitutional limits on the power of the elected. The assumption is that political weight and authority can shift from one group to another, and that any group or party seeking power will have to enlist the cooperation of other groups. In other words, pluralism is assumed.

The values of democracy are often debated. Some authors consider democracy to be essentially equivalent to certain fundamental values such as the protection of individual liberty or equality or other goals. In this volume we shall describe, analyze and assess the Canadian political system as a *means* or *technique* of government. It is the methods of democracy that will be in question, not the substance of the policies produced. For example, it may be possible to have a democratic political system with either a capitalist or a socialist economy.

Since public policies are not scientifically determinable, we are best advised to put our faith in free and fair elections with the concomitant necessary values.[40] Placing such high hopes in the "system" of democracy is best defended by Winston Churchill's well-used maxim that it is the "least worst" system of government. If it were possible to determine scientifically the best government policies, then the obvious conclusion of intelligent citizens should be to agree with Plato

---

[39]See Seymour Martin Lipset, "Some Social Requisites of Democracy: Economic Development and Political Legitimacy," *APSR* vol. 53, no. 1 (March 1959), pp. 69-105.

[40]Henry B. Mayo, *An Introduction to Democratic Theory* (New York: Oxford, 1960).

and set up an élite of philosopher kings to rule. However, this contention is difficult to uphold. The ruler of present-day Bahrain,[41] the smallest and least prosperous of the independent Gulf states, personally makes the rules or laws for his citizens. Citizens merely appear on Friday morning, make a verbal appeal, hand in a written petition and wait for the judgement to come down from on high. While there may be some merit – such as efficiency – in such a process, it is certainly not procedurally democratic. There is no institutionalized way for the citizens to change their ruler. The outstanding worth of democracy appears in that it allows citizen participation in the orderly succession of rulers. Governments elected by the people will more likely produce government *for* the people. As Aristotle put it, an expert cook knows best how to bake a cake, but the person who eats it is a better judge of how it tastes.

Countries are "more" or "less" democratic. While the level of democracy which a country possesses changes over time, cross-national (diachronic) comparisons indicate that Canada always appears high on a list of nation-states on this criterion. Yet within the sub-set of developed democracies, Canada has been placed first on an index of democratization by two authors, but ninth and eleventh out of twelve respectively, by two others.[42] Therefore, although Canada is usually complimented in a global perspective, our ability to be "as democratic" as some other developed countries has been challenged by a few serious scholars.

In adopting a democratic system, Canada did not shed its ties to the monarchy, as occurred in the United States where a republic was established. The number of monarchies in the world has steadily decreased. Even members of the Commonwealth, such as India, have opted to become republics. Canada, on the other hand, like the United Kingdom, continues to adopt a garb of constitutional monarchy – monarchical because Queen Elizabeth II sits on the throne of Britain and presides as the Queen of Canada. The symbols which historically indicated this attachment – "God Save the Queen" as our national anthem and the Union Jack as our flag – have disappeared, but our monarchical origins have had a lasting impact on the system of central government and administration. Symbols such as those on the Great Seal badges of the Royal Canadian Mounted Police and the reverse side of coins and some bills illustrate the monarchical ties that remain.

Canada is further, a **constitutional democracy**, because the Constitution shapes and limits political power. The documents and behaviour which comprise the Constitution limit the powers of the government by specifying the form of involvement of elected representatives and the division of authority among the partners in the federation. The Constitution also defines the power of those cho-

---

[41]Sheikh Isa ben Sulman al-Khalifa.

[42]Compare, Lipset, *op. cit.*; Phillips Cutright, "National Political Development: Its Measurement and Social Correlates," in N.W. Polsby, R.A. Dentler, P.A. Smith, eds., *Politics and Social Life* (Boston: Houghton Mifflin, 1963), pp. 569-82; Deane E. Neubauer, "Some Conditions of Democracy," *APSR* Vol. 61, No. 4, (December 1967), pp. 1002-9; and Robert A. Dahl, *Polyarchy: Participation and Opposition* (New Haven: Yale University Press, 1971).

sen to govern us. The choice of a parliamentary system rather than a presidential one followed logically from the adoption of a monarchical form. In the presidential system of the United States, the chief executive and symbolic head is the elected president. In the parliamentary system the monarch retains the latter honour and the chief political executive officer is relegated to a lower status for purposes of protocol. In other words, in the presidential system the president is both the nominal and political head of state, whereas parliamentary systems usually have a nominal head of state whose functions are chiefly ceremonial and whose influence is marginal.

Throughout this volume (particularly in Chapters 5 and 6), we shall describe and analyze these constitutional mechanisms. The basic form rests on British parliamentary traditions, but the Constitution also divides power by a federal principle. The essential difference between a unitary and a federal form of government is simply that a **unitary system**, such as that found in France, has a central government which possesses total authoritative power, whereas a **federal system** divides such power among jurisdictions and over geographical areas.

OVERVIEW

In eleven decades of independent existence Canadians have shown the vision required to master the huge desolate spaces of the wide northern hemisphere, to exploit the riches of the land and to solve the puzzles of a bilingual and multicultural society. The Fathers of Confederation created a structure of government which has met the tests of viability and flexibility under stress. In the decades ahead the tests may be more difficult, but they will nonetheless relate to past Canadian crises and to the way politics is played in Canada.

To describe, analyze and explain contemporary politics in Canada requires an understanding of the origin, territorial expansion and development of the Canadian nation-state. In the next chapter, a brief developmental history will introduce this subject and illustrate the major importance of the growth of the state.

The four parts of the volume which follow study those dimensions of politics in Canada which the authors regard as the most significant: political culture, institutions, behaviour and public policy. All four have an impact on the Canadian people, directing daily life and shaping the future.

Part II (Chapters 3 and 4) describes the Canadian political culture and how it is transferred from generation to generation. Part III (Chapters 5, 6, 7, 8, 9) outlines and dissects the institutions, such as the Constitution, federalism, the executive and the legislature, which give structure to the culture and to political options. Part IV (Chapters 10, 11, 12) assesses the activities of individuals within these formal institutions and other organizations in the political process. The last section, Part V (Chapters 13 and 14), evaluates the impact of Canadian culture, institutions and behaviour on public policy-making. Woven throughout the discussion is the importance of the development of the Canadian nation-state, and its divisions over the allocation of the resources of the territory – in brief, politics.

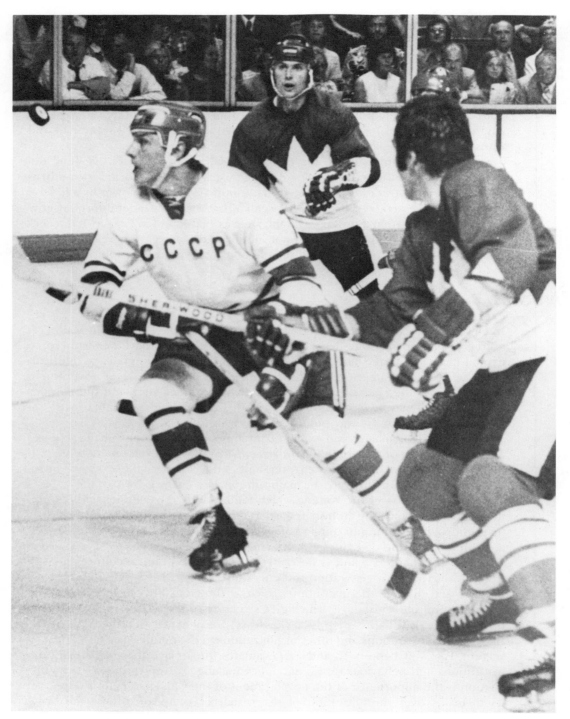

chapter 2

The Canadian Nation-State
Yesterday and Today

POLITICAL SCIENTISTS are sometimes accused of being "ahistorical" in that they attempt to portray contemporary politics without a due appreciation of how and why present cultural attitudes, institutions or modes of behaviour developed as they did. This is not to suggest that the political life of a nation-state is nothing more than a product of past and present conflict in the domestic and international arenas. Nonetheless, contemporary politics is circumscribed by these broad constraints. In fact, without at least some understanding of Canada's economic, social and political history, it is impossible to grasp how Canadians forged a positive and dynamic system of government when the country was vulnerable to dangers on all sides. In this chapter, therefore, we seek to develop an historical framework as a context for an appreciation of contemporary politics in Canada.

In chronological terms, Canada is one of the world's older nation-states. With the passage of the *British North America (BNA) Act* in 1867, Canada became the 45th of the present members of the United Nations to receive its independence. It is therefore one of the minority group of nation-states which can claim continuous existence as an independent entity for over a century. Yet Canada is considerably younger than the majority of current West European countries, many of which were established sovereign states before the first European settlers set foot on North American shores. It also postdates most of the countries of South and Central America, which gained their independence from the Spanish Empire largely between 1810 and 1840 and many of which are still considered to be part of the developing, as opposed to the developed, world. Unlike these Latin American examples, however, Canada has established a highly stable political system based upon the Western European norm of parliamentary democracy, and has become very much a part of the "developed world" of advanced industrial societies, as evidenced by its membership in the Organization for Economic Cooperation and Development (OECD), the Atlantic Alliance

(NATO) and the "Group of Seven" summits attended by the leaders of selected major western economies.

Other aspects of contemporary political life in Canada, however, are more reminiscent of the problems faced by newer nation-states. Until 1982, concerns were voiced over political and constitutional dependence upon the United Kingdom. Economic dependence upon the United States is an ongoing issue. And internal linguistic, nationalist and regional conflicts are suggestive of a lack of political integration also more typical of countries in the developing world.

Thus, Canada may justifiably be labelled one of the "first new nations",[1] inasmuch as it shares with many developing countries the past experience of European colonization and colonial rule before gaining independence as a sovereign state. Furthermore, its high level of economic development notwithstanding, Canada continues to face many of the problems of nation-state building and national integration suffered by newer, less affluent, states in the Third World. Canada is therefore something of a paradox. A stable parliamentary democracy, with over a century of self-government and a highly industrialized economy, it still faces some of the difficulties of much younger nation-states. How Canadians have attempted to cope with these problems constitutes much of the subject-matter of this book and comprises the source of key issues in Canadian politics.

In this chapter, we link the past and the present, the history of yesterday with the politics of today. Taking an historical perspective, we outline the origin of the Canadian nation-state from early colonial settlement to Confederation and examine its expansion and development since 1867. Then, we discuss the growth of the state and the present role of its institutions in the everyday lives of Canadians, concluding with an illustration of some of the current issues which demonstrate the impact of Canada's history upon contemporary politics.

ORIGIN: FROM COLONY TO CONFEDERATION

The development of Canada as a modern nation-state began with the act of Confederation, which united three British North American colonies, New Brunswick, Nova Scotia and Canada, in 1867. But that act of union, and the federal nature of the new political entity founded thereby, must itself be placed within an historical context.

For over 250 years, between the establishment of the first permanent European settlements on the North American mainland and the time of Confederation, parts of what is now Canada were governed as colonies, primarily through laws made on the other side of the Atlantic Ocean. From the founding of the first French colony at Port Royal in 1605 until the British conquest of Québec

---

[1] For use of the term "new nation" to apply to former colonies which are now mature and affluent nation-states, see Seymour M. Lipset, *The First New Nation: The United States in Comparative Perspective* (New York: Basic Books, 1963).

in 1759, much of the future Dominion (together with the Ohio and Mississippi River valleys) was in French hands. Although many settlers established themselves in the St. Lawrence valley and on the coasts of Nova Scotia and Cape Breton, the primary function of these colonies was to provide raw materials (especially fish and fur) to the economy of mainland France.

In serving this purpose, the colonies of New France and Acadia (now Nova Scotia) were no different from most others. A *colony*, in general terms, is an area of land geographically remote from the metropolis (the centre of the colonial power) and incorporated into the colonial empire either by right of first possession or by conquest. Its laws are usually made in the metropolis and are administered by either a civilian governor or the military authorities. Colonies serve three major functions for a colonial power. First and most importantly, they are exploited for their natural resources, which are exported to serve the interests of the metropolitan economy. Second, they may be used for settlement, especially for surplus population (for example, during the great famine in Ireland in the 1840s) or, occasionally, as a means of getting rid of undesirable elements (an example is the penal settlements of Australia). Third, their possession acts as a symbol of the international importance of the colonial state, and they are therefore frequent subjects of international dispute and war between rival powers.

For the British in the mid-18th century, the French colonies of North America offered substantial natural resources. They also posed a threat to both the British colonies on the eastern seaboard of what is now the United States and the rich fur-bearing interior then owned by the Hudson's Bay Company. As an extension of repeated wars between Britain and France in Europe, Britain gradually acquired, through treaty concessions and by conquest, the French colonies in North America. Along with access to the natural resources of the region, the British acquired the problem of how to deal with the French-speaking population that had settled there, a problem which grew in complexity as the number of British merchants and English-speaking immigrants into the colonies increased.

A further generalization to be made about colonies is that their inhabitants, whatever their origin, tend to develop their own interests separate from those of the imperial economy and may eventually rebel against the imposition of laws made in the colonial metropolis. Since World War Two, many new nation-states have been created as a result of armed uprisings, usually by indigenous populations against their European colonial masters. But over 200 years ago, the first challenge to British supremacy in North America came not from a previously conquered native population, nor from a rival power, but from descendants of British settlers who had become disaffected with the policies of George III and his administrators. Following the success of the American Revolution and the establishment of the world's first post-colonial state, the major threat to Britain's remaining North American colonies was posed by the danger of invasion from or absorption by the United States. As well, resistance to colonial rule emerged inside the future Canada, as demands developed within the colonies for some degree of self-determination and responsible government.

Thus, the origin of the Canadian nation-state, from colony to Confederation, must be traced with reference to at least three major sets of historical relations: the trilateral relationship between the British North American colonies, the United States and the United Kingdom; the relations amongst the colonies themselves; and the conflict, particularly within the colony of the United Canadas, between the English- and French-speaking populations which constituted the two founding nations of the Canadian nation-state.

Early Settlement

Archaeologists have discovered traces of human life in Canada dating back as far as 30 000 years, but relatively little is known about this early pre-history. We do know that the native Indian and Inuit populations are descended from Asiatic nomads, who probably crossed on foot from Siberia into Alaska and northern Canada during the last Ice Age to become the oldest of Canada's many ethnic groups. The Vikings, around 1000 A.D., were the first Europeans to discover and briefly settle on the Canadian east coast, which they called "Vinland", but not for another five centuries did permanent European settlements tentatively begin and eventually thrive.

John Cabot first arrived on the Atlantic shores in 1497, five years after Columbus' historic "discovery", and within seven years St. John's, Newfoundland, was established as an English fishing port. The French, Portuguese and Spanish also began to use east coast harbours as bases for the exploitation of the rich North Atlantic fisheries. Thirty years later, in 1534, Jacques Cartier explored the coastal area of what he contemptuously described as "the land God gave to Cain". The following year, however, he discovered the Indian settlements of Hochelaga (Montréal) and Stadacona (Québec) in the St. Lawrence valley and established a French interest in this more promising region. Yet it was not until 1605 that the first French colony was established at Port Royal in Acadia. Three years later, Samuel de Champlain, the first governor of New France, founded Québec City. In the next century and a half, approximately 10 000 French immigrants arrived to settle along the shores of the St. Lawrence.

Early English settlement in North America was primarily restricted to what is now New England and the eastern seaboard of the United States, although the area around Hudson Bay was also claimed by London-based commercial interests. In the early 18th century, successive wars in Europe between England and France began to spill over into North America. In 1710, a combined force of British troops and American colonial militia captured Port Royal; the Treaty of Utrecht (1713) subsequently recognized British possession of Hudson Bay, Newfoundland and the new colony of Nova Scotia. The French retained the rest of eastern mainland Canada, Isle St. Jean (now Prince Edward Island) and the Isle Royale (Cape Breton) which was defended by the newly constructed fortress of Louisbourg.

In 1754, war broke out again in North America. In rapid succession the British expelled the French-speaking Acadians from Nova Scotia, shipping them off to the southern colonies, and captured both Louisbourg and the Lake Ontario stronghold of Fort Frontenac. In 1759, the forces of Wolfe and Montcalm met on the Plains of Abraham outside Québec City and the capital of New France fell into British hands. A year later, the remnants of the French army surrendered at Montréal, ending military resistance to the British conquest. The French colony was formally ceded to Britain in 1763 as part of the Treaty of Paris, which ended the Seven Years War in Europe. The British now controlled all of North America north and east of the Mississippi, except for the tiny islands of St. Pierre et Miquelon, which remain part of France to this day. But British domination was not to endure.

The American Revolution

In 1776, the southern colonies of British North America seized the reins of their own destiny and revolted against the British crown in order to found the United States of America. In the wake of the revolution, 40 000 Empire Loyalists, American colonists loyal to the crown, sought refuge in the remaining British colonies, particularly in the Maritimes (where their influx resulted in the creation of the colony of New Brunswick in 1784) and in what was then western Québec, now Ontario.

The boundaries between the newly sovereign United States and the British colonies were gradually settled over the next century. The Treaty of Paris had established an approximate southern border for the new British acquisition of Québec between the Atlantic Ocean and the western tip of Lake of the Woods (now the Ontario-Manitoba border). Large parts of this border were subsequently adjusted by Jay's Treaty in 1794 and the Webster-Ashburton Treaty of 1842. The Rush-Bagot Treaty of 1817, the world's oldest disarmament agreement, clarified the boundary through the Great Lakes. In 1818, the Treaty of London fixed the westward border along the 49th Parallel to the Rockies and paved the way for western settlement. The final step, to the Pacific Ocean around the southern tip of Vancouver Island, was determined by the Oregon Treaty of 1846. This formalized the bulk of the borders well before Confederation, but two remaining treaties settled smaller land disputes: in 1872 the San Juan Islands were ceded to the United States, and the boundary between Alaska and British Columbia was finally agreed upon in 1903. British dominion over the Arctic Islands had been passed to Canada in 1880.

These boundary agreements were often preceded by dispute, but were always achieved without violence. The single major hostile outbreak between the United States and Canada was occasioned less by overt dispute over territory than by America's desire to teach Britain a lesson and demonstrate the complete nature of the break from its former colonial masters. Although some American leaders may have hoped that the colonists to the north would throw off British rule in order to join the United States, the War of 1812-14 was mostly an affirmation of American sovereignty against what was seen as continued British interference. First, the U.S. resented the seizure of neutral American ships on the suspicion that they were trading with the French, with whom Britain was once again at war. Second, British traders were accused of arming and inciting a potential Indian rebellion in the American Midwest. Despite incursions by each side into the territory of the other – among other incidents, the Americans sacked the colonial capital of York, now Toronto, and the British burned the Capitol Building in Washington by way of retaliation – the Treaty of Ghent of 1814 left the pre-war boundaries intact. If the war achieved anything on the Canadian side, it was to lay the basis for a future Canadian nationalism that would come to fruition with Confederation, as well as for the periodic upsurges of anti-Americanism that manifest themselves within Canadian political culture.

The Founding Nations

The cessation of hostilities with the United States allowed the British colonial administrators in Canada to return to the long-term problem of relations between the two founding nations of British North America. The history of French/English relations leading up to Confederation illustrates the agonizing indecision of the British government about how to deal with the conquered French population, the original settlers.

The intention of the British government in 1763 was to promote immigration by English-speaking Protestant settlers and to assimilate the French-speaking Roman Catholic population as rapidly as possible. However, in the first few years, only about 200 English families, mostly merchants, settled in the new colony. For this reason, neither of the first two British Governors was prepared to establish in the new colony the representative assembly promised in the Royal Proclamation of 1763. They both considered that such a body would have represented only the 600 English settlers and not the 90 000 French who, as Roman Catholics, were excluded from the franchise under British law at that time.

With the failure of the assimilation strategy and the growing realization that French Canadian loyalty might prove vital as the southern colonies became increasingly restive, Governor Carleton persuaded the British government to revise its policy towards Québec. The *Québec Act* of 1774 withdrew the provision for an assembly, placing full authority in the hands of the governor and an appointed advisory council consisting of both English and French speakers. The French culture was to be preserved. Neither language was specifically guaranteed, but Roman Catholics were allowed freedom of worship and the right to hold civil office. The Catholic Church was given official sanction, and both French civil law and the seigneurial landholding system were retained to protect the property rights of individuals.

The decision to respect the cultural heritage of French Canada was clear, and the French population warmly approved of the *Act*. Many English Canadians, on the other hand, resented it. The break in the tradition of representative government in the British colonies arising from the special circumstances of a French-speaking majority was anathema to many English-speaking colonists, who felt unjustly deprived of their right to a representative assembly and British civil law, rights to which they had grown accustomed. The English merchants were slightly mollified by the expansion of the colony's boundaries to encompass the rich fur-trading area between the Ohio and Mississippi Rivers – but most of that gain was lost under the Treaty of Versailles in 1783 which finally settled the American War of Independence.

Partly in response to demands from the Empire Loyalists who had settled in what is now Ontario, the British next attempted to satisfy both ethnic communities with the *Constitutional Act* of 1791. This *Act* maintained the commitment to the French culture established by the *Québec Act*, but within a new political context. The old colony of Québec was divided in two: Upper Canada, west of the Ottawa River, which was predominantly English-speaking, and Lower Canada, which was predominantly French. The right of representative government was now granted to each group and, whereas French civil law and seigneurial landholding were retained in Lower Canada, English common law and freehold land tenure were established in Upper Canada. Thus, English Canadians outside Montréal were placated and the French Canadians were largely protected from absorption and conflict.

This promising new arrangement deteriorated over the next few years as the representative assemblies grew increasingly frustrated by their lack of control over the executive. The appointed members of the Governors' legislative councils often abused their privileged positions in order to enhance their own wealth and power, and paid scant attention to the elected members of the assemblies. Political and social agitation began against Upper Canada's "Family Compact" and Lower Canada's "Chateau Clique". Finally, open rebellion under the leadership of Mackenzie and Papineau forced Britain to re-evaluate its policies. In 1838 Lord Durham was dispatched to report on the situation and recommend a course of action. In Lower Canada he found all the problems of the other British colonies, plus an ethnic war. Britain's approach, he decided, had been wrong; the colony of Canada should have remained united so that the French population would have been gradually assimilated. Consequently, his recommendations included a reversion to the pre-1791 union and the granting of responsible government which he believed would, given the first condition, function effectively.[2]

The British government did not see fit to accept Durham's philosophy wholeheartedly; instead, it took a middle course. The *Union Act* of 1840 re-established the two Canadas as one political unit (although each was to retain its own version of the law), with English as the sole official language of record. Although Durham had recommended representation by population, which would have given the more populous Canada East (formerly Lower Canada) a majority, the two former colonies were each granted 42 members in the assembly. Canada West, with its lesser numbers, graciously accepted this equality of representation. Not surprisingly, however, Canada West was to declare the allocation grossly unfair a decade later, after rapid immigration had elevated its population to majority status. Durham's other major recommendation, that the government be made responsible to the elected assembly, was not implemented in 1840, though it became effective in practice some eight years later. Also at this date, the English-only language policy was deemed unworkable and the two basic languages were declared officially equal.

---

[2]Gerald M. Craig, ed., *Lord Durham's Report* (Toronto: McClelland and Stewart, 1963).

Perhaps because of the half-hearted adoption of Durham's recommendations, or because of the separation of the two Canadas fifty years earlier, relations between the two founding nations did not unfold according to Durham's desires and predictions. Repeated attempts to find a workable solution to the ethnic problem showed the leadership's great determination to satisfy both cultures. From about 1849, Cabinets in the colony included representatives from both ethnic groups. Rather than a single Prime Minister at the head of government, there were two party leaders, one from each group, as well as separate attorneys-general to mirror the dual legal system. Some legislation applied to one or both; sometimes dual legislation was enacted. For a number of years, even the capital of the colony alternated between Toronto and Québec City until Queen Victoria settled the problem by deciding on the (then) backwoods lumbering town of Ottawa.[3]

The theory of cooperation was excellent, but the practice impossible. Discord stemmed partly from the fact that one group could enact legislation relating to the other even if the latter did not give it majority support. Soon, Montréal merchants in Canada East were openly supporting union with the United States, while George Brown's Reformers in Canada West demanded "Rep by Pop" and, eventually, a federal solution to the colony's governmental problems. Ethnic and religious antagonisms were exacerbated under these circumstances until it became almost impossible for any government to retain the confidence of the assembly. By about 1857 the government had reached a virtual impasse, which representatives of both ethnic groups sought a way to break. It was in this common search for a solution to political deadlock that both French and English leaders came to embrace the goal of British North American unity.

Confederation

A handful of men from the colony of Canada took their vision to Britain for approval as early as 1858, but the concept of "a British North America united from sea to sea" had not yet penetrated British government circles and the Canadians were sent home. Nevertheless, they kept sight of their goal and in 1864 they gatecrashed a meeting of Maritime representatives in Charlottetown in order to sell their idea there. Over the next three years they laboriously patched together a successful proposal for an Act of Union involving three of the five colonies – Canada, New Brunswick and Nova Scotia – and paved the way for the later accession of other colonies and territories.

It should be noted that Confederation was not directly approved by the people. There was no referendum or election to determine public sentiment, nor was the omission deemed significant at the time. Confederation grew out of the gentlemanly agreement of a few men united by a noble ideal regarding the type

[3]David B. Knight, *Choosing Canada's Capital: Jealousy and Friction in the Nineteenth Century* (Toronto: McClelland and Stewart, 1977).

of political system most appropriate to achieving their common goals. In the final analysis, it was a series of external circumstances which eventually allowed the Fathers of Confederation to marry their ideals with practical necessity and proceed on the path to nationhood. Had these men not clung tenaciously to their dream and acted when they did, it is questionable whether the Canadian nation-state would ever have existed. The Canadian colonies would almost certainly have been annexed or absorbed by the United States by the turn of the century. As one historian has observed, "perhaps the most striking thing about Canada is that it is not part of the United States".[4]

In many ways the fulfilment of the Canadian dream at that particular time was a response to events in the United States; such decisions have since become commonplace in Canadian history. In the mid-1860s, Anglo-American relations were at a new low and the Canadian colonies were isolated and vulnerable to attack. The American Civil War was drawing to a close and the army of the northern states would soon be available for an attack on Canada. Westward migration in the United States had become a threat to the political vacuum west of the colony of Canada. Furthermore, Britain had neither the resources nor the desire to protect these colonies from American aggression.

In 1864, therefore, after having discouraged for several years the efforts by those few Canadians (notably Macdonald, Cartier, Galt, Tupper, Tilley, Brown and McGee) who wished to have the issue of a federal union of British North America taken seriously, the British government suddenly deemed it propitious to encourage Canadian unity and independence. It was recognized that if British North America were united it would be not only more economically viable and easier to defend, but also, as a self-governing dominion, more responsible for the cost of its own defence. The colonies of New Brunswick and Canada, which shared long boundaries with the United States, supported a union, but Nova Scotia, with no American land border, was less easily persuaded.

The 1864 Charlottetown Conference, instigated by Nova Scotia Premier Dr. Charles Tupper, was originally called to discuss the prospects for Maritime union. The Canadians invited themselves and had the agenda changed to deal with their proposals for a larger entity. The Québec and Maritime leaders were adamant that the new arrangements should be federal in order to prevent Canada West from dominating the future Dominion by virtue of its size. Sir John A. Macdonald was willing to accept federalism as a second choice rather than delay or thwart the project on this point. Thus, Charlottetown concluded with a basic agreement that the new larger union would be a federal, not a unitary, arrangement and that another meeting be held to discuss proposals in more detail.

The Québec Conference which followed in October 1864 was very brief. Within three weeks the leaders had produced the 72 resolutions which were to provide the basis for Confederation. Since the Conference had no official status,

---

[4]J.B. Brebner, *Canada: A Modern History* (Ann Arbor: University of Michigan Press, 1960), p. ix.

one of the resolutions was the proposal that "the sanction of the Imperial and Local Parliaments shall be sought for the Union of the Provinces on the principles adopted by the Conference."[5]

The future provinces acted on this item in very different ways. Prince Edward Island and Newfoundland rejected any association with the Conference or its proposals. The legislature of Canada debated at length and finally adopted the 72 resolutions by a three-to-one majority (with most of the "nays" coming from Canada East). Canada was the only colony which ever formally approved the project. The government of New Brunswick called a general election on the question and was soundly defeated, while Premier Tupper, afraid of similar unpopularity in Nova Scotia, avoided an assembly vote on the resolutions by introducing a motion to approve a Maritime Union. The Canadian group again persevered and took the results of the Québec Conference to London where, this time, they received a more sympathetic audience.

Although the colonies were by then internally self-governing, Britain retained direct influence over their policies through its colonial governors. Britain refused to consider Nova Scotia's stated preference for a Maritime Union, and the governors of the Maritime colonies were instructed to sway their respective political executives in favour of the wider confederation. By 1866, the legislatures of both Nova Scotia and New Brunswick (the latter now under threat of invasion from the United States by the Fenians)[6] had reconsidered their earlier dismissal of the Québec Resolutions and sought a renewal of consultations towards a union with the Canadas.

In December 1866, delegates from the three participating colonies incorporated the essence of the Québec Resolutions into an Act of Confederation at the Westminster Palace Conference in London. The *British North America Act* was given Royal Assent on March 29, 1867, and came into effect three months later on July 1, 1867, without any of the colonies having had further opportunity to discuss or approve the birth of their future nation-state.

The *British North America Act* brought into formal existence the Dominion of Canada. In the light of the continuing tensions between English and French Canada, it is somewhat ironic that it was the combined leadership of the United Canadas which provided the direct impetus for Confederation. The French Canadian leaders at that time fully supported the federal union, although there was some disquiet within the newly created province of Québec on the part of those who feared that the addition of the largely English-speaking Maritimes would further exaggerate the minority status of French Canadians within Canada. However, it was Nova Scotia, not French Canada, that welcomed Dominion Day in 1867 by draping the streets in black!

The union of 1867 provided immediate solutions for three major problems facing the former colonies and the British government. The reorganization of

---

[5]Quoted in R. MacGregor Dawson, *The Government of Canada*, 5th ed., revised by Norman Ward (Toronto: University of Toronto Press, 1970), p. 32.

[6]The Fenian Brotherhood, an organization of Irish-Americans, sought to pursue the cause of Irish independence by provoking war between Britain and the United States.

the internal government of the United Provinces of Canada, in the form of the creation of the separate provinces of Ontario and Québec provided relief from the political impasse there. The threat of American invasion was allayed once Nova Scotia and, particularly, New Brunswick were joined with Canada and arrangements had been made to connect the provinces by rail. Lastly, the provisions made in the act of Confederation to bring other territories into the union enabled the political vacuum west of Ontario to be filled and laid the basis for a "Dominion from sea to sea".

However, nation-states are not born overnight. These tentative steps towards the development of a Canadian nation-state were merely the beginning of a long and sometimes arduous process of territorial consolidation, national integration and state building, which may not be complete even today.

THE EXPANSION OF THE CANADIAN NATION-STATE

The concept of a nation-state embodies four interrelated ideas: a clearly defined area or territory; a set of state (or political) institutions which govern that territory and maintain both internal and external sovereignty; a given population which is subject to the state; and a sense of community or common identity ("nationhood") amongst that population. The Dominion of Canada founded by the act of Confederation in 1867 was considerably smaller, in both area and population, than the present nation-state. Consequently, before we examine the problems encountered by the new Dominion in developing a sense of "nationhood" and attaining sovereign status, we will outline in the next pages the expansion of the Canadian nation-state with regard to territory and population.

Territorial Expansion

The territorial outline of the nation-state formulated at Confederation was gradually filled in over the succeeding years. In 1670, England's King Charles II had granted all the lands which drained into Hudson Bay to a company of that name. Proceedings were initiated in 1867 to bring this territory under Canadian control, and eventually the Company sold it to the Canadian government for £300,000. In 1870, both Rupert's Land and the North-western Territory were formally annexed to the Dominion. In the same year, the Red River Colony (under the new name of Manitoba) became the first additional province in the union, although it was much smaller then than today (see Figure 2.1). Lured by the promise of permanent railway communications with eastern Canada, British Columbia was admitted by Imperial Order-in-Council in 1871. Two years later, the previously uninterested Prince Edward Island also decided to join.

The next major jurisdictional change occurred in 1905, when Alberta and Saskatchewan were carved out of a large portion of the Northwest Territories and granted provincial status. Seven years later, Manitoba, Ontario and Québec were allowed to annex more land from the Territories to assume more or less their current forms. The tenth and final province, Newfoundland, entered the

FIGURE 2.1 The Growth of Confederation from 1867 to 1949

Stamps reproduced courtesy of Canada Post Corporation.

federation in 1949, over eighty years after the original invitation and even then only after two referendums to decide its future.[7] The rest of the land within the boundaries of the Canadian nation-state, the Yukon Territory (created out of the Northwest Territories in 1898) and the Northwest Territories, currently remains under federal jurisdiction.

Canada's external boundaries have therefore changed very little since shortly after Confederation. Except for the tardy addition of Newfoundland, all of Canada's current territory was formally part of the Dominion by 1873. Thus,

---

[7]See Henry B. Mayo, "Newfoundland's Entry into the Dominion," *Canadian Journal of Economic and Political Science,* vol. XV, no. 4 (November 1949), pp. 505-522; Richard Theoret, "The Uses of the Referendum in Canada," in D.C. Rowat, ed., *The Referendum and Separation Elsewhere: Implications for Quebec* (Ottawa: Carleton University, 1978), especially pp. 26-29.

the territorial development of the Canadian nation-state has been primarily a process of internal adjustment: creating or admitting new provinces or extending the boundaries of existing ones. But, as a number of contemporary political issues would suggest, this process is not necessarily complete. There is, for example, a lingering boundary dispute between Québec and Newfoundland over the status of Labrador. Québec has never accepted the 1927 decision of the Judicial Committee of the (British) Privy Council which gave more than 100 000 square miles (260 000 square kilometres) of Labrador to Newfoundland. As well, maritime boundaries have taken on new importance in recent years, with ownership of potentially huge reserves of offshore oil and natural gas at stake. At the time of writing, all of Canada's six maritime boundaries – four with the United States, one with France and one with Greenland – are in dispute.

In addition, Canada has been and continues to be subject to the regionalist and nationalist territorial strains often observed in states with multi-ethnic populations. Pressures for provincial status for both territories (especially the Yukon), or for the division of the Northwest Territories into two separate regions, indicate that the membership of the Confederation may yet increase.[8] Provincial status is likewise the goal of a small group of Acadian nationalists, who wish the predominantly francophone northern part of New Brunswick to separate from the rest of the province.

On the other side of the coin, the secessionist aspirations of the Parti Québécois and of separatist elements in Western Canada, such as the Western Canada Concept, have imposed a certain degree of doubt on the long-term integrity of Canada's external boundaries.[9] After a century of growth it is possible, but currently very unlikely, that the number of provinces and the amount of territory encompassed by the Canadian federation may one day decline.

Population Growth

At the time of Confederation, the population of the four member provinces totalled approximately 3.5 million people. The number of Canadians has steadily increased, to over 25 million in 1984. As the size of the population has grown, so too has its ethnic diversity. Today, Canada is regarded as a multi-ethnic or multicultural society, a view given formal recognition by the federal government in its creation of a separate post of Minister of State for Multiculturalism in 1971. But this was not always so.

In 1763, when the French Empire in North America was officially ceded to Britain by the Treaty of Paris, the total population of what is now Canada was

---

[8]In 1979, for example, Progressive Conservative leader Joe Clark promised to speed up the acquisition of provincial status for the Yukon, but his government was defeated before it could implement the proposal. In April 1982, a referendum was held in the Northwest Territories on a proposal to divide the Territories in two – Nunavut in the eastern and northern Arctic and Denendeh in the west. It produced no clear result, with a sizeable majority in favour in the east being counterbalanced by a net no-vote in the west.

[9]For further discussion of both movements, see Chapter 6, below.

fewer than 100 000. The vast majority were French Canadian descendants of immigrants from the Old France to the New. By 1812, partly "as a result of one of the highest birth rates in recorded history",[10] the French Canadian population of Lower Canada had reached about 330 000; but the number of English-speakers had also increased rapidly, swelled by immigration from Britain and by the large influx of Loyalist settlers from the United States into Upper Canada and the Maritimes. After further immigration from Britain, the United States and Ireland, the English-speaking population reached parity with the French and then surpassed it. In 1867, the new province of Ontario was the most populous of the four founding members of Confederation, and the predominantly French-speaking majority in Québec constituted only about one-third of the total population of Canada.

Even when referring to the time of Confederation, however, it may be a misleading oversimplification to see Canada's population purely in terms of the two founding nations or, as John Porter labelled them, "the charter groups" of the society.[11] For one thing, the English-speaking segment was by no means homogeneous, consisting as it did of immigrants from England, Scotland and Ireland and their descendants, the descendants of the Empire Loyalists, and many subsequent settlers from the United States who had migrated north in search of farmland or employment offered by the economic expansion of Canada West. Even among those who had migrated directly from the British Isles there were profound differences.

For instance, many of the Scots and Irish settlers were Catholic, not Protestant, a distinction which proved a source of conflict in Ontario and the Maritimes. Religious division was reflected in the creation of denominational schools and "a whole network of colleges, newspapers, hospitals and charitable and welfare institutions" which served to separate Catholics of both language groups from Protestants in everyday life.[12] Some current analyses of Canadian electoral behaviour posit that religious affiliation is still the best predictor of individual voting habits in General Elections.[13]

Furthermore, many of the Scots and Irish immigrants originally spoke Gaelic rather than English, and although their descendants have long been assimilated into the English Canadian linguistic majority, small enclaves preserving the Gaelic language and culture have survived, especially in Newfoundland and Cape Breton.

Second, as the census of 1871 illustrates, although members of the two charter groups constituted over 90 percent of Canada's population at that time,

---

[10]Ramsay Cook *et al.*, *Canada: A Modern Study* (Toronto: Clarke, Irwin and Co., 1963), p. 21.

[11]John Porter, *The Vertical Mosaic: An Analysis of Social Class and Power in Canada* (Toronto: University of Toronto Press, 1965), p. 60 ff.

[12]Kenneth D. McRae, "Consociationalism and the Canadian Political System," in McRae, ed., *Consociational Democracy: Political Accommodation in Segmented Societies* (Toronto: McClelland and Stewart, 1974), p. 243.

[13]John Meisel, *Working Papers on Canadian Politics*, 2nd enlarged edition (Montréal: McGill-Queen's University Press, 1975), p. 255. See also Harold Clarke *et al.*, *Political Choice in Canada* (Toronto: McGraw-Hill Ryerson, 1979), pp. 100-103, and our Chapter 11, below.

representatives of other ethnic groups were already becoming established in the new Dominion. In addition to the Native peoples, both Indian and Inuit, (about 0.7 percent of the total population), there were nearly 30 000 Dutch (0.9 percent), over 200 000 Germans (5.8 percent), and a smattering of other ethnic minorities, including some American Blacks (chiefly in Nova Scotia and southwestern Ontario) who had first arrived with the Loyalists.

Since Confederation, the population of the Canadian nation-state has grown rapidly through a combination of natural increase (the excess of births over deaths in any given period), a generally high rate of immigration and, to a lesser degree, the incorporation of new territory (for instance, approximately 360 000 people were added to Canada's population by the accession of Newfoundland in 1949).

As in most western societies, the death rate in Canada has declined consistently since the mid-19th century and is now less than one percent per annum. The birth rate, while always exceeding the death rate, has fluctuated more wildly, following economic circumstances and contemporary fashion. It declined, for example, during the depression years of the 1930s and accelerated rapidly during the so-called "baby boom" in the more prosperous period after World War II. In recent years, natural increase has slowed to below one percent per year and this downturn is expected to continue.[14]

Immigration and Ethnicity

Canada, like other settler societies, depended upon immigration for its very beginnings. The colonists were naturally all immigrants: the French settled Québec, the British colonized the Maritimes and what is now Ontario, the Loyalists followed. Each group multiplied; the population of Canada in 1867 consisted largely of their descendants. Although much of Canada's population growth may be ascribed to natural increase, after Confederation the new Dominion sought more immigrants to settle the vast uninhabited western spaces.

Approximately 11 million immigrants have entered Canada since Confederation, but not all have stayed. In the second half of the 19th century, especially in the 1870s and 1880s, and again in the depression years of the 1930s, there was net emigration from Canada – that is, the number of people leaving the country between census years exceeded the number of new arrivals. But waves of mass immigration in other periods have tilted the overall balance of population flow in Canada's favour. For example, between 1895 and 1913, over 2.5 million immigrants entered the country and another one million arrived in the decade immediately following the Second World War.

In the last few years, stricter immigration policies have reduced the influx of new Canadians. From a high of 218 000 in 1974, the annual figure dropped to 86 000 in 1978. The slight upswing since then has been due largely to the num-

---

[14]See Statistics Canada, *Population Projections for Canada and the Provinces, 1972-2001* (Ottawa: Queen's Printer, 1974), Catalog No. 91-512.

ber of refugees, especially from South East Asia, admitted under special procedures. In 1982 the total number of immigrants was 121 147.[15] However, although the absolute volume of immigration has declined, predictions of a continued low level of natural increase suggest that immigration could constitute an increasingly important component of Canada's future population growth.

As new immigrants and their descendants helped swell Canada's population after Confederation, the ethnic composition of the Canadian populace began to change. Although English-speaking immigrants from the British Isles and the United States continued to form the largest groups, other Europeans arrived in increasing numbers. Significant concentrations of Germans, Dutch, and Scandinavians were present by 1900; they were joined in the early decades of the 20th century by Eastern Europeans, chiefly from Poland and the Ukraine. After 1945, large numbers of new Canadians came from countries devastated by the Second World War, especially Germany, Italy, the Netherlands and Eastern Europe.

It was not until after 1962, when the regulations were changed to eliminate explicit discrimination on the basis of race or nationality, that the preponderance of English-speaking and European immigrants began to decline. Previously, the only significant groups of non-white Canadians were Chinese and Japanese immigrants and, of course, the Native peoples. By the late 1970s, over one-quarter of new immigrants came from Asian countries (Hong Kong, India and the Philippines among them), and there had also been significant increases in the numbers entering from Africa, South and Central America and the West Indies.

As a consequence of changes in immigration patterns over the last century, Canada is today a truly multicultural society. The component from the British Isles, which in 1871 was 61 percent of the population, dropped to about 40 percent by the 1981 census.[16] The French element, comprising 31 percent of the total in 1871, was 27 percent in 1981. The remaining population could in 1981 be categorized into over seventy small but well-defined ethnic groups, the most significant of which were Germans (5%), Italians (3%) and Ukrainians (2%). Native people formed the sixth largest group.

Furthermore, despite the bicultural image projected by conflict between the two major language groups, Canada is a "nation of many tongues". Although the 1981 census showed that 21 million Canadians had English or French as their mother tongue (the language first learned in the home), the remaining 3.2 million cited over seventy other languages, each one claimed as the mother tongue by at least a thousand, and in some cases by up to half a million people. The integration of this multicultural and multilingual population into Canadian society

---

[15]See Department of Employment and Immigration, *Annual Statistical Report* (Ottawa: Queen's Printer, various years) and Department of Employment and Immigration booklet *Background paper on future immigration levels* (Ottawa: Supply and Services, 1983), p. 28.

[16]The 1981 census was unique in its methodology in that it allowed respondents to identify more than one ethnic background. Therefore, 1 838 615 persons can be assigned more than one ethnic origin. Approximately 76% of this group reported British as one component of their ethnic origin. Data for this section was provided by Statistics Canada. Not all of the data for the 1981 census has appeared in print as of the time of writing.

and the creation of a sense of national identity and political community amongst them have posed additional problems for the development of a Canadian nation-state.

THE DEVELOPMENT OF THE CANADIAN NATION-STATE

In the mid-1960s, political scientists evinced a growing concern with the problems of developing countries which in turn led them to focus on the twin themes of "nation-building" and "state-building". Particular emphasis was placed on identifying patterns in the historical evolution of established nation-states which might serve as models for comparison with contemporary processes of political development. The majority of historical analyses concentrated on the experience of Western European countries, although some also investigated the process of nation-state formation in older "new nations" such as Canada and the United States.[17]

Most authors agreed that two factors – successful national integration and a clearly defined and legitimate role for the state – are prerequisites for the emergence of stable political systems. In ideal terms, the development of a sense of national identity among the inhabitants of a territorial state – otherwise known as **nation-building** – serves to increase the sense of loyalty and legitimacy accruing to that nation-state. The nation-state thus replaces region, church or ethnic group as the primary focus of citizen allegiance and consequently reduces the number and intensity of potential sources of conflict within the population.

The establishment of the second factor – called **state-building** – similarly involves integration and consolidation. Again in ideal terms, the imposition of the supreme authority of state institutions and laws throughout the land serves to integrate the various parts of its territory into a single cohesive unit and to guarantee its domestic sovereignty – that is, its authority over and above the rival claims of other internal sources of political influence. In addition, the state ideally requires external sovereignty, which frees it to manage its own domestic and international affairs, independent of constraints imposed by any other country.

We have already made reference to the regional, religious and ethnic conflicts, and the problems of geographic diversity and external influence which hampered the processes of forming a sense of national integration and building a sovereign state in Canada. The remainder of this chapter will examine the impact of these factors on the progress Canada has made since Confederation towards the "ideal-typical" model of an integrated and sovereign modern nation-state.

---

[17]For example, Gabriel Almond and G. Bingham Powell, *Comparative Politics: A Developmental Approach* (Boston: Little Brown and Co., 1966); Karl Deutsch and William J. Foltz, eds., *Nation Building* (New York: Atheston Press, 1966); Samuel Eisenstadt and Stein Rokkan, eds., *Building States and Nations*, two volumes (Beverly Hills and London: Sage Publications, 1973). For studies of older "new nations", see Kenneth D. McRae, "Empire, Language, and Nation: The Canadian Case," in Eisenstadt and Rokkan, eds., *op. cit.*, volume II, pp. 144-176; S.M. Lipset, *op. cit.*

Problems of Nation-Building in Canada

The concept of national identity is rather like a coin in that it bears two sides which are related but which present different pictures of the whole. The "heads" of the national identity coin consists of a sense of belonging together in a single political community, while the "tails" represents a sense of distinctiveness from all other peoples. In different countries and different periods, one side or the other will appear to predominate. It sometimes seems that in the case of Canada there is a distinct bias in favour of "tails". According to Kenneth McRae, "the segregative or differentiative aspects of [nation-state] building in Canada are at least as important as the aggregative or combinatory ones."[18] That is to say, the Canadian national identity is characterized as much by its distinctiveness from other peoples as by its own internal solidarity.

No discussion of the development of the Canadian nation-state can ignore the effects of what J.B. Brebner has called the "North Atlantic Triangle", the trilateral relationship between Canada, the United Kingdom and the United States.[19] The emergence of a separate Canadian identity has largely involved a process of differentiation from these two major influences. The need for Canadians to cut the colonial ties that bound them to the United Kingdom, paramount in the 19th and early 20th centuries, has more recently been transformed into the problem of establishing a Canadian identity and culture distinct from that of the United States.

The other side of the coin, the development of a sense of belonging together, has been hindered by three potential obstacles: the historically conflictual relationship between English-speaking and French-speaking Canadians; the problems attendant on integrating minority ethnic groups into the community; and the pervasive effects of regionalism, exacerbated by the federal nature of the political system, the uneven distribution of economic activity and the peculiar configuration of settlement in Canada. Certain aspects of each of these problems will be examined in greater detail in other parts of the book (notably, Chapters 3, 4 and 6), but an overview linking the various obstacles to nation-building in Canada will be useful here.

A Distinct Canadian Identity?

A Canadian, or rather "Canadien", identity distinct from that of Metropolitan France had already emerged in Québec before the British conquest, but the British colonies in North America were relatively indistinguishable before 1776. However, the events of the American Revolution and the entry of the Empire Loyalists into the northern colonies marked the initial differentiation of Canada

---

[18]Kenneth McRae, "Empire, Language, and Nation: The Canadian Case", p. 146.

[19]J.B. Brebner, *North Atlantic Triangle: The Interplay of Canada, the United States and Great Britain* (Toronto: McClelland and Stewart, 1966).

from the United States, based on loyalty to the British Crown and Empire. The identification with Britain was further strengthened by the successful defence of Canada in the War of 1812 and by massive immigration from Britain in the next few decades. As McRae argues, "the literature of the period suggests that they [the newcomers] did not see migration as involving a change of allegiance. They remained simply British subjects who lived in the colonies."[20]

The formation of a separate Canadian Dominion in 1867 owed much to relationships within the triangle. Canadian Confederation was "largely a response to the American presence; as a defence strategy, as imitation, and as a general alternative."[21] Faced with a potentially expansionist United States, the Fathers of Confederation were motivated by "the fear of slow death by absorption and a quick one by annexation [which] hung over Canadian constitutional debates."[22] The British, for their part, were increasingly unwilling to devote resources to the

Credit: Rodewalt Illustration, originally appeared in Policy Options.

[20]Kenneth McRae, "Empire, Language, and Nation: The Canadian Case", p. 149.

[21]John H. Redekop, "Continentalism: The Key to Canadian Politics," in Redekop, ed., *Approaches to Canadian Politics*, 2nd edition (Scarborough, Ontario: Prentice-Hall Canada Inc., 1983), p. 35.

[22]Janet Morchain, *Sharing a Continent* (Toronto: McGraw-Hill Ryerson, 1973), p. 108.

defence of their North American colonies and were happy to give self-govern-ment to a new Dominion whose inhabitants remained loyal to the Crown and the Empire. Indeed, for many Canadians of British stock, there appeared to be little conflict in values between the new Canadian nationality created at Confederation and continued loyalty, as British subjects, to the Empire – a dual allegiance which remained widespread among English Canadians up to the First World War.[23]

Since 1920, this duality has declined in favour of a more exclusive identi-fication with Canada, especially among those born here. Growing national con-sciousness has been bolstered by the adoption of specifically Canadian national symbols, such as the Maple Leaf flag to replace the Red Ensign (which bore a Union Jack in one quarter), the substitution of "O Canada" for "God Save the Queen" as Canada's national anthem and, most recently, the patriation of the "made-in-Canada" Constitution. As the famous "Flag Debate" of 1964 illus-trates, the process of differentiation from Britain has not been without conflict. A degree of imperial and monarchical sentiment lives on, partly because of rein-forcement by continued immigration from the United Kingdom and by the activ-ities of organizations like the Orange Order and the Monarchist League, and partly because remnants of the Tory and Empire Loyalist traditions remain a component of Canadian political culture. But these elements aside, the sepa-ration of the Canadian national identity from British influence is more-or-less complete. In the eyes of many Canadians, a far more pressing need in the second half of the 20th century has been to emphasize Canada's distinctness from the United States.

The relationship with the United States is hardly a new factor in the devel-opment of the Canadian nation-state. But the major source of anxiety has changed over time. Although Canadians no longer fear direct military annexa-tion by the Americans, concern is now directed towards economic and cultural penetration of Canada by its much larger neighbour. Economic relations, includ-ing Canada's trade dependence on the United States, American ownership of Canadian industry and natural resources and the impact of economic interde-pendence are among the major foreign policy issues examined in detail in Chap-ter 14. But, just as important for many Canadians, and more pertinent to the present discussion, is the issue of cultural independence from the United States.

It is, of course, difficult to divorce entirely the economic and cultural di-mensions of Canada/U.S. relations, since the concern for cultural independence seems to mirror economic realities. Before the First World War, when the emer-gence of a Canadian identity appeared to be hindered by the continuing British heritage, over 70 percent of foreign investment in Canada was via British port-folio or direct capital investment. Since World War Two, it is the United States that has been responsible for over 70 percent of foreign investment and has been simultaneously viewed as the major cultural threat. The culture/economy dis-tinction is further complicated by the fact that some foreign investment has been

---

[23]Carl Berger, *The Sense of Power: Studies in the Ideas of Canadian Imperialism, 1867-1914* (Toronto: University of Toronto Press, 1970).

in the so-called "cultural industries" – publishing, broadcasting and the cinema. Moreover, economic nationalism *vis-à-vis* the United States may at times be coated with the more respectable veneer of "defending Canadian culture". Nonetheless, concern over assimilation into America, or continental North American culture, is real.

The proximity of most Canadians to the border with the United States, the existence of a shared language, the relative size of the two populations and the penetration of Canadian society by American mass media and other culture-bearers are all viewed as potential threats to the emergence or maintenance of a distinct Canadian identity. Canadian governments have responded by attempting to impose "Canadian content" regulations on domestic television and radio broadcasting and on certain types of publications. Similarly, educational authorities have urged the inclusion of more Canadian studies in school curricula. Yet studies have revealed that Canadian schoolchildren often know more about the history, politics and cultural symbols of the United States than about their own country (see Chapters 3 and 4). Nevertheless, some observers suggest that a determination to resist total cultural assimilation remains a fundamental component of the Canadian national identity. As one writer has put it, despite a tendency to embrace many aspects of popular American or continental culture,

> "being 'non-American', and at times quite pointlessly anti-American, is part and parcel of the Canadian forms of patriotism and nationalism. Such negation is perhaps a somewhat weak basis for a national sentiment to focus on, nevertheless it is integral."[24]

Internal Obstacles to Nation-Building

If distinctiveness from outside cultures, notably British and American, is held to be an important component of the Canadian national identity, the various obstacles to developing a sense of belonging together *inside* Canada may well form the cause.

First, the traditional conflict between English and French Canadians has resurfaced on numerous occasions since Confederation. The execution of Louis Riel, the conscription crises of 1917 and 1944, the October Crisis of 1970 and the exclusion of Québec in the constitutional settlement of 1981 are among the low points in relations between the two charter groups. (For details, see Chapters 5 and 6). But even at other periods, no satisfactory long-term *modus vivendi* has ever been apparent between the founding nations. The incomplete nature of the nation-building process was vividly demonstrated in Québec by the 1976 surge to power of the Parti Québécois, a party officially espousing separation from the Canadian nation-state and the foundation of an independent, sovereign state of Québec.

---

[24]George Heiman, "The 19th Century Legacy: Nationalism or Patriotism?," in Peter Russell, ed., *Nationalism in Canada* (Toronto: McGraw-Hill, 1966), pp. 337-338.

Next is the question of the integration of other, non-charter, ethnic groups into Canadian society. Government policies and popular support in favour of multiculturalism have allowed each ethnic minority to preserve its own cultural identity and heritage, while becoming integrated in Canada's social mosaic. Admittedly, there are certain minority groups, such as the Sons of Freedom sect of the Doukhobors, who have refused to acknowledge the sovereignty of the Canadian nation-state, but the general pattern among immigrants has been one of willingness to concur with the norms of their host society. In turn, the host society has been for the most part willing to accept them. However, there exist examples of both institutionalized (governmental) racial discrimination and public racism, even racial violence, in various periods of Canadian history, chiefly directed in the past at Chinese and Japanese minorities and more recently at Asian and West Indian immigrants in certain large cities.[25]

Perhaps the most disruptive impact of minority ethnic groups on nation-building in Canada has occurred with respect to the French-English relationship. The fact that the majority of new immigrants, even in Montréal, have tended to learn English rather than French as their first official language has exaggerated the minority status of French-speaking Canadians in Canada and exacerbated relations between the two charter groups.

Special mention must be made here of Canada's Native groups, since, for a long time, they were deliberately excluded from the nation-building process. Whereas, following the conquest of Québec, the British authorities made repeated attempts to accommodate the interests of the French-speaking population, they demonstrated little regard for the rights and customs of Canada's aboriginal peoples. Successive colonial and, later, Dominion administrations deprived the Indians of their land (by fair means or foul) as a means of opening up western Canada for settlement and railway construction, herding them onto reservations and subjecting them to the draconian measures of the 19th century *Indian Acts*. Although some of the more discriminatory provisions of the legislation pertaining to Native Indians have since been relaxed – for example, after 1960 Indians on reserves were at last allowed to vote in federal elections – status Indians still occupy a dependent, quasi-colonial, position *vis-à-vis* the federal government.[26] Non-status Indians and Métis, excluded from the reservations and thus forced to attempt integration into mainstream (white) society, also find themselves largely amongst the poorer and under-privileged sections of the Canadian population, often being subject to discrimination and racial stereotyping.[27]

---

[25]Alan B. Anderson and James S. Frideres, *Ethnicity in Canada: Theoretical Perspectives* (Toronto: Butterworths, 1981), pp. 200-202 and Chapter 9 *passim*; D. Hill, *Human Rights in Canada: A Focus on Racism* (Ottawa: Canadian Labour Congress, 1977); Evelyn Kallen, *Ethnicity and Human Rights in Canada* (Toronto: Gage, 1982), Chapters 1 and 6.

[26]See, for example, Mel Watkins, ed., *Dene Nation: The Colony Within* (Toronto: University of Toronto Press, 1977).

[27]For a critical view of the situation of the Indian population from a human rights perspective, see James Wilson, *Canada's Indians*, MRG Report No. 21 (London: Minority Rights Group, n.d.), especially Parts Three and Four.

The current situation of the Indian population is a product of the expansion of the Canadian colonies and nation-state in the 19th century, which brought the Native and the white man into direct competition for possession of land. In contrast, because of their geographical isolation – mainly in the Northwest Territories, northern Québec and Labrador – the Inuit were largely by-passed by the processes of nation-building and modernization until perhaps three decades ago. Like status Indians, the Inuit were for a long time – until 1950 – explicitly excluded from the federal franchise. However, many Inuit living in the high Arctic could not actually exercise their right to vote until 1963, following the creation of a new parliamentary riding covering the entire Northwest Territories.[28]

During these three decades, the Inuit have been forced into coexisting with an advanced industrial society within the Canadian nation-state. Their traditional lifestyle has been encroached upon by modernity in the form of attempts to develop Arctic energy and other mineral resources and the construction of the Distant Early Warning (DEW) line of radar stations and other military installations. Many Inuit, like the Indians, are resentful of the disruption of their customary mode of life by modernization and economic development. But, unlike Canadians elsewhere in the country, the inhabitants of the Northwest Territories (where Natives, including Métis, constitute a majority of the population) and the Yukon Territory (approximately one-quarter Native) have no provincial government to manage their natural resources and to speak on their behalf at intergovernmental conferences or constitutional negotiations.[29]

For Native organizations like the Inuit Tapirisat of Canada or the Dene Nation, minority status and the lack of institutionalized channels make it difficult to compete within the established mechanisms of federal/provincial negotiation. It is perhaps not surprising that some Native groups feel themselves to be non-participants in the Canadian nation-state, and actively oppose further modernization and development.

Last in this examination of the obstacles to nation-building in Canada comes regionalism. Regionalism, or provincialism, is not a new phenomenon in Canada. Even in pre-Confederation days there was little contact between the colonies of British North America. The events leading up to the establishment of the Dominion suggest profound regional differences in attitudes towards the founding of the Canadian nation-state. Today, well into the second century of Confederation, the differences and interests continue to exist.

The persistence of regionalism within the Canadian nation-state can be ascribed to several factors. First among them is the sheer size of the country. The second, the uneven development of economic activity across Canada, has meant that the different regions have separate economic interests to advance and pro-

---

[28]From 1953 to 1962, there was a constituency of "Mackenzie River", which excluded the territorial districts of Keewatin and Franklin. From 1963 to 1979, the "Northwest Territories" riding covered all three districts. Since the 1979 General Election, the N.W.T. has been represented by two MPs, one for "Western Arctic" and one for "Nunatsiaq". In addition, the N.W.T. and Yukon were finally given representation in the Senate, one Senator each, in 1975.

[29]On the constitutional status of the Territories, see Chapter 5, below.

tect. Thus, there are several economic bases for regional conflicts: oil producing *vs.* oil consuming regions, agricultural *vs.* industrial areas, resource-rich *vs.* poorer provinces, among others.

The next two factors are connected. Canada's peculiar pattern of settlement, with 90 percent of the population clustered within a strip 320 km wide extending along the American border (see Figure 2.2), has already been noted. One result is that, unlike in many western societies, there is no single centre of population concentration to serve as a cultural and economic core.

An additional result is that there is no dominant city in Canada. Rather, Canada has a "polycephalic" city network,[30] with several regional centres (Halifax, Montréal, Toronto, Winnipeg, Calgary, Vancouver, *etc.*) as the political, economic, social and cultural foci for the populations clustered around them. Instead of possessing a single metropolis dominating and easing the integration of the peripheries of the nation-state (examples are Paris and London), Canada thus consists of a series of "core/periphery" (or "city/hinterland") relationships which divide the country into more-or-less self-contained regions and communication networks (see Figure 2.3).

Even within central Canada (that is, Ontario and Québec), which is sometimes portrayed as the "centre" in relation to the "peripheries" of east and west, no dominant city emerges. Ottawa is the political capital of Canada, but little else; Toronto is the economic and cultural centre of Ontario, as well as the provincial capital; Montréal is the economic core of Québec and the cultural centre for French Canadians; Québec City is increasingly viewed as *the* political capital by Québec nationalists. Clearly, none of these can claim to dominate central Canada, let alone the whole country.

The effect of this core/periphery network is compounded by the federal system of government adopted at Confederation, whereby regional interests are primarily articulated by provincial governments in competition with each other or with the federal government. It is this fifth factor which is chiefly responsible for the frequent equation of "regions" with "provinces" in Canada. But the representation of regional interests by provincial governments tends to lead to an exaggeration of differences between regions and to understate intra-regional variatons. Richard Simeon has argued that the provincial governments have "vested interest in maintaining and strengthening the salience of the regional dimension . . . ."; each one, therefore, "is motivated to accentuate the degree of internal unity, and to exaggerate the extent of difference with Ottawa. . . .".[31] Thus, while Canada's federal system was intended to reflect and take into account the

---

[30]On the impact of "polycephalic" city networks on nation-building, see Hans Daalder, "On Building Consociational Nations: The Cases of the Netherlands and Switzerland," in McRae, ed., *Consociational Democracy,* pp. 107-124; or Stein Rokkan, "Cities, States and Nations: A Dimensional Model for the Study of Contrasts in Development," in Eisenstadt and Rokkan, eds., *op. cit.,* Volume 1, pp. 73-97.

[31]Richard Simeon, "Regionalism and Canadian Political Institutions," in J.P. Meekison, ed., *Canadian Federalism: Myth or Reality,* 3rd edition (Toronto: Methuen, 1977), pp. 301-302.

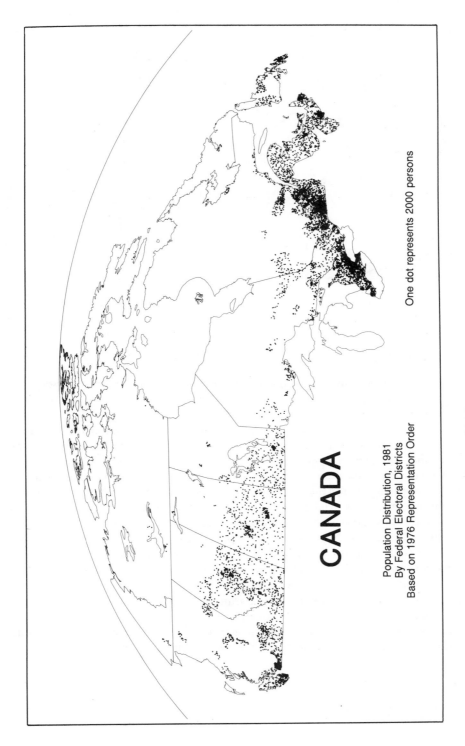

CANADA

Population Distribution, 1981
By Federal Electoral Districts
Based on 1976 Representation Order

One dot represents 2000 persons

FIGURE 2.2 Population Distribution, 1981 by Census Divisions

Source: 1981 Census of Canada

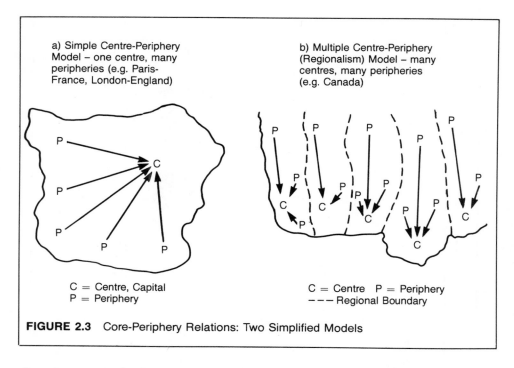

a) Simple Centre-Periphery Model – one centre, many peripheries (e.g. Paris-France, London-England)

b) Multiple Centre-Periphery (Regionalism) Model – many centres, many peripheries (e.g. Canada)

C = Centre, Capital
P = Periphery

C = Centre   P = Periphery
– – – Regional Boundary

FIGURE 2.3   Core-Periphery Relations: Two Simplified Models

diversity among the four original provinces, it has since served to perpetuate, institutionalize, and perhaps exacerbate regional differences and conflicts among the members of the now much larger Canadian federation.

Last among the factors contributing to the persistence of regional particularism in Canada is the absence of nationally-oriented mass media which, according to some nation-building theorists, often serve as an integrative force. Where the media focus is upon local news and political or social issues, there is little opportunity for the consumer to acquire knowledge about other parts of the country or to learn what people elsewhere think about his or her own region. Despite the best efforts of the CBC and the aspirations of *The Globe and Mail* to become "Canada's National Newspaper", no nationally integrative force has emerged among the Canadian mass media (see Chapter 4). As one recent discussion suggests, ". . . the present national [media] system has been only moderately successful at best in fostering interregional communication."[32]

We have therefore seen that a number of factors combine to ensure the persistence of regionally based attitudes and interests in Canada: the sheer size of the country; variations in economic activity and wealth; uneven population distribution and the polycephalic city network; the institutionalization of regional

---

[32]Frederick J. Fletcher and Daphne F. Gottlieb, "The Mass Media and the Political Process," in M.S. Whittington and G. Williams, eds., *Canadian Politics in the 1980s* (Toronto: Methuen, 1981), p. 149.

differences by the federal system and the vested interests of provincial governments; and the lack of information and awareness of the regions of Canada about one another and about national affairs. The results are that Canadians often do not share a strong sense of belonging together, and regional or provincial interests frequently take precedence over those of the nation.

Nation-Building and Contemporary Politics

Canadians today have, on the whole, accepted that theirs is a nation of differences. This willingness to accept diversity may well be one of the distinguishing marks of the Canadian national identity – a contrast to the pressures towards conformity that characterize other national cultures. However, potential dangers lie in store for the Canadian nation-state when these latent cleavages become politicized.

Some of the most bitter recent debates among Canadian politicians, including the long-drawn-out wrangling over constitutional patriation, reflect the persistence of divisions among regions and between the two founding nations. Memories, real or reconstructed, of anglophone oppression fuelled the nationalist aspirations of the Parti Québécois as it launched its quest to lead Québec out of Confederation. Though based on a sense of physical and political marginality rather than ethnic discontent, similar resentment against "the Centre" or "the East" underlies a potential separatist threat in the West, where the Western Canada Concept represented the most extreme form of a generalized feeling of "western alienation".[33] Further, a combination of regional economic disparities, perceived historical grievances and (in some cases) a sense of physical remoteness often exacerbates tensions among the provinces and between the provinces and the federal government.

Relations between the various levels of government and the Canadian Native populations also reflect the impact of what might be called "the unfinished nation-building process" on contemporary politics. The relative isolation of most of the indigenous groups, whether on reservations or in the far north, is gradually being broken down by the expansion of state activity and by the ongoing process of economic development. Whether they wish it or not, the Native people have increasingly been drawn into the mainstream of economic and political life. As they have become more politicized, they have introduced new political issues with which governments are inadequately prepared to cope. Consequently, pressures for and conflict over increased self-government in the North and the settlement of Native land claims are likely to intensify over the coming decades.

In a country as large and diverse as Canada, it may be unrealistic to expect the process of nation-building to have eradicated all differences or integrated all disparities. As Chapter 3 will argue, certain overarching values and attitudes

---

[33]See various articles in Larry Pratt and Garth Stevenson, eds., *Western Separatism: The Myths, Realities and Dangers* (Edmonton: Hurtig, 1981).

shared by all Canadians have developed which partially counterbalance the potentially disintegrative effects of regionalism and ethnic differences. But the historic rivalries remain. Chapter 6 will discuss in detail the continued impact of these divisions upon the contemporary politics of Canadian federalism. Perhaps, when all is said and done, one of the fascinations of Canadian politics for political scientists and outside observers lies in the fact that Canada has survived for as long as it has, despite the persistence of strains and conflicts left unresolved by the nation-building process.

Problems of State-Building: The Acquisition of External Sovereignty

We have already outlined, in "The Expansion of the Canadian Nation-State" above, the enlargement of Canada's territory in the years immediately following Confederation. By 1873, Canada's borders were established virtually as they are today, with the exception of the Alaska/British Columbia boundary, settled in 1903, and the addition of Newfoundland in 1949. But while the boundaries of the Canadian Dominion were defined early in its history, the acquisition of sovereignty over the territory enclosed by them was a somewhat slower process.

The major task was the establishment of external sovereignty. This process was naturally linked to Canada's gradual acquisition of independence from Britain, the former colonial power. The quest for external sovereignty in fact began even before Confederation, as the elected assemblies of the British North American colonies strove for some measure of responsible self-government within the context of Britain's colonial administration. Progress was slow. Between 1758 (in the case of Nova Scotia) and 1791 (Lower Canada), each of the colonies was granted what might be called a popularly elected assembly. The early years of these assemblies saw them dominated by the respective Governors and their appointed Executive and Legislative Councils. By the time Lord Durham recommended the political union of Upper and Lower Canada under "responsible government" in his Report of 1838, the power of the Governors was under strenuous attack. Although the first of Lord Durham's recommendations, the Act of Union, was implemented by the British government, the second, responsible government, was initially ignored. But the first Governor of the new united colony of Canada, Lord Sydenham, combined his gubernatorial duties with those of Prime Minister and leader of his own party of adherents, appealing directly to the population to provide his followers a majority in assembly elections. This practice was also followed by other colonial Governors, but eventually proved to be counter-productive since the "appeal to the electorate worked in the end to confirm that power resided, in part at least, in the people, and not solely in the crown."[34]

---

[34]Thomas A. Hockin, *Government in Canada* (Toronto: McGraw-Hill Ryerson, 1976), p. 6.

In 1846, a change in the British government produced an administration more sympathetic to responsible government in the colonies, and newly appointed Governors of Canada and Nova Scotia were instructed in 1847 to select their Councils from the leaders of the majority factions or parties in their respective assemblies. Within a year, non-confidence motions passed in the popular assemblies resulted in changes of ministries in united Canada, Nova Scotia and New Brunswick.

In this fashion, the principle of responsible government, whereby the Governor retained his advisors only as long as they were collectively able to retain majority support in the assembly, became established in British North America. The next stage in the development of representative and responsible self-government occurred over the next decade with the effective separation of the political executive ("Cabinet") from the formal executive (the Governor). Governors increasingly absented themselves from the deliberations of their political advisors, while acting upon their recommendations.

Thus, even before Confederation, the Canadian colonies had achieved a moderate degree of self-government through the development of responsible government and parliamentary democracy. But their assemblies and governments were not sovereign; there were constraints upon their autonomy and on the supremacy of their parliamentary institutions. When the British North American colonies were each granted assemblies in the 18th century, they were given the power to legislate on local matters, subject to two conditions: first, that they did not attempt to enact laws having effect outside their territorial boundaries and second, that their laws did not contravene the established law of England. The latter restriction was alleviated by the *Colonial Laws Validity Act* of 1865, which stated that only those British statutes which applied specifically or by implication to the colony concerned could invalidate local legislation.

Obstacles to the outright independence of governmental institutions obtained, even after the creation of the new Dominion in 1867. First, legislative competence within Canada was divided and apportioned to two different levels of government: some powers were given to the federal or Dominion Parliament; others were allotted to provincial governments or legislatures. Although this in itself did not directly affect the external sovereignty of the Canadian state, it did have an indirect impact, in that neither the federal division of powers nor any other provisions of the *BNA Act* could be amended by any Canadian legislature, but only by the British Parliament. Moreover, the creation of separate fields of legislative competence had important consequences for internal state-building.

As well, certain matters were withheld from all levels of government in Canada. In particular, legislation having extraterritorial effect (such as laws pertaining to copyright or to merchant shipping) was reserved exclusively for the United Kingdom Parliament. In similar vein, the Canadian government was not regarded as an independent actor in the world of international relations. For over fifty years after Confederation, Canada was effectively an appendage of the United Kingdom when it came to the conduct of diplomatic affairs, which remained the exclusive preserve of the British government.

Third, even within the legal competence of Canadian federal or provincial legislatures, parliamentary supremacy could be overridden by the powers of reservation given to the Governor General and the Lieutenant Governors (as representatives of the Crown in Canada) and by the powers of disallowance retained by the British government.

These factors and others (for example, the retention until 1949 of the Judicial Committee of the Privy Council in the United Kingdom as the highest court of appeal, a device which permitted substantial outside meddling in Canada's internal affairs) combined to maintain Canada in a quasi-colonial relationship with Britain long after the nominal achievement of self-government at the time of Confederation.

In the present century, however, two major periods of constitutional change, some fifty years apart, have served to secure Canada's *de facto* and *de jure* independence from the United Kingdom.

The first series of events revolved around the Imperial Conferences of 1926 and 1930, culminating in the 1931 Statute of Westminster. At the Imperial Conference of 1930, the disallowance and reservation powers of the British government and the Governor General were declared constitutionally obsolete. They had, in any case, long ceased to be of much practical relevance. The Statute of Westminster paved the way for the Dominions to emerge as independent foreign-policy actors by stating that a Dominion Parliament had full power to make laws having extraterritorial operation. (It should be remarked that, a few years earlier, Canada had already negotiated and signed its first treaty with the United States, the Halibut Treaty of 1923, after the King gave specific permission to do so.) A further provision of the Statute laid down that the United Kingdom Parliament no longer had the right to legislate for any Dominion except at the request of the Dominion concerned – for example, by way of a petition to amend the *BNA Act.*

These changes highlight the role of the Statute of Westminster as the watershed between the effective ending of colonial status for the Dominions and their emergence as more-or-less independent nation-states. According to the historian A.R.M. Lower,

> "The Statute of Westminster came as close as was practicable without
> revolutionary scissors to legislating the independence of the 'Dominions'.
> There is good ground for holding December 11, 1931 as Canada's
> Independence Day, for on that day she became a sovereign state."[35]

However, Lower slightly exaggerates the significance of the Statute of Westminster. There is no doubt that it was important for all the Dominions, but in the case of Canada reminders of the colonial heritage lingered, despite Canada's emergence as an international actor in its own right.

Some more colonial remnants were removed in 1949. The Supreme Court

---

[35]Arthur R.M. Lower, *Colony to Nation: A History of Canada,* 4th edition revised (Don Mills, Ontario: Longmans Canada, 1964), p. 489.

replaced the Judicial Committee of the British Privy Council as Canada's highest court of appeal. In addition, the *British North America (No. 2) Act* of 1949 permitted the Parliament of Canada to amend certain portions of the *Act* without recourse to Westminster. However, in order to achieve Constitutional reforms, it was still necessary for the Canadian government to go cap-in-hand to Westminster to seek amending legislation from the United Kingdom Parliament. While Westminster was traditionally willing to accede to any such requests from Canada, the necessity remained a limitation to Canada's self-determination.

Thus, one of the dominant political issues of the 1970s was Prime Minister Pierre Trudeau's almost personal crusade to patriate the Canadian Constitution – a quest which finally came to fruition with the passage of the *Canada Act* by the British parliament in 1982. At last, Canada, like other sovereign states, had its own Constitution and was able to determine its internal political structure without reference to external authorities. In formal terms at least, it was the year 1982, over half a century after the Statute of Westminster and 115 years from Confederation, which marked the final stage in Canada's evolution from colony to sovereign nation-state.

External Sovereignty and Contemporary Politics

The final, formal severance of ties with the United Kingdom does not mean, however, that Canadian governments can now do just as they please. In the modern era, increasing interdependence among nation-states and national economies has severely constrained the capacity of governments to act independently of all external pressures. This is especially the case for countries which have a high degree of economic integration with a larger, more powerful neighbour.

While Canada is a genuinely sovereign nation-state in international law, the nature of its relationship with the United States imposes limits upon government policy-making. Canada's defence policy is conducted within the context of the NATO alliance, in which the United States is the largest single actor – a position it uses to attempt to sway the policies of its partners. Canadian fiscal and budgetary policies are heavily influenced by American interest rates and by capital flows between the two countries. Energy and industrial policies have to take into account American ownership of Canadian branch-plants and American investment in Canadian resources. The success of Canadian environmental policy is partly dependent upon the extent to which American governments can be persuaded to impose their own controls on the emission of industrial pollutants which cause acid rain. Even attempts to formulate a "made in Canada" cultural policy are hampered by the accessibility of Canadian homes to American television and radio stations and by American domination in the fields of film production and book and magazine publishing. Thus, contemporary issues of external sovereignty now revolve, not around Canadian/British, but around Canadian/American relations (to be further examined in Chapter 14).

Internal State-Building in the 19th Century

In contrast to the long, drawn-out process of Canada's acquisition of external sovereignty, the initial stages of internal state-building were quite rapid. After the political unification of the four original provinces in 1867 and the subsequent expansion of Canada's territory, it was imperative to integrate this vast area as far as possible into a cohesive, governable political entity. The three major components in this late-19th century integration process were the imposition of law and order over the entire territory; the development of means of communication; and attempts to create a viable national economy.

One of the key characteristics of the modern state is the government's ability to ensure that its laws are obeyed and, where necessary, to utilize its "monopoly of the legitimate use of physical force" in order to maintain its authority. Since the birth of the Dominion, Canadian governments have not been averse to using large-scale coercion when deemed necessary. On at least four occasions – the Riel Rebellions of 1870-71 and 1885, the Winnipeg General Strike of 1919, and the 1970 October Crisis – large numbers of police and troops have been mobilized to crush perceived or actual uprisings against the Canadian state.

However, the major symbol of central authority in much of Canada in the late 19th century was the red coat of the Mountie. Four years after the annexation of lands from the Hudson's Bay Company in 1869, the North West Mounted Police force (later, the Royal Canadian Mounted Police or RCMP) was created to impose a uniform code of law on the territories. For this reason, unlike the United States at the same period, Canada never had a "wild west" frontier. The Mounties were responsible for keeping the peace in all the federally administered lands stretching from the American border to the Arctic and between Hudson Bay and the Rocky Mountains. To a more limited degree, the RCMP still maintains a federal presence throughout Canada today. In addition to its tasks of enforcing federal laws everywhere, acting as the sole police force in the two remaining territories, and until recently providing for Canada's internal security, the force is under contract to perform provincial policing functions in every province except Ontario and Québec.

The second medium of internal state-building in the new Dominion was the improvement of communications among its provinces and regions. In such a large state, an efficient system of transportation was necessary – for security purposes, for the movement of mail and other sources of information and for economic reasons. In the second half of the 19th century, the most efficient form of transport for all such purposes was the railway. Thus, one of the conditions under which New Brunswick and Nova Scotia were willing to join Confederation was that a railway be built linking Halifax and the Saint John valley to the St. Lawrence. The construction of this "Intercolonial Railway" was actually enshrined in the original *BNA Act* as one of the duties of the Dominion government.[36]

---

[36]*British North America Act,* section 145 – repealed in 1893 after the government had fulfilled its duty.

Communications became even more of a challenge as the Dominion grew from sea to sea, with vast distances separating eastern Canada from the new province of British Columbia (which had also been promised a railway connection as a means of luring it into Confederation). The building of a transcontinental railway consequently became one of the most important political issues and objectives of Canada's first twenty years. Through a mixture of governmental intervention and private enterprise, Canada's railway system slowly took shape, highlighted by the completion of the transcontinental Canadian Pacific Railway when the famous "last spike" was driven in 1885.[37]

In contemporary Canada, when air travel and instantaneous communications are taken for granted, it may be easy to underestimate the importance of the railway system to the economic and political integration of the 19th century Dominion. But, although we have given it separate emphasis, railway construction was also very much a part of the third aspect of 19th century state-building. The so-called "National Policy", first publicized by John A. Macdonald in the general election campaign of 1878, became the basis for Canada's economic development for the next fifty years. The National Policy consisted of three interrelated objectives: the development of a comprehensive railway system (already discussed); the opening up of western Canada through the encouragement of immigration, settlement and agriculture on the prairies; and national economic development through protection of Canadian industries by means of an external tariff.

In order to realize the dream of a Dominion stretching *ad mare usque ad mare*, and also to forestall the danger of United States expansionism into western Canada, it was deemed necessary for Canadians to populate the vast open plains between Manitoba (at that time little more than the area around Winnipeg) and British Columbia. The government therefore opened the door to immigrants, largely from Central and Eastern Europe, who were willing to settle and farm on the prairies, and gave them land grants and financial aid to help them become established. Of course, the railways were of great importance to such settlement, particularly for the transportation of wheat and other prairie products to consumer markets in the east and to the coasts for export abroad.

At the same time, the Macdonald government attempted to develop other sectors of the Canadian economy. In particular, the high rate of emigration from Canada in the 1870s brought home the realization that Canada required secondary or manufacturing industries in order to provide jobs for its non-agricultural labour force. But such emerging industries required protection from more advanced foreign competition. Interprovincial tariffs had already been removed to aid the free flow of raw materials and goods within Canada. Now, as the third plank of the National Policy, the government imposed an external tariff designed to reduce the flow of imports (especially certain manufactured products) into the

---

[37]See Pierre Berton's detailed history of the transcontinental railway in *The National Dream: The Great Railway 1871-1881* and *The Last Spike: The Great Railway 1881-1885* (Toronto: McClelland and Stewart, 1970 and 1971).

country. Ironically, while this move was intended to increase Canada's economic independence, it may have had the opposite effect in the long run. British and American companies, faced with a tariff on goods sold to Canada from outside, started to set up branch plants inside the country. So began the pattern of foreign ownership of Canadian industry which has become a major political and economic issue in the present day.[38] However, the abolition of internal trade barriers and the creation of the tariff did aid indigenous economic development in certain industries. As well, in combination with the new railways, it increased the volume of east-west trade within Canada at the expense of north-south trade with the United States. These measures taken together therefore represented a major step towards the emergence of Canada as a national economic community.

The National Policy was an explicit attempt by Canadian governments of the late 19th century to enhance the economic and political integration of the Dominion. To a certain extent, it was as important for its symbolic contribution to nationalism and independence as for its contribution to Canada's economic development;[39] in fact, its economic impact has recently come under critical re-evaluation by historians and political scientists.[40] But the National Policy is also noteworthy in that it represented the first major incursion of the state into economic life in Canada, an influence of increasing importance to Canadians in the 20th century.

THE GROWTH OF THE STATE IN THE 20TH CENTURY

One of the traits of the nation-state in the 20th century has been the seemingly inexorable growth of the role of the state in the lives of its citizens. Whether this phenomenon is referred to as the growth of the state, the expanding sphere of government or the enlargement of the public sector, it appears to be common to all nation-states, particularly the industrial societies of the western world. The author of a recent study of increasing government expenditure in sixteen western democracies introduces his subject with this observation:

> "Government, it seems safe to say, is one thing that has been growing rapidly in the West. Wherever governments were once small they have become big and wherever they were big they have become bigger. Nothing is so rare as a shrinking government."[41]

---

[38]Micheal Bliss, "Canadianizing American business: the roots of the branch plant," in Lumsden, ed., *Close the 49th Parallel,* pp. 26-42.

[39]Craig Brown, "The nationalism of the national policy," in Russell, ed., *Nationalism in Canada,* pp. 155-163.

[40]For an overview of some of the critiques of the National Policy, see Michael Bliss, " 'Rich by Nature, Poor by Policy': The State and Economic Life in Canada," in R.K. Carty and W.P. Ward, eds., *Entering the Eighties: Canada in Crisis* (Toronto: Oxford University Press, 1980), especially pp. 78-81.

[41]Warren G. Nutter, *Growth of Government in the West* (Washington, D.C.: American Enterprise Institute for Public Policy Research, 1978), p. 1.

In the second half of the 19th century, when the Canadian state began to take shape, the role of government was everywhere considerably more limited than today.[42] The main functions of central state institutions were providing for external defence and for the maintenance of internal law and order, conducting foreign policy and trade relations, managing the currency and the national debt and perhaps overseeing a few services such as the postal system and harbour and navigation facilities. Additional tasks were performed by local or municipal authorities: building and maintaining roads, ensuring a water supply and employing local law enforcement officers. Municipalities might also provide for some elementary education and minimal health care and social services, although these were more often the preserve of private, charitable or religious organizations. In brief, in the 19th century, there were no major welfare state programs.

In many contemporary societies, the state now offers free education to all students under eighteen and often subsidizes university and college education; provides massive medical care, unemployment and old age pension programs; and has become involved in a wide variety of other social welfare policies ranging from family allowances to low-cost public housing. In addition, it has become increasingly important in the economic sphere: as an owner and entrepreneur in resource development, transportation and other nationalized industries; as a regulator of both the public and the private sector; and as a manager of the national economy, through economic and regional planning, intervention in the capital and credit markets, budgetary policy and its own spending decisions. Consequently, in many western societies, total government expenditure *per annum* is fast approaching, and in some cases (for example, Sweden and the Netherlands) actually exceeds 50 percent of the GNP.

This last point – government expenditure as a percentage of GNP – raises the question of how the growth of the state can be measured in real terms. As the state has expanded its activities, so government expenditure has grown. Of course, even if a government continued to perform exactly the same functions over time, expenditure in money terms would increase as the cost of goods, labour and services purchased by the government also grew, especially in inflationary times. Therefore, when an attempt is made to measure the growth of government expenditure (and the growth of the state) in real terms, it is usually expressed as a proportion of the country's GNP or some other indicator of national income, expenditure or product. As well, the growth of the role of the state can be measured in terms of the increase in governmental activities: the number of new programs adopted by the government, the number of new laws and regulations; the statutes establishing new public corporations or nationalized industries. A third way of expressing the growth of the state is in terms of the actual size of government, that is, either the number of governmental organizations or the percentage of the labour force employed by the state. Lastly, these government activities and employees must be paid for; the state must have revenues in

---

[42]See, for example, the very limited number of functions listed under federal and provincial jurisdictions in the original *British North America Act* (1867), Sections 91 and 92.

order to meet its expenditures (despite the tendency towards budgetary deficits displayed by many governments in recent years). Thus, a final indicator of the growing role of the state is the size of government revenues, especially those accruing from the taxation of individual and corporate citizens. Once more, this is usually expressed as a percentage of the GNP or other national income statistics.

The Extent of the State in Canada

To this point, we have been using the terms "government" (in the singular) and "state" more or less interchangeably. Doing so is quite reasonable when discussing "the state" in abstract terms, or when referring to centralized unitary countries like Britain, France or Sweden in which most state activities are performed by a single level of government and the majority of public expenditure is centrally funded and controlled. In the Canadian context, however, things are slightly different. As in other federal systems, the functions of the state in Canada are shared among two major levels of government, federal and provincial, and a third, minor, tier, local or municipal government. Thus, a definition of the extent of the Canadian state, and the measurement of its growth, must take into account activities, expenditures, organizations and employment in all three government levels.

Once it is accepted that the Canadian state consists of multiple layers of government, rather than a single hierarchical structure, an additional problem arises: How much of each layer are we to take into consideration as part of the state?[43] In order to get a complete picture of the growing role of the state or the size of the public sector in contemporary society, we must include not only the regular government departments in each tier (in other words, the "civil service" component), but also the numerous federal and provincial regulatory boards and commissions, Crown corporations and other public enterprises, as well as the so-called "parapublic" service, in particular the health care and educational sectors. Indeed, as suggested earlier, the very proliferation of these "non civil service" bodies may be used as one indicator of the expansion of state influence.

Before we attempt to measure the growth and current extent of state activities in terms of the various indicators suggested above, it will be useful to outline briefly the ongoing process of state-building in Canada in the 20th century which has given birth to the present "interventionist state".

The Interventionist State

Internal state-building in Canada since the National Policy has been more complex than in many nation-states because of the federal nature of the political system. Rather than a simple one-to-one relationship between unitary state and

---

[43]The problem, even for government policy-makers, of specifying the boundaries of the state (or the "public sector") is well-illustrated by the discussion in Dan Butler and Bruce D. Macnaughton, "Public Sector Growth in Canada: Issues, Explanations and Implications," in Whittington and Williams, eds., *Canadian Politics in the 1980s,* especially pp. 87-89.

society, Canadian state-building has consisted of a trilateral relationship between society, federal institutions and the set of provincial governments. Thus, while the term "defensive expansion" was coined to describe the growing role of the Canadian state to defend Canada's political autonomy and economic independence *vis-à-vis* external rivals[44], it is equally applicable to the expansion of provincial government activity in the face of potential federal encroachment. Competition between the particularistic objectives of province-building and the centralizing bias of federal state-building has served to aggravate existing regional conflicts and the broader context of federal/provincial relations. Despite these complexities, political institutions have assumed an increasingly activist role in Canadian society and the economy.

The initial thrust of state intervention in Canada was primarily economic. As the example of the National Policy indicates, the role of the state was originally conceived as one of indirect intervention (through taxes, land grants, *etc.*) to provide the infrastructure and other conditions conducive to private sector economic development. In the 20th century, however, the state has intervened more directly in the economy, especially through public ownership of Crown corporations. The federal government takeover of Canadian National Railways in 1917 was followed in the 1930s by the establishment of the Canadian Radio Broadcasting Committee (now the CBC), the Bank of Canada and Trans Canada Airlines (later Air Canada); more modern examples include Atomic Energy of Canada Limited (1952), Telesat Canada (1969) and Petro-Canada (1976). Public ownership has also played a major role in provincial "state-building", beginning with Ontario Hydro (1906) and other provincial utility companies. Now, provinces are involved in transportation (Alberta's Pacific Western Airlines), natural resources (Québec's National Asbestos Corporation or the Potash Corporation of Saskatchewan) and, with mixed success, the promotion of industrial development (Nova Scotia's Industrial Estates Limited, New Brunswick's ill-fated Bricklin sportscar enterprise).

But while Canadian state institutions have a long history of intervention in the economic sector, the development of social policies leading to the current welfare state system occurred relatively late. This tardiness has been attributed to the delayed nature of Canada's industrial revolution; to the weakness and late emergence of the working class as an organized political force; to the strength of the business community in restricting the role of the state to promotion and protection of its own interests; and to the peculiarly Canadian form of conservatism, which reconciled strong state leadership of the economy with private responsibility (through family or community) for individual social welfare. With the last point in mind, it is perhaps not surprising that many innovations in social policy have been led by provincial governments in the prairies, where frontier isolation created a somewhat more collectivist culture.

---

[44]Henry G.J. Aitken, "Defensive Expansion: The State and Economic Growth in Canada," in W.T. Easterbrook and M.H. Watkins, eds., *Approaches to Canadian Economic History* (Toronto: McClelland and Stewart, 1967), pp. 183-221.

Although some programs had already been introduced earlier (for example, Workmen's Compensation in almost every province by 1920 or the federal government's Old Age Pension legislation of 1927), it was not really until the period between 1930 and 1945 that the Canadian welfare state began to take shape.[45] The combined impact of the depression and the Second World War created a climate more conducive to social intervention by both federal and provincial governments. A number of factors have been cited as contributing to this change: the growing militancy of western farmers and industrial workers in the depression; the threat posed to government parties by the electoral successes of the CCF in the early 1940s; the inability of municipalities and private welfare agencies to cope with the demand for relief during the depression; the emergence of a more collectivist national spirit induced by the shared tribulations of economic disaster and world war; and reduced opposition from a business community which saw that its interests might be served, rather than hampered, by welfare legislation. At first, the federal government provided a series of temporary relief measures to alleviate poverty in the depression, but more permanent legislation followed, especially in the fields of unemployment insurance (1940) and family allowances (1944).

Since the Second World War, both federal and provincial governments have introduced many programs into the welfare state system, including Medicare and hospital insurance, the Canada and Québec Pension Plans, housing policies, grants for higher education and guaranteed income supplements, among others. Total government spending at all levels on welfare state policies (health, education and social welfare) has risen from less than 10 percent of the GNP in the mid-1940s to approximately 25 percent in 1980. But from a state-building perspective, it may be argued that it was in the decade preceding 1945 that the major shift in perception of the role of the state occurred, allowing Canada to join the ranks of the "welfare societies". Canadians began to view poverty less as a sign of individual weakness, and more as a social problem whose alleviation could be beneficial to the rest of society and which therefore came to be regarded as a responsibility of the Canadian state.

Once governmental responsibility for social welfare functions was accepted, as it had already been for economic development, the last major step in the state-building process was accomplished. Since that time, the role of the state (or "government", or "public sector") in Canadian society has never ceased to expand.

The Growth of the Canadian State: Some Indicators

The most commonly employed measure of the growth of the state in Canada and elsewhere is the percentage of Gross National Expenditure (equivalent to GNP) spent by the various levels of government and associated organizations which constitute the state or the public sector. As the graph in Figure 2.4 indicates, this

---

[45]Support for this view comes from Alvin Finkle, "Origins of the Welfare State in Canada," in L.V. Panitch, ed., *The Canadian State: Political Economy and Political Power* (Toronto: University of Toronto Press, 1977), pp. 344-370.

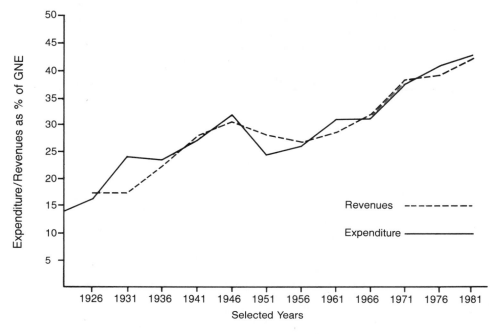

FIGURE 2.4 The Growth of Public Expenditure and Government Revenues as Proportions of GNE – Selected Years, 1926 - 1981

Source: Adapted from Tables 2.1 and 2.2, below.

proportion has increased from 15.7 percent in 1926 to 42.5 percent in 1981. However, this rate of growth has been by no means constant. There have been distinct periods of growth, when the increase in government spending clearly outdistanced the rise in GNE – for example, in the period from 1926 to 1931 when GNE actually declined during the depression, in the war years and in the late 1960s and early 1970s. On the other hand, public expenditure decreased as a percentage of GNE in the mid-1930s and in the postwar years, while in the late 1970s a large increase in public expenditure in money terms was counterbalanced by a similar rise in GNE to produce a levelling off in "real" government spending.

As Table 2.1 demonstrates, the growth in overall public expenditure disguises substantial shifts in the relative importance of different levels of government. Fifty years ago, local and municipal governments were the biggest spenders, since they were primarily responsible for financing education and the limited social welfare functions which then existed. With local and provincial governments unable to cope with demands on their budgets during the depression, the federal government began to expand; it continued to do so in order to meet the costs of the war effort. Since the mid-1960s – somewhat ironically in view of the harsh criticism of federal spending habits recently voiced by provincial politicians – it has been at the provincial level that the largest increase in expenditure has occurred. However, it is also true that in recent years federal

TABLE 2.1 The Growth of Public Expenditure by Level of Government (excluding intergovernmental transfers), as Percentage of GNE – Selected Years, 1926-1981

Year	Level of Government					Total
	Federal	*Provincial*	*Local*	*Hospitals*	*CPP/QPP*[1]	
1926	5.9	3.2	6.6	—	—	15.7
1931	7.5	6.4	9.9	—	—	23.8
1936	7.9	8.0	7.5	—	—	23.5
1941	18.1	4.6	4.3	—	—	27.0
1946	22.7	4.6	4.2	—	—	31.6
1951	13.6	5.6	5.0	—	—	24.2
1956	14.4	5.5	5.8	—	—	25.6
1961	15.3	6.1	7.4	2.0	—	30.8
1966	13.1	7.3	8.2	2.2	0.0	30.8
1971	13.8	11.1	9.3	2.8	0.2	37.2
1976	15.8	12.1	8.7	3.1	0.6	40.2
1981	17.5	12.4	8.5	3.0	1.0	42.5

[1]CPP/QPP — Canada and Québec Pension Plans

Source: Calculated from Statistics Canada, *National Income and Expenditure Accounts,* various issues, (Ottawa: Information Canada or Supply and Services, various dates).

spending has risen substantially in dollar terms. In 1984-85 the federal government spent $98 billion, compared with $13 billion in 1971, and the federal deficit of $20.4 billion was nearly three times the entire federal budget of about 23 years earlier.

Of course, government expenditure has to be paid for out of revenues. Table 2.2 demonstrates that the growth of the state can also be indicated by the share of GNE which is received by governments through taxation, public enterprise earnings or other revenues. Like expenditures, the revenues of all levels of government have more than doubled as a percentage of GNE over the last half century, from 16.8 percent in 1926 to 41.8 percent in 1981. Again, there was a much slower growth rate in the 1970s. The federal government's decision to index the personal income tax structure in 1973 may help explain this period's reduced rate of growth in public expenditure.

Not all state activity is measurable in terms of public expenditure. While many public policies do require the outlay of money, others need very little – particularly those which seek to regulate or control the behaviour of either individual or corporate members of society. Thus, as the state has become more involved in its citizens' lives, the volume of legislation, statutes and regulations has increased. This aspect of the growth of the Canadian state was aptly summarized by former Conservative Justice Minister Senator Jacques Flynn in a speech to the Canadian Bar Association in 1979.

"We recently published a consolidation of federal regulations – 15,563 pages of them. Add to that 10,000 pages of Revised Statutes (Canada's

TABLE 2.2 Government Revenues by Level of Government (excluding intergovernmental transfers), as Percentage of GNE — Selected Years, 1926-1981

Year	Level of Government					Total
	Federal	*Provincial*	*Local*	*Hospitals*	*CPP/QPP[1]*	
1926	7.6	3.0	6.3	—	—	16.8
1931	5.3	4.0	7.8	—	—	17.2
1936	9.1	5.8	7.9	—	—	22.2
1941	18.4	4.7	4.7	—	—	27.7
1946	22.1	4.6	3.7	—	—	30.4
1951	19.2	5.3	3.4	—	—	28.0
1956	17.8	4.9	3.8	—	—	26.5
1961	17.1	6.4	5.0	0.1	—	28.7
1966	16.1	9.4	4.8	0.1	1.2	31.6
1971	18.3	12.5	5.0	0.1	1.6	37.4
1976	18.6	13.6	4.5	0.1	1.7	38.5
1981	19.5	15.6	4.5	0.1	2.0	41.8

[1]CPP/QPP – Canada and Québec Pension Plans

Source: Calculated from Statistics Canada, *National Income and Expenditure Accounts,* various issues, (Ottawa: Information Canada or Supply and Services, various dates).

Statutes were last revised and consolidated in 1970) and 8,000 to 10,000 pages of Statutes since the revision, plus hundreds of thousands of pages of provincial laws and regulations to say nothing of municipal by-laws, orders and regulations. Now you begin to realize that we've come a long way from 10 clauses on a slab of stone."[46]

Finally, as the state has increasingly intervened in social and economic life and accounted for a growing proportion of Canada's Gross National Expenditure, so the actual machinery of government has become more complex. The number of federal government departments and branches quadrupled between 1870 and 1985. There are now well over 400 federal government Crown corporations and agencies, of which almost 50 percent have been created since 1970.[47] Even local government has become increasingly complex, as residents of cities like Vancouver, Toronto and Montréal will readily acknowledge. One study of Metropolitan Toronto identified 101 different agencies and units involved in the administration of the area.[48] Similarly, the number of people employed by the

---

[46]Quoted by Donald John Purich, "Too Many Laws? There may not be enough!," *The Chronicle-Herald,* Halifax, February 2, 1980.

[47]Allan Tupper and G. Bruce Doern, *Public Corporations and Public Policy in Canada* (Montréal, Institute for Research on Public Policy, 1981), Chapter 1.

[48]Dominic Del Guidice and Stephen M. Zachs, "The 101 Governments of Metro Toronto," in L.D. Feldman and M.D. Goldrick, *Politics and Government of Urban Canada,* 3rd edition (Toronto: Methuen, 1976), pp. 285-295.

Reprinted with permission, Alan King, The Citizen, Ottawa.

The controversial recommendations of the 1985 Royal Commission on the Economic Union and Development Prospects for Canada (the Macdonald Commission) will help structure the debate on Canada's economic development in the coming decades.

state has also grown: in 1961, there were an estimated 337 000 civilian employees in federal departments and Crown agencies, compared with over half a million twenty years later. As in the case of public expenditure, however, the "real" growth in terms of the percentage of total employment in the public sector has been relatively much smaller.[49]

Whichever indicators we may choose, it is unarguable that the state has grown in Canada over the last century – or even the last twenty years – although when measured in real terms this expansion is by no means as large as some critics of government intervention would suggest. Still, the question remains, How do we account for the growth of the state?

---

[49]Richard M. Bird *et al.*, *The Growth of Public Employment in Canada* (Scarborough, Ontario: Butterworths, for the Institute for Research on Public Policy, 1979), p. 43.

The Growth of the State: Some Explanations

Why has the state, or government in general, or the public sector, grown in Canada? So many authors have attempted to explain the growth of the state in Canada that, according to Richard Bird,

> "the problem is not that there are *no* explanations of the growth of government in Canada since the war: it is rather that there are too many explanations, each one of which probably contains both some truth and some misleading elements."[50]

In the following discussion, we focus on the more pertinent among this plethora of potential explanations advanced by numerous authors.[51]

Many accounts of the growth of the state are essentially apolitical in that they view the expansion of the role of government as a product of exogenous (externally determined) forces. For example, it may be posited that the growth and changing age structure of the population call for increased state activity. More expenditure and more government personnel are needed to provide even a fixed level of services to a larger number of people, and the fact that more people are living longer necessitates more services to provide old age pensions and health care for the aged. Alternatively, the vast technological development undergone by Canadian society in the last century may be said to have increased the scope for government intervention. At the time of Confederation, the invention or discovery of the automobile, airplane, nuclear power and television, for instance, was undreamed of. The coming of the motor vehicle alone has given rise to a great variety of government activity: road building and maintenance, traffic laws, seatbelt legislation, driver and vehicle licensing, exhaust emission controls, vehicle safety regulations, regulation of the trucking industry and much more.

But the growth of the state is *not* the direct consequence of demographic change or technological innovation; these are background factors at best, which merely create increased potential for state intervention. The current extent of state activity *is* the result of an extensive series of political decisions – to increase public expenditure on a particular item, to move into a new functional area, to create another regulatory agency – each one taken by politicians or senior bureaucrats acting in the context of the political process. Therefore, although the number of people over 65 already exceeded 5 percent of the population in 1901 (compared with around 9 percent today), it was another quarter-century before pensions were introduced for some people over the age of 70, and fifty years be-

---

[50]Richard M. Bird, *Financing Canadian Government: A Quantitative Overview* (Toronto: Canada Tax Foundation, 1979), p. 82. (Emphasis in original.)

[51]For a more comprehensive discussion, see Richard M. Bird, *The Growth of Government Spending in Canada* (Toronto: Canada Tax Foundation, 1970), Part II, Chapters 4-7. For briefer overviews, see Bird, *Financing Canadian Government*, Chapter 7; Bird *et al.*, *The Growth of Public Employment in Canada*, Chapter 8; Butler and Macnaughton, "Public Sector Growth in Canada", pp. 97-102; James Gillies, *Where Business Fails: Business-Government Relations at the Federal Level in Canada* (Montréal: Institute for Research on Public Policy, 1981), pp. 5-7.

fore pensions were granted to those over 65. Similarly, while the introduction of legislation making the wearing of a seat belt compulsory would be senseless if the automobile had not been invented, people had been driving cars on Canadian roads for over half a century before being instructed to "belt up".

Since the state is first and foremost a political phenomenon, many attempts to explain its growth focus on the bureaucratic and political forces which underlie its activities.

It is sometimes argued that bureaucrats judge their success by the growth rate of their departments, as regards budgets, number of employees and volume of programs administered. Although the proposition smacks of individual self-interest or "empire-building", such may not be the case. A more benevolent view might ascribe it to genuine concern for a bureaucracy's target population or to a response to political pressures. The dominant modes and structures of policy-making in state bureaucracies may also play a part, especially with respect to the growth of public spending. Incremental decision-making, in which "this year's budget is based on last year's budget, with special attention given only to a narrow range of increase or decrease"[52] has predominated in the budgetary process over much of the past century. Consequently, consideration is rarely given to abolition of or serious cutbacks in programs. The nature of the incremental budgetary process also militates against a department's accepting even a minor decrease in its allocation or leaving any portion of its budget unspent, for fear that those funds will be permanently lost in future years. While attempts have been made to reform the budgetary process in recent years it has proven difficult to counterbalance the natural tendency towards continued expansion of public expenditure. (Budgetary reform is covered extensively in Chapters 9 and 13.)

Unfortunately, the role of political ideas or ideologies is sometimes overlooked in explorations of the political decisions underlying the growth of the state. First, it may be argued that an interventionist role for the state has traditionally been considered legitimate in the diffuse attitudes towards government which comprise Canadian political culture. Canadians do not share the anti-statist liberalism and the free enterprise ethic which predominate in the United States. Even the business community, in other countries often the opponent of state intervention, has tended to "reject free-enterprise *laissez-faire* liberalism in favour of sheltering under the wing of an expansive, interventionist, paternalist government."[53] Thus, according to one author, Canada "is a public enterprise country, always has been, and probably always will be."[54] In the 19th century, the Canadian versions of "Toryism" and nationalism motivated state intervention in the interests of private enterprise and national economic development through the National Policy. Since the Second World War, the acceptance of Keynesian

---

[52]Otto A. David, M.A.H. Dempster and Aaron Wildavsky, "A Theory of the Budgetary Process," *American Political Science Review,* vol. LX, no. 3 (September 1966), pp. 529-530.

[53]Bliss, "The State and Economic Life in Canada," p. 87.

[54]Herschel Hardin, *A Nation Unaware: The Canadian Economic Culture* (Vancouver: J.J. Douglas, 1974), p. 140.

economics (by the general public and, particularly, by policy-makers) and the embracing of a "welfare state ideology" imported from western Europe have served to legitimate an even more interventionist role for the state.

At the more overtly political level of elections, political parties vie with one another to provide the best package of state services for voters. Like detergent manufacturers who rarely cut prices but do offer "20 percent more for the same cost", parties generally tend to offer the electorate more services rather than fewer taxes. In particular, it is suggested that government parties introduce expansionary and expensive programs in the latter stages of their term of office in order to maximize votes, deferring the problem of payment through increased taxation or borrowing until after they have (hopefully!) been re-elected.

Why do political parties compete to expand government services and public expenditure rather than to reduce state intervention and cut tax-rates? One possible answer lies in public expectations of the role of the state in Canada, although, as Richard Bird points out, "The popular postwar ideology that government can – and should – solve most problems is now, however, increasingly being questioned in the face of the strong evidence that it cannot."[55] An alternative suggestion is that support for tax cuts is much more diffuse than opposition to reductions in services – that reductions are more deeply felt and are more likely to be translated into votes against the party proposing such measures. This may especially be the case in Canada where, it has been estimated, approximately 40 percent of the electorate are employed in some way by government and are therefore in favour of public sector expansion and opposed to any reduction of the role of the state.[56]

Last among the political factors is the proposition that the very structure of key political institutions in Canada, expressly the Cabinet system of government and federalism, may militate in favour of the growth of the state. Just as in the bureaucracy "success" may be measured in terms of departmental expansion, so in Cabinet the success or influence of individual ministers may be evaluated by the extent to which they have defended or enhanced the budgets and programs of their departments. Consequently, even if a Cabinet were collectively to commit itself to reducing public expenditure or cutting government services, it would be difficult to find any minister who would say "let us start with my department." Moreover, the federal nature of the Canadian political system may be a contributory factor in accelerating the growth of government as a whole. The apparently competitive relationship between federal and provincial governments leads one to suspect that, as new areas of potential public sector growth have opened up, governments have rushed in, motivated as much by desire to upstage the other level of government as by their concern for the public welfare.

With so many alternatives to choose from, it is perhaps not surprising that no universally accepted explanation of the growth of the Canadian state has emerged. One point upon which a number of authors are agreed is that, while

---

[55]Bird, *Financing Canadian Government*, p. 85.

[56]Don McGillivray, "40% of Canadian Voters are on Government Payroll," *Financial Times of Canada*, Toronto, June 27, 1977.

demographic, technological and economic factors provide the contextual background to the growth of the state, "the key to any satisfactory explanation lies more in the political than in the economic process."[57] However, since the discipline is not yet committed to a commonly accepted general theory of the political process, it is impossible to conclude with certainty which political factors best explain the level of government activity and intervention in any nation-state. Clearly, the solution lies in the complex interaction of political and bureaucratic cultures, institutions and behaviour which together constitute the public policy processes in Canada.

The Politics of the Interventionist State

The growth and the absolute size of the Canadian state both condition contemporary politics and are themselves topics of political debate. As the sphere of government activity expands, so more aspects of everyday life become "political" and greater numbers of individuals and organizations are directly affected by public policies and the political process. In return, popular expectations of what governments can do may be raised, which leads to increased demands on the political system. A consequence, some observers suggest, is that there is a danger that the Canadian political system may become "overloaded", with a resultant inability of its institutions (collectively or individually) to cope with the pressures being placed upon them. Indeed, it may be argued that many of the institutional reforms discussed elsewhere in this book have been undertaken or proposed with a view to enhancing the capacity of the policy-making process to deal with the greater volume of demands and the expanded role of the state.

Other critics argue that the growth of the state has stifled individual initiative and redirected resources away from the private sector, thereby endangering Canada's prospects for economic growth. They demand a reduction in public expenditure and deregulation of the economy so that private enterprise can prosper, unfettered by government controls.

Finally, even where the actual size of the state or the overall rate of growth of the public sector has not been directly at issue, a persistent source of federal/provincial conflict over the years has concerned the relative distribution of state activities among the levels of government in Canada. Thus, provincial critics of federal government spending or involvement in certain fields are often not so much condemning government intervention *per se* as claiming interference in provincial jurisdiction. Once again, the politics of the present is haunted by the unresolved conflicts of Canada's past.

OVERVIEW

Politics is more than the product of historical, social and economic forces. But these forces do influence political life, and the historical development of the Ca-

---

[57]Bird, *Financing Canadian Government*, p. 94.

nadian nation-state has had and continues to have a profound impact on Canadian politics.

Many of the major issues and conflicts emerging from the processes of nation-building and state-building in Canada have been only partially resolved. Consequently, some of the most contentious subjects of debate in the political arena today have their origins in the strains and antipathies created by the evolution of the nation-state. Furthermore, these same strains often hamper the reconciliation of other, apparently unrelated, disputes among actors in the Canadian political system.

Even the settlement of Canada's sovereign status *vis-à-vis* the United Kingdom served to exacerbate tensions elsewhere. The proclamation of Canada's new Constitution on April 17, 1982 was accompanied by political controversy and acrimony in other parts of the country. Some 20 000 Québécois joined René Lévesque in a Montréal demonstration to protest the exclusion of Québec from the constitutional accord between the federal government and the nine other provinces. Meanwhile, Native Indian organizations, whose demands for the entrenchment of Native rights in the Constitution had not been fulfilled, also boycotted the ceremonies in Ottawa and declared that any Indians celebrating the event were committing treason against their nation.

Although the major question of external sovereignty has now been resolved, relations with the third actor in the North Atlantic Triangle are still at issue. Fears of assimilation into a U.S.-dominated North American culture and the impact of American economic influence in Canada remain important topics of political debate.

With regard to internal nation-building, conflicts among regions or provinces and between the two founding nations continue to intrude on the political agenda. The threat of separation by Québec or by parts of Western Canada, while not great, cannot be totally ignored. Jurisdictional disputes, especially over ownership and control of natural resources, exacerbate federal/provincial relations. Attempts to reduce regional economic disparities are frequently declaimed as unfair by the "have" provinces and inadequate by the "have-nots". The recent politicization of the Native movements adds another new dimension to contemporary ethnic politics in Canada. Despite all these differences, however, the country stays together, united by the almost indefinable sense of "being Canadian".

Lastly, the growth of the Canadian state from the 19th century National Policy to the present day has also provided a subject for political debate. Today, conservatives argue that governments are too interventionist, while socialists condemn them for not being active enough. Meanwhile, provincial governments criticize the expansion of federal spending and budgetary deficits, simultaneously protesting cutbacks in federal contributions to provincially managed programmes such as Medicare and higher education. Concern over the size of government in general is widespread and growing among the public. A Gallup Poll published in December 1981 reported that 44 percent of respondents felt that "big government" would provide the greatest threat to Canadians in future years. This figure is to be compared with 28 percent who viewed "big labour" as a threat and 16 percent who opted for "big business". It also marked a substantial increase over the 29 percent who feared "big government" in a similar poll in 1980.[58]

Many of the major issues in contemporary Canadian politics have their source in the origins, expansion and development of the nation-state over the past three hundred years. Furthermore, the attitudes, myths and grievances which evolved from the nation- and state-building experience profoundly affect the approach of contending sides to other, less directly related questions. Those attitudes and myths will be examined in more detail in the next two chapters; other issues raised above will receive further attention elsewhere in the book. The purpose of this chapter has been to draw together various strands of Canadian historical evolution in order to provide a base from which to commence the exploration of present-day politics in Canada.

---

[58]Findings of the Gallup Poll, published in *The Gazette,* Montréal, December 2, 1981.

Part II
Culture

MACDONALD

chapter 3

Political Culture
The Fabric of Society

CERTAIN MYTHS ABOUT CANADA and Canadians are common in foreign countries, some based on reality, some not. These include conceptions of Canadians as a solid, stolid, northern, reliable, prosperous, tough, not sexy people blessed by good government and policies and one of the world's greatest police forces.[1] This chapter is not concerned with quaint myths held by others, nor even with whether such notions are based on fact. Rather, it looks at the attitudes and values that Canadians hold about themselves, their country and their system of government, all of which in turn affect their political behaviour.

Traditionally, the focus of Canadian political science was on government and political institutions, but gradually this scope expanded to include the relationship between these institutions and their cultural and social milieu. Political scientists have attempted to replace impressionistic generalizations or myths about "national character" such as those cited with scientific studies of the beliefs and values of citizens of nation-states.

Every society has a distinctive political system which fosters a particular set of attitudes in its citizens. The citizens, in turn, develop certain perceptions and expectations of what their political system can and should do for them and what obligations they have in return. This invisible interaction provides the value structure within which political decisions are made, delineates the accepted bounds of government and individual political activity and enables organizations and institutions to function coherently.

We can compare Canada's political culture to a colourful tapestry. When examined closely, a tapestry can be separated into three strands or elements: warp, woof and appliqué. Only when these basic units are interwoven and viewed together as a whole is the unique design of the tapestry visible. Similarly, Canadian

---

[1]See for example, "The Maiden Aunt Among Nations," *International Herald Tribune*, Paris, November 1, 1979.

political culture consists of three distinct strands or elements. Sometimes one of the parts is mistaken for the whole, and then the view of the country's political culture is incomplete. This chapter aspires to identify and separate the three strands of political culture in order to achieve a more meaningful view of Canada. The next chapter deals with political socialization – how political culture is learned. But first, the concept of political culture must be clarified.

WHAT IS POLITICAL CULTURE?

Political culture is a relatively new concept in political science, and certainly one of the most controversial. The term was first coined in the United States in the 1950s and only later applied in Canada.[2] It has been defined in a multitude of ways. One leading scholar, Sidney Verba, considered political culture to be "the system of empirical beliefs, expressive symbols, and values which defines the situation in which political action takes place."[3] Gabriel A. Almond and G. Bingham Powell excluded specific mention of values and concentrated on attitudes and orientations in defining political culture as "the pattern of individual attitudes and orientations toward politics among the members of a political system."[4]

Combining elements of both these definitions, and using "orientations" and "attitudes" synonymously, we use the term **political culture** in this book to refer to the broad patterns of individual values and attitudes toward political objects. These may be concrete objects such as government institutions or national symbols such as the flag, but they may also be intangibles like power. In the latter case, it is important to understand how Canadians perceive the distribution of power between themselves and government, and what institutions or positions they view as the greatest sources of political power. Students of political culture therefore attempt to determine the degree of the individual citizen's knowledge and awareness of the political system, as well as the attitudes held about politics and political objects and the perceptions of the personal role in societal affairs.

Political culture, though but a small part of the general culture of a society, serves many purposes: it draws individuals together; supports thought, judgement and action; constitutes the character and personality of a community; differentiates it from other communities; and encourages its members to seek

---

[2]The concept was first introduced by Gabriel Almond in "Comparative Political Systems," *Journal of Politics*, vol. 18 no. 3 (August 1956), pp. 391-409; reprinted in Gabriel Almond, *Political Development* (Boston: Little, Brown, 1970). For a concise history of the term "political culture", see David Bell and Lorne Tepperman, *The Roots of Disunity* (Toronto: McClelland and Stewart, 1979), Chapter 1.

[3]Sidney Verba, "Comparative Political Culture" in Lucian W. Pye and Sidney Verba, eds., *Political Culture and Political Development* (Princeton: Princeton University Press, 1965), p. 513.

[4]Gabriel A. Almond and G. Bingham Powell, *Comparative Politics: A Developmental Approach* (Boston: Little, Brown, 1966), p. 50.

common objectives.[5] What citizens know and feel about their political system will affect both the number and kinds of demands they make on the system and their response to laws, political leadership and the outputs of the political system. In addition, political culture renders the government's decision-making processes acceptable by demarcating the boundaries within which it can legitimately act.

A clear understanding of this relationship between the nature of political culture and the performance of the political system assists in identifying and appreciating the means by which political change can be effected. Political leaders often appeal to the appropriate values and standards of citizens in creating and justifying policies. For example, when Pierre Elliot Trudeau used the campaign slogan "the just society", he was appealing to fundamental values in the electorate and trying to link the Liberal Party platform to those values. Furthermore, the degree to which values and beliefs are shared greatly affects the degree of national cohesion and stability in a country. Deep cleavages within a nation-state over such issues as language or economic well-being obstruct the sharing of values and beliefs and contribute to political instability. The more is known about the political attitudes of individual citizens the better their political reactions can be explained and predicted, including participation not only within the system through such means as voting, but also outside the electoral process through demonstrations, strikes and even violence.

Perhaps the most important contribution made by studies of political culture has been the integration of research on political systems and on individual behaviour, previously unrelated by scholars. The study of political culture is a multi-disciplinary endeavour to which political science, sociology and psychology all contribute. Citizens' beliefs and values which were formerly ignored by political scientists are now scrutinized to determine their effect on voting behaviour and other forms of political participation or non-participation.

Political culture studies in Canada have been stimulated and strongly influenced by the empirical work of Gabriel Almond and Sidney Verba, American pioneers in the field. These political scientists conducted the first statistically-based cross-national study of political beliefs, symbols and values in an attempt to measure and compare national political attitudes.[6] In the course of their study they encountered many difficulties, which have not been resolved. For example, large-scale opinion surveys and interviews are extremely expensive to administer and difficult to interpret. The answers elicited are not always truthful or thoughtful, and can be affected by temporary events or personalities and so may not reflect deeply-held beliefs on which people will act. As well, an empirical approach to comparing nations is limited because it lacks an historical or contextual dimension and therefore fails to recognize the constantly changing nature of politi-

---

[5]For a general discussion of the concept of culture, see *The Task Force on Canadian Unity: Coming to Terms – The Words of the Debate* (Hull: Minister of Supply and Services, 1979), p.41.

[6]Gabriel A. Almond and Sidney Verba, *The Civic Culture* (Boston: Little, Brown, 1965). For comments on the above study see Gabriel A. Almond and Sidney Verba, eds., *The Civic Culture Revisited* (Boston: Little, Brown, 1980).

cal culture. Despite such limitations upon this type of study, Almond and Verba effectively demonstrated that national cultures vary considerably with regard to beliefs about government and politics and that these beliefs affect essential aspects of political behaviour.

As we shall see, social scientists have studied Canadian political culture in quite different ways. Some have followed this empirical methodology, using surveys and questionnaires to learn about mass attitudes and behaviour. Others have chosen to carry out more impressionistic research on the historical development of political ideas. Although they cannot be directly compared, and each has its shortcomings, both methods contribute to an understanding of the Canadian political system.

THE THREE STRANDS OF CANADIAN POLITICAL CULTURE

We now return to our analogy of Canadian political culture as a tapestry composed of three separate but interwoven strands. Each strand is valid and important but, if taken in isolation, gives only one part of the picture. In this chapter the subject of political culture is divided, for the sake of simplicity, into three sections, each of which corresponds to one of the strands.

The first section defines Canadian political culture in terms of the values and attitudes common to all citizens of the nation-state, searching out the roots of the Canadian heritage. It attempts to determine whether there is a common ideology behind Canadian political thought, and, if so, what its origins are. This *nation-state* level of interpretation also seeks to establish the elements of Canada's political culture that distinguish Canadians from citizens of other countries. Studies in this field reveal one strand of Canadian political culture.

The second section identifies Canadian political culture by examining the most important subcultures created by *ethnic* and *linguistic* cleavages in the country. The literature dealing with this strand focuses on two distinct groups: the French Canadian community, whose cultural and linguistic differences were reinforced by geographical and economic circumstances; and the English Canadian sector, as it is generally called because of the official bilingual status of the country. However, the latter is much less uniform than its French Canadian counterpart. Although the two founding groups represent the main cultural division in Canada, we have seen that other ethnic groups make up over a quarter of the total population. To varying degrees, these ethnic groups have cherished their languages and traditions and, rather than face absorption into a national "melting pot", have fought for an independent existence. Their perseverance has created a distinctive Canadian social mosaic of different languages and cultures that is an important aspect of the Canadian political culture.

The third strand of Canadian political culture arises from the *regional* diversity of the country. Generally, those scholars who regard the system as relatively evenly balanced between provincial and federal interests stress the importance of regional differences. The regions are not always the same in each study, but they often coincide with political boundaries and encompass certain ethnic and linguistic groups. According to this interpretation, Canadians' values and beliefs about their political system are conditioned by the distinct geographic and economic characteristics of the region in which they live. People of different origins and interests settled in areas which offered greatly varied resources and potential for industrial development. Furthermore, the federal system of government helps to reinforce and perpetuate these regions and the attitudes related to them. It is inevitable that, given these conditions, individuals within the different regions will maintain different attitudes toward national problems. This third section will examine how distinctive the regions are and what evidence exists that there are several territorially-based political cultures in Canada.

The fact that political values and beliefs are far from uniform across the nation-state leads some scholars to argue that there is no such thing as a Canadian political culture, but rather many cultures based on ethnic or regional divisions. In this book, we maintain that a multitude of regional and ethnic political subcultures exist, tied together by the overarching values of a national culture. Subcultures can, and do, affect the dominant culture of the political community, sometimes acting as a disruptive force when group ties are stronger than loyalty to the whole. But they are only one strand of the country's cultural fabric. Canadian political culture has been shaped by the environmental and historical factors described in Chapters 1 and 2. Distinctive Canadian values are derived from geographical, historical and economic determinants, and are institutionalized in areas such as religion, education, class relations and family structure. Many of them are unstated values such as traditions of liberty, respect for the law and coexistence of heterogeneous communities which underlie the political system. These are the heart of Canada's political culture.

The rest of this chapter examines the three strands of Canadian political culture under the headings: nation-state political culture, ethno-linguistic political cultures and regional political cultures.

NATION-STATE POLITICAL CULTURE

Nation-state political culture encompasses values and attitudes which pertain to the entire Canadian political system. Before examining some of these values and attitudes and the symbols in which they are embodied, we will first consider the broad historical roots of the political thought which forms the parameters of mainstream political culture in Canada.

Historical Roots

A few classic arguments about what traditional attitudes, if any, form the base of Canada's political system underlie all discussions of political culture. Before we look at these arguments in detail, it is important to clarify a confusion that sometimes arises between the terms "political culture" and "ideology". Both refer to political attitudes, values and beliefs, but ideologies are more coherent and explicit.[7] As used in this book, **ideology** is narrower in scope than political culture and refers to an explicit doctrinal structure which provides a particular diagnosis of the ills of society and prescribes a solution for them. Within Canadian society, for example, we can identify certain ideologies, socialism, conservatism and liberalism among them. Political culture, on the other hand, refers to vaguer, more implicit orientations which may include more than one ideology. Political culture studies are concerned with the views and values of citizens whether or not they embrace any explicit, formal ideology.

The source of many ideas concerning the traditional attitudes which underlie Canadian political culture is Professor Louis Hartz's *The Liberal Tradition in America*.[8] This volume was published before the popularization of the concept of political culture and consequently the word "ideology" is used in this and subsequent writing on the topic in a way that differs from the usage in the present text – not as an action-oriented system of ideas, but as a relatively vague set of attitudes which form the foundation of political culture. Had the discussion begun a decade later, Hartz and other authors might have substituted "political culture" for "ideology". As it is, much of the literature which followed Hartz, and which is discussed here, uses the latter term in the loose sense of a set of general principles.

The thesis put forward by Hartz and later expanded by Kenneth McRae[9] is that North America, like other societies founded by European settlement, is a "fragment society". According to Hartz, the New World societies based their political cultures on single European ideologies brought as "cultural baggage" during colonization. Immigrants to the new land did not represent all elements of the society which they left. Institutions and myths set up and passed on by the founding peoples perpetuated those beliefs and values. McRae argues that, because it has two founding nations, Canada is a classic instance of a "two-fragment" society.

The settlers in New France represented one fragment, the feudal strain from France. As a result, a kind of "feudal catholicism" dominated rival ideologies there, and excluded others through expulsion or assimilation. The second fragment, English Canada, was very similar to its liberal American counterpart. English-speaking immigrants were predominantly liberal. In the pre-revolutionary United States, the liberalism of the philosopher John Locke

---

[7]See Bell and Tepperman, *op. cit.*, Chapter 1, for a brief examination of the concept of ideology as used by Karl Marx and Karl Mannheim.

[8]Louis Hartz, *The Liberal Tradition in America* (New York: Harcourt Brace, 1953).

[9]Louis Hartz, ed., *The Founding of New Societies* (New York: Harcourt Brace, 1964). See McRae's analysis in "The Structure of Canadian History" in Chapter 7. See also Kenneth D. McRae, "Louis Hartz's Concept of the Fragment Society and Its Applications to Canada," *Etudes Canadiennes*, vol. 5 (1978), p. 17-30. For a strong argument that the Hartz framework is too abstract, see Walter C. Sodurlund, Ralph C. Nelson and Ronald H. Wagenberg, "A Critique of the Hartz Theory of Political Development as Applied to Canada," *Comparative Politics*, vol. 12, no. 1 (October 1979) pp. 63-85.

became the prevailing ideology. The beliefs of which Locke was the primary spokesman were based on the importance of the individual, free enterprise and the right of the individual to pursue personal interests without government interference. Loyalists who flooded into Canada at the time of the American revolution brought these liberal values with them – along with strong anti-American sentiments.

The differences that developed between English Canada and the United States were subtle and minor, according to Hartz and McRae. In both cases, the liberal ideology "congealed" before socialism developed in Europe; therefore, socialism did not take hold in North America. Liberal thought, with its belief in maximizing individual freedom and satisfaction of private desires, is widely diffused and dominant in the political culture of English North Americans. However, Hartz, McRae and others argue, Canadian thought is more conservative and collectivist than that of the United States.[10] For instance, Canadians feel strongly that the state is responsible for its citizens and is obligated to provide for their collective well-being. Americans, on the other hand, believe in non-interference by the government and the primacy of individual liberties.

George Grant, writing on this matter, lamented the widespread diffusion of liberal thought in Canada. He warned that the triumph of liberalism over conservatism and socialism in Canadian society represents the defeat of Canadian nationalism because it brings total conformity with the ideological structure of the United States.[11] Others have argued that Canadian anglophones have never been able to accept liberal ideology totally, because it was the natural culture of the Americans. They see the tension between adhering to the British connection and the fostering of antipathy toward the American culture, which was ideologically very similar to Canada's own, as the origin of a serious identity crisis for Canadians.[12]

Hartz's "fragment" theory of political culture considers the culture of founding groups as a kind of "genetic code", one which does not determine, but rather imposes boundaries on, later cultural developments. This approach offers the advantage of historical depth, since political thought is viewed as a phenomenon which develops over time, rather than being static. A drawback is that it fails to explain how fragment cultures survive, how they are transmitted to new immigrants and new generations. Why, for example, did new immigrant groups not establish new competing cultures? This question is considered in the next chapter.

Part of the Hartz and McRae thesis has been challenged by Gad Horowitz, who maintains that the respective heritages of Canada and the United States are indeed very different because Canadian liberalism did not "congeal" before Brit-

---

[10]Gad Horowitz, "Conservatism, Liberalism and Socialism in Canada: An Interpretation," *CJEPS*, vol. 32 no. 2 (May 1966), pp. 143-171. See also Horowitz, "Notes on 'Conservatism, Liberalism and Socialism in Canada'," *CJPS*, vol. XI, no. 2 (June 1978), pp. 383-399.

[11]George Grant, *Lament for a Nation; the Defeat of Canadian Nationalism* (Toronto: McClelland and Stewart, 1965) and also *Technology and Empire* (Toronto: Anansi, 1969).

[12]Bell and Tepperman, *op. cit.*, ch. 3.

ish and European immigrants arrived in Canada in the late 19th and early 20th centuries, bringing with them newer ideas from the old societies.[13] The fact that a socialist movement grew, especially in Saskatchewan, illustrates that, unlike the United States, Canada has had an enduring, though small, socialist "fragment". Thus, political thought in Canada was not totally buried beneath an unqualified liberal nationalism. Even among the English-speaking group, Horowitz maintains, there is no single dominant ideology.

Other authors, such as S.M. Lipset, conversely stress the conservative inheritance of the Canadian political culture.[14] Using census data and a comparative framework comprising the United States, Britain, Australia and Canada, he concluded that Canadian values are generally conservative, closer to those of Europeans than Americans. He based this conclusion on evidence that Canadians are more elitist than their American neighbours, who place a higher value on egalitarianism and achievement. For example, he found deferential attitudes in Canada, evidenced by a widespread respect for political leaders, the law and public authority. He noted that compliance forces such as the RCMP and the military are generally viewed with respect, not as symbols of oppression as in many countries. Finally, Lipset found that, compared to the United States, Canada has a much lower *per capita* crime rate, and less political corruption – both of which facts, he believed, might be traced to elitist values.[15]

These and other Canadian/American differences, Lipset posited, are the result of very different "formative events" in the history of the two countries. Canada became independent through evolution, the United States though revolution. Canada had a relatively civilized westward expansion, not a "wild west". The religious traditions too, differed: Canada was settled predominantly by Anglicans and Roman Catholics rather than by Calvinists and fundamentalists.

Colin Campbell and William Christian[16] have added to the debate by rejecting the view that the Canadian ideological system congealed in the way suggested by either McRae or Horowitz. They maintain that the Loyalists introduced strains of Tory thought into English Canada. Their presence shifted the patterns of settlement so that more liberally inclined immigrants went to the United States, while more conservative individuals chose to remain under the British Crown. Close ties with Britain reinforced this Tory strain. As for Canadian socialism, Campbell and Christian contend that it was indigenous, a natural product of the post-First World War depression.

---

[13]Horowitz, "Conservatism, Liberalism and Socialism in Canada."

[14]Seymour Martin Lipset, "Revolution and Counterrevolution: Canada and the United States," in O. Kruhlak *et al.*, eds., *The Canadian Political Process: A Reader* (Toronto: Holt, Rinehart and Winston, 1970), pp. 13-38. This article was first published in 1965. See also by the same author, *The First New Nation: The United States in Comparative Perspective* (New York: Basic Books, 1963).

[15]Lipset, "Revolution and Counterrevolution," p. 19.

[16]William Christian and Colin Campbell, *Political Parties and Ideologies in Canada: liberals, conservatives, socialists, nationalists* 2nd ed., (Toronto: McGraw-Hill Ryerson, 1983).

All these interpretations suggest that Canadian political culture, unlike its American counterpart, was open to both conservative and socialist thought. It is our contention, however, that liberal values, based on belief in a capitalist society, a market economy and the right to private property, dominate in Canada, but not to the exlusion of other perspectives. Liberalism is, as David Bell and Lorne Tepperman aptly phrase it, "the ideology of the dominant class; it has the full force of the state, Church, media and educational system behind it: it has been trained into all of us."[17]

Overarching Values and Their Symbols

The political values of a country form the broad base of its political system. Though generally taken for granted and not articulated, they set the parameters of acceptable behaviour and underlie citizens' attitudes toward specific political objects. They are reflected in political symbols such as national emblems or institutions, and are often enshrined in the country's constitution.

In April 1982, the *Canadian Charter of Rights and Freedoms* was proclaimed. It became the first comprehensive statement of the fundamental values of Canadians to be passed by Parliament. The preamble sets out the premise that "Canada is founded upon principles that recognize the supremacy of God and the Rule of Law". The *Charter* then proceeds to guarantee the fundamental rights of Canada's "free and democratic society". The implicit values of Canadians, as formalized in the *Charter*, are rooted in the western political tradition and the Judeo-Christian religious tradition.

Democracy, as we have discussed in Chapter 1, is such an ambiguous concept that it has become a cliché to claim it as a basic value of a country. It is espoused by all types of political systems. Democracy is, in fact, a process rather than a system of values. In Canada it takes the form of representative democracy rather than direct democracy, which is rule by the people as a whole. The democratic right of citizens to vote in elections for their political representatives, and the basic rules governing those representatives, are outlined in the *Charter of Rights and Freedoms*. Embedded in the process of representative democracy are a great many values. One is the individual right to *liberty* or, as it is put in the *Charter*, fundamental freedoms, among them freedom of conscience and religion, of belief and expression, including freedom of the press and freedom of association. Another is *equality* before and under the law, without discrimination. In the political sphere, equality presumes associated values such as *universal suffrage* and elections contested by competing political parties that give voters alternatives from which to choose. Another associated value is acceptance of the *rule of law*, with civil rights for all citizens. (These and other constitutionally approved values

---

[17]Bell and Tepperman, *op. cit.*, p. 232. For a discussion of dominant ideologies and counter-ideologies, see M. Patricia Marchak, *Ideological Perspectives on Canada* 2nd ed., (Toronto: McGraw-Hill Ryerson, 1981).

will be detailed in Chapter 5.) Still another implicit value of representative democracy is *majority rule*. Governments are elected by majority, and once elected they enact laws with majority approval. Basic democratic values are generally considered inviolable, beyond even the right of the majority to change.

The political values of a country are symbolized by flags, anthems, leaders, national holidays and historical heroes, among other things. Such symbols help enforce respect for and emotional attachment to political institutions, and can be a focal point for national unity. Canada's passage from colony to nation is clearly reflected in the country's changing national symbols. In the early stages, they manifested a dual allegiance to Britain and Canada, but were gradually transformed to reflect national pride and unity without reference to Britain.

The evolution of the Canadian flag is perhaps the best illustration. At Confederation in 1867, Canada was granted permission to fly the red ensign, the flag of the British Merchant Navy. Attempts to replace it with a uniquely Canadian flag began as early as 1925 but did not succeed until four decades later. The transition was difficult. There were bitter debates both within and outside Parliament, concerning not only the specific choice of a replacement but also the basic question of whether Canada should jettison the flag which represented its historical attachment to Britain. In the end, of course, a flag was selected which features a red maple leaf, a distinctively Canadian symbol which had been adopted quite separately by both English and French Canadians well before Confederation and which has deep historical roots in heraldic arms, regimental colours and literary publications.[18] The choice was one with which the entire nation-state could identify. Today, in addition to its official status on the flag and other national symbols, the red maple leaf is used by Canadian manufacturers to identify their products, from clothing to maple syrup, and many tourists would not leave the country without a tiny facsimile on their lapels.

A similar evolution is evidenced in the acquisition of a Canadian coat of arms. Following World War I, representation was made to the Crown for a coat of arms which was uniquely Canadian. For years a controversy simmered over whether Canada should be symbolized by living green leaves or dead red ones. (Sir Robert Borden, then Prime Minister, thought green far more appropriate). The dispute was not settled until 1957 when it was agreed that three red leaves would adorn the base of the shield, and a lion would proudly display a fourth.

Another progression to a specifically Canadian symbol occurred in the choice of the national anthem. At Confederation, the English version was "The Maple Leaf Forever", which was quite unacceptable to French Canadians for the good reason that it referred to the French defeat at Québec. "God Save the Queen" took over as the unofficial anthem until the music for "O Canada", a song written by Calixa Lavallée in 1880, was officially adopted in 1967. The revised lyrics were finally adopted by the Canadian Parliament in 1980, but disagreement over the wording remained intense. Rather than inspiring loyalty and

---

[18]Strome Galloway, "Why the Maple Leaf is Our National Emblem," *Canadian Geographic* (June 1982) pp. 30-35.

devotion, such words as "native land", "sons command", "true North" and "God" gave rise to resentment among immigrants, women, westerners, easterners and atheists. Of course, there were royalists who still preferred "God Save the Queen". The French version of "O Canada", whose lyrics resemble the English only in that they refer to the same country, also contained some offensive wording, but it too was accepted.

It is important that a symbol of unity cause as little friction as possible, and the efforts to compromise and please were evident at the formal adoption ceremony. There had been hot debate over whether the choir should sing first in English or in French. What was later called a typically Canadian solution was found: the choir was divided in two and sang both versions simultaneously.

Other minor conflicts and reminders of the British heritage have emerged from time to time with regard to other symbols. The first of July, Canada's national holiday, was known as Dominion Day until November 1982. Although the word "dominion" had been chosen explicitly by the Fathers of Confederation to mean sovereignty from sea to sea, many Canadians came to feel that it smacked of colonial dependence. With some trepidation because of the controversy the topic engendered, the Canadian Parliament finally changed the title of the holiday to Canada Day.

In many countries, the constitution provides a concrete focus for pride and unity. In Canada this has only recently been the case. As with the other symbols we have discussed, the process of wrenching away from British ties and establishing a uniquely Canadian symbol was not easy. The *British North America Act*, Canada's written constitution, was passed as an ordinary *Act* of the British Parliament. As a national symbol it was increasingly embarrassing to Canadians in the 20th century, both because it could not be amended without British approval and because it contained no formal guarantee of rights. The remedy finally came in the spring of 1982 when the revised constitution was patriated. Like the American constitution, the new document is likely to provide a focus for citizens' homage.

Two other predominant political symbols deserving of mention here, although they are discussed extensively in Chapter 5, are the monarch and her representative, the Governor General. Canada is a constitutional monarchy, and the role of the Queen as head of state is ceremonial. Canadians do not support the royal family financially. The monarch has always been a questionable symbol for French Canadians and, since an overtly hostile reception for the Queen during a Royal visit to Québec in 1964, officials of the Québec government have taken increasingly great pains to disassociate themselves and their constituents from the monarchy. It is evident that the ability of this institution to serve as a unifying symbol for Canada's two founding cultural groups is limited.

By convention, the monarch's portrait adorns Canada's currency and postage stamps, but even this practice has led to occasional debate. For example, there is a tradition in Canada that members of the Royal Family should be the only living persons portrayed on postage stamps. Public controversy was heated when the custom prevented the issuing of a stamp featuring Marathon of Hope runner Terry Fox while he was still alive.

The role of Governor General has evolved considerably from its British origins. The Queen's representative to Canada was originally selected by Britain. However, since 1936, the Governor General has been appointed only after consultation with the Canadian Cabinet, which means, in effect, that the Prime Minister makes the choice. The appointment of the first Canadian, Vincent Massey, came in 1952. This final transition to a Canadian Governor General nominated in Canada has increased the potential of the position as a unifying symbol for Canadians.

Finally, we must allude briefly to historical heroes as symbols of national pride and unity. Gradual evolution to nationhood, as opposed to dramatic revolution, does not produce charismatic hero material. And independence on the installment plan has no glamour as a national event. To compound the difficulties, French and English Canadians each tend to cultivate their own heroes, based on different interpretations of history. In fact, Canadian heroes often gained reputations in their own communities by resisting or defeating their counterparts. The dearth of common national heroes and events around which to rally has undoubtedly encouraged substitutions from south of the border, a problem discussed more fully in the following chapter. F.R. Scott aptly described this situation in a satirical poem entitled "National Identity":[19]

> The Canadian Centenary Council
> Meeting in Le Reine Elizabeth
> To seek those symbols
> Which will explain ourselves to ourselves
> Evoke unlimited responses
> And prove that something called Canada
> Really exists in the heart of all
> Handed out to every delegate
> At the start of the proceedings
> A portfolio of documents
> On the cover of which appeared
> In gold letters
> >   not
> A Mari Usque Ad Mare
> >   not
> E Pluribus Unum
> >   not
> Dieu et Mon Droit
> >   but
> COURTESY OF COCA-COLA LIMITED.

Attitudes: Cognitive, Affective and Evaluative

The overarching values just discussed set the general parameters of political behaviour. Also important to political culture are the specific attitudes of citizens towards political objects. These attitudes may be less widely accepted than basic

---

[19]From *The Collected Poems of F.R. Scott*, John Newlove, ed. Used by permission of the Canadian Publishers, McClelland and Stewart Ltd., Toronto.

values and more fleeting, but they may be more immediate determinants of political behaviour, depending upon the intensity with which they are held. Three types must be distinguished: cognitive, affective and evaluative.[20] *Cognitive* attitudes reflect the degree of knowledge, accurate or otherwise, which citizens have about political objects. *Affective* attitudes reflect the degree of citizens' attachment to or rejection of the political objects which surround them: how do Canadians feel about their country, their government or the political symbols we have discussed? *Evaluative* attitudes reflect the moral judgements made by individuals about the goodness or badness of political objects. The three types of attitudes are interrelated, and often difficult to distinguish in practice.

Attitudes towards specific political issues of the day, as opposed to more permanent political objects, are ephemeral. Issues change and so do people, but institutions and symbols remain. These transient attitudes are defined as public opinion, and although they can be important in determining short-term behaviour they are less helpful in understanding the political culture of a country.

Very little research has been done on political attitudes in Canada. The major contribution to date has been a large attitudinal survey undertaken by Clarke, Jenson, Leduc and Pammett as part of the 1974 National Election Survey.[21] This survey looked at the cognitive, affective and evaluative attitudes of Canadians to the federal system of government. The type of cooperative federalism which has evolved is a particularly complicated system in which policies and programmes are often negotiated by both federal and provincial levels of government, and the potential for conflict is therefore high. Attitudes toward the federal system are an important element of Canadian political culture.

With respect to cognitive orientations to the federal system, Clarke *et al.* concluded that most respondents understood "in a reasonably accurate way the workings of the federal political system, at least in terms of its formal division of powers", and therefore that Canadians have the basic information necessary to allow them to operate effectively at both levels of government.[22] This conclusion indicates that federalism might be one of the better understood aspects of the Canadian political system, a finding which seems to contradict the traditional view that most Canadian citizens have only a superficial understanding of their government and politics, that they tend to recognize prominent leaders but know little about political issues or party positions.

The examination of affective attitudes toward the federal system in the Clarke study shows no evidence of strongly conflicting loyalties between country and province. Canadians exhibit a high degree of affect for both their country and their province of residence. Respondents to the survey were asked to write five words or phrases on a map of Canada. Their remarks provide an interesting

---

[20]Almond and Verba identified and elaborated on these three types of political orientations in their study of *The Civic Culture*.

[21]Harold D. Clarke, Jane Jenson, Lawrence LeDuc and Jon H. Pammett, *Political Choice in Canada* (Toronto: McGraw-Hill Ryerson, 1979). This section draws heavily on conclusions from Section One of their study.

[22]*Ibid.*, p. 79.

insight into how Canadians from coast to coast view themselves and their country. Comments on Canada were generally positive, with such words or phrases as "fortunate" and "a good place to live" recurring. In another part of the same survey respondents were asked to rank on a thermometer the degree of warmth they felt for Canada and for their province; 50, the centre of the scale was "luke-warm". The data indicated considerable warmth toward Canada, the mean score being 84. Overall, the respondents also demonstrated considerable affect for their own provinces, though somewhat lower than for Canada. These findings were confirmed by similar surveys at the time of the 1979 and 1980 elections.

Despite these positive orientations to the federal system, certain disquieting findings about the affective nature of attitudes toward objects in the Canadian political system did surface. Clarke *et al.* subdivided the political system into three areas – political community (the country itself), regime (the government and Constitution) and authorities (political parties, politicians and leaders) – in order to classify the affective attitudes of Canadians toward the system.[23] Attitudes toward the Canadian political community were mixed, neither strongly positive nor negative. Towards both regime and authority objects, however, they were decidedly negative. When asked to inscribe "five words or phrases which best describe politics in Canada", respondents' general comments on politicians, parties and government were overwhelmingly negative. When asked specifically which of their governments they felt closer to, federal or provincial, respondents from all provinces except Ontario said they felt closer to their provincial government.

These negative attitudes were tempered somewhat when specific individuals or parties were mentioned; nonetheless, they indicate a lack of faith or trust in the capability of politicians and the political system to respond positively to citizens' interests. Of course, specific criticisms of the workings of the political system do not imply that there is not at the same time diffuse support for the particular form of government. Moreover, these attitudes can fluctuate over a relatively short period and are not uniform across the population.

Evaluative attitudes toward the federal system reflect the assessment by Canadians of the impact of federal institutions in their lives. The survey by Clarke *et al.* concluded that Canadians see the impact of both levels of government as being relatively equal in this respect. Evaluative scores in which the respondents gave judgements about the relative importance of the two levels of government indicated that Canadians awarded reasonably equal weight to each. Not surprisingly, however, they were likely to see their own province as being unfairly assessed for the financing of federalism, particularly with regard to the distribution of costs and benefits. The authors of the study speculated that perhaps this gen-

---

[23]*Ibid.*, Chapter 3. The authors use David Easton's breakdown of the political system into three major components. David Easton, *A Systems Analysis of Political Life* (New York: John Wiley, 1965), pp. 171-219. This breakdown is adapted by Pammett and Whittington to depict different foci for attitudes about the political system. They add a second dimension to construct a nine-fold system of classification. See Jon H. Pammett and Michael S. Whittington, *Foundations of Political Culture: Political Socialization in Canada* (Toronto: Macmillan, 1976), pp. 14-17.

eralized feeling of injustice *vis-à-vis* the federal system underlies the negative feelings expressed by much of the population toward the political system.

This evaluation of the federal system as unjust reflects the competitive nature of federal/provincial bargaining, but it does not, as we shall see, hamper participation at either level. Neither does it indicate a rejection of government authority. Individual Canadians are quite willing to comply with basic political laws, and major political groups rarely offer unconditional resistance. Acts of Parliament are automatically considered legitimate and are carried out voluntarily by citizens without the need for coercive security forces.[24] Crimes against the state are rare, even when laws are unpopular. Only about 7 percent of Canadians have deliberately disobeyed what they considered to be an unjust law. Canadians very rarely join protest movements: only about 6 percent have marched in a legal protest rally, and 2 percent in an illegal one. On the other hand, it would be naive to accept unquestioningly the popular conception of Canada as a docile "peaceful kingdom". In a study of politically motivated violence in Canada, the empirical data suggest that Canada experiences an incidence of violence comparable to that of most industrialized democracies.[25]

Behaviour: Participation and Efficacy

As we have seen, values and attitudes are often difficult to ascertain. Impressionistic studies and survey research are helpful, but both have limitations in the answers they can provide. Another approach is to deduce from people's behaviour the attitudes and values that made them act in a certain way. One of the best deductive methods is to examine the extent to which people *participate* in the political world about them. Next we will consider various aspects of political efficacy, that is, the extent to which citizens believe that they can or cannot produce a desired effect on their political environment, as well as the degree to which they ac-

---

[24]Jon H. Pammett, "Public Evaluations of the Canadian Federal System." Paper prepared for delivery at the Canada-India Workshop on Federalism, Hyderabad, India, August 1981.

A good deal of research is being done on support for the Canadian political community and the national political regime. See especially Allan Kornberg, Harold D. Clarke and Marianne C. Stewart, "Public Support for Community and Regime in the Regions of Contemporary Canada," *American Review of Canadian Studies*, vol. 10, no. 1 (Spring 1980), pp. 75-93. See also Michael M. Atkinson, William D. Coleman and Thomas J. Lewis, "Studying Political Support in Canada: An Evaluation of Indicators." Paper presented at the annual meeting of the CPSA, Montréal, Québec, June 1980.

There is an interesting exchange between these authors in the following publications. Michael M. Atkinson, William D. Coleman and Thomas J. Lewis, "Regime Support in Canada: A Comment," *British Journal of Political Science*, vol. 10, no. 3 (July 1980), pp. 402-409. Allan Kornberg, Harold D. Clarke and Lawrence LeDuc, "Regime Support in Canada: A Rejoinder," *British Journal of Political Science*, vol. 10, no. 3 (July 1980), pp. 410-416.

[25]Robert J. Jackson, Michael J. Kelly and Thomas H. Mitchell, "Collective Conflict, Violence, and the Media in Canada," Ontario Royal Commission on Violence, in the Communications Industry, Report. Volume 5: *Learning from the Media* (Toronto: Queen's Printer, 1977). Another interesting article is by Judith Torrance, "The Response of Canadian Governments to Violence," *CJPS*, vol. 10, no. 3 (September 1977), pp. 473-496.

tually participate in that environment. The individual's self-perception as a political object is an important factor here, because self-esteem can affect the degree and intensity of participation.

Relative to most democratic countries, Canadians participate very readily in electoral politics; about 74 percent vote regularly in federal and provincial elections. This is one of the highest rates of voter turnout in the western world. French Canadians are less active politically at the national level than English Canadians, but more active at the provincial level.[26] Corresponding to a high level of electoral participation, feelings of political efficacy with regard to voting are very high: Canadians feel that their individual vote is important. Their reasons for feeling they should vote are mixed. Some are committed to the principles of democracy and a feeling of civic duty; others feel it important to render judgement on a government or certain politicians, perhaps seeking to punish parties or politicians by voting them out of office.

Apart from this factor, however, overall feelings of political efficacy are low. As a result, Canadians are said to have a "quasi-participant" political culture:[27] Canadians are not confident that they can understand and affect the political process. Questions designed to measure political efficacy in the 1974 election survey centred on attitudes toward the responsiveness of decision-makers, the utility of potential political action and difficulty in understanding the political system. In the responses, 52 percent believed the government cared what they thought, 44 percent felt they had a say in what the government does, 33 percent believed that Members of Parliament were concerned with their electorates and 33 percent thought government and politics were not too complicated for them to follow.[28] British Columbia was at the "most efficacious" end of the scale, Newfoundland at the "least efficacious". In general, however, Canadians expressed feelings of distrust, cynicism and powerlessness in the face of government domination by powerful interests.

But Canadians are not alone in expressing these sentiments. Comparative analysis of responses to similar questions raised in surveys undertaken in Canada and the United States shows that, on most items, Canadians had as high a sense of efficacy as Americans and similar levels of trust in government. The major difference lay in the fact that Canadians were particularly cynical about government being run by big business interests, while Americans were most concerned about their government wasting money.[29]

---

[26]William Mishler, "Political Participation and Democracy," in Michael S. Whittington and Glen Williams, eds., *Canadian Politics in the 1980s* (Toronto: Methuen, 1980), pp. 128, 131 and 140.

[27]See Robert Presthus, *Elite Accommodation in Canadian Politics* (Toronto: Macmillan, 1973). Rick Van Loon uses the term "spectator-participant" in "Political Participation in Canada," *CJPS*, vol. III no. 3 (September 1970), p. 397.

[28]Clarke *et al.*, *op. cit.*, pp. 31-32.

[29]Nathaniel Beck and Jon Pierce, "Political Involvement and Party Allegiances in Canada and the United States," *International Journal of Comparative Sociology*, vol. 18 (March-June, 1979), p. 29.

Active participation in politics beyond casting a ballot is low in Canada. Only 4 or 5 percent of the electorate participate regularly in political parties or hold elected office at either the federal or provincial level. Unless the level of interest is artificially high because of colourful personalities or issues, Canadians retain only a vague spectator interest in politics and rarely show strong ideological commitment. Political protest, even peaceful demonstration as opposed to breaking the law or violence, is engaged in by a very small percentage of Canadians. Moreover, political participation aside from voting is very uneven across different groups in Canadian society. The higher an individual's social status, the more likely he or she is to participate politically. The most active participants tend to be wealthy, well-educated and male, middle-aged Protestant members of the English "charter group". Lower socio-economic and less well-educated groups participate only infrequently. Participation in parties and elections is discussed further in Chapters 10 and 11.

Table 3-1 shows a drastic drop in political participation when voting is excluded, but it must be noted that only 25 to 30 percent of Canadians confine their participation exclusively to casting a ballot. About 60 percent of the public

Table 3.1   The Extent of Reported Canadian Political Participation*

Type of Activity	Percentage
1. Voting	
(a) Voted in 1974 federal election	85
(b) Normally votes in federal elections	83
(c) Normally votes in provincial elections	82
2. Worked with others to solve community problems	26
3. Contacted public officials	24
4. Participation in Electoral Campaign	
(a) Tried to influence how others vote	22
(b) Attended political rally	19
(c) Displayed political sign on car	16
(d) Acted as Scrutineer	10
5. Political Protest	
(a) Disobeyed unjust law	7
(b) Marched in legal protest rally	6
6. Active party member	4
7. Member of political club	4
8. Contributed money to party or campaign	3

*All of the data here are based on responses to survey research and are not necessarily accurate representations of how Canadians "actually" participated. (Compare the average voter turnout of 73 percent to the 83 percent reported in 1 (b)).

Source: Adapted from William Mishler, "Political Participation and Democracy", in M.S. Whittington and G. Williams, eds., *Canadian Politics in the 1980s* (Toronto: Methuen, 1981), Table 7.1, p. 129.

participate in at least one political activity in addition to voting. Although Canadians are less active in political life than would befit the democratic ideal, they are considerably closer to that goal than citizens of the majority of the world's states.[30]

ETHNO-LINGUISTIC CLEAVAGES AND POLITICAL CULTURE

Under the veneer of national political culture in Canada, as in all societies, there are many political subcultures which, because of economic, geographic, religious, occupational, ethnic and other differences, do not share the values and attitudes discussed above. Among the most significant of these subcultures are ethnic groups.

Until 1971, the Canadian government determined ethnic origin for census purposes by identifying the mother tongue spoken by an individual or his/her father, or by tracing patrilinear descent for a family belonging to an ethnic group or region outside of Canada. This definition was changed for the 1981 census to include maternal descent, so that an individual may have more than one ethnic origin. Ethnic group members maintain their distinctiveness through such means as preserving their mother tongue, attending an ethnic-oriented church or maintaining certain customs. Different groups place different emphasis on retaining these cultural elements. Ethnically, of course, there is no such thing as a Canadian race. If an original decision had been made to engulf minorities in a unitary rather than a federal system of government, cultural diversity might not have been sustained, and ethnic groups would perhaps not have the political significance they do today. In Canada, cultural pluralism has also been encouraged by the size of the country, its sparse population and, particularly, the federal system of government.

There are two major ethno-linguistic cleavages in Canada, which have a profound effect on the country's political culture. The most significant of these cleavages, that between the two founding nations, French and English, is based on the conception of Canada as a bicultural, bilingual nation-state. The other important division, within the large non-francophone majority itself, is based on the conception of Canada as a multicultural country. We shall consider each in turn.

Reprinted with permission – The Toronto Star Syndicate.

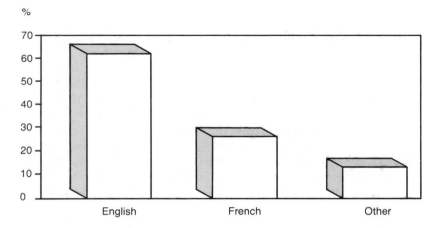

%

FIGURE 3.1 Percentage Distribution by Mother Tongue of the Population, Canada 1981

Source: 1981 Census of Canada. From *Language in Canada*, (Statistics Canada, Minister of Supply and Services, 1985), Catalogue 99-935, Chart 1.

French-English Cleavage

At the time of the 1981 census, over six million Canadians – about 27 percent of the total population of Canada – claimed French as their ethnic origin. Over 80 percent of these people lived in Québec, with other significant groupings residing in Ontario and New Brunswick. French was claimed as the mother tongue by 26 percent of Canadians, compared to 61 percent for English.

One fundamental difference between French and English lies in each group's understanding of the term "nation", as discussed in Chapter 2. To French Canadians the word "nation" means "people" or "society". To English Canadians it means "nation-state". Leon Dion's description of this difference is tripartite: francophones see Canada as two distinct societies or nations, one French-speaking and the other English-speaking; these two societies are qualitatively equal in every way; and the Canadian constitution should accordingly give special status to francophones within federal political institutions and also to the province of Québec.[31] Thus, while many anglophone Canadians are thought to view Canada as one nation, with an enclave of French Canadians in Québec, francophones begin with the dualistic conception of a political system composed of "Québec" and "the rest of the country". This conception of Québec as a separate "nation" can be traced in the history of the province. Whether Canada is one

---

[30]William Mishler, *op. cit.*, pp. 131 and 140.

[31]Leon Dion, *Québec: The Unfinished Revolution* (Montréal: McGill-Queen's University Press, 1976), p. 180.

nation or two is obviously a matter of definition. Constitutional expert Eugene Forsey expressed the situation this way: "In the ethnic, cultural, sociological sense, Canada is 'two nations' . . . In the political, legal, constitutional sense, Canada is one nation."[32]

We have discussed Hartz's and McRae's concept of New France as a feudal fragment founded by bearers of a feudal tradition who had left France before the liberal revolution. From 1663 on, when it came under royal control, the political development of the colony was dominated by French-style absolutism, modified somewhat by circumstances in the New World. When the British conquest ended French rule, most merchants and officials returned to France, and the forces for modernization and change departed with them. Isolated from the turmoil of the French Revolution, the culture of New France was enveloped and preserved by a few remaining institutions: the Catholic church, the French language and civil law and the feudal landholding system. So tightly sealed was French Canadian society in Québec that most of the francophone population there today are descendants of the original 10 000 French colonists who arrived before 1760.[33] From this fundamental difference in inheritance of political thought, historical events deepened divisions and produced a political culture very different from its English Canadian counterpart.

In direct contrast to the encapsulated and preserved feudal fragment in New France, Canadian anglophone society was open to outside influences. An extremely high percentage of the early inhabitants of the northern British colonies were Loyalists who fled the American Revolution; indeed, their numbers – 30 000 to 60 000 – submerged the fewer than 15 000 English colonists already in Canada. The Loyalists brought with them certain attitudes still prevalent in English Canadian society: some aspects of the liberal American tradition, but also anti-American sentiments and a corresponding loyalty to the British Crown. Some authors have termed this bond with Britain a colonial mentality, "an artificial loyalty to the Crown that grew ever more strained as new Canadians without British origins poured into the population."[34] Certainly the net effect was to delay the development of a unified and coherent nation.

French Canadian Cultural Development

Until the 1960s, the Roman Catholic church was fairly successful in directing and fostering attitudes of withdrawal and non-participation among French Canadians in Québec. The strategy was to ignore, avoid and deny activities and values foreign to their traditional culture. French Canadians were encouraged to remain an agrarian society and avoid "sinful" urban commercial enterprises. Politically, the

---

[32]Eugene Forsey, "Canada, One Nation or Two?" in *Le Canada, expérience ratée ... ou réussie?* (Québec: Congrés des affaires canadiennes, 1962), pp. 55-57.

[33]Jacques Henripin and Yves Peron, "The Democratic Transition in the Province of Quebec," in D.V. Glass and Roger Revelle, eds., *Population and Social Change* (London: Edward Arnold, 1972), pp. 213-231.

[34]Bell and Tepperman, *op. cit.*, p. 63.

result was that French Canadians neither participated as a group in the political affairs of the country nor even exploited to any degree the control that they, the majority, could have wielded within the provincial jurisdiction. They were concerned mainly with *survivance*, cultural preservation, which necessitated resistance to change and withdrawal from external influences that would alter the composition of francophone society. French Canadians were content, even within their provincial government, to resist change rather than control it. The English community took full advantage of this situation and dominated both federal politics and economic activity in Québec and elsewhere. In part, as we have seen, the federal system had been adopted in Canada to cope with the problem of how the two charter groups could coexist without ceasing to be distinct communities. The withdrawal and non-participation of the French Canadian majority in Québec were significant factors in the relative dominance of the federal over the provincial government for many years.

The situation began to change in the early 1960s, when the election of the Jean Lesage government on a *"maîtres chez nous"* platform revealed a change in the character and aspirations of French Canadian society – the beginning of the "Quiet Revolution". The influence of the Catholic church declined dramatically. One precise indication of this fact was a drop in church attendance from about 70% in 1957 to only 30% in 1975 in Montréal's Roman Catholic community. The culture of self-preservation was still strong, but Québec francophones had come to believe that the old method of withdrawing rather than actively resisting change was not working and that, if they were to maintain their identity, they had to take control of their own destiny and initiate, rather than submit to, innovations by others. The cultural spectrum of Québec politics expanded from defensive, conservative nationalism to ideologies of liberalism, socialism and more radical thought.

The commitment to a federal regime is, as one author succinctly stated, "commonly based on a rational calculation of the needs and interests of one's own community, and a judgement that they are best served by an association with other groups".[35] The Quiet Revolution soon became a challenge to Canadian federalism. The Royal Commission on Bilingualism and Biculturalism set up by the federal government to study the matter confirmed that the state of affairs established in 1867, and never before seriously questioned, was now being rejected by the Québécois. The strategy of *survivance* had been replaced by *épanouissement* – a desire to blossom and fulfill oneself; in this case, a desire to develop French culture to its full extent. Since the inception of the Quiet Revolution, Québec francophones have wanted to participate actively in determing the political, social, economic and cultural arrangements that would best fulfill their aspirations. Thus, the relationships between francophones and anglophones and between the federal and Québec governments have changed over time. Until the Quiet Revolution, the needs and aspirations of both communities and governments were relatively congruent; since then they have often diverged or conflicted.

---

[35]David Cameron, *Nationalism, Self-Determination and the Quebec Question* (Toronto: Macmillan, 1974) p. 109.

During the 1960s, the federal Liberal government responded to the Quiet Revolution by declaring Canadian federal institutions to be officially bilingual. It made great efforts to increase the number of bilingual civil servants in the government and to improve government services in both languages. In 1973, many public service positions were designated bilingual. In the 1981 census, only about 5 percent of English-speaking Canadians outside Québec claimed they were bilingual, but this represented a 78 percent increase in a decade. The increase was highest among young people. Today, the stereotype of "two solitudes" existing side-by-side within the Canadian nation-state but not communicating is far from true at the political level; there is a healthy and often vociferous political dialogue between the two cultural groups, especially whenever the minority French group has an interest to defend. Though Québec public opinion is volatile, there is, as we shall see, a remarkable degree of convergence between the political attitudes of the citizens of that province and the rest of Canada.

Political Attitudes of French Canadians

What attitudes do Québec francophones hold about their province, country and federal and provincial governments? Attitudinal surveys of French Canadians have for practical reasons generally been confined to citizens of Québec. In this unique province, where political and ethnic boundaries more or less coincide, Canadians often hold political attitudes quite distinct from those of any other region or province. A recent study found French Québec to be furthest from the national average in five of the eight ideological measures used.[36] Québec francophones scored much higher than all other regional populations on prejudice against immigrants and favouring restrictions on foreign economic control, rights of labour, redistribution of income and more social welfare. Both English and French Québécois also showed above-average support for aid to minority groups and for political protest. French respondents in the same study were also "more satisfied than average with both the federal and provincial governments but . . . far less likely to approve of federal treatment of their province(s) or to support increased federal powers".[37]

Measurements of affect in the province also reveal distinctive results. When Québec residents were asked in the course of the 1974 National Election Study how they felt about Canada and their province, thermometer scores for both questions were relatively low compared to those in other provinces, 71 and 75 percent respectively, but still quite positive. Québec anglophones showed levels of affect for Canada similar to other anglophone Canadians, but substantially lower levels for their province. Québec francophones showed slightly lower af-

---

[36]See Michael D. Ornstein, H. Michael Stevenson and A. Paul Williams, "Region, Class and Political Culture in Canada," *CJPS*, vol. XIII no. 2 (June 1980), p. 267.

[37]*Ibid.*, p. 253.

fective ratings for both. However, another attitudinal survey, administered in Québec at the time of the 1980 referendum, clearly indicated that the major reason for the defeat of the referendum was support for Canada.[38]

Surveys which measure the relative attachment of French Québécois to Canada and Québec all indicate an attachment to Québec which is somewhat or much stronger than attachment to Canada. Maurice Pinard, who has researched extensively in this area, examined the system of dual loyalties in Québec in terms of attachment to, perceived importance of and interest in the two levels of government. He concluded that "in ethnically segmented societies, precisely because of this segmentation, people tend to develop a system of dual loyalties".[39] In a 1970 survey of Québec he asked, "What degree of attachment do you feel towards Canada – do you feel a very strong attachment, a fairly strong attachment, a rather weak attachment, or a very weak attachment?" About 80 percent of francophones respondents felt very strong or fairly strong attachment to Canada. Asked whether they regarded the two levels of government as equally important, or one as more important than the other, 71 percent of French Canadians judged them to be equally important; 15 percent chose the provincial government and 9 percent the federal government. In terms of interest, Québec francophones demonstrated considerably more in provincial than in federal politics. As for attachment to governments, Pinard concluded that Québec francophones feel the provincial government looks after their interests better than the federal government, and that they are correspondingly more loyal to the former. His surveys show that, in any conflict between the two governments, 40 percent of the francophone population favour the Québec government, compared to 15 percent who support the federal government. Therefore, "if there is a system of dual loyalties, loyalty to Quebec nevertheless seems often much stronger than loyalty to Ottawa."[40]

The intensity and forms of loyalty among French Canadians appear to have changed in recent years. Between surveys done in 1970 and 1977, the group's self-identification increased substantially from "French Canadian", in which identification was with all French in Canada, to "Québécois", limited to the francophone population in the province of Québec. In light of these results, it is not surprising that Québec francophones have increasingly supported greater autonomy for Québec. Since 1962, Québec residents have frequently been polled on how they feel about independence as an option for their province. Examined

[38]Jon H. Pammett, Harold D. Clarke, Jane Jenson and Lawrence LeDuc, "Political Support and Voting Behaviour in the Quebec Referendum." Paper presented at the Conference on "Political Support in Canada: The Crisis Years", Duke University, November 1980, and Conference on "Le comportement élèctoral au Québec ", Université Laval, March 1981.

[39]See Maurice Pinard, "Ethnic Segmentation, Loyalties, Incentives and Constitutional Options in Quebec," p. 4. Paper presented at twinned workshop organized by the Canadian Political Science Association and the Israel Political Science Association at Sde Boker, Israel, December 11-16, 1978.

[40]*Ibid.*, p. 12.

longitudinally, the results reflect the strategy of *épanouissement*. Pinard's data show that the French Canadians in Québec favouring independence have always been a relatively small minority, but that the total grew from 10 percent in 1962 to 20 percent in 1978. The number of French Canadians who opposed independence in 1978 was virtually as large (70 percent) as it was in 1962, in spite of fluctuations downward, especially around 1976. However, the level of support for independence declined after the referendum in 1980. By early 1981, opposition to independence had returned to a level as high as that of the early 1960s.

An October 1983 opinion poll in Québec concluded that a large majority of francophones supported the maintenance of a vital English-speaking community in that province. Ninety-three percent of the francophones and 72 percent of the anglophones interviewed said that knowing a second language did not compromise their cultural identity. Ninety-four percent of the francophones and 96 percent of the anglophones also thought it was important that their children learn to speak the other official language.[41] In the same vein, the 1981 census showed that 32 percent of the Québec population is bilingual (French-English), a considerably higher percentage than in any of the other provinces, or in Canada as a whole (only 15 percent).

Nevertheless, bilingual policies promoted and adopted by the federal government in the late 1960s and 1970s failed to satisfy the rising tide of Québec nationalism. Even more important to Québec nationalists than bilingual services across Canada was a strong francophone society within Québec which would ensure the cultural survival of their community on an English-speaking continent. This desire was at least partially fulfilled by making French the principal language of work in Québec. Between 1971 and 1981, the number of residents in the province of Québec who declared English as their mother tongue decreased by approximately 10 percent, so that by 1981 they formed only 11 percent of the population. Québec residents, French and English, rejected sovereignty-association in the 1980 referendum, but few supported the *status quo*. Hope for the peaceful and cooperative coexistence of the two communities has been said to reside in constitutional change and a renewed federalism which would meet francophone social and political aspirations. This matter is discussed in Chapters 5 and 6.

Political Attitudes of Non-French Canadians

When Acadian author Antonine Maillet was awarded the prestigious *Prix Goncourt* for French literature in 1979, she attracted great interest in France. In a televised interview she was asked how she regarded herself – as Acadian, French, French Canadian, French Acadian, Canadian or some other. She replied that she considered herself to be all of them in different proportions. This response is perhaps a

---

[41]The poll was carried out for Alliance Québec by Sorecom Inc, Reported in *The Globe and Mail*, Oct. 26, 1983, p. 10.

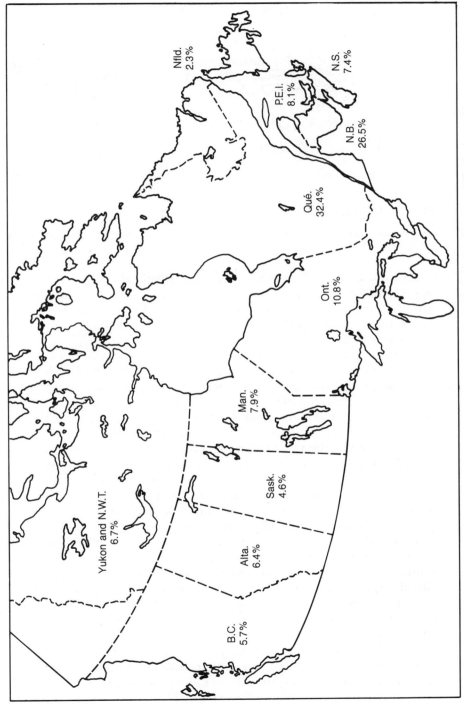

FIGURE 3.2 Bilingual Population as a Percentage of the Total Population, Canada, Provinces and Territories, 1981

Source: 1981 Census of Canada. From *Language in Canada*, (Statistics Canada, Minister of Supply and Services, 1985) Catalogue 99-935, Chart 5.

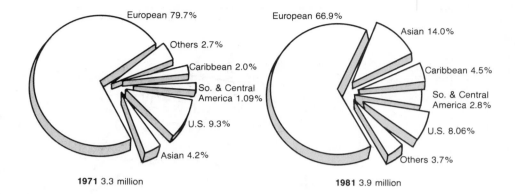

FIGURE 3.3 Canadian Residents Born Abroad

Source: Adapted from *Canada Today*, vol. 15, no. 2 (Ottawa: K.G. Campbell Corp., 1984) p. 9. Percentages are based on 1971 and 1981 census data.

good summation of the views of many Canadians who feel that belonging to an ethnic group does not detract from their self-image as Canadians. Not all Canadians fit neatly into the framework of the two founding nations. The English-speaking "nation" includes a diversity of ethnic groups, and it is with these that we are concerned in this section.

As we noted in Chapter 2, over 70 ethnic groups have been identified in Canada, the largest being German (5%), Italian (3%) and Ukrainian (2%). The 70 ethnic groups are very unevenly mixed throughout the population. According to the 1981 census, people with non-official mother tongues represent about 13 percent of the population. More than half of that number live in five large cities: Toronto, Montréal, Vancouver, Edmonton and Winnipeg.

After 1867, the Canadian population became increasingly heterogeneous. In 1871, 61 percent of Canadians were of British origin; only 8 percent were neither English nor French. During the 19th century, in spite of high rates of immigration, the size of the anglophone community remained relatively constant because of high emigration and death rates. The ratio of immigrants to total population remained constantly high. There was therefore no large stable group to absorb the newcomers, and heterogeneous communities and ideological diversity flourished. From the end of the 19th century till 1981, non-British immigration flourished to the point that only 40 percent of Canadians claimed solely British origin, 27 percent French and 33 percent other ethnic background.

Three large waves of immigration occurred in Canadian history. The first was between 1896 and 1914, and was composed mostly of British labourers, American farmers and East European peasants. The second wave was in the mid-1920s, when more hands were desperately needed, particularly in the West, to clear marginal land and increase settlements. The majority of newcomers in the second wave were central and eastern Europeans. Many were refugees, and most were very poor. Immigration died almost completely during the depression in the 1930s. The third wave did not begin until after the Second World War; it lasted until 1960. Predominantly European in origin, it included significantly more well-educated professionals than the earlier waves.

Over the years, the attitude of the welcoming majority towards the reception and accommodation of newcomers changed considerably.[42] Though the tendency was always towards assimilation, three quite different conceptions of assimilation succeeded one another during Canada's relatively short history. They corresponded approximately in time to the three major waves of immigration.[43] These fluctuations were attributable to various factors, perhaps the most important being prevailing economic conditions, the number of new arrivals and the origin of the newcomers.

The first conception of assimilation held that immigrants should renounce their old culture and adopt the patterns of behaviour and values established by Anglo-Canadians. This anglo-conformity view was based on the belief that the English Canadian nation should be patterned exclusively on the British model because it was superior to any other model. Consequently, non-British and non-French groups in Canada were relegated by this conception of assimilation to the bottom of the social, economic and political ladder.

After World War I, as Canadians began to loosen their ties to Britain, a new conception of assimilation replaced anglo-conformity. This "melting pot" view also held that conformity was necessary, but it saw assimilation as a relatively slow process in which immigrant groups should intermarry and blend with the established population in order to create a distinctive new society. The difference between this attitude and anglo-conformity was that the former acknowledged that the British way was not always innately superior and that other cultures might have something to offer Canadian society. Often, however, advocates of the melting pot could not rid their thinking of Anglo-Saxon biases. For example, one western historian advised readers in 1924 that "there is enough Anglo-Saxon blood in Alberta to dilute the foreign blood and complete the process of assimilation to the mutual advantage of both elements."[44] During the depression years of the 1930s, when competition for jobs was severe, there was considerable discrimination and overt prejudice toward ethnic groups, and the melting pot approach to assimilation was more talked about than practised.

During the high immigration period of the later 1940s and the 1950s, (a period of economic recovery marked by a rising tide of Canadian nationalism), a

---

[42]Howard Brotz, "Multiculturalism in Canada: A Muddle," *Canadian Public Policy*, vol. VI, no. 1, 1980, pp. 41-46. See also Lance W. Roberts and Rodney A Clifton, "Exploring the Ideology of Canadian Multiculturalism" in *Canadian Public Policy*, vol. VIII, no. 1 (Winter 1982), pp. 88-94 and Allan Smith, "The Ascendancy of the Ethnic Idea in North America," *CJPS*, vol. XIV, no. 2 (June 1981), pp. 227-257.

[43]See Howard Palmer, "Reluctant Hosts: Anglo-Canadian Views of Multiculturalism in the Twentieth Century," in *Multiculturalism as State Policy: Conference Report, Second Canadian Conference on Multiculturalism* (Ottawa: Minister of Supply and Services, 1976), pp. 81-119.

[44]John Blue, *Alberta Past and Present*, Vol. I (Chicago: Pioneer Historical Publishing Co., 1924), p. 218.

third conception, cultural pluralism or, more commonly, multiculturalism, gained popularity. It postulated that within the context of Canadian citizenship and economic and political integration, ethnic customs and cultures should be valued, preserved and shared.

There are many reasons for the growth of more liberal views toward ethnic groups at this time. Economic prosperity eased cultural conflicts, and the new wave of immigrants (many of whom were educated or professionals) helped break down the rigid correlation between class and ethnicity. Britain was declining as a world power and therefore provided a less attractive model; at the same time, rising Canadian nationalism required a new self-image to distinguish Canada from the American melting pot. Perhaps the most immediate reasons for the advance of pluralist ideas at this time were the dramatic changes brought about by the Quiet Revolution in Québec. Many ethnic groups found the dualist image conveyed by the recommendations of the Royal Commission on Biculturalism and Bilingualism offensive and sought official assurance that their own aspirations and interests would not be overlooked. In response to their pressures, the Royal Commission produced a fourth volume dealing with the role of "other ethnic groups" in Canada.[45] Subsequently, in the early 1970s, the federal government and the provincial governments of Ontario, Manitoba, Saskatchewan and Alberta formally adopted a policy of multiculturalism. In 1971, the federal government defined Canada as being multicultural within a bilingual English-French framework, and established a Ministry of State for Multiculturalism within the federal government. Services on which ethnic groups could draw were steadily increased throughout the 1970s.

The current policy of the federal government is to promote the retention of characteristic cultural features of ethnic groups which want to maintain their identity, and to encourage the sharing of these features with all Canadians. The basic assumption of this policy is that confidence in one's own cultural foundations helps to break down prejudice and discrimination between ethnic groups. To this end, Ottawa spends millions of dollars to fund projects such as ethnic group histories and language schools designed to further the objectives of multiculturalism in the country.

Cultural Tolerance

Unfortunately, cultural tolerance of ethnic diversity is a self-congratulatory ideal that Canadians have not always lived up to. There have been many incidents of racial bigotry in Canadian history, including the shameful internment of Japanese Canadians during World War II and the often shabby treatment of Native peoples. Racist ideologies have repeatedly been condemned, but still persist. Some sociologists even maintain that "racism is a virulent ideology held by Canadians.

---

[45]*Report of the Royal Commission of Bilingualism and Biculturalism*, Book 4, (Ottawa: Queen's Printer, 1970).

There is a belief that certain groups (non-Whites) are inferior to Whites and this justifies invidious distinctions and behaviours directed toward them."[46]

Immigration policies are a good measure of cultural tolerance. Canada's immigration regulations were traditionally based on the principle that all immigrants should be assimilated into the dominant French and English ethnic groups, with the result that less easily assimilable groups were restricted. Since the early days of the country, when white immigrants were actively sought by the Canadian government, immigration policies have been consistently restrictive toward non-white groups. For instance, the federal government took the position after 1900 that non-whites, specifically Asians, would not fit into Canadian society and would be a disruptive element.

Since 1952, there have been consistent attempts to broaden admission policies, but they have been tempered by the notion of "ethnic balance" – that is, that no new immigrant group should disturb the existing ethno-racial balance of Canada. In practice, this concept has tended to ensure that ethnic groups that are not already well-represented remain that way. A point system introduced in 1967 was designed to restrict entry to individuals who might not adapt quickly to Canadian society; these obviously tended to be poorly educated non-whites from developing countries.

By 1978, the new multicultural policies were finally reflected in a more liberal *Immigration Act*, which declared that immigration policy was to be founded on principles of non-discrimination, family reunion, humanitarian concern for refugees and promotion of national goals. Provincial and federal governments now consult to provide an annual forecast of how many immigrants can be absorbed. This forecast is a global limit, rather than a quota system for specific countries or areas. The humanitarian move to consider family reunion and refugees in particular is an attempt to make the multi-ethnic ideal of the cultural mosaic more than merely a platitude. Whether interpretation of the new principles will be liberal or restrictive remains to be seen, but, as we noted in Chapter 2, immigration figures do show increasing percentages of Asian, Caribbean, Central American and African immigrants. It must be noted, however, that merely by advertising and making more immigration offices available in some areas than in others, the government subtly affects who will immigrate. For example, in 1981 there were over 30 offices in Europe and 13 in the United States, but only five in Africa and eight in Asia. Preferred immigrants are still entrepreneurs or those with particular skills who can fit quickly into the labour market, and people who meet these qualifications are preponderantly from developed countries.

Federal immigration policies have a significant impact on a wide range of matters under provincial jurisdiction, especially on health and community services. The selection and entry of immigrants is of particular concern to French Canadians in Québec, who fear the prospect of becoming a minority in their own

---

[46]Alan B. Anderson and James S. Frideres, *Ethnicity in Canada*, (Toronto: Butterworths, 1981), p. 229. Compensation for interned Japanese Canadians was one of several controversial recommendations made by an all-party Commons committee on visible minorities in 1983.

province. Whether or not an ethnic minority maintains its separate identity may well depend on the degree to which it is replenished through continued immigration. In the past two decades, the number of people speaking French in their homes has decreased, while English speakers have gained numbers relative to speakers of French and other languages. This trend has been attributed to increased anglicization of French-speaking communities outside Québec, and even within the province of Québec as migration to cities from the rural areas has increased. Moreover, Québec's overall birth rate is declining and in 1982 was slightly below the national average. Immigrants, even in Québec, show a marked preference to learn English as their new language. In the face of this perceived cultural threat, the Québec government in 1968 established a separate Department of Immigration to deal with recruitment and settlement of immigrants, and launched a series of programs and regulations to encourage immigrants in Québec to become integrated into the francophone community. However, some of the stringent regulations may have been premature, since there has been no major change in the composition of the Québec population. Ethnic gains in Montréal until 1981 were balanced by the loss of anglophone population. Outside the city over 93 percent of the population was French-speaking in 1981; within Montréal, over 68 percent.

The discrimination evident in the history of Canada's immigration policy can also be traced in the social, economic and political development of the country. John Porter's *The Vertical Mosaic* revealed the existence of a pecking order for various ethnic groups which allowed them unequal chances to move between classes and succeed in Canadian society.[47] The ethnic pecking order which existed in immigration policy was identical to the "vertical mosaic" of ethnic stratification. The British were on top, in establishment positions; Chinese and blacks, on the bottom rung, held the most menial occupations. Before World War II, members of ethnic groups other than British or French were poorly represented even in middle-echelon jobs in politics, education or the civil service, and almost none had penetrated elite positions.[48]

A survey of attitudes in 1974 concluded that the vertical mosaic described by John Porter in the 1960s still existed but was significantly diminished.[49] An ethnic pecking order was still part of the mental baggage of Anglo-Canadians inasmuch as northern European groups were more highly regarded than southern Europeans or non-whites. The same survey showed a correlation between the attitude towards a group and how that group feels it is being treated. However, a

---

[47]See John Porter, *The Vertical Mosaic* (Toronto: University of Toronto Press, 1965) and W. Clement, *The Canadian Corporate Elite* (Toronto: McClelland and Stewart, 1975).

[48]*Report of the Royal Commission on Biculturalism*, Chapter 2. Also see Dennis Olsen, *The State Elite* (Toronto: McClelland and Stewart, 1980). For an analysis of the various causes of ethnic stratification see Book IV of the *Report*.

[49]A good summary of this survey was published in the Report of the Second Conference on Multiculturalism: J.W. Berry, R. Kalen and D.M. Taylor, "Summary – Multiculturalism and Ethnic Attitudes in Canada," in *Multiculturalism as a State Policy*, pp. 149-168.

Table 3.2 Percentage Distribution by Mother Tongue of the Population,
Provinces and Territories, 1981

Mother Tongue	Nfld.	P.E.I.	N.S.	N.B.	Qué.	Ont.	Man	Sask.	Alta.	B.C.	Yukon	N.W.T.
	%	%	%	%	%	%	%	%	%	%	%	%
English	98.8	94.0	93.6	65.1	10.9	77.3	71.7	79.7	81.1	81.9	87.4	54.1
French	0.5	4.9	4.2	33.6	82.4	5.5	5.1	2.6	2.8	1.6	2.3	2.7
Other	0.7	1.1	2.2	1.2	6.7	17.2	23.1	17.7	16.2	16.5	10.3	43.2

Source: 1981 Census of Canada. From *Language in Canada* (Statistics Canada: Minister of Supply and Services, 1985) Catalogue 99-935, Table 1.

great deal of evidence suggested that these attitudes were in the process of breaking down. The 1974 survey further revealed that, despite the fact that knowledge about the federal multicultural policy was very limited (only 19 percent of Canadians indicated they had heard about it), Canadians demonstrated a mild acceptance of a policy of multiculturalism. The results varied by province, with the greatest acceptance in Ontario and the prairie provinces, the least in Québec and the maritime provinces.

Except in Québec, minority groups are most valued where they are most concentrated. The 1981 census results showed Ontario to be by far the largest centre for nearly all ethnic groups, followed by the prairie provinces and British Columbia. At the other extreme, just over 1 percent lived in all four maritime provinces combined. In terms of percentage of total provincial population claiming non-official mother tongues, the maritime provinces again were lowest in the country, followed by Québec. As Table 3.2 shows, Manitoba, Saskatchewan and Ontario have the highest percentage of individuals claiming non-official mother tongues. Low acceptance of minority groups by Québec respondents reflects the tendency of French Canadians to regard the existence of other cultures and languages as a threat. Any acceptance of other ethnic claims, it is argued, undermines the concept of dualism for the country and reduces the French claim to that of the largest of the minority cultures. This problem was studied by the Task Force on Canadian Unity set up in the wake of the November 1976 election victory of the Parti Québécois in Québec. To ensure that ethnic pluralism remained subordinate to dualism, it recommended that "the provincial governments should assume primary responsibility for the support of multiculturalism in Canada."[50] So far, there has been no significant move in that direction.

---

[50]The Task Force on Canadian Unity, *A Future Together: Observations and Recommendations* (Ottawa: Ministry of Supply and Services, 1979), pp. 55-56. A study of attitudes towards minority groups is found in J.W. Berry, R. Kalen and D.M. Taylor, *Multiculturalism and Ethnic Attitudes in Canada* (Ottawa: Minister of Supply and Services, 1977).

Besides the French Canadians' fear that their place as a founding nation will be undermined, there are two other criticisms of multiculturalism as a government policy. First, it is argued that it will only perpetuate the vertical stratification of Canadian society and decrease social and economic mobility. However, stratification by ethnicity is losing its rigidity and today there are numerous examples of ethnic diversity of personnel in middle level and establishment positions.

Another common criticism of multiculturalism is that it fragments Canadian society. There is, however, no evidence that this is the case. To date, Canadian society has proven remarkably resilient in accommodating large numbers of immigrants with relatively little social stress. Since World War II, only Australia and Israel have accepted comparable numbers of immigrants in proportion to their populations. Inevitably, a rapid influx of immigrants into urban areas results in competition for housing, jobs and social facilities which can create a high degree of social tension. Nonetheless, as we noted, positive attitudes toward multiculturalism are strongest in areas where other ethnic groups are most concentrated.

Ethnicity and Political Culture

Does ethnic diversity fragment the nation-state political culture and make the country less cohesive? The existence of significant subcultures within a country can be disruptive to the dominant political culture if group ties are stronger than loyalty to the country. In extreme situations, ethnic crises can raise doubts about the efficacy of a federal system of government in meeting the needs of an ethnically diverse country, and even about whether the country should stay united. Canada has experienced several ethnic crises in which group loyalties conflicted strongly with larger community loyalty, though these were confined to the two founding groups. However, it would be pessimistic to regard such crises as the norm.

Optimistic conclusions about the multi-ethnic nature of Canadian society can be drawn from research by David Elkins which reinforces the suggestion of the Bicultural and Bilingualism Commission that multiculturalism is a strengthening feature of Canadian unity. Elkins concluded that ignorance of one's own and other nations is associated with parochial, localist sentiments, while knowledge about and appreciation of other nations is an enriching experience that encourages individuals to feel warmer toward their own country.[51] A partial explanation, he suggested, lies in the fact that most immigrants to Canada are from countries with strong central governments. For example, the largest single group of immigrants comes from Britain, which has a unitary system of government. It is logical that these newcomers would support the familiar idea that the central government is the strongest and most important voice for the country.

---

[51]David Elkins, "The Sense of Place," in David J. Elkins and Richard Simeon, eds., *Small Worlds*, (Toronto: Methuen, 1980) pp. 1-30.

Elkins found that native-born Canadians are more provincially oriented than immigrants, and that, the longer immigrants are in the country, the more provincial they become.

Another interesting finding about immigrants to Canada is that they are on average slightly more efficacious in their political attitudes than native-born Canadians. Elkins speculates that individuals who act positively to improve their personal environment by emigrating demonstrate self-reliant efficacious behaviour, which might explain their higher score on political efficacy.[52]

As well as having warmer feelings toward the country as a whole than do native-born Canadians who remain in one region, immigrants and internal migrants adopt norms and patterns of behaviour characteristic of the province in which they settle. Immigrants adapt to and perpetuate provincial political cultures. Assimilation to provincial values and attitudes appears to be a function of both length of residence and type of background. Relatively recent or first generation immigrant minorities tend to be concerned primarily with problems of adjustment to their new circumstances, whereas well-established minorities are less concerned with the persistence of their ethnicity than with increasing their collective economic and political strength.[53] When language, religious affiliation and adherence to custom are used as criteria, ethnic identity is not static, but changes steadily from one generation to the next as individuals adapt to Canadian circumstances. The 1981 census, for example, showed that 10 percent of those with a mother tongue other than English or French are able to speak not one but *both* official languages – 2 percent higher than those whose mother tongue is English.

The Canadian commitment to cultural diversity in the form of bilingualism and multiculturalism serves to unite Canadians by helping to combat two threats: American cultural domination and threats of separation by any province or region. Bilingualism and multiculturalism are uniquely Canadian responses adopted to deal with uniquely Canadian circumstances. To date, research supports the positive effect of the cultural mosaic and indicates that multiculturalism is not to be feared, but encouraged. Some, however, question whether enough effort is being made to do so. One author questions bluntly whether Canadians genuinely aspire to cultural diversity. What, he asks, does multiculturalism amount to other than folk-dancing on the weekends? The "rhetoric of the Canadian mosaic may be no more than sugar coating on the bitter pill of assimilation."[54]

There is no doubt that ethnic cultures are eroding: the studies of language, religion and customs as indicators of ethnic strength all support this view. Language is the easiest of these indicators to measure. Except in Québec, from 1941

---

[52]*Ibid.*, and David Elkins, "The Horizontal Mosaic: Immigrants and Migrants in the Provincial Political Cultures," in Elkins and Simeon, eds., *Small Worlds*, pp. 106-130.

[53]Wsevolod Isajiw, "Immigration and Multiculturalism – Old and New Approaches." Paper presented at the Conference on Multiculturalism and Third World Immigrants in Canada, University of Alberta, Edmonton, September 3-5, 1975, p. 2.

[54]D. Forbes, "Conflicting National Identities Among Canadian Youth," in Pammett and Whittington, eds., *Foundations of Political Culture*, pp. 288-315.

to 1981 there was a steady increase in the number of Canadians who named English as their mother tongue, and a corresponding decrease in the number who named French and other languages. The 1981 census showed that while 61 percent of Canadians claimed English as their mother tongue, 68 percent spoke English most at home. With the exception of Québec and New Brunswick francophones, most French Canadians now speak English in the home because it is the working language of the community. It can be expected that non-use of a given mother tongue will eventually result in loss of ability. Even where it is used in the home, the maternal language is not often used outside a very small community of friends and family, so that linguistic assimilation becomes inevitable over time. Many factors hasten language assimilation. Provincial legislation restricts the use of languages other than English and French in schools. Migration from rural to urban areas also erodes former bastions of ethnic culture. Intermarriage, too, weakens ethnic ties, although it is not a major factor in Canada, where in-group marriages are characteristic.

Given this dilemma, we would argue that multiculturalism is indeed a form of assimilation. In fact, the term "multicultural" is misleading: multi-ethnic describes the Canadian reality more accurately. Whether or not one views multiculturalism as a viable policy depends on how it is defined. Jean Burnet addressed the issue by saying, "Multiculturalism within a bilingual framework can work, if it is interpreted as is intended – that is, as encouraging those members of ethnic groups who want to do so to maintain a proud sense of the contribution of their own group to Canadian society."[55] In this way, it becomes something very Canadian: voluntary marginal differentiation among peoples who are equal participants in society. Cultures cannot be preserved in their entirety: immigrants do adapt to the language and customs of the majority. But in doing so they add a richness, variety and depth to the cultural tapestry that makes it unique. The formal adoption of bilingual and multicultural policies by the government enshrines ethnic tolerance among the other important values of Canadian political culture.

The concept of multiculturalism presupposes a number of subcultures based on ethnic identities. Some authors suggest instead that the different cultures within Canada are based on regional identities.

THE REGIONAL DIMENSION OF POLITICAL CULTURE

There is widespread acceptance in the theoretical literature of comparative politics of the thesis that strong regional interests are incompatible with mature statehood, that nation-building involves a gradual reduction of conflict between regional and national interests. While this contention is not without its critics, it remains one of the primary hypotheses about the growth and development of na-

---

[55]Jean Burnet, "The Policy of Multiculturalism within a Bilingual Framework: An Interpretation," in A. Wolfgang, *The Education of Immigrant Students: Issues and Answers* (Toronto: Ontario Institute for Studies in Education, 1975).

Reproduced with permission (Bas. – Tachydromos, Greece/Rothco).

tion-states and their legitimacy.[56] In this section we shall address the question, How strong is regionalism in Canada, and is it increasing or decreasing?

To be sure, impressive factual data exist about regional forms of social behaviour in Canada. Canadians, for example, are insular even in their preferred way of spending leisure time. Three-quarters of vacation travel in 1980 was not only within Canada, but mainly in the province of residence. Regional behaviour is strong in the economic sphere, too, especially in the area of natural resources where the issue of revenue-sharing between federal and provincial coffers arises.[57] The industrial heartland of Ontario and Québec has long been the source of friction and jealousy elsewhere, and Alberta's oil wealth has resulted in country-wide contention.

---

[56]See Almond and Powell, *Comparative Politics*; Clarke *et al.*, *op. cit.*, p. 43; Robert Alford, *Party and Society* (Chicago: Rand McNally, 1963); Seymour M. Lipset and Stein Rokkan, "Cleavage Structures, Party Systems and Voter Alignments: An Introduction," in Lipset and Rokkan, eds., *Party Systems and Voter Alignments* (New York: The Free Press, 1967); Mildred A. Schwartz, *Politics and Territory: The Sociology of Regional Persistence in Canada* (Montréal: McGill-Queen's University Press, 1974); Raymond Breton, "Regionalism in Canada," in David Cameron, ed., *Regionalism and Supranationalism* (Montréal: Institute for Research on Public Policy, 1981).

[57]See Garth Stevenson, "Federalism and the Political Economy of the Canadian State," in Leo Panitch, ed., *The Canadian State: Political Economy ad Political Power* (Toronto: University of Toronto Press, 1977) and Kenneth Campbell, "Regional Disparity and Interregional Exchange Imbalance," in Daniel Glenday, Herbert Guindon and Allan Turowetz, eds., *Modernization and the Canadian State* (Toronto: Macmillan, 1978).

Provincial boundaries promote unique regional, social and political behaviour because each province has its own institutional focus, sometimes with regional political parties. On a practical level, educational and professional standards, as well as licensing requirements, differ from province to province and are often not easily transferable. One author comments in this regard that "it may even be easier to transfer professional qualifications between two member countries of the European Community than between Canadian provinces."[58] The provinces also restrict mobility of individuals through numerous other variations in standards, laws and services such as driver's licences, pension plans and medical insurance. Such regionally-based behaviour may be caused by differences in political culture between regions or may be the cause of regional differences in values and attitudes.

Not surprisingly, therefore, researchers have produced interesting evidence that Canada may have not merely one or even two "political cultures", but several which are regionally based. In view of the distinctions made earlier, we see these, not as "cultures" *per se*, but rather as important subcultures existing within the overarching Canadian political culture along with the various ethnic subcultures. The establishment of a federal form of government gave a structural guarantee that some form of regionalism would flourish in Canada; indeed, it was chosen partly because it would allow regional diversity. This is well illustrated by provincial political parties which are, for the most part, inclined to place provincial issues ahead of party solidarity with their counterparts in the rest of the country. Even the federal parties are often unable to bridge regional and linguistic cleavages. The most prominent feature of the federal party system for most of this century has been the dominance of the Conservative Party in the West and (until 1984) the Liberal Party in Québec.

Numerous factors promote and sustain regionalism.[59] People of varying cultural and linguistic backgrounds settled in different parts of the country. Geographical and economic disparities among the regions fostered distinct viewpoints, loyalties and attitudes toward national political problems. As one author put it, Canada became "a country displaying a complex of political cultures which are regionally based . . . the extent of the diversity of Canada's political cultures and its scope . . . are quite astonishing."[60] There is no doubt that differences in institutions and policies of the various provincial governments reflect differences in the values and attitudes of their citizens.

The term "regionalism" is particularly obtuse. It implies a socio-psychological dimension in that the population displays an emotional identification with or attachment to a given territory. There is also a political dimension in that specific

---

[58]Garth Stevenson, *Unfulfilled Union* (Toronto: Macmillan, 1979), p. 125.

[59]For an economic explanation see D. Glenday *et al.*, eds, *Modernization and the Canadian State* (Toronto: Macmillan, 1978).

[60]John Meisel, *Working Papers on Canadian Politics* (Montréal: McGill-Queen's University Press, 1972), p. 25.

interests – cultural, economic and political – can be defined and articulated for a particular area. There is thus general agreement that regions are more than purely scientific artifacts, but many different opinions surface about exactly what they are, how many there are or what their boundaries might be. The previous section in this chapter took the viewpoint that there are two dominant political cultures, derived from the two founding nations. Some researchers, however, have postulated that the boundaries of the ten provinces demarcate regions having separate political cultures.[61] Others prefer to think in terms of three regions (eastern, central and western Canada); four (Atlantic Canada, Québec, Ontario and the West); or five (here British Columbia is separated from the prairie provinces).[62] There seems to be no limit to where regional boundaries could be drawn. Respondents in the 1974 National Election Survey provided approximately 700 different combinations of regions.[63] Obviously, they drew boundaries for strictly idiosyncratic reasons. Similarly, academic researchers often define regions according to the nature of their particular study.

In the following pages, we have adopted a popular conception of Canadian regional boundaries wherein six regions are identified: the Atlantic provinces (Newfoundland, Nova Scotia, New Brunswick and Prince Edward Island); Québec; Ontario; the Prairies (Manitoba, Saskatchewan and Alberta); British Columbia; and the North (comprising the Yukon Territory and the Northwest Territories). However, the reader should be aware that basing regions on provincial boundaries (or groups of provinces) is largely a convenience, and that significant variations in cultural patterns may well occur within these borders – for example, between northern and southern Ontario.

Four main categories of regional differences lead researchers to expect cultural diversity: physical factors (such as climate, terrain and land quality); demographic factors (including ethnic and religious composition and urbanization); economic development (including natural resources and type of economy); and services which affect the quality of life (such as transportation, health and welfare). The following brief regional profiles illustrate some of these important differences.

Six Regional Profiles

As Table 3.3 shows, the *Atlantic provinces* possess 9 percent of the population of Canada. The inhabitants are largely of British and Irish ancestry, with pockets of Acadian French in New Brunswick. The majority are Protestant, but Roman Catholics constitute the largest single denomination. Their formal educational level is relatively low, they are relatively poor (refer to Figure 3.3), and they usually

---

[61]John Wilson, "The Canadian Political Cultures: Towards a Redefinition of the Nature of the Canadian Political System," *CJPS*, vol. 7, no. 3 (Sept. 1974), pp. 438-483.

[62]Mildred A. Schwartz, *op. cit.*

[63]Clarke *et al.*, *op. cit.*, Chapter 2.

TABLE 3.3 Percentage Distribution of Canadian Population by Province and Region, 1981

	Province	*Region*
Newfoundland	2.3	
Prince Edward Island	0.5	
Nova Scotia	3.5	9.2
New Brunswick	2.9	
Québec	26.4	26.4
Ontario	35.4	35.4
Manitoba	4.2	
Saskatchewan	4.0	17.4
Alberta	9.2	
British Columbia	11.3	11.3
Yukon Territory	.1	
Northwest Territories	.2	.3
	100.0	100.0

Source: 1981 census data supplied by Statistics Canada.

have the highest unemployment levels in Canada.[64] Most reside in rural areas and small towns. Economically, the major contribution comes through the fisheries, of which more than half Canada's total are located here. The region is seriously deficient in secondary industries and contributes less than the other regions to the national wealth in proportion to the population. Both internal and external communications are relatively inadequate. Low immigration and a tendency towards outward migration have often meant a net loss of inhabitants for the region as a percentage of the country's total population.

Québec houses just over one quarter of the Canadian population. It is the bastion of French language and culture and of Roman Catholicism. Eighty-two percent of Québécois were French-speaking at the time of the 1981 census. The fertility rate in Québec is declining; in 1982 it was the lowest among the provinces, at 14 live births per thousand population. In the 1970s and 1980s, the province increased efforts to attract more French-speaking immigrants in order to keep the balance between the French and English populations in the province relatively stable. Although between 1976 and 1981 Québec lost 12 percent of its anglophone population, the total population grew by nearly 7 percent. Economically, Québec and neighbouring Ontario are the most industrialized regions, with major contributions to agriculture, mining, forestries, electric power, manufacturing and construction. Québec has a rapidly growing urban population which is mainly located in a few major cities; 78 percent of its population was classified as urban in 1981.

---

[64]Bernard R. Blishen, "A Socio-Economic Index for Occupations in Canada," *Canadian Review of Sociology and Anthropology*, vol. 4, no. 1 (February 1967), pp. 41-53.

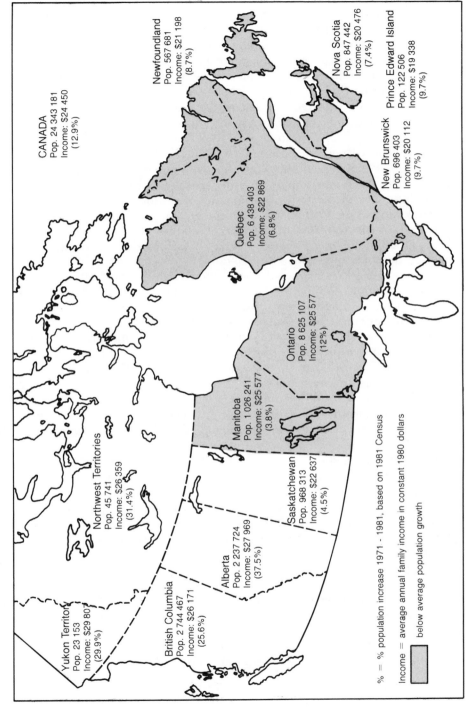

FIGURE 3.4 Population and Family Income in Canada by Province, 1981

Source: Adapted from "Money and Migration," in *Canada Today*, vol. 15, no. 2 (Ottawa: K.G. Campbell Corp., 1984), pp. 6–7.

Ontario contains 35 percent of the Canadian population. Although still predominantly of British stock, Ontarians include large groups of French, German and Dutch, in that order, and many other ethnic groups in lesser numbers. In 1981, 46 percent of the Canadian population with non-official mother tongues resided in Ontario. They are particularly concentrated in Toronto, Canada's largest metropolitan area.[65] Roman Catholic and Protestant denominations dominate, but many other religious groups are also represented. As we noted above, Ontario, along with Québec, forms the industrial heartland of Canada. Urban, well-educated and well serviced medically, with more televisions, telephones and automobiles *per capita* than most of their fellow Canadians, Ontario residents increased by 12 percent between 1971 and 1981, a figure close to the national average of 12.9 percent, but down from the province's peak growth rate in 1971.

The three *Prairie Provinces* are ethnically extremely diverse and still reflect the influence of the European peasants who flocked to settle the prairie farmlands in the late 19th and early 20th centuries. The first settlers in the region were Scottish crofters in the Red River valley in Manitoba. Today, the largest single group in the prairie region is still of British origin, but there are exceptionally large numbers of German and Ukrainian descent, a large percentage of Native Indians, as well as many citizens of Polish, Dutch and Scandinavian origin. No single religion dominates. Economically dependent on natural resources for their above-average wealth, the prairie provinces make outstanding contributions in agriculture, particularly wheat, mining and oil and gas production. Development of the Alberta oil fields has dramatically increased the prosperity and prestige of that province in recent years.

Since World War II, the agrarian nature of the prairie region has been changing and an increasing percentage of the population is urban, although Saskatchewan is still one of the least urbanized Canadian provinces. Alberta, the richest and most urban of the prairie provinces, and the most attractive for immigrants because of the expanding oil and gas industries, accounts for much of the significant increase in net migration in the prairie region during the past two decades. It sustained the most rapid population growth of all the provinces and territories between 1971 and 1981 – 37.5 percent. Manitoba and Saskatchewan grew least – only 3.8 and 4.5 percent, respectively.

British Columbia is relatively isolated from the rest of the country, cut off by the Rocky Mountain chain. Immigrants in the early years were primarily British but today the ethnic composition is very diverse because of high immigration and internal migration. In 1981, British Columbia had 11 percent of the total Canadian population, but 14 percent of those who were foreign-born. Religious affiliation is also diverse; however, the United and Anglican churches make up the majority. Economically prosperous, British Columbia makes major contributions through fisheries and forestry and to some extent through its manufacturing and construction industries. Despite reliance on primary resource industries, the region is relatively urban, with a number of heavily populated centres.

Canada's largest region, the vast *Northland* of the Northwest Territories and

---

[65]The figures were supplied by Statistics Canada.

the Yukon Territory, comprises 39 percent of the country's total land mass. However, the thinly scattered population, which includes the Dene (Indian) nation, several Inuit peoples and a small white population, constitutes only .3 percent of the Canadian population, in spite of rapid growth in percentage terms since 1971. The economy of the Yukon Territory has grown rapidly over the past decade largely because of demand for certain minerals, but the economy of the Northwest Territories remains precarious. Communications in the entire region are tenuous. For Canada's Native peoples, living conditions are difficult. For example, Indian babies have a much higher mortality rate than the national average, and the death rate for young adult Indians is two to four times the national average.

In November 1982, the federal government agreed to reshape the political boundaries of the Northwest Territories, so that eventually the inhabitants will not have to rely on a single regional government in Yellowknife. Once the land claims of the Native peoples are settled, it is proposed that the Northwest Territories be divided into two or three smaller units, each with its own capital and territorial government. It should be noted that the change will not confer full provincial status.

The differences in historical development, ethnic and demographic make-up and economic structure within Canada are very evident in these brief profiles of the six regions. However, since provincial governments provide the only institutional focus through which regions can mobilize, it is questionable whether particular groups of provinces can ever be as effective as individual provinces in political terms. Indeed, it is not even clear that they want to be. Premier Alex Campbell of Prince Edward Island said publicly that "We in Atlantic Canada have not yet made the decision to develop as a region. We are four separate competitive, jealous and parochial provinces."[66] Furthermore, a study commissioned by the Task Force on Canadian Unity in 1978 concluded that attachment to either region or province does not threaten national integration.[67]

The prairie region, particularly Alberta and Saskatchewan, holds the attitude that their region is exploited. This feeling is based on the perceived economic and political domination of the rest of the country by the tiny Golden Horseshoe area of southern Ontario, and Montréal. Former Alberta Premier Harry Strom's imagery illustrates it well: "We have always had a sense of economic exploitation. This notion has marked all political parties in the West. The cartoon that has captured these sentiments is one of a large cow standing on a map of Canada munching grass in Alberta and Saskatchewan, with milk pouring from a bulging udder into the large bucket in Ontario."[68]

[66]Quoted in Roger Gibbins, *Regionalism: Territorial Politics in Canada and the United States* (Toronto: Butterworths, 1982), p. 178.

[67]Relevant findings from the Atlantic Provinces Study conducted for the Task Force on Canadian Unity can be found in Roger Gibbins, *op. cit.*, pp. 179-180.

[68]Quoted in David Elton and Roger Gibbins, "Western Alienation and Political Culture," in R. Schultz *et al.*, eds., *The Canadian Political Process*, 3rd edition. (Toronto: Holt, Rinehart and Winston, 1979), p. 85.

The main thrust of western discontent, however, has been integrative rather than separatist, and may "reflect frustration at the lack of national integration as much as it does resistance to integration".[69] A survey of the four western provinces in October 1980 revealed that about 35 percent of that population thought the West was ignored in federal political decision-making. About 61 percent also felt that the federal government discriminated against the West in economic terms. At the same time, however, 90 percent of westerners said they would prefer to remain part of Canada, even though 60 percent believed the West had sufficient resources to thrive on its own.[70] The problem of Western alienation is further discussed in Chapter 6.

It has been suggested that regional discontent may be more a fabrication of elites than a strong feeling of the mass public.[71] It is often to the benefit of the political elite to exacerbate differences between provinces or regions and the federal government. Provincial premiers can play on regional sentiments to gain support in striking tough financial bargains with the federal government.

It is important to note, however, that regional economic disparities and the manner in which they are dealt with are distinguishing features of Canadian politics. Since Confederation, the belief that the rich provinces and regions should help the poorer ones has been a fundamental part of the Canadian political culture. Sharing through redistribution is built into the political system and is viewed by Canadians as the "just" way to cope with differences in wealth.[72] The disparities are levelled to a degree through equalization payments designed to raise the economic standards of the have-not provinces. Disputes over formulas and provincial jostling for a fair share of the economic pie take place within this basic redistribution framework.

Regional Political Cultures

Richard Simeon and David Elkins are among those who argue that Canada embraces several regional political cultures.[73] Basing their argument on survey data collected in 1965 and 1968, they compared the provinces, examining differences

---

[69]R. Gibbins, *op. cit.*, p. 181. See also J.F. Conway, *The West: The History of a Region in Confederation* (Toronto: James Lorimer, 1983).

[70]Reported in *The Globe and Mail*, November 25, 1980, p. 9. The results were from a three-part survey by a non-political, non-profit research group that studies Western Canada and its position in Confederation.

[71]See, for example, Richard Simeon and Donald E. Blake in "Regional Preferences: Citizens' Views of Public Policy," in David J. Elkins and Richard Simeon, *Small Worlds* (Toronto: Methuen, 1980), pp. 77-105.

[72]See, for example, Herschel Hardin's concept of "The Canadian Redistribution Culture," in H. Hardin, *A Nation Unaware: The Canadian Economic Culture* (Vancouver: J.J. Douglas Ltd., 1974), especially Chapter 13.

[73]Richard Simeon and David J. Elkins, "Regional Political Cultures in Canada," *CJPS*, vol. 7, no. 3 (September 1974), pp. 397-437. The revised version of this article is "Provincial Political Cultures in Canada," in *Small Worlds*, pp. 31-76.

among their populations as regards pattern of political orientations, and explanations of these differences. They identified twelve province/language regions: the non-French-speaking populations in the ten provinces and two French groups – those within Québec and those elsewhere. The aim of the study was to determine whether distinct political orientations existed in three areas: a sense of efficacy, trust in government, and political participation. Their findings demonstrated that provincial variations in political culture do exist. Canadians were polarized in terms of both efficacy and political trust. The highest levels of these orientations were found in British Columbia, Ontario and Manitoba. Alberta, Saskatchewan and Québec anglophones were not far behind. The Maritime provinces were at the opposite extreme, with very low levels of trust and efficacy, and French-speaking Québécois were not far from that extreme.

When Simeon and Elkins combined the factors of efficacy and political trust to determine the degree of disaffection in the various provinces, they concluded

> "In Newfoundland, New Brunswick and Nova Scotia, a majority of respondents are disaffected. About 45 percent of French Canadians, in or out of Québec, are in this category. The figure drops to about 37 percent in Alberta and Saskatchewan, 26 percent in Ontario and Manitoba, and to only 15 percent in British Columbia. The order is reversed among the supporters: British Columbia has the greatest proportion, at 38 percent, and the Maritimes, especially Newfoundland and New Brunswick, the least."[74]

Such discontent, however, does not lead to apathy. According to the same study, despite their cynicism, Maritimers and French Canadians participate about as readily as others in the political system. The differences in attitudes found in the data do, however, reflect important socio-economic characteristics of provincial populations, including education, income and occupational distributions. Class and education had a strong independent effect on basic orientations of citizens, but class, party identification and other control variables did not wash out the wide variations between regions. Simeon and Elkins concluded that "there are indeed differences between the provinces which may be called cultural, which are rooted in the matrix of historical and sociological factors unique to each province."[75]

It is interesting to speculate on the possible sources of the cultural variations among the provinces. Some of the factors outlined in the regional profiles are undoubtedly significant. Levels of industrialization and economic development are extremely low in the Maritime provinces, high in Ontario and British Columbia. Emigration from the Maritime area is high, immigration low. The extreme weakness of the economy and the consistent historical inability of governments to solve the problem would likely engender lack of political trust and feelings of inability to change their situation in the Maritime population. The

---

[74]Simeon and Elkins, "Provincial Political Cultures in Canada," *op. cit.*, pp. 44-46.

[75]*Ibid.*, p. 68.

provinces that scored highest in the efficacy/political trust scale have the opposite of these characteristics. As well, the peculiar pattern of settlement along the American border and the polycephalic city network discussed in Chapter 2 help perpetuate regionally based interests and attitudes.

The six regions profiled above might well exhibit differences of which their residents are unaware. But if there is little or no regional consciousness, it can be argued that residents cannot be politicized into action over regional interests or problems. If there is no regional consciousness, "regionalism" cannot be treated as an explanatory variable for analytical purposes, but must be limited to the role of "container" for other variables. Researchers would have to let Canadians themselves describe the regions in which they live and articulate their feelings about these regions in order to demarcate lines of regional consciousness.

To determine whether or not regional boundaries form part of the perception of Canadians, Clarke, Jenson, LeDuc and Pammett asked respondents in the 1974 National Election Survey "whether they thought of the country in terms of regions, and if so, what region they lived in and what the other regions were."[76] Of the sample interviewed, 59 percent said they thought of the country in regional terms. However, the word "region" clearly meant different things to different people. In not one of the provinces did over 46 percent of the respondents agree about what region they belonged to, and in most provinces the percentage was considerably lower. The answers varied from very local designations such as Gaspésie to single provinces or parts of provinces, to different combinations of provinces or vast designations of East,Centre and West. The three prairie provinces, called "the West" by most, constituted the best-defined regional unit in Canada. In no province did more than one-third of the respondents say that their regional and provincial boundaries coincided.

The authors of the 1974 study argued that regional consciousness exists in Canada and is increasing. They found it to be highest among young, highly educated, economically well-off English-speaking Canadians who are geographically mobile. Regional consciousness appears to be highest in the four western provinces; Prince Edward Island and Nova Scotia represent the national average; Ontario, Québec and New Brunswick are lower than average and Newfoundland is the lowest. However, the data were not conclusive, and when individuals were asked what they perceived as the other regions of the country besides their own, the responses were even more complex and difficult to interpret.

The "self-assigned" concept of regions causes theoretical problems of the highest order. The term is used in so many ways by Canadians that it may have little causal effect on behaviour. Clarke *et al.* concluded that the diversity of responses about what the regions are" . . . makes it unlikely that regional consciousness will provide a major explanatory variable in the definition of Canadian party politics and in the explanation of Canadian electoral behaviour . . .". However, they stated that enough regional feeling was discovered to indicate that the

---

[76]Clarke *et al.*, *op. cit.*, p. 49.

"*potential* exists for both politicization of regional cleavages and for region to be an explanatory variable in itself."[77]

Thus, although it has become widely accepted among Canadian political scientists that regionalism is an important facet of Canadian life, the salient spatial boundaries of the regions have not been determined. Nor has the theoretical explanation of their persistence been satisfactorily developed. Some argue that it is premature to conclude that Canadian politics is largely regional, because there has been no thorough study of class structure in Canada, or of the socio-economic issues dividing right and left branches of public opinion. After analyzing a national sample survey conducted in 1971, one study, for example, concluded that Canadian politics is regional only if political views are narrowly defined as attitudes towards electoral politics and governmental institutions.[78] Other researchers show that regional variations in opinions are neither strong nor consistent on topics that have no readily apparent territorial connotations, and that Canadians have been, over the past 30 years, becoming more alike in their responses to important public policy issues, regardless of region.[79]

Regional cleavages are not necessarily detrimental: they can be normal and healthy, and non-threatening to national cohesiveness. Analysis of 1974 data showed that although regional loyalty is often high in Canada, it is not at the expense of national loyalty.[80] In fact, feelings toward province and nation are strongly correlated: positive feelings toward the province are usually accompanied by positive feelings for the country. In addition, the more knowledgeable Canadians are about their country, and the more sensitive they are to regionalism, "the more they favour the federal government over their provincial governments and the higher they score on the measure of national identity, regardless of provincial, linguistic or social backgrounds."[81] Canadian nationalists tend to be not only well-informed about Canada but also cosmopolitan people who feel warmly about other countries.

In conclusion, then, the divisive effect of regional differences should not be exaggerated. Not enough is known about whether territorial identities are compatible with strong national identification. But it is clear that strong regional identities alone do not prove that national identification is weak or threatened. There is enough evidence to indicate that, in the case of ethnic identities, multiple loyalties alone need not be feared; in fact, they make Canada richer as a nation. However, when strong regional loyalties are linked to general perceptions of injustice, regionalism becomes a potent political force. The federal government must be sensitive enough to relieve tensions on these occasions. Canadians should not be forced by governments to choose whether they prefer to be Aca-

---

[77] *Ibid.*, p. 64.

[78] M. Ornstein *et al.*, "Region, Class and Political Culture in Canada," p. 267.

[79] R. Gibbins, *op. cit.*, p. 184 and Simeon and Blake, "Regional Preferences," p. 100.

[80] David J. Elkins, "The Sense of Place," in *Small Worlds*, p. 23.

[81] *Ibid.*, p. 25.

dians, French Canadians or Canadians first. David Elkins expressed the matter this way: "Multiple loyalties can have . . . a civilizing result, since they encourage us to reject absolute choices and teach us to give assent and express dissent in graduated and qualified terms."[82]

OVERVIEW

Canadians have a rich variety of perceptions and cognitions about their country, their provinces and their regions. The very nature of the country, with its geographical, historical, economic and demographic differences, dictates that this will be so. Surely it is this very diversity that is at the heart of a distinctive Canadian political culture.

Canadians did not create an ideologically based nation. Ideological diversity resulted naturally from a combination of such factors as strong American influence, a high rate of population turnover and strong regional, economic and ethnic differences. Canadians also suffered a prolonged condition of colonial mentality which delayed the development of national symbols and pride. With the Constitution home from Britain, Canada finally matured politically. Perhaps social and cultural maturity will follow.

It is difficult to measure something as elusive as a sense of political community. However, while we must recognize that regional and ethnic variations do exist, we can say that the models of governing that Canada inherited from Britain and the United States have fostered certain types of values, attitudes and behaviour toward the political system and government-related activities. The collective heritage of beliefs, opinions and preferences shared by Canadians is greater than the rhetoric of provincial autonomy and regional cleavages would lead one to believe. The federal structure and the party system, with their apparent inability to bridge regional and linguistic cleavages, exaggerate differences that exist among Canadians. In fact, it is often in the interests of the provincial or federal political elites to frame issues so that their own interests and ambitions are accommodated. In a successful federal system, citizens should feel positively about both federal and provincial levels of government. We know that Canadians do. Those who feel strongly about their province also generally feel strongly about their country. The two are not mutually exclusive; rather, they are strongly correlated.

The most basic values and attitudes demonstrated by Canadians are democratic attitudes toward political participation and governmental authority. Canadians participate very readily in electoral politics but otherwise participate only

---

[82]*Ibid.*, p. 26.

passively – only 4 or 5 percent participate on a continuous basis. Concomitantly, authority patterns exhibit a strong element of deference toward political elites, and there is a reasonably high level of trust in government. Canadians in all regions are becoming increasingly similar in their expectations and preferences with respect to most areas of public policy. They want equity in government services and programs.

The Earl of Balfour wrote in 1927 in his introduction of Bagehot's book on the British constitution that "our whole political machinery presupposes a people so fundamentally at one that they can safely afford to bicker: and so sure of their own moderation that they are not dangerously disturbed by the never-ending din of political conflict."[83] It is not clear exactly what the British people were "fundamentally at one" about, nor is it clear today for Canadians, but the cohesion in the Canadian political culture has been strong enough to permit division and conflict without the eruption of widespread and continual violence. Politicians and government officials can rely on deep-seated attitudes to maintain the authority of government in Canada.

There is a distinctive Canadian political culture. Within the country, provincial political cultures are strong, and provide an assimilative framework for immigrants and internal migrants. However, this should not be seen as subversive of the whole. The provinces also have many features in common. There is unity in diversity, just as the strength and beauty of a tapestry is determined by the very different strands of which it is composed.

---

[83]Introduction by the Earl of Balfour to Walter Bagehot, *The English Constitution* (London: World's Classics edition, 1955), p. xxiv.

Photograph courtesy of the CBC.

chapter 4

Political Socialization
Acquiring Political Orientations

IN EVERY COUNTRY, the citizens harbour unique feelings and beliefs about their political leaders and institutions. In one country fatalistic resignation and apathy may be the norm; in another, a sense of trust and personal power. Whatever the attitudes and beliefs, they form the political culture of the nation and both reflect and shape its politics.

In Canada, the overarching political culture is fragmented by strong linguistic, ethnic and regional subcultures and the powerful influence of a gigantic neighbour. Many values and beliefs are shared by Canadians, but not strongly enough to entirely prevent threats of separation and some fear of disintegration of the nation-state. An awareness of the existence and significance of political culture evokes the underlying question of how it is acquired.

Certain political orientations are learned by children in their informal relations with family and peers. Schools teach political values more directly and explicitly. Later in life, political values and attitudes are initiated and reinforced by other means such as universities, the communications media and even government institutions.

Centralized and abundant communication links facilitate the development of a strong national political culture. Various media, dispensing the same general information and positive opinions about common concerns, help break down regional and ethnic barriers. But communications in this vast country have always been difficult. Do the CBC and *The Globe and Mail*, to take only two examples, provide adequate national links – or do they exacerbate regional and ethnic divisions?

Other media – films, books, magazines and records – also have an important role in shaping Canadian culture. But to a great extent these industries are all dominated by the United States; the values, attitudes and concerns they convey into this country originate south of the border. This fragments and retards the development of a vibrant Canadian culture, reinforcing regional and ethnic diversity. There are many examples; pop stars and other figures who dominate the entertainment world in English Canada are primarily American, very rarely French Canadian; international news is presented to Canadians from the perspective of the large American networks; schools in English Canada are inundated by American textbooks with their United States examples, orientations and values.

There are powerful economic reasons for this situation. However, it must also be noted that Canadians tend to be complacent about the invasion of their culture, preferring the glitz and glamour of American productions and stars, and the presentation of even domestic public affairs as theatre and gossip rather than thoughtful analysis. Clearly, there is a need for the federal government to exercise some control in the areas of public policy which help to shape Canadian culture. What can, and does, the federal government do to safeguard and strengthen Canadian culture by such means as regulating the content and standards of Canadian broadcasting or the distribution of movies and records? Technological advances are revolutionizing communications and making centralized control of broadcasting more physically and economically feasible. Should the government choose that path, or would more centralization only deepen existing cultural cleavages?

The federal government has done much in recent years to improve communications between Ottawa and individual citizens. Does it do enough to ensure that information is adequately distributed to all Canadians? Situated far from the population centres of Toronto, Montréal and Vancouver, the capital, Ottawa, is not even a large economic centre. Are citizens well informed about federal initiatives and activities? Is this communication two-way, so that the government can respond adequately to the needs of those on the periphery as well as those close to the hub of power?

In this chapter, we shall examine some of the major agents which transmit political orientations to Canadians. In particular, we shall analyze and assess the role of public policy in the political socialization of citizens through the agencies of education, the mass media and government information. Throughout, the focus is on how public policy deals with the regional and ethnic divisions within Canadian political culture, and on how it copes with the special problem of American influence. But first we will briefly discuss the concept of political socialization and some of the less explicit means by which it is accomplished.

WHAT IS POLITICAL SOCIALIZATION?

The process by which political culture is learned and transmitted at both the individual and community levels is known as **political socialization**. It comprises casual, informal learning from peers and family as well as calculated political indoctrination by the state. The latter, for example, includes any deliberate manipulation of the school curriculum to instill pride in one's country or, conversely, to foster ignorance about or disdain for political adversaries. Through the political socialization process, political culture is maintained, transformed or created.[1]

Interest in the question of how citizenship values are best instilled has long been of interest to political theorists. In ancient Greece, for example, Plato outlined an ideal state where citizens would be fitted with the appropriate attitudes and values to maintain a stable and productive society. Anthropologists, sociologists, social psychologists and psychiatrists have all studied different aspects of the wider socialization process of which political socialization is a part. In the late 1920s, anthropologist Margaret Mead effectively turned the tide in the famous "nurture versus nature" controversy over whether human beings are shaped mainly by environment or heredity. Her study of Samoan people gave critical support to the cultural determinists who believed that culture rather than heredity determines personality.[2] It was not until the early 1950s, however, that political scientists, borrowing from the other behavioural sciences, introduced the specific term "political socialization" into their discipline.[3]

Talcott Parsons and David Easton were among the most significant pioneers in political socialization theory.[4] Like many social scientists, they were eager to account for political order and disorder. Parsons and Easton reasoned that the process of political socialization which builds citizen support for the state is a major ingredient of political stability. Unfortunately, the connection between socialization and political stability has not been satisfactorily established. Political socialization literature has been plagued since its inception by uncertainty over what constitutes socialized citizen support as well as lack of proof for the direct causal relationship between socialization and stability. Even political scientists who initially viewed the relationship with certainty have modified their thinking. David Easton, for example, in his early writing on the topic, considered that political socialization helped the system maintain itself. A few years later he subtly revised his thesis, rendering system maintenance no longer paramount. "Fundamentally," he said, "the theoretical significance of the study of socializing processes in political life resides in its contribution to our understanding of the

---

[1]See Richard E. Dawson, Kenneth Prewitt and Karen S. Dawson, *Political Socialization*, 2nd edition (Boston: Little Brown, 1977), Chapter 1.

[2]Margaret Mead, *Coming of Age in Samoa* (New York: Morrow, 1928). Mead's research has recently been severely challenged, and the nature/nurture controversy revived, by Derek Freeman in *Margaret Mead and Samoa: The Making and Unmaking of an Anthropological Myth* (Boston: Harvard University Press, 1983).

[3]Fred I. Greenstein, a pioneer in the field, dates the study of political socialization from the late 1950s and early 1960s in David L. Sills, ed., *The International Encyclopedia of the Social Sciences*, vol. 14 (New York: The MacMillan Co., 1968), p. 55.

[4]See T. Parsons, "Family structure and the socialization of the child," in T. Parsons and R. Bales, *Family, Socialization and Interaction Process* (Glenco, Illinois: Free Press, 1955), pp. 35-131 and D.E. Easton, "The function of formal education in a political system," *School Review*, vol. 65 (1957), p. 309.

way in which political systems are able to persist, even as they change, for more than one generation."[5]

The relationship between the socialization process and the workings of the political system is extremely complex, containing many intervening variables. Other techniques, such as military force, are also used by states to maintain political stability and may be just as effective as political socialization. However, if through the political socialization process norms are internalized which structure appropriate behaviour, it should be possible, as one political scientist concluded, "to count on a reservoir of support for the status quo that does not depend upon the offering of bribes or the employment of sanctions."[6] The active support of a majority of citizens must still be considered a firm base for stability.

Political socialization studies are carried out at both individual and community levels. Studies of individual learning are based on the premise that the "political self" is made, not born. Particular attention is paid to children and how and when the "political self" is acquired. Concern centres on such matters as how and when individuals develop their feelings of patriotism, their identification with parties or political groups, their feelings about their rights and responsibilities as citizens and their opinions on political issues and personalities. Political socialization is a continuous, life-long process, but some stages are normally more important than others. For example, basic political loyalties, identifications and values are acquired very young, before specific facts and knowledge, and rarely change abruptly.

Stages and Means of Political Socialization

Important developments of the political self occur in early childhood.[7] Many studies have concluded that children in Western societies acquire emotional attachments to the political community to which they belong by five or six years of age, often before schooling begins, and that these attachments are nearly always positive. Authority figures are seen as benevolent "helpers"; personal and concrete symbols of the political community such as the Queen and the flag are regarded very positively. Concurrently, children also identify with a social and economic class and an ethnic or racial group, though again with little or no factual information. Laws are regarded as absolute and unchanging; authority is seen as people such as policemen or teachers, rather than in abstract terms such as law or responsible government. Political orientations learned at this time are less likely to change than those learned later which involve more information. This fact is important for the political culture and the political system inasmuch as it allows a high degree of continuity and intergenerational agreement about

---

[5]D. Easton and J. Dennis, "The child's image of government," *The Annals of the American Academy of Political and Social Science*, no. 361 (September 1965), p. 41.

[6]Ted Tapper, *Political Education and Stability: Elite Responses to Political Conflict* (London: John Wiley and Sons, 1976), p. 9.

[7]One of the best studies of childhood socialization is R.D. Hess and J.V. Torney, *The Development of Political Attitudes in Children* (Chicago: Aldine 1967).

basic values to be taken for granted by the Canadian government, making it relatively easy to predict citizen reactions and expectations on many topics. The same may not be true in newly developing countries, where changes in basic attachments are constantly taking place.

Between the ages of seven and thirteen, children increasingly understand and relate to more abstract political symbols. As they develop the capacity to see political leaders more critically, and their factual knowledge increases, they gain a better understanding of their political system and its leaders. Ages eleven to thirteen are the most significant in terms of the ability to reason and grasp abstractions. This stage is followed by a gradual and steady increase in political participation and involvement in the remaining adolescent years.[8] Of course, political learning and the development of political orientations continue during adulthood, but it is less likely that changes in basic loyalties and identifications will occur. Adults may alter their opinions towards specific government policies and develop evaluations of new national roles in world affairs, but they are less likely to change national or group loyalties, broad ideological goals or their conception of the legitimate means of selecting political rulers.[9]

Though basic political attitudes are formed early and tend to persist, they may be held to different degrees by individuals as a result of discontinuities in their political socialization. If, for example, socialization agents are inconsistent in their lessons, or a long time elapses between socialization and the assumption of a political role, then attitudes may be weakly held. The greater the number of agents of political socialization to which an individual is exposed, the greater the likelihood that contradictory messages will be received and changes or discontinuities in attitudes occur. Experiences at one stage of life can clash with those at a different time. Pioneer research findings that learning experiences in American children were cumulative and harmonious and resulted in well-rounded citizens were seriously challenged after student radicals in the mid-1960s clashed with authorities on campuses across the United States. Subsequent studies concluded that these students were not deviants from the norm in terms of political socialization but were perhaps over-socialized. They were motivated by their perception of a great disparity between the values which they had internalized during childhood and the realities of American society which they perceived as they grew older.[10]

Complex societies provide more discontinuities or contradictory messages than simple ones where the family is the major, perhaps the sole, agent of socialization. As well, the more socially and geographically mobile an individual is, the more discontinuities there will be in his or her political learning. The strong regional and ethnic subcultures in Canada ensure that the minority of Canadians

---

[8]The early development of political orientation is discussed more fully in Dawson *et al.*, *op.cit.*, Chapter 4.

[9]*Ibid.*, Chapter 5.

[10]Proponents of the view that learning experiences are cumulative and harmonious were R. Hess and J.V. Torney, *op.cit.*, pp. 20-22. This view was modified by K. Keniston, *The Young Radicals: Notes on Committed Youth* (New York: Harcourt Brace and World, 1968), Chapter 2.

who move between particular provinces will be exposed to very different influences.

A final condition causing discontinuity in political learning is the amount of change in the structure and process of government. In Canada institutions have changed very little since Confederation, but in newer, politically unstable countries, discontinuities are enormous as children who have been socialized to tribal or local loyalties are engulfed by a larger state.

Political learning occurs in a variety of ways. Some forms of socialization are indirect in that they are not aimed at specifically political objects, but subsequently influence the development of the political self. Others are direct because they transmit or develop specifically political orientations. Dawson *et al.* outline several types of indirect and direct political learning which are applicable to a study of political socialization in Canada.[11]

One form of indirect political socialization is the transference of attitudes learned about one authority figure to another one. Young children, for example, form relationships with authority figures in their families and schools and establish patterns of interaction with these adults which they transfer to encounters with other authority figures later in life or even to abstract figures beyond their experience. Thus, a child with benevolent parents in a democratic household would tend to regard other authority figures as benevolent and would have democratic political orientations. A second indirect form occurs through what has been termed "apprenticeship". Canadian schoolchildren participate in many non-political activities which provide experiences and skills that may be transferred into the political world. Boy Scouts or Girl Guides, 4-H Clubs and school and work activities are examples. Yet another form of indirect socialization occurs through generalization from social values to political objects. For example, a person who has learned to be cynical and distrustful may well generalize these orientations to political objects such as Parliament or elections.

Direct forms of political socialization are more specific in their goals. In one, role models are important because children learn political orientations through imitation. We have already seen, for example, that young children often take on the party identification of their parents. Another direct form is effected through anticipatory socialization. This term is used to describe learning which occurs when people look ahead to the values and positions of a certain role before they actually achieve it. John Turner or Brian Mulroney might, for example, have anticipated very early a future career as Prime Minister of Canada and have adopted the appropriate mannerisms and style for that position. On a humbler level, a child or immigrant might anticipate becoming a good citizen and try to act accordingly.

Direct, deliberate attempts are often made to transmit certain political attitudes through education. An agent such as family, school, church, political party or club might formally or informally try to propagandize, to teach certain political attitudes or behaviour. Government financial support of student exchanges

---

[11]See Dawson *et al., op.cit.,* Chapter 5.

between English and French cultural environments is an example of a government attempt to promote positive political attitudes between the two language groups. Likewise, after the patriation of the Constitution in 1982, the government distributed miniature copies of the document to schoolchildren from coast to coast.

Political experiences which result from contact with the political process are also a means of direct political socialization. The teenager whose MP intercedes to get him a part-time job in the Post Office at Christmas time is developing certain attitudes toward political figures. Young people who worked for Action Trudeau in the 1968 election campaign had such a learning experience, with regard to both politics and themselves.[12]

Studies of political socialization at the community level concentrate on cultural transmission from one generation to another and on the means of achievement of intergenerational continuity in political attitudes and values. The unstinting Canadian appreciation of democratic government, competitive elections and majority rule is an example of a supportive political attitude perpetuated from generation to generation and not necessarily found in all other countries. Other community studies might examine such topics as political violence and racial injustice and how they are perpetuated in a society.

At both the individual and the community level, political socialization is continuous. Whether or not the country in question is stable, cultural values are constantly being transformed and new ones introduced. Usually the process happens slowly, but sometimes events such as war or economic crisis can rapidly transform the political perspectives of the community. The defeat of the Third Reich, for example, required a radical change in the political outlook of the German community. Governments of newly independent countries generally place great significance on their role as agents of political socialization and work actively to create a new political culture from important elements in the past and aspirations for the future.

PRIMARY AGENTS OF POLITICAL SOCIALIZATION

Having examined the means by which political socialization occurs, we shall turn to the agents that shape individual and community orientations, imparting norms and values and forming political attitudes. We have seen that childhood socializing agents are generally non-political and do not devote much effort to explicit political training. But there are also deliberate agents of political socialization. These two types of agent can be classed as primary or secondary according to the form of relationship between the individual and the agent. Primary relationships are informal and highly personalized; family, friends, peer groups and work associates are thus classed as primary agents. Secondary relationships

---

[12]Jon Pammett, "Adolescent Political Activity as a Learning Experience: The Action Trudeau Campaign of 1968," in Jon Pammett and Michael Whittington, eds., *Foundations of Political Culture* (Toronto: MacMillan, 1976), pp. 160-194.

Reprinted with permission – The Toronto Star Syndicate

are more structured and impersonal. Some of the most important secondary agents in political socialization are educational institutions, the communications media and the government itself. Primary agents form the subject-matter of this section; secondary agents are discussed in the following section of this chapter.

Primary agents are rarely specifically political in their aims. The political learning they offer is therefore likely to be sporadic and incomplete and does not adequately prepare an individual for participation in the political world. Primary agents are a conservative force, not easily manipulated by leaders wishing to change the political culture of a nation. This is beneficial in countries like Canada which wish to maintain the *status quo*, but other countries such as China which have deliberately tried to alter their political culture have found it necessary to break down primary relationships in order to diminish their power.

The Family and Peer Groups

The family, as a key agent affecting basic political orientations, is generally very important in determining the extent and direction of political learning.[13] Orientations such as love of country and certain political structures learned in childhood tend to be the most intensely held and lasting of all political views.

Families maintain their influence in three main ways. First, although political training is not one of its main functions, the family does provide examples or role models and sometimes even direct teaching about politics. It has been found that children from families which are actively concerned with partisan party politics are likely to be politically active when they grow up.[14] The family is also important in indirect socialization, *i.e.*, in instilling other social attitudes and personality traits that will eventually be significant in influencing how the child reacts to the political world. Finally, the family provides social and economic sur-

---

[13]See M. Kent Jennings and Richard Niemi, "The Transmission of Political Values from Parent to Child," *APSR*, vol. 62, no. 1 (March 1968), pp. 169-84. Also see Russel J. Dalton, "Reassessing Parental Socialization: Indicator Unreliability Versus Generational Transfer," *APSR*, vol. 74, no. 2 (June 1980), pp. 421-431.

[14]Kenneth Prewitt, "Political Socialization and Leadership Selection," *The Annals of the American Academy of Political and Social Science*, no. 361, (September 1965), pp. 105-108.

roundings, determines social class, educational values and language and often even directs which other socialization agents will reach the child.

It has long been established that, even in Western societies where as a rule family ties are weaker than in more traditional cultures, individuals tend to hold the same attitudes and values as their parents. A 1970 study of elementary school children in Québec is a case in point. It demonstrated that the majority of the children viewed the government in personal rather than institutional terms. This proportion was especially high for children from French-speaking families.[15] The children also viewed authority as vested in people rather than in institutions. These conceptions of personalized authority support the hypothesis that children's perceptions of social and political authority are shaped by the early home environment. Another finding was that these children viewed political authority as a masculine rather than feminine attribute (not a surprising attitude in a country where men were, at the time, considered to be the traditional "head of the household" even on census forms). The study also indicated a difference between French and English children's attitudes toward government: francophones conceived of political authority as belonging to one man; anglophones saw it as being vested in a group of men. In both groups, older children were more likely to depict government authority as shared rather than belonging to an individual. This latter finding again supports the hypothesis that attitudes toward authority are transferred from the family to other structures. A further interesting conclusion was that anglophone children tended to have an input-oriented view of government functions, to see the government as a problem-solver, while francophone children viewed government functions more in terms of output functions such as welfare cheques, children's allowances, unemployment insurance, *etc.*

A strong correlation also exists between the general views of children and their parents concerning partisanship and party affiliation. Early political socialization studies in the United States indicated a high level of party identification among children and concluded that party orientations pass from parents to children.[16] The process was viewed as an important source of stability to political parties and electoral systems. Although the findings were essentially correct, they were later proven to be culture-bound and subject to qualifications. For example, a major comparison of France and the United States revealed that in France there was very low party identification, and considerable discontinuity in the transmission of party orientations from parents to children.[17] Only 29 percent of the French sample could name their father's party affiliation. In the United States, on the other hand, party identification was high; 91 percent knew their father's party affiliation. Later research in Canada by Jabbra and Landes

---

[15]Jean-Pierre Richert, "Political Socialization in Quebec: Young People's Attitudes toward Government," *CJPS*, vol. 6, no. 2 (June 1973), pp. 303-313.

[16]See Herbert Hyman, *Political Socialization*, 2nd edition (New York: Free Press, 1969).

[17]P. Converse and G. Dupeux, "Politicization of the Electorate in France and the United States," *Public Opinion Quarterly*, vol. 26, no. 1 (Spring 1962), pp. 1-23.

found that 95 percent of their sample of Grade 7 students in Nova Scotia expressed a partisan party choice.[18] It had previously been assumed that there was little transmission of partisan identification from parents to children in Canada; however, the Nova Scotia study revealed a high correspondence between the parents' preference as perceived by their children, and the children's own preferences. Over two-thirds of the children who preferred the Liberals or Conservatives identified their parents' national party preference as being for the same party. (A much lower level of parent/child continuity was observed for the NDP). A further interesting observation was that the data supported earlier tentative findings that mothers have a "slightly greater impact than fathers on the development of political orientations in their children".[19]

Variance from country to country, and even within countries, with regard to the continuity of party affiliations indicates that several factors can interfere with the transference of knowledge and loyalties. For example, when there are several parties rather than two, or when parties spring into prominence and then disappear, greater uncertainty can be expected in the transference process. Nevertheless, as a rule, research indicates that the more stable the party loyalties of the parents, the more stable will be the preference patterns passed on to children.[20]

Although there is some disagreement as to the extent of family influence in later, adult political behaviour, there is general agreement among social scientists that the family helps to perpetuate traditional values, attitudes and behaviour patterns. This influence, which is essentially conservative, is beneficial to countries that wish to maintain the *status quo*, but is a problem for nations wanting to instigate radical changes in society. In the latter case the family unit can come under attack, as it did in China, as previously mentioned, and in the early years of the Soviet Union when it was maligned as a "bourgeois institution".[21]

Friends, associates, sports teams, clubs and groups of all sorts comprise the peer group, a category which acquires increasing significance as the child's dependence on the family wanes. It is especially important at about age 13 or 14, and continues to be influential throughout adulthood. Political socialization by peers resembles that by the family. First, it is haphazard because it is usually not the primary aim of the relationship. Again, the individual relationships are highly personal and emotionally involved. Peer group socialization can alter or reinforce the earlier political learning that has taken place in the family, or, in cases where family socialization was weak, provide fundamental political learning.

---

[18]J.C. Jabbra and R.G. Landes, "Political Orientations among Adolescents in Nova Scotia: An Exploratory Analysis of a Regional Political Culture in Canada," *Indian Journal of Political Science*, vol. 37, no. 4 (Dec. 1976) pp. 75-96.

[19]*Ibid.*, p. 77. Also see Kenneth P. Langton, *Political Socialization* (New York: Oxford University Press, 1969), p. 83.

[20]See, for example, Tapper, *op.cit.*, p. 5.

[21]The changing Soviet attitude toward the family is outlined in K. Millett, *Sexual Politics* (London: Rupert-Hart Davis, 1971), pp. 217-19.

Peer groups often assume greater importance in complex urban societies which are normally more depersonalized and less family oriented than simpler societies. They use blatant or subtle tactics such as ostracism and ridicule to pressure individuals to conform to group norms and attitudes. Peer group socialization can be given much credit for the persistence of minority groups in Canada. The Doukhobors are an extreme example of a minority group that attempts to limit close personal relationships to group members so that traditional values will constantly be reinforced.

SECONDARY AGENTS OF POLITICAL SOCIALIZATION

While primary agents only implicitly socialize individuals into political values and orientations, secondary agents are less personal, closer to the governing process and involved to varying degrees in the process of direct, explicit political learning. We shall now examine three agencies – educational institutions, the media and the government itself – to determine their effects on Canadian political culture. There are indications that these agencies support all three strands of culture examined in Chapter 3. Education and the media in Canada initiate and reinforce attitudes and beliefs about Canada as a nation-state divided by cleavages of language and region. While the educational institutions maintain a modicum of national preference, the structures and the curricula, as we shall see, ensure domination by provincial interests and languages and cultures. The media, which are somewhat more national in outlook today than formerly, respond to the unique linguistic and regional divisions in the country in a manner that reinforces historical and cultural divisions. The federal government's efforts to cut across these divisions by asking for centralized standards in education, broadcasting and television, and even through direct government information programs, have been only partially successful. In this regard, the federal government labours under two handicaps: first, the linguistic and regional cleavages are deep and well entrenched; second, government efforts to communicate directly with the public are often regarded as propaganda for the party in office.

The roles of these three agencies in the socialization process are extremely complex. We shall therefore examine them one by one.

Education

Educational institutions constitute an important agent of political socialization. Unlike families and peer groups, schools are directed by the state and are therefore able to transmit political messages explicitly. Obviously, no educational system is limited to the role of agent of political socialization, but, as in other modern societies, classrooms in Canada are the focus of comprehensive and deliberate attempts not only to instill the 3 Rs but also to shape the social and political outlooks of young citizens. Schools carry a heavy responsibility for preparing young people for the political world by providing them with relevant facts, values, predispositions and skills. Moreover, in Canada they are the main community facility in which numbers of immigrant children learn one or both of the two official languages and also acquire basic citizenship training.

For convenience, the Canadian educational system and its contributions to political socialization will be examined under the headings formal structure, curriculum and subject content.

FORMAL STRUCTURE

Education during Canada's early colonial years was dominated by the church. Not until the mid-1800s was a public system of education developed in each colony, supplemented in Québec by the schools and colleges operated by Roman Catholic orders. The Fathers of Confederation awarded education to the provincial sphere of jurisdiction, but tried to protect English and French minority schools. Section 93 of the *British North America Act* placed education "exclusively" under the control of each province, recognizing provincial differences that existed at the time of entry into Confederation. The federal government retained direct control over the education of persons beyond the jurisdiction of the provinces: the Native peoples, armed forces personnel and their families and inmates of federal penal institutions. Today, Ontario, Québec, Saskatchewan and Alberta allow religious groups to establish their own schools, but these remain under the authority of the provincial education department and must conform to departmental regulations on curriculum, textbooks and teacher certification. The other provinces have unique local arrangements for sectarian schools. There is also a small number of private schools, which operate independently of the public system and are attended by 3 to 4 percent of elementary and secondary students. Government grants for these schools vary considerably from province to province. Under the new *Charter of Rights and Freedoms*, children whose parents have been educated in Canada in English or French have a right to instruction in that language. (Chapters 5 and 6 address this very complicated subject.)

In spite of the relatively clear division of powers between the federal and provincial governments, education has often been a divisive issue for English and French in Canada. Conflicts have particularly arisen when provincial governments passed laws which conflicted with the Constitution or with federal policy on language rights. Manitoba, for example, entered Confederation in 1870 through the *Manitoba Act*, which specifically acknowledged French language rights in the courts and legislature. Since Catholic and French language schools were already in existence they were to be guaranteed by the *BNA Act*. Twenty years later, however, following an influx of English-speaking immigrants, the Manitoba legislature declared English to be the province's only official language and stopped public funding of Catholic schools. The federal Conservative government of the time belatedly introduced legislation to overturn this ruling but it was never passed. Then, in 1916, the Manitoba legislature banned teaching in any language but English, thereby closing not only French language but also German and Ukrainian schools. Decades later, second language teaching and public support for private and parochial schools were quietly resumed, but a legacy of uncertainty remained among the Franco-Manitoban community (and all linguistic minorities in Canada). Manitobans' minority rights in education, the courts and the provincial legislature will eventually be clarified under the new *Charter*. The Québec situation is even more complex. The historical and legal problems in that province are discussed in Chapters 5 and 6.

In the early 1980s, elementary and secondary schools consumed about two-thirds of all educational spending in Canada. They were originally financed largely from municipal real estate taxes but, as rapid postwar expansion increased the need for educational services, the bulk of the financing was taken over by the provincial governments. Today, provincial assistance is determined by a formula intended to provide minimum standards and to minimize disparities in wealth among the various municipalities. The federal government contributes a very small amount for primary and secondary education. In all, the federal share was about 5 percent of the total expenditure on these services in 1982-83, and was directed at such programs as the development of bilingualism in schools.[22]

Post-secondary education in Canada has had a similar historical development. By Confederation there were a few degree-granting institutions in Canada which were largely supported and controlled by religious groups for the primary purpose of training clergy. At about that time, in a reaction against this religious domination, English language institutions began to offer practical and scientific studies under secular control; the French language sector continued to emphasize classical studies under clerical control. Demands for university education escalated, particularly after the Second World War, coming to a head in the 1960s when "baby boom" children graduated from high school in record numbers. As the demand increased, the provincial governments became increasingly involved in planning university development.

During the 1950s, in a deliberate attempt to build a world-class educational system, the federal government inaugurated a system of grants which were distributed to the provinces according to population. The provinces in turn distributed the funds to the universities based on full-time enrollment figures. In this manner the universities, which had operated as private institutions, became heavily dependent on public support. Religious sponsorship and control diminished. By 1976-77 the federal and provincial governments contributed the bulk of university finances, with about half coming from Ottawa.

Canada ranks among the very top countries in the world in the amount it spends on education as a percentage of the GNP.[23] In 1981-82, education claimed 7.5 percent of the GNP in Canada. On the other hand, Canada spends less on research and development than many leading western democracies. In 1978, the

---

[22]*Support to Education by the Government of Canada* (Ottawa: Minister of Supply and Services, 1983), p. 7. The federal government also sponsors programs in vocational and technical training. The extent of their involvement is reflected in the report of the Skill Development Leave Task Force, *Learning a Living in Canada*, vols. 1 and 2 (Ottawa: Minister of Supply and Services, 1983).

[23]G.T. Kurian, *The Book of World Rankings* (New York: Facts on File, 1979), pp. 308-336. Federal contributions to post-secondary students are outlined in *Federal Source of Financial Aid* (Ottawa: Minister of Supply and Services, 1983).

federal government set the goal that 1.5 percent of Canada's GNP should be devoted to research and development by 1983. This target was not reached, and the date was later revised to 1985. Figures for 1978 released by the Organization for Economic Cooperation and Development (OECD) indicated that at the time France spent 1.8 percent of its GNP on research and development; Japan 1.9 percent, Britain and West Germany 2.2 percent; and the United States 2.3 percent.[24]

In the past decade, the federal government has grown increasingly restive over two education-related problems: the lack of recognition for its support of Canadian universities; and a feeling that some provinces exploit the federal/provincial financing agreement by diverting money to other sectors and hence under-finance post-secondary education. In early 1983, when new federal funding was being renegotiated, there were suggestions that some federal revenue might be distributed directly to colleges and universities if the provinces did not increase their support to these institutions. The provincial governments, of course, claimed federal interference in their jurisdiction. This type of dilemma, which is recurrent because the federal government supplies much of the funding with little or no central control except through the bargaining process, illustrates the difficulty in maintaining consistent educational services and standards across the country.

It is clear, therefore, that the fact that education is a provincial responsibility allows great diversity within the Canadian educational system in terms of curriculum content, standards and administration. Variations occur in such areas as compulsory attendance, course offerings, graduation prerequisites and the number of years required to complete elementary, secondary and post-secondary requirements. Ontario is the only province to offer a Grade 13 (although it is no longer compulsory), and Québec has a unique intermediate level of education (CEGEPs) between high school and university. Provincially funded grants and scholarships are generally restricted to provincial residents, and evaluation of high school records is difficult even within provinces because of the lack of standardized examinations in most of them. Such differences often make interprovincial transfers difficult for students.

The diverse historical developments, cultural traditions and geographic, social and economic conditions within the provinces and territories are reflected in twelve unique educational systems. Provincial and regional political cultures are nurtured and perpetuated by this structural fragmentation.

Nonetheless, some generalizations can be made about political socialization throughout Canada's educational institutions. New nation-states are always faced with the difficult decision of whether to structure an educational system which will concentrate on improving mass literacy or one which will create an elite to run the state. In Canada the direction has fallen somewhere between the two. Since the government is firmly established, political socialization in the educational system is generally implicit and indirect. The educational base is egalitarian in that education is universal and funded by the state. All children must

---

[24]For comparative figures see A.Abonyi and M. Atkinson "Technological Innovation and Industrial Policy: Canada in an International Context" in M. Atkinson and M. Chandler, eds., *The Politics of Canadian Public Policy* (Toronto: University of Toronto Press, 1983) Table 1, p. 99.

attend school until the age of 15 or 16. Most flow through the state elementary and secondary schools. Composite high schools at the secondary level generally offer a choice of vocational and academic programs. Canadian students are not, as in some European countries, for example, rigidly streamed at an early age by academic or socio-economic criteria with a view to educating them (not explicitly, of course) for a particular station in life.

Although free and compulsory education is provided by the state to all Canadian children until university level, the length of attendance in school is closely related to factors such as class, wealth and occupation of the family. Significant inequalities in opportunities for education exist among children of different class backgrounds for such reasons as family interest, financial need or variation in quality of schools in different municipalities. The disparity becomes extreme at the post-secondary level where children from middle-class homes whose parents are business owners, managers or professionals are greatly over-represented. In the early 1970s R. Manzer found inequalities in access to education not only by social class but also by status groups, ethnicity and sex groups. He concluded that the "opportunity to secure educational advantages based only on a person's ability to profit from them" is still a long way from being realized in Canada.[25] That situation has not changed since Manzer's study.

Higher education in Canada falls somewhere between the extremes of Britain and the United States: it is much less exclusive than in Britain, but not as accessible as in the United States. In 1982-83 there were over 70 universities across Canada, as well as about 200 specialized colleges and institutes. In 1975, Canada placed third in world ranking of post-secondary enrollment; in 1977 it ranked ninth in terms of literacy rate.[26] Yet in 1983 about four million adults could neither read nor write at a Grade 9 level, the minimum standard for being considered functionally literate by the United Nations Educational Scientific and Cultural Organization (UNESCO). These figures are important because of the significant correlation between general political knowledge, political participation and education. The higher a citizen's social status, the more likely he/she is to actually participate in politics beyond merely voting or campaigning. Education, together with occupation and income, is a principal determinant of social status. It thus "conveys important political advantages, increasing political interest and awareness, expanding opportunities and developing the political skills necessary for effective participation."[27] Post-secondary education has become a virtual necessity for holding high public office.

CURRICULUM

The curriculum in educational institutions is potentially a major instrument of political socialization. Topics can be included or ignored to reinforce the basic values and beliefs desired. Curriculum content reflects both social values and

---

[25]R. Manzer, *Canada: A Socio-Political Report* (Toronto: McGraw-Hill Ryerson, 1974), p. 192.

[26]G.T. Kurian, *op.cit.*, pp. 309, 323.

[27]W. Mishler, "Political Participation and Democracy," in M.S. Whittington and Glen Williams, eds., *Canadian Politics in the 1980's 2nd edition* (Toronto: Methuen, 1984), p. 183.

structural constraints. Some political and educational values, such as the fundamental right to an education and basic political rights, discussed in the previous
chapter, provide a common bond across provincial boundaries. John Dewey, an
American educationalist, argued that democracies should pursue a type of education which instills an interest in social relationships and control, as well as habits of mind which allow social change without disorder.[28] That this philosophy
underlies the administration of education in Canada is evident in a 1976 directive
of the Ministry of Education for Ontario which said that the goals of the curriculum "must" include providing the child with "the knowledge and . . . the attitudes that he or she needs for active participation in Canadian society". It was
further deemed that the teachers' duty was to develop in the child values "that
reflect the priorities of a concerned society".[29] Just what these specific values *were*
was left rather vague, to be determined at a later date. What values actually are
taught remains uncertain, but the list undoubtedly includes obedience, honesty,
fair play, democracy, and honour of Queen, flag and country, among others. Theoretically at least, these values are taught and reinforced through teacher example, informal social situations and formal curriculum in an attempt to shape the
orientations of the pre-adult.

Deliberate attempts are made in the educational system to have children relate emotionally to their country from an early age. As an example of the political
socialization of Canadian schoolchildren, let us look briefly at the public school
curriculum of Ontario, which is similar to those of the other nine provinces. The
Ontario Ministry dictates that national symbols are to be brought to the children's attention daily and the proper reverence instilled. "O Canada" is to be part
of the daily opening or closing exercises in the schools, and every school must fly
the Canadian flag when the board directs. Currently, in Ontario, Canadian history is introduced in Grade 6 and continues in Grades 7 and 8, and it is only
through these courses that anything of government or politics is taught. Even at
the secondary level there is no compulsory "civics" or Canadian government
course. Course offerings are, for the most part, at the individual discretion of
each school, with final approval from the Ministry in Toronto, with the result that
a "Canadian Politics" course may be optional in one school but not offered at all
in another.

Analysis of formal education as a socializing agent has been plagued by the
problem of measurement. Whether they define education as curriculum content
or length or type of education, academic studies have generally been unable to
exclude non-educational variables (such as socio-economic environment) or
other school-based influences (such as teachers) in order to isolate the impact of
strictly educational variables on the acquisition of values and attitudes.

---

[28]John Dewey, *Democracy and Education* (New York: Macmillan, 1916).

[29]*Education in the Primary and Junior Divisions* (Toronto: Ontario Department of Education,
1976), pp. 7 and 20. In 1984 the Ontario Ministry of Education issued its first detailed
description for teaching values in the schools in a document called *Personal and Societal Values*, to
be used in kindergarten to Grade 6.

For this reason, researchers have been unable to demonstrate that schooling contributes directly to the development of democratic values in children, although this has long been inferred to be the case. We have noted that an important aim of the Canadian educational system is to strengthen the cooperative social conscience that underlies our concept of democracy. But there is no agreement on how the goal is to be achieved. Doubts have even been expressed as to whether schoolchildren can learn freedom and equality from schools which enforce constraint, hierarchy and inequality. According to one theory, the undemocratic nature of schools provides a "hidden curriculum" which undermines the values the schools profess to teach. In other words, the basic attitudes toward authority learned by children at school may have an impact on the attitudes they develop toward political authority; and, because schools are not democratic, children do not learn democratic values in schools.

As a concrete manifestation of the acceptance of the "hidden curriculum" notion, the 1960s saw a general democratization within Canadian schools and universities. Compulsory courses were minimized or eliminated and "interest" courses, many of which were designed to teach "life skills", were widely expanded at the expense of core courses such as mathematics, English and history. Although the move had no visible impact on democratic values, it did lower standards sufficiently to raise an outcry from universities about the growing illiteracy of their students. The 1980s are witnessing a tentative reversal of this policy, with a general reimposition of basic core subject requirements for graduation.

Other countries have tried to solve the dilemma of teaching democratic values within authoritarian institutions in equally unsatisfactory ways. According to Richard Merelman,

> American schools adapt to demands that they transmit the democratic values of popular sovereignty and political equality by deemphasizing the academic competence of their teaching staffs, by setting their grading standards at levels which insure that the majority of students perform acceptably, if perhaps poorly, by glossing over the difference between facts and values in politics. In short, American schools adapt by reducing the quality of education.[30]

This type of adaptation to demands to teach democratic values, Merelman claims, causes many of the most promising students to become disillusioned and alienated and actually limits the transmission of democratic values in schools.

Political instruction can be divided into two broad categories, civic education and indoctrination. The first imparts models of how a good citizen participates in the political life of his/her country. There are no conclusive studies to

---

[30]Richard M. Merelman, "Democratic Politics and the Culture of American Education," *APSR*, vol. 74, no. 2 (June 1980), pp. 319-332. For a somewhat comparable view of the state of Canadian universities see David J. Bercuson, Robert Bothwell and J.L. Granatstein, *The Great Brain Robbery: The Decline of Canada's Universities* (Toronto: McClelland and Stewart, 1984).

date which show that formal civics classes have any significant effect on political attitudes.[31] In any case, civics courses as such rarely appear on the curriculum in Canadian schools. On the other hand, courses in politics, history, perhaps even literature and geography also have as an indirect aim the political education of children. In Canada, where bilingualism and multiculturalism are federal policy goals, the teaching of a second official language or a foreign language may also provide a degree of political socialization.

The general assumption made in educational policy is that learning the history, geography, literature and language of one's country is very important in creating citizens with strong positive attitudes and beliefs about their nation-state. The 1970s saw a marked increase in "Canadian Studies" courses in most Canadian educational institutions. At the same time, however, language requirements, which had been dropped in most schools and universities, were not reinstated, and enrollment drastically declined – a situation which bodes ill for a society which prides itself on bilingual and multicultural institutions. Immersion French programs multiplied in cities across the country, but even in Ottawa, the leading city for immersion, only about 10 percent of high school students in 1983 enrolled in them. Outside of that elite program, children were increasingly dropping French after elementary school. There are, of course, provincial differences. In 1983 only three provinces, Ontario, New Brunswick and Prince Edward Island, required even minimal French language training to graduate from secondary schools. Admission or degree requirements for second languages in the universities are almost non-existent. In all of Canada only the University of Ottawa required a knowledge of both official languages for all undergraduate degrees as of 1983. Meanwhile, in Québec, the provincial government, concerned that the majority of new immigrants to the province were joining the English rather than the French community, introduced its controversial language legislation, Bill 101. The thrust of this bill was to force immigrants from abroad as well as those moving to the province from elsewhere in Canada to adhere to French schools and therefore (it was hoped) to strengthen the French-speaking community. Bill 101 was, however, partially overruled by a 1984 Supreme Court decision which allows the children of anyone educated in English in Canada to attend English schools in Québec.

Apart from the two official languages, foreign languages are almost extinct in the regular school program, having often been confined to special heritage language programs designed to meet the needs of ethnic communities. These programs help ethnic groups retain their language and culture but are not designed to encourage other Canadians to share or appreciate the achievements or contributions of these groups to Canadian society.

The second type of political instruction, indoctrination, is a more extreme situation which carries pejorative connotations. In this case there is a deliberate aim to impart a specific ideology designed to rationalize or justify a particular

---

[31]For a discussion of American and British studies of the use of formal civics classes as instruments of political socialization, see Ted Tapper, *op.cit.*, pp. 49-55.

regime or political party. Teaching propaganda slogans is an obvious method of indoctrination; others can be more subtle. For example, a Cuban mathematics workbook for adult education in 1962 contains the following type of problem:

> There have been 3,000 lynchings in the United States in the last 20 years. What has been the average number of lynchings per year in that country?[32]

There is a certain amount of political indoctrination in all educational systems – every Canadian child is taught at some point that democracy is good. However, deliberate policies of indoctrination are generally more prevalent in societies which are trying to establish a new political order and are concerned to legitimate and justify their regime. This approach is quite different from the diffused *ad hoc* nature of political socialization in Canada, where the nation-state is firmly established and the federal nature of the political system fragments political socialization in formal schooling by placing it under provincial jurisdiction.

Subject Content

Since the relationship between curriculum and attitude formation is not fully established, we do not know whether curriculum shapes political attitudes or reflects orientations already learned. However, an important aim of the subjects taught in schools, especially history, is to impart an awareness of a common heritage and build national pride. This goal has not always been realized in Canada.

When Marcel Trudel and Geneviève Jain conducted a national history project for the Royal Commission on Biculturalism and Bilingualism in 1967, they surveyed ten thousand Grade 12 students and compared fourteen representative Canadian history textbooks. They found that English and French texts, were very different from each other in organization, themes and objectives.[33] These significant differences in school history texts across Canada corresponded to the wide attitudinal and political cleavages between the French and English. The Trudel-Jain study concluded that in Canadian history courses the French Roman Catholic schools in Québec were preoccupied with survival of their own society, while the English schools across the country neglected the interests and development of French Canada. The textbooks expounded different political myths and different historical memories. The English books stressed economic interpretations, whereas the French texts stressed the importance of religion and the survival of the French ethnic group.

Key figures and common historical experiences in Canadian history were depicted quite differently. For example, the French saw Lord Durham as a great assimilator; the English considered him a great decolonizer. Riel was a defender of minority rights to the French, but a traitor and murderer to the English. Similarly, the early period of French colonization to 1663 was covered at great length

---

[32]Richard R. Fagan, *Cuba: The Political Content of Adult Education* (Stanford, Calif.: The Hoover Institution on War, Revolution and Peace, 1964), pp. 68-69.

[33]Marcel Trudel and Geneviève Jain, *Canadian History Textbooks: A Comparative Study,* Studies of the Royal Commission on Bilingualism and Biculturalism, no. 5 (Ottawa: Queen's Printer, 1970), Chapter 4.

in French texts, but very briefly in English texts. The periods of the British regime and Confederation were handled so differently that the authors concluded that the two groups did not even seem to be talking about the same country. Books used by francophones attempted to give the students a moral education, while the anglophones' books attempted to convey a political and social education. Elementary school children in French Roman Catholic Schools developed strong identification with their own ancestors. At the secondary school level, the interpretations tended to become bitter, resentful and vindictive, with frequent references to resistance and, in the economic field, to revenge.[34]

In the light of these Royal Commission findings, many textbooks have been revised to eliminate blatant biases, as well as other glaring stereotypes such as the portrayal of Canada's Native peoples as "savages and heathens" and "fiends".[35] Students learn the nature and glory of the established order through a combination of facts and myths, and the very significant differences in subject content which the 1967 study exposed illustrate that Canada's two founding nations never shared a common national mythology.

Conflicting interpretations of Canadian history are not unique to the English- and French-speaking communities. There are regional variations as well. Very different theses have been developed by leading historians from western and central Canada. Donald Creighton, for example, saw Canada as an extension of Ontario. The "Laurentian thesis" which he expounded holds that Canada developed around the extension of trade routes.[36] Creighton argued that the crucial drive behind Confederation was the commercial development of the St. Lawrence, and that the annexation of the West was an extension of this drive. W.L. Morton, on the other hand, gave a western interpretation when he stated that Creighton's thesis does not take account of regional experience and history, but distorts local history and confirms "the feeling that union with Canada had been carried out against local sentiment and local interest."[37] Morton contended that the study of Canadian history has been limited to the history of the economic and commercial development of Upper and Lower Canada, with little regard for the vigour of regional sentiment. For Morton, the prairie provinces, unlike British Columbia or the Maritimes, had no option but to join Canada, as the colony of a colony, and have never existed outside that subordinate position. According to Barry Cooper, the result of this emphasis on commercial develop-

---

[34]*Ibid.*

[35]Garnet McDiarmid and David Pratt, *Teaching Prejudice* (Toronto: Ontario Institute of Education, 1968). Also David Pratt, "The Social Role of School Textbooks in Canada," in Robert M. Pilke and Elia Zureik, eds., *Socialization and Values in Canadian Society,* vol. 2 (Toronto: Macmillan, 1978), pp. 100-126.

[36]Donald G. Creighton, *The Commercial Empire of the St. Lawrence, 1760-1850* (Boston: Houghton Mifflin, 1958).

[37]W.L. Morton, "Canadian History and Historians," in A.B. McKillop, ed., *Contexts of Canada's Past: Selected Essays of W.L. Morton* (Toronto: Macmillan, 1980), pp. 33-4. See also David Jay Bercuson, Philip A. Buckner, eds., *Eastern and Western Perspectives: Papers from the Joint Atlantic Canada/Western Canada Studies Conference* (Toronto: University of Toronto Press, 1981).

ment and economic exploitation of the West by the "loyalist heartland" has led to a split between political allegiance and local identity. "That split appeared and still appears, as a sense of sectional or regional injustice."[38] Often, political movements or minor political parties such as Social Credit or the United Farmers of Alberta have served to channel such regional grievances and provided a Western sense of identity.

The cleavages within Canadian political culture are revealed not only in historical interpretations but also in the works of the novelists and poets whose writings comprise much of the subject content in Canadian schools. These works become instruments of political socialization as they mirror and reinforce attitudes about such issues as national unity and regional identity. Literary critic Northrop Frye wrote that the literature of one's own country can provide the cultivated reader with "an understanding of that country which nothing else can give him".[39] He found in Canadian literature signs of a closely-knit, beleaguered society held together by unquestionable morals and authority – what he termed a "garrison mentality". Margaret Atwood expanded this theme, basing her conclusions on a survey of both English and French Canadian literature. The aim of garrison life is survival, and survival, she claimed, is "the central theme for Canada".[40] Literary critic Dennis Duffy further concluded that the strong garrison will of central Canada was reinforced by political strength. The Canadian identity, he argued, has been restricted to the Loyalist heartland and does not extend to the Maritimes or the West.[41] Such literary analyses correspond to the emphasis by historians on the importance of central Canada and may, as Cooper speculates, help to explain contemporary Western political consciousness. If national unity is a symbol expressing "Canadian" identity, and that identity is limited to the Loyalist heartland, then Westerners will distrust national unity "because it appears as the manifestation of the garrison will".[42]

Ethnic and regional interpretations of Canadian history within central and western Canada exhibit subtle differences which contribute to or reflect regional political consciousness. Such differences are even more apparent in the education of the Native peoples in the Canadian north. Course requirements and subject content rarely foster or reflect northern or Native interests; nor are courses taught in Native languages. Education of the country's registered Indian and Inuit population is, as we have mentioned, the responsibility of the federal government, and is administered by the Department of Indian Affairs. The litany of problems is extensive. Many teachers are trained in the south and know little

---

[38]Barry Cooper "Western Political Consciousness" in Stephen Brooks, ed., *Political Thought in Canada* (Toronto: Irwin Publishing, 1984), p. 228. See also Howard and Tamara Palmer, "The Alberta Experience," *Journal of Canadian Studies*, vol. 17, no. 3 (Fall 1982), p. 23.

[39]Northrop Frye, *The Bush Garden: Essays on Canadian Imagination* (Toronto: Anansi, 1971), p. 183.

[40]Margaret Atwood, *Survival: A Thematic Guide to Canadian Literature* (Toronto: Anansi, 1972), p. 32.

[41]Dennis Duffy, *Gardens, Covenants, Exiles: Loyalism in the Literature of Upper Canada/Ontario* (Toronto: University of Toronto Press, 1982), pp. 131-2.

[42]Barry Cooper, *op.cit.*, p. 235.

about Native culture and history. Native students must generally leave their homes at the end of Grade 8 if they wish to continue their education. All too often these factors combine to instill in students neither national nor ethnic pride, but alienation and disillusionment which contribute to high drop-out rates and social and economic problems. Moreover, the tacit goal of the school system has been to provide Native children with the knowledge and skills of the southern Euro-Canadian culture and encourage them to identify with southern values. This dated approach is incompatible with the preservation of a vibrant multicultural society and has encouraged Indians and Inuits to demand more input into government programs which directly concern them.

Political socialization in Canada's educational institutions is fragmented not only by the ethnic and regional divisions within the country but also by pressures from the United States. Textbook markets are so much larger and more lucrative south of the border that it is financially advantageous to adopt American texts rather than use Canadian-written and -published material. Factors of major concern are the limited availability of Canadian books in the school system and the small amount of Canadian content in textbooks, both of which contribute to a stunted knowledge of Canada and Canadians. One study, for example, found only 91 of 9000 books in a Toronto high school library to be Canadian; most of the rest were published in the United States by American authors. A more thorough study by Statistics Canada determined that 45 percent of school texts used across Canada are Canadian.[43] As would be expected, Canadian content is much higher in French texts than in English. A considerable effort is being made to rectify this situation in English Canada. In Ontario a book must now have Canadian authors and be manufactured in Canada to be approved as a text, and every province has a "Canada First Policy" which means that if a Canadian text is available it must be given priority.

Similarly, at the university level, rising nationalist feeling in the 1960s and 1970s unleashed widespread concern for the high percentage of both foreign texts and professors and their possible influence on higher education in Canada.[44] In 1975, a Report of the Committee on Canadian Content conducted for the Canadian Political Science Association revealed concern by political scientists across the country that introductory courses in their field (with the exception of Canadian government courses) relied too heavily on American texts and were therefore overloaded with American examples.[45] The study emphasized the vulnerability of Canadian education to influences from the United States as yet

---

[43]Quoted in *The Globe and Mail*, October 20, 1976, p. 1. Statistics Canada, *The English Elementary and High School Report on Canadian Education and Publishing in Canada* (Toronto: Pepper Wood Inc., 1982) p. 92.

[44]The Nationalist arguments are expounded at length in Robin Matthews and James Steele, eds., *The Struggle for Canadian Universities*, (Toronto: New Press, 1969). See also Alan Cairns, "Political Science in Canada and the Americanization Issue," *CJPS*, vol. 8, no. 2 (June 1975), pp. 191-234.

[45]R. Drummond, P. Clarke and R. Manzer, "Report of the Committee on Canadian Content," meetings of the CPSA, June 1975.

another factor contributing to the fragility of the political socialization process in Canadian educational institutions.

The Canadian educational system, fragmented from within by regional and ethnic interests, and pressured from without by American cultural influences, still strives to impart to students an awareness of a common heritage and to instill national pride. It is a difficult struggle in which the federal government has serious concerns and responsibilities. Working within the parameters allowed by the federal political system, and recognizing special regional and ethnic educational needs, it must assure a minimum national level of political socialization in educational institutions. Recently, the federal government stated as one of the objectives of its educational programs "to increase through formal learning the knowledge and understanding Canadians have of themselves and their environment, with particular concern for the cultural diversity of Canada, and to stimulate and maintain a sense of Canadian citizenship."[46] It can accomplish this end by maintaining strong financial and moral support for bilingual programs in the schools and generously funding research agencies such as the Social Sciences and Humanities Research Council. It can also encourage the universities to require a degree of competence in both official languages as a prerequisite for admission or graduation and support some universities in the establishment of degree programs in both official languages. These types of influence and assistance by the federal government in the educational field are vital to strengthen and reinforce Canadian political culture.

The Media

The mass communications media are an increasingly important socializing force both within and across national borders, as they break down the traditional barriers of distance and national frontiers. Concern about the effects of this phenomenon was expressed in the 1982 international debate wherein the United Nations General Assembly endorsed a curb on the free flow of information, declaring that all nations had the right to veto any incoming television broadcasts by satellite from abroad. The resolution, which was sponsored by 18 African, Asian and Latin American nations, as well as Rumania, reflected concern about new technology which relays satellite telecasts directly to residences without going through a ground receiving station. Delegate after delegate expressed the fear that direct satellite broadcasting from abroad implies enormous threats from stronger cultures. Like all General Assembly motions, the resolution was a recommendation and not binding; the debate over free flow of information is far from over.

Traditional societies which are trying to "modernize" recognize the value of controlling their own mass media in order to standardize messages, set community goals and educate and unify a scattered population. Efficient internal communications among a whole people is considered one of the basic re-

---

[46]*Support to Education by the Government of Canada*, p. 12.

quirements of nationhood. Canadians, with a huge and quite sparsely populated territory, depend heavily on mass communications for disseminating both internal and external political information, and must be concerned about the effects that the free flow of information across their borders can have on their culture.

The media reflect the values and tastes of the society they serve. But they do much more. They act as gatekeepers for the citizenry by selecting which beliefs and perspectives will be presented. In doing so, they help to shape the values of society and influence the political process. At their best, the media offer citizens a broad range of information and informed commentary and provide a voice for the government and opposition parties. At their worst, they offer a distorted selection of facts and unbalanced, biased viewpoints. The media constitute a powerful tool because they can potentially reach vast audiences and manipulate content to either reinforce or challenge the norms of society.

Prior to 1950, scholars credited the mass media with vast influence over the values, attitudes and beliefs of the public. More recently, with the application of long-term studies and more sophisticated methods, scholars have modified that

Reprinted with permission – The Toronto Star Syndicate.

Government regulations on Canadian content are a constant source of controversy.

view to conclude that the mass media have a limited but important effect on the general public. Their most significant role in this respect is in setting the agenda for public discussion and debate; that is, in determining the issues and individuals that people think and talk about. To date there are no studies in Canada dealing directly with agenda-setting, but a study of public opinion trends in Canada from 1960 to 1978 verified that headlines affect what the public perceives to be the most important problems facing the country.[47] Most researchers agree that the subtle and indirect influence of the media on public perception helps, over time, to bring about changes of attitude. By concentrating on one character or event at the expense of another they focus public debate, help legitimize actors or issues and confer or withhold status. They build and destroy the public images of political figures by reporting selectively and commenting on specific events, awarding such labels as "wimp", "awkward", "swinger" or "poor debater", which become indelible. Investigative journalism also exposes issues that invite strong public reactions. However, there are many restraints on media attempts to set the agenda for public debate, among them editorial policy, financial constraints and the need to attract middle class readers and therefore substantial advertising.

Below we shall examine the various media in terms of how they, as agents of political socialization, cope with three major challenges: American influence, ethnic relations and regional divisions. In each case, the primary focus is whether or not the media help reinforce the Canadian political culture, and specifically, whether they foster or fragment the Canadian national identity. Particular emphasis is placed on television and newspapers, the two media which reach virtually all Canadians. There is at least one television set in 97% of Canadian households; 84% of adults, 87% of teens and 90% of children watch it every day.[48] Television is primarily an entertainment medium in which impressions and images are more influential than issues, and so is limited as an agenda-setter. Newspapers on the other hand were originated to inform and persuade rather than entertain. They have a more restricted but also more attentive public. Data show that "the most politically attentive individuals regard newspapers as the single most important source of political information."[49]

THE AMERICAN CHALLENGE

To build a strong national identity it is important that citizens of any political unit exchange ideas and information within that unit more than with other people outside it. In this respect it is unfortunate that Canada shares the North American continent with one of the most powerful countries in the world, a country which not only is English-speaking, but which extends along the most densely populated border of almost every Canadian province. North/south communications between the proximate English groups in Canada and the United States

---

[47]See Frederick J. Fletcher, *The Newspaper and Public Affairs*, vol. 7, Research Publications, Royal Commission on Newspapers (Ottawa: Minister of Supply and Services, 1981), p. 17.

[48]*Ibid.*, p. 103.

[49]*Ibid.*, p. 106.

flow naturally, while internal communications between French and English regions as well as the widely separated provinces of English Canada are artificial and must be protected and nourished.

The development of modern communications systems since the early 1840s has facilitated the natural north/south communication links between English-speaking Canadians and Americans and increased the threat of cultural domination from the south. At the same time, improved mass communications have helped integrate Québec into international society after a long period of isolation. Unfortunately they have done little to unite the two official language groups within Canada.

The history of media development in Canada is to a great extent the record of a struggle by the Canadian government to counter the influences of foreign penetration and bind the country together through better internal communications. Canadians are outnumbered by Americans by almost ten to one, and nearly all live within easy reach of the American mass media and other cultural influences. That any form of distinct Canadian identity or culture exists at all in light of the strong influence of the United States is contrary to the expectations of most theories of national integration. As one author noted, it is surprising that

> two centuries of contiguous territory, common language and culture (for English-speaking Canadians at least), intermigration, trade, travel, and communication have *not* produced formal political integration.[50]

Interprovincial communications links have always been a challenge for Canadians. While all the principal cities of the United States were linked by telegraph by 1846, the first Canadian line between Toronto and Montréal was not complete until 1847. The most important centres in the Canadas and the Maritime colonies were linked by 1861, but by then north/south channels of information were already established.

The 1850s were a great growth period for newspapers because of the high interest in war reports. However, from the beginning Canadian newspapers found it easier and cheaper to fill their pages with news from the United States than to hire their own reporters. And the competition from established American newspapers was already intense. In the Maritimes in 1865, Canadian newspapers were "a rarity where the foreign and certainly not superior sheets of New York have established a regular circulation."[51] Rather than reading news from the provinces, Canadians of the time devoured the shocking and gory events, mainly murders, lynchings and riots, that filled the American papers.[52]

Canadian radio services, and later television, were also founded as a direct response to American infiltration of the Canadian market. From radio and television channels, through cable and pay television and, finally, to satellite transmis-

---

[50]Kenneth D. McRae, "Empire, Language and Nation: The Canadian Case," in S.N. Eisenstadt and S. Rokkan eds., *Building States and Nations*, vol. II (Beverly Hills: Sage, 1973), p. 151.

[51]*Montreal Gazette*, November 15, 1865; reprinted from a British periodical, *Saturday Review*.

[52]R. Brunskill, *A Newspaper Content Analysis of Canadian Integration 1845-1895*, Carleton University Ph.D. Dissertation, 1976, Chapter 1.

sion, the issue has been how best to protect Canadian cultural sovereignty from massive U.S. media penetration. In November 1981, for example, Secretary of State for Communications Francis Fox warned that Canada would be "an occupied land, culturally" by 1985 unless action were taken against the spread of American television channels, and urged his government to adopt a national cultural policy similar to its National Energy Program.[53] However, steps to achieve such a policy have been slow and uncertain, particularly in the face of the new technological advances.

How real is the danger of assimilation into the dominant American cultural milieu? Selected facts and figures from the current scene give some indication of the degree of American penetration into Canadian popular culture.[54] Over 80 percent of Canadians have access to American television channels. Not only are American channels readily available, often without cable, but both of Canada's national networks, the CTV and CBC English networks, show a preponderance of American programs – and surveys show that Canadians overwhelmingly prefer them to Canadian alternatives.[55] For example, in a 1973 survey only 9 percent of Toronto viewers reportedly watched Canadian programs during the evening prime time period. In 1978, CBC President A.W. Johnson expressed his concern as follows:

> The plain truth is that most of our kids know more about the Alamo than
> they know about Batoche or Chrysler's Farm. They know more about
> Davey Crockett than they do about Louis Riel. They talk about "taking the
> fifth" rather than about Canada's Bill of Rights.[56]

Public opinion surveys show that anglophone Canadians agree that American television is a prime ingredient in American cultural penetration. Francophones are less likely to identify it as such, an indication that linguistic difference operates as an effective screen for American influence.[57]

Entertainment shows are cheaper to import than to produce domestically because their costs have already been recouped in the U.S. market which is ten times the size of Canada's. Consequently, CTV, Canada's only private national English television network, "is the only national television network in the industrialized world that does not produce a single dramatic series".[58] The bright spot

---

[53]See the *Toronto Star*, Sunday edition, November 29, 1981, p. 1.

[54]For more detailed discussion, see S.M. Crean *Who's Afraid of Canadian Culture?* (Don Mills, Ont.: General Publishing, 1976); John S. Dickey, *Canada and the American Presence* (New York: New York University Press, 1975); Janet Morchain, *Sharing a Continent*, (Toronto: McGraw-Hill Ryerson, 1973).

[55]R. Manzer, *op.cit.*, p. 110.

[56]A.W. Johnson, *Broadcast Priorities for the 1980's*, CBC Corporate Statement to the CRTC, 1978, p. 3. Quoted by Frederick J. Fletcher and Daphne P. Gottlieb, "The Mass Media and the Political Process," in M.S. Whittington and G. Williams, eds., *Canadian Politics in the 1980's op. cit.*, p. 201.

[57]John H. Sigler and Dennis Goresky, "Public Opinion on United States-Canadian Relations," *International Organization*, vol. 28, no. 4 (Autumn 1974), p. 660.

[58]Fletcher and Gottlieb, *op.cit.*, p. 201.

is that Canadians do show preference for Canadian documentaries, news and public affairs programs, which now operate with a budget surplus. Moreover, Gallup polls over the last 30 years indicate that Canadians want Canadian programming to be available, even if they do not watch it.[59]

Over the years serious efforts have been made by the government to increase the quantity and quality of Canadian programming. In 1932, the government of R.B. Bennett created the publicly owned non-profit radio network which evolved into the CBC and now broadcasts nationally in English and French. In the 1950s the CBC also took on a national television service. The CBC's primary concern is Canadian content. The extent to which it has succeeded in its mission as a public service is controversial. The general pattern since 1953 has been one of underfunding, on a year to year basis. This situation undermined effective planning at a time when the CBC faced severe competition from a rapidly expanding private television broadcasting system. Until the present, the CBC has been forced to remain dependent on advertising revenue. As Paul Audley notes, "These two factors, combined with insecure and inadequate financing, have resulted in CBC schedules that continue to include a substantial amount of foreign content. . ."[60]

First the Board of Broadcast Governors, and later the Canadian Radio-Television Commission (which now covers telecommunications) were established to regulate both the CBC and all private broadcasting in Canada. The stated goal of the CRTC is to safeguard, enrich and strengthen the cultural, political, social and economic fabric of Canada by broadly regulating the content and standards of Canadian programming. Through the CRTC the Prime Minister has special access to the broadcast media. Of course, he can ask for time on CBC television and radio at any time, but through an instruction from Cabinet, the CRTC can invoke section 18(2) of the *Broadcasting Act* and gain access to all stations. Such an invocation constitutes a directive to all licencees to broadcast any program deemed to be "of urgent importance to Canadians generally".[61]

CRTC recommendations have often been highly controversial. For example, a policy statement issued by them in January 1983 argued that if the domestic communications system "serves only for the importation of foreign programs, there is a real and legitimate concern that the country will ultimately lose the means of expressing its identity." It proposed tougher Canadian content rules which were ultimately rejected by the Cabinet on the grounds that such an interventionist approach seemed obsolete since satellite television and video cassettes allow viewers to watch what they please. Also, stiff regulation of programming

---

[59]*Ibid.*

[60]Paul Audley, *Canada's Cultural Industries* (Toronto: James Lorimer and Co., 1983), p. 255.

[61]Martha Fletcher and Frederick J. Fletcher, "Communications and Confederation: Jurisdiction and Beyond," in R.B. Byers and R.W. Redford, eds., *Canada Challenged: The Viability of Confederation* (Toronto: Canadian Institute of International Affairs, 1979), p. 171-2. See also Robert E. Babe, *Canadian Broadcasting Structure, Performance and Regulation* (Ottawa: Minister of Supply and Services,. 1979), Chapters 2 and 3 and Leslie Seidel, "The Regulation of Political Advertising on Canadian Television", unpublished paper, Aug. 1983, p. 9.

and scheduling might mean loss of audience and advertising revenue – and there are other options. The CBC could, for example, give up advertising dependence and become a genuine national medium, reducing its American content and increasing Canadian programs of high quality. As well, cable and satellite networks could be more strictly controlled.

At the time of writing, Canadian television stations must provide at least 60 percent Canadian content in their programming between 6 AM and midnight, calculated on an annual basis. The CRTC has also promulgated Canadian content regulations for radio. What constitutes Canadian content has, however, been subject to controversy, and at times the CRTC has been arguably too lax in implementing and enforcing its regulations. A further requirement is for cable systems carrying American signals to give priority to Canadian stations. This restriction on the free-flow of U.S. programming, supplemented by the cancellation of tax exemptions for advertisements carried by foreign media, has been particularly controversial both in Canada and across the border. The objective of such restrictions is not to censor American programming but rather to guarantee a minimum level of Canadian content and encourage the Canadian industry. In the same vein, when the CRTC licensed several pay-TV channels in 1982, it stipulated that the licencees must convert a significant amount of their revenues into Canadian programs. Unfortunately, the one national culture-programming channel which might have done most to develop quality Canadian productions for a national audience went bankrupt within months.

The publishing industry in Canada is also American-dominated; American publishers produce about 60 percent of all books sold. The percentage of Canadian-published sales actually dropped from 34 percent in 1969 to 27 percent by 1980. American publishers also produce about 90 percent of magazines sold in Canadian stores. The weak Canadian magazine industry is particularly affected by American competition: of the 10 best selling magazines in Canada in 1980 only four – *Maclean's, Chatelaine*, the Canadian edition of *Reader's Digest* and *TV Guide* – were Canadian. Almost two-thirds of English-speaking Canadians surveyed in 1969 preferred American to Canadian magazines. In fact, at that time, a Special Senate committee reported that Canadians spent more money buying American comic books than they did on the seven leading Canadian-owned magazines.[62] Basically, American magazines can be sold cheaply in Canada because Canadian sales are only a small fraction of their total circulation. A Canadian publisher trying to compete by producing a magazine of comparable quality would have much higher costs.

This situation was improved considerably in 1975 when the federal government passed legislation to eliminate tax exemptions for advertising by Canadian companies in Canadian editions of foreign owned publications. Bill C-58 set rigid standards of Canadian content on magazines published in Canada in an attempt to forcibly remove large American magazines, particularly *Time* and *Read-*

---

[62]Special Senate Committee on Mass Media, *Report, Volume 1: The Uncertain Mirror*, (Ottawa: Queen's Printer, 1970), p. 152.

er's Digest, from direct competition with Canadian magazines for advertising dollars. [63] However, the legislation did not affect the massive circulation of American magazines in Canada. With a significantly smaller Canadian operation than previously, *Time* continues to publish profitably in Canada with an advertising base that is about 80% Canadian. *Reader's Digest* developed what is in effect a separate Canadian operation, and, under a compromise agreement with the Canadian government, articles obtained from the American parent qualify as Canadian provided that they are edited or condensed in Canada. The magazine's content thus remains at least 80% Canadian. The legislation did somewhat improve the situation of English language periodicals in Canada by generating more advertising revenue for them and creating an intangible atmosphere of confidence.

The scenario is similar in the record industry except that the concern is less for editorial expression than cultural and financial losses. The industry is overwhelmingly dominated by foreign owned and controlled companies which manufacture and distribute mainly proven hit music from outside of Canada. In 1980, Canadian-controlled manufacturers accounted for only 16 percent of all records sold in Canada, and only 8 percent of total industry sales had any Canadian content. [64] Currently, the most effective policy of the federal government to encourage the Canadian record industry is the CRTC Canadian content rule which ensures that a minimum amount of air time is allotted to Canadian musical compositions and performances.

The movie industry is also foreign dominated. Feature films primarily entertain, but they have social, cultural and propaganda value which can be very significant both at home and abroad. A few U.S. film companies which dominate their home industry have been able to provide big budget movies to foreign audiences at relatively low cost because of their large domestic market. Their movies have never been restricted in Canada, and as a result American productions also dominate the Canadian market place. Fewer than 2 percent of the movies shown in Canada in 1979 were Canadian made; most were from the United States, then Britain. Until 1968 the Canadian film industry concentrated on non-commercial, non-competitive productions, and it still has not established a solid industrial base from which to produce and distribute feature films. One bright light is the National Film Board (NFB), established by the federal government in 1939 and given the ambitious task of interpreting Canada to Canadians and other nations. It is the largest single producer of Canadian film and confines its production mainly to quality documentary and educational films, though recent forays into feature films have included some major successes.

Another effort by the federal government to promote a feature film industry in Canada was the creation of the Canadian Film Development Corporation (CFDC) in 1968. This corporation was to provide financial and other assistance

---

[63]To be Canadian for tax purposes, periodicals (in addition to being Canadian-owned, edited and published) must be at least 80% different in content from periodicals published outside Canada.

[64]Audley, *op.cit.*, chapter 4.

to producers who worked with Canadian talent. By 1977 it had succeeded in increasing the number of Canadian films produced but not in breaking American control of production and distribution systems even in Canada. The exception was in Québec, where producers exercised greater control over distribution and where most French language features were purchased for television as well as being shown in theatres. Other federal attempts to boost the Canadian film industry through such means as tax incentives to encourage investment in films have had very limited success.[65]

It is clear from this discussion that economics constitutes a powerful factor in American influence on all Canadian media. Its effects are particularly evident in news reporting. The relative cost of "made in Canada" news gathering is prohibitive, so that Canadian news, in all the media, relies heavily on U.S. agencies and wire services. This is particularly true in international news, where American news chains sponsor teams abroad, and where national daily newspapers such as the *Washington Post* and the *New York Times* have considerable prestige and influence on the American political scene. No Canadian newspaper has nearly the equivalent influence in Canadian foreign policy discussions. At least part of the reason is that most news from outside North America is taken from American sources. One study showed that even U.S. domestic national news occupied nearly one and a half times more space in our dailies than Canadian-reported international news.[66] On television, U.S. foreign reports tend to displace not only Canadian foreign reports, but also Canadian domestic news. Another study, for example, revealed that CTV devoted 67 percent of its national news programs to foreign events, of which 42 percent was about the United States.[67]

Canadian news is therefore distorted in the amount of coverage accorded to U.S. domestic news, and the selection and perspectives of foreign news is heavily influenced by the U.S. Topics of interest to Americans automatically become of interest to Canadians, and American viewpoints and justifications are well aired in Canada. It has also been argued that another possible effect of the pre-eminence of U.S. sources in Canadian news is that it could undermine the NDP support in Canada in subtle ways by lending a right-wing bias.[68] It must be noted, however, that studies have been unable to prove that the media have a direct affect on citizen behaviour. The Ontario Royal Commission study on Violence and the Media, for example, could not find an empirical relationship between violence portrayed on television and the amount of violence in society.[69]

What concrete effects does a high degree of American exposure have on Canadian political culture? The lack of systematic research on the topic leaves us

---

[65]*Ibid.*, chapter 6.

[66]Joseph Scanlon, "A Study of the Contents of 30 Canadian Daily Newspapers," (Ottawa: Special Senate Committee on Mass Media, October 1969), p. 29.

[67]Conrad Winn, "Mass Communication," in Conrad Winn and John McMenemy, *Political Parties in Canada* (Toronto: McGraw-Hill Ryerson, 1976), p. 143.

[68]*Ibid.*, p. 148.

[69]Robert J. Jackson, Michael J. Kelly, Thomas H. Mitchell, "Collective Conflict, Violence, and the Media in Canada," Ontario Royal Commission on Violence in the Communications Industry, *Report, Volume 5: Learning from the Media*, (Toronto: Queen's Printer, 1977).

with generalizations and speculation. Canadians have shown a predilection for domestic news and public affairs programs, but like other media programming these rely heavily on American sources. Since the main effect of the mass media on the public is to set the agenda for public discussion and debate and thereby influence public priorities and attitudes about policy issues, it is reasonable that a society which depends on another for its view of the world will absorb some of the latter's norms. The inevitable effect of this American influence is to encourage attitudinal integration with the United States. Clearly this fact has a bearing on the fragility of the Canadian national identity. American influence must be controlled to allow a vibrant, independent Canadian culture to develop.

A study of Canadian public opinion about U.S./Canadian relations revealed considerable resentment among Canadians during the 1960s and early 1970s over the issue of American economic and cultural influence. Nationalist feelings, which at the time were high among English-speaking Canadians, were accompanied by a negative view of American cultural and economic penetration. Those who were most negative were also most nationalistic: residents of Ontario, NDP followers, businessmen, professionals and the university educated. The least anti-Americanism was evidenced east of Ontario, particularly in the Atlantic region and Québec. Residents of the latter were more concerned that excessive concern with the U.S. detracted from Québec problems. Ontario was the most consistently opposed to American cultural and economic penetration and also the most supportive of Canadian nationalism. However the authors of the study pointed out that even during this period of intense nationalist feelings there was clearly no "rampant anti-Americanism in the Canadian mass public. Canadians continued to feel closer to the United States than any other country, and esteem, while diminished, remained high."[70]

The question of American cultural penetration through the mass media presents a serious dilemma for Canadians. If Canadians believe in a free press and free information flow, then they should leave the borders open to any communications without restriction, no matter what their country of origin. Yet this philosophy clearly operates against the development of a distinctive Canadian culture and identity. One author described the Canadian solution to the dilemma this way: in Canada, we "follow a classical liberal ideology and let the media directors, advertisers and people choose the media and the media content they wish." This "reinforces U.S. influence and presumably weakens Canadian identity as such."[71]

ETHNICITY AND THE MEDIA

The primary barrier to the development of a "national" political agenda in Canada is that the two founding communities live in separate media worlds which

---

[70]Sigler and Goresky, *op.cit.*, pp. 665 and 666.

[71]Frederick Elkin, "Communications Media and Identity Formation in Canada," in B.D. Singer, ed., *Communications in Canadian Society* (Toronto: Copp Clark, 1975), p. 232. For a recent evaluation of the effects of government intervention in cultural activities, see Steven Globerman, *Cultural Regulation in Canada* (Montréal: The Institute for Research on Public Policy, 1983).

reinforce the linguistic and cultural differences in Canadian society. In Canada in 1983, eleven daily newspapers were published in French, ten of them in Québec. In Québec, as in the rest of Canada, newspapers are the major source of news for top decision makers. Research shows that the newspapers serving anglophone and francophone communities focus on different headlines and stories, and often view events from quite different perspectives.[72] There is also a degree of stereotyping of French Canadians in the English press, and of insularity in the French press, although coverage of issues outside Québec by francophone newspapers has improved since the mid 1970s.[73]

In television and radio broadcasting as well the two communities are isolated one from the other even though they are served by the same Crown corporation. The CBC operates AM radio networks in the two languages with near-national distribution. It also operates two nation-wide television networks, one in English, one in French. However, the English CBC and its French counterpart, Radio-Canada operate independently of each other. The only other network to provide national television service from coast to coast is the English CTV, which also has a French subsidiary, TVA. Like the newspapers, French and English television and radio newscasts focus on their own language group and often carry few items in common. Even the entertainment shows spotlight different personalities representing the separate communities. English programs often feature Americans but very rarely francophone Canadians. Attempts to bridge the gap with bilingual radio stations have been unpopular and short-lived.

Different agendas in the French and English media are often evident in political biases. For example, while English CTV is judged to be neutral and the CBC to be establishment-oriented in political leanings, Radio-Canada is more partisan to the left and to the Parti Québécois. In one study, the NDP received almost 70 percent more news exposure from Radio-Canada than from English networks. And while both language networks provided high coverage of the Liberals, the Conservatives received considerably less attention in Québec – less than half that accorded the NDP.[74] Such a bias against the Conservative Party may have accentuated the bicultural cleavage in the political system by reducing the electoral prospects of that party in Québec during some periods of Canadian history.

Apart from the relative inability of the national media to provide an integrative service between the two official language communities, there is another communications issue which has generated considerable bitterness and distrust between federal authorities and ethno-cultural groups other than French and English. In spite of considerable pressure from ethnic organizations, the CBC has

---

[72]Elkin, *op.cit.*, p. 235. See also Arthur Siegel, *Politics and the Media in Canada* (Toronto: McGraw-Hill Ryerson, 1983), chapter 10.

[73]André H. Caron and David C. Payne, "Media and Canadian Politics; General and Referendum Applications," paper presented at the Duke University Conference on Political Support in Canada: The Crisis Years, Durham, North Carolina, 1980.

[74]See Winn, *op.cit.*, p. 137.

often not accepted the spirit of federal multicultural policy by providing minority language programs in areas of high ethnic concentration. Some independent networks in areas such as Toronto, as well as certain cable channels in Ottawa provide a limited amount of this type of programming. However, when the Secretary of State announced funds for multicultural programs to four federal cultural agencies in 1972 a notable exception was the CBC. In 1973 and 1974 the CBC actually eliminated multilingual broadcasts in Manitoba, Nova Scotia and Alberta when it purchased three private radio stations which served minority language groups. In the ensuing years the Ukrainian Canadian community, in particular, has expressed fear that the refusal of the CRTC and the CBC to accept the multilingual implications of multiculturalism indicates the tenuousness of the scope and depth of the federal commitment to multicultural policy.[75]

Another group that feels its needs are not being adequately met by available programming is the Native audience of the far north. That problem is gradually being solved by technological advances and increased funding. East-west radio and television networks were understandably the government's first priority. Until recently, services in isolated communities depended on such improvisations as CBC circulation of recorded television programs to low-powered northern television transmitters. This situation has been revolutionized by satellite technology. CBC's Northern Television Service (NTS) began live satellite transmission in 1973, and their stations receive programming by satellite, mainly from CBC networks in southern Canada. Fewer than 2 percent of Canadians were without radio and television service in the early 1980s, and that was due mainly to distance and topography. All communities of 500 or more are already getting, or in the process of getting, radio and television services. In 1982, the Inuit Broadcasting Corporation (IBC) began on a modest scale to air television programs across the Northwest Territories and northern Québec. This has assured more community control of northern broadcasting, but decisions about policy and funding are still made in the south. As with education in the North, much needs to be done to develop programs which are relevant to northern communities, the Native peoples in particular.

REGIONALISM, NATIONAL UNITY AND THE MEDIA

In many ways, Canada represents a triumph of communications. The pattern of the lines of communication is, as Walter Young commented, an "armature on which the figure of Canada as a political community has been shaped".[76] Rivers, lakes, canals and railways were not only avenues of commerce and transportation but also vital means of communication. Communities developed along these lines, and communication links between them were gradually strengthened by technological advances. The network of communications moved steadily out-

---

[75]See Bohdan Bociurkiw, "The Federal Policy of Multiculturalism and the Ukrainian-Canadian Community," in Manoly R. Lupul, ed., *Ukrainian Canadians, Multiculturalism, and Separatism: An Assessment* (Edmonton: University of Alberta Press, 1978), p. 120.

[76]Walter D. Young, "The Voices of Democracy: Politics and Communication in Canada," *CJPS*, vol. 14, no. 4 (Dec. 1981), p. 685.

ward, from centre to periphery, conquering enormous distances and facilitating political, social and economic movement. The central Canadian elite which directed the development of the media also formulated national goals and aspired to preserve establishment values. That interlocking group, which John Porter described as the ideological elite at the top of the mass media, the educational system and the churches, ensured that its central, national perspective dominated the development of the communications system.[77] The various federal commissions from the Aird Report in 1929 to the Davey Report on the mass media in 1970, which were set up to study and direct the course of broadcasting in Canada, have all agreed that national goals and values should be pursued and preserved through the media. The values they referred to were predominantly those of the anglophile elite of central Canada.[78]

In late 1982, the controversial Applebaum-Hébert report added a new dimension to discussions of cultural policy in Canada. It was the first major federal document on culture since the Massey-Lévesque Commission in 1951. Among the Applebaum-Hébert's many wideranging recommendations on broadcasting, film, publishing, heritage and other topics, the report proposed that the CBC continue as a broadcasting outlet but that its own productions be limited to news, and that all commercials should be eliminated. It strongly supported a federal system of "arm's-length" funding for all major cultural agencies including the CBC, to avoid political interference in independent agencies. The report has set the agenda for discussions of federal cultural policy in the coming decades.

Unfortunately, little evidence concerning the impact of the mass media on national cohesion is available. However, it is generally accepted that the extent to which the media provide common images and a cross-regional flow of information, as well as the way in which they present regional and ethno-linguistic conflict, have a significant bearing on national unity. In Canada, with its federal structure there is danger in a communications system that is either too strongly centralized or one that is too fragmented. Regional and ethnic cultures may be strong enough so that centrally controlled media which are not sufficiently attuned to such differences might, as one media specialist suggests, "produce alienation and hostility rather than assimilation to a national culture".[79] Certainly, as we have already noted, the domination of the Ontario heartland in areas other than communications has been an important facet of regional alienation. Although the Canadian communications system, like the federal political system, aims to foster Canadian identity but also support regional diversity, central Canadian domination of national media remains a problem.

We noted in the section above that the media help set the agenda for public debate. The advent of nation-wide television, and the CBC in particular, as well

---

[77]The ideological elite is described in John Porter, *The Vertical Mosaic* (Toronto: University of Toronto Press, 1965), p. 460, and later elaborated on by Wallace Clement in *The Canadian Corporate Elite* (Toronto: McClelland and Stewart, 1975).

[78]Young, *op.cit.*, p. 687.

[79]Fletcher, *op.cit.*, p. 25.

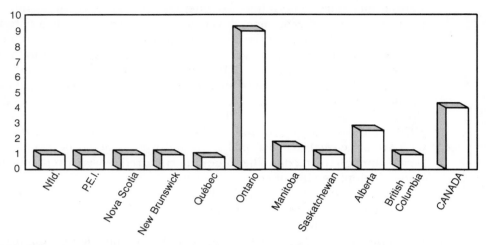

FIGURE 4.1 *Globe and Mail* Circulation in Canadian Provinces in Proportion to Households: Penetration per 100 Households*

*As of Sept. 30, 1981

Source: Arthur Siegel, *Politics and the Media in Canada* (Toronto: McGraw-Hill Ryerson, 1983) p. 128.

as the relatively recent achievement of national newspaper status by *The Globe and Mail*, have contributed greatly to the development of a national agenda. In the print media two other newspapers help set the agenda for national and public affairs: *The Toronto Star* and *Le Devoir*.

The Globe and Mail is read by nearly three-quarters of the country's top decision makers, and more than 90 percent of media executives read it regularly for ideas and trends. It proclaimed itself "Canada's National Newspaper" just after the turn of the century, but distance prevented simultaneous publication from British Columbia to the Atlantic provinces until satellite transmission made the scheme practical in the 1970s. Since it finally became available on a nation-wide, day-of-issue basis early in the 1980s *The Globe* has gained considerable strength as a national newspaper, although its share of the newspaper market outside of Ontario is still very small, as Figure 4-1 shows. It is Toronto-based and, although it does carry regional, national and international material, it is still strongly biased to central Canada coverage and reviews the periphery and the whole from a central perspective. *The Toronto Star*, Canada's largest independent daily, can be considered national only by virtue of a few widely syndicated articles. *Le Devoir* is comparable to *The Globe and Mail* for the francophone community. The Canadian Press (a cooperative news agency owned and operated by Canadian dailies which provides information to more than 100 media outlets), Southam News (the largest Canadian newspaper chain) and a few national magazines must also be included as part of the national scene.[80] In the broadcast media, CBC radio and television and CTV offer national services which filter and define the world of politics for most Canadians.

---

[80]Fletcher, *op.cit., passim.*

Because of factors such as distance, time and also the federal political structure, these national networks of communication are supplemented by a wide range of regional daily newspapers and television networks which carry both local and non-local news. Their contribution is limited to the regions concerned, and their influence on the national capital is small. Their dependence for national and international news on centre-oriented agencies such as the Canadian Press reinforces the influence of the central establishment on content and values. The steadily improving quality of the Canadian Press (CP) and increased regional coverage by *The Globe and Mail* and Southam News appears to contribute to a better cross-regional flow of information, as does the development of major newspaper chains at the expense of independent dailies.

Two major chains, Thomson and Southam, dominate the newspaper market, controlling over 50 dailies with more than half the total circulation in Canada. This domination poses serious questions about both lack of competition and conflict of interest. The Thomson newspapers, for example, are part of an international conglomerate which includes insurance, television, oil, real estate

TABLE 4.1 Number of Daily Newspapers, and Circulation by Ownership, 1970 and 1980

	Number of Daily Newspapers		*Aggregate Weekly Circulation (000's)*		*% of National Newspaper Circulation*	
	1970	*1980*	*1970*	*1980*	*1970*	*1980*
Independent	45	29	11 567	7 412	41.5	22.8
Thomson	30	40	2 398	6 865	8.6	21.2
Southam	11	14	4 965	8 693	17.8	26.8
Quebecor	2	2	526	2 762	1.9	8.5
Sun Group	—	3	0	2 197	—	6.8
Desmarais	4	4	1 920	1 711	6.5	5.3
Unimedia	—	2	0	871	—	2.7
Irving	5	5	623	793	2.2	2.4
Armadale	2	2	633	715	2.3	2.2
Sterling	—	11	0	292	—	0.9
Bowes	3	3	64	93	0.2	0.3
James Johnston	—	2	0	41	—	0.1
FP Publications	8	—	5 039	0	18.1	—
Dingman	2	—	126	0	0.5	—
Green	2	—	91	0	0.3	—
Total	114	117	27 851	32 445	99.9	100.0

Source: Adapted from Royal Commission on Newspapers, Research Studies, vol. 1, *Newspapers and their Readers* (Ottawa: Supply and Services, 1981).

and import companies, among other holdings. It is questionable whether the running of a newspaper is compatible with such interests. The Kent Royal Commission on Newspapers recommended that the government limit further concentration of media ownership, but no action has been taken.[81] Although it would reasonably appear to be in the national interest to maintain diversity of news sources, as the Commission claimed, their researchers were able to find little evidence that chain ownership affects newspaper quality, news or editorial coverage, although it obviously does affect their credibility.[82] Chain ownership does not even automatically guarantee national coverage. Southam News, for example, ensures that articles on the federal government are available, but regional papers need not publish them.

Despite centralized coverage it is often lamented that Canada still has no "national" agenda because of the regional and ethnic divisions in the country; a national agenda is temporarily created by events such as national elections but then fragments when regional conflict arises. This is certainly true in that there are regional differences in the selection of stories and the amount of local coverage for specific events, but these variations do not tend to be based on explicit differences of interpretation.[83] Studies conducted since the mid 1960s have found consistent regional differences in news selection to be based largely on geographical proximity to given events as well as on cultural preferences. For example, a study of 29 daily newspapers for the Biculturalism and Bilingualism Report showed great regional differences in amount of coverage and subjects stressed; this difference was more pronounced between French and English newspapers, which tended to be preoccupied with the affairs of their own language-group.[84] Similarly, the amount of news coverage of Québec-related issues, such as language policy a year after the election of the Parti Québécois, corresponded to the results of public opinion surveys: there was most coverage and most concern for these issues in Québec, somewhat less in Ontario and the Atlantic region and least in the West. Press content, Fred Fletcher speculates, prob-

---

[81]The Kent Commission was set up after the Ottawa Journal, owned by Thomson Newspapers, and the Winnipeg Tribune, owned by Southam Inc., shut down on the same day in August 1980. Government legislation to freeze the size of the two largest chains and restrict the size of developing chains to 20% of national circulation, among other changes, died at the end of the parliamentary session in late 1983. In order to ensure editorial quality and diversity, the government, during the same period, directed the CRTC, which grants licences to broadcasters, to restrict cross-ownership between broadcasters and owners of daily newspapers. In December 1983, Southam Inc. and Thomson Newspapers Ltd. were acquitted in the Ontario Supreme Court of criminal charges for conspiracy and merger in the closing of the *Ottawa Journal* and the *Winnipeg Tribune* and undue lessening of newspaper competition in Vancouver.

[82]Royal Commission on Newspapers (Ottawa: Minister of Supply and Services, 1981). See especially Fletcher, *op.cit.*, Chapter 3.

[83]See, for example, Walter C. Soderlund *et al.*, "Regional and Linguistic Agenda-Setting in Canada: A Study of Newspaper Coverage of Issues Affecting Political Integration in 1976," *CJPS*, vol. 13 no. 2. (June 1980), p. 356.

[84]See, for example, Donald Gordon, *National News in Canadian Newspapers*, Report to the Royal Commission on Biculturalism and Bilingualism, 1966.

ably both reflects and reinforces regional differences.[85] Media emphasis and public concern about issues generally correspond, so that regional differences in public opinion also correspond to differences in newspaper emphasis.

The way in which issues are presented is another important factor in promoting or discouraging national unity. Concentration by the media on divisive stories and issues is destructive. A 1976 study of editorials on Québec language issues showed the Ontario and Québec press to be generally integrative, stressing compromise, as opposed to editorialists in the West and the Atlantic region, who tended to condemn Québec nationalist aspirations.[86] Public opinion data show that public attitudes closely parallel this same regional division.[87] Whenever provincial newspapers support their provincial governments in conflicts with the federal government they are in fact promoting regional cleavages: for example, during federal/provincial disagreements when regional coverage is most complete about the regional personalities involved. As might be expected where local cultures exist, inter-regional conflicts occasionally surface in editorials which can fairly be described as parochial, hysterical and combative. These are generally about regionally-based issues such as western alienation or language rights, and although as Fletcher points out, they are unlikely to create new tensions, they often do reinforce existing ones.[88]

Studies of recent elections show that news coverage of election campaigns tends to be more nationally oriented and homogeneous now than in the past. Since 1974, for example, coverage of election campaigns in all regions (including the French press) has tended to emphasize the same themes, focusing on the leaders' campaigns rather than on regional problems. This apparent decline in regional differences may reflect the growing influence of television on election campaigns. The media cannot deliberately swing elections, but they certainly do help to form images of leaders and perceptions of issues. Political campaigns are increasingly designed for the medium of television, which constitutes the primary source of campaign information for most voters. (Better informed, issue oriented citizens prefer newspaper coverage, but they are in the minority.) The general homogenization of election coverage seems to reflect increased reliance on the Canadian Press and Southam News and a few syndicated columnists, as well as the influence of chain-owned newspapers.

VALUES AND THE MEDIA

Canadian newspapers reflect community norms and generally support the *status quo*, tending to reinforce the prevailing institutional and cultural patterns of authority and orientation. Most newspapers are anti-union. Rarely do they chal-

---

[85]Fletcher, *op.cit.*, p. 26. The studies were by W.C. Soderlund *et al.*, *op.cit.*, The public opinion poll study was by F. Fletcher and R. Drummond, *Canadian Attitude Trends 1960-1978* (Montréal: Institute for Research on Public Policy, 1979).

[86]Soderlund *et al.*, *op.cit.*, p. 320.

[87]Fletcher and Drummond, *op.cit.*, pp. 22-35.

[88]Fletcher, *op.cit.*, p. 29.

lenge dominant community interests or endorse political parties other than the Liberals or Conservatives. The Southam group, for example, makes political contributions to the federal party in power and also to the official opposition party. It does not give money to the NDP. According to Southam's president, the reason is "Because we believe in the Canadian two party system."[89]

This "middle of the road" tendency has been explained by two factors. First, the media are appealing to mass audiences so they tend to reinforce community values rather than challenge them. Second, as the Special Senate Committee on the Mass Media suggested, many newspapers may be unwilling to challenge the existing power structure in their community because of "lassitude, sloppiness, smugness and too chummy a relationship".[90] Underlying both of these situations is the fact that, with the exception of the CBC (and some minor stations), the print and electronic media are all privately owned, in many cases by large monopolies and conglomerate enterprises. They are run primarily to make profits, not to inform the public or challenge the *status quo*. To accomplish their financial goals they must compete for advertising revenue, which necessitates maximizing their audience or readership by such methods as packaging their news as entertainment and conforming with existing values.[91] Of course, they must also keep their commercial sponsors happy, which allows advertisers to wield indirect influence on the content and direction of news and programming. Editors or station managers would certainly hesitate, and probably decline to run, a story which was adverse to the interests of a generous sponsor.

Some researchers have noted a trend toward judgemental journalism in recent years, with an increase in commentary which focuses on certain aspects of the news, thereby extending and accentuating certain issues. Both this and the predominantly negative tone of political coverage may have negative consequences for the political system. Surveys have shown a widespread lack of respect for politicians, civil servants, government agencies and Parliament. Some studies attribute these negative attitudes to critical media coverage.[92] Media concentration on fault-finding and crisis might also be a factor in alienating citizens from the political process. At the same time, Canadian newspapers and public affairs programs are considerably less influential than their counterparts in other countries because policy-makers tend to lack respect for the expertise of columnists and commentators. There is no Canadian equivalent of the *New York*

---

[89]Quoted in Audley, *op.cit.*, p. 29.

[90]The Special Senate Committee on the Mass Media, *The Uncertain Mirror*, vol. I of the Report (Ottawa: Information Canada, 1970), p. 87.

[91]For a recent study of the structure of radio, television and cable television markets and its impact on the pricing of advertising and profitability, see Stuart McFadyen, Colin Hoskins and David Gillen, *Canadian Broadcasting: Market Structure and Economic Performance* (Montréal: The Institute for Research on Public Policy, 1980).

[92]Allan Kornberg and Judith D. Wolfe, "Parliament, Media and the Polls," in Harold D. Clark, *et al*, eds., *Parliament, Policy and Representation*, (Toronto: Methuen, 1980) pp. 35-58; and James P. Winter and Alan Frizzell, "The Treatment of State-Owned vs. Private Corporations in English Canadian Dailies," *Canadian Journal of Communications*, vol. 6 (Winter 1979-80), pp. 1-11.

Times, Washington Post or *Times of London*. The relationship between former Prime Minister Trudeau and the press was notoriously poor in at least the final half of his tenure, partly as a result of the Canadian journalistic tendency to treat public affairs as theatre and gossip, stressing personalities rather than social issues, style rather than substance. This orientation is not, however, entirely the fault of the journalists. As one study noted, "The vast majority of viewers/listeners/ readers want all things on their information menu to be black or white, true or false, good or bad – preferably seasoned with a pinch of sensationalism and intimate personal detail of the famous, and served on a platter of conventional belief."[93]

Communications in Canada are at a vital juncture. The current revolution in information technology is fraught with social and political implications. Distances are becoming meaningless, and the sheer volume of information available to individuals is overwhelming. In the decades ahead who will select and supply the information that Canadians will receive? Will the government find ways to control the flow of information without outlawing private direct broadcast satellite receivers, thereby depriving Canadians of the lower costs and vastly improved communications they offer? The nature of new technology makes it highly suitable for centralized control. Will such centralization increase the already established domination of a central Canadian elite? Will the free flow of information increase American cultural domination? What will the overall effect be on Canadian political culture? There are still many questions unanswered.

Government Services

The federal government plays a major role in shaping and reinforcing the political culture of Canada. It constantly taps citizens' reactions and attempts to inform, educate or propagandize as the case may be, in order to increase public support and loyalty. We have noted that public information about government affairs stems mainly from the mass media. Governments time their political announcements and broadcasts for peak exposure, advertise their parties and policy positions, televise parliamentary debates and record statements in Hansard, all in an effort to inform and thereby socialize the public. They attempt to reach citizens directly: mothers often find messages from the Minister of Health and Welfare enclosed with their Family Allowance; citizens who respond to government urgings to switch from oil heating to more energy efficient fuels may receive a congratulatory note from the Minister of Energy with their subsidy cheque. But there are many other ways to inform citizens and influence their attitudes. Governments advertise in the various media; public servants answer questions and distribute information; MPs deliver speeches and attempt to maintain personal contact within their constituencies; schools often use government booklets on a variety of subjects. As well, government ceremonies are held with tradi-

---

[93]Michael J. Trebilock *et al.*, *The Choice of Governing Instruments*, (Ottawa: Minister of Supply and Services, 1982), pp. 16-17.

tional pomp and dignity, instilling feelings of respect and a sense of historical continuity.

Government communications have increased dramatically in recent years, for a variety of reasons. One is the perceived need to refurbish the image of Parliament and federal institutions; another is an attempt to promote national unity and combat the centrifugal forces of regionalism. These concerns among political leaders came to a head in the late 1960s as youthful protest movements and vocal separatists underlined the growing cynicism and hostility of Canadians toward their federal government and its works. Why was the federal government not reaping credit for its programs? Was the problem a breakdown of communications between the government and its citizens? Should the federal government be doing more to create a national consciousness?

INFORMATION CANADA

To address these problems, the Federal Government set up a Task Force on Information to study government information services and offer suggestions for improvement. It reported in 1969 that in a national public opinion survey a majority of the respondents could not recall having seen any federal advertisements. This same group tended to be ill-informed about the responsibilities of their provincial and federal governments. On the other hand, the minority who remembered having been exposed to government advertising were relatively knowledgeable. The report noted, however, that exposure of the informed group to federal advertising did not appear to have favourably influenced their attitudes toward the federal government. Mass media were by far the most common source of public information; other sources of government information, such as direct contact with government representatives or publications, were used infrequently, and then primarily by the middle class. Those who used government services held the most positive attitudes towards government officials, finding them helpful and friendly.[94]

The same study found that the public obtained far more government information from the public service than from their MPs. However this communication was one-way, in that information from the public to the government passed not through public servants but mainly through MPs or MLAs.

This Task Force report ushered in a controversial era in government information programs. Modern Canadian governments have always advertised to inform the public about such topics as new unemployment regulations, or to increase sales of agricultural products such as eggs, which are marketed by a government board. Each government department has a budget for this purpose. In response to the report however, a new agency, Information Canada, was set up in 1970 to provide a direct information service by selling and distributing government pamphlets and other information across the country. It included a small "federalism" section, the aim of which was "a defence in depth of Confederation". This section was to render government more understandable by

---

[94]"To Know and To Be Known," Report of the Task Force on Information (Ottawa: Queen's Printer, 1969).

setting up information centres run jointly by the federal and provincial governments and generally to help provide easier access to government departments and better service. However, the agency was immediately viewed with suspicion as a partisan government party propaganda device by both the media and the opposition parties. It was inadequately defended by the government, and under pressure it was disbanded in 1976.

FURTHER INITIATIVES

Nevertheless, the problem of negative public attitudes to government remained, and a year after the demise of Information Canada a Task Force on Service to the Public was established. Located within the Department of Supply and Services in Ottawa, it prospered where Information Canada failed. By 1984 it had service bureaus in more than a dozen cities across the country, as well as toll free numbers for every province. Its mandate was to improve access to federal programs and help government departments advertise their services. To this end it initiated such changes as a telephone referral service designed to help citizens cut through red tape and negotiate the confusing maze of government bureaucracy by directing inquiries to the proper contact. To assist departments in meeting citizens' needs the Department conducts surveys, collects data, conducts workshops, and trains department personnel so that they can implement changes. It has also set up a computerized system, Telidon, in public places, so that citizens can instantly draw on information concerning the government.

The government has, in a word, gone into the marketing business; the product it is trying to sell is itself. The facilities it offers the public are widely used, and press reaction remains friendly. However, it is uncertain whether the current task force reforms, which are pilot projects subject to review, will be maintained; they could yet fall victim to either budgetary restraint or political manoeuvring. The greatest danger for this type of information service is that it can be viewed, justifiably or not, as a vehicle for publicizing programs, policies and views of the governing party – as a partisan political instrument.[95] Such criticisms would be unfortunate because the type of services offered represent a positive, long-term response to the problems of growing isolation and consequent alienation of the government and bureaucracy from the citizens, especially those who are distant from Ottawa.

The federal government has taken other concrete steps in recent years to improve communications. One, during the twilight Trudeau years when the government was widely accused of arrogance and insensitivity, was the setting up of a Cabinet Committee on Communications. Committee Chairman Gerald Regan declared at the time that the government had never been "more determined to communicate better, listen attentively to the public, and to make visible the work and worth of national government."[96] Another Liberal initiative was the estab-

---

[95]See Bob Phillips, "Opening Up," *Policy Options*, vol. 4, no. 2 (March/April, 1983), pp. 34-35.

[96]Gerald Regan, quoted in Duncan McDowall, ed., *Advocacy Advertising: Propaganda or Democratic Right?*, Study 73 (Ottawa: The Conference Board of Canada, 1982), p. 38.

lishment of the Canadian Unity Information Office (CUIO) in 1977, a year after the election of the Parti Québécois in Québec. This office was intended to organize major advertising campaigns and handle media contracts and payments. Initially, it coordinated publicity about the federal government's position on the 1980 Québec referendum; subsequently, it directed advertising supporting the government's views in the bargaining with the provinces that led to the patriation of the Constitution. The CUIO conveyed the federal government's message through both the print and the electronic media, making certain that the federal viewpoint reached citizens in all provinces.

While the Conservatives were in opposition, they consistently accused the Liberals of using the CUIO to build an image for their own political ends. One of the first Conservative acts on assuming power in September 1984 was to disband the CUIO. The Secretary of State retained responsibility for promoting national unity, and the Minister of Supply and Services was given responsibility for government advertising. It is not yet clear how the Conservative government will handle the latter function; however, there remain two important controversies about government advertising as it was conducted by the CUIO. One is the use of advocacy advertising techniques; the other is the large financial cost to the taxpayer.

In essence, advocacy advertising means selling ideas rather than products or services. Such advertisements attempt to build the legitimacy of their sponsor by sustaining or changing public attitudes concerning long term fundamental values which underlie social and political institutions.[97] Liberal government spokesmen viewed advocacy advertising as a means of building national unity and ensuring that Canadians were informed without the intermediary interpretation of the press. Their advertisements therefore did not contain much information but were designed to underline what the federal government saw as basic national values, and to promote understanding of national goals. For instance, ads extolling the virtues of Canada's multicultural society carried logos like "Growing Together" and "We have a lot to offer each other."

This type of service becomes controversial when advertisements extol clearly partisan policies. One of the best examples was government advertising over patriating the Constitution. In October 1980 contracts were awarded (without competition) to three agencies which had filled contracts for the Liberal Party in the previous election campaign. The advertisements they generated were designed to convince Canadians that the Constitution should be rewritten and patriated despite the differing opinions of provincial premiers and political parties. This aggressive approach, the government declared, was necessary for informing the public on a matter of national interest. Many of those opposed to the government viewpoint felt that the powerful political sales effort before the passing of the bill weakened Parliament and democracy in Canada by undermining traditional relations between MPs, the electorate and the government. One widely

---

[97]See Duncan McDowall, "And Now a Word from Our Sponsor: Ottawa Turns to Advocacy Advertising," *The Canadian Business Review,* vol. 9, no. 3 (Autumn, 1982), p. 30.

criticized television commercial featured Canada geese as the backdrop for a constitutional message. A federal member complained at the time, "I'll never be able to look at Canada geese or a beaver in quite the same way again. I'll see them as Liberals in disguise."[98] There is little doubt however that the advertisement contributed to setting a national agenda and ensuring that the federal message was heard in all provinces. Given the regionalization of the press, which often allows provincial premiers and opponents of the federal government to monopolize news coverage, federal government advertising may well be necessary for informed debate to take place and for redressing any distortions in the information received by the public.

The federal government's rising tendency to use advocacy advertising on controversial issues has stimulated occasional ad wars between the federal and provincial governments. The most notable occurred when the Parti Québécois spent $600 000 on an ad campaign to counter Prime Minister Trudeau's constitutional proposals. The eye-catching advertisements, entitled *"Minute: Ottawa!"*, showed a "federal" hand crushing the provincial flag. Such ad wars exacerbate federal/provincial differences, the very thing the federal government says it aspires to eliminate. At the same time, however, the parochialism and anti-federal bias of much of the press demonstrate the need for the national or federal viewpoint to be expressed across the country.

The second major criticism of government advertising concerns its cost. The federal government does not release a comprehensive figure for all advertising expenditures, but industry experts estimated the total for 1982-83 to be $70 million. This figure does not include advertising for such Crown corporations as Air Canada, CN, Petro-Can or for agencies which are not required to advertise through the Department of Supply and Services.[99] Such huge outlays made the government the largest single advertiser in Canada by the early 1980s, up from 17th position just over a decade earlier. Expenditures are particularly high compared to American figures. The federal government of the United States was the 28th largest advertiser in that country in 1980, spending only 65 cents *per capita*, compared to about $1.66 per capita spent by the Canadian government in the same year.[100] The discrepancy could, of course, be due to better portrayal of national issues and federal government positions by the American media.

Advocacy advertising clearly needs close regulation. Even when money is spent for advertising less controversial topics, it is sometimes debatable whether the sum could not be put to better use. For example, to show the federal government's concern about high unemployment in the 1980s, the Department of Employment and Immigration spent $46 million on billboards depicting men and women working. The only print was "Helping Canada Work" and, in smaller

---

[98]Quoted in Frances Phillips, "And Critics Have a Go at Ottawa," *The Financial Post,* May 13, 1982, p. 16.

[99]*Ibid.*

[100]*The New York Times,* November 2, 1980, p. 17.

type underneath, "Employment and Immigration Canada". It may perhaps not be unduly sceptical to suggest that the money might have been better spent on creating jobs.

The question of government advertising promises to play a conspicuous role in the years ahead. The federal advertising budget is high compared to private sector advertising, but given the size of the country, two major languages and the cultural divisions within it, as well as the high number of social programs in which the government is involved, much of it is justifiable.

The federal government has a responsibility to inform Canadians about its policies and programs and yet refrain from using its resources to disseminate partisan propaganda. The ethnic and regional divisions in Canada's political culture can be alleviated to a degree by ensuring that all citizens are exposed to views which represent the country's interests, not just those of a particular region, province or ethnic group. It is the responsibility of the opposition parties to ensure that the government does not abuse this right, and to date they have shown a marked ability to detect and publicize infractions.

OVERVIEW

Political socialization in Canada is a haphazard affair, far from the calculated indoctrination of authoritarian political systems. Early socialization through families and peer groups is casual and informal with minimal interference by the state. The three important secondary agents of socialization which we have examined, educational institutions, the mass media and the federal government are all closer to the political process and are the object of deliberate attempts by the federal government to influence the values and beliefs of Canadians. But even then, the state direction is severely limited. Education for example is not within the federal jurisdiction, and the mass media, including broadcasting, television and the press, all act independently, to varying degrees.

We have discussed many powerful obstacles to building a strong Canadian nation-state political culture. American influences are pervasive. French and English language media in Canada, through their selection and treatment of news, reinforce the linguistic and cultural differences between the two official language groups. Educational institutions display significant regional and French-English differences with respect to both structure and curriculum. Both the media and education as agents of political socialization reflect and reinforce the regional, linguistic and ethnic cleavages in the political culture. Such obstacles are to be expected given the constraints of a democratic federal political system and a society which is bilingual and multicultural. In liberal democratic societies basic freedoms must be respected. The state cannot assume direct control of the agents of socialization. Would Canadians want totally centralized government socialization in order to attempt to instill a stronger national culture? Or would too much centralization have the opposite effect and simply deepen regional and ethnic cleavages? Such weak centralization as exists is already at the root of regional discontent. The federal government has moved in the last two decades to combat strong divisive forces in the Canadian political culture. It continues to build on the goals of strengthening communications, facilitating access to government and improving the circular flow of information between government institutions and the public. Its methods, though often controversial, are geared to bring government closer to the people.

The Canadian political culture, initiated and reinforced as it is by the socialization process described in this chapter, contains at least the minimal level of national identity required to legitimize the Constitution and the democratic political process. Canadians expect to live in a liberal society free of government control and indoctrination. They have learned to value the assumptions and processes of parliamentary democracy and to expect the political system to manage the tensions caused by linguistic and regional cleavages – and to do so democratically.

In the next part of the book, and the next two chapters in particular, we shall examine how the institutions of the Canadian political system are based upon, and reflect, the essential characteristics of Canadian political culture.

Part III
Institutions

Reprinted with permission – The Toronto Star Syndicate.

chapter 5

The Foundations of Constitutional Order
From the *B.N.A. Act* to the *Canada Act*

ONE OF THE PERSISTENT GOALS of all societies is the establishment of stability and order. Among the various means of achieving this end is the creation of a set of laws and principles embodying the aspirations of the society and at the same time providing guidelines for political life. Although it may take an infinite variety of forms, such a set of rules and procedures is commonly referred to as a *constitution*. Some societies choose to depend on a constitution in the form of a single written document which is both a statement of principles and a detailed explication of the relative authority and jurisdiction of the various actors in the political process. In other societies, values and political traditions are so firmly rooted in the political culture that no attempt to codify them is considered necessary. The true test of the significance of a constitution, be it written or unwritten, is the nature of its relationship to the society that produced it. Some constitutions are nothing but a set of lofty platitudes which are rarely observed, while others play an integral role in political affairs.

In this chapter we will explore the meaning of the term "constitution", and trace the evolution of the Canadian Constitution since 1867. Of particular interest will be the provisions for the formal executive in Canada and the problems and difficulties inherent in constitutional amendment and change.

While matters of fundamental law and legal procedure can be complicated for those unfamiliar with the principles of jurisprudence, this chapter will attempt to approach the subject in a non-technical manner, yet remain sensitive to the political implications of constitutional institutions. As we shall determine, the various efforts to patriate the Constitution and develop an amendment procedure acceptable to all the provinces were the source of enormous controversy in the past half-century. Though the 1982 *Canada Act* brought the Constitution home from Britain, the controversy is far from ended, and arguments over the nature of the Canadian Constitution remain a lively political pastime.

WHAT IS A CONSTITUTION?

All societies, primitive or modern, require some regularized patterns of interaction. Rules imposing obligations and assuring structures for the solution of
conflict must be adopted. In primitive societies these rules are developed
through custom and usage; in modern societies they have been regularized and
formalized, yet rendered capable of adapting to change. Such fundamental rules
delineate the authority structures of society and grant leaders the legitimacy to
act in authoritative ways.

Early societies tended to be dominated by individuals who sought to establish traditions and rules to govern their people. In more recent times, there has
been a tendency for basic rules to be formalized into what is commonly referred
to as a "constitution". The origin of the concept can be traced to Greek and Roman times. Further significant constitutional development flourished during the
18th and 19th centuries. Since then it has become practically universal for political power to be organized by some form of constitution.

In any political system, political leadership requires guidelines for action –
the supreme law or constitution of the state, which defines and limits political
power. The concept of law is nebulous but very important. As W.H. Auden described it in "Law Like Love",

> . . .Law is the clothes men wear
> Anytime, anywhere,
> Law is Good-morning and Good-night.
>
> Others say, Law is our Fate;
> Others say, Law is our State;
> Others say, others say
> Law is no more
> Law has gone away.
>
> And always the loud angry crowd
> Very angry and very loud
> Law is We,
> And always the soft idiot softly Me.[1]

The major difficulty with the concept "constitution" arises in distinguishing the fundamental constitutional aspects of political order from less significant parts of political organization. Clearly, the fundamental aspect of a
constitution states the guiding principles of a society. However, in modern times
the word **constitution** has been used both empirically and normatively: to depict
the organization of government, and to advise restraints on its action.

Though many constitutions are the product of historical development, they
also tend to reflect current conditions. In absorbing contemporary elements,
constitutions are able to help shape the future through their incorporation of

---

[1]W.H. Auden, "Law Like Love," in *The Collected Poetry of W.H. Auden.* (New York: Random
House, 1945), p. 75.

norms of political life. Constitutional authorities in most countries have particularly insisted on the need to incorporate individual rights into the supreme law as well as to set the parameters for government action. The vast majority of contemporary written constitutions contain a discussion of natural rights and the goals of universal liberty, peace and prosperity. Even the most repressive regimes are likely to make reference to these objectives in their constitutions.[2] The French Declaration of the Rights of Man and Citizens, the American Constitution with its Bill of Rights and the Soviet Constitution all include quite similar statements supporting the principle of the natural rights of humankind. Of course, the fact that such rights are incorporated into a constitution is no guarantee of their actualization. In situations of real or perceived emergency, such statements may carry little weight in even the most liberal societies.

Above all else, the existence of a constitution embodies the *rule of law*. In addition to setting out a commitment to certain general goals, a constitution is intended to provide a guarantee of impartiality and fairness. The authority of the state is to be exercised rationally and without malice, with all citizens being protected from the abuse of power. The rule of law means that the citizen, no matter what his/her transgression, cannot be denied the due process of law. It therefore regularizes the relationship between citizens and their government. Whether or not it is formally included, the rule of law is a fundamental principle without which any constitution, written or unwritten, would be meaningless.

The two main sources of law in Canada are *statutory enactments*, legislation passed by the Parliament of Canada and the provincial legislatures, and case law developed by the courts, also known as *common law* or unenacted law. While Canada's Constitution grants legislative authority to the eleven legislatures, the legislative competence of each is specifically limited to certain classes of matters.

Common law is based upon the rule of precedent, *stare decisis*. That is, the judiciary is bound by previous decisions in deciding current cases. Application of precedents has resulted in the development of a body of case law that acts as a guide for judges in rendering decisions. As new problems are brought before the courts, judges refer to previous decisions that are deemed relevant, and apply the deciding arguments when making their own judgements. If there is a lack of precedents, judges rely on common sense and reason. Existing principles are thereby broadened and the body of case law is expanded. Thus, judicial interpretation is an important source of our law.

The relationship between these two major sources of law is defined by the doctrine of *parliamentary supremacy*, a basic premise of parliamentary democracy. Parliament has the authority, in theory, to repeal or modify any principle set out in common law. This power is not absolute, however. The courts' ability to declare an Act *ultra vires* (beyond a legislature's powers) on the basis of Canada's federal division of power is an important qualification. The entrenchment of some individual and group rights in Canada's *Charter of Rights and Freedoms* also

---

[2]For a discussion of the history of constitutionalism, see Charles M. McIlwain, *Constitutionalism: Ancient and Modern*, second edition (Ithaca, New York: Cornell University Press, 1947).

limits the extent of parliamentary supremacy by placing that body of rights beyond the reach of Parliament.

As well as stating fundamental principles, written constitutions detail the nature of the organization of government. Some are remarkably complicated documents outlining the entire government structure and the relative powers and limitations of the various institutions in the political process. It seems to be a general belief that the greater the detail in explicating these relationships, the less the likelihood for abuse of power. At the least, most written constitutions discuss the powers and duties of the executive, the legislature, the judiciary and sometimes other institutions such as the bureaucracy or the military. However, the functions of the three major bodies are not so easily assigned to any one of them, since they are multi-functional. The courts, for example, adjudicate the law, but, as we have seen, in their accumulated judgements they also legislate.

However detailed the various legal restraints on the exercise of power, nearly all constitutions contain provisions for emergency situations. War, civil unrest or natural disaster may require a government to act in a way that under normal conditions would be illegal. The real test of a constitution is whether, after such a crisis, there is a speedy return to compliance with constitutional structures. The case of the late Indian Prime Minister Indira Gandhi's invocation of certain emergency provisions of her country's constitution and the subsequent return to normal legal procedures after the perceived crisis is a vindication of India's constitutional democracy. The use of the *War Measures Act* to suppress civil rights in Québec in 1970 by the Liberal government of Prime Minister Trudeau is another pertinent example of how constitutions allow governments to handle crises. We need not search far to find examples of other countries, in which constitutional restraints on the exercise of power have been easily subverted by phony crises. Once a group obtains a power base in society, either through the institutional structure or outside of it, the potential always exists to manipulate the provisions of the constitution or even suspend it entirely. As we have said, a constitution alone is no guarantee that fundamental principles will be upheld. Unless a constitution is congruent with the prevailing political culture, it stands little chance of having any lasting effect.

One form of government in which a written constitution is almost a necessity is *federalism*. The establishment of federalism usually requires some sort of "federal bargain",[3] in which the constituent elements of the union agree to give up a degree of autonomy in exchange for certain benefits which they perceive as arising from being part of a more powerful political entity. It is difficult to imagine a federalism that is not based on some sort of written document which enshrines guarantees and concessions to the various subordinate governments. This is not to say that a federal constitution cannot be altered at a later point by judicial interpretation or by amendment. What is important to remember is that federal states are, for the most part, initiated through the adoption of written constitutions, and that their provisions and limitations help shape the nature of federalism in the given states.

---

[3]See the detailed discussion in Chapter 6.

We mentioned earlier that some societies possess what are referred to as "unwritten constitutions". This is not a contradiction in terms; rather, the existence of such a constitution indicates that certain fundamental principles may be so firmly entrenched in the political process of the given state that no formal document outlining them is considered necessary. The United Kingdom is perhaps the best-known example of a nation with an unwritten constitution.[4] There may in these cases exist certain documents and precedents which, taken as a whole, resemble a written constitution. In the case of Britain, such documents are the *Magna Carta* of 1215, the *Habeus Corpus Act* of 1679 and the *Reform Bill* of 1832. Despite these and other documents and legal precedents, the real core of Britain's unwritten constitution is the set of values and norms embedded in the political culture: the right of opposition, the right of freedom of speech and assembly, the right to participate in the political process, among others. The existence of an unwritten constitution provides certain advantages for a nation. For instance, it makes it possible for a society to adapt more readily to change without the constraints of a formal constitutional straight-jacket.

THE EVOLUTION OF THE BRITISH NORTH AMERICA ACT

This section examines how the Canadian constitution evolved over time from the passing of the 1867 *British North America Act* to the 1982 *Canada Act*.[5] The Canadian constitution was always something of a hybrid of the written and unwritten types. While many Canadians have automatically assumed that the *BNA Act* was the Canadian Constitution until 1982, this assertion must be severely qualified.

In reading the *BNA Act* it is wise to follow the French adage, "Read between the lines; it's less fatiguing on the eyes." Important elements of Canada's unwritten constitution evolved in Britain for many centuries before Confederation.[6] Common law precedents and the parliamentary form of government are examples. As British colonists emigrated to Canada they brought with them basic constitutional principles such as the rule of law and the right of opposition. The *BNA Act*, with its provision that Canada was to have a form of government "similar in principle to that of the United Kingdom", intended not only that certain institutional arrangements with respect to the formal executive were to be reproduced in Canada, but also that the parliamentary system, with all its implicit values, was to be transplanted. Important elements of the Canadian Constitution were therefore already implicitly in place when the Fathers of Confederation met at Charlottetown.

---

[4]See R.M. Punnett, *British Government and Politics*, fourth edition, (London: Heinemann, 1980), pp. 163-193.

[5]Two copies of the original *BNA Act* to which Queen Victoria gave Royal Assent on March 29, 1867 can be seen in London, England; one in the Victoria Tower of Westminster Palace and the other in the Public Records Office. Reproductions are now at the Public Archives of Canada.

[6]See W.P.M. Kennedy, *The Constitution of Canada, 1534-1937* (London: Oxford University Press, 1938) and E. Russell Hopkins, *Confederation at the Crossroads: The Canadian Constitution* (Toronto: McClelland and Stewart; 1968).

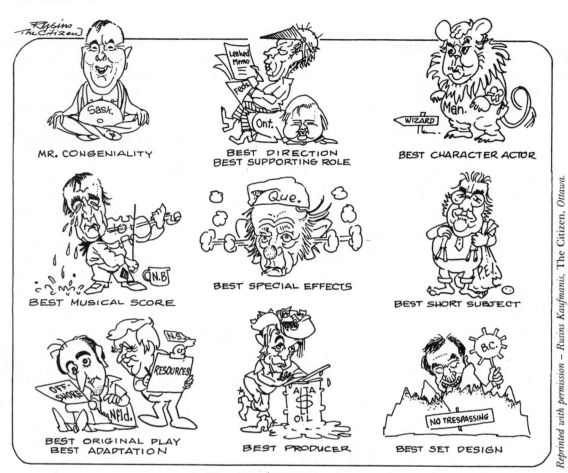

MR. CONGENIALITY

BEST DIRECTION
BEST SUPPORTING ROLE

BEST CHARACTER ACTOR

BEST MUSICAL SCORE

BEST SPECIAL EFFECTS

BEST SHORT SUBJECT

BEST ORIGINAL PLAY
BEST ADAPTATION

BEST PRODUCER

BEST SET DESIGN

Reprinted with permission – Rusins Kaufmanis, The Citizen, Ottawa.

The 1980 BNA Awards

As Professor Ronald I. Cheffins phrased it, "A literal reading of the Act itself is not only of little value in understanding the realities of political life, but is in fact dangerously misleading."[7] Many issues that preoccupy governments today were not included in the document. All levels of government responded by finding ways to expand their responsibilities without constitutional authority. Even certain vital procedural matters bearing on the governing of the country go unmentioned in the *BNA Act*; for example, the Prime Minister and Cabinet are not mentioned explicitly. Rules that are accepted practice or tradition without being enshrined in the constitution are called "conventions". The country would not be able to govern itself without conventions such as the one requiring the government to resign when it is defeated in Parliament.

---

[7]Ronald I. Cheffins, *The Constitutional Process in Canada* (Toronto: McGraw-Hill, 1969), p. 9.

Given these elements of the unwritten Canadian Constitution, what is the significance of the *British North America Act?* Simply put, it is that the *Act* set out the basic terms of federalism and outlined the machinery of government, based on the British model.[8] As we have already suggested, the establishment of a federal form of government calls for the adoption of a written constitution to enshrine the "federal bargain". The *BNA Act* was thus the product of lengthy, complex negotiations between the political leaders of the period over the terms of the federal union. The various leaders had differing expectations of what federalism would mean for their regions. Efforts were made to obtain concessions and guarantees which would protect matters of vital local concern. For example, Québécois sought protection for the French language as the price for joining the union, while Nova Scotians were concerned about economic concessions and subsidies.

The *BNA Act* is a relatively simple, straightforward document. It lacks the stirring rhetoric of the American Constitution, and whatever commitment it has to the fundamental rights of individuals is merely implicit. In some respects the statute is as significant for what it does not say as for what it does say. The *BNA Act* was a document designed to enable the provinces to join in a political union. It was not intended to establish a truly independent state, since it provided that the formal executive of Canada was to continue to be the British monarch and that the *Act* itself could be amended only by the British Parliament.

The established provinces continued to adhere to their colonial constitutions, and the provinces added after Confederation were later to receive their constitutions from the Ottawa government. The heritage from the United Kingdom in English-speaking provinces included the common law tradition. However, since Confederation did not change existing law, Québec continued and still continues to have a system of civil law, based on French traditions such as the *Code Napoléon,* and in turn on Roman civil law. Criminal law was to be similar in all provinces, however, as a federal responsibility. Principles such as liberty and the rule of law were considered to be protected by common law and hence were not included in the *BNA Act.*

With respect to the machinery of formal executive power, the *Act* is reasonably detailed, but on matters concerning the division of authority between the federal and provincial governments it is notably vague.[9] The intent of the authors of the document was the creation of a strong central government. Jurisdiction over education, welfare and other matters perceived to be insignificant in 1867 was left to the provinces. The federal government was given responsibility for trade and commerce, defence and foreign affairs. As we shall see in the next chapter, over time the responsibilities of the provinces became relatively more important, and when legal disputes did ensue between the two levels of government, the British Law Lords usually seemed to side with the provinces. At times,

---

[8] W.H. McConnell, *Commentary on the British North America Act* (Toronto: Macmillan, 1977).

[9] See Garth Stevenson, *Unfulfilled Union: Canadian Federalism and National Unity,* revised edition (Toronto: Macmillan, 1982).

therefore, the *BNA Act* has been a very restrictive document and has created an impasse in federal/provincial relations.

We have said that the *BNA Act* did not contain a procedure for being amended, save by the passage of a bill in the British Parliament. This occurred 18 times.[10] It is on the last of these occasions that the *Canada Act* was passed, ending forever this link between Canada and the United Kingdom. Over time, the role of the British Parliament in amending the *BNA Act* became more limited. In 1931 the *Statute of Westminster* established the principle that the British Parliament could not legislate for Canada except at the request of the Canadian government. In 1949 Louis St. Laurent's government secured an amendment to the *BNA Act* which widened the scope of the Canadian Parliament's authority to undertake amendments: it was empowered to amend the Canadian Constitution on its own except with reference to provincial matters, the five year term of Parliament and the language and educational rights of minorities. Despite these changes, the *BNA Act* remained an *Act* of the British Parliament, serving to raise the ire of Canadian nationalists.

Although the *BNA Act* was the centrepiece of Canada's written Constitution, there were other relevant documents. Besides the various amendments to the *BNA Act*, and the *Statute of Westminster*, the Canadian Constitution before 1982 could be said to include the Royal Proclamation of 1763; the *Colonial Laws Validity Act* of 1865; the various Acts admitting new provinces to the federal union; letters patent concerning the office of the Governor General; and a whole range of common law precedents and Orders-in-Council.

Whether a constitution originates as a single written document or as a cluster of laws and agreements, there is no question that major changes to it occur through interpretation. In any federal system, there is always the need for a court or an arbitration process to resolve disputes over jurisdictional authority. For most of Canadian history the court of final appeal was the Judicial Committee of the Privy Council (JCPC) of the United Kingdom. For the most part, as we noted, it tended to define federal authority as narrowly and provincial authority as widely as possible. The so-called emergency powers of the federal government, expressed in the clause "Peace, Order and good Government", granted extensive residual power to the federal government, but were interpreted in a way that virtually nullified the apparent centralizing intentions of the drafters of the *BNA Act*.[11]

The rulings of the JCPC on the law of Canadian federalism were the source of considerable controversy. It was widely felt that the Law Lords were too far removed from the political realities of Canada to render appropriate decisions.[12]

---

[10]See Paul Gerin-Lajoie, *Constitutional Amendment in Canada* (Toronto: University of Toronto Press, 1950) and Alan C. Cairns, "Recent Federalist Constitutional Proposals: A Review Essay," *Canadian Public Policy*, vol. 5, no. 3 (Summer 1979), pp. 348-365.

[11]See Peter J.T. O'Hearn, *Peace, Order and Good Government* (Toronto: Macmillan, 1964).

[12]See Alan C. Cairns, "The Judicial Committee and Its Critics," *Canadian Journal of Political Science*, vol. 4, no. 3 (September 1971), pp. 301-345.

The reign of the JCPC as the court of last appeal ended in 1949 with the establishment of the Supreme Court of Canada as the arbiter of constitutional review. Consisting of nine federally-appointed judges, the Supreme Court is the highest court for civil, criminal and constitutional cases (The Federal Court of Canada, a separate body, oversees matters of law, equity and admiralty.) The Supreme Court has been somewhat hampered by the nature of the parliamentary system and the absence of an entrenched bill of rights until 1982.[13] It has been concerned mainly with jurisdictional disputes, and has not taken the activist role for which the American Supreme Court is widely known. In recent years, the provinces have displayed notable reticence to take jurisdictional matters to the Supreme Court, because of an alleged pro-centralist bias. Disputes between the federal and provincial governments increasingly tend to be resolved outside the judicial process through the mechanism of federal/provincial conferences. The rise of a modern style of federalism has meant that the terms of federalism can be adjusted by methods other than judicial interpretation.[14]

This is not to argue that the Supreme Court is irrelevant. On the contrary, there have recently been important decisions by the Court on matters such as offshore oil and mineral rights and the question of resource taxation, not to mention its ruling on the federal government's plan of unilateral patriation of the Constitution. Of late, the court also seems to be taking an interest in cases involving civil rights and liberties. After over thirty years, the Supreme Court of Canada is beginning to assert itself within the constraints imposed on it.

The second important determinant of power in any federal system between federal and provincial governments rests on the financial strength of the two jurisdictions. In a federal state, revenue sources must be divided between the two levels of government. If not, the federal reality will quickly wither. The key question concerns how to distribute funds to the provinces and at the same time maintain federal control of the national economy.

The *BNA Act* conferred on the federal government the ability to raise money by any system of taxation, while at the same time it gave over most areas of growing financial responsibility to the jurisdiction of the provinces. Provincial authorities are still restricted to collecting revenue through direct taxes or the sale of natural resources. (Direct taxes must be paid by the individual or firm assessed, but indirect taxes may be passed along to other persons or institutions.) Thus, it appeared from strict interpretation of the 1867 *Act* that the provinces could not levy a sales tax (indirect) on commodities which would be passed along to consumers. However, by the ingenious device of making vendors tax collectors for the provincial governments, the rules of the *BNA Act* were evaded and

---

[13]For a review of the Supreme Court's recent interpretations on federalism, see Paul C. Weiler, "The Supreme Court and the Law of Canadian Federalism," *University of Toronto Law Journal*, vol. 23, no. 3 (Summer 1973), pp. 307-367; James Lorimer, ed., *The Supreme Court Decisions on the Canadian Constitution* (Toronto: James Lorimer and Company, 1981); and Peter Russell, *et al.*, *The Court and the Constitution* (Kingston: Queen's University Institute of Intergovernmental Relations, 1982).

[14]See Richard Simeon, *Federal-Provincial Diplomacy: The Making of Recent Policy in Canada* (Toronto: University of Toronto Press, 1972).

the provinces were able to employ both types of taxation. But even such ploys as this do not suffice to alleviate provincial budgetary needs.

The *British North America Act* was an attempt to graft a federal system of government onto a British heritage of representative and responsible cabinet government. Its authors had to take into account two dissimilar linguistic groups, a federal system and complex financing regulations. The result was a division of jurisdiction between the two levels of government, federal and provincial. While the Crown, Government and Parliament are the central governmental institutions, they are therefore not totally sovereign in Canada as they are in the United Kingdom. In the following section, we look at the institutions which make up the formal executive in Canada.

THE FORMAL EXECUTIVE: CROWN, MONARCHY AND GOVERNOR GENERAL

The *British North America Act* set out in detail the powers and prerogatives of formal executive power in Canada. While there is no question that the powers of the formal executive are largely ceremonial, it would be incorrect to dismiss them as trivial and meaningless. There have been situations in which the formal executive has proven a very important element of the political process.

In British tradition, the supreme authority of the state resides with the Sovereign. Government functions are carried out in the name of the *Crown.* The term "Crown" refers to the composite symbol of the institutions of the state. Government property is held in the name of the Crown. The Crown may be involved in court proceedings,[15] and it assumes a variety of duties and responsibilities. In Britain the Crown has been defined as "the sum total of governmental powers synonymous with the Executive".[16]

The Crown retains some rights from common law, but most of its present authority comes from statute law. The so-called "prerogative powers" can be traced to an earlier period of authoritarian rule in Great Britain when the Crown possessed wide discretionary authority. With the rise of Parliament and the gradual movement toward popular sovereignty, the authority of the Crown has been eroded to a very few reserve powers. Although Parliament and the political executive still govern in the name of the Crown, there is little question that the monarch is severely limited. Even the ability of the monarch to stay on the throne is no longer a right. In the cases of both James II and Edward VIII in Britain it was clear that the monarch could not remain on the throne unless the ministers and Parliament were prepared to accept him.

The reigning monarch is the personal embodiment of the Crown. The contemporary functions of the monarch are largely ceremonial and non-partisan.

---

[15]Since the passage of the *Crown Liability Act* of 1952, the Crown can be sued like any other litigant.

[16]E.C.S. Wade and A.W. Bradley, *Constitutional Law,* eighth edition (London: Longman, 1970), pp. 171 ff., 678 ff.

The monarch reigns, but does not govern. As Walter Bagehot put it, the monarch's functions are mainly of the "dignified", not of the "efficient" , type.[17] By this Bagehot meant that the monarch does not actually govern the country, but rather carries out a myriad of ceremonial responsibilities which generate mass support for government, while the ministers carry out the "efficient" procedures which operate the machinery of government.

Except in francophone Québec, the present monarch, Queen Elizabeth II, is the object of considerable admiration and respect. While the Queen serves to unify English Canada, the antipathy felt in French Canada towards this symbol of anglophone domination is a matter for concern. One poll showed that 60% of French Canadians felt that the monarchy should be abolished; only 30% of English Canadians agreed.[18] René Lévesque, former Premier of Québec, once declared at a federal/provincial conference, "Long live the Queen – until further notice." Recently, the Québec government introduced a bill which would put an end to swearing allegiance to the Queen by future members of the National Assembly. The oath to Canada's sovereign would be replaced by a solemn promise of loyalty to the "people of Québec", and to conduct oneself "with honesty and justice and with respect for the constitution of Québec".

Since the monarch could not be permanently based in Canada, a Governor General was appointed after 1867 by the British government. As Canada evolved out of colonialism towards nationhood, this executive link was modified. After the end of the First World War there was a gradual movement toward autonomy from Britain. The Imperial Conference of 1926 sought to make the Governor General a representative of the Crown, not of the British government. In 1947, new Letters Patent completed the process by allowing the Governor General the power to exercise the powers of the sovereign. However, the Queen continues to be Canada's monarch: she makes royal tours to Canada and acts as the symbolic head of the Commonwealth of which Canada is a member.

The Governor General, in performing only the Queen's "dignified" roles in Canada, does not provide much practical input into the political process. As the Queen's representative, the Governor General is appointed by Her Majesty on the recommendation of the Canadian Prime Minister and the Cabinet. In 1952 the office was further Canadianized by the appointment of Vincent Massey, the first Canadian to hold the position. It has since become customary to alternate the position between English- and French-speaking Canadians. The appointment of Edward Schreyer in 1978 changed the trend, since he is an English-speaking Canadian from neither charter group. The next appointee, Jeanne Sauvé, a French Canadian, in 1984 became the first woman appointed to this high office. Governors General have often been selected from outside the partisan political sphere, mainly from the diplomatic or military establishment. The appointment of former Manitoba Premier Edward Schreyer and Liberal Speaker Jeanne Sauvé marked a departure from this pattern.

---

[17]Walter Bagehot, *The English Constitution* (London: World's Classics, 1928).

[18]John Meisel, *Papers on the 1962 Elections* (Toronto: University of Toronto Press, 1964), p. 159.

The tenure is usually five years, but the officially recognized term is six years, which has on occasion been extended to seven. In the event of death, incapacity, removal or absence of the Governor General, the Chief Justice of the Supreme Court, Canada's leading judge, acts as the Administrator, and may carry out all duties of the office.

The functions of the Governor General as head of state provide the official monarchical structure of Canadian government on an everyday basis. First, many purely ceremonial functions such as conferring Order of Canada awards or reviewing troops may be carried out by the appointee. In order to fill these roles, the Governor General presides over Rideau Hall Estate, a staff of about 100, a budget near $5 million annually and a secondary residence in Québec City. Second, the Governor General acts as a representative for the state. In studying loyalty in regimes, theorists have found that individuals are socialized into acceptance of authority through their attachment to authority figures such as the Governor General.

The Governor General is bound to act on nearly every piece of advice given by his/her ministers. Nevertheless, certain functions are the Governor General's alone. The most important of these stem from prerogative powers left to the monarch – powers which have not been by-passed by statute law. The Letters Patent provide the Governor General with all the powers of the Queen "in respect of summoning, proroguing or dissolving the Parliament of Canada". Clearly the most significant of these powers is the duty to appoint a Prime Minister. In order to exercise this significant prerogative power, the Governor General must have a reasonably free hand to make a decision based on the circumstances. In a case where there is a leader of a party who can command a clear majority of the seats in the House of Commons, the Governor General has nothing to do but follow the rules in selecting the obvious candidate. Since the 1890s, when Sir John Abbott and Sir Mackenzie Bowell held the prime ministership from the Senate, all Prime Ministers have held seats in the House of Commons. In 26 of the 33 elections since Confederation, one of the two major parties has obtained an absolute majority of the seats in the House. However, after an election in which the results are confused or which produces no majority in the House, or when a Prime Minister dies in office, the Governor General could exercise this prerogative in an independent manner. Such discretionary power would always be subject to controversy, and it has not been exercised in the selection of the Prime Minister during any of the seven minority governments. However, in 1979 Governor General Edward Schreyer did make outgoing Prime Minister Joe Clark wait two hours before agreeing to his request for a new election. This action was legitimate because the Governor General must consider whether or not an opposition leader can form a government.

While the dissolution of Parliament is often separated from the appointment of the Prime Minister for purposes of discussion, the two are logically related. It is generally agreed that only a Prime Minister can ask for and obtain a dissolution of Parliament, although a Governor General once refused such a request. This incident was the famous Byng-King case. A Prime Minister who is defeated, or feels he may be, can ask to have Parliament dissolved rather than submit his resignation. Liberal Prime Minister Mackenzie King did so in 1926. The Governor General, Lord Viscount Byng, declined King's request for dissolution and instead called on Arthur Meighen to form a new administration. However, the Progressives were unable to give their continued support to the new Conservative government and within four days the government fell. Meighen, in turn, had to ask the Governor General for a dissolution.[19] In the election which ensued, the Liberals charged that the Governor General had favoured the Conservatives and that the British were again interfering in Canada. The electoral victory of the Liberals demonstrated that, although the Governor General may have had the constitutional power to dissolve Parliament, the people were the final arbiters of whether or not the action was practical.

The precedent is now firm. In December 1979, Conservative Prime Minister Joe Clark, who headed a minority government, was defeated on the Budget. Although theoretically the Liberals, New Democrats and Créditistes could have been asked to try to form a government, the Governor General consulted Mr. Clark and dissolved Parliament without discussing the matter with any of the opposition parties.

Can a Governor General force a dissolution of Parliament? It has always been assumed that this would prove impossible when one party controlled a majority in the House. However, the Australian "Canberra case" of November 1975 has upset the certainty of this contention. While the Australian constitutional structure differs from that of Canada in many respects (especially in the fact that the upper house is an elected body), it has generally been assumed that the Governors General of both countries were unable to dissolve Parliament. The Australian Senate continually held up supply bills from the lower House, until a financial crisis threatened the country. The Senate was controlled by the Liberal and Country parties, while the lower house was controlled by the Prime Minister, Gough Whitlam, and his Labour party. The Governor General asked Whitlam to dissolve both Houses. Whitlam refused, and the Governor General dismissed him. The Governor General asked the leader of the opposition to form a government, on the condition that the new Prime Minister would then request a dissolution. In the bitter election campaign which followed, the Liberal/Country coalition was elected – the Governor General's recommendation was electorally upheld. The effect of this on Canada and even Britain is difficult to determine, since nothing equivalent has occurred in either country during this century. In view of the changing nature of the Commonwealth and the weakening bonds between the members, constitutional precedents are likely to prove inconsequential. It is thus fairly safe to say that no Governor General should act in Canada following the manner chosen in Australia, but the matter is not entirely settled.

Perhaps more important than formal constitutional power is the Governor General's opportunity to advise ministers. The Governor General meets regularly with the Prime Minister to discuss general points, personnel or appoint-

---

[19]See Eugene A. Forsey, *The Royal Power of Dissolution of Parliament in The British Commonwealth* (Toronto: Oxford University Press, 1943).

ments, and on such occasions Prime Ministers have been known to solicit advice on policy matters as well. In other words, the Governor General has a degree of access which is denied to most individuals, and therefore has a chance to influence the course of events. Sir Wilfrid Laurier confided: "The Canadian Governor General long ago ceased to determine policy, but he is by no means, or need not be, the mere figurehead of the public image. He has the privilege of advising his advisers, and if he is a man of sense and experience, his advice is often taken."[20]

BASIC ELEMENTS OF THE FEDERAL CONSTITUTION

We have seen that federalism was a key element in the Canadian system of constitutional monarchy. The federal dimension was necessitated by the exigencies of the Confederation period and developed through two forces subsequently: judicial interpretation of the constitutional documents; and the evolution of financial relations between the federal and provincial governments. Today, federalism is central to the way Canadians think about their politics. The winning entry in a 1967 contest for Canadian jokes was a Canadian version of the ancient elephant joke: Of three students, the American wrote his essay on "The President and Elephants", the French student discussed "Sex and the Elephant", while the Canadian's topic was "Elephants: A Federal or Provincial Responsibility?".

The need for a "federal bargain" which would apportion powers between the central and the regional governments was obvious in the 19th century. There had been a tradition of local government in the colonies, and the lack of adequate transportation routes and communication among the provinces meant that, no matter what type of system was adopted, some independence had to be granted to the local entities. Moreover, Sir G.E. Cartier and other French Canadian leaders demanded an element of isolation from central government authority as part of the bargain to be struck with those Fathers of Confederation who favoured a more centralized system of government – John A. Macdonald, for example, would actually have preferred a unitary to a federal form of government.[21] The federal principle was therefore accepted as necessary for the unity of the political system and as protection for provinces and language groups. Since then, for better or worse, the federal dimension has pervaded the history and development of Canada.

Provincial constitutions follow the federal pattern. In each of the provinces, the Queen is represented by a Lieutenant Governor appointed by the Governor General in Council. The Lieutenant Governor acts on the advice and with the assistance of his ministry or Executive Council, which is responsible to the legislature and resigns office under circumstances similar to those for the federal government. The legislature of each province is now unicameral, and is elected for a maximum of five years.

---

[20]O.D. Skelton, *Life and Letters of Sir Wilfrid Laurier*, vol. II (Toronto, 1921), p. 86n.

[21]P.B. Waite, *The Life and Times of Confederation, 1864-1867* (Toronto: University of Toronto Press, 1962).

Two vast territories remain under the legal control of the federal government. The government of Yukon is based on two federal statutes – The *Yukon Act* and the *Government Organization Act* of 1966. The *Yukon Act* provides for a Commissioner to be head of government and for a legislative body called the Council. Under the *Act* the Minister of Indian and Northern Affairs directs the Commissioner. Members of the Council are elected for four years but have no power over resources or budgets. Although the *Acts* have not been amended for Yukon, the federal government has begun to treat the Council as the real political authority for the area and the Commissioner as responsible to the Council. The 1970 *Northwest Territories Act* provides for executive, legislative and judicial structures in that region. Its Commissioner, appointed by the federal government, is chief executive officer and is again responsible to the Minister of Indian and Northern Affairs. As in Yukon, there is a Council, elected for four years.

As well as being under the laws of the federal and provincial governments, Canadians are regulated by local governments. Whether designated as city, town, village or township, these authorities are created by the provinces and territories to provide such services as transportation, public health, garbage disposal and recreation. Local school boards, are usually empowered to administer education at the primary and secondary levels.

The constitutional status of the provinces appeared insignificant in the earliest period of Canadian history. The Constitution provided such disproportionate power to the national government that some experts have even referred to the period as one of "quasi-federalism", that is, one whose appearance is federal (i.e., with divided jurisdictions), but whose reality is unitary because no significant power rests in the sub-units. This assertion is based on certain constitutional facts. First, the central government could *disallow* provincial legislation even when the subject matter of the legislation was assigned to the provinces by the *BNA Act*. This unlimited power has rarely been used but could be employed in what were seen as extreme circumstances. For instance, it was used effectively during the depression years to stop several Acts of William Aberhart's Social Credit government in Alberta. The federal government of the time argued that Aberhart's proposal to print money would destroy the banking system.[22] Altogether, the power was employed 112 times after Confederation but has not been used since 1943. However, though the federal government could negate provincial laws, it could not legislate in provincial fields.

The second and third major powers were those of *veto* and *reservation*. The Lieutenant Governors may at one time have had the ability to employ the royal prerogative of vetoing legislation. Since they did not exercise this power, however, it has atrophied as a weapon. On the other hand, the constitutional ability of Lieutenant Governors to reserve provincial legislation for federal approval has been employed quite often: some 70 bills have been reserved since 1867.[23] The

---

[22]For a discussion of the power of disallowance, see J.R. Mallory, *Social Credit and the Federal Power in Canada* (Toronto: University of Toronto Press, 1954) especially chapters 2 and 9.

[23]R. MacGregor Dawson, *The Government of Canada* fifth edition, revised by Norman Ward (Toronto: University of Toronto Press, 1970), pp. 213-217.

most recent case occurred in 1961, when the Lieutenant Governor of Saskatchewan, Frank Bastedo, without first consulting the federal government, reserved provincial legislation concerning the alteration of certain mineral controls. It seems unlikely, however, that such extreme power will be wielded again in Canada, except perhaps in a circumstance as grave as the secession of a province from the federal union. Moreover, while the federal government may have the legal authority to block any provincial legislation initiating secession, a "technical" solution of this type would hardly be satisfactory in such a circumstance. A movement toward secession by any province, if it were clearly supported by a popular mandate, could not be contravened by legal devices alone.

The *BNA Act* also included a residual clause which might have allowed the federal government to interfere in any matter except those specifically assigned to the provinces under section 92 of the *Act*. The basis of federal power rests in section 91, which states that "It shall be lawful for the Queen, by and with the Advice and Consent of the Senate and the House of Commons, to make Laws for the Peace, Order, and good Government of Canada, in relation to all matters not coming within the Classes of Subjects by this Act assigned exclusively to the Legislatures of the Provinces. . . ." In addition to granting this sweeping authority, section 91 specified 29 items as belonging exclusively to the federal government, among them trade, commerce, banking, credit, currency, taxation, navigation, citizenship and defence. Section 92 delineates 16 areas of provincial jurisdiction, including direct taxation, hospitals, prisons, property and civil rights. These subjects, though of limited and local concern in 1867, were later to become much more important than the Fathers of Confederation could have foreseen in their era of more-of-less *laissez-faire* government. They regarded the American Civil War as an example of what could happen if a central government did not have strong powers, and certainly did not fail to refer to this during Canada's Confederation debates.

While the *BNA Act* was a centralist document, it is important to note that the definitions of its certain key words have changed over time. Leaving aside for the moment the matter of how judicial interpretation has changed the document, it is clear that certain terms were not defined precisely enough or took on new meanings. Certain matters, of course, could not have been foreseen by the Fathers of Confederation. These omissions created a void which both federal and provincial authorities have sought to fill to their own advantage. For example, section 109 gave control over natural resources to the provinces – but did this control include off-shore resources and the taxation of resources? Section 93 gave power over education to the provinces, but today it is a matter for debate whether education, as a provincial responsibility, encompasses cultural matters, broadcasting, occupational training and research.

The conflict over division of powers is well illustrated by resources. The *BNA Act* clearly assigned "ownership" of resources to the provinces, but gave the federal government a major voice in sales of resources through its control of inter-provincial and international trade. Moreover, through use of the "declaratory" power (*BNA Act* s. 92.10(a)), the federal government can assume jurisdiction over any "work" that is for the benefit of Canada as a whole. In the 1920s the Parliament, for example, declared that every grain elevator was under federal control but it did not assume ownership. Control over uranium exploration is a more recent example. The provinces have always contested this declaratory power, but the courts have continually backed the federal authorities. Thus, in summary form, the provinces own the oil because it is under the ground; the oil wells are in the hands of private or public companies; and the Parliament of Canada exercises some control over oil through taxation and jurisdictional powers.

Breakthroughs in technology permitting exploitation of off-shore resources have resulted in hot disputes in recent decades. In 1967 the Supreme Court ruled in an advisory opinion that Ottawa, not British Columbia, owned the resources off the west coast. In 1977 the federal government proposed temporary arrangements with three Maritime Provinces which would have given Ottawa 25 percent and the provinces 75 percent of their off-shore resources. Newfoundland never accepted this bargain, and Nova Scotia quickly backed out after a provincial election. In 1979 the Conservative government of Joe Clark offered to give complete control of off-shore resources to the provinces; however, the return of the Liberals in 1980 left the situation in limbo. Disputants on both sides of the east coast question finally applied to the courts for settlement: Newfoundland to the provincial Court of Appeal, Ottawa to the Supreme Court of Canada. After a long-running battle, the courts awarded ownership of off-shore resources to the federal government.

It is clear that the *BNA Act* has been inadequate in determining most jurisdictions. As Garth Stevenson has pointed out, there are now very few areas of policy which are handled exclusively by one level of government. "The only exclusively federal areas appear to be military defence, veterans' affairs, the post office and monetary policy. The only exclusively provincial areas appear to be municipal institutions, elementary and secondary education and some areas of law related to property and other non-criminal matters."[24] In all other areas, there is either tacit or explicit agreement by the two major levels of government to engage in activities in the same fields. Sometimes this is harmonious, as for example when the federal government allows the provinces to regulate inter-provincial highway transport. In other areas such as external trade, manpower training, communications, language and culture, the two levels are in constant warfare.

Another aspect of the division of powers which continues to cause controversy is the delegation of joint responsibilities. Section 95 of the *BNA Act* declared joint jurisdiction between the Parliament of Canada and the provinces in the areas of agriculture and immigration. Moreover, *de facto* concurrent powers have arisen in some fields because of the federal government's control of spending power. While the federal government may have little or no jurisdiction over a particular matter such as education, consumer protection or the environment, this does not prohibit Ottawa from spending money in these areas. The provinces have had great difficulty in saying "No" to such largesse. Although not mentioned in the *BNA Act*, scientific research, recreational activities, tourism and

---

[24]Garth Stevenson, "Federalism and Intergovernmental Relations," in M.S. Whittington and G. Williams, eds., *Canadian Politics in the 1980's* second edition (Toronto: Methuen, 1984), p. 378.

protection of the environment all seem to be handled as areas of concurrent jurisdiction.

Conflicts over jurisdictional boundaries are to be expected in federal systems. Canada certainly has been no exception to this rule. Successive court decisions by the Judicial Committee of the Privy Council of the United Kingdom and later the Canadian Supreme Court have cleared up some, but by no means all, questions about jurisdiction in various policy fields.The precise lines of authority remain blurred in many areas. Dissent has risen mainly over the fact that matters which have grown in significance over the years, such as property and civil rights, are within the provincial sphere, whilst the "Peace, Order and good Government" clause conveys competing authority to the federal government in the same fields in a case of emergency. With changes in the nature of social and economic policy, this federal power has increasingly conflicted with the specific powers accorded the provinces.

In such disputes, decisions have varied from being very restrictive interpretations which left the federal government with very little authority except in the gravest of emergencies (*e.g., Local Prohibition*, 1896; *Hodge v. The Queen*, 1883; *Board of Commerce*, 1922; and *Toronto Electric Commissioners vs. Snider*, 1925) to granting the federal government such wide scope that the specific powers which appeared to fall exclusively in the provincial field were undermined (*e.g., Canada Temperance Act*, 1878; and *Russell v. The Queen*, 1882). Even such major events as the Great Depression were not considered significant enough to offset clearly and permanently the arguments that, first, social legislation was under provincial jurisdiction because of the property and civil rights clause and second, that Canada's federal Parliament was restricted to those fields in its specific jurisdiction (*Snider*, 1925). Thus, even in the face of this supreme test of government authority, the federal government could do no more than supply funds to the provinces for fighting the effects of the depression. Prime Minister R.B. Bennett's legislation for social insurance, marketing schemes and minimum wages was struck down by the JCPC in 1937, an action which seriously undermined the federal government's ability to provide any relief in the crisis.[25]

This constitutional position was short-lived. During the Second World War a surge of nationalism made it possible to circumvent restrictive interpretation of the *BNA Act*. The federal government assumed almost unlimited powers, and the JCPC, apparently sensing the national mood, seemed to shift its position. The result in the 1946 *Canada Temperance Federation* case, for example, was a judgement which declared that laws going beyond local interests could be the concern of the federal authorities. This decision revised the concept of federalism dictated by earlier cases.

An amendment to the *Supreme Court Act* in 1949 gave the power of final arbitration over jurisdictional authority to the Supreme Court. The federal government can refer either its own legislation or that of a province to the Supreme Court, while a provincial government can refer either its own or federal legislation to the superior court of the province, from which the case may proceed to the Supreme Court on appeal. Since it appoints not only federal judges but also

---

[25]See Mallory, *Social Credit and Federal Power in Canada*, p. 51.

all judges to provincial superior and county courts, the federal government exercises great power in the judicial field.

The belief that a wholly Canadian court would be somewhat more inclined to take into account Canadian reality and adopt a broader interpretation of federal powers seems to have been borne out by history. Since the ascendancy of the Supreme Court the federal government has obtained authority over radio, telecommunications and nuclear energy. A classic example of the centralist orientation of the Court is indicated by the 1952 *Johannesson* case, in which the Court upset earlier judgements by proclaiming that since aeronautics was of "national importance" it belonged to the federal authority. James Mallory concluded from this case that the Supreme Court "has begun to develop a more generous interpretation of the federal power than has existed, except in wartime . . . ."[26]

In a 1975 *Anti-Inflation* case the Supreme Court interpreted the federal division of powers in Canada in a similar way. It ruled that the federal government could impose pay restraints if a national emergency existed. The British Privy Council had limited the use of this power to emergencies such as war, pestilence and famine, but the Canadian Court now added economic factors to the list and thus broadened the interpretation of the "Peace, Order and good Government" clause. The Court did not approve the federal government's contention that controlling inflation concerned all of Canada, ruling only that the federal Parliament could enact legislation in the field of economic regulation during an emergency.

Thus, as mentioned earlier, since the Second World War the terms of federalism have increasingly been adjusted through the mechanism of federal/provincial conferences rather than through the judicial process. A feeling has arisen among the provinces that if matters of federal/provincial jurisdiction were to reach the courts for a resolution, they might lose. This subject is more fully discussed in Chapter 6.

RHETORIC OVER CONSTITUTIONAL AMENDMENT

Changing the "federal bargain" struck in 1867 has been extremely difficult.[27] In political science jargon, a *rigid* constitution is one which is difficult to amend, whereas a *flexible* constitution can be more easily adapted to changing circumstances. Though arguments exist both for and against the use of either type of amending formula, it is clear that all constitutions must provide some means to adapt themselves to new circumstances.

The 1931 Statute of Westminster declared that the Parliament of the United Kingdom could no longer legislate for Canada except at the latter's request. At the time of its passage, the British government attempted to persuade Canada to

---

[26]J.R. Mallory, *The Structure of Canadian Government* (Toronto: Macmillan, 1971), p. 354.

[27]See R.D. Olling and M.W. Westmacott, eds., *The Confederation Debate: The Constitution in Crisis* (Toronto: Kendall/Hunt, 1980); Richard Simeon, "Constitutional Development and Reform," in M.S. Whittington and G. Williams, eds., *Canadian Politics in the 1980's* (Toronto: Methuen, 1981) pp. 243-259; and David Milne, *The New Canadian Constitution* (Toronto: James Lorimer, 1982).

accept a specific amending formula and cut the tie with the United Kingdom altogether. Unfortunately, Canadian politicians could not agree on how the mechanism should work. The British Parliament therefore remained responsible for constitutional amendment in Canada. On several occasions after this date, then, the Constitution was amended in the United Kingdom. Provincial compliance was obtained, for example, in the 1940 amendment which gave the federal Parliament jurisdiction over unemployment insurance; the 1951 amendment which gave the federal Parliament shared power over old-age pensions; and the 1960 amendment dealing with the retirement of judges. On the other hand, no provincial agreement had to be found (nor was it!) when representation in the Senate was amended in 1915 or when representation in the House of Commons was altered in 1946, 1952 and 1974.

In view of the practices adopted on these occasions, it was clear that a constitutional convention or protocol had developed with regard to the amendment of the *BNA Act*. The British Parliament accepted each of the 18 amendments which emanated from a Joint Address of both Houses of the Canadian Parliament. On significant amendments which affected the federal balance, the provinces were always consulted and had to agree to the proposals. On the other hand, no substantial amendment was ever made at the request of any province or group of provinces, since only communications which arrived by way of the federal Parliament were accepted as legitimate by the British Parliament.

Many aspects of the Constitution could be changed within Canada itself, however. From the beginning, the provinces were allowed to amend their own constitutions in all spheres except those concerning the powers of the Lieutenant Governor. With the passage of the *BNA Act* (No. 2) in 1949, the federal Parliament was empowered to amend the Constitution, except with regard to provincial powers, rights and privileges; the rights of minorities with respect to schools and language protection; the extension of the life of Parliament beyond five years; and the necessity to call at least one session of Parliament per year. These were extensive exceptions, however, as they prevented Ottawa from amending anything which touched on the nature and division of federal/provincial responsibilities, the fundamental cornerstone of the Canadian political system. Moreover, some institutions like the Senate and the Supreme Court may be considered to be either purely in the federal sphere or to belong to both Ottawa and the provinces. The Senate has a regional basis to its representation and the Supreme Court is the final arbiter of federal-provincial disputes. It is not surprising therefore that the Supreme Court ruled as unconstitutional Prime Minister Trudeau's unilateral attempt to change the Senate in 1980.

From 1931 until 1981 strenuous efforts were made to patriate the Constitution to Canada. The question in Canada had never been *whether* we should have our own Constitution, but *how* we would get it. Patriation involved two seemingly insoluble conundrums: how much provincial participation there should be before an agreement to patriate the constitution; and what type of amendment process should ensue. Only when Canadians came to an agreement over these two matters were they able to amend their Constitution without recourse to Britain.

Changing a constitution is an amazingly complex process. Senator Eugene Forsey put it forcefully:

". . . let us never forget that, because a constitution is what it is, pervading and shaping every human being in the community, changing it by formal amendment is an immensely serious business. It is not like getting a new hair-do, or growing a beard, or buying new furniture or new clothes, or putting in a new bathroom. It is more like marriage – In the words of the Anglican Prayer Book – 'not by any to be enterprised, nor taken in hand unadvisedly, lightly or wantonly . . . but reverently, discretely, advisedly, soberly, and in the fear of God.' What we are dealing with in constitutional change is not paper or things. It is human lives."[28]

Though efforts to find an acceptable agreement started in the 1930s, only in the 1960s did public debate take place between the federal government and the provinces. Two of the resulting proposals almost succeeded: the Fulton-Favreau formula of 1964 and the Victoria Charter of 1971. The former is significant in Canadian constitutional development because it was the first and only mechanism that ever received the unanimous support of all ten provincial premiers. Nevertheless, it was bitterly criticized in Québec, and the Liberal government of Premier Jean Lesage did not ask the Assembly to concur with it. The Fulton-Favreau formula proposed drawing up a set of amending mechanisms which would change depending on the issue at stake. The federal Parliament of Canada would be able to amend the Constitution subject to approval of the provinces, which approval would vary in detail issue-by-issue. Matters such as the powers of the provinces, the use of French and English and the number of senators, for example, could be amended only if all the provinces agreed with the federal Parliament. Changes in education, on the other hand, could be effected with the consent of all the provinces except Newfoundland. Still other portions of the Constitution could be changed if the federal Parliament could obtain the agreement of two-thirds of the provinces, representing at least 50% of the population of Canada. The reality of this proposal was that either Ontario or Québec would have had to concur with all changes in this domain. Further, certain aspects of the Constitution directly related to the functions of the federal government could be changed by Parliament acting alone. For a time it appeared that the Fulton-Favreau formula might gain acceptance and thus form the basis of patriation of the *BNA Act*. However, the opposition in Québec vetoed the arrangement.

In the summer of 1971 another federal/provincial conference came to a tentative agreement on an amending formula.[29] Unlike the Fulton-Favreau formula, the Victoria Charter proposal required *not* the unanimous consent of the provinces for any amendment, but rather the agreement of the federal Parliament and a majority of the provinces, including all provinces with over 25% of Canada's population, at least two Atlantic provinces, and two Western provinces having 50 percent of the population of the West. As with the Fulton-Favreau formula, it seemed for a time that the Victoria Charter might gain acceptance, but it too failed to receive the support of Québec.

---

[28]*Senate Debates*, May 4, 1976, p. 2080.

[29]See Simeon, *op. cit.*

The essential stumbling block to finding an amendment formula was always Québec's desire to be treated as a province unlike the others ("*pas comme les autres*"). To many Québécois, the idea that federalism refers to a process involving all ten provinces and the federal government working in one system is unacceptable. They argue that Canada is a union of two "founding peoples". The basis of this view is the premise that the Canadian Constitution is basically a "compact" between two cultural groups or between English and French provinces.[30]

By extension, some Québécois argue that it is the Québec state which is best able to protect their interests. From this standpoint they develop one of two possible strategies. Some accept the federal system, but with special status for Québec, in which cultural fields such as education and communications are totally left to Québec, and in which the federal government does not intervene in such matters as social welfare. In practice, all premiers of Québec since Maurice Duplessis have taken this stand as a minimum position. Premiers Lesage, Johnson and Bourassa have all argued that Canada consists of "two nations". In 1976, for example, Robert Bourassa, then Premier of Québec, called for increased constitutional powers for Québec in the key areas of communications, immigration, cultural activities, and appointments to the Supreme Court and Senate.[31]

The second strategy advocated by some Québécois is separation from Canada. The rise to power of the Parti Québécois in November 1976 made this strategy a possibility. The Parti Québécois argued that it was not possible for Québec francophones to protect their language and culture within the federal system, and that separate status was essential. The history and detailed development of this option are discussed in the next chapter; however, a word on the right of constituent states to secede from their nation-state may be useful here. As a general rule, such a right does not exist in any of the democratic federal states – Canada, the United States, Australia, the Federal Republic of Germany or Switzerland. On one occasion the state of Western Australia did attempt to secede from Australia, and actually passed a referendum to this effect, 136 653 votes to 70 706. The Parliament of the United Kingdom, however, would not allow the case to go forward as British legislation and the proposal died.

PATRIATION OF CANADA'S CONSTITUTION

The long and at times bitter debate over patriation and constitutional change ended in 1982 with passage of the *Canada Act* by the British Parliament. While patriation of the Canadian Constitution was primarily symbolic in that it did not represent any changes in jurisdiction that would affect Canadians in any funda-

---

[30]See Ramsay Cook, *Provincial Autonomy, Minority Rights and the Compact Theory, 1867-1921*, Study no. 4, Royal Commission on Bilingualism and Biculturalism (Ottawa: Queen's Printer, 1969).

[31]See Edward McWhinney, *Quebec and the Constitution 1960-1978* (Toronto: University of Toronto Press, 1979) and E. McWhinney, *Canada and the Constitution, 1979-1982* (Toronto: University of Toronto Press, 1982).

mental sense, the inclusion of an entrenched *Charter of Rights and Freedoms* and an amending formula will have substantial effects.

The events leading up to patriation are crucial to an understanding of the features of Canada's present Constitution. The catalyst responsible for what became the final round of constitutional negotiations leading to patriation was the Québec referendum on sovereignty-association.

In May 1980 Premier René Lévesque's Parti Québécois *indépendantiste* government sought sovereign political status but continued economic association with the rest of Canada for Québec.[32] Federalist opponents of this proposal – including the federal Liberal party – pledged during the referendum campaign that Canada would begin a process of "renewal" and constitutional change to address the concerns of Québec citizens if they rejected the referendum. Québec voters ultimately did reject Lévesque's plan by a convincing margin, 60 to 40 percent. Patriation of the Constitution was thereby given new momentum, with Prime Minister Trudeau and the Liberal party exhorting Canadians and their political leaders to renew federalism in order to reciprocate Québec's gesture of confidence in Canadian federalism. The concept of renewed federalism, while vague, allowed Trudeau to ride his favourite hobby-horse of patriation, a goal he had pursued since his first election as Prime Minister in 1968.

That summer, the federal government and the provinces conducted a series of meetings culminating in a major conference in September 1980 in Ottawa. However, government leaders made no progress on the agenda items, which included patriation, an amending formula, a *Charter of Rights and Freedoms*, the principle of equalization, reform of the Senate and the Supreme Court and redistribution of powers between the two levels of government. At length, Prime Minister Trudeau, faced with an intransigent group of provincial premiers and frustrated by the many previous attempts of constitutional negotiation, decided that the federal government would proceed unilaterally.

Trudeau's unilateral patriation "package" proposed an entrenched *Charter of Rights* as well as equalization and amendment formulas. Of the ten provincial governments, however, only New Brunswick and Ontario supported the federal government's unilateral course of action, agreeing with Trudeau that unanimous provincial agreement had proven impossible. The federal government justified its action on the premise that, as the representative of all Canadians, it legitimately spoke for the interests of all Canadians. A special Joint Committee of the Senate and the House of Commons was formed to review the government's resolution. Over 1200 briefs and letters from interested groups and individuals across the country were received by the Committee. After prolonged debate and more than 70 substantial changes, the government's resolution was adopted. The federal Conservative party opposed the government's unilateral action. The NDP, however, supported the package after it won amendments guaranteeing provincial ownership of natural resources.

---

[32]See Québec's White Paper on sovereignty-association, *Quebec-Canada: A New Deal* (Québec: Gouvernement du Québec 1979).

The Role of Britain

The federal government's decision to act unilaterally moved the site of the political battle from the Canadian to the British Parliament (since the Liberals had a majority, ensuring passage of the resolution), a situation which strained relations between the two countries. British MPs became the targets of intensive lobbying efforts. In London, Prime Minister Trudeau and several of his cabinet ministers attempted to ensure quick passage of the request, suggesting that failure would have serious international repercussions. Dissenting groups and provinces, especially Alberta, Saskatchewan and Québec, also sent representatives to argue their case. One Labour front-bencher was quoted as saying: "I could have dined out for weeks at a time on the invitations I was getting from various Canadians."[33]

The 1949 amendment to the *BNA Act* had made it clear that the federal Parliament could amend only those provisions which were already under federal jurisdiction. The procedure for constitutional change required a joint address from the House and Senate to the British Parliament. While Britain had always acted automatically on receiving a Joint Address, Britain's role in this particular crisis was uncertain. Canada had seldom made requests affecting the division of powers without first obtaining provincial consent. British parliamentarians were faced with a dilemma, since either accepting or rejecting the Canadian federal government's unilateral request for patriation would leave many Canadians unhappy. Prime Minister Trudeau's remark that British MPs should "hold their noses" and pass the request made their task no easier.

The British House of Commons Select Committee on Foreign Affairs decided to hold hearings on the subject. Its report questioned Trudeau's assertion that Westminster had no choice but to pass any request from the Canadian Parliament, arguing instead that some measure of provincial consent was required for any constitutional changes affecting provincial powers. Though it did not define the extent of provincial support needed, the committee recommended that it should be the same as that required in the amending formula proposed in the patriation package. The Trudeau government naturally attacked the Committee's conclusions, charging that it was suggesting that Britain should assess the merits of the request and that Britain was therefore interfering in Canadian internal affairs.

The Supreme Court's Decision

British politicians hoped to escape their dilemma by telling their Canadian counterparts that, given such strong provincial opposition, Westminster would be reluctant to pass the request without a ruling by Canada's Supreme Court on the legality of unilateral patriation. By this time, six of the provinces had brought the question before the Court. However, the Supreme Court's ruling, delivered September 28, 1981, offered both sides a measure of support. By a vote of 7 to 2, the judges ruled that the federal government could "legally" and "unilaterally" sub-

---

[33] *The Globe and Mail,* April 15, 1982, p. 9.

Reprinted with permission – The Toronto Star Syndicate.

mit the constitutional resolution with its entrenched *Charter of Rights* to the British Parliament for passage. However, by a 6 to 3 vote, the Court also ruled that a constitutional convention requiring provincial consent existed, and that the process embarked upon by Ottawa "offended the federal principle". The extent of provincial consent required by this convention was left vague: the consent of more than the two supporters (Ontario and New Brunswick) was needed, but unanimity was not essential. The Court further noted that conventions are not enforceable by law. Federal Justice Minister Jean Chrétien agreed, arguing that it is not up to the courts but rather to politicians to decide what political conventions should be.[34]

The patriation package was thus tossed back into the political arena. As a result, another First Ministers' Conference was held in November. The federal government was adamant that its patriation package include a *Charter of Rights*, and an amending formula similar to that offered at the Victoria Conference in 1971. It proposed that constitutional change should require the consent of Parliament and a majority of legislatures in Canada's four major regions: two in Atlantic Canada; Québec; Ontario; and two in the West. The two largest provinces' veto power would thereby be guaranteed. This formula was opposed by almost all the provinces.

Earlier in 1981 those Premiers who were opposed to the federal plans had argued for a patriation package of their own. They had proposed that constitutional change should require the consent of Parliament and seven provinces, representing 50 percent of the population.[35] This proposal would have allowed a province to "opt out" of any amendment which took away existing provincial rights or powers, and would further have entitled any such province to fiscal compensation.

The "Gang of Eight", as the opposing provincial Premiers were dubbed, was also against much of the *Charter of Rights*. The eight Premiers feared that it

---

[34]*The Globe and Mail*, December 29, 1981, p. D1.

[35]Acceptance by Québec of this plan was the basis for later federal efforts to discredit arguments that traditionally Québec had a constitutional veto.

would give new powers to federally-appointed judges and reduce provincial authority. Their other concerns included the prospect of an expensive and time-consuming redrafting of provincial legislation to comply with the new *Charter*; the hint of importation of American jurisprudence in the language of the legal rights section; and the direct recourse to the courts which the *Charter* would grant to wronged individuals, allowing them to avoid the human rights commissions of all the provinces.[36]

The most general provincial opposition to the entrenched *Charter of Rights* was based on the contention that it would be difficult to amend it in order to adapt it to changing circumstances or particular regional problems. While most provincial Premiers did favour the inclusion of basic democratic and fundamental rights, they opposed the more controversial mobility, legal and equality rights, which they feared would conflict with provincial legislation. Newfoundland, New Brunswick, the Northwest Territories and Yukon were particularly concerned that provincial legislation allowing preferential local hiring policies for their disadvantaged jobless would be challenged. Québec had similar reservations concerning its language requirements and job programs.

Federal/Provincial Constitutional Agreement

The November 1981 federal/provincial conference, unlike most of those of the previous 54 years, ended in agreement between the federal government and nine out of ten of the provinces (Québec was the exception). The major compromise responsible for this success was the inclusion of a *notwithstanding* clause which allowed Parliament or a provincial legislature to override specific *Charter* provisions (fundamental freedoms and legal and equality rights) by declaring that they were doing so when passing legislation. However, a "sunset clause" requiring renewal of this exemption every five years was included. In the absence of renewal, the Charter's provisions would take precedence. Supporters of the notwithstanding clause argued that it provided an important check maintaining the pre-eminence of the provincial legislatures in the event of an "awkward" court ruling.

The idea of a notwithstanding clause is of long duration in Canada. It is found in the *Canadian Bill of Rights* passed by the federal Parliament in 1960, as well as in the provincial Bills of Rights passed by Alberta, Québec, Saskatchewan and Ontario. The federal government used it only once, during the October Crisis in Québec in 1970. The Québec Assembly has used it several times, but in non-controversial ways only. An example is a law passed "notwithstanding" the provincial charter provision regarding discrimination against the elderly: it required motorists seventy-five years old or older to take driver's tests every year.

Critics of the notwithstanding provision argue that it circumvents the very purpose of an entrenched *Charter*, which is to give the courts the authority to protect fundamental individual freedoms in the event that legislative and governmental restraint fail. According to one constitutional expert, "If legislatures are given the power to cancel . . . judicial authority they are most likely to use it when

---

[36]*The Globe and Mail*, October 31, 1981, p. 14.

there is a failure of restraint."[37] Constitutional guarantees are not as necessary to protect the rights of the majority as they are the rights of minorities. The case of the Native peoples provides a pertinent example. Recognition of their treaty rights was originally excluded from the *Charter* at the insistence of those provinces which were concerned that Native land claims might impede provincial control over natural resources. It was only after intense lobbying by Native groups that recognition of these rights was later included.

The second reason for the success of the November 1981 conference was that a compromise concerning the provision of an amending formula was reached between the two levels of government. Instead of the federal Liberal proposition, the formula preferred by the "Gang of Eight" was adopted. It called for amendments to be made by a joint resolution of both the Senate and the House of Commons, as well as by a resolution of the legislative assemblies of at least two-thirds of the provinces, representing at least 50 percent of the population of Canada.[38] In addition, it granted dissenting provinces the right to opt out of all amendments which affected their status and powers. The first such amendment to the new Constitution, an accord on aboriginal rights, was proclaimed in 1984, after the federal government and all the provinces except Québec had agreed to its provisions.

Further compromises were made by the federal government. For instance, provinces where the unemployment rate is above the national average may restrict mobility rights, allowing affirmative hiring programs. The search for a compromise over minority language rights caused considerable bitterness. The final agreement (described below) was complicated and subject to passage by the Québec legislature and to court decision. Finally, in order to appease the regions, the new Constitution confirmed the right of provincial ownership of natural resources and the principle of equalization.

While federal/provincial agreement on a patriation package removed much of the hesitancy of British politicians to grant the federal government's request for patriation, Native Indian groups continued to press their opposition in the British courts, arguing that the British Crown was still responsible for them. The British courts rejected this claim, however, finding that while no government should derogate the Indian rights guaranteed in treaties signed with the British and Canadian governments, responsibility for Native groups had long since passed from the Crown in Britain to the Crown in Canada.

The British Parliament was finally presented with the Canada Bill in mid-February of 1982. The Bill was speedily passed at every stage by large majorities.[39] On March 29 the Queen gave Royal Assent to the *Canada Act*, 115 years to the day after the *BNA Act* received Royal Assent. In Ottawa, on April 17, 1982, the Queen proclaimed the *Constitution Act*, 1982, completing the patriation process.

---

[37]Noel Lyon, *The Globe and Mail*, November 17, 1981, p. 8.

[38]According to the latest general census. The Senate does not possess an absolute veto on constitutional change. After 180 days an amendment may be concluded without its agreement.

[39]All the major British parties supported the bill.

Québec's Opposition

The dissent of Réné Lévesque, as the lone Premier opposing the patriation agreement, caused grave concern in the rest of Canada. Québec's opposition prompted some to question whether the Supreme Court's call for "a substantial measure of provincial consent" had been achieved, given Québec's position as representative of French Canadians. Lévesque opposed several elements of the patriation agreement. He argued first, that Québec's cultural security was threatened by the restriction of its exclusive rights in linguistic matters. The *Charter's* guarantee of access to English-speaking schools contradicted Québec's Bill 101, which restricted admission to English schools in that province to children who had at least one parent educated in Québec's English system.[40] Lévesque felt that the Charter tampered with his province's exclusive right to legislate on education and was therefore a threat to French dominance in Québec. He also objected that the measure of bilingualism imposed on Québec was not imposed on Ontario, although the latter has the largest minority French-speaking population of any province.

The Québec government also opposed the mobility rights clause which guaranteed Canadians the ability to move freely from one province to another in search of jobs, in the belief that policies developed by a provincial government to create and protect employment for Québec citizens could thereby be declared unconstitutional.

Lévesque criticized the Constitution's failure to recognize "in any tangible way" the character and needs of Québec as a distinct national society. The document treated Québec as merely another province of Canada, like all the others, he alleged. Finally, Lévesque disliked the amending formula's removal of what Québec considered its traditional veto over constitutional changes. While the Constitution does provide financial compensation in the important areas of education and culture, the amending formula does not guarantee financial compensation for provinces that choose to opt out of other programs initiated by constitutional amendments.

The Québec government's extreme displeasure with the new federal Constitution was demonstrated by its strategy to circumvent it. Legislation (Bill 62) was introduced and passed in the Québec Assembly which attempted to ensure that Quebeckers' fundamental freedoms and legal and equality rights would be subject only to the provincial charter of human rights, not to its new federal counterpart. According to the provisions of Bill 62, which came into force in June 1982, a new clause is to be appended to each Québec law, stating that it will operate "notwithstanding" the provision of the *Charter*. However, the notwithstanding clause does not apply to language-of-education articles in the federal Constitution. To by-pass this obstacle, Québec relied on section 1 of the federal

---

[40]Section 23 states that citizens whose first language learned and still understood is that of the English or French linguistic minority population of the province in which they reside possess the right to have their children receive primary and secondary school instruction in that language in that province.

Constitution, which states that the federal *Charter of Rights and Freedoms* guarantees the liberties it sets out "subject only to such reasonable limits prescribed by law as can be demonstrably justified in a free and democratic society." The Québec government hoped to prove in court that Bill 101's provisions could be justified on these grounds. However, in 1984 the Supreme Court rejected the Québec government's argument that the threat to the survival of the French language in North America justified Bill 101's restrictions on English school enrollment. The Court ruled that the section of Bill 101 (Charter of the French Language) limiting eligibility to English language schools to children one of whose parents had received his/her primary education in English in Québec was "incompatible" with the constitutional guarantees set out in the *Canadian Charter of Rights and Freedoms*.

THE CANADIAN CHARTER OF RIGHTS AND FREEDOMS

The desirability of an entrenched *Charter of Rights and Freedoms* in Canada has been a subject of debate since Confederation and no doubt will remain so despite its constitutional adoption in 1982. The entrenchment of rights can be said to have two primary functions, one symbolic, the other procedural. Symbolically, such a charter is a statement of the principles and ideals valued by a society. While it is not always observed in practice, protection of these rights is the final test by which a polity is judged. A more tangible impact of a charter of rights lies in its restraint of the actions of a government *vis-à-vis* its citizenry, preventing the government from violating rights of individuals and groups as defined in the charter. It is this restraint which makes the entrenchment of rights contentious, especially in a parliamentary system such as Canada's where it constitutes a reduction in parliamentary supremacy. As we discussed above, concern over these limitations was an important element in provincial opposition to adoption of the *Charter*.

Why does Canada need an entrenched *Charter of Rights*? Critics have posed this question in light of the fact that Canada existed as a relatively free society for more than one hundred years without such a document, relying instead on the traditional rights provided by British common law. During the Constitutional debates, some Premiers noted that every province already protected the rights of its citizens, going on to argue that the federal government was merely seeking to assert further authority over the provinces.

However, Canada's record of ensuring the protection of its citizens' rights is not without blemish. For example, in the early 1950s Québec City passed a city by-law prohibiting the distribution of religious pamphlets on the streets without a special permit, thereby limiting the freedom of religious expression. A more celebrated example was the Québec Padlock law of 1937. At that time the Québec government enacted legislation banning the propagation of "Communism and Bolshevism" by padlocking any premises allegedly used for such purposes. The law allowed Premier Duplessis to arbitrarily move against groups opposed to his regime.

Although both pieces of legislation were subsequently overturned by the courts, the rationale cited by the judges in their decisions strengthened the argument for entrenchment. The courts based their majority rulings not on the fact that these instances represented violations of fundamental rights (although this view was expressed by some of the presiding judges), but rather on the contention that a provincial government did not have the right to restrict civil liberties because of the federal division of power. In both cases the court declared the actions *ultra vires*. Under the new constitutional provisions it is the recognition of inviolable rights which will be the basis for making such decisions.

Another notable example of a violation of basic rights in Canada's history was the internment of Japanese Canadians during World War II. Thousands of people were uprooted from their communities and placed in camps for the duration of the war for "security" reasons under the *War Measures Act*. Decades later, in 1970, Prime Minister Trudeau again invoked the *War Measures Act*, this time in response to FLQ terrorist activities in Québec. This action, which suspended civil liberties and allowed the arbitrary detention of hundreds of suspects, is the most recent major example of government violation of basic human rights in Canada. Both cases raised concern that such violations of basic democratic rights could not be prevented without written constitutional guarantees.

The *Charter* in its final form is the result of a long process of extensive discussion and amendment of the Liberal government's initial constitutional proposal, tabled before the House of Commons in 1980. The process took 267 hours of arduous parliamentary debate.[41]

The *Charter* consists of a short preamble – "Whereas Canada is founded upon principles that recognize the supremacy of God and the rule of law. . ." – followed by 34 sections. It is the first section that actually defines the limits of Canadians' rights and freedoms, stipulating that they are "subject only to such reasonable limits prescribed by law as can be demonstrably justified in a free and democratic society".

The *Charter* protects fundamental freedoms, including those of conscience and religion, of thought, belief, opinion and expression, and of peaceful assembly and association. The basic democratic rights named in the document include the right of every citizen to vote; a five-year limit on the terms of federal and provincial legislatures, except in time of real or apprehended war, invasion or insurrection; and the requirement for legislatures to meet at least once every twelve months.

Also in the Charter is the protection of mobility rights, *i.e.*, the right of Canadian citizens to enter, remain in and leave Canada, and to move to and work in any province. These rights are limited, however, by recognition of provincial residency requirements as a qualification for the receipt of social services. Affirmative action programs, whose purpose is to ameliorate the conditions of a province's socially or economically disadvantaged are also allowed if the rate of employment in that province falls below the national employment rate.[42]

---

[41]Tom Kelley, *Canada Today*, No. 4 (Ottawa: K.G. Campbell Corp., 1982).

[42]Section 6(4)

Legal rights such as the traditional right to life, liberty and security are listed, along with new legal rights provisions. For example, unreasonable search or seizure and arbitrary detention or imprisonment are prohibited. A detained individual is guaranteed the right to be informed promptly of the reasons for detention, to have counsel without delay and to be instructed of that right, as well as to have the validity of the detention determined and to be released if detention is not justified. Individuals charged with an offence have the right to be informed without delay of the specific offence and to be tried within a reasonable time, have a right against self-incrimination and are to be considered innocent until proven guilty by an impartial and public hearing. Individuals are not to be deprived of bail without just cause, are permitted trial by jury where the maximum punishment for the offence is imprisonment for five years or more, except in the case of a military offence tried before a military tribunal and are not to be punished for an action that was not illegal at the time of commission. If acquitted, an individual may not be tried for the same offence again, or, if found guilty and punished, may not be tried or punished again. Finally, if the punishment for the offence has changed between the commission of the crime and the time of the sentencing, the individual will be subject to the lesser punishment.

Individuals are also protected against cruel and unusual treatment or punishment. Witnesses who testify in any proceedings have the right not to have any incriminating evidence they might give used against them in any other proceedings, except in prosecution for perjury. Evidence obtained in a manner that infringes upon an individual's rights and freedoms shall be excluded, but only if its admission would "bring the administration of justice into disrepute".

The *Charter* further provides equality rights guaranteeing that every individual is equal before and under the law without discrimination, particularly without discrimination based on race, national or ethnic origin, colour, religion, sex, age or mental or physical disability. However, affirmative action programs aimed at improving the conditions of groups discriminated against are allowed.

The importance of linguistic rights is acknowledged in the *Charter*. English and French are recognized as Canada's official languages and have equal status in all institutions of Parliament and the federal government. Both languages are also recognized in the province of New Brunswick. Thus, in Parliament and New Brunswick's legislature, both languages may be used in debates and other proceedings. Parliamentary statutes and records, as well as proceedings of the courts, are published in both languages. Individuals have the right to communicate with any head or central office of Parliament or government of Canada in either official language, and the same right is extended to other offices where there is significant demand. Official language rights for Manitoba were included in the Manitoba Act of 1870, but their practical effect was in dispute until various legal judgements beginning in 1979. They await further clarification by the Supreme Court of Canada.

Under the *Charter*, all citizens of Canada who received their primary education in Canada in either French or English have the right to have their children educated in the same language if it is the minority language of the province in which they reside. This right, however, is applicable only "where numbers warrant", *i.e.*, where the number of children warrants the provision of public funds for minority language instruction. Minority language education rights are also guaranteed to the children of Canadian citizens whose first language learned and understood is that of the English or French linguistic minority of the province in which they reside, whether or not the parents were able to receive their primary education in that language. This latter guarantee is not applicable to Québec until it is approved by the Québec government or the Assembly.

The *Charter* includes a variety of other specific rights. The rights of the Native peoples are not to be diminished by the *Charter's* provisions; for example, the provision that guarantees language education rights in French and English may not be interpreted to deprive the Indian people of James Bay of their right to educate their children in Cree. More broadly, the *Charter* may not be used to deprive anyone of existing rights and freedoms, and its interpretation must recognize Canada's multicultural heritage. The *Charter's* provisions are to be applied equally to males and females. Significantly, in recognition of Canada's federal nature the *Charter* states that neither level of government gains power as a result of its provisions. Section 33 also recognizes this fact by allowing the provinces and Parliament to enact laws overriding *Charter* provisions on fundamental freedoms and legal and equality rights.

The courts are given responsibility for enforcing the provisions of the *Charter* in the event that legislative and governmental restraint fail. As a result, the role of the judiciary has the potential of becoming more active in the creation of positive law. This possibility was a source of concern to many provincial government representatives who feared that their ability to amend or adapt *Charter* rights would be limited. The reader should recall the earlier discussion of the conflict between parliamentary supremacy and the role of the judiciary. Yet the purpose of entrenching fundamental rights in the Constitution is to remove them from the whims of transient government majorities.

Nonetheless, some critics remain fearful that the *Charter of Rights and Freedoms* will push the judiciary to a position similar to that of its American counterpart, making it more independent and interventionist. It is not likely, however, that the role of Canada's judiciary will change suddenly. Judicial tradition, based on common law, will continue to influence the conduct of judges. While opportunity for a more active, and, some might argue, more creative, role for the judiciary now exists, this will not bring about sudden changes. It will take considerable time for precedent-setting cases to be brought before the courts and for judges to determine the nature of their role.

Many groups are worried about the *Charter's* potential effects. Law enforcement representatives, for example, wonder how its provisions will affect their ability to deal with criminals. Politicians had the significance of the Charter in political affairs brought home to them during a dispute in 1983 over cruise missile testing in Canada. A coalition of union and peace groups, led by Operation Dismantle, challenged the government's authority to test unarmed United States missiles in Northern Alberta on the grounds that the decision violated the right to life, liberty and security of the person as guaranteed by section 7 of the *Charter*. The Federal Court of Appeal upheld the government's authority to make decisions on matters of defence and national security such as missile testing. Four of the five judges declared that the coalition had failed to prove that the decision to test the missiles was a break with principles of fundamental justice. According to one of the most persuasive arguments of the Court, the *Charter's* guarantees "are not, and cannot be, absolute. We all must die, and many are, at one time or another in their lives, imprisoned or made insecure."[43]

It is likely that in the future the Québec government will once again challenge the *Charter*, especially with reference to the province's law on French language. The response of the Québec government to the Supreme Court's decisions, as well as Québécois perceptions of the *Charter*, will help to determine the legitimacy of the document in Canada.

The *Charter of Rights and Freedoms* will not have an immediate impact on the average Canadian since many of its provisions have been taken for granted by Canadians for years. However, the *Charter* does provide a new avenue, through the courts, for seeking redress for any perceived violation of individual or group rights, thereby strengthening the safeguards against arbitrary or misguided government action. The *Charter of Rights and Freedoms* will ultimately be judged on the effectiveness of this protection.

OVERVIEW

It is clear from the short description in this chapter that the Canadian Constitution is not a single document which provides clear and precise direction to the political process. As in most democratic countries, in Canada the Constitution is both a product of the political system and a significant factor in shaping it. The Canadian Constitution can be said to include both written and unwritten dimensions. Among the unwritten elements are the British parliamentary heritage and the democratic norms and values inculcated in the Canadian political culture. The written dimensions of the Canadian Constitution include the well-known *British North America Act* of 1867 and the *Canada Act* of 1982, as well as a number of other *Acts* and documents. The *BNA Act* has been altered or expanded numerous times since 1867 by formal amendments and by legal interpretations by the Judicial Committee of the Privy Council or the Supreme Court of Canada. At the time of writing, the 1982 *Canada Act* is still largely untested as a constitutional document.

The *Canada* and *BNA Acts* provide the legal basis for the federal division of power. For over a century the *BNA Act* provided a relatively serviceable Constitution for Canada, although rising economic power in the West and a militant separatist movement in Québec sparked contemporary challenges. The *Canada Act* allows possibilities for amending the Constitution, but rapid and comprehensive change over jurisdictions cannot be expected. Most tinkering with the Constitution will only demonstrate once more the wisdom of the Italian maxim: "If things are going to remain the same around here, there are going to have to be some changes made."

In the next chapter we will examine in greater detail the meaning of federalism in Canada and how it has been the product of constitutional imagination.

---

[43]Justice James Hugessen, cited in *The Globe and Mail*, November 29, 1983.

Dimensions of Federalism
Authorities and Divided Loyalties

ALTHOUGH TO SOME STUDENTS federalism has the reputation of being a dry subject, this assessment is certainly not accurate in Canada. Far from being an obscure topic for academics and constitutional lawyers, federalism is an active force that helps shape the issues and priorities of contemporary politics. In a general sense, Canadian politics can be said to be the politics of federalism.

The threat of Québec separation, the sense of grievance in several western provinces, the controversies over language and educational rights for minorities, the disputes over resource control and many similar troublesome matters – all are political issues which can be considered as being conflicts over the authority and jurisdiction of the federal system in Canada. Whether one is conscious of it or not, developments in federalism reach into everyone's lives. The vast array of social services and programs available to Canadian citizens today is the outgrowth of federal/provincial interaction. While certain programmes may be supported by only one level of government, the majority require the financial cooperation of both Ottawa and the provinces. The procedures and priorities which lead to the smooth interaction of the federal and provincial governments in these activities reveal much about Canadian politics. On the other hand, the federal system makes more difficult the handling of many traditional issues such as economic planning and control of inflation, and modern problems such as job creation, pollution, safety, women's rights and the overall impact of large cities. These concerns are not easily transferable into questions about legal jurisdiction.

In Chapter 5 we outlined the constitutional provisions which formally define the relationship between the federal and provincial governments. However, the conduct of politics within Canada's federal structure is also affected by the dynamic social and economic realities in which it operates. Therefore, to comprehend Canadian federalism more is required than a discussion of the legal division of powers and jurisdictional niceties: of great importance is an understanding of fiscal relations, since this matter animates much of federal/provincial conflict.

In this chapter we will explore the meaning of federalism and its implications for Canadians. One conclusion is already obvious. Rather than being a fixed, immutable institutional structure, Canadian federalism has changed dramatically over the years. It is not a simple static division of powers, but a process whereby the two levels of government adapt and change their nature in order to reduce tensions within the political environment. Further, the present chapter explains why federalism was initiated in the first place, and how it has been adapted to Canadian realities.

Although the Canadian federal structure has proven remarkably resilient, during the past three decades powerful pressures have emerged which threaten to overwhelm the system. The ultimate outcome of what is often referred to as the "crisis of Canadian federalism" is by no means certain. Whether these forces result in a truncated Canada or serve to strengthen the federal system will depend on an array of factors, including leadership and political circumstances. The concluding portions of the chapter survey the contemporary regional challenges, both territorial and nationalistic, which operate against federalism, and outline possible scenarios for the future.

WHAT IS FEDERALISM?

In his influential book on the subject, William Riker contends that the 20th century is an "age of federalism" and proceeds to list numerous federal countries, including the United States, the Soviet Union, Australia, West Germany and Canada.[1] Federalism, he argues, has replaced empire as a means of governing diverse peoples over a large land mass.[2] This statement is partially correct. Approximately two dozen of the world's states are federal, including most of the large ones. About half the world's territory and one-third of the global population are ruled by federal governments. However, it is apparent at the same time that there are approximately seven times as many unitary as federal states, and that even within the systems labelled "federal" the term means quite different things to different people. Except in name, there is little similarity in the federal aspects of countries such as the USA and the USSR, or Australia and Brazil, or Mexico and Canada. We shall have to be precise in our use of the term.

Simply put, federalism refers to a division of jurisdiction and authority between at least two levels of government. It is usually characterized by the existence of one central government and two or more regional governments operating simultaneously over the same territory and people. Therefore, **federalism** can be defined as "a political organization in which the activities of government are divided between regional governments and a central government in

---

[1] William H. Riker, *Federalism: Origin, Operation, Significance* (Boston: Little, Brown, 1964), p. 1.

[2] *Ibid.*, pp. 3-5.

such a way that each kind of government has some kind of activities on which it makes final decisions."[3]

This definition further implies that each level of government has more-or-less complete authority over specific spheres of activity, while on a few other matters there may be a degree of concurrent jurisdiction. There is certainly no single, ideal way in which this authority is divided. What is important is that each level have a degree of autonomy. In the federal form the various levels of government obtain their respective powers from the country's constitution, not from each other. Citizens owe loyalty to more than one level of government, and both levels may act directly on the citizens.

The history of the concept of federalism has been traced back to the fusion of ancient Israelite tribes. In North America its first occurrence has been ascribed to the Five Nations of the Iroquois Indians. Its modern meaning, however, is best dated to the 18th century. During that period the United States Constitution provided a system of government which has been emulated ever since. The dual essence of the theory of American federalism was the idea of distribution of government power on an area basis, and the philosophy that unity and diversity can coexist.

Concepts of Federalism

Since the beginning, one problem has dominated debate about the meaning of federalism. It concerns those systems which have a federal constitutional structure, but whose political and social forms reduce the significance of the bargain between the central and regional governments. Examples are Mexico and the USSR, where the one-party system links the political forces together in such a way as to produce a state very similar to those which are unitary. On the other hand, some unitary states are highly decentralized. In summary, therefore, federal states may be *centralized* or *decentralized* – and so may unitary systems.

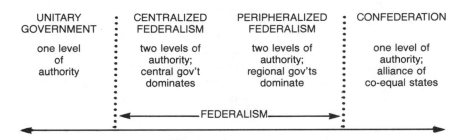

FIGURE 6.1 Continuum of the Degree of Centralization of Authority

Source: Adapted from concepts proposed by William H. Riker in *Federalism: Origin, Operation, Significance* (Boston: Little, Brown, 1964).

---

[3]William H. Riker, "Federalism," in Fred I. Greenstein and Nelson W. Polsby, eds., *Handbook of Political Science, Vol. 5: Government Institutions and Processes* (Reading: Addison and Wesley, 1975), p. 101. (Emphasis added.)

Reproduced with permission, Alan King, The Citizen, Ottawa.

William Riker offers a useful continuum by which to measure various federalisms.[4] This continuum ranges from centralized federalism, in which the central government dominates or encroaches on the sub-units, to what is referred to as peripheralized or decentralized federalism, in which the sub-unit governments dominate (see Figure 6-1). For a variety of reasons, most federal states today are of the centralized variety. The requirements of national security, the welfare state and in general the growing complexity of society are all factors conducive to a centralization of power at the national level. There are, however, states in which the various regional sub-units retain significant powers. Furthermore, there are countries in which it is possible to discern pendulum swings along the continuum over a period of decades. Although centralized federalism is the more common form today, there is nothing intrinsically superior or inferior about the arrangement.

While considering the continuum of federalism, it is important to note its polar ends: the *unitary* and *confederation* forms of government. As its name implies, **unitary** government is characterized by one level of political authority. In this form the central government grants and amends the powers of local or provincial

---

[4]Riker, *Federalism: Origin, Operation, Significance*, pp. 5-10. See also K.C. Wheare, *Federal Government*, fourth edition (New York: Oxford University Press, 1963), pp. 31-32.

authorities. The archetype of this form may well be France, where virtually all significant decisions about political life are made at the national level, in Paris. On the other hand, except in Canada and Switzerland, **confederation** government refers to a loose alliance of sovereign states which band together for very narrow reasons. The United States in the period of the Articles of Confederation, 1781–1787, is a good example of this form. Even earlier, in 1643–1648, the New England Confederation was founded solely for reasons of defence and external relations. Admittedly, there may be a fine line between certain peripheralized federalisms and unitary states. Perhaps the only way to differentiate between the two types is to ascertain whether the various "regional" units are completely, as opposed to partially, sovereign. Despite its imprecision, Riker's continuum is useful for exploring the federal phenomenon.

Many authors dislike the apparent formalism in these legal, political and territorial definitions of federalism. Economists[5] and some political scientists speak of a "federal society", defined as a society in which economic, religious, racial or historical diversities are territorially grouped. W.S. Livingston, for example, believes that certain societies are intrinsically federal because they are pluralist, and that federalism is simply the institutional outcome of the forces which exist in these societies.[6] The inherent difficulty with such definitions is that they concern more than federal unions and could just as well apply to any state composed of more than one ethnic group. Other authors believe that non-territorial federalism can exist. They cite examples such as Estonia in 1925 or Cyprus in 1960. In these instances, legal jurisdiction over cultural and educational affairs was accorded to groups wherever they lived, and was not based on a geographic division of the state.[7] These kinds of examples lead researchers away from rigid, formalistic definitions of federalism; however, at the same time, the concepts become so loose that any form of delegation of power can be included, with the result that the definitions become so general that federalism can mean practically anything to anybody.

Evaluations of Federalism

Why is federalism adopted? What are its advantages? On these questions there is much disagreement among scholars. Some argue that federalism is synonymous with liberty, that it is a protection for minority rights. Others believe it to be chosen essentially to achieve unification without the loss of separate identities for the

---

[5]See, for example, Wallace Oaks, *Fiscal Federalism* (New York: Harcourt, Brace, 1977).

[6]See W.S. Livingston, "A Note on the Nature of Federalism," in J. Peter Meekison, ed., *Canadian Federalism: Myth or Reality*, second edition (Toronto: Methuen, 1971), p. 24.

[7]See Karl Aun, "Cultural Autonomy of Ethnic Minorities in Estonia: A Model for Multicultural Society?," paper presented at the Third Conference of Baltic States in Scandinavia, Stockholm, 1975; Carl J. Friedrich, "Corporate Federalism and Linguistic Politics," paper delivered at IPSA, Montréal, 1973; and Kenneth D. McRae, "The Principle of Territoriality and the Principle of Personality in Multilingual States," *International Journal of the Sociology of Language*, vol. 4 (1975), pp. 33-54.

units. On the other hand, Graham Maddox has argued that many of the so-called altruistic objectives often attributed to federalism are inaccurate and perhaps even misleading.[8] Britain, perhaps one of the world's most liberal democracies, is a unitary state, while a number of non-democratic countries have, on paper at least, adopted the federal form. Maddox finds the popular argument that federal governments are "closer to the people" also to be questionable when carefully examined.[9] William Riker, too, dismisses the notion of lofty motives, and suggests that federalism is ultimately the result of a rational political bargain.[10] Franz Neumann concludes simply that federalism may be good, bad or indifferent, depending on other circumstances.[11]

We have stated earlier that the federal form is characteristically adopted because the leaders of the constituent units become convinced that they have something to gain which they could not achieve if they were to remain completely separate and autonomous. The two most often-cited motivations underlying federal unions are the desire for military security, and the desire for economic or political expansion.[12] A large geographic unit with a degree of coordination of resources provides a more effective defensive unit than a collection of smaller, independent states. And, of course, such a unified entity stands a good chance of being able to expand economically and politically. The possibility for self-aggrandizement, rather than lofty idealism, seems to be a more accurate assessment of the motivations for federalism.

While the various sub-units may perceive gains from a federal union, they must also take certain drawbacks into consideration: in order to realize their objectives, the sub-units will be obliged to give up some privileges and powers to the central government. Before doing this, they may seek certain guarantees and safeguards so that they may maintain at least a modicum of separate authority. These guarantees are usually in the form of a written constitution clearly dividing political authority and jurisdiction and spelling out certain limitations and restrictions.[13]

A constitution is therefore often referred to as the "umpire" of federalism, acting as a protection as well as a limitation. Whether the constitution is a single written document or an unwritten collection of statutes and understandings, what is important is that the "federal principle" be enshrined in a way that recognizes the diversity of the country and at the same time provides a check on arbitrary rule by the central government. The component units are usually given equal or disproportionately strong representation at the centre. This is often

---

[8]For a critique of some of the justifications often cited in the adoption of federalism, see Graham Maddox, "Federalism: Or Government Frustrated," *Australian Quarterly*, vol. 45, no. 3 (September 1973), pp. 92-100.

[9]*Ibid.*, pp. 93-94.

[10]Riker, *Federalism: Origin, Operation, Significance*, p. 12.

[11]Franz Neumann, *The Democratic and the Authoritarian State: Essays in Political and Legal Theory* (Glencoe: Free Press, 1957).

[12]Riker, *Federalism: Origin, Operation, Significance*, pp. 12-16.

[13]Wheare, *op. cit.*, pp. 15-34.

achieved by having two legislative chambers – one based on population, the other based on a recognition of regionalism.[14] The importance of federal constitutions is demonstrated by the controversy over how they may be amended or altered. Much of the evolution of federalism depends on how a given constitution is interpreted, in particular by the judiciary.

To establish a federal union at all, to make the necessary promises and concessions, requires remarkable salesmanship. Once the union is achieved, it will inevitably evolve on the basis of many, perhaps unforeseen, factors. But to establish the union itself is an extraordinarily complex and difficult task. Individuals who accomplish the task usually end up enthroned in history as near-mythical figures, like the Canadian "Fathers of Confederation".

Many apparently stable federal constitutional systems have endured stresses and strains, and on occasion even failure. Ronald Watts has found four common conditions of failure: regional divergences of political demands; weak communications; a diminution of the original impetus for union; and external influences.[15] All these conditions are present in Canada to some degree; in fact, they are present in all federations to some degree – both those which have failed and those which have succeeded. Since the Second World War there has been no example of a solidly-based sovereign federal state which has had a peaceful secession. The only examples of peaceful secessions invariably involved very loose confederations such as Malaysia (Singapore was virtually expelled) and the tenuous arrangements of Syria-Egypt and Senegal-Mali. The other cases involved violence, or the termination of colonial regimes without contiguous territories with the parent countries, such as Algeria's breakaway from France. We have to go back to the turn of the century, when Norway divided from Sweden, to find an example of peaceful dissolution of a solid federal system. The lesson is clear – civil war has been the usual means by which federal states divide.

Thus far, we have described federalism in terms of constitutions which divide the authority of the central and sub-unit governments, and balance regional interests. Nonetheless, readers must be careful not to take too legalistic an approach and overlook the fact that federalism is fundamentally based on a sociological reality.[16] Were it not for societal diversity, federalism would not be as prevalent in the world as it is today. While federal states may be formed for essentially narrow, pragmatic reasons, this political arrangement is ultimately a recognition that the various sub-units are different and that there is something

---

[14]*Ibid.*, pp. 10-14. Dispute rages on this topic because both the Cameroons and Pakistan have had federal constitutions with unicameral legislatures. For a discussion of the relevant examples with different facts, see Ivo D. Duchacek, *Comparative Federalism: The Territorial Dimension of Politics* (New York: Holt, Rinehart and Winston, 1970), chapter 8, and Daniel J. Elazar, "Federalism," in David L. Sills, ed., *International Encyclopedia of the Social Sciences*, Vol. 5 (New York: Macmillan, 1968), pp. 353-367.

[15]R.L. Watts, "Survival or Disintegration," in Richard Simeon, ed., *Must Canada Fail?* (Montréal: McGill-Queen's University Press, 1977), pp. 42-60.

[16]See Michael Stein, "Federal Political Systems and Federal Societies," in Meekison, ed., *Canadian Federalism: Myth or Reality*, second edition, pp. 30-42.

about them which should be preserved and protected. Keeping this in mind, let us now turn to a consideration of how federalism came to be adopted in Canada and how it has evolved over the years.

THE ORIGIN AND EVOLUTION OF CANADIAN FEDERALISM

The Origin of Federalism

Throughout the first half of the 19th century, Britain's Canadian colonies moved toward a type of political union. The creation of a united Upper and Lower Canada (the present Ontario and Québec) in 1841 was the first step. However, all the legislation in the Province of Canada, as it was then called, had to be enacted by the legislatures of both Upper and Lower Canada. As the population of Upper Canada grew in relation to that of Lower Canada, there was a corresponding demand by the former for more political influence. Meanwhile, Lower Canada was steadfastly insisting on non-interference with the French, Catholic way of life. As a political deadlock developed, tension mounted and the experiment of joining the two Canadas failed. It was obvious that a more broadly based union was necessary.

The motivations for the establishment of a federal union in Canada in the 1860s were mixed. Both military security and economic expansion were central themes of the speeches and political programs of the contemporary leaders. The persuasiveness and political acumen of the Fathers of Confederation on these topics was very impressive. Foremost among them was Sir John A. Macdonald, who played the leading role in establishing the federal union in 1867 by placating the objections of the smaller Maritime provinces and holding forth the prospect of a glorious national destiny.[17] By the 1860s, Macdonald, among others, was keenly aware of the need for greater military security. The victory of the Northern States in the American Civil War had sent a shiver up the spines of Canadian leaders. British interests in Canada had made no secret of their support of the American Confederacy and, after Appomattox, there was some expectation that Canada might be annexed as part of the spoils of war. Raids by fanatical Fenians across the border into Canada further served to add a note of urgency to plans for some type of national unification. The British, for their part, were tired of the burden of defending their colonies in North America and were not adverse to the prospect of turning over to Canadians the responsibility for their own defence.

At the same time, Macdonald recognized the great potential of the unsettled western territories for the development of a transcontinental nation. The possibility of economic development and expansion was therefore another significant motivating factor in establishing federalism. A political union would not

---

[17]See Donald Creighton, *John A. Macdonald: The Young Politician* (Toronto: Macmillan, 1952), *John A. Macdonald: The Old Chieftain* (Toronto: Macmillan, 1955) and *The Road to Confederation: The Emergence of Canada, 1863-1867* (Toronto: Macmillan, 1964); and Peter Waite, *The Life and Times of Confederation, 1864-1867* (Toronto: University of Toronto Press, 1967).

only improve internal trade between the Maritime provinces and Upper and Lower Canada, but would also help in the drive to settle the prairies and the far west before the Americans moved into the vacuum.

Each of the British colonies in North America saw certain specific advantages for itself in the enterprise. The leaders from Upper Canada, a growing and prosperous area, looked forward to further economic expansion and development. Those from Lower Canada, while uneasy about their English Canadian neighbours, were willing to consider a federal union if their language and culture could be protected by law. The sparsely populated Maritime colonies of Nova Scotia and New Brunswick were perhaps the most reluctant, but at the same time were attracted by economic advantages, namely the building of a transcontinental railway and various subsidies from the future federal government. The Charlottetown and Québec conferences, discussed in detail in an earlier chapter, culminated a long process of negotiation resulting in the Dominion of Canada.

The Evolution of Federalism

While the *BNA Act* authorized the establishment of a type of government in Canada "similar in principle to that of the United Kingdom", the resulting form of government necessarily differed in that jurisdiction and authority were divided between the central government and the provinces. We have seen that the architects of the federal system sought to establish a strong central government, mindful as they were of the threat posed by the movement for states' rights to the American union, leading to the bloody Civil War of 1861–1865. Even cursory reading of the *BNA Act*, revealing the sweeping jurisdiction given the central government, confirms the impression that it was meant to be predominant. Reversing the American example, it was the federal government in Canada that was to be the beneficiary of the residual "Peace, Order, and good Government" clause. The limited jurisdiction of the provinces was meant to underscore their subordinate position in the federation. While reference is often made to the "Confederation Agreement" and the "Fathers of Confederation", it is clear that the authors did not intend Canada to be a confederation in a genuine political sense, but rather a centralized federation.

In a summary article, Howard Cody has traced the evolution of federal/provincial interaction in Canada since 1867.[18] While his argument lacks a rigorous definition of "interaction", the précis does provide a short history of federal/provincial relations. Cody identifies four eras, and suggests that there have been several pendulum swings between centralization and decentralization. While Canada clearly began as a centralized federation, during the latter part of the 19th century the relative power of the provinces was growing, due to a series of judgements by the Judicial Committee of the Privy Council. We have noted that, in jurisdictional disputes referred to the JCPC, there was a consistent pattern of

---

[18]Howard Cody, "The Evolution of Federal-Provincial Relations in Canada: Some Reflections," *American Review of Canadian Studies*, vol. 7, no. 1 (Spring 1977), p. 55-83.

interpretation favouring provincial rights.[19] Led by such forceful provincial leaders as Sir Oliver Mowat and Honoré Mercier, the original dominance of the central government was eroded to the point that the *BNA Act* was being interpreted by the JCPC as an international treaty rather than as the founding document of a nation.[20] This period of decentralized or peripheralized federalism, lasting into the early 20th century, has been roundly condemned by Garth Stevenson: "This peculiar situation, which even the Australians had the foresight largely to avoid, had the effect that for almost a century the most influential concepts of Canadian federalism were largely defined by outsiders, men who had no practical knowledge of Canada, or of federalism, and who were not even required to live in the society that to a large degree was shaped by their opinions."[21]

According to Cody's historical summary, the pendulum began to swing back toward a centralization of authority with the introduction of what became known in the funding system for provinces as "conditional grants". Under the *BNA Act*, the provinces assumed jurisdiction over such matters as education and social welfare, which originally required very little expenditure. As the demand for social services grew in the 20th century, the provinces found themselves starved for funds, since the provisions of the *Act* made it virtually impossible for them to raise the revenues needed to meet public needs. To help them escape from this impasse, the central government in Ottawa offered various grants to the provinces on the condition that the money be spent in a specified manner. The provinces, for their part, resented this intrusion but had no choice. The Depression further deepened the dependency of the provinces on the federal government.[22]

In addition, the necessity for placing Canada on a war footing in 1914 and again in 1939 naturally tended to centralize power in Ottawa. Except perhaps in Québec, where there was considerable opposition to the two World Wars and especially to the policy of conscription, the national government became a focus of patriotism and loyalty for most Canadians, endowing it with enormous prestige and symbolic influence.

The factors contributing to centralization of power continued for some time into the postwar era, but there were signs that the provinces would seek to regain their lost ground. The dominance of Ottawa can be said to have continued until the late 1950s, when the most recent pendulum shift occurred. The current

---

[19]See Alain C. Cairns, "The Judicial Committee and its Critics," *Canadian Journal of Political Science*, vol. 4, no. 3 (September 1971), pp. 301-345; V.C. MacDonald, "The Privy Council and the Canadian Constitution," *Canadian Bar Review* (December 1951). pp. 1021-1037; and Martha Fletcher, "Judicial Review and the Division of Powers in Canada," in Meekison, *op. cit.*, pp. 100-123.

[20]See Donald Swainson, ed., *Oliver Mowat's Ontario* (Toronto: Macmillan, 1972), especially Bruce W. Hodgins, "Disagreement at the Commencement: Divergent Ontarian Views of Federalism, 1867-1871," pp. 52-68 and Christopher Armstrong, "The Mowat Heritage in Federal-Provincial Relations," pp. 93-118.

[21]Garth Stevenson, *Unfulfilled Union*, revised edition (Toronto: Gage Publishing, 1982), p. 43.

[22]Cody, "The Evolution of Federal-Provincial Relations in Canada," pp. 66-67.

era of relative decentralization actually began in 1937, with the recommendations of the Royal Commission on Dominion-Provincial Relations, perhaps better known as the Rowell-Sirois Commission.[23] This Commission was charged with investigating the reasons for the near-bankruptcy of the provinces and with recommending ways in which to revitalize the federation. While its suggestions could not be implemented until after the Second World War, the Rowell-Sirois Commission came out strongly against the conditional grants procedure. In addition, it recommended that Ottawa take over such expensive responsibilities as unemployment insurance and pensions and generally seek to equalize the financial resources of the provinces.

As the provinces began to obtain relief from their heavy financial burdens through new fiscal mechanisms, important changes were also occurring in postwar society. Beginning in the 1960s and with increased momentum through the decade, Québec underwent a "Quiet Revolution" in which traditional French Catholic values and occupational patterns were transformed. A new, confident French Canadian élite, epitomized perhaps by the government of Jean Lesage, led the assault on Ottawa's paternalism.[24] Ottawa countered with the introduction of what were referred to as "shared cost programs", which nonetheless tended to be regarded as distorting provincial spending priorities and therefore still engendered antagonism. In the spirit of Mowat and Mercier, Québec politicians insisted on the right to exercise their independence by "opting out" of certain programs so that they could go their own way. Ottawa had no coherent or effective response with which to meet this challenge. Québec's agitation in the 1960s for "special status" only served to give the other provinces ideas.

The longstanding sense of grievance against Ottawa in the western provinces also began to erupt during this period. Made confident by their enormous resource revenues, the provinces of Alberta and British Columbia in particular sought greater political clout within the federation to match their recent wealth. While they were not sympathetic to the cultural and linguistic aspirations of the Québécois, the western provinces shared with them a degree of antipathy toward the perceived paternalism of the federal government in Ottawa.

FEDERAL/PROVINCIAL MECHANISMS FOR CONFLICT RESOLUTION

The constant interplay of federal/provincial relations has brought into being numerous institutions for coordinating policies and resolving disputes. As we pointed out in the previous chapter, most fields of public policy are managed by both levels of government, and many are jointly financed. Both facts necessitate much federal/provincial interaction.

---

[23]See D.V. Smiley, ed., *The Rowell-Sirois Report: An Abridgement of Book 1 of the Royal Commission Report on Dominion-Provincial Relations*, The Carleton Library No. 5 (Toronto: McClelland and Stewart, 1963).

[24]See Claude Morin, *Quebec versus Ottawa: The Struggle for Self-Government, 1960-72* (Toronto: University of Toronto Press, 1976), pp. 12-28.

Reprinted with permission – The Toronto Star Syndicate.

In the early days of confederation, there was not much need for formal fed-eral/provincial consultations, and what meetings did occur were of an *ad hoc* na-ture, convened to discuss specific problems. However, increased financial power expanded the fields of influence and concern of both levels of government. Com-mitment to economic policies aimed at full employment, growth and trade liber-alization, as well as to a wide range of social policies, resulted in a dramatic increase in intergovernmental relations. Effective intergovernmental consulta-tion has thus become a basic requirement for the maintenance of Canadian fed-eralism. This development is perhaps best indicated by the establishment, within the federal government and within almost all provincial governments, of depart-ments or offices whose sole purpose is dealing with federal/provincial issues.

Intergovernmental relations immediately after the Second World War were characterized by constant, reasonably harmonious exchanges of ideas, financial decisions and policies. This period has been labelled one of *cooperative federalism*, albeit with a decided federal predominance. Economic times were good as a re-sult of the post-war boom, and federal/provincial relations were primarily con-cerned with social programs which did not necessarily involve regional conflict.[25] As a rule, bureaucrats from both levels of government dominated intergovern-mental relations, resolving problems before they reached the political agenda.

The 1960s and 1970s, however, were characterized by less cooperation and more confrontation between the two levels of government. Economic downturns and the ascendancy of provincialism – concern for the jurisdictional integrity of the provinces – changed the conduct of federal/provincial relations. The term coined to describe this relationship, *executive federalism*, represents an attenuation of federal power. The clearest sign of the change from cooperative to executive federalism was the movement of intergovernmental talks from among public ser-vants behind closed doors to among politicians in the full glare of publicity. The most public institution in intergovernmental relations today is the First Minis-ters' Conference, during which the leaders of the eleven governments meet in the former Ottawa railway station to hammer out deals, recently under the scru-

---

[25]Timothy B. Woolstencroft, *Organizing Intergovernmental Relations*, Institute Discussion Paper No. 12 (Kingston: Queen's University Institute of Intergovernmental Relations, 1982), p. 12.

tiny of television cameras. Some of the most important of these meetings have lately been named Constitutional Conferences.

While Ottawa may have thought that it could placate opposition through such conferences, some have argued that the meetings have in fact provided an instrument for the expression of provincial discontent and resistance.[26] The conferences have increasingly become political forums in which each Premier appeals not to the other heads of government, but directly to his own electorate. Richard Simeon has argued that intergovernmental bargaining has become more like the diplomatic relations between nation-states than the usual politics within a single state.[27] Responsible only to the people who elected them, provincial leaders today are well organized and prepared to take on the federal government through counter-proposals and independent programs. Moreover, a dangerous new practice has developed: the ten provincial premiers are tending to meet in advance of First Ministers' Conferences and approach the final bargaining table as a unified group opposed to the federal government. Ottawa is no longer able to overwhelm its partners in the federation.[28] Explicit delegation of responsibility to the provinces for such matters as resources and education in the *BNA Act* put them in many respects on an equal footing with the federal government. As the resource-rich provinces have expanded their tax revenue in recent years, they have been in a better position to challenge the dominance of Ottawa.

There is little question that the era of executive federalism has been one of decentralization characterized by intergovernmental conflict. D.V. Smiley, for example, argues that the result of the rise of intergovernmental specialists has made federal/provincial conflicts more intractable, perhaps to the point of being irreconcilable.[29] Representatives of each level of government, jealous of their position, promote their own narrow interests, thereby impeding compromise.

Yet this argument confuses the process of intergovernmental relations with the causes of conflict. Intergovernmental specialists have in fact facilitated cooperation and compromise between governments. As Simeon points out, intergovernmental interactions promote consultation between governments and thus contribute to the effectiveness and harmony of intergovernmental cooperation.[30] The appearance of intergovernmental specialists is more a consequence of the

---

[26]Don Stevenson, "The Role of Intergovernmental Conferences in the Decision-Making Process," in Richard Simeon, ed., *Confrontation and Collaboration – Intergovernmental Relations in Canada Today* (Toronto: The Institute of Public Administration of Canada, 1979), p. 94 and Gordon Robertson, "The Role of Interministerial Conferences in the Decision-Making Process," in Simeon, *Confrontation and Collaboration*, pp. 28-88.

[27]Richard Simeon, *Federal-Provincial Diplomacy: The Making of Recent Policy in Canada* (Toronto: University of Toronto Press, 1972) and Donald V. Smiley, *Canada in Question.; Federalism in the Eighties*, third edition (Toronto: McGraw-Hill Ryerson, 1980).

[28]See Donald V. Smiley, "Federal-Provincial Conflict in Canada," in Meekison, ed., *Canadian Federalism: Myth or Reality*, third edition (Toronto: Methuen, 1977), pp. 2-18.

[29]D.V. Smiley, "An Outsider's Observations of Federal-Provincial Relations Among Consenting Adults," in Simeon, ed., *Confrontation and Collaboration*, pp. 109-111.

[30]Simeon, *Federal-Provincial Diplomacy, passim.*

need for consultation than a source of conflict. As well, the concern for jurisdictional integrity has not displaced the ability of government officials to resolve conflicts as, for instance, in the oil pricing agreements of 1973–1974, the Alberta/Ottawa energy agreement of 1979 and the constitutional accord of 1981. Intergovernmental interaction provides a means of communications between governments, encouraging an awareness of the views of their respective Cabinets and bureaucracies – a necessary precondition to achieving compromise.[31]

Thus, since relations between the federal and provincial governments are often characterized by disagreement, the mechanisms of conflict resolution are important for the functioning of federalism. The ability of the Canadian federation to cope with fundamental divergences of interest which animate federal/provincial conflict is largely based on the continued effectiveness of these mechanisms.

As the preceding discussion of the evolution of Canadian federalism has demonstrated, an understanding of federalism requires an awareness not only of the formal divisions of responsibility and powers, but also of the economic and social context in which the political contest takes place. While relations between the levels of government are defined by the Constitution, they are subject to the pressures of the day and so are far from static.

The constitutional details described in Chapter 5 and this general review of the evolution of federalism reveal the basic patterns of political interaction. Figure 6-2 portrays the pendulum swings which we have been describing, and illustrates some developments in federal/provincial interaction. While specific dates are given, in reality changes of this nature take place very gradually, and we have simply used some specific event or individual as marking a turning point when in fact the transformation may have been building for some time.

Despite the imprecision with respect to time, it is important that federalism be perceived as something other than a static phenomenon. Of utmost concern today is the fact that the pendulum has been moving towards decentralization with such intensity that it has threatened to overwhelm the Canadian federal system. While change is to be expected as the normal course of events in any federation, such pressures threaten to terminate federalism in Canada. In the next sections we shall examine what may be referred to as the dual crises of Canadian federalism: federal/provincial fiscal relations; and regional challenges to federalism.

FEDERAL/PROVINCIAL FISCAL RELATIONS

From the beginning, money and ways of obtaining it have been a crucial aspect of federal/provincial interaction in Canada, the source of considerable difficulty for the federation. While certain conflicts within a federal union revolve around highly symbolic issues, much of what governments actually do is enormously expensive and ways must be found to finance it.

---

[31]Woolstencroft, *Organizing Intergovernmental Relations*, p. 80.

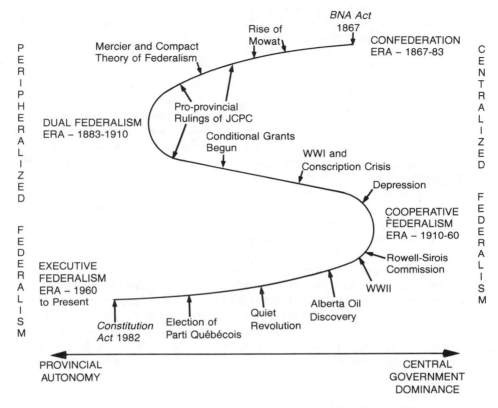

FIGURE 6.2 The Evolution of Canadian Federalism from 1867 to the Present, Indicating Swings of Centralization and Peripheralization

Source: Based on material from Howard Cody, "The Evolution of Federal-Provincial Relations in Canada," *American Review of Canadian Studies,* vol. 7, no. 1, (1977), pp. 55-83.

Four general economic problems have been identified by J.C. Strick as being at the root of this difficulty.[32] In his opinion, all four are constantly interwoven with political sensitivities and historical exigencies. In this section we will examine these problems, tracing the conflict they have engendered from 1867 to the current era.

The first and most obvious problem of federal/provincial financial relations, according to Strick, is that there has always been a fundamental incongruence between responsibilities and sources of revenue at the different levels of government. As we have pointed out, at the inception of the federal union the central government acquired the most significant revenue sources while agreeing to pay some limited subsidies and annual grants to support the obligations of the

---

[32]J.C. Strick, *Canadian Public Finance,* second edition (Toronto: Holt, Rinehart and Winston, 1978), pp. 100-101.

provinces. The Constitution entitled the federal government to raise money "by any mode or system of taxation" (BNA 91.3), while the provinces were limited to direct taxation (BNA 92.2). Since provincial expenditure continued to grow rapidly, the provinces' need to find more revenues became a constant source of tension and political conflict.

The second problem can be traced to the fact that the provinces themselves differed widely in fiscal capacities. In the early years, a relatively prosperous province like Ontario or Québec was fortunate in having a strong tax base in the form of a concentration of corporate activities and personal fortunes and, therefore, the ability to raise adequate funds to provide social services. Poorer and relatively depressed provinces like Prince Edward Island were plagued with the problem of being unable to obtain sufficient tax revenue: excessive provincial taxation would only lower individual incomes and undermine economic growth. While in any federation some regions may be better off than others, in Canada the discrepancies have been extraordinarily sharp. Over time, the ability to obtain high tax revenues has shifted from province to province – for example, from Ontario to Alberta during the period of high energy prices.

The third problem has resulted from a certain degree of joint occupancy of the tax fields. As mentioned above, the *BNA Act* gave the provinces control over direct taxation, while the federal government was granted a more-or-less blanket authorization to tax. "Direct taxation" refers to individual income tax, corporate income tax and succession duties, among others. The problem lay in the fact that the federal government could levy indirect taxation through customs and excise duties, but could also institute its own direct taxation in competition with the provinces. To a considerable degree, therefore, both the provinces and the federal government could levy taxes on the same sources. This ongoing competition for revenue sources has not been conducive to a stable and equitable tax policy, and has remained one of the most contentious aspects of federal/provincial fiscal relations.

The fourth problem of note relates to the implementation of fiscal policy. In an age of Keynesian economics, with its long-term budgetary manipulation of the economy, the possibility exists that, without close cooperation between federal and provincial taxation and spending policies, the overall economy will not be effectively controlled. If, for example, the federal government were seeking to cut taxes to stimulate the economy, while at the same time the provinces were deciding to increase taxation, the impact of the federal initiative would be negated. Without some degree of cooperation there is a danger that federal and provincial policies could be working at cross-purposes. The era of executive federalism has sought to introduce a degree of coordination and consultation between the federal government and the provinces, although certainly not all difficulties of this type have been resolved.

Bearing in mind these four problems, we shall next survey the historical evolution of federal/provincial financial relations in Canada. Before doing so, however, we shall reiterate that, in terms of its degree of centralization (as measured by the proportion which the federal government spends of *all* government expenditures), Canada ranks last among western liberal federal states such as

Australia, USA and the Federal Republic of Germany. As W.H. Riker put it, "Among the more or less centralized federations of the modern world, most writers would agree that Canada is about as decentralized as one can get."[33]

A Brief History of Fiscal Federalism

At the inception of the federal union in 1867, the federal government took over existing provincial debts and agreed to pay *per capita* subsidies and annual grants to the provinces to support their activities. Almost from the beginning, however, the provinces were hard pressed for revenue sources. As early as the 1870s one province began enacting personal and corporate income taxes as well as estate taxes.[34]

While the provinces did acquire revenue from direct taxation, their obligations were escalating rapidly. In the period between 1896 and 1913 there was an enormous increase in public expenditure. The various federal subsidies promised in 1867 were helpful, but never sufficed to meet the growing need. Federal subsidies continued to decline as a proportion of provincial revenue – from 58 percent in 1874 to 8 percent in 1929. Also, as time went on, the economic disparity between the provinces widened.

The First World War period was characterized by strong economic regulation by Ottawa. Increased military expenditures required the imposition of additional taxes to cover the federal debt, which exceeded two billion dollars at the end of the war. Not surprisingly, the federal government soon took up direct taxation in the form of personal and corporate income taxes to meet its own obligations.[35]

The early 20th century saw an important development in federal/provincial fiscal relations: the use of **conditional grants.** The federal government was willing to provide funds to the provinces for specific programs *on condition* that the money was spent in accordance with federal standards. These grants closed the provincial budgetary gap somewhat but did little to redress the fundamental problem of unequal fiscal capacity. The money was typically offered on a "take-it-or-leave-it" basis and, while tempting for most provinces, it could be disruptive of budgetary planning and priorities. Perhaps more significantly, the provinces grew increasingly annoyed at the paternalistic way in which the grants were set up and administered.

Before 1930, then, the provinces were already straining under various new obligations. The Great Depression had a devastating impact on their fragile finances. Their tax base was eroded, yet the demand for services, especially in the

---

[33]Riker, "Federalism," in Greenstein and Polsby, eds., *Handbook of Political Science, op. cit.*, pp. 132-133.

[34]British Columbia introduced a personal income tax in 1876; Prince Edward Island followed suit in 1894. By 1896 all provinces were levying estate or succession taxes. See A. Milton Moore, J. Harvey Perry and Donald I. Beach, *The Financing of Canadian Federation: The First Hundred Years* (Toronto: Canadian Tax Foundation, April 1966), pp. 3-4.

[35]Strick, *Canadian Public Finance, op. cit.*, p. 102.

welfare field, increased dramatically. Federal conditional grants were stepped up but were not sufficient and led to a certain amount of heavy-handed federal intervention. The 1930s have become known as the "decade of the tax jungle". Uncoordinated joint occupancy of tax fields, duplication of administrative bureaucracy and high regressive taxation (sales taxes) all served to exacerbate the effects of the Depression. While other countries were able to launch coordinated assaults on economic stagnation, Canada was caught in a serious bind. The Depression served to reveal that the division of federal/provincial fiscal jurisdictions was inadequate for the 20th century; some major restructuring would be necessary to let the country survive as a coherent federal system.

The Royal Commission on Dominion-Provincial Relations (the Rowell-Sirois Commission) was established in 1937 to study the matter. Experts in several fields were assembled and given a sweeping mandate to examine the operations and problems of the federal system, and to offer recommendations which would bring about a degree of congruence between obligations and revenue sources. The Commission presented its recommendations, based on considerable study and review, in 1940. It suggested that the federal government assume responsibility for personal and corporate income tax collection, the accumulated debt of the provinces and the support of the unemployed through a social security program.[36] In addition, the Commission recommended a system of national adjustment grants to subsidize the poorer provinces so that the level of social services could be standardized across the nation. The latter proposal ran into immediate opposition, especially from some of the wealthier provinces, which did not wish to support their poorer fellows. The outbreak of the Second World War served to divert everyone's attention from the issue. Finally, as R.M. Burns concluded: "Patriotism accomplished what financial reasoning could not."[37]

The wartime period of relative economic prosperity somewhat eased the burden of the provinces. Citing the emergency, the federal government usurped the income tax and succession duty fields for itself. In return, the provinces were given compensatory payments. Thus began a complicated series of *tax-rental* and *tax-sharing* agreements.[38] The federal government in effect took over virtually all provincial sources of revenue from direct taxation in exchange for a payment of "rent". It is clear from this why the federal government in the war years and in the postwar decade was in a position of considerable dominance over the provinces.

By the end of the Second World War, the federal government was spending approximately three-quarters of the money spent by all governments in Canada. It had built up an impressive bureaucratic infrastructure and was intent on implementing its vision of Canada's future. As the war emergency disappeared, the federal government began to assume responsibility for the problems of postwar

---

[36]Moore, Perry and Beach, *The Financing of Canadian Federation*, pp. 11-13.

[37]R.M. Burns, "Recent Developments in Federal-Provincial Fiscal Relations in Canada," *National Tax Journal*, vol. 15, no. 3 (September 1962), p. 228.

[38]See Stevenson, *Unfulfilled Union*, pp. 136-141 and Strick, *Canadian Public Finance*, pp. 106-112.

reconstruction. At this time, a distinct change in attitude arose concerning the role of government in society. The concept of the balanced budget was replaced by Keynesian economic theory: the federal government committed itself to maintaining a high and stable level of economic growth and employment throughout the country. To do so, the federal government had to adjust federal tax rates and levels of expenditure. It was able to obtain provincial agreement for an extension of the tax rental arrangement until at least 1952.[39] The pre-eminence of the federal government began to erode during the later 1950s, as the various tax rental agreements between it and the provinces began to engender opposition. Québec, for its part, began to resent both this arrangement and the conditional grants scheme.

As the 1960s approached, there was an accentuation of Strick's first perennial problem in fiscal relations: the lack of correlation between revenue sources and expenditure responsibilities. The welfare state was entering the "big money" era. The provinces began to feel the financial pinch from education and health care again. The federal government was virtually left out of these important jurisdictional areas. Increased provincial responsibilities were matched by the increasing competence and aggressiveness of provincial bureaucrats, perhaps seen most clearly in Québec. The federal government seemed to be losing its grip on the economy as the country began to experience a recession and slow economic growth. Sensing weakness, the provinces began to claim more responsibility for their own economies and questioned the feasibility of a national economic policy. The most obvious indication of provincial self-assertion was in the area of tax-sharing.[40] Tax-sharing was a continuation of the tax-rental program; however, instead of *per capita* grants, the provinces were to get a fixed percentage of three standard taxes: personal income tax, corporation tax and federal succession duties. Tax-sharing protected provincial autonomy to some extent and was supplemented by a payment in the form of an unconditional grant. Despite this apparent liberalization of federal policy, Ontario and Québec objected to the arrangement, and the federal government introduced a tax abatement system for the two provinces. This meant that the federal government moved out of the tax field to a considerable degree so that the provinces could levy their own taxes. This agreement only encouraged agitation by all the provinces for a better deal.

During the 1960s, the abatement system was gradually extended to all provinces. The federal government thus withdrew somewhat from the personal and corporate income tax field. Although the federal government continued to collect the tax, as long as the provincial tax base remained the same as the federal tax base, the provinces had more room for increasing their taxes. In 1966 the tax arrangements were opened up for periodic review, with the provinces asking for even more tax room and more federal money. At the time, Ottawa was not in a mood to compromise and the arrangement was extended virtually unchanged. By 1972, however, the abatement system was practically at an end. The federal

---

[39]Strick, *Canadian Public Finance*, p. 107.
[40]*Ibid.*, pp. 110-112.

government introduced a guarantee program to prevent provincial loss of revenues resulting from a rationalization of their tax base with that of the federal government. Today, Ottawa still collects taxes for all the provinces except Québec (at rates set by the provinces); Québec takes in its own personal and corporate income taxes.[41]

Basic Concepts of Fiscal Federalism

Before outlining the most recent federal/provincial financial agreements, we shall examine in greater detail two of the most important elements of the financial relationship: conditional and unconditional grants; and equalization programs. The two are, of course, related, and under various formulas have been a major part of overall federal/provincial policy for decades. Since Ottawa collects more than its expenditure needs, these funds are shared with the provinces.

CONDITIONAL AND UNCONDITIONAL GRANTS

As mentioned earlier, conditional grants were one of the means by which the financial gap of the 1930s was bridged. Such transfers between the central and the regional governments occur in most federations because of the need to provide equal standards in services. In Canada, they are essential because of the imbalance of resources across the country. The first conditional grants in Canada were given in 1912 for agricultural instruction.[42] Larger-scale grants of this type were offered in 1927 to help finance old age pensions. After the Second World War vast expenditures on health and welfare necessitated another major expansion. Over the years, these conditional grants were made available under the provisions of Ottawa's spending power.

The federal government was able to act in these fields because of this spending power. **Spending power** refers to the federal government's blanket authority to spend money for any purpose in any field even if it has no legal jurisdiction over the area. In most cases Ottawa offered to pay half the costs of a certain program, with the province paying the rest. While these so-called "50 cent dollar" programs were an attractive proposition for some provinces, they had the effect of enticing provincial legislatures to spend their limited resources on programs chosen by the federal government.

On certain occasions provincial leaders might have wished to spend their money on other programs, but there was no way to shift resources unless Ottawa agreed. Budgetary priorities were inevitably affected. Québec was particularly dissatisfied, because it was left with reduced powers in what were felt to be important matters of provincial concern.

As a result of criticism, the federal government in 1964 decided to allow any province which did not want to be involved in a joint-cost venture to receive

---

[41]*Ibid.*, pp. 112-119.

[42]Cody, "The Evolution of Federal-Provincial Relations in Canada," p. 66.

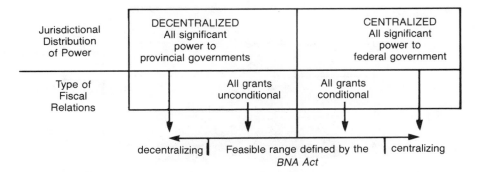

FIGURE 6.3 Federal/Provincial Transfers and the Distribution of Power

Source: Adapted from Thomas J. Courchene, "The New Fiscal Arrangements and the Economics of Federalism," in *Options,* Proceedings of the Conference on the Future of the Canadian Federation (Toronto: University of Toronto Press, 1977), p. 315.

an equivalent sum of money either by way of a federal tax withdrawal or in another form. Only Québec took up this offer, thereby highlighting its claim to special status within Confederation. Québec's "different" status was also confirmed by the development of its own hospital and old age pension schemes.

As the provinces grew in financial health, it was inevitable that they would seek a revision of these fiscal arrangements. Led by militant Québec, and to some extent Alberta and Ontario, they now seem to have won the struggle to end the restrictive conditional grants system. Ottawa is increasingly offering **unconditional grants,** which the provinces can spend in any way they wish because they are not designated for any specific expenditure program. This shift can be considered an indication of the current decentralization of the federal system. The influence exercised by the federal government's spending power is being reduced. Figure 6-3 highlights the correlation between conditional and unconditional grants, and constitutional centralization and decentralization.

EQUALIZATION GRANTS

We have already pointed out that a continuing problem of federal/provincial financial relations has been the different fiscal capacities of the various provinces. In 1867 the financial gap between the provinces was already wide; it has been growing ever since. A primary objective of post-Second World War fiscal policy has been to narrow this gap and to provide a degree of economic stabilization. The instrument for accomplishing this is the provision of equalization payments to the provinces. **Equalization payments** are unconditional transfer payments to the provinces from the federal government calculated on the ability of each province to raise revenue. (See Figures 6-4 and 6-5.) They enable less affluent provinces to provide an average level of public services without the need to resort to excessively high levels of taxation. Until 1957, such grants were tied to the tax rental scheme. Since then they have been calculated by bringing provinces up to an average based on a number of provincial revenue sources.

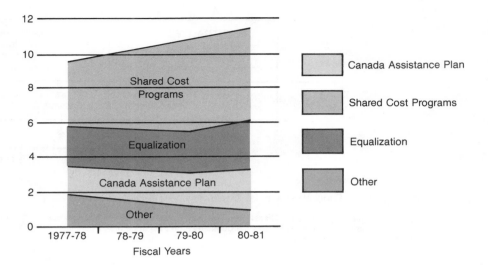

FIGURE 6.4   Federal Transfers to the Provinces, 1977-78 to 1980-81 (Billions of dollars)

Source: David L. Emerson, "The Tightrope of Fiscal Federalism," *The Canadian Business Review,* vol. 8, no. 4 (Winter 1981), p. 38.

How successful have the equalization efforts been? In terms of increasing *per capita* provincial expenditures, they can be considered successful because they brought the "have not" provinces up to the level of the "have" provinces. However, they have not erased interprovincial and interregional disparities. In recent years the federal government has had to resort to a variety of special grants for depressed areas in order to improve the situation. Tax incentives and grant and loan guarantees have been offered to industries to encourage them to locate in economically deprived areas. For example, a Department of Regional Economic Expansion was established under Prime Minister Trudeau to coordinate federal programs in this field.[43] The ultimate objective of equalization policy, of course, is to strengthen federalism by meeting the needs of the weaker elements in the union, establishing a national standard for social services. While its intentions are undoubtedly noble, the federal government has not been able to convey much sense of urgency to this endeavour. For their part, the so-called "have" provinces seem to object loudly to any increase in their financial commitment.

Yet the impact of the equalization program is substantial. In 1980-81, the program contributed from 21 to 26 percent of the general revenues of all governments in the Atlantic provinces, as well as lesser but significant proportions of the government revenues of Manitoba and Québec.[44] Table 6-1 shows the equalization payments offered in 1975-76 and 1980-81 to support the so-called "have

[43]Stevenson, *Unfulfilled Union,* pp. 141-145.

[44]Economic Council of Canada, *Financing Confederation: Today and Tomorrow* (Ottawa: Supply and Services, 1982), p. 11.

not" provinces in their budgetary process. Apart from the equalization program, federal transfers to all but the two poorest provinces are mostly paid by federal taxpayers in the province concerned.[45] Thus, the equalization program is critical for attainment of *horizontal equity,* the reduction of disparities between provinces in the treatment of persons in similar economic circumstances, as well as *vertical equity,* the reduction of inequalities in real income among individuals. It should come as no surprise, then, that the concept of equalization was enshrined in the Canadian Constitution of 1982 with the unanimous consent of all the governments.

Contemporary Fiscal Arrangements

We have said that in the 1970s conditional grants came under attack in Canada for neither providing economic justice nor allowing provincial initiative and independence. Some critics also argued that regional economic policies cannot always be made to harmonize with national objectives. In view of these and other difficulties the entire payments system was changed in 1977. In that year federal transfers, as a percentage of a province's own resources, provided a low of 17 percent for Alberta and a high of 90 percent and above for the four Atlantic provinces.

Thus, in 1977 a *Federal/Provincial Fiscal Arrangements Act* ended the most expensive shared cost programs and offered the provinces a more-or-less unconditional block grant to be earmarked for the health and educational fields:[46] hospital insurance, medicare and post-secondary education. The federal government surrendered some of its tax points as a means of financing the transfer. The amount of the transfers was determined by a formula which included the average

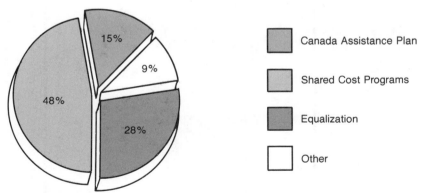

FIGURE 6.5 Composition of Federal Transfers, 1980-81 (Percent average for all provinces)

Source: David L. Emerson, "The Tightrope of Fiscal Federalism," *The Canadian Business Review,* vol. 8, no. 4 (Winter 1981), p. 38.

[45]D.O. Sewell and D.W. Slater, "The Case for Equalization," *Policy Options,* vol. 3, no. 3 (May/June, 1982), p. 17.

[46]David B. Perry, "The Federal-Provincial Fiscal Arrangement Introduced in 1977," *Canadian Tax Journal,* vol. XXV, no. 4 (July/August, 1977), pp. 429-440.

TABLE 6.1 Equalization Payments: Summary Data for 1975-76 and 1980-81

Province	Equalization Payments ($000) (1)		Provincial Share of Equalization Payments (%) (2)		Provincial Share of Federal Taxes (%) (3)		"Net Benefits" Col. 2 - Col. 3 (4)	
	1975-76	1980-81	1975-76	1980-81	1975-76	1980-81	1975-76	1980-81
Newfoundland	197 119	376 000	10.34	11.07	1.41	.91	8.93	10.16
Prince Edward Island	47 553	88 000	2.49	2.59	0.28	.24	2.21	2.35
Nova Scotia	254 865	449 000	13.37	13.22	2.45	2.53	10.92	10.69
New Brunswick	200 198	379 000	10.50	11.16	1.99	1.71	8.51	9.45
Québec	987 045	1 721 000	51.76	50.68	23.80	21.55	27.96	29.13
Ontario	0	0	0	0	41.35	43.20	-41.35	-43.20
Manitoba	137 945	343 000	7.23	10.10	3.83	3.42	3.40	6.68
Saskatchewan	82 065	40	4.30	1.18	3.27	3.53	1.03	-2.35
Alberta	0	0	0	0	8.63	11.45	-8.63	-11.45
British Columbia	0	0	0	0	12.88	11.45	-12.88	-11.45
Total	1 906 791	3 396 000	100	100	100	100	0	0

Source: Adapted from Thomas J. Courchene, "The New Fiscal Arrangements and the Economics of Federalism," in *Options,* Proceedings of the Conference on the Future of the Canadian Federation (Toronto: University of Toronto Press 1977) p. 323, and Economic Council of Canada, *Financing Confederation: Today and Tomorrow* (Ottawa: Supply and Services, 1982), p. 19.

rate of *per capita* GNP growth. While the federal government interpreted the *Act* as giving more autonomy to the provinces, it also placed the burden of two of the most expensive areas of social services squarely in the lap of the provincial governments. The provinces' point of view was that the federal government got them into these expensive fields and, since costs were rising rapidly, it wished to disengage itself from the responsibilities.[47]

Changes were also made in the equalization programs in an attempt to limit the net cost to the federal government. The number of revenue sources in the formula was increased and a limit placed on the use of provincial revenues from non-renewable resources in the calculation. With revenues from energy and minerals escalating rapidly, it was necessary to do the latter because the rise in the level of equalization payments was draining federal revenues. If the old formula had not been amended, many more provinces would have become "have not" provinces, thus qualifying for equalization payments.

However, even with these changes, Ontario, the only province which has never received equalization payments, would have become eligible for equalization transfers. To prevent Ontario from qualifying, legislation known as the "Ontario rider" was introduced by the federal government. It disallowed the payment of equalization grants to any province in which personal *per capita* income had been above the national average in both the current and two previous years. Although this legislation was not passed until 1981, regulations were enacted to prevent Ontario from receiving equalization grants in the years 1977 to 1980. The resultant savings to the federal government have been substantial. It has been estimated that Ontario would have received nearly $500 million in equalization payments in just the fiscal year 1979-80.[48] Figure 6-6 illustrates the effect of these restrictions on the growth of equalization payments.

The latest round of negotiations over the renewal of fiscal arrangements for 1982-87 ended with passage of federal legislation despite provincial opposition. Although Ottawa has exclusive jurisdiction over fiscal arrangements, an informal consensus clearly existed that decisions would be made in consultation with the provincial governments. However, in these negotiations Ottawa was less accommodating to provincial demands for increased transfers.

The atmosphere of the negotiations was strained. The federal government sought to correct what it perceived to be two fundamental problems.[49] First, the growing fiscal imbalance between the federal and provincial governments had to be arrested. While the federal government's deficit was increasing, there was an overall surplus in provincial revenues. Second, the federal government was concerned with maintaining a proper "political balance". Ottawa argued that its contribution to provincial government services was not sufficiently visible and that

---

[47]Marsha Chandler and William Chandler, *Public Policy and Provincial Politics* (Toronto: McGraw-Hill Ryerson, 1979), p. 165.

[48]Economic Council of Canada, *Financing Confederation*, p. 15.

[49]Allan J. MacEachen, Deputy Prime Minister and Minister of Finance, "Federal-Provincial Fiscal Arrangements in the Eighties: A Submission to the Parliamentary Task Force on the Federal-Provincial Fiscal Arrangements," (Ottawa: Supply and Services, April 23, 1981), pp. 8-11.

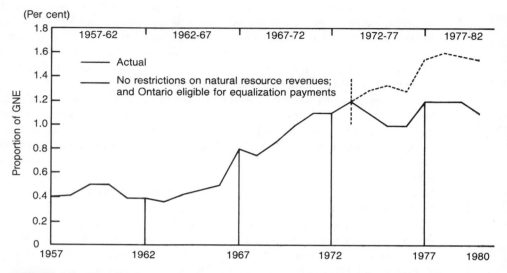

FIGURE 6.6 Equalization payments as a Proportion of Gross National Expenditure, Fiscal Years 1957-58 to 1980-81

Source: Economic Council of Canada, *Financing Confederation: Today and Tomorrow* (Ottawa: Supply and Services, 1982), p. 15.

this fact hindered proper government accountability for taxes and expenditures and deprived the federal government of recognition for its assistance. Thus, the federal government sought to cut back the level of transfers to the provinces in order to reduce the growth of its own deficit and determined to be more assertive in ensuring the integrity of national programs, including the national health system and post-secondary education.

The provinces, on the other hand, generally favoured maintenance of the *status quo*. The federal deficit, they argued, was due not to federal transfers to the provinces, but rather to federal policies of indexation, tax expenditures, the subsidization of oil and gas prices and interest rate policies. The provinces also noted that the overall provincial revenue surplus was the result of the resource wealth of a few provinces and did not reflect the general provincial fiscal capacity. Thus, provincial leaders rejected the concept of "fiscal imbalance". The Report of the Parliamentary Task Force on Federal-Provincial Fiscal Arrangements agreed, stating that "The mere existence of deficits at one level of government does not indicate the existence of such a structural imbalance nor does it mean that such deficits have to be rectified at the expense of another level of government."[50] The "have not" provinces were especially concerned with the future of the equalization program. The wealthier provinces, for their part, sought to protect the money they received from established programs.

Nonetheless, Ottawa was determined to reduce federal transfers. After four months of inconclusive bargaining, the federal government enacted the new set

[50]*Fiscal Federalism in Canada*, Report of the Parliamentary Task Force on Federal-Provincial Fiscal Arrangements (Ottawa: Supply and Services, August 1981), p. 33.

of fiscal arrangements. According to federal estimates, the provinces will receive $105.54 billion in cash and tax points during the term of the agreement, representing a saving for the federal government over the five years of almost $6 billion, compared to the terms of the previous arrangements.[51]

Changes were made in the calculation of equalization payments. The federal government had proposed Ontario as the standard for determining eligibility for equalization payments, thereby ensuring that province's continued exclusion from receiving such grants. However, the poorer provinces (and Ontario) objected to having their level of receipts contingent upon Ontario's economic performance, especially in light of that province's stagnation in recent years. Ottawa therefore dropped the so-called "Ontario standard", replacing it with a formula based on an average revenue of five provinces. This change is important in that Ontario could become eligible for payments if its economic performance were to decline before the agreement expires in 1987. The federal government also provided special payments to Québec, Manitoba and the Atlantic provinces to ease the transition to the new formula.

While the outcome of the negotiations is relevant, a larger question remains concerning the state of intergovernmental relations demonstrated by these meetings. The postponement of federal consultation with the provinces, as well as the eventual passage of fiscal legislation over provincial opposition, was a departure from the norms of "cooperative federalism". On the other hand, another initiative, the 1981 appointment of a Parliamentary Task Force on Fiscal Arrangements, was innovative and beneficial. This Task Force heard from over 100 groups concerning the effects of federal/provincial fiscal arrangements upon them.[52] Such task forces may play an increasingly important role in facilitating future federal/provincial relations.

REGIONAL CHALLENGES TO FEDERALISM

In recent years, there has been a proliferation of books, articles and editorials expressing alarm at the possible break-up of Canada.[53] In an atmosphere of apprehension a Task Force on National Unity was established in 1977 to examine once again the question of why the Canadian federation was in peril.[54] The smugly confident view that Canada was breaking down old barriers and divisions and progressing toward a unified federal state was replaced by profound anxiety and pessimism. The immediate cause of this crisis of Canadian federalism was the

---

[51]*The Globe and Mail*, March 20, 1982, p. 1.

[52]Sheilagh M. Dunn, *The Year in Review 1981: Intergovernmental Relations in Canada* (Kingston: Queen's University Institute of Intergovernmental Relations, 1982), p. 107.

[53]See R.B. Byers and Robert W. Reford, eds., *Canada Challenged: The Viability of Confederation* (Toronto: Canadian Institute of International Affairs, 1979); Gilles Lalande, *In Defence of Federalism: The View from Quebec*, translated by Jo LaPierre (Toronto: McClelland and Stewart, 1978); and Richard Simeon, ed., *Must Canada Fail?*

[54]See the Report of the Task Force on Canadian Unity, *A Future Together: Observations and Recommendations* (Ottawa: Queen's Printer, 1979).

election of the separatist Parti Québécois to power in Québec in 1976. However, while the rise to power of René Lévesque was certainly disturbing to the federalist cause, it represented only one element of a much larger and more complex problem. In the rest of this chapter, we shall describe and diagnose the challenges to federalism. From the beginning, though it may seem obvious, we wish to emphasize that the institutional arrangement called "federalism" is not necessarily synonymous with "the nation", although for some individuals the terms are interchangeable. The essence of Canada is not federalism but rather a nation-state governed by a federal system.

In the discussion of the concept in Chapter 1, **ethnic nationalism** was defined as the collective action of a politically conscious ethnic group (or "nation") in pursuit of increased territorial autonomy or sovereignty. In a federal system, especially in one as decentralized as Canada, an option for nationalist movements in their quest for self-determination is to gain control of provincial government power. Ethnic nationalist groups in Canada, especially in Québec, have pursued varying degrees of autonomy, up to and including independent statehood. Often, they utilized the mechanisms of federalism to challenge the federal *status quo.* However, since federalism institutionalizes territorial divisions through its political structures, provincial power may also be employed to express regional conflicts which lack an ethnic dimension. In the last two decades provincial government power has been used to press both ethnic nationalist and regionalist demands on Ottawa. The discussions which follow trace the development of these territorially-based conflicts, first with regard to French Canadian and Québécois nationalism; and second, to the expression of regional discontent.

The French/English Dimension

At the time of Confederation, there were approximately 1 200 000 French-speaking and 2 300 000 English-speaking Canadians. It was between about 1840 and 1845 that the French had, for the first time, become a minority. As we noted in Chapter 3, the Roman Catholic Church was a powerful influence in determining the initial strategy for minority survival. After the conquest in 1760 the Church successfully encouraged its flock to remain socially separate from the English in the province, maintaining an essentially agrarian society. French Canadians generally remained aloof from political affairs, and even after Confederation the English minority within Québec dominated urban and political economic life. It was not until much later, in the late 1950s and the 1960s, that change became apparent in the character and aspirations of Québec francophones. French Canadians began to initiate, rather than submit to, the events around them. This "Quiet Revolution" eventually blossomed into an outright challenge to Canadian federalism and the very existence of the Canadian nation state.

French/English relations in the years leading up to this challenge have sometimes been stormy. However, the discord has not been constant; rather, periods of unrest have been interspersed with more-or-less prolonged periods of quiet. The several crises trace the breakdown of good will between the two communities and the growth of the separatist movement. It will be helpful to examine these events before detailing the growth of modern nationalism within Québec. The history is not a particularly proud one for English Canadians.

The ethnic conflicts which periodically erupted had their roots in the linguistic and educational rights of the provinces. Manitoba, with its large French-speaking community, was created in 1870 on the same basis as Québec, with Roman Catholic schools and bilingual education. In the other provinces, the languages to be used locally were left as a matter of solely provincial concern.

By 1885, French-speaking Métis in the West were being swamped by English-speaking settlers. To protest land losses they rallied around the Métis leader Louis Riel, who returned from exile in the United States to lead a rebellion against the government. Eastern Canada viewed his action as treason and sent troops to quell the disturbance. Riel was defeated and executed. French Canadians grieved for Riel as a patriot who died in the struggle to preserve the "Frenchness" of his people. English Canadians saw him as a traitor or a madman. The ethnic groups were thus polarized, and the stage was set for the limitation of French language rights in Manitoba.

Only five years after the Riel rebellion, the government of Manitoba established a completely non-sectarian educational system in which Roman Catholic schools no longer received provincial aid. The situation posed a unique problem for French Canadians inasmuch as it divided them over whether to support their ethnic group or their church. To have the legislation removed they had to support federal disallowance of provincial leglislation, and French Québec was against the principle of federal veto power. An election ensued in which the French Canadians of Manitoba stood by the Roman Catholic Church and the Conservative party demanded federal disallowance. Québec francophones supported the Liberal Party, which demanded provincial autonomy and opposed the federal use of the disallowance power. The Liberals won. Québec francophones thus prevented legislation which would have protected French Canadian interests in Manitoba.

The language division appeared in another guise in the conscription crises of both the First and Second World Wars. French Canadians were strongly opposed to conscription. André Bernard in his book *What Does Québec Want?*[55] maintains that one of the main reasons behind this opposition was the fact that the recruiting officers and the military hierarchy were English-speaking. The 1917 federal election on the conscription issue divided the country along linguistic lines: every riding in which French was the majority language voted against the government and conscription. Fortunately, the war ended before conscription could be enacted, and the issue died. The legacy of bitterness remained, however, and its residue in federal politics and parties has not yet been fully erased. In the federal election campaign which followed the conscription bill, the pro-conscription Conservatives and English Liberals united to run Union candidates. They won the election, but captured only three seats in Québec. In the first post-war election in 1921, the Liberals formed the government, this time winning all

---

[55]André Bernard, *What Does Quebec Want?* (Toronto: James Lorimer, 1978).

the Québec seats. Provincially as well as federally, the Conservatives were decimated and, except for the Diefenbaker sweep in 1958 and the Mulroney landslide in 1984, the party never regained the confidence of French Canadians. In the 1979 election, for example, the Conservatives formed the new federal government but won only two seats in the province of Québec.

In 1942, during World War II, there was a second conscription crisis which closely resembled the first. This time the government held a plebiscite, an expression of opinion by the voters which was not legally binding. The campaign was bitter.[56] French-speaking Québec voted by a huge majority of 85 percent against conscription, while English-speaking Canada was overwhelmingly in favour. Liberal Prime Minister Mackenzie King employed delaying tactics in an attempt to avoid, or at least postpone, the imposition of conscription in order to allay the fears of French Canadians. This served to minimize the crisis since the war ended before the conscripts were sent into battle. However, the apparent impotence of the French in face of the English majority decision remained as a humiliating residue of the affair.

The Confederation arrangement allowed Québec to legislate in the field of education and gave constitutional protection to the French language community in that province. English was also a legal language in the Québec legislature and courts. In the other provinces, however, the practice until the 1940s was for English-speaking Canadians, wherever they were in the majority, to deprive French-speaking minorities of public school facilities in their native language, and to refuse them the use of their language in government institutions. Even within the federal government, where the *BNA Act* had stated the right of both groups to function in debates, records, journals and courts in their own language, government employees were largely unilingually English.

French Canadian nationalist and historian Abbé Lionel Groulx in 1935 published the following summary of French language and school rights (or lack of rights) outside Québec.

1864 NOVA SCOTIA: French-speaking Catholic Acadians are forbidden to have French schools.

1871 NEW BRUNSWICK: Catholic schools are closed and teaching of French (and in French) is forbidden in public schools.

1877 PRINCE EDWARD ISLAND: Catholic and French schools become outlawed.

1890 MANITOBA: Separate (Catholic) schools are outlawed and teaching of French (and in French) is forbidden at the secondary level.

1892 NORTHWEST TERRITORIES (including what is now Alberta and Saskatchewan): Teaching in French is outlawed in public schools and Catholic schools are prohibited.

---

[56]See Richard Théoret, "The Uses of the Referendum in Canada," in D.C. Rowat, ed., *The Referendum and Separation Elsewhere: Implications for Quebec* (Ottawa: Carleton University, 1978), pp. 19-34.

1905 ALBERTA AND SASKATCHEWAN: The regulations of 1892 (Northwest Territories) are confirmed.

1915 ONTARIO: By regulation (regulation No. 17), French is outlawed in Ontario schools.

1916 MANITOBA: Teaching of French is forbidden at all levels.

1930 SASKATCHEWAN: Teaching of French is prohibited even outside school hours.[57]

Abbé Groulx argued that each of these rulings deprived French Canadians of what they considered to be their basic human rights. This succession of ethnic crises formed the history of the loss of French rights outside of Québec. The result was abandonment by the Québécois of French Canadians outside their province, and the gradual assertion of Québec nationalism.

NATIONALISM IN QUÉBEC

Québec nationalism in some form has been present since the British took Québec in 1760. Over the following century, it took the form of resistance to assimilation by the English; what mattered was *survivance*. As a conquered people, the French did not become integrated with their victors, but formed an isolated and basically rural society, for the most part living in small parish units where economic activity centred on the family farm. The French elite, especially the clergy, maintained control over the masses through the Church, the educational system and the continuation of the French language. It can thus be said that in general the English dominated politics and commerce, while the French elites controlled the cultural institutions.

After Confederation, two strains of nationalism developed in *"La Belle Province"*.[58] The first, depicted by the historian Abbé Lionel Groulx, was based on earlier French Canadian history. It called for a rural vision of Catholic, anti-materialist values, and on occasion resulted in proposals for an inward-looking, corporatist and authoritarian solution to the Québec situation. The second, led by Henri Bourassa, politician and editor of *Le Devoir*, called for a pan-Canadian vision and an equal partnership between English and French Canada. For Bourassa, the Canadian dilemma was to be resolved by building a state which was both bicultural and bilingual.

The inward-looking strain was characterized by the Union Nationale governments of Maurice Duplessis, 1936-39 and 1944-1960. A rurally-based party, the Union Nationale founded its philosophy on the older-style nationalism and

---

[57]Bernard, *op. cit.*, p. 27, taken from Abbé Lionel Groulx, *L'Enseignement Français au Canada* (Montréal: Granger Frères, 1935).

[58]See Léon Dion, *Quebec: The Unfinished Revolution* (Montréal: McGill-Queen's University Press, 1976); Herbert Guindon, "The Modernization of Quebec and the Legitimacy of the Canadian State," in D. Glenday, *et. al.*, *Modernization and the Canadian State* (Toronto: Macmillan of Canada, 1978), pp. 212-246; Denis Moniere, *Le Développement des idéologies au Quebec: des origines a nos jours* (Montréal: Editions Québec/Amérique, 1977); Marcel Rioux, *Quebec in Question* (Toronto: James, Lewis and Samuel, 1971).

its action on patronage and intimidation. The modern period of Québec nationalism is often dated from the 1949 Asbestos Strike. The strike of 5000 workers lasted four months and consisted of an alliance between the American-owned asbestos company and the Duplessis government against the workers, who were supported to a large extent by Québec's developing intelligentsia. The 1950s in Québec were characterized by widespread reaction to both clerical influence and Duplessis manipulation. Industrialization and urbanization helped erode the bases of Union Nationale support, and values in the province changed rapidly from rural to urban, from religious to secular.

The outward-looking strain was typified by the Québec Liberal Party, which Jean Lesage led to victory in 1960 after 16 years of opposition. In the subsequent period of "Quiet Revolution", Lesage's government reversed the guiding philosophy of previous governments in Québec. Drastically increasing the role of government in society, the Liberal government secularized the school system, nationalized hydro-electricity in the province and reformed the civil service. Led by a new middle class, French Canadian nationalism gave way to Québec nationalism. Technological and economic changes had already altered the educational and social structure of the province; now a new administrative elite managed the state machinery of education, welfare and medicare.[59]

Nationalists were struck by the fact that French usage was on the decline in Canada and that Québec's share of the Canadian population was dropping. The *"épanouissement"* or flowering of Québec-based nationalism was encapsulated in the 1960 political phrase *"maîtres chez nous"* (masters in our own house).

Québec's challenges to Canada came in many guises – judicial, social and political. Objections ranged from precise attacks on centralizing mechanisms such as the power of disallowance to general claims that the *BNA Act* did not define a true federal system. On the latter subject, Marcel Faribault stated, "Our present Constitution is at variance with a genuine conception of federalism, which alone can keep Canada united."[60] And Claude Ryan, later leader of the Liberal Party of Québec, argued when he was a journalist that "It is the document [the *BNA Act*] as a whole, the general ideas underlying the text, that must be revised."[61]

The division of powers between the federal and provincial governments was also claimed to discriminate against Québec. Marcel Chaput summarized the situation in *Why I Am A Separatist*: "The Federal government has exclusive legislative authority in the main fields of administration. . . ."[62] The grievance was expressed in more detail by André Allemagne in *Le Colonialisme au Québec*: "By virtue of the BNA Act, which serves as Canada's constitution, the Ottawa government retains powers of which the Québec government is deprived within its own territory. These powers are enormous. They give the federal state supremacy in

---

[59]See Kenneth McRoberts and Dale Posgate, *Quebec: Social Change and Political Crisis*, revised edition (Toronto: McClelland and Stewart, 1980) for a discussion of this period and the impact of economic development on Québec nationalism.

[60]*Le Devoir*, June 30, 1967.

[61]*Le Devoir*, June 30, 1967.

[62]Cited in Lalande, *op. cit.*, p. 63.

economic matters and allow it considerable scope for intervention in socio-cultural affairs.''[63]

Some Québec francophones saw the federal union as lacking the free consent of the contracting parties – in other words, self-determination. The following serve as a sample of representative opinions: "No referendum enabled the people to express their will in 1867." (Raymond Barbeau).[64] "This system [confederation] . . . was not established by the express will of the people affected, but imposed by statute by an imperialist mother country." (Le Ralliement pour l'Indépendence Nationale).[65] "Once Confederation had been voted by the House and approved by London, in complete disregard of popular opinion, Québec, which thirty years earlier, under the influence of the Patriots, had dreamed of becoming a republic, was *de facto* turned . . . into a minority. . . ." (Pierre Vallières).[66] "The Canadian state is a purely political and artificial entity formed originally by armed forces and maintained by a submission of the French-Canadian to the Federal Government."(Marcel Chaput).[67]

These viewpoints were underpinned by real economic injustices. Kenneth McRoberts and Dale Posgate, in their volume on Québec, showed that the province's economy was characterized by a predominance of non-French capital and ownership in large corporations. According to their data, only 26 of 165 enterprises with an annual production worth $10 million were owned by French Canadians. The export-oriented, resource-based corporations tended to be under American and multinational control. Modern light industry (such as electronics) tended to be owned by Anglo-Canadians. As McRoberts and Posgate demonstrated, French Canadians predominated in the ownership of labour intensive, lower productivity industries such as textiles, leather products and food processing. Finally, the financial institutions were predominantly controlled by Anglo-Canadians.[68]

At the individual level as well, Quebeckers have fared worse than many other Canadians. In *What Does Quebec Want?*, André Bernard found that since 1926 the gap between Québecois and Canadian *per capita* incomes has oscillated around an average of 15 percentage points lower for the former. The rate of unemployment in the province was regularly over 25% above the Canadian average, and Québec rates for standard taxes were 10% to 15% above the Canadian average.[69] Sceptics, however, will discover in Bernard's book more arguments about why Quebeckers deserve independence than evidence that they will choose it ahead of other options.

The 1958 Report of the Québec Royal Commission of Inquiry on Constitutional Problems (The Tremblay Report) summed up Québec's cultural and economic situation: "Because of the religion, culture and history of the majority of

---

[63]Cited in *ibid.*, p. 63.

[64]Raymond Barbeau, *J'ai choisi l'indépendance*, cited in *ibid.*, p. 67.

[65]RIN, *L'Action nationale*, February 1961, cited in *ibid.*, p. 67.

[66]Pierre Vallières, *White Niggers of America*, cited in *ibid.*, p. 71.

[67]Marcel Chaput, *Why I am a Separatist*, cited in *ibid.*, p. 76.

[68]McRoberts and Posgate, *op. cit.*, p. 4 and *passim*.

[69]Bernard, *What Does Quebec Want?* p. 48.

its population, the Province of Québec is not a province like the others. . . . The 1867 Constitution made the Province of Québec, which was already historically its national focus, the French-Canadian centre *par excellence*, and the accredited guardian of French-Canadian civilization."[70]

Québec increased its political pressure on the federal government throughout the 1960s. For the first time, an ethnic crisis seriously threatened the unity of the country. The phrase *maîtres chez nous* became a serious option for some French Canadians, who adopted separatism for Québec as their goal, maintaining that only with their own government could they preserve their culture and fulfill the aspirations of their community. Their slogan "Vive le Québec libre" drew international support from French President Charles de Gaulle. Opposition focused on the use of English in Québec in Crown corporations, banks and the federal public service.

The Front de la Libération du Québec (FLQ), representing the most extreme separatists, initiated terrorist activities which culminated in the October Crisis of 1970, with the kidnapping of a British diplomat and the murder of the Québec Minister of Labour, Pierre Laporte, and a direct confrontation with the federal government. The *War Measures Act* was proclaimed to deal with what Prime Minister Trudeau considered to be an acute emergency; in legal terms, it was an "apprehended insurrection". It was the first and only time that the statute had been invoked in peace-time. The basic freedoms of Canadians, mostly French-speaking, were infringed, and hundreds of Québécois were arrested. When the atmosphere of crisis faded, its residue was uncertainty among many Canadians that the crisis had been of sufficient proportion to necessitate such large-scale repression.[71] Prime Minister Trudeau labelled critics of the *War Measures Act* "bleeding hearts".

As Québec nationalism grew in the 1960s and 1970s, Québécois intellectuals became divided. Pierre Elliott Trudeau and his friends Jean Marchand and Gérard Pelletier moved into federal politics, where they offered a policy based on a bicultural and a bilingual state, but with no special status for the province "pas comme les autres". As Prime Minister of Canada, Trudeau became the major spokesman for Henri Bourassa-style nationalism and a unified state. According to Trudeau, the Parti Québécois simply replaced the traditional Québec clericalism with the "clericalism of nationalism".[72]

---

[70]See David Kwavnick, ed., *the Tremblay Report, The Report of the Royal Commission of Inquiry on Constitutional Problems*, The Carleton Library No. 64. (Toronto: McClelland and Stewart, 1973), p. 45.

[71]See Denis Smith, *Bleeding Hearts . . . Bleeding Country: Canada and the Quebec Crisis* (Edmonton: Hurtig, 1971).

[72]For Trudeau's position see Pierre Elliott Trudeau, *Federalism and the French Canadians* (Toronto: Macmillan of Canada, 1968), pp. 207-209. For an overview of the challenge and response see Robert J. Jackson and Abbie Dann, "Quebec Foreign Policy? Canada and Ethno-Regionalism." in Werner Link and Werner J. Feld, eds., *The New Nationalism* (New York: Pergamon, 1979), pp. 89-106 and Robert J. Jackson, "Federal Government Strategy and Response To the Victory of the Parti Québécois," in *La Vie Politique au Canada, Etudes Canadiennes*, Numero Spécial, 1979, pp. 103-119.

Meanwhile, in Québec the separatist challenge grew. In the 1966 provincial election the Ralliement National (RN) and Le Ralliement pour l'Indépendence Nationale (RIN) gained 10% of the vote. Former provincial Cabinet minister René Lévesque left the Liberal party in 1968 and formed the Parti Québécois. This new party brought together the left-wing RIN, the right-wing RN and other nationalists under a new umbrella organization.

Such nationalist organizations with aspirations for provincial independence were not new in Québec history. The first, the Parti Patriote of the first half of the 19th century, was elected to office with a large majority under its very popular leader Louis-Joseph Papineau. In an attempt to win parliamentary control over government expenditures and other concessions the party instigated an armed rebellion in 1836-37. It was quelled by the troops of the British governor. The second, the Parti Nationale led by Henri Mercier, was elected in 1886. It was defeated in 1892 because of financial problems, corruption and lack of support for constitutional change. Then in 1936 the Union Nationale, led by Maurice Duplessis, came into office as the third successful nationalist party. It played the nationalist game within the context of Canadian rules. Gradually, however, the more progressive element split off because the party promoted nationalism, not wholesale independence.

In the 1970 election, the Parti Québécois received only 24% of the popular vote, and Liberal leader Robert Bourassa formed the government. The October Crisis intervened between this election and that of 1973. Playing on the fear of separatism and on his success with the James Bay Hydro development, Bourassa won another landslide victory despite an increase in PQ votes to 30%.

In the face of these defeats the Parti Québécois softened its stand from political independence to sovereignty-association, political sovereignty with economic association. The party did not, however, give up its vision of a Québec in which no tax would be paid to the federal government and no citizen would be subject to federal law. In the 1976 election, Lévesque ran on a platform of "good government" and offered a referendum on sovereignty-associaiton. This approach worked.[73] Forty-one percent of Québec voters cast their ballots for the Parti Québécois on November 15, 1976, and so the PQ became the fourth nationalist party to gain control of the government in Québec.

While the new government proved to be moderate in fiscal and monetary policies, it managed to nationalize the Asbestos Corporation and frighten the business community. The election of the Parti Québécois also escalated the tension in French/English relations within the province. Bill 101, the Charter of the French language in Québec, was introduced in the Québec legislature in April 1977, declaring the intention to make the province unilingual. The May 1980 referendum on sovereignty-association proved a setback for Lévesque, however. The PQ initiated a vote which forced Québec residents to choose between *"oui"*

---

[73]For a summary see John Saywell, *The Rise of the Parti Québécois* (Toronto: University of Toronto Press, 1977) and Vera Murray, *Le Parti Québécois* (Montréal: Editions Hurtubise HMH, Ltée., 1976). For the official position, see Government of Québec, *Québec-Canada: A New Deal* (Québec: Editeur Officiel, 1979).

– to negotiate sovereignty-association, and *"non"* – not to negotiate. On even this mild resolution the government proposal was defeated by almost six out of ten votes. The *"non"* forces captured the majority in Québec with their slogan *"Je suis fier d'être Québécois et Canadien."*

The threat of independence did not die with this vote. Lévesque knew that his support came overwhelmingly from voters under age 35 and that he could afford to wait. In the 1981 election the Parti Québécois promised *not* to call a referendum before another election and received 47% of the vote and 80 of 122 seats in the National Assembly. The challenge was to continue. After all, according to PQ strategists, Québec had all the ingredients necessary to form an independent state: both people and resources. If Québec had been independent in the 1970s, it would have had a geographical territory greater than 90% of the states already members of the United Nations and a population in the top one-third of UN member states.

The Centre/Periphery Dimension

If the greatest challenge to federalism in the 1970s was Québec separatism, the next greatest was undoubtedly decentralization in some of the regions. Newly acquired economic power in several provinces has drastically altered the regional distribution of power in Canada in the past two decades.

Large reserves of coal, oil and gas exist west of Manitoba; in addition, Saskatchewan possesses half the country's reserves of uranium. The scarcity and higher cost of non-renewable energy in the form of oil and gas spurred western economic development. Once among the weak partners of the federal union, the West began to acquire enormous economic power through its sale of natural resources. As this economic wealth was exploited, migration to the West increased. Since the end of World War II, Alberta and British Columbia, for example, have doubled their populations. The West finally found itself capable of challenging what it considered the insufferable domination of central Canada. As we pointed out in Chapter 3, a central component of Western Canada's political culture is alienation.[74] Throughout the West's history there has been a strong belief that the resource-rich prairie provinces were exploited by federal government policies which represented central Canadian interests. Perennial issues of contention centre on federal freight-rate and tariff policies, which are held responsible for making the West a captive market for higher-priced manufactured goods from central Canada. These policies concomitantly increase the cost of exporting

---

[74]David Elton and Roger Gibbins, "Western Alienation and Political Culture," in Richard Schultz, *et al.*, eds., *The Canadian Political Process*, third edition (Toronto: Holt, Rinehart and Winston, 1979), p. 85. On the concept of "western alienation" see Roger Gibbins, "Western Alienation and the Alberta Political Culture," in Carlo Caldarola, ed., *Society and Politics in Alberta* (Toronto: Methuen, 1979), pp. 143-167; Robert R. Gilsdorf, "Western Alienation, Political Alienation and the Federal System," in Calderola, ed., *op. cit.*, pp. 168-192; and Larry Pratt and Garth Stevenson, eds., *Western Separatism* (Edmonton: Hurtig, 1981).

products from the West. Thus it is argued that such policies have allowed the East to remain the industrial heartland of Canada while the West has carried a disproportion of the costs.[75]

Current economic issues dividing western and central Canada have continued to be interpreted within this context of alienation. In the 1970s regional criticism of the political and economic dominance of central Canada was expressed in a desire for constitutional reform. During the 1975-81 disputes, the Western provincial governments refused to compromise over patriation of the Constitution unless the federal government would reduce its power, especially on economic issues. In other words, the jurisdictional issue of whether the provinces or the federal government should control resource development flowed over into the constitutional arena.

Conflicts over Western natural resources are essentially about public finances. Garth Stevenson describes the situation clearly: "Provincial efforts to collect larger 'royalties' from their minerals in the early seventies were viewed by the federal government as surreptitious efforts to violate the arrangements for sharing tax revenue from corporations, while federal efforts to keep the price of oil below international levels are resented by Alberta and Saskatchewan as depriving them of revenue that would otherwise be available from their provincial treasuries."[76] The western provinces seek to secure not only a measure of financial independence from the federal government, but also to use the wealth generated from the development of their natural resources to diversify their economies so that, when the non-renewable resources are depleted, economic prosperity will continue. The federal government, on the other hand, is concerned about its own fiscal needs, as well as about ensuring an equitable sharing of Western resource wealth throughout Canada. Many Westerners perceive the redistribution of this wealth as an attempt to keep the West in a position of permanent subordination.

The most recent public expression of Western alienation was the formation in the early 1980s of various groups and political parties dedicated to the separation of the western provinces (Manitoba, Saskatchewan, Alberta, British Columbia, and possibly the Northwest Territories and Yukon) from Canada. The rise of Western separatism was ignited by the re-election of the federal Liberal party to government in 1980, an event which resulted in the political disenfranchisement of Western Canada, since the Liberals captured no seats west of Manitoba. Subsequently, the Liberal government initiated two aggressive federal policies: unilateral patriation of the Constitution despite provincial objections; and implementation of the National Energy Program, which many Westerners perceived as an attempt to rob them of their resource wealth.

---

[75]For an alternative view, See Kenneth H. Norrie, "Some Comments on Prairie Economic Alienation," *Canadian Public Policy*, vol. 2, no. 2 (Spring 1976), pp. 211-224.

[76]Garth Stevenson, "Federalism and Intergovernmental Relations," in M.S. Whittington and G. Williams, eds., *Canadian Politics in the 1980s*, second edition (Toronto: Methuen, 1984), p. 381.

The two leading separatist groups were the Western Canadian Federation (West-Fed) and the Western Canada Concept (WCC). Frustrated by a lack of political power within the federal government, Westerners felt powerless against "centralist" policies, including bilingualism, metrication and immigration. One author summarized the separatist rationale as follows: "Without political power, this line of reasoning seems to go, there is nothing that can protect the [resource] wealth that exists. The national government can, if it so wishes, drain the West of its wealth and leave it both economically and politically impoverished within a few years."[77] Therefore, separatist leaders argued, separation was the only solution.

Separatist meetings attracted hundreds of supporters (mostly in rural Alberta), climaxing with a November 1980 Jubilee Auditorium rally where 2700 gathered in Edmonton. Yet the popularity of Western separatism dissipated as quickly as it had risen. As one observer noted: "The spontaneity of the separatist movement was both the most important reason for its success and its greatest handicap in developing into a solid, permanent politician movement."[78] While the movement provided an outlet for the expression of frustration, there was little agreement among the groups, let alone within them, concerning what strategy to follow. "Western separatism" provided an effective rallying cry, but masked the differing degrees of commitment to separatism within the movement. For example, the founder of West-Fed saw his group as an interest group composed of members from all parties, while the leader of the WCC sought to build a unique separatist party. Infighting within the WCC as well as between West-Fed and WCC exposed long-term political and organizational differences, as well as the inability to mobilize Western frustration.[79]

Nevertheless, the separatists did win a stunning victory in an Alberta provincial by-election when a WCC candidate was elected to represent the rural riding of Olds-Didsbury. He received 42 percent of the vote, with the Social Credit and Progressive Conservative candidates gathering 28 and 25 percent respectively. Success, however, was short-lived; he was defeated nine months later in a General Election.[80] Although the WCC polled 10 percent of the total vote province-wide in this election, it received no seats. Their one sitting MLA had alienated separatists by his moderate stand on separatism, preferring to stress "free enterprise" and "good government." In a reflection of the fractious nature of separatist supporters, he was challenged by other separatist candidates. Similar internal dissension plagued the founder of the WCC in British Columbia. He was expelled from Alberta's WCC by the party's executive committee because of differences about the form of regime an independent West should adopt.

---

[77]Doug Owram, "Reluctant Hinterland," in Pratt and Stevenson, eds., *Western Separatism*, p. 61.

[78]Denise Harrington, "Who are the Separatists?," in Pratt and Stevenson, eds., *Western Separatism*, p. 24.

[79]*Ibid.*, p. 31.

[80]The candidate switched ridings, contesting a seat outside Calgary.

Still, to dismiss Western separatism out of hand may be premature. The rapid slide into obscurity of West-Fed and the WCC does not necessarily signal the end of Western grievances and alienation. Many Westerners, wealthy and independent of hand-outs from Ottawa, feel that they put more into the federation than they receive in benefits. If Ottawa is not able to accommodate the ambition of Western Canadians, the potential for continued separatist challenge in the West remains – perhaps awaiting only a very unpopular federal government decision.

OVERVIEW

This chapter has explored the meaning of federalism in Canada. Rather than being an obscure or esoteric phenomenon, federalism is one of the basic structures shaping the issues and controversies of contemporary Canadian politics. We began with a general definition of federalism and examined some of the motives and justifications offered for the adoption of the federal form. As we stressed, there is nothing intrinsically good or bad about this arrangement. At a minimum, federalism is simply a means of dividing authority. In practice, however, federalism can assume a number of other meanings and implications which may lead one to believe that the phenomenon is synonymous with "the nation".

The institutional mechanism of federalism is a reflection of societal diversity, and it has provided a framework for the interplay of economic and political forces in Canada. A careful review of the history of federalism in Canada reveals pendulum swings of centralization and decentralization. The history of federal/provincial fiscal relations, for example, has been characterized by the waxing and waning of federal dominance. These shifts have been due to interpretations of the *BNA Act* as well as to the impact of particular individuals and historical events, such as the depression and the Second World War.

The best known Father of Confederation, Sir John A. Macdonald, thought of federalism as a means of subordinating provincial governments in the national system. His has been called a "quasi-federalist" position. At certain times in Canadian history, federalism has been interpreted as an agreement or "compact" between the English and French. At other periods, it has been described as a clear-cut or "classical" division of powers between the federal and provincial governments.[81] Over time, the original financial and legislative powers have had to change with the realities of Canadian life. Adjustments to economic reality and societal concerns forced the constitutional system to adapt from a strict separation of financial powers to a period of "cooperation". In this period, the federal government dominated in the financial aspects of government, but the provinces were consulted and agreed to cooperative arrangements. In recent

---

[81]See Edwin R. Black, *Divided Loyalties; Canadian Concepts of Federalism* (Montréal: McGill-Queen's University Press, 1975) and J.R. Mallory, *The Structure of Canadian Government* (Toronto: Macmillan of Canada, 1971), pp. 325-369.

years, some authors have characterized the system as one of federal/provincial "diplomacy" rather than "cooperation" to indicate how the process evolved and how much the provinces are asserting their power in the state. The First Ministers Conference, which has brought together the Prime Minister of Canada and the ten premiers at least once a year since 1963, is the most public manifestation of this form of federalism. By the end of the 1970s, two conferences per year occurred on average, and an Ottawa Conference Centre had been set up as a permanent meeting place with a substantial secretariat. Also inseparable from all modern concepts of federalism have been the proliferation of ministerial conferences, interprovincial coordinating meetings and the development of entire departments devoted to federal/provincial relations.

The five models of federalism (quasi-federalism, compact, classical, cooperative, diplomatic) help explain various aspects of federal/provincial relations. While they are often put forward as if they refer to the evolution of federalism, they more adequately depict which relationships between the federal and provincial governments predominate at any one time. Moreover, there are many other ways to define federalism.

In order to understand Canadian federalism we must also bear in mind how it is buttressed by social and political forces. The federal dimension provides both advantages and disadvantages to Canada. It decentralizes some decision-making and allows a degree of cultural and linguistic autonomy. Its disadvantages show up when too much weight is given to either the federal or the provincial governments. In the former case there can easily be an erosion of prerogatives, as when the federal government is required to aid the provinces in new, but essentially localized, matters such as pollution regulations, environmental protection, consumer rights and so on. Too much provincial control makes it difficult to handle nation-wide problems: unless the federal government makes inroads into provincial activities, it cannot disseminate national standards and values.

Despite a few difficult periods, federalism in Canada has proven remarkably resilient and adaptable. A degree of movement along the centralization/decentralization continuum is to be expected and is not in itself a matter for much concern. However, Québec and, to some extent, the western provinces continue for quite different reasons to seek changes in the present relationship. The possibility that provinces or regions of Canada may eventually break away from the federal union is not to be totally discounted. The problem, as we have suggested, is not so much with federalism as it is with the deep cleavages and divisions in our society. There is nothing very new in regional pressures. Such challenges go back a long way in Canadian history. Economic historian Harold Innis commented shortly after the Second World War:

> "The hatreds between regions in Canada have become important vested interests. Montreal exploits the hatred of Toronto and Regina and that of Winnipeg and so one might go through the list. A native of Ontario may appear restive at being charged with exploitation by those who

systematically exploit him with their charges of exploitation, but even the right to complain is denied him."[82]

In the search for a creative compromise, politicians will have to enunciate and examine Canada's fundamental problems. The redefinition of federal arrangements will rest between national and provincial aspirations. Reconciliation must be built on a recognition that Canada has two linguistic groups and several cultures which are often in conflict, as well as heterogeneous socio-economic regions. The first fact demands constitutional and institutional guarantees; the second, a proper division of the public purse and power. While provincial distinctiveness is the fundamental reason for all federal systems, a sense of positive consensus among the different regional groups is also imperative.

---

[82]Harold A. Innis, *Political Economy in the Modern State* (Toronto: Ryerson, 1946), p. xi.

chapter 7

The Inner Circle
Policy-Making at the Centre

OUR INTENT IN THIS CHAPTER is to describe and explain the nature of executive power in Canada and to shed light on how government policy is established. In one respect, executive power is comparable to a Shakespearean drama: there is a world of difference in both between appearance and reality.

The nature of political power and its exercise are exceedingly complex and fascinating phenomena. The analysis of leaders and their policies has always been one of the favourite pursuits of political scientists and pundits, regardless of country or type of political system. Perennial debates and studies consider who really exercises power, what the machinery of leadership is and whether power is shifting in some fashion. A factor complicating the analysis is that political power is an abstract commodity, changing in response to the dynamic political and social environment in which a variety of issues, problems and personalities come and go. It is difficult to isolate power analytically from social influence. Political power is, in a manner of speaking, like a complex mathematical equation in which there are a few constant values and many indeterminate ones.

In nation-states the task of applying and interpreting the rules of society is concentrated in an **executive**. This broad term is used to depict the institutions, personnel, and behaviour of governmental power. Generally, there are two kinds of rules in a society – constitutional laws or the basic rules of the game, and the less fundamental laws, policies and resolutions. Both types of rules are implemented by the executive, which, in performing this function, plays a vital role in the political system.

In this chapter, we shall place emphasis on the political executive and the realities of power in contemporary Canadian politics. Canada's constitutional heritage from Britain has bequeathed a formal executive, the Governor General, discussed in Chapter 5. Here we shall begin by examining the heritage of parliamentary government and its effects on executive power in Canada. Next, we shall outline the role of the Prime Minister and the structure of Cabinet decision-making. The policy-making relations between the budget and expenditures will be analysed, followed by the increasing number of government ministries and agencies, which offer executive support through specialized research and advice and provide assistance in policy formation and implementation. We shall conclude the chapter by evaluating the ongoing debate about the expanding role of the Prime Minister and its implications for Canadian politics.

The reader should be conscious of how much easier it is to describe the machinery of government and what it can accomplish than it is to assess the nature of political power itself. One should also be aware that much important information about the *modus operandi* of the executive is shrouded in mystery. Important parliamentary traditions, as well as such legal devices as the *Official Secrets Act* have, for the most part, shielded the executive from penetrating scrutiny by the press or the public. Canada has never experienced anything quite like the Crossman Diaries affair, in which the inner workings of the British Cabinet in the late 1960s were laid bare through the posthumous publication of the daily journal of a high-ranking Cabinet minister. Nevertheless, despite certain obvious gaps in understanding, a reasonable amount is known or can safely be surmised about the executive and the determination of policy in Canada.

WHAT IS THE CANADIAN EXECUTIVE?

Apart from the ceremonial functions of government discussed in Chapter 5, the main task of the executive is providing leadership. The determination of which bodies constitute government is complex, as there is no accepted view about how it should be organized.[1] As a result, executive leadership may refer to formal roles, to individuals, to types of activities or to the results of such activities. The executive leaders discussed here have been selected on the basis of their formal roles. They include the Prime Minister, the Cabinet and the immediate staff of these individuals.

In modern times, executives have become the organizational centre of the political system.[2] The traditional areas of executive action, such as foreign policy and defence, have been augmented by the growing role of governments in managing the economy and social policy. These newer functions have added immensely to the complexity of the policy process, increased the size of bureaucracies and made it difficult to coordinate government activities.

The central feature of any survey of Canada's political heritage must be the pervasive impact of the British model of parliamentary government. Though other aspects of Canadian life have been strongly influenced by the United States, the parliamentary form of government is firmly entrenched and has pro-

---

[1]See Jean Blondel, *The Organization of Governments* (London: Sage, 1982).

[2]Richard Rose and Ezra N. Suleiman, eds., *Presidents and Prime Ministers* (Washington: A.E.I., 1980).

ven remarkably resistant to change.[3] As discussed in Chaperts 5 and 6, the 1867 *British North America Act* established a type of government based on the British example, with the exception that there was to be a federal division of legislative powers in recognition of the diversity of the country. Canada was to be governed by a parliamentary system with British historical traditions and procedures, and by a constitutional monarch represented by an appointed Governor General. Although the Governor General is the country's formal executive, his or her powers and prerogatives are in fact severely limited.[4] Only in extraordinary situations has a Governor General attempted to interfere directly in the political process. It is clear that executive power, though carried out in the name of the Governor General, resides elsewhere in the political structure.

The provisions of the *BNA Act* also established the Queen's Privy Council for Canada. This body was created to assist and advise the Governor General, in the performance of duties. The members of this largely ceremonial body are appointed for life and include most current and former Ministers of the Crown, as well as a few other politically prominent individuals.[5] In reality, a committee of the Privy Council known as the Cabinet and comprised of current Ministers of the Crown constitutes the real executive power in Canada.[6]

The term "Governor-in-Council" refers to the formal executive authority of the Governor General carried out upon the advice and consultation of this committee of the Privy Council. The decisions rendered by the Cabinet on specific matters carrying legal force are referred to as *orders-in-council*. Technically speaking, any Cabinet directive is an agreement arrived at in Council with the Governor General absent. However, the Governor General is obliged by convention to grant approval to virtually any Cabinet decision or legislative bill. While Canada does have a monarchical form of government embodied in the Governor General and certain legal procedures, there is no doubt that real executive power belongs to the Cabinet. Its authority, in turn, comes from maintaining at least a plurality of supporters in the House of Commons.

The foregoing passage has described the largely ceremonial role of the formal executive in the parliamentary system. There are other, more significant, features of this form of government which to some extent impinge upon the operations and powers of the political executive in Canada. Perhaps most significant is the fact that, as in the British parliamentary system, the executive and legislative powers are combined. The Canadian people vote for the 282 Members of the House of Commons, and the Prime Minister and Cabinet emerge

---

[3]Leon D. Epstein, "The Comparative Study of Canadian Parties," in O. Kruhlak, *et al.*, eds., *The Canadian Political Process: A Reader*, revised edition (Toronto: Holt, Rinehart and Winston, 1973), p. 335.

[4]For a thorough discussion of the formal executive in Canada see J.R. Mallory, *The Structure of Canadian Government* (Toronto: Macmillan, 1971), pp. 32-68.

[5]For example, all provincial premiers were made Privy Councillors in 1967 to celebrate Canada's Centennial.

[6]See R. MacGregor Dawson, "The Cabinet – Position and Personnel." *Canadian Journal of Economics and Political Science*, vol. 12, no. 3 (August 1946), pp. 261-281.

from this body of representatives. Earlier in Canadian history, during the 1890s, Sir John Abbott and Sir Mackenzie Bowell were in the Senate at the time of their appointment as Prime Minister, but convention now demands that the Prime Minister be elected to the House of Commons either before or shortly after investiture.

The Prime Minister and the personally selected Cabinet constitute the government; they formulate policy and direct administrative operations as long as they are supported by Parliament. When they no longer receive such support they are replaced, or Parliament is dissolved and elections are called. The crucial point is that both the Prime Minister and the Cabinet ministers are simultaneously members of the legislature and the executive. In contrast is the American Presidential form of government, wherein there is a clear separation of executive and legislative powers. The Presidential/Congressional system of checks and balances creates an atmosphere of public political bargaining not found in Canada. For example, in the United States the executive must rely on congress to authorize funds to implement policy, and the Senate must ratify presidential appointments to Cabinet, the diplomatic service, federal courts and other boards and commissions.

Also in contrast to the Canadian Constitution, the American chief executive is elected independently by the people at large, and his tenure in office is in no

In Canada:

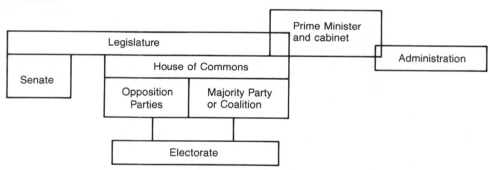

In the United States:

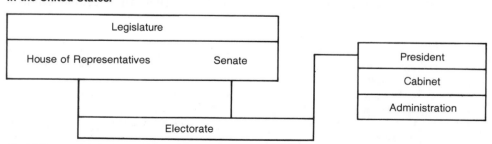

FIGURE 7.1   Legislative-Executive Relations in the Canadian Parliamentary System and in the American Presidential System

way dependent on the fate of his legislative program. The executive can frustrate Congress because, for instance, Congress is dependent on the President to implement its policies, and the executive often controls the information needed to formulate effective policies in Congress. On the other hand, the American legislature can and often does reject executive proposals, an exceedingly rare event in Canada, where such rejection could cause the government to fall and a new election to take place.

Both houses of the American Congress share fully in legislative activity, and there is often rivalry between them. Unlike their Canadian counterparts, national parties in the United States have little power as organizations over the Congressmen they may help to elect. Once in office, Congressmen have greater latitude on issues and are much more independent than Canadian MPs, who belong to disciplined, tightly controlled parties. Figure 7-1 illustrates the fusion of power in the Canadian system, where the Prime Minister is both the leader of the majority party in the legislature and the leader of the administration, and compares it to the American Presidential system, which was constructed on the premise that such concentration of power is undesirable and that law-making and implementation should be separated by preventing the overlap of key personnel. One familiar with the parliamentary system and its relatively smooth flow of operations resulting from the fusion of executive and legislative powers may well wonder how the American system with its built-in conflict and rivalry can possibly work effectively.

Whereas in the United States it is forbidden for an individual to hold a post in Congress and an executive position at the same time, precisely the opposite is true in Canada, for all members of Cabinet must be elected to the House of Commons or at least be appointed to the Senate. What is perhaps most important to remember in considering the implications of different types of governmental structures is that the principle of fusion of powers creates, at least theoretically, a form of government which is more coherent and responsive to the will of the people. The Canadian executive, assuming it is backed by a parliamentary majority, can be assured of legislative support on most bills and programmes it wishes to enact. It will of course be held accountable by the people at the next election, but during the interim it is relatively free to pursue its goals.

THE PRIME MINISTER'S POWERS

The Prime Minister is unquestionably the central figure in Canadian politics. As we have already suggested, the pre-eminence of the Prime Minister and the Cabinet has evolved more from tradition than from any specific statute. What is the basis of the power of the Prime Minister and Cabinet? How is this power exercised? After these questions are answered, we can turn to examine whether Canada has developed a unique system of government.

The basis of the Prime Minister's power and authority is leadership of the party (or coalition of parties) which commands at least a plurality and normally a majority of the seats in the House of Commons.[7] The Prime Minister is above all else an elected Member of Parliament, who has been chosen national leader of the party at a leadership convention. As leader of the party which has been victorious at the polls, the Prime Minister is able to claim that the "right" to govern is based on a popular mandate, The link with the people gives the Prime Minister enormous legitimacy and authorizes, the pursuit of his or her programs and policies under the cloak of popular support, at least until the next election. This is not only important in dealings with the bureaucracy and the press, but it also helps in controlling the party. As leader of the party and the holder of this mandate, the Prime Minister can command obedience and support from Cabinet ministers and backbenchers alike.

Another major source of the Prime Minister's power is control over appointments.[8] The Prime Minister selects the members of the Cabinet from the membership of the parliamentary caucus. This may well be the most difficult task. Once, in signing a visitors' book, Sir John A. Macdonald entered his occupation as "Cabinet-Maker".[9]

A number of factors may influence the Prime Minister's choice of ministers. First, there is an obvious advantage in appointing Cabinets which reflect the regional and ethnic diversity of the country. A persistent effort seems to be made to have at least one Cabinet minister from every province and from every significant ethnic and religious group in the country. This practice can be frustrated, of course, if the party does not hold any seats in a particular province or has not attracted any candidates from a specific ethnic or religious group.

A second factor in the selection process is that Cabinet posts are sometimes used as a reward for favours or services rendered to the Prime Minister or the party. Conversely, Cabinet positions may be withheld as a punishment for some misdemeanour. On occasion, a talented but troublesome member or a rival for the party leadership may be included in the Cabinet (especially in a difficult but not too prestigious portfolio) in order to silence his or her opposition to the leader. The Prime Minister may also make an appointment on the basis of the ability and popular appeal of a particular MP. It is evident that the Prime Minister wants a certain number of energetic and effective ministers to run the key portfolios of the government, because there could be political repercussions if Cabinet ministers are perceived as bumbling and incompetent. On the other hand, the Prime Minister must not allow himself to be constantly upstaged and overshadowed by ministers who appear more capable than himself. The power to make and shift Cabinet appointments thus gives the Prime Minister great power over

---

[7]See Fred Schindeler, "The Prime Minister and the Cabinet: History and Development," in Thomas A. Hockin, ed., *Apex of Power: The Prime Minister and Political Leadership in Canada*, second edition (Scarborough, Ontario: Prentice-Hall, 1977), pp. 22-47.

[8]R.M. Punnett, *The Prime Minister in Canadian Government and Politics* (Toronto: Macmillan, 1977), p. 56-85. See also R.J. Van Loon, "Choosing the Cabinet: The Prime Minister's Dilemma," *Quarterly of Canadian Studies for the Secondary School*, vol. 3, no. 3, (1974), pp. 131-140.

[9]Cited in Punnett, *op. cit.,* p. 56.

the political careers of colleagues. Journalist Doug Fisher likes to tell a story about Jack Pickersgill's view of Cabinet appointments during Prime Minister Lester B. Pearson's term of office. Apparently Pickersgill told Fisher that there "must be some slow members in every Cabinet or nothing would ever get accomplished."

The Prime Minister and his ministers share the responsibility for appointing parliamentary secretaries. The first two were appointed by order in council in 1916, and thereafter their numbers slowly increased until proper legislative recognition was given them with the 1959 *Parliamentary Secretaries Act*. That *Act*, as amended in 1971, provides for the appointment of the same number of parliamentary secretaries as there are ministers. The are appointed by the Prime Minister for twelve months and aid ministers in their duties, but have no statutory authority. As one parliamentary secretary put it, "There's no rule; it depends entirely on the Minister you are dealing with. Some are given considerable responsibility, others very little. It depends on the understanding between the two people concerned."[10] Usually, parliamentary secretaries have at least the agreement of their minister before being appointed, but even this is not always the case. The Prime Minister may make an appointment without any consultation whatsoever.[11] The Prime Minister, in addition to choosing the members of the executive, also makes a great many other crucial appointments: senators, judges, Lieutenant Governors and the senior staff of the public service. Through these selections he or she can again make his or her influence felt throughout the governmental structure. Legally, the Prime Minister's appointments are mere recommendations of appointment, forwarded to the Governor General for formal approval. However, despite the Governor General's apparent power of discretion, a Prime Minister's appointees are never rejected. In fact, as we have seen, the Prime Minister plays the vital role in the selection of the Governor General.

Yet another significant basis of the Prime Minister's authority is the power to dissolve Parliament. The Prime Minister alone can determine the timing of an election within the five-year term of Parliament. This power can be used to impose discipline or solidarity on a fractious Cabinet or caucus. Fraught with uncertainty, election campaigns are expensive and exhausting for most MPs. If the government is clearly defeated on a major bill due to breakdown of party discipline or the unravelling of an inter-party coalition, the Prime Minister has little choice but to call an election to seek a new mandate. This is a rare occurrence, except in minority situations such as the defeat of Joe Clark's Conservative government in December 1979. Normally, Parliament is dissolved only when the Prime Minister believes that the party has a good chance of victory at the polls, though he or she may be constrained by the five-year limit, or even misjudge the

---

[10]Quoted in Claude Majeau, "The Job of a Parliamentary Secretary," *Parliamentary Government,* vol 4, no. 3 (1983) p. 3.

[11]Judy La Marsh, *Memoirs of a Bird in a Gilded Cage* (Toronto: McClelland and Stewart, 1969), p. 57.

popular mood. Nonetheless, for the most part, the Prime Minister's power of dissolution is a potent weapon, helping to maintain the discipline and solidarity of the party and the stability of the Cabinet system.

A final major basis of the Prime Minister's pre-eminence is his or her power to control the organization of government. Nearly every Prime Minister has had plans for some new organizational structure to streamline or modernize the government. Crown corporations can be created, Cabinet portfolios modified, bureaucratic agencies abolished and Royal Commissions appointed – all on the initiative of the Prime Minister. However, while the power to make these changes certainly exists, the Prime Minister must be mindful that unwarranted or unnecessary modifications may generate significant opposition. The Prime Minister's power to initiate organizational changes extends across the entire government, but there is a tendency to focus on the various executive coordinating agencies which fall directly under his or her jurisdiction. Each Prime Minister can therefore be expected to make some changes in the Prime Minister's Office and the Privy Council Office to reflect his or her own interests or special needs.

The Prime Minister is the chairman of the Cabinet and the pivotal figure in the Cabinet committee system. No Prime Minister, however, can possibly deal with all matters needing attention. The Prime Minister must therefore to some extent delegate authority and responsibility to Cabinet. Before turning to a consideration of the operations of the Cabinet and its methods of arriving at policy decisions, we shall briefly examine the history and style of Canada's Prime Ministers.

THE PRIME MINISTERS IN PRACTICE

Canada has had eighteen Prime Ministers since 1867, seven Liberal and eleven Conservative. Joe Clark became the youngest Prime Minister in Canadian history at the age of 39. As of Brian Mulroney's election in 1984, the average age of a new Prime Minister was 56. Mulroney's election continued the tradition of highly educated leaders; every appointment since the First World War has gone to a university graduate. With regard to residence in adult life, there have been three Maritimers as Prime Ministers, five Québécois, six Ontarians and four Westerners. Three provinces – Prince Edward Island, Newfoundland and New Brunswick – have never had a Prime Minister elected in one of their provincial ridings. John Turner became a British Columbia Member of Parliament only three and a half hours before he was replaced as Prime Minister.

The regional electoral support of parties in Canada is illustrated by the fact that all seven Liberal Prime Ministers have come from Ontario or Québec (John Turner's western credentials notwithstanding), whereas the Conservatives have come from more varied parts of the country. On the other hand, the Liberals have balanced Canada's religious and ethnic diversity better than the Conservatives in their choice of Prime Ministers. Of the eighteen Prime Ministers, six have been Roman Catholic, and twelve Protestant; the Liberals have had four Roman Catholics and three Protestants. Moreover, since the 1880s Liberal Party

TABLE 7.1 The Prime Ministers of Canada

Prime Minister	Party	Tenure	Birth	Adult Life	Age As PM	Occupation
Sir John A. Macdonald	Lib.-Con.	July 1st, 1867–Nov. 5th, 1874	Britain	Ontario	52-76	Law
Alexander Mackenzie	Lib.	Nov. 5th, 1873–Oct. 9th, 1878	Britain	Ontario	51-56	Journalist/Stonemason
Sir John A. Macdonald	Con.	Oct. 9th, 1878–June 6th, 1891				
Sir John Abbott	Con.	June 15th, 1891–Nov. 24th, 1892	Québec	Québec	70	Law/Lecturer
Sir John Thompson	Con.	Nov. 25th, 1892–Dec. 12th, 1894	Nova Scotia	Nova Scotia	48-50	Law/Lecturer
Sir Mackenzie Bowell	Con.	Dec. 13th, 1894–April 27th, 1896	Britain	Ontario	70-72	Journalist
Sir Charles Tupper	Con.	April 27th, 1896–July 8th, 1896	Nova Scotia	Nova Scotia	74	Doctor
Sir Wilfrid Laurier	Lib.	July 9th, 1896–Oct. 6th, 1911	Québec	Québec	54-69	Law
Sir Robert Borden	Con.	Oct. 7th, 1911–July 10th, 1920	Nova Scotia	Nova Scotia	57-65	Law
Arthur Meighen	Con.	July 10th, 1920–Dec. 29th, 1921	Ontario	Manitoba	46-52	Law/Business
W.L. Mackenzie King	Lib.	Dec. 29th, 1921–June 28th, 1926	Ontario	Ontario	47-73	Civil Service
Arthur Meighen	Con.	June 28th, 1926–Sept. 25th, 1926				
W.L. Mackenzie King	Lib.	Sept. 25th, 1926–Aug. 7th, 1930				
R.B. Bennett	Con.	Aug. 7th, 1930–Oct. 23rd, 1935	New Brunswick	Alberta	60-65	Law/Business
W.L. Mackenzie King	Lib.	Oct. 23rd, 1935–Nov 15th, 1948				
Louis St. Laurent	Lib.	Nov. 15th, 1948–June 21st, 1957	Québec	Québec	66-75	Law
John Diefenbaker	Con.	June 21st, 1957–April 22nd, 1963	Ontario	Saskatchewan	61-67	Law
Lester B. Pearson	Lib.	April 22nd, 1963–April 20th, 1968	Ontario	Ontario	65-70	Civil Service
Pierre Elliott Trudeau	Lib.	April 20th, 1968–June 4th, 1979	Québec	Québec	48-65	Law/Lecturer
Joseph Clark	Con.	June 4, 1979–March 3rd, 1980	Alberta	Alberta	39-41	Journalist
Pierre Elliott Trudeau	Lib.	March 3rd, 1980–June 30th, 1984				
John Turner	Lib.	June 30th, 1984–Sept. 17th, 1984	Britain	Ontario	55	Law
Brian Mulroney	Con.	September 17th, 1984–	Québec	Québec	45-	Law/Business

Source: Government of Canada, *Guide to Canadian Ministries Since Confederation 1867-1957* (and Supplement 1957-67) (Ottawa: Public Archives of Canada, 1957 and 1967).

J.K. Johnson, ed., *The Canadian Directory of Parliament 1867-1967*(Ottawa: Public Archives of Canada, 1968).

R.M. Punnett, *The Prime Minister in Canadian Government and Politics* (Toronto: Macmillan, 1977).

leaders have been drawn alternately from English Canada (Blake, 1880; King, 1918; Pearson, 1958; Turner, 1984) and French Canada (Laurier, 1887; St. Laurent, 1948; Trudeau, 1968).

Until recently, Conservative Prime Ministers have had much more parliamentary experience than their Liberal counterparts. Except for Clark and Mulroney, every Conservative PM had ten years' or more legislative experience at the federal or provincial level before his appointment. Experience in Cabinet before becoming PM, however, has been minimal for both parties in Canada; all but four had only two years' experience or less. Sir Charles Tupper had the most experience in federal and provincial Cabinets, but he lasted as PM for only two months. Pierre Trudeau, by contrast, with no provincial experience and only one year of Cabinet experience, survived eleven years in his first period as Prime Minister and after a defeat was re-elected to a further mandate. Brian Mulroney had no Cabinet experience when he became Prime Minister in 1984.

The durability of Canadian Prime Ministers varies enormously. Unlike American Presidents, who may serve only two terms, a Canadian Prime Minister may, in theory, be elected for as long as the public and House of Commons support him. In actual practice, Prime Ministers in Canada have lasted longer than those in almost all Anglo-American and continental European countries: according to Malcolm Punnett's data, only Swedish Prime Ministers tend to serve longer average terms.[12]

The eighteen Canadian Prime Ministers can be divided into three broad groups on the basis of their tenure in office. The shortest careers were those of Meighen, Thompson, Abbott, Bowell, Tupper, Clark and Turner, who all served for less than two years (the very shortest periods were held by Sir Charles Tupper – 69 days and John Turner – 80 days). Six Prime Ministers stayed in office for five to eleven years: Borden, St. Laurent, Mackenzie, Bennett, Diefenbaker and Pearson. Four have towered above the rest: King, 22 years; Macdonald, 20 years; Trudeau, 15 1/2 years; and Laurier, 15 years. Laurier's fifteen consecutive years in office was the longest continuous term enjoyed by any PM; Trudeau's 15 1/2 year term was broken into two periods. These four individuals held the office of Prime Minister for well over half of Canada's history since Confederation: 72 out of 118 years, as of 1985.

How are Prime Ministers' terms ended? Few of Canada's Prime Ministers retired of their own choice; their careers were usually ended by defeat in a General Election. Abbott, Borden, King, Pearson and Trudeau retired. Eleven PMs lost their positions through defeat in a General Election; one (Mackenzie Bowell) because of a Cabinet revolt, two (Macdonald and King) through defeats in Parliament. Only Macdonald, King, Meighen and Trudeau have managed to win another General Election after being defeated as Prime Minister. Macdonald and Thompson died in office. Getting rid of a Prime Minister, even via the electoral route, is extremely difficult. The statistics show that in just over one-third of all elections the Prime Minister was defeated, whereas in about two-thirds he was returned, albeit half the time with a reduced majority in the House of Commons.

---

[12]Punnett, *op. cit.*, pp. 141-2.

THE CABINET

We have said that the Prime Minister determines which individuals will serve as ministers, as well as the extent of their duties. In some parliamentary countries, such as Australia and New Zealand, particular caucuses select the ministers and the PM merely assigns the portfolios. In Canada the Prime Minister has a free hand, but traditionally he selects most of his Cabinet from the House of Commons, and, more rarely, the Senate.

In selecting his future colleagues on the front bench, the Prime Minister takes into consideration a number of factors, one of them overall size. The size of Cabinets has gradually increased over the years. By the end of the second Trudeau administration in 1984, the Cabinet included 37 ministers. John Turner's appointments temporarily reduced the size of the Cabinet, but this situation was

Reproduced with permission – The Globe and Mail, Toronto.

immediately reversed when Brian Mulroney was appointed Prime Minister. He named 40 ministers, the largest number in Canadian history.

The composition of Cabinet is determined by merit and factors of representation. Since the idea of coalition governments does not seem to appeal to Canadian politicians,[13] Cabinet positions are all doled out to members of the Prime Minister's own party. There have been a few exceptions. General McNaughton was Defence Minister in 1944-5 without holding a position in either house. After being defeated twice he gave up the post. On the other hand, Lester Pearson was appointed Minister of External Affairs in 1948, then stood for election in a by-election and won.

As noted earlier, the Prime Minister's choice of ministers is limited essentially by certain considerations, foremost among them regional, ethnic and religious representation. Regional representation is the first of these, but not necessarily the most important. There is usually a Cabinet member from each province (with the frequent exception of Prince Edward Island) and from the largest cities, with the more important urban regions receiving extra seats.

It has been shown that the correspondence between distribution of Cabinet ministers and provincial population has been almost exact since Confederation.[14] As a general principle, Ontario has had more members in Cabinet than any other province, with Québec second. However, in recent years the principle has changed somewhat. In his governments, Trudeau usually had one more Cabinet member from Québec than from Ontario. Mulroney awarded an abnormally large number of Cabinet seats to the West: upon his election in 1984, his Cabinet consisted of thirteen from the four Western provinces and the North, eleven from each of Ontario and Québec and five from the Atlantic provinces.

Ethnicity is also significant. According to Malcolm Punnett, of the total number of Cabinet ministers serving between 1867 and 1965, 28% were French Canadians, a figure which is remarkably close to the French Canadian percentage of the population.[15] Prime Ministers also attempt to appoint their chief lieutenant from the opposite official ethnic group. The most successful alliance, for example, may have been that between Macdonald and Cartier. On the other hand, Clark found it necessary to appoint three French-speaking members of the Senate to his Cabinet to rectify his weak support in Québec. Brian Mulroney, a Quebecker, appointed his chief lieutenant from Yukon. Smaller groups have usually been under-represented in Cabinet. In recent years the new post of Minister of State in charge of multiculturalism has been used to some extent to fill this vacuum. Religion has also been balanced in Cabinet composition. "Between Confederation and 1965, there were almost equal numbers of Anglican, Presbyterian

---

[13]Only twice – in 1867 under Macdonald and in 1917 under Borden – have Canadian Cabinets been formed from more than one party.

[14]Richard J. Van Loon and Michael S. Whittington, *The Canadian Political System* (McGraw-Hill Ryerson, 1981), p. 455.

[15]R.M. Punnett, *op. cit., passim.*

and United Church or Methodist cabinet ministers while about 35% of cabinet ministers were Catholics."[16]

Certain posts are distributed according to traditional rules. The post of Minister of Agriculture usually goes to a Westerner. When this is difficult, as in the Trudeau Cabinet, a Western minister may receive control of the Wheat Board. Either a Maritime province or British Columbia usually gets the Ministry of Fisheries. The distribution of seats which the government has obtained throughout the country is also important in determining many assignments. In the case of the Liberals, the department of Finance has usually been held by an Ontarian, but in the 1980 Trudeau government a French Canadian was appointed to that post to bolster Québec's strength in Cabinet. Joe Clark was even more daring – in 1979 he went to Newfoundland to find his Finance Minister. But Brian Mulroney returned to tradition when he appointed Michael Wilson from Toronto to the position.

Unrepresented in Cabinet, or under-represented, are practically all of Canada's minority groups, as well as one majority group – women. Six women, the largest number ever, were appointed to Cabinet in 1984 – out of a total of 40 Cabinet members. No significant room has been made in Cabinet for the Native Peoples, for workers and unskilled labourers or for the poor. They and their interests have been consistently under-represented. Over-represented are those with higher education and high social status occupations. The most over-represented group are lawyers, who have held approximately half the positions in Cabinet since Confederation; they are an elite, extremely well educated, financially successful group representing less than 1 percent of the population. Historically, about one-fifth of Cabinet members have been businessmen; fewer than one-tenth, farmers; and fewer still from the public sector.

Since the enactment of the *Ministries and Ministers of State Act,* five categories of Ministers of the Crown can be identified. The first of these comprises the ministers of regular government departments such as the Minister of Justice or Agriculture. The second includes ministers who have parliamentary responsibilities, such as being House Leader, but who are not in charge of any department or ministry. The third category comprises Ministers of State who might head a junior department which has generally been created for certain short-term purposes. An example would be the Minister of State for Science and Technology. The fourth type includes Ministers of State appointed to assist a regular department minister. An example would be the Minister of State for Forestry. The final category includes ministers without portfolio, those selected for Cabinet duty without a specific department or bureaucracy to administer. Needless to say, nearly all Cabinet ministers are chosen from the Commons, although in some historical periods a number have been appointed from the Senate, particularly when the governing party lacked elected representatives from a particular region – as the Conservatives did from Québec in 1979 and the Liberals did from the West in 1980-84.

---

[16]Van Loon and Whittington, *op. cit.,* p. 458.

The Prime Minister and Cabinet as a whole are aided in their tasks by the central agencies discussed in the following section. Individual ministers are supported by their departments and by their political appointees. The overall personnel budget for each Minister's office (approximately $250 000) is used to employ a chief of staff, an executive assistant, special assistants, a private secretary, and other support personnel. In total there are over 200 of these aides in Ottawa, not including those in the Prime Minister's Office. In addition, ministers sometimes second departmental employees to their offices and hire individuals under contract.

These aides are part of what Blair Williams has called the "para-political bureaucracy".[17] They are hired by ministers on an individual basis in order to perform largely partisan tasks. They are not subject to the regulations of the public service (and hence are called "exempt staff") and, under provisions of the 1967 *Public Service Employment Act,* they are allowed permanent positions in the administration after a period of political service.

The importance of these staffs is debatable. Depending on the minister's views and confidence they are engaged on any number of personal concerns. Liaison work with the department, constituency, party and Parliament is perhaps the most important. Their work on policy is underdeveloped, possibly because, with some exceptions, they usually do not have the necessary competence or experience. Their partisan work for the ministers is clearly significant. If competent, they strengthen both the minister and the party in power. In the 1974-79 Trudeau Cabinet, one-third of all the ministers had at one time been members of another minister's exempt staff. As Williams concludes, "there is little doubt today that ministerial exempt staffs play a fundamental and legitimate role at the executive level of the government process."[18]

Most appointees to the Cabinet are responsible for administering a department of government and must accept statutory responsibility for it. While they may delegate authority to their officials, they remain at the apex for appeals of administrative decisions and must be involved in the initiation and defence of new policies. The complexity of a minister's task can be illustrated by the work of the Minister for Industry, Trade and Commerce and Regional Economic Expansion. In 1982 his department took 4700 decisions – the Minister kept control of only 190 of them, but these constituted well over half the department's expenditures.[19] The minister's world involves frenetic activity in the department, in Cabinet and Parliament, before the media and on the hustings.

---

[17]Blair Williams, "The Para-Political Bureaucracy in Ottawa," in Harold D. Clarke *et al.,* eds., *Parliament, Policy and Representation* (Toronto: Methuen, 1980), p. 218. See also J.R. Mallory, "The Minister's Office Staff: An Unreformed Part of the Public Service," *Can. Pub. Admin.,* vol. 10, no. 1 (March 1967), pp. 25-34; K.G. Tilley, "Ministerial Executive Staffs," in Paul Fox, ed., *Politics: Canada* (Toronto: McGraw-Hill, 1977); Brooke Jeffrey, *A Comparison of the Role of the Minister's Office in France, Britain, Canada,* Research Branch, Library of Parliament, Ottawa, Oct., 1978.

[18]Williams, *op. cit.,* p. 225.

[19]Ian Clark, "A 'Back to Basics' Look at the Government Decision-Making Process," unpublished paper, Nov. 4, 1983, p. 13.

As we shall see in Chapters 13 and 14, public policy derives from a multitude of sources, but it is the individual minister who puts the final stamp of approval on departmental initiatives. As Jackson and Atkinson put it, "Politicians cannot duplicate the expertise which derives from administration, nor the information which comes from permanent contact with interest groups. And yet only a minister may carry forward departmental requests to the Cabinet or defend departmental policies in the House of Commons."[20] This iron-clad relationship between minister and department places approval or disapproval upon the appropriate and responsible political official. The ministers act collectively in Cabinet to develop policy, approve draft legislation, manage the country's finances and adopt orders-in-council. Cabinet deliberations are held in secret, individual opinions are not publicly voiced, and ministers are not supposed to speak or act except in the name of the entire Cabinet.

In theory, therefore, the Cabinet system of government is premised on both collective and individual ministerial responsibility. As a group the ministers are supposed to be held accountable for their government's actions. In this sense, they are to speak about policy only after it has been agreed to in private by their colleagues. The convention of collective responsibility, however, is so pervasive that ministers are expected to support each other even if the issue has not yet been discussed in Cabinet. At the individual level they should receive confidential advice from the public service, make the important decisions, then be held accountable for these decisions in Parliament and the country. In other words, there is a trade-off: the civil servant foregoes public praise in order to avoid public blame, while the minister accepts both credit and criticism.[21]

In practice it is nearly impossible to adhere at all times to these constitutional doctrines. Where is the line to be drawn between ministerial and departmental responsibility? Ministers do not even know most of the detailed decisions which are carried out in their names. They cannot be held responsible for every activity, and, increasingly, ministers have been voicing this problem openly. One even claimed he could not be held accountable for the "shabby research" in his department. The main check on ministerial responsibilities, therefore, is not the minister's will or his public servants' activities, but the free and open debate which takes place in Parliament and society about ministers' actions.

CABINET AND POLICY-MAKING

In recent years, the Cabinet has been making major alterations to its internal organization. In the 1963 Pearson administration, full Cabinet was the major vehicle for Cabinet decision-making: it reviewed almost every decision taken in

---

[20]Robert J. Jackson and Michael M. Atkinson, *The Canadian Legislative System*, revised edition (Toronto: Macmillan, 1980) p. 63.

[21]See T.M. Denton on the history of ministerial responsibility in "Ministerial Responsibility: A Contemporary Perspective," in Richard Schultz, *et al.* eds., *The Canadian Political Process*, third edition, (Toronto: Holt, Rinehart and Winston, 1979) pp. 344-362.

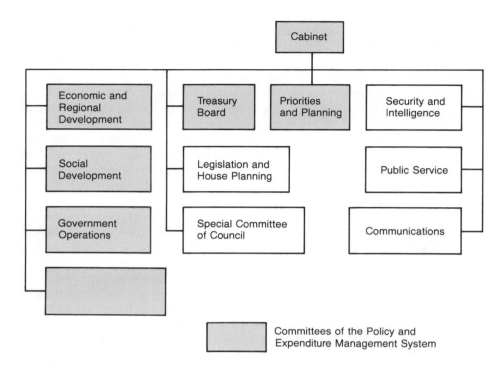

FIGURE 7.2   The Cabinet Committee System (as of September, 1985)

committee. After Trudeau came to office in 1968, Cabinet and committee meetings were scheduled on a more regular basis and committees became much more powerful. The 1979 Clark and 1980 Trudeau Cabinets decentralized decision-making even further with the introduction of a Policy and Expenditure Management System. Today, committees make most important decisions, but all decisions are ratified by the full Cabinet or by the Committee on Priorities and Planning, both chaired by the Prime Minister.

At the time of writing, Cabinet is divided into eleven committees, each chaired by a minister who holds the Cabinet portfolio or ministry most directly associated with the subject matter. Of these, four are policy sector committees, each of which handles general policy issues: Economic and Regional Development, Social Development, Government Operations, and External Affairs and Defence. Two special committees – Security and Intelligence and the Public Service – meet irregularly. Other special committees or sub-committees are established for particular purposes, and usually atrophy once their relevance is over. In the past, there have been up to ten such sub-committees at a given time.

Under Mulroney, as under Trudeau, coordinating committees include such important committees as Priorities and Planning and the Treasury Board, as well as Legislation and House Planning. Priorities and Planning, chaired by the Prime

Minister and composed mainly of the chairpersons of Cabinet's other committees, is concerned with providing overall coordination for government activities. Its status as the Prime Minister's committee gives it overall domination of long-term policy development. Priorities and Planning is multi-functional; its duties differ from one period to the next. In the Trudeau governments it was assigned wide fields of responsibility, including the articulation of broad policy objectives, the Speech from the Throne, the legislative programme, the fiscal framework, macroeconomic policy, federal/provincial relations and the public debt. It also handled major energy and constitutional matters.

The most conspicuous change in Cabinet structure came in 1979 with Joe Clark's concept of an "inner" and "outer" Cabinet. It had generally been accepted until that time that a division of senior and junior ministers in Canada would not be possible because of the need for regional and ethnic balance in the Cabinet. G. Bruce Doern even predicted that "such a full-blown inner and outer cabinet system will never occur in Canada, given the strength and importance of regional and ethnic representation in the cabinet. . ."[22] In fact, Canada has naturally always had some ministers who were more important than others; Clark merely institionalized this division of status.[23] Clark appointed twelve members to an "inner Cabinet" and thirty to full Cabinet. The Inner Cabinet's potential for usurping Cabinet's power was quickly exaggerated. In reality, however, it functioned similarly to the old Priorities and Planning Committee of Cabinet. When Trudeau returned to office in 1980, he abolished the name "Inner Cabinet" and replaced it with the former system. In 1984, Mulroney too simply retained the old name.

The coordination of policy is primarily the responsibility of Priorities and Planning. But the Cabinet committees on Legislation and House Planning and Treasury Board must also be included in policy coordination because of their general supervision of parliamentary affairs and government spending. Treasury Board is chaired by the President of the Treasury Board. It is the only Cabinet committee which is statutory, and which does not position itself in a circle during meetings. Instead, it sits like a jury, facing the petitioners, and hears arguments from within the government, acting more like a tribunal than a committee. The Leader of the Government in the House of Commons, who is often given the title of President of the Privy Council in order that a place may be secured for him in Cabinet, chairs Legislation and House Planning. In the Mulroney administration, the Government House Leader, Ray Hnatyshyn, was first appointed as a Minister of State within the Prime Minister's portfolio. Together, these three committees provide ministers with the opportunity to plan and to coordinate the bureaucracy. During some administrations, a further committee, Communications, was re-

---

[22]G. Bruce Doern, "The Development of Policy Organizations in the Executive Arena" in G. Bruce Doern and Peter Aucoin, eds., *Structures of Policy-Making in Canada* (Toronto: Macmillan, 1971), p. 74.

[23]See Jackson and Atkinson, *op. cit.*, Chapter 4. On PEMS see Richard Van Loon, "The Policy and Expenditure Management System in the Federal Government," *Canadian Public Administration*, vol. 26, no. 2 (Summer 1983), pp. 255-285.

sponsible for information, publicity and propaganda about Cabinet's activities and conclusions. At first, Mulroney changed this by giving its responsibility to his Deputy Prime Minister, Erik Nielsen; he later revived the committee.

The eleventh Cabinet committee is the Special Committee of Council. This committee, usually chaired by the President of the Privy Council, meets weekly to deal with regulations and routine issues requiring Governor-in-Council approval. That is, it passes uncontroversial orders-in-council which require the government, not a single minister, to make the decision. In practice, only four ministers need be present.

Orders-in-council are, in most cases, authorized by provisions contained in statutes. They are used to carry out government rule-making and administration. Some orders, however, such as the appointment of Ambassadors and High Commissioners, fall under the Royal Prerogative. Upon passage, they are all published in the Canada Gazette. The number of orders-in-council has increased yearly. In 1982, 4379 were passed, ranging from the most trivial to the most urgent. Almost a third of them consisted of regulations for administering the country; the next greatest number had to do with FIRA (Foreign Investment Review Agency – acquisitions and establishment of new businesses). The most visible, however, are generally those for appointments. By convention the Prime Minister recommends about a hundred deputy head positions on his own authority. The other 2000 full time Governor-in-Council positions involve Cabinet deliberation or decision.

In principle, Cabinet and its committees are assembled at least once a week during parliamentary sessions. In 1956, under St. Laurent, Cabinet met 91 times. In 1969, under Trudeau, full cabinet met 73 times, and there were 369 meetings of its committees. Under Clark's "Inner Cabinet" system, the number of full Cabinet meetings was further reduced to approximately twice a month, while the Inner Cabinet met weekly. By 1982 this number was reduced to 50 full Cabinet meetings and 232 meetings of committees.

Ministers are expected to bring substantial policies to their Cabinet colleagues for resolution. The formal process for Cabinet approval of a document is illustrated in Figure 7-3. The minister's memorandum is forwarded to the Privy Council Office, which distributes it to the Cabinet members. The memorandum is then discussed by the appropriate Cabinet committee and forwarded to full Cabinet or Priorities and Planning for final determination. As Figure 7-3 indi-

TABLE 7.2 Cabinet Workload* (1982)

Cabinet Meetings	50
Cabinet Committee Meetings	232
Memoranda to Cabinet and Discussion Papers	747
Draft Bills	68
Cabinet Decisions	716

Derived from private communication from the Privy Council Office, December 1, 1983.

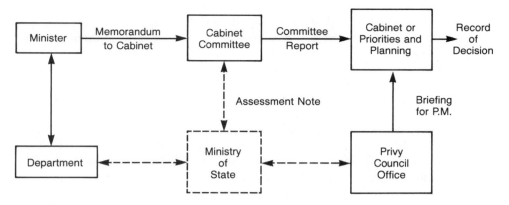

FIGURE 7.3 The Formal Cabinet Policy Process

(*Note:* The dotted lines (---) indicate structures and processes which were deleted in the September 1984 system.)

cates, during most of the Trudeau years either of the two ministries of state (Economic and Regional Development or Social Development), the Privy Council Office or the Interdepartmental Secretariat on Foreign and Defence Policy also provided an independent assessment to the Cabinet committee of a minister's Cabinet document. In 1984 the two ministries of state were eliminated and the process simplified. The PCO briefs the Prime Minister, as does the Prime Minister's Office. This series of actions completes the process and Cabinet gives final approval or disapproval in a record of decision. Of course, private conversations about government policies, over the telephone and in person, add immeasurably to the complexity of Cabinet business.

Every Cabinet document is numbered and awarded a security classification. Their number increased rapidly after World War II. In 1982, there were 1533 documents: 747 memoranda, 68 draft bills and 716 Cabinet decisions.

As Jackson and Atkinson show, ministers are allowed to place some major policy areas and legislative proposals on Cabinet's list of priority problems. "Cabinet cohesiveness, like that of any group, is maintained by encouraging each minister to believe that he will succeed in persuading his colleagues to accept some of his proposals."[24] If serious Cabinet dissent emerges over a minister's ideas, he or she will be asked to reconsider and resubmit them. Each minister is made to feel part of a team which values his or her proposals. The participants are united for their own survival – and they know it!

How successful the Cabinet will be depends to a large extent on its management of several critical factors, including taxation, expenditures and the legislative program. By controlling these, as well as the machinery of government

---

[24]Jackson and Atkinson, *op. cit.,* p. 63.

and senior personnel, the government is able to effect major decisions in Canada. Strategic planning is the government's attempt to accomplish its goals and to resolve policy issues by employing all these resources. In theory the government attempts to place all the goals and issues into a hierarchy of interests, but in practice this rarely works. For one thing, long-term policy requirements often have to give way to short-term administrative matters. Second, the issues change over time, and the government must be prepared to adjust its targets. Finally, ultimate determination occurs within the ephemeral world of politics, where politicians come and go, change their opinions and are themselves divided over policies, with the result that a slight change in personnel may affect the distribution of power which first caused the priority. Nevertheless, the idea of strategic planning comes from the desire to achieve comprehensive, non-urgent policy-making to help counter the piecemeal policies emanating from individual departments.

The Policy and Expenditure Management System

In 1979 and 1980, a Policy and Expenditure Management System (PEMS) was introduced into government. It is still being refined. Its general purpose was to integrate the processes of policy-making and fiscal and expenditure planning within the Cabinet committee system. As well, the PEMS had three specific objectives: to decentralize decision-making, giving it over to Cabinet committees; to increase ministerial direction; and to provide a longer period for the integration of policies and expenditures.

The PEMS is designed to ensure that the government's decisions on priorities and policies are integrated closely with the allocation of resources. Before 1980 a considerable problem existed in this regard: the ideas for policies and their projected costs were worked out by separate Cabinet committees and at different times. The result was an increased probability that ministers would accept new programs without considering the overall costs to the government. With the introduction of the PEMS, policy decisions are made and expenditure limits set simultaneously by the same Cabinet committee. In addition, the new system ensures that priorities and expenditure limits are set before expenditure plans are developed. The intent is to allow sufficient time for ministers and officials to change policies and reallocate resources.

The PEMS involves the addition of two new features to the Cabinet system. First, a five-year fiscal plan is to be developed to set out the overall financial constraints within which policy choices must be made. This plan is to be revised each year. Second, specific expenditure limits, called "resource envelopes", are to be set. At the inception of the PEMS, there were ten of these envelopes. In 1984, the Mulroney government reduced the number of envelopes from ten to eight by combining the Energy envelope with Economic and Regional Development, and Justice and Legal Affairs with Social Affairs. As of September 1984, therefore, the expenditures for a five-year period were to be divided into eight envelopes for the eight policy sectors. Responsibility for managing these within the expenditure limits is assigned to the four Cabinet policy committees, and Priorities and Planning. The ministers on a policy committee allocate the money in the envelope among themselves. In this way, they are forced to choose the policies to support, and to make trade-offs. If a department wishes to spend more money, on either an old or a new program, it must delete programs or convince the ministers on the appropriate Cabinet policy committee to reduce allocations elsewhere in that policy sector.

It is the Prime Minister's committee, Priorities and Planning, that determines overall government priorities, establishes the multi-year fiscal plan and sets the size of the resource envelopes. In recent years the funding decisions have been taken at ministerial deliberations at so-called "Lakes and Lodges" meetings. These annual Cabinet retreats are used to develop the highlights of the government's expenditures, the Budget and the Speech from the Throne.

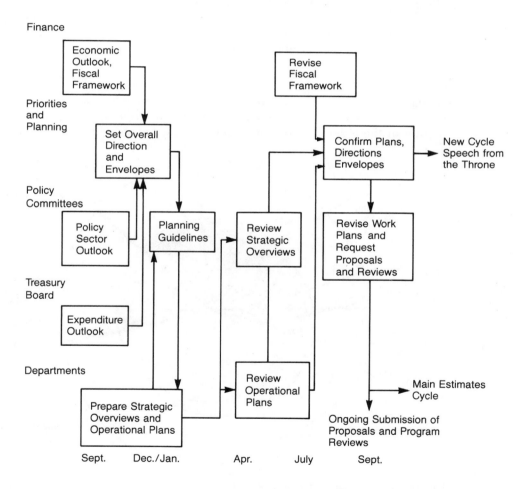

FIGURE 7.4 Policy and Expenditure Planning Cycle

Source: Privy Council Office, The Policy and Expenditure Management System (1981), p. 16.

The development of these items is based on advice from the central agencies (the Prime Minister's Office, the Privy Council Office, Finance and Treasury Board) and the chairpersons of the Cabinet policy committees. The Treasury Board remains responsible for the preparation of the Main Estimates (spending proposals for the upcoming fiscal year), which are based on decisions of the policy committees. It reviews departmental plans in the late fall and in February. The Main Estimates are then tabled in Parliament for the next fiscal year (April 1 – March 31).

At the departmental level, strategic overviews, multi-year operational plans and budget-year operational plans are made and circulated to the policy committees and central agencies as a basis for decisions on departmental requests for policies, programs and funds. Refer to Figure 7-4.

The final result of the PEMS is the annual government expenditure plan. Figure 7-5 indicates the size of the government's expenditures by policy sector; it should be examined carefully.

Policy and Budget

The days are long gone when Ministers of Finance could present their Budget from a few notes written on the back of an old envelope. In earlier periods, the activities of the federal government were so few that they had far less effect on

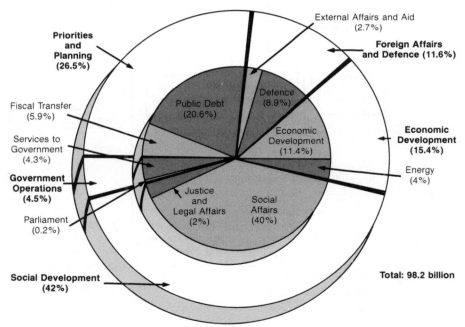

FIGURE 7.5 Cabinet Committees and their Spending Envelopes 1984-85 Fiscal in Percentages

Source: 1984-85 Government *Estimates.*

(*Note:* In Sept 1984 Energy was combined with Economic Development, and Justice and Legal Affairs with Social Affairs.)

the Canadian economy than today. Total federal expenditures in 1984-85 exceeded 98 billion dollars.

The Canadian Budget shares with others in parliamentary systems of British origin the peculiar characteristic of containing no detailed proposals for spending: the spending estimates are tabled separately, prior to the Budget. This feature is in contrast to the budgets of some other political systems and to those of private businesses, where budgets are targets for both spending and revenues.

The Budget and its proposals are subjects of a lengthy process of preparation. Preliminary discussions are held in the Department of Finance to fix an approximate level of expenditures for the fiscal year. These talks also establish estimates of revenues expected to be realized from existing tax rates. From these two estimates, expenditure and revenue, emerges a surplus or a deficit. In recent years the government has usually had to borrow money by issuing securities in order to finance its deficits. In 1984-85 the accounts show that the government had to spend about 20.4 billion dollars to service the public debt.

To help in determining the appropriate fiscal stance, the Minister of Finance receives an analysis of the economic situation and outlook from departmental officials. These deliberations are also aided by information from the Governor of the Bank of Canada on general economic conditions, conditions in the money markets, monetary policy and the market's capacity to absorb government bonds. The result is an indication of the appropriate budget surplus or deficit, and, in the latter event, the size of deficit that can be financed. Further, an idea of the proper taxation strategy to employ should emerge – whether direct or indirect taxes should bear the burden of change, and on what scale.

In matters of taxation, departmental officials advise the Minister of tax loopholes which may be closed, public reactions concerning taxes, tax reform proposals from external sources and proposals for changes in the customs tariff. From these discussions a general pattern of taxation policy emerges. Costs of tax reduction and revenues from tax raises are totalled and compared with the estimates and the desired fiscal stance. The road is then clear to begin drafting the Budget speech. As well, the Minister can begin consulting Cabinet colleagues to obtain their agreement to the proposals. The timing of the latter process depends on the individual whim of the Minister of Finance and, to a lesser extent, on his relations with fellow Cabinet members. Some Finance Ministers spring the Budget proposals upon the Cabinet at the last possible moment before Budget Day. Recently, however, there has been a tendency (first developed by Walter Gordon and Mitchell Sharp) to undertake more lengthy consultation. Mitchell Sharp, for example, has stated that he began discussions with the Prime Minister some three weeks before Budget Day and approached his Cabinet colleagues at three successive Budget meetings, as follows:

> Two weeks before Budget Day, he presented his economic outlook and its implications for fiscal policy.
>
> One week before Budget Day, he gave a broad indication of the nature of tax changes under consideration, and the possible alternatives.
>
> One day before Budget Day, he described in detail the tax changes that would be proposed to Parliament.

But Sharp admitted that, although Cabinet had an opportunity to discuss the broad objectives and the alternative tax proposals, it had little chance to discuss the details of tax change that would appear in the Speech itself.[25] At the same time, departmental officials prepare the budget papers (especially the detailed economic analysis underlying the rationale of the final proposals) to be tabled in the House by the Minister of Finance along with the Budget.

The actual address and the debate are regulated by the Standing Orders of the House. The Budget speech is usually delivered in the evening after the markets have closed and little time is left for opposition comment at the end. Mitchell Sharp commented about these speeches that in his career "as a Minister of Finance the most uncomfortable times were when I was delivering the Budget Speech. I found all of those speeches excessively long and incredibly dull. On one occasion I was so overwhelmed, I read so fast that a member of the opposition called out 'whoa'! I wanted to get it over with and did not think anyone was any more interested than I was in the presentation, except for the final paragraphs."[26] The speech reviews the state of the national economy and the financial operations of the government over the past fiscal year, and provides a forecast of spending requirements for the year ahead, taking into account the estimates as determined by the Policy and Expenditure Management System.

THE CENTRAL COORDINATING AGENCIES

In response to the growing scope of the government's role in Canadian society in recent years and to the corresponding need for innovative and effective policy formation and implementation, certain executive agencies have been either created or expanded. These central coordinating agencies have a special responsibility to support the Prime Minister and Cabinet and are not part of the regular departmental infrastructure. They have little legal authority, but for the most part are organized under the Prime Minister's prerogative for machinery of government. While their stated purpose is to streamline the governmental process, the executive agencies have recently received much public attention and have drawn accusations that Canada is being run by a cabal of "superbureaucrats" who have become powers unto themselves. The closed nature of these agencies makes them a target for criticism. To some extent they have become recruiting grounds for senior positions in the public service.

The centralization of power in the hands of the Prime Minister and Cabinet as well as in these coordinating agencies appears indisputable. It is also clear, however, that this development has probably been inevitable, given the range of demands for government action in Canada. We shall evaluate the nature of this

---

[25]Remarks by Mitchell Sharp at Seminar on *The Budgetary Process* (Ottawa: Queens Printer, 1977). See also Douglas G. Hartle, *The Expenditure Budget Process in The Government of Canada* (Toronto: Canadian Tax Foundation, 1978) and Richard W. Phidd and G. Bruce Doern, *The Politics and Management of Canadian Economic Policy* (Toronto: Macmillan, 1978).

[26]Sharp, *ibid.*, p. 1:8.

controversy in the concluding section of the chapter, "Prime Ministerial Government". For now, we shall discuss briefly the duties and responsibilities of five important executive agencies: the Prime Minister's Office; the Privy Council Office; the Federal-Provincial Relations Office; the Treasury Board; and the Department of Finance. The first three report directly to the Prime Minister; the other two have their own ministers.

It is important to bear in mind that it is individuals within these agencies who are important, not necessarily the institutions themselves. One of Campbell and Szablowski's interviewees listed the basic ingredients for success at the top:

> "Both senior officials and ministers are candidates for the inner circle.
> With respect to officials, there are three important elements. First, the
> person has to have an excellent knowledge of government procedure, the
> 'rules of the game'. Second, he has to be persuasive, the logical force of his
> arguments has to come across. Third, he has to be a team player, willing to
> help his colleagues."[27]

The Prime Minister's Office

Of the various executive support agencies, the Prime Minister's Office (PMO) appears to be the most overtly political. The upper echelon of the PMO is composed of personal appointees of the Prime Minister and sometimes includes those referred to as "Ottawa's best and brightest". On the advice of ministers and other advisors the PMO drafts the Speech from the Throne. Perhaps the most crucial task of the PMO, however, is to act as a monitoring agency tracing political developments and their implications for the Prime Minister and his career.

An official explained the PMO's role as follows:

> "We are just a valve at the junction of the bureaucratic and the political.
> We add a little of the political ingredient when it appears that it has been
> overlooked. For instance, if I know that an official in PCO is working on a
> briefing note to the PM on an issue which I am responsible for, I'll go to
> him and express the political point of view. – I guess we are sort of a
> Distant Early Warning System for things that are going to cause trouble
> politically."[28]

While the PMO lacks the statutory authority of some other executive agencies, it became important because of the style and personality of Pierre Elliott Trudeau. Consistent with Trudeau's quest for rationality and the scientific analysis of political problems, the PMO was enlarged and staffed with technocrats and so-called "whiz kids".

The Prime Minister's Office has grown immensely. Near the end of the Trudeau years (1983-84), the office had a budget of just over $4 million *per an-*

---

[27]Cited in Colin Campbell and George J. Szablowski, *The Superbureaucrats: Structure and Behaviour in Central Agencies* (Toronto: MacMillan, 1979), p. 172.

[28]Cited in *Ibid.*, p. 66.

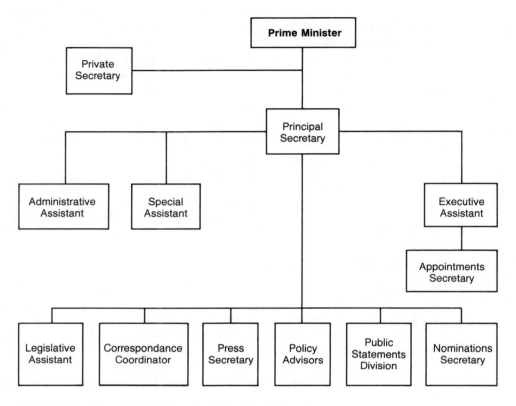

FIGURE 7.6 The Prime Minister's Office (Basic Form)

num, and in the first year of Mulroney's government over $6 million.[29] The importance of the Office is determined solely by the Prime Minister's personality and needs. Yet, as Blair Williams points out,

> "Today in its advisory, administrative, and political functions the PMO is the most significant element of the para-political bureaucracy in Ottawa. Indeed, as the events of August, 1978 [when Trudeau announced economic initiatives which have been alleged to have been wholly devised by his advisors] seemed to reflect, the PMO might, in many respects, be the most important element of the total governmental policy-making apparatus."[30]

In concert with the Privy Council Office, the PMO provides the Prime Minister with a range of technical and political advice that may not be available from

---

[29]*Main Estimates,* 1983-84 and *Toronto Star,* Oct. 6, 1985.

[30]Williams, "The Para-Political Bureaucracy in Ottawa," p. 218. Material in parenthesis added.

the more established bureaucratic structures. The emphasis of the PMO is on the development of practical policy suggestions relevant to the political fortunes of the Prime Minister and his party. In addition, the PMO does much public relations work. It gathers surveys on the popularity of the Prime Minister and specific policy initiatives, and helps in preparing press conferences and in dealing with the media generally. As a rule, officials in the PMO know and understand the marketing maxim that "It's the sizzle not the steak which sells." Other related responsibilities include answering the Prime Minister's mail, coordinating his daily appointment schedule and searching for candidates for nomination and awards.

The organization and structure of the PMO remain the prerogative of each Prime Minister. Throughout most of Canada's history, the PMO has been a small, relatively insignificant body. However, under Trudeau it achieved unprecedented importance.[31] The most significant position in the PMO is that of Principal Secretary. In 1968 Trudeau appointed Marc Lalonde, who had been with the Pearson administration, to this position. Lalonde, a friend and confidant of Trudeau's, came to hold a very sensitive position at the apex of decision-making and was in control of information flowing to the Prime Minister. In 1984 Brian Mulroney appointed his law school friend, Bernard Roy, as his Chief of Staff. The extent of the power and influence of this position depends in large measure on the ability of the individual and on the amount of authority the Prime Minister is willing to delegate.

Other changes of interest have occurred in the Prime Minister's Office. The "regional desks" concept was introduced in 1968 but was abandoned after the Liberals' near defeat in 1972. The regional desks were designed to provide the Prime Minister with up-to-date information from the significant regions of the country. While the idea of a regional monitoring apparatus may have been sensible from the point of view of rational decision-making, it nonetheless revealed a certain insensitivity to the role and prerogatives of local MPs, as it was perceived to undermine their jealously guarded positions. Somewhat more successful than the regional desks idea was the creation of an office to monitor developments in foreign affairs.[32] Through his personal rapport with the Prime Minister, Ivan Head came to take on a crucial role in external affairs analogous to that of Henry Kissinger in the first years of the Nixon Administration. In delegating many important foreign policy matters to Head, Trudeau indicated a desire to control more directly the country's foreign affairs. In bypassing External Affairs, the traditional source of foreign policy advice and coordination, Trudeau indicated his distrust of older bureaucratic structures and his desire to create alternative sources of policy and information.

Joe Clark's PMO was less hierarchically arranged than Trudeau's. While the

---

[31]Thomas d'Aquino, "The Prime Minister's Office: Catalyst or Cabal? Aspects of the development of the office in Canada and some thoughts about its future." *Canadian Public Administration*, vol. 17, no. 1 (Spring 1974), pp. 55-79.

[32]*Ibid.*, pp. 63-64.

chief of staff had an overall coordinating role, the positions of policy advisor and patronage secretary were given to professional politicians who would have been in the Cabinet had they won election in the Conservative victory of 1979. Clark also placed one of his closest advisors in the Senate rather than in his personal office.

Though as we have said the PMO was for many years an organization of little power, it has achieved considerable importance and is likely to continue to be extremely influential in policy-making at the political apex.

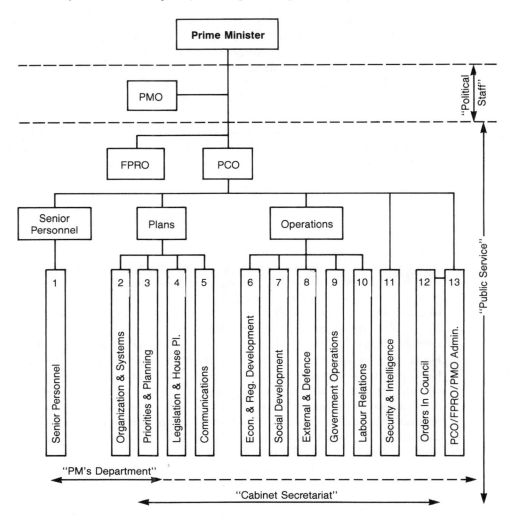

FIGURE 7.7 Simplified Organization Chart of Prime Minister's Staff (1983)

Source: Adapted from Ian Clark, "A 'Back to Basics' look at the Government Decision-Making Process", unpublished paper, Nov. 4, 1983.

The Privy Council Office

The Queen's Privy Council for Canada was established by the *BNA Act* to advise the Governor General. It is a largely ceremonial body comprised almost exclusively of current and former Ministers of the Crown. The Cabinet is, in fact, a committee of the Privy Council. The main organization supporting the Cabinet and Prime Minister is the Privy Council Office. The top position in the Office is held by the Clerk. This position has existed since 1867, and was combined with the function of Secretary to the Cabinet in 1940.

The PCO performs some of the same functions as the PMO but is staffed by career bureaucrats seconded from various government departments. The PCO has responsibility for the development and coordination of overall government policy. Although the top echelon staff of the PCO is appointed by the Prime Minister, there is little emphasis on partisan politics. Under recent Prime Ministers the PCO, like the PMO, has flourished in size and scope of responsibility.[33]

The Privy Council Office possesses an impressive research capability and acts as the "eyes and ears" of the Cabinet in coordinating the numerous governmental departments and agencies. With a staff of over 300 officers and support personnel, the PCO's overall budget in 1983-84 was $22 million.[34] The PCO is divided into three principal divisions: Plans, Operations and Senior Personnel. Each of these divisions has its own staff and is responsible for advising the Prime Minister, the plenary Cabinet and the various Cabinet sub-committees on matters of national policy. To achieve this, the PCO employs a wide range of talent – from clerical staff and legal counsel who prepare documents, to technical and scientific experts.

The Clerk of the Privy Council is in charge of coordinating Cabinet activities by setting agendas, taking the minutes of Cabinet meetings and conveying Cabinet decisions to the bureaucracy. This position ranks at the top of Canada's civil service. The role and stature of the Clerk of the Privy Council, like those of the officers of the PMO, depend to a great extent on his rapport with the Prime Minister. Any Prime Minister would likely consider the Clerk of the Privy Council to be one of his most crucial appointments.

The relationship between Cabinet ministers and officers of the PCO is for the most part cordial and constructive. There is, of course, always the possibility of a rift or tension. Although the staff of the Privy Council may be expert on specific matters of policy, in the end it is the elected ministers, whatever their knowledge or qualifications, who must make decisions. In principle, the PCO exists to advise and suggest alternatives in an objective and dispassionate manner, since the weight of public responsibility is not on its members' shoulders.

In an article describing developments in the PCO, a former Clerk, Gordon Robertson, suggested that it should be non-partisan, politically sensitive and governed by four principles.[35] The first is that the PCO should act as a source of

---

[33]See Thomas A. Hockin, *Government in Canada* (Toronto: McGraw-Hill Ryerson, 1976).

[34]*Main Estimates*, 1983-84.

[35]Gordon Robertson, "The Changing Role of the Privy Council Office," *Canadian Public Administration* vol. 14, no. 4 (Winter 1971), pp. 487-508.

policy ideas and should not construe its role as that of an administrative body.[36] Responsibility for implementation and action lies with the various departments headed by the ministers of the Crown. The PCO may play a coordinating role or provide specialized assistance, but should do nothing to undercut the authority of departments charged with specific responsibilities. The second principle is that the three divisions within the PCO should work together and provide mutual assistance.[37] In Robertson's opinion, unless there is coordination within the PCO itself, it will not be able to impart coherence to overall governmental policy. The third principle is that the PCO should be maintained as a non-career agency.[38] As indicated earlier, the PCO is for the most part currently staffed by career bureaucrats on loan from various government departments. Robertson suggested that there be a continual turnover of staff in order to provide fresh talent and prevent anyone from becoming too settled or perhaps too deeply identified with a particular line of goverment policy. In his opinion, the task of liaison and coordination is far too sensitive to be left in the hands of a true believer. The fourth principle, Robertson argued, is that the PCO should be kept small in size.[39] While it has grown dramatically since the Second World War, the present staff of approximately 300 is probably adequate for meeting its current needs and objectives. A further increase in staff would likely be counterproductive.

The PCO has a difficult task to perform within the Canadian government. It must be able to offer expert advice to the Prime Minister on a wide range of problems and policies. Given such expectations, it is not surprising that the PCO is considered one of the most prestigious agencies of the government.

The Treasury Board

Another central coordinating agency is the Treasury Board, which is by statute a committee of the Privy Council. In 1966, following recommendations of the Glassco Royal Commission on Government Organization, the Treasury Board was removed from the jurisdiction of the Department of Finance and elevated to the legal status of a separate government department. This agency is headed by a Cabinet minister appointed by the Prime Minister and referred to as the President of the Treasury Board. The Treasury Board includes five other Cabinet ministers, one of whom is usually the Minister of Finance. Aided by its own Secretariat, the Treasury Board is charged with two broad areas of responsibility: review of government expenditures and personnel management.[40]

---

[36]*Ibid.*, p. 505.

[37]*Ibid.*, p. 505.

[38]*Ibid.*, pp. 505-506.

[39]*Ibid.*, pp. 506.

[40]See A.W. Johnson, "The Treasury Board of Canada and the Machinery of Government in the 1970s," *Canadian Journal of Political Science*, vol. 4, no. 3 (September 1971), pp. 346-366 and Michael Hicks, "The Treasury Board of Canada and its Clients: five years of change and administrative reform 1966-1971," *Canadian Public Administration*, vol. 16, no. 2 (Summer 1973), pp. 182-205.

Responsibility for the review of expenditures means that the annual budgets of all government departments are screened and approved by this agency. The Treasury Board monitors all requests for money, evaluates them and provides an overall budget in keeping with the priorities and objectives expressed by the Prime Minister and Cabinet. There is continuous consultation and negotiation between the Treasury Board and the spokesmen for each department, usually senior level bureaucrats and the minister. Each department attempts to maximize its share of the government's budget, and it is up to the Treasury Board to assess these requests and make its recommendations.

The task of the Treasury Board would be exceedingly difficult, if not chaotic, were it not for improvements in policy-making techniques during the past two decades. The first major reform came in the 1960s with the introduction of a Program, Planning and Budgetary System (PPBS). The second was the 1979 introduction of the PEMS system mentioned earlier. In theory, these procedures force departments to frame their budgetary requirements in terms of government goals and objectives. Whether the Treasury Board has been fully able to meet its heavy responsibility in budgetary control is a matter of contention for various disgruntled department heads and, of course, for the loyal opposition. In fairness, it should be noted that the task it faces is complex. It is continually faced with pressure from both within and without Cabinet. Inevitably, no matter how worthwhile certain programs may be, there is only a finite amount of money to pay for them. It is the task of the Treasury Board to maximize the return.

The second major responsibility entrusted to the Treasury Board is management of civil service personnel. In 1967 the Treasury Board replaced the Public Service Commission as the official employer of government personnel; it is thus the responsible party in any collective bargaining negotiations.[41] It exerts control over salaries and job classifications across the civil service, and its purpose is to expand the application of the merit principle. Motivating the Treasury Board above all else should be a desire to encourage the effective utilization of human resources.

To assist the six official members of the Treasury Board there is a small, highly qualified staff – the Treasury Board Secretariat. Among the staff of the TBS are some of the brightest and most efficient members of the public service. Its economists, statisticians and efficiency experts conduct much of the preliminary analysis of departmental budgets. The TBS often makes various preliminary budgetary adjustments and other decisions which may be challenged by department heads or ministers at the formal meetings of the Board itself. Needless to say, the specialized staff of the TBS can also play an important role in policy-making.

The Department of Finance

The fourth central coordinating agency of the executive is the Department of Finance. While it is a regular government department, by virtue of its subject mat-

---

[41]On collective bargaining see chapter 9.

ter it is one of the most sensitive. Created in 1867 out of the financial bodies which predated Confederation, its authority is assigned under the *Financial Administration Act*. The Department of Finance shares some of the general concerns of the Treasury Board, but its chief preoccupation is analyzing taxation policy and the impact of government activity on the economy. That is, the Department is concerned with monitoring Canada's economic prospects and with predicting the probable level of tax revenues available to the government. It also engages in long range economic forecasting and suggests ways to maximize the performance of the economy.

The Department of Finance provides most of the information on the performance of the economy which reaches the Cabinet. It is on the basis of these facts that Cabinet committees weigh and sift various programs and proposals in order to establish priorities. The accuracy of its predictions and analyses greatly assists other policy-makers in their goal of achieving maximum use of available resources. Public servants employed by the Department of Finance concentrate on the analysis of four areas which comprise the Department's statutory authority: taxation policy; economic development and government finance; fiscal policy and economic analysis; and international trade and finance.

The first major concern, taxation policy, is handled by individual units within the Department. Specialists analyze existing tax measures from the perspective of the business community. A personal income tax unit examines proposals relating to personal taxation, deferred income plans such as retirement savings plans and trusts and partnerships. Other tax units attempt to determine the effects of taxation on the distribution of income, on the long-term growth of the economy and on the behaviour of individuals and corporations. Finally, the Department of Finance maintains an international tax policy unit which negotiates tax treaties with foreign countries and examines the effects of foreign taxation on the Canadian economy.

With respect to the second topic examined by the Department of Finance, economic development, the Department seeks to devise policies and strategies encouraging the overall growth of the Canadian economy. For instance, policy analysts study plans to foster the development of Canada's natural resources and to promote industrial growth in such diverse fields as communications, transportation, nuclear energy and manufacturing. The Department of Finance is also involved in providing government loans to promote economic development and in negotiating financial guarantees to Crown corporations.

The third responsibility of the Department of Finance is fiscal policy and economic analysis. The Department monitors all indicators of the overall economic conditions of the country and prepares forecasts used in the development of the annual government budget. This involves establishing the annual fiscal framework and maintaining a close link with the Treasury Board Secretariat.

The fourth concern of the Department of Finance is international trade. One unit investigates and reports on proposals concerning the Canadian customs tariff and its relation to the General Agreement on Tariffs and Trade (GATT) and various bilateral trade agreements. Recommendations on international trade policy, particularly imports, are formulated. The Department maintains a liaison with international financial organizations and, of course, seeks to promote export development. The international finance section is also concerned with the balance of payments and foreign exchange matters.

The Department of Finance maintains a relatively high profile among government departments. Its Minister is more than a spokesman for economic decisions made by the Cabinet. While he or she must carry out Cabinet's directives, other ministers become involved so late in the budget planning process that in effect the Finance Minister has the dominant voice. It is the Minister who presents the government's budget to Parliament and is inevitably the object of criticism or praise by the press and the Opposition. Because taxation policy is usually the target of public scorn, however, the Finance portfolio has traditionally been considered the graveyard of many a political career.

The Federal-Provincial Relations Office

Issues of concern to Ottawa and the provinces are periodically negotiated and adjusted through the mechanism of federal/provincial conferences. As we discussed in Chapter 6, this "executive" federalism has recently been characterized by a strong challenge to federal power, particularly from the richer provinces. The holding of numerous federal/provincial meetings on a wide range of issues necessitates intensive planning and preparation on the part of Ottawa. Within the Privy Council Office a new central agency has developed to carry out this responsibility. The Federal-Provincial Relations Office (FPRO) was established in 1974 and was designated a separate department under the Prime Minister in 1975.

The small but increasingly important FPRO is responsible for conducting research and analysis to help in coordinating Ottawa's interaction with the provinces and in anticipating provincial reactions.[42] In particular, the FPRO has had a special mandate to monitor events in Québec and prepare scenarios for action *vis-à-vis* its government and the issue of independence. The Office also has ongoing duties in the areas of aboriginal rights and constitutional planning. Given the continuous challenges to federalism, it is likely that the duties of the Federal-Provincial Relations Office will continue to increase.

A Profile of Superbureaucrats

The combined weight of the five organizations discussed above in bolstering the Prime Minister and Cabinet is beyond dispute. Their interactions with ministers and each other are extensive. For example, Campbell and Szablowski found that 39 percent of the sample of "superbureaucrats" in these agencies had had contact with the PM, 60 percent with their own minister, 73 percent with other ministers, and 62 percent with MPs (see Table 7-3). They also found that 72 percent of their respondents attended Cabinet committee meetings on a fairly regular basis.[43]

---

[42]*Main Estimates*, 1983-84.

[43]Campbell and Szablowski, *op. cit.*, p. 167.

TABLE 7.3   Personal Interactions of Central Agents (In Percentages)

Type of Contact				With Whom			
	PM	Own Minister	Other Ministers	Own Deputy Minister/ Secretary	Other Deputy Ministers/ Secretaries	MPs	Senators
Personal							
Any Kind	39.1	59.8	72.8	88.0	84.8	62.0	29.3
Frequency							
Once a month	34.8	66.7	67.4	75.0	79.3	44.6	23.9
twice a month	22.8	56.7	56.5	67.4	65.2	34.8	16.3
Telephone	7.6	15.2	20.7	42.4	48.9	32.6	10.9
Personal Visit	21.7	41.3	22.8	68.5	41.3	15.2	10.9
Letters/Memos	18.5	17.4	12.0	32.6	25.0	13.0	8.7
Official Meetings	30.4	40.2	64.0	72.8	66.3	23.9	13.0
Hallway	0.0	0.0	0.0	2.2	1.1	0.0	0.0
Social	1.1	0.0	2.2	1.1	3.3	7.6	4.3
About Policy	37.0	48.9	62.0	69.6	67.4	37.0	15.2

Source: Colin Campbell and George J. Szablowski, *The Superbureaucrats* (Toronto: Macmillan, 1979). p. 163.
Copyright © Colin Campbell and G.J. Szablowski, 1979. Used by permission of the authors and Gage Educational Publishing Company (a division of Canada Publishing Corporation).

Who serves in these central agencies? Perhaps surprisingly, it has been found that superbureaucrats do not come from a social elite. Campbell and Szablowski's sample of central agents in 1976 showed that their socio-economic backgrounds were more similar to those of the country's general populace than were the backgrounds of bureaucratic elites in other western democracies.[44] The study also revealed that central agents averaged 45 years of age. Québécois were the most under-represented proportionately, as they obtained only 15 percent of the positions. Ontario had 38 percent, Westerners 22 percent and the Maritimes only 4 percent. A full 21 percent came from outside Canada. It was found that 80 percent were of English or French origin; 20 percent came from other ethnic groups. Catholics and Protestants were equally repesented with 38 percent each, while 9 percent were Jewish and 15 percent were of no religious affiliation. The backgrounds of the parents of superbureaucrats were startling – many members of the bureaucratic elite were found to come from reasonably humble origins. "Only 37 percent of central agents' fathers attended university, while 29 percent never even attended high school. In addition, although 30 percent of central agents' fathers had professional or technical occupations and 36 percent were businessmen or managers, a fairly large 34 percent had clerical or blue-collar jobs."[45]

What distinguishes central agents from the general populace, and indeed from the average bureaucrat, is their level of education. Like the majority of min-

[44]*Ibid.*, p. 105 and *passim.*
[45]*Ibid.*, p. 116.

isters and Prime Ministers, members of the central agencies are highly educated. Nine out of ten graduated from university, seven out of ten received graduate degrees and many obtained foreign degrees. Many central agents began their careers outside the federal public service. The largest single group, 23 percent, came from the universities; 15 percent came from private corporations, 11 percent from Crown Corporations, 9 percent from provincial government, 9 percent from media backgrounds, 8 percent from law firms and 4 percent from high school teaching.[46] Educational achievement has clearly been a prime factor in rapid upward mobility. Such backgrounds, especially those in the social sciences and law, account for much of the pragmatism and professionalism found in the central agencies.

PRIME MINISTERIAL GOVERNMENT?

Considerable disquiet exists today among observers of the Canadian political scene. One basis for this uneasiness is the suggestion that the political executive has overstepped its proper authority; such encroachment is seen as portending grave consequences for responsible government and the parliamentary system. Changes in the rules of House of Commons procedure and the expanding jurisdiction of the central coordinating agencies have lessened the effectiveness of Parliament in its role of scrutiny and deliberation. The result is that the Prime Minister is beginning to exercise a scope of authority analogous to that of the American President.

In an early article discussing this issue, Denis Smith suggested that Parliament had surrendered its important roles of providing a forum for serious public debate and developing public policy.[47] He argued that the establishment of a presidential-style control of government had been evolving well before the election of Pierre Trudeau in 1968. Rather than establishing the trend, Trudeau merely refined and consolidated it. According to Smith, the source of the Prime Minister's predominance is that the system is devised in such a way that a great deal ultimately depends on him. The Prime Minister appoints his ministers, and their tenure depends almost solely on him. Although Cabinet may include some unusually dynamic and persuasive figures such as C.D. Howe, John Turner and Joe Clark, in the end, the decisions it reaches depend on the priorities and orientations of the Prime Minister. Cabinet policy becomes government policy, and backbenchers have little choice but to vote in obedience to the party and their Prime Minister. The recent reforms in House rules permit the government to guide legislation through with a minimum of delay or modification. The opposition parties, lacking adequate research and basic information, may resort to fiery oratory but are rarely able to conduct thorough scrutiny and effective criticism.

---

[46]*Ibid.*, p. 262.

[47]Denis Smith, "President and Parliament: The Transformation of Parliamentary Government in Canada," in Hockin, ed., *Apex of Power* pp. 308-325.

Richard Row Illustration, Toronto.

A very strong executive certainly appears to exist in Canada today. Whether the current situation is beneficial for the country and its political process is a matter that will continue to be debated for years to come. Without taking sides in the argument, we can consider what has given rise to this kind of executive leadership. While Canada's total population has been rising gradually, demands for services of all kinds have risen exponentially. To meet these needs, the government developed large departments and bureaucracies. Their size and the variety of needs they must address made it increasingly difficult to control government spending. Faced with this cumbersome and ever-expanding government sector, Prime Ministers Trudeau and Clark introduced aspects of systematic planning to replace the somewhat haphazard, *ad hoc* policy-making of previous administrations. While pushing for the reform of House procedural rules to streamline the legislative process, Trudeau simultaneously expanded the size and functions of the central coordinating agencies, especially the PMO, PCO and Treasury Board. In so doing, he brought together some talented individuals and made them responsible for rendering the government's program more rational and coherent.[48]

This delegation of exceptional policy-making authority to central executive agencies was resented by the middle and upper echelons of the civil service and

---

[48]T. d'Aquino, *op. cit.*

distrusted by the press and opposition. Journalistic reports abounded of the existence of a coterie of insiders who, being outside the bounds of parliamentary control, were able to manipulate the levers of power in Canada. While the descriptions of flagrant abuse of power may have been overstated,[49] the potential for its occurrence has been very real indeed. The power of the Prime Minister and the executive staff has become enormous and pervasive. Once elected, a Prime Minister can shape the direction and content of policy, and, except in extraordinary situations, can count on dominating the political process until he decides to call an election.

While our discussion has justifiably focused on the powers and advantages of the Prime Minister's position, at the same time we must not overlook certain limits upon it. It is our contention here that, in fact, Canada does *not* have Prime Ministerial government. The political resources of the Prime Minister are undeniably potent and broad. But the power of the Prime Minister is not exercised in isolation. The Prime Minister and his colleagues must take care to guide the Cabinet and caucus toward policies which avoid hostile reactions from Parliament and the public. As well, the Prime Minister must secure the loyalty of his followers or he will soon be out of office. As Jackson and Atkinson summarize:

> "The Prime Minister's influence stems from an ability to command the maximum possible amount of information about the political environment and to use this resource in persuading political actors to follow his policy initiatives. Administrative secrecy and collective ministerial responsibility permit the executive to acquire requisite political knowledge without revealing conflicts or divisions which may occur within its ranks. However, the ability to conceal the process of decision making at this level in government has sustained the erroneous idea that the executive works in isolation from parliamentary influence and has contributed significantly to the impression that the government acts independently of public opinion."[50]

The Prime Minister's power differs from issue to issue. At certain times, he will be able to act independently; at others, he will be forced to rely on his party colleagues. Malcolm Punnett has provided the most succinct criticism of the thesis of Prime Ministerial government. After a detailed examination of the governing style of Canada's Prime Ministers, he concluded that the argument is not justified "because of the fundamental distinction that exists between the seeming concentration of power in the hands of the Prime Minister of the day and the realities of his position."[51] The Prime Minister is constrained in his choice of ministers by the difficulties of holding a Cabinet together, of directing a complex government machine and of securing agreements to his proposals from the Cabinet, backbench and often other parties.

---

[49]Walter Stewart, *Shrug: Trudeau in Power* (Toronto: New Press, 1971).

[50]Jackson and Atkinson, *op. cit.*, p. 56.

[51]Punnett, *op. cit.*, p. 157.

There are four basic models of executive government in the political science literature:

(a) Prime Ministerial, in which decisions are taken by Prime Minister acting alone.
(b) Ministerial, in which decisions are taken by individual ministers in their own spheres of interest.
(c) Cabinet, in which Cabinet under the direction of the Prime Minister collectively takes decisions.
(d) Inner-Group, in which decisions are taken by a sub-group of Cabinet along with the Prime Minister.[52]

In view of the constraints listed above, it is our view that the first model does not apply to Canada. No Canadian Prime Minister can really act alone. Of course, some have tried to do so more than others. R.B. Bennett simultaneously held the posts of Prime Minister, Minister of Finance and External Affairs, and is said to have acted independently of his Cabinet colleagues. A splendid joke was told about him in the 1930s:

Visitor to Ottawa – "Who is that man coming toward us?"
Ottawa Resident – "Mr. R.B. Bennett, the new Prime Minister."
Visitor to Ottawa – "Why is he talking to himself?"
Ottawa Resident – "He is holding a Cabinet meeting."[53]

However, even Bennett had to avoid coalitions of conflicting interests and often ran into difficulties.

Prime Ministers obtain much of their strength from holding their team together. This must be done with conciliation, tact and only rarely with force. Most Prime Ministers bring particular skills to bear on this responsibility. For example, Pearson was a master chairman-of-the-board type of leader; Mackenzie King was a master electioneer. Mulroney appears to combine both talents. The skills required are so varied that no Prime Minister can be said to have had all of them. What all Prime Ministers must demonstrate is the ability to coordinate their colleagues, and hence policy. The primary ingredient of this ability is anticipation of the actions of all the major actors in the political system. Recent Prime Ministers have accomplished this by relying on a small coterie of ministers to help them come to compromises and conclusions. Prime Ministers Trudeau and Mulroney have employed a Priorities and Planning committee of Cabinet to obtain information and consensus. Clark constructed an Inner Cabinet to accomplish the same end. On this evidence, the usual Prime Ministerial pattern could therefore be described as setting up an informal partial Cabinet to help run the government. This is a far cry from the arrangement suggested by those who contend that Canada now has Prime Ministerial government.

---

[52] *Ibid*. p. 86.
[53] Ernest Watkins, *R.B. Bennett: A Biography* (London: Secker and Warburg, 1963), p. 167.

OVERVIEW

The centralization of power in the hands of the executive and its specialized agencies is a matter for serious attention. While some will find even the appearance of presidential-style government difficult to accept, it is likely inevitable. The centralization of power is a political reality, although at the same time critics, in their zeal, should not overlook the obvious constraints and limitations within which the Prime Minister must operate. An extraordinary apparatus and structure of power has been built over the years; fortunately for Canada, its Prime Ministers have thus far been enlightened figures.

This chapter has sought to illuminate the nature of executive power in Canada. While the *British North America Act* established a formal executive in the person of the Governor General, there is no question that real political power is exercised by the Prime Minister and his Cabinet and is based on the possession of an electoral mandate. The fusion of powers principle, along with other aspects of the British parliamentary tradition such as party discipline and Cabinet solidarity, confers upon the political executive the opportunity to carry out its program knowing that it can count on consistent legislative support. The Prime Minister has extraordinary powers at his disposal, such as the authority to make Cabinet appointments, reorganize the government structure and dissolve Parliament at his discretion. In order to run the government apparatus efficiently the Prime Minister must delegate some authority to the members of Cabinet. In recent years the Cabinet has evolved into a reasonably elaborate system of committees and sub-committees, all of which are ultimately responsible to the Prime Minister. In the last two decades the various executive coordinating agencies have grown greatly in size and authority. Unquestionably, power is becoming centralized as never before in the hands of the executive. Whether this is necessary or inevitable will probably be debated for years to come.

✦The Canadian Legislative Process✦

POLICY ALREADY IN PLACE

WHAT THE FEDERAL
GOVERNMENT WANTED

WHAT THE PROVINCES
WANTED

LEGISLATION INTRODUCED

AS AMENDED IN
COMMITTEE

AS PASSED IN
COMMONS

AS AMENDED
IN SENATE

AS FUNDED IN
ESTIMATES

AS IMPLEMENTED
BY BUREAUCRACY

WHAT WAS ACTUALLY
NEEDED

Richard Row Illustration, Toronto.

chapter 8

Legislative Politics
Symbolism or Power?

IN A PARLIAMENTARY DEMOCRACY, it goes almost without saying that the federal legislature, or Parliament, should be one of the most important institutions in the political life of the nation. But a certain degree of dissatisfaction exists in Canada among academic and media observers, sections of the general public and even parliamentarians themselves about the role of Parliament. There is perennial debate on the subject of parliamentary reform. At times, dissatisfaction with Parliament verges on outright cynicism. During a so-called "bell-ringing episode" which brought the House of Commons to a standstill over the Liberals' omnibus energy bill in March 1982, the *Toronto Sun* published the headline "WHO NEEDS 'EM! EVERYBODY'S DOING FINE WITHOUT PARLIAMENT." The answer, which the newspaper did not provide, is that "We all need 'em!" While we have to get along without Parliament from time to time, especially during recesses when Parliament is adjourned or during election campaigns, we would not "do fine" without Parliament for very long.

In a parliamentary democracy, as opposed to a presidential system, the political executive receives its authority to govern from the legislature. The government needs the approval of Parliament to legitimate its policies and activities, particularly for the expenditure of public funds. In return, the Prime Minister and Cabinet must hold themselves accountable to Parliament, and may continue to govern only as long as they retain the "confidence" of Parliament, or, more correctly in the case of Canada, at least the tacit support of a majority of the House of Commons. Thus, while Parliament gives the executive the authority to govern, it also serves as a check on the absolute or irresponsible use of government power.

Parliament, moreover, provides an arena for debate in which the major political issues of the day may be aired – and subsequently relayed to the public by the mass media. As such, it is a public forum for opposition parties to criticize the government of the day and to demonstrate why they, not the governing party, should be returned with a majority of seats at the next General Election.

Last, but not least, Parliament serves important functions on behalf of Canadian citizens. In the theory of parliamentary democracy, Parliament is the "repository of popular sovereignty" – in making laws and ensuring the responsibility of government, Parliament exercises power on behalf of the general public, power vested in it through the electoral process. It is not possible in a country the size of Canada for all citizens to participate directly in the legislative process. Instead, Canada is a *representative* democracy in which, from time to time, we choose certain individuals (Members of Parliament) to represent our interests in the making of national policies. But on a more practical level, a significant part of the role of parliamentarians is catering to the needs of their constituents. Members of Parliament and their staff spend much of their time taking up the problems of citizens with ministers, public servants or representatives of government agencies – attempting to ensure, for example, that old M. Simard gets his full pension entitlement, or that Mrs. Smith has equal access to a government retraining program. Such problems may seem prosaic compared with inflation and the nuclear bomb, but they are important to the people they affect. All Canadians, and perhaps especially those with no well-organized business lobby or trade union to represent them, need Parliament.

Thus, Parliament is indeed an important institution in Canadian political life. The ongoing debates about parliamentary reform reflect its significance. But it is not always easy to determine whether the importance of Parliament is derived from its *power* to enact legislation, hold the government accountable and control the public purse-strings, or from its perceived *symbolic* role as the repository of popular sovereignty, an arena for political debate and the legitimator of the actions of government and perhaps of the entire policy process.

Like other legislatures, the Parliament of Canada is a multifunctional institution. It plays several roles of importance to the political process and to the Canadian people. Accordingly, its members have a multitude of tasks to perform – as Senators and MPs, as members of Cabinet and opposition, as members of party caucuses and parliamentary committees and as individual representatives of their constituents. There is a constant tension, visible in many of the reform debates, among the various roles of Parliament and among the tasks that members are expected to carry out.

In this chapter, we examine how these tensions are reconciled through the process of *legislative politics*. We look at several aspects of this reconciliation: how the parliamentary timetable and procedures reflect the competing demands of a government wishing to govern and an opposition seeking to air public issues and criticize the government's method of handling them; how the working subgroups of parliamentarians in committees and party caucuses contribute to the overall work of Parliament; how individual MPs attempt to manage the competing demands on their time; how the Senate continues to make a positive contribution; and how adherence to the parliamentary "rules of the game" generally imposes a workable peace on an adversarial system of politics. We shall commence our examination by defining what a legislature is. Then, in the section that follows, we shall consider the role of legislatures in comparative perspective, with particular reference to the concepts of the *power* and *symbolism* of Parliaments and to the various meanings which may be attached to the term *"legislative politics"*.

WHAT IS A LEGISLATURE?

Legislatures are among the most pervasive of political institutions. At the beginning of 1984, approximately 130 of the independent states had some kind of parliamentary chamber; many of these also had assemblies at the sub-national level such as the state legislatures of the United States, the provincial assemblies in Canada, and so on. The very ubiquity of the institution makes the definition of a "legislature" and the specification of its functions difficult. It was once common, if not entirely correct, to base such a definition on the characteristics of the American Congress or the British Parliament. However, easy conceptualization has been hindered by the development, particularly in the Third World, of many institutions which call themselves "legislatures" or "parliaments" but which possess methods of recruitment, powers and relations to other political structures widely divergent from those of the two traditional models.

Some authors avoid this matter of definition altogether – apparently taking for granted that their readers already know what a legislature is – and plunge directly into their analyses.[1] An alternate strategy to such avoidance *and* to offering a precise definition is the presentation of a checklist of characteristics which, taken together, are both necessary and sufficient to distinguish legislatures from other political institutions. Thus, Nelson Polsby argues that a

> . . . mélange of characteristics – officiality, a claim of legitimacy based on
> links with the people, multi-memberedness, formal equality, collective
> decision-making, deliberativeness – typifies and distinguishes legislatures in
> a wide variety of settings.[2]

While Polsby's approach is primarily structural, an alternative is the functional perspective, which defines legislatures in terms of their tasks or the purpose they serve in the political system. The latter approach shows legislatures performing a multitude of functions – in addition to the apparently tautological "legislative" or "law-making" role – which vary in salience from country to country and even over time within the same political system. The role of the Supreme Soviet in the U.S.S.R., for example, is very different from that of the American Congress; and the functions of the British Parliament today have changed considerably since its so-called "Golden Age" over a century ago. Furthermore, the fact that many of the functions attributed to legislatures are also performed by other political institutions merely adds to the terminological confusion.

---

[1]For example, Jean Blondel, *Comparative Legislatures* (Englewood Cliffs; Prentice-Hall, 1973).

[2]Nelson Polsby, "Legislatures," in F. Greenstein and N. Polsby, eds., *Handbook of Political Science*, vol. 5 (Mass.: Addison-Wesley, 1975), p. 260.

Reprinted with permission – The Globe and Mail, Toronto.

The *Globe and Mail* paid its tribute to the end of the record-setting First Session of the 32nd Parliament.

A recent comparative study of legislatures by Michael Mezey offers a personal perception of the concept in which both structural and functional elements are combined:

> I think of a legislature as a predominantly elected body of people that acts collegially and that has at least the formal but not necessarily the exclusive power to enact laws binding on all members of a specific geopolitical entity.[3]

---

[3]Michael L. Mezey, *Comparative Legislatures* (Durham: Duke University Press, 1979), p. 6. (Emphasis added.)

There is one major problem with Mezey's conceptualization in the Canadian context. In applying his definition individually to each chamber or "house" of bicameral parliaments, he specifically excludes the Canadian Senate from consideration as a legislature, since its members are appointed rather than "predominantly elected". On the other hand, he does not tell the reader just what the Senate *is*, if it is not a legislature or at least a part of one. Of course, there would be no problem in the Canadian case if the definition were applied to the whole Parliament of Canada (*i.e.*, the Senate and the House of Commons) since it is "predominantly elected"; but the usage could not then be extended to the British Parliament, wherein the membership of the House of Lords, recruited by appointment or by heredity, exceeds that of the popularly elected House of Commons. The application of Mezey's definition may therefore be broadened to cover bicameral parliaments if both chambers collectively are considered to constitute the legislature, as long as the lower house (or, in parliamentary systems, the house to which the government is officially responsible) is predominantly elected. With the addition of this proviso, the simplicity and clarity of Mezey's conceptualization make it a suitable working definition for this chapter.

THE ROLE OF LEGISLATURES

A frequent source of confusion in the study of parliamentary institutions is the notion that "Legislatures must legislate." Given the similarity between the two words and the mythology surrounding the role of legislatures, this assumption is not surprising. But neither is it to be strongly encouraged, since it may lead to unfulfilled expectations of what legislatures ought to do and to overly simplistic criticisms of parliamentary institutions. For this reason, one author justifies his usage of "parliament" as a generic term for national legislative assemblies in preference to "legislature" in that the latter is "too restrictively an implied definition of what these bodies do".[4] On the other hand, most legislatures do spend a substantial portion of their time in consideration and passage of legislation. For instance, approximately one-third of all oral debates in the Canadian House of Commons are devoted to discussion of government legislation, and between one-quarter and one-half of all Commons committee meetings are on the same subject.[5] The essential point is that a distinction must be drawn between the legislative function – the task of initiating, formulating and enacting bills or statutes – and the legislature as an institution. The legislative function is a complex one which involves various other actors in the process of devising and drafting bills

---

[4]David M. Olson, *The Legislative Process: A Comparative Perspective* (New York: Harper & Row, 1980), p. 11.

[5]See Thomas A. Hockin, "Adversary Politics and Some Functions of the Canadian House of Commons," in R. Schultz *et al.*, eds., *The Canadian Political Process*, 3rd ed. (Toronto: Holt, Rinehart & Winston, 1979), p. 318; and Robert J. Jackson and Michael M. Atkinson, *The Canadian Legislative System*, 2nd rev. ed. (Toronto: Macmillan of Canada, 1980), p. 187.

before the legislature gives them consideration and decides whether the proposals are to become part of the law of the land. As institutions, legislatures are multifunctional and the passage of legislation is but one of a number of roles which they perform.

The delineation of the roles of legislatures has a long history in the study of political institutions, with the result that a bewildering array of functions now appears in the literature. Over a century has passed since the famous English constitutionalist Walter Bagehot described the major roles of the British House of Commons as *elective, expressive, teaching, informing* and *legislative.*[6] Given the reputation of the British legislature as "the mother of parliaments", it is perhaps not surprising that many subsequent classifications have been based more or less loosely upon Bagehot's classic formulation, although his categories have often been re-labelled with more current terminology or jargon. However, after the Second World War, as political scientists increasingly oriented their research to non-western societies, it became apparent that some legislatures had no real power to make laws, to constitute or remove governments or to articulate the grievances of the population. New functions had to be added to the list to describe the roles of what were little more than "rubber stamp" assemblies; as a result, attention was drawn to the more symbolic functions of parliaments, such as *legitimation* of the regime and *integration* of the political community.

So numerous have the proposed functions of legislatures become that some scholars have turned to a process of consolidation. To take one example, Mezey suggests that, "with only a modest amount of pushing and shoving", all the activities of legislatures and their members "can be grouped into three broad categories: policy-making activities, representational activities, and system-maintenance activities".[7] From this perspective, **policy-making activities** include not only the traditional legislative function (the initiation and passage of legislation), but also all attempts to influence the content of government policy, the publication of political issues through parliamentary debate and the scrutiny or control of the activities of government and bureaucracy. The **representational activities** of parliamentarians consist largely of expressing the interests and opinions of their respective electorates and dealing with the problems of constituents, particularly with regard to mediating with the bureaucracy on their behalf. Finally **system-maintenance activities** are the often primarily symbolic functions which contribute to the viability and legitimacy of other parts of the political system or the regime itself. Hence, legislatures often participate in the recruitment and socialization of future members of the political elite; they aid in the regulation and management of conflict and may serve to integrate and build consensus among rival political elites; they frequently elect and thus help to

---

[6]Walter Bagehot, *The English Constitution,* 1st ed. 1867 (London: Fontana/Collins, 1963), pp. 150-154.

[7]Mezey, *op. cit.,* p. 7 ff. For an application of these broad categories to the literature on the Canadian House of Commons, see Allan Kornberg and Colin Campbell, "Parliament in Canada: A Decade of Published Research," *Legislative Studies Quarterly,* vol. III, no. 4 (November 1978), pp. 555-580.

legitimate governments; and through their participation in the decision-making process they legitimate public policies.

The relative importance of the various activities of legislatures and their members varies from country to country, and over time within individual systems. As a consequence of erroneous preconceptions of what legislatures *ought* to do, this change in the relative salience of different functions over time has led some commentators to lament the "decline of legislatures". Here, "decline" refers to a waning of the power vested in the more established parliaments of Western Europe and the old members of the British Commonwealth. Particular attention is given to the dominance of Cabinet and the bureaucracy in the legislative process. Much of the blame for this situation has been placed upon the growing volume and increasingly technical nature of legislation in the modern nation-state and the lack of resources available to parliamentarians for coping with this complexity, or on the adverse effect of the emergence of cohesive, disciplined political parties upon the role of individual parliamentarians.

The bemoaning of a decline in the powers of parliaments is largely based on an inappropriate comparison of their present roles with an ideal-typical yardstick, the so-called "Golden Age of Parliament" in Britain. Admittedly, there was a time when much legislation was either initiated or introduced by private members; when the volume of parliamentary business was sufficiently small to allow members to spend long hours in debate and individual displays of grandiose rhetoric; when legislators were virtual independents and formed *ad hoc* majorities on an issue-to-issue basis; and when governments were frequently removed and replaced by Parliament without resorting to General Elections. But this situation existed only in a few countries and only for a short period during the mid-19th century. It was an era in which the business of the state was minimal and parliaments were well-suited "to operate by competition between political parties responsible to a non-democratic electorate".[8] But, although a dominant executive has historically been the norm in Britain, it was in this brief and rather exceptional interlude that many of the myths currently surrounding legislatures had their origin. Not unnaturally, given the time at which the Parliament of Canada was established, on British principles, some idealistic views entered the mythology of Canadian parliamentary democracy.

Although, as we have said, the activities of legislatures have changed over time in response to alterations in the political and socio-economic environment, it must be pointed out that the decline of some functions has been matched by an enhancement of others. As one author has remarked of the legislature as a political institution, "decline, in short, is in the eye of the beholder and depends upon his analytical perspective."[9]

To talk of the "strength" or "weakness" of a legislature is difficult in any case. The concept of power is extremely complex, particularly as it relates to the

---

[8]C.B. Macpherson, *The Real World of Democracy* (Toronto: CBC Publications, 1965), p. 35.

[9]Gerhard Loewenberg, "The Role of Parliaments in Modern Political Systems," in Loewenberg, ed., *Modern Parliaments: Change or Decline?* (Chicago: Aldine-Atherton, 1971), p. 15.

legislative process. If a given parliament accepts the vast majority of the legislation placed before it by the government, it is not possible to be sure whether this demonstrates the weakness of the legislature *vis-à-vis* the executive or its strength in forcing the government to introduce only those measures which have a high probability of success.

Similarly, *power* and *symbolism* are often posed as dichotomous concepts: a legislature is *either* powerful *or* its weakness makes its role primarily symbolic. While this may be partly true in the short term, it may also be argued that in the long run only a powerful or effective legislature will have sufficient efficacy to perform a symbolic role in maintaining the legitimacy of the policy process and its outputs. All too often, the power of a legislature is equated with the extent of its involvement in the legislative process, especially with the initiation of legislation or the frequency of rejection of government policies. But legislatures are multifunctional institutions, and many of their activities other than law-making are symptomatic of their importance in the political system and contribute to their public image and symbolic capabilities. Thus, the characteristics "power" and "symbolism", rather than constituting polar opposites, are parallel concepts which may be applied to each of the many activities undertaken by legislatures.

Legislative Politics

As the title of this chapter suggests, legislative behaviour in an assembly such as the Parliament of Canada is highly political. But what is meant by the term **legislative politics**? Perhaps the closest analogy we can draw is to the concept of politics as it appears in the popular phrase "office politics" – that is, the interaction and competition among workers in the same organization for status, influence and power in the life of that institution. Whether in the form of opposition parties seeking to influence or change the policy of the government, or the legislature as a whole seeking greater opportunities for effective participation in the decision-making process, or members of the same party vying for advancement in the legislative or government hierarchy, there is constant politicking in the life of a legislature.

Nonetheless, all members of the legislature are bound together by their common participation in the institution and by codes of ethics and behaviour that are often the source of incomprehension to the outsider. Political foes on the floor of the House may be the best of friends outside the chamber, while colleagues from the same party may be fiercely antagonistic. This phenomenon is well explained by the experienced but fictional Minister in the BBC comedy series *Yes Minister*:

> "Strange though it may seem it is much easier to be friends with a member of the opposite party than a member of one's own party – for one is not in direct personal competition for office with members of the Opposition in the way that one is with one's colleagues."[10]

---

[10]Jonathan Lynn and Anthony Jay, eds., *Yes Minister: The Diaries of a Cabinet Minister by the Rt. Hon. James Hacker MP*, Volume I (London: British Broadcasting Corporation, 1981) p. 101.

Similarly, members from polar extremes of the political spectrum may join forces in defence of the sovereignty of Parliament in the face of encroachment by the government or some other institution. Or, as occurred when Stanley Knowles was made an honorary officer of the Canadian House of Commons for life, all members of the legislature, partisan allies and foes alike, may put aside their differences to unite in paying tribute to one of their number for long and distinguished service. Meanwhile, through it all may rage a fierce war of rhetoric between rival parties and competing ideologies. Such is the stuff of legislative politics.

THE LEGISLATIVE PROCESS IN PARLIAMENT

The *British North America Act* established the Parliament of Canada as a bicameral legislature consisting of an appointed upper house, the Senate, and a popularly elected lower house, the House of Commons. In addition, the Monarch plays a formal role in the legislative process through his or her representative, the Governor General, inasmuch as all bills must receive Royal Assent before becoming part of Canadian law.

In strictly legal terms, the two chambers of the Parliament of Canada have coequal legislative powers in that all bills must be passed in their entirety by both houses in order to receive Royal Assent, and neither chamber has the power to override the veto or the amendments of the other. In this regard, the Senate appears to be stronger than its British counterpart, the House of Lords, because the former can defeat legislation, whereas the latter can only exercise a suspensory veto.[11] However, the Senate rarely employs its amendment powers on the substance of bills and no longer uses its veto; it usually backs down in the case of dissension between the two chambers. As a result, many commentators view the Senate as the junior partner in the parliamentary process and often virtually ignore the upper house in analyzing the Canadian legislature. The fact remains, however, that all bills must be passed by both chambers before becoming law. The Senate should therefore not be overlooked in an examination of the legislative process.

The Parliamentary Life-Cycle

The Senate and the House of Commons may meet as legislative bodies only during a parliamentary session. Parliaments are labelled by consecutive numbers, changing after each general election. For example, the 282 MPs returned in the September 1984 election collectively constituted the 33rd Parliament. In each Parliament there may be one or a number of sessions, depending upon the wishes of the government of the day and its ability in managing its legislative program, and upon the length of the Parliament – that is, how much time elapses between general elections.

---

[11] In contrast to this view see Thomas A. Hockin, *Government in Canada* (Toronto: McGraw-Hill Ryerson, 1976), p. 173.

A parliamentary session begins with the Governor General summoning the MPs and Senators to Parliament at the request of the Prime Minister. Members of both Houses come together in the Senate Chamber, amid great pomp and ceremony, to hear the Governor General deliver the Speech from the Throne, outlining the government's proposed legislative program for the forthcoming session. They then return to their respective chambers to commence business. In the Commons, the debate on the Throne Speech usually occupies the first few days of the session; afterwards, the normal timetable of the House comes into effect.

Another ceremonial occasion, known as the *prorogation of Parliament,* brings a session to a close. The Governor General again acts upon the advice of the Prime Minister; therefore, the length of a session is really determined by the government's ability to tidy up the loose ends in its legislative program. Any legislation which has not successfully completed all the stages of the process automatically dies when Parliament is prorogued: if the government is still committed to it, the bill must go through the entire process again in the next session. This fact explains the phenomenon of so-called "trial-balloon bills", which governments sometimes introduce close to the end of a session to test parliamentary and public reactions before the bill is redrafted for introduction in the next session.

At one time, each session of Parliament lasted a year or less, but sessions have generally become longer in recent years. Thus, the first session of the 32nd Parliament lasted an unprecedented three years and eight months. Also in the past, MPs and Senators used to enjoy a break between sessions, in addition to their vacations from Ottawa when Parliament was adjourned or in recess. Today, prorogation of one session is often followed immediately by the summoning of the next. However, at least once every five years, there has always been and continues to be a proclamation by the Governor General announcing the dissolution of the House of Commons. *Dissolution,* which occurs at the request of a Prime Minister who seeks a new mandate or whose government has been defeated in the House,[12] brings in its wake a General Election. For most MPs, it is a sign to disperse and begin campaigning for re-election to the next Parliament.

As we have noted, one of the reasons for which MPs and Senators are summoned to Ottawa is to participate in the legislative process through which bills must pass before being promulgated by Royal Assent. The parliamentary stages are only the final elements of a much longer process which begins with the initiation, formulation and drafting of bills by a number of institutions, "such as the Prime Minister, Cabinet subject-matter and legislation committees, the Privy Council Office, the drafting office of the Department of Justice and other departments."[13] Given that most legislation originates from outside the parliamentary chamber, what happens to bills once they enter the parliamentary deliberation

---

[12]In theory, the Governor General retains some discretionary power in the matter of dissolution; see Chapter 5.

[13]Jackson and Atkinson, *op. cit.,* p. 22.

stage of the legislative process? Before examining this question, we shall make a brief but necessary aside.

Types of Bills

For a better understanding of the legislative process it is necessary to distinguish between the various types of legislation, since the nature of a bill helps determine its route through Parliament. Parliamentary procedure distinguishes among bills on constitutional and legal grounds on three major levels (see Figure 8-1). First, legislation may be divided into **private** and **public bills**. Private bills are those which confer special powers or rights upon specific individuals, groups or corporations, rather than upon society as a whole. They are often utilized to incorporate companies or certain religious and charitable organizations, and, until 1964, were required for granting divorces for residents of Québec and Newfoundland. Most private bills are first introduced into the Senate and receive relatively little discussion. They constitute a small proportion of total legislative activity.

Second, public bills, which seek to change the law affecting the public as a whole, are themselves divided into two types: **government bills**, those introduced by the Cabinet as government policy; and **private members' bills**, those introduced by individual Members of Parliament. In the 19th century, when the business of government was relatively limited, private members' bills were an important component of legislative activity. Today, with a restricted number of specific slots in the parliamentary timetable, few even come to a vote, and, except for those changing the name of a constituency, for example, it is quite unusual for Parliament to pass even one private members' bill during a session.

Finally, government bills are further divided into **financial** and **non-financial bills**. Under the *BNA Act*, "money bills", those which authorize taxation and appropriations or expenditures, must be introduced first into the House of Commons, and then only by a Minister of the Crown. These special provisions relate to the traditional right of Parliament to demand that the Crown hear grievances from the people before the granting of supply – that is, before approving the funds necessary to conduct the Crown's affairs. The consideration of fi-

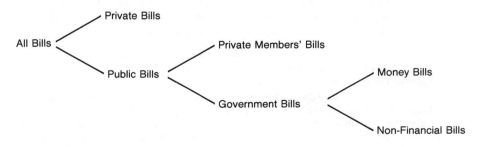

FIGURE 8.1 The Types of Bills

nancial measures is therefore intended to be a time when the Cabinet accounts for its management of the economy, listens to complaints brought forward by private members of Parliament and (usually but not always) survives an opposition motion to the effect that the government has failed in its responsibilities. To accentuate the importance of financial matters, many of the procedures employed in the consideration of money bills differ from those used to examine other legislation.

Before we leave the subject of the types of legislation, some comment should be made upon **delegated** or **subordinate legislation**. This type of legislation refers to the power to make decisions, called "regulations" or "statutory instruments", having the force of law, which are delegated by Parliament under various statutes to the Governor-in-Council (the Cabinet), to ministers of individual government departments and to a number of agencies and boards such as the CRTC and the CTC. Delegated legislation constitutes a large and ever-increasing proportion of all government legislative decisions. The Special Committee on Statutory Instruments reported in 1969 that, of 601 Acts of Parliament examined, 420 provided for delegated legislation, and that an average of 530 regulations *per annum* had been published in the Canada Gazette over the previous twelve years.[14] An enormous volume of legislation (much of it admittedly trivial and technical) is therefore not subjected to the full parliamentary legislative process. However, one of the consequences of the Special Committee Report was the establishment in 1973 of the Standing Joint Committee on Regulations and Other Statutory Instruments, whose purpose is to review delegated legislation and report possible abuses to Parliament.[15]

The Stages of Legislation

The vast majority of bills passed by the Canadian Parliament are government bills. Although government legislation may be introduced first in the Senate, this is an increasingly rare occurrence, and money bills are constitutionally prohibited from this route. Figure 8-2 illustrates the following brief overview of the major stages in the passage of a typical government bill originating in the lower house.

After the pre-parliamentary processes of policy formulation are over, the minister responsible for the legislation asks the House for leave to introduce the bill. This motion is not debatable. A short description of the aims of the bill may be given. Acceptance of the **First Reading** motion "that this bill be read a first time and be printed" is usually a matter of course. It allows the bill to be printed,

---

[14]House of Commons Special Committee on Statutory Instruments, *Third Report* (Ottawa: Queen's Printer, 1969).

[15]See James R. Mallory, "Parliamentary Scrutiny of Delegated Legislation in Canada: A Large Step Forward and a Small Step Back," *Public Law* (Spring 1972), pp. 30-42; Graham Eglington, "Scrutiny of Delegated Legislation in the Parliament of Canada," *The Parliamentarian*, vol. 59 (October 1978), pp. 271-275; and Gary Levy, "Delegated Legislation and Standing Joint Committee on Regulations and other Statutory Instruments," *Canadian Public Administration*, vol. 22, no. 3 (Fall 1979), pp. 349-365.

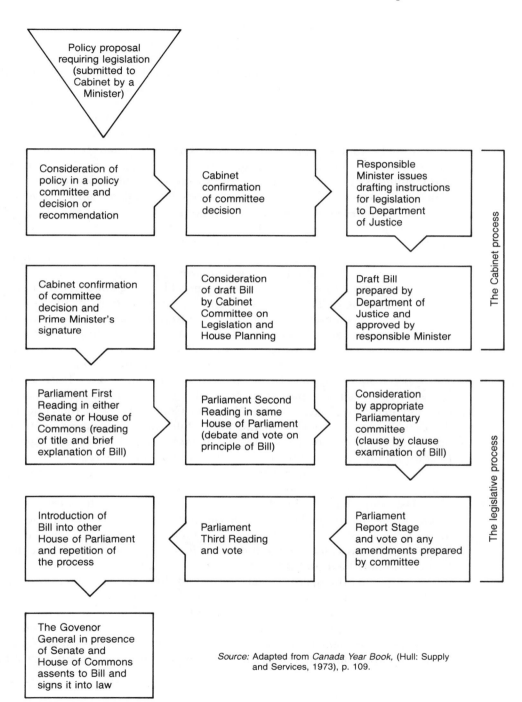

FIGURE 8.2 How a Bill Becomes Law

numbered (with a 'C' prefix if it originates in the House of Commons, 'S' if in the Senate) and distributed to MPs. The bill is now on the *order paper*, the schedule of pending parliamentary business. The **Second Reading** motion, usually proposed by the sponsoring minister, permits debate upon the principle of the bill; no amendments are accepted by the Speaker. The debate is monopolized by the government and opposition front benches. The opposition strategy is usually restricted to moving that the bill "be considered six months hence", a tactic known as "the hoist" which would effectively kill the bill for that session.

After Second Reading, the Standing Orders stipulate that "unless otherwise ordered" a bill must be sent directly to a standing, special or joint (Senate and Commons) Committee. This is the **Committee Stage**. Most bills go to the appropriate standing committees. For money bills and certain other legislation upon which the House agrees, the Committee Stage is undertaken by the Committee of the Whole, the whole chamber sitting in committee chaired by the Deputy-Speaker. At this stage, the bill undergoes detailed clause-by-clause consideration. Amendments may be moved by both government and opposition members. The amended bill is then voted on as a whole.

Except in the case of those bills examined by the Committee of the Whole, which go straight to **Third Reading**, the recommendations of the appropriate committee are presented to the House at the **Report Stage**. Debate is allowed on both the principle and the details of the bill, amendments proposed by the committee are voted on and further amendments may be introduced. Sometimes the opposition reintroduces amendments defeated in committee or the government seeks to reinstate original clauses altered by the committee. "During the 28th and 29th Parliaments, report stage consumed between 10 and 25 percent of the time devoted to legislation in the House of Commons."[16] At the conclusion of the debate, a vote is taken on the whole bill, including amendments. Unless unanimously agreed otherwise by the House, after the Report Stage, Third Reading commences with the motion "that the bill be now read a third time and passed". Debate is not unknown at this point, but usually takes place only at the insistence of the opposition. A final vote is now taken on the bill.

Assuming that the bill has successfully negotiated the various debates, amendments, attempted hoists and divisions (formal votes) in the House of Commons, it has to begin the whole process again in the Senate. However, the upper house usually provides a smoother path for government legislation than the lower chamber. First and Second Readings are quickly over. It is at the Committee Stage that the major legislative work of the Senate is done. While the upper house rarely uses its powers to amend the substance of a bill, "it does do considerable work 'cleaning up' sloppily drafted bills."[17] The Senate is not allowed to increase taxation or spending; in fact, there is some debate as to whether it is constitutionally permitted to amend financial legislation at all.[18] As in the House of Commons, the bill as amended in committee is reported back to the

---

[16]Jackson and Atkinson, *op. cit.*, p. 95.

[17]Hockin, *op. cit.*, p. 174.

[18]See F.A. Kunz, *The Modern Senate of Canada 1925-1963: A Re-Appraisal* (Toronto: University of Toronto Press, 1965), pp. 338-339.

Senate for debate, possible further amendment and acceptance. After the final consideration of the bill by the Senate and the Third Reading vote, word is sent to the House of Commons reporting whether the Senate has rejected, amended or passed the bill.

If the bill is defeated by the Senate (which is extremely unlikely), it is lost and must pass through the entire process from the start. A bill passed by the Commons but amended by the Senate returns to the lower house for consideration of the amendments. Since such changes are more often to the wording or to a minor detail of the bill (rather than its substance), they are often accepted by the responsible minister. Once this has happened or if the bill is passed intact by the Senate, it is ready for Royal Assent. In this final stage of the process the Governor General, sitting in the Senate before the assembled members of both houses, puts the final seal of approval on the bill. The bill thereby becomes an Act of Parliament of Canada, and henceforth is law unless other arrangements for formal proclamation in the future are contained within it.

Money bills follow the same general process as other government legislation, but are unique for four reasons. First, as noted above, they must originally be introduced in the House of Commons. Second, revenue-raising bills are not considered in standing committees in the Commons but by the Committee of the Whole. Third, there are political limitations upon the Senate's ability to amend such bills. Finally, they tend to have a longer gestation period than other bills, because they are not themselves the only, or even the most important, basis for debate. In the case of tax bills, much debate centres on the Budget speech delivered by the Minister of Finance, which outlines the government's economic policy and summarizes the changes that will subsequently appear in tax legislation. With appropriation bills – those which authorize the spending of public money by government departments and other agencies – the key debates occur during the consideration of departmental estimates by standing committees. Once the estimates are examined, appropriation bills are usually passed quickly to give legislative effect to the government's spending proposals.

The entire legislative process is thus complex and variable. The time taken by a bill to pass and its likelihood of success depend upon a number of factors: the importance or controversiality of the given bill and of the other legislation under consideration at the same time; the partisan composition of the two chambers and the presence or absence of a government majority; the willingness of the government to impose, and of Parliament to accept, procedural devices to shorten debate and speed passage of the bill; and last, but not least, because Parliament is necessarily composed of human beings, the mood of the House at a particular moment.[19] Despite the apparent dominance of governments over the legislative process, the whole procedure looks very much like an obstacle course to the minister introducing a piece of contentious legislation.

Having briefly reviewed the legislative process, it is time for us to focus on

---

[19]On the last point, in particular, one study evaluating Canadian legislative activity suggests that "in each parliament the lowest performance levels appear during the final session . . . Parliaments, it seems, become cantankerous as they get older.. . ." Jackson and Atkinson, *op. cit.*, p. 181.

the component parts of the legislature. The role of the Monarch, through his or her representative the Governor General, has already been examined in Chapter 5. There remains the analysis of the legislative politics of the two chambers, the House of Commons and the Senate.

THE HOUSE OF COMMONS

It is probably not unreasonable to suggest that, when most Canadians talk about "Parliament", they really mean "The House of Commons". After all, when people vote for a Member of Parliament, they are electing a member of the House of Commons, not the Senate. And when they write to their MP about some personal or public matter, they expect their constituency representative in the Commons to take action on their behalf. Moreover, media attention is focused mainly on the House of Commons, because it is the chamber to which the government is responsible and because the more newsworthy and dramatic confrontations in Canadian legislative politics occur there.

Conflict and Compromise

The tone of legislative politics in the House of Commons is profoundly affected by two key inheritances from the British political tradition: first, an adversarial system of party politics, with a clear dichotomy between government and opposition; second, a code of rules and procedures governing the behaviour of members which serves to counteract, to some extent, potential hostility arising from the partisan nature of the House.

The adversarial pattern of relations between government and opposition is clearly reflected in, and perhaps reinforced by, the physical layout of the House. In many legislative chambers, such as the U.S. House of Representatives or the West German Bundestag, all elected members sit in a semicircle facing the Speaker of the House. However, the seating plan of the Canadian House of Commons follows the British model in forcing government and opposition to face one another across the floor of the House, the government to the Speaker's right and the opposition on the left. The leaders of the two major parties confront each other like old-time gunfighters, each surrounded by his immediate lieutenants and backed by the rest of his supporters. This "head-to-head" confrontation, separated only by the open floor of the House, serves to demarcate clearly the government from the opposition and to reinforce the sense of political identity and party cohesion on both sides of the Commons.

In the central area of the chamber, between the two main rivals, sit the officials of the House. Most conspicuous among them is the Speaker who, under the *BNA Act*, "shall preside at all meetings of the House of Commons." Although nominated by the Prime Minister, the Speaker is officially an impartial arbiter chosen by the whole House and is usually elected without opposition. The position has become increasingly independent or non-partisan: since 1963, the Leader of the Opposition has seconded the Prime Minister's nomination and, in 1979,

Liberal James Jerome became the first Speaker to serve under two different parties when Prime Minister Joe Clark nominated him to continue the role he had fulfilled under the previous Liberal administration. The Speaker is not permitted to vote in House divisions, except for casting the deciding vote in the event of a tie, when convention dictates that he or she support the government of the day.[20]

Apart from the main function of presiding over the work of the House, the Speaker is in charge of the administration of the chamber. First, he or she oversees the staffing of the House in the form of secretaries, clerks and so on. As well, the Speaker is jointly responsible with the Board of Internal Economy, a body composed of the Speaker and House representatives, for the economic management of the House and prepares and steers through the annual estimates of the costs of running the House of Commons. In the political function of chairing the House, the Speaker is aided by a Deputy Speaker, also elected by fellow MPs at the beginning of each Parliament. In the exercise of administrative duties, the Speaker is assisted by the chief permanent employee of the Commons, the Clerk of the House. The Clerk is responsible for ensuring that relevant documents are printed and circulated to all members of the House and advises the Speaker on the day's business. The Clerk also bears the rank of Deputy Minister as head of the permanent staff of the House of Commons.

In keeping with the Westminster model, the Speaker is simultaneously an ordinary member of the House of Commons and an impartial arbiter removed from the political struggle in the rest of the House both by the conventions and traditions which surround the office and by the elevated position of the chair on a dais at one end of the chamber. In the midst of the potential chaos and conflict engendered by the partisan nature of the Commons, the Speaker is responsible for enforcing the rules designed to permit the orderly functioning of the House. The Speaker must therefore be a skilled parliamentarian, well versed not only in the formal rules contained in the Standing Orders of the House but also in unwritten conventions established by past practice.

Certain rules of the House are explicitly designed to reduce the temperature of party politics in the legislature by limiting the direct personal interaction of the members. Verbal confrontations during debate are somewhat constrained by the requirements that no member may speak officially without recognition by the Speaker and that all statements must be addressed to the Chair. Thus, members do not speak to one another directly. Neither may they speak *of* one another directly, inasmuch as individuals are referred to not by name but through more impersonal titles, such as "The Prime Minister", "The Leader of the Opposition", or "The Honourable Member for Constituency X".

---

[20]The casting vote of the Speaker "is not to be construed as an expression of opinion upon the merits of the question. According to tradition the Speaker endeavors to vote in such a way as to provide a further opportunity to consider the question . . ." Sir John George Bourinot, *Bourinot's Rules of Order*, 3rd ed., revised by Geoffrey H. Stanford (Toronto: McClelland & Stewart, 1977), p. 27. For a full discussion of the roles and traditions of the Speakership, see W.F. Dawson, *Procedure in the Canadian House of Commons* (Toronto: University of Toronto Press, 1962), Chapter 4.

If all else fails and the debate becomes heated, as it does on occasion, the dignity of individual members and of the House as a whole is protected by the proscription of certain terms deemed to constitute "unparliamentary language".[21] It is not permitted, for example, to use expressions which cast doubt upon the legitimacy of a member's birth, nor to allege that a speech has been inspired by intoxicating substances. One of the most common infringements of the rule is the suggestion that another member is "lying" to the House. Shortly before the time of writing, Progressive Conservative MP Gord Taylor faced expulsion from the Commons after refusing to withdraw an accusation that New Democrat MP Dan Heap was telling "complete lies". When an attempt to substitute "fabrications" for "lies" was also ruled out of order, Conservative House Leader Erik Nielsen came to Taylor's aid with the synonym "mendacities", which also means "lies" but has not been placed on the parliamentary list of proscribed words.[22]

As this example demonstrates, the rules of "unparliamentary language" often have the effect of testing the verbal ingenuity of members in order to convey the sense of a particular epithet without the actual use of forbidden terms. There may also be other ways of getting one's point across without breaching the rules. Former Conservative MP Gordon Aiken reports the clever and entirely legitimate device employed by one member exasperated by criticism from the other side of the House:

> "Mr. Speaker," he asked, properly addressing the Chair, "would it be out of order if I called the honourable Member a son-of-a-bitch?" The Speaker nodded his head. "I thought so," said Clancy, resuming his seat.[23]

Outspoken members are, however, sometimes called to order by the Speaker and may even be suspended from the House for refusing to retract derogatory remarks. Ironically, in view of his own experience two months previously, Dan Heap himself was expelled from the Commons in June 1984 after accusing Liberal Jean-Luc Pépin of lying to the House. But in general it is assumed that MPs are quite capable of taking care of themselves in debate, although those outside the House cannot do so; therefore, the rules protect certain persons (especially the Royal Family, the Governor General and the Senate) from explicit attacks in the Commons.[24]

Also among the conflict-regulating devices in the House of Commons are the Standing Orders, the procedures and regulations adopted by members for their internal self-government, and the rules of debate. Perhaps, most important among the latter is the principle that, once recognized by the Speaker, every MP has the right to speak for a certain length of time without interruption, as long as

---

[21]See the discussion of "Parliamentary Language" and "Parliamentary Behaviour" in Dawson, *Procedure in the Canadian House of Commons*, pp. 110-117.

[22]"Lies are unacceptable, mendacity OK," *Montreal Gazette*, April 22, 1982.

[23]Gordon Aiken, *The Backbencher* (Toronto: McClelland & Stewart, 1974), p. 66.

[24]Through precedent established by past Speakers, the protection of S.O. 35 has been extended to the judiciary, lieutenant-governors and others of "high official station".

the speech remains relevant to the motion before the House. The Speaker has to ensure that members from both sides of the House get a fair hearing – a difficult task which is facilitated by Party Whips providing the Speaker with a daily list of members who wish to speak on various motions – but it is not unknown for the opposition parties to complain that the Chair is favouring the government side.

Once a member has the floor, his colleagues or opponents are not always capable of containing themselves; thus, some expressions of support and disagreement are, within certain bounds, sanctioned by the Speaker. Outbursts of laughter and cheering or antagonistic remarks are accepted as part of the debate; the euphemistic reporting in Hansard of "hear-hear!" or "oh-oh!" may disguise a multitude of sins.

All of these formal devices help in maintaining peace and reducing conflict emanating from the partisan composition of the House. Other effective mitigating factors are the sense of corporate identity shared by members of the Commons, and the extent to which MPs from both sides of the House interact in informal situations outside the chamber, often forging friendships across party lines. In the midst of the rhetoric, the struggle is, after all, "often carried on more in the spirit of a game than a war".[25]

The Business of the House

Once the currents of conflict and compromise within the House of Commons are appreciated, the way in which the House works can perhaps best be understood with reference to the business of a typical day in the House and to the weekly timetable presented in Figure 8-3.[26] The timetable of the House of Commons reflects a compromise between the competing demands for time of the various groups within it. The business of the House may be arranged, on the basis of practical usage rather than procedural formality, into five broad categories: routine business, urgent business, government business, private members' business and opposition business.

The **routine business** of the House usually begins after the daily Question Period and consumes fifteen to twenty minutes. The Speaker reads through a list of routine proceedings, not all of which will arise on any particular day: announcements and the raising of questions of privilege;[27] the presentation of reports from standing and special committees; the tabling of documents and government papers for the notice of members; statements by ministers regarding government policy; the introduction and First Reading of Commons bills and the First Reading of public bills originating in the Senate (in both cases, formalities

---

[25]R.M. Dawson, *The Government of Canada*, 5th ed., revised by Norman Ward (Toronto: University of Toronto Press, 1970) p. 356.

[26]The discussion of House of Commons proceedings and procedures is based upon the new procedures originally adopted for a trial period of one year in December 1982 and renewed.

[27]See the discussion of "Privilege," in Dawson, *Procedure in the Canadian House of Commons*, Chapter 3.

on which no debate is allowed and no formal divisions occur); government notices of motions to be introduced later in the Orders of the Day; and other motions, particularly those requesting concurrence in committee reports and those pertaining to special arrangements for the sittings and proceedings of the House.

Next, the Speaker calls upon the Parliamentary Secretary to the Government House Leader to notify the House regarding government responses to Questions on the Order Paper (written questions which, after a minimum forty-eight hours' notice, are usually answered in print in the day's *Debates*) and, on occasion, to reply to requests from members for the tabling of government papers in the House.[28] The Commons is then ready to proceed with what the government regards as the main business, the Orders of the Day, unless there is first an interjection under Standing Order 30, one of the items of **urgent business**.

Standing Order 30 is a procedural device which permits any member to move "that this House do now adjourn" in order to discuss "a specific and important matter requiring urgent consideration". This motion could, at one time, exhaust considerable time in the House, even if not eventually granted. As a result, "it became the practice for members to discuss the matter proposed for discussion if leave were given under the guise of discussing the urgency of discussing it."[29] Since 1969, the Speaker rules immediately upon the validity of the request but, in order that the entire day may not be wasted, gives leave to the member to introduce the adjournment motion. Standing Order 30 is primarily utilized by the opposition to introduce debate on an issue which is not on the government Order Paper or to criticise the government.

The other procedure classified as urgent business is the opportunity for MPs to make statements to the House under Standing Order 21, immediately preceding the Question Period (see Figure 8-3). This provision has replaced the old S.O. 43 which permitted private members, usually from the opposition, to introduce without prior notice a motion relating to a matter of "urgent and pressing necessity". Since the unanimous consent of the House was required for debate to take place, the "necessity" was rarely established, and most members making use of S.O. 43 were, in fact, primarily concerned with focusing attention on themselves or on some particular issue in the presence of a packed House and a crowded press gallery gathered for the upcoming Question Period. The new S.O. 21 effectively recognizes this fact; it was introduced to prevent the widespread abuse of House time and patience that occurred under S.O. 43. Thus, S.O. 21 permits members to make only a 90-second statement to the House, allowing them to make a point or gain the desired media exposure without going through the pretence of formulating a motion or of attempting to establish "urgent and pressing necessity". It is an excellent example of sensible and pragmatic innovation in House rules to satisfy the needs of individual members

---

[28]For a detailed explanation of each of the "routine proceedings", see John B. Stewart, *The Canadian House of Commons: Procedure and Reform* (Montréal: McGill-Queen's University Press, 1977), pp. 57-67.

[29]*Ibid.*, p. 68.

HOUR	MONDAY	TUESDAY	WEDNESDAY	THURSDAY	FRIDAY
11:00 AM	Government Business	Government Business	(Party Caucus Meetings)	Government Business	S.O. 21 ——————— Question Period ——————— Routine Government Business
12:00 NOON					
1:00 PM	Suspension (Lunch)	Suspension (Lunch)		Suspension (Lunch)	Suspension (Lunch)
2:00 PM	S.O. 21 — — — — Question Period	S.O. 21 — — — — Question Period	S.O. 21 — — — — Question Period	S.O. 21 — — — — Question Period	Government Business
3:00 PM	Routine	Routine	Routine	Routine	
4:00 PM	Government Business	Government Business	Private Members' Business	Government Business	
5:00 PM					
6:00 PM	Adjournment Debate (Late Show)	Adjournment Debate (Late Show)		Adjournment Debate (Late Show)	
Evening	Possible Emergency Debates OR Sittings Beyond Normal Hour of Adjournment (Mondays, Tuesdays, Thursdays)**				

* The daily and weekly timetable outlined in this Figure is that which operated under the experimental Standing Orders adopted by the House of Commons to take effect in December 1982 (subsequently renewed in December 1983).

** See *Standing Orders* 9 (1).

FIGURE 8.3 A Week in the House*

without making a mockery of the formal proceedings of the Commons.

The bulk of the time of plenary sessions of the Commons is consumed by the Orders of the Day, during which the House deals with the public business placed before it. The greater part of this period – three mornings and four afternoons in most weeks – is devoted to **government business** in the form of motions dealing with the passage of bills and the referral of legislation, estimates and investigatory tasks to standing and special committees. *Orders* are the prime means through which the House of Commons formulates instructions in response to motions. They serve to guide the Speaker and other members and to direct the officers of the House to pursue particular courses of action. Some orders, for example Standing Orders, are general and more or less permanent, applying mainly to the procedure of the House. Others are more particular: for example, that a bill "now be read a second time", or that it be sent to committee. In the long run, of course, these latter cases result in a change in public policy through new laws. However, some motions result not in orders but in *resolutions*. Herein lies a source of confusion for many observers of Parliament. From time to time, the House makes a resolution on a particular issue, on which the government subsequently takes no action. This is because resolutions are not binding on anybody: they are simply expressions of the *opinion* of the Commons, as opposed to orders, which express the *will* of the House. While orders reflect the power of the Commons to impose its will on others, resolutions are the primarily symbolic outputs of "Parliament as rhetoric", although they may often be influential in legitimating policies for which the government wants a public expression of support from the House.

Not all of the business conducted during the working week is instigated by the government. On Wednesday afternoons, following routine proceedings, the House turns to **private members' business**. Items under this heading are listed in the order in which they are raised by members, under four categories: requests for the tabling of papers and documents; private members' bills; private members' motions; and private bills, although very few of the latter are now introduced in the Commons. The prospects for private members' motions and bills are particularly gloomy, since there is no time limit (after which a vote must be taken) on debate of these items. If the question has not been put to the House by the end of the time allocated on Wednesday afternoons, the matter drops to the bottom of the relevant list and is extremely unlikely to get another hearing in that session. Thus, both motions and bills proposed by private members can be "talked out" each time they come up for debate and, since most represent views contrary to government policy, that is usually their fate.

On certain sitting days during the year, the Orders of the Day are not dominated by government motions. These are the days officially designated for **opposition business**, when the opposition has a chance to lead major debates on government policy. At the start of the session, the House is permitted eight days to debate the Address in Reply to the Speech from the Throne: since the Throne Speech contains only vaguely-worded policy outlines, rules of relevancy are relaxed and debate takes a very general course. A further six days are allocated for the Budget Debate – officially, to discuss the Finance Minister's proposals, but effectively, again, to articulate broad criticism of the government's record. As well, after the abolition of the old Committee of Supply in 1968, the opposition parties have been compensated by the allocation of twenty-five Supply (or Opposition) Days, spread unevenly over the three supply periods of the session, on which opposition motions can be debated. Such debates rarely focus specifically on government expenditures, although that was the original intention. Instead, Opposition Days provide time for individual opposition parties to mount their own attacks on the government, to propose alternative policies and, on a maximum of six occasions in the session, to introduce motions of non-confidence in the government. There are, however, both practical and political limitations on the ability of the opposition parties to effect radical criticism of government activities or produce startlingly different policy proposals. Hence, Opposition Days serve more as a symbolic recognition of the opposition's right to criticize the government than as a forum for policy initiation.

Far more effective as an instrument for the opposition – primarily because of the amount of media attention devoted to it and because no notice of content is required – is the Oral Question Period. This is invariably the high point of the sitting day in the Commons. It provides an opportunity for any member who can catch the Speaker's eye to ask a question of the Prime Minister or one of his Cabinet colleagues. Although, technically, questions should be for the purpose of eliciting information and be "concise, factual and free of opinion and argument which might lead to debate",[30] the Question Period in fact provides a forum for the Opposition parties to embarrass the government, criticize its policies and force discussion (but not, officially, debate) on issues of the day, frequently based "on news stories, on leaks by indiscreet or disaffected public servants, and on complaints from the public".[31]

As a mechanism for surveillance and accountability of the government, the Oral Question Period has many advantages. Still, it is not perfect. Although supplementary questions are permitted by the Speaker, no formal debate is allowed, and ministers can often manoeuvre to avoid the main substance of a question. The time limit of 45 minutes each day is often too short for the number of questions which members wish to raise, and opposition members are highly critical of the fact that government backbenchers use up some of the period to ask questions of "minor" constituency interest or to feed "friendly" queries to their own front bench. Finally, the division of the opposition into two parties has frequently resulted in a lack of structure or continuity to the proceedings. As one former New Democratic MP complained a few years ago:

> "You've got Otto Lang on the ropes and someone else stands up and asks a question to the Minister of State for Small Business. You're left with a feeling of frustration. . .There are so many loose ends at the end of Question Period."[32]

[30]Ruling given by then-Speaker of the House, Roland Michener, cited in *House of Commons Debates*, February 26, 1959, p. 1393.

[31]Stewart, *op. cit.*, p. 56.

[32]Former New Democrat MP Bob Rae, cited in the *Globe and Mail*, Toronto, November 14, 1978, p. 8.

To surmount this problem, after 1980 the Conservatives carefully orchestrated their efforts at Question Period to provide a more focused and sustained attack on certain government ministers. Despite the ongoing problems, well-directed opposition tactics make the daily Question Period into an important occasion for calling the executive to account for its actions, for effective participation by backbenchers and for the general public to see responsible government at work in the House of Commons.

Occasionally during the Question Period, a member who is dissatisfied with the response from a minister will shout "six o'clock" across the floor of the chamber. This refers to what is commonly known as "The Late Show", more formally the Daily Adjournment Debate, which takes place three days a week at 6:00 PM. Unless the House has agreed to sit beyond the normal hour of adjournment for some special purpose, the Speaker proposes at 6:00 PM on these days "that this House do now adjourn", then recognizes in turn a maximum of three members who have made it known that they wish to perform. Members usually take up unresolved issues from the Oral Question Period; they are permitted to speak for up to seven minutes, addressing their point to a minister or parliamentary secretary, who is given three minutes in which to reply. By half-past-six, the Late Show is over; the Speaker then adjourns the House until the next sitting.

Under contemporary rules, the House has a minimum working week of 28-1/2 hours, which may well be increased by emergency debates or long series of divisions continuing after the normal hours of adjournment. The House is by no means full for the whole of this time: in fact, it is usually crowded only for the Oral Question Period, for important divisions on major items of government legislation and for non-confidence motions. The public has been made aware of empty spaces in the chamber by the televising of House proceedings since October 1977, despite occasional attempts by members to arrange themselves around and behind whoever is on camera. But the average voter or TV viewer may not always be aware of the fact that attendance at plenary sessions of the House of Commons is only a part of the total workload of MPs. Apart from their role as members of the House, MPs must serve on parliamentary committees, are members of parliamentary parties or caucuses and are also elected representatives with large caseloads of constituency duties to perform. An analysis of procedure and legislative politics in the House of Commons is therefore only a part of the story of how Parliament works: the next three sections provide a more complete picture by discussing the role of committees, party competition and individual MPs in the life of the House.

MPs IN GROUPS: THE COMMITTEE SYSTEM

Since 1969, when major reforms of the committee system were implemented, an increasing proportion of the time most MPs devote to parliamentary duties has been spent outside the plenary sessions of the House in meetings of the various Commons committees. There are three kinds of committees in which MPs may be involved.

First is the **Committee of the Whole,** in which the entire complement of MPs sits in the chamber itself in one large committee under the chairmanship of the Deputy Speaker or the Deputy Chairman of Committees, and uses committee rules rather than House procedures to govern its activities. At one time, the majority of bills were considered by the Committee of the Whole rather than being sent to smaller, more specialist, standing committees, but enormous pressures on the timetable of the House and the workload of MPs have resulted in much more limited use of this procedure. Today, it is largely reserved for money bills.

The second type, the **Standing Committees** of the House, are relatively permanent bodies of three kinds. The thirteen specialist standing committees each cover a substantive area of government policy: examples are the Standing Committee on Agriculture or the Standing Committee on External Affairs and National Defence. They are all multifunctional bodies, with the ability to consider legislation, review estimates and investigate particular problems or future policy alternatives. All are empowered to form sub-committees, especially for investigative purposes, and "to send for persons, papers and records" to aid them in their deliberations. The seven general standing committees are responsible for the procedural and miscellaneous administrative concerns of the House; an example is the Standing Committee on Procedure and Organization. General standing committees are more restricted in scope than specialist standing committees, being empowered to study legislation, scrutinize estimates or conduct investigations, but not all three. The three joint standing committees are composed of members of both the House of Commons and the Senate. They are primarily responsible for the "housekeeping" duties of Parliament which af-

TABLE 8.1   Standing Committees in the House of Commons

A. *Specialist Committees*
(with Departmental Responsibilities)

Agriculture
Broadcasting, Films and Assistance to the Arts
External Affairs and National Defence
Finance, Trade and Economic Affairs
Fisheries and Forestry
Health, Welfare and Social Affairs
Indian Affairs and Northern Development
Justice and Legal Affairs
Labour, Manpower and Immigration
National Resources and Public Works
Regional Development
Transport and Communications
Veterans' Affairs

B. *General Committees*

Miscellaneous Estimates
Miscellaneous Private Bills and Standing Orders
Privileges and Elections
Procedure and Organization
Public Accounts
Management and Members' Services
Northern Pipelines

C. *Joint Committees (Commons and Senate)*

Library of Parliament
Printing
Regulations and Other Statutory Instruments

fect both chambers; an example is the Joint Committee on the Library of Parliament.

The third type of committee is the **Special Committee.** Unlike the relatively permanent standing committees, special committees (which include, since 1980, the Parliamentary Task Forces) are established on an *ad hoc* basis to investigate specific issues or, very occasionally, to conduct the Committee Stage of bills for which there is no appropriate standing committee. They are disbanded as soon as they have completed their appointed task. Some special committees, too, are joint committees.

Committee Recruitment, Composition and Staffing

Memberships in the various standing committees are allocated by the Committee of Selection, more commonly known as the "Striking Committee", which is composed of seven MPs, including the Chief Whip of each party and one representative of the Cabinet. The partisan composition of each committee is roughly in proportion to that of the Commons as a whole, although a majority government will always claim more than 50 percent of the members and the official Opposition is usually over-represented compared with any minor parties. Individual MPs are appointed to committees on the basis of their Chief Whip's recommendations, although these often reflect the personal preferences of the member and, in the case of the Conservative and Liberal parties, are usually in accordance with membership in party caucus committees. At one time, if an MP was unsuccessful in obtaining membership in a first-choice committee, there was always the opportunity to act as a substitute for an original member who could not, or did not, attend. However, it was widely recognized that frequent substitutions and fluid membership detracted from the "specialist" role foreseen for the standing committees. Consequently, the procedural changes instituted in 1982, in addition to reducing the number of MPs on each committee from twenty or more to between ten and fifteen, permitted only pre-selected alternate members to substitute for absentees.

The chairmen and vice-chairmen of standing committees are elected at the start of each session by the committee members and, since 1968, have almost all been members of the governing party. By convention, however, the opposition always provides the chairmen of the Public Accounts Committee and the Management and Services Committee, as well as the vice-chairman of the Standing Committee on Procedure and Organization.[33] Given the preponderance of government members filling these offices, committee chairmen are frequently placed in an ambiguous position by conflicting expectations of their roles: while their responsibility for presiding over committee meetings requires them to be as impartial as the House Speaker, their selection by the government majority re-

---

[33] The apparent monopoly of government members in committee leadership positions is not solely the fault of the party in power. In 1972, the minority Liberal government offered the Official Opposition half the standing committee chairmanships – an offer which was refused by the Conservatives.

sults in pressure to serve the interests of the government in pursuance of its policy goals.[34]

Committee deliberations are expedited by the work of several parliamentary organizations. The Committees and Private Legislation Branch of the Commons staff provides procedural and administrative support. Research assistance comes from two other sources: the Research Branch of the Library and outside consultants. Some commentators have insisted that Canadian committees should have the high level of staffing and research resources enjoyed by the Congressional committees in the United States, but such an increase is unlikely, in itself, to enhance the influence of committees in the legislative process:

> "Until committees are given an independent capacity to influence public policy, it is unlikely that the addition of even the most competent of research assistants will do more than contribute to the frustrations of MPs and researchers alike."[35]

As this quotation suggests, there have long been doubts among both politicians and academic observers whether the committee system in the House of Commons is effectively fulfilling its major functions.[36] Despite recent innovations in the form of the Parliamentary Task Forces and the changes introduced after the Report of the Special Committee on Procedure in 1982, many misgivings persist.

Committees at Work – An Evaluation

Committees in the Canadian House of Commons have three principal areas of operation: detailed consideration of legislation after a bill has passed its Second Reading in the House; scrutiny of the financial aspects of government and bureaucracy; and investigation of reports, policy proposals and other items by both special and standing committees.

CONSIDERATION OF LEGISLATION

The Committee Stage of the legislative process is designed to provide an opportunity for the clause-by-clause examination of the details of each bill by a small

---

[34]A recent article suggests that there has been some increase in committee autonomy in that members of the (Liberal) majority on committees shared, through discussions in caucus, in the nomination of committee chairmen and vice-chairmen. See Michael Atkinson and Kim Nossal, "Executive Power and Committee Autonomy in the Canadian House of Commons: Leadership Selection, 1968-1979," *Canadian Journal of Political Science*, vol. 13, no. 2 (June 1980), pp. 287-308.

[35]Jackson and Atkinson, *op. cit.* See also Peter Dobell, "Committee Staff: What else is necessary," paper presented to the Second Conference on Legislative Studies, Simon Fraser University, Burnaby, B.C. February 1979.

[36]For the views of politicians on the committee system, see the results of surveys of MPs reported by Paul Thomas, *The Role of Committees in the Canadian House of Commons*, (unpublished Ph.D. Thesis, University of Toronto, 1975) or by Michael Rush, "Committees in the Canadian House of Commons," in J. Lee and M. Shaw, eds., *Committees in Legislatures: A Comparative Analysis* (Durham: Duke University Press, 1979).

group of relatively specialized MPs, as well as for the proposal of amendments which, if accepted by the committee, will subsequently be recommended for adoption by the whole House at the Report Stage. Sometimes, the Opposition members of a committee will try to investigate further the general policy behind a bill, especially since they have an opportunity, denied them during debates in the House, to question public servants and other witnesses. However, amendments of principle or major policy differences introduced by the Opposition have little hope of adoption in committee, especially if party divisions have been reinforced by heated debate at the Second Reading. Hence they are usually presented solely for propaganda purposes. Other amendments may be introduced to force the government to explain or defend a particular provision in the bill. Finally, it must be noted, many amendments constitute genuine attempts to improve the bill – either by making substantive changes to its provisions or by altering technical details, wording or the administration of the legislation. Amendments may be introduced by the government itself, in response to problems which have become apparent in committee, or sometimes as a result of second thoughts in the light of interest group pressure, provincial government responses to the bill or departmental reactions after the initial drafting of the legislation. Thus, although some observers have suggested that the number of amendments accepted at this stage may be an indication of the influence of the standing committees,[37] the sources of amendments are so many and varied that the measure is at best imprecise.

Once adopted by a committee, the fate of amendments in the House usually depends upon the minister's willingness to accept them at the Report Stage. The government is more likely to agree to amendments when they are supported by influential groups or by provincial governments, are technical rather than substantive in content and relate to bills of minor or relatively non-partisan nature rather than to central items in the government's legislative program.[38] Some notable amendments to government legislation have been achieved, but in general the standing committees do not permit a significant increase in the ability of the opposition parties to exert influence upon the executive's legislative program. The more usual situation is that a "majority government exerts tight control over what amendments will be accepted within the committees, and most of the successful amendments originate with the government."[39]

SCRUTINY OF PUBLIC EXPENDITURE

The second main function of the standing committee system is the scrutiny of public expenditure. It is performed through two mechanisms: first, detailed examination of the main estimates of individual departments by the appropriate

---

[37]See, for example, Thomas A. Hockin's study of the 1968 Broadcasting Act in Hockin, "The Advance of Standing Committees in Canada's House of Commons: 1965 to 1970," *Canadian Public Administration*, vol. 13, no. 2 (Summer 1970), pp. 185-202.

[38]Paul Thomas, "The Influence of Standing Committees of Parliament on Government Legislation," *Legislative Studies Quarterly*, vol. 3, no. 4 (August 1978), p. 700.

[39]*Ibid.*, p. 699.

standing committees each spring;[40] second, investigation of the government's spending practices by the Standing Committee on Public Accounts at the end of each session.

With regard to the first mechanism, the estimates represent the government's projected spending patterns for the forthcoming financial year. They are drawn up by the Treasury Board Secretariat and tabled in Parliament each February in the so-called "Blue Book". Before 1968, the main estimates were considered in Committee of Supply (*i.e.*, the whole House), wherein the supply motion gave the opposition a chance to criticize the government's policies and management of the nation's finances. In 1968, the supply procedure was replaced by the introduction of Supply or Opposition Days and the referral of estimates to the newly established standing committees. Today, main estimates are referred to committees by March 1st and must be reported back by May 31st. If a committee has not reported by that date, the Standing Orders provide that the estimates "shall be deemed to have been reported" anyway.

According to Jackson and Atkinson, theoretically, "the opportunity for parliamentary scrutiny of government policy is best afforded by consideration of departmental estimates."[41] Since the government cannot spend money for any purposes not specifically approved by Parliament, and since the estimates procedure allows MPs to investigate closely the aims of public expenditure before appropriation bills are introduced, the process should permit the legislature (through its committees) to scrutinize and influence the direction of government policy. However, this opportunity is by and large not realized to its full potential. Since only ministers of the Crown can propose public spending, no committee can recommend an increase in estimated funding for any program which it considers desirable – committees can only accept, reduce or reject outright the proposed amounts. The opportunity is further limited by infrequent attendance at committee sessions on the part of many ministers responsible for departmental estimates, and by the considerable information gap that exists between MPs and the departmental officials defending their proposed expenditures.

Then there is the attitude of MPs themselves. To many committee members, the estimates procedure is a boring, routine task, devoid of publicity and offering little political mileage. Hence, many meetings are conducted in the absence of a quorum, and it is "by no means unusual for committees to approve votes at the outset of the meeting – when a quorum is present – and then proceed to question witnesses on the millions of dollars that have just been approved."[42] Those who do participate are most likely to use the estimates process to relay the complaints of constituents to the departmental bureaucrats attending or to gain information which may be of use in their constituencies or in embarrassing the

---

[40]Supplementary estimates, which detail additional funds required to meet unforeseen circumstances or to compensate for inflation, are tabled later in the financial year and are referred to the Miscellaneous Estimates Committee.

[41]Jackson and Atkinson, *op. cit.*, p. 99.

[42]*Ibid.*, p. 101.

government at some future time in the House. Even where there does exist "that rare bird, 'the economy hawk', who swoops down on the plentiful bait of departmental spending . . . (he) . . . saves his attacks for the minor items, like trips and potted plants, that indicate waste and extravagance."[43]

In general, therefore, it appears that MPs, by their actions, show little commitment to reducing public expenditure or to increasing the efficiency of government departments, however much lip-service they may pay to these aims. But even if such goals were widely shared, their achievement has been hampered by the fact that each committee considers the estimates of only one government department at a time, with few opportunities for comparing spending patterns among departments or evaluating the total projected expenditure. One recent change in the publication of estimates has helped: the "Blue Book" is now accompanied by an overall government expenditure plan. But there is need for a separate committee to review the finances of Crown corporations[44] and for a General Estimates Committee which would undertake a comparative analysis of all departments for a more comprehensive view of government expenditure.[45]

Despite its many weaknesses as a mechanism for parliamentary surveillance of government, the current estimates procedure does have some redeeming qualities. Its very existence may lead government departments to take extra care in the preparation of estimates and to eliminate potential excesses before they are spotted by MPs. It also provides an opportunity for members to meet bureaucrats face-to-face and to carry out representative functions on behalf of their constituents. As well, committee debate provides an additional forum for the opposition to criticize the government policies and program priorities implicit in the projected spending patterns. But the overall impression is that the standing committees, in their estimates function, are incapable of exercising adequate control over government finance or substantially influencing the content of government policy.

The second mechanism for overseeing public expenditure is the "post-audit" function of the Standing Committee on Public Accounts. This committee is somewhat unusual in that, since 1967, it has always been chaired by a member of the opposition. As well, it receives expert assistance from the Auditor-General, an independent officer of Parliament. The Committee's examination of the annual Public Accounts has often resulted in criticisms of government inefficiency and recommendations for improvements in spending practices. However, the Committee does have two major problems. First, there is no automatic referral of the Public Accounts to the Committee; instead, the government sometimes releases the Accounts very late. Second, there is no mandatory debate on the Committee's report, and its recommendations are frequently ignored by the

---

[43]Paul Thomas, "Parliament and the Purse Strings," in H.D. Clarke *et al.*, eds., *Parliament, Policy and Representation* (Toronto: Methuen, 1980), pp. 166-167.

[44]Thomas d'Aquino, G. Bruce Doern and Cassandra Blair, *Parliamentary Democracy in Canada: Issues for Reform* (Toronto: Methuen, 1983), pp. 69-70.

[45]Thomas, "Parliament and the Purse Strings," pp. 175-176.

government. Elimination of these stumbling blocks would considerably increase the Committee's capacity as a mechanism of accountability.

INVESTIGATION

Part of the conventional wisdom concerning legislative committees is that, as small groups, they permit MPs to interact in a manner rather different from their behaviour in the House.[46] In particular, it posits that the less formal environment and the relative absence of publicity surrounding committee deliberations permit the development of a less partisan atmosphere and enhance corporate identity, thereby facilitating the objective criticism of government policies and increasing the opportunity for meaningful participation by members. It is in the performance of their third responsibility, the investigative function, that Canadian parliamentary committees most often live up to the conventional wisdom by displaying non-partisanship, group cohesion and autonomy from party and government control.

Investigations may take place at three stages in the policy process. First, a committee may hear evidence from interested parties and formulate recommendations to help the government establish priorities on an issue for which no policy has yet been formulated. Alternatively, a committee may be utilized to establish reactions to a particular set of policy proposals, usually contained in a government "white" or "coloured" paper.[47] Or, a committee may evaluate the strengths and weaknesses of existing policies and their administration, especially in an extension of its estimates scrutiny role.

In most policy areas, investigatory tasks are referred to the appropriate standing committee, but certain complex or contentious issues require the establishment of an *ad hoc* special committee. In this regard, one of the most interesting recent innovations in the committee system was the experiment with small special committees, popularly known as "Parliamentary Task Forces", initiated by the Liberal government in 1980. Each committee consisted of only seven members (nine in the case of the Task Force on Pension Reform) selected from all parts of the country, who could each claim expertise and keen interest in their respective subject areas.

The Task Forces were directed to explore future policy alternatives in relatively new issue areas on which political parties had not yet established firm partisan positions. They carried out studies of such subjects as the Disabled and Handicapped, North/South Relations, and Regulatory Reform. They were given all the powers normally accorded to standing committees – and some additional

---

[46]On the application of small group theory to legislative committees, see Malcolm Shaw, "Conclusion," in Lees and Shaw, eds., *Committees in Legislatures: A Comparative Analysis,* esp. pp. 412-418.

[47]For example, the review of the White Paper on Tax Reform by the Standing Committee on Finance in the 28th Parliament, or the hearings by Special Joint Committee on the Government Green Paper on Immigration Policy Perspectives in 1975. On the latter, see Douglas C. Nord, "MPs and Senators as Middlemen: The Special Joint Committee on Immigration Policy," in Clarke *et al.,* eds., *Parliament, Policy and Representation,* pp. 181-193.

advantages: virtually unlimited budgets (the average report cost almost one million dollars); the authority to travel and to hire staff without having to seek permission from the House; and the ability to publish their reports whether or not the Commons was sitting.[48] The Task Forces travelled extensively throughout Canada, conducting hearings and making contact with the general public and organized interest groups. In one year, seven of them held 728 meetings, more than the number held by all twenty standing committees together in the same period.[49]

For the MPs directly involved, membership in a Task Force proved to be a rewarding experience. The small size of the committees, the extensive travel, the intensive workload in the face of early report deadlines, the absence of previously entrenched party positions on what in most cases were "motherhood" issues, all combined to reduce partisan conflict far more than work in the House or even on standing committees. As one MP, New Democrat Neil Young, commented,

> "Travel was useful not only because of the public input we were able to get
> . . . but also because we got to know each other as people, not as Tories or
> Liberals. A great sense of *esprit de corps* developed. This really helped when
> we came to write the report . . ."[50]

The working relationships thus established were evident in the remarkable degree of unanimity found in most of the reports.[51]

Despite the apparent success of the Task Force experiment, described for example by veteran New Democrat MP Stanley Knowles as "one of the better things to happen around here in a long time",[52] only one (that on Pension Reform) was established after the initial spate in 1980-81. This may have stemmed partly from the preoccupation of the House with extremely divisive issues, such as energy policy and constitutional patriation, from 1981 onwards. The Task Forces were criticized as being too expensive and as benefitting only a few MPs because of their small size. But, perhaps most importantly, the independence and consensus displayed by these committees, many of which were extremely critical of existing policy (or its lack), worried the Liberal government which was already unpopular in the country and under heavy criticism in the House of Commons.

---

[48]Parliamentary Centre for Foreign Affairs and Foreign Trade, "Task Forces: A Model for the Future?" *Parliamentary Government*, vol. 2, no. 3 (1981), pp. 3-6.

[49]Robert J. Jackson, "The Unreformed Canadian House of Commons," *Les Cahiers de Droit*, vol. 26, no. 1 (March 1985) pp. 161-173.

[50]Cited in Parliamentary Centre . . . "Task Forces: A Model for the Future?" p. 6. See also the discussion among four of the Task Force Chairmen in "Round Table: The Chairman's Job," *Parliamentary Government*, vol. 2, no. 3 (1981), pp. 7-10.

[51]Thus, the government responded quickly to the report of the Task Force on the Disabled and Handicapped by adopting 102 of the 142 recommendations almost at once. See Robert J. Jackson, "Models of Legislative Reform: Diagnosis and Prescription," in *Le Contrôle de l'Administration et la Réforme Parlementaire* (Sainte-Foy: Université du Québec, Ecole Nationale d'Administration Publique, 1984).

[52]Cited in Parliamentary Centre . . . "Task Forces: A Model for the Future?", p. 6

As previously noted, Task Forces are not the only committees which conduct investigations. A number of larger special committees have also been created over the years to examine future policy alternatives in areas for which there is no appropriate Standing Committee. An example is the eighteen-member Special Joint Committee on Senate Reform, which reported in January 1984. Meanwhile, some of the most influential studies of current social problems have come from sub-committees of the Commons standing committees (such as the unanimous 1977 report of the Sub-Committee on Penitentiaries), which share some of the benefits of small size, less intense partisanship and strong corporate identity enjoyed by the Task Forces.[53]

Committees: Problems and Reforms

Certain of the problems experienced by the House of Commons committee system since its inception in the late 1960s have been resolved by reforms introduced in December 1982. First, a reduction in the number of members of each committee has decreased the overall burden of committee work and permitted individual MPs to become more specialized. It was further hoped that smaller committees could operate more efficiently than their larger predecessors, and that any partisan conflict might be reduced.

The 1982 reforms also introduced the practice of drawing up a list of alternate members for each committee. Now, when a committee member is unable to attend a meeting, only one of the designated alternates may substitute for the missing MP. Previously, any member of the House could be called upon to substitute in committee hearings, usually for the purpose of maintaining the government's majority when votes were held on amendments or clauses of a bill. This resulted, according to one opposition MP, in

> "roving squads of Members whose chief ability is to sit on committees,
> read newspapers, sign letters and at the same time raise their right hands
> in approval of matters on which they have no previous experience. These
> members have not participated in the committee discussions and are
> merely present to fill a seat or fill out a quorum."[54]

Today, alternate members are kept informed of the business before the committee, so they at least know which piece of legislation they are voting on!

A criticism of the committee system unresolved by the reforms relates to the lack of autonomy of Commons committees. Committees cannot operate unless their activities are specified in the Standing Orders or unless they receive a reference from the House instructing them to pursue a particular topic. This referral process is effectively controlled by the government through its majority in

---

[53]For a comparison of Task Forces and sub-committees from the perspective of participants, see Parliamentary Centre for Foreign Affairs and Foreign Trade, "Looking Toward Committee Reform: What Have the Task Forces Proved?" *Parliamentary Government*, vol. 2, no. 4 (1981), pp. 3-7.

[54]Marcel Lambert, *House of Commons Debates*, October 15, 1970, p. 156.

the House. Thus, the government may limit the number of referrals to a given committee, or so overburden it with work that there is insufficient time for detailed consideration of any item. In the last resort, the government may create a hand-picked special committee to investigate particularly contentious legislation or issues, or simply to bypass a committee which is displaying too much independence. However, the reforms did go so far as to give committees the power to generate their own references for investigations based on the annual reports of the Crown corporations and government departments, without referral from the House.

Lack of autonomy is further complicated by the fact that committees do not enjoy an even workload throughout the year. At the beginning of a session, the workload is usually light. The major bills in the government's program usually reach the committees in the spring, just at the time when they are supposed to be carefully scrutinizing the spending proposals in the main estimates. The expenditure scrutiny function is therefore undermined: reports on the estimates are often brief and hastily written, and some committees never do report to the House.[55]

Another aspect of lack of autonomy left unchanged by the 1982 reform is that, unlike the Task Forces, the standing committees do not have their own budgets, but have to go "cap-in-hand" to the House of Commons to seek permission to spend funds for the purposes of travel or engaging staff. It is evident that the Task Forces benefitted considerably from the expertise of their staff and from the extent to which public participation was facilitated by the committee's mobility. Nonetheless, some MPs are opposed to granting financial autonomy to committees, fearing the prospect of what one Conservative described as "travelling circuses . . . crossing the country for one reason – not for the sake of participatory democracy . . . [but] to build up a political image and aura for the Liberal Party."[56]

Also among the traditional problems faced by committees has been the fate of their final reports. Prior to 1982, there was no guarantee that a report, produced after many months of work and perhaps containing substantial recommendations about or criticisms of government policy, would ever get a hearing in the House or provoke any government reaction. The frustrations of a committee member were well expressed by a former New Democrat MP, Stanley Knowles:

> "What is the point of talking about the committee system and matters being referred to a committee for detailed study if, after all this is done and a thoroughly researched report is tabled, the government takes no action . . . Surely there comes a time when pleading which is consistent, unanimous and responsible ought to have some effect on the cabinet."[57]

---

[55] In the 3rd session of the 28th Parliament, for example, the main estimates of ten departments or agencies were "deemed to have been reported" in the absence of committee reports – see Thomas, "Parliament and the Purse Strings," p. 170.

[56] Eldon Woolliams, *House of Commons Debates,* October 30, 1970, p. 761.

[57] *House of Commons Debates,* December 11, 1975, pp. 9930-9933.

Under the new House rules adopted in 1982, however, at the request of a committee the government must now table a comprehensive response to its report within 120 days. In the past, it was too easy for the government to ignore committee proposals and criticisms. Now, even if it is not obliged to adopt recommendations put forward by committees, the government does have to explain its reaction to Parliament.

The procedural reforms of 1982 have thus gone part of the way toward resolving the problems experienced by committees in the House of Commons and alleviating some MPs' deep-seated dissatisfaction with the committee system.[58] But problems do remain. First, in order to function effectively, committees require professional research staff, their own annual budgets for financial autonomy and more generalized references in the Standing Orders to reduce the extent of government control over referrals and committee workloads.

In addition, as the Task Forces demonstrated, committees can have most impact on the content of public policy at the pre-legislative phase, rather than at the Committee Stage of a bill, when parties have already established firm stands in the debate on principles at Second Reading. Consequently, there is a strong case for strengthening the investigatory role of committees and perhaps also for referring all but the most controversial legislation to committees after First Reading, before conflicting party positions have been staked out.

But the area of committee work most in need of reform may well be the expenditure scrutiny function. The paper prepared for the Special Committee on Procedure by MPs Ron Huntington and Claude-André Lachance made specific proposals (not subsequently adopted) for increasing financial accountability, as did the Final Report of the Lambert Royal Commission in 1979.[59] We have already mentioned proposals for the establishment of a General Estimates Committee whose major task would be to develop an overview of total government spending. Perhaps reform needs to go even further – to provide for a National Finance Committee, similar to that proposed by the Lambert Commission, which would analyse both revenues and expenditures in order to bridge the current gap between standing committees' consideration of individual departmental estimates and the debate in the whole House on the Finance Minister's economic review and taxation proposals in the Budget.[60] Pressures for reform of the committee system continue. At the time of going to press, the fall of 1985, the Reports of the Special Committee on House of Commons Reform (the McGrath Committee) were largely accepted by the government. When implemented, new legislative committees will take over the function of studying bills from the old standing committees and be chaired by MPs selected from a Panel of Chairmen.

---

[58]See, for example, the comments by a selection of MPs interviewed in Parliamentary Centre . . . "Looking Toward Committee Reform."

[59]House of Commons Special Committee on Procedure, *Seventh Report* (Ottawa: Queen's Printers 1982); Royal Commission on Financial Management and Accountability ("Lambert Commission"), *Final Report* (Ottawa: Ministry of Supply and Services, 1979), esp. Chapter 22.

[60]"Lambert Commission," *Final Report,* Ch. 21; and Jackson, "The Unreformed Canadian House of Commons," p. 11.

The new standing committees will be enhanced by more responsibilities and resources.

MPs IN PARTIES: GOVERNMENT AND OPPOSITION

In contrast to earlier times, it is now rare for an Independent member in the House of Commons to survive very long amid the ranks of party representatives in the chamber. The only Independent member of the 32nd Parliament, William Yurko, who resigned from the Conservative caucus in 1982 because "he could not abide his party's stand on the Constitution",[61] failed to retain his seat in the 1984 general election. The sole Independent elected in September 1984 was Anthony Roman, who defeated a Conservative right-winger only to announce after the election that he might be seeking admission to the Conservative caucus in the 33rd Parliament. In recent years, no Independent MP who has maintained that status has successfully defended a seat in the subsequent election.

Today, political parties are an inescapable fact of life in the Canadian House and have a profound effect upon legislative politics in the chamber and its committees. The government relies on cohesion among its backbenchers to keep it in office and to secure the passage of its legislative proposals. Effective opposition likewise depends on the ability of minority party leaders to mobilize their own MPs in certain directions. In both cases, individual members often have to compromise their own short-term interests and aims in order that party goals may be achieved.

Intra-Party Relations

Some observers argue that cohesion is imposed upon MPs through party discipline; that backbenchers, especially on the government side, are forced to adhere to the directives laid down by the party leadership. Others portray cohesion as the product of a commonality of views among members of the same party and as the result of consensus arrived at through regular meetings of the party caucus.

Former Conservative MP Gordon Aiken has asserted that party discipline is imposed equally on both sides of the House to turn opposition backbenchers as well as government supporters into what he calls "trained seals".[62] Certainly, party leaders, especially of the governing party, have a number of sanctions at their disposal to ensure or at least encourage backbenchers to toe the party line. On the negative side, individual members who consistently oppose the party leadership or fail to vote with their colleagues on important issues may be coerced in a number of ways, culminating in the threat of expulsion from the party. Without the official backing of the party, the rebellious MP would have to contest

---

[61]"Independent's decision good news for Grits," *Globe and Mail,* Toronto, July 14, 1984.

[62]Aiken, *The Backbencher,* passim. For anecdotal description of the life of an MP, there are few studies to match this book.

the next election as an Independent candidate with, as we have seen, little probability of success. More sizable revolts within the governing party may be met by the threat of dissolution of Parliament. Given the high turnover of seats at every General Election, this may serve to quell dissent, especially among those backbenchers who represent marginal constituencies. But the dissolution of Parliament on these grounds is something of a double-edged sword, since it constitutes a public admission of division within the government party.

While these negative sanctions are the "sticks" in the enforcement of party discipline, party leaders also have a number of "carrots" available. The Prime Minister particularly has a large fund of patronage which may be used to reward the loyal, well-behaved member: promotion to Cabinet minister, parliamentary secretary or committee chairman; appointment to the Senate; and numerous positions in public corporations and Crown agencies. Although all are potentially in the grasp of the leadership of the major opposition party, the government generally has more disciplinary sanctions at its disposal.

The discussion of party discipline tends to imply a *conflict approach* to the maintenance of party unity according to which inherent divisions exist between leaders and backbenchers which can be overcome only through coercion. On the other hand, it may equally be argued that party cohesion is based primarily upon the existence of consensus (rather than conflict) amongst MPs in each parliamentary party.[63] According to the latter view, party unity may thus be based upon a "value-consensus", a commonality of opinions on major issues shared by members of the same political movement and reinforced by regular meetings of the party caucus. However, while political parties in Canada do not have the organized political tendencies found in parliamentary parties of some other countries, it should not be forgotten that they are broad "brokerage" coalitions of a variety of regional and other interests. Another view is that unity may be based upon the deference of backbenchers toward party leaders – a willingness to accept the decisions of those who derive their legitimacy from selection by national conventions and who, in the era of "personality politics", may be perceived as largely responsible for the electoral success of the party. It may be also argued that peer group pressure from fellow party-members serves to reinforce party solidarity. But potentially the most effective instrument of party cohesion in the House of Commons is the regularity of party caucus meetings.[64]

The party caucus is a uniquely Canadian institution. Every Wednesday morning when Parliament is in session, all members of the House of Commons (together with any Senators who wish to attend) meet in their respective party groups. Caucus meetings are held in private, away from the press and public.

---

[63]The consensus view of party cohesion is emphasized by Allan Kornberg, "Caucus and Cohesion in Canadian Parliamentary Politics," *American Political Science Review,* vol. 60, no. 1 (March 1966), pp. 83-92.

[64]On the origin of the caucus, see Mark MacGuigan, "Backbenchers, The New Committee System, and the Caucus," in Paul Fox, ed., *Politics: Canada,* 4th ed. (Toronto: McGraw-Hill Ryerson, 1977), pp. 431-438.

Commentators feel that there are differences in the extent to which each party caucus permits backbenchers to participate in and influence the formulation of a common party position. In the opposition parties, there is relatively little distinction in status between leaders and backbenchers: consequently, all MPs feel equally entitled to their point of view, and debate is often quite heated. Within this context, a majority of opposition members consider that the caucus meeting does indeed allow them to influence the direction of party policy.[65]

In the governing party, however, the situation is often perceived to be different. Since the prevailing attitude is that the primary task of government backbenchers is to support the executive and its legislative program, and since members are often consulted only after policies have already been decided by Cabinet, it might be expected that the major function of the government caucus is to enforce party discipline and ensure Cabinet control of the policy process. Thus, according to former Liberal MP Mark MacGuigan, there is "little doubt that the government caucus is of greater utility to the ministry than to the members, and that it is in effect the chief instrument of government control of the House of Commons".[66]

Elsewhere, however, while re-emphasizing his view of the caucus as an instrument of party discipline, MacGuigan admitted that "strong caucus opposition to any government proposal imposes an absolute veto on that proposal. The government has shown time and again that it does not act in the face of clear caucus opposition".[67] On numerous occasions the government caucus has challenged, and sometimes persuaded its leaders to amend or reject, policy proposals agreed upon by Cabinet.[68] Such cases, added to evidence drawn from surveys of MPs,[69] suggest that government backbenchers, like their opposition counterparts, view their caucus as a major opportunity to influence the content of party policy.

Inter-party Relations

Whatever its source, whether enforcement by sanctions or consensus based on common values and agreement in caucus, there can be little doubt that the existence of a strong degree of party cohesion in the House of Commons is an integral part of representative and responsible government. The emergence of responsible parliamentary government has produced and is in turn reinforced by an adversarial relationship between government and opposition. The government requires cohesive, unified support from its backbenchers to retain office and to realize its policy goals; at the same time, the opposition has to mobilize all

---

[65]Allan Kornberg and William Mishler, *Influence in Parliament: Canada* (Durham, N.C.: Duke University Press, 1976) pp. 171-181.

[66]MacGuigan, "Backbenchers, The New Committee System, and the Caucus," pp. 436-437. See also Aiken, *The Backbencher,* pp. 114-123.

[67]Mark MacGuigan, "Parliamentary Reform: Impediments to an Enlarged Role for the Backbencher," *Legislative Studies Quarterly,* vol. 3, no. 4 (November 1978), p. 676.

[68]For examples, see Jackson and Atkinson, *op. cit.,* pp. 50, 80.

[69]Kornberg and Mishler, *op. cit.,* pp. 177-187.

its resources to criticize the government and to portray itself to the public as a viable alternative administration.

Although the relationship between government and opposition is basically one of confrontation, both sides of the House developed certain behavioural norms in order to make Parliament work and to restrain unbridled competition. Opposition members recognize the government's responsibility to carry on the business of governing and will sometimes lend their support to that end; simultaneously, they retain the right to criticize government policy. The government, in turn, recognizes the opposition's right to criticize, but denies it the right to obstruct. The debates on the Budget and the Throne Speech, and the allocation of Supply Days on which the opposition parties may choose the topics for debate, constitute formal recognition of the right to criticize the government's record in general. The rules of debate, the committee system and the Oral Question Period permit criticism of individual items of policy or administration. Less formally, although the governing party has final control over the timetable of the House, both government and opposition recognize the value of agreements between respective House Leaders or party whips concerning the disposal of parliamentary time in order to foster a spirit of cooperation.[70]

Occasionally, however, cooperation breaks down, usually when the government, confronted with what it views as obstruction by the opposition, attempts to push through a bill with what the opposition regards as unseemly haste. When this occurs, both sides of the House have various procedural weapons at their disposal. The government may seek to terminate debate by resorting to *closure*, an extremely unpopular measure whereby all outstanding discussion and divisions on a particular stage of a bill must be completed within the next sitting day instead of being adjourned from one day to the next, as unfinished business usually is. Closure is a device to which governments turn with the greatest reluctance because of its procedural complexity and political ramifications.[71] As one author has commented, notice of closure "resembles so much a death sentence and a public execution that ministers shrink from using it; and when they do, the opposition, regardless of their true sentiments, feels obliged to lament the end of a thousand years of freedom and democracy."[72] A less drastic alternative to closure as a means of limiting debate lies in a pre-arranged allocation of time to a particular bill or its various stages under the Standing Orders. Here, a balance of power is maintained between government and opposition by three alternative rules which respectively become more complex procedurally as they require less inter-party cooperation.[73]

---

[70]See Paul G. Thomas, "The Role of House Leaders in the Canadian House of Commons," *Canadian Journal of Political Science*, vol. 15, no. 1 (March 1982), pp. 125-144; Martin W. Westmacott, "Whips and Party Cohesion," *Canadian Parliamentary Review*, vol. 6, no. 3 (Autumn 1983), pp. 14-19.

[71]On the origins, procedural details and use of "closure" see Dawson, *Procedure in the Canadian House of Commons*, pp. 121-130.

[72]Stewart, *The Canadian House of Commons*, p. 244.

[73]For a detailed explanation see *Ibid.*, pp. 250-258.

In the 32nd Parliament particularly, the opposition found dramatic weapons to confront an uncooperative government. In March and April 1981, the Progressive Conservatives tied up the business of the House of Commons with a collective "filibuster" – an apparently endless series of "point of order" and "questions of privilege" in order to prevent further discussion of the resolution on patriation of the Constitution until after it had been ruled upon by the Supreme Court. For two weeks in March 1982, the division bells were left ringing on Parliament Hill as the opposition boycotted the House in protest against the Liberals' omnibus bill on Energy Security. In both cases, the government was forced to compromise its original proposals in order to get the House back to work.

In its adversarial relationship with the government, the opposition is placed at a disadvantage by the former's control over the parliamentary timetable and access to departmental information. But, as events in the 32nd Parliament demonstrated, the opposition does have sanctions to prevent what it sees as abuse of the parliamentary process. Even the complaint that the opposition parties lack the research facilities to compete with the government's monopoly on bureaucratic information has been partly blunted by the provision of public funding for partisan activity by caucus research groups: in 1982-83, between 3 and 4 million dollars.

Indeed, many of the difficulties encountered by the opposition in formulating effective criticism of government policy have less to do with House of Commons procedures or research facilities than with more fundamental problems which also afflict parliamentary oppositions in the other western democracies.[74] One is that the official Opposition in Parliament often has difficulty in making itself heard above the "hubbub" coming from other political actors. Major interest groups and private research institutes frequently offer articulate and well-publicized criticisms of government policy, and, in a federal context such as Canada, "there is little doubt that the clashes between the provinces and the federal government...detract attention from the federal parliamentary opposition on some of the most important issues in Canadian politics."[75]

Sometimes, too, it may be difficult for the opposition parties to offer clear-cut alternatives to government policy. Some issues do not lend themselves to a confrontational style of politics, since they cut across party lines and strain party cohesion on both sides of the House. This is especially true of moral issues such as abortion, capital punishment or nuclear weapons. On other social and economic policy issues, the development of an ideological consensus supportive of the mixed-economy and the welfare state in most western societies has tended to preclude the presentation of radical policy alternatives by a "loyal" opposition.

---

[74]For an extended discussion, see Andrew J. Milnor and Mark N. Franklin, "Patterns of Opposition Behaviour in Modern Legislatures," in A. Kornberg, ed., *Legislatures in Comparative Perspective* (New York: David McKay, 1973), pp. 421-446.

[75]Jackson and Atkinson, *op. cit.*, p. 119.

Oppositions have increasingly had to be content with criticizing the specifics of government policy and its administration rather than developing comprehensive alternatives, and with presenting themselves as an alternative source of leadership and government personnel. In this regard, the opposition parties have been greatly aided by the introduction of television cameras into the House of Commons. The broadcasting of Question Period and major debates not only supplies them with a wider audience for their criticisms of the government, but also gives nation-wide exposure to the leaders of the opposition parties and their "teams". Direct communication with the electorate via the medium of television may in fact have greatly facilitated the major task of contemporary parliamentary oppositions – that of presenting themselves as a viable alternative. Increasingly, the chief efforts of parliamentary oppositions are directed "not to defeat the government, nor to amend or improve its laws, but to keep explaining to the electorate outside parliament why the government is making mistakes and why the opposition should be returned to power at the next election."[76]

THE PRIVATE MEMBER: LEGISLATOR OR OMBUDSMAN?

In parliamentary systems, where cohesive political parties are the main actors and the mass media focus upon leading personalities from the government and opposition front benches, it is easy to lose sight of the private member. Furthermore, the myths of "legislative decline" and "executive dominance" have tended to stress the political impotence of the individual backbencher. In contrast to the 19th century, private members' bills today constitute a tiny fraction of the total legislative output of the House of Commons, but the narrow view of the member of a legislature as an initiator of legislation must be revised to take into account the many other demands on an MP's time.

Former Liberal MP and Cabinet Minister Mark MacGuigan has provided us with a guide to the workload of an average member of the House of Commons. As a freshman backbencher in the 28th Parliament, MacGuigan found that "parliamentary demands on my time were considerable, and the burden of constituency cases staggering."[77] His catalogue of responsibilities and activities included:

> ...at least three half-days each week duty service in the House to ensure
> that a quorum was always maintained; attendance at major debates and
> divisions; attendance at the Oral Question Period "for both excitement and
> information"; membership of two standing committees and, later, the
> chairmanship of the Special Committee on Statutory Instruments; caucus
> meetings for three hours each Wednesday morning and caucus committee
> meetings in lunch and dinner breaks; twice-weekly French classes, "being

---

[76]John P. Mackintosh, "The British Parliament," paper presented to the European Parliament Symposium on European Integration and the Future of Parliament in Europe, Luxembourg, May 2-3, 1974, p. 2.

[77]MacGuigan, "Parliamentary Reform. . .," p. 673.

Reprinted with permission – The Toronto Star Syndicate.

determined to become bilingual''; a one thousand mile round trip each weekend to constituency and home in Windsor; approximately 200 public functions and 200 visits to the homes of constituents in each year; and a large volume of constituency business (some 5500 cases a year) which arrived by mail and by telephone.[78]

Even a list of this length excludes attendance at the routine proceedings of the House and attempts to develop expertise in one or more policy areas! Furthermore, new MPs are expected to become familiar with the rules and procedures governing behaviour in the House.

Complaints concerning the inadequacy of staffing and research resources for legislators are neither new nor restricted only to Canada.[79] However, with regard to the former, the lot of private members has improved considerably over the last two decades.[80] In earlier days, when parliamentary sessions were much shorter, permanent assistance for MPs was considered unnecessary. Today, most MPs have a couple of full-time assistants in their Ottawa offices, and at least one more to manage inquiries at their constituency office. Still, for most members, this increase has barely kept pace with the immense caseload of constituency business in the form of correspondence, telephone calls and personal contacts. Thus, a former Clerk of the House of Commons has suggested that, while most MPs are adequately staffed for their role as constituency representative, they are not "over serviced" with respect to either their legislative functions or active participation in the committee system.[81]

---

[78]*Ibid.*, pp. 673-675.

[79]A comparative appreciation of the problem is offered by James A. Robinson, "Staffing the Legislature," in A. Kornberg and L. Musolf, eds., *Legislatures in Developmental Perspective* (Durham: Duke University Press, 1970), pp. 366-390.

[80]On the development of legislative staffing for MPs, see Alistair Fraser, "Legislators and their Staffs," in H.D. Clarke *et al.*, eds., *Parliament, Policy and Representation, op. cit.*, pp. 230-240.

[81]*Ibid.*, p. 240.

We have said that the job of an MP is multifunctional. In theory at least, members of the Commons are constituency representatives, caucus members, orators, law-makers and watchdogs over the government and bureaucracy. In practice, time constraints and limitations on personal stamina force most members to select one particular role or concentrate on certain activities at the expense of others.[82]

Some recent reforms and innovations have enhanced the ability of individual MPs to perform their parliamentary tasks more effectively. The Task Forces provide the opportunity for a minority of MPs to have real input into the pre-legislative stages of policy formulation. Even government backbenchers in the 32nd Parliament took advantage of the new Standing Order 21 to voice independent opinions and mild criticism of Cabinet policy.[83] Reduction of the maximum length of speeches to the House from forty minutes to twenty allows more members to take part in debates. But, by and large, effective participation in debate or in the scrutiny of government legislation and estimates is hampered by lack of information, resources and policy expertise.

Of course, there are exceptions – MPs who carve out a particular area of specialization or who adopt some issue as their own. Stanley Knowles achieved prominence for his encyclopaedic knowledge of House procedure. Perrin Beattie made a thorough but brilliant nuisance of himself to the Liberal Minister of National Revenue by heading a Conservative Task Force examining the excesses of Revenue Canada officials. And the late Tom Cossitt gained much publicity, and generated some amusement, in his self-assigned role of watchdog over the cost to taxpayers of former Prime Minister Trudeau's swimming pool and daily fresh rose.

But for every activist backbencher in Parliament, there are many more who, however diligently they may serve their constituents, play a minimal part in the legislative process. Lack of opportunity is clearly one factor involved in this syndrome. But it may also be true that, as one study alleges, "private members do not seem to take full advantage of the opportunities available to them" to introduce legislation and initiate criticism of the government.[84]

The attitudes of MPs themselves, and their relations with constituents, are also responsible for the concentration upon representational activities. The electorate is becoming more demanding. With the ever-increasing volume of government legislation and the seemingly omnipresent role of the government, there is real pressure from constituents for MPs to act as intermediaries on their behalf in disputes with departments and other central agencies. Such "ombudsman" work

---

[82]For a broader review of the literature on Canadian legislative behaviour, see Jackson and Atkinson, *op. cit.*, pp. 159-167.

[83]See "Liberal seals are showing some bite," *Globe and Mail*, Toronto, February 15, 1983.

[84]Kornberg and Mishler, *op. cit.*, p. 311. See also John M. Reid, "The Backbencher and the Discharge of Legislative Responsibilities," and subsequent comments (especially those of Paul G. Thomas) in W.A.W. Neilson and J.C. MacPherson, eds., *The Legislative Process in Canada: The Need for Reform* (Montréal: Institute for Research on Public Policy, 1978), Chapter 5.

usually involves simple concrete problems, readily solved by a telephone call to a department or a brief negotiation with a minister. Policy-making, on the other hand, requires abstract, generalized conceptualization of an issue and a long-term commitment to pursue a particular solution. In terms of results for effort expended, the role of ombudsman is more rewarding than that of law-maker for the majority of members. Furthermore, the bottom line is that the political future of many MPs may depend upon satisfying their constituents:

> In any conflict of roles I believe it is fair to say that they will always give their representational function priority over their legislative one....The MP...is certainly aware that, if he does not succeed in pleasing his constituents, he will not stay around long to grapple with the problems of the nation.[85]

The development of a heightened role for the backbencher in the legislative process requires more than procedural reform of the House of Commons.

SYMBOLISM OR POWER? OBJECTIVES OF HOUSE OF COMMONS REFORM

> The reform of parliamentary procedure should be an ongoing process. Parliament is in a constant state of evolution, and if its practices are to be effective, they must be adapted when necessary to meet the changing needs of Parliament and reflect the changing conditions of society and the nation.[86]

As this passage from a report by a recent Special Committee on Standing Orders and Procedures illustrates, members of the House of Commons appear to be perfectly aware of the necessity to reform the roles, procedures and customs of the chamber in order to maintain Parliament as a central institution in Canadian society. Yet it has also been observed that possibly the most enigmatic feature of parliamentary democracies is that ordinary members know that they possess limitless authority to change the structures of their legislatures but nevertheless persist in ignoring this power.[87]

Only periodically do Canadian MPs undertake systematic reform of the way in which they conduct their activities. After a wave of reforms in the late 1960s, notable among them the establishment of the modern system of standing committees, more than a decade elapsed until the next round of innovation and experimentation. But there is constant debate, both within and outside Parliament, about the "urgent" need to reform legislative institutions.

---

[85]MacGuigan, "Parliamentary Reform. . .," p. 677.

[86]House of Commons: Special Committee on Standing Orders and Procedures, *Third Report* (Ottawa: 1982), p. 5.

[87]Jackson, "Models of Legislative Reform. . .," p. 4.

Consequently, a voluminous body of literature exists on proposals for House of Commons reform.[88] This is not the place to add to it, although we have drawn attention in the preceding pages to areas in which reform may be desirable, and made some specific proposals. It may even be justifiably argued that little new or innovative can be added to the catalogues of recommendations. What may be more useful is to provide some criteria for evaluating existing and future reform proposals.

First, it should be emphasized that one cannot turn back the clock to the so-called "Golden Age of Parliament" in the mid-19th century. Former Progressive Conservative leader Robert Stanfield, in a keynote address to a Conference on Legislative Reform a few years ago, asserted that

> ...we no longer have parliamentary responsible government in Ottawa. I assert that parliamentary government is not fitted for what it is being asked to do: that both the government and the Parliament are overloaded to the point that we have poor government and Parliament cannot cope with government.[89]

Stanfield prescribed a reduction of the "all-pervasive" influence of government through the decentralization of decision-making. Only by cutting the workload of the federal government and Parliament, he argued, could parliamentary control over the executive be restored while policy-making efficiency was maintained. However, though it is clear that the expansion of federal government activities has influenced the role of Parliament, there is little reason to believe that a reduced role for government in society is either necessary or sufficient for re-establishing parliamentary control.

Those who cling fondly to the myth that Parliaments were once more important only because governments were less so appear to forget that the growth of the public sector and state intervention are not the only things that have changed. Constituents today expect more of both their governments and their Members of Parliament, and there are more of them to bring more problems to each MP. Even traditional federal government responsibilities, such as defence policy, have become increasingly technical in nature, placing additional burdens on parliamentarians who wish to grasp their complexities. Television and other mass media have created direct channels of communication between government and the general public which have altered the representative, intermediary func-

---

[88]Among the many comprehensive "reform designs", the reader may wish to consult the following academic discussion: Robert J. Jackson and Michael M. Atkinson, *The Canadian Legislative System* 1st and 2nd eds. (Toronto: MacMillan, 1974 and 1980). At the time of press a plethora of reforms were suggested by the Special Committee on Reform of the House of Commons, *Reports 1, 2 and 3* (Ottawa: Queen's Printer for Canada, 1985).

[89]Robert L. Stanfield, "The Present State of the Legislative Process in Canada: Myths and Realities," in Neilson and MacPherson, eds., *The Legislative Process in Canada*, p. 42. See also the reply to Stanfield by Robert J. Jackson in "Point . . . Counterpoint," *Public Policy Options*, no. 1 (March 1979) pp. 4-6.

tions of MPs. Such trends cannot be reversed. Nor, in the absence of substantial realignment in the perceptions of Canadian citizens about the role of government in society, can the scope of federal government activities be significantly reduced. Realistic proposals for reform of the House of Commons must therefore be formulated within this context.

The objectives of parliamentary reform may be grouped under the two broad headings "power" and "symbolism" – the central themes of this chapter. Some reforms are oriented towards increasing the power of Parliament – to strengthening the House of Commons *vis-à-vis* other institutions and to increasing its ability to control, criticize and hold government accountable for its actions. Other proposals are primarily symbolic in nature inasmuch as they seek to enhance the image of the House of Commons as a key institution in the democratic process. As we noted earlier, these two categories are not necessarily mutually exclusive, since a Parliament that is perceived as weak and ineffective will not be able to sustain, in the long run, the degree of legitimacy necessary to fulfill its symbolic functions. However, the concepts "power" and "symbolism" do serve as useful organizing devices.

When it comes to a measure designed to increase the power of the House of Commons, the probability of success depends upon various implicit norms and constraints that result from the realities of legislative politics in the chamber. First, as Jackson and Atkinson have observed, "no government will accept organizational or procedural changes...unless it is assured that changes favourable to the government will also be adopted."[90] Thus, reform packages must be designed in such a way that they maintain a balance between the competing needs of government and opposition. If, for example, the opposition is to gain increased opportunities for surveillance and criticism of the administration, the government must be guaranteed certain concessions with regard to limiting debate without fearing outbreaks of bell-ringing or other such measures. Political reality dictates that the government will simply deploy its majority in the House to defeat unbalanced reform proposals.

And we may be sure that governments will continue to deploy their forces in a cohesive fashion on matters affecting their interests. Proposals which seek to enhance the influence of backbenchers by advocating, for example, that "leaders of both government and opposition parties recognize and adopt in practice a less stringent approach to the question of party discipline and the rules governing confidence"[91] are politically naïve and based upon misleading comparisons with the United States, where members of Congress are deemed to be more powerful because they work in a state of partisan anarchy.

As we have already pointed out, the principle of responsible party government in Canada is different from that in the United States, where the President is directly elected and not dependent upon a majority in Congress in order to stay in office. Therefore, pressures in favour of party cohesion are much stronger in

---

[90]Jackson and Atkinson, *The Canadian Legislative System*, 2nd ed., p. 192.

[91]d'Aquino *et al.*, *Parliamentary Democracy in Canada*, p. 30.

Canada – and not only in the government party, since opposition party leaders also rely on support from their MPs to maintain pressure on the government and to present themselves to the electorate as a responsible alternative administration. If decreased partisanship is considered desirable, then aspiring reformers should perhaps focus on strengthening the committee system, with particular emphasis on increased use of sub-committees and Task Forces, which have already demonstrated their value in lowering inter-party barriers and in providing genuine opportunities for backbench participation.

Finally, with respect to measures to enhance the power of the House of Commons, it must be emphasized that it is much easier to alter procedures and institutions than to effect changes in the attitudes and behaviour of politicians. Many reformers criticize the lack of opportunities for ordinary members to participate in the policy process or to effectively control government spending, without acknowledging that many MPs fail to take advantage of the opportunities that already exist – either because they choose not to, or because pressures of work and competing commitments prevent them from doing so. Thus, if members do not take the scrutiny of government estimates very seriously, because much of it is boring, routine work, more committees or more powers for committees will not help; rather, there must be some perceived reward for effective participation, such as exposure to constituents through the televising of committee hearings. If MPs are too overworked to fulfill all expectations of them, giving them more powers will have little effect on their performance. A far better solution might be to enlarge the membership of the House of Commons in order to spread the workload more thinly.

Reforms designed to increase the power of Parliament *vis-à-vis* other actors such as the government and the bureaucracy may well have a beneficial effect on the symbolic functions of the House of Commons in legitimating the policies of the government and many other aspects of the political system. But other reforms might also enhance the symbolic role of the House by raising the level of esteem in which it is held by the Canadian public. Thus, although the members of the 33rd Parliament and the government they sustain are more representative of Canadian voters across the country than their recent predecessors, electoral reform might assure the integrative capacity of the House as a representative institution.[92] Increased travel by committees and country-wide consultation would serve to bring Parliament closer to the people. So too would more interesting televising of House proceedings – for example, letting cameras range around the Chamber to capture the full flavour of debate instead of focusing on one talking head at a time; or, following the popular precedent set with the Special Committee on the constitution, allowing cameras into committee meetings, where so much of the work of the House is done. As reformers seek to strengthen the House of Commons – to increase its power to control the executive – all too often the other potential strengths of the House, as a representative institution, as a symbol of societal integration, as a link between government and citizens, are neglected.

---

[92]See the discussion of the impact of the electoral system in Chapter 11.

THE SENATE

Canada is one of approximately 50 countries in the world with a bicameral legislature – that is, with a second chamber or upper house in addition to the (usually) popularly-elected lower house. Second chambers have been adopted or retained for a number of purposes, among them, the representation at the national level of the constituent parts of a federal system and the representation of a particular class (or estate) to act as a conservative restraint upon the potentially unbridled liberalism of the lower house.

> But the essential case has always been that the formulation of legislation and policy issues ought to receive a second consideration, and possibly might be rejected, or delayed, by a chamber different from the first in character and composition.[93]

While the notion of the second chamber as a provider of "sober second thought" concerning legislation from the lower house is almost universal, the other functions of upper houses can often be related to their mode of selection. In federal systems, all of which give their sub-national territorial units some representation in the national legislature, the upper house is sometimes directly elected by the public, as in the United States, Australia and the Soviet Union. It sometimes consists of delegates from the state governments or legislatures, as in West Germany. Elsewhere, members may be appointed as representatives of various economic, occupational or cultural associations, as in the Portuguese Corporative Chamber before 1975. In still other countries (notably Belgium, Italy and Japan), the upper house is popularly elected, but is designed to give rise to a chamber with a political complexion different from that of the lower house. Finally, the predominantly conservative and upper class mood of the British House of Lords has been only partly modified by the appointment of Life Peers recommended by successive governments.

Recruitment and Formal Roles

The Senate of Canada appears, at first glance, to fit none of these models. It is the only legislative chamber in the western world whose members are all appointed; this is done by the Governor General at the behest of the government of the day. Thus, Canadian Senators cannot claim to represent directly, or to be delegates of, any electorate, any subordinate level of government or any interests within society.

Admittedly, there is a regional basis to the appointment system. Since 1975 the membership of the Senate has been fixed at 104, with 24 each from four main regions – Ontario, Québec, the West (six from each of the four provinces west of Ontario) and the Maritimes (ten each from New Brunswick and Nova Scotia, four from Prince Edward Island) – together with six from Newfoundland and one each

---

from Yukon and the Northwest Territories.[94] A Senator nominally "represents" the province for which he or she was appointed and, unlike a member of the House of Commons, must actually reside and own property in that province. Thus there is a clear regional or provincial underpinning to the composition of the Senate, and it would appear that the Fathers of Confederation did perceive the Second Chamber as a "federal" institution. According to Sir John A. Macdonald:

> In order to protect local interests and to prevent sectional jealousies, it was found requisite that the great divisions into which British North America is separated should be represented in the Upper House on the principle of equality.[95]

As we have stated, however, Senators are not elected by the voters in the provinces which they nominally represent; nor do provincial governments formally play any part in the selection process. Furthermore, most federal systems give their constituent states equal representation in the upper house or at least some modified form of representation by population.[96] But although the "great divisions" of Canada are equally represented in the Senate, there are obvious inequities in representation among Canadian provinces, particularly to the detriment of the West.

Senators were originally appointed for life, but since 1965 they have retired at age seventy-five. One observer noted, with a touch of black humour, that this formal change had little practical relevance:

> "Senators, on the average, die at the age of 74...Therefore, the introduction of a compulsory retiring age at 75 would by no means seriously affect the existing situation in the Senate; it would rather formalize a practice already present."[97]

But neither tenure provision permits Senators, once appointed, to subsequently be held accountable or responsible to either the provinces or to the regions they were originally intended to represent. Instead, the representation of provincial or regional interests in the federal policy-making process has become increasingly institutionalized in the form of Federal-Provincial Conferences and, to a lesser extent, in the regional composition of the Cabinet.

If the Senate does not actually fill the role of guardian of regional or provincial interests in a federal system, neither does it seem necessarily oriented toward providing a more mature or conservative restraint upon the youthful enthusiasm

---

[94]There was also provision in the *British North America Act* for the appointment of an additional four or eight Senators (drawn equally from the four main regions) to allow for the breaking of a deadlock within the Senate and the Commons, but this has never been invoked.

[95]*Parliamentary Debates on Confederation of the British North American Provinces*, Québec City 1865 (Ottawa: 1951), p. 29.

[96]The United States and Switzerland for example permit each state and full *canton*, respectively, two members in the federal chamber. The West German *Länder* send three, four or five members, weighted according to population, to the federal *Bundesrat*.

[97]Kunz, *The Modern Senate of Canada*, p. 71.

of the House of Commons. Senators must be at least thirty years of age, but this is well below the average age of new MPs entering the lower house. And although the *BNA Act* determined that Senators must own property exceeding $4000 in value, which in the mid-19th century limited potential membership to a fairly narrow and privileged minority, this figure has not been revised since 1867. Thus, the constitutional requirements for membership in the Senate are no longer of great relevance to its composition or perceived role within the legislative process.

One potential advantage of the process of appointment is that it can be used to give recognition to economic, ethnic and religious groups which are under-represented in the House of Commons. Thus, organized labour has been given special notice – though not nearly as much as its numbers in the population would warrant – as have farmers. The Protestant minority in Québec and English-speaking Catholics elsewhere have tended to be over-represented in the Senate to compensate for their relative lack of seats in the Commons.[98] The first woman Senator, Mrs. Cairine Wilson, was appointed in 1930, after a long constitutional wrangle which was resolved by a decision from the Judicial Committee of the Privy Council that women were equally "persons" under the relevant sections of the *BNA Act*.[99] However, the fact that only fourteen women were appointed to the Senate between 1930 and 1975[100] demonstrates that Senate appointments have not been systematically used as a means of redressing inequities of representation in the House of Commons. Rather, selection of leading figures from minority groups has been a symbolic act, "a token of recognition of their relative importance in the social and political system of the country".[101] Often, it has been motivated by purely partisan interests in an attempt to win electoral support from certain groups.

This last point underlines the true nature of the system used in appointing Senators. Although in formal terms "qualified persons" are "summoned" to the Senate by the Governor General, in practice, as with other such appointments, the real power of selection rests with the Prime Minister. The truth is therefore that the primary basis of appointment to the Senate is unashamedly partisan. "Senatorships have been invariably regarded as the choicest plums in the patronage basket, and they have been used without compunction as rewards for faithful party service."[102] There have been few more blatant examples of this than former Prime Minister Trudeau's nomination of four of his former ministers, three Liberal MPs, a Liberal party fundraiser and two former employees to

---

[98]Robert A. Mackay, *The Unreformed Senate of Canada*, rev. ed., (Toronto: McClelland & Stewart, 1963), pp. 148-149.

[99]On the question of women in the Senate, and the development of minority group representation in the upper house, see Kunz *op. cit.*, pp. 46-56.

[100]Brodie and Vickers, *Canadian Women in Politics: An Overview* (Ottawa: Canadian Research Institute for the Advancement of Women, 1982), p. 42.

[101]Kunz, *op.cit.*, p. 46.

[102]Dawson, *The Government of Canada*, p. 283.

the Senate as part of a veritable orgy of patronage appointments upon his retirement in 1984.[103]

It must be acknowledged that the partisan nature of Senate appointments may have some positive value for the political system. It does allow Cabinet ministers and other long-serving party members to be "promoted" to secure, well-paid Senate seats rather than being "relegated" to the backbenches. In this way, the Prime Minister can give himself room to manoeuvre – to reshuffle the Cabinet and introduce new blood without appearing to demote old colleagues. It also sometimes occurs that a party candidate regarded as potential ministerial material fails to win or retain a seat in the House of Commons. The Senate provides two alternative strategies for a Prime Minister wishing to have such an individual available for inclusion in the government. One is to elevate to the Senate a member of the caucus who holds a safe seat into which the promising candidate can be "parachuted" at the ensuing election. Otherwise, the potential minister may be directly appointed to the Senate and hold a ministerial portfolio as a member of the upper house. Thus, when Robert René de Cotret failed to get elected in 1979, he was appointed to the Senate and the federal Cabinet by Prime Minister Clark.

Although this "renewal" function tends to give rise to a Senate composed mainly of semi-retired party faithfuls, the upper house is far from being a geriatric retreat. The number of appointments of relatively young Senators has increased in recent years, and some members have played important roles within their national party organizations. Senators are, for example, in an ideal position to direct election campaigns, since they are close to the centres of power in Ottawa but do not have to seek personal re-election. Thus, Senators Keith Davey (Liberal) and Lowell Murray (PC) served as their respective parties' chief strategists in the 1980 election campaign; Davey was recalled to help John Turner partway through the 1984 campaign.[104]

From the foregoing discussion, it is apparent that the Senate fulfills only imperfectly many of the formal roles normally ascribed to second chambers. It is not manifestly a representative of provincial rights nor of minority groups; neither is it a straightforward champion of a particular class, nor a sanctuary for aging politicians. Therefore, to ascertain the place of the upper house within the Canadian legislative process, we need to consider the actual work done by the Senate and Senators' own perceptions of their task.

Legislative Politics in the Senate

The status of the Senate as an independent and non-partisan counterweight to the Commons has been challenged. According to this view, Senators are partisan

---

[103]"Farewell postings number 225," *Globe and Mail*, Toronto, July 7, 1984; and "One-sixth of Trudeau caucus gets plums," *Globe and Mail*, July 10, 1984.

[104]See John McMenemy, "Influences and Party Activity in the Senate: A Matter of Conflict of Interest," in Fox, ed., *Politics: Canada*, pp. 460-461; and McMenemy *et al.*, "Party Structures and Decision-Making," in C. Winn and J. McMenemy, eds., *Political Parties in Canada*, pp. 184-185.

appointments; as such, they are by no means independent of external pressures and vested interests. According to R. MacGregor Dawson,

"The fact that they are still associating with their old colleagues and are only a few feet away from the thickest of the fight, makes party detachment and independence little more than a fanciful aspiration which has lost contact with the facts of life."[105]

A contrary view is posited by F.A. Kunz in his study of the Senate. While admitting that "it would be rather naïve to expect a person who is summoned to the Senate at the (average) age of fifty-eight to forget his entire political background,"[106] he argues that strongly-held partisan convictions are counterbalanced by the process of socialization into the norms of the upper chamber that a new Senator undergoes.[107]

Certainly, the career backgrounds of Senators show them to be highly political. One survey of Senators in the early 1970s reported that over half had held public office before appointment to the upper house; one-third were former MPs. Strength of partisanship is also demonstrated by the fact that two-thirds of Senators had held party office, including one-third who had at some time served in their party's national executive.[108]

However, there is also strong evidence that, once institutionalized into the norms and values of the upper house, Senators forego overt displays of partisan attachment in favour of other roles. Many cling to perceptions of themselves as independent elder statesmen placing their expertise and experience at the service of the country as a whole rather than serving particular party interests. The higher incidence of cross-voting, voting across party lines, in the upper house on important issues of government legislation would suggest that partisanship is lower in the Senate than in the House of Commons.[109]

But, of course, the Senate rarely rejects government legislation in any event.[110] Despite the fact that the Canadian upper house is one of the few second chambers to retain a full set of legislative teeth (including absolute veto over bills passed by the Commons), it has consistently failed to make full use of them. On the few occasions when the upper house has thrown caution to the winds and blocked government initiatives, it has been threatened with dire consequences,[111] and most Senators are fully aware of the erosion of powers, and in some cases abolition, of second chambers elsewhere. Moreover, the self-perceived role of elder

---

[105]Dawson, *The Government of Canada*, p. 285.

[106]Kunz, *op. cit.*, p. 113.

[107]*Ibid.*, p. 115.

[108]Colin Campbell, *The Canadian Senate: A Lobby from Within* (Toronto: Macmillan, 1978) p. 53 and Appendix II.

[109]Several examples are offered by Kunz, *op. cit.*, Table XIX, p. 118, and Chapter 4, *passim*.

[110]*Ibid.*, Tables XV-XVIII, pp. 116-117.

[111]See Henry S. Albinski, "The Canadian Senate: Politics and the Constitution," *American Political Science Review*, vol. 57, no. 2 (June 1963), pp. 378-391.

statesmen would appear to forbid the obstruction of legislation passed by a House of Commons mandated by popular will. Instead, one of the most important legislative functions performed by the Senate consists of the detailed scrutiny of bills with a view to removing ambiguities of interpretation in the original wording and amending technical items which fall within the particular expertise of individual members.

The second major critique of the independence of members of the upper house suggests that the expertise and experience of individual Senators is not always employed in the interests of the general public; rather it is placed at the disposal of a particular segment of the population, namely the business community. In the most detailed of the studies addressing this matter, Colin Campbell argues that the system of appointment to the Senate has tended to favour those who have not only lengthy party service but also high standing in the business world. Campbell alleges that while partisan loyalties may be eroded by immersion in Senate politics, a core group of Senators continues to represent the interests of business in their consideration of government legislation. He labels the upper house "A Lobby from Within" and posits that "business review" is now one of the two major functions of the Senate.[112]

As in many other legislative chambers, a large proportion of the everyday work of the Senate, including the detailed scrutiny of legislation, is carried out by its standing committees. Of the thirteen standing committees established at the beginning of each session, seven specialize in a particular issue area or field of legislation (for example, Agriculture or National Finance). Others are concerned with the internal management of the chamber. Senators also participate with members of the House of Commons in joint standing committees concerned mainly with the housekeeping duties of Parliament.

Some critics allege that the Senate committee on Banking, Trade and Commerce is the key actor in the Senate's defence of the interests of major industrial corporations, established commercial banks and other financial interests. The tactics employed by the Banking Committee, the business connections of its members,[113] their lack of public accountability, and the absence of publicity surrounding their work, all led Colin Campbell to question whether "...the current Senate does not provide too much institutionalized protection for business interests" and whether there is not a danger that certain Senators "...perform their tasks in a way that is antipathetic to democracy."[114]

Other aspects of Senate committee work, however, have often been cited as beneficial to Canadian society and have increased the status of the upper house.

---

[112]Campbell, *op.cit., passim.* See also McMenemy, "Influence and Party Activity in the Senate," pp. 455-460.

[113]"An examination of public records by the Canadian Press in 1973 showed that eight of 22 members of the Senate's committee on banking held 130 company directorships. These 22 senators accounted for 75 percent of reported directorships of the then 93 senators." McMenemy, "Influence and Party Activity in the Senate," p. 547.

[114]Campbell, *op. cit.*, pp. 26, 32.

From time to time, the Senate establishes special committees to investigate key social issues and to make recommendations for new policy initiatives. In the 1960s and early 1970s, Senate Special Committees on such diverse issues as Poverty, the Mass Media, Aging and Science helped to build social consensus around particular problems and alternative responses. But, like the recent House of Commons Task Forces, these special committees were frequently critical of existing government policy. In fact, they were probably too critical and non-partisan for their own good, because there has been a tendency in recent years for Government House Leaders in the Senate to allocate investigatory tasks to standing committees, which can be more easily controlled.[115]

Prior to the 1984 General Election, it appeared that the Senate was developing a new role in the legislative process – that of a supplier of ministers. Ministers from the Senate have ensured regional and linguistic balance in the Cabinet to governing parties denied House of Commons representation from major regions of the country. In 1979, Prime Minister Clark, with only two Conservative MPs elected in Québec, recruited three ministers from the Senate to bolster francophone representation in his Cabinet. Similarly, after the 1980 General Election, with no Liberal MPs from the three western provinces, Prime Minister Trudeau included three Senators in his government. Although the appointments were criticized by opposition MPs on the grounds that these ministers held no popular mandate, they did provide the Senate with an enhanced opportunity to oversee the work of government and to participate more fully in legislative/executive relations.

In the 33rd Parliament, with 211 Conservative MPs elected from all parts of the country, Prime Ministery Mulroney had little need of Senators to build his Cabinet. With all eyes focused on the new government in the House of Commons, there is a possibility that the Senate may be relegated to the obscurity to which some observers have long, but inaccurately, confined it.[116] On the other hand, it is also possible that the Liberal Opposition, decimated in the House of Commons, may utilize its majority in the Senate to amend, delay or obstruct government policies – although this tactic would almost certainly add fuel to the many demands for Senate reform.

SYMBOLISM OR POWER? OBJECTIVES OF SENATE REFORM

Like the House of Commons, the Senate is the subject of ongoing debate on parliamentary reform. As Henri Bourassa claimed half a century ago, such debate is something that "comes periodically like other forms of epidemics and current fe-

---

[115]For a discussion of investigatory committees in the Senate, see *Ibid.*, pp. 19-26.

[116]See, for example, the dismissal of the Senate as unworthy of attention in Kornberg, "Parliament in Canadian Society," in Kornberg and Musolf, eds., *Legislatures in Developmental Perspective*, p. 83.

vers."[117] However, in the last fifteen years or so, a qualitative shift in the motivation for reform has occurred. With reference again to the central concepts of this chapter, it might be said that the objectives of change have altered from increasing or decreasing the power of the Senate as part of the parliamentary system to enhancing the symbolic value of the upper house within the context of Canada's federal system.

In the past, demands for restrictions on the power of the upper house came, not surprisingly, from governments confronted by a "hostile" Senate. Both Mackenzie King in 1927 and Diefenbaker in 1962 sought or threatened Senate reform after government legislation had been blocked by an opposition majority in the second chamber. It is also unsurprising that proposals designed to enhance the effective functioning of the upper house or to reassert its legislative significance have largely come from within the Senate itself.

Some critics of the role of the Senate as presently constituted have not contented themselves with proposing minor reforms or even a diminution of its powers. The Progressive Party of the 1920s, the CCF and its descendant the NDP have all advocated nothing less than abolition of the second chamber, arguing that an unelected body has no place in the legislative process of a democratic society. But total abolition of the upper house is not only constitutionally unfeasible for at least 180 days, according to a 1979 Supreme Court decision and to *The Constitution Act*, 1982,[118] but also politically impractical.

At one time, both demands for abolition and attempts at reform derived from dissatisfaction with the role and powers of the Senate as second chamber in the parliamentary system. More recent proposals, from the 1969 federal government White Paper which set out Prime Minister Trudeau's draft for a new Canadian Constitution through the various constitutional discussions of the late 1970s and early 1980s,[119] were predicated upon the assumption that the upper house could be reshaped into a primarily symbolic institution designed to correct perceived deficiencies elsewhere in the political system. As federal/provincial and regional tensions became more acute, and as changes in voting behaviour created pronounced regional imbalances within party caucuses in the House of Commons, reform of the Senate, together with patriation of the Constitution was viewed as a panacea for all manner of perceived ills afflicting Canadian society.

---

[117]*House of Commons Debates*, 1926, p. 648.

[118]In December 1979, the nine judges of the Supreme Court ruled unanimously that the existing power to amend the Constitution in Canada "was not intended to include the power to eliminate the Senate or the House of Commons".

[119]The major "official", i.e., governmental and parliamentary proposals included Pierre Elliott Trudeau, *The Constitution and the People of Canada* (Ottawa: Queen's Printer, 1969); Special Joint Committee of the Senate and of the House of Commons on the Constitution of Canada, *Final Report* (Ottawa: Information Canada, 1972); Government of Canada, The Constitutional Amendment Bill (C-60), (Ottawa: Queen's Printer, 1978); *The Task Force on Canadian Unity, A Future Together: Observations and Recommendations* ("The Pepin-Robarts Report") (Ottawa: Ministry of Supply & Services, 1979).

The many reform designs produced a variety of schemes for a more equitable geographical distribution of seats in the upper house, usually to the potential benefit of Western Canada.[120] They ranged from allowing some provincial input into the existing appointment system,[121] through joint selection by the federal Parliament and the provincial legislatures in a proposed "House of the Federation",[122] to having an upper house consisting of delegates chosen by and representing provincial governments in a so-called "House of the Provinces" modelled after the West German *Bundesrat*.[123]

When the Constitution of Canada was finally patriated in 1982, the Senate was left intact. With enthusiasm for constitutional reform dampened by other concerns such as the depressed economy, the issue of Senate reform reverted, at least temporarily, to making the upper house a more effective and representative participant in the legislative process.

Thus, the Report of the Special Joint Committee on Senate Reform in January 1984 recommended that Senators be directly elected by the citizens of Canada.[124] It also proposed amendments to the traditional powers of the Senate. In particular, it suggested that the present absolute veto be replaced by a suspensive veto of up to 120 days by which legislation passed by the House of Commons could be delayed but not rejected outright. Only on legislation of linguistic significance would the absolute veto power be retained. The Report argued that, while this may represent a diminution of the formal powers of the upper house, Senators might in fact be more willing to exercise lesser powers in exchange for playing a more effective role in the legislative process. Other proposals, however,

---

[120]Exceptions to this general rule are to be found in Canada West Foundation, *Regional Representation: The Canadian Partnership* (Calgary: Canada West Foundation, 1981); and d'Aquino *et al., Parliamentary Democracy in Canada.*

[121]The 1969 White Paper and the 1972 Special Committee Report proposed that the provinces would submit short-lists of nominees from which the Prime Minister would choose one-half of the future appointees.

[122]Half of the members for any particular province were to be chosen, following a federal General Election, by the House of Commons in proportion to the votes received by parties represented in the Commons after that election. Similarly, the other half would be chosen by the relevant provincial legislature, immediately subsequent to a provincial election, in proportion to popular support received by parties in that legislature.

[123]The "*Bundesrat* model", first discussed by academics in the 1960s, was subsequently endorsed by some provincial governments and other public bodies. See, among others: Canadian Bar Association, *Towards A New Canada* (Ottawa: Canadian Bar Association, 1978); Government of British Columbia, *Reform of the Senate: Paper 3: British Columbia's Constitutional Proposals* (Victoria: Government of British Columbia, 1978); Task Force on Canadian Unity, *A Future Together.*

[124]Special Joint Committee of the Senate and of the House of Commons on Senate Reform, *Report* (Ottawa: Queen's Printer, 1984). For the authors' more detailed views on Senate reform, see Robert J. Jackson, "Remarks to the Special Joint Committee of the Senate and of the House of Commons on Senate Reform," June 23, 1983.

for instance, that no Cabinet ministers may be recruited from the Senate, might weaken the ability of the upper house to scrutinize the work of government. And the proposed direct election of Senators for a non-renewable term of nine years would do little to enhance the accountability of Senators: since they could not seek re-election, there would be no mechanism with which they could be held responsible by the electorate.

And so the debate continues![125] While the internal organization and procedures of the Senate have evolved over the last twenty-five years, and one minor adjustment has been made to Senate tenure, the objectives of Senate reform have changed, perhaps rendering the task more difficult. The principle of producing an effective second chamber within the context of the efficacy of Parliament as a whole has largely been abandoned in favour of creating an institution valued more for its symbolic contribution to Canadian unity and maintenance of the federal system than for its role in the legislative process. However, as long as federal/provincial wrangling over the Constitution continues, and until an accepted means of amendment can be found, the Senate will maintain its role as a usually cooperative, sometimes cantankerous, but invariably dignified part of the legislative process. And as long as the Senate continues, so too will demands for its reform or abolition.

OVERVIEW

Throughout this chapter we have used the twin concepts of *power* and *symbolism* as reference points in describing the various roles performed by the two chambers of the Canadian Parliament and as an organizing device to evaluate certain proposals or directions for future reform. But we have also stressed that these two concepts are not mutually exclusive. In a relatively open society such as Canada, where the activities of Parliament and its members are subjected to fierce, often critical, scrutiny by the mass media, only a legislative body that is perceived to be powerful will be able to maintain sufficient legitimacy to fulfill its symbolic roles. Reform designs must therefore be packaged in such a way as to maintain the delicate balance between power and symbolism if Parliament is to continue to fulfill the many functions demanded of it as a key institution linking citizens with their federal government. Proposals which threaten to upset this balance are effectively doomed to failure.

---

[125]See, for example, Don Braid, "Elected Senate Just A Dream," *Toronto Star*, June 3, 1984. There has even been concern with corruption in the Canadian Parliament. See Michael M. Atkinson and Maureen Mancuso, "Do we need a code of conduct for Politicians? The Search for an Elite Political Culture of Corruption in Canada", *CJPS*, vol. XVIII, no. 3 (Sept. 1985) pp. 459-480.

Thus, for example, demands that Parliament be made more like legislatures which are deemed to be "more powerful", such as the American Congress or the West German Bundestag, must take into account the fact that the Canadian legislature performs different symbolic roles. In the United States, members of Congress are perceived to be more influential because they are relatively independent of party ties: but Congress does not have the same symbolic importance in sustaining the political executive in office and legitimizing its policies. Hence, any attempt to reduce the level of discipline in the Canadian House of Commons must be accompanied by a careful reconsideration of the concept of government responsibility, which is currently based on the assumption of cohesive party behaviour.

Similarly, the West German Bundestag is perceived to be influential in part because much of its work is carried out by parliamentary committees working in relative isolation from media and public scrutiny: but debates in the legislative chamber itself are often quite stilted and boring affairs, since most issues have already been decided elsewhere. The Canadian House of Commons could grant increased powers and delegate much heavier workloads to committees, but only at the risk of reducing the current importance of plenary sessions to the House both as a forum for debate and as a place where the business of government and opposition is *seen* to be done.

The same delicate balance between power and symbolism must also appear in attempts to reform the upper house. Admittedly, the Senate as currently constituted has rather more formal power than legitimacy in the eyes of most Canadians. But many of the reform designs would tilt the balance too far the other way. The proposed "House of the Federation", for example, would almost certainly have a constantly shifting membership, which would undermine many of the traditional strengths of the upper house such as the expertise and parliamentary skills accumulated by experience in the legislature. Under this scheme, the upper house would become an empty shell, full of short-term symbolism, but lacking any real political clout. With no meaningful powers and, in all likelihood, composed of defeated candidates biding their time until they could win a seat at the next election, it is highly improbable that such a chamber could become the symbol of societal integration envisaged by its proponents.

Some actual and proposed reforms do manage to maintain the balance. The Parliamentary Task Forces of the early 1980s, as we have suggested, temporarily increased the influence of their backbench members and strengthened the investigative and policy-making roles of the House of Commons while enhancing the representative and symbolic functions of the legislature by taking Parliament to the people. It is not always so easy to kill two birds with one stone. However, more comprehensive reform packages can be designed that take into account both the need to strengthen Parliament and the requirement that it continue to serve as the representative and symbolic cornerstone of the governmental process. And such reforms are required, and most of the suggestions for reform from the 1985 Special Committee are in the right direction. As society continually evolves in complexity, as the state plays an ever-expanding role in the lives of its citizens, as technological advances provide new links between government and the people, Parliament is struggling to keep up. If Parliament is to maintain its status as the most important institution in Canadian political life, it has to amend both its internal procedures and its external relations with other political actors.

chapter 9

The Public Service and the Administrative Process
Bureaucracy and Democracy

IN CANADA, AS IN MOST DEMOCRATIC SOCIETIES, there is a distinction between transient politicians who come and go on the winds of electoral change, and permanent administrators whose role is to carry out the goals and purposes of their political masters, no matter which party may be in power. Constitutionally, it is the elected executive of the federal government that is responsible for formulating policies relevant to the needs of all Canadians. The administrative process of implementing government policies is entrusted to permanent state officials employed by the departments, agencies and Crown corporations that constitute the federal bureaucracy.

In the modern state, however, the traditional dichotomy between "politics" and "administration" is no longer as clear as it once appeared. First, the vastly expanded scope and complexity of contemporary public policy have rendered politicians increasingly dependent upon permanent administrators for information and advice on the formulation, as well as the execution, of government policy. Furthermore, as we noted in Chapter 8, Parliament has delegated to the bureaucracy substantial decision-making autonomy in many areas of technical policy-making in the fields of regulation and administrative procedure. Fears have consequently been expressed about the increasingly "political" role of the bureaucracy and about a perceived lack of bureaucratic accountability to either Parliament or the general public in many areas of government policy-making.

At the same time, expansion of the responsibilities and activities of the Canadian state has effected a commensurate growth in the size and scope of public administration. The sheer size and complexity of what has been called a "bureaucratic leviathan" give cause for concern. As well, administrative secrecy, the apparent impenetrability of bureaucratic processes and lack of open accountability have been cited as threats to responsible, democratic government.

In this chapter, our primary focus is on the administrative machinery of the Canadian government and on the major issues relating to the efficient implementation of government policy. However, since it is not always easy to separate the administrative process of policy implementation from the political process of policy formulation, it is impossible for us to ignore the controversy surrounding the role of bureaucracy and the influence of public servants in contemporary Canadian politics. Thus, we begin with a general discussion of the concept of bureaucracy: its so-called "ideal" characteristics, its development and role in modern society and some central questions concerning the relationship between bureaucracy and democracy.

WHAT IS BUREAUCRACY?

For centuries, political rulers have relied upon permanent officials to carry out the routine daily tasks of administering government policies. From tax-collectors and magistrates of old to modern inspectors of nuclear power plants and Unemployment Insurance Commission officials, public administration is as old and ubiquitous as government itself.

Bureaucracy, on the other hand, is a relatively new and more limited phenomenon. The term originated as a satirical combination of the French *bureau* (desk) and the Greek *kratein* (to rule), on the analogy of "democracy" and "aristocracy".[1] In popular parlance, it has come to signify depersonalization, inefficiency and inflexibility. But, while anyone who has encountered the "red tape" often said to be associated with bureaucracies may feel that such characterizations are appropriate, it is nevertheless an inescapable fact that these organizations are central to the effective management of numerous aspects of modern life.

Similarly, "bureaucrats", those individuals who comprise and carry out the functions of bureaucracies, are regularly condemned as overpaid, under-employed, inefficient and self-serving.[2] They are the objects of numerous anecdotes and popular jokes – witness this quip by the Honourable Member from Kicking Horse Pass (alias Dave Broadfoot of the Royal Canadian Air Farce):

Q: "How many civil servants does it take to screw in a light-bulb?"
A: "One, but he's been promoted three levels by the time it's all screwed up."[3]

---

[1] Florence Elliott, *A Dictionary of Politics*, 7th ed. (Harmondsworth: Penguin Books, 1973), p. 71.

[2] For an overview and examples of the widespread negative attitudes to bureaucracy, see Robert F. Adie and Paul G. Thomas, *Canadian Public Administration: Problematical Perspectives* (Scarborough: Prentice-Hall, 1982), pp. 50-55.

[3] From the Royal Canadian Air Farce Album, "Air Farce Live" (CBC Enterprises, 1983).

Yet Canadians turn to public servants to solve the toughest of problems on society's behalf. Politicians routinely run for office on promises of reducing big bureaucracy, then discover that they cannot do without its officials when the public demands increased social services and a managed economy.

Weber's Concept of Bureaucracy

The term **bureaucracy** as a socio-political concept may be applied to complex organizational forms in a variety of contexts – business corporations, large social institutions such as churches, political structures such as party organizations, among others. But it is with the administrative machinery of government that the term is most clearly and most often identified in people's minds. The size of contemporary nation-states and the myriad of governmental responsibilities entailed in the management of modern societies necessitate the adoption of complex structures which can routinize the administrative decision-making process.

The starting point for most studies of bureaucracy is the "ideal-type" of bureaucratic organization formalized by the German social scientist Max Weber. His ideal-typical bureaucracy was to be characterized by

(a) the specialization of official duties;

(b) the hierarchical organization of authority;

(c) operations governed by a consistent application of abstract rules to particular cases;

(d) impersonal detachment toward subordinates and clients;

(e) employment based on merit and protection from arbitrary dismissal; and

(f) maximization of technical and organizational efficiency.[1]

In theory, organizations adopting the characteristics of Weber's model would maximize administrative efficiency and the rationalization of social activity. In reality, however, no bureaucracy conforms exactly to this ideal-type: indeed, the concept of "ideal-type" implies an abstraction from reality, a near-perfect standard against which examples in the observable world can be evaluated. Nonetheless, all these characteristics are found to a greater or lesser degree in Canadian federal administrative structures and, as Weber predicted, they have been developed partly as a result of "the increasing complexity of civilization", which encourages bureaucratization.[5]

Ironically, in view of current perceptions of bureaucratic power as a threat to democracy, some of the characteristics of bureaucracy developed as a consequence of the emergence of democratic forms of government. As the idea of alternation of power between competing parties became accepted under the

---

[1]Summarized by Peter M. Blau, *Bureaucracy in Modern Society* (New York: Random House, 1956), pp. 28-31, *passim*. See also Max Weber, *The Theory of Social and Economic Organization*, ed. and trans. by A.M. Henderson and Talcott Parsons (Glencoe: Free Press, 1947), pp. 329-341.

[5]H.H. Gerth and C. Wright Mills, eds. and trans., *From Max Weber: Essays in Sociology* (New York: Oxford University Press, 1946), p. 212.

doctrines of parliamentary democracy and representative government, it became necessary to separate the bureaucracy from the political executive. Thus, Henry Parris describes the emergence of what he termed "constitutional bureaucracy" in the United Kingdom: "From being one strand in the unified executive, the civil service has become a distinct entity, at the service of each successive cabinet."[6] The bureaucracy has thus been able to maximize rational administration free from political concerns, and individual public servants are protected from arbitrary dismissal on political grounds (*i.e.,* when government changes hands) as long as they maintain an air of overt partisan neutrality.

The development of liberal democracy also saw demands for the substitution of *merit* for patronage as the primary method of recruitment to government service and subsequent promotion within it. Whereas appointments to administrative office were once made on the basis of family and "old school tie" networks or as a reward for political services rendered, attempts to "democratize" the public service have resulted in the establishment of a merit system involving examinations or other forms of open competition.

Finally, certain characteristics of bureaucracy identified by Weber – the making of decisions through "the constant application of abstract rules to particular cases" and the display by bureaucrats of "impersonal detachment toward . . . clients" – serve to enhance administrative efficiency by routinizing the decision-making process. They also coincide with the fundamental constitutional principle of democracy, the concept of the rule of law, inasmuch as they protect individuals from arbitrary decisions and ensure that all clients are treated equally: where there may once have been one law for the rich and another for the poor, the operations of the ideal-type bureaucracy apply the same rules to all citizens.

Thus, a neutral, professional public service based on the organizational principles of modern bureaucracy has emerged alongside, and partly as a consequence of, the development of liberal democracy. Yet it has been suggested that a fundamental contradiction exists in the coexistence of bureaucracy and democracy in a society such as Canada.

Bureaucracy versus Democracy

Bureaucratic and democratic structures are, in part, founded upon different organizing principles: bureaucracy is based primarily on a clearly defined hierarchy of authority established in the interests of efficiency; democracy is based on the principle of fundamental political equality which permits majority rule while respecting minority rights and freedom of dissent. But as Peter Blau points out, democratic values also demand that social goals determined by majority decision (*i.e.,* through the democratic process) be implemented by the most effective means available so that the "will of the majority" may be seen to de done. Such effective methods, suggests Blau, are more likely to be governed by the dictates

---

[6]Henry Parris, "The Origins of the Permanent Civil Service, 1780-1820," *Public Administration,* vol. 46, no. 2 (Summer 1968), p. 164.

of bureaucracy than by those of democracy.[7] Since bureaucratic efficiency is aided by the routinization of decision-making through consistent application of abstract rules to particular cases, the quest for effective implementation may result in the application of uniform standards which reflect the will of the majority but neglect the minority interests which represent "exceptions to the rule". In a country like Canada, where minority ethnic, linguistic and regional interests are particularly sensitive, the result may be the exacerbation of potential conflicts and a loss of legitimacy for both the bureaucracy and the entire policy-making process.

This problem has become particularly acute in the modern era, since many areas of government policy are now so complex that the means of implementing public policies are often as important to their outcomes as the choice of goals. Therefore, although as Blau suggests "bureaucratic efficiency is expected to prevail in specialized government agencies, but not in the political arena,"[8] it is becoming increasingly difficult to maintain the distinction between administrative and political processes.

We have pointed out that in Canada, ultimate decision-making power in many fields resides constitutionally with the federal government; the bureaucracy is designated as the neutral, professional administrator of policy. But in practice it is difficult to separate the political and administrative dimensions of government action. While not political *per se*, the bureaucracy influences the actual formation of public policy in a number of ways.

First, Cabinet ministers who are formally responsible for defining public policies rarely enjoy sufficient tenure to permit the development of a high degree of expertise in the affairs of their respective ministries. Not only does government occasionally change hands from one party to another at general elections, but there are also periodic Cabinet shuffles in which ministers are moved from department to department and hence from one policy area to another. Each time this occurs, it takes a while for a minister to get to grips with his/her new role. The former British Labour Cabinet minister Anthony Crosland reckoned that "It takes you six months to get your head properly above water, a year to get a general drift of most of the field, and two years really to master the whole of a department."[9] Since the average departmental tenure of Canadian Cabinet ministers has been approximately thirty months in recent years (refer to Table 9-1), and assuming that Canadian politicians are no quicker on the uptake than the highly analytical and erudite Mr. Crosland, it is clear that the average federal minister spends a considerable portion of his/her time in office learning to master the workings of the department.

---

[7]Blau, *op. cit.*, pp. 106-107.

[8]*Ibid.*, p. 107.

[9]Anthony Crosland in M. Kogan, ed., *The Politics of Education* (Harmondsworth: Penguin Books, 1971), pp. 157-158. See also, on the trials and tribulations of being a new minister among experienced civil servants, Flora MacDonald, "The Minister and the Mandarins," *Policy Options*, vol. 1, no. 3 (September/October 1980), pp. 29-31.

TABLE 9.1 Ministerial Tenure in Four Federal Governments

Prime Minister	Duration of Tenure	Number of Major Cabinet Shuffles[1]	Average Departmental Tenure of Cabinet Ministers
St. Laurent	1948-1957	1	5 years, 2 1/2 months[2]
Diefenbaker	1957-1963	2	2 years, 4 months
Pearson	1963-1968	2	2 years, 2 months
Trudeau	1968-1979	8	2 years, 6 months[3]

Notes:

1. Major cabinet shuffles are defined as those involving at least 20 percent of Cabinet ministers.

2. Many of St. Laurent's ministers had previously served in the same departments under the former Prime Minister, Mackenzie King. Their previous experience in those departments is included here.

3. Previous experience in the Pearson government is included here.

In contrast, the permanence of public servants allows them to develop expertise and practical knowledge on which politicians can draw in formulating policies. Consequently, if, as Max Weber maintained, "knowledge is power,"[10] then the bureaucracy in a complex technical society may have great political power. It may screen the data furnished to its political masters, and such filtered information may be fundamental to the direction of government policy.

The relative permanence and access to information enjoyed by bureaucrats may influence the policy process in a number of other ways as well. Bureaucratic tenure permits public servants to develop a more long-term view of policy formulation than that of politicians, who must remain more sensitive and responsive to short-term shifts in public opinion. Also, administrative personnel in certain departments may have close links with "client" interest groups and thus would be in a better position than politicians to identify certain public needs.

Furthermore, the bureaucracy (or its components) may even be considered to constitute an "interest group" in its own right.[11] Thus, certain policy proposals generated within the bureaucracy may be advocated in such a way that they influence the government's subsequent choice among competing alternatives. Most government departments contain a policy analysis unit which monitors and evaluates the impact of ongoing policies. Here again bureaucrats may be in a better position than politicians to recommend fine-tuning or wholesale changes in existing policies. Finally, even after a political choice has been made by the government, a degree of discretion has to be left to public servants with regard to policy implementation.

The bureaucracy therefore has numerous opportunities to influence the policy-making process in Canada. But why should the bureaucracy, and especially

---

[10]Gerth and Wright Mills, *op. cit.*, pp. 232-235.

[11]See the discussion in Chapter 13 on Public Choice Theory.

its expanded role in the policy-making process, be viewed as a threat to democracy? Critics of bureaucratic influence propose several arguments.

First, they allege that the bureaucracy is unrepresentative of the general public and is therefore not sensitive to the requirements of citizens. If various minority groups and interests are not adequately represented within the bureaucracy, it is argued, their needs will be neglected.

The second argument is a more serious accusation extending the logic of the first – that the bureaucracy is steered by a narrow and cohesive elite which seeks to impose its own vision of society and the role of the state on the rest of the country. This argument is sometimes linked to "elite" or "class" theories of politics, which posit that the elitist family and educational backgrounds of bureaucrats render them sympathetic to the interests of friends, relatives and former colleagues in the business world and the upper class.[12]

Third, the growth of the state, the rise in public expenditures and the tax increases to pay for them and the escalating budgetary deficits incurred by most western governments are all blamed upon the expansionary tendencies of bureaucracy and the "empire-building" of individual bureaucrats.[13] Supporters of this line of argument aver that new government programs, and the budgets to pay for them, serve the interests of administrators rather than those of the general public. Furthermore, they allege that the inefficiency of the bureaucracy and the public sector results in the waste of economic resources. These critics demand that measures be initiated to increase financial accountability and bureaucratic efficiency.

Fourth, these arguments about the lack of financial accountability are often extended to more general criticisms of the lack of popular, parliamentary or governmental control over the actions of the bureaucracy. Politicians may be held accountable for their behaviour through the ballot box: if they have not served the needs of the public then they may be removed at the next election. However, in Canada there are no such mechanisms by which permanent public servants may be held accountable. For this reason, too, critics regard bureaucracy as inimical to the democratic process.

In later sections of this chapter, we shall examine various aspects of the bureaucracy and the administrative process in Canada in relation to these arguments. By examining the social and economic backgrounds of public servants, we may gauge the extent to which they are representative of the Canadian public. In outlining the budgetary process and the techniques designed to enhance administrative efficiency and effectiveness, we shall discuss their efficacy in ensuring the responsiveness and responsibility of the bureaucracy.

But first it should be noted that most critics of bureaucracy tend to view it as an undifferentiated, monolithic monster. Nothing could be further from the

---

[12]See, for example, Ralph Miliband, *The State in Capitalist Society* (London: Weidenfeld & Nicholson, 1969), Chapter 5, esp. p. 111.

[13]See, for example, Thomas E. Borcherding, ed., *Budgets and Bureaucrats: The Sources of Government Growth* (Durham: Duke University Press, 1977).

truth. The Canadian administrative apparatus is a complex hierarchy of different types of government departments, Crown corporations, agencies and other bodies serving a wide range of functions. Since some of the fears pertaining to bureaucracy are derived from minimal knowledge of its internal composition and operation, the next section provides a brief guide to the major structures of the administrative apparatus and their respective roles and responsibilities.

STRUCTURES OF THE FEDERAL BUREAUCRACY

The two formal structures of government with which Canadians most frequently come into contact are government departments and Crown corporations (or public enterprises). Few citizens escape encounters – some pleasant, some less so – with institutions such as the Department of National Revenue. Revenue Canada, of course, collects taxes and customs duties. Its employees may embarrass us by searching our luggage for contraband at the airport; but it may also provide a welcome windfall in the form of a tax rebate just in time for the next summer vacation. Most Canadians deal with Crown corporations every day – when buying gas at Petro-Canada service stations, listening to CBC Radio or travelling by Air Canada, CN Ferries or Via Rail.

But departmental officials and public enterprises which interact directly with the public are merely the most visible tip of the administrative iceberg. Three basic organizational forms are found in the Canadian federal bureaucracy: departments, Crown agencies and advisory bodies. Government **departments** are each headed by a Cabinet minister and are largely responsible for the administration of programs serving the public (*e.g.*, Employment and Immigration, Transport) or for the provision of services to the government itself (*e.g.*, National Revenue, Supply and Services). **Crown agencies** include public enterprises (*e.g.*, Air Canada, Canadian National, Petro-Canada), other Crown corporations (*e.g.*, National Museums of Canada) and regulatory commissions (*e.g.*, the Canadian Radio-Television and Telecommunications Commission and the Atomic Energy Control Board). The third group of structures, **advisory bodies**, consists of Royal Commissions, government and departmental task forces and a range of advisory councils, which collectively provide alternative sources of research and advice for the political executive.

Because of their special role in the policy process and their often exaggerated elite status, it may be tempting to classify **central agencies** (introduced in Chapter 7) as a fourth type of bureaucratic organization. However, with the exception of the Prime Minister's Office (PMO), these agencies are staffed almost exclusively by career public servants appointed under the aegis of the Public Service Commission. They are all formally headed by a Cabinet minister, and in all structural and legal respects closely resemble the departmental form of organization. For the purposes of this discussion, therefore, central agencies are viewed as a sub-category of government departments (see Table 9-2 below).

Federal Departments

According to J.E. Hodgetts, a department is "an administrative unit comprising one or more organizational components over which a minister has direct management and control".[14] Each government department is created by its own statute, which outlines generally the reason for the department's creation and its administrative duties. However, the *Transfer of Duties Act* of 1918 allows the Cabinet considerable latitude in altering internal structures and reallocating departmental responsibilities.

Reprinted with permission –
J. Beutel, New Brunswick.

One symptom of the expansion of the role of the state in Canada is the growing complexity of the institutional structures of government, which has been accompanied by an increase in the number of federal departments responsible for administering proliferating government functions. In the early years following Confederation, the work of the federal government was carried out by only thirteen ministries. The titles and duties of these first departments reflected what were then perceived to be the dominant functions of the federal government: the maintenance of law, order and security (Justice, Militia and Defence); the coordination of government policy and service (Privy Council, Secretary of State, Secretary of State for Provinces, Finance, Receiver General, Customs, Inland Revenue); and the provision of communications networks and some limited encouragement to economic development (Public Works, Post Office, Agriculture, Marine and Fisheries). Most of these have survived to the present day, albeit with many alterations and additions to their duties and functions. But four have disappeared, the most recent casualty being the Post Office Department upon the transformation of Canada Post into a Crown corporation in 1981.[15]

---

[14]J.E. Hodgetts, *The Canadian Public Service: A Physiology of Government 1867-1970* (Toronto: University of Toronto Press, 1973), p. 89.

[15]The three other original ministries which have disppeared as separate entities are Secretary of State for Provinces, Receiver General and Customs.

New responsibilities acquired by the federal government were often added to the duties of existing government departments, until the latter became so unwieldy that reorganization was imperative. The major expansion in the number of departments occurred between 1966 and 1971, in part reflecting the continuing growth of state activities in the post-war period. But it was also a product of attempts by Prime Ministers Pearson and Trudeau to modernize the policy-making process and further, a possible response to the recommendations of the Glassco Report on Government Organization.[16] This five-year period witnessed the establishment of the Treasury Board (formally separated from the Department of Finance in 1966), Manpower and Immigration (1966), Consumer and Corporate Affairs (1967), Communications (1968) and Energy, Mines and Resources (1970). Lastly, 1971 saw the emergence of a new type of department, the ministry of state. The Ministries of State for Urban Affairs (MSUA) and for Science and Technology (MOSST) were created in that year to provide research, information and policy planning and to encourage the coordination of policies and programs administered by other departments concerning these issue areas.[17]

Even after this period of intense activity, the process of reorganizing existing departments, creating new ones and juggling their responsibilities continued. In 1978 the Urban Affairs ministry disappeared again, but a new type of ministry of state was being discussed. As part of the new Policy Expenditure Management System (PEMS), the Ministry of State for Economic Development (MSED) and the Ministry of State for Social Development (MSSD) were established in December 1978 and June 1980 respectively. Like their predecessors, they were intended to be small departments aiding the coordination of other departments' efforts. But unlike the earlier versions, the two new ministries of state had genuine budgetary clout. In addition to their policy development roles, they also acted as "quasi-central agencies", providing advice and support to the Cabinet committees on economic development and social development which establish priorities and allocate monies among the various departments and programs in the expenditure envelopes under their control.[18] Nevertheless, Prime Minister John Turner disbanded MSERD (by this time, "Regional" had been added to its title) and MSSD during his brief stay in power during the summer of 1984.

Meanwhile, other changes had occurred. We have already noted the transformation of Canada Post from a government department into a Crown corporation in 1981. In the same year, the government announced plans to merge parts of the Department of Regional Economic Expansion (DREE) and of Industry, Trade and Commerce (IT&C) into a new Department of Regional and Industrial Expansion (DRIE); the "trade" component of IT&C was to be transferred to the Department of External Affairs. And so the process continues. Sometimes new

---

[16]Royal Commission on Government Organization, *Report* (The "Glassco Report") (Ottawa: Queen's Printer, 1962, 1963).

[17]On the origins and rationales of the new ministries of state, see Peter Aucoin and Richard French, *Knowledge, Power and Public Policy* (Ottawa: Science Council of Canada, 1974).

[18]See the discussion of Cabinet Committees, envelopes and their roles in Chapter 7.

departments are created or duties are shuffled among existing departments, in the interest of policy-making effectiveness and administrative efficiency. But, on occasion, political and symbolic motivations prevail in that the reorganization of departments is designed to display the government's sensitivity to particular problems or to the concerns of special interest groups.[19]

As of August 1985, there were twenty-five government departments.[20] Table 9-2 presents a typology of federal government departments which divides them into three major categories – Vertical "Constituency", Horizontal "Administrative Coordinative" and Horizontal "Policy Coordinative" – on the basis of their major functions and the clienteles which they serve.[21]

Of the twenty-five departments, sixteen may be classified as **Vertical "Constituency" Departments**, those ministries whose primary function is the provision of services directly to the general public as a whole (*e.g.*, National Health and Welfare, Transport) or to some particular constituency or clientele (*e.g.*, Indian Affairs and Northern Development, Veterans' Affairs). These departments are described as "vertical" because they represent direct links between government and citizens, while the two "horizontal" categories primarily serve the government. Often, "constituency" departments are also referred to as "line" or "program-oriented" ministries since their administrative structures are chiefly geared towards a kind of assembly-line delivery of programs or services to Canadian citizens.

The second category, **Horizontal "Administrative Coordinative" Departments,** are those ministries whose main function is providing services to other departments or to the entire governmental structure. Duties performed by these departments include the collection of taxes and other government revenues by Revenue Canada; management of the government's real estate and office buildings by Public Works; and the wide variety of financial, management, consulting, purchasing, printing and publishing services provided to government agencies by the twin administrative structures under the Minister of Supply and Services.

The chief roles of the third group, **Horizontal "Policy Coordinative" Departments,** consist of developing a broader policy framework within which other governmental functions are carried out and of coordinating policies and programs across all departments, rather than administering services to the public or

---

[19]Sometimes, rather than creating a new department, the Prime Minister may instead appoint Ministers of State with special responsibilities within an existing department – for example, the Minister of State for Small Business, the Minister of State for Multiculturalism and the Minister of State for Forestry.

[20]The figure of 25 government departments, effective August 31, 1985, includes the Privy Council Office, but excludes some examples listed in Table 9-2, specifically the three disbanded ministries of trade (MSUA, MSERD, MSSD) and the "functional equivalents" of departments (the Public Service Commission and FPRO).

[21]Our typology of government departments is a revised and updated adaptation of an approach to classifying ministerial portfolios suggested by G. Bruce Doern, "Horizontal and Vertical Portfolios in Government," in Doern and Wilson, eds., *Issues in Canadian Public Policy* (Toronto: MacMillan, 1974), pp. 310-336.

TABLE 9.2 A Typology of Federal Government Departments

Vertical "Constituency" or "Line" Departments	Horizontal "Administrative Coordinative" Departments	Central Agencies	Horizontal "Policy Coordinative" Departments Other
Agriculture	National Revenue	Finance	External Affairs
Communications	Public Works	Privy Council Office (PCO)	Justice
Consumer and Corporate Affairs	Supply and Services	Treasury Board Secretariat (TBS)	Ministry of State for Science and Technology (MOSST)
Employment and Immigration	¹Public Service Commission	¹Federal-Provincial Relations Office (FPRO)	²Ministry of State for Economic and Regional Development (MSERD)
Energy, Mines and Resources			²Ministry of State for Social Development (MMSD)
Environment		¹Prime Minister's Office (PMO)	²Ministry of State for Urban Affairs (MSUA)
Fisheries and Oceans			
Indian Affairs and Northern Development			
Labour			
National Defence			
National Health and Welfare			
Regional and Industrial Expansion			
Secretary of State			
Solicitor General			
Transport			
Veterans' Affairs			

Notes: 1. Agencies which serve as functional equivalents to departments in coordinative roles but which are not recognized a government departments in legal or other terms.

2. Three ministries of state, now disbanded, included in the table for the purpose of illustration. All other departments extant as of August 1984.

Source: Adapted from original distinction between "vertical" and "horizontal" functions made by G. Bruce Doern, "Horizontal and Vertical Portolios is Government," in G.B. Doern and V.S. Wilson, eds. *Issues in Canadian Public Policy* (Toronto: MacMillan, 1974).

to the government itself. Thus, in addition to the Department of Finance and other central agencies such as the Privy Council Office and Treasury Board Secretariat, Policy Coordinative departments include the former MSERD and MSSD (whose Cabinet support functions made them something like quasi-central agencies), the sole surviving ministry of state, MOSST and the Departments of External Affairs and Justice which respectively provide the foreign policy and legal frameworks for the program and policy activities of other departments.

The primary function of a government department, as revealed in this typology, is a key determinant of its internal structure. Each department is formally headed by a Cabinet minister appointed to that particular portfolio by the Prime Minister. But while the minister is politically responsible for the activities of the department and for formulating general policy, the administrative and managerial head of each ministry is its senior public servant, the Deputy Minister or DM.[22] The Deputy Minister is at the apex of a pyramidal structure of authority and organizational agencies. Two or more Assistant Deputy Ministers (ADMs), heading branches or bureaus, report directly to the DM. There may also be a Senior Assistant Deputy Minister in charge of policy coordination and corporate planning for the whole department. Below the ADMs are directorates or branches, each headed by a Director or Director General. These directorates are in turn composed of divisions, headed by Directors or Divisional Chiefs; the divisions are further broken down into sections, offices and units. The exact titles of departmental sub-units and their respective senior officials vary from department to department.

The number of senior officials, and the range of sub-units and employees for which they are responsible, will tend to vary according to the type of department. Vertical Constituency or Line departments generally consist of a large number of sub-units and employ more staff to deal with the general public. Agriculture Canada, for instance, with a wide variety of programs under its administration, employs more than 10 000 people across the country. The Administrative Coordinative ministries also tend to be large, complex structures. However, the Policy coordinative departments, with the exception of External Affairs, are generally much smaller and have more simplified organizational forms, in part because they have few, if any, program- or service-delivery functions. They tend to have only four or five main branches concerned with research and policy coordination in different policy areas or may be divided into "research", "planning", and "policy coordination" functions.[23] Thus, while the hierarchical chain of command is common to both program-oriented and policy-

---

[22]In departments where the minister's official designation is "Secretary of State for. . .," as in "Secretary of State for External Affairs", the senior public servant is known as the "Undersecretary of State. . ." rather than the "Deputy Minister". Similarly, in Ministries of State, such as MOSST or the late MSSD, the senior public servant is known as the "Secretary".

[23]See, for example, organizational charts in the Annual Reports published by MOSST and other Ministries of State, or the stylized diagramatic presentation of a "model" policy-oriented department in Audrey Doerr, *The Machinery of Government in Canada* (Toronto: Methuen, 1981), Figure 4-2, p. 90.

oriented departments, the Policy Coordinative type tends to have a much more cohesive, streamlined structure than the rather ramshackle and apparently unwieldy typical Vertical Constituency or Administrative Coordinative ministry.

Crown Agencies

We have said that the second basic organizational form in the federal bureaucracy is the Crown agency. This category includes a wide variety of non-departmental organizations including Crown corporations, regulatory agencies, administrative tribunals and, strictly speaking, some of the advisory bodies discussed separately below. The rationale for distinguishing the latter from Crown agencies is that they are primarily involved in the process of policy formulation, while Crown agencies are charged directly with attaining government policy objectives – through public owernship, regulation of the private sector and so on. The notion that Crown agencies are largely "instruments of public policy" was incorporated into the definition of these bodies by the 1979 Royal Commission on Financial Management and Accountability:

> Crown agencies are distinct entities established as instruments of public policy that have been directly delegated by Parliament, the Government, or another Crown agency specified continuing responsibilities and decision-making powers that assure them a degree of autonomy from Parliament and the Government in the pursuit of their tasks.[24]

A number of characteristics serve to distinguish Crown agencies from government departments. A.M. Willms identified four of the more obvious differences:

1. Departments are answerable directly to a Cabinet minister and that minister takes responsibility for their actions. Agencies usually have a minister designated to them through whom they report to Parliament but the degree of supervision and accountability varies and is much smaller than that with departments. . .
2. Departments are all subject to the estimates system of budgeting, that is, revenues coming from the Crown must be spent exactly as directed by Parliament and Treasury Board, and receipts must be returned to the Receiver-General. Agencies vary widely in their budget practices.
3. The personnel of departments are generally recruited by the Public Service Commission and their promotion and transfer is closely supervised by the Commission. Only a few of the agencies recruit through the Public Service Commission. Generally speaking they are responsible for their own personnel matters.
4. Departments have deputy ministers as the administrative heads while agencies vary widely in the nature of their management. Some have

---

[24]Royal Commision on Financial Management and Accountability, *Final Report* (Ottawa: Minister of Supply & Services, 1979), p. 271.

boards of directors, others have chairmen, commissioners, or directors.[25]

Depending upon the exact definition employed, there are between 400 and 500 federal Crown agencies.[26] They have been developed over time to cope with new roles and new demands engendered by the growth of federal government activities. Thus, Crown corporations have been established to provide transportation and communication infrastructures; to ensure a Canadian presence in certain key sectors; to save jobs by bailing out declining private companies; and to supply financial and other aid to private sector manufacturing, agriculture and resource development.[27] Regulatory agencies have been created to control "natural monopolies" and to remedy other market failures; to effect redistribution; and to meet social and cultural objectives of the federal government.[28] Similar goals may be achieved in both cases by less direct forms of government intervention, such as subsidies, taxation or legislation, without the creation of separate agencies. What characterizes most Crown agencies and distinguishes them from departmental forms of organization is their relative independence of direct governmental or ministerial control.

Most agencies report to Parliament through a minister, but they are usually headed by an independent board appointed by the government. Agencies are generally given considerable amounts of delegated authority and are permitted to function in a quasi-independent manner with regard to budget expenditure, staffing, policy-planning and ministerial control, compared with government departments. There are several reasons for legitimizing the independence of these bureaucratic entities. The nature of their tasks necessitates a degree of expertise not usually found in government bureaucracies; as well, traditional bureaucratic structures do not permit the flexibility or continuity of policy necessary for the experimental and innovative functions of the agencies. Finally, such agencies, in all their guises – administrative tribunals, appeal boards, regulatory bodies and Crown corporations – require an arm's length relationship with government in order to insulate their policies and decisions from partisan or other political pressures.

But many observers have demonstrated concern over the independence and perceived non-accountability of Crown agencies. J.E. Hodgetts labelled

---

[25]A.M. Willms, "Crown Agencies," in W.D.K. Kernaghan and A.M. Willms, eds., *Public Administration in Canada: Selected Readings*, 2nd. ed. (Toronto: Methuen, 1971), p. 103.

[26]According to the Lambert Commission, "As of January 1979 the official count was 426." Royal Commission on Financial Management. . ., *Final Report*, p. 277.

[27]See the discussion of "public ownership" as a policy instrument in Chapter 13. Discussion of the rationale for Crown corporations or public enterprises may be found in: Marsha Gordon, *Government in Business* (Montréal: C.D. Howe Institute, 1981); John Langford, "Crown Corporations as Instruments of Policy," in G.B. Doern and P. Aucoin, eds., *Public Policy in Canada: Organization, Process and Management* (Toronto: Macmillan 1979), pp. 239-274.

[28]See the further discussion of "regulation" as a policy instrument in Chapter 13, and Economic Council of Canada, *Interim Report: Responsible Regulation* (Ottawa: Minister of Supply & Services, 1979), Ch. 4.

them "structural heretics" within the Canadian political system because of their non-departmental form, and argued that to varying degrees they do "violence to the constituted form of ministerial responsibility".[29] In response to questions in Parliament about the functioning of agencies nominally under their jurisdiction, it is too easy for ministers to disclaim responsibility by stating that "this is a matter involving an independent agency and one can only answer in so far as the agency sees fit to provide one with the information."[30]

The late 1970s saw mounting criticism of the degree of autonomy enjoyed by Crown agencies from both parliamentary and government control. The proliferation of regulatory agencies and their functions gave rise to a comprehensive study by the Economic Council of Canada of the problems of regulation and the need for regulatory reform.[31] But the major attacks were reserved for Crown corporations. The 1976 Report of the Auditor General argued that Parliament had effectively lost control of the public purse in Canada. Both in the 1976 Report and in subsequent ones, a large part of the blame was attributed to insufficient financial control over the activities of Crown corporations. At the same time, certain allegations were made public concerning serious mismanagement of some of the major public enterprises which were supposed to be serving as policy instruments on behalf of the federal government. According to the Lambert Royal Commission Report,

> these events included the revelation by a Commission of Inquiry of unorthodox practices within Air Canada with respect to the establishment, operation and reporting of subsidiaries; Polysar's purchase . . . of an interest in Sentrachem of South Africa; the contradictory advice from auditors as to invoicing practices in a more recent and highly publicized Polysar affair; the inquiry into claims of separatist influence in CBC programming; AECL's cost overruns and payments to sales agents; and the complaints by certain ministers that they had lost control of the regulatory agencies and Crown corporations in their portfolios.[32]

Despite such concerns, a number of formal mechanisms do exist by which Parliament and Cabinet can seek to control these quasi-independent agencies. Many of their incorporative statutes require agencies to respond to ministerial or Cabinet policy directives. Cabinet may appoint and dismiss top management and board members and determine the number of years an appointee may serve. The regulatory power of some agencies, such as the National Energy Board (NEB), is subject to veto by the Governor-in-Council. In other cases, such as the Foreign Investment Review Agency (FIRA), Cabinet itself is the formal regulatory authority, making the final decisions based on recommendations from the Agency.

---

[29]Hodgetts, *The Canadian Public Service*, p. 141 and Chapter 7, *passim.*

[30]J.E. Hodgetts, "The Public Corporation in Canada," in Hodgetts and D.C. Corbett, eds., *Canadian Public Administration* (Toronto: Macmillan, 1960), p. 199.

[31]Economic Council of Canada, *Interim Report: Responsible Regulation, op. cit.*, and *Final Report: Reforming Regulation* (Ottawa: Minister of Supply & Services, 1981).

[32]Royal Commission on Financial Management. . ., *Final Report*, p. 272.

In addition, a degree of financial control is exercised: at least part of most agencies' proposed spending is subject to Parliamentary scrutiny in the estimates process. Furthermore, agencies are subject to audit by the Auditor General, who reports his findings to Parliament, and they must usually submit to Parliament an annual report which is now automatically referred to the appropriate standing committee for investigation. Perhaps most important, all agencies ultimately receive their powers either from Orders-in-Council or from statutes, either of which may be amended or revoked by politicians if an agency abuses its independent status.

Thus, while much reform debate has revolved around the need to strengthen parliamentary and Cabinet control over the activities of Crown agencies, there have also been arguments in favour of reducing the extent of government intervention via the regulatory process and public ownership. Some of these ideas have received active political support; for example, the Conservative government of 1979-80 was officially committed to the "privatization" of Petro-Canada and other public enterprises, and the subsequent Liberal government took some tentative steps towards the deregulation of the airline industry. We shall give more attention to proposed reforms later in this chapter; more immediately, we shall discuss in detail the different types of Crown agencies.

CROWN CORPORATIONS

According to John Langford, "a crown corporation is (or should be) a wholly-owned, semi-autonomous agency of government organized under the corporate form to perform a task or group of related tasks in the national interest."[33] Despite the relative precision of this definition, the exact delineation of the universe of Crown corporations at the federal level is a difficult task. The usual starting place for defining and classifying these agencies is the *Financial Administration Act*, (FAA), which sets out the financial relationship between different types of Crown corporations and the federal government. The *FAA* classifies Crown corporations into three categories – "departmental", "agency" and "proprietary" – according to their main functions and degree of financial autonomy.[34]

A **departmental corporation** is a "servant or agent of Her Majesty in right of Canada and is responsible for administrative, supervisory or regulatory services of a governmental nature." In March 1984, the *FAA* listed seventeen departmental corporations. These organizations are in many respects branches of their parent departments. They are financed out of the Consolidated Revenue Fund, and their expenditures are subject to control by the Treasury Board and scrutiny by Parliament. The employees of many departmental corporations are appointed by the Public Service Commission under the same terms of classification, pay and tenure as their colleagues in the departmental hierarchy. Fur-

---

[33]Langford, "Crown Corporations as Instruments of Policy," p. 242.

[34]Quotations from the FAA and the number and examples of Crown corporations under its Schedules are taken from Government of Canada, *Financial Administration Act, Office Consolidation, March 1984* (Ottawa: Minister of Supply and Services, 1984), pp. 30-35 and Schedules B-D, pp. 46-48.

ther, the board, council or commission of these bodies is generally less of a collegial corporate executive than an advisory group to the departmental minister who exercises most managerial control.

So similar are most departmental corporations to the regular departments that, in the words of one critic, "there seems to be no compelling reason to have given them Crown corporation status in the first place."[35] However, the functions of some departmental corporations could render them susceptible to allegations of political or bureaucratic interference if they did not enjoy at least a minimal degree of autonomy from the departmental structure. The regulatory function of the Atomic Energy Control Board; the need for fresh thinking from corporations with advisory roles such as the Economic Council of Canada and the Science Council of Canada; and the potentially sensitive disbursal of funds by the three research councils (Medical Research Council, Natural Sciences and Engineering Research Council, Social Sciences and Humanities Research Council) – all require some independence from ministerial pressure.

An **agency corporation** is defined by the *FAA* as a Crown corporation that is "responsible for the management of trading or service operations on a quasi-commercial basis, or for the management of procurement, construction or disposal activities" on behalf of the Crown. Agency corporations are rather like private trading companies in structure. Legally, they are autonomous agencies which may be held responsible for their actions in court. However, their shares are held in trust for the Crown; therefore, their directors are appointed by the Governor-in-Council. Unlike in most departmental corporations, the managers of agency corporations appoint their own staff rather than relying on the Public Service Commission. The finances of agency corporations are subject to fairly rigorous scrutiny by the appropriate minister and by Parliament, although their financial dependence on public funding varies widely. Among the thirty agency corporations listed by the *FAA*, Canada Patents and Development Limited, for example, operates at a profit; others are funded wholly by appropriations voted by Parliament; while better-known cases such as Atomic Energy of Canada Limited and the Canada Post Corporation receive income both from appropriations and from their own trading revenue.

Members of the third category, **proprietory corporations**, are "responsible for the management of lending or financial operations, or for the management of commercial or industrial operations involving the production of or dealing in goods and supplying of services to the public." In March 1984 the *FAA* listed twenty-five proprietory corporations, including some of Canada's best-known Crown corporations: Air Canada, the CBC, Canadian National, Petro-Canada and Via Rail. Many of them are in competition with private sector companies for sales, viewers, listeners or customers. Consequently, they are forced to reveal fewer details of their operations in their annual reports to Parliament than the other two types and may therefore have greater autonomy from political supervi-

---

[35]Langford, "Crown Corporations as Instruments of Policy," p. 244.

sion, especially since some, such as Air Canada, do not have to submit their accounts to the Auditor General. According to the *FAA*, proprietary corporations are ordinarily required to conduct operations without Parliamentary appropriations; but it is not uncommon for Parliament to help out in balancing their budgets, especially for the pursuit of certain cultural or political objectives which may not be commercially viable. Despite this partial financial dependence, the proprietary corporations are, with the exception of quasi-administrative agencies like the Canada Mortgage and Housing Corporation, the most independent agencies listed by the *Financial Administration Act*.

The schedules of the *FAA* listed 72 Crown corporations in March 1984. It has been estimated that these constitute only about one-third of all federal Crown corporations.[36] Some so-called "unscheduled corporations" are governed by their own Acts of Incorporation and are thus exempt from the provisions of the *FAA* except for the requirement that they subject their books to audits. Such agencies as the Bank of Canada, the Canada Wheat Board and the National Arts Centre Corporation are wholly owned by the federal government, and in all functional and other respects appear to satisfy most definitions of Crown corporations. The *FAA* schedules also exclude the many subsidiaries of those Crown corporations which are listed; Canadian National, for example, has over fifty subsidiaries not covered by the *Act*.

To complete the picture, it should be noted that the federal government is also involved in a number of intergovernmental or mixed enterprises in which it is a joint shareholder either with other governments (e.g., Canadian-American co-management of the Roosevelt Campobello International Park Commission) or with private investors (*e.g.*, Canada Development Corporation). While these enterprises may not conform to the above definition of Crown corporations, since they are not wholly owned by the federal government, they cannot be ignored in discussions of public policy and financial accountability because they serve as instruments of government policy and involve the expenditure of public funds.

REGULATORY AGENCIES

Regulation, according to the Economic Council of Canada, is "the imposition of constraints, backed by government authority, that are intended to modify economic behaviour of individuals in the private sector significantly."[37] Regulation may be conducted through any of three mechanisms: **direct regulation**, in which constraints on behaviour are clearly specified in legislation, leaving little discretion to implementing authorities (usually government departments); **delegated self-regulation**, in which private actors such as the medical and legal professions or agricultural marketing boards are given substantial power to reg-

---

[36]Allan Tupper and G. Bruce Doern, "Understanding Public Corporations in Canada," *Canadian Business Review,* vol. 9, no. 3 (Autumn 1982), p. 35.

[37]Economic Council of Canada, *Interim Report: Responsible Regulation*, p. xi.

ulate their own activities, subject to certain conditions; and **independent regulatory commissions**.[38] Our concern here is with the last of these, the independent regulatory agency or commission, another non-departmental bureaucratic structure or "structural heretic".

Among other functions, regulatory agencies may be required by government to influence private or corporate behaviour with respect to prices and tariffs, supply, market entry and conditions of service, product content and methods of production. In order to meet their objectives, agencies may be granted a variety of powers. Most agencies have quasi-judicial power, "that is, the power to judge specific cases involving the granting, denial or removal of licenses, the approval of rates or fares and the censuring of failure to comply with terms of licenses."[39] Thus, the Canadian Transport Commission (CTC) can control the degree of competition in the air passenger transport market by granting or withholding licenses to carriers and by adjudicating the fares they are allowed to charge. Furthermore, some agencies have developed legislative powers which permit them to formulate general rules applicable to all cases under consideration: an example is the "Canadian content" regulations applied by the Canadian Radio-Television and Telecommunications Commission (CRTC). Most agencies also enjoy investigative powers allowing them to use their expertise to undertake research and pursue inquiries within their field of competence. The investigative function is, in fact, the primary role of agencies such as the Foreign Investment Review Agency which have no adjudicative powers of their own, but rather act as "screening agencies" making recommendations for regulatory decisions to Cabinet or the responsible official. Finally, some agencies manage expenditure programs on behalf of the government: for example, the Railway Transport Committee of the CTC approves compensation to railway companies operating uneconomic lines.[40]

Independent regulatory agencies receive their major powers from enabling legislation which also sets out agency objectives. In many cases, regulatory mandates are extremely vague – the CTC, for example, is charged with promoting "an economic, efficient and adequate transportation system".[41] Such imprecision permits considerable discretion to commission members. They are appointed by the Governor-in-Council, usually for fixed terms of from five to ten years, although members of FIRA or the Atomic Energy Control Board hold office "at pleasure". While most agencies are subject to ministerial directives, ministers usually are loathe to infringe upon the traditional arm's-length relationship. Regulatory bodies are required to submit their budgets to the Treasury Board

---

[38]See Michael J. Trebilcock *et al.*, *The Choice of Governing Instrument* (Ottawa: Minister of Supply and Services, 1982), pp. 88-92.

[39]Richard Schultz, "Regulatory Agencies," in M.S. Whittington and G. Williams, eds., *Canadian Politics in the 1980s*, 2nd ed. (Toronto: Methuen, 1984), p. 438.

[40]Hudson N. Janisch, "The Canadian Transport Commission" in G.B. Doern, ed., *The Regulatory Process in Canada* (Toronto: Macmillan, 1978), pp. 176-177.

[41]*Ibid.*, p. 169.

(and usually, also, to the Auditor General) for review, and to present annual reports to the responsible minister and to Parliament.

The autonomy enjoyed by many regulatory commissions – the consequence of broad mandates, tenure of office, lack of ministerial direction and often inadequate Parliamentary scrutiny – leads some observers to question whether these agencies always act in the public interest. Most prevalent among these arguments is the so-called "capture thesis" which suggests that regulatory bodies often end up serving the interests of the industries and firms they are supposed to regulate. The capture thesis was first popularized in the United States, where regulatory commissions are even more independent of government than their Canadian counterparts;[42] but, while there are undoubtedly exceptions, there appears to be little evidence of its general applicability to Canadian federal agencies.[43] Rather, writers from various perspectives have suggested that regulatory agencies are effectively coordinative organizations which link the government with business by simultaneously regulating and representing the interests of regulated industries.[44] Nonetheless, other concerns continue to be voiced: the continuous growth in the volume and scope of regulation; perceived lack of accountability and ministerial direction; the reform of the internal decision-making and hearing processes of regulatory agencies; and the costs and inefficiencies allegedly associated with regulatory regimes. Consequently, regulatory reform is on many people's lists of pet reform topics.

Advisory Bodies

Federal departments and Crown agencies are designed to deal primarily with the implementation and administration of government policies. There are other federal structures, however, whose activities are more closely related to the formulation of public policies. This third group, advisory bodies, is comprised of Royal Commissions, government and departmental task forces and advisory councils.[45]

Royal Commissions and task forces are widely employed as sources of public policy advice to the executive. They are generally asked to investigate an area of critical public concern and to issue a subsequent report recommending a suitable course of action. Typical issues in recent years have included the economy (the Macdonald Royal Commission on the Economic Union); federalism (the Pepin-Robarts Task Force on National Unity); business and corporate policy (the

---

[42]See Marver H. Bernstein, *Regulating Business by Independent Commission* (Princeton: Princeton University Press, 1955).

[43]See the discussion in Schultz, "Regulatory Agencies," pp. 435-437; and G. Bruce Doern, *The Regulatory Process in Canada*, esp. pp. 26-29.

[44]Adie and Thomas, *Canadian Public Administration: Problematical Perspectives*, p. 275; Rianne Mahon, "Regulatory Agencies: Captive Agents or Hegemonic Apparatuses," *Studies in Political Economy*, vol. 1 (Spring 1979), pp. 162-200.

[45]"Governmental" task forces should not be confused with the small Special Committees of the House of Commons, otherwise known as "Parliamentary Task Forces" described in Chapter 8.

Bryce Royal Commission on Corporate Concentration); and cultural policy (the Applebaum-Hébert Federal Cultural Policy Review Committee).

Such bodies attempt to encourage wide public understanding of serious national problems and at the same time to provide an informed basis for future policy-making by the government. Their investigations are in part carried out by soliciting outside views through public hearings and inviting individuals, groups and organizations to submit briefs. But they also initiate programs of directed and commissioned research, employing *ad hoc* research staff and retaining academics and other outside experts as consultants.

ROYAL COMMISSIONS

Royal Commissions are established by the executive through an Order-in-Council under the *Public Inquiries Act*. Policy-oriented commissions are established under Part I of the *Act*, but the *Act* also provides for the formation of Royal Commissions of a strictly investigatory nature, inquiring into alleged wrong-doings; an example is the Estey inquiry into recent bank failures established in 1985. The latter type are usually conducted by a single commissioner. Policy-oriented Commissions, on the other hand, are normally headed by three commissioners, although there are exceptions: the 1966 Royal Commission on the Status of Women had seven.

There is no consistent policy governing the procedure of Royal Commissions, although a time limit is sometimes set for their report to the government. Royal Commissions have some advantages over standing committees and most special committees of Parliament, in that they are given their own budgets and may meet and travel when and where they wish (but recall that similar facilities were also given to the Parliamentary Task Forces in 1980-83). Governments are not legally bound to release Commission reports, though it would generally be politically unwise to refuse to do so. With few exceptions, the work of a Commission is solely of an advisory nature and does not confer any power or responsibility regarding implementation of recommended policy. This characteristic is frequently cited as the greatest weakness of Royal Commissions. At the same time, it permits them the latitude to formulate progressive policy positions which are visionary yet could not possibly be legislated by the government under existing political conditions. Commission proposals are generally incorporated into government action as incremental policy change, the Royal Commission process having allowed the executive to sound out the limits of intended action.[46]

TASK FORCES

Some so-called "task forces", such as the Task Force on National Unity, are little more than a variation on the Royal Commission theme. They, too, are appointed by Order-in-Council and may be awarded powers under the *Inquiries Act*. They usually do less research than Royal Commissions, concentrating primarily on ob-

---

[46]Vincent S. Wilson, "The Role of Royal Commissions and Task Forces," in G.B. Doern and P. Aucoin, eds., *The Structures of Policy-Making in Canada* (Toronto: Macmillan, 1971), pp. 119-120.

taining public input into the consultative process.[47] As *ad hoc* bodies, they suffer from the same problem as Royal Commissions in that, once their reports are published, no entity is empowered to force follow-up discussion in either Parliament or the mass media.

Other task forces are constituted on a less grandiose scale within the bureaucracy, consisting of representatives from a single department, from a number of ministries or from the public and private sectors. Bureaucratic task forces were introduced in the first Pearson government in the 1960s, but their use expanded rapidly under Trudeau. The rationales for employing these advisory bodies to tackle particular policy problems are that they require less staffing and funding than Royal Commissions and, most importantly, that they tend to produce results much more quickly than their formal counterparts.[48] Critics question the use of task forces rather than Royal Commissions because the former are more prone to interference from ministers and because there is no requirement for their reports to be made public. However, for quick responses in "trouble-shooting" situations, the flexibility of executive task forces gives them an advantage over the more formal, public and stately Royal Commissions.

ADVISORY COUNCILS

Frustration with the *ad hoc*, short-term work of Royal Commissions and task forces has caused the Canadian government to create a number of permanent advisory councils whose purpose is to study public policy questions, offer appropriate advice and monitor ongoing policies in their area of expertise. Thus, the Advisory Council for the Status of Women (ACSW) is charged with producing "recommendations to the Government on legislation on programs to improve the status of women; research on matters pertaining to the status of women in Canada; and publications of reports on areas of concern and an annual report on the progress being made in improving the status of women."[49]

Several advisory councils, such as the Economic Council of Canada and the Science Council of Canada, are also Crown corporations. This dual nature enhances their independence as sources of policy advice. Others, such as the ACSW and the Advisory Committee on Multiculturalism, are extremely vulnerable to changes in departmental or financial priorities. All advisory councils are given permanent research staffs to assist the full-time and part-time board members, who are appointed for fixed terms by the Governor-in-Council.

Most advisory groups representing specific constituencies or sub-groups of the population act as both government policy advisors and interest groups lobbying government departments on behalf of their respective clienteles. Consequently, they have to tread a fine line between being co-opted into the

---

[47]Doerr, *The Machinery of Government in Canada*, p. 151.

[48]Wilson, "The Role of Royal Commissions and Task Forces," pp. 121-122.

[49]Government of Canada, *Estimates for the Fiscal Year Ending March 31, 1985* ("The Blue Book") (Ottawa: Minister of Supply and Services, 1984), Sections 24-32.

bureaucratic process and taking too independent a stance which might alienate them from their access to government policy.

Organizing Principles and Linkages

An inventory of the main organizational forms within the Canadian federal bureaucracy may serve to illustrate the diversity of bureaucratic structures but does not in itself provide a complete picture of the way the bureaucracy operates. One also requires an appreciation of the the basic principles on which the bureaucracy is organized as well as of the various linkages that exist, first, among different structures within the bureaucracy and, second, between the bureaucracy and the more overtly political institutions of Cabinet and Parliament.

The chief organizing principle of the bureaucracy itself is the concept of **departmentalization**, whereby, at least in theory, every administrative function in the federal government is allocated to a single government department. Two reasons may be cited for a clear apportionment of duties among government departments or agencies: it avoids financial waste and administration confusion; and it helps to clarify lines of accountability for administrative actions and thus strengthens another principle of bureaucratic organization in Canada – ministerial responsibility and accountability.

The allocation of duties to government departments may be based on one or more of the following criteria: common purpose, clientele, territory or place, expertise, process.[50] Thus, for example, the Departments of Labour and Veterans' Affairs cater largely to specific clienteles, as their names suggest. So, too, in part does the Department of Indian Affairs and Northern Development, although that ministry's traditional responsibility for overseeing the administration of government in Yukon and the Northwest Territories has also been based on the criterion of "place". The Department of Supply and Services is organized around the use of common facilities – "process" – in acting as a printing and publishing house for almost the entire federal government structure.

In many cases, however, there is no perfect correspondence between these organizational criteria and the activities of individual departments. Consequently, some departments have a semi-schizophrenic existence; different organizational criteria force them to pursue internally contradictory goals. In the case of the Department of Indian Affairs and Northern Development cited above, it has been argued that the function of protecting and enhancing the interests and way of life of Native people in the North is irreconcilable with the objective of promoting northern resource development.[51] Furthermore, the absence of a consistent application of the criteria has ensured that some jurisdictional disputes do arise between federal departments and agencies. Such conflicts may be exacer-

---

[50]See Hodgetts, *The Canadian Public Service*, p. 112.

[51]Simon McInnes, "The Policy Consequences of Northern Development," in M. Atkinson and M. Chandler, eds., *The Politics of Canadian Public Policy* (Toronto: University of Toronto Press, 1983), pp. 247-266.

bated by the different philosophies of policy-making and administration within various structures in the bureaucracy.[52]

The processes of policy-making and conflict resolution between government departments and agencies are often referred to as **bureaucratic politics**. This term is usually associated with the work of Graham Allison, who argued in his book on the 1962 Cuban Missile Crisis that the conventional model of foreign policy decision-making, the so-called "rational actor" model, did not adequately explain the actions of policy-makers in that situation. The rational actor model suggests that government is effectively a unitary, monolithic actor, with a single set of goals or objectives, which selects from a range of alternatives the policy that best serves its perception of the national interest. Allison contended instead that the choice of policy decisions in the Missile Crisis might better be explained by the "bureaucratic politics" model, which assumes that government consists of a variety of individuals, groups and agencies, pursuing divergent interests and policy goals, which compete with one another to have their respective values and objectives reported in the final policy outcome.[53]

Most studies of bureaucratic politics and policy-making in Canada have focused, as Allison did, on foreign and defence policy decisions.[54] But there have also been applications of, and support for, the model in the domestic policy arena.[55] Conflict between bureaucratic agencies can often be settled relatively amicably through discussions at the ministerial level in Cabinet or Cabinet committee, or at the "official" level in interdepartmental committees of senior public servants, or sometimes by resorting to the creation of a bureaucratic task force. On other occasions, however, the failure to reconcile competing agency philosophies or interests has effectively paralyzed the policy-making process. Richard French, for example, has demonstrated how the attempt to develop a rational approach to economic and industrial planning in the 1970s was undermined by the existence of three competing planning philosophies in the federal central agencies most closely involved.[56] Richard Schultz, like Allison, found that the failure to implement all of the 1967 *National Transportation Act* could not be explained by the "rational actor" model, but was due mainly to in-

---

[52]See Peter Self, *Administrative Theories and Politics* (Toronto: University of Toronto Press, 1983), Chapter 3.

[53]Graham T. Allison, *Essence of Decision: Explaining the Cuban Missile Crisis* (Boston: Little, Brown & Co., 1971).

[54]For a useful overview of the applicability of Allison's arguments to Canadian foreign policy, see Kim Richard Nossal, "Allison through the (Ottawa) Looking Glass: bureaucratic politics and foreign policy in a parliamentary system," *Canadian Public Administration*, vol. 22, no. 4 (Winter 1979), pp. 610-626.

[55]Not all applications of the "bureaucratic politics" models to domestic politics have been entirely successful. For a discussion of some of the problems, see J.C.H. Jones, "The Bureaucracy and Public Policy: Canadian Merger Policy and the Combines Branch, 1960-71," *Canadian Public Administration*, vol. 18, no. 2 (Summer 1975), esp. pp. 272-273.

[56]Richard D. French, *How Ottawa Decides: Planning and Industrial Policy Making 1968-1984* 2nd. ed. (Toronto: Lorimer, 1984), esp. Chs. 2 and 8.

ternecine struggle between different agencies of the federal government, in particular the irreconcilable discord between the Department of Transport and the Canadian Transport Commission.[57]

The principle of departmentalization and its side effect of bureaucratic politics may also have contributed to the failure of the federal government's experiments with ministries of state. The creation of the Ministries of State for Urban Affairs and Science and Technology in the early 1970s ran directly counter to the existing logic of departmental organization. Unlike vertical constituency departments, the new ministries had few, if any, of their own programs to implement, and they lacked an identifiable or unified clientele to lobby government or other departments on their behalf. Moreover, unlike traditional central agencies such as Finance or the Treasury Board, they had little impact on the expenditure/budgetary process which might otherwise have given them leverage to persuade or compel other departments to cooperate with their objectives.

The newer ministries of state, MSERD and MSSD, did enjoy greater financial clout than their predecessors through their role as support agencies for Cabinet committees involved in the financial system as well as through their research and policy-planning functions. But although the official reason given for their dissolution in the summer of 1984 was the restoration of the primacy of elected politicians over expenditure allocations (one of the rationales for the establishment of the new financial system in the first place), it is clear that their privileged position in the policy process upset many traditional departments and their ministers who were used to lobbying directly for funds in Cabinet rather than negotiating through intermediary agencies. In addition, the new ministries tended to both duplicate and conflict with the advisory and policy-planning roles of the traditional central agencies. The experience of the ministries of state would appear to suggest that in the Canadian federal bureaucracy, contrary to Weber's maxim, knowledge does not, in itself, equal power. Attempts to impose greater rationality on the policy-making and administrative processes ignore at their peril the alternative conceptions of bureaucratic rationality, fostered by the principle of departmentalization.

Clearly, the Canadian federal bureaucracy is far from being a homogeneous, monolithic entity. The diversity of structural forms found in departments and agencies; the different philosophies of policy-making and administration that develop in each agency; the periodic conflicts that arise between agencies with regard to policy objectives, jurisdictions and modes of implementation – all suggest a view of the Canadian bureaucracy as relatively pluralistic. On the other hand, Ottawa is not a world of anarchy. Inter-agency competition and bureaucratic infighting are not always as destructive as some of the above examples might suggest. Disputes between agencies or departments may be constrained by parameters established by Cabinet on the range of possible policy alternatives

---

[57]Richard J. Schultz, *Federalism, Bureaucracy and Public Policy: The Politics of Highway Transport Regulation* (Montréal: McGill-Queen's University Press, 1980), esp. Chapters 5 and 6.

that may be considered on a particular issue.[58] It might even be argued that bureaucratic politics has its advantages, since agencies in competition with one another must reveal more information in support of their respective causes than would otherwise be available to politicians. In other words, the greater the degree of competition between agencies, the more information and alternative choices Cabinet has at its disposal in making policy decisions and hence, the greater the extent of political control over the policy-making process.

But what control does Cabinet have over the administrative process to ensure that policies, once made, are implemented in accordance with its collective wishes? The second major principle of government organization in Canada – and the primary link between the bureaucracy and the overtly political realm of Cabinet, Parliament and the people – is the doctrine of **ministerial responsibility.**

The Prime Minister appoints members of the Cabinet to assume responsibility for particular ministries or portfolios, and their associated departments, commissions, boards and corporations. Even semi-autonomous agencies like proprietory Crown corporations and regulatory commissions, which are headed by board members appointed by the government from outside the public service, report to Parliament through an appropriate minister. Ministers are constitutionally responsible for all of the operations of their departments. Thus, legally, it is ministers who are assigned the powers and duties to be exercised by their departments. Departmental officials, on the other hand, are given scant attention in the law and are responsible exclusively to their ministers, not to Parliament. They are supposed to be non-partisan, objective and anonymous – shielded from the glare of public attention and from the partisan political arena of Parliament by their minister – in order to safeguard their neutrality and ensure their ability to serve faithfully whichever government is in power. In the event of a serious error in the formulation or administration of policy within a department, therefore, convention dictates that the minister, rather than the officials, be held responsible to Parliament; and if the minister cannot account for failures to the satisfaction of Parliament, then convention dictates that the minister should resign.

Experience has shown, however, that there are limitations to the full realization of the doctrine of ministerial responsibility.[59] The individual responsibility of ministers for the operations of their departments is often sacrificed in favour of another principle of responsibility, the collective responsibility of the Cabinet to Parliament. Unless political expediency dictates otherwise, as long as

---

[58]See, for example, Michael M. Atkinson and Kim Richard Nossal, "Bureaucratic Politics and the New Fighter Aircraft Decisions," *Canadian Public Administration*, vol. 24, no. 4 (Winter 1981), pp. 531-562.

[59]See the examples cited in discussion of ministerial responsibility by T.M. Denton, "Ministerial Responsibility: A Contemporary Perspective," in R. Schultz *et al.*, eds., *The Canadian Political Process*, 3rd. ed. (Toronto: Holt, Rinehart & Winston, 1979), pp. 344-363; and Kenneth Kernaghan, "Power, Parliament and Public Servants in Canada: Ministerial Responsibility Reexamined," in H.D. Clarke *et al.*, eds., *Parliament, Policy and Representation* (Toronto: Methuen, 1980), pp. 124-144.

a minister retains the confidence and support of the Prime Minister, resignation is extremely unlikely. Another problem is the fact that ministers cannot be held personally responsible for administrative matters occurring before their current appointments. Thus, when questions were raised in the House of Commons in the late 1970s about RCMP wrongdoings (such as barn-burning and illegal break-ins), the then-Solicitor General took refuge behind this convention, saying that the events had taken place prior to his appointment; but neither could three former Solicitor Generals sitting in the House be called to account for the activities of a department for which they were no longer the minister!

Perhaps it is reasonable that ministers should not be held responsible to the point of resignation for the administrative errors of public servants. The relative impermanence of Cabinet ministers and their multifunctional roles make it impossible for ministers to involve themselves extensively in the management of their departments. Ministers are expected to direct their attention to policy matters rather than to the details of departmental administration. For this reason, one observer argues, it is "unrealistic to expect a minister to accept personal responsibility for all the acts of his departmental officials. Why should a minister 'carry the can' when he has little or no knowledge of its contents?"[60]

If Cabinet ministers cannot, will not, or should not be held responsible to Parliament for the administrative functioning of their departments, then who can? The Lambert Commission proposed that "the minister's responsibility must be shared with the deputy [minister], who should be accountable to Parliament through the Public Accounts Committee as the chief administrative officer for the day-to-day operations which are, in practical terms, beyond the minister's control."[61] This recommendation is suspect in that it reflects adherence to the distinction between policy matters and administrative tasks, which is at best fuzzy and at worst likely to distort an understanding of the role of the bureaucracy. Moreover, the Commission may well have underestimated the extent to which some ministers seek to participate in the internal administration of their departments, while others might use a bifurcated system of accountability to deflect criticism and deny their own responsibility for policy failures by laying blame on the implementation of policy, for which the Deputy Minister might be considered responsible.[62] Though sound reasons exist for re-evaluating the doctrine of ministerial responsibility, there appears to be little point in adding to existing ambiguities surrounding the role of the Deputy Minister.

If the minister is the key link between the bureaucracy and Cabinet for the purposes of formal political accountability and policy direction, the Deputy Minister's role is equally crucial to effective administration and the coordination and direction of policy implementation. As we stated earlier, the exact nature of the Deputy Minister's duties is not clearly specified in law. Certain financial and man-

---

[60]Kernaghan, "Power, Parliament and Public Servants. . .," p. 128.

[61]Royal Commission on Financial Management and Accountability, *Final Report*, p. 57.

[62]See Doerr, *The Machinery of Government*, p. 201; also the discussion in Paul Thomas, "The Lambert Report: Parliament and Accountability," *Canadian Public Administration*, vol. 22, no. 4 (Winter 1979), esp. pp. 561-562.

agerial responsibilities are laid down by the *Financial Administration Act* and the *Public Service Employment Act*, or are delegated to the DM by the Treasury Board and the Public Service Commission. Otherwise, the DM possesses only that power which the minister chooses to delegate. In fact, the *Interpretation Act* indicates that ministers may delegate any and all of their powers under the law to their Deputies, except for the power to make regulations and, of course, their Parliamentary duties.[63] Exactly how much a minister chooses to delegate is a personal decision.

The main function of the Deptuy Minister, outside the administrative responsibilities of managing the department, is to act as the minister's chief source of non-partisan advice on public policy. The problem for the DM is how to initiate policy proposals and studies without appearing to undermine the ultimate policy-making responsibility of the minister.[64] In their policy-advisory roles, Deputies have to strike a delicate balance between political sensitivity and bureaucratic objectivity – especially when they are led by their experience and expertise to disagree with policies put forward by the minister for primarily partisan reasons. In such cases, the DM may stress the potential difficulties which might be encountered in implementing the policy – although perhaps not in the forthright fashion attributed to a senior British civil servant who reportedly told his minister that

> "he could not stop his political master taking a damn silly decision but thought it justifiable to question whether he need carry it out in such a damn silly way."[65]

Deputy Ministers are appointed by the Governor-in-Council on the recommendation of the Prime Minister. Their office is held "during pleasure", which means that they can be dismissed or transferred at any time without assigned cause and that they are not protected by the provisions of the *Public Service Employment Act.* This insecurity of tenure naturally creates further ambiguity about the role of the Deputy Minister. Deputies who try to save ministers from themselves by advising against "damn silly decisions" may soon come to be viewed as obstacles to the government in pursuit of its partisan political objectives and accordingly be removed.

On the other hand, Deputies who are perceived as being too successful in administering certain government policies may become personally identified with programs unpopular with the opposition, and therefore risk losing their jobs when the reins of government change hands. The principle of "rotation in office", whereby Deputy Ministers and other senior public servants are replaced with each change of government, is not as widely accepted in Canada as in, for example, the United States. The political neutrality and relative permanence of

---

[63]Denton, "Ministerial Responsibility."

[64]See A.W. Johnson, "The Role of the Deputy Minister," in Kernaghan, ed., *Public Administration in Canada: Selected Readings*, 4th ed., pp. 262-263.

[65]Cited in Herbert R. Balls, "Decision-making: the role of the deputy minister," *Canadian Public Administration*, vol. 19, no. 3 (Fall 1976), p. 419.

Deputy Ministers is viewed as both a safeguard against a return to political patronage and partisan bureaucracy and a source of continuity in administration amid political changes.[66] Thus, after dismissing several senior bureaucrats in 1979, then-Prime Minister Joe Clark felt bound to reassure those remaining that there would not be a wholesale "blood-letting". But another former Conservative Prime Minister, John Diefenbaker, publicly regretted that he had not fired certain senior officials who had served the previous Liberal government, and prior to their electoral success in 1984 a number of leading Conservative politicians had been threatening a far-reaching purge among the higher echelons of the federal bureaucracy.

While the primary tasks of Deputy Ministers relate to matters concerning their own departments – including managerial functions and advisory roles – they also participate in coordinating the activities and policies of government. Most important issues discussed by Cabinet or its committees involve more than one department. Consequently, Deputy Ministers can advise and prepare their Ministers effectively only if there has been prior interdepartmental consultation. This may take place in an informal way, or it may be routinized through regular meetings of interdepartmental committees. Such committees at the Deputy Minister level include the sectoral deputies committees, which paralleled the various Cabinet committees established under the Trudeau government, and the Coordinating Committee of Deputy Ministers (CCDM), which is chaired by the Secretary to the Cabinet and, through him, serves as an important source of policy advice for the Prime Minister. Other committees of Deputy Ministers help coordinate and advise on administrative, rather than policy, concerns. The Treasury Board Senior Advisory Committee (TB-SAC) discusses issues arising out of the Treasury Board's role as employer of the public service, and the Committee of Senior Officials on Executive Personnel in the Public Service (COSO) advises the Prime Minister on the management, performance and recruitment of senior officials appointed by the Cabinet. Lastly, there is a host of interdepartmental committees and working parties at the level of Assistant Deputy Minister and below which help coordinate the work of government departments and solve common problems.

Thus the cycle of organizing principles and linkages is more-or-less complete. The Canadian federal bureaucracy is an extremely complex and diverse organization whose historical development reflects constant tension between the competing demands of democracy and efficiency. The fragmentation of the bureaucracy into many departments and Crown agencies in the interests of efficiency somewhat impedes policy coordination. At the same time, the principle of departmentalization underlies the doctrine of ministerial responsibility which, ideally, should enhance the democratic process by providing a line of ac-

---

[66]On this and related issues of bureaucratic neutrality, see, for example: Mitchell Sharp, "Neutral Superservants," *Policy Options*, vol. 3, no. 6 (November/December 1982), pp. 32-34; Gordon Robertson, "The Deputies' Anonymous Duty," *Policy Options*, vol. 4, no. 4 (July/August 1983), pp. 11-13; Thomas D'Aquino, "Political Neutrality is Right," *Policy Options*, vol. 5, no. 1 (January/February 1984), pp. 23-26.

countability to Parliament and the people. And between the Cabinet and the great mass of the bureaucracy, the Deputy Ministers and other senior officials play key pivotal roles. They not only advise their respective ministers on how best to serve the interests of the people and attempt to ensure the efficient management and functioning of their own departments, but also play an important part in the coordination of policy advice and effective policy implementation throughout the bureaucracy as a whole.

The importance of Deputy Ministers and other senior officials in the administrative and policy-making processes is recognized by those who express concern that Canada is governed, in effect, by a narrow bureaucratic elite. It is true that in the 1940s and 1950s, a small and closely-knit group of "Ottawa Mandarins" had an enormous influence on the development of the Canadian bureaucracy and on Canadian politics in general.[67] However, even during that period, bureaucratic influence may have been counterbalanced by the experience accumulated by Cabinet ministers through longer tenure in departmental office. Today, it is argued that "there is no such thing as a public service dominated by class, family, and tradition . . ."; instead, modern federal bureaucrats come from "a wide range of social and educational backgrounds".[68] In the next section, we shall investigate this claim in more detail.

THE PUBLIC SERVICE

While the word "bureaucracy" tends to be used to refer to the structures and principles of organization in the administrative arm of government, **public service** is the collective term in Canada for the personnel employed in those structures. Like other political institutions described in this book, the public service of Canada has undergone many profound changes since Confederation. During this time it has evolved from a loosely organized, patronage-based service in which most people were recruited on the basis of political connections to a modern professionalized bureaucracy appointed on the principle of merit; from a predominantly anglophone and almost exclusively male preserve to an equal opportunity employer which consciously attempts to reflect Canada's ethnic and linguistic diversity and which has recently introduced affirmative action programs designed to promote the participation of women, indigenous peoples and handicapped persons.

In the discussion which follows, we first examine the development of the federal public service, with particular reference to the evolution of the merit principle and employee/employer relations in the government sector. Next we

---

[67]See J.L. Granatstein, *The Ottawa Men: The Civil Service Mandarins 1935-1957* (Toronto: Oxford University Press, 1982).

[68]J.L. Granatstein, "Once but not Future Kings," *Policy Options*, vol. 3, no. 3 (May/June 1982), p. 46. See also Colin Campbell and George Szablowski, *The Superbureaucrats* (Toronto: MacMillan of Canada, 1979).

turn to public servants themselves, evaluating the extent to which the public service has become representative of the society it serves.

The Growth of the Public Service

Since 1867 the federal public service has gone through many major transitions, partly in reflection of the changes occurring in the society it serves.[69] The civil service which became operant upon Confederation involved a loose coordination of existing bureaucratic structures from Upper and Lower Canada, and did not include a central personnel agency. Appointment to the civil service at this time was exclusively on the basis of political patronage. In the 1880s, a Board of Civil Service Examiners was created to help select candidates, but this had a negligible impact on the prevailing mode of recruitment.

Largely as a response to pressures arising out of the modernization of Canadian society, the *Civil Service Act* of 1908 sought to replace patronage with the merit principle. The **merit principle** is actually based on two interrelated principles: first, that all Canadian citizens "should have a reasonable opportunity to be considered for employment in the public service" and, second, that selection must be based "exclusively on merit, or fitness to do the job".[70] The 1908 *Act* formally divided the bureaucracy into two services: the Inside Service, which consisted of all persons employed at headquarters in Ottawa, and the Outside Service, comprised of federal employees outside the national capital. The *Act* also created a Civil Service Commission (CSC) to enforce the merit principle in the recruitment and promotion of government employees. However, at the time of its creation, the Commission controlled only the Inside Service; the Outside Service, which comprised about five-sixths of all federal civil servants, was still governed by patronage. Thus, thousands of Outside civil servants were dismissed when the Conservatives ousted the Liberal government in the 1911 election.[71]

In 1918, the *Civil Service Act* extended the method of appointment by competitive examination to the entire service and re-emphasized the role of the CSC in enforcing implementation of the merit principle. To aid its task, the Commission was required to reorganize the whole service on the basis of a classification of all positions within the bureaucracy. Over the next four decades the CSC had considerable success in enforcing the merit principle, although the task of classification proved awesome and the Commission experienced increasingly difficult relations with the Treasury Board and with the growing staff associations of government employees.

---

[69]For a comprehensive examination of the historical evolution of the federal public service see J.E. Hodgetts, William McCloskey, Reginald Whitaker and V. Seymour Wilson, *The Biography of an Institution: The Civil Service Commission of Canada 1908-1967* (Montréal: McGill-Queen's University Press, 1972).

[70]R.H. Dowdell, "Public Personnel Administration" in Kernaghan, ed., *Public Administration in Canada: Selected Readings*, 4th ed., p. 196.

[71]Robert B. Best, "The Meaning of 'Merit' in Canadian Public Administration," in Adie and Thomas, *Canadian Public Administration: Problematical Perspectives*, p. 197.

The *Civil Service Act* of 1961 came about largely as an effort to resolve a power struggle over common areas of responsibility which had built up between the CSC and the Treasury Board. By this *Act*, the Treasury Board was given sole responsibility for pay determination and administrative organization. The CSC kept its merit-related responsibilities with regard to staffing, appointments, promotions, conditions of employment and classification. It was also charged with administering a new appeals function, where its decision would be final except in the area of dismissals. Perhaps most important, this *Act* provided the context within which collective bargaining could develop, since final decisions on pay "now lay squarely between Treasury and the organized public servants", without any CSC activity as an independent arbiter.[72]

Two *Acts* were passed in 1967 which further affected the role of the CSC and permitted it to become a more specialized staffing body. These *Acts* incorporated recommendations of the Glassco Royal Commission on Government Organization, which suggested the need to re-evaluate the CSC role *vis-à-vis* the Treasury Board and federal employees.[73] The *Public Service Staff Relations Act* (1967) created a collective bargaining regime in the public service, and through amendments to the *Financial Administration Act* (1951) the Treasury Board has since 1967 acted as general manager of the bureaucracy, with the power to enter into collective agreements in the name of the government. Responsibility for classification, pay determination and most conditions of employment rests with the Board. The *Public Service Employment Act* (1967) gave the renamed Public Service Commission (PSC) ultimate responsibility for all elements of the staffing process, including administration of the appeals process (an important component of staffing, given competition under the merit principle) and staff training, especially language training. The Commission is formally an agency reporting to Parliament, not to the executive – a status which permits it a degree of independence in investigating complaints and hearing appeals against the government with regard to appointments and promotions, discrimination or harassment in the workplace. However, its independent status is somewhat compromised by the fact that the three PSC Commissioners are appointed for a set term by the Cabinet. Moreover, the Commission is expected to carry out government or Treasury Board directives with regard to staffing priorities, particularly in relation to the promotion of bilingualism.

The 1970s were a challenging period for the Public Service Commission as it sought to make its new mandate operational. In general, the division of labour between the PSC and the Treasury Board introduced by the two 1967 *Acts* appears to have been successful in providing for more efficient staffing practices in the federal bureaucracy. Even so, two major reports recommended further changes in the management of the public service in the late 1970s. The 1979 Lambert Commission recommended an end to the division of labour in the inter-

---

[72]Hodgetts, *et al.*, *The Biography of an Institution*, p. 274.

[73]Royal Commission on Government Organization, *Report, Volume I – Management of the Public Service.*

ests of efficiency and centralized control, with a new Board of Management taking over the Treasury Board's existing functions and the PSC's staffing role.[74] In the same year, the D'Avignon Report recommended the creation of a Personnel Management Secretariat which would combine the PSC's staffing function with the Treasury Board's personnel management tasks. In return, the monitoring and adjudicative functions of the Public Service Commission were to be broadened in order to strengthen its role as an agency of Parliamentary scrutiny of the bureaucracy.[75]

Although changes have occurred in other areas of the bureaucracy and the public service which might be attributed to the influence of these reports, neither the D'Avignon Committee proposals nor those of the Lambert Commission have been implemented. In the 1980s, with its role and powers intact, the Public Service Commission faces new challenges which focus attention on its original, and some say most important, function as guardian of the merit principle.

The Merit Principle in the 1980s

There are two sides to the merit principle. One is that all appointments to, and promotions within, the public service are to be based on ability to do the job, in the interest of creating a qualified and efficient public service. The other, which guards against patronage and helps safeguard the neutrality of the bureaucracy, is that public servants are expressly forbidden to engage in partisan political activities.

With respect to the first aspect, the role of the Public Service Commission in implementing government directives to promote participation by under-represented groups has threatened to compromise its application of the merit principle. This is not a new issue in public service staffing. Both the 1918 and the 1961 *Civil Service Acts* entrenched absolute preference in hiring for war veterans. Then, following the passage of the *Official Languages Act* of 1969, which required the provision of minority language services in areas where numbers warranted, the designation of many public service positions as bilingual brought accusations of "reverse discrimination" and "contravention of the merit principle" from unilingual employees and from public service unions.[76] At the same time, the PSC became responsible for providing language training programs. In 1983, over 12 000 public servants were enrolled in language education courses.[77]

The *Public Service Employment Act* forbids discrimination in hiring or promotion on the basis of "race, national or ethnic origin, colour, religion, age, sex,

[74]Royal Commission on Financial Management and Accountability, *Final Report*, p. 14.

[75]Privy Council Office, *Report of the Special Committee on the Review of Personnel Management and the Merit Principle in the Public Service* (Ottawa: Minister of Supply and Services, 1979), pp. 154-155 and Appendix E.

[76]See P.K. Kurivilla "Bilingualism in the Canadian Federal Public Service," in K. Kernaghan, ed., *Public Administration in Canada: Selected Readings*, 3rd ed. (Toronto: Methuen 1977), pp. 81-90; and Kenneth Kernaghan, "Representative Bureaucracy – the Canadian Perspective," *Canadian Public Administration*, vol. 2, no. 4 (Winter 1978), pp. 489-512.

[77]Public Service Commission of Canada, *Annual Report 1983* (Ottawa: Minister of Supply and Services, 1984), Tables 54, 55, p. 107.

marital status, disability, or conviction for an offence for which a pardon has been granted." However, it is evident that certain groups have remained persistently under-represented in the public service, especially in senior positions. Thus, following a successful pilot project begun in 1980 in a limited number of departments, the Public Service Commission in 1983 introduced a service-wide affirmative action program designed to promote the employment and advancement of women, handicapped persons and indigenous peoples.

Affirmative action should not automatically be equated with quota systems or negative discrimination. Much of the affirmative action program is oriented towards education, training and career counselling through such agencies as the Office of Equal Opportunities for Women, rather than towards providing special treatment in hiring or promotion. In a small number of cases, the public service provisions have been waived to permit preferential access for members of under-represented groups, but the PSC insists that these measures "must be treated as special and limited in coverage and duration" and that, in general, "the affirmative action program implemented in 1983 does not conflict with merit, which requires that only qualified persons be appointed."[78] The fact that the Commission feels compelled to justify its programs in such terms reveals its sensitivity to potential criticisms that affirmative action might "unwisely and unnecessarily undermine the merit system of recruitment and promotion and the efficiency of the public service."[79] In the 1980s, therefore, the PSC must continue the vital task of increasing the participation by groups currently under-represented without allowing opponents of affirmative action to use the merit principle as a weapon to prevent the achievement of a more representative Canadian bureaucracy.

The enforcement of the other side of the merit principle (the limitations imposed on political activity to safeguard the neutrality of the public service) has become a sensitive issue because of one much-publicized case. Public servants are permitted to be members of political parties, to contribute money to them and to attend meetings, but not to stand for public office nor to indulge in overtly partisan activity. Such transgressions may result in suspension or, ultimately, dismissal. Most cases are fairly straightforward. For example, in 1980, a customs inspector from New Brunswick was fired after a number of letters, indicating his party affiliation and attacking another party's candidate in the 1980 general election, were published under his name. Upon appeal to the Public Service Staff Relations Board (PSSRB), the employee was reinstated after a period of suspension with a warning that "if he continues to test the limits of proscribed political activity he will be doing so at his own peril."[80]

According to the PSSRB, Neil Fraser, a senior tax auditor with Revenue Canada, went well beyond the limits of proscribed political activity. In 1982, after two suspensions and repeated warnings from senior officials, Fraser was dismissed from his job for criticizing the federal government's compulsory metric con-

---

[78]*Ibid.*, p. 16.

[79]One of the potential criticisms reported but dismissed by P.K. Kurivilla in "Still Too Few Women," *Policy Options*, vol. 4, no. 3 (May/June 1983), p. 55.

[80]Public Service Staff Relations Board, File: 166-2-8889, para. 71.

version program and the proposed *Charter of Rights*, and for accusing the government and its officials of abusing the democratic process. When Fraser appealed to the PSSRB, the Board quashed one of his suspensions, upholding the right of public servants to speak out on political issues not directly connected with their own department or jobs. However, the other suspension and his dismissal were confirmed since, according to the Board, "...Mr. Fraser engaged in rhetoric that was vitriolic in the denunciation of his Government and its leaders" to the extent that he "had assumed the mantle of a 'politician' and as such was acting in a manner incompatible with his duties as a public servant."[81]

The Fraser case provoked a storm of protest in the press. Calling his dismissal "unjustified", an editorial in the Ottawa *Citizen* complained, "It is obvious rights don't have the sanctity in practice they seem to have in speeches."[82] Another observer argued that, among democratic societies, "Canada imposes the severest restrictions on political activities of civil servants" and proposed an end to the "deadly muzzling of the public servant".[83] No government will relish the prospect of being criticized by its own employees – whatever the issue. Even if the issue concerned is not directly related to the employee's job, a public servant's criticisms may well receive more press attention and be accorded more credibility than those of "ordinary" citizens. Consequently, substantial liberalization of the rules governing the political activities of government employees is unlikely, even though demands for enhanced political and civil rights for individual public servants will continue to resurface.

Collective Bargaining in the Public Service

From the current debate over the civil rights of individual public servants we turn to the evolution of their collective rights as employees. In comparison with workers in the private sector, employees of the public service have always been in a unique position in relation to their employer. Traditionally, it was held that the federal government was a sovereign employer and, consequently, its employees could not be given the statutory right to make demands. Employee/employer relations within the public service were thus expected to be conducted in an atmosphere of information cooperation – the so-called "association-consultation" model of industrial relations – rather than through institutionalized collective bargaining between union and employer.[84]

Staff associations representing Canadian civil servants were in existence before the First World War. They lobbied the government for improvements in pay and employment conditions but were not permitted to contribute in any signif-

---

[81]Extracts of the decision rendered by David Kates, Deputy Chairman of the PSSRB, reported in Public Service Staff Relations Board, *PSSRB Decisions (1982) Volume I*, pp. 52-53.

[82]"The rights to speak out," *The Citizen*, Ottawa, March 24, 1982.

[83]Joseph E. Magnet, "The deadly muzzling of the public servants," *The Globe and Mail*, Toronto, October 26, 1982.

[84]See Allen Ponak, "Public-Sector Collective Bargaining," in J. Anderson and M. Gunderson, eds., *Union-Management Relations in Canada* (Don Mills: Addison-Wesley, 1982), pp. 343-378.

icant manner to the formulation of decisions which inevitably affected them. It became increasingly apparent that the association-consultation method was not working.

Unrest grew among public servants in the 1950s, and the staff associations began to lobby for collective bargaining rights. At the same time, they assumed many of the characteristics of modern mass-based unions, excluding management personnel from association membership, hiring full-time officers, rationalizing their fragmented structures and, in many cases, affiliating with the Canadian Labour Congress.

The 1961 *Civil Service Act* met some of their demands by giving the associations the statutory right to be consulted in pay determination, with the Treasury Board acting as "management" on behalf of the government and the CSC serving as a consultant. But the major breakthrough came in 1967 with the passage of the *Public Service Staff Relations Act* (PSSRA). The staff associations were empowered to negotiate directly with the Treasury Board, eliminating the cumbersome consultation procedures with the CSC. The associations were granted the legal status of trade unions, with the right of full collective bargaining on behalf of their members in bargaining units certified by the Public Service Staff Relations Board, the agency which administers the *Act*.

In August 1984, 203 417 employees in 135 bargaining units were represented under the PSSRA by fifteen certified bargaining agents. By far the largest bargaining agent or "union" was the Public Service Alliance of Canada, representing 164 651 employees, followed by the Professional Institute of the Public Service (18 337). Two other well-known unions, the Canadian Union of Postal Workers (CUPW) and the Letter Carriers Union (LCUC), with around 22 000 members each, were no longer covered by the PSSRA after the Post Office became a Crown corporation in 1981. The vast majority of employees covered by the PSSRA are in government departments or other agencies for which the Treasury Board is officially the employer, but some employees in other agencies are also included.

Despite predictions of the havoc which collective bargaining in the public service would wreak on Canada, labour relations in the public service have been remarkably peaceful. Approximately 97% of contract negotiations have been settled without a strike, through voluntary settlement, binding arbitration or acceptance of conciliation agreements. Between 1967 and 1981, there were twenty-seven legal strikes in pursuance of collective bargaining.[85] Two major reports in the mid-1970s concluded that the 1967 *Act* was basically sound, and that public servants should retain their collective bargaining rights, including the right to strike.[86]

---

[85]See Jacob Finkelman and Shirley Goldenberg, *Collective Bargaining in the Public Service: The Federal Experience in Canada*, vol. 2, (Montréal: Institute for Research in Public Policy, 1983), pp. 741-742.

[86]Jacob Finkelman, *Employer-Employee Relations in the Public Service of Canada: Proposals for Legislative Change*, vol. I (Ottawa: Information Canada, 1974); and Special Joint Committee of the Senate and of the House of Commons on Employer-Employee Relations in the Public Service of Canada, *Report* (Ottawa: Queen's Printer, 1976).

Since 1981 there have been no official strikes in the public service, although this is not necessarily a reflection of either a more conciliatory attitude among unions or of the changed status of the Post Office, but is rather a product of the Liberal government's *Public Sector Compensation Restraint Act* (Bill C-124) of 1982. By abrogating previously negotiated contract agreements and unilaterally extending all contracts due to expire after June 28, 1982 as part of its "6 and 5" program, the government suspended collective bargaining and effectively withdrew the right to strike from all public sector employees for a period of two years. Bill C-124 and the increase in the number of designated employees who are forbidden to strike under any circumstances (for example, virtually all operational air traffic controllers) have been viewed by the unions and some academic critics as part of a concerted assault on the collective bargaining rights won by public servants in 1967.[87]

It would appear that these events have resulted in a more militant approach to collective bargaining by public servants. In 1984, for the first time, the number of bargaining units opting for the conciliation-strike path (81 units representing 165 000 employees) is greater than the number opting for binding arbitration (52 units with 37 000 employees), and informed guesses have suggested that the trend would continue.[88] If greater public sector union militancy does materialize, provoked in part by the suspension of collective bargaining in 1982-84, then the PSSRA may soon come in for re-examination.

A Sociological Profile of the Public Service

The federal government is a major employer in the Canadian economy. In December 1983, the federal government employed over 580 000 people, approximately one out of every twenty people in the labour force. But not every person employed by government is regarded as a public servant. In the discussion of the characteristics of public servants which follows, we shall refer only to those employed under the auspices of the Public Service Commission. In December 1983, these totalled 222 044 persons or 38.2 percent of all government employees. The remaining federal employees include such individuals as uniformed personnel in the Armed Forces and the RCMP, as well as others not covered by the *Public Service Employment Act*.

The present public service is divided into six major occupational categories:

(a)   Management (formerly called Senior Executive)
(b)   Scientific and Professional

---

[87]See Leo. V. Panitch and Don Swartz, "From Free Collective Bargaining to Permanent Exceptionalism: The Economic Crisis and the Transformation of Industrial Relations in Canada," in M. Thompson and G. Swimmer, eds., *Conflict or Compromise: The Future of Public Sector Industrial Relations* (Montréal: Institute for Research on Public Policy, 1984), pp. 403-435; and, for example, Ed Finn, "Bill C-124 – Anti-Union Legislation," *The Facts* (Canadian Union of Public Employees), 4(7), August-September 1982, pp. 12-14.

[88]Figures courtesy of Public Service Staff Relations Board, October 1984.

(c)   Administration and Foreign Service
(d)   Technicians
(e)   Administrative Support
(f)   Operational

In 1983, the first four of these (the "officer" categories) accounted for 108 850 employees. A slight majority of all public servants, 113 194 individuals, were employeed in the two remaining categories.[89]

The PS classification system organizes employees in a uniform manner, permitting rational staffing and appointment within the public service in accordance with the guiding merit principle. Regardless of the department in which an employee works, the same classification and level carry identical remuneration. The hierarchical system, with its explicit job descriptions, also fosters a definitive chain of responsibility within the bureaucracy. Within each department a descending order of command is evident, with each employee responsible to a superior. This chain of command, which ultimately begins with a government minister, protects against the arbitrary assumption of power by individuals within the bureaucracy. Bureaucratic "red tape" in the guise of triplicate copies, codes, memos and standard forms is in fact a necessary part of the process of horizontal and vertical communication among employees and departments in the federal government. Given the immense number of people within the public service and the diversity of their duties, it becomes easier to appreciate why the bureaucracy's primary goal of efficiency is sometimes difficult to achieve.

Entrance into the public service is open and carries no restrictions as to age, race, sex, religion, colour, national origin or marital status. Recruitment is carried out across Canada on the basis of merit. Qualifications are determined through an entrance exam, the results of which determine the applicant's capabilities and job placement. Recruitment programs are sponsored by the Public Service Commission.

Once within the public service, the competition and appeal procedures ensure that virtually every employee can elevate his/her status. When a position is created or becomes vacant it is advertised, and prospective applicants are invited to apply. Depending upon the job, the competition will be "open" (available to candidates from both within and outside the public service) or "closed" (available only to those already in the public sector). Once a suitable candidate has been selected the appeal procedure allows complaints and criticisms against the appointment to be formally voiced; a board is convened to consider the appeal. In 1983, 2400 such appeals were lodged with the Public Service Commission. The PSC prides itself on this procedure, which in combination with the competition process provides an assurance of unbiased hiring and promotion practices.

To some extent, the bureaucracy is expected to be representative of the society it serves. Yet factors such as region, religion, ethnicity, social class, education, language and sex all render Canada a highly heterogeneous society. This

---

[89]Unless otherwise acknowledged, figures relating to Public Service employees are drawn from the Annual Reports of the Public Service Commission.

situation might potentially hinder egalitarian representation. In what follows, we outline and assess the composition of the public service with reference to these factors in order to illuminate the patterns of employment found in the bureaucracy.

REGIONAL DISTRIBUTION

It is commonly assumed that most federal employees work in Ottawa, or, more properly, in the National Capital Region (NCR). In 1983, however, only 32 percent were located in Ottawa-Hull. Approximately 64 percent of all federal employees are located in Ontario and Québec, a statistic roughly approximating these two provinces' share of the total Canadian population. A further 13 percent of public servants are based in the Atlantic Provinces; about 23 percent work in the western provinces and in Yukon and the Northwest Territories. In relation to regional populations, this means that the Atlantic area has rather more than its fair share of federal employees, while the West is slightly under-represented. By and large, these figures reflect the success of a deliberate attempt by the federal government to decentralize the bureaucracy away from Ontario in general and Ottawa in particular.

RELIGION AND ETHNICITY

Recent government reports do not provide information on the religious affiliation of public employees; therefore, knowledge about the religious background of bureaucrats is limited to infrequent surveys of samples of federal public servants. John Porter's 1953 survey of 132 senior bureaucrats found that Roman Catholics were greatly under-represented in the upper echelons of the public service.[90] Twelve years later, an analysis of middle-level public servants for the Royal Commission on Bilingualism and Biculturalism found that Roman Catholics were still disadvantaged, constituting 36 percent of the sample as compared with 46 percent of the population, while Protestants remained relatively over-represented. It may be argued that the under-representation of Roman Catholics shown by these studies was due to the relative absence of *French* Catholics. Given that 94 percent of French Canadians are Roman Catholic, the traditional under-representation of francophones in the bureaucracy contributed to the under-representation of their dominant religious affiliation.[91]

With respect to ethnicity in the middle and upper levels of the bureaucracy, the 1965 study found that 61 percent were of British origin, 18 percent of French and 21 percent of other origin (mostly from Northwestern and Central Europe).[92] Porter's earlier sample had found that British ethnicity predominated in the bureaucratic elite (84 percent), with only 13 percent being French Canadian.[93] Olsen's 1973 survey of a similarly small group showed that 65 percent were

---

[90]John Porter, *The Vertical Mosaic* (Toronto: University of Toronto Press, 1965), p. 443.

[91]Christopher Beattie, *Minority Men in a Majority Setting* (Toronto: McClelland, 1975), pp. 17-20.

[92]*Ibid.*, p. 17.

[93]Porter, *op. cit.*, pp. 441-442.

from the British Isles, 24 percent were of French origin, and 11 percent other.[94] These studies demonstrate that French Canadians have been persistently under-represented, especially in senior positions in the bureaucracy. However, a concerted attempt to attract more francophones into the service over the last decade and a half is reflected both in Olsen's data and in the growing covergence in Catholic and Protestant representation, at least in the central agencies, where Campbell and Szablowski reported in their 1976 survey that there were as many Catholic as Protestant respondents.[95]

SOCIAL CLASS AND EDUCATION

John Porter's *Vertical Mosaic* survey of senior public servants indicated that the bureaucratic elite was composed mainly of individuals from the middle and upper classes – 87 percent – a figure more or less confirmed by Olsen's study twenty years later, although the latter's data show a moderate increase in middle-class background at the expense of the upper class.[96] The class background of senior public servants in Canada is thus similar to that of bureaucratic elites elsewhere.[97]

However, the middle and lower levels of the bureaucracy seem to be considerably more open than the top level to people from lower- and working-class backgrounds. A 1965 study of middle-level anglophone and francophone public servants indicated that the public service presents an avenue for upward mobility for Canadians of both linguistic communities. The middle level of the public service was not the preserve of the economically privileged; in fact, fewer than six out of ten from both language groups were from middle- or upper-class origins.[98] Similarly, in 1968, Presthus and Monopoli found that only 40 percent of their public service respondents came from middle- or upper-class families.[99] What, then are the criteria for appointment and promotion?

Higher education, which has traditionally provided an avenue of upward mobility for the middle class, appears to be of crucial importance for advancement in the public service. In 1953, according to Porter, 79 percent of the bureaucratic elite had university degrees, and 44 percent had completed post-graduate training.[100] The 1965 survey of middle-level public servants revealed that 71 percent had earned at least one degree, and that disproportionate numbers had attended reputedly "elitist" universities such as Laval, McGill, Queen's

[94]Dennis Olsen, *The State Elite* (Toronto: McClelland and Stewart, 1980) pp. 77-78.

[95]Campbell and Szablowski, *The Superbureaucrats*, p. 115.

[96]Porter, *op. cit.*, p. 445; Olsen, *op. cit.*, pp. 78-79.

[97]See Robert Putnam, *The Comparative Study of Political Elites* (Englewood Cliffs: Prentice-Hall, 1976), pp. 24-25.

[98]Beattie, *Minority Men in a Majority Setting*, pp. 23-25.

[99]Robert Presthus and William Monopoli, "Bureaucracy in the United States and Canada: Social, Attitudinal, and Behavioral Variables," in Presthus, ed., *Cross-National Perspectives: United States and Canada* (Leiden: Brill, 1977), pp. 177-179.

[100]Porter, *op. cit.*, p. 433.

and Toronto.[101] By 1973, 92 percent of Olsen's respondents had at least a bachelor's degree (compared with 8 percent of the male Canadian labour force) and 61 percent had graduate degrees.[102]

Increasingly, possession of a university degree has become necessary to even apply for admission to officer categories in the public service. The competition for places is fierce. In 1983, the university recruitment program elicited 19 821 applicants, of whom only 522 were successful. As public service salaries and working conditions become more attractive in comparison with those in the private sector, Porter's observation that the upper levels of the bureaucracy contain "what is probably the most highly trained group of people to be found anywhere in Canada" is becoming applicable to the middle levels as well.[103]

LANGUAGE

In the area of language differences, the public service demonstrates significant weakness as a representative bureaucracy and as an open institution permitting vertical mobility based on merit. The failure to acknowledge the French fact in Canada has been seen by some commentators as the most damning indictment of the recruitment methods of the public service.

Below, we shall present a brief history of francophone participation in the public service, in order to place in perspective present-day francophone representation and to underline the importance of "bilingualization" in the public service.

Prior to 1918, at least adequate francophone representation was assured through patronage appointments made by French-speaking Cabinet ministers. But with the rationalization of the bureaucracy on the basis of merit, no procedure evolved to replace the patronage system's assurance of adequate representation based on language. The majority of the public service tended to define "merit" and "efficiency" in accordance with its own cultural and educational values; the result was that "with few francophones in the guiding councils of the public service, its explicit qualifications and its implicit assumptions tended to become more unfavourable to francophones."[104]

Thus, while in 1863 36 percent of government employees were French-speaking, by 1918 only 22 percent were.[105] By 1936 the number had fallen to 20 percent, and by 1945 to only 12 percent.[106] In 1965, only 5 percent of senior executives appointed by the Public Service Commission were French, while 16.5 percent of bureaucratic political appointees were francophone. It was only in the 1960s, after the Glassco Report and the 1965 B & B Commission, that there was

---

[101]Beattie, *op. cit.*, pp. 36-37.

[102]Olsen, *op. cit.*, pp. 71-72.

[103]Porter, *op. cit.*, p. 433.

[104]From the Report of the Royal Commission on Bilingualism and Biculturalism as quoted in Vincent Seymour Wilson, *Staffing in the Canadian Federal Bureaucracy.* (Unpublished Ph.D. dissertation, Kingston, Ont.: Queen's University, 1970), p. 244.

[105]Hodgetts, *et at., op. cit.*, p. 473.

[106]Wilson, *Staffing in the Canadian Federal Bureaucracy,* p. 236.

widespread recognition of the need to increase francophone representation in the federal government. In reaction, a tendency developed to "parachute" French-speakers into top-level political appointments in the bureaucracy.

Many factors combined during these years to reduce levels of francophone recruitment in the federal bureaucracy. The public service became less attractive for French Canadians because, despite post-1918 efforts to cultivate efficiency, no provisions were made for language representation which would ensure efficient service to French Canadians. Nor were francophones' bilingual skills included in an assessment of their qualifications. Francophones were also hindered by the merit system's examinations and interviews. Even when translated into French, these reflected the patterns of thought and cultural style of English-speaking Canada.[107] The competitions emphasized the technical and commercial skills taught in the English educational system, placing French-Canadians, with their classical education, at a disadvantage. It is sometimes argued that it is because of this "unsuitable" education that French Canada did not produce the type of administrator who could be used in the public service.[108] However, as Nathan Keyfitz has pointed out, it is precisely such a classical curriculum which equipped many an "empire-builder" with the skills to become an effective "generalist" administrator.[109]

In finally assuming responsibility for language training in the late 1960s, the Public Service Commission found itself at the centre of one of the most significant transformations ever attempted in the bureaucracy.[110] The Commission was directed to aid the government in achieving full and equal participation of anglophones and francophones in the public service while preserving the merit principle in recruitment and promotion.[111]

Progress is slowly being made towards this goal. The 1983-84 Public Service Commission budget allocated around one-third of its funds to official language activities. In 1983, 2944 public servants were enrolled part-time or full-time in English language training, and 9263 in French language training. Meanwhile, the percentage of francophone employees in the public service has increased, so that now participation is more comparable to their distribution in the national population: by 1983, their numbers had increased to 27 percent of all public servants.

However, closer examination of the distribution of anglophones and francophones within the public service shows that French-speaking Canadians are still relatively disadvantaged. In terms of salary, for example, francophones constituted only 17 percent of public servants earning over $50 000 *per annum* in

---

[107]Hodgetts, *et al., op. cit.,* p. 475.

[108]Porter, *op. cit.,* p. 442.

[109]Nathan Keyfitz, "Canadians and Canadiens," *Queen's Quarterly*, vol. 70, no. 2 (Summer 1963), p. 173.

[110]Hodgetts, *et al., op. cit.,* p. 479.

[111]P.K. Kurivilla, "Bilingualism in the Canadian Federal Public Service," in K. Kernaghan, ed., *Public Administration in Canada*, 3rd. ed. (Toronto: Methuen, 1977), p. 81.

1983, but 31 percent of those earning less that $20 000. Similarly, francophones are somewhat under-represented in the officer categories of employment (25 percent), especially in the management category (20 percent), and somewhat over-represented in the Administrative Support group (33 percent). There may, however, be grounds for optimism regarding a public service more representative in terms of language. In 1983, approximately 35 percent of all public servants under the age of 30 were francophones, and 36 percent of university graduates appointed in 1982 and 1983 under the university recruitment program were also French-speaking.

Through a number of measures, successive federal governments have made concerted efforts to reduce the under-representation of French Canadians in the federal bureaucracy. While there is still room for improvement, especially at higher salary levels and ranks, the federal public service is gradually becoming more representative of the official language composition of the Canadian population.

Women in the Public Service

If the federal government is to be congratulated on its progress in creating a public service more representative of Canada's two main language communities, it has little reason for complacency with regard to its representation of the gender division in Canadian society. Although the federal government is Canada's largest single employer of women, with over 90 000 female employees in 1983, women have long faced both institutional and attitudinal barriers to advancement in the bureaucracy which are only slowly being broken down by more sensitive recruitment, training and affirmative action programs.[112]

In contrast to the informal bias, which has affected francophone mobility in the public service, discrimination against women in the bureaucracy was officially endorsed in varying degrees until 1967. In direct contradiction of the merit principle, anti-female prejudice was built into the very fabric of civil service legislation and personnel practice.[113] As early as 1908, the CSC admitted that "there are women who have as good executive ability as men, and who might, on the *mere* ground of personal qualifications, fill the higher positions in the service.[114]

In order to "protect the merit principle from itself", deputy heads were instructed to segregate occupational categories into male and female groups, with women being limited to the lowest clerical levels. Since inequality of opportunity thus became a foregone conclusion, and women were not given access to middle-level positions, the issue of equal pay for equal work could not arise. As Kathleen Archibald points out, this occupational sex-typing of jobs was later used as "evidence" to show why women were not capable of filling higher executive posi-

---

[112]On institutional and attitudinal barriers to female employees, see the critical review by Kurivilla, "Still Too Few Women," pp. 54-55.

[113]Hodgetts, *et al., op. cit.,* p. 483.

[114]*Ibid.,* p. 485 (Emphasis in original.).

tions.[115] In the 1917 *Civil Service Act*, sex was mentioned as a "limiting" factor on an individual's qualifications, and in 1921 formal restrictions were placed on employing married women.

Over the next five decades, the concentration of women in the lower white-collar ranks provided the CSC with a cheap labour supply. During World War II, however, it became the patriotic duty of women to fill "male" jobs, so that while in 1938 only 17 percent of public service appointees were female, by 1943 this figure had risen to 65 percent. With the enforcement of the "veteran's preference" in 1946 the proportion of female appointees was halved, and restrictions were once again placed on employing married women.

In 1955, when one-third of all Canadian working women were married, the CSC finally lifted restrictions on the appointment of members of this group. The 1950s also witnessed the appointment of the first female Civil Service Commissioner, Ruth Addison. But it was only with the promulgation of the 1967 *Public Service Employment Act* that "sex" was added to "race, national origin, colour and creed" as grounds upon which an individual could not be discriminated against.

Legally, the federal administration's position on sex discrimination has altered; but the real situation of women in the bureaucracy is little improved. While women have constituted an increasingly large percentage of public servants over time, from 27 percent in 1943 to 41 percent in 1983, they are still slightly under-represented in proportion to their participation in the labour force, and more so in relation to their proportion of the total population. More importantly, effective segregation by occupational category is still occurring. In 1983, close to 70 percent of all female public servants worked in the Administrative Support and Operational categories compared with less than 40 percent of male employees. Within these categories, they tended to be concentrated in the traditionally "female" job ghettos within Administrative Support, serving as clerks, secretaries, stenographers and typists. In fact, women have constituted a growing percentage of the Administrative Support category over the last decade. In the officer categories, on the other hand, while their numbers have certainly increased since 1974, women are still seriously under-represented in proportion to their total employment in the public service.

Not surprisingly, given their concentration in lower-paid categories, women tend on average to earn less than male public servants. In 1983, women constituted 69 percent of all employees earning less than $20 000 a year but only 5 percent of those earning over $50 000. In addition, female employees provide the majority of short-term contract workers and part-time employees.

There are signs of potential improvement in the position of women in the public service. Women constituted 59 percent of all public servants under thirty years of age in 1983, and also accounted for 45 percent of new appointments from outside the public service. But it is also clear that the current lines of occupational segregation must be broken down if women are to achieve genuine

---

[115]Kathleen Archibald, *Sex and the Public Service: A Report to the Public Service Commission of Canada* (Ottawa: Queen's Printer, 1970), pp. 18-23.

equality of opportunity in the bureaucracy. While the just application of the merit principle might permit women to increase their representation very gradually in the long term, in the short term there is manifestly a need in the public service for serious commitment to continued and expanded affirmative action programs.

In summary, the Canadian public service has, over the last twenty years, become more representative of the society it serves. The reports of the Royal Commissions on Bilingualism and Biculturalism and on the Status of Women created increased sensitivity to the under-representation of francophones and women in the bureaucracy. At the same time, the advent of more readily available university education helped to enhance opportunities for the appointment and advancement of individuals from middle- and lower-class backgrounds. But there is still room for improvement – a fact which has been recognized by the government in its launching of affirmative action programs oriented towards groups which continue to be disadvantaged.

BUDGETS AND BUREAUCRATS: THE QUEST FOR EFFICIENCY

If the general public has a single dominant image of the federal bureaucracy it is perhaps that of a rather large drain down which their hard-earned tax dollars are poured. In one sense, this view is not entirely inaccurate. No government can govern without spending money, whether it be in the form of direct transfers such as pensions or unemployment insurance payments to Canadian citizens, the provision of subsidies and grants to Canadian entrepreneurs, or the payment of salaries to public servants who administer these and other programs. But, since most of the money expended by government finds its way back into the Canadian economy, boosting the demand for goods and services, the drain might be more accurately described as a well, which in many periods of Canadian history has helped to irrigate the economy, providing a stimulus to economic growth.

This having been said, the government is also responsible to Parliament and to the Canadian taxpayer for ensuring that there is not too much seepage from the well. Consequently, a major focus of political and administrative reform

Reprinted with permission – The Toronto Star Syndicate

over the past quarter-century has been the search for increased efficiency in government spending and greater control over it. During this period, the federal government has gone through three different expenditure-budgetary systems: from the traditional "incremental" process prior to the mid-1960s, through the Planning Programming Budgeting System (PPBS), to the current Policy and Expenditure Management System, otherwise known as "PEMS" or "the envelope system". In the two sections which follow, we shall examine the evolution of the budgetary process up to and including PEMS, and discuss the efficacy of some of the techniques introduced to monitor public spending.

The Budgetary Process

As we noted in the two preceding chapters, the finances of the federal government are managed through two separate but interrelated processes, involving two different sets of actors. The first, the expenditure budget process, is centred on the consolidation of the estimated spending requirements of all government departments and most agencies for the next fiscal year, under the watchful eye of the Treasury Board, a Cabinet committee. These estimates are subsequently submitted to Parliament and its committees for scrutiny and approval via Appropriations Bills which grant the government the requisite permission to spend public funds. The second, the revenue budget, concerns the means by which those funds are to be raised – taxation and other measures – and is largely the responsibility of another central agency, the Department of Finance. Its Parliamentary focal point is, of course, the Budget Speech delivered by the Minister of Finance, in which the government's economic policy outlook and revenue-raising proposals are announced to the House of Commons amidst great media attention. The revenue budget and the role of its primary actor, the Finance Department, have been briefly outlined in Chapter 7; the discussion which follows focuses on the detailed changes in the expenditure budget process, which have had far-reaching implications for the entire federal bureaucracy.

Before the mid-1960s and the quest for more "rational" policy-making under Prime Ministers Pearson and Trudeau, the expenditure budget process could best be described as a department-centred, "bottom-up" process. Individual departments determined their own spending requirements, usually based on an incremental increase over the previous year's budget for ongoing programs plus additional resources for new commitments, then sent their respective ministers to bat for them in Cabinet. The departmental estimates presented to the government and the House of Commons were aggregated into "standard objects" of expenditure (*i.e.*, administrative inputs such as salaries and supplies) for the whole department, rather than being broken down into the costs of individual programs, functions and objectives. Consequently, Parliamentary and auditing control emphasized strict legal accounting for the correct expenditure of funds according to the standard objects, rather than the elimination of potential waste caused by the duplication of programs or functions among departments. Any centralized control exercised by Cabinet was largely over the total level of spending across all government departments, reflecting a concern arising out of Keynesian economic principles for the assumed impact of aggregate public expenditure on the economy. But, given the relative lack of information about the objectives served by aggregated input expenditures, political decision-makers in the traditional process could not easily impose rational reductions; rather, they had to "either make cuts blindly or refrain from making them altogether – a most difficult choice."[116]

The "control" aspect of this traditional budget process was strongly criticized in the report of the Glassco Commission, which urged that public service managers be allowed increased autonomy to manage their departments and programs within guidelines established by the Treasury Board which, it was also recommended, should be separated from the Department of Finance. Furthermore, the Glassco Report proposed the adoption throughout the federal bureaucracy of a number of new managerial and administrative techniques designed to enhance flexibility and efficiency, including the preparation of departmental estimates on the basis of programs and their objectives.[117]

An approach that would more effectively link expenditure to the outputs of government was found in the Planning Programming Budgeting System (PPBS), first popularized in the United States by Secretary of Defence Robert McNamara. Starting with an experimental period in four departments in 1963, PPBS was gradually adopted by the government until the whole federal bureaucracy was committed to this model by 1968. As its name implies, PPBS marked a deliberate step towards a more "planned" approach to government, with estimates for various departmental programs being evaluated by the newly-created Treasury Board in the light of policy priorities to be drawn up by the new Cabinet Committee on Priorities and Planning. Thus, in place of the "bottom-up" approach of the traditional expenditure budget, PPBS was supposed to be a "top-down" system, providing for a more rational allocation of resources to departments, or rather programs, according to the priorities and objectives determined by the Cabinet.[118]

As it happened, PPBS was little more effective than its predecessor in either restraining the overall growth in government expenditures or ensuring that funds were allocated according to Cabinet priorities. In part, this was due to political failures. At no time was the Cabinet able to produce a sufficiently detailed and comprehensive list of government objectives by which departmental programs could be evaluated. The one serious attempt to do so, the so-called "Priorities Exercise" of 1974-75, collapsed amid the OPEC Oil Crisis, rising inflation

---

[116]David Siegel, "The Evolution of the Expenditure Budget," in Kernaghan, ed., *Public Administration in Canada*, 4th ed., p. 167.

[117]Royal Commission on Government Organization, *Report, Volume I, Management of the Public Service* (Ottawa: Queen's Printer, 1962).

[118]For a description of the key elements of the PPB system, see Doern, "The Budgetary Process. . ."; Government of Canada, *Planning, Programming Budgeting Guide*, rev. ed. (Ottawa: Information Canada, 1969); and A.W. Johnson, "Planning, Programming, and Budgeting in Canada," *Public Administration Review*, vol. 33, no. 1 (January-February 1973), pp. 23-31.

and growing disillusionment with the whole concept of "planned" government.[119] But the PPBS experiment also suffered from the fact that departments and program managers learned quickly "how to work the system". In preparing annual expenditure plans, departments were initially required to divide their estimates into three categories. The "A" budget specified the cost of maintaining programs at their current levels, with allowances made for inflation, population growth, *etc.*; the estimated cost of expanding existing programs or introducing new ones was to comprise the "B" budget; and the "X" budget was to provide a forecast of savings that would accrue from curtailing or eliminating those programs which had lowest priority in the department. But so few departments were willing to identify "X" budget items (largely because there was no guarantee that the savings would be reallocated to other programs in the same department) that this part of the system soon became unworkable.

Moreover, departments soon learned that it made little sense to promote expanded or new programs ("B" budget items) during the preparation of main estimates, when all new proposals could be compared for their contribution to overall government objectives. Because in a number of fiscal years during the early 1970s government revenues exceeded original expectations, it was easier to introduce new programs later in the budgetary year, when competition for funds was less and special requests could be made to the Cabinet. By the time of the next annual review, new or expanded programs would have become existing programs protected by the "A" budget: thus, as a former senior Treasury Board official put it, "the marshmallows of the current fiscal year become the bricks of the next fiscal year" and government expenditures continued to grow unabated.[120]

By the mid-1970s, less than a decade after PPBS was adopted on a government-wide basis, it was being argued that "While the coroner's report is not yet in ... there seems little doubt that PPB is dead."[121] Bedevilled by a host of problems – some basically technical in nature (for example, "What, exactly, is a program?"), others resulting from the different forms of rationality pursued by politicians and bureaucrats and from inter-agency rivalries – PPBS failed to live up to the overly optimistic accolades that welcomed its introduction.[122]

Amid growing criticism of the federal government's financial management, PPBS gradually faded into history. In attempts to strengthen financial accountability and control, the Office of the Auditor General (a persistent critic at

---

[119]See French, *How Ottawa Decides*, Ch. 4.

[120]D.G. Hartle, "Techniques and processes of administration," *Canadian Public Administration*, vol. 19, no. 1 (Spring 1976), p. 30.

[121]*Ibid.*, p. 24.

[122]Expectations that a technical system could impose rationality on a complex political process may have been the greatest problem in implementing the PPB system. As one author suggests: "It might well be the case that PPB has not failed, but rather that some people expected (and others promised) more than PPB could ever deliver." Siegel, "The Evolution of the Expenditure Budget," p. 172.

this time) was strengthened; a new Office of the Comptroller General (OCG) was created in 1978 to report directly to the President of the Treasury Board on financial practices and to develop government-wide procedures to ensure efficient, effective use of public funds; and the (Lambert) Royal Commission on Financial Management and Accountability was launched in 1977. The last nails were hammered into the PPBS coffin in late 1978 and early 1979 when, first, the Liberal government made drastic spending cuts of 2.5 billion dollars without any apparent reference to PPBS principles, and then, just prior to the Liberals' defeat in the 1979 General Election, the highly critical Lambert Report was published, recommending a sweeping overhaul of the federal government's financial procedures.

In the last months of the 1974-79 Liberal government, work was already underway on a new expenditure budget process. First announced publicly in a paper accompanying the ill-fated Conservative government budget in December 1979, the **Policy and Expenditure Management System** came into full operation during the fiscal year 1981-82.[123] The elements of this new "envelope" system, chiefly as it pertains to Cabinet, have already been covered in Chapter 7; what follows is a more general overview of the PEMS process.

The first point to emphasize is that PEMS operates under a much longer time frame than its immediate predecessor. Under PPBS, departmental plans submitted to the Treasury Board were supposed to provide estimates of operations and expenditures for future years. However, in practice, as we have seen, forecasting rarely went beyond the eighteen-month period to the end of the next fiscal year. Under the new PEMS approach, the fiscal year in which spending actually occurs marks the final stage in a continuous, rolling five-year planning cycle. Hence, as Table 9-3 illustrates, the first step towards planning expenditures for 1988-89 should have occurred in September 1984.

The expenditure planning process begins three and one-half years before the beginning of the fiscal year. This so-called "Multi-Year Fiscal Plan" provides the broad framework of resource availability for both the government as a whole and the various sectoral policy envelopes. The Fiscal Plan is updated every September, when necessary adjustments are made to envelope allocations and to policy and program forecasts. Nine months before the fiscal year begins, targets are established for the formulation of departmental and program estimates within each envelope (see Table 9-4). Once estimates have been formulated within these targets, they are consolidated by the Treasury Board into the Blue Book and presented to Parliament for scrutiny by the standing committees. At the be-

---

[123]On the origins of the envelope system, see Sandford F. Borins, "Ottawa Expenditure 'Envelopes': Workable Rationality at Last?" in G.B. Doern, ed., *How Ottawa Spends Your Tax Dollars . . . 1982* (Toronto: Lorimer, 1982), esp. pp. 64-66; The Government of Canada, Privy Council Office, *The Policy and Expenditure Management System* (Ottawa: Minister of Supply and Services, 1981), pp. 3-5; and Richard Van Loon, "Stop the music: the current policy and expenditure management system in Ottawa," *Canadian Public Administration*, vol. 24, no. 2 (Summer 1981), pp. 175-199.

TABLE 9.3 Expenditure Management — Major Steps Relating to 1988-89 Fiscal Year

Calendar Year		Stage of Expenditure Planning for 1988-89	Action for 1988-89
1984	September	Planning-Year 3	–Initial establishment by P & P Committee of total expenditures and policy sector envelope levels in Fiscal Plan for 1988-89
1985	September	Planning-Year 2	–Review of Fiscal Plan –Initial establishment of departmental levels within policy sector envelopes –Policy and program changes initiated as required.
1986	September	Planning-Year 1	–Review of Fiscal Plan –Policy and program changes initiated as required.
1987	June	Upcoming Year	–Targets established for formulation of 1988-89 Estimates.
	September	Upcoming Year	–Review of Fiscal Plan –Policy and Program changes initiated as required.
	November	Upcoming Year	–Main Estimates approved by Treasury Board and Cabinet.
1988	February	Upcoming Year	–Main Estimates tabled in House of Commons.
	April	Current Year	–1988-89 Fiscal Year begins (April 1).
	September	Current Year	–Review of Fiscal Plan including status report and outlook for Current Year
	November	Current Year	–First regular Supplementary Estimates tabled.
1989	March	Current Year	–Final regular Supplementary Estimates tabled. –Fiscal Year ends (March 31)

Source: Adapted from Government of Canada, *Guide to the Policy & Expenditure Management System* (Ottawa: Minister for Supply & Services, 1980), Table 2, p. 25.

ginning of the fiscal year, on April 1, departments and program managers start making the current expenditures, which have been planned for the last three years or more, drawing on funds approved by the annual Appropriation Bills. But before the end of the financial year on the following March 31, it may be necessary for departments to request extra funds for unforeseen circumstances or for coping with changing economic conditions such as a rise in unemployment. Assuming that the extra funds can be found, either from existing revenues or by increasing the deficit, these additional requests for spending power are placed before Parliament in the form of Supplementary Estimates. Meanwhile, the final stages are being undertaken in a partially overlapping multi-year planning cycle for the next "Upcoming Year".

A number of new instruments have been devised to support this longer-term planning process under the PEMS approach.[124] At the government level, reference has already been made to the Multi-Year Fiscal Plan, which serves as the framework within which the government makes future expenditure planning decisions. To aid Cabinet, its sectoral committees and the Treasury Board, government departments are required to prepare each year a long-term Strategic Overview and a Multi-Year Operational Plan. The primary role of the Strategic Overview is to relate the department's objectives and programs to the overall and sectoral priorities of government, while the focus of the Operational Plan is on the efficiency and effectiveness of departmental programs and expenditures in achieving those objectives. In addition, departments also submit a Budget Year Operational Plan each October; it sets out in more detail the key operational goals and targets for the upcoming year and serves as a basis for analyzing departmental estimates and subsequently evaluating its expenditure management practices.

The second major feature of PEMS is that it is a much more explicitly top-down approach than PPBS. Instead of all departments competing in a free-for-all for whatever resources may be available, the Cabinet Committee on Priorities and Planning now imposes advance limits on aggregate government spending. Furthermore, it imposes expenditure limits on each of the sectoral policy envelopes in accordance with government priorities. Each envelope level is calculated on the basis of estimated costs for continuing existing programs plus a possible "policy reserve" for the initiation of new programs.

However, the allocation of funds to the various departments and programs within each envelope (refer to Table 9-4) is the task of the appropriate sectoral policy committee of Cabinet. Thus, as we noted in Chapter 7, the ministers responsible for the spending departments within each envelope are forced to choose which programs or departments should receive additional shares of funding and, if necessary, where reductions have to be made.

The new system can therefore be interpreted as an attempt to strengthen collective government control over aggregate government expenditure. This is accomplished in part through the centralization of overall limit setting and envelope allocation in the Priorities and Planning Committee, chaired by the Prime Minister. At the same time, the decentralization of expenditure decision-making to the sectoral policy committees is designed to enhance individual ministerial responsibility for departmental expenditure management and planning.

But has PEMS succeeded in imposing order on the expenditure budget process? The present verdict appears to be a qualified "Yes." According to one observer, there is no doubt that "the envelope system has increased the workable rationality of the decision process over the pre-1979 system",[125] while another

---

[124]For a more detailed description of these planning instruments, see Government of Canada, Treasury Board, *Guide to the Policy and Expenditure Management System* (Ottawa: Minister of Supply and Services, 1980), pp. 19-22.

[125]Borins, "Ottawa's Expenditure Envelopes. . .," p. 84.

TABLE 9.4 The Policy Sector Resource Envelopes: Selected Contents (as of January 1985)

Responsible Cabinet Committee	Envelope	Main Contents of Envelope
Priorities and Planning	Fiscal Arrangements	Fiscal transfer payments (Dept. of Finance) Municipal grants (Public Works)
	Public Debt	Public debt, interest and amortization
	External Affairs and Aid	Dept. of External Affairs, Canadian International Development Agency, plus devlopment assistance programs (Dept. of Finance)
	Defence	Dept. of National Defence
Economic and Regional Development	Economic Development (including Energy)	Depts. of Agriculture, Consumer and Corporate Affairs, Fisheries and Oceans, Labour, Regional Industrial Expansion, Science and Technology, Transport, Plus Communications programs (Dept. of Communications), Minerals and earth sciences programs (EMR), Forest programs (Dept. of Environment), Export development programs (External Affairs). Plus Crown Agencies, including Canadian Dairy Commission, Canada Labour Relations Board, Foreign Investment Review Agency, National Research Council, NSERC, Science Council of Canada, Canada Development Investment Corporation, Canadian Transport Commission
		Energy Programs (EMR) plus Northern Pipeline Agency, Atomic Energy Control Board, Atomic Energy of Canada Ltd., National Energy Board, Petro-Canada
	Social Affairs (including Justice and Legal Affairs)	Departments of Employment and Immigration, Environment (excluding forestry), Indian Affairs and Northern Development, National Health and Welfare,

		Secretary of State, Veterans' Affairs Plus
Social Development		Arts and culture programs (Dept. of Communications) Plus
		Crown agencies, including Canada Council, CBC, CRTC, Canada Mortgage and Housing Corporation, Immigration Appeal Board, Medical Research Council, Social Sciences and Humanities Research Council, Advisory Council on the Status of Women
		Dept. of Justice plus Canadian Human Rights Commission, Supreme Court, *etc.*
		Dept. of Solicitor General, plus Correctional Service, National Parole Board, RCMP
Government Operations	Parliament	The Senate, House of Commons, Library of Parliament
	Services to Government	Depts. of Finance, National Revenue, Public Works, Supply and Services, Privy Council Office, Treasury Board Secretariat Plus
		Canada Post Corporation, Governor General, Economic Council of Canada, Public Service Staff Relations Board, Public Service Commission, Office of the Auditor General, Office of the Comptroller General, Statistics Canada

argues that the PEMS procedures "are an improvement over their predecessors ... (since) ... they do impose a general budgetary discipline upon the development of most new proposals and because they genuinely decentralize responsibility for a significant part of the policy management process to sectoral Cabinet committees."[126]

On the other hand, the PEMS approach is not perfect. Its first years have revealed a number of weaknesses, some of which may be capable of resolution; others, however, may not be because, to a greater or lesser extent, they are common to all budgetary systems. Among the problems peculiar to PEMS is the fact that it

[126]Richard Van Loon, "Ottawa's Expenditure Process: Four Systems In Search of Coordination," in G.B. Doern, ed., *How Ottawa Spends . . . 1983* (Toronto: Lorimer, 1983), pp. 116-117.

may not be a single integrated system at all. According to Richard Van Loon, there are actually *four* systems for policy and expenditure management in the federal government, played out among different sets of actors in different arenas:

1. the budgetary and macro-economic management system, including the revenue budget process, dominated by the Department and Minister of Finance;
2. the A-base management system for ongoing programs, under the control of Treasury Board and its Secretariat;
3. the macro-policy or major governmental priorities system, in which the Cabinet Committee on Priorities and Planning is the major actor; and
4. the system for managing new policies and expenditures, involving the sectoral policy committees of Cabinet and their constituent departments.[127]

The existence of these four systems or sub-systems within PEMS results in competition among the various central agencies involved and gives rise to immense problems of coordination which, if left unresolved, may result in an apparent lack of overall direction of government policy, "as if the government had jumped upon its horses and ridden off in all directions".[128]

Second, the early years of PEMS implementation were bedevilled by inaccurate economic forecasting. While this problem may be common to most budgetary systems, PEMS is particularly dependent upon long-range economic forecasting because of the central importance of the Multi-Year Fiscal Plan as a basis for all planning. The early planning of the 1980-84 Liberal government was based on the erroneous assumptions that economic recovery from the recession of the late 1970s had already begun and that public coffers would be sweetened by additional energy revenues accruing from rising world oil prices. Instead, economic conditions deteriorated so rapidly in this period that even short-term forecasting was a risky business and "forecasts further ahead than one year could have been as accurately divined from reading the entrails of small birds as from reading the printouts of anyone's computers."[129] Inaccurate economic forecasting can also make nonsense of estimates for statutory programs whose expenditure levels are determined by the demand for the programs from Canadian citizens rather than the government's willingness to supply them. For example, payments under the government's Petroleum Incentives Program were dictated by the number of companies undertaking exploration for new energy reserves in the Canada Lands.[130] Thus, as government revenues failed to meet expectations

---

[127]See *Ibid.*, pp. 100-101 and, for a more extensive discussion, Van Loon's concluding chapter to French, *How Ottawa Decides*, 2nd ed.

[128]Richard Van Loon, "The Policy and Expenditure Management System in the federal government: the first three years," *Canadian Public Administration*, vol. 26, no. 2 (Summer 1983), p. 284.

[129]Van Loon, "Ottawa's Expenditure Process," p. 106.

[130]See the discussion of "demand-driven programs" in the energy sector in G. Bruce Doern, "Energy Expenditures and the ENP: Controlling the Energy Leviathan," in A.M. Maslove, ed., *How Ottawa Spends . . . 1984* (Toronto, Methuen, 1984), pp. 51-59.

in the early 1980s, and the recession brought growing demand for unemployment and other social welfare expenditures, the long-range planning process was undermined and the federal deficit escalated to alarming proportions.

Like most other budgetary systems, PEMS is not immune to "end-runs" – techniques used by departments and politicians alike to circumvent the process or the spirit of the approach.[131] A number of financial instruments do not appear in, or are poorly integrated with, the PEMS process – for example, non-governmental borrowing by Crown corporations; tax expenditures; loan guarantees; and the practice of "netting", whereby departments discount revenues received from programs in calculating their costs.[132] Departments have learned a number of new techniques, including the inflation of A-base estimates to provide stock funds later in the year; these may be reallocated without the need to compete with rivals in the sectoral policy committees. They have also realized that their chances of getting new expenditures are increased if they flood the system with demands, one or two of which may be satisfied, rather than putting up a single proposal.[133] Moreover, Cabinet ministers have demonstrated an understandable reluctance to assume responsibility for cutbacks in their departments and programs; it has consequently been difficult to achieve redistribution of funds within policy sectors or to reallocate funds to policy reserves for the financing of new programs. Instead, most major new projects have been announced as "special allocations" by the P & P Committee, with little reference to envelope ceilings or to the appropriate sectoral policy committee. While special allocations do permit some flexibility to deal with pressing circumstances, they also do violence to the PEMS process, both as a recognized process of policy management and as a system of expenditure control.

In summary, then, given the trying economic circumstances under which it was introduced, the Policy and Expenditure Management System may be labelled a qualified success. It has by and large increased both collective and individual ministerial responsibility for public spending. However, it has not yet entirely succeeded in restraining the escalation of public spending and government deficits. Departments have learned to play by the rules to get what they want – and, on occasion, to bend the rules – but that is a feature of all budgetary systems. The key question, perhaps, is whether PEMS provides less opportunities for end-runs than its predecessors. Much depends upon the collective will of Cabinet to

---

[131]On the phenomenon of "end-runs" in general, see Aaron Wildavsky, *How to Limit Government Spending* (Los Angeles/Berkeley: University of California Press, 1980), Ch. 6. See also Wildavsky, "From chaos comes opportunity: the movement toward spending limits in American and Canadian budgeting," *Canadian Public Administration*, vol. 26, no. 2 (Summer 1983), pp. 163-181.

[132]On loan guarantees as "end-runs", see Allan M. Maslove, "Loans and Loan Guarantees: Business as Usual Versus the Politics of Risk," in Doern, ed., *How Ottawa Spends . . . 1983*, pp. 121-132; and on "netting", see Rod Dobell, "Pressing the Envelope: The Significance of the New, Top-Down System of Expenditure Management in Ottawa," *Policy Options*, vol. 2, no. 6 (November-December 1981), pp. 13-18.

[133]Van Loon, "The Policy and Expenditure Management System. . .," pp. 269-272.

impose and adhere to more stringent limits on both aggregate spending and envelope levels if expenditure growth is to be curtailed.

The current PEMS process is not engraved in stone. There has already been one major change in its institutional apparatus: the abolition of the Ministries of State which lent support to the Cabinet policy committees. In addition, energy expenditures, formerly accorded their own envelope to reflect the importance of the National Energy Program in the policy priorities of the Trudeau government, have been subsumed within the Economic Development envelope. More changes may be required, including further adjustments to the envelopes themselves as government priorities change over time. It may be that a government committed to restraint may introduce new techniques within the PEMS process – such as Zero-Base Budgeting (discussed in detail below) – to force departments to justify their current A-base program budgets.

The PEMS process is still relatively new. Because of the long-term nature of the planning process, to date only two fiscal years of government expenditures have been preceded by the full cycle. Some of the key central agencies are still seeking a clear definition of their roles in the new system.[134] These roles may require further redefinition in the light of priorities expressed by the Conservative government elected in 1984. Therefore, it may be some time yet before a full assessment can be made of Ottawa's latest experiment in budgeting and expenditure management.

Efficiency Techniques

Along with the expenditure budget process reforms of the last two decades, the federal government has experimented with various managerial and administrative techniques designed to enhance bureaucratic efficiency. Part of the impetus for these experiments came from the Glassco Commission's recommendation in the early 1960s that the federal public sector should avail itself of some of the modern tools of management which had proven successful in raising efficiency levels in private sector organizations. But, before we mention some of these techniques, it is worthwhile to examine whether management practices can be adopted uncritically from the private business sector by the governmental bureaucracy.

In a brilliant article stimulated by reflections on the Glassco Report, A.W. Johnson distinguished between two kinds of efficiency, "policy efficiency" and "administrative efficiency".[135] **Policy efficiency** refers to making the right policy decisions, correctly identifying needs and selecting the appropriate programs to achieve government priorities in satisfying those needs. **Administrative efficiency**, on the other hand, assumes that the right policy decisions have been

---

[134]See W. Irwin Gillespie, "The Department of Finance and PEMS: Increased Influence or Reduced Monopoly Power?" and Douglas J. McCready, "Treasury Board: Lost Influence?" in Maslove, ed., *How Ottawa Decides . . . 1984*, pp. 189-214 and 215-239 respectively.

[135]A.W. Johnson, "Efficiency in Government and Business," *Canadian Public Administration*, vol. 6, no. 3 (September 1963), pp. 245-260.

made and that the concern is then with delivering programs in the most cost-effective manner. In both business and government, Johnson argues, policy efficiency is vastly more important than administrative efficiency, since the benefits of

> ... 'policy efficiency' greatly outweigh the savings that can be achieved by 'administrative efficiency'. One bad policy decision – for example, the construction of an uneconomic railway or road – will cost the taxpayer more than can possibly be saved by better control over the purchase of underwear for the armed forces.[136]

Where government differs from business, however, is with respect to a third aspect of efficiency, which Johnson labels "service efficiency". Business has a simple, clearly identifiable bottom line which is served by both policy efficiency and administrative efficiency – the profit margin. In government, however, efficiency cannot be measured in economic terms alone: the search for economic efficiency has to be tempered by other considerations such as service to the public, responsiveness to public opinion and the preservation of parliamentary control – all aspects of **service efficiency.** If a business fails to serve the public adequately or to respond to changes in consumer tastes, then that failure will soon be reflected in its profit and loss figures. In government, however, failures in service efficiency may result in different, non-economic penalties – electoral defeat of the governing party, erosion of constitutional principles or general loss of confidence in the ability of government to serve the needs of the people.[137]

The widespread but sadly mistaken assumption in the 1960s that "rational" planning and the implementation of PPBS techniques would lead inevitably to the making of the "right" policy decisions created a preoccupation with improving administrative efficiency, rather than policy or service efficiency, in the public service. For this reason, the introduction of PPBS into the federal government was closely allied to two administrative techniques borrowed from the private sector – Management by Objectives (MBO) and Operational Performance Measurement Systems (OPMS).[138]

In contrast to the authoritarian approach to management that one might expect in a highly stratified bureaucracy, MBO stresses that effective management is based not on "directives" from superiors to subordinates but on "objectives" agreed upon after consultation between them. At each level within the administrative hierarchy, subordinates meet with their managers to discuss what contribution they will make to the achievement of organizational or sub-organization goals. Job responsibilities are thereby clarified and acceptable performance criteria established which can be used at the end of the year as a basis for

---

[136]*Ibid.*, p. 248.

[137]*Ibid.*, pp. 248-249.

[138]On the linkages between PPBS, MBO and OPMS, see J.S. Hodgson, "Management by Objectives: the experience of a federal government department," *Canadian Public Administration*, vol. 16, no. 3 (Fall 1973), pp. 422-431.

performance review and evaluation.[139] The success of MBO as a general philosophy of management, was dependent, like PPBS, on the clear articulation by Cabinet of overall priorities and goals for departments and programs. In the absence of clearly prescribed goals, critics have argued, MBO-determined objectives can too easily be redefined or watered down, as the "rationality" of the management philosophy gives way to the dictates of office politics, which are typical of any complex organization but which may be more pronounced in one where there is no economic bottom line.[140]

As a second tool of administrative efficiency, in the early 1970s the Treasury Board also introduced Operational Performance Measurement Systems (OPMS), designed to monitor the performance of public servants by measuring changes over time in the unit costs (or labour productivity) of programs or activities. OPMS has been widely deployed throughout the federal bureaucracy despite a number of serious limitations to its applicability.[141] One of the most important among these is that OPMS can only measure changes in efficiency over time *within* programs; it cannot cope with cross-program efficiency and productivity, since programs which are inefficient to begin with can display remarkable reductions in unit costs, while others with little fat to trim have to struggle to show any rise in productivity. Another limitation is that while operational performance measurement may demonstrate the increasing "efficiency" of a program in converting (labour) inputs into the attainment of certain goals, "it is not ... capable of determining whether the objectives of the program remain appropriate or whether there are alternative approaches to meeting those stated objectives."[142]

Such criticisms flow naturally from the fact that OPMS, like MBO, is a technique oriented towards administrative rather than policy efficiency. However, there are a number of other mechanisms designed to ensure that "the objectives of the program remain appropriate" or to determine whether there are in fact "alternative approaches to meeting those stated objectives".

An example of the first type is Zero-Base Budgeting (ZBB), a budgeting system which requires managers or departments to defend existing programs and levels of expenditure as rigorously as they lobby for new ones.[143] Instead of tak-

---

[139]The stages of MBO procedure are discussed in detail by Walter Baker, "Management by Objectives: A Philosophy and Style of Management for the Public Sector," *Canadian Public Administration*, vol. 12, no. 3 (Autumn 1969), pp. 427-443.

[140]Douglas G. Hartle, *The Expenditure Budget Process in the Government of Canada* (Toronto: Canadian Tax Foundation, 1978), pp. 91-93.

[141]See Henning Frederiksen, "Operational Performance Measurement Systems," in K. Kernaghan, ed., *Public Administration in Canada*, 3rd ed., *op cit.*, pp. 185-186; and Hartle, *The Expenditure Budget Process*, pp. 89-91.

[142]J.M. Jordan and S.L. Sutherland, "Assessing the results of public expenditure: program evaluation in the Canadian federal government," *Canadian Public Administration*, vol. 22, no. 4, (Winter 1979), p. 588.

[143]For a full explanation of ZBB, see Porter M. Pyhrr, "The Zero-Base Approach to Government Budgeting," *Public Administration Review*, vol. 37, no. 1 (January-February 1977), pp. 1-8. Pyhrr was the architect of the system in the private sector.

ing ongoing programs as given, the ZBB process involves the examination of objectives and relevance to government priorities of all current programs as well as new proposals, since managers are forced to justify "every dollar spent from zero up".[144] Therefore, ZBB is advocated as a method of increasing the amount of information that policy-makers have at their disposal and as a basis for eliminating programs which have outlived their usefulness.

A few federal departments have experimented with ZBB on a trial basis, but there appear to be obstacles to its universal adoption. It is claimed that, like other "rational" approaches, ZBB cannot contend with the entrenched "political rationality" to be found among bureaucrats, politicians and program clienteles. Moreover, many programs involving statutory expenditures or long-term agreements with the provinces cannot be abolished or reduced overnight, whatever the prerequisites of the ZBB process. Successful implementation of ZBB is more likely to be achieved as part of a more general cycle of "program evaluation" within the PEMS process, in which the programs of each government department are reviewed on a periodic basis to determine both their efficiency and their effectiveness.[145]

In establishing whether there might be more appropriate ways to achieve particular program objectives, the Treasury Board has, for a number of years, advocated Benefit/Cost Analysis (B/CA).[146] As its name implies, this technique involves the systematic comparison of all measurable costs incurred by, and benefits derived from, the selection of one course of action over other alternatives. In this sense, B/CA encourages policy-makers to evaluate alternative courses of action which might meet the same goals; hence, it may be a guide to policy efficiency. The major problem with the technique is that many of the priorities of government are not immediately tangible, nor measurable in strictly economic terms.[147] Since there is no single bottom line, economic or otherwise, in the public sector, the utility of Benefit/Cost Analysis is limited by the lack of common agreement on measures of the benefits and costs associated with government programs. Consequently, B/CA, like other measures, is not a panacea. It is useful only if it is applied alongside others of "the best current empirical methods of investigation in the social sciences",[148] as part of a comprehensive system of program evaluation.

---

[144]Siegel, "The Evolution of the Expenditure Budget," p. 173.

[145]On the prospects and problems of program evaluation, see Jordan and Sutherland, "Assessing the results of public expenditure"; and W. Irwin Gillespie, "Fools' gold: The Quest for a Method of Evaluating Government Spending" and Harry Rogers, "Program Evaluation in the Federal Government," in G.B. Doern and A.M. Maslove, eds., *The Public Evaluation of Government Spending* (Montréal: Institute for Research on Public Policy, 1979), pp. 39-59 and 79-89 respectively.

[146]See, for example, Government of Canada, Treasury Board, *Benefit-Cost Analysis Guide* (Ottawa: Information Canada, 1976).

[147]On the limitations of Benefit/Cost Analysis, see, among others, Gillespie, "Fools' Gold. . ., pp. 48-49; Hartle, *The Expenditure Budget Process*, 86-89.

[148]Rogers, "Program Evaluation in the Federal Government," p. 81.

New techniques to enhance administrative efficiency or policy efficiency in the federal bureaucracy should not be dismissed as irrelevant. Efficiency is important in the public sector – after all, it is the taxpayers' money that is wasted if the wrong decisions are made or if programs are administered inefficiently. But the uncritical adoption of efficiency measures that have proven successful in the private sector ignores the fundamental differences between the private sector and government. While the private sector has a single bottom line that may be called "economic rationality", government has no unique bottom line. Responsiveness to the needs of the public, demands for redistribution, equity and access to government programs, politicians' natural desire for re-election, "bureaucratic politics" among and within government departments and agencies, accountability and control within the democratic process – all may constitute higher forms of "rationality" than the quest for economic efficiency in the public sector. Efficiency is important, but the overriding concern must be with the effectiveness of the governmental process: that government programs effectively serve the needs of the public and that departments effectively account for their expenditures and activities in accordance with the priorities established by Cabinet and Parliament. In a liberal democracy such as Canada, these factors, which Johnson grouped together under the heading of "service efficiency", are vastly more important than the savings which might accrue from pursuing economic efficiency in the federal bueaucracy.

EFFICIENCY *VERSUS* CONTROL: BUREAUCRACY *VERSUS* DEMOCRACY REVISITED

The Weberian concept of bureaucracy posited an organizational form ideally suited to providing the most efficient means to achieving a given end. In a parliamentary democracy such as Canada, the selection of "ends" or policy objectives should be the task of the political executive, responsible through Parliament to the people. The bureaucracy's role, in theory, should be primarily that of implementing the goals chosen by politicians through the most efficient and effective means possible.

However, as we noted earlier in this chapter, in a complex modern society governed by a highly interventionist state, the distinction between means and ends or administration and politics is at best unclear and at worst virtually untenable. The relative permanence and immense organizational resources of the bureaucracy confer upon public servants considerable influence in the policy-making process. Moreover, considerable discretionary power has been given to the bureaucracy in many areas of policy implementation, especially in those areas where Parliament has delegated regulatory or administrative decision-making authority to government departments, agencies and tribunals. Given these trends, peaceful coexistence between bureaucracy and democracy cannot be maintained by seeking an impractical restoration of the distinction between politics and administration. The policy-making or policy-influencing activities of the bureaucracy have to be controlled by representative political institutions such as

Cabinet or Parliament in such a way that the bureaucracy can be held accountable for its operations. With this in mind, we consider below some of the mechanisms through which the bureaucracy may be controlled in a parliamentary democracy.

Ministerial Responsibility

Although, as we have seen earlier in this chapter, a number of authors have expressed concern over the decline of both individual and collective ministerial responsibility for the work of the federal bureaucracy,[149] many recent reforms have been directed towards restoring ministerial control over the public service. For example, the newly-introduced Policy and Expenditure Management System was explicitly intended to increase the collective responsibility of Cabinet over resource allocation. In addition, by decentralizing decision-making on allocations *within* sectoral envelopes to the appropriate Cabinet committees, PEMS has ensured that the ministers responsible for spending departments are also responsible for spending decisions. And, by forcing departments to compete for limited resources within pre-set spending limits, the PEMS process has helped to increase the flow of information from bureaucrats to politicians. In large measure, therefore, the new system has shifted the balance of power in the expenditure budget process from departments to Cabinet ministers.

Cabinet control over government spending and bureaucratic operations has also been enhanced by the creation of the Office of the Comptroller General in 1978. The Comptroller General reports directly to the President of the Treasury Board, and thus to Cabinet, on the three main functions of the Office: monitoring the financial administration practices of departments and agencies; implementing performance measurement systems to enhance operational efficiency; and evaluating the effectiveness of government programs. The OCG will not only provide an additional mechanism of control over spending practices, but, if the evaluation process is fully implemented, will also serve to increase the availability of information upon which operating and financial decisions can be made.

The last point raises the crucial importance of information in the relationship between bureaucracy and the democratic process. In ideal terms, democracy depends upon a free flow of information in all parts of the political system. If one element of the political process, such as the bureaucracy, is able to monopolize information, it can exercise disproportionate weight in the policy-making process and make it virtually impossible for representative institutions to check or control potential abuses of its power. Consequently, governments have increasingly made an effort to counteract any tendencies towards a bureaucratic monopoly on research and policy advice. In part, the function of the various central agencies described in Chapter 7 is to provide information from a different perspective from that of the vertical line departments. However, their importance has raised

---

[149]See, for example, Denton, "Ministerial Responsibility: A Contemporary Perspective"; Kernaghan, "Power, Parliament and Public Servants. . .".

concerns that Cabinet may merely have exchanged one kind of bureaucratic influence for another.[150] Among non-bureaucratic inputs, Royal Commissions, Commissions of Inquiry, advisory councils and research councils, parliamentary standing and special committees all serve as alternative sources of research and policy recommendations, as do non-governmental policy organizations such as the Business Council on National Issues, the C.D. Howe Institute and the Institute for Research on Public Policy.

In addition to these primarily non-partisan or cross-party bodies, the Cabinet also has at its disposal more explicitly partisan advisors who furnish information geared towards the government's own "political", rather than "bureaucratic", rationality; *i.e.*, towards the formulation of policies designed to maximize its chances of re-election. The PMO, of course, serves the political needs of the Prime Minister, and individual ministers have their own "kitchen cabinets" of aides and policy advisors to reduce their dependence on departmental sources. Indeed, one of the first actions of the newly elected Mulroney government was the announcement of a considerable increase in funding for ministerial staff, and the creation within each minister's office of a post of Chief-of-Staff with rank and salary equivalent to that of a departmental Assistant Deputy Minister. This enhancement of what we earlier called the "para-political bureaucracy" marks a clear attempt to increase collective and individual ministerial responsibility for and control over the public service.[151]

To offset the possibility of bureaucratic screening or filtering of the information furnished to the bureaucracy's political masters, successive federal governments have developed a wide range of alternative sources of policy advice. Given that "knowledge equals power," individual ministers and Cabinet as a whole can use these diverse sources of information to reduce their dependence on the bureaucracy.

Parliamentary Controls

Parliamentary reforms enacted over the last two decades have in part been oriented toward reducing the preponderance of the bureaucracy as a source of information and policy advice. The effectiveness of parliamentary committees is increasing, and their reports necessarily present a view of government policy which differs from that of the public service. Opposition parties are now given research funds to assist them in making more effective policy input or, at least, in developing more informed criticism of existing policy-making and implementation. Increased staff support for individual MPs, while still not sufficient, does provide them with some research potential and enables them to question more effectively bureaucratic decisions on behalf of their constituents.

---

[150]See the concerns raised by Campbell and Szablowski in *The Superbureaucrats*.

[151]Blair Williams, "The Para-political Bureaucracy in Ottawa," in Clarke, *et al.*, ed., *Parliament, Policy and Representation*, pp. 215-230. See also Donald J. Savoie, "The Minister's Staff: the need for reform," *Canadian Public Administration*, vol. 26, no. 4 (Winter 1983), pp. 509-524.

Perhaps the most important role of Parliament in scrutinizing the work of the bureaucracy and attempting to ensure accountability arises in the expenditure budget process. Here, too, parliamentary and administrative reforms have enhanced the potential for democratic control. The presentation of estimates in program format (rather than by standard objects of expenditure) facilitates the comparison of spending with policy outputs and government priorities. The development of multi-year fiscal plans and departmental supporting documents under the PEMS process provides a broader and more long-range context for the evaluation of both overall spending plans and individual estimates. The enhanced role of the Auditor General, since the strengthening of that office in 1977, permits a more critical appraisal of the effectiveness of both public spending and accounting practices by the Public Accounts Committee.

There remain some problems, however. One is the perceived lack of accountability to Parliament of Crown corporations identified by the Lambert Commission. Although the reports of public enterprises and regulatory agencies are now referred automatically to the appropriate standing committees, inadequate auditing provisions and difficulties in imposing ministerial responsibility for these semi-autonomous agencies hinder effective parliamentary control over their activities. Although a number of measures have been proposed for strengthening the accountability of Crown agencies,[152] legislation introduced by the Clark and Trudeau governments failed to secure passage before their respective electoral defeats.

With this exception, the mechanisms for parliamentary control of the bureaucracy are largely in place. The key question thus remains, as we suggested in Chapter 8, whether MPs have the inclination or the time to devote themselves to ensuring bureaucratic accountability. The Lambert Commission called on parliamentarians to "treat their surveillance role with the same seriousness they accord their political responsibilities"[153] but, in the absence of structural and/or widespread attitudinal change in the House of Commons, it seems that MPs have little inclination to utilize fully the opportunities available to them.

Alternative Mechanisms for Control

Other means of controlling the bureaucracy's role in policy-making have been proposed over the years. Given the proliferation of legislation delegating the authority to make rules and regulations to government departments and other administrative agencies, and given the absence of effective parliamentary control over delegated legislation, the judicial process might be called upon to play a greater role in protecting citizens against arbitrary bureaucratic decisions. But, although there will undoubtedly be an increase in court challenges to bu-

---

[152]See Government of Canada, Privy Council Office, *Crown Corporations: Direction, Control and Accountability* (Ottawa: Queen's Printer, 1977); and Royal Commission on Financial Management and Accountability, *Final Report*.

[153]Royal Commission on Financial Management and Accountability, *Final Report*, p. 388.

reaucratic decisions as the new *Charter of Rights* is implemented, we have to agree with the conclusion drawn by one opponent of judicial review of the bureaucracy:

> It would be wrong to abandon democratic processes working through Parliament to check bureaucratic power in favour of a more elitist approach based upon courts, lawyers and tribunals as the primary mechanisms for safeguarding the rights of individuals.[154]

As an alternative means of protecting individual citizens against arbitrary decision-making, there has been some debate concerning the establishment of a federal "ombudsman", an officer who would be responsible to Parliament for the investigation of citizens' complaints against the bureaucracy.[155] The establishment of an ombudsman at the federal level (most provinces already have provincial ombudsmen) was recommended by an investigatory committee in 1977,[156] but legislation introduced the following year failed to pass beyond Second Reading.[157] However, although the ombudsman might provide an additional mechanism of overall surveillance of the bureaucracy, it should be noted that Canada already has a number of more specialized ombudsman-like officers, including the Commissioner of Official Languages, a Privacy Commissioner within the Canadian Human Rights Commission and the Correctional Investigator for Penitentiary Services, who all act as watchdogs over certain aspects of bureaucratic activity.

Even if the time of the ombudsman has not yet arrived, the federal government has taken one step in recent years to provide for more open government. In 1983, the *Access to Information Act* was finally promulgated after over twenty years of debate within and outside Parliament.[158] With a number of controversial exceptions, Canadian citizens and permanent residents now have the right to obtain or examine records which were previously kept secret by federal government institutions. At stake in many cases is the individual's right to know why certain government decisions were taken, or to determine whether they were fairly arrived at or whether mistakes were made. The *Act* is intended to make government

---

[154]Paul Thomas, "Courts Can't be Saviours," *Policy Options*, vol. 5, no. 3, (May/June 1984), p. 27.

[155]A major advocate of the "ombudsman" concept for Canada has been Donald C. Rowat; see D.C. Rowat, "An Ombudsman Scheme for Canada," *Canadian Journal of Economic and Political Science*, vol. 28, no. 4 (November 1962), pp. 543-556, and his comparative survey in D.C. Rowat, ed., *The Ombudsman*, 2nd ed. (Toronto: University of Toronto Press, 1968).

[156]Government of Canada, Committee on the Concept of the Ombudsman, *Report* (Ottawa: Queen's Printer, 1977).

[157]For a critique of the proposed *Ombudsman Act*, see K.A. Friedmann and A.G. Milne, "The Federal Ombudsman Legislation: A Critique of Bill C-43," *Canadian Public Policy*, vol. 6, no. 1 (Winter 1980), p. 63-77.

[158]On the history of the "Freedom of Information" debate, see Adie and Thomas, *Canadian Public Administration* . . . Ch. 9, esp. pp. 321-331; and the brief overview in Donald C. Rowat, "The Right of Public Access to Official Documents," in O.P. Dwivedi, ed., *The Administrative State in Canada: Essays for J.E. Hodgetts* (Toronto: University of Toronto Press, 1982), p. 177-192.

more accountable for its actions and to reverse whatever public image exists of public servants scheming to hide blunders or alleged corruption from innocent victims.

Nonetheless, some observers are skeptical of the value of the *Act* in its present form. Donald Rowat, long an advocate of public access to government information, has argued that some of the exceptions to access "go against the whole spirit of a freedom of information act by absolutely prohibiting certain types of records from being released, thus turning these exemptions into an extension of the Official Secrets Act."[159] Also disturbing is the long list of subjects on which discretionary exemptions can be made by bureaucrats, which may well "limit the accountability of the government to Parliament."[160] Moreover, if the government refuses to disclose information on request, although appeal can be made first to an Information Commissioner, ultimate recourse is via the Federal Court – an expensive procedure, and one which raises the undesirable prospect of having the judicial process replace Parliament as the primary mechanism for ensuring bureaucratic accountability.

In the final analysis, public confidence will depend on how well the mechanics of releasing information work and on whether information which should be released is actually made public. This in turn, will depend upon the extent to which the Cabinet and the bureaucracy are willing to comply with the spirit rather than the letter of the new law.[161] The issue of freedom of information will undoubtedly remain on the agenda of public debate in the 1980s as the *Act* is evaluated.

OVERVIEW

It is an unfortunate fact of life that many Canadians are extremely suspicious, if not downright cynical, about the federal bureaucracy. In part, as we have argued, this suspicion stems from fear of the unknown, or, at least, the inadequately understood. The bureaucracy is not a single monolithic entity whose size and organizational structure automatically present a threat to democratic government. Rather it is a complex of competing departments, corporations and agencies established to meet the perceived economic, social and political goals of the public. Neither is the bureaucracy an elite group, dominated by a single class or ethnic/linguistic group and thereby unrepresentative of and unresponsive to the Canadian population. Concerted efforts have been made over the last two decades to make the bureaucracy more representative, although there is still substantial room for improvement, especially with regard to increasing opportunities for wo-

---

[159]Rowat, "The Right of Public Access . . .," pp. 185-186

[160]*Ibid.*, p. 187.

[161]For a pessimistic view of government's willingness to comply with the *Act*, see Jeff Sallot, "Is Ottawa pulling the blinds on what Canadians should see?" *The Globe and Mail*, Toronto, Monday, December 5, 1983, p. 7.

men and native people. Nor is there an absence of mechanisms through which control or accountability might be imposed on the bureaucracy by elected institutions. Rather, if there is a problem it may well be described as a lack of political will to make use of these control mechanisms. Since elected politicians in both Cabinet and Parliament feel bound to respond to the immediate demands of constituents and voters in order to secure their own re-election, and since voters and interest groups rush immediately to the defence of threatened programs from which they benefit, reduction of the size of the bureaucracy and public spending levels appear to be relatively low in the political priorities of Canadians. As long as the bureaucracy continues to serve the needs of most segments of Canadian society, there will not be sufficient impetus for a serious assault on the public service and its programs. Ultimately, as with governments, it may be argued that societies get the bureaucracies they deserve.

Part IV
Political
Behaviour

CanaPress Photo Service

chapter 10

Political Parties
Agents of Representation

POLITICAL PARTIES are a vital part of the Canadian political system; they have become uncontested agents of representative democracy in Canada. With very rare exceptions, candidates for election are selected by local party organizations; the Prime Minister, although formally named by the Governor General, is invariably leader of the party which holds the greatest number of elected representatives and is therefore most likely to form a viable government. In short, the party system provides essential organizing, stabilizing and legitimating functions in a large bureaucratic state.

In spite of their important role in political systems, organized political parties are relatively recent historical phenomena. As natural vehicles of mass participation in politics, they became increasingly formalized and significant as the franchise was extended, providing voters with progressively clearer alternatives. The Liberal and Conservative parties have assumed an important place in Canadian political culture for roughly a century, while the New Democratic Party's historical roots go back about half that length of time.

The federal parties provide a common political focus for Canadians, including a national soap opera complete with a roster of heroes, rogues and villains. Loved or hated, party leaders are the object of rapt media attention; their political views and personal foibles provide fodder for discussion of issues and personal gossip from coast to coast. The dramatic saga of the rise and fall of Joe Clark as Conservative leader, for example, was broadcast live into millions of living rooms across the nation. Politics reached dramatic heights in 1983 when Clark, surrounded by his tearful and emotionally exhausted supporters, conceded defeat to Brian Mulroney. Today, more than ever, federal party leaders play major roles on the national stage of Canadian politics.

Yet, for many decades, federal political parties have had a divisive influence on Canadian unity, as federal leaders proved powerless to prevent the growing regionalization of their bases of party support. The claims of the two major parties to the status of national parties have often been tenuous, as Conservative representatives were consistently excluded from Québec and Liberals increasingly from the West. The New Democratic Party, as the only third party in Parliament since 1980, has never been able to make significant inroads beyond some western provinces and Ontario. The failure to build strong national bases of support remains the most serious problem facing modern Canadian political parties, although the Progressive Conservative Party made a major breakthrough in this respect in the 1984 General Election.

In this chapter, we examine the origins and development of Canadian parties and their organization and structure outside of Parliament. How representative of the Canadian public are political parties, and how democratic are they, particularly in terms of formulating party policy? We also look at the role of the party leader and consider the selection process which thrusts individuals into that prestigious and potentially powerful position. First, however, in order to achieve a better perspective on the existing party system, we shall examine briefly the definition and role of parties, and survey the wide range of party types and party systems that exist as possible alternatives to our own.

WHAT ARE POLITICAL PARTIES?

Political parties have been defined in a number of ways. Marx, for example, considered them to be a manifestation of class conflict and struggle. Disraeli saw them as organized opinion. However, perhaps the most useful definition for our purposes is simply that parties are organizations designed to secure the power of the state for their leaders. The goal of political parties is to gain control of the levers of government and therefore to be able to realize their policies or programs. In democratic systems this end is achieved through open competition in the electoral process. The voluminous literature on political parties provides general (though not unanimous) agreement that parties constitute a crucial link between society and government.[1]

Party Functions

Political parties have certain tasks or functions to perform in society; these vary according to the political system in which the parties operate.[2] It has already been mentioned that political parties add an important element of stability to the political system by legitimizing the individuals and institutions which control po-

---

[1]Parties are relatively modern phenomena, playing a major role in Britain for the first time in the 18th century. There has been considerable controversy over their desirability, epitomized in the classic works of M.I. Ostrogorski, *Democracy and the Organization of Political Parties*, 2 vols., trans. by Frederick Clarke (New York: Macmillan, 1902) and Robert Michels, *Political Parties: A Sociological Study of Oligarchical Tendencies of Modern Democracy*, trans. by Eden and Cedar Paul, with introduction by S.M. Lipset (New York: The Free Press, 1966). Modern classics include Leon D. Epstein, *Political Parties in Western Democracies* (New York: Praeger, 1967).

[2]See a comprehensive article by Anthony King, "Political Parties in Western Democracies," *Polity*, vol. II, no. 2 (Winter 1969), pp. 111-141.

litical power. In addition, they help to organize the electorate by recruiting candidates, organizing campaigns, encouraging partisan attachments, helping individual voters get their names on polling lists and generally stimulating voter participation. As well, they help to organize the government by providing a degree of policy direction and supplying party leaders who are potential Prime Ministers and Cabinet ministers. The winning party serves to fuse the executive and legislative branches of government in Canada, and constitutes the foundation of Cabinet government.

Within the broad task of organizing the electorate and the government, there are several specific party functions which deserve elaboration.

RECRUITMENT, NOMINATION AND ELECTION OF POLITICAL OFFICEHOLDERS

It is the task of every political party to enlist suitable candidates for the positions of MPs, government ministers and Prime Minister, then to get them elected to form a government. In order to achieve this, every party must select and present candidates and mobilize voters to support them by waging a campaign to present the merits of its platform. The winning party forms the government and largely decides who will occupy the policy-making posts; in so doing it claims the most powerful tool a party can control. At the same time, it gains control of numerous patronage appointments throughout the government structure, rewarding its own supporters while extending its power and influence. Party leaders therefore recruit public appointees such as Senators and members of crown agencies, as well as elected representatives.

INTEREST ARTICULATION AND AGGREGATION

A vast number of interests are articulated in modern, complex societies. Political parties perform the very valuable function of reducing and simplifying this morass to manageable sets of policy alternatives. By appealing to the many classes, regions, and interest and ethnic groups that make up the country, political parties modify conflict and facilitate decisions. This process is known as aggregation of interests. It is performed by a variety of structures in our society, but political parties may be the most important. In addition, parties articulate interests in many ways; they help educate and form public opinion by debating important issues; and they provide a legitimate outlet for dissent and pressure for change. The latter is particularly important, since it allows regional or sectional interests to be articulated. It is, however, the aggregation function which is crucial. In fact, parties are often referred to as "gatekeepers" in the political system because they allow certain demands to pass directly to decision-makers, while they eliminate or combine others. Success in interest aggregation is a significant factor in electoral success in Canada. Parties constantly monitor the electorate for ideas and conduct opinion polls to help them transform public concerns into vote-winning policies.

FORMULATION OF PUBLIC POLICY

By winning elections, parties determine which partisan team will form the government and therefore have the initiative in the formulation and presentation of public policy. Once a party forms the government, the Cabinet, along with senior civil servants who have an important role in drafting policies, leads the policy-making function in the legislative process. Parties provide platforms for election campaigns, but these are rarely restrictive in terms of policy decisions.

Party organizations play only a limited role in the policy process, although when their parties are elected they do provide support for policies generated within the inner circles of government.

POLITICAL SOCIALIZATION

In stable democracies, political parties normally play a conservative role of rein-forcing the established system in order to keep the political process running smoothly. A revolutionary party would of course play the opposite role. In a parli-amentary democracy such as Canada, which lacks a strong national political cul-ture, there is a need for political parties to play special roles as "agencies for the creation of national symbols, experiences, memories, heroes, and villains".[3] Un-fortunately, at the present time, Canadian parties contribute little toward de-veloping and fostering a national political culture. The failure of Canadian parties to bind regional cleavages by building strong national bases of repre-sentation limits their effectiveness in this area.[4] They do, however, inform and educate the public, enlisting a high percentage of Canadians to participate in the electoral process through volunteer work as well as through voting.

OTHER FUNCTIONS

Parties sometimes participate in community activities outside the political arena in an attempt to influence constituents indirectly. They also provide a training ground for future political leaders, giving them the opportunity to hold minor of-fices. This is especially important in countries where local governments, for ex-ample, are based on party competition. For those who do not aspire to leadership positions there are possible economic rewards or other social and psychological benefits which accrue to association with the powerful and to participation in party decisions.

Party Types

Political parties within the system can be classified in a great number of ways. Maurice Duverger formulated a widely used and simple scheme dividing political parties into three categories: mass, cadre or devotee.[5] **Mass parties** are those

---

[3]John Meisel, "Recent Changes in Canadian Parties," in Hugh Thorburn, ed., *Party Politics in Canada,* 2nd ed. (Scarborough: Prentice-Hall, 1967), p. 34. This volume, now in its 5th ed., 1985, provides the best collection of articles on Canadian political parties.

[4]Alan Cairns was one of the first to challenge the idea that Canadian political parties are effective nationalizing agencies, arguing that the party system "conditioned by the electoral system, exacerbates the very cleavages it is credited with healing". Alan C. Cairns, "The Electoral System and the Party System in Canada, 1921-1965," *CJPS,* vol. 1, no. 1 (March 1968), p. 62.

[5]The classic discussion of party organization is found in Maurice Duverger, *Political Parties: Their Organization and Activity in the Modern State* (London: Methuen, 1954).

which have open membership and which recruit members across class lines to achieve the largest possible membership. The theoretical rationale behind these parties is that a large membership across social class lines helps to counter the power of establishment parties, whose leaders are mainly from the economic, political and social elite of the society. **Cadre parties**, on the other hand, are highly centralized and recruit only from the politically active elite. They are often associated with developing nations but are found throughout the developed world as well. The third category, **devotee parties**, are those built around a charismatic leader; an example is the Nazi party under Adolf Hitler.

Using Duverger's scheme, Fred Engelmann and Mildred Schwartz have formulated a typology by which to classify parties.[6] They suggest the use of eight categories in which political parties might be placed, depending on the following factors: (a) the degree to which they obtain support from the population; (b) the degree to which "principles are invoked as the underlying rationale for party existence and activities," *i.e.,* whether or not the party is based on an ideology or political philosophy – parties would thus be categorized as either "pragmatic" (often called "catch-all" because they are non-ideological) or "principled"; and (c) whether the organizational form of the party is cadre or mass.

Under this Engelmann-Schwartz categorization, the Liberal and Conservative parties were both broadly-based, pragmatic cadre parties before World War I, at which time they were the only significant parties. After 1921, Liberal support was eroded by the upsurge of third parties; since then the party has generally failed to obtain one-third of the prairie farmers' votes. Thus, the Liberal Party after World War I can be categorized as "restricted", even though it mobilizes across social groups. In the same vein, the Conservative Party lost its "broad" support categorization following the Conscription Crisis in 1921. Since that time, with the exception of the 1930 election, the Diefenbaker sweep of Québec in 1958 and the Mulroney breakthrough in 1984, the Conservatives have had an essentially English population support base. However, the extent of their 1984 electoral victory in Québec indicates that they may have regained a firm base in French Canada and moved back to the "broad" category. The Liberals, on the other hand, have done progressively worse in Western Canada and remain solidly lodged in the "restricted" category.

The NDP, like the CCF before it, is ideologically based. It has a restricted support base, being generally confined to Ontario and the western provinces, and is labour dominated, with a mass party organization. The Social Credit Party, which lost all representation in the federal Parliament in 1980, is difficult to classify because Alberta, British Columbia and perhaps Québec are the only provinces in which it has been relevant. However, it can tentatively be classified as a mass principle party with a restricted support base – restricted mainly to small urban areas, blue collar workers and small businessmen in rural areas.

There are some obvious difficulties with the Engelmann-Schwartz typology. Depending on the historical period and on the interpretation of the degree of

---

[6]F.C. Engelmann and M.A. Schwartz, *Canadian Political Parties: Origin, Character, Impact* (Scarborough: Prentice-Hall, 1975), pp. 19-21.

support required to be called a national party, parties can change from one category to another. Moreover, the typology is best suited for cross-national comparison of parties. Restricted to Canada, it contains too many empty cells to be an ideal categorization mechanism; the number and type of Canadian parties is simply too limited. It does, however, draw attention to and summarize some of the key concepts used for distinguishing the characteristics of parties in Canada.

Party Systems

The series of relationships between parties in a political system constitutes the party system. One way to categorize party systems is by the number of active parties. Around the world there are one-party, dominant party, two-party and multi-party systems.[7]

In the **one-party** state, a single party – which is the only legal party – controls every level of government. Authoritarian regimes such as the Soviet Union, the People's Republic of China and some African states are examples.

A **dominant party** system exists when a single party regularly wins almost every election, though opposition parties are allowed to function freely. An example is in India, where the Congress Party under Indira Gandhi, and after her death, under her son Rajiv Gandhi has dominated since Independence in 1947, or in Mexico, where the Institutional Revolutionary Party (PRI) invariably defeats the three minor parties in congressional and presidential elections.

The **two-party** system is characteristic of much of the English-speaking world. In this system, two major parties dominate; others have only minor political strength. The United States has a classic two-party system. Great Britain, Australia, New Zealand and Canada all have two dominant parties which vie for power as well as one or more weaker third parties. The main advantage claimed for this system is that it offers the electorate a choice of policies and leaders, and at the same time promotes governmental stability by making it possible for one party to win a majority or near-majority in the legislature.

In the **multi-party system**, popular support is divided among several parties, so that the party in power must generally form coalitions with one or more other parties to retain its position. This system, of which present-day Italy, the Third and Fourth French Republics and Weimar Germany are major examples, is often criticized as being unstable. However, there are many examples of multi-party systems with stable governments – notably Switzerland, the Netherlands and France since the beginning of the Fifth Republic. Advocates of this type of system argue that it allows a wide expression of the many interests of a complex society.

More sophisticated classification systems for parties have been devised to distinguish with greater precision among party systems. Joseph LaPalombara and

---

[7]Of course, there are more complex definitions and typologies of party systems. See, for example, Giovanni Sartori, *Parties and Party Systems: A Framework for Analysis* (London: Cambridge University Press, 1976).

TABLE 10.1 Party Systems

Non-competitive Systems	(1) Totalitarian (Soviet Union)
	(2) Authoritarian (Franco's Spain)
	(3) Pluralistic (Mexico)
Competitive Systems	(1) Dominant One-party (France under de Gaulle)
	(2) Two-party (United States)
	(3) Multi-party dominant (three or more parties; one receives at least 40% of the vote) (Canada) or Multi-party loose (three or more parties; none regularly receives 40% of the vote) (Italy)

Source: Adapted from Joseph LaPalombara and Myron Weiner, eds. *Political Parties and Political Development* (New Jersey: Princeton University Press, 1966) and Joseph LaPalombara, *Politics Within Nations* (Englewood Cliffs, N.J.: Prentice Hall, 1974), Ch. 13.

Myron Weiner, for example, introduced a competitive/non-competitive classification of party systems which has since been expanded by others.[8]

Competitive systems are classified by the number of parties that compete for and have access to legislative power. In the dominant one-party system only one party polls more than one-third of the vote. In the two-party system, no third party polls more than 15% of the total vote; if three or more parties poll more than 15%, a multi-party system exists. Non-competitive systems, in which one party dominates, are classified by other variables, such as how repressive their governments are.

THE CANADIAN PARTY SYSTEM

Classification systems are intended for gross comparisons between nation states, and not all countries fit neatly into any one category. Canada is a prime example of this situation. It has a competitive party system, but, partly because this system has changed over time, Canada does not clearly belong in any of the above categories. Until the rise of third parties in 1921, when the Progressives suddenly won 23% of the federal vote, the Canadian party system was developing along the lines of a classic two-party system. Since that time, and particularly since the advent of the NDP in 1961, third parties in the form of the NDP and Social Credit have fairly consistently captured 25% to 28% of the federal vote. They never come very close to winning power in Ottawa, but nine times altogether (six times since World War II) they have prevented one of the major parties from winning a clear majority in a General Election. This situation causes the Canadian system

[8]Joseph LaPalombara and Myron Weiner, eds., *Political Parties and Political Development* (Princeton: Princeton University Press, 1966), pp. 33-41

to fall somewhere between the two-party and multi-party systems in the classification scheme set out above. Because of this, the arrangement in Canada has often been called a "two-and-a-half party" system.

There are both pros and cons to this kind of system. In general it works quite smoothly. The two major parties in Canada are lodged firmly in the centre of the political spectrum. They are often portrayed as Tweedledum and Tweedledee (two "brokerage" parties) because they appeal to the same middle-of-the-road electoral supporters, shifting their principles in search of electoral success. The Liberals are often considered centre-left and the Progressive Conservatives centre-right, because of a few alleged historical differences such as the Conservative support of free enterprise and the Liberal leadership in social legislation and public ownership. However, they both display remarkable flexibility within this broad range.

The third parties allow more radical voices to be represented in the federal Parliament, thus widening the scope of the expression of opinion. The NDP, which is on the moderate left of the political spectrum, has often acted as a social conscience, initiating innovative ideas for social programs which are too extreme for the major parties but which over time may be taken into the Liberal or Conservative party platforms and eventually implemented in watered-down form. A case in point was Medicare. The Social Credit Party has been the furthest right on the spectrum in Canada. Still, neither of these two minor parties is very extreme. There is no doubt that the precursor of the New Democratic Party, the Co-operative Commonwealth Federation (CCF), was a militantly ideological party out to eradicate capitalism and establish a new socialist society, but the NDP has moderated such aims considerably. The need for a broader electoral base has pressured it gradually to adopt a moderate-left reform position which at times overlaps with centre-left Liberal positions. Similarly, Social Credit was unquestionably a party of the extreme right in the beginning. Electoral success provincially in Alberta and British Columbia and the desire to enlarge its electoral base eventually contributed to an abandonment of its most radical proposals and a movement left toward more progressive policies. The "middle of the road" tendency of all the parties is evident, but the historical relationship between the parties is still sufficient to warrant their relative positions on the left-right continuum.[9]

By helping to broaden the spectrum of political views represented in Parliament, minor or third parties provide a legitimate outlet for political dissent, giving a voice to minority opinion that might otherwise be forced to work outside the system. They are particularly effective in this respect at the provincial level when they espouse regional concerns. Although they have not had significant electoral success federally, they often form the government provincially. For example, the CCF-NDP has governed in Saskatchewan, Manitoba and British Co-

---

[9]On problems encountered in placing Canadian parties on an ideological left-right spectrum, see David Elkins, "The Perceived Structure of the Canadian Party System," *CJPS*, vol. 7, no. 3 (September 1974), pp. 502-524. See also Hugh C. Thorburn, "Interpretations of the Canadian Party System" in Thorburn, *op. cit.*, 5th ed., pp. 20-40.

lumbia; Social Credit in Alberta and British Columbia; the Union Nationale and the Parti Québécois in Québec.

On the debit side, minority governments tend to be short-lived, relatively unstable and slow-moving, because the governing party constantly needs to negotiate with the minor party or parties for support in order to pass legislation. By crude empirical measures, such as number of bills passed or number of pages of enacted legislation, minority governments are less efficient than majority governments.[10]

Another possible classification for the Canadian party system is "multi-party dominant", a system in which three or more parties exist, but one party receives at least 40 percent of the vote. Only four times since 1878 has the Liberal party fallen below 40 percent of the vote in a federal election: in 1958, 1962, 1972 and 1984. In only two of those cases – the 1958 Diefenbaker sweep of the country and the 1984 Mulroney victory – has the Conservative party received a significantly higher percentage of the vote than the Liberals. When votes are translated into seats, the Liberals have won all but eight elections since 1896, all but two since 1962 – the Clark government that lasted less than a year, and the Mulroney landslide in 1984. Until 1984, therefore, the Liberals monopolized bureaucratic and Senatorial appointments and all the other advantages of holding power, including the psychological advantage of being perceived as the government party. The Conservatives, and to an even greater extent the New Democratic Party, have been much less successful in the 20th century; this has made them more prone to factionalism, which has further decreased their chances of electoral success.

In spite of its relative stability and the flexibility afforded by the presence of minor parties, the Canadian party system is plagued by certain problems. Party funds have traditionally come largely from businesses and corporations; over time, the non-government elite has thereby gained a strong influence on the political system. Ownership and control of corporations in Canada by foreign investors, preponderantly from the United States, magnifies the problem. Another concern is the strong relationship which has necessarily developed between the Liberal Party, as the dominant party, and the bureaucratic elite in the civil service. These and other problems within the system are discussed more fully below.

Federalism, Regionalism and the Party System

In addition to the facts that it is competitive, and arguably either a two-and-a-half or one-party-dominant system, the prime characteristics of the Canadian party system are that it is both federal and highly regional. While they parallel the federal organization of government, the provincial party systems are not necessarily identical to their federal counterpart. The classic two-party system is found consistently only in the Maritimes, where third parties rarely win more than 5 percent of the vote. Even more bizarre is the fact that federal and provincial parties

---

[10]Robert J. Jackson and Michael Atkinson, *The Canadian Legislative System,* 2nd rev. ed. (Toronto: Macmillan, 1980), pp. 179-81.

of the same name have separate elites, organizations, financial support and often platforms.[11] Only in the Atlantic provinces do federal-provincial party ties remain fairly integrated. A Conservative government in Ottawa thus cannot assume ideological congruence or policy support from its provincial counterparts; nor can a Liberal government. Provincial governments generally win support by pugnacious behaviour and strong stands for provincial concerns against the federal government. Garth Stevenson speculates that this "peculiar separation of the party system into federal and provincial layers is perhaps in part a consequence of the intensity of federal-provincial conflict, which makes it difficult for a party affiliated with the federal government to appear as a credible defender of provincial interests."[12] For whatever reason, voters do not always support the same parties federally and provincially. The Liberal Party has dominated federal politics for most of this century, but, since the Second World War, it has gradually been losing support at the provincial level. By the late 1970s it was reduced to the role of major opposition party provincially, or even to that of third party, as in Alberta and British Columbia. In fact, at the time it was defeated federally in 1979 and again in 1984, not a single Liberal provincial government existed anywhere in Canada. On the other hand, provincial success does not necessarily carry over into the federal sphere. Despite their mediocre federal record, the Conservatives have a strong record of provincial governments in Atlantic Canada, Ontario, Manitoba and Alberta. As we shall see in the following chapter, on electoral behaviour, Ontario voters are somewhat more likely to elect Conservatives in provincial elections and Liberals in federal elections (although they voted strongly Conservative in the 1984 federal election and marginally Liberal in the 1985 provincial election). Third parties have also done well at the provincial level. In 1985, Social Credit held British Columbia; the NDP, Manitoba; and the Party Québécois, Québec.

The federal structure encourages the establishment of new parties at the provincial level. Some of them remain unique to one or to very few provinces and never move into the federal system, while others do enter the federal contest but never come close to power. The Parti Québécois, for example, is likely to remain a one-province party, but after a decade-and-a-half in provincial politics it took the tentative step of supporting the new Parti Nationaliste, formed in 1983, at the federal level. The Social Credit Party, which has never expanded beyond three provinces, won no seats in the 1980 or 1984 elections. Its western wing from Alberta and British Columbia was never effectively integrated with the Québec wing. At the provincial level, Alberta's Social Credit Party, which by 1979 had shrunk to a handful of seats in the provincial legislature, changed its name to the Alberta Party, although in the same year the Social Credit Party under Bill Bennett won a majority government in British Columbia. The NDP has the widest

[11]Donald V. Smiley, *Canada in Question: Federalism in the Eighties* 3rd ed. (Toronto: McGraw-Hill Ryerson, 1980), pp. 83-113.

[12]Garth Stevenson, *Unfulfilled Union: Canadian Federalism and National Unity*, rev. ed. (Toronto: Gage, 1982), p. 182.

federal support of the minor parties, but even it won no seats in six of the ten provinces in the 1984 election.

Its strong regional character is perhaps the most interesting, but also the most worrisome feature of the Canadian party system. In recent years, with the exception of 1984, General Elections have increasingly produced governments

TABLE 10.2 Percentage of Seats in Each Region Won by Governing Party in Canadian General Elections, 1867 – 1984

Election	Governing Party	% Seats Won by Governing Party in Each Region				
		Canada	West	Ontario	Quebec	Atlantic
1867	CONS	55.8	—	56.1	69.2	29.4
1872	CONS	51.5	90.0	43.2	58.5	48.6
1874	LIB	64.6	20.0	72.7	50.8	79.1
1878	CONS	66.5	90.0	67.0	69.2	55.8
1882	CONS	66.2	72.7	59.3	73.8	67.4
1887	CONS	57.2	93.3	56.5	50.8	55.8
1891	CONS	57.2	93.3	52.2	46.2	72.1
1896	LIB	54.9	47.1	46.7	75.4	43.6
1900	LIB	62.0	70.6	39.1	87.7	69.2
1904	LIB	65.0	75.0	44.2	83.1	74.3
1980	LIB	60.2	51.4	41.9	81.5	74.3
1911	CONS	60.2	51.4	83.7	41.5	45.7
1917	UNIONIST (CONS)	65.1	96.5	90.2	4.6	67.7
1921	Lib	49.4	8.8	25.6	100.0	80.6
1925	Lib	40.4	33.3	13.4	90.8	20.7
1926	Lib	47.3	34.8	28.0	92.3	31.0
1930	CONS	55.9	44.9	72.0	36.9	79.3
1935	LIB	69.8	48.6	68.3	84.6	96.2
1940	LIB	72.7	59.7	67.1	93.8	73.1
1945	LIB	51.0	26.4	41.5	83.1	69.2
1949	LIB	72.5	59.7	67.5	90.4	73.5
1953	LIB	64.2	37.5	58.8	88.0	81.8
1957	Prog Cons	42.3	29.2	71.8	12.0	63.6
1958	PROG CONS	78.5	91.7	78.8	66.7	75.8
1962	Prog Cons	43.8	68.1	41.1	18.7	54.5
1963	Lib	48.7	13.9	61.2	62.7	60.6
1965	Lib	49.4	12.5	60.0	74.7	45.5
1968	LIB	58.7	40.0	72.7	75.7	21.9
1972	Lib	41.3	10.0	40.9	75.7	31.2
1974	LIB	53.4	18.6	62.5	81.1	40.6
1979	Prog Cons	48.2	73.8	60.0	2.7	56.3
1980	LIB	52.1	2.5	54.7	98.7	59.4
1984	PROG CONS	74.8	76.3	70.5	77.3	78.1

LIB/PROG CONS — Majority Government   Lib/Prog Cons – Minority Government
(*Note:* "West" includes NWT and Yukon)

with great regional distortions because the parties were unable to build strong national bases. In the 1980 election, for example, the Liberals won 99 percent of the seats in Québec, 55 percent of those in Ontario, 59 percent in the Atlantic region, but just under 3 percent in the West. Translated into seats, 74 of the Liberal government's 147 seats came from Québec, 52 from Ontario, 19 from Atlantic provinces and only two from the West (both in Manitoba). This meant that the four Western provinces were virtually excluded from the government caucus: they had just over one percent of the membership. They have been severely under-represented in virtually all the Liberal caucuses since 1963, sinking to a low in 1980 and remaining there in 1984. In fact, from 1921 until 1984, the West was mildly or severely under-represented in almost all government caucuses. The only exceptions were during three Progressive Conservative governments, which lasted in total only about six years. Conversely, Québec was highly over-represented in all Liberal government caucuses during the same period. The 1984 Conservative electoral breakthrough in Québec has, at least temporarily, given Canada a government with a strong national mandate. One can only speculate at this time whether it can be maintained, but, as Table 10-3 shows, for the first time since 1958 the percentage regional composition of the PC caucus in 1984 is extremely close to the percentage regional composition of the House of Commons.

It is evident that the Liberal Party has increasingly become the party of central Canada, winning 85% of its seats there in the 1980 election, and 78% in 1984. Prime Minister Trudeau summarized the condition of the Liberal Party in a speech at a Liberal Conference in 1976:

> West of the Manitoba border we exist as a third party and not a strong one at that. We have in a sense almost local representation amongst the French-speaking part of New Brunswick but very little, just one member, in the English-speaking part of the province. Just one member out of four in PEI, two members in Nova Scotia. So, you know, I think we have to worry as Liberals about our future as a national party.

He went on:

> Indeed, the governments of Canada for a large part of the period of Liberal holding of office have been the governments of a majority of French-speaking Canada, plus a minority of English-speaking Canada.[13]

The Progressive Conservatives, for their part, won 50 percent of their seats in 1980 in the Western provinces, and only one seat in Québec. This situation changed radically in 1984, to 27 percent in the West and 27 percent in Québec. The NDP won 80 percent of its seats in the West and none in Atlantic Canada or Québec in 1980 , and 57 percent in the West and the rest in Ontario in 1984.

These severe regional imbalances in the party system make it difficult for the parties to perform many of their important functions, discussed above. Recruitment for political patronage positions has been distorted by Liberal Party

---

[13]*The Globe and Mail*, Toronto, Oct. 4, 1976, p. 7.

TABLE 10.3 Regional Composition of Government Caucus and House of Commons, Canadian General Elections, 1867-1984

Election	Governing Party	% Regional Composition of Government Caucus				% Regional Composition of House of Commons			
		West	Ont.	Qué.	Atl.	West	Ont.	Qué.	Atl.
1867	CONS	—	45.5	44.6	9.9	—	45.3	35.9	18.8
1872	CONS	8.7	36.9	36.9	17.5	5.0	44.0	32.5	18.5
1874	LIB	1.5	48.1	24.8	25.6	4.9	42.7	31.6	20.9
1878	CONS	6.6	43.1	32.8	17.5	4.9	42.7	31.6	20.9
1882	CONS	5.8	38.8	34.5	20.9	5.2	43.3	31.0	20.5
1887	CONS	11.4	42.3	26.8	19.5	7.0	42.8	30.2	20.0
1891	CONS	11.4	39.0	24.4	25.2	7.0	42.8	30.2	20.0
1896	LIB	6.8	36.8	41.9	14.5	8.0	43.2	30.5	18.3
1900	LIB	9.1	27.3	43.2	20.5	8.0	43.2	30.5	18.3
1904	LIB	15.1	27.3	38.8	18.7	13.1	40.2	30.4	16.4
1908	LIB	13.5	27.1	39.8	19.5	15.8	38.9	29.4	15.8
1911	CONS	13.5	54.1	20.3	12.0	15.8	38.9	29.4	15.8
1917	UNIONIST (CONS)	35.9	48.4	2.0	13.7	24.3	34.9	27.7	13.2
1921	Lib	4.3	18.1	56.0	21.6	24.3	34.9	27.7	13.2
1925	Lib	23.2	11.1	59.6	6.1	28.2	33.5	26.5	11.8
1926	Lib	20.7	19.8	51.7	7.8	28.2	33.5	26.5	11.8
1930	CONS	22.6	43.1	17.5	16.8	28.2	33.5	26.5	11.8
1935	LIB	20.5	32.7	32.2	14.6	29.4	33.5	26.5	10.6
1940	LIB	24.2	30.9	34.2	10.7	29.4	33.5	26.5	10.6
1945	LIB	15.2	27.2	43.2	14.4	29.4	33.5	26.5	10.6
1949	LIB	22.6	29.5	34.7	13.1	27.5	31.7	27.9	13.0
1953	LIB	15.9	29.4	38.8	15.9	27.2	32.1	28.3	12.5
1957	Prog Cons	18.8	54.4	8.0	18.8	27.2	32.1	28.3	12.5
1958	PROG CONS	31.7	32.2	24.0	12.0	27.2	32.1	28.3	12.5
1962	Prog Cons	42.2	30.2	12.1	15.5	27.2	32.1	28.3	12.5
1963	Lib	7.8	40.3	36.4	15.5	27.2	32.1	28.3	12.5
1965	Lib	6.9	38.9	42.7	11.5	27.2	32.1	28.3	12.5
1968	LIB	18.1	41.3	36.1	4.5	26.5	33.3	28.0	12.1
1972	Lib	6.4	33.0	51.4	9.2	26.5	33.3	28.0	12.1
1974	LIB	9.2	39.0	42.6	9.2	26.5	33.3	28.0	12.1
1979	Prog Cons	43.4	41.9	1.5	13.2	28.4	33.7	26.6	11.3
1980	LIB	1.4	35.4	50.3	12.9	28.4	33.7	26.6	11.3
1984	PROG CONS	28.9	31.8	27.5	11.8	28.9	33.7	26.6	11.3

LIB/PROG CONS–Majority Government   Lib/Prog Cons–Minority Government

(*N.B.* Rows may not add up to 100.0%, because of rounding.)

(*Note:* "West" includes NWT and Yukon.)

domination of the government, as has recruitment to Cabinet, since recent Liberal governments were virtually locked out of representation in the West. Interest aggregation and articulation by the parties is also distorted when regions are severely over- or under-represented in governments on a regular basis over several decades. Even the socialization function is distorted, because regional cleavages are exacerbated instead of smoothed over. The politics of each region are very introverted. The different political traditions and social and economic cleavages in the regions make Canada difficult to govern, and tend to encourage viewpoints which are parochial and narrow rather than national. Since the national parties are federal organizations based on provincial components, regional conflicts are often the cause of internal dissension within the parties as well.

THE ORIGIN AND DEVELOPMENT OF CANADIAN PARTIES

History and traditional loyalties, rather than logic or ideology behind party platforms, are the distinguishing features of Canadian political parties.[14] The names of the parties are not necessarily significant, as even a cursory examination of party electoral platforms reveals. The many cleavages in the country – ethnic, geographic, economic and demographic – have forced parties to be "middle of the road" in their attempts to win majorities. Radical parties have been able to do no more than flicker on the sidelines while the major parties vie for the middle ground.

It is difficult to pinpoint the date of origin of political parties in Canada. Initially, they were loosely organized and even less encumbered by ideology than they are today. In their early years, Upper and Lower Canada, Nova Scotia and Prince Edward Island were all governed by oligarchies. The Family Compact, the Chateau Clique, the Halifax Compact and the landed proprietors in Prince Edward Island controlled the economic and political power in their particular areas. Any opposition that existed was fragmented and factional. The prime requisite for the emergence of parties was, in each case, increased competition for power within the legislature. Nowhere did the factions and interest groups mature into parties until the advent of responsible government. In fact, the formation of parties occurred even later in the case of PEI, where religious rights and land settlement problems cut across party lines. Only after the executive became responsible to the legislature was there a genuine need for political parties to develop. As legislative responsibilities were extended and the franchise expanded, the pressures for party cohesion increased and recognizable political parties emerged.[15]

---

[14]Paul W. Fox, "Political Parties in Canada," in Paul W. Fox, ed., *Politics: Canada*, 4th ed. (Toronto: McGraw-Hill Ryerson), pp. 253-357.

[15]See J.M. Beck, "Nova Scotia, the Party System in Nova Scotia: Tradition and Conservatism," in Martin Robin, ed., *Canadian Provincial Politics*, (Scarborough: Prentice Hall, 1972). Also J.M. Beck, *The Government of Nova Scotia* (Toronto: University of Toronto Press, 1957); and Frank Mackinnon, *The Government of Prince Edward Island* (Toronto: University of Toronto Press, 1951).

The origin and development of parties are directly influenced by the system of government. Thus, Canadian parties developed within the framework of a democratic parliamentary system and, after 1867, a federal constitutional arrangement. Party origins and development are also very much affected by internal factors such as national and industrial development, and external stimuli such as, in Canada's case, historical precedents and ideological influences from Britain and the United States.

Until shortly after Confederation, politics in Canada were characterized by factionalism and disparate interests. Party structures had not had time to form, and in any case the problems of the day did not require a comprehensive set of policies. As electoral reforms were introduced, including the secret ballot and simultaneous balloting in federal elections, party lines solidified. Until these developments took place candidates often did not commit themselves to a party until they had determined who would win. Western Canada did not have simultaneous elections until much later; this is often thought to be one reason why strong party traditions did not develop there, and third party movements are more successful in Western than in Eastern Canada.

Until the 1920s the two major parties were able to aggregate the various interests in Canada, which were not very complex. The economy prospered; regional and rural-urban cleavages were minimal. It is after this date that the first minor parties appeared on the political scene.

The support base of the parties has been relatively stable in terms of numbers; the two major parties have consistently won about 80 percent of the vote, the NDP about 20 percent. It is more difficult to determine who has regularly constituted these support bases. Voting patterns in Canada, as we shall see in the following chapter, have been sufficiently fluid to make most demographic factors largely irrelevant in terms of predictive value.[16] Socio-economic status, for example, as well as age, sex and community size correlate only weakly with voting behaviour. Certain correlations are, however, based on regional, religious and ethnic groups. We have already noted clear regional bases of support for each of the parties. Studies also confirm fairly persistent preferences of metropolitan voters, Roman Catholics and French Canadians for the Liberal Party.

As for the Conservative support base, there are modest correlations to show that Conservative voters have tended to include disproportionate numbers of non-Roman Catholics, older voters and those in rural areas. Canadians of Anglo-Celtic origin have been divided between the two major parties. Voters from ethnic groups other than the two charter groups have disproportionately supported the Liberals, to varying degrees across the different regions.

The only demographic variable to correlate strongly with NDP voters has been region, and, to a small degree, working class status. A high percentage, but not the majority, of NDP voters have been working class, but it is also true that only a small percentage of the working class has tended to vote for the NDP. Con-

---

[16]Lawrence LeDuc, Harold D. Clarke, Jane Jensen and Jon H. Pammett, "Partisan Instability in Canada: Evidence from a New Panel Study," *APSR* vol. 78, no. 2 (June 1984), pp. 470-484.

siderable NDP support has come from metropolitan areas. Social Credit support, on the other hand, has proved greatest in towns and small cities.

The Progressive Conservative Party

The oldest party in a country is often the party of established interests, and this is certainly the case in Canada. The privileged elements of Canadian society banded together as early as 1854, when John A. Macdonald brought together a working coalition of various interests under the label Liberal-Conservative. It was an alliance which included eastern commercial interests, conservative French Canadians and Ontario Tories. Their objectives were to bring about Confederation and then work toward a National Policy; the means of achieving these ends were basically encouraging national unity and developing the country by promoting a national railway, industry and commerce. Maintenance of the British connection was fundamental to the early Conservatives, as was the establishment of relatively high tariffs. The Conservative Party was traditionally disliked by farmers in the West because of its empathy for big business, and French Canadians were wary of it because of its strong British interest. These latter attitudes were consolidated by both the execution of Riel and the Conscription Crisis of 1917. Conservative support in French Québec disintegrated, and the Conservative party structure became centralized in Ontario. In the West as well, where there was no strong party tradition, voters withheld support from the Conservatives. After World War I, Westerners formed the Progressive Party, which allied itself uneasily with the Liberals.

Another misfortune for the Conservatives was that they happened to be in power during the Depression, a situation which assured further unpopularity and even more erosion of support. Their adversities were compounded by a serious leadership vacuum; Arthur Meighen and R.B. Bennett showed promise, but neither could make inroads in Québec. Then, in the 1940s, the party wooed Progressive support in the West and chose John Bracken, the Liberal-Progressive Premier of Manitoba, as its leader, renaming the party the Progressive Conservatives. George Drew became leader in 1948, but still the party remained in the political wilderness.[17] Not until John Diefenbaker, another Westerner, emerged as leader did Tory fortunes improve. The Conservatives formed a minority government in 1957, followed by a landslide victory in 1958.

John Diefenbaker's charismatic personality and his appeal to diverse Canadian ethnic, economic, religious and regional groups brought not only his native Prairies into the fold but also 50 seats from Québec. The Progressive Conservative Party was on the rise, and appeared to take over the Liberal stand of moderate reform. However, Diefenbaker's capricious leadership in difficult times ultimately alienated French Canada, the large urban centres, business and industry and the intellectual community. Only the West, his gift to the party, remained

---

[17]See W.L. Morton, *The Progressive Party in Canada* (Toronto: University of Toronto Press, 1950).

loyal. Diefenbaker's electoral defeat in 1963 left the Conservatives floundering and unable to re-enlist the Québec votes they had briefly recaptured; the charismatic leader who had reunited and led the party to victory had lost his magic.

When Diefenbaker failed to resign in the light of this disillusionment with his leadership, Dalton Camp, the party president, engineered his removal at the party convention of 1967. The conflict over "the Chief's" leadership and forced retirement created deep factions within the party which plagued the Stanfield era which followed.[18] Enough local party members abandoned active politics to seriously weaken party organization at the local level. The six years of power under Diefenbaker's leadership preceded the Conservatives' second longest continuous period as the major opposition party. Diefenbaker's successor, Robert Stanfield, with his honest but plodding image, lost his third and final campaign in 1974 by advocating wage and price controls. He was replaced by thirty-six year old Joe Clark, Member of Parliament for Rocky Mountain, Alberta, who assumed the leadership after a photo-finish win against Québec's Claude Wagner in the 1976 leadership convention. This move consolidated Western support, but by then the other bases of strength had dwindled to the Atlantic provinces and rural and small-town Ontario.

The 1979 election gave the Progressive Conservatives their first hold on power in sixteen years, but the prize was snatched from their hands just eight months later when their minority government was defeated on a vote on the budget. Joe Clark accepted the vote as want of confidence in the government and advised the Governor General to dissolve Parliament. The consequence of that combination of events was a severe Conservative defeat in the 1980 election and Clark's own ultimate rejection and defeat as party leader. At the ensuing party policy convention in Winnipeg, Clark submitted to a routine vote of confidence. Although he won 67 percent of the delegate vote, which was technically more than adequate, he asked the executive to call a leadership convention and declared he would be a candidate. His defeat by Brian Mulroney at that spring convention was a personal humiliation. Mulroney, who had run unsuccessfully against him in the 1976 convention, had had no experience in public office. He was, however, an extremely astute politician who had diligently paved the way to this leadership position over many years.[19] As a bilingual Québécois of Irish-French descent, with family connections to the Yugoslavian community, his qualifications were tailor-made to win support from the two major constituencies the Conservatives desperately needed: French Canadians in Québec, and ethnic groups, particularly in key Toronto ridings.

Mulroney's challenge was to build a significant and durable electoral base in French Canada. In the 1984 General Election he won handsomely and relatively evenly across the entire country, gathering between 42 percent and 69 per-

---

[18]See, for example, Peter Newman, *The Distemper of Our Times: Canadian Politics in Transition, 1963-1968* (Toronto: McClelland and Stewart, 1968).

[19]Patrick Martin, Allan Gregg and George Perlin, *Contenders: The Tory Quest for Power* (Scarborough: Prentice-Hall, 1983).

cent of the popular vote in every province – 50 percent in Québec. By the time of the election, PC membership had increased impressively in that province, engendering party hopes that they might be able to consolidate electoral support there.

The Tory party in Canada is not doctrinaire and has never sought ideological purity. The early Conservative Party under Macdonald was dominated by themes of Canadian nationalism and support for British imperialism with its "innate assumption of moral and racial superiority".[20] Years in the political wilderness and the pressures resulting from expanding American influence in Canada as well as the growing anachronism of British imperialism undermined these Tory traditions. Conservatives themselves agree that their modern party is "hampered by its public image of being pro-big business and anti-labour, anti-ethnic, anti-women and anti-youth, as well as reactionary on most social issues".[21]

This harsh assessment is, as Charles Taylor comments, a formidable burden. In broad general terms, however, the modern Progressive Conservative Party represents a "conservative-radical mix which is based on a sense of community and order, a feeling for the land, a respect for human diversity and human rights, a concern for social justice, and a non-ideological approach to the problems of political and economic organization".[22] The party is committed to upholding the private enterprise system, but it is willing to have the government intervene in the economy to protect broad collective interests.[23] It has traditionally been less sensitive to francophone positions than the Liberals, but with a leader from Québec that may change. Historically, it has been wary of American influence (this also has changed under Mulroney), as well as pro-British and supportive of agricultural interests. Ideological differences between the "progressive" and "conservative" wings which are often underlined in the press, especially during leadership conflicts, are probably exaggerated.[24] They are based on disagreements within the party over the scope and need for government action in different areas such as business and welfare, and have been exacerbated by successive electoral disappointments.

The Liberal Party

The Liberal Party was much slower than the Conservatives to develop as a national force. Its predecessors were the early reformers who generally advocated a radical transformation of society and wanted to solve major inequities through governmental reform. The opposition to Sir John A. Macdonald's first govern-

---

[20]Charles Taylor, *Radical Tories: The Conservative Tradition in Canada* (Toronto: Anansi, 1982), p. 211.

[21]*Ibid.*, p. 211.

[22]*Ibid.*, p. 213.

[23]See Robert Stanfield, "Conservative Principles and Philosophy," in Paul Fox, ed., *op. cit.*, pp. 260-264.

[24]George C. Perlin, *The Tory Syndrome: Leadership Politics in the Progressive Conservative Party* (Montréal: McGill-Queens University Press, 1980), p. 101.

ment consisted of Clear Grits from Ontario, Le Parti Rouge from Québec, and anti-Confederation Nova Scotia MPs. It was generally considered a more egalitarian grouping than the Conservatives. However, there was no real unity until Wilfrid Laurier became leader in 1887 and transformed these disparate interests into the national Liberal Party. As Canada's first French Canadian Prime Minister, Laurier firmly entrenched the Liberal Party in Québec, with assistance from people like Honoré Mercier and Israel Tarte. Laurier still holds the record for the longest continuous term in office as Prime Minister – from 1896 to 1911.

After Laurier, the Liberal Party endured a decade of discontent which climaxed with the bitter division over the Conscription Crisis in Québec. In 1919, the party elected William Lyon Mackenzie King as party leader. The Liberals won the 1921 election, and King rebuilt the party into a strong organization which dominated Canadian government for most of the next six decades. Mackenzie King set a record for total years in power; he was Prime Minister for 21 years and 5 months. During his early years in office he astutely tried to accommodate the agrarian protest from the West by forming an alliance with the Progressives, but that initiative collapsed. Louis St. Laurent, who succeeded King (and who was defeated by John Diefenbaker in 1957), his successor Lester Pearson (party leader from 1958-68, Prime Minister from 1963-68) and Pierre Trudeau (Prime Minister 1968-1979 and 1980-1984) who followed Pearson all more or less successfully accommodated Québec discontent but gradually lost the West.

Trudeau's ascent to the leadership in April 1968 was dramatic – a victory by an attractive political neophyte over well-known, experienced Liberal leaders. It spurred a wave of "Trudeaumania" which swept the country and gave his party a large majority in the ensuing election. Throughout the 1960s the Liberal popular vote had increased in the West and, although the 1968 sweep was not as large there as in Ontario and Québec, it represented a Liberal high point. Following that election, the party endured an unrelenting decline in support west of Ontario. As the initial wave of Trudeaumania wore thin, apathy in the party grew and Liberal support began to fluctuate. In the wake of accusations of arrogance and insensitivity, the Liberals suffered near-defeat in the 1972 election. A new professional approach refurbished Trudeau's tarnished image by the next election, and the party won a fresh, strong mandate in 1974. But again the glow wore off. Five years later the Liberals received another rebuff at the polls. It was not a crushing defeat, just severe enough to allow the Conservatives a tenuous minority hold on power; the Liberals still had 4 percent more of the popular vote than the Conservatives, and 40 percent of the seats. The most serious problem was not the electoral loss itself but the fact that half of the Liberal MPs were elected from one province – Québec. That November, Trudeau publicly stated his intention to resign as leader, but within weeks the Conservative government was toppled and a new election was called. To the chagrin of many pretenders to his mantle Trudeau stayed on to fight the campaign. Endowed with a new mandate in 1980, Trudeau's stated intent to resign dissolved. Record lows in public opinion polls for both his personal popularity as leader and the party in 1983 did not dislodge his firm grip on the Liberal leadership. As he was fond of saying, he would leave when he was ready.

In the spring of 1984, having led his party for over 16 years, with all but nine months as Prime Minister, Pierre Trudeau took his leave of party politics. John Turner dominated the ensuing party leadership convention and within days, called an election. He won his own seat, but the Liberal Party won only 28 percent of the popular vote, the worst result ever for the federal Liberals in a General Election.

The philosophical base of the Liberal Party derives mainly from British liberalism, but Canadian Liberal leaders have tended to adopt a distinctively pragmatic approach to issues as they arise. Traditional liberal themes such as reform, individual rights, state intervention to enhance the individual liberty of the underprivileged, national and international conciliation have recurred in various concrete forms in Liberal Party platforms and policies. However, practical politics in Canada tend to be ideologically fuzzy and opportunistic.[25] As one observer put it, "Certainly there have been sporadic tremors of small 'l' liberalism. But whether the unemployment insurance or the National Energy Program, the tremors have usually been in isolation, a reflection of an individual minister rather than concerted Government policies."[26]

Successive Liberal governments since the last World War have gradually expanded their influence in the social and economic spheres. Following the war they introduced considerable social welfare legislation and assumed more responsibility for directing the Canadian economy. The latter tendency increased considerably when the Liberals decided to enforce wage and price controls in 1975. In the 19th century, when the Liberal Party was generally in opposition in Ottawa and in government in the provinces, it was a staunch defender of provincial rights. Since the party has dominated power in Ottawa, however, it has gradually moved into the position of the major opposition party or worse in the provinces, and correspondingly has espoused strong centralizing policies. In foreign affairs, Liberal policies have been judged to be selectively continentalist.[27] Internally, bilingualism, broad commitment toward Québec and individual rights, both linguistic and legal, were perhaps the most coherently pursued liberal policies under Trudeau.

Having been the dominant party for most of the period since the 1920s, the Liberals have benefited from their monopoly on patronage appointments and have built strong ties with the mushrooming mandarinate of the public service. However, somewhat ironically, the massive patronage appointments made by Trudeau as he left office raised the ire of the electorate against John Turner and the Liberal party and became a major campaign issue in 1984. There is also a negative side to the Liberal Party's strong ties to the federal bureaucracy: Liberal Party members and observers alike have deplored the extent of government de-

[25]William Christian and Colin Campbell, *Political Parties and Ideologies in Canada* (Toronto: McGraw-Hill Ryerson, 1974), p. 41.

[26]John Gray, "Who will be the Liberals' New Skipper," *The Globe and Mail*, Toronto, Jan. 6. 1982, p. 7.

[27]See Chapter 14 for a bibliography on Canadian foreign policy.

pendence on the bureaucracy and the diminishing relevance of the political party in policy-making.[28]

The CCF/NDP

The historical origins of the NDP are based in the Co-operative Commonwealth Federation (CFF), which met for its founding convention in 1933. It was an assortment of Fabian socialists, Marxists and farm and labour groups under the leadership of J.S. Woodsworth.[29] The party they formed had a predominantly Western rural backing, and in the ensuing 28 years never attracted more than 14 to 16 percent of the popular vote. When organized labour decided to openly espouse a political party the CCF was the logical choice, and in 1958 the Canadian Labour Congress (CLC) made formal overtures to the party, proposing the need for a broadly-based people's movement which would embrace the CCF, the Labour movement, farm organizations and professionals. The CCF approved of the invitation and set up a joint committee with the CLC to create a new party.

Thus in 1961, the CCF was dissolved and the New Democratic Party, with its democratic socialist platform, was born. The new party retained many of the CCF leaders, but the participation of organized labour caused difficulties, and tensions between farmers and workers often ran high.[30] The extent to which the party should be influenced by trade unions is still a divisive issue.

Internal dissension in the form of a faction called the "Waffle" group grew within the party in the late 1960s. The group argued for a stronger socialist position and greater Canadian economic independence. James Laxer, the Waffle spokesman, was a serious challenge to David Lewis at the 1971 leadership convention. However, under pressure to disband, the faction finally dissolved shortly after the convention. A few Wafflers remained in the party; others founded the Movement for an Independent Socialist Canada.[31]

Vigorous leadership by Tommy Douglas in the early years and then by David Lewis and Ed Broadbent was never enough to overcome the lack of funds and the ideological divisions which kept the New Democratic Party limited to third-party status at the federal level. In 1980 it achieved its best results to date: 32 seats in the House of Commons and 20 percent of the vote. It has never been able to expand its restricted territorial base, however.

---

[28]Joseph Wearing, *The L Shaped Party: The Liberal Party of Canada 1958-1980* (Toronto: McGraw-Hill Ryerson, 1981), p. 241. Also see John Meisel, "The Decline of Party in Canada," in Hugh Thorburn, ed., *Party Politics in Canada*, 5th ed., *op. cit.*, pp. 98-114.

[29]W.D. Young, *The Anatomy of a Party: The National CCF 1932-61* (Toronto: University of Toronto Press, 1960). See also S.M. Lipset, *Agrarian Socialism: The Cooperative Commonwealth Federation in Saskatchewan* (New York: Anchor Books, Doubleday, 1968).

[30]Gad Horowitz, *Canadian Labour in Politics* (Toronto: University of Toronto Press, 1968), pp. 143-44.

[31]See, for example, N. Penner, *The Canadian Left* (Toronto: Prentice-Hall, 1977), Ch. 7; and Robert A. Hackett, "The Waffle Conflict in the NDP," in Hugh Thorburn, ed., *Party Politics in Canada*, 4th ed. (Scarborough: Prentice-Hall, 1979), pp. 188-205.

Reproduced with permission, the Toronto Star Syndicate

There are several reasons for the failure of the NDP to become a national winner. As a left-wing party, it has had no strong position or impact on the country's major French/English cleavage. In the early years it attracted the votes of discontented Westerners, but since the 1960s the Conservatives have encroached on that base.

At the provincial level, on the other hand, the NDP has remained successful in British Columbia, Saskatchewan, Manitoba and to a lesser extent in Ontario, where it has on one occasion been the official Opposition. Following the 1985 Ontario provincial election, NDP support allowed the Liberals to oust the minority Conservative government of Frank Miller and end over four decades of Conservative rule. The NDP has used the issue of medicare, or hospital insurance, as well as foreign domination of the economy to its advantage in these provinces. Federally as well, the NDP has played a larger role in Canadian politics than its success at the polls would indicate. Its effects, for example, were very apparent during the 1972 minority government, when NDP support was vital to the Liberals.

In general, the NDP platform is based on democratic socialist goals. The NDP is the closest thing Canada has to an ideologically-based party. It advocates policies which support government regulation of the economy, including more government control of private enterprise, higher taxes for big business and industry, increased social welfare and protection from American influence.[32]

The Social Credit Party

The only other minor party of national significance in Canada also originated in the West. The Social Credit Party has always been a regional party, never more than a third party federally, and never a serious alternative to government. During the Depression and the agricultural failures of the 1930s, a charismatic

---

[32]For further reading on the NDP, see N.H. Chi and George Perlin, "The New Democratic Party: A Party in Transition," in Hugh Thorburn, 4th ed., *op. cit.,* pp. 177-187; Desmond Morton, *The Dream of Power* (Toronto: Hakkert, 1974); and Janine Brodie and Jane Jensen, *Crisis, Challenge and Change: Party and Class in Canada* (Toronto: Methuen, 1980).

preacher, William Aberhart, captured the political imagination of Albertans with the unorthodox financial theories of Major C.H. Douglas (which were often labelled "funny money"). Under Aberhart's leadership the Social Credit Party advocated the principle of monetary reform, or more explicitly, the right of the provinces to issue money and credit. In 1935 the party flooded the Alberta legislature with members and sent fifteen to Ottawa as well. The party's attempts to institute their radical financial reforms in the late 1930s in Alberta were declared unconstitutional by the Supreme Court, but Social Credit persisted as a populist conservative party.

At about the time that Social Credit appeared in Alberta, the same financial policies appealed to voters in Québec. La Ligue du Crédit Social de la Province du Québec was established, a party which changed its name to L'Union des Electeurs, and finally joined the Western Social Credit Association to become the Social Credit Association of Canada. The Québec wing was a failure and opted out of electoral politics until the fiery orator Réal Caouette revived it as Le Ralliement des Créditistes. In 1961 the Créditistes joined the national Social Credit Party, but the two groups were never fully integrated. The Ralliement was much more successful than its counterparts outside of Québec, and within a short time broke away from the more pragmatic national Party led by Robert Thompson. Thompson continually urged the Conservatives to join them in a coalition against the Liberal and NDP "socialists" until he eventually abandoned Social Credit himself and joined the Conservatives.

Since 1965, no Social Credit member has been elected to the federal Parliament from Western Canada, but the Ralliement maintained a small representation of fourteen or fifteen MPs until 1974.[33] Then, in the 1974 election, the number dropped to eleven seats. The failure to meet the required minimum twelve-seat representation in Parliament deprived them of the financial rewards of a leader's salary and a research budget, on which they relied very heavily. The party won only six seats in 1979, and none since then.

Maurice Pinard, in his extensive research on the rise of third parties in Québec, contends that the success of Social Credit in that province was due mainly to the long dominance of the Liberals provincially, combined with the extreme weakness of the Conservative Party. He hypothesizes that the single-member constituency system, coupled with various cleavages and tensions (regional, economic, ethnic, religious), results in the dominance of one of the major parties; continued tensions facilitate the rise of minor parties. Third parties, according to him, develop first outside of urban centres, because small-town and rural voters

---

[33]The best discussion of the Ralliement in Québec is in Michael Stein, *The Dynamics of Right-Wing Protest: A Political Analysis of the Social Credit in Quebec* (Toronto: University of Toronto Press, 1973). See accounts of the Social Credit Movement in Alberta in C.B. Macpherson, *Democracy in Alberta: The Theory and Practice of a Quasi-Party System* (Toronto: University of Toronto Press, 1953); J.R. Mallory, *Social Credit and the Federal Power in Canada* (Toronto: University of Toronto Press, 1954); and J.A. Irving, *The Social Credit Movement in Alberta* (Toronto, University of Toronto Press, 1959).

tend to think in terms of their district issues and campaigns rather than the national campaign.[34] The increasing role of the media in recent elections has, however, meant that national issues have been communicated far more widely than before, so this particular factor may have changed.

The Social Credit Party has had very minimal impact on the Canadian party system. Only on rare occasions during a minority government have Social Credit's few votes been important in the federal Parliament. One such occurred during the short-lived Clark government of 1979, when the five remaining Social Credit members were vital to the Conservatives because the Progressive Conservative and Social Credit votes combined equalled the Liberal and NDP votes in Parliament.

Long-term prospects for a Social Credit revival are bleak. Nevertheless, the party is still significant at the provincial level. In British Columbia it returned to government under Bill Bennett in 1975 after a short period of NDP rule. In Alberta, it remained the official Opposition party with four seats, until the 1983 election.

The Progressive Party

Of strictly historical interest is the Progressive Party, which appeared briefly on the national scene in the 1920s. It consisted of a loose coalition of provincial United Farmers, and was based largely in the western provinces of Manitoba, Saskatchewan and Alberta, and also in Ontario. The Progressive Party made a startling appearance in the 1921 election, in which it sent no less than 65 MPs to Ottawa, fifteen more than the Conservatives. However, they refused to form the official Opposition, and with no organization the party quickly disintegrated as a national movement. Four elections later, it disappeared on the federal scene; its adherents drifted into other parties. In the early 1940s, John Bracken, former Progressive Party leader from Manitoba, became the national leader of the Conservatives and, to take advantage of the potency of the Progressive label in the West, the Conservatives adopted "Progressive" as part of their party's name.

Other Minor Parties

There have been and continue to be several minor parties on the fringes of the party system in Canada which never win enough support to gain any influence or credibility. The Communist Party of Canada (CPC), formerly called the Labour Progressive Party, fields several candidates in every General Election but has

---

[34]Maurice Pinard, "One Party Dominance and the Rise of Third Parties," *CJEPS*, vol. 33, no. 3 (August 1967), pp. 358-373. See also Pinard, *The Rise of a Third Party: A Study in Crisis Politics* (Englewood Cliffs: Prentice-Hall, 1971); and "Third Parties in Canada Revisited: A Rejoinder and Elaboration of the Theory of One-Party Dominance," *CJPS*, vol. 6, no. 3 (September 1973), pp. 439-460; Graham White, "One Party Dominance and Third Parties: The Pinard Theory Reconsidered," *CJPS*, vol. 6, no. 3 (September 1973), pp. 399-421; and A. Blais, "Third Parties in Canadian Provincial Politics," *CJPS*, vol. 6, no. 3 (September 1973), pp. 422-438.

never claimed any significant electoral strength. Only once did it have a federal member elected, and he was subsequently arrested as a Russian spy.

Socialism was introduced in Canada in the late 19th and early 20th centuries, at a time when the world socialist movement was dominated by the ideas of Karl Marx. This fact was strongly reflected in Canadian socialist organizations until 1921. The Russian Revolution and Lenin's restrictive definition of Marxism split Canadian socialists into those who favoured the social democratic ideas of the British Labour Party and those who preferred the revolutionary path and close association with the Communist International. After 1921 the Communist Party of Canada (CPC) represented Marxist thought in Canada. Since Stalin's death, many small Marxist groups have flourished, but the CPC remains an important wing of the Marxist movement.

There have been many other attempts to form parties, some more serious than others, but none of any lasting significance. Paul Hellyer's Action Canada was one such effort which disintegrated shortly after it was formed. Included in the official list of parties for the 1980 election besides the two major parties, the NDP and Social Credit were the CPC, the Marxist-Leninist Party, the Libertarian Party, the Union Populaire and the frivolous Rhinoceros Party. Most of their candidates lost their deposits.

By January 1984, fifteen political parties had officially recorded their names with the Chief Electoral Officer for the next federal election.[35] Only eleven fielded the 50 candidates required to be officially recognized as a political party (nominations must be completed 30 days before polling day). Again, no candidates from the fringe parties won in the September 1984 election, but some of the parties showed small pockets of strength. The Confederation of Regions Western Party, for example, captured 8.5 percent of the popular vote in Manitoba, coming second in three ridings. This proliferation of new parties is new in Canada, and one reason for it is the rise of powerful single-interest lobbies. Some groups which support issues such as ecology or feminism are increasingly choosing not to work through the traditional parties but are turning their movements into new parties instead. Most of them do not attempt to develop policies on a cross-section of issues, but, like the Pro-Life Party of Canada, field candidates on a single issue only.

PARTY STRUCTURE AND ORGANIZATION

We have already noted that one outstanding feature of the system within which Canadian parties operate is its confederal nature. Parties at the federal and provincial levels may bear the same name but act quite independently. They share facilities and often personnel at the lower levels, but communication between federal and provincial wings of each party at the higher levels is generally weak, though this is less true of the NDP than of the two major parties. Parties may or

---

[35]*The Globe and Mail,* Toronto, Jan. 27, 1984, p. 3.

may not even exist at both federal and provincial levels in any given province.

All three federal parties have constitutions outlining their formal structures. These documents reveal little about power and influence and do not necessarily even mention all of the most important committees. All do, however, set out the general structure of the party and describe the basic functions of each part. As well, the constitutions authorize the appointment of bureaucracies and the establishment of standing committees with appointed memberships, and guarantee regional and bicultural party representation at the executive level.[36] They also indicate the basic philosophical leanings of the parties.

The New Democratic Party, for example, states its philosophy and purposes this way:

> The social, economic and political progress of Canada can be assured only
> by the application of democratic socialist principles to government and the
> administration of public affairs.

Its constitution goes on to downgrade the role of profits and encourage the use of "social ownership" when necessary.

The Progressive Conservative constitution states that "our national progress depends on a competitive economy", and stresses the freedom of the individual and the subordination of the state to the citizens. It explains the compatibility of the words "progressive" and "conservative" in the party name by stating that

> ...progress and stability can best be achieved by building on the firm
> foundations of those things proved good by experience.

The Liberal Party constitution is the least explicit in expressing a philosophy. It stresses the dignity of the individual, the need for "constant adaption to the changing needs of modern Canadian society", and the need for free access to government information:

> ...human dignity in a democratic system requires that all citizens have
> access to full information concerning the policies and leadership of the
> state.

Each of the three parties represented in Parliament consists of two wings: the parliamentary wing, comprised of the party leader and caucus; and a very large, three-tier extra-parliamentary wing. Both are dominated by the party leader, whose role and selection are discussed later in the chapter.

The basic pyramidal structure of the extra-parliamentary party, which is linked at the upper levels to the parliamentary wing, is similar for both federal and provincial parties, although here our concern is only with the federal organization. As Figure 10-1 shows, an executive body and a small permanent office stand at the apex of the federal parties; a very wide but fluid base of party voters is at the foundation. Between elections, virtually all of the structure below the

---

[36]John McMenemy, John Redekop and Conrad Winn, "Party Structures and Decision-making," in C. Winn and J. McMenemy, eds., *Political Parties in Canada* (Toronto: McGraw-Hill Ryerson, 1976), pp. 167-190.

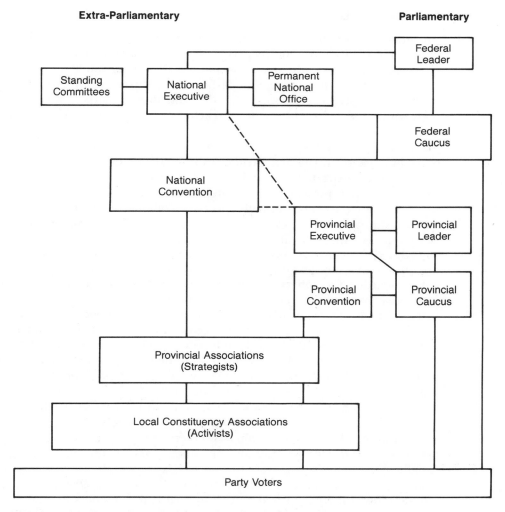

FIGURE 10.1 Canadian Political Parties: General Structure

apex dissolves, and communication with the party must be through the national organization or the parliamentary wing. This is quite different from the situation in Britain and other Western parliamentary democracies, where the extra-parliamentary party continues to function, mobilizing citizens and participating in the dialogue between citizen and state. As well, none of the Canadian parties has a permanent office or professional staff which can compare in size or sophistication with those of British parties. The major parties in Canada have had permanent offices only since the mid-1940s. Until their establishment, the entire extra-parliamentary wing of each party was virtually dormant until an election was called, when it would arise spontaneously to coordinate the campaign. The extra-parliamentary wing was therefore even more cut off from dialogue with the parliamentary wing at one time than it is today.

Constituency Level

The grassroots organization of each of the federal parties is the constituency party, which not only represents its party in the constituency, but also nominates federal candidates, recruits party workers and raises funds for constituency campaigns. The activity level and dedication of this basic unit are vital to party fortunes, but despite its importance the constituency party is a relatively weak body within the party. The quality and activity of local organizations varies greatly. Most Progressive Conservative constituency associations in Québec, for example, have been only "paper organizations" in French-speaking areas. Instead, the party has relied on regional structures embracing several constituencies. One can, however, expect this situation to change following the dramatic Conservative win in that province in the 1984 General Election.

The national office normally sets out a code of procedures governing party membership and the selection of delegates, but formal decisions fall under the jurisdiction of the provincal party organizations.[37] Therefore, the rules about who can vote in the meetings held in each riding to elect delegates vary from province to province and often within provinces. Neither of the two major parties has standardized membership qualifications or dues, although on their own initiative many associations do charge a small fee. Constituency organizations in the two major parties issue membership cards easily – indeed, on rare occasions, they have been known to sign up children and derelicts when the need for votes was pressing! The NDP is slightly different, as one would expect of a mass party. It has dues; it also prohibits members from belonging to another party and requires them to pledge support to the constitution and principles of the NDP. An individual who joins the provincial wing of the NDP automatically becomes a member of both the federal and provincial constituency organizations. Fees are shared by the constituency, provincial and federal levels of the party.

In spite of large membership bases there are generally very few active members in each of the parties, and the constituency associations meet infrequently – usually only when it is necessary to elect the executive, choose delegates for conventions or prepare for an imminent General Election. In 1984, for example, the federal Liberal Party launched a drive to double its membership in the province of Québec before the next election; it was the first drive of its kind in a decade in that province and required considerable constituency activity.[38] One reason for the usual lassitude between elections is that parties do not normally contest municipal elections, and cannot draw on the forum of local government for support. As well, there is little congruence between provincial and federal party constitu-

---

[37]Recruitment drives are often innovative. In 1982 the Liberal Party headquarters prepared a controversial guide for local associations on how to recruit new members. The manual urged party associations to sponsor Canadian citizenship classes, preparing flyers in different languages and inviting immigrants to speak with a citizenship judge. This procedure would, it noted, encourage Canadian citizenship and bring "potential members of the Liberal Party into contact with established associations". *The Globe and Mail,* Toronto, Dec. 15, 1982.

[38]*The Globe and Mail,* Toronto, Feb. 7, 1984.

ency boundaries, so there is little reinforcement at that level either, although the same party workers are often active at both levels. Another factor which hampers party activity at a local level is that constituency units are often very large and their members widely scattered. If the party is weak electorally in a particular constituency, funds are inevitably scarce, and it becomes difficult to hold activities and attract new members. Finally, constituency associations are sometimes inadequately represented at party conventions because they cannot afford to cover delegates' expenses.

Provincial Level

At the intermediate level of the extra-parliamentary party pyramid is the provincial organization of each federal party. Individuals at this level coordinate and plan strategy and activities for implementation at the constituency level. The provincial executive has the ultimate responsibility for all federal constituencies in the province. In some provinces there are regional organizations within the provincial structures. The Liberal Party, for example, has a "Toronto and District" regional organization in Ontario. These associations remain under the control of the provincial associations.

The unique feature of the federal parties' provincial level organization is that it is generally shared with provincial party counterparts, although the relationship varies from party to party and province to province. As we have seen, provincial parties in Canada are very independent, and generally like to keep their distance from their federal partners particularly when those partners are in power in Ottawa. This is especially true in Ontario, Québec and Alberta, where the federal Liberals maintain their own party organizations separate from the provincial party and concern themselves with federal political activity only.[39] In Québec, where there has been no provincial Progressive Conservative Party from the mid-1930s to 1984 (no candidates and no provincial leader) the federal Conservative Party has relied on informal association with the provincial Union Nationale Party to assist it at general election time.

National Level: Conventions

At the upper level of the extra-parliamentary party pyramid is the national organization of each party which unites the individual provincial associations. About every two years, the national association holds a convention in order to elect party officials and debate policy resolutions. These resolutions have no formal authority and are not binding on the party. However, the debates do give delegates the opportunity to air their views and communicate their policy concerns to the political wing; further, they allow the party to benefit from free media publicity. Party leaders are elected during conventions; these occasions are important in marshalling enthusiasm to help heal a divided party, particularly following a diffi-

---

[39]Wearing, *op. cit.*, p. 138.

cult leadership contest. Conventions also have an important centralizing influence on the Canadian political system.

Party conventions are large, widely representative gatherings of several thousand delegates who are, for the most part, elected at local public meetings in the various constituencies. On occasion, they have been appointed by the local executive or chosen by the MP concerned, but keen competition for delegate votes has made these options rather rare for recent conventions. Most constituency meetings are composed of the local party faithful, and the average delegate is someone who has already invested considerable time and energy for the party as an executive officer or active member of women's or youth's associations.

In both major parties, Senators, MPs and defeated candidates attend party conventions. As well, there are a number of delegates-at-large from the provinces, including those from women's and young people's organizations, and people who are prominent in party affairs but are not eligible to become delegates in one of the other categories. Both the Liberals and Conservatives have always allowed a number of appointed delegates-at-large and appointed committee members to attend their National Conventions, often in the face of vociferous objections that it was elitist and undemocratic to allow a small committee to name delegates. It is worth noting that the voting strength of the constituency delegates in both cases (though less so for the Liberal Party) is affected indirectly by the relative strength of the parties provincially and nationally at the time of the convention. The Conservatives send all of their provincial legislators, while the Liberal delegation includes only one-fourth of the party's provincial legislators and defeated candidates.

As a mass party, the NDP places great emphasis on the importance of the individual member; not suprisingly, it has the longest history of regular meetings. The NDP's National Conventions include broad representation from Parliament, constituencies, youth groups and affiliated organizations such as trade unions and farm groups. Unlike in the other two parties, the number of delegates who attend from any particular constituency is based on how many members it has. This rewards active associations but does not help make inroads into areas where the party is weak. Compared to the major parties, there are very few delegates who attend purely by virtue of their position. Table 10-4 presents a more detailed comparison of the representatives at national party conventions.

Party conventions are clearly not designed to be representative of Canadian society, but of the party in society. They are normally more inclusive of the various age, sex, occupational and religious groups than are the party caucuses, but, as John Courtney indicates, there are glaring deficiencies in comparison to the total population.[40] Delegates are much better educated and are economically better off than the total population; they are typically active in various local and national organizations, especially political groups. In no sense are they instructed

---

[40]John Courtney, *The Selection of National Party Leaders in Canada* (Toronto: Macmillan, 1973), p. 106. Also see J. Lele, G.C. Perlin and H.G. Thorburn, "The National Party Convention," in H.G. Thorburn 5th ed., *op. cit.*, pp. 89-97. For more detail on the attendance at party conventions, see John Courtney, "Leadership Conventions and the Development of the National Political Community in Canada," paper presented at CPSA meeting, June, 1983.

TABLE 10.4 Comparison of Convention Attendance Rules, 1983

LIB	PC	NDP	Position
7	6	v	Delegates per constituency
7	6	–	Alternates
–	3	–	Delegates per post-secondary club
–	3	–	Alternates per post-secondary club
L	P	–	Delegates-at-large
–	v	–	Other party organizations
4 per	–	–	Executive members of each provincial party association
2 per	–	–	At-large from each womens' club (federal and provincial)
–	–	32	Council members not listed elsewhere
–	–	v	Associate members
–	–	v	Other youth delegates
v	v	–	Privy Councillors
v	v	–	Senators (Lib.: incl. retired senators)
v	v	v	Members of Parliament
v	v	–	Official candidates
12	12	12	Leaders of the provincial/territorial parties
*	all	–	Provincial/territorial elected members of the party
*	–	–	Defeated candidates in provincial/territorial elections
–	v	–	Past federal Leaders
1	v	2	Past-Presidents (and Association)
–	5	2	Honorary Officers
12	12	12	Presidents of each provincial/territorial Association
12	12	–	Presidents of each provincial/territorial Womens' Association
12	12	–	Presidents of each provincial/territorial Youth Association
1	1	1	Leader
1	1	2	President (and Association)
4	5	8	National Vice-Presidents
1	1	2	Secretary (and Association)
1	1	1	Treasurer
–	2	1	National Director (and Association)
6	10	–	National Womens' President and officers
6	10	–	National Youth President and officers
10	3	–	Committee Chairman
–	22	24	Provincial Secretary/Treasurer/Directors
–	12	36	Provincial representatives on the National Executive/Council
v	40	–	Standing Committee members
–	15	–	Provincial/territorial fund-raising chairmen

v – numbers may vary
* – defeated or elected members equalling up to one-quarter of total number of seats
L – Lib: youth equalling 10 percent of constituency delegates per province
P – PC: delegates equalling one-half the number of ridings, with a minimum of 5 per province (and 2 for each of the Yukon and the NWT), 20 percent of whom must be youth, and 50 percent female.
(*Note:* Numbers given are maximum figures.)
Adapted from an unpublished paper by Tema Frank, "Political Party Constitutions: A Comparison", Ottawa, 1983, prepared for the Parliamentary Internship Programme.

by their constituency association to support a particular resolution or candidate – and since voting is by secret ballot, such instruction would be useless anyway.

Conventions cannot, therefore, be defended as representative in any strict sense. Terms such as "democratic" and "representative" are merely part of the rhetoric used by parties and commentators to generate respect and approval for party conventions. Still, there is much in favour of the wider participation that conventions afford over the former method of basing party decisions entirely on "informal soundings".

National Level: Executives

The national executive appears in a different form in each of the parties, but it consists basically of a small group of executives who conduct party business on behalf of the mass party. The Liberals have a relatively simple structure, with one National Executive Committee which has 44 members including the party leader, the president and other elected party officers. They meet at least four times a year. The Liberal Party also has six standing committees which do specialized work on Finance, Policy, Organization, Communications, the Constitution and Legal Affairs and Native and Original Peoples' Affairs. All standing committees report to the National Executive, which has the authority to establish further *ad hoc* committees as needed.

The Progressive Conservative Party has a more elaborate three-tiered executive consisting of the National Executive, Steering Committee and Executive Committee. The National Executive is large, and meets infrequently. More functional are the two smaller committees branching from it. The Executive Committee meets at least twice a year; the even smaller Steering Committee is the most active. The Steering Committee is the only executive body at the national level which does not include specifically designated representatives from the provincial parties. The Conservative committees comparable to the Liberal standing committees are the Policy Advisory Council, the PC Canada Fund and the National Campaign Committee.

The NDP equivalent of the National Executive is the Federal Council. It is a large body which includes representatives of provincial parties and meets at least twice a year. The NDP elects party officers in convention and they, as well as others chosen by and from the Federal Council, comprise a smaller group of Executive Members who meet frequently. The only two committees enshrined in the constitution of the party are those for the Participation of Women and Constitutional Affairs.

National Offices

As we have already noted, each party also maintains a small permanent office or headquarters at the national level. This body contains a handful of bureaucrats and staff who are responsible to the executives from the extra-parliamentary organization and also to the party leader. The National Office of each major party is headed by a National Director, or, in the case of the NDP, a Federal Secretary.

It functions as the link between the provincial organizations and the elected Members of Parliament; it is a clearing house for intra-party communications. Despite its permanent position at the top of the extra-parliamentary party, this body has few real levers of power and is engaged mainly in service and coordinating functions: it organizes conventions, helps conduct federal by-elections, and helps prepare for General Elections. As Wearing commented about the Liberal National Office, the duties of a National Office are

> chiefly those of keeping the party alive between elections ... The leader
> tends to see it as being less responsive to his own needs than his personal
> staff on Parliament Hill; the fund raisers see it as a drain on elections
> funds; the parliamentary caucus want to use it as an MPs' re-election office;
> and the provincial organizations see it as yet another manifestation of
> distant, insensitive Ottawa.[41]

The National Office of the Liberal Federation was expanded to about 21 permanent employees in the late 1960s to enable it to provide more service to the parliamentary wing of the party. It has a number of divisions engaged in programs and public relations, the largest being Communications, which is the headquarters of a speakers' bureau, information officers and the editor of the national Liberal Party magazine. The luxury of power has allowed a modest central office; the governing Liberals were able to rely on a wide variety of resources including the Prime Minister's Office, political aides, Senate and party committees, and did not need a large central office. Members of the Liberal Youth Association complained vehemently, particularly at the 1983 convention, about this effective gutting of the National Office. Trudeau's reliance on his own chosen advisors including Senator Davey and Jim Coutts rather than party workers in the National Office caused much bitterness in the party. It also left Trudeau's successor, John Turner, with a less effective National Office to handle his election campaign.

The Conservative National Office has a considerably larger permanent staff of about 72 (in 1984), and is supplemented by temporary help as needed. It too has several divisions, including a huge printing and distributing centre. In both offices volunteer help is very significant in pre-election periods. The NDP maintains the most modest permanent federal headquarters, with only six professionals and ten support staff in 1984.

Women and Youth

Women were relative late-comers to Canadian politics. They did not have the right to vote federally until 1917 (much later in some provincial elections), nor did they have a representative of their own sex in the federal Parliament until 1921. Until the 1950s political parties were male preserves. Women, and also youth, were gradually acknowledged and accepted, but certainly not as full partners. In the Liberal Party, for example, young people were hived off into affiliated organizations, the Young Liberal Federation and the Canadian University Liberal

---

[41]Wearing, *op. cit.*, p. 214.

Richard Row Illustration, Toronto.

Federation.[42] Women, who even then did much of the background work licking stamps and providing tea in the ridings, were diverted to the Women's Liberal Federation (WLF). Both groups were effectively barred from any significant part in the National Federation. As the novelty of such low-grade participation gradually wore off, the demand grew for women and youth to be integrated into the main organizations. By the 1960s, the old organizations were faltering for lack of participants; fewer than one-third of the ridings had youth organizations left. Finally, in 1973, the affiliated organizations were replaced by two new ones, the Liberal Commission (for women) and the National Youth Commission. These are no longer separate, affiliated units, but elect their own executives and "are responsible to caucuses of women or youth delegates respectively at national meet-

---

[42]Reginald Whitaker, *The Government Party: Organizing and Financing the Liberal Party of Canada, 1930-1958* (Toronto: University of Toronto Press, 1977), pp. 78-79 and 194-195.

ings".[43] They are intended to represent and promote the interests of students, youth and women in the party and encourage their participation and party activities.

In time, special organizations which are designed to encourage women to participate in the parties may be abandoned because their participation can be taken for granted. In the meantime, however, to ensure female participation, both the PC and Liberal constitutions guarantee officials of the women's groups positions on the party executive committees, and specify that a certain number of voting delegates at the conventions must be female. The PCs require that at least one of six constituency delegates and one-half of the delegates-at-large from the provinces be female. One of the two directors representing each province on the National Executive must also be a woman. The Liberals require that two of seven constituency delegates, and two of the four national Vice Presidents, be women. The NPD constitution has guaranteed least with respect to female participation, on the general understanding that there is no need for such measures. The NDP was the first party to address such issues as daycare and pensions for widows. By 1981, however, the party had an internal affirmative action program, and two years later approved a requirement for equal representation of men and women on its executive and council.

Partly because of these guaranteed positions, women have achieved higher visibility within all three party organizations in recent years. For the first time in Canadian history a woman, Iona Campagnolo, was elected Liberal Party President in 1983, and there was a strong movement within the party encouraging her to run as a leadership candidate the following year. Two of the major contenders for the Conservative Party presidency in 1983 were women. Another high-profile woman, Lorna Marsden, Liberal Vice President and long-time party worker, was rewarded with a Senate appointment in 1984.

This trend to more active female participation and leadership in parties reflects prevalent changes in the role of women in society. Females constitute 52 percent of the Canadian population, but are a relatively disadvantaged group in Canadian society. Their average pay is about three-fifths that of men, and a majority of those living below the official poverty line are women – particularly single mothers and seniors. Women's groups are becoming increasingly vocal and forceful in ensuring that these items appear on the political agenda. Issues of special concern to women, including pensions for homemakers, daycare, affirmative action and eliminating pay differentials between men and women, are rapidly moving up the scale of political priorities. They were major issues in the 1984 election campaign, and for the first time there was a major debate, sponsored by the National Action Committee on the Status of Women (NACSW), between the three party leaders specifically on so-called "women's issues" to clarify the party positions. It is important to note that women are not strongly aligned with any particular party as they often are in the United States.

---

[43]Wearing, *op. cit.*, p. 218.

Despite such measures to encourage female participation, women continue to be poorly represented in the parliamentary wings of all three parties. The record is dismal. Between 1917 and 1970 less than 11 percent of all elected members of the federal and provincial legislatures were women.[44] In 1980, only fifteen females, or 5 percent of the federal representatives elected that year were women; that number increased to 27 women, or nearly 10 percent in 1984. More women are competing for office in Canada than ever before (65 ran in 1980, 131 in 1984) but the proportion of women in the legislature remains lower than in most liberal democracies.[45] Since about 1979 there has been a greater willingness on the part of the three major parties to accept and even search for and assist women as candidates, but they still run primarily in "lost cause" ridings where party popularity is lowest. Few retiring members are succeeded by female candidates, although the Québec Liberals have, in recent years, nominated several women to run in safe federal seats in that province.[46] Most women candidates continue to be merely standard-bearers nominated to fly the party colours in hopeless races. Women frequently run as independents for fringe parties (as many as 106 of the 195 female candidates in 1979). Yet in terms of social characteristics, female candidates are generally similar to their male counterparts – married, middle-aged, well-educated professionals.

One can only speculate on the reasons for this dismal but improving record. The role of women in society generally has changed rapidly over the past two decades. The traditional family structure is changing, with more women working outside of the home. Women are also increasingly represented in universities and professional schools. Society's views about the acceptability and ability of women to seek roles of active political leadership are more positive, while the socialization of girls into passive roles is widely criticized and diminishing.

Youth, too, have a fairly prominent role in all three parties, but the attempt to recruit active young members has its problems. It has sometimes been argued, for example, that youth are being guaranteed more voting delegates than would seem reasonable based on their membership numbers, or that they can vote for the party leader even though they may be too young to vote in a federal election. None of the party constitutions establishes a minimum age for young members, though the Liberals have 25 as a maximum, and the PCs 29. The Liberal and Conservative parties both have elaborate structures guaranteeing youth representation at conventions at the constituency association level, among the provincial delegates-at-large and from recognized student clubs. There were, for

---

[44]M. Janine Brodie and Jill Vickers, "The More Things Change – Women in the 1979 Federal Campaign," in Howard R. Penniman, ed., *Canada at the Polls, 1979 and 1980* (Washington D.C.: American Enterprise Institute, 1981), p. 323.

[45]Jill McCalla Vickers and June Adam, *But Can You Type?* (Toronto: Clarke, Irwin and Co., 1977), p. 90.

[46]*Ibid.*, p. 326. Also see Jill McCalla Vickers, "Where are the Women in Canadian Politics?" *Atlantis,* vol. 3 (Spring 1978), pp. 40-51.

example, significantly more youth delegates at the 1984 Liberal Leadership Convention than in 1968, and their concerns influenced the issues debated at that time: youth unemployment, education and party reform.

PARTY FINANCE

Political parties require funds for three basic purposes. The first and most widely recognized is that they must support expensive election campaigns. Second, they must maintain a small permanent staff between elections. Third, they need money to support research and advisory services for the party leader and elected representatives.

Where do these funds come from, and who collects them? In the early years of two-party politics in Canada, both major parties were financed largely from the same corporate contributors. Provincial and federal parties received allotments from central party funds; this highly centralized organization of party finance had an integrative effect which helped counter the centrifugal forces of the federal system. Party leaders played a key role in collecting and distributing campaign funds because there was no special fund-raising structure or permanent party organization.

With the advent of third parties and the increased economic and political strength of the provinces *vis-à-vis* the federal government, the centralized nature of party financing began to change. After the Second World War the concentration on resource and extractive industries, which are under provincial jurisdiction, increased provincial wealth. Large corporations began to seek direct access to provincial governments and to make party contributions directly at the provincial as well as the federal level. Provincial parties in Western and Central Canada in particular were adept at gathering funds. As the provincial governments and provincial parties increased their wealth and power, they were able to compete more and more successfully with their federal counterparts. Gradually, party financing became decentralized; today, it retains little of its traditional role of supporting Canadian federalism.

The *Election Expenses Act* which came into effect in 1974 had a profound effect on the fund-raising patterns of all Canada's parties.[47] The new law was intended to bring party financing into the open and at the same time cap election spending. Until that time, parties were reluctant to admit the extent of their financial dependence on specific sources. There was always a suspicion that those who contributed might have undue influence on the selection of leaders or the determination of party policies. The motivation of donors was suspect even though their reason for contributing might have been as innocent as a desire to do their civic duty.

---

[47]See F. Leslie Seidle and Khayyam Zev Paltiel, "Party Finance, the Election Expenses Act, and Campaign Spending in 1979 and 1980," in Howard Penniman, *op. cit.,* pp. 226-279.

There were two early political scandals in Canada resulting from parties accepting money from "unsavoury" sources: the Pacific Scandal of the 1870s in the Conservative party, and the Beauharnois affair of the 1930s in the Liberal party. The 1960s brought more scandals, particularly the Rivard affair, in which a narcotics smuggler, Lucien Rivard, was linked to the Liberal "old guard" in Québec. These publicized events increased the pressure for full disclosure of sources and amounts of party funds so that parties would be free of the danger of hidden manipulation by contributors. It was hoped that the *Election Expenses Act* would prevent further financial scandals. The resultant changes in campaign spending practices and reimbursements to the parties from public funds are discussed in the following chapter; here we are concerned primarily with party fund-raising.

Since the passage of the *Election Expenses Act*, contributors are named publicly if they donate more than $100 to a party, and those making contributions up to $500 may claim a tax deduction. Each national party must now file a detailed expenditure and revenue report within six months of the end of its fiscal year. It also must submit to the Department of National Revenue an annual report of contributions received and income tax receipts issued. Before 1974, businesses often donated 60 percent of their total political contribution to the party in office and the balance to the official Opposition, a decision which favoured the Liberal Party because of its dominant position. The belief behind the 1974 legislation was that it would encourage corporations to contribute relatively equal amounts to the major parties, both of which relied heavily on corporate contributions. Since disclosure has been made mandatory, equal contributions have been the general rule; only a few private companies, such as Eaton's, which has supported the Conservative party exclusively since 1975, do not feel obliged to provide equal treatment.[48] A few donors, particularly multinational corporations, stopped contributing once their actions were made public. Corporate donations are illegal in the United States, and since the Watergate investigations in that country many multinationals stopped making political contributions anywhere. IBM is an example of one large multinational corporation which ceased donating in Canada.

The Liberal and Conservative parties have traditionally been financed by businessmen, trade associations and, most importantly, by the corporate financial structures of Toronto and Montréal. Only a few donors and collectors, or "bagmen" as they are known, used to be involved. K.Z. Paltiel estimated in 1970 that "the collectors and contributors together number no more than several hundred."[49] Two years after the new regulations were introduced, Prime Minister Trudeau expressed concern that the large sources of funds were "drying up", and said that the major parties needed to broaden their bases of financial support. He complained to a meeting of Liberals in Ontario that the party was not well organized: "Your fund-raising efforts in Ontario since the new *Election Expenses Act* are pitiful, and they are even worse in almost every province with a cou-

---

[48]Wearing, *op. cit.,* p. 232.

[49]Khayyam Z. Paltiel, *Political Party Financing in Canada* (Toronto: McGraw-Hill, 1970), p. 14.

ple of exceptions." Whether as a result of his chastisement or of the longer-term effects of the new *Act*, the party's fund-raising base broadened considerably, although a discussion paper issued by the party reform commission in 1984 claimed that the Liberals have the "most anemic" fund-raising effort of all three major parties.[50] Certainly the almost seven million dollars in donations received by the Liberals in 1983 amounted to only about half that of the Conservative total and even one million less than the NDP collected. Most, as usual, was collected by party bagmen who approached individuals and corporations for funds. Individual donors in the $100 to $1000 range have become the most important source of funds for the Liberal party. The NDP was less affected by the new legislation because it had always relied to a considerable extent on smaller donations from many sources. It continues to collect substantial amounts from membership fees and individual donations as well as affiliation fees from some large trade unions.

The 1974 *Election Expenses Act* also altered the internal financial situation in the two major parties. Since the provincial and constituency organizations are able to raise more money than ever before from small donations, they have become far more independent of central authorities. For example, the Liberal Treasury Committee, which is appointed by the party leader, used to control the bulk of the funds for election campaigns, a decidedly non-democratic procedure. Now it collects only the large donations from corporations, and since these have decreased in importance it has lost some of its pivotal role in the campaign funding operation. It still retains final financial authority in approving the annual party budget, but that power too is under review. By 1983, when Iona Campagnolo became party President, the Liberal National Office was deeply in debt because it received no donations of its own and the National Executive had no control over party finances. Campagnolo's first tasks were to devise a system which would give headquarters an automatic share of all donations to the party and to establish the right of the party's elected executive to decide how the party's funds would be shared.[51] The Conservative and NDP National Offices both receive part of the funds raised locally (outside of election periods), so their immediate problems are not so severe. From the party executive's view, however, powerful riding associations could turn into political Frankenstein monsters. As one Conservative put it: "Individual candidates will need the party less and less. The local guys don't need the national headquarters . . . In fact they are far more solvent than headquarters."[52]

PARTY PROGRAM FORMULATION

In discussing the roles of political parties, we pointed out that their main function is to aggregate or sift various interests in society. Somehow, parties must rank and articulate claims of interest in the competition for votes and decide

---

[50]*The Globe and Mail,* Toronto, Feb. 4, 1984, p. 2.

[51]Those reforms were underway at the time of publication. *The Globe and Mail,* Toronto, March 28, 1984.

[52]*Ibid.,* Nov. 29, 1980.

which to present to the electorate as their party platform. Party election platforms have contributions from both intra- and extra-parliamentary branches of the parties; they are generally what R.M. Dawson called "conspicuously unsatisfactory documents".[53] Of necessity, items must be vague enough to carry wide appeal – examples are "social reform" or "improved education" – and so end up reading rather like a list of New Year's resolutions. And because Canadian parties must obtain substantial support from at least two of the five regions – Atlantic, Québec, Ontario, Prairies, British Columbia – in order to win, the platforms also appeal to sectional interests such as fisheries and maritime rights or wheat exports. Party platforms are therefore deliberately vague, broadly appealing documents of compromise that will unite their parties nationally. Between the three major parties there is often a degree of policy overlap as they vie for the middle ground.

At the national level, the extra-governmental party structure takes part in drafting policy resolutions at national conventions. As has been noted, these meetings are currently held at least every two years by all three parties. One of the main preoccupations at these gatherings is revising the party platform. The trend in recent years has been to keep leadership and policy conventions separate because of their complexity. Before a policy convention assembles, party associations are invited to send in suggestions to a resolutions committee which sorts and prepares them for consideration by the convention. The resolutions presented to the delegates are, theoretically, debated and passed item by item. However, because of the difficulty of effectively debating long, comprehensive resolutions in the limited time available, the resolutions committee often, in fact, determines the success of resolutions.

Even after the platform is drawn up and approved by the national convention, it is little more than a guide, or, as Mackenzie King was fond of stating, a chart and compass for the party leader to interpret and follow as he deems opportune when steering the ship of state. The party constitutions give no official status to policy resolutions emanating from the National Associations; this situation has been reinforced by successive party leaders. In the 1957 election John Diefenbaker often disregarded party decisions and relied heavily on personal advisors in his election campaign. Lester Pearson, in response to a resolution passed by the Liberal Policy Conference of October 1966 on bilingualism in the federal civil service, stated in the House that

> resolutions themselves do not establish policy, and in respect of the
> resolution on bilingualism, which we undoubtedly will consider, I would
> like to point out that the policy of the government in that matter was laid
> down in the House on April 6.[54]

---

[53]R.M. Dawson, *The Government of Canada*, 5th ed. revised by N. Ward (Toronto: University of Toronto Press, 1970), p. 504.

[54]*Debates of the House of Commons*, Oct. 14, 1966, p. 8656.

In 1971, the Trudeau Cabinet refused to grant the party policy group any role in determining the 1972 election platform. Predictably, party activists were appalled by their lack of influence. A typical reaction was "I don't think the Parliamentary Wing of the Government gives a damn about the party or what it thinks."[55] The low party morale may have been a factor in the Liberal government's electoral setback to minority status in 1972.

The issue of extra-parliamentary involvement with policy decisions has been a contentious one for several decades. Until the late 1950s, party memberships were generally docile, content to provide services at election time. However, by the 1960s both major party federations were demanding to be involved in party affairs on a continuing basis. We have already noted several concrete steps that were taken to make the parties more democratic. Full-time national directors were hired, and National Offices were established to operate between elections. Conventions gradually became more regular, and measures were taken to bring women and youth into the main body of the parties. The philosophical justification for conventions continues to be that their decisions are representative of the party, and consequently are more democratic than those reached by the parliamentary caucus.

One innovation whose intent was to allow wider policy input was the "Thinkers Conference". These meetings were attended by MPs, MLAs, academics and other invitees who wished to contribute to policy initiatives. The Liberals held their first one in 1933, but the most notable were held in 1960 by the Liberals at Kingston and the Conservatives at Montmorency Falls in 1967. Both these conferences made recognized contributions to party policy, and were followed by others. A Liberal meeting at the elegant mountain resort of Harrison Hot Springs in British Columbia in 1969 was to be the first phase in a more ambitious operation intended to stimulate floods of public participation, but the public showed little interest in the follow-up meetings. When the steam went out of that particular participatory experiment, the Thinkers Conference became unfashionable and has not been revived on the same scale.

During that same period, the Liberals made other structural changes geared to improve communications between the leader, caucus and federation, particularly to allow wider consultation about policy and patronage decisions. In late 1968 an Advisory Group or Troika was instituted for every province. Each consisted of a representative from the Cabinet, caucus and provincial party organization. The task of these Groups was to facilitate coordination and communications between the three bodies represented in them.[56] In practice, the Advisory Groups found their formal consultative role in the constituencies cumbersome and time-consuming. They were extremely varied in quality, and no longer exist as formal structures, but operate on an informal basis.

---

[55]Stephen Clarkson, *Feedback from Active Liberals: Survey of 1,000 Most Prominent Members of the Liberal Party in Ontario* (Toronto: Liberal Party in Ontario, July 1973), p. 29.

[56]Wearing, *op. cit.*, p. 149.

In the same vein, the Liberal National Policy Convention in 1970 established a Consultative Council which was to provide continuity of policy and issue discussions between conventions and keep the National Executive in touch with constituency views. At the 1980 National Convention the Council was dissolved and brought under the umbrella of the Standing Committee on Policy. A steering committee of the Policy Committee now consults regularly by mail with the whole committee.

In 1966 the Liberal Party added a new clause to its constitution requiring the leader to report to future policy conventions upon "the consideration given, the decisions made and the reasoning therefore regarding resolutions passed at the previous Convention". This has become known as an "accountability session" at which, theoretically at least, the leader is peppered with difficult questions about the conduct and policies of the parliamentary wing for which the leader is responsible. In fact, the sessions usually produce little serious dialogue and more accolades than criticisms.

Despite such attempts to keep the parliamentary party in touch with the grass roots of the party and allow wider participation in policy discussions, the locus of party power remains in the leader and a small group of his chosen associates. Liberal activists in 1984 expressed the same frustration as their predecessors two decades earlier when, fearful of the consequences of a long period of miserable showings in opinion polls, they complained that the Liberal Party had become a closed elitist organization which was out of touch with ordinary Canadians.

The extra-parliamentary wings of the major parties have slowly strengthened their hand, but the leader and parliamentary caucus remain by far the dominant partners. The extra-parliamentary wing still largely evaporates between elections; only an elite executive group (which has a symbolic share in party decisions) remains, and it is dominated by the party leader. All party appointments are made by the leader or on his approval. The National Director, for example, is the principal administrative officer, appointed by the steering committee of the National Association – on the recommendation of the leader. The party President, who is elected by convention delegates, occupies another key position of the extra-parliamentary wing. But neither of the two major parties restricts MPs from occupying that position. In 1983 the PCs elected Peter Elzinga, MP for Pembina, as the President. In the same year, Iona Campagnolo, a former MP and Cabinet Minister, was elected Liberal President; the result is that both parties had individuals with strong ties to the parliamentary party as head of the extra-parliamentary party.

Another factor which increases the dominance of the parliamentary party is that, particularly when in government, it has a large support staff which it prefers to consult over the National Party Office. As described in earlier chapters, the Prime Minister's Office, the Privy Council Office, the Ministers' Exempt Staffs and the Parliamentary Research Office all have specialized personnel at the disposal of the parliamentary party and cabinet.

In many ways, the NDP is the most democratic, as would be expected of a mass party. Party members are asked to make a commitment both through standardized membership dues and a pledge to support the party. As well, the NDP does not allow MPs to head the extra-parliamentary party as either President or Associate President. It has the longest history of regular conventions, and unlike the major parties does not have lists of delegates appointed by the party elite. NDP policy conventions are also the most serious and binding on the leadership, a situation which may well change if the party ever comes to power.

PARTY LEADERSHIP

The Role of the Leader in the Party

The party leader has a pre-eminent role as figurehead and spokesperson of both the parliamentary and extra-parliamentary branches of a party. The image a leader projects is extremely important because it provides a simple, personal differentiating feature between the parties, which otherwise often appear very similar to the electorate. A leader with a poor image can ruin the electoral chances of even the most vital party; this fact encourages enormous preoccupation with image building and the appearance and personality of the leader, to the detriment of policy issues. The leadership position is a prestigious one carrying considerable powers in the parliamentary system. National party leaders are symbols of unity, figures above sectional interests.

Much of the prestige of the official Leader of the Opposition lies in the fact that he or she is a potential Prime Minister, and could inherit the superior status and authority of that coveted position. The Prime Minister's position at the apex of government and the civil service was discussed in Chapter 7. Here it is sufficient to note that the office includes a large support staff and many other perquisites.

The Prime Minister's political patronage powers are second to none. As top member of the government hierarchy he has Cabinet, government bureaucracy and Senate positions to fill, as well as party appointments. During his leadership campaign Brian Mulroney dangled the prospect of patronage, should he become Prime Minister, in front of hungry Conservative audiences. "You dance with the lady what brung you," he announced repeatedly, claiming that the fact that one is of Conservative persuasion should not, and would not, be a deterrent from getting a government appointment.[57] Soon after Mulroney won the leadership, his team established a committee headed by Finlay MacDonald, former aide to Joe Clark, to plan appointments for the day the Conservatives would take office. The committee discovered about 3300 Liberal appointees on federal boards, commissions and Crown corporations, some appointed "at pleasure" – meaning that their appointment could be revoked at any time – and others for fixed periods of time. "If we're in office long enough every one of these will come up for reappointment and we'd change every one of them," claimed one Conservative MP.[58]

---

[57]Martin, Gregg and Perlin, *op. cit.*, Ch. 3.

[58]*The Globe and Mail*, Toronto, Feb. 3, 1984, p. 4.

This attitude did not, of course, prevent scandalized outcries from Tories and the public when retiring Prime Minister Trudeau left massive patronage appointments for his successor to implement in 1984.

We have already noted the extensive authority the leader has over the extra-parliamentary wing of his party, including the power to approve or disapprove the budget for the activities of the party organization and therefore to control the allocation of resources within the party. Another power arises from the right not only to make key appointments on the national executive, but also to create *ad hoc* committees whose authority may supersede that of the officers elected by the National Association. For example, the leader determines the appointments to the election campaign committee. Within the parliamentary party the Opposition leader appoints a "shadow cabinet", and in many ways enjoys more flexibility than the Prime Minister does in choosing his Cabinet.

The Leader of the Official Opposition has special status at official functions and in parliamentary ceremonies and even an international standing with foreign governments, but this position is nevertheless inferior compared to that of the Prime Minister.[59] Though his or her functions are not governed by statute, the role is officially recognized in the procedures of the House of Commons. Canada first officially recognized the existence of the Leader of the Opposition in 1905 by granting the occupant of that position a salary equal to that of a Cabinet minister. Surprisingly, Canada was well ahead of Britain in doing so, for it was not until 1937 that the British Parliament officially recognized their Opposition leader along with their Prime Minister.[60]

While the Prime Minister enjoys the many perquisites of government and 24 Sussex Drive, the Opposition leader receives, in addition to his salary and expense allowance as a Member of Parliament, a sum as Opposition leader, a car allowance and an official residence – Stornoway in Rockcliffe Park. As for facilities on Parliament Hill, the Opposition leader is provided with a set of offices in the Centre Block of the House of Commons identical to that allocated to the Prime Minister. In addition, he is entitled to a suite of offices as a Member of Parliament and to a constituency office with a full-time staff of three in Ottawa and one in his riding.[61]

One aspect of the party over which the leader does not have exclusive control is party nominations. This area is a carefully guarded prerogative of the riding associations. The only formal nomination requirement is the procedural one that the candidate must be chosen according to the rules of the party constitution. A leader obviously does have some influence in nominations, however. At a by-election in Toronto's Broadview-Greenwood riding in 1982, party leader Joe Clark influenced the local riding association to nominate an ethnic candidate rather than a popular journalist, Peter Worthington. As it turned out, Worthing-

---

[59]R.M. Punnett, *Front-Bench Opposition* (London: Heinemann, 1973), p. 99.

[60]Ghita Ionescu and Isabel de Madariaga, *Opposition: Past and Present of a Political Institution* (London: C.A. Watts and Co., Ltd., 1968), p. 69.

[61]Alastair Fraser, "Legislators and their Staffs," in Harold Clarke *et al.*,eds., *Parliament, Policy and Representation* (Toronto: Methuen, 1980), p. 232.

ton ran as an independent candidate, and drew sufficient support away from the Conservative candidate that the NDP won the by-election.[62] Another interesting nomination case occurred earlier, in 1974, when Robert Stanfield refused to allow the name of the party to appear on the ballot beside the name of candidate Leonard Jones, ex-mayor of Moncton. Jones, who held strong views against bilingualism, subsequently ran as an independent and won. He received no party support while in office, however, and did not endeavour to seek re-election.

The party leader is accountable to the caucus, yet this fact is not mentioned in any of the party constitutions. Without the support of both the caucus and the National Association the leader cannot hope for enough party unity to achieve electoral victory. The relationship is complicated because the caucus represents federal interests, while the National Association represents a great variety of provincial interests. As Conservative leaders can testify, this task is especially difficult for an opposition leader who has general responsibility for the conduct of the members of his caucus but little power over them. Internecine battles over the leadership during Joe Clark's tenure contributed to and reinforced the Conservative image of a fragmented party in electoral decline.[63] As well, because their job is to lead the offensive against the party in power, opposition leaders are often accused of carping and sometimes even unpatriotic behaviour for attacking the government.

Nonetheless, the power of the parliamentary caucus is limited *vis-à-vis* the leader because regular meetings are held only a half day each week, and even then no votes are taken. The leader simply interprets the general mood in the party's best interests. The leader appoints committee chairpersons and their deputies, including the chair of the caucus. This means, as George Perlin notes, that there is in fact no recognized independent body within the caucus that can challenge the leader.[64]

The superior status of the party leader in the Canadian system is deeply rooted in parliamentary tradition. The leader is the only party member who can claim broadly based legitimacy. Chosen by the National Convention but also the voice of the parliamentary caucus, the party leader is the most powerful individual in the creation of party policy. The position is, at least theoretically, a symbol of coherence and cohesion for the party.

National Party Leadership Selection

Until 1919, the normal procedure of leadership selection in Canada followed the British model. Members of the parliamentary caucus and the retiring leader selected the new leader, occasionally with the advice of the Governor General, then

---

[62]Worthington subsequently won the party nomination in 1984 for the same constituency but lost the 1984 election.

[63]George Perlin, *The Tory Syndrome* (Montréal: McGill-Queen's University Press, 1980), p. 103.

[64]*Ibid.*, p. 26.

presented him to the party. The Liberal Party was the first national political party in Canada to break this tradition and select a leader with the active participation of its extra-parliamentary wing. It happened almost accidentally. The 1919 convention was not originally intended to be a leadership convention; it was instigated by Laurier as a policy convention to help reunite his badly divided party, and there is no evidence that he intended to have his successor chosen by the convention. However, his sudden death, "combined with the peculiar internal conditions of the parliamentary Liberal party, made the convention appear to be a natural way of selecting the next leader of the Liberal party".[65] Mackenzie King became the first party leader selected by a national convention, and he consolidated his position by leading the party to electoral victory within two years.

The Conservatives chose one more leader – Arthur Meighen – by the caucus method in 1920, but when the party was defeated and Meighen subsequently resigned in 1926 the party felt compelled to follow the democratic precedent set by the Liberals and call a leadership convention. In 1927 they elected R.B. Bennett leader at a national convention; he went on to lead the party to electoral success three years later. The British leadership selection model whereby party leaders "emerged" after consultations generated by the retiring leader and the party caucus with the parliamentary party was thus abandoned. Open, more American-style conventions were established. Liberals have subsequently held leadership conventions in 1948, 1958, 1968, and 1984; the Conservatives in 1938, 1942, 1948, 1956, 1967, 1976 and 1983: and the NDP in 1971 and 1975.

The appeal of the convention method is that it gives the impression, justified or not, that the party is "open", "democratic" and "representative" in making its decisions. A drawback is that it was not designed for parliamentary government, but rather for a system with separate legislative and executive offices. It has been adapted to Canada's unique federal, parliamentary needs, but not without leaving inevitable contradictions in the Canadian system. For example, leadership candidates must support their party in Parliament at the same time that they appeal for delegate support – something very difficult to do when Cabinet solidarity is at stake. There is often a legacy of bitter feelings that makes it difficult for the new leader to command the full support of the caucus. The adoption of the convention system has also increased the incidence of lateral entry into leadership positions, minimizing the significance of parliamentary experience in favour of extra-parliamentary career routes in becoming party leader – Prime Minister Brian Mulroney is a classic example.

Don Smiley pointed out in 1968 that the nature of the convention was changing, that a new "openness" was being established. He cited five examples. There were many more serious candidates than in early conventions; the major candidates conducted elaborate competitive campaigns across Canada; mass media coverage was extensive; the rank and file of the parties was more involved and influential; and token candidates were treated generously.[66] These changes

---

[65]Courtney, *The Selection of National Party Leaders*, p. 78.

[66]D.V. Smiley, "The National Party Leadership Convention in Canada: A Preliminary Analysis," *CJPS*, vol. 1, no. 4 (December 1968), pp. 373-397.

have all been confirmed; to them must be added the beneficial effect of the secret ballot on leadership selection. It would be unthinkable for outgoing leaders today to designate their successors and have the convention duly annoint them, which happened as recently as 1942 for the Conservatives and 1948 for the Liberals. At the same time, however, as we have already noted, conventions are far from representative of Canadian society, and the establishment within each party has a relative advantage because of the large number of delegates it can appoint.

Leadership conventions are similar to policy conventions in terms of basic organization and participation, and their general rules are common to all three parties, although specific details vary. Leadership conventions are called when a leader resigns or dies, and sometimes even against his wishes if he does not score sufficiently high on a leadership review vote. Rules about when a leadership review will be held differ from party to party. Currently, the Liberal constitution states that a leadership review will be held only during the first national convention after a General Election. In practice, Liberal convention delegates have always voted against a leadership convention, but the procedure remains a significant reminder that the leader is responsible to the party.

The Conservative Party amended its review procedure at the 1983 convention to reduce the opportunities for a leadership review vote. Reviews are now held only at the first convention after a federal General Election in which the party did not form the government. Leadership reviews had been a focus of Tory party factionalism since they were first initiated to assess John Diefenbaker's performance in 1967, and later became a regular feature of party conventions.[67]

Technically, a Tory leader needs to win only 50 percent of the leadership review vote. In 1983, however, Joe Clark resigned as Conservative leader after he failed to secure more than 67 percent of the voting delegates' support. He felt he could not continue with the party and caucus badly split, and submitted himself as a leadership candidate in a final effort to consolidate his party support. The caucus chose a temporary leader, Erik Nielsen, from its own membership, and the party elected a new leader, Brian Mulroney, at a subsequent leadership convention.

The NDP has no leadership review procedure as such, but requires its leader to seek re-election automatically at biennial meetings. In practice, an incumbent has never been defeated.

Leadership conventions take several months to organize once a leader announces his decision to step down. Delegates are quickly chosen, and it is obvious that the manner in which this is done has important consequences for the leadership candidates. Most delegate positions are fixed. The Conservative convention in 1983 allowed each of the 282 ridings to send four senior and two

---

[67]Diefenbaker's leadership was in dispute following his defeat in the 1963 General Election, and party President Dalton Camp seized the opportunity to argue for the need to "democratize" the party by assessing the leadership. After a bitter struggle, the Camp faction won and a leadership convention was called in 1967, even though the constitution was not amended to make leadership reviews a regular occurrence until two years later, a regulation which was further clarified in 1974.

youth delegates. All Conservative MPs or candidates, Tory members of provincial legislatures, executive officers and a fixed number of delegates-at-large were included, for a total of about 3000. One category of delegates still allowed considerable flexibility and distortion: each university campus club was allotted three delegates, but the number of clubs was not fixed, so that in some instances students were highly over-represented.[68]

Once the delegates arrive at the convention, the procedure is relatively simple. Voting is by secret ballot. To discourage "nuisance" candidates, contestants must file nomination papers with a minimum number of signatures and make a financial deposit. Eight candidates ran in the 1983 PC leadership race; nine when Trudeau won the Liberal leadership in 1968; and seven when Liberal delegates chose his successor in 1984. Balloting continues at a rapid pace, with the bottom candidate automatically being dropped off in each successive ballot until someone receives a majority of the votes cast.

Recent leadership conventions have adopted the festive atmosphere of American conventions, with flamboyant speeches, entertainment and full national television coverage. There are some important differences, however. Balloting at U.S. conventions is by states rather than individuals, and the votes are announced openly, making the event quite ritualistic and predictable. The American primary system and open delegate selection process tend to produce a winner long before the convention. In Canada, the secret ballot (and the not so genteel tendency of some delegates to vote differently than they have promised candidates) lends a degree of suspense that is missing in the American process. Nuisance candidates, though kept to a minimum, are not totally discouraged in either system because of the colour and democratic element they add. In Canada, the existence of weaker candidates also allows the serious ones to learn the absolute voting figures and gain time to bargain between ballots while the token candidates are being eliminated. Delegates normally give little, if any, indication ahead of time about how they will act if their first choice is eliminated, and their voting behaviour is often unpredictable.

At the end of each session of balloting, the votes are counted and results announced as a total – there is no provincial breakdown which could be potentially divisive. Victory on the first ballot does not necessarily indicate the eventual winner; Clark won the first ballot in 1983, well ahead of Mulroney. That lead narrowed in the next two ballots and was finally reversed on the fourth and final vote. With the withdrawal or elimination of a candidate, coalitions shift and delegates disperse, some candidates being unable to deliver a block of votes to their next preferred candidate.

Leadership campaign costs have escalated dramatically in recent years. In order to keep costs low, and also to discourage candidates from relying on large sums of money from one or two donors who hope for future considerations, the Liberal Party constitution provides for the appointment of a Leadership Expens-

---

[68]Martin, Gregg and Perlin, *op cit.,* p. 109.

es Committee whenever a leadership convention is called. The committee is empowered to set a maximum limit for candidates' spending prior to and at the convention, to enforce compliance with that limit and to ensure complete disclosure of all contributions to leadership campaigns. Candidates at the 1984 Liberal convention were required to disclose the source of all donations over $500 and to observe a $1.6 million spending limit. The Conservative Party had no such provisions at its 1983 convention, claiming that they are unenforceable. Candidates in both conventions were left with large debts, and the Tory party received negative publicity from accusations that "offshore" financing had been used to defeat the incumbent leader.

Leadership conventions give parties precious hours and pages of media coverage. The Liberal convention of June 1984, for example, was an entertainment extravaganza. In the initial phase, amid great speculation about who would run, seven candidates entered the contest, timing their declarations to receive optimum publicity. Then came the stampede by candidates and their teams to influence the election of nearly 2000 riding delegates. The highly competitive courting of potential delegates by the candidates was intended to assure that as many delegates as possible would arrive at the convention solidly committed. Modern technology radically transformed delegate tracking procedures from the previous leadership convention in 1968. Computers replaced the traditional filing cards and typing pools; detailed delegate records were kept showing daily delegate counts, trends and shifts, second choice preferences, *etc.*

In the next phase, policy rallies were held across the country to introduce the candidates and gain more media attention. Meanwhile, pollsters and candidates showered delegates with attention by mail, telephone and personal contact. At the same time, Liberal candidates were concerned to firm up the support of fellow MPs and raise funds (about $1.5 million) for each three-month campaign.

On convention weekend, the Lansdowne Park site in Ottawa was crammed with about 3500 registered voters, 2000 alternates and several thousand observers and media representatives. Delegates, particularly the uncommitted, remained the focus of candidate attention. The wooing included free drinks, food, parties, boat rides and a plethora of souvenirs including scarves, pins, hats, T-shirts and even periscopes for seeing over the crowd on the convention floor. As one delegate commented afterwards, "I feel sorry for delegates who immediately jumped on somebody's bandwagon. I wouldn't have missed it for anything." Candidates rented small hospitality suites in most major hotels in addition to their well-stocked home-base suites. Competing television networks produced their best-known anchors and sought to capture as much of the convention drama and gossip as possible as they fought for a larger share of the viewing audience. Amid the hoopla, the candidates each made a major speech, poll results were "leaked" to help candidate campaigns gain momentum and politicking was intense.

John Turner went into the convention ahead in the polls, followed by Jean Chrétien. Turner campaigned as the candidate of change. Having resigned from

TABLE 10.5 1984 Liberal Convention Balloting Results

First Ballot percentages		*Second Ballot percentages*	
John Turner	46	John Turner	54
Jean Chrétien	31	Jean Chrétien	40
Donald Johnston	8	Donald Johnston	6
John Roberts	5		
Mark MacGuigan	4		
John Munro	3		
Eugene Whelan	2		

the Cabinet and returned to the private sector ten years earlier, he was the only candidate who was not a minister at the time, and therefore did not have to defend the government's record. The others were in the very difficult position of having to maintain Cabinet solidarity while demonstrating why they were the most capable to lead the party. Ironically, Turner had the support of most establishment figures in the party as well as of a significant number of Liberal MPs whose ambitions had been frustrated by the outgoing Trudeau regime. Chrétien, in contrast, ran as "the little guy from Shawinigan", an anti-establishment candidate – although, ironically, he was the closest of all the candidates to establishment policies under Trudeau. Most Liberal Cabinet ministers opted for Turner or remained neutral (even those from Québec), leaving Chrétien with no strong regional base.

Most of the remaining five claimed to be the third candidate – a favoured spot since Joe Clark won from that position in 1976. The first ballot results were fairly predictable, as Table 10-5 shows. Mark MacGuigan immediately threw his support to Turner; John Roberts, John Munro and Eugene Whelan went to Chrétien. None could be certain that his delegates would follow. In spite of overtures from Chrétien, Don Johnston stayed on for the second ballot, all but assuring a Turner victory. There was no need for a third ballot.

The candidate who wins a leadership convention is likely to exhibit certain characteristics which depend on the party to which he or she belongs. Virtually all who enter the fray are university educated professionals. In the past the typical Conservative leader was a lawyer, a Protestant and from one of the Prairie Provinces, Ontario or the Maritimes. Today, it is increasingly likely that he or she will be bilingual. Brian Mulroney is the party's first elected leader from Québec; Joe Clark was the first to master the French language. The average Liberal leader was a lawyer – though this is less likely than for the Conservatives – a Roman Catholic and bilingual. The Liberals have never had a leader who was not from Ontario or Québec; normally they have alternated between French and English leaders, a tendency which has become a matter of principle for many Liberals. "I voted for Trudeau in 1968 because I thought it was important for the party," commented an anonymous delegate at the 1984 Liberal convention, "but it doesn't matter if it's Christ Himself, I won't vote for a francophone this time."

Prior to the introduction of leadership conventions, leaders of both parties were likely to have been experienced career parliamentarians, but since that change previous parliamentary experience has become less significant for leaders of both parties. Brian Mulroney was the first leader of either party to win the position with no legislative experience whatsoever. Not until he won a seat in a by-election several months after the convention was Mulroney sworn in as Member of Parliament and therefore able to become Leader of the Official Opposition as well as Leader of the Progressive Conservative Party. Mackenzie King and Pierre Trudeau had both been in Parliament less than three years when they were elected leader. At recent conventions Stanfield, Clark, Mulroney and Trudeau were all relatively unknown even by party activists until shortly before the conventions at which they were chosen. John Turner had been out of politics and disassociated from the Liberal government for years, but still remained the darling of the media while he waited in the wings. It would appear that a fresh image counts more at a leadership convention than does the experience of a party veteran.

OVERVIEW

At the beginning of the chapter we outlined the essential functions of political parties. Upon closer examination of the history and organization of the parties, some conclusions about how Canadian parties function within the Canadian political system have become evident.

In terms of recruitment, nomination and election of political officeholders, there are certain limitations. All three federal parties have a relatively small membership core and rely on the direct participation of dedicated party workers, many of whom are actively interested in politics only at election time. In the New Democratic Party their number is supplemented by indirect membership of trade union affiliates, but neither it nor any other minor party has ever received more than one-quarter of the votes cast in a federal election. The two major parties have supplied the managers and decision-makers of Canadian federal politics.

Another idiosyncracy of the Canadian party system is that it strongly reflects the decentralized nature of the federal system of government within which it operates. The relationship between the constituency and the provincial and federal structures are relatively weakly articulated in all parties, although NDP party workers tend to participate at both provincial and federal levels. Provincial and federal leaders of the same parties occasionally assume opposing policy positions because of different provincial and federal interests. A significant number of voters support one party at the provincial level and another federally.

Important functions of an electorally successful party are the effective aggregation of demands from society and the articulation of practical and systematic policy contributions. The two major parties have maintained their dominant roles by bringing together coalitions of ethnic and regional interests, thereby allowing a means of expression to those interests and providing an integrative force in Canadian society. In recent years, major distortions in regional representation in the two parties have called into question their ability to be truly national parties representing all regions. Minor parties have been even less successful in aggregating interests, however, basically because they have attempted to capture votes by presenting a program based on a single ideology or principle.

With regard to interest articulation, political parties are more limited. They are effective "gatekeepers", allowing certain demands, and not others, to reach decision-makers. But party programs, which are expressions of coordinated and consistent politics aimed at achieving certain goals with which parties are associated, are virtually non-existent in the Canadian system. The two major political parties could (and sometimes do) exchange large parts of their party programs with no visible effect. Because they attempt to mediate diverse interests they cannot afford the rigidity of firm policy commitments. The NDP is much less extreme in this regard, but is also less successful electorally. Issues are discussed and developed for election campaigns, but, as we shall see in the next chapter, elections are a very poor source of policy communication, with policies often being advanced in a random fashion as *ad hoc* responses to specific problems. Even after winning an election, parties can rarely claim clear policy directives from the electorate, or even that the electorate supports one or all of their policies.

Party organizations are designed to achieve electoral victory for their party, and their members are concerned with policy-making mainly as a means to achieve that goal. Between elections they hold policy conventions to agree on policies that are generally designed to win electoral support where they are weak. Other policies are favoured as a means of recruiting new personnel into the organization; thus, controversial policies which might alienate weak party identifiers are avoided. However, Canadian political parties are not organized very well for policy formulation, and the impact of policy decisions made at conventions on the party leadership is uncertain. Convention policy statements are not binding on the leadership, and, although steps are taken to avoid embarrassing contradictions or inconsistencies in party and government policies, such gaffes still happen. The mass party does not have much influence over policy formation; senior party bureaucrats and members of the parliamentary party have more. This is especially true in the majority party, because the government caucus, or private meeting of the parliamentary party, has the opportunity to discuss most policy matters before they reach the House of Commons.

By their very nature, political parties are flawed, as Lord Macaulay pointed out in this irreverent analogy:

> Every political sect . . . has its altars and its deified heroes, its relics and its pilgrimages, its canonized martyrs and confessors, and its legendary miracles.[69]

Political parties in this electronic age still use all the devices of superstition to win converts and maintain their loyalty: conventions are but pilgrimages; heroes and

---

[69]Quoted by Neil A. McDonald in *The Study of Political Parties* (New York: Random House, 1955), p. 20.

martyrs provide the spiritual glue of the party; relics are the venerated policies and records that provide the proof of vision and ideas of substance. Along with the manipulation, patronage and distortions, however, parties in Canada allow for the orderly election of representatives and leaders to government and the means by which thousands of Canadians can actively participate and express themselves in the process. In short, parties are a colourful and important part of the democratic process in Canada, and even with their shortcomings it is difficult to conceive of political representation in this country without them. The next chapter will examine the electoral system within which the parties vie for power.

chapter 11

Elections and Electoral Behaviour
The Voice of the People

ELECTIONS, like parliamentary assemblies, are almost universal. Of the 159 members of the United Nations, only 27 have failed to hold a national election to choose either an assembly or a head of state in the past decade, as of the time of writing. These 27 countries included traditional societies in which heredity or family ties determine political office (*e.g.*, Saudi Arabia, Oman, the United Arab Emirates), long-term military dictatorships (*e.g.*, Chile, Upper Volta) and relatively new communist or socialist states such as Angola, Ethiopia and Laos. In the vast majority of countries which held elections during the same period, including all liberal democracies (*e.g.*, Canada, the United States) and most of the older communist regimes (*e.g.*, the Soviet Union), the citizens have gone to the polls at least once in the past five years. Admittedly, some countries have fallen by the wayside as far as elections are concerned, especially those where the military have intervened in the last few years. But others have recently restored elections after long periods without an opportunity for citizens to vote: Iraq in 1980 and Nepal in 1981 both held their first General Elections in 22 years!

Although elections are held under a wide variety of political regimes, they assume special significance in liberal democracies. Here, they afford citizens the opportunity to choose their political representatives from competing candidates and, in principle at least, they give citizens a voice in the governance of their society. Through elections, voters may have a chance to express their acceptance or disapproval of decisions made by government. The electoral process aggregates various demands in society into a limited number of choices and assures the representation of diverse opinions in the policy-making arena. As a result, the process accords political leaders a degree of legitimacy on which to base their policies. Elections also have a more immediate strategic political importance, namely their impact on the formal allocation of political power and influence within the political system.

Electoral outcomes are shaped by many factors. Electoral law defines who has the right to participate in the electoral process, both as candidate and as voter. Legal constraints may also limit the financial resources which can be mobilized by those seeking elected positions, with regard to both absolute sums and the actual means of spending the funds.

The electoral system in use in a particular society is also significant. The method by which the popular preferences of the voters are translated into representation in political institutions may have a long-term impact on the nature of the party system (which in turn defines the nature of competition in electoral politics), as well as a more immediate effect on the outcome of any one election.

Since the electoral process involves an aggregation of individual decisions – i.e., the choices made by each voter, first, whether or not to vote; then, which party or candidate to vote for – patterns of individual electoral behaviour clearly determine electoral outcomes. Further, to the extent that individual voting choices may be influenced by the mass media and by election campaigns, these factors too may play a role in shaping the final result.

Elections in Canada, as elsewhere, are thus determined by the interplay of a number of different forces. In this chapter, we shall examine the mechanics of the Canadian electoral process, including the franchise, the means by which candidates are selected, and the legal constraints on election spending; the factors which shape individual electoral behaviour; the role of the media; and a brief case-study of the 1984 election campaign. First, however, we shall consider the topic of elections in comparative terms, looking at their role in the overall political process and the ways in which other countries elect their political representatives.

REPRESENTATION AND ELECTIONS

In large nation-states such as Canada, it is clearly not possible for everyone to be directly involved in the policy-making process. In earlier times, when societies consisted mainly of small, more-or-less autonomous communities, direct democracy could function: all citizens in a community could have the opportunity to participate personally in collective deliberation and decision-making about the way in which they were to be governed. To some political thinkers, this represented the ideal form of democracy. The famous 18th century philosopher Jean-Jacques Rousseau believed that true political freedom could exist only in societies small enough for all citizens to meet together to govern themselves.[1]

Today, town meetings in some small New England communities and the *Landesgemeinde* in certain Swiss communes are legacies of a time when collective self-government was a simpler process. But as societies grew larger and more complex, direct democracy was replaced by representative democracy, wherein certain individuals are selected to represent the interests of their fellow citizens

---

[1]A.H. Birch, *Representation* (London: Pall Mall, 1971), p. 35.

in the policy-making process. In most societies, the means by which such representatives are chosen is the electoral process. For the most part, democratic government now means government by representatives of the people, chosen by their peers in elections. However, there are occasions on which citizens can participate more directly in policy-making.

Referendums

The major exception to the general rule of indirect representation in modern democracies is the political device known as the "referendum". A **referendum**, sometimes known as a **plebiscite** (there appears to be no clear universally-accepted distinction between the two), is a means by which a policy question can be submitted directly to the electorate rather than being decided only by their elected representatives. A referendum may consist of a single direct question or statement requiring a simple "Yes" or "No" vote from the public, or of alternative policy proposals from which the voters may make a choice.

Referendums may be used in various ways. Some are merely *consultative*, providing a kind of official public opinion poll on an issue in order to guide politicians in their own deliberations, but not forcing them to adopt the majority view. Others are *binding* in that they do force the government to follow the majority decision when enacting legislation. Still others are essentially *instruments of ratification*, the final seal of approval on a course of action chosen by the government; this is particularly the case in those countries where proposed constitutional amendments must be ratified by the electorate before they can come into effect.

It should be noted that not all referendums are designed with a view to permitting the electorate a genuine voice in how their country is governed. Especially in non-democratic systems, referendums may be used primarily as symbolic devices which give the illusion of popular participation without any meaningful choice. Such referendums may be useful in lending an air of legitimacy (perhaps more in the eyes of undiscriminating external observers than the domestic population) to decisions upon which the ruling elite is already agreed. Not surprisingly, their results are often suspiciously close to unanimous support for the government's policies – for example, in nine referendums held in Egypt between 1956 and 1976, not one yielded a "Yes" vote of less than 99.8 percent.[2]

Where referendums do allow a meaningful choice, however, they may be considered to enhance the democratic process. Proponents of the referendum as a political device argue that it represents a form of direct democracy – an example of popular participation in government policy-making. Voters are given an opportunity to have a much more immediate influence on public decisions than is possible through the election of representatives. Advocates also point out that the widespread consultation referendums provide increases the legitimacy of po-

---

[2]David Butler and Austin Ranney, eds., *Referendums: A Comparative Study of Practice and Theory* (Washington, D.C.: American Enterprise Institute for Public Policy Research, 1978), p. 9 (fn. 9) and Appendix A, p. 232.

litical decisions. This legitimizing function is particularly important when it comes to fundamental changes in the political system such as, for example, the aforementioned ratification of constitutional amendments.

Notwithstanding these apparent advantages, referendums are not widely used in most liberal democracies, though there are exceptions such as Switzerland and Australia. Other countries clearly demonstrate that the use of the referendum is not necessarily addictive: Belgium has used it only once (on the Monarchy, in 1950); the United Kingdom once (on whether to remain in the European Community, in 1975); West Germany never (perhaps because the referendum was used by Hitler to gain ratification of his dictatorial rule in the 1930s); and the United States has never held a national referendum, although the device is employed widely at the state level.[3]

The infrequent use of the referendum in most countries suggests that there are drawbacks associated with it. Critics argue that it detracts from the sovereignty of Parliament: that legislators are elected to make decisions on behalf of their constituents and that bypassing Parliament by appealing directly to the voters downgrades the importance of the sovereign law-making body. Others argue that it is unreasonable to ask relatively uninformed citizens to make decisions, especially on technical or legal matters; the average citizen has neither the time nor the expertise to evaluate complex issues. Furthermore, it is impossible to consult the citizens on every issue which might be regarded as fundamental – although some futurologists foresee the day when every home has its own computer terminal and people may vote on issues as they arise. Another criticism of referendums concerns their inflexibility – they usually require a straight Yes/No decision which may oversimplify complex political problems and make subsequent compromise difficult. In a country as diverse as Canada, such finality might be divisive. As well, there is always the danger that unscrupulous politicians could use the referendum, as Hitler did, to appeal to populist sentiments and gain support for extremist and non-democratic measures. Finally, it is argued that referendums, especially if used frequently, pose a threat to minorities. Majority rule, while a central component of democracy, must be tempered by the protection of minorities, lest it turn into "the tyranny of the majority".

Most countries therefore tend to use referendums with extreme caution and only under certain circumstances. The most frequent application, perhaps, is associated with the process of constitutional amendment which requires a referendum to ratify changes. Referendums are also widely employed in deciding questions of national importance, whether they be matters of sovereignty, secession or autonomy. The third common use of referendums is in allowing citizens to decide what might be called "moral" isues over which political parties (and, hence, usually governments) are internally divided. Thus, a number of countries have held national or local referendums on such matters as prohibition, licensing laws and drinking hours, divorce and nuclear energy. On such sensitive issues politicians often appear only too happy to allow parliamentary sovereignty to be bypassed and let the citizens decide for themselves!

---

[3]*Ibid.*, various chapters and Appendix A, pp. 227-237.

Referendums in Canada

Federal politicians in Canada share the mistrust of referendums and concern for parliamentary sovereignty displayed by their counterparts elsewhere. There have been only two referendums at the national level in Canada, and both were consultative; that is, they were not necessarily to result in legislative action.[4]

The first was held in 1898, when the federal government was contemplating prohibition of alcohol. Although a small majority voted in favour of prohibition (51 percent), there was a very low turn-out (44 percent) and Prime Minister Wilfrid Laurier did not believe that support was strong enough to go ahead. It should be noted that the proposal was massively rejected in Laurier's home province of Québec; this fact undoubtedly influenced the government's decision not to proceed.

The second national referendum was during the famous Conscription Crisis of 1942. Prime Minister Mackenzie King proceeded with conscription after a referendum, which asked whether the federal government could overturn its previous pledge not to institute a draft, received the support of 65 percent of the voters. Québec, however, voted heavily against conscription (71 percent), thus exacerbating relations between English and French Canadians. Fortunately for Canada and for the Liberal government Canadian conscripts were never used in battle.

Referendums have also been used by other levels of government in Canada. Newfoundland held a referendum on the question of joining Confederation – in fact, it held two.[5] In the first, in June 1948, Newfoundlanders were given three choices as to their future status: responsible self-government was supported by 45 percent of the voters; joining Canada by 41 percent; and remaining under the control of a board of commissioners appointed by the British government by 14 percent. Six weeks later, the choice having been narrowed to self-government or Confederation, 52 percent voted in favour of joining Canada.

The only other province to hold a referendum relating to the question of sovereignty was, of course, Québec. In May 1980 the Parti Québécois government held a referendum asking the voters of that province for a mandate to negotiate sovereignty-association with the rest of Canada. However, 60 percent of the voters voted "non", and the *status quo* was maintained.

In general, the referendum has not been widely used in Canada,[6] although practically every province has had at least one vote on alcohol regulations, and many municipalities have asked their residents to vote "wet" or "dry" – i.e., to decide whether or not they wanted liquor outlets in their area. In addition, muni-

---

[1]On federal referendums in Canada see Richard Theoret, "The Uses of the Referendum in Canada," in D.C. Rowat, ed., *The Referendum and Separation Elsewhere: Implications for Quebec* (Ottawa: Carleton University, 1978), pp. 23-26. For criticisms see Robert J. Jackson, "Referendums," *Ottawa Citizen,* July 13, 1978. Data taken from Butler and Ranney, *op.cit., passim.*

[2]See Henry B. Mayo, "Newfoundland's Entry into the Dominion," *Canadian Journal of Economics and Political Science,* vol. 15, no. 4 (November 1949), pp. 505-522.

[3]Theoret, *op. cit.,* pp. 19-23.

cipalities hold votes on other issues, sometimes even on matters outside their jurisdictions, as was the case over the establishment of "nuclear-free" zones. Finally, during the discussions on constitutional patriation, Prime Minister Trudeau suggested that a referendum might be used as a means of ratifying amendments on which the federal and provincial governments were unable to agree, although no such provision was included in the amending formula in the new Constitution.

The Functions of Elections

At the most basic level, the primary function of elections is to provide a mechanism for selecting the individuals who will occupy seats in representative institutions. Hence, in Canada, the federal electoral process is the means by which the voters in various constituencies throughout the country choose which men and women will represent their interests in the House of Commons.

But, in liberal democratic societies such as Canada, elections fulfill an even more important function: they "provide for orderly succession in government, by the peaceful transfer of authority to new rulers when the time comes for the old rulers to go, because of mortality or because of failure."[7] Elections held at regular intervals provide the citizens with periodic opportunities to review the record of the government, to assess its mandate, and to replace it at will with an alternative administration. In certain countries such as the United States, the political executive (the President) is elected, reconfirmed or replaced by the people directly through the electoral process. In Canada and other parliamentary democracies, however, the election of constituency representatives to the House of Commons assumes additional significance in that the government arises out of the majority within the legislature and is subsequently responsible to it for the exercise of executive power until the next election.

Once a government has been elected, directly or indirectly, it may claim a mandate from the voters to rule on their behalf. Thus, the electoral process helps to legitimate the government of the day and, although this may be exaggerated, to legitimate the policies that the government has been elected to carry out. Furthermore, elections legitimate not only the immediate government but also the entire system of government. To the extent that Canadians, for example, turn out in relatively large numbers at the polls (on average, around 74 percent of the electorate have voted in federal General Elections in this century), they are expressing confidence in the system by their very participation.

It is this function of legitimation of the system which makes elections so common around the world, not just in liberal democracies, but also in communist regimes and other forms of government where there is no real element of choice put before the voters. Elections in all countries provide an opportunity for citizens to participate in the political process and to express their support for the system. But they serve an additional role in many countries, since "in non-com-

---

[7] W.J.M. Mackenzie, *Free Elections* (London: George Allen and Unwin, 1958), p. 14.

petitive state-controlled systems, international legitimation counts for at least as much as national legitimation. Elections are signs of good conduct to the outside world."[8]

In all societies, elections also serve as agents of political socialization and political integration. For a few weeks at least, the whole society is joined together in one common enterprise, the election of a new government or the reaffirmation of an existing one. The extensive media coverage given to election campaigns in most countries and the efforts of political parties and leaders to maximize their popular support give rise to mass exposure to political issues, especially to national issues which transcend local or regional concerns, and to widespread dissemination of information about current politics.

Especially in competitive elections – *i.e.,* those involving more than one party with a chance of forming a government – political parties are forced to aggregate as many interests as possible in their search for a political majority. Through campaign literature, speeches and personal contacts, the candidates attempt to "educate" the voters and to persuade them to vote the "right" way. But even where there may be only a single slate of candidates for the voters to ratify, as in Soviet elections, election campaigns provide "an immediate and solemn occasion for the transmission of orders, explanations and cues from the government to the population."[9]

Finally, in competitive systems at least, elections provide a forum for airing views not regularly heard in everyday political debate. Widespread media coverage, all-candidates meetings and institutionalized access to private homes to distribute unsolicited political literature all allow minor parties, interest groups supporting particular candidates, independent politicians and the occasional "odd-ball" an unrivalled opportunity to air their ideas and opinions. Thus, while in the normal course of events political debate at the federal level in Canada is dominated by the Liberal, Conservative and New Democratic Parties, an election campaign exposes Canadians to the views of, among others, the Communists, the Marxist-Leninists, the Libertarians and the Rhinoceros Party. To the extent that some people (3 percent of Canadians in 1984) vote for minor parties and independent candidates, elections may be viewed as a kind of safety valve providing voters with an opportunity to express dissatisfaction with the major parties and to lend support to ideas not generally represented in the federal political arena.[10]

Before leaving the subject of the functions of elections, we should also briefly mention the role of by-elections; they are discussed in more detail later in the chapter. In parliamentary systems like Canada's, by-elections are used to fill vacancies in Parliament caused by the death or resignation of a sitting member. Again, at the most basic level, they provide a mechanism whereby the voters in a

[8]Guy Hermet, "State Controlled Elections: A Framework," in G. Hermet, *et al.,* eds., *Elections Without Choice* (London: Macmillan, 1978), p. 15.

[9]*Ibid.,* pp. 13-14.

[10]Andrew J. Milnor, *Elections and Political Stability* (Boston: Little Brown & Co., 1969)

particular constituency can choose their representative in the legislature. But they also provide a useful indicator between General Elections of public opinion concerning the record of the government of the day. Since by-elections involve only one seat in Parliament and therefore rarely have a major impact on the overall distribution of seats, they permit voters to show displeasure with the government (or with any other party) without drastically altering the balance of power.

TYPES OF ELECTORAL SYSTEMS

There is a tendency to believe that one's own established electoral system is the best way of choosing a government. But history reminds us that there are many perceptions of what is best among political arrangements; different electoral systems may be viewed as institutional expressions of these competing values.

According to one observer of electoral practices around the world, there are four primary objectives of elections, which may be regarded as the principles upon which different electoral systems are based:

(i) A parliament reflecting the main trends of opinion within the electorate.
(ii) Government according to the wishes of the majority of the electorate.
(iii) The election of representatives whose personal qualities best fit them for the function of government.
(iv) Strong and stable government.[11]

Some electoral systems place a higher premium on the concept of "representation", inasmuch as they are designed to ensure that all significant shades of public opinion are represented in Parliament. Others appear to be concerned more with providing majority governments which, by conventional wisdom, are commonly assumed to be stronger and more stable than minority or coalition governments.

To illustrate these points, we shall briefly outline the major types of electoral systems and their effects on party competition and government outcomes. In essence, two factors are determined by electoral systems: how many candidates are elected in each geographical district (usually known as "constituencies" or "ridings"); and how votes are translated into parliamentary seats. Using these criteria, we can identify four basic varieties of electoral systems: single-member plurality, single-member majoritarian, multi-member proportional representation, and mixed systems.

Single-Member Plurality

The single-member **plurality** system is used primarily in what are often called the "Anglo-American" democracies, among them the United Kingdom, the United

---

[11]Enid Lakeman, *How Democracies Vote: A Study of Electoral Systems*, 4th rev. ed. (London: Faber and Faber, 1974), p. 28.

States, New Zealand and Canada. Under this system, one member or representative is elected from each constituency. Each elector has one vote, which is cast by indicating (usually with an "X") one's favourite candidate. The translation of votes into seats is based on the achievement of a plurality – that is, the candidate with the most votes wins. It is important to note that the victorious candidate is not required to gain an absolute majority of votes, but merely to receive more votes than anyone else. For this reason the system is sometimes known by other labels, such as the "simple majority" or "relative majority" (as opposed to "absolute majority") system.

In Canada, all members of the House of Commons are now elected by plurality voting in single-member constituencies, as are the members of most provincial legislatures. But it is also possible to conduct elections under the plurality formula in districts returning more than one member. The rules are essentially the same, except that the voter has as many votes as there are seats to be filled. Thus, in a two-member constituency, each voter marks two names, and the two candidates with the most votes are the winners. As recently as the 1965 General Election there were federal constituencies returning two members to the Canadian House of Commons.[12] Even today, the 32 members of the provincial legislature of Prince Edward Island are elected in 16 two-member ridings, and many municipal councils and school boards are still elected "at large" or in multimember districts using the plurality formula. However, most contemporary national elections, including those in Canada, use the plurality formula in single-member constituencies.

Single-Member Majoritarian

In plurality systems, the candidate receiving the most votes is the winner whether or not he or she has an absolute majority of all votes cast. Other electoral systems based on single-member constituencies are designed to increase the likelihood of the winning candidate's receiving an absolute majority of votes cast in the constituency. These "majoritarian" formulas are essentially of two types, the alternative vote (AV) and the second ballot.

Under the **alternative vote** system, used for example in elections to the federal House of Representatives in Australia, voters are given the opportunity to rank candidates in order of preference – *i.e.*, to place "1" beside their favourite candidate, "2" beside their second choice, and so on. When the votes are counted, each ballot paper is assigned to the candidate it ranks first. If one candidate has an absolute majority of votes, that candidate is declared elected. Otherwise, the candidate with the least votes is excluded and his or her supporters' ballots are transferred to the remaining candidates according to their second preferences. This process of excluding candidates and transferring votes continues until one candidate has an absolute majority over all other remaining contenders.

---

[12]See T.H. Qualter, *The Election Process in Canada* (Toronto: McGraw-Hill, 1970), pp. 118-123, for a discussion of single-member and multi-member constituencies in Canadian elections.

Another variation on the single-member constituency format is the **second ballot** system, until recently used in all public elections in France. Here, as in the plurality system, electors initially opt for a single candidate, but if no one obtains an absolute majority on this first vote, a run-off election is held, usually a week or two later. On this second ballot, candidates failing to get a specified proportion of the votes the first time round are excluded; usually, only the two leading candidates reappear and, therefore, the elected representative normally claims the support of a majority of voters in the constituency.

The second ballot system has never been used in Canada, but the alternative vote has, though not at the federal level. In the provincial elections of 1952 and 1953, the entire legislature of British Columbia was elected by the AV system, although plurality voting was subsequently reintroduced. In Alberta from 1926 to 1959, rural MLAs were returned from single-member ridings using the AV, while those from Calgary and Edmonton were elected by the multi-member proportional representation (PR) system described below. Similarly, rural MLAs in Manitoba were elected by the AV from 1927 to 1936, while members from Winnipeg were again elected under a PR formula.

Multi-Member Proportional Representation (PR)

Multi-member proportional representation systems provide an opportunity to elect two or more members from each constituency. They are designed to ensure that parties, or groups of voters, are represented more fairly than is often the case under the single-member plurality or majoritarian formulas. In other words, PR formulas attempt to ensure that parties receive representation in parliament more-or-less in proportion to their respective shares of the popular vote. PR systems are essentially of two types: party list systems and the single transferable Vote (STV) formula.

Party list systems of PR are used extensively in Western Europe. In its simplest form, the **party list** system involves electors in a multi-member constituency voting for a party or a slate of candidates, rather than for one or more individuals. Seats are then allocated to each party roughly in proportion to its share of the popular vote. Assume, for example, that a constituency sends ten members to the parliament and that 100 000 people turn out to vote. Theoretically, if Party A receives 50 000 votes, Party B 30 000 and Party C 20 000, the resulting seat distribution will be 5, 3 and 2 respectively – *i.e.*, each party will receive exactly the same percentage of seats as votes. In real life, the percentages of voters are rarely distributed so conveniently, and a number of different procedures exist whereby seats are allocated. But the general effect is that parties receive representation approximately proportional to their popular support.

In party list systems, seats are usually awarded to individual candidates on the basis of their position on the party's slate. Before the election, each party publishes a list of candidates in order of rank and, under normal circumstances, if Party A receives five seats in our hypothetical constituency, the top five names on the party list will be declared elected. In some countries, however, the electoral rules permit the voters to express preferences for one or more individuals within the party list and, therefore, perhaps to effect a change in the rank order-ing of candidates.[13] But whatever freedom of choice among individual candidates is given to the voters, the basic principle of party list systems still obtains – that is, seats are awarded in the first instance to political parties according to their rel-ative shares of the popular vote; the actual representatives who will occupy those seats are essentially a secondary concern. This is in direct contrast to single-member constituency systems, where the election of individual members is the immediate objective, and the relative strengths of the parties in Parliament is the product of the individual constituency races.

The second variety of proportional representation places greater emphasis on individual candidates than does the party list system. The **single transferable vote** formula is used in all public elections in the Republic of Ireland and also for electing the Australian Senate. Again, representatives are elected from multi-member constituencies, but electors vote for individual candidates rather than for a party list.

In the STV, as in the alternative vote system, voters rank candidates in or-der of preference, and ballot papers are initially assigned to the first-choice can-didate. In order to be elected, a candidate must obtain a specified number of votes known as the "quota". Candidates receiving first preference votes in excess of the quota are declared elected and their "surplus" votes (those in excess of the quota) are transferred to the remaining candidates according to subsequent preferences. If no candidate receives a quota on the first count, or if seats remain to be filled after any surpluses have been distributed, the least popular candidate is excluded and his or her votes are transferred. This process continues until all seats have been allocated.[14] Although the STV system need not be used with proportional representation of political parties in mind, its effect in countries such as the Irish Republic is very similar to electoral outcomes under other PR formulas.

Unlike the party list form of PR, the STV system has been used in Canada, though again not at the federal level. Members of the Alberta legislature from Calgary and Edmonton were elected by this system from 1926 to 1959, as were Winnipeg's representatives in the Manitoba provincial assembly from 1920 to 1953. STV was also used for municipal elections in Winnipeg until 1972.

Mixed Systems

Mixed systems or **additional member** systems (AMS) represent a combination of plurality and PR formulas. In these types a certain percentage of the seats is filled by plurality voting in single-member constituencies, while the remainder are awarded to parties according to their popular support in order to achieve an

---

[13] For details of alternative methods of allocating seats among parties and of degrees of candidate choice given to voters in PR party list systems, see Lakeman, *op. cit.*, Chapter 5.

[14] For a more detailed account of the STV system and its operation in the Irish Republic, see James Knight and Nicolas Baxter-Moore, *The Republic of Ireland General Elections of 1969 and 1973* (London: Arthur MacDougall Fund, 1973), pp. 31-36 and *passim*.

approximately proportional representation of each party in the legislature.

Such a system is used in West Germany for electing both the federal *Bundestag* (analogous to Canada's House of Commons) and the provincial (*Land*) legislatures. Under the West German system, each elector has two votes, one for a constituency candidate and one for a party list. The "first" votes, those for candidates in single-member constituencies, determine half the seats in the *Bundestag*. The "second" votes, cast for a party list, determine the share of total seats each party will obtain. Parties are awarded additional seats if the number of representatives directly elected in the constituencies is less than their overall proportional entitlement based on their shares of the "second" votes.

While the West German system represents a pure mix of the plurality and PR party list systems, the AMS places greater emphasis on the plurality formula. Here, the majority of seats in the parliament are still elected in single-member constituencies, but a small reserve of seats is allocated to parties according to their share of the popular vote in order to alleviate some of the disproportional effects of the plurality system. Variations on the AMS have been proposed by several contributors to the debate on electoral reform in Canada.

THE EFFECTS OF ELECTORAL SYSTEMS

There is a large body of literature on the effects that different electoral systems have on the politics of their respective countries.[15] It is necessary to recognize that many of these works are highly polemical since they are contributions to debates on electoral reform, either defending the existing system or propounding the adoption of an alternative method. In the following brief discussion, therefore, we outline what might be called the "conventional wisdom" on the effects of different electoral systems, keeping in view three main criteria: their impact on representation at the constituency level; the representation of political parties and effects on the party system; and the type of governmental outcome that each system typically produces. These effects are summarized in tabular form in Table 11-1.

With respect to constituency representation, one of the advantages claimed for single-member formulas (whether plurality or majoritarian) is that they maintain the traditional link between the individual MP and the constituents. Since the constituency has elected only one member, there is no ambiguity about who

---

[15]Among many others, see Maurice Duverger, *Political Parties*, translated by B. and R. North (London: Methuen, 1954), Book II, Chapter 1; F.A. Hermens, *Democracy or Anarchy?* (Notre Dame, Indiana: University of Notre Dame Press, 1941); Lakeman, *op. cit.*; Douglas Rae, *The Political Consequences of Electoral Laws* (New Haven: Yale University Press, 1967). On Canada, see also Alan C. Cairns, "The Electoral System and the Party System in Canada, 1921-1965," *Canadian Journal of Political Science*, vol. I, no. 1 (March 1968), pp. 55-80; William P. Irvine, *Does Canada Need a New Electoral System?* (Kingston, Ontario: Queen's University, Institute of Intergovernmental Relations, 1979), especially Chapter 3; J.A.A. Lovink, "On Analyzing the Impact of the Electoral System on the Party System in Canada," *Canadian Journal of Political Science*, vol. 3, no. 4 (December 1970), pp. 497-516.

TABLE 11.1 Types of Electoral Systems and Their Effects

Electoral System (Examples)	Constituency Representation	Representation of Parties	Governmental Outcome
Single-Member Plurality (U.K., U.S., New Zealand, Canada)	Maintains traditional link between MP and constituents. MPs often elected on a minority of total votes.	Distortion of votes/seats ratio. Minor parties disadvantaged unless support is regionally concentrated. Discourages multiplication of parties – tendency towards two-party system.	Tends to "over-represent" largest party. Usually single-party majority government. Some alternation of government between two dominant parties.
Single-Member Majoritarian (a) Alternative Vote (AV) (Australia, House of Reps.) (b) Second Ballot (France)	Both maintain traditional link between MP and constituents. Representatives usually elected by a majority.	Distortion of votes/seats ratio. "Wasted vote" thesis does not apply – therefore, small parties survive even if unsuccessful. Tendency towards multi-party system.	Tends to "over-represent" largest party (parties). Usually single-party majority government or stable coalition.
Proportional Representation (PR) (a) Party List (Italy, Netherlands, Switzerland) (b) Single Transferable vote (STV) (Rep. of Ireland) (Australia, Senate)	(a) Individual representatives usually owe election more to party than to voters. (b) Representatives forced to compete for "first preference" votes.	Approximate congruence between vote shares and seat allocations. Minor parties usually gain "fair" representation – easy entry for new parties. Tendency towards multi-party systems.	Coalition governments – may be stable (Sweden) or unstable (Italy). Alternation of government rare.
Mixed Plurality/PR (West Germany)	Maintains traditional link between MP and constituents.	Approximate congruence between vote shares and seat allocations. Minor parties usually gain "fair" representation, unless measures are adopted (as in W. Germany to prevent representation of "splinter" groups.	Reasonably stable coalition government.

is designated to represent the interests of the voters, and since the representatives owe their election as individual candidates to the voters rather than to their positions on a party list, it is in their own interest to represent their constituents if they wish to be re-elected. Furthermore, the representatives' task is made easier because, even in relatively large and populous countries, division into a large number of single-member districts keeps the size of both the area and the electorate of each constituency manageable. These generalizations apply equally to representatives elected in single-member constituencies under a mixed or AMS formula.

In party list systems of PR, on the other hand, it may be argued that MPs owe their election more to their party (especially to their position on the party list) than to their constituents. Furthermore, particularly where large numbers of members are elected from each district, constituencies may be too large for individual representatives to maintain contact with all constituents and it is often difficult to establish clear lines of representative responsibility. Thus, there may be a tendency for members to focus their attention on maintaining their popularity within the party, and hence their high standing on the party list, rather than on representing the interests of their constituents. However, this is less true with the STV system of PR, especially as it operates in Ireland. There, each candidate attempts to gain as many first preference votes as possible in order to maximize the chances of being (re-)elected. The members therefore do have to pay considerable attention to constituency interests, since they are in competition for first preference votes not only with candidates from other parties, but also with candidates from their own party within the same constituency.

What effect do electoral systems have in the representation of political parties and the nature of party competition within a society? First of all, proportional representation systems are by definition designed to achieve a more-or-less proportional allocation of seats to parties according to their respective shares of the popular vote. However, the degree of congruence between the percentage of votes and the number of seats won by each party tends to vary from country to country. A key factor here is the number of members returned by each constituency. The Netherlands, which elects its legislative chamber, the *Tweede Kamer*, by treating the whole country as if it were a single constituency returning 150 members, achieves an almost perfect correspondence between votes and seats for each party. However, where constituencies are smaller, returning, say, three or four members each, it is more difficult to achieve congruence when allocating seats according to popular votes: there is the likelihood that some parties will be persistently over- or under-represented in each constituency, and thus overall in the legislature.

If we take the argument concerning constituency size to its logical conclusion, it follows that the proportional allocation of seats according to shares of the popular vote is least likely to occur in systems where electoral districts return only one member each – *i.e.*, in single-member plurality and majoritarian systems. This can easily be illustrated with reference to the 1979, 1980 and 1984 General Elections in Canada (see Table 11-2), all of which were conducted under single-member plurality voting rules. In 1979, the Progressive Conservatives

TABLE 11.2 Canadian General Election Results 1979, 1980, 1984:
Shares of Votes and Seats by Party

	1979			1980			1984		
	% Votes	*% Seats*	*No. of Seats*	*% Votes*	*% Seats*	*No. of Seats*	*% Votes*	*% Seats*	*No. of Seats*
LIB	40	40	(114)	44	52	(147)	28	14	(40)
PC	36	48	(136)	32	37	(103)	50	75	(211)
NDP	18	9	(26)	20	11	(32)	19	11	(30)
SC	4.5	2	(6)	2	0	(0)	0.1	0	(0)
Other	1.5	0	(0)	2	0	(0)	3	0.4	(1)

(*N.B.* Percentages may not add up to 100%, because of rounding.)

gained more seats than the Liberals and thus formed the government, although they received a smaller share of the popular vote, 36 percent to the Liberals' 40 percent. This outcome was rather exceptional, and the normal pattern reasserted itself in 1980, with the Liberals getting the most votes and the most seats. In 1984 the Conservatives returned with a massive majority of both votes and seats. Table 11-2 demonstrates some of the negative characteristics typically associated with the plurality system: a tendency to favour the two largest parties, with an additional "bonus" of seats for the largest party; and, conversely, a tendency to under-represent third or minor parties, especially those whose support is spread fairly evenly but thinly across the country.

As a consequence of the tendency to under-represent minor parties,[16] the plurality system is often said to favour the development or maintenance of a two-party system of electoral competition. It is argued that people who might otherwise support a persistently under-represented minor party will refrain from voting for it for fear of "wasting" their votes – in other words, of casting votes which have no effect on the election of individual representatives or on the formation of a government. Thus, the French scholar Maurice Duverger suggested that the association between the plurality electoral formula and the two-party system was close to being a "true sociological law",[17] although he noted that Canada was one of the exceptions to his general rule.

The other types of electoral system outlined above are more often associated with multi-party forms of party competition. Like the plurality system, the alternative vote and second ballot formulas both tend to result in severely dispro-

---

[16]An exception to this general rule may occur when a minor party has its support strongly concentrated in a particular region. Then, as with the Social Credit and Créditiste parties in certain Canadian elections, a minor party may on occasion be relatively "over-represented" (see Table 11-2).

[17]Duverger, *op. cit.*, p. 217. For a test of Duverger's hypothesis regarding the plurality formula and bipartism, see Rae, *op. cit.*, pp. 93 ff.

portional allocations of seats, often in favour of the largest parties.[18] But they do not tend to "squeeze out" minor parties to the same extent as the plurality formula. Voters do not have to worry about wasting their votes, as the majoritarian formulas effectively give them a "second bite at the cherry". Electors can give their first preferences (under the AV) or their "first ballots" (under the second ballot system) secure in the knowledge that, if their favourite candidate is unsuccessful, subsequent preferences or the "second ballot" can be used to choose between the major protagonists in the constituency.

Under PR formulas where all parties, including the minor ones, receive seats more-or-less in proportion to their shares of the popular vote, there is also a tendency towards a multiplicity of political parties. Some countries attempt to counteract this tendency by imposing a threshold – a certain proportion of votes which small parties must exceed before they are allotted seats. West Germany, for example, has modified the proportional element of its mixed system to make things more difficult for new or splinter parties by insisting that they gain at least 5 percent of the popular vote or win seats in three single-member constituencies before being allotted seats on a proportional basis.

Lastly we come to the impact of the electoral system on the formation of governments. Because the plurality formula favours the development of a two-party system (or at least of two dominant parties) and because the largest single party in any election usually receives a "bonus" of seats, elections conducted by single-member plurality voting usually result in the creation of relatively stable single-party governments. Frequently these governments enjoy majority support in Parliament, although, as the results of the 1972 and 1979 Canadian General Elections demonstrate, minority governments may sometimes occur.

A further characteristic of the plurality system is that relatively small swings in votes between parties often result in large numbers of seats changing hands. Perhaps the most outstanding example in Canada occurred in the 1935 General Election, when the Liberals swept triumphantly back into power. Although their share of the popular vote increased by less than one percent, their number of seats nearly doubled, from 91 to 173.

Such amplification of small voting shifts across the country into large-scale changes in seat allocation causes the plurality system to tend to encourage alternation in government between the two dominant parties; for example, eleven General Elections in Britain since the Second World War have produced six changes of government between Conservative and Labour administrations.

Most of the typical characteristics ascribed here to the plurality system are also true of the majoritarian AV and second ballot formulas. The major exception is that, because the majoritarian formulas do not discriminate to the same extent

---

[18]In particular, both the alternative vote and the second ballot tend to "over-represent" parties which can reach agreements or alliances with other parties regarding the destination of second preferences or second ballots. Thus centrist or moderate parties are often "over-represented" compared with extremist parties of either the right or left, since the latter often cannot persuade supporters of other parties to transfer allegiance to them in the latter stages of voting.

TABLE 11.3 General Election Results by Region 1945-1984

	1945	1949	1953	1957	1958	1962	1963	1965	1968	1972	1974	1979	1980	1984
Atlantic														
LIB	19	25	27	12	8	14	20	15	7	10	13	12	19	7
PC	6	7	5	21	25	18	13	18	25	22	17	18	13	25
SC	—	—	—	—	—	—	—	—	—	—	—	—	—	—
CCF-NDP	1	1	1	—	—	1	—	—	—	—	1	3	—	—
Other	1	1	—	—	—	—	—	—	—	—	1	—	—	—
Total	27	34	33	33	33	33	33	33	32	32	32	33	32	32
Québec														
LIB	54	66	66	63	25	35	47	56	56	56	60	67	74	17
PC	1	2	4	9	50	14	8	8	4	2	3	2	1	58
SC	—	—	—	—	—	26	20	—	—	15	11	6	—	—
CRED	—	—	—	—	—	—	—	9	14	—	—	—	—	—
CCF-NDP	—	—	—	—	—	—	—	—	—	—	—	—	—	—
Other	9	5	5	3	—	—	—	2	—	1	—	—	—	—
Total	64	73	75	75	75	75	75	75	74	74	74	75	75	75
Ontario														
LIB	34	56	50	20	14	43	52	51	64	36	55	32	52	14
PC	48	25	33	61	67	35	27	25	17	40	25	57	38	67
SC	—	—	—	—	—	—	—	—	—	—	—	—	—	—
CCF-NDP	—	1	1	3	3	6	6	9	6	11	8	6	5	13
Other	—	1	1	1	1	1	—	—	1	1	—	—	—	1
Total	82	83	85	85	85	85	85	85	88	88	88	95	95	95
*West**														
LIB	19	43	27	10	1	7	10	9	2	7	13	3	2	2
PC	11	7	9	21	66	49	47	46	26	43	50	59	51	61
SC	13	10	15	19	—	4	4	5	—	—	—	—	—	—
CCF-NDP	27	10	21	22	5	12	11	12	16	20	7	18	27	17
Other	—	—	—	—	—	—	—	—	—	—	—	—	—	—
Total	71	71	72	72	72	72	72	72	70	70	70	80	80	80

*including the Northwest Territories and Yukon
Sources: Adapted from the *Canadian Parliamentary Guide, 1980 and 1984.*

against minor parties and therefore tend to encourage a multiplicity of parties, coalition governments are more frequent than under the plurality system. Australia was ruled by a coalition of the Liberal and Country Parties from 1975 to 1983, and most recent French governments have had to rely on support from more than one party in the National Assembly.

Since PR systems do not give significant bonuses of seats to any party, and since they are usually associated with multi-party systems, it often happens that no single party is in a position to form a majority government. In such cases, coalition or minority governments often result. Sometimes such governments can be highly unstable, as in Italy, which has had over 40 governments since the Second World War. Elsewhere, however, PR formulas may be associated with stable coalitions or even single-party governments, as in Austria, Holland or Sweden. To the extent that the mixed West German system can be considered a variety of PR, it also provides an example of a stable coalition government.

Because PR formulas do not exaggerate vote swings to the extent that single-member systems do, alternation of government between major parties or blocs of parties is less frequent in the former. Changes of administration usually result from changes in the alliance strategies of parties in and around the governing coalition, rather than from mass changes in voter allegiance at elections. Thus, for example, the replacement of Social Democratic Chancellor Helmut Schmidt by Christian Democrat Helmut Kohl in West Germany in October 1982 resulted partly from the decision of the small Free Democratic (Liberal) Party to abandon its coalition with the Social Democrats and seek a new alliance with Kohl's party.

Electoral systems do not determine the nature of party systems, nor the type of government, majority or minority, single-party or coalition, in any country. Governmental outcomes are largely a function of the balance of party forces: the party system, in turn, is largely shaped by a country's political culture and social structure and by the electoral behaviour of its citizens. However, the electoral system – the way in which votes are translated into seats – is a powerful intermediary force, modifying the competition among parties, distorting or faithfully reproducing the electoral preferences of the voters. Since elections are key institutions in modern democracies and provide the chief mechanism of political participation for most people, the means of translating individual votes into political representation is naturally an important factor in a country's political system. Having provided a general, comparative introduction to elections and electoral systems, we can now examine in detail the mechanics of the electoral process in Canada.

ELECTIONS IN CANADA

The Franchise

Canadians have enjoyed a universal franchise only since 1960. The attainment of this level was gradual, and at certain stages even retrograde as different groups were explicitly disenfranchised.

At the time of Confederation, the federal franchise was based on provincial laws and was restricted to male property owners. These were years of flagrant discrimination in favour of the upper classes and the ruling Conservative Party. The property qualification was doubly discriminatory because of plural voting; that is, citizens were allowed to vote in each area in which property was owned. Instead of being on a single election day, voting was staggered, so the government could control the timing of elections in each region. Elections were held first in those areas where the government was most popular, moving to areas of lesser support only later. The government benefited from this arrangement, since areas in which government support was not as prevalent were encouraged to fall into line, supporting the likely "winner" in order to gain favours from the future government.

In 1885, balloting was brought under federal jurisdiction, but the former restrictions remained and a new one, the disenfranchisement of Asians, was added. The two World Wars also affected the development of the franchise. In 1917, Canadians of Central European descent lost their vote. On the other hand, females, if they were relatives of soldiers, were given the right to vote, along with Native Indians serving in the Armed Forces, in the expectation that they would support the Union government's call for conscription. The following year all women were granted equal voting rights. Canadians of Asian descent, however, were not granted normal voting privileges until 1948 and the Inuit, who were disenfranchised in 1934, did not have that right restored until 1950. Religious conscientious objectors, mainly Mennonites, who had been disenfranchised as early as 1920, were not to receive voting rights until 1955. The last group to receive voter status was reservation Indians, and that as late as 1960.

The present federal franchise laws are contained in the *Canada Elections Act*, as amended by the *Election Expenses Act* of 1974. Persons who are still specifically prohibited from voting include the Chief Electoral Officer, the Assistant Electoral Officer, judges appointed by the Governor-in-Council, returning officers, inmates of penal institutions, the certified mentally incompetent and individuals disqualified by law for corrupt or illegal practices. In the light of the *Charter of Rights*, which states that every citizen of Canada has a right to vote, the Chief Electoral Officer recommended in 1983 that Parliament reconsider the status of the approximately 80 000 Canadians who are denied that right. He proposed 150 changes to the electoral system, many of which would alleviate injustices to the above-mentioned groups or individuals, and also allow Canadians living or working abroad to vote. Suggested changes include proxy votes for the latter group, mobile polls, easily accessible polls in nursing homes and hospitals and even elimination of the law prohibiting the sale of alcohol on voting day. It is up to the government to consider which, if any, of these recommendations should be presented to Parliament for approval.

Electoral Procedure

According to the Constitution, the Prime Minister must ask the Governor General to dissolve Parliament and call an election at least once every five years. The opposition parties may, as they did in 1974 and 1979, defeat the government and force the Prime Minister to call an election at an earlier date. Otherwise they have no part to play in the choice of election date. The Prime Minister's decision is usually taken some time in the fourth year, at the most favourable opportunity for the governing party. The Cabinet (officially the Governor-in-Council) formally instructs the Chief Electoral Officer, an independent official responsible to the House of Commons, to set the election machinery in motion. The Chief Electoral Officer issues the writs of election to the Returning Officers in all constituencies or ridings, who in turn supervise the collation of voters' lists, appoint Deputy Returning Officers for each polling subdivision and receive nominations of candidates.

The government assumes the responsibility for enrolling the voters. In the seventh week before an election, an army of canvassers, in couples representing the two leading parties in each constituency (except in rural areas, where one enumerator suffices), visits every residence to register the names of eligible voters. There follows a period where voters missed or wrongly included in the blitz may apply to the courts of revision. Finally, seventeen days before election day, the voting lists are closed. From the issuing of the writ to the closing of the polls the 1984 election campaign lasted 57 days. This is generally considered to be too long, but probably cannot be cut by much without changing the current system of enumeration.

The enumeration process is slow and expensive. The length of this pre-election period could be reduced, but only at the expense of accuracy. Leaving the lists open until seventeen days before the election ensures that extremely few eligible voters are left off the lists. Other types of systems present different problems. Britain, for example, has a "permanent voters' list" which allows shorter campaigns – about three weeks. Citizens are required by law to register once a year, and the voters' list is revised only at this time. Thus, it can be quite out-of-date when an election is called, eliminating many voters who move, marry or divorce.

Voting procedure is carefully controlled. Each Returning Officer designates the locations of the polling stations in his or her constituency, usually church basements or schools. On election day, the balloting is overseen at each polling station by Deputy Returning Officers and their polling clerks, and two scrutineers for each candidate. The voter identifies himself or herself to the polling clerk, who has a list of eligible voters for that polling station, and gives the voter an official, bilingual ballot listing in alphabetical order the official candidates and their party affiliations. Candidates not representing a registered party are listed as independents, unless they request the Returning Officer to show no designation. The voter marks the ballot in a private booth, then returns it to the Deputy Returning Officer, who verifies that it is the valid ballot and deposits it in the official box. When the polling booth closes, the Deputy Returning Officer, with the polling clerk and party scrutineers, counts the ballots, seals them in the box and delivers them to the Returning Officer. An unofficial result is made public immediately, but the official count by the Returning Officer is not made until later, in some cases not for several days when the military vote from overseas is in. In the very rare event of a tie vote, the Returning Officer casts the deciding ballot.

When a seat is vacated by any party for any reason during a Parliament, it is up to the Prime Minister to call a by-election to elect a new representative. This is a political tool. If it is an opposition seat, the Prime Minister can hold it vacant for many months, as Trudeau did in 1975, leaving St. John's West with no representative for 13 months and 10 days.[19] Or, if a vacancy represents an opportunity

---

[19]This has been the longest vacancy to date.

to place a colleague in the House of Commons, a by-election can be held very quickly. Obviously, governments often use by-elections as barometers to measure popularity, and, as with General Elections, they attempt to time them to their best advantage.

Electoral Irregularities

We have noted that Canadians did not benefit from a universal franchise until 1960. Gerrymandering and malapportionment were not brought under control until 1964, with the *Electoral Boundaries Commission Act.* While different patterns of boundaries clearly produce different electoral outcomes, mischievously redrawn boundaries were not necessarily illegal acts. However, there are other ways in which elections in this country have been, and, in some cases, remain, less than just.

In the past, fraudulent election irregularities have included multiple voting (ballot stuffing), impersonating, bribing, intimidating and either excluding real names from (false enumeration) or adding fictitious names to (padding) voters' lists. None of these actions is an accepted part of the national political culture today, and, if discovered, would damage the popularity and credibility of the candidate involved. Two of the most recent examples of false enumeration were in Toronto in 1957 and 1962, when blocks of names were left off the voters' lists. In both of these instances court cases led to prosecutions. Most irregularities that do occur now are at the provincial rather than the federal level. Gifts of money or liquor to voters, for example, have been an accepted part of the Maritime political culture, though the practice is much less common than even a generation ago. In any case, the secret ballot renders such favours almost meaningless.

The Candidates

Virtually any elector can become a candidate.[20] All that is necessary is to file nomination papers with the signatures of 25 other electors and deposit $200 with a Returning Officer. The deposit is intended to discourage nuisance candidates, but at the same time is low enough to encourage participation by interested citizens.[21] A prospective candidate need not have the backing of a political party, or even reside in the constituency he or she would like to represent. However, it is extremely difficult, though not impossible, for a candidate without party endorsement to be elected in Canada.[22]

As we noted in the preceding chapter, as soon as a Parliament is dissolved, party organizations spring to life and rush to legitimate their candidates through the nomination process. The procedure varies from one constituency to the next.

---

[20]Persons convicted of certain crimes, mental patients, and those holding certain public offices or appointments are excluded.

[21]Local party organizations usually pay the deposit fee for their candidates.

[22]Robert J. Williams, "Candidate Selection," in Howard R. Penniman, ed., *Canada at the Polls, 1979 and 1980* (Washington D.C.: American Enterprise Institute, 1981), pp. 86-120.

Local party organizations generally take the initiative in candidate recruitment, and, although automatic renomination of candidates sometimes occurs, particularly in Québec, locally controlled delegate conventions are the usual procedure for nominating candidates. It has been exceptional for national party headquarters or the party leader to interfere with local nominations. However, Robert Stanfield's veto in 1974 of the nomination of Leonard C. Jones, mayor of Moncton, because of his alleged anti-French prejudices set a precedent.

If the leader of a winning party is defeated in his own constituency, an apparently safe seat is quickly found for him. When Tommy Douglas, then NDP leader, was defeated in Regina in 1962, the member for Burnaby-Coquitlam in British Columbia resigned his seat for the party leader. When Brian Mulroney became PC leader in 1983 he had not yet been elected to the House, and the Member from Central Nova in Nova Scotia resigned to let him contest and win that seat in a by-election. On occasion, a Prime Minister wants an "outsider" in his Cabinet and uses his influence to get the national party to obtain the appropriate nomination. Another occasion for interference with local control arises when a seat is considered hopeless for the party and candidates are difficult to find. Then the provincial organization of that party generally takes on the task of finding someone and "parachutes" a candidate in from an outside riding. This practice is very common in Québec, where the Conservative constituency organization has traditionally been so weak that such recruitment has been necessary to provide a full slate of candidates. In 1977, Conservative Stanley Schumacher, who had refused to give up his constituency to leader Joe Clark following boundary and redistribution changes, was defeated at the nominating meeting of Bow River by a last-minute nominee who had run provincially for another party. Clark's supporters claimed to be innocent of influence in the affair.

Changes in the *Canada Elections Act* have also increased the role of the federal party leaders in the nomination process at the local level. As a result of the 1970 electoral revisions, each candidate's party affiliation appears on the ballot; it is therefore necessary for the parties to identify their own candidates so that they will qualify for benefits under the revised legislation, such as expenditure reimbursements. Thus, a statement signed by the party leader or his designated representative confirming the party's endorsement must now be filed with a candidate's nomination papers. Although local party associations for the most part continue to have the main responsibility for candidate recruitment, this requirement for endorsement allows the party leader to reject candidates nominated by the local riding association, furthering the protection of "national" party interests. As we note in the case study at the end of the chapter, Brian Mulroney took advantage of this rule in the nomination of Conservative candidates in 1984.

A study of candidates in federal elections over 20 years reveals different characteristics for the candidates of the four parties.[23] Although all parties have

[23]A. Kornberg and Hal H. Winsborough, "The Recruitment of Candidates for the Canadian House of Commons," *American Political Science Review*, vol. 62, no. 4 (December 1968), pp. 1242-1257.

recruited candidates of increasingly higher status since 1945, major party candidates, particularly the Liberals, have had a higher socio-economic standing than did those of minor parties. Urban candidates have had a higher socio-economic standing than did their rural counterparts. The occupational status of candidates has corresponded to the electoral success of the parties: Liberals highest, then Conservatives, NDP and Social Credit relatively lower. Surveys of candidates in the 1972 and 1974 elections also revealed that the two major parties differ from their foremost competitor, the NDP, in that their candidates are more apt to be older and male and to have religious affiliations, and are less likely to have been involved for very long in the party bureaucracy.[24] As noted earlier, there has been a dramatic increase in the number of minor party candidates since World War II; in 1984 eleven parties claimed official status in the federal election.[25]

We pointed out in the last chapter that, although Canadian women gained the right to vote and hold office in federal politics in 1921, few have become candidates for the major political parties, and fewer still have been elected.[26] Nonetheless, during the past decade the number of women elected to the House of Commons has increased, and the number of women contesting federal constituencies has risen even faster.[27] According to Janine Brodie and Jill Vickers, there is a greater willingness on the part of the three federal parties to permit women to run as candidates; still, they run primarily in "lost-cause" ridings.[28] Of the three, it is the Liberals who seem most likely to recruit female candidates in competitive contests. For example, in the 1979 and 1980 elections the success rates of Liberal male and female candidates were quite close: 43 percent of women compared to 53 percent of men were elected. The success rate for women in the NDP was half that of men – 6 percent and 12 percent respectively. But it was the Conservative Party which had the greatest imbalance: 38 percent of male, but only 14 percent of female candidates were successful.

We also noted in the previous chapter that many women are contesting elections as independents or, more often, as candidates for fringe parties such as the Green, Marxist-Leninist, Libertarian or Communist parties.[29] The chance of

---

[24]See Joachim E.-C. Surich and Robert J. Williams, "Some Characteristics of Candidates in the 1972 Canadian Federal Election," paper presented to the Annual Meeting of the Canadian Political Science Association, June 1974.

[25]According to one analyst, revisions to the *Canada Elections Act* in 1970 which allowed candidates' party affiliation to appear on the ballot increased the visibility of minor parties, increasing their activity. Second, both the 1970 amendments and the 1974 financial provisions provided more incentives to minor parties. They granted, for example, free television time or a share in the time allocated by all broadcasters, as well as expenditure reimbursements. See Robert Williams, "Candidate Selection," p. 90.

[26]See M. Janine Brodie and Jill Vickers, "The More Things Change ... Women in the 1979 Federal Election," in Howard R. Penniman, ed., *Canada at the Polls, 1979 and 1980*, p. 323.

[27]*Ibid.*

[28]Between 1921 and 1967, the proportion of women among federal candidates was below 3 percent. However, it doubled between 1972 and 1979, from 6.4 to 13.8 percent. *Ibid.*, p. 324. In 1984, there were 131 women candidates, 27 of whom were successful.

[29]*Ibid.*, p. 326.

success of the vast majority of these female candidates is marginal to say the least, given the nature of Canada's parliamentary, single-member constituency system.

Campaigning

With the announcement of an election, the national headquarters of the three major parties become nerve centres of nation-wide campaigns. Their various functions include coordinating the meetings and tours of party leaders, issuing literature, arranging broadcasts, employing public relations firms, issuing news releases and collecting public opinion data.[30] All major parties have two focuses during an election campaign: the national campaign, whose aim is electing the party; and 282 separate constituency campaigns, whose aim is electing the party's individual candidates.[31]

In all parties, the leader's role in the campaign is paramount. The personal charisma and flamboyant campaign style exhibited by Diefenbaker in 1958, Trudeau in 1968 and Mulroney in 1984 are given credit for the large majorities won by their parties. Leaders and their families are paraded before party gatherings from coast to coast and photographed shaking hands with as many people as possible in an effort to have some of the leaders' charisma rub off onto the local candidates.

The candidates, meanwhile, are busy making themselves as visible as possible in their constituencies. Speeches, door-to-door canvassing, coffee parties and media appearances fill each day. The appointment of a campaign manager has become mandatory to make efficient use of the candidate's time and to organize financing and other details. It has become increasingly true that party advisors recruited during the campaigns include a large percentage of media people: communications strategists, advertising personnel, public relations experts and public opinion pollsters. It is their job to plan strategy, obtain maximum media coverage for their candidate, communicate the party's promises and build images. Fred Engelmann and Mildred Schwartz comment that these functions have become so professional in many centres that the old-fashioned party worker has "increasingly less influence on the planning of overall strategy", although of course he or she is still important in delivering the vote at the local level.[32] The basic duties of phoning constituents, distributing literature and organizing babysitting and rides to and from the polling boths on election day all fall to volunteers.

A candidate plans campaign strategy with two goals in mind: holding onto normal party supporters, and attracting as many undecided and opponent votes

[30]Frederick C. Englemann and Mildred A. Schwartz, *Canadian Political Parties: Origin, Character, Impact* (Scarborough: Prentice-Hall, 1975), *passim*.

[31]George Perlin, "The Progressive Conservative Party in the Election of 1974," in H.R. Penniman, ed., *Canada at the Polls: The General Election of 1974* (Washington, D.C.: American Enterprise Institute, 1974), p. 116.

[32]Frederick C. Englemann and Mildred A. Schwartz, *Canadian Political Parties: Origin, Character, Impact*.

as possible. To achieve both these aims, a knowledge of the various voting groups in the constituency is essential; these include class, ethnic and geographic blocs. Their importance to the candidate depends on their size, turnout on election day and party commitment.[33] What percentage of time should a particular candidate spend wooing the farm or trade union vote? What issues should be emphasized or avoided in his or her particular constituency? Voting behaviour studies obviously have important practical applications here.

At the party level, the same knowledge is essential in planning a competent overall campaign strategy. Here again, the growing complexity of campaigns has correspondingly increased the amount of professional help necessary to win an election. What areas does a party have little chance of winning? What issues should be stressed? How should financial and other resources be allocated? There are many such questions for party campaign strategists to answer.

Under Trudeau, the most proficient party leader at winning elections in recent years, electoral planning was effective but not necessarily democratic. Liberal election strategy in 1979 and 1980 was devised primarily by his personal advisors and Trudeau himself, and the National Campaign Committee was the key body engaged in putting the strategy into operation. For the 1980 campaign Senator Keith Davey (a former National Director and Trudeau's close advisor) and Marc Lalonde acted as co-chairmen of that committee. To increase extra-parliamentary involvement in response to widespread criticism from the party after the 1979 election, two new committees, the Platform Committee and the Strategy Committee, were created. The latter was chaired by Prime Minister Trudeau as was the campaign committee. The Platform Committee was created mainly to consider and avoid repetition of the mistakes of the previous campaign. It was a relatively large group consisting of 20 members from caucus, 20 extra-parliamentary members and the leader's staff. This allowed extra-parliamentary members to contribute to policy development for the election campaign. The Strategy Committee had five regional representatives and was also intended to open up the old closed circle of advisors. It did undoubtedly widen debate, although their ultimate degree of influence on decisions is uncertain.

Conservative Party election strategy in 1979 and 1980 under Joe Clark was considerably less elaborate: it was directed by Senator Lowell Murray from the party leader's office. By the 1984 General Election both parties had new leaders and, as we shall note in the case study below, the campaign organizations reflected that change.

Public Opinion Surveys

The first psephologist, R.A. McCallum, remarked after completing his study of the 1945 General Election in Britain that election studies should cease, or they

---

[33]For an excellent American study, see Robert Axelrod "Where the Votes Come From: An Analysis of Electoral Coalitions, 1952-1968," *APSR*, vol. 66 (March 1972), pp. 11-20. See also Nelson W. Polsby and Aaron B. Wildavsky, *Presidential Elections: Strategies of American Electoral Politics*, 3rd ed. (New York: Chas. Scribner's Sons, 1972), which relates party strategy to the behaviour of the electorate.

would take all the mystery out of voting.[34] His advice, of course, went unheeded, and survey research now plays a large role in both pre- and post-election analyses in most western countries.

A great fund of election data is available in Canada. Major opinion surveys have been conducted by academics in most elections since 1965; these continue to provide valuable material for studies of voting behaviour. Recent elections have seen a proliferation of pre-election polls, which are commonly used to predict election outcomes and probe specific issues. Perhaps the most widely known research organization is the Canadian Institute of Public Opinion, the Canadian Gallup affiliate which publishes its results in syndicated newspapers across the country. But the media compete by offering their own polls as well. Both major television networks, the CBC and CTV, conduct their own national surveys. Local stations, not to be outdone, often do their own polls at the town or city level. Besides these sources, there exist many private surveys, done for various groups by either Canadian or American firms.

Canada's immense size and uneven population distribution causes pollsters two major problems. First, it is expensive to sample an adequate number of Canadians to represent the whole population. Second, regions often differ dramatically in their opinions, and are often at variance with the national patterns. Whereas in a smaller country like Britain it is usually possible to measure the swing of votes for or against the government as a uniform movement across the country, it is sometimes impossible in Canada. This situation is mainly caused by strong regional differences, but it is compounded by the fact that minor parties which are important in certain regions are virtually non-existent in others. These and other factors make Canadian election forecasters extremely reluctant to predict the distribution of seats in Parliament from the national opinion trend. Gallup polls, for example, deal only with national voting percentages, not with the distribution of parliamentary seats. As we see below in the case study of the 1984 General Election, the polls reflecting voter opinion immediately before that election were extremely accurate with regard to the outcome.

Media and Voters

The relationship between the campaign and media coverage is reciprocal: each affects the conduct of the other. Party strategists structure their daily campaign itineraries around the demands of television, and, to a lesser extent, radio. For example, the timing and presentations of policy pronouncements are made to ensure inclusion on network evening newscasts. Policy statements are delivered early in the day to allow reporters enough time to meet their news report filing deadlines. Television crews accompanying the leaders' campaign tours are provided with the best vantage points at rallies and other "media events", as well as with good "visuals"; that is, photogenic background scenes highlighting the

---

[34]R.B. McCallum and A. Readman, *The British General Election of 1974* (Oxford: Macmillan, 1974).

theme of party pronouncements, whether tours of mines, factories, shipyards or supermarkets, depending upon the topic of the day. The desire of candidates to receive maximum coverage is best demonstrated by the media events staged by party organizers. "Advance men" are sent ahead to the various campaign stops to ensure a proper expression of support for their candidate.

The importance that parties attach to the role of the media is reflected by the amounts they spend on broadcast and print advertising. For example, the 1979 Liberal advertising campaign was estimated at $2.25 million; the PCs spent

$2.5 million; and the NDP $1.2 million.[35] Even more instructive is the percentage that advertising comprised of the parties' total campaign expenditures: 71 percent, 62 percent and 61 percent, respectively.[36] In 1980, candidates and parties spent a total of $11.5 million on campaign expenses, most of which went for advertising and travel costs.

While the conduct of the campaign is structured around the needs of the media, albeit for the parties' purposes, party strategists do have an impact on the nature and extent of coverage. By highlighting or avoiding certain issues in campaign speeches, policy pronouncements and advertising, party tacticians influence the tone and substance of the media's coverage. During the 1979 election, for example, the Liberals sought to maintain the electorate's focus on the need for strong leadership, hoping that comparisons between their leader and Conservative Joe Clark would win them support. By the same token, the Liberals attempted to deflect attention from their past record because of the poor state of the Canadian economy. Trudeau helped ensure that reporters covering his campaign would focus on his attacks on Clark by using one basic speech throughout the campaign, varying only the quips about the Opposition leader. Reporters, looking for a new lead item when filing their reports, were therefore fed characterizations of Clark as a "tumbleweed", in reference to PC policy shifts; as a "headwaiter", who would only acquiesce in face of provincial demands; or as the "7 billion dollar man", referring to the Liberal estimate of the cost of his campaign promises. Little in the way of Liberal policy was offered, leaving reporters to headline their reports with such one-liners. The Clark campaign also featured personal attacks on Trudeau, reinforcing the acerbic tone of much of the media coverage.

The mass media therefore play a crucial role in helping voters choose among the parties at election time. There is, however, growing concern about how well they are performing this role. Many observers resent the excessive concentration the media place on campaign style rather than on the substantive content of the campaign. How the campaign is portrayed to the citizenry is very important. As one political observer noted, "The media's depiction of the campaign shapes the amount and quality of information acquired by voters while influencing the perception of elections held by both the public and the politicians."[37]

Many campaign observers have noted that Canadian election coverage is analogous to that of a horserace or a game. Emphasis is placed on polls, campaign strategies and party prospects in individual ridings, in an attempt to determine which party is "winning". Serious analysis of party pronouncements or investigation into areas of voter concern are for the most part ignored. Thus the

---

[35]Frederick J. Fletcher, "Playing the Game: The Mass Media and the 1979 Campaign," in H.R. Penniman, ed., *Canada at the Polls, 1979 and 1980,* p. 281.

[36]*Ibid.*

[37]R. Jeremy Wilson, "Media Coverage of Canadian Election Campaigns: Journalism and the Media Campaign," *Journal of Canadian Studies,* vol. 15, no. 4 (Winter 1980-81), p. 56.

voter is provided little information on which to base his or her decision. Fred Fletcher traces the origins of this "horserace" coverage of Canadian elections back to the 1974 election. It is his contention that the media have been reacting to what they perceived as manipulation by the Liberals during that campaign. To prevent recurrence of such events, journalists were instructed not only to convey what the parties said, but also to report on the tactics and purposes underlying media events. The result of this brand of "judgemental journalism" was not without its disadvantages. Penetrating the motives of the party campaigns, and thereby focusing on the campaign style of each party was done at the expense of analyzing campaign issues.

Emphasis on style also resulted in a "leader fixation", since the parties' campaigns were based around their leader's tour. In the daily newspapers, 54 percent of all front-page campaign headlines mentioned a party leader (more than twice the number that mentioned a party).[38] Polls conducted throughout the campaign also focused on leadership in an attempt to predict the outcome of the election and to explain it in terms of leader appeal. The polls were presented as measures to gauge how the leaders' campaigns were faring. In this sense the media coverage "...misrepresented the political system, narrowed the focus of public debate, and denigrated political leaders and institutions."[39]

We noted earlier in this book that the media are highly political instruments. Their role became far more important with the development of television because of the vast number of voters who can be reached. The extent to which voters rely on the media is indicated by the findings of a 1979 election poll. Fifty-two percent of the respondents said they obtained most of their campaign information from television; 30 percent mentioned newspapers; 11 percent radio.[40] The recruitment of technically qualified people in the field of media relations clearly assumes great importance.

Television and radio coverage tends to be partisan toward the established parties. The bias against minor parties is evident in newspapers as well, where editors propagandize through editorials and influence the contents of the headlines and news pages.[41] Minor parties are thus at a severe disadvantage, especially if no alternative sources of information are available. Many newspapers are under the same ownership – and that ownership sometimes extends to the local radio and television stations as well.

Media time for parties during election campaigns is strictly governed by law. According to the *Election Expenses Act*, all broadcasters are required to sell up to a maximum of six-and-one-half hours of prime-time spots to registered political parties. The number of hours is divided among the parties according to a for-

---

[38] Frederick Fletcher, "Playing the Game," p. 295.

[39] *Ibid.*

[40] *Ibid.*, p. 285.

[41] T.H. Qualter and K.A. MacKirdy, "The Press of Ontario and the Election," in John Meisel, ed., *Papers on the 1962 Election* (Toronto: University of Toronto Press, 1964), pp. 151-154.

mula based on the number of seats held in the House of Commons at the time the election is called and the number of seats each party is contesting in the election. Often, only a fraction of the time is actually used because it is so expensive.[42] Free time is allocated on the same basis; naturally, it is all used. These regulations were designed to provide registered political parties with a reasonable opportunity to present themselves directly to the public.[43] They helped equalize access to the airwaves, especially in the case of the NDP. While the Liberal and Progressive Conservative parties continued to have a decided advantage in 1979 after the law was enacted, the NDP was able to triple its share of all advertising expenditure.[44] However, it is important to note that, while this law establishes some equity for the three federal parties, it too reinforces the bias against minor and new parties and independent candidates.

The timing of political advertising is also restricted. In 1984, none was allowed during the first four weeks of the campaign, nor on the day before the election or on polling day itself. The object is to prevent a last-minute "ad blitz".[45]

Elections have become big business, with the establishment of public relations firms whose primary purpose is to build the leaders' images and direct political campaigns. Typically, these public relations experts determine the voters' key prejudices by means of public opinion polls, then tailor the campaign to avoid unpopular subjects that might alienate large voting blocs. They devise catchy slogans like "The Canadian Vision" or "The Just Society" that fix a name and personality in the voters' minds in connection with a positive proposal.

According to K.Z. Paltiel, the Liberal and Conservative Parties first used advertising agencies to plan their campaigns in the 1940s. The Walsh Advertising Agency wrote in *A Formula for Liberal Victory* in 1948, " ...we stripped away all the mysticism of political campaigns and 'sold' Liberalism as we would sell any other product or service ... by modern merchandising methods... ."[46] Of course, the opposite effect can occur if the slogan is badly chosen. The 1972 Liberal slogan "The Land is Strong" drew the widely repeated comment in rural areas that "What makes my land strong is horse shit."

While there is something degrading about politicians being packaged and sold like soapflakes, all this advertising activity does have positive aspects. Despite evident media distortions, the simplification of issues and the personalization of the political campaigns arouse wide interest, and therefore probably increase awareness and participation in the political process. The media may also bring about a nation-building effect, as parties and issues are presented with a minimum of regional variation at the same time to the entire country. The media, deservedly or not, claimed considerable credit for the Conservative victory in Al-

---

[42]Fletcher, "Playing the Game" pp. 282-283.

[43]*Ibid.*, p. 283.

[44]*Ibid.*

[45]See section on 1984 Election Case Study.

[46]See R. Whitaker, "The Liberal Party Enters the Age of the Ad Man: Advertising Agencies and the National Liberal Party 1943-58," unpublished paper.

berta in 1971 after years of Social Credit control, on the theory that they reached rural communities and broke down traditional ties and sources of communication.[47]

Election Financing

The rising costs of financing a General Election campaign raise questions about political competitiveness. Does the expense hinder or exclude individuals and groups from active involvement in the election process? The 1974 enactment of the *Election Expenses Act*, discussed in the previous chapter, represented an important attempt to address such questions.[48] The concept of the *Act* began in the Task Force on Election Expenses and received its main thrust from Privy Council Office President Allan MacEachen and his aides during 1970 to 1974. According to its provisions, which were embodied in a series of amendments to the *Canada Elections Act*, the *Broadcasting Act*, and the *Income Tax Act*, federal candidates were for the first time required to give a detailed accounting of money received and spent. They were also compelled to observe spending limits, and candidates who received 15 percent of the votes were eligible for subsidies from the national treasury.

F. Leslie Seidle and K.Z. Paltiel[49] ascribe the motivating forces behind the adoption of the *Election Expenses Act* partly to financial difficulties encountered by political parties: between 1957 and 1965 Canada experienced a rapid succession of five elections, which taxed the fund-raising capabilities of the major parties. Compounding this problem was the increasing expense of elections, arising mainly from the accelerated use of television advertising. Another reason was the party financing scandals which aroused the ire of the public. Seidle and Paltiel note that:

> Party leaders since Confederation have attempted to overcome through financing the problems created by the absence of cohesive parliamentary factions and extra-parliamentary organizations. They were faced with the task of raising and allocating funds to finance campaigns as well as to weld together a loyal and disciplined legislative following. As a result, they were inevitably vulnerable to the temptation of fund-raising abuses and to their subsequent exposure.[50]

Continued concerns about party fund-raising activities and the influence of the Watergate scandal in the United States encouraged politicians to take steps to prevent further mistrust on the part of the public.

---

[47]See John Rolfe, "The Impact of Television on Rural Alberta Voters," *The Globe and Mail*, Toronto, September 7, 1971, p. 7.

[48]Twenty-four days after the 1974 federal election.

[49]F. Leslie Seidle and K.Z. Paltiel "Party Finance, the Election Expenses Act and Campaign Spending in 1979 and 1980," in H.R. Penniman, ed., *Canada at the Polls, 1979 and 1980*, pp. 229-230.

[50]*Ibid.*, p. 227.

Perhaps the most important aspect of the *Election Expenses Act* is that it recognizes the parties as legal entities, thereby rendering them publicly accountable. They can therefore be prosecuted for an infraction of the *Act*.[51]

The *Act* controls election spending by limiting the campaign costs of both candidates and parties to a base formula linked to the consumer price index and adjusted before every election. It also encourages the parties to develop broader financial bases by granting generous tax credits, primarily for small donations, as a balance against reliance on corporate funds.[52] A further provision to reduce the reliance of political parties and their candidates on large contributors is the refunding of deposits and partial reimbursement of election expenses for candidates: a candidate who obtains 15 percent of the valid votes cast in his or her electoral district is refunded the $200 deposit and partially reimbursed by the Receiver General of Canada for election expenses. Provided that they comply with the requirements concerning the filing of a return of election expenses,[53] registered parties can be reimbursed for one-half the costs incurred in the purchase of permitted radio and television advertising time.

We stated in the previous chapter that the *Election Expenses Act* requires the parties to make financial statements in order to expose fund-raising practices and election expenses to public scrutiny, thereby promoting a greater sense of public trust in the electoral process. Under the *Act*, all expenses and the amount and sources of contributions must be disclosed. Six months after the end of the party's fiscal year, an audited return containing a detailed statement of the party's contributions and operating expenses must be sent to the Chief Electoral Officer. The names of those who contributed $100 or more during the fiscal year must be included. Candidates are also required to file detailed, audited returns after each general or by-election. These returns are public documents and are thus available for scrutiny.

General Election Results, 1867-1984

Since Confederation, Canada has held 33 General Elections. One of the two major parties has won each time. However, the fortunes of the Liberal and Conservative parties have altered with time. The Conservative Party dominated federal politics from 1867 until nearly the turn of the century (1896), with the exception of the Liberal victory of 1874. The Liberal Party has been in the ascendant since

---

[51]A "registered" political party is defined as a political party which was either (a) represented in the House of Commons on the day before the dissolution of Parliament, immediately preceding the General Election, or (b) thirty days before polling day at the General Election, had officially nominated candidates in at least fifty electoral districts in Canada. The Chief Electoral Officer maintains a register of political parties.

[52]F.L. Seidle and K.Z. Paltiel, *op. cit.*, pp. 227-228.

[53]Only "registered" political parties can take advantage of these income tax credits. However, a contribution during a federal election made directly to a candidate allows the contributor to claim a tax credit whether or not the candidate represents a registered political party.

that time, holding power for most of the present century. The most important element in the Liberals' success, as we have already noted, was the capture and maintenance of Québec support until it disintegrated in 1984 and moved to the Conservative Party.

The competition for votes has therefore been much stronger in the rest of the country than in Québec. The Atlantic provinces have maintained a two-party loyalty to the extent of almost excluding third parties. Ontario, for the most part, has divided its support between the two major parties, although the NDP has captured a significant proportion of its seats there since the 1950s. Ontario is important in determining the outcome of federal elections although, unlike Québec, it rarely allies itself as closely to one party at the federal level. Ontario's influence on party fortunes was evident in the results of the 1979, 1980 and 1984 federal elections. In 1979, the Conservatives gained 57 seats in Ontario compared to 32 for the Liberals, forming a minority government. However, the results of the 1980 election were almost the reverse, with the Liberals collecting 52 seats and the PCs 37, resulting in a Liberal majority government. In 1984, the pendulum swung back again and the Liberals won only 14 seats, the PCs 67 in a massive Tory sweep of the province.

The Western provinces have shown a greater willingness to support third parties. Still, the Conservatives have captured large percentages of Western federal seats, especially since 1958. The Liberals, on the other hand, saw their portion of Western seats dwindle almost to extinction in the 1980 election, when they fell to two seats. They were unable to raise that total in 1984, even with Prime Minister Turner running in Vancouver. Nevertheless, strong support in the West as well as in the Atlantic provinces is not enough to make the Conservatives the governing party when the Liberals have control of Québec and strong support in Ontario.

New Democratic Party support has been based heavily in the Western provinces, although its image as a working class party has led some to believe that it could gain more support in industrial Ontario. While receiving some seats in Ontario, the NDP has been shut out of Québec and has made little headway in the Atlantic provinces.

By-Elections

As mentioned earlier, by-elections are held to fill vacancies of legislative seats which occur between General Elections. The timing of federal by-elections is at the discretion of the Prime Minister, who, within six months from the date the Speaker issues the notification warrant acknowledging the vacancy, may name any date. By-elections may be held soon after a vacancy appears, a year or more later, or not at all, if the writs for a General Election are issued before the by-election takes place.

While much fanfare and attention, at least on the part of the media, accompanies most by-elections, their significance is limited as a predictor of party fortunes in General Elections. The reason is that by-elections tend to be idiosyncratic because of a variety of factors, including the small number contested at any given time (and therefore the lack of regional representativeness), their inability to alter the government's status, changing political conditions between the time of the by-election and General Election and the absence of national campaigns by the political parties.[54] The lack of congruence between by-election and General Election results is demonstrated by a recent example. In 1978 the federal Liberal government lost thirteen of fifteen by-elections, yet the Conservatives failed to win a majority government in 1979.

Nevertheless, by-elections are an important part of the democratic process, providing an outlet for voters to air their frustrations and send the government a message. They also are important in maintaining representation. It is in the performance of this latter function that Canada's election laws are lacking. Outrageous delays have occurred between the time seats became vacant and the subsequent by-elections. The Prime Minister and his advisors are not anxious to call a by-election if they believe its result will be perceived as unfavourable. This hesitancy is reinforced by the tendency of governments to lose by-elections. However, most reformers agree that political considerations should not be allowed to overshadow the basic right of citizens to representation in Parliament.

ELECTORAL BEHAVIOUR

As we have noted, virtually every Canadian eighteen years of age and over has the right to vote. However, certain citizens are more apt to exercise their franchise than others. Comparative studies in the United States[55] and Canada[56] show that there are several standard factors involved in whether a person votes or not. First, some individuals are by nature more socially at ease and gregarious and find interaction with others rewarding. Such people are more likely to have a psychological predisposition to participate actively in the electoral process.

The poor and the uneducated are much less apt to vote than are individuals in the higher income levels with a college education.[57] The wealthy are more apt to vote because they feel they have more at stake in an election outcome, and the more highly educated people are the more interested and better informed they tend to be. The difference in voting patterns also reflects the feeling of efficacy, which increases from the lower to upper middle classes. In general, lower class workers have a low feeling of efficacy; that is, they don't feel their vote matters, while corporation presidents, at the other extreme, tend to believe that they can further their interests by electing the right candidate.

It is also known that voter turnout in Canada is higher in the middle-aged range; the youngest and the oldest tend to abstain. Men still cast their vote more

---

[54]See Barry J. Kay, "By-Elections as Indicators of Canadian Voting," *CJPS*, vol. XIV, no. 1 (March 1981), pp. 37-52.

[55]W. Mishler, *Political Participation in Canada* (Toronto: Macmillan of Canada, 1979), pp. 88-97.

[56]*Ibid.*

[57]See Anthony Downs, "The Causes and Effects of Rational Abstention," in his *Economic Theory of Democracy* (New York: Harper and Row, 1957), pp. 260-275.

often than women, though this gap is narrowing. Again, there are a great number of reasons for non-voting. Accidental factors such as issues and campaigns are important, and so is the sense of civic responsibility that has been instilled in the voters through the various agents of socialization.

Interestingly, no significant difference between ethnic groups in terms of their overall index of electoral activity has been found at the federal level.[58] Moreover, levels of participation in the various regions are roughly similar across the country.

Although meaningful generalizations about political participation are difficult to make with precision, it would appear that socio-economic factors are significant in motivating participation, but there appears to be no substantial variation based on ethnicity or regionalism. A stereotype of the Canadian voter, then, would be middle-aged, white collar and college educated. The counterpart, the typical non-voter, would be a young person with little formal education. These are of course crude generalizations, but they support the studies in political socialization which show that political participation is a middle-class affair.

Let us now turn to a consideration of the factors that have been posited as influences on Canadian voting behaviour. These factors include regionalism, class, religion, urban/rural environment, ethno-linguistic identity, party identification and campaign issues.

Regionalism

As we have shown in Chapters 3 and 4, regionalism is very important in Canada. What does regional identity mean for voting behaviour? In order that voting behaviour may be explained by regionalism, there must exist both a regional identity and a politization of that identity. Mildred Schwartz argues that the physical aspects of territory have attained a social significance in Canada.[59] Each region has become associated with particular groups (cultural or economic) facing common problems. Thus, both problems and acceptable solutions are to a large extent defined by indigenous forces resulting in regional distinctiveness. However, as we have seen in Chapter 3, although Canadians recognize the existence of various regions, they tend to differ on what the boundaries are, and, more importantly, what the regions mean politically. As one recent work states, "the near absence of regional political institutions in western Canada, coupled with the growth of strong provincial governments, has fragmented the prairie region along the lines of provincial boundaries and the effect of this fragmentation has been to reduce the regionalization of politics in the Canadian west."[60] Thus, as an explanatory variable, regionalism fails to account for voting behaviour. It appears to be a "container" concept for several other variables.

---

[58]Richard Van Loon and Michael S. Whittington, *The Canadian Political System: Environment, Structure and Process*, 2nd ed. (Toronto: McGraw-Hill Ryerson, 1976), p. 112.

[59]Mildred A. Schwartz, *Politics and Territory* (Montréal: McGill-Queen's University Press, 1974).

[60]Roger Gibbins, *Prairie Politics and Society: Regionalism in Decline* (Scarborough: Butterworth, 1980), p.3.

Class

The search for class-based voting patterns has long preoccupied researchers into Canadian voting behaviour. One of the most famous studies of class-based voting, *Party and Society: The Anglo-American Democracies*, by Robert Alford,[61] prompted a major debate on the subject by concluding from a comparative study of four countries that Canada had a relatively low level of class-based voting in the 1950s. His method for determining its degree was to lump the Liberal Party in with the labour-oriented Co-operative Commonwealth Federation as representing the "left" – a fundamental misjudgement of the Canadian case. Alford's critics are legion.

Those who support the view that class is an important factor motivating Canadian voters agree that its impact has not been appropriately measured. Moreover, "class" has been defined in several different ways, adding confusion to the analysis of the phenomenon. For some it refers to the occupation of the head of the household; for others, support for a particular brand of politics; for still others, a level of educational attainment. There is also the contention that class-related voting behaviour is obscured by the strength of regional interests or that the absence of a significant working class party, and not voter support, explains the lack of class influence.

However, although there may or may not be objective grounds on which to argue for the presence of different "classes" in Canadian society, the study by Clarke *et. al.*[62] does not establish class as being a significant determinant of Canadian voting behaviour. Canada's two leading parties are clearly of the mass-oriented cadre variety, while the NDP also appears to be diluting its ideological commitment in favour of wider electoral support. Although it may well be argued that the results of opinion polls show a degree of class awareness in Canada, there is no evidence to indicate that it has made a significant impact on Canadian electoral choice. Finally, Alan Cairns has suggested that it is Canada's electoral system itself and its homogenizing effect that works against the emergence of class-based politics.[63] As class orientations are spread relatively evenly across the country, their political impact is effectively nullified by the single-member district electoral system.

Religion

Unlike class orientation and regionalism, religion does seem to have had an impact on voting behaviour in Canada. While in recent years, religious issues have not surfaced in national politics, at least not explicitly, it can be determined that some parties have indeed derived an extraordinary degree of electoral support

---

[61]Robert Alford, *Party and Society: The Anglo-American Democracies* (Chicago: Rand McNally, 1963).

[62]See Harold D. Clarke, Jane Jenson, Lawrence LeDuc and Jon Pammet, *Political Choice in Canada*, abridged edition (Toronto: McGraw-Hill Ryerson Limited, 1980).

[63]A. Cairns, "The General Election and the Party System".

from particular religious groupings in Canadian society. Perhaps the most striking feature of Canada's religious cleavage and its effect on voting behaviour has been that Catholics have proven more likely to support the Liberal Party. Mildred Schwartz's research has confirmed this finding across all regions of Canada.[64] Ontario, in particular, has stood out as a province characterized by strong religious divisions. Ontario Catholics have tended to vote very strongly Liberal, while Protestants have lined up consistently behind Conservative or NDP candidates.

No simple logic is adequate to explain the impact of religious affiliation on voting preference. The answer is perhaps intertwined with the historical evolution of Canada. For years the Catholic Church was identified as a protector of French Canadian interests. In the period after Confederation, French Canadian Catholics became increasingly alarmed by what they perceived to be a distinctly anti-French and anti-Catholic attitude on the part of various Conservative governments. A string of events, from the Manitoba Schools Question to the two Conscription Crises, put French Canadian Catholics strongly in the Liberal column. An anti-Catholic sentiment on the part of some Tories during the last century may have alienated English Canadian Catholics as well, but the fact is that French Canadians are overwhelmingly Catholic and, with a few exceptions, have tended to vote strongly Liberal. The association between Catholics and Liberals and between Protestants and Conservatives may make no objective sense in light of today's problems and political issues, but it has nonetheless proven to be an ingrained aspect of voting patterns in Canada for a large part of Canadian history.

Urban/Rural Environment

Despite its relatively small population and its enormous land mass, Canada is a remarkably urban country. Although to some people "urban" may connote a particular viewpoint rather than a place of dwelling, for our purposes the term is defined as habitation in a town or city of at least 5000 people. As we noted in Chapter 1, the Canadian population is overwhelmingly concentrated in several urban regions in the provinces of Ontario, Québec and British Columbia. In recent years there has been a significant shift of population to the sparsely settled Western provinces, particularly to oil-rich Alberta. The Maritime provinces remain relatively under-populated and rural. How do these facts translate into electoral results?

A consistent finding of many electoral studies is that the Conservatives receive a significant degree of rural support, while the Liberals tend to attract a disproportionate number of urban voters.[65] Support for the New Democratic Party

---

[64]Mildred A. Schwartz, "Canadian Voting Behaviour," in Richard Rose, ed., *Electoral Behaviour: A Comparative Handbook* (New York: Free Press, 1974), pp. 571-574.

[65]Harold D. Clarke, Jane Jenson, Lawrence LeDuc and Jon Pammett, *Political Choice in Canada* (Toronto: McGraw-Hill Ryerson, 1979), ch. 4.

also tends to be urban. However, in most 20th century federal elections, the Liberals, while receiving considerable urban support, have appeared to be the party best able to attract a variety of voters by cutting across urban/rural lines.

The impact of community size on voting is likely to be associated with several other cleavages and voting influences. In order to prove its independent effect, the researcher would have to control for the various historical influences and factors in the political demography of the constituencies being examined. Moreover, the impact of middle-class suburbia on Canadian voting patterns has not been fully addressed in the literature.

Ethno-Linguistic Cleavage

The history of Canada is, in many ways, the history of the interaction of French and English and their quest for a workable accommodation. As we indicated in Chapters 3 and 4, a number of political culture and socialization studies have documented the degree to which French Canadians and English Canadians hold quite different attitudes and values. What complicates the analysis of voting behaviour in this regard is that ethnicity, language and religion are interrelated.

Nearly all election studies have reached the same conclusions. Traditionally, the Liberal Party has received a consistently high level of support from French Canadians while simultaneously attracting a significant proportion of English Canadian and post-World War II immigrant voters. The Progressive Conservatives, on the other hand, have received more support from Canadians of British descent. Ethnic voting support for the NDP has been confined primarily to non-French Canadians. The ability of the Liberal Party to bridge the two founding ethnic groups and at the same time to appeal to immigrant voters was the principal reason for its dominance in Canadian politics during most of the 20th century – a dominance which may have been destroyed in the 1984 General Election.

Party Identification

One of the most controversial topics in the field of electoral studies is the role of party identification – the degree to which citizens identify with a particular party. It is thought by some that parental party identification is transmitted to children through the socialization process and that the resulting attachment has a long-term effect on voting behaviour, filtering the effects of short-term factors such as party leaders or campaign issues. While in the preceding analysis we have discussed essentially "group" phenomena such as region, class, religion and ethnic identity, the question of party identification directs us to the level of the individual voter. How important is this factor in influencing voting behaviour?

Studies of electoral behaviour indicate that party identification is widespread in Canada but is relatively low in intensity. The impact of specific issues and the image of the leader are credited with many recent defections from party loyalty. While there continues to be a relatively stable core of loyalists, a significant proportion (20 percent in 1979)[66] shifts from one party affiliation to another. Thus the stabilizing effect of party identification on Canadian voters is questionable, suggesting at least the possibility of pendulum swings of political support over time.

Campaign Issues and Election Outcomes

Issues, too, may play an important part in influencing the individual voter's decision. Nearly half of all those who voted in the 1979 election cited issues as the primary basis for their voting choice.[67]

For an issue to have an impact on the outcome of an election it must meet three conditions.[68] First, it must be salient to voters; that is, voters must have an opinion on it and they must consider it relatively important. Second, the issue must be linked with partisan controversy. It will have little impact on election outcomes if all the parties are perceived to have the same position on it. Third, opinion must be strongly skewed in a single direction and not simply reflect the usual degree of attachment to the various political parties.

The perception that issues are an important factor in a voter's choice leads strategists to rely heavily on public opinion surveys. Party planners identify those groups which contain possible supporters and strive to mobilize their support through appeals and policies tailored to a winning electoral coalition. The measure of success, of course, is the election result. The following brief case study illustrates these relations between strategies and outcomes. The 1980 federal election, was the last Liberal victory of the Trudeau era and demonstrated the party's electoral machine at peak form. In the 1984 General Election, with new leaders in both major parties, the situation was reversed and the Conservatives, with meticulous, sophisticated planning and organization won a massive majority.

From this brief survey it is obvious that a number of factors influence voting. The turnout rate in Canadian elections is relatively high, and for many the act of voting is the most direct means of participating in the political process. Votes themselves are precise and measurable entities, carefully counted on Election Day and duly recorded by an army of clerks and statisticians. The contradictory perceptions and influences weighing on voters' minds as they enter the polling booths are indeed difficult to disentangle. We have identified a number of the leading factors in an attempt to understand electoral choice, and have drawn some conclusions about each in an attempt to place them within the wide spectrum of potential influences on voting behaviour. It goes without saying that while these factors have been evaluated separately there is undoubtedly a degree

---

[66]Jon Pammett, Harold Clarke, Jane Jenson and Lawrence LeDuc, "The Politics of Limited Change: The 1979 Federal Election," Occasional Paper no. 8, Department of Political Science, Carleton University (April 1981), p. 43.

[67]*Ibid.*, p. 20.

[68]*Ibid.*

of interaction and reinforcement among them which makes the precise independent effect of each difficult to determine.

While we have learned much about Canadian society through voting studies over the past few years, it is obvious that many gaps and puzzles remain. For example, the impact of the federal system itself on voting perceptions and preferences is one area where further research is needed. Provincial and municipal elections remain largely unexplored. There is an obvious need to test and re-test some of the leading theories and assumptions in the field to determine whether they hold up, given the improvements in data collection and analysis. Much has been learned, but much remains to be explored in order that we may understand this most fundamental of democratic procedures.

CASE STUDY OF THE 1984 GENERAL ELECTION

When Prime Minister Pierre Trudeau officially resigned in June 1984 in the fifth year of his current term, he left his successor, John Turner, very limited options for seeking a new mandate – none of them good. As possible dates for an election there remained late summer or autumn or the gamble of accepting whatever conditions might exist at the fifth-year deadline.[69] To complicate the decision, the Queen's scheduled visit to Canada in July could not proceed during a political campaign. Turner had just finished a demanding leadership race after eight years away from politics, and needed time to take stock, reorganize, rest and allow wounds in the party to heal. (see Chapter 10)

In retrospect, Turner would probably have decided on a different date. However, when he officially became Prime Minister on June 30, 1984 his party was still enjoying the glow of the leadership convention; it was leading in the opinion polls for the first time in three years. The Liberals appeared to have emerged at last from what Mackenzie King might have called their "valley of humiliation", a slump in popular support which had reached record depths the previous July when the Gallup poll gave them only 27 percent compared to the Conservatives' 55 percent.

September is traditionally a black month for a ruling party in Canada to call an election; on all three such occasions since Confederation the government which did so lost power (not counting Macdonald's first election). However, Turner ignored the omens and, encouraged by an eager caucus and assured personally by the Queen that she would postpone her tour, he called the election for September 4. It was an error of judgement; he and his advisors had misinterpreted the polls. As a Liberal pollster admitted afterwards, Liberal strategists could not determine the reason for the party's high standing in the early part of the campaign and thus could not take advantage of it by appealing to its source.[70]

---

[69]Trudeau had waited until the fifth year on two previous occasions. On one, in 1979, he lost; on the other, in 1972, he won only two seats more than the Conservatives. By the time Turner was elected, the fifth year of the Liberal mandate was already well underway.

[70]*The Globe and Mail*, Toronto, Sept. 20, 1984, p. 4.

The reason, almost certainly, was the change of leadership. The same shifts in party support were evident following the Tory leadership changes in 1976, 1983 and also after Lester Pearson resigned in 1967 and Trudeau became leader in 1968. On the latter occasion, the Liberals vaulted ahead of the Conservatives in the polls, but their lead going into the ensuing election was much larger – 21 points in the Gallup poll, not 9 as it was for Turner.[71]

Whatever the reason for the higher polls – the leadership convention, John Turner personally, Trudeau's peace initiative or some other phenomenon – it was temporary. By mid-campaign opinion had returned to its pre-convention condition. Had Turner waited to show more "prime ministerial" qualities with a new team, new policies and a statesmanlike image from hosting the Queen and the Pope in Canada, things might have turned out differently.

Campaign Strategy: "Media-ocracy"?

The Liberal campaign began behind and was plagued by disorganization and errors which the media publicized and magnified. Trudeau's election committee, headed by Senator Keith Davey and Finance Minister Marc Lalonde, had stopped working when he resigned, and no-one on the party executive had taken over the job. This vacuum was inherited by Bill Lee virtually as the election was being called. Lee had orchestrated Turner's very successful leadership campaign and stayed on to direct the election campaign. Candidates had to be nominated and policies and strategies formulated, but the machinery was not in place: the party personnel were not on hand; the National Office was but a skeleton. Strategists put on a brave face telling workers in Toronto, for example, that it was an advantage that their candidates were not yet nominated because the publicity from the nominating conventions would spill over into an enthusiastic campaign. However, it did not work that way. In Ontario and Québec, where the Liberals had been strongest, patronage appointments and retirements drastically reduced the number of strong candidates and there was little time to search for more.

Turner personally got off to a very shaky start and never recovered. He had won his leadership campaign on the theme that he represented change from the Trudeau years, but from the time he became Prime Minister that plank lost credibility. When he named his first Cabinet many familiar faces reappeared. Then, the same day as he announced the election, he made several controversial patronage appointments for Trudeau, cementing his connection to the former regime. By mid-campaign the polls were showing a rapid Liberal decline and, under a cloud, Bill Lee left. He was replaced by Senator Keith Davey, a veteran of six Liberal campaigns whom Turner had vowed to replace. The appointment compounded the impression that the campaign was in desperate trouble. Then even more familiar faces started to reappear, among them Trudeau's main speechwriter, press secretary and executive assistant. Themes from the Trudeau era also began to appear in Turner's speeches – the Constitution, medicare and appeals to low-income Canadians.

---

[71] *Ibid.,* Toronto, July 30, 1984, p. 4.

In the early days of the campaign Turner's strategy was to encourage a Liberal revival in the West by running in the riding of Vancouver-Quadra. He stressed competence and trust, contrasting his national and international experience with Mulroney's inexperience. However, reports of disorganization and mistakes eroded his image of competence, and the strategists were increasingly forced to rely on promises as a lure for voters.

With 21 days to go in the campaign Davey's strategy was to get Turner more on the attack, to move him more to the left of issues and to unveil new issues at an accelerated pace. He wanted Turner to concentrate on southern Ontario and be less accessible to the media. Advertising was reshaped to stress that Turner was a new leader. In the last days, Trudeau was brought into the campaign in his old constituency of Mount Royal, as well as in Spadina and Outremont where old friends needed help. But relations between Turner and the former Prime Minister were strained and the value of such forays limited because Turner had tried from the beginning to distance himself from his predecessor.

The Progressive Conservative campaign provided a startling contrast with the Liberal disorganization. It was, as Liberal Senator Davey himself commented after the election, the "slickest election campaign in Canadian history". The ingredients for success were all there – organization, communications and commitment. While Turner was unable to sell himself as the agent of change, Mulroney was the very personification of it.

The Conservative campaign had begun when Mulroney took his seat in the House of Commons the previous June. One of his first actions was to divide his caucus into task forces to develop policies for an election. The freeze that had been placed on nomination meetings when he was elected in June was lifted in October, and each constituency was asked to coordinate its selection of potential MPs with a representative of the leader. This direct show of interest in traditionally autonomous constituency affairs was part of an attempt to recruit and place "star" candidates in specific ridings. It was a particularly effective tactic in Québec, where Mulroney had an active candidate selection committee. The party had about 90 percent of its new candidates taking "how-to" classes by the time the election was called. By that point the Conservative leader had also conducted campaign trial runs in March and April to raise funds and iron out problems before the media began to scrutinize them. The staff was ordered to maintain a low profile. The plan for the first half of the campaign was to reinforce the desire for change; for the second half it was to sell Mulroney as Prime Minister. Promises would be made, but not costed until the end of the campaign, when it would be too late to inflict serious damage.

With the advice of his campaign co-directors Norman Atkins (who had run four successful provincial campaigns for Bill Davis in Ontario) and Jean Bazin (who had been working hard on the campaign for six months before Turner was even elected leader), Mulroney quickly called for several regional debates. These, along with two nationally televised debates, one in French, one in English, gave the Mulroney campaign a significant boost. The Conservative strategy in Québec was to sell Mulroney as the person best able to represent Québec interests now that Trudeau was gone. His polished, strong performance in the

French television debate plus the fact that he had decided to run in Québec, in Manicouagan, gave that claim credibility. In the English debate Mulroney scored by pressing arguments over the controversial patronage appointments, thus tying Turner to the old regime and forcing him to say repeatedly that he had "had no option".

Mulroney proved to be a master at enlisting skilled help; perhaps the best illustration was in Ontario, where he had the full backing of Premier Bill Davis and his notoriously competent "Big Blue Machine" (a favour which had never been bestowed on Clark). It was in Québec, however, that he moulded an impressive *"tonnerre bleu"* machine. When he became leader, there was virtually no party organization in Québec. Mulroney, Bernard Roy and Rodrigue Pageau put together a coalition of Mulroney's friends, old Union Nationale politicians and organizers, former Créditistes and disaffected Liberals and Parti Québécois supporters. By the last weeks of the campaign the Tories were confident of victory.

The NDP also conducted a remarkably successful campaign. Ed Broadbent had been unanimously reconfirmed as leader at the Regina convention the previous summer and his critics silenced. Like the PCs, the NDP began to prepare for the election at least a year in advance. However, despite poor economic conditions, Canadians were not looking to the NDP for solutions. The party entered the campaign with only 11 percent in the opinion polls, plagued by media speculation that they might lose all their seats in the West and perhaps fall below the figure needed for official recognition as a party in Parliament.

Armed with a new staff at party headquarters, including a new tour director and direct mail specialist, NDP party strategists met the 31 sitting MPs to develop tactics for holding onto their seats. They were told to "sandbag", to work furiously for the next year. A new pollster was commissioned to conduct a poll to find out why the party was doing so badly. Among other things, he learned that NDP support was strongest on social policies such as medicare and weakest on long-term economic planning, and that there was a strong perception of the NDP as an honest fighter for the "little guy". From this came their new campaign strategy: to concentrate on "ordinary Canadians" and forget about trying to run the country. One strategist put it this way: "We decided to cut out the B.S. We would admit candidly that we didn't stand a chance of forming the government and you haven't seen us scaring anybody with plans for some grand industrial design."[72]

It was agreed that the MPs could spend more time in their constituencies and less in travel, and in return they would not have to attend party functions and unimportant House of Commons committee meetings.[73] Broadbent too spent more time travelling to constituency events. His experience and relaxed manner won him wide respect throughout the campaign, particularly during the televised debates.

As in 1980, the Canadian Labour Congress rallied behind the NDP but stayed out of sight because they had no solid vote at their command and because

---

[72]Quoted by Hugh Winsor in *The Globe and Mail*, Toronto, Aug. 23, 1984, p. 5.

[73]See Bob Hepburn, "Rejuvenated NDP Fights Uphill Fight," *Toronto Star*, Nov. 27, 1984.

they were afraid they might frighten away some voters. They did, however, make targeted telephone calls and mailings to emphasize the need for "working people" to stick together.

During the last few weeks of the campaign, when the polls showed a surge of Tory strength, the NDP stressed the threat of a huge Tory majority: "Would you trust the Tories if they won 200 seats? Keep them honest by sending some New Democrats to Ottawa to stick up for the ordinary Canadians."[74]

The 1984 campaign illustrated once again the powerful role of the media in modern Canadian elections. Above all, campaign strategists must be capable of harnessing the media, employing them for their own purposes. Turner began his first press conference on becoming Prime Minister by saying he would remain open and accessible to the media. But midway through his chaotic campaign the chumminess was gone; familiarity had eroded trust. Contact was, as in the Mulroney campaign, limited to sending out only the words and images he wanted transmitted. No spontaneous remarks were allowed to distract the media. Instead of becoming more open with the help of the media, the two major parties became more controlled and secretive.

The media subjected political leaders to what amounted to Hollywood-style screen tests. Characteristics such as "blue eyes", "silvery hair" and a "deep voice" were extolled. Incidents such as a spilled cup of coffee and an inadvertent pat on the *derrière* of a female colleague were more widely discussed than policy issues. Since media competition is intense, and such titillations attract significantly larger audiences than do serious discussions about unemployment or the economy, they were dwelt upon at great length. It was a prime example of what might be termed "media-ocracy". Turner had re-entered political life with an image that was larger than life. He emerged from the election with that image badly tarnished.

The three parties aired slogans in a series of commercials from early in the campaign until two days before the election. They followed the same general pattern: a concentrated series in prime time at the start followed by a relatively calm period, then saturation the last few days. The Liberal ads emphasized traditional liberal values and their new leader. However, in the final days they became desperately negative, saying the Tories could not be trusted, reminding voters of the closing of Schefferville by Iron Ore of Canada when Mulroney was President of that company. The Tories prepared three types of ads – leader-oriented, issue-oriented and negative, but the negative ones were not needed. The content of their advertising focused primarily on the need for change. The NDP's advertisements concentrated on the theme "We speak for the ordinary people."

Special interest groups were able to continue spending freely and promoting or opposing candidates at will, since the government, shortly before the election, had accepted a court ruling against restrictions on their activities and spending.[75]

---

[74]*The Globe and Mail,* Toronto, Aug. 23, 1984.

[75]Restrictions incorporated into the *Canada Elections Act* in 1983 were immediately challenged by the Toronto-based National Citizens' Coalition as an infringement on free speech provisions in the *Charter of Rights.*

1984 Campaign Issues

The most serious issues in the campaign were economic: the projected $30 billion federal deficit and unemployment. The first of these topics elicited wide generalizations and few specific proposals from the parties; the second, a variety of electoral promises.

The Progressive Conservatives maintained that they could not be specific on economic matters until they were in power and could "see the books". Initially Mulroney called the deficit "shameful", but later he maintained that it must be reduced while conceding that it might have to be increased temporarily to fulfill some of his other objectives. He offered no specific target. The Liberals, on the other hand, said there would be a reduction of about $15 billion in the deficit over the next five to seven years, but did not say how it would be accomplished and refused to make public any new economic forecasts about the size of the deficit. Instead, they warned that Mulroney had a secret agenda to slash social services. The NDP made no specific promises about deficit targets, but said they would raise it the first year, after which it would probably fall. On economic issues generally, Broadbent contrasted his concern for the ordinary man with that of the "Bobbsey Twins of Bay Street", stressing the similar "boardroom approach" of the Liberal and Tory leaders. All three parties offered some version of a minimum tax on the rich in order to aid the poor.

With 497 000 young Canadians out of work, the unemployment issue centred largely on youth. All three leaders named youth unemployment the most pressing issue of the campaign, and all three presented slightly different schemes to improve it. The Conservatives offered a refundable tax break for any employer who created a job for an unemployed young person and promised that loans would be made available from the unemployment insurance fund for young people wanting to start businesses. The Liberals offered a "first choice" program to create training positions that would give youth job experience. Among NDP promises was a $1.5 billion youth initiative fund to provide jobs in projects designed by young people.

Women's issues, too, were widely publicized in each party's campaign, reflecting society's new sensitivity to topics such as women's pensions, reproductive choice, daycare and the wage gap. A national television debate between the leaders revealed (not surprisingly) a common concern to improve the lot of women in all of these areas, and a wide range of policy proposals to that end. The NDP (which had been first to address these types of issues, as far back as the 1960s) was the most progressive, endorsing, for example, equal pay for work of equal value and mandatory affirmative action programs in the federal public service and in companies doing business under federal jurisdiction or with the federal government. The Liberals, at the other extreme, were sympathetic but steered away from the most difficult promises and offered instead such concrete proposals as increasing the child-care deduction, strengthening laws on pornography and prostitution and doubling the number of jobs available for women in part-time retraining programs. The Conservatives supported equal pay for work of equal value within the federal civil service and affirmative action programs for companies dealing with the federal government.

There was general agreement that action should be taken on women's issues, but like many other election promises they were not expected to be acted on very vigorously. According to pollsters at Decima Research, people reacted positively to so-called "women's issues" as long as the solutions remained vague. Support dropped dramatically when details of implementation were fleshed out.[76]

Foreign policy was not a major issue during the campaign, but the Conservatives urged stronger support for US foreign policies and NATO, an increase in the defence budget and distinctive uniforms for the three branches of the Armed Forces. The Liberals went into the election still basking in the glow of Trudeau's popular peace initiative, but they did not maintain a united front. Iona Campagnolo, Liberal Party President, was the first to jump off the bandwagon and call for a mutual and verifiable nuclear freeze. Turner said, "Personally I believe in arms freeze," but simultaneously maintained that Canada had to be loyal to NATO and move in concert with it. The NDP, as usual, supported getting out of NATO.

Another widely discussed issue was one generated by the departing Prime Minister. In his last two days in office Trudeau handed out well over 200 patronage rewards to his political friends. He also extracted a written promise from John Turner to name several more when he called the election. Turner agreed to this demand because the appointments included several MPs; he wanted to keep his majority in the Commons and thus have a free hand to determine the election date without the possibility of one being foisted on him by a defeat in the House. The day he announced the election, Turner revealed Trudeau's seventeen appointments. There was an immediate public outcry about hands in "the public trough". Turner refused to make public the correspondence between himself and Trudeau on the matter, even though the issue plagued him throughout the campaign and he was portrayed as Trudeau's partner or stooge in the affair. Whether he indeed had "no option" in making the appointments as he maintained or whether he should have refused and accepted the consequences was a matter of intense public debte.

Another related issue which all three parties tried to use to their advantage was the need for change. On the whole, however, discussion of issues in the campaign was often secondary to public fascination with the images of the leaders coined and promoted by the media, and to gossip about minor accidents and gaffes, particularly those which plagued the Liberal campaign.

1984 Election Outcome

The Progressive Conservatives were swept to power with the largest number of Tory MPs in Canadian history: Conservatives 211, Liberals 40, NDP 30 and Independent 1.[77] It was the first Conservative majority victory in 26 years. They won

---

[76]*The Citizen*, Ottawa, June 9, 1984.

[77]The Independent candidate had stated that if he won he would probably quickly join the Conservative Party.

Illustration by Barbara Spurll.

three seats more than Diefenbaker had captured in 1958, but there were fewer seats in the Commons then, so Diefenbaker's majority was relatively larger. The Liberals' 28 percent of the vote was their worst showing ever. Many high-profile MPs were lost, with the result that almost three-quarters of the new Liberal caucus arrived with no experience on the front bench either as Cabinet members or as shadow Cabinet critics in opposition. A record high of 27 women was elected (10 percent of the House), nearly double the 1980 record of 14.

     The regional distribution in the government caucus was ideal yet how truly representative of the Canadian electorate was the ratio of MPs in the newly elected Parliament? The Conservatives won 75 percent of the total seats on the basis of 50 percent of the popular vote; the Liberals 14 percent on 28 percent of the vote; and the NDP 11 percent on 19 percent of the vote. Under a system of proportional representation the Mulroney government would have had 141 seats, the Liberals 79, the NDP 54 and all others 8.

     Many factors contributed to the massive Conservative victory: the desire for change; the new Conservative weapon – a leader from Québec; the breakdown of

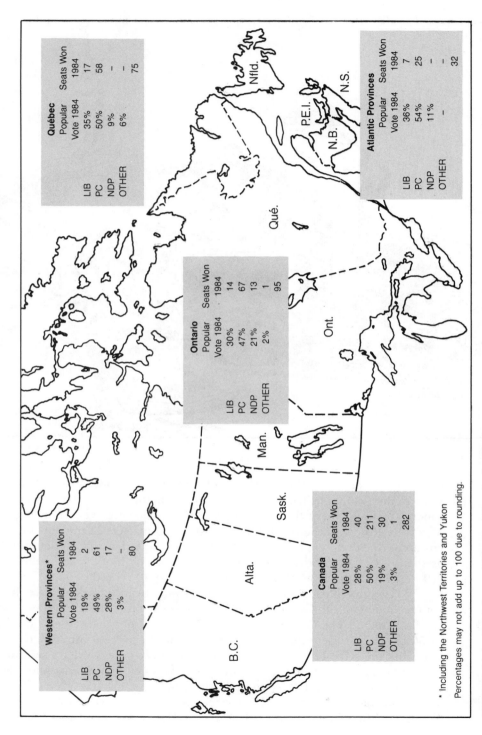

Québec

	Popular Vote 1984	Seats Won 1984
LIB	35%	17
PC	50%	58
NDP	9%	–
OTHER	6%	–
		75

Atlantic Provinces

	Popular Vote 1984	Seats Won 1984
LIB	36%	7
PC	54%	25
NDP	11%	–
OTHER	–	–
		32

Ontario

	Popular Vote 1984	Seats Won 1984
LIB	30%	14
PC	47%	67
NDP	21%	13
OTHER	2%	1
		95

Western Provinces*

	Popular Vote 1984	Seats Won 1984
LIB	19%	2
PC	49%	61
NDP	28%	17
OTHER	3%	–
		80

Canada

	Popular Vote 1984	Seats Won 1984
LIB	28%	40
PC	50%	211
NDP	19%	30
OTHER	3%	1
		282

Nfld.
P.E.I.
N.S.
N.B.
Qué.
Ont.
Man.
Sask.
Alta.
B.C.

* Including the Northwest Territories and Yukon

Percentages may not add up to 100 due to rounding.

FIGURE 11.1 1984 General Election Results by Region

the Liberal electoral machinery; a series of strategic and tactical minor events and errors during the Liberal campaign that caused the media to saddle John Turner with an accident-prone image, much as they had done to Joe Clark in the previous election; and a superbly orchestrated Conservative campaign. To this list must be added the fact that Trudeau lingered so long that he severely limited Turner's options for choosing an election date.

Québec provided the most dramatic aspect of the electoral outcome; it gave the Conservatives their first popular majority there since Diefenbaker's victory in 1958, and, before that, 1891. This sudden change of preference, giving the Conservatives just over 50 percent of the popular vote in Québec, reflected Mulroney's success in portraying himself as Trudeau's successor. The Liberals were reduced to 35 percent of the Québec vote from 67 percent in 1980. The Liberal campaign in Québec, organized by André Ouellet, was late in starting and disorganized, and suffered from overconfidence on the basis of previous easy victories. Ouellet's reasoning after the vote was that Québec voters "smelled victory with Mulroney and went there. I think people wanted change and they made up their mind early in the campaign that the Mulroney team represented more change than the Turner team."[78] The Québec campaign was also hurt by internal feuding between supporters of Ouellet and Jean Chrétien, a legacy of the leadership convention. The NDP clung to the 9 percent popular vote it had won in Québec in 1980; 6 percent voted for the remaining minor parties, especially the Parti Nationaliste and the Rhinoceros Party.

The Conservatives won an absolute majority in each of the Atlantic provinces and Alberta, and in Ontario their popular vote rose to 48 percent, up 12 percent from 1980. The NDP weathered the campaign extremely well. They did well in Ontario, where the strong Conservative showing eroded the traditional Liberal base, and created three-way races. Their popular vote fell in three of the four Atlantic provinces but they fared well in the West, increasing their support slightly in both Alberta and Saskatchewan.

National polls are, it must be remembered, a snapshot of public opinion, not a prediction. However, the polls released just before the election provided a startlingly accurate reflection of the final results. The Gallup Poll taken August 28-29 gave the exact percentage of popular vote outcomes for all three parties: PC 50, Liberals 28, NDP 19, and Other 3, with 10 percent undecided. The Globe-Crop polls plotted on Figure 11.1 showed the dramatic changes in relative position of the three parties in public opinion from the 1980 election to 1984. The Conservatives peaked just before their leadership convention; Liberal fortunes improved with Trudeau's impending resignation, peaked during the Liberal leadership convention and then, after the leaders' debates of July 24 and 25, rapidly dropped back to their 1982 and early 1983 level.

The publication during the election campaign of polls which showed a rapid decline in Liberal support raised questions once again about whether polls can cause a bandwagon effect, particularly when they generate the type of head-

---

[78]*The Globe and Mail,* Toronto, Sept. 5, 1984.

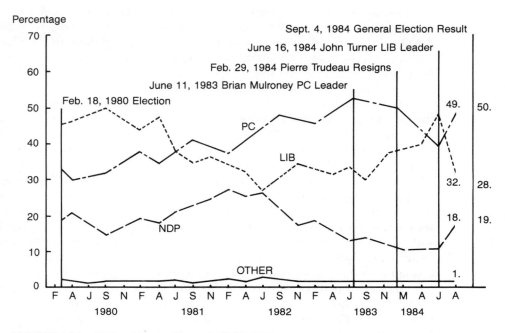

FIGURE 11.2 Federal Party Support, 1980-1984

Source: Adapted from Globe-Crop polls conducted from Feb. 18, 1980 to Aug. 19, 1984.

line publicized in *The Citizen* on August 25: "Liberals Tumbling Toward Destruction". Some commentators and candidates asked whether polls should be banned in the final two weeks of a campaign, as they are in France and briefly were in British Columbia. However, until there is greater proof that polls do, in fact, prejudice opinion, the law is unlikely to be amended, particularly since the *Charter of Rights and Freedoms* protects freedom of expression.

OVERVIEW

Elections have an important role in Canadian politics. By providing a stable means of transferring government office between contesting political parties as well as an opportunity for voters to express their acceptance of or displeasure with the decisions of the government, elections legitimate the exercise of political power. Furthermore, the mobilization of voters' interest in electoral contests confers legitimacy on the political regime itself, as well as on the individual office-holders.

Through the party organizations based upon them, elections are vital in reconciling diverse interests within society. They provide a national forum for discussion and allow issues to be raised and compromises to be arrived at, leading thereby to a measure of consensus. However, there are grounds to question the performance of this role in the case of Canada. The results of Canadian General Elections often appear to be more divisive than consensual, pitting region against region and eroding the legitimacy of the "national" government. This concern has motivated calls for electoral reform. Yet elections continue to generate support for Canada's political system. It may even be that the viability of elections themselves may in the long run be more significant than the actual partisan results.

Elections also have an impact on government decision-making. By determining which party will form the government, elections influence the choices made by policy-makers. Elections also help to establish the broad policy parameters of political parties and the government. Issues perceived as important during the campaign must usually be addressed in some manner; otherwise, the government will run the risk of defeat in the next election. Defeated parties may also adjust their behaviour and policy positions both to prevent repetition of what they conclude were their mistakes and to broaden their support. To this extent, therefore, elections help provide politicians with a reference for guiding their actions.

In summary, the main importance of elections in Canada stems from the legitimacy they confer on government and its actions. Because of the democratic and consistent nature of elections, most voters perceive that the government is representative of their interests. Although few would express unqualified support of government, most Canadians are committed to Canada's basic electoral structures and their results.

CanaPress Photo Service

chapter 12

Interest Groups
Lobbying and Public Policy

CANADIANS ARE ORGANIZED IN NUMEROUS AND NOVEL WAYS. There are organizations to represent business, labour, loyalists, separatists, nature lovers and economic developers. In short, practically everyone belongs to some organization or other. Large or small, these groups are active in pressing their needs, principles and demands on other Canadians. When they act in the political arena they are called interest groups, or, more pejoratively, pressure groups.

Such groups are an important element in the political life of all modern societies, but their form and importance varies from one country to the next. In Japan, for example, the *chingodan*, a group of rural petitioners, often bearing gifts of fruit, traditionally visits Tokyo when the national budget is being prepared in order to present their arguments to government officials and politicians.[1] In countries such as the Soviet Union, on the other hand, where citizens have few legal rights to organize associations, unauthorized interest groups attempt to influence the government by means of dramatic events such as hunger strikes intended to attract international publicity.[2] These cases illustrate that the structure and behaviour of interest groups is closely related to the political system in which they operate.

In Canada, such groups can organize legally to petition and cajole the government. They operate in and help to mould the federal political system. They are ubiquitous, representing interests as varied as business (Canadian Manufacturers Association), labour (Canadian Labour Congress), agriculture (Canadian Federation of Agriculture), professionals (Canadian Medical Association), consumers (Consumers' Association of Canada), women (National Council of Women), religious groups (Canadian Council of Churches), ethnic groups (Canadian

---

[1]Nathaniel Thayer, *How the Conservatives Rule Japan* (Princeton: Princeton University Press, 1969).

[2]F.C. Barghoorn, *Politics in the USSR* (Boston: Little, Brown, 1966) Chapter 5.

Jewish Congress) and even public interests such as a clean environment (Greenpeace or Energy Probe).

Thousands of individuals work in Ottawa today to represent these multifarious interests. Some organizations are powerful; others are practically insignificant. Some employ experts such as professional lobbyists, public relations firms or highly paid lawyers to promote their interests. Others occasionally send their local officials or chief executive officer to Ottawa to argue their cases. Still others spend their time and energies trying to attract public attention through the media. What they all have in common is the desire to influence government policy, legislation, regulation or expenditures.

Much of the public is dismayed by the power of these interest groups. Citizens' groups complain about big business; businessmen admonish the special pleading of narrowly formed organizations. Some skeptics complain that interest groups are associated with unethical means such as bribery or blackmail in influencing government decisions in their favour. Many citizens even harbour the suspicion that they are "evil because they conflict with the fundamental attributes of democracy".[3] Political scientists, on the other hand, usually counter that such groups are inevitable and important for the political process.

WHAT ARE INTEREST GROUPS?

There are many sociological meanings to the word "group". But in this volume, "interest groups" are simply distinguished from others by their orientation to the political system.[4] We are not interested in those groups with no relation to the political system or those with no organizational element. Thus, an **interest group** is here defined as an "organized association which engages in activity relative to governmental decisions".[5]

This is a very wide definition which includes many types of groups, from those which are relatively transient and issue-oriented to others which are institutionalized, with many general as well as specific interests. The common denominator is, as the definition states, that they are non-publicly accountable organizations which attempt to further their common interest by affecting public policy.

In *Pressure Group Behaviour in Canadian Politics*, Paul Pross identifies four prime characteristics of interest groups.[6] First, they have a formal structure of organization which gives them continuity. Organization is essential to allow them

---

[3]Harmon Zeigler, *Interest Groups in American Society* (Englewood Cliffs: Prentice-Hall, 1964), p. 33.

[4]Mildred A. Schwartz, "The Group Basis of Politics," in John A. Redekop, ed., *Approaches to Canadian Politics*, 2nd ed. (Scarborough: Prentice-Hall, 1983), p. 316.

[5]Robert H. Salisbury, "Interest Groups," in Fred I. Greenstein and Nelson W. Polsby, eds., *Handbook of Political Science*, Vol. 4 (Reading, Mass.: Addison-Wesley, 1975), p. 175.

[6]A. Paul Pross "Pressure Groups: Adaptive Instruments of Political Communication" in A. Paul Pross, ed., *Pressure Group Behaviour in Canadian Politics* (Toronto: McGraw-Hill Ryerson, 1975).

to determine their objectives and strategies for action. Second, interest groups are able to articulate and aggregate interests. Third, they attempt to act within the political system to influence policy outputs. Fourth, they try to influence power rather than exercise the responsibility of government.

Mobs are not interest groups because they lack organizational structure. Political parties too are excluded, although the first three of these criteria apply equally to them. However, parties have different goals than interest groups; they seek political power by having their candidates elected to government offices, whereas interest groups try to influence political parties and government officials toward certain policies rather than enacting these policies themselves. Interest groups can, and often do, try to win the support of all parties. The similarities between parties and groups have led to different opinions about how the two are related. Some analysts, for example, believe that a rise in interest group power has been at least partially responsible for the decline in the role of political parties. In countries like Canada where there are two dominant political parties, the distinction between parties and interest groups is evident. However, it is interesting to note that in countries where many small parties compete, minority parties often represent the very narrow interests of one group, and the distinction becomes less clear.

ANALYZING INTEREST GROUPS: AN ART IN ITS INFANCY

The study of interest groups by the political science community grew out of a sociological revolt against the narrow and somewhat sterile confines of formal institutional analysis. The change represented a necessary stage in the maturation of political science, in which "politics" finally came to be viewed as something associated with, but much larger than, "government".

Of seminal importance to a theory of politics which centred around the interaction of social groups was the work of A. F. Bentley. His *Process of Government*, published in 1908, cited the "group" as the basic unit of all political life.[7] Rejecting the concept of the state as "no factor in our investigation" and the idea of sovereignty as a "piteous, threadbare joke",[8] Bentley put the case for identifying the group as *the* fundamental point of departure for the study of politics:

> All phenomena of government are phenomena of groups pressing one another, forming one another, and pushing out new groups and group representatives (the organs or agencies of government) to mediate the adjustments. It is only as we isolate these group activities, determine their representative values, and get the whole process stated in terms of them, that we approach a satisfactory knowledge of government.[9]

[7]Arthur F. Bentley, *The Process of Government, A Study of Social Pressures,* edited by Peter H. Odegard (Cambridge: Harvard University Press, 1967).
[8]*Ibid.,* pp. 263-264.
[9]*Ibid.,* p. 269.

While Bentley displayed a disinclination to indulge in precise definitional rigour, the ambiguity of his terminology did not serve to undermine his position in the development of political science. Even a cursory review of monographic group studies from the 1930s onwards serves to illustrate the power of his influence.

In their concern to reduce ideological presuppositions and expose the underlying dynamics of the political process, many of these works found themselves in fundamental agreement with Ambrose Bierce's definition of politics as "a strife of interest masquerading as a contest of principles".[10] Earl Latham's research on the evolution of anti-trust legislation before the eighty-first American Congress, for example, began with the assertion that organized groups, as "structures of power", are the vehicles through which social values cherished by individuals are realized, and concluded that one of the ways in which politics can be properly understood is as "the struggle of groups to write in their favor the rules by which the community is governed".[11]

It is indicative of Bentley's influence on American political science that works such as Latham's, published in the early 1950s, actually represent comparatively late research on interest group activity. As early as the late 1920s books such as Peter Odegard's on the prohibition movement and Pendelton Herring's on interest group representation in Congress[12] had laid the foundation of a rich body of interest group literature very much within the Bentley tradition. The work of greatest theoretical importance to the contemporary study of interest groups, however, is unquestionably David Truman's monumental work on political interest and public opinion, *The Governmental Process.*[13] For Truman, the fundamental justification for emphasizing groups as basic social units lay in "the uniformities of behaviour produced through them".[14] Uniformity of behaviour, he pointed out, does not deny the existence of individual will; on the contrary, the nature and frequency of interaction between individuals determine the existence or nonexistence of a group:

> If a motorist stops along a highway to ask directions of a farmer, the two are interacting, but they can hardly be said to constitute a group except in the most casual sense. If, however, the motorist belongs to an automobile club the staff of which he and the other members more or less regularly resort to for route information, then staff and members can be designated as a group.[15]

---

[10]Ambrose Bierce, *The Devil's Dictionary,* (New York: Dover, 1958), p. 101.

[11]Earl Latham, *The Group Basis of Politics: A Study in Basing-Point Legislation* (Ithaca: Cornell University Press, 1952), p. 12, p. 1, p. 209.

[12]Peter H. Odegard, *Pressure Politics: The Story of the Anti-Saloon League* (New York: Columbia University Press, 1928); E. Pendelton Herring, *Group Representation Before Congress* (Washington: Brookings Institute, 1929).

[13]David B. Truman, *The Governmental Process: Political Interests and Public Opinion* (New York: Alfred A. Knopf, 1951).

[14]*Ibid.,* p. 23.

[15]*Ibid.,* p. 24.

Truman studied both formal and informal groups, but his primary concern centred upon the functioning of groups in the political process. In his effort to examine not only existing but also potential interest groups, Truman arrived at an unusually broad definition of the object of study: "interest group" referred to "any group that, on the basis of one or more shared attitudes, makes certain claims upon other groups in society for the establishment, maintenance, or enhancement of forms of behaviour that are implied by the shared attitudes".[16] At the same time, he inveighed against the popular inclination to credit interest groups with inherently sinister instincts or intentions – an inclination typified by the use of terms such as "vested interest", "special interest" and "pressure group".

Indeed, the concept of interest group as found in Bentley, Truman and their theoretical disciples can be said to be an indispensible component of later pluralist theories.[17] To pluralist scholars interest groups represent highly functional cogs in the variegated machinery of the participatory democratic process. As aggregators and articulators of the needs of their constituent membership, interest groups serve to place issues on the political agenda of society, predigest the disparate views of individual members and formulate coherent demands for insertion into the legislative process.[18]

Yet no matter how political scientists have come to evaluate the role of interest groups in contemporary politics, most have found it necessary to begin with a definition of "interest group" which is more discriminating than the one offered by Truman. The majority of writers on interest groups do not, unlike Truman, anticipate future organizations but limit themselves to existing associations while conforming fairly closely to the characterization of an interest group as defined above: an "organized association which engages in activity relative to government decisions".[19] The narrow political activity of an interest group thus defined we call **lobbying**, which constitutes activities aimed at securing favourable policy decisions or the appointment of specific government personnel.

---

[16]*Ibid.*, p. 33.

[17]See Robert A. Dahl, *Who Governs? Democracy and Power in an American City* (New Haven: Yale University Press, 1961) and *Polyarchy: Participation and Opposition* (New Haven: Yale University Press, 1971); Gabriel A. Almond and G. Bingham Powell Jr., *Comparative Politics: A Developmental Approach* (Boston: Little, Brown and Co., 1966); and Gabriel A. Almond and Sidney Verba, *The Civic Culture: Political Attitudes and Democracy in Five Nations* (Princeton: Princeton University Press, 1963). See also the brief critique of pluralism in Chapter 13.

[18]Terms such as "aggregation" and "articulation", "input", "output" and policy "process" have become standard vocabulary in scholarly literature on interest group activity and public policy formation. Systems theory and structural-functional analysis, as formulated by David Easton and Gabriel Almond respectively, can be credited with arriving at a terminology which permeates all political science writing. Even the most vehement critics of Easton and Almond frequently adopt their nomenclature. See David Easton, *The Political System: An Inquiry into the State of Political Science* (New York: Alfred A. Knopf, 1953); David Easton, "An Approach to the Analysis of Political Systems," *World Politics*, vol. 9 no. 3 (April 1957), pp. 383-400; Almond and Powell Jr., *Comparative Politics: A Developmental Approach, op. cit.*

[19]This is the definition offered by Robert H. Salisbury in Fred I. Greenstein and Nelson W. Polsby, *op. cit.*.

Any text on Canadian politics would clearly be incomplete without a discussion of interest groups and political lobbying. There are two reasons why this statement is increasingly valid. The first is that government, not only in Canada but also in all the industrialized democracies, has come to consume an ever-greater share of the national economic pie. In fact, political life in Canada has always featured a very active and effective state; one scholarly inquiry into the growth of Canadian government activities placed "the high point in the influence of the doctrine of laissez-faire and the low point in government intervention" at a date preceding Confederation itself, "somewhere about 1850".[20] In the contemporary Canadian welfare state eleven governments jointly account for 43 percent of the Gross National Expenditure, while the federal government alone has grown by more than 250 percent between 1970 and 1980.[21]

Second, the relationship between public and private has become one of mutual rather than asymmetrical dependence. By furnishing politicians and bureaucrats with invaluable information through the communication of consolidated attitudes, interest groups lower the aggregate information costs of the legislative system. Put in the simplest terms, interest groups collect information, predigest it and process it so that coherent demands can be made on political actors. At the same time, organized interests put a reservoir of technical skills and expert personnel at the disposal of political decision-makers. In the words of one official at the Department of Transport, "We're often as anxious to meet them as they are us."[22] And, he continued, "on an important policy matter it's vital that we get industry's ideas and criticisms. If we don't understand what they say and why, we only open ourselves up to trouble later on."[23] In other words, an effective bureaucrat must acquire the skill of consultation.

Political science has identified the following as the contributions of interest groups to liberal democratic politics. First, interest groups are a major source of mediation between the government and the individual, articulating aggregated opinions and protecting the individual from undue control by the state. Second, they provide a mechanism for political representation which supplements the electoral process, assisting the political system by marshalling support for issues and providing ideas for public policy. Third, interest groups allow the political process to be more responsive than the electoral process to social and economic differences in society.[24] Next, such groups feed the government valuable informa-

---

[20]J.A. Corry, "The Growth of Government Activity Since Confederation," A Study Prepared for the *Royal Commission on Dominion-Provincial Relations*, Ottawa, 1939, p. 1.

[21]See Robert J. Jackson, "An Underdeveloped Art: Analysing Interest Groups and Lobbying in Canada," paper prepared for Conference on Foreign Lobbies, Johns Hopkins University, 15-16 June 1983.

[22]Quoted in Ron Blunn, "The Lobbyists: They're Discreet, Don't Twist Arms and Affect Almost all of Ottawa's Rules," *Financial Times of Canada*, January 30-February 5, 1978.

[23]*Ibid.*

[24]Adapted from a list by Amitai Etzioni, "Making Interest Groups Work for the Public," *Public Opinion*, vol. 5, no. 4 (August/September 1982), pp. 53-55.

tion, both facts and opinion, which can be used to help formulate policies and test policy proposals. This circular process of communication provides a valuable link between citizens and public policy by helping to keep the government in touch with shifts of opinion in society.

Groups also supplement government agencies: bureaucrats delegate administrative responsibilities to certain groups. For example, in the case of the Canadian Medical Association, they actually regulate their own professional activity. This largely unpaid service can be an enormous assistance to the government bureaucracy. As well, professional groups indirectly help the civil service to disseminate information by publishing explanations of government policy in their journals.

Finally, interest groups have valuable internal functions. Membership in a group offers benefits won through communication with government such as tax incentives or other legislation. Of course, not only the membership at large benefits from the organization; there are also tangible career benefits for those who hold leadership positions within subgroups. David Kwavnick has shown, for example, that the Québec-based Confederation of National Trade Unions' "leadership risked and ultimately sacrificed the most vital interests of the Lapalme drivers in a dispute which ultimately concerned only those leaders' ambitions for organizational aggrandizement."[25]

Today, the influence of group theorists is clearly visible in all aspects of political science. At the same time, it has been and remains subject to revision, modification and debate. The dominant arguments about interest group manoeuvring and such groups' contribution to public policy will be the object of discussion later in this chapter. Elementary descriptions, however, should precede analysis. The following section will therefore address itself to the institutions and organizations of Canadian interest groups.

THE UNIVERSE OF CANADIAN INTEREST GROUPS

Interest groups in Canada reflect a wide range of issues and concerns, both economic and non-economic. The number of interest groups is extraordinarily large and has not been fully catalogued. In Ottawa alone there are over 300 trade and professional organizations. It has been estimated that these 300 groups, representing only the tip of a giant iceberg, employ over 2000 staff to improve "public relations" with the government.

Few individual corporations can afford to have full-time employees in Ottawa. Instead, their interests are "protected" by their public relations departments

---

[25]David Kwavnick, "Pressure Group Demands and Organizational Objectives: The CNTU, the Lapalme Affair and National Bargaining Units," *CJPS*, vol. VI, no. 4 (December 1973), p. 583. For a perceptive analysis of the broader question raised here, see David Kwavnick, *Organized Labour and Pressure Group Politics: The Canadian Labour Congress: 1956-1968* (Montréal: McGill-Queen's University Press, 1972).

"What was it the Opposition was saying about the poor, the weak and those least able to defend themselves?"

and chief executive officers. There is no doubt that these officers expend considerable effort attempting to influence government. According to one survey,[26] 27 percent of chief executive officers had been before a parliamentary committee at least once; 33 percent had direct regular contact with the government; 29 percent were on a government board or advisory group; and 42 percent had made a personal representation to the government.

If all these types of activities were summed one would obtain a complete list of the interest group universe. Doing this would be so difficult, however, that political scientists have attempted to avoid the problem of tabulation by classifying the types of interest groups instead.

---

[26]James Gillies, *Why Business Fails* (Montréal: Institute for Research on Public Policy, 1981). On business and politics, see Robert J. Jackson and R. van Schendelen, "Politics and Business: Partners and Antagonists," unpublished paper, delivered at ECPR meetings, Barcelona, Spain, March 1985.

Classification of Interest Groups

Only two typologies of interest groups have had lasting acceptance in Canadian political science. Engelmann and Schwartz divide interest groups into economic and non-economic categories, then sub-divide the first into agriculture, labour and business groups. The non-economic category is further sub-divided into nine sub-types.[27] Such distinctions, based on the primary basis of affiliation for their members, do help to explain the basic differences in origin, activities and goals of the groups. This typology was used, for example, by W. Blair Dimock and later by Elizabeth M. Dixon to provide stimulating discussions of the impact of groups on Canadian foreign policy.[28]

The economic/non-economic distinction, however, does not convey any information about the activities or relative importance of the various groups. There is a wide disparity in their powers. They range from relatively transient issue-oriented groups to others which are well-established and assert a strong influence on political and economic life. They differ not only in terms of structure but also resources, tactics and goals. These differences seem to affect the success or failure of groups in reaching their goals.

Paul Pross has addressed this omission in offering the most satisfactory categorization of Canadian interest groups to date, a model that embraces all of them within a single framework.[29] His typology is designed to relate the groups to one another and to the policy system at large. Groups are classified as issue-oriented, fledgling, mature or institutionalized; each is then categorized according to its objectives, organizational features and levels of communication with government. It should of course be kept in mind that the distinction between the categories is not clear-cut, and any one group may not conform exactly to this pattern.

Institutionalized groups are relatively well-structured and enduring. In Pross' definition they have five main characteristics: organizational continuity and cohesion; exclusive knowledge of the appropriate sectors of government and their clients; stable membership; operational objectives that are clear and concrete; and organizational imperatives on which the credibility of the organization is based which are generally more important than any particular objective. At the opposite extreme of institutionalized interest groups are **issue-oriented** groups. Their organizational continuity and cohesion are weak, their knowledge of government poor and their membership fluid. They also have trouble formulating

---

[27]F.C. Engelmann and M.A. Schwartz, *Political Parties and the Canadian Social Structure,* 2nd ed. (Scarborough: Prentice-Hall, 1975).

[28]W. Blair Dimock, "The Involvement and Influence of Domestic Interest Groups in Canadian Foreign Policy Making," (M.A. Dissertation, Carleton University, 1980); and Elizabeth Riddell-Dixon, *The Domestic Mosaic: Domestic Groups and Canadian Foreign Policy,* (Toronto: CIIA, 1985). For general studies of interest group growth see K. Paltiel, "The Changing Environment and Role of Special Interest Groups," *Canadian Public Administration,* vol. 25, no. 2 (Summer 1982), pp. 198-210.

[29]Paul A. Pross, "Pressure Groups...", *op. cit.,* pp. 9-18.

and adhering to long-range objectives, and maintain a low regard for their own organizational mechanisms. What issue-oriented groups lack in size and organization they make up for in flexibility; they can be excellent vehicles for generating immediate public action on specific issues. They are little constrained by fear of disturbing their relationship with government officials. Good examples were the early environmental groups and some peace organizations in Canada that were short-lived but very active publicly. The **fledgling** and **mature** groups fall, in that order of organization, between these two extremes.

Canadian Groups: A Catalogue

In order that readers become aware of some of the main groups which participate in the political area, we summarize here the activities of some of the largest and most active. It is not an exhaustive list but does indicate the multiplicity of groups in Canada. Because of the federal political structure of the country, most of the major interest groups have federated organizations. Interests in the economic sphere, for example, are regulated by both federal and provincial governments; as a result, groups representing the various agriculture, labour and business interests require federated organizations with bureaucracies in Ottawa and the provincial capitals.

BUSINESS

Business groups are especially active in political persuasion, since the economic viability of the businesses they represent is very often directly dependent on government policies and contracts. Large organizations like the Canadian Manufacturers Association and the Canadian Trucking Association retain offices in the national capital, while others have public relations officers in their headquarters who make regular or irregular visits to Ottawa.

The largest business association in Canada is the Canadian Chamber of Commerce, with 650 local charters and boards of trade, 125 000 affiliated members and 5000 corporations. It is funded by the business community. While its headquarters is in Montréal, its President is constantly in Ottawa representing the business community. Another large organization which aims at influencing government policy in such fields as corporate regulation and taxation is the Canadian Manufacturers Association. Representing 80 percent of Canadian manufacturing, its membership is between 8000 and 9000 companies. It is funded by this corporate membership.

Business interests in domestic affairs are also defended and promoted by associations representing particular sectors. These include the Canadian Industries Association, which represents 120 manufacturing companies, and the Canadian Nuclear Association, representing over 200 companies and organizations interested in the development of nuclear energy. The interests of manufacturing groups can often be recognized by their names: examples are the Automobile Industries Association, the Canadian Chemical Producers Association, the Mining Association of Canada, the Canadian Pulp and Paper Association, and even the

Confectionery Manufacturers' Association and the Shoe Manufacturers' Association.

The petroleum industry is represented by the huge Canadian Petroleum Association, which has 66 member companies involved in the exploration and production of oil and gas, as well as by the far smaller Independent Petroleum Association.

The various financial interests are also well organized. The Canadian Life and Health Insurance Association represents all companies in the insurance business. The Canadian Bankers' Association represents all 58 banks. Small business is centralized as an interest group by the Canadian Federation of Independent Business which consists of 70 000 private enterprises.

Business groups also try to influence government foreign policies. Probably the most significant of these groups is the Canadian Business and Industry International Advisory Committee. The CBIIAC is an umbrella organization which includes the Canadian Chamber of Commerce, the Canadian Manufacturers Association, the Canadian Export Association, the Canadian Import Association, and other organizations concerned with trade policy. Of course, this means there can be incongruities in the CBIIAC. The CIA, representing 840 firms, wants the reduction of tariffs and non-tariff barriers, while the CEA, representing 500 corporations, wants to increase access to foreign markets and obtain government assistance and tax concessions.

AGRICULTURE AND FISHERIES

The Fisheries Council of Canada is the largest organization representing fishing interests. It is comprised of twelve provincial associations of companies in fishing and fish processing.

Agriculture has two major organizations. The largest, the Canadian Federation of Agriculture, enrolls two-thirds of the country's 300 000 farmers. It is composed of provincial federations of agriculture and many commodity organizations such as the Canadian Pork Council. The CFA makes representations to the federal government, but is somewhat less willing to engage in direct confrontation with the government than is the smaller National Farmers' Union.[30]

LABOUR

Labour can be a powerful force in Canadian politics. Approximately one out of every three paid workers outside agriculture is a member of a labour union. The major umbrella organization is the Canadian Labour Congress. It consists of affiliated trade unions representing 2 300 000 workers. The CLC is a federation with twelve regional offices and 120 local councils. Representation is geograph-

---

[30]See Elizabeth M. Dixon, *op. cit.,* p. 25. For this section as a whole also see Helen Jones Dawson, "The Consumers Association of Canada," *Canadian Public Administration,* vol. 4, no. 1 (March 1963), pp. 92-118; W.T. Stanbury, *Business Interests and the Reform of Canadian Competition Policy* (Toronto: Carswell, 1977); and Jonah Goldstein, "Public Interest Groups and Public Policy," *CJPS,* vol. 12, no. 1 (March 1979), pp. 137-156.

ically dispersed: the Ottawa office deals with issues at the national or international levels, and the regional and local branches focus on issues under provincial jurisdiction. Unlike most interest groups, the Canadian Labour Congress supports one political party – the NDP.

A second major worker association, the Canadian Federation of Labour, is comprised of ten building-trade unions. It differs from the CLC in emphasizing cooperation with the government and in being non-partisan; it does not uniquely support the NDP.

Québec has its own major labour organization, the Confederation of National Trade Unions, which represents 220 000 members in a number of Québec labour unions.

Workers are also affiliated with their particular sector of the economy or trade; examples are the Québec Woodworkers Federation and the United Automobile Workers of America. Government employees are represented by organizations such as the Canadian Union of Public Employees (CUPE) and the Canadian Union of Postal Workers (CUPW).

Other Economic Groups

Another prominent category of economic interest groups comprises those representing consumers. The Consumers Association of Canada, consisting of 170 000 individual members, represents the interests of consumers to government. This function often brings it in conflict with both business and labour.

In a separate category are professional workers. The Canadian Bar Association, the Canadian Association of Broadcasters and the Canadian Council of Professional Engineers, among others, attempt to secure government policies conducive to their professional interests. Perhaps the best-known group in this category is the powerful Canadian Medical Association; another prominent organization is the Canadian Dental Association.

Non-Economic Groups

This category is possibly the largest; it is certainly the most diffuse. As indicated in the classification earlier, such groups may be transitory or permanent. Religious interests are fostered by the Canadian Council of Churches, the Canadian Conference of Catholic Bishops and the Christian Movement for Peace. Ethnic representation is made by groups such as the Canadian Jewish Congress, the Arab Palestine Association, the Ukrainian National Association, and the Canadian Polish Congress. Women are represented by the National Council of Women, the Voice of Women and the YWCA.

Weaker and more transitory than the above-named are public interest groups. Motivated by a mixture of principle and ideology, these groups usually see themselves as representing the unrepresented or under-represented. Usually they are dependent on favourable media coverage. Of course, all groups believe they represent the "public interest", but these particular groups specialize in this approach rather than in one based on occupation, nationality, religion, sex or ethnicity. They include such vocal advocates as the Friends of the Earth, Greenpeace, Energy Probe, Amnesty International and Operation Dismantle.

Ingredients For Interest Group Success

Perhaps the most fundamental ingredient for political success is that the values, goals and tactics of an interest group be compatible with the country's political culture and therefore be perceived as legitimate. Without public support a group has very little chance of receiving government recognition. Such recognition is vital to group leaders because it imparts legitimacy to the group, demonstrating that the government feels that the group has a right to have its views considered.[31] Groups which use the tactic of violent demonstration rather than the standard practice of negotiation of individual claims meet rigid resistance in the Canadian system, as do those which approve goals foreign to the Canadian political culture such as, say, state control of family planning.

Another ingredient for success is an appealing issue – one which will gather very broad public sympathy, and, if not increase the size of the group, at least increase its support. Good leadership is also important, a strong, vocal and prestigious leader brings the group valuable publicity and direction. A high-status general membership further increases the chance of success, since distinguished, influential people bring contacts and other resources, and have easier personal access to bureaucrats and politicians. Similarly, large budgets naturally assist in achieving and maintaining access to policy-makers. Prosperity does not guarantee success, but it certainly increases its possibility.[32]

A permanent organizational structure is very important because it helps the group act cohesively. Internal divisions weaken any political force the group might have. Sections of society which have common interests but are unorganized, such as housewives or pensioners, can have little long-term impact on public policy because of their lack of unity.

Flexibility is a further important factor in achieving success: it is often necessary to compromise one part of a demand to achieve another. As one lobbyist said, "We are often forced to ask ourselves should we shoot for the moon or try to give suggestions politicians might accept. It is an important calculation in our work." Successful groups will often band together at least temporarily with other groups to bolster each others' claims. Interest groups must also be flexible enough to make use of all the areas of access available to them. To assist them, they must have a good knowledge of where to "plug into" the policy-making system. An important condition of success consists of knowing where and at what stage access to policy-makers can be achieved.

Attempts to measure success have had only limited utility. In both the Canadian and American political science literature, observations of the frequency

---

[31]David Kwavnick, *Organized Labour and Pressure Group Politics op. cit., passim.*

[32]An interesting case against this is made by Francis Piven and Richard Cloward in *Poor People's Movements* (New York: Pantheon Books, 1977). In a study of four large mass movements of the poor lower class in the US, they conclude that one of the main reasons the poor are unsuccessful in winning concessions is that their leaders are overconcerned with organizations and so lose the anger, spontaneity and solidarity that could force government response. Concessions to the poor are not made through established political channels, but to placate mass defiance.

and nature of the contact between interest groups, legislators and bureaucrats have frequently led to disappointing assessments that border on truisms. One such study of Canadian interest group activity concluded that

> Legitimate, wealthy, coherent interests having multiple sources of access to the legislative process would *tend* to be much more influential than less legitimate, poor, diffuse interests having few sources of access to the legislative process.[33]

It is true but regrettable that interest group politicking is a well-practiced but little understood art.[34] Part of the problem has stemmed from insufficient rigour in defining the object of analysis in the first instance. David Truman's definition of "interest group", for example, does not specify a political content to "interest",[35] while, at the other extreme, the state of Texas has found it necessary to designate as a political lobbyist anyone who comes in contact, however casual, with a legislative representative. Political lobbying is a poorly studied phenomena generally, and has been the victim of misunderstanding on a number of levels.

LOBBYING IN CANADA

The term "lobby" comes from the corridor in the British House of Commons where constituents may meet their MPs to cajole or pressure them about policy or legislation. We have said that in Canada hundreds of professional lobbyists are based in Ottawa and the provincial capitals to represent interest groups and bring their concerns before politicians and public servants. These lobbyists exert pressure whenever they find receptive personnel or access points. Some are unscrupulous and powerful; others are not. Most major organizations retain these professionals, who "know how to throw their weight around", but many interest groups use law firms which defend their interests for a large retainer.

One of the more useful texts on the subject of political lobbying in Canada begins with the observation that interest groups "live in the half-light of politics."[36] For all too many Canadians, including academics, the "half-light" is in fact a shroud of suspicion. While nothing is more proper in a democratic process

---

[33]Fred Thompson and W.T. Stanbury, *The Political Economy of Interest Groups in the Legislative Process in Canada* (Reprinted by permission of the Institute for Research on Public Policy, May 1979), p. 48. (Emphasis in original.)

[34]For a sophisticated effort see Harmon Zeigler, "The Effects of Lobbying: A Comparative Assessment," in Norman R. Luttbeg, ed., *Public Opinion and Public Policy* (Homewood: Dorsey, 1974), pp. 225-251.

[35]For Truman "Interest Group" refers to "any group, that on the basis of one or more shared attitudes, makes certain claims upon other groups in the society for the establishment, maintenance, or enhancement of forms of behaviour that are implied by the shared attitudes." See David B. Truman, *The Governmental Process, op. cit.*, p. 33.

[36]A. Paul Pross, "Pressure Groups...", *op. cit.*, p. 1.

than for individuals to attempt to organize to influence their government, social taboos endure which construe such activity as embarrassing and imprudent. In the realm of interest group politics, Canadian lobbyists have historically had greater pretentions to political virginity than their American counterparts, often cultivating the image of a certain spiritual aloofness from partisan politics. Lobbying is, in effect, a rose by any other name.

Yet, for all the prudery, Ottawa and the provincial capitals *are* full of lobbyists. It is worth noting that while businessmen, for example, make frequent and ostentatious display of their contempt for the dirty world of politics, they exhibit remarkable ability to hold their noses and socialize when something is to be gained. These relationships are both accommodating and antagonistic. Government regulates business and yet also subsidizes and protects it.

Nevertheless, unlike in the United States, where registration of lobbyists is compulsory, there are absolutely no rules regulating political lobbying in Canada. In 1978 private member's bill C-255, entitled "An Act to Register Lobbyists" failed to secure passage through the House of Commons. The lobbies break down roughly into two groups: those primarily focused on general government policy, such as the Business Council on National Issues, and those with a more specific focus, typified by the Pharmaceutical Manufacturers Association or the Mining Association of Canada. Trade and umbrella groups send scores of lawyers before regulatory tribunals to secure the modification of regulations, while voluntary groups press their causes with MPs, Cabinet ministers and bureaucrats. One organization, the Canadian Federation of Independent Business, with a permanent staff of more than one hundred people, used its resources to considerable effect: it secured the creation of a Ministry of State for Small Business. Yet the entire scene remains in a limbo of unregulated obscurity and a substantial portion of Ottawa's work force describes its occupation simply as "public relations".

Common Tactics and Strategies

The lobbying strategy chosen by an interest group depends largely on the type of group it is, its resources and the type of issues involved. Some groups concentrate on the pre-parliamentary stages of government, while others prefer buttonholing MPs. In all cases, the strategies used must include more than an attempt to influence legislators and bureaucrats. Public opinion must be aroused too. No amount of persuasion of the government will be effective unless public opinion is in agreement with a lobby, or at least not hostile to its demands.

In his study of the Canadian Medical Association, a very well established pressure group, Bernard Blishen notes the major ways in which that group promotes its interests. Positive relations with the press and personal contact are considered very important. Both formal and informal contacts between the profession and government are pursued. The close relationship that has been built up is evidence of the fact that many senior officials of the federal and provincial government health departments, as well as Ministers of Health, have been physicians. In addition to these contacts, "institutional patterns" are well established between the group and the government. For example, close contacts are fostered between the profession and the public service by the "medical care pre-payment" plans in the area of health insurance. A final significant tactic used by this group is referred to as the "tie-in-endorsement", which refers to the effort to "tie members in" with related groups such as other health professionals, hospital associations, insurance industries, and other health programmes in an effort to protect similar interests and policies. In all its activities, group members make every effort to act in unison, in the knowledge that their influence depends to a large degree on the cohesion of the Association.[37]

Thus, many lobbyists establish friendly relationships with legislators, bureaucrats and media or other group contacts, in order to present their cases in informal, friendly ways. Robert Presthus' research showed that about 75% of MPs of all parties had frequent or occasional contact with interest groups. This contact generally concerned interests which the MPs already supported, and was aimed at convincing them to influence their colleagues.[38] Lobbyists also disseminate literature, present briefs, provide research results, promote letter writing campaigns, support groups at committee hearings and entertain. At the same time, they must keep close track of what is happening in Parliament, so that they and the group they represent will know when and where to take appropriate action. In the United States, interest groups often influence appointments to important government posts by approving or disapproving Cabinet nominees in their areas of interest. The Canadian system rarely provides this opportunity, but it does occur with certain appointments.

Lobbying MPs is probably least effective when the policy concerned is already before Parliament. Policies are made before they reach Parliament, and by then it is very difficult for any group to have an effect on them. At this stage, legislation is more apt to be blocked or delayed than changed. It is therefore common for groups to lobby or encourage write-in campaigns to MPs when they want to initiate new policy, but they are more likely to be successful if they attempt to block government proposals.

Occasionally, interest groups will use the judicial process to pursue their goals. It is possible for group leaders to initiate suits directly on behalf of their group. Or they may support another individual who seeks to achieve the same goals. For example, a housewife might obtain the support of a women's organization in the matter of certain rights because the interest group considers that her case provides the best opportunity to have the law interpreted in its favour. Or parents who take court action against a provincial government because their child is not allowed to attend the school of their choice might be supported by a group whose cause is thereby represented.

We have pointed out that public relations campaigns are expensive, and, as a result, groups with a large membership, extensive financial resources and influ-

---

[37]Bernard R. Blishen, *Doctors and Doctrines: The Ideology of Medical Care in Canada,* (Toronto: University of Toronto Press, 1969) p. 101.

[38]Robert Presthus, "Interest Groups and Parliament Activities, Interaction, Legitimacy and Influence," *CJPS,* vol. 4, no. 4 (December 1971), p. 460.

MINISTER, IT'S THOSE LOBBYISTS FROM THE LEARNED SOCIETIES

P. BLANEY

Reproduced with permission: Peter Blaney, Social Science Federation of Canada.

ential connections often have a major advantage. Direct advertising or program sponsorship are often too expensive for many groups, but some such advertisements, for example, those by monopolies such as Bell Telephone, will be familiar to most Canadians. Because it is the function of the media in a democratic system to inform the public, active interest groups often take advantage of this to create newsworthy events so that information about their group and their activities will be publicized without charge.

Some groups employ other tactics to get free media coverage. For example, they may stage employee strikes directly against the management to halt production and force the government to listen to their demands through the media. Picketers intend not only to affect management but also to appeal to public opinion. Or an angry consumer group may picket a business to protest high prices or poor services and thereby gain publicity.

Non-violent demonstrations are yet another means of seeking publicity. The tactic has become increasingly popular since the non-violent US civil rights movement in the 1950s and 1960s. It is especially popular with minority and low income groups.[39] But neither non-violent nor violent protest fits within the norms of mutual accommodation between interest groups and policy-makers in Canada. Such a tactic presents an ultimatum that precludes negotiation of individual group claims; on the whole, groups which use this strategy are likely to be ignored, discredited or placated with purely symbolic action.

---

[39]Michael Lipsky, "Protest as a Political Resource," *APSR*, vol. 62, no. 4 (December 1968), pp. 1148-58.

Access Points

One lobbyist has commented that "Our political system is great if the government is doing what you like – otherwise there are never enough access points." To be successful, most groups must be flexible enough to approach and adapt to all of the available access points. "We throw out our line everywhere," is the usual approach.

We have seen that within the policy process, access is available through individual MPs via the committee system or caucus and, of course, the Cabinet. But interest groups also operate outside the narrow confines of Parliament. The government bureaucracy is concerned with policy in its earliest formation and is often the most important focus of lobbying. Such activity has been known to provoke complaints that interest groups bypass Parliament and the elected representatives.

In both arenas, the interaction between pressure group leaders and politicians or bureaucrats is characterized by a spirit of cooperation that has been termed an "ethos of mutual accommodation".[40] This ethos is evident in the following remark by an interest group leader: "We are concerned to always give full and accurate information to bureaucrats because if we don't create a confidence and they depend on advice which is biased towards us – they have a long memory and will hold it against us later." Two-way communication is an important aspect of this accommodation in that all parties receive benefits and therefore value the interaction.

It is important for interest groups to use the access points provided within the political system and establish interaction of mutual consultation. Once a pattern is established, it indicates that the group has obtained recognition or legitimacy as the representative for its particular interests. The interaction is also a symbol of the compatability of their goals and tactics with both Canadian political culture and the goals of the government.

Successful access to the policy-making process is, of course, greatly enhanced by knowledge of the institutional and procedural structures of government and the legislative system, such as, for instance, how a bill originates and what affects its passage. The early stages are particularly important for interest groups because, as we noted in an earlier chapter, Parliament passes laws but is less involved in originating them: legislation and expenditures are generally approved by the executive as a package. By the time a particular package reaches Parliament, the government has publicly committed itself to the policies therein, and little can be done to change the details of single bills or estimates without destroying the delicate compromises on which the "deal" has been constructed.

If we trace the course of a bill through the pre-parliamentary to the parliamentary stages, the relative importance of the various access points becomes clearer. The interaction process can be very complex, and most of it is on an informal and secret basis.

---

[40]Robert J. Jackson and Michael M. Atkinson, *The Canadian Legislative System* 2nd rev. ed. (Toronto: Gage, 1980), p. 36.

The bureaucracy and Cabinet are the significant access points in the pre-parliamentary stages of a bill. Many political analysts believe that the bureaucracy is the most widely used arena for successful pressure group activity. There is a close relationship between civil servants and pressure groups for many reasons. Civil servants are often required by their ministers to initiate and draft or to research and evaluate policy proposals for Cabinet, to give advice on the public acceptability of these policies and even to help educate and inform the public about them. Interest groups, which do much information gathering in their given areas, are often approached by bureaucrats for their expertise. For this reason, groups that do little research and have only marginal expertise are likely to have relatively low prestige *vis-à-vis* the civil service. Thus, their specialized knowledge provides pressure groups with the opportunity to affect policy formulation.

This opportunity exists again during the drafting and amendment of a bill. One lobbyist stated his preferences this way, "After a bill is printed it is almost impossible to have a great effect. We prefer the white paper process so that the minister is not married to his bill." The Canadian Medical Association and the Canadian Federation of Agriculture are excellent examples of recognized established groups offering expert advice at the different stages.[41] Professional lobbyists are particularly critical about the lack of pressure points in the closed atmosphere around taxation legislation: "Too few people get involved in the final projects ... We prefer the American system where there is a greater airing of views on each bill."

Since responsibility for initiation and control of legislation is in the hands of the government, the Cabinet is a natural target for interest group activity. In the pre-parliamentary stages of a bill the minister behind a new policy is responsible for gathering information from interest groups. At the same time, government secrecy requires that the groups not be informed about the government's intentions regarding decisions or policy details. It can also happen that only the minister directly concerned is aware of the groups' demands. We have remarked that relationships between ministers and certain interest groups are often extremely close: when Mitchell Sharp and C.M. Drury entered the Pearson Cabinet they were both members of the Canadian Manufacturers Association. An interest group leader's approach to a Cabinet minister may be illustrated by an incident in 1977. A Toronto lobbyist asked an acquaintance who was a friend of Cabinet Minister A.C. Abbott to tell the Minister over lunch that he wanted to be sure that an insurance company would have the opportunity to present a brief at the committee stage of a certain bill (The *Borrowers and Depositors Protection Act*, 1977). Abbott assured him that they would be heard, and they were.

Some interest groups' relations with Cabinet are more formalized. Every year certain large national groups are invited to present an annual brief to the whole Cabinet. This recognition, which has been achieved by only a few organi-

[41]Malcolm Taylor, "The Role of the Medical Profession in the Formulation and Execution of Public Policy," *CJEPS*, vol. 26, no. 1 (February 1960), pp. 108-26; and Helen Jones Dawson, "Relations Between Farm Organizations and the Civil Service in Canada and Great Britain," *Canadian Public Administration*, vol. 10, no. 4 (December 1967), pp. 450-70.

zations, such as the CLC, is greatly valued. Apart from publicity and prestige, it gives these groups an opportunity to air their views directly to ministers, including the Prime Minister.

Interest groups seek access to individual MPs more for their long-term political influence than because the groups need immediate assistance. Because legislation is approved and passed, rather than initiated, in the House of Commons, unless an MP has special information or interest (or is strategically located in a minority government situation) he can be of little direct help. Also, interest group leaders complain that "it is almost impossible to get backbenchers involved in the technical details of bills" and that "there has to be public appeal in order to get backbenchers involved." On the other hand, it is always possible that a friendly member may bring an issue to the attention of the appropriate Cabinet minister, become a Cabinet minister himself or, together with his fellow backbenchers, force desired change in Cabinet decisions. In addition, opposition MPs may, after the next election, gain key positions; they therefore cannot be ignored altogether. As a rule, however, opposition MPs get most interest group attention during minority governments, when their vote is more significant.

An MP may take up the cause of an interest group for various reasons. It could be politically expedient for him to do so because his constituents support the issue. Or he might be given information and research help that would enable him to put forward a well-informed question or speech in the House, earning him credit and recognition within his party caucus.

Caucus, the private meeting of the parliamentary party, gives individual MPs an opportunity to express their views. The outline of a bill which is ready to be introduced in the House is presented first to the caucus. Weekly meetings follow in which the MPs have an opportunity to express the interest of groups who have approached them. If Cabinet and interest groups' opinions diverge, it is usual for interest groups to attempt a coalition of anti-government forces. Caucus continues to debate a bill even after it has been introduced in the House, and, on occasion, can even prevent the moving of second reading. Jackson and Atkinson note that

> Generally cabinet opinion prevails when the caucus, the provinces, or the relevant interest groups can be attracted to cabinet's side. Cabinet has the least chance of imposing its views where all three of these elements resist its direction.[42]

The committee system is yet another attractive access point for interest groups because the very purpose of committees is to gather information. In fact, Presthus found that committees were the most frequent site of interest group impact on legislators. It is not uncommon for interest groups, both in Ottawa and the provincial capitals, to have their own representatives on legislative committees. The Royal Canadian Legion, for example, is usually well represented on the committee for Veterans' Affairs.

---

[42]Robert J. Jackson and Michael M. Atkinson, *op. cit.,* p. 40.

Some lobbyists prefer Senate committees over House committees as a lobbying forum. Senate committees often handle testimony from corporations less politically than do House of Commons committees. Businesspeople often find dealing with Standing Committees of the House of Commons unsatisfactory because the deliberations are unsystematic and politically partisan.[43]

When legislation is before a House Standing Committee, all interests are invited to present briefs. But Van Loon and Whittington downplay the usefulness of this in that "the real policy-makers tend to seize upon briefs favourable to their position as tangible evidence of support for their policies and to ignore briefs which are against them."[44] However, as we have already noted, even after bills are before the House a great many devices exist for slowing down their progress. Passage of legislation is at best a very lengthy process, often taking several years, thereby giving interest groups extensive opportunities to lobby and conduct public relations campaigns.

Although organized groups normally prefer to transmit their demands directly through the bureaucracy or legislative system, political parties constitute a further possibility for access to decision-making. Interest groups attempt to influence party policy resolutions because it is political parties which supply the government leaders; party decisions therefore may become government policy decisions. However, being identified with one political party is a two-edged sword that many groups prefer to avoid. Fearing that such an attachment will close their routes of access to other parties, many groups declare non-partisanship. The Canadian Manufacturers Association is often singled out as a classic example of a group that has achieved success by avoiding identification with a party. Although over the years it has favoured Conservative tariff policies and opposed those of the Liberals, it has not openly supported the Conservatives. On the other hand, some interests, particularly labour associations, not only openly identify themselves with specific political parties, but also affiliate with them, providing both financial and political support. For example, the Canadian Labour Congress first openly identified with, then directly associated with, the CCF/NDP. In 1943 it endorsed the CCF as "the political arm of labour in Canada", and in 1961 the joint CLC-CCF Committee founded the NDP.

ANALYZING THE BARELY DESCRIBED

The absence of formalized rules for lobbyists has doubtlessly contributed to their remaining in the "half-light" of politics as well as on the periphery of Canadian political science – "If we ignore it, maybe it will go away." The inclination of Canadian political scientists to form generalizations from deductive reasoning

---

[43]Colin Campbell, *The Canadian Senate: A Lobby From Within* (Toronto: Macmillan, 1978), *passim*.

[44]R. Van Loon and M. Whittington, *The Canadian Political System* (Toronto: McGraw-Hill, 1971) p. 311.

based on the structural features of the legislative process in Canada has done little to shed new light on these dark corners of the discipline. The following serves as just a single example of this attitude, though perhaps an extreme one:

"Viewed from the standpoint of the supply and demand for political (legislative) decisions, the contrast between Canadian and American federal political systems is striking. This is particularly true of the supply side where Cabinet has a virtual monopoly in Canada. Legislative decision-making in Canada is highly centralized and party discipline is almost complete."[45]

The supposedly greater concentration of political authority in Canada is usually assumed *a priori* to possess enormous explanatory power in analyzing Canadian politics. From this observation about the Canadian legislative process, a leap is made to the conclusion that, because of the "more restricted role", interest group representation does not have the same power to explain legislative outcomes that it possesses in the United States.[46]

This inference is sweeping and somewhat misleading. As a whole, Cabinet is closely involved in the lobbying process and it is true that this large body of ministers pivoting around the Prime Minister is a very large cog in the overall legislative machinery. It is not, however, a monolithic block of power, but rather the sum of its ministerial parts. While the whole Cabinet is involved in major issues because of the principle of collective responsibility and collegiality, its committee system forms the nexus of the most significant decisions. In fact, the majority of Cabinet decisions are made in committee; they are merely ratified by Cabinet. For the lobbyist, access to the committee system involves contact with the relevant minister, often via the ministerial bureaucracy. Thus, it is our contention that Cabinet *is* closely involved with the lobbying process.

However, reinforcing the myth of Cabinet monopoly is the handy commonplace that, while the members of the House of Commons pass legislation, very few of them initiate it. At face value the statement is true; however, on close examination of the workings of the House, it is revealed as an unscholarly distortion. To be sure, lobbyists spend less time approaching MPs than their American counterparts do Congressmen. Nevertheless, Members of Parliament are now more significant in terms of briefings, committee hearings and new task forces than ever before. Proof of this assertion can be found in a recent survey which showed that some 75 percent of the chief executive officers of Canadian business corporations or their representatives have frequent contact with Members of Parliament. The August-September 1982 open hearings on the tax laws were a primary example of the new direct approach in lobbying.[47]

Depending on their styles and resources, certain groups are consistently moved to place particular stress on one link of the legislative process over others.

---

[45]Fred Thompson and W.T. Stanbury, *op. cit.*, p. 25.

[46]*Ibid.*, p. vii.

[47]Robert J. Jackson, "Lobbying and the Political Process," paper prepared for the Social Science Federation of Canada, October 22, 1982, p. 12.

According to Robert Presthus, religious, educational and business groups focus most frequently on Cabinet, welfare groups on the bureaucracy and labour organizations on the legislature.[48] While the financial capacity of certain lobbies may enable them to wage a long-term campaign at a high level, one should be careful of the assumption that wealthy lobbies are necessarily the most influential. An aide to the Minister of Energy, Mines and Resources is on record as having described the tactics of oil interests as "unbelievably bad". Their attempts at dramatizing first Canada's oil wealth, and later her relative poverty, contributed to a substantial erosion of their credibility in government circles.[49] Moreover, even enormous financial resources have difficulty in offsetting salient political factors:

> While the industry in general lacks credibility, there are exceptions. Dome Petroleum Ltd. and Nova, both large Calgary-based companies, and many of the medium and smaller companies are both heard and listened to in Ottawa.
>
> The primary reason for this is that they can drape themselves in the maple leaf flag. Canadian companies are treated differently than foreign companies, a treat that was extended by the former Conservative government as well as the present one.[50]

Members of Parliament have a small staff. Lobby groups therefore become a source of information to the backbencher. In a period of a week, a total of two hundred briefs, magazine articles and letters was forwarded to one MP from groups eager to inform backbenchers of their points of view and perhaps win support. Thus, the backbenches often become a barometer of the political climate:

> ... special interest groups can give an MP a reading of the political pros and cons of a particular proposal. This is very important to the MPs who are often more concerned about public attitudes on legislation than are members of the bureaucracy or the Cabinet. Moreover, MPs usually have more time to see lobbyists than do Cabinet ministers or senior bureaucrats.[51]

Consequently, interest groups or their representative public relations firms often distribute responsibility for the 282 legislators among members of their organizations in order to provide a consistent and geographically based influence. For organizations that can afford such a broad and sustained effort, doing this represents a calculated investment in the future. As we said earlier, Cabinet ministers are, to a large degree, recruited from the ranks of the government backbench,

---

[48]Robert Presthus, *Elite Accommodation in Canadian Politics* (Toronto: Macmillan, 1973), Chapter 6.

[49]James Rusk, "Powers in the Oil Lobby Cull Clout from the Flag," *The Globe and Mail,* Toronto, October 27, 1980, p. 9.

[50]*Ibid.*

[51]J. Gillies and J. Pigott, "Participation in the Legislative Process," *CPA,* vol. 25, no. 2 (Summer 1982), p. 256.

and neither they nor opposition backbenchers can be allowed to feel isolated or ignored.

Yet even in the short term the skilful lobbying of backbenchers can have considerable impact on the legislative output of the government. The primary forum for backbench influence is in caucus. When a substantial coalition of backbenchers with the support of one or more concerned interest groups opposes the Cabinet's position, the likelihood that the government's proposals will be reviewed increases. Further leverage is often available via a three-way alliance between lobbyists, backbenchers and a disgruntled provincial government.

Thus, backbench MPs provide a substantial link to the executive. Unfortunately, many scholars underestimate this feature of the Canadian legislative process, because of the inclination to oversimplify the structural features of Canadian government and its points of contrast with the American system. In just one example, Robert Presthus asked nearly one thousand directors of interest groups in Canada and the United States which arm of government received the most attention in their lobbying efforts.[52] The results are presented in Table 12-1.

From these data Presthus drew the unjustified conclusion that Canadian interest groups direct the greater part of their lobbying efforts at the Cabinet and federal bureaucracy. The error emanates from making a distinction between "Cabinet" and "legislators". While this division is certainly valid for the American figures, Canadian Cabinet ministers are also legislators, in spite of their special status. According to Presthus' statistics, therefore, Canadian lobbyists target legislators, defined in general terms, 51 percent of the time. This results in a difference of only 8 percent in interest group contact with legislators between the US and Canada – a figure of little statistical significance. Presthus' table represents an effort to explain differences in lobbying activity in two countries through quantification without sufficient regard for the subtle relationships between the executive and legislature in Canada.

Zero-Sum Reasoning: Power as a Football

Presthus' findings indicate that Canadian interest groups seem more inclined to petition the federal bureaucracy than are their American counterparts. Certainly business groups exhibit a tendency to approach lower- and middle-level bureaucrats "on the premise that policy becomes more set and less easy to change the higher up it moves and that the lower level bureaucrats rely on business for information."[53] Hence there exists a reciprocity of dependency. Effective lobbying of the public service presupposes, of course, a fairly sophisticated understanding of the bureaucratic process and sufficient knowledge about the best timing and point of contact. In the perception of one former lobbyist, the campaign to influence legislative outputs cannot possibly begin too early "because

---

[52]Robert Presthus, *Elite Accommodation*, p. 255.

[53]Elizabeth Dixon, *op. cit.*, p. 7.

TABLE 12.1   Interest Group Activity

Target of Interest Group	Canada	US
Bureaucracy	40%	21%
Cabinet and Executive Assistants	24	7
Legislators and Legislative Committees	27	59
Judiciary	3	3
Other	6	9
	100%	100%
	N=393	N=604

Source: Robert Presthus, *Elite Accomodation in Canadian Politics* (Toronto: Macmillan, 1973), p. 255.

you don't even see the tip of the iceberg until there's a hell of a lot of ice down there."[54]

The effectiveness of focusing on public servants for the articulation of interests at the pre-parliamentary stage of the process is augmented at later stages. Legislation is often returned to departments for further consideration; thus, the entire process is reopened to groups which seek to block or stall disadvantageous proposals. The complexities of the legislative system and the rough landscape of Canadian politics give some indication of why it is often "considered easier to block or slow down proposals than to initiate them".[55]

The increased salience of bureaucracy is a phenomenon general to all advanced industrial societies. There is, however, a regrettable tendency on the part of students of Canadian politics to overstress the political significance of the bureaucratic process. This is especially true of members of the press, for whom the use of the word "mandarin" in reference to senior civil servants carries an aura of omnipotence. All-knowing observations to the effect that "Any lobbyist who is worth either the handsome retainer or the comfortable salary that goes with the title will tell you that the real levers of power in Ottawa lie within the bureaucracy" abound.[56] Those wasting their time with MPs and Cabinet ministers, so the reasoning goes, are simply not in the know.

The habit of using language such as "the real levers of power" stems from the mechanization of the concept of political "power". The competition for access to government decision-makers is seen as a zero-sum game. Power is viewed as a kind of football in the lobbyists' free-for-all; if one group has it, other groups do not.

The fact is that while certain interests single out specific components of the legislative system for special attention consistent with their goals and resources, no successful group fosters illusions about "power" having a single address.

---

[54]Quoted in John Gray, "Insiders go to Mandarins Before Minister," *The Globe and Mail,* Toronto, October 25, 1980.

[55]Robert J. Jackson and Michael M. Atkinson, *op. cit.,* p. 39.

[56]John Gray, *op. cit.*

Flexibility and a concern to touch all the bases are, without exception, the hall-marks of the most seasoned practitioners of the art of lobbying. When business groups suspect, for example, that their efforts at the mid-level of bureaucracy are too late or simply insufficient, chief executive officers from the major relevant corporations will engage jointly in discussions with members of Cabinet – an activity which is frequently coordinated by a large umbrella organization. All groups appreciate the importance of monitoring developments in Ottawa very closely and making regular contact with government officials. The Canadian Trucking Association maintains offices in the capital, while executive officers from the Canadian Association for Latin America and the Caribbean commute to Ottawa on a regular basis. The Canadian Manufacturers Association, representing an interest constituency with impressive financial and organizational resources, is capable of both methods of liaison.[57]

Despite this common characteristic, it is no exaggeration to say that no two groups are identical in goals or resources, organization or methods, even when their general interests coincide. The National Farmers' Union (NFU) has a history of activity somewhat analogous to that of an agricultural labour union; it does not hesitate to employ confrontational tactics when they are deemed necessary. The larger Canadian Federation of Agriculture (CFA) makes representations to the federal government on matters of macro and micro agricultural policy, paying special attention to the development of export markets. While the NFU has placed greater emphasis on the economic viability of the family farm and the dignity of the Canadian farmer, it does have a community of interest with the CFA in promoting trade policies which will increase exports and protect domestic producers generally.[58]

The Canadian Business and Industry International Advisory Committee (CBIIAC) represents a major umbrella organization responsible for the interests of the Canadian business community in matters of foreign policy. Its members include some of the most respected business groups in the country, including the Canadian Chamber of Commerce and the Canadian Manufacturers Association. The CBIIAC has traditionally worked closely with the Department of Industry, Trade and Commerce, but recent departmental reorganizations will require it to give greater attention to the Department of External Affairs in the future. While this group's broad membership dictates that it will concern itself with a very wide range of issues pertinent to business and industry, other groups feature more exclusive membership and a concomitantly narrower focus, stressing a specific geographic area or a particular sector of the economy.[59]

Regionalism has a considerable impact in Canada, especially when federalism affords interest groups differing areas of opportunity. David Kwavnick has noted how competition between the Canadian Labour Congress and the Québec-based Confederation of National Trade Unions demonstrates that "rival

---

[57]Elizabeth Dixon, *op. cit.*, pp. 6-7.

[58]*Ibid.*, p. 24.

[59]*Ibid.*, p. 6-7

groups representing the same interest, but having access to different levels of government in a federal system, will attempt to shift power to the level of government to which they enjoy access."[60]

All these groups recognize the multi-faceted nature of the legislative process as well as the reality that a long-term, systematic yet flexible effort exerted at as many points of access as possible is a prudent lobbying strategy. Lobbyists are aware that political power is not some finite substance that necessarily ebbs in the legislature as it flows in the bureaucracy. They know that government structures are not held together by nuts and bolts; a search for the "real lever of power" is for bare-handed amateurs. Government, like a growing onion, continues to change size; the political process features so many different but similar layers that it is impossible to distinguish which of them really counts. Successful lobbyists have learned that they *all* count – in fact, each layer has meaning only because of its relation to the others.

The relative utility of any one facet of the legislative system to lobbyists can and does change over time. This is true in regard to backbench MPs, who are now considered more suitable targets for lobbying than in the past, as well as to Cabinet ministers. Here again, zero-sum assumptions about the exercise of influence and political authority have tended to cloud an understanding of the subtleties of relations between administrative and legislative branches of government. Rare indeed is the contemporary political science text which does not make much ado about the increasing importance of specialized, bureaucratized expertise to government in the contemporary welfare state. Students of politics often seem to regard knowledge held by the bureaucrat to be knowledge lost to the politician; elected representatives are held to be overshadowed by civil service technocrats. Whatever political analysts may have accused politicians of having been in the past two decades, few elected representatives would claim to have been the artless victims of manipulative bureaucrats or lobbyists.

This does not mean that MPs, either the backbench or Cabinet variety, cannot unwittingly be manipulated. Consider, for example, the story of an official attached to a certain foreign embassy in Ottawa who thought that an issue concerning some aspect of his country's relation with Canada should have an airing in the House of Commons. This official contacted an opposition member and armed him with a particularly contentious question with which to confront the government. When the Minister of External Affairs asked his staff to brief him on the substance of the matter they of course required information from a foreign embassy – information they received from the very man who had originally formulated the question and inserted it into the system. Yet politicians are neither unaware of such manoeuvring nor unappreciative of the perceptions and ideas

---

[60]David Kwavnick, "Interest Group Demands and the Federal Political System: Two Canadian Case Studies," in A. Paul Pross, *op. cit.*, p. 77. For a broader perspective see Stephen McBride, "Public Policy as a Determinant of Interest Group Behaviour," *CJPS*, vol. XVI, no. 3 (September 1983), pp. 501-523.

which filter through this way. To paraphrase Senator Duff Roblin, former Conservative Premier of Manitoba, I've never had an original idea in my life, but I know one when I see it!

When substantive legislation rather than the publicity about a particular issue is the target of interest group activity, the utility of clever cut-and-thrust must give way to the sustained campaign. It is perhaps in endurance that well-financed lobbies have great advantages. The controversial Drug Bill was tabled in the House of Commons in 1962, yet by the time all concerned interests had aired their views and conducted their public relations blitzes two governments had been in power, and the bill did not become law until 1968.[61] The legislation, which was designed to reduce the retail cost of pharmaceuticals by encouraging druggists to substitute generic alternatives for more expensive brand-name products, never sat well with foreign-based multinationals. The law's provision that Canadian pharmaceutical manufacturers be granted licenses to produce the drugs of foreign companies domestically after just four years of patent protection had provoked the accusation that the Trudeau government's "hatred of American multinationals" was the equivalent of Central European anti-Semitism. One of the more hysterical voices went so far as to claim that the principle of private property in Canada was being subverted by "Godless Consumerism." Yet after years of counteroffensive the law may be changed yet again, this time in favour of the multinationals.[62]

LOBBYING IN CANADA: CASTING THE WIDE NET

It should by now be apparent that the relatively unregulated practice of lobbying in Canada is an art of enormous complexity. Far from operating in a "restricted" environment, interest groups have the advantage of multiple access points to the legislative process. It is also obvious that scenarios which speak of the "virtual monopoly" of Cabinet clash with those that view federal bureaucrats as the unseen power brokers in Ottawa and that, in fact, both are misrepresentations of a complicated reality.

The relationship of lobbyists, bureaucrats and politicians in Canada is not one of zero-sum games or of sinister cabals in the corridors of power. The interaction of interest groups with the political system is at all points permeated by an ethos of mutual accommodation involving a recognition by each party involved in the process that all other parties have an investment in the outcome of the legislative process and hence a legitimate share in the formulation of public policy. The spirit of accommodation thrives where no party is seen to dominate all of

---

[61]Donald Coxe, "A License to Loot: How Ottawa Promotes Drug Piracy and Drives Away R & D," *Canadian Business,* March 1982, p. 142.

[62]"Critics Say Ottawa Drug Changes Will Add Millions to Consumer Cost," *The Globe and Mail,* Toronto, May 28, 1983, p. 1.

the time and when each party receives sufficient satisfaction from the process to justify further participation.[63]

Yet recognition of the legitimate claims of others and the ultimate interdependence of public and private actors does not guarantee success in, or satisfaction from, the political process for interest groups. A successful and fruitful relationship with government actors begins with a group's recognition of the complexity of the contemporary democratic state and the opportunities rather than the obstacles that such complexity offers. A concern to leave no point of contact or influence untried, to cast one's net in as wide an arc as possible, is the cardinal rule of serious interest group politics. This means that while certain components such as Cabinet and the bureaucracy may be more significant than others, no facet of the process can be dismissed as unimportant.

The Canadian Senate, for example, is popularly considered to be the inconsequential artefact of a British political heritage, the pasture of political has-beens. We have remarked that this contention is incorrect from the point of view of the lobbyist. Indeed, one author has called the Senate "a lobby from within", by which he meant that most Senators already represent lobbying interests before they are appointed to the upper house.[64] Formally, the Senate is responsible for detailed amendments to legislation from the House of Commons, a task for which it possesses a committee system capable of analyzing the impact of details of legislation on the business community. Moreover, both Prime Ministers Trudeau and Clark "recruited" Cabinet ministers from the Senate in order to make up for weak representation in specific regions of the country. Consequently, in recent years the Senate has been a more significant base of operations for the lobbyist than in the past.

Often the key to lobbying success is not so much the amount of effort exerted to articulate a specific position as it is a sense of timing. Clause-by-clause consideration of bills, for example, almost always takes place in one of the several committees of the House of Commons after the Second Reading. Membership of these committees consists of MPs representing all parties. And, while the government side of each committee is "whipped" to ensure the bill's passage at this stage, lobbyists have a good chance to secure amendments at this time either in functioning as witnesses or prompting initiatives by backbenchers. In the first session of the thirty-second Parliament, 631 witnesses were heard by special committees, 2370 by standing committees, and 325 by sub-committees.

An adjunct to the committee system which has contemporary relevance to interest groups is the development of "task forces". These do not handle legislation, but they do undertake important investigations on subjects of concern and are consequently endowed with a steady membership as well as a considerable budget for research, travel and publication. In 1980, lobbyists were called to all of them: 2500 witnesses were heard from the 796 interest groups participating.

---

[63]Robert J. Jackson and Michael M. Atkinson, *op. cit.*, pp. 36-37.

[64]Colin Campbell, *op. cit.*

The more successful interest groups will monitor the evolution of these new committees closely.

Finally, it should be stressed that interest group activities do not occur in a social vacuum. "Casting a wide net" can also involve the careful nurturing of broad public support or opposition to certain policies by interest groups. The size of the social constituency sought will of course depend on the nature and substance of the issue. The past record and perceived social "legitimacy" of an interest group affects its ability to harness social support. Oil interests operating in Ottawa no longer nurture any delusions about how the Canadian public views them. Their lobbying strategies have changed accordingly. John Bullock, representative of the interests of Canadian small business and a very successful lobbyist himself, estimates that 90 percent of lobbyists are ineffectual because they either lack the necessary knowledge to articulate their case or sufficient public support to legitimate it.[65]

OVERVIEW

Lobbying in Canada is a well practised but poorly studied art. Simplistic interpretations of the relationship between government and interest groups stem from a lack of appreciation of the complexity and evolution of the Canadian legislative process. It is quite likely that if government were to finally establish formal rules for lobbying and partly draw back the veil of obscurity and suspicion, social scientists would be enabled to bring greater sophistication to their study of the phenomenon. Above all, resort to tired clichés, conspiracy scenarios, and zero-sum characterizations of power and influence should be abandoned. This does not mean that all is well in the universe of interest group politics or that inequalities do not abound. It does mean, however, that a greater appreciation of the multi-faceted and changing relationship between public and private must accompany future study of interest groups in Canada. Sensitive description must precede analysis. Accurate diagnosis must precede prescription.

How well do interest groups serve the average Canadian? We have seen that interest groups in this country are a widely accepted part of the political culture. The interaction between groups and the political system is characterized by an ethos of mutual accommodation or cooperation in which the interaction is deemed mutually worthwhile. The fact that interest groups are accepted within the political culture means that there is a legitimate channel for complaints and frustrations; an opportunity for citizens to articulate viewpoints and defend them, so that citizens do not have to resort to extra-legal behaviour to be heard. Once they are part of such a legitimized group, the members are committed to acting within the system. Interest groups in this sense act as a safety valve for individual frustrations by allowing the possibility of joining with others to influ-

---

[65]Quoted in *The Globe and Mail,* Toronto, October 25, 1980, p. 11.

ence legislation. They thus provide a crucial and culturally acceptable link between citizen and public policy.

Interest groups widen the range of interests that are taken into account in the legislative process. On the premise that more information can help achieve fairer laws, this is good – but what assurance is there that the most worthy groups are heard? Deserving groups might be ignored because of lack of funds or prestige, or competition from more powerful groups. And where is the fine line between information and propaganda in the expert advice offered to lawmakers? Groups can be expected, even within the realm of mutual accommodation to give selective information, making their own cases as strong as possible and not making the cases for their competitors. We know too that interest groups are elite dominated. People with higher status participate more, and groups tend to be dominated by the most active and vocal members. And what of unorganized interests? Who is to press the urgent claims of old age pensioners, children or non-working mothers? To be fair the system must be responsive to those who do not have the resources to sustain mass organization.

Representation in the Canadian political system is sought through the electoral process. It is clear that interest groups in the role we have described constitute another legitimate form of political representation. Yet these representatives seek influence on their own initiative and are responsible only to themselves. Some seek the good of the whole, but never to the detriment of their own interests. Interest group supporters say that extra representation through interest groups is good because the constituency form of representation cannot meet all the demands of groups in the political system, and that the modern welfare state makes interest group representation a necessary adjunct to government activity. Physicians are a prime example here. Medicare could not operate without the cooperation of the majority of that particular group.

However, should interest groups play such an important role in making public policy? Surely the representation allowed to interest groups may erode political responsibility in a representative democracy. This problem within the system is aggravated even further when one political party has dominated the government for a long period of time, and relationships become well ingrained. It is then that we find more highly placed and experienced bureaucrats leaving the public service to sell their knowledge and contacts to interest groups through private consulting services. If interest groups are to exist as representative bodies complementary to the elected representatives, steps should be taken to eliminate some of these injustices.

Part V
Public Policy

PETRO-CANADA

Full
Serve
Service
Complet

43.9

PETRO-CANADA

VISA

MasterCard

Gulf

Self Serve

43

CanaPress Photo Service

chapter 13

Public Policy-Making in a Federal State
Rationalism or Muddling Through?

NO STUDY OF POLITICS is complete without some examination of what governments actually do. Thus, in the last decade or so, one of the burgeoning fields within the discipline of political science has been the study of public policy. In fact, it would appear from the titles (if not always from the contents) of books, articles and courses on Canadian government and politics that research and writing about public policy has become a major growth industry.

In the world of social science, as one author puts it, "Concepts, like clothes, are trendy."[1] Consequently, as a particular concept, theme or area of study becomes fashionable, there is often a tendency to dress up rather dowdy subjects in more colourful and popular attire. Courses and books can be made to appear more relevant and attractive by incorporating a trendy term into the title, or by utilizing a fashionable analytical approach which may be ill-suited to the subject matter at hand. Like most other "chic" topics, the concept of public policy has occasionally endured such a fate – an unfortunate occurrence, because much insightful research has been done under the rubric of public policy analysis, and it has greatly augmented our understanding of politics in Canada and elsewhere.

In Chapter 2, we examined the expansion of the role of the government or public sector in Canada, and noted that the degree of intervention by governments at all levels has increased considerably in most western industrialized nations, especially since the Second World War. Inasmuch as the study of public policy is concerned primarily with what systems analysts would call "the output side of the political system" – *i.e.*, what governments actually do in response to

---

[1]The 'fashion' metaphor is employed by Leo Panitch, "Corporatism in Canada," *Studies in Political Economy*, no. 1 (Spring 1979), p. 43 ff.

both the manifold challenges which confront them and the demands emanating from their society – the current popularity of public policy studies stems from the realization that governments or the public sector have come to play an ever more important role in the social and economic life of the nation.

Thus, when politicians or policy-makers decide to increase public spending, or raise taxes or create a new Crown corporation in pursuit of certain objectives, we want to know what aims they have in mind, why they have chosen one course of action in preference to competing alternatives and which factors or interests have helped to influence and shape their decisions.

Sometimes, however, governments apparently fail to take action on a particular issue, even where there may be concerted demands for them to intervene in a certain direction. This, too, is of interest to students of public policy, since explanation of the inaction of government may be just as illuminating for our understanding of politics as the analysis of a host of more "positive" actions.

In particular, the study of non-decisions , or situations in which the government fails to act on public demands, helps one to understand some of the constraints within which policy-makers have to operate. The options open to policy-makers may be limited by the availability of resources in the physical and economic environments, but constraints may also be related to other aspects of Canadian politics, to the cultural, institutional and behavioural patterns examined in earlier chapters.

It is in the policy process that these other elements – culture, institutions and behaviour – all come together. The **culture** of a society shapes the demands placed before policy-makers and imposes constraints on the range of possible responses. Some forms of government activity may be legitimized by prevailing ideas and cultural norms, others precluded.

The **institutional structure** of Canadian politics also has a crucial influence on the policy-making process. Policy-makers' room for manoeuvre may be limited by the federal nature of the political system, by other aspects of the Canadian Constitution, by the dictates of governmental responsibility and accountability to Parliament – as well as by non-institutional factors such as relations with the United States and the available levels of financial and other resources.

Political **behaviour**, manifested through parties, interest group activity and the electoral arena, is one important means whereby the demands of citizens are articulated and channelled to policy-makers. Moreover, in a liberal democracy such as Canada, the electoral process is of significance in determining who will occupy some of the formal policy-making positions. But the electoral process requires that governments display a measure of responsiveness to public opinion and may also influence the timing of key policy initiatives which may please or dissatisfy certain segments of the electorate.

In this chapter, we shall attempt to demonstrate the nature and extent of linkages between culture, institutions, behaviour and public policy. Our first task, however, is to define what we mean by the term "public policy", ideally, in such a way that the concept may be used to encompass both the actions and the inactivity of governments.

WHAT IS PUBLIC POLICY?

One of the most common problems in the development of any new field of study is the task of securing common agreement on the definition and scope of its subject matter. This has certainly been the case in the emergence of public policy analysis. One part of the term "public policy" presents relatively little difficulty. The "public" half of the concept merely points to the fact that what is in question is policy initiated and carried out by "public authorities" – those involving the state or government, or the "public" sector – as opposed to the policies of "private" institutions such as commercial banks, private sector corporations and churches or other social organizations. The primary distinguishing feature of "public" policy, therefore, is that it is ultimately backed by the force of public law and the use, or threat, of the coercive sanctions of the state.

It is the second half of the concept, the word "policy", which has proven more difficult to delineate. As one author complained in a review of new books on public policy analysis: "No term in social science has suffered more ambiguity and abuse in the 1960s and the 1970s than 'policy'."[2] This ambiguity stems largely from the many contexts in which the term is employed by social scientists, politicians and the general public. "Policy" is from time to time misapplied to phenomena ranging from the narrowness of individual decisions, such as building an airport in a particular location, to broad philosophical precepts such as a vague commitment to "the just society". However, policies are not the same thing as decisions in that policy-making "involves a long series of more-or-less related activities, rather than a single discrete decision",[3] while the large scale of social engineering that would have to be undertaken to attain grandiose objectives like former Prime Minister Trudeau's "just society" would involve changes in a wide range of public policies.

Between these two extremes, it has been argued, "policy" is used more-or-less indiscriminately in everyday political debate in at least three contexts: "to refer to the *intentions* of politicians...to the *actions* of government...or to the *impact* of government..."[4] Rather than constituting adequate alternative definitions of the concept, these three usages are in fact different dimensions of public policy. A policy, whether public or private, is first and foremost a program or course of action pursued in response to a particular problem or issue.[5] But it is also, in most

---

[2]Eliot J. Feldman, "Review Article: Comparative Public Policy: Field or Method?," *Comparative Politics*, vol. 10, no. 2 (January 1979), p. 288.

[3]Richard Rose, "Introduction," in Richard Rose, ed., *Policy-Making in Britain: A Reader in Government* (London: Macmillan, 1969), p. x.

[4]Richard Rose, "Models of Change," in Richard Rose, ed., *The Dynamics of Public Policy: A Comparative Analysis* (Beverly Hills, California: Sage Publications, 1976), p. 9. Emphasis added.

[5]Cf. the definitions of "policy" as "A purposive course of action followed by an actor or set of actors in dealing with a problem or matter of concern," James E. Anderson, *Public Policy Making*, 2nd edition (New York: Holt, Rinehart and Winston, 1979), p. 3; or "A cluster of related activity organized around some general purpose," Marsha A. Chandler and William M. Chandler, *Public Policy and Provincial Politics* (Toronto: McGraw-Hill Ryerson, 1979), p. 2.

cases, linked to particular goals or objectives ("the intentions of politicians"). Further, the study of public policy is concerned with the effects of policies on society ("the impact of government"), whether such results are intended or are the unintended consequences of pursuing a certain course of action.

There is one further dimension of policy which is not revealed by any of the above interpretations of the term. On occasion, a government or some other actor may decide *not* to take action on a given problem. In this case, "policy" takes the form of inaction or non-intervention rather than a positive series of activities. This aspect of policy is well illustrated by Thomas Dye's much-quoted one-line definition of public policy as "whatever governments choose to do or not to do".[6]

Thus far, we have argued that policy is something larger in scope than an individual decision, but smaller than a universalistic prescription for society; that it involves action or inaction in relation to some issue or problem; and that it is usually conducted within the context of certain goals or objectives (whether explicitly stated or not). In addition, we noted previously that the term "public" when applied to "policy" refers to the activities of public authorities or governments backed by the force of "public law".

Therefore, we are now in a position to propose a definition: **Public policy** is the broad framework within which decisions are taken and action (or inaction) is pursued by governments in relation to some issue or problem. Thus, when we examine Canadian foreign policy in the next chapter, we shall be outlining the broad framework of goals, objectives, decisions, activities (and occasional inaction) of the federal government with regard to Canada's place in the world and its relations with other states and international actors. Similarly, when we discuss recent developments in Canadian energy policy later in this chapter, we shall refer to the changing priorities of government, the series of decisions and agreements which constituted the National Energy Program and the many subprograms and activities which Canadian governments have pursued in order to safeguard energy supplies and develop and exploit indigenous energy resources.

Mention of these two examples raises a further dimension of public policy analysis. How many "broad frameworks" are we talking about? How can we divide the total activities of government into more manageable chunks for the purpose of analysing public policy? A number of classifications of types of public policy may be proposed.

The most obvious division is the traditional separation of foreign policy from domestic public policy. **Foreign policy** shapes Canada's place in the international political system and determines Canada's relations with other nation-states and with international organizations such as the United Nations and NATO. **Domestic public policy**, on the other hand, is directed towards the internal economic, social and political environment.

As national economies and national political systems become more interdependent, it may be argued that a sharp distinction betweeen domestic and foreign policy is increasingly difficult to maintain. This is especially the case for a

---

[6]Thomas R. Dye, *Understanding Public Policy*, 3rd ed. (Englewood Cliffs: Prentice Hall, 1978), p. 3.

country like Canada whose national economy is closely integrated with that of a much larger and more powerful neighbour. Thus, for example, policy measures like the Foreign Investment Review Act of 1973 and the 1980 National Energy Program, which attempted to enhance domestic control over the Canadian economy, had important repercussions for Canada's external relations. On the other side of the coin, while national defence is usually considered to be an adjunct of foreign policy, politicians may attempt, for example, to utilize an expansion of defence spending and domestic procurements to boost a sagging economy. But, despite the grey areas created by growing interdependencies, there remains a sufficiently clear distinction between domestic and foreign policy, and the respective policy-making processes, to justify the division of these two types of government activity. Therefore, we shall conform to conventional usage by restricting our discussion of public policy in this chapter to the domestic activities of government, and look at foreign policy separately in Chapter 14.

As the umbrella term "foreign policy" covers a number of government activities – ranging from functional areas such as defence, foreign aid and trade policy to policies toward specific regions or countries – so, too, may the domestic activities of government be divided into different policy areas. Again, here, there occurs a much-used dichotomy – social policy and economic policy – which does serve as a basic organizing device, but may also reveal some grey areas when applied to specific activities and programs of government.

"Social policy" is perhaps the more easily defined. In general terms, **social policy** encompasses those activities oriented toward the education, health and welfare of the population. The term "economic policy", on the other hand, may be applied to two different levels of government activity. From a macro perspective, **economic policy** refers to the overall management and stabilization of the nation's economic environment; that is, to government attempts to control the money supply and interest rates, manage government spending and taxation and foster balanced economic growth without incurring the "twin evils" of rampant inflation and mass unemployment. Social policy cannot be divorced totally from economic policy in this broad sense, because public spending on social programs has often been manipulated to increase or deflate aggregate demand in the economy, and social expenditure is therefore one of the tools available to governments in implementing macroeconomic policy.

On another level, **economic policy** is also a generic term for a number of sectoral policy frameworks to develop or conserve national resources, promote industrial growth, reduce regional disparities or provide communications and transportation systems. In this sense, "economic policy" and "social policy" are more easily distinguished. Even so, some grey areas persist. The objectives of regional development or transportation policy may be as much social as economic, insofar as they attempt to ensure access to services in all parts of the country. Some authors include certain aspects of social policy in their considerations of Canadian economic policies. Education, for instance, may be closely linked to the provision of adequately trained personnel for the labour market.[7]

---

[7] See, for example, Ingrid Bryan, *Economic Policies in Canada* (Toronto: Butterworths, 1982).

However, in addition to the two levels of economic policy and the traditional application of social policy to such issues as education, health, income security and social welfare, there remain a number of policy areas or frameworks in which governments have become active in Canada and elsewhere. These include the subsidization of performing arts (ballet, opera, theatre, *etc.*), the regulation of the mass media (especially broadcasting), the preservation of the physical environment and the enhancement of the multicultural fabric of Canadian society. To the extent that these policies are not directly linked to economic development, they appear to be more closely related to the "social" concerns of society. But they are clearly of a different nature than the traditional concerns of social policy and the priorities of the welfare state. Rather than pertaining to standards of living (in quantitative or material terms), they are oriented toward preserving or enhancing the quality of life of Canadian citizens.

In Figure 13-1, we have therefore classified the multiplicity of domestic activities under four main headings. "Macroeconomic Policy" comprises those activities which pertain to the national or federal government's role as the central manager of the overall domestic economy, including control of the currency and money supply, manipulation of interest rates via the Bank of Canada, managing public expenditures and taxation and so on. Since priorities established under this general heading will influence the resources available for, or the constraints upon, the attainment of other public objectives, "Macroeconomic Policy" is placed at the centre of the table; dotted lines indicate its relation to other policy fields.

The other two general categories, "Social Development Policies" and "Economic Development Policies" reflect more or less the division of responsibilities between the federal Cabinet Committees on Social Development and on Economic and Regional Development in managing their respective envelopes under the PEMS process.[8] The category "Economic Development Policies" includes a wide range of sectoral and regional frameworks designed to deal with different aspects of the Canadian economy. In keeping with our earlier discussion, we have divided "Social Development Policies" into two sub-categories. "Social Policies" reflect the traditional concerns of the welfare state with providing adequate minimum standards of education, health care, housing and income security for all citizens. "Quality-of-Life Policies", on the other hand, are oriented toward preserving and enhancing the nation's artistic, cultural and environmental heritage and with civil liberties, human rights and opportunities for individuals and groups.

Even with this comprehensive four-fold classification of the activities of government, some problems and possible omissions remain. The government's relatively recent interventions on behalf of certain designated groups, such as youth, Native peoples, handicapped persons and women, do not fit easily into any classification since they clearly entail both social and economic activities. For exam-

---

[8]For a similar division of public policies at the provincial level in Canada, see Chandler and Chandler, *Public Policy and Provincial Politics.*

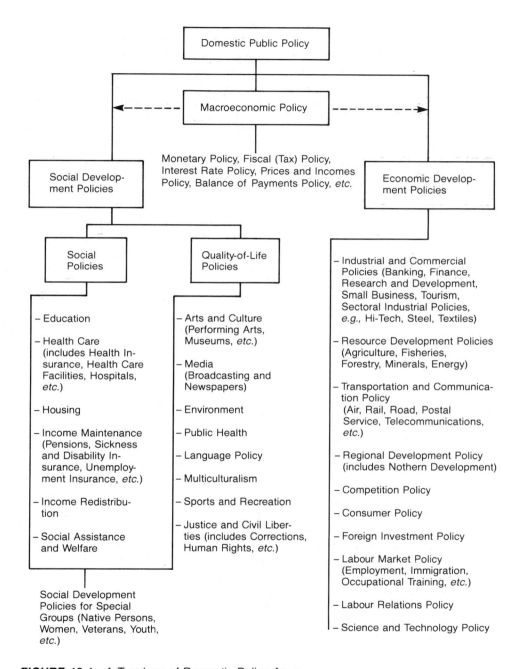

FIGURE 13-1 A Typology of Domestic Policy Areas

ple, in tackling the disadvantaged position of women in Canadian society, public policy has to be directed toward reforming traditional social policies (such as the provision of adequate pensions for elderly single women), providing new social programs (such as day care, maternity leave and perhaps, parental insurance), taking into account quality-of-life issues (such as the elimination of sexist bias in advertising, media reporting and publishing) and promoting equal employment and training opportunities for women as part of labour market policy. Since the overall goal of such policies is to enhance the human dignity and social equality of women (and the other designated groups), we have included them under the general heading of "Social Development Policies", but the reader should note that these policy frameworks may well include an economic policy component.

These caveats aside, the typology of government activities or policy areas in Figure 13-1 provides a fairly comprehensive guide to many major policy concerns of governments in Canada while grouping them into more manageable bundles to facilitate analysis. In a later section of this chapter, we shall undertake three short case studies of specific policy areas to illustrate some of the problems of policy-making in a federal state such as Canada. Our selection of policy areas for the case-studies is in part guided by the classification in Figure 13-1 inasmuch as we shall examine one area from each of three categories: energy policy from economic development, health care from social policy, and broadcasting policy from the quality-of-life group. First, however, some further theoretical and conceptual discussion is necessary to provide a context for the analysis of the case studies.

PUBLIC POLICY AND THEORIES OF POLICY-MAKING

The study of public policy may be defined in simple terms as "the study of *how, why* and *to what effect* different governments pursue particular *courses of action and inaction*".[9] As the literature on public policy has grown, analysts have embraced a number of alternative theoretical models and approaches in attempts to explain how individual policy decisions were made and how public policy frameworks developed, why various governments (at national and sub-national levels) have adopted different courses of action and inaction in response to apparently similar problems and issues, and to what effect governments have intervened or refrained from acting to resolve the problems which confront them.

These models and approaches may be distinguished from one another with regard to their respective levels of analysis; their portrayal of the major actors in the policy process; their assumptions regarding the nature of society and politics and the role of government/state; and their evaluation of the interests served by public policy outputs. We should point out that, in explaining how or why public

---

[9]Arnold J. Heidenheimer, Hugh Heclo and Carolyn Teich Adams, *Comparative Public Policy: The Politics of Social Choice in Europe and America,* 2nd ed. (New York: St. Martin's Press, 1983), p. 4. (Emphasis in original.)

policies are made, as in other areas of political science, there is no universally accepted theory. Consequently, in the pages which follow, we shall outline some of the more frequently used approaches and note some of their respective strengths and weaknesses. Later in the chapter, we shall demonstrate how selected approaches may be applied to empirical examples of public policy development in the Canadian context. To organize our discussion, we have divided the contending theories into two categories: micro-level models, which focus mainly on the making of individual policy decisions; and macro-level approaches, which are more concerned with accounting for broader patterns of public policy as part of the relationship between the state and society.

Micro-Level Approaches to Policy-Making

Micro-level models or theories of decision-making are intended to explain how individual decisions are taken within a broad framework of public policy. It must first be made clear that, in our terms, policy-making and decision-making are not the same thing. Rarely will a policy consist of a single decision. If **decision-making** is defined as the process whereby one course of action (or inaction) or one objective is chosen from a number of competing alternatives, then each public policy will involve, at the barest minimum, the following:

1. a decision whether or not government should intervene in a particular issue area;
2. a decision with regard to the goals or objectives of governmental involvement;
3. a decision on the best available means of achieving those goals and the instruments to be used; and
4. a decision to maintain, alter, or discontinue the chosen course of action once some evaluation of its effectiveness can be undertaken.

Decision-making therefore is clearly a part of the policy-making process, but it is not the whole process. Decision-making models, by and large, concentrate on the third of the four minimal stages oulined above – the selection of the best available means of achieving the goals of governmental intervention. They assume that governmental priorities and objectives have already been established via the political process, and tend to focus instead on the choice of means to attain those goals via the administrative process.

Over the years, a number of debates on the relative merits of different theories of decision-making have appeared in the literature of public administration. For example, we referred in Chapter 9 to Graham Allison's application of the *rational actor, organizational process*, and *bureaucratic politics* models to the events surrounding the Cuban Missile Crisis and to the subsequent testing of these models in both foreign and domestic policy contexts.[10] But the most widely-known de-

---

[10]See Chapter 9, above and Graham T. Allison, *Essence of Decision: Explaining the Cuban Missile Crisis* (Boston: Little, Brown, 1971).

bate has centred on the confrontation between advocates of the *rationalist* and *incrementalist* approaches to decision-making.[11]

The Rational-Comprehensive Model

The usual point of departure for this debate is the so called *rational-comprehensive* model of decision-making. This model can best be described by listing the following elements or stages of the process:

1. The rational decision-maker is presented with a problem that can be distinguished from other problems, or at least compared meaningfully with them.
2. The values, goals and objectives that guide the decision-maker are reviewed and ranked in order of priority.
3. A list of alternative means of achieving these goals is compiled.
4. The consequences (costs and benefits) that would ensue from each alternative are estimated.
5. Each alternative, and its likely consequences, is then compared with all other alternatives.
6. Finally, the rational decision-maker will select the course of action, and its consequences, which offers maximum attainment of the values, goals or objectives identified in Step 2.[12]

According to the advocates of this model, the end product of the process will be a "rational" decision – that is, one which selects the most effective and efficient means of achieving a given end.

Under ideal conditions, the rational-comprehensive process may be the way that some decisions ought to be made; but does it describe accurately the way in which all, or even most, decisions are actually taken? According to its critics, the rationalist model is wrong on both counts – it neither describes reality nor represents an ideal to be emulated.[13] First, it is argued that in a complex industrial society, very few of the issues confronting governments are simple, concrete problems that can be easily singled out for this kind of comprehensive analysis. Second, such a process makes totally unreasonable demands on decision-makers, with regard to both the information they must have at their disposal and the time and resources they must consume in evaluating the costs and benefits of all pos-

---

[11]See, especially, Charles E. Lindblom, "The Science of 'Muddling Through'," *Public Administration Review,* vol. 19, no. 2 (Spring 1959), pp. 79-88; the critique by Yehezkel Dror, "Muddling Through – 'Science' or Inertia?"; and Lindblom's response, "Contexts for Change and Strategy: A Reply," both in *Public Administration Review,* vol. 24, no. 3 (September 1964), pp. 153-157 and 157-158.

[12]Adapted from Anderson, *Public Policy-Making,* pp. 9-10.

[13]See, among others, Lindblom, "The Science of 'Muddling Through' "; and the reviews by Anderson, *Public Policy Making,* pp. 10-11; and G. Smith and D. May "The Artificial Debate between Rationalist and Incrementalist Models of Decision-Making," in A.G. McGrew and M.J. Wilson, eds., *Decision-Making: Approaches and Analysis* (Manchester: Manchester University Press, 1982), pp. 116-124.

sible alternative courses of action. Thus, the model is claimed to be impractical and, perhaps, not entirely "rational". The costs of undertaking a search for the most efficient means of implementation may well be greater than the savings realized by deploying it. Furthermore, as Smith and May point out, "Even if the savings of a novel policy option do exceed the search costs there is no way of knowing about that before the search begins."[11]

Lastly, it is argued that the rational-comprehensive approach is a normative or prescriptive model: it does not *describe* how decisions are actually made; rather, it *prescribes* how some people think policies and decisions *ought* to be made. Thus, there is a danger for policy analysts and governments alike that means become confused with ends, that the ultimate objectives of government become less important than the quest for the most efficient or rational means of achieving those goals. When technocratic models of decision-making or policy-making come to value rationality and efficiency as ends in themselves, the outcome may be as Theodore Lowi trenchantly expressed it with reference to a convicted war criminal: "There is neither politics nor political science left when we can look at Eichmann and ask only whether his policy-making system was as good as it could have been."[15]

THE INCREMENTALIST MODEL

Charles Lindblom has advocated an alternative to the technocratic and prescriptive rational-comprehensive model which, he argues, is more descriptive of the way decision-makers actually proceed. This approach has been variously labelled "disjointed incrementalism", "policy-making by successive limited comparisons", "the science of muddling through" or, in its simplest form, "incrementalism".[16]

The **incrementalist** model assumes that the majority of problems facing decision-makers are complex and interrelated, and allows for the fact that decision-makers operate in a climate of uncertainty and limited resources. In contrast to the rationalist approach, the point of departure for incremental decision-making is not some ideal goal to be attained in the most efficient manner but the policies and programs already in place in a given issue area. From that basis, only a limited number of policy alternatives (*i.e.*, changes to existing programs) is considered, and only a few foreseeable consequences (estimated costs and benefits) are evaluated for each alternative. Incrementalism therefore results in alterations at the margins of existing policies, rather than fundamental changes, in a manner in which maximum agreement can be achieved among the various interests involved.

---

[11]Smith and May, *ibid.*, p. 118.

[15]Theodore Lowi, "Decision Making vs. Policy Making: Toward an Antidote for Technocracy," *Public Administration Review* vol. 30, no. 3 (May 1970), p. 319.

[16]Lindblom, "The Science of 'Muddling Through' "; David Braybrooke and Charles Lindblom, *A Strategy of Decision* (New York: Free Press, 1963), especially Chapter 5; and Lindblom, "Still Muddling, Not Yet Through," *Public Administration Review*, vol. 39, no. 6 (November/December 1979), pp. 517-526.

The incrementalist model, it is claimed, resolves the matter of inadequate information and uncertainty since marginal adjustments to policies and programs can easily be reversed or altered if they are unsuccessful, if new information comes to light or if circumstances change. Thus, according to its proponents, incrementalism may in fact be the more "rational" way to proceed, because it avoids the making of serious, lasting errors. Moreover, the strategy of successive limited comparisons consumes less time, money and other resources than the exhaustive search process of the rational-comprehensive model. Finally, since there is rarely general or permanent agreement on the values and objectives of government intervention, an incremental approach to decision-making offers endless opportunities for a redefinition of goals and the adjustment of both the means (programs, activities) and ends (values, priorities) of public policy-making.

Like the rational-comprehensive model, the incrementalist approach has been criticized on a number of grounds. Many criticisms of incrementalism are essentially subjective in nature, arguing that, whether or not the model is empirically valid, it is just not the way that decisions *should* be made. Given the preoccupation of advocates of rationalism with "improving" the decision-making process in the interests of technical efficiency, it is perhaps not surprising that they are appalled by the prospect of decision-makers "muddling through" on most issues. Yehezkel Dror, for example, has labelled Lindblom's model an inherently "conservative" recipe for maintaining the *status quo* since it provides an "ideological reinforcement of the pro-inertia and anti-innovation forces prevalent in all human organizations, administrative and policy-making."[17]

A much more important problem, in our view, is the fact that although the incrementalist model is supposed to provide a general description of how policy decisions are made by making marginal adjustments to the policies and programs already in place, it quite clearly cannot account for occasional radical departures from existing patterns of activity or inactivity. Thus, it cannot explain the entry of governments into new areas of policy intervention such as the federal government's decision to begin regulating foreign ownership, nor can it account for drastic alterations to or innovations in existing policy such as the National Energy Program.

RESOLVING THE RATIONALIST *VERSUS* INCREMENTALIST DEBATE

In an attempt to overcome both the descriptive shortcomings of incrementalism and the impracticality of the rational-comprehensive model, Amitai Etzioni has proposed a third theory of decision-making known as **mixed-scanning**.[18] Etzioni differentiates two kinds of decisions: "contextual" or "fundamental" decisions, which establish or review the broad framework of goals and long-term action in a given policy area and which are made through a modified, more realistic, form of

---

[17]Dror, "Muddling Through – 'Science' or Inertia?", p. 155.

[18]Amitai Etzioni, "Mixed-Scanning: A 'Third' Approach to Decision Making," *Public Administration Review,* vol. 27, no. 5 (December 1967), pp. 385-392.

the rationalistic process; and "incremental" decisions, which are based on marginal adjustments and which fill in the short-term details of policy implementation within the contexts set by fundamental decisions. It is doubtful, however, whether this type of compromise solution to the debate is really viable, since "rationalism and incrementalism embody diametrically opposed principles which are not reconciled by 'mixed scanning' sampling of either side."[19]

The central problem in the rationalist/incrementalist debate, which effectively precludes any reconciliation or middle ground, is that the two sides have different conceptions of the term "model" and the functions ascribed to it. In political science, as in everyday language, "model" is sometimes used to refer to a normative ideal which all should seek to emulate, as in "She is a model citizen." But "model" is more commonly used in both contexts in the sense of a simplified and scaled-down version of reality designed to show how various components fit together and work, as in a "working model" of a car or steam engine. The rational-comprehensive model is of the former type, since it assumes that general agreement can be reached on long-term values and goals and prescribes how decisions ought to be made in the interests of technical efficiency. It is, therefore, a prescriptive model to which decision-makers and policy analysts may aspire, but which is strictly impractical for routine decision-making. Incrementalism, on the other hand, is a simplified "working model" which purports to explain and describe how decision-makers actually proceed, given the economic and political constraints (including lack of consensus on goals and values) within which they operate. Critics of rationalism argue that, from a realist's perspective, it is empirically inaccurate, that "This is not the way things are actually done." For technocratic idealists, on the other hand, although incrementalism may describe how some decision-making takes place, there is a strong suspicion that "This is not the way things should be done." To a great extent, therefore, the two sides are advocating totally different things, and the whole discussion between incrementalists and rationalists is an artificial debate based on differing conceptions of the roles and purposes of decision-making models.[20]

As a theoretical approach to aid our understanding of how decisions are made within the broader framework of public policy, the rational-comprehensive model is faulty in many respects, although it may be argued that it is the kind of normative ideal to which the Canadian federal government aspired in its attempts to develop a more "rational" approach to policy-making in the late 1960s and early 1970s. Incrementalism, on the other hand, is a more descriptive model (admittedly with some normative overtones of its own) which may accurately portray the tendency of governmental decision-makers to "muddle through" from day to day on many issues. But it also has limitations, inasmuch as it cannot account for certain key decisions such as government involvement in a new issue area, where no clear policy positions or programs existed previously. Neither of

---

[19]Smith and May, "The Artificial Debate . . .", p. 121.

[20]*Ibid.*, pp. 121-123.

these contending models, nor any attempt to develop a middle ground between them, has yet provided a comprehensive and generally accepted theory of decision-making. However, we have argued that decision-making is only a part of the overall process of public policy activity. Therefore, to the extent that any model can tell us *how* policy decisions are made, it still could not provide guidance as to *why* governments pursue particular directions in public policy, nor *to what effect*. In order to get closer to these dimensions of policy analysis, we require a broader perspective on the role of the state and its relationship with society than decision-making theories can provide.

Macro-Level Approaches to Public Policy Analysis

Macro-level approaches are those which focus on the wider relationship between state and society, and therefore on the general direction of broad patterns of public policy, rather than on the details of how individual policy decisions are made within the government or bureaucracy. These theories tend to differ from one another with respect to both the relative emphasis they place on economic, social and political factors in the determination of public policy and their views of the interests served by the state or government in its policy activities. In the pages which follow, we outline briefly four of these approaches, "environmental determinism", "pluralism", "public choice theory" and "neo-Marxism", together with some of their respective strengths and weaknesses as frameworks for analysing Canadian public policy. The reader should be warned, however, that space permits merely an overview of what are, in some cases, highly complex and contentious theoretical arguments. Although we shall illustrate the application of these models at various points in this chapter, some further reading and discussion may be necessary before the subtleties of some of these approaches are fully appreciated.[21]

ENVIRONMENTAL DETERMINISM

The **environmental determinist** approach to the study of public policy is the least political of the four macro-level frameworks considered in this chapter. Its methodology is based upon "the systematic comparative analysis of public policies the objective of which is to discover the relationship between various environmental factors and public policy".[22] The approach calls for the study of a number of national political systems or sub-national political units (*e.g.*, Canadian provinces or American states) in order that sufficient data may be obtained for statistical analysis of the relationships between public policy outputs (usually measured in terms of public expenditure) and socio-economic variables such as economic or technological developments, affluence or the demographic structure of populations. At the same time, it tends to ignore or downplay the impor-

---

[21]For further reading, see the references in Footnotes 23-56.

[22]Peter Aucoin, "Public Policy Theory and Analysis," in G.B. Doern and P. Aucoin, eds., *Public Policy in Canada: Organization, Process and Management* (Toronto: Macmillan, 1979), p. 11.

tance of both explicitly political actors such as parties or interest groups, and other major political variables such as ideology or the distribution of power in society.

The theoretical origins of this approach lie in the functionalist and systems-analysis frameworks which were popular during the so-called "behavioural revolution" in the study of politics in the late 1950s and the 1960s. These models viewed the political system as a sub-system of society as a whole, as the complex of roles and structures concerned with the "authoritative allocation of values" for a society.[23] From this perspective, public policies are "authoritative allocations" designed to maintain or restore an equilibrium between the political system and its environment. Policies, therefore, are largely determined by changes in the economic, physical, social and technological environments, both domestic and external, as well as in the international political system.

A number of studies in the United States provided support for this thesis by showing that public policy outputs were more strongly related statistically with socio-economic environmental variables than with political factors such as the nature of party competition or the extent of electoral participation, both in cross-national analyses[24] and in intra-societal comparisons among the American states.[25] Attempts to reproduce these findings in the Canadian context met with mixed results. While, for example, Falcone and Whittington found that political variables were less relevant than socio-economic factors in predicting federal policy outputs over time,[26] studies of provincial policy innovation by Poel and Chandler re-emphasized the importance of political characteristics such as the partisan complexion of government, the size of the public service, constituency representation and the nature of party competition.[27]

However, even where statistical analyses do suggest a strong relationship between socio-economic and other environmental factors on the one hand, and

---

[23] Hence, the environmental determinist model is sometimes labelled, especially by its critics, the "sociological" approach to politics and public policy. See, for example, Francis G. Castles and R.D. McKinlay, "Public Welfare Provision, Scandinavia and the Sheer Futility of the Sociological Approach to Politics," *British Journal of Political Science*, vol. 9, no. 2 (April 1979), pp. 157-171; or Ian Gough, "Theories of the Welfare State: A Critique," *International Journal of Health Services*, vol. 8, no. 1 (1978), pp. 27-40.

[24] For example, Phillips Cutright, "Political Structure, Economic Development, and National Security Programs," *American Journal of Sociology*, vol. 70, no. 5 (March 1965), pp. 537-550; Harold Wilensky, *The Welfare State and Equality* (Berkeley: University of California Press, 1975).

[25] For example, Thomas R. Dye, *Politics, Economics and the Public: Policy Outcomes in the American States* (Chicago: Rand McNally, 1966); Richard I. Hofferbert, "The Relation Between Public Policy and Some Structural and Environmental Variables in the American States," *American Political Science Review*, vol. 60, no. 1 (March 1966), pp. 73-82.

[26] David Falcone and M.S. Whittington, "Output Change in Canada: A Preliminary Attempt to Open the 'Black Box'," unpublished paper delivered to the Canadian Political Science Association, Annual Meeting, Montreal, June 1972.

[27] Dale H. Poel, "The Diffusion of Legislation among the Canadian Provinces: A Statistical Analysis," *Canadian Journal of Political Science*, vol. 9, no. 4 (December 1976), pp. 605-628; William M. Chandler, "Canadian Socialism and Policy Impact: Contagion from the Left," *Canadian Journal of Political Science*, vol. 10, no. 4 (December 1977), pp. 755-780.

public policy outputs on the other, their explanatory power is limited. As one critic observes, "The fact that socio-economic variables are closely associated with political or policy variables does not in itself show that one 'causes', 'shapes', 'determines', or 'accounts for' the other."[28] This is not to say that environmental factors are unimportant to the study of public policy. It may reasonably be expected that broad social and economic changes such as the changing age structure of the population, urbanization, industrialization or a recession may generate new demands for government intervention. But we need to know how those demands become mobilized and why public policy-makers respond to them in a particular fashion – if indeed they respond at all. We need to know which social groups are affected by environmental changes, whether these groups have the political resources to channel demands to policy-makers, as well as the factors which determine why governments appear willing to respond to some interests and not to others. In the absence of these vital linkages, Richard Simeon has argued,

> ...environmental variables alone have only limited explanatory value. They probably explain more about the variance in the scope of government than they do about either the means selected or the distribution of benefits involved. To the extent they do shape policy, it is as they interact with cultural and ideological predispositions, with the distribution of political resources among groups, and the like.[29]

In our view, the vast majority of economic, geographical, social and technological factors in the environment of the policy-making process should be regarded not as causal determinants of public policy but as strictly environmental variables – that is, as part of the broader context of resources and constraints (including the cultural, ideological, institutional and political context) within which policy-makers operate and make political choices. To be sure, economic growth may lead to an expansion of the government's tax base, thereby providing greater revenues to finance public expenditure, but it will not in itself cause governments to spend more, nor determine which programs, if any, will benefit from increased resources. In a recession, the revenue base may shrink, placing constraints on the government's freedom of action but not necessarily determining that the government will reduce spending in general or on any particular program. To take another example, Canadian energy policy has been influenced by international political and economic factors, including the Arab-Israeli War of 1973, the subsequent policies of OPEC and the changing world price of oil. But the government's responses have been conditioned at least as much by the domestic political realities of interest group activity, federal-provincial relations and partisan and bureaucratic manoeuvring as by these external environmental factors.

---

[28]Joyce M. Munns, "The Environment, Politics and Policy Literature: A Critique and Reformulation," *Western Political Quarterly*, vol. 28, no. 4 (December 1975), p. 658.

[29]Richard Simeon, "Studying Public Policy," *Canadian Journal of Political Science*, vol. 9, no. 4 (December 1976), pp. 567-568.

Environmental factors do have some influence, because policy-making does not take place in a vacuum. Canadian policy-makers have to take into account the state of the economy, the multicultural, linguistic and demographic composition of Canadian society, Canada's economic interdependence with the United States, the availability of natural resources, among many other factors. But exactly how these variables affect the policies of government is largely left unexplained by the environmental determinist approach. The next model, pluralism, attempts to fill some of the gaps.

PLURALISM

The **pluralist** approach to the study of public policy places much more emphasis on political actors in the policy process, especially on the role of parties and interest groups, than does the environmental determinist model. For pluralists, politics is the process whereby individuals and groups seek to promote their interests through organization, political mobilization and alliance-building on an issue-to-issue basis, in order to influence the policy outputs of government. Political parties are seen as more-or-less broad coalitions of interests, seeking legislative majorities in the electoral arena, while the pluralist views government as a neutral arbiter which referees the group struggle, adjudicates among competing group demands, and implements and enforces public policies in the national interest or, at least, according to the wishes of the majority on each issue.

Thus, pluralists regard public policies as the outcomes of competition between groups and parties (coalitions of groups). According to Earl Latham, "What may be called public policy is the equilibrium reached in this struggle at any given moment, and it represents a balance which the contending factions or groups constantly strive to weight in their favor."[30]

The essence of the pluralist approach is the assumption that power is widely dispersed in society. Since in its extreme forms pluralism does not admit to the existence of structural inequalities within society, all individuals and groups are seen as having approximately equal access to the policy-making process. Therefore, they all have potentially equal influence on public policy outputs as long as they organize themselves and play by the "rules of the game" – that is, as long as they abide by the underlying consensus on political values and procedures. The tendency for coalitions and alliances of groups to change composition from one issue to another – for example, workers and managers in the steel industry may be opposed on matters of occupational health and safety legislation but allied in lobbying the government for protectionist measures to keep out foreign steel – means that there are no permanent winners and losers in the group struggle. Power, defined in simple terms as "the ability to get things done", therefore shifts from coalition to coalition according to the issue at stake and is never the exclusive preserve of any one group or elite.[31]

---

[30]Earl Latham, *The Group Basis of Politics* (New York: Octagon Books, 1965), p. 36.

[31]The classic pluralist statement of the diffusion of political power is found in Robert A. Dahl, *Who Governs?* (New Haven: Yale University Press, 1961).

It is this vision of widely dispersed power based on equality of access to the policy process that has provoked some of the strongest criticisms of the pluralist approach. First, it is argued that some groups can never get a fair hearing for their interests because obstacles exist to placing certain issues on the agenda of political debate. To quote E. E. Schattschneider,

> All forms of political organization have a bias in favor of the exploitation of some kinds of conflict and the suppression of others because organization is the mobilization of bias. *Some issues are organized into politics while others are organized out.*[32]

To take a simple example, it may be argued that the federalist organization of Canadian political life is more conducive to the expression of linguistic and regional issues than to the mobilization of redistributional issues based on social class. Since many class-based issues such as labour legislation and welfare policies fall under provincial jurisdiction, it is more difficult to mobilize these interests across provincial boundaries. Thus, they are partially "organized out" of federal politics, while cultural and regional issues are "organized in".

In any case, suggests Schattschneider, it is harder for the poor and the working class to become politically organized than for the rich or for business interests. The latter groups have more political and economic resources to bring to bear and their relatively small numbers facilitate mobilization.[33] Consequently, he argues, "The flaw in the pluralist heaven is that the heavenly chorus sings with a strong upper-class accent. Probably about 90 percent of the people cannot get into the pressure (group) system."[34]

The idea that some issues are "organized out" of politics by the "mobilization of bias" inherent in all political systems is taken a step further in the concept of *non-decision-making*, associated particularly with the writings of Peter Bachrach and Morton Baratz. In their now-classic article, "The Two Faces of Power", Bachrach and Baratz condemned the pluralists for emphasizing one aspect of power, "the ability to get things done", to the exclusion of "the ability to stop things getting done", which is the power of non-decision.[35] They argued that elite groups (sometimes called "veto groups") within or outside government can take advantage of the "mobilization of bias, a set of predominant values, beliefs, rituals and institutional procedures ('rules of the game') that operate systematically and consistently to the benefit of certain persons and groups at the expense of others" in order to prevent some issues contrary to their interests

---

[32]E.E. Schattschneider, *The Semisovereign People: A Realist's View of Democracy in America* (Hinsdale: Dryden Press, 1975), p. 69. (Emphasis added.)

[33]Schattschneider's arguments about the effects of group size on political mobilization are supported by Mancur Olson, Jr., *The Logic of Collective Action* (Cambridge; Harvard University Press, 1965).

[34]Schattschneider, *The Semisovereign People*, pp. 34-35.

[35]Peter Bachrach and Morton S. Baratz, "The Two Faces of Power," *American Political Science Review*, vol. 56, no. 4 (December 1962), pp. 947-952.

from ever reaching the agenda of political debate or, once there, to prevent effective action from being taken.[36]

Obviously, non-decisions present serious methodological problems for study since by their very nature they cannot be readily identified, especially where issues have been successfully suppressed or excluded from the political agenda.[37] To a certain extent, the term "non-decision" itself is a misnomer, since many of the examples cited by Bachrach and Baratz and other non-decision theorists involve actual decisions by policy-makers either to suppress an issue or to take no action on a particular problem. However, this critical approach does serve to sensitize us to the facts that some interests and issues are more easily organized than others and that various groups do not have equal political resources or enjoy equal access to the policy-making process.

To be sure, a wide array of interest groups do organize themselves in attempts to influence policy-makers, and it is necessary to examine their effects when studying public policy, especially in a liberal democracy such as Canada where governments must maintain a degree of responsiveness to pressures from society. But, for a variety of reasons, some groups have greater influence on policy-making than others. The next two macro-level approaches attempt to explain why this is the case.

PUBLIC CHOICE THEORY

"Public choice can be defined as the economic study of non-market decision-making or simply the application of economics to political science."[38] The basic premise of **public choice** theory, borrowed directly from classical liberal economics, is that each individual is essentially a self-interested, rational, utility-maximizing actor. Thus, when people come together to engage in collective non-market decision-making in the political arena (making "public" choices), they behave in exactly the same way that many economists believe they do when making market-oriented choices in the economic sphere – that is, they act in a rational and calculating fashion to maximize their own interests. Voters will give electoral support to that party which offers a package of programs most likely to maximize their individual well-being.[39] Interest groups will naturally lobby for their particular concerns. And, when politicians and bureaucrats make decisions and formulate policies, they do so not according to some vague notion of "the public interest" or even "the will of the majority" but largely to satisfy their own narrow individual interests.

---

[36]Peter Bachrach and Morton S. Baratz, *Power and Poverty: Theory and Practice* (New York: Oxford University Press, 1970), p. 43 ff.

[37]See Geraint Parry and Peter Morriss, "When is a Decision not a Decision?" in McGrew and Wilson, eds., *Decision-Making: Approaches and Analysis*, pp. 19-35.

[38]Dennis C. Mueller, *Public Choice* (Cambridge: Cambridge University Press, 1979), p. 1.

[39]Anthony Downs, *An Economic Theory of Democracy* (New York: Harper and Row, 1957), esp. Chapter 3.

Not all individuals have an equal opportunity to realize their respective interests in the public choice model, however. The average voter, for example, is fairly peripheral to the public choice view of the policy process. Voters are important only when they have the periodic opportunity to choose, through elections, which politicians will have most influence in government. Otherwise, except when they participate in an effective special-interest group, ordinary citizens are little more than passive consumers of public policies.

According to public choice theorists, the central actors in the policy-making process are special-interest groups, bureaucrats and politicians (especially the leaders of the governing party).[40] But this is not just pluralism in disguise. First, in the public choice approach, the primary unit of political action is the individual, not the group. Although individuals may join forces in pursuit of their interests, for example, by forming an interest group, they do so only when collective action promises greater rewards than acting alone and when the benefits of collective action outweigh the costs of group participation (such as time spent at meetings, payment of membership dues or having to compromise some individual goals). When the benefits of group action are uncertain, or when they might possibly be derived without paying the costs of group membership (the so-called "free rider" problem), it is often more rational for the individual not to participate in collective action.

As a result of the free-rider situation it is much more difficult for some groups to organize and mobilize supporters than it is for others. Small, relatively homogeneous groups with much to win or lose from public policy changes, such as specific business interests, are more easily mobilized and enjoy proportionately greater resources than larger, disparate groups like consumers or environmentalists.[41] Thus, in contrast to the pluralists, who consider that all groups have equal access to and potentially equal influence upon the policy-making process, public choice analysts argue that "There is no reason to believe that the pressure exerted on decision-makers by special interest groups ... is in any sense balanced or fair or offsetting."[42]

The third major departure from pluralism is that public choice views government not as a neutral arbiter refereeing the group struggle in the public interest, but rather as a complex process of interaction and bargaining among bureaucrats and politicians seeking to maximize their own individual (and, sometimes, mutual) self-interests. Thus, for example, it is assumed that politicians will support policies which confer benefits upon marginal voters in order to maximize the likelihood of their election or re-election to office. Bureaucrats, on the

---

[40]Some public choice writers also include the media as a fourth influential actor in the policy process, because the media helps to structure the agenda of political debate. See, for example, Douglas G. Hartle, *A Theory of the Expenditure Budgetary Process* (Toronto: Ontario Economic Council/University of Toronto Press, 1976), Chapter 3; and Michael J. Trebilcock, *et al.*, *The Choice of Governing Instrument: A Study Prepared for the Economic Council of Canada* (Ottawa: Minister of Supply and Services, 1982), Chapter 2.

[41]Olson, *The Logic of Collective Action*, pp. 53-57 and Chapter 7.

[42]Trebilcock, *et al.*, *The Choice of Governing Instrument*, p. 10.

other hand, will use the information at their disposal, on which politicians depend, to push for policies which will expand their departmental budgets, increase the number of programs or staff under their responsibility or enhance opportunities for promotion and influence in the policy process.

A major weakness of the public choice approach at present is the absence of common agreement on the definition of the central concept of "self-interest". Some authors view it in very narrow terms as financial reward and material well-being.[43] But such an interpretation rather cynically dismisses the possibility that some individuals are motivated by altruistic concerns or certain moral values or ideas. At the other extreme, Douglas G. Hartle's concept of self-interest as "subjective net worth", the net inflow of all rational and psychological benefits, including status and self-esteem,[44] is so broad and all-encompassing as to be tautological.

From the perspective of policy analysis, a further problem is exemplified by these questions: "Given that various individuals and group actors are all pursuing their respective interests, who will prevail? Which factors determine who wins and who loses on each issue?" Public choice theorists have yet to produce a systematic set of propositions which place their assumptions of self-interested behaviour within the context of these questions of power relations in society and the ideological and institutional constraints on government.

Although it draws upon the long-established traditions of classical economic theory, public choice as an approach to politics and public policy analysis is still a young and relatively underdeveloped art. Its application has produced some interesting insights into the policy-making process[45] – especially, in contrast to the environmental determinist and pluralist approaches, in its recognition that politicians and bureaucrats are not mere servants of external pressures, but rather have their own interests and objectives. However, its focus remains rather restrictive. Despite its ambitions toward formulating a more general theory of the political process (hence its inclusion among the macro-level approaches), public choice theory is, at best, only a partial aid towards understanding how and why public policies are made.

NEO-MARXIST ANALYSIS

Public choice theory is sometimes also referred to as "liberal political economy" because it attemps to apply the precepts of liberal economics to the study of politics. An alternative political economy approach is **neo-Marxist analysis**. "Neo-Marxism" is a generic label for various contemporary theories and propositions

---

[13]The narrow view of self-interest as material or financial advancement underlies most of the arguments put forward in Thomas E. Borcherding, ed., *Budgets and Bureaucrats: The Sources of Government Growth* (Durham, N.C.: Duke University Press, 1977).

[14]Hartle, *A Theory of the Expenditure Budgetary Process*, Chapter 2.

[15]See, for example, Trebilcock, *et al.*, *The Choice of Governing Instrument*; Allan M. Maslove and G. Swimmer, *Wage Controls in Canada 1975-1978: A Study of Public Decision-Making* (Montréal: Institute for Research on Public Policy, 1980).

which seek to develop a systematic conceptualization of politics and the role of the state in capitalist society based upon assumptions originally formulated by Karl Marx concerning the relationship between economic, social and political structures. There are, at present, a number of strands of neo-Marxist theory; the following brief overview attempts to simplify some fairly complex concepts and arguments.[46]

The essence of Marxist theory is that, at all stages of historical development, social and political relations are largely determined or constrained by the economic basis of society. In the present era, the capitalist mode of production, two main social classes are differentiated by their respective economic roles: the capitalist class, or bourgeoisie, which owns and controls the means of production (factories, machines, financial capital, *etc.*) and the working class, or proletariat, which sells its labour to the capitalists. But, according to Marx's economic theory, the dynamics of capitalism also require that capitalists extract "surplus value" from labour – that they effectively exploit the working class – because this is the chief mechanism whereby they make profits for further investment and the accumulation of capital. This exploitative economic relationship between capital and labour forms the basis for unequal, conflictual class relations in social and political life.

The primary function of the state in capitalist society (the state being defined as a complex of political, administrative, judicial and coercive institutions, at both the national and sub-national levels) is to serve the interests of capitalism by creating and maintaining conditions favourable to profitable capital accumulation. However, in order to reduce conflict between classes and to forestall the possibility of revolution by the exploited working class, the state also has to create and maintain conditions of social harmony by providing policies which legitimize capitalist society.[47]

Most public policies, in the neo-Marxist view, may be roughly categorized according to their intentions or effects as serving either the *accumulation* or *legitimation* functions of the capitalist state. Examples of accumulation-oriented policies in the Canadian context include the provision of industrial infrastructure (*e.g.*, transportation networks, public utilities such as hydro), subsidies or tax expenditures for private sector businesses and fiscal and monetary policies aimed at creating a healthy climate for investment. Legitimation policies would include most social welfare programs (*e.g.*, unemployment insurance, social assistance), occupational health and safety regulations, environmental pollution controls and language and cultural policies. Some programs or policies, however, may serve both accumulation and legitimation roles; hence these two functions are not necessarily mutually exclusive. For example, the introduction of free mass education in response to working class demands may enhance the legitimacy of the state in

---

[46]For useful surveys of the different strands of Neo-Marxist analysis, see David Gold, *et al.*, "Recent Developments in Marxist Theories of the Capitalist State," Parts I and II, *Monthly Review*, vol. 27, no. 5 (October 1975), pp. 29-43 and vol. 27, no. 6 (November 1975), pp. 36-51.

[47]See James O'Connor, *The Fiscal Crisis of the State* (New York: St. Martin's Press, 1973), p. 6.

the short term but, by providing a better-trained, more skilled labour force, it may also aid capital accumulation.[48]

The key question in neo-Marxist analysis, of course, is why does the state pursue particular public policies and courses of action. The **instrumentalist** view of the state suggests that it serves the interests of the capitalist class because of the strong links in the form of common class backgrounds, family ties and old school networks that exist between political and bureaucratic elites on the one hand and the business community on the other.[49] An alternative line of reasoning, the **structuralist** view, argues that the capitalist class is itself internally divided into a number of competing elements or *fractions* (finance capital, manufacturing capital, resource capital, *etc.*) which have different interests. Hence, the state must be *relatively autonomous*, or independent of the dominant class, so that it can serve the long-term interests of capitalism rather than the short-term profit-maximizing interests of individual capitalists.[50] Therefore, the state often pursues policies such as social welfare programs which respond to working class demands, in the long-term interests of legitimation and social harmony, even if these policies are opposed by much of the capitalist class. According to structuralist neo-Marxists, the capitalist state operates in this apparently contradictory way because it is the political expression of the conflictual, but unequal, relationship between social classes.

If one can accept the premises on which their arguments are based, neo-Marxist analyses can be seen to account for broad patterns in public policy in different societies and for the expanding economic and social activities of the state over time. For example, since Marxist economics predicts that the rate of return on capital investment (*i.e.*, the rate of profit) will tend to fall as capitalism progresses, it becomes increasingly necessary for governments to underwrite some of the costs of production (*e.g.*, by subsidizing research and development expenditures). Neo-Marxist analysis is also explicitly oriented towards matters of inequality and distribution of power in Canadian society. In addition, more than any other approach considered here, it addresses issues of external constraints on Canadian policy-making, especially in an era of extensive foreign ownership, multinational corporations and the interdependence of capitalist economies. But, despite numerous attempts to get inside the policy process and to develop a neo-Marxist approach to public policy analysis[51] rather than a more general the-

---

[48]For further discussion of the functions of the Canadian state, see Leo Panitch, "The Role and Nature of the Canadian State," in Panitch, ed., *The Canadian State: Political Economy and Political Power* (Toronto: University of Toronto Press, 1977), pp. 3-27.

[49]See, for example, Ralph Miliband, *The State in Capitalist Society* (London: Weidenfeld and Nicolson, 1969).

[50]The state is only "relatively" autonomous because its activities are constrained by the underlying social and economic (class) relations in society. See Nicos Poulantzas, *Political Power and Social Classes* (London: New Left Books, 1973).

[51]See especially, Rianne Mahon, "Canadian Public Policy: the Unequal Structure of Representation," in Panitch, ed., *The Canadian State*, pp. 165-198; and Mahon, *The Politics of Industrial Restructuring: Canadian Textiles* (Toronto: University of Toronto Press, 1984).

ory of the relationship between state and society, neo-Marxism remains unclear on exactly how the state makes specific policy choices or decisions at particular moments in time. Like public choice theory, the neo-Marxist approach is still relatively underdeveloped; much more work, both theoretical and empirical, needs to be done for a comprehensive theory of policy-making to emerge within it.

The Approaches Compared

In his excellent article, "Studying Public Policy", Richard Simeon has argued that a comprehensive approach to the study of public policy must involve at least three levels of analysis.[52] According to Simeon, although the policy process (that is, the bargaining among politicians, bureaucrats and interest groups) itself has "some independent effect on policy outcomes", it also reflects and is shaped by a broader framework which imposes constraints on the alternative policies considered by policy-makers and on their freedom of action. This broader framework consists of two sets of factors. Furthest removed from the policy process are the resources and constraints flowing from the social and economic environments. But the effects of these environmental influences are profoundly shaped by a number of important intervening factors, including the system of power relations, the dominant values and ideas of society and the structure of political institutions. The combination of these three levels of analysis "suggests a sort of funnel of causality".[53] In this model of policy analysis, all three groups of factors are considered relevant, but the relative importance of factors in determining actual policy outputs increases as the "funnel" narrows from left to right (see the graphic portrayal in Figure 13-2).

In the introduction to our summaries of the various models or theories of policy-making, we stated that no single approach to policy analysis has gained overall acceptance among those who study public policy. One reason is that the various approaches tend to focus on particular aspects of the policy process – on different parts of the "funnel". For example, micro-level models such as incrementalism and rationalism, and, to a lesser extent, the public choice approach, are more concerned with the process of policy-making inside government than with the wider relationship between government and its socioeconomic environment or broader questions of the distribution of power, ideas and institutions. At the other extreme, the environmental determinist approach also ignores both these distributional questions and the decision process, since it seeks to link public policy outputs directly to aggregate economic and social variables.

The neo-Marxist and pluralist approaches succeed in bringing together more elements from the "funnel". Neo-Marxists explicitly address the influence of the economic and social environments, inasmuch as they link the role of the state to changes in the social structure and the economy which result from the

---

[52]Simeon, "Studying Public Policy", esp. pp. 555-556 and pp. 566-578.

[53]*Ibid.*, p. 556.

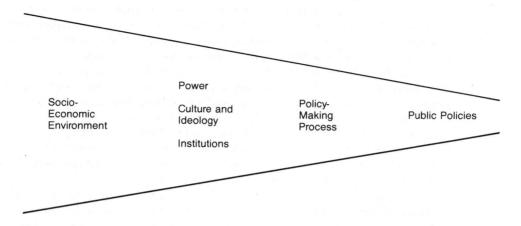

FIGURE 13.2   Policy "Funnel of Causality"

Source: Graphic adaptation of ideas discussed in Richard Simeon, "Studying Public Policy," *Canadian Journal of Political Science,* Vol. 9, no. 4 (December 1976), esp. p. 556.

ongoing development of the capitalist mode of production. In addition, inequalities in power, income and resources between social classes, and the role of ideology and values supportive of capitalism in the process of legitimation are central themes in neo-Marxist analysis. However, as we have already noted, this approach has not yet fully come to terms with the independent influence of actors within the policy-making process in determining public policy outcomes – notwithstanding the acknowledged "relative autonomy" of the state.

The pluralist approach at least implicitly takes into account the socio-economic environment, since the growing complexity of industrial society gives rise, in the pluralist view, to more and more issues and interests around which groups may be mobilized. The pluralists, of course, emphasize the interaction of interest groups with the policy-making process; they also stress the mediating effects of institutions such as the electoral process. However, the traditional pluralist view has often been criticized for its failure to recognize inequalities of power and influence and for its emphasis on government as a reactive agent – as a neutral arbiter which responds only to the balance of group pressures. Recent contributions have attempted to come to terms with these difficulties, but have not really succeeded. The admission by Dahl and Lindblom that business enjoys a privileged position in the interest group struggle does not go far enough for critics who argue that they are unwilling to acknowledge that inequalities in power and resources are structurally based.[54] Pluralist conceptions of the decision

---

[54]See Robert A. Dahl and Charles E. Lindblom, *Politics, Economics and Welfare* (Chicago: University of Chicago Press, 1976); Charles Lindblom, *Politics and Markets* (New York: Basic Books, 1977); and the critique by John F. Manley, "Neo-Pluralism: A Class Analysis of Pluralism I and Pluralism II," *American Political Science Review,* vol. 77, no. 2 (June 1983), pp. 368-383.

process have usually drawn on Lindblom's incrementalist model, in which politicians and bureaucrats marginally adjusted policies in accordance with what could be agreed upon by contending interest groups. Today, some authors in the pluralist tradition are willing to allow that the modern state possesses its own dynamic in the policy process.[55] But, while the granting of "autonomy" to the state or government frees it from being a mere cipher of group demands, the argument fails to develop a coherent analysis of how, why and to what effect the state takes advantage of its newly discovered freedom.

A second problem in developing a general theory of the policy process is the contention that there may be different types of public policy, each involving different interests, actors and procedures, and each therefore appearing to fit the assumptions of a different theoretical approach. Theodore Lowi, for example, has proposed that three major types of public policy – distributive, regulatory and redistributive – are each characterized by a distinctive policy process.[56] **Distributive** policies are those which confer benefits on particular individuals or groups, but where the costs are shared widely through the population (*e.g.*, through the general revenue system). Therefore, there are no clear losers, but the recipients of distributive policies such as patronage or regional development grants are easily identified. This type of policy appears to be explained best by the assumptions of public choice theory, in that politicians can use distributive policy outputs to confer benefits on marginal voters or marginal constituencies in order to secure re-election. **Regulatory** policies (which, for Lowi, include most legal and statutory constraints on behaviour) involve clear winners and losers, but only on an issue-to-issue basis. Thus, groups and coalitions of groups organize around each regulatory issue, only to disperse again once the issue is resolved. The regulatory policy-making arena portrayed by Lowi is very similar to the competitive group struggle of the pluralist model. **Redistributive** policies also involve clear winners and losers, but here the lines of battle are more permanent, according to Lowi: "The categories of impact are much broader, approaching social classes. They are, crudely speaking, haves and have-nots, bigness and smallness, bourgeoisie and proletariat."[57] Redistributive policies, whether they involve social welfare programs or tax-breaks to big business, centre on conflicts between more permanent social aggregates such as classes – categories which are central only to the neo-Marxist approach.

---

[55]Eric A. Nordlinger, *On the Autonomy of the Democratic State* (Cambridge: Harvard University Press, 1981).

[56]Theodore J. Lowi, "Distribution, Regulation, Redistribution: The Functions of Government," in R.B. Ripley, ed., *Public Policies and Their Politics* (New York: W.W. Norton, 1966), pp. 27-40. In later writings, Lowi also adds a fourth type of policy, "constituent" policies, which include symbolic and other policy outputs which do not fit easily into the other three categories; see Lowi, "Four Systems of Policy, Politics and Choice," *Public Administration Review*, vol. 32, no. 4 (July 1972), pp. 298-310.

[57]Lowi, "Distribution, Regulation, Redistribution . . .", p. 28.

A further problem that has served to inhibit the emergence of a generally accepted approach to public policy analysis lies in the ideological and political rhetoric associated with some of the theories sketched out above. Too often, theoretical models of public policy are used in the same way as a drunk uses a lamppost – for support rather than illumination. This problem is particularly acute in the case of the two so-called "political economy" approaches – public choice and neo-Marxism.

The public choice argument that politicians and bureaucrats pursue their own interests in formulating public policies rather than some vague notion of the public interest makes this approach an attractive vehicle for those who think that government has grown too large and that public expenditures have risen out of control. By providing a theoretical rationale for allegations of bureaucratic empire-building or for the supposed self-serving actions of politicians, public choice lends additional weight to the arguments of neo-conservatives who wish to lower tax rates, reduce the size of the bureaucracy and social programs and generally "get government off the backs of the private sector".

While public choice theory may reinforce the prejudices and negative views that many people hold toward bureaucrats and politicians, the assumptions of neo-Marxism tend to challenge the way most citizens think about politics, especially in North America. Indeed, one of the attractions of the neo-Marxist approach is that it provides a critical alternative way of looking at the role of the state in Canada and makes us question our assumptions about the way government operates. However, neo-Marxist analysis is also often difficult to disentangle from ideological rhetoric. Many critics believe that it is impossible to use neo-Marxist concepts as an approach to analysis without also adhering to Marxism as an ideology, with its prescription for the revolutionary overthrow of capitalist society. Others quite simply refuse to accept the premises of class division and conflict on which neo-Marxist theories of the state are based. In either case, strong opposition is further reinforced by the economic determinist and hypertheoretical nature of some neo-Marxist writings.

Rather than promoting research which will enhance the understanding of the policy process and the role of the state or government in formulating and implementing public policies, both public choice and neo-Marxist analysis may be reduced to facile sloganeering. By attributing every perceived evil of the modern state to the self-interest of bureaucrats or to the iniquities of capitalism, political economy becomes reduced to polemical economy.

For a variety of reasons, therefore, it is extremely unlikely that any of the approaches outlined in this section will emerge as a universally accepted theory of public policy-making. But these models do represent the dominant frameworks of analysis found in the current literature on public policy. Each approach has its strengths and weaknesses in explaining how, why and to what effect governments choose to act on certain issues. Students of public policy should be conversant with these models and be able to apply them to specific policy decisions and broader policy frameworks, so that, from the strengths of each approach, they may derive a broader understanding of public policy phenomena.

POLICY INSTRUMENTS AND PROCESSES

The processes of public policy-making and decision-making are not restricted only to the setting of governmental objectives and priorities; they also entail the selection of means by which these ends are to be achieved. The concept of **policy instruments** (sometimes also called "governing instruments") relates to the methods used by governments to attain their policy goals. The purpose of this section is to illustrate the range of instruments which governments have at their disposal in attempting to put policy proposals into effect.

Many early studies of public policy and the growth of the state in Canada focused on the financial instruments of governing: expenditure and taxation. In the mid-1970s, however, G. Bruce Doern applauded the rediscovery of the "other half of government", its regulatory activities, which had hitherto been ignored, Doern argued, because they did not go through a regular and well-publicized cycle such as the annual expenditure and revenue budgeting processes.[58] Scholars have more recently drawn attention to other policy instruments in addition to the financial and regulatory activities of government, notably exhortation and symbolic policy outputs, and public ownership through Crown corporations and other public enterprises.

These instruments of policy implementation are often portrayed as part of a continuum of governing instruments, on which they are arranged according to the degree of legitimate coercion each one implies. Thus, exhortation is viewed as the least coercive instrument, since it entails requests for voluntary compliance with government policies in the absence of any explicit sanctions. Expenditures attempt to secure compliance through the provision of financial inducements – with, perhaps, the implied threat that funding will be withdrawn if government objectives are not met. Although taxation may be viewed for some purposes as a separate policy instrument, Doern's latest formulation groups it together with regulation, in that both impose rules of behaviour on citizens "backed up directly by the sanctions (penalties) of the state".[59] Finally, public ownership is considered the most coercive form of policy instrument (see Figure 13-3). We shall return to the idea of the continuum and its utility for analyzing public policies at the end of this section. But first, it is necessary to discuss briefly the various policy instruments and their application in the Canadian context.

Exhortation and Symbolic Outputs

According to Doern and Phidd, exhortation and symbolic policy outputs together constitute a "residual category" of governing instruments into which "one puts everything that does not quite fit into the other processes" of policy

---

[58]G. Bruce Doern, "The Concept of Regulation and Regulatory Reform," in G.B. Doern and V.S. Wilson, eds., *Issues in Canadian Public Policy* (Toronto: Macmillan, 1974), p. 8.

[59]The most detailed consideration of governing instruments by Doern, *et al.* may be found in G. Bruce Doern and Richard W. Phidd, *Canadian Public Policy: Ideas, Structure, Process* (Toronto: Methuen, 1983), Chs. 5 and 12. (Quotation from p. 112.)

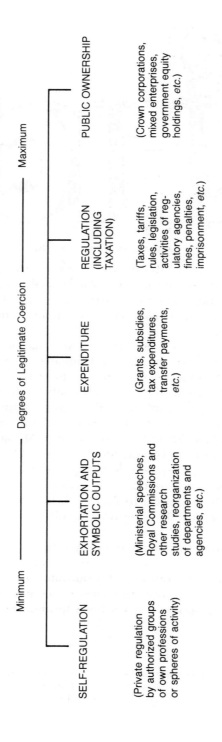

FIGURE 13.3 Instruments of Governing

Source: Adapted from G. Bruce Doern and Richard W. Phidd, *Canadian Public Policy: Ideas, Structure, Process* (Toronto: Methuen, 1983), Figure 5.1, p. 111 and Figure 5.3, p. 134.

Reproduced with permission, Rusins Kaufmanis, The Citizen, *Ottawa.*

implementation.[60] Because of the disparate, less clearly defined nature of this category, it has not been studied as systematically as the regulatory process or the use of Crown corporations as policy instruments. In fact, there may even be a case for arguing that we have here two discrete groups of instruments rather than a single broad category.

Exhortation (or, as it is sometimes called, "suasion") consists of a variety of attempts by policy-makers to induce individuals and groups to comply voluntarily with government objectives in the absence of other policy instruments. Whatever the examples cited – from fireside chats by the Prime Minister urging restraint in the battle against inflation, through government-sponsored advertisements extolling the benefits of "Participaction" or warning against drinking and driving, to former Health and Welfare Minister Monique Bégin's attempt in 1983 to pressure provincial governments to end extra-billing by doctors – exhortation is widely used by government in trying to change patterns of private behaviour.[61] In a sense, exhortation may be seen as a mirror-image of interest group lobbying, since "the state . . . seeks to alter the behaviour of firms and individuals in the private sector, rather than the reverse, which is characteristic of interest group politics."[62]

Exhortation is often used in pursuit of specific objectives when, for a variety of reasons, the government is unable to resort to other policy instruments such as taxation or regulation. **Symbolic policy outputs**, on the other hand, are mainly ways of demonstrating government concern over an issue; they are often used when no clear policy response has yet been formulated, although the govern-

---

[60]*Ibid.*, p. 317.

[61]For further discussion of these and other examples of suasion or exhortation, see William T. Stanbury and Jane Fulton, "Suasion as a Governing Instrument," in A.M. Maslove, ed., *How Ottawa Spends 1984: The New Agenda* (Toronto: Methuen, 1984), pp. 282-324.

[62]*Ibid.*, p. 283.

ment must be seen to be "doing something" about the perceived problem. Examples of symbolic policies include ministerial speeches and resolutions on pressing issues, the reorganization of departments and ministerial portfolios to express symbolic recognition of particular interests or the establishment of Special Committees or Royal Commissions on matters of public concern. Sometimes, these symbolic acts are accompanied or quickly followed by more substantive policy responses, such as the allocation of new public funds to deal with a problem area. But they may also be used as a form of "non-decision-making", to defuse or deflect public opinion and to delay action on an issue of perceived importance. Thus, symbolic politics has its limitations, inasmuch as too much "smoke and mirrors" may eventually alienate rather than placate the electorate.

Expenditure Instruments

To a certain extent, all actions of government involve public expenditure – for example, advocacy advertising for the purposes of exhortation must be paid for, as must the staffing and administrative costs of regulatory agencies. As a distinct category of policy instruments, however, **expenditures** refer to those funds which are explicitly directed toward achieving government objectives. With expenditures so defined, there are a number of ways in which the federal government can use its spending power to attain policy goals. The most obvious is the provision of direct transfers to individuals in the form of old-age pensions, child allowances or unemployment insurance, in order to redistribute income and provide a measure of security against various social contingencies. Second, the federal government also makes fiscal transfers to provinces, to ease regional disparities and to contribute to the funding of desirable social programs such as Medicare, social assistance (welfare) and post-secondary education. Social transfer expenditures (directly to individuals or via transfers to provinces under Established Programs Financing, the Canada Assistance Plan, *etc.*) accounted for about one-third of total estimated spending by the federal government in 1984-85.

But expenditure instruments may also be used in other policy areas. In recent years, the federal government has employed a broad array of subsidies, grants, loans and loan guarantees to aid new enterprises, to bail out troubled firms (*e.g.*, Chrysler, Dome), to encourage exploration for energy resources (Petroleum Incentive Payments), to promote small business and so on. Further, the government's own capital expenditures not only attain immediate objectives such as the modernization of port and rail facilities, but may also serve indirectly to approach other goals, for instance, through the awarding of contracts to firms from depressed areas or to equal opportunity employers.

Also of interest to policy analysts is a less visible sub-category of expenditure instruments, the phenomenon known as "tax expenditures". **Tax expenditures** are the revenues foregone by the government through the provision of tax deductions or tax credits to individuals and corporations. Some allowances for individual tax-payers are intended to encourage personal spending on "socially desirable" purposes such as deductions from taxable income for charitable donations and Registered Retirement Savings Plans (RRSPs) while others, including medical expense deductions, child care deductions and child tax credits for low income families, are part of the social safety nets of the welfare state.[63] In the corporate tax sector, too, there are two major categories of tax expenditures: those which give preferential treatment to certain kinds of income (*e.g.*, small business tax credits), and those which reward certain objectives of corporate spending; examples of the latter are investment tax credits, allowances for research and development expenditures and tax incentives to encourage the installation of pollution control devices in industrial plants.

Since tax expenditures are revenues foregone by the government rather than funds collected and subsequently disbursed, they are less easily quantified than ordinary expenditures, which must be accounted for in the expenditure-budgetary process. However, various studies estimate that the volume of tax expenditures has been growing rapidly in recent years, as federal governments have come under fire for escalating public spending.[64] At the same time, there has been concern that tax expenditures tend to favour upper-income earners and more profitable corporations, thereby counteracting redistributive effects elsewhere in the expenditure and tax processes.

Regulation

A regulation, suggests G. Bruce Doern, "can be viewed *politically* as a rule of behaviour backed up more directly by the legitimate sanctions of the state".[65] From this rather broad perspective, the concept of **regulation** comprises all rules of conduct imposed by government on its individual and corporate citizens. It encompasses statutory legislation (including, for example, the *Criminal Code*), since such laws establish general rules of behaviour, the tax system, which imposes special rules concerning the payment of money to government, as well as the activities of semi-autonomous regulatory agencies which lay down more restricted codes of conduct within their respective spheres of operation. In this broad sense, in addition to regulatory agencies, the actors in the regulatory process include Parliament and Cabinet, which formulate regulations, and bureaucratic departments, the police and the court system, which administer and enforce them.

However, much of the emphasis in the public policy literature on regulation is on the more limited area of regulation of private economic activity. Thus, one article on the subject of regulatory reform in Canada defines regulation as "the

---

[63]For a more extensive discussion of personal tax expenditures, see Allan M. Maslove, "Tax Expenditures, Tax Credits and Equity," in G.B. Doern, ed., *How Ottawa Spends Your Tax Dollars: Federal Priorities 1981* (Toronto: Lorimer, 1981), pp. 232-254.

[64]See the review by Kenneth Woodside, "The Political Economy of Policy Instruments: Tax Expenditures and Subsidies in Canada," in M.M. Atkinson and M.A. Chandler, eds., *The Politics of Canadian Public Policy* (Toronto: University of Toronto Press, 1983), esp. pp. 176-178.

[65]G. Bruce Doern, "Regulatory Processes and Regulatory Agencies," in Doern and Aucoin, eds., *Public Policy in Canada*, p. 150. (Emphasis in original.)

imposition by government of rules, backed by the use of penalties, that are intended specifically to modify the economic behaviour of firms and individuals in the private sector".[66] From this narrower perspective, **regulation** is a policy instrument which is aimed at forcing private economic actors to adopt behaviour which they would not normally choose to follow in the absence of regulation, that is, in a completely *laissez-faire*, free-market economy. The study of economic regulation therefore focuses on "public intervention by way of non-market controls in a mixed but primarily market-oriented economy".[67]

In what circumstances, and to what end, do governments intervene to impose "non-market controls" on private economic behaviour? In the area of direct economic regulation, government may act to control prices and rates of return (*e.g.*, telephone rates, local utilities, airline fares, wage and price controls); entry to the market (*e.g.*, broadcasting licences for television and radio stations, commercial fishing licences); market exit (*e.g.*, ensuring that railways or public utilities serve remote communities); and output (*e.g.*, supply management by agricultural marketing boards). In addition, governments may also regulate economic behaviour in pursuit of social objectives of "health, safety and fairness". Social regulations include controls over occupational health and safety and other conditions of employment, the contents of food and other consumer items, product labelling and misleading advertising, and environmental controls over air and water pollution or land-use.[68]

Typically, governments use regulation as a policy instrument for one of three purposes: to remedy market failures, especially to control natural monopolies such as telephone services or local utilities and to prevent destructive competition which might lead to cost-cutting measures by firms which endanger health and safety; to serve as an instrument of redistribution, by constraining monopoly profits or by requiring transportation companies to service unprofitable routes in return for licences to operate profitable ones; and to meet social and cultural objectives, as in CRTC Canadian content requirements in broadcasting or FIRA's screening of foreign investment (now Investment Canada).[69]

However, to the extent that some of these objectives might be met by other policy instruments such as expenditures or public ownership, there may be, in addition to economic, social and cultural objectives, a political rationale for the choice of regulation to achieve policy goals. Regulation may be managed directly by government departments, as in the case of most forms of social regulation; it may be delegated to semi-autonomous agencies such as the Canadian Radio-television and Telecommunications Commission, the Canadian Transport Commis-

---

[66]Gil Reschenthaler, *et al.*, "Whatever Happened to Deregulation?" *Policy Options*, vol. 3, no. 3 (May-June 1982), p. 36. A similar definition was adopted by the Economic Council of Canada for its studies of regulatory reform — see Economic Council of Canada, *Responsible Regulation* (Ottawa: Minister of Supply and Services, 1979), p. 43.

[67]Richard J. Schultz, *Federalism and the Regulatory Process* (Montréal: Institute for Research on Public Policy, 1977), p. 8.

[68]Economic Council of Canada, *Responsible Regulation*, pp. 43-45.

[69]*Ibid.*, pp. 45-52; Schultz, *Federalism and the Regulatory Process*, pp. 9-12.

sion and the National Energy Board; or powers of self-regulation may be granted to professional associations like medical and bar associations. In any event, regulatory regimes are remarkably inexpensive. According to the Economic Council of Canada, in 1979 "the total budgetary cost of all federal regulatory programs amount[ed] to less than 2 percent of the total federal budget."[70] In an era of widespread criticism of growing federal spending and budgetary deficits, regulation is therefore an attractive option for governments seeking an instrument to realize policy goals. The major cost of regulation, it is argued, is that of compliance, borne not by government, but by businesses, shareholders and consumers in the private sector. Consequently, there has been growing support in Canada for "deregulation", for a lessening of constraints on private behaviour in certain sectors of the economy – recently evidenced, for example, by partial deregulation of air passenger transport, the relaxation of metric conversion rulings and the abandonment of regulated oil and gas pricing. At the same time, however, it is apparent that powerful vested interests (often the regulated industries or professions themselves) support the continuation of regulatory regimes. As a result, governments will be able to maintain this weapon among their array of alternative instruments for the implementation of public policies. At the time of writing, the same may be less true of the next, and last, policy instrument considered here.

Public Ownership

Public Ownership or **public enterprise** – the direct provision of goods and services by corporations owned partly or wholly by the government – has a long history in Canada at both the federal and provincial levels. Indeed, some observers have labelled Canada a "public enterprise culture".[71] Among major contemporary federal enterprises, the oldest is the Canadian National Railways, established soon after World War One by the merging of three existing state-owned railways with three privately owned networks; but the CNR was predated by more than a decade by provincially owned enterprises such as Ontario Hydro and publicly owned telephone systems in the Prairie provinces. From these early beginnings, public ownership has expanded to other transportation, energy and communications facilities, as well as resource development, manufacturing, finance and a number of other sectors of the economy. Today, several public corporations may be found among Canada's largest business enterprises (see Table 13-1).[72]

---

[70]Economic Council of Canada, *Responsible Regulation*, pp. 43-44.

[71]Herschel Hardin, *A Nation Unaware: The Canadian Economic Culture* (Vancouver: J.J. Douglas Ltd., 1974).

[72]For more extended discussion of the origins and growth of public enterprise in Canada, see Allan Tupper and G. Bruce Doern, eds., *Public Corporations and Public Policy in Canada* (Montréal: Institute for Research on Public Policy, 1981), especially Chapter 1; and Marsha Gordon, *Government in Business* (Montréal: C.D. Howe Institute, 1981).

TABLE 13.1 Major Public Enterprises in Canada, 1983[1]

Corporation	Government Ownership	Sales 1983 $M	Rank[2]	Assets 1983 $M	Rank[2]	Employees 1983
Canada Wheat Board	Federal Government 100%	5,469	9	4,297	19	543
Canadian National Railways	Federal Government 100%	4,624	12	6,790	12	63,496
Petro-Canada	Federal Government 100%	4,124	15	8,239	6	6,601
Canadian Development Corporation	Federal Government 48%	3,835	17	7,559	10	18,605
Ontario Hydro	Ontario Government 100%	3,805	19	23,194	2	31,233
Hydro-Québec	Quebec Government 100%	3,656	20	25,199	1	18,975
Air Canada	Federal Government 100%	2,298	35	2,191	29	21,584
Canada Post Corporation	Federal Government 100%	2,258	37	2,216	38	62,202
B.C. Hydro & Power Authority	B.C. Government 100%	1,528	54	8,910	5	8,667
Alberta Government Telephones	Alberta Government 100%	893	90	2,311	36	11,924
Société Générale de Financement du Québec	Quebec Government 100%	853	92	1,031	85	24,724
Saskatchewan Power Corporation	Saskatchewan Government 100%	705	107	2,356	34	3,105
Via Rail Canada Ltd.	Federal Government 100%	625	124	652	113	3,474
New Brunswick Power Commission	New Brunswick Government 100%	546	134	2,744	31	2,600
Canadian Commercial Corporation	Federal Government 100%	507	140	368	166	121

[1]Major industrial enterprises only - excludes financial institutions, and subsidiaries included under parent corporation.

[2]"Rank" shows corporation's ranking among all private and public corporations in terms of sales and assets.

Source: Adapted from *The Financial Post 500* (Toronto: Maclean Hunter, Ltd., 1984), "Industry's 500", pp. 70 ff.

The realm of public ownership partly overlaps that of Crown corporations, discussed in Chapter 9, but the two are not identical. Some federal agencies classified as Crown corporations are mechanisms for policy implementation via other instruments, such as the distribution of grants and expenditures by the Medical Research Council or the regulatory activities of the Atomic Energy Control Board. Others, such as the Economic Council of Canada and the Science Council of Canada, are advisory bodies which contribute to the formation of public policy, as opposed to public enterprises used as instruments of policy implementation.

On the other side of the coin, public ownership need not entail 100 percent government ownership and control. Apart from wholly-owned Crown corporations and their subsidiaries, governments may turn to mixed (public-private) enterprises or to equity- (share-) holding in a private company in their attempt to realize certain policy goals. Perhaps the best-known example of mixed enterprise at the federal level is the Canada Development Corporation (CDC), established by the government in 1971 to "help develop and maintain strong Canadian-controlled and Canadian-managed corporations in the private sector" and to "give Canadians greater opportunities to invest and participate in the economic development of Canada". Although, at the time of writing, the federal government owns 48 percent of CDC shares, the Corporation has fiercely resisted any Cabinet encroachment on its autonomy in investment decision-making. Thus, while the CDC has, generally speaking, been a commercial success, its intractability as an instrument of public policy led the federal government to create in 1982 a more easily controlled, wholly-owned Crown corporation, the Canada Development Investment Corporation (CDIC), to manage its holdings in a number of commercial and industrial ventures considered too risky by the profit-oriented CDC.[73]

As these examples illustrate, the objectives of public ownership as a policy instrument are many and varied. Some early public enterprises, such as state-owned railways and Trans-Canada Airlines (later Air Canada), were established to develop essential economic infrastructure in situations where "the private sector was unwilling or unable to take the initiative."[74] These transportation facilities also played a part in nation-building or national integration; a similar motive lay behind the creation of the Canadian Radio Broadcasting Commission (now the CBC) in 1932. Other public enterprises have been founded to provide financial infrastructure for the Canadian economy. Thus, the Canadian Business Development Bank, the Export Development Corporation and perhaps also the CDC were designed to "fill gaps in the financial system and to assist interests whose financial needs were only partially met by established (private) lenders".[75] As well, public ownership has been used to develop pioneer enterprises involv-

---

[73]See Stephen Brooks, "The State as Entrepreneur: From CDC to CDIC," *Canadian Public Administration*, vol. 26, no. 4 (Winter 1983), pp. 525-543.

[74]John W. Langford, "Crown Corporations as Instruments of Policy," in Doern and Aucoin, eds., *Public Policy in Canada*, p. 248.

[75]Allan Tupper and G. Bruce Doern, "Understanding Public Corporations in Canada," *Canadian Business Review*, vol. 9, no. 3 (Autumn 1982), p. 34.

ing high costs or commercial risks which were deemed to be in the long-term public interest. Federal government involvement in Atomic Energy of Canada Ltd., Eldorado Nuclear Ltd., the Polymer Corporation (now Polysar) and the Syncrude project was intended to foster the development of new technologies and processes and to encourage diversification of the Canadian economy.[76]

In all these cases, public enterprises complemented, rather than competed with, the interests of the private sector. In recent years, however, more controversial examples of government ownership have brought the public sector into conflict with private enterprise over market shares and investment resources. Petro-Canada's commercial and retailing activities have aroused strong opposition (more so than its exploration role), as has the government's involvement with a number of unprofitable ventures such as Canadair, de Havilland and Massey-Ferguson, which have been taken over or bailed out largely to save jobs or in pursuit of more-or-less vaguely articulated goals of a federal industrial strategy.

Opposition to public ownership has crystallized around two major issues: first, the growing concern about a perceived lack of accountability of Crown corporations; second, the losses suffered in recent years by Canadair and de Havilland, for example, which have lent extra ammunition to arguments that resources devoted to public enterprise might be more profitably and efficiently allocated in the private sector. Critics of public ownership have adopted as a solution to both problems the concept of "privatization" of a number of Crown corporations[77] – an idea which has met with some favour in the federal Conservative Party. The short-lived Clark government promised to privatize Petro-Canada, among others, yet found the proposal unpopular with the electorate. The Conservative government elected in 1984 has been committed to more wide-ranging privatization; immediately upon election, it announced the intention to seek private sector buyers for the aircraft companies and other assets held by the Tories' *bête-noire,* the CDIC.

Public ownership, as perhaps the most direct form of public policy implementation, is currently under fire from that new breed, neo-Conservatives, who view any and all forms of government intervention as an infringement upon the supremacy of the free market economy. Thus, while it is improbable that privatization will be carried as far as it has in some countries, it seems likely that public ownership will be less prominent in the next few years within the government's arsenal of public policy instruments.

Policy Instruments and the Policy Process

Given the range of instruments that policy-makers have at their disposal, a natural task for public policy analysts is to attempt to explain how and why particular instruments are chosen by governments in pursuit of their objectives. Three

---

[76]Gordon, *Government in Business,* Chapter 6.

[77]T.M. Ohashi and T.P. Roth, *Privatization: Theory and Practice* (Vancouver: Fraser Institute, 1980). See also Tom Kierans, "Commercial Crowns," *Policy Options,* vol. 5, no. 6 (November/December 1984), pp. 23-29; Paul E. Martin, "Why and How to Privatize," *Policy Options,* vol. 5, no. 2, (March/April 1984), pp. 22-25.

main approaches to the selection of policy instruments may be identified from the existing literature.

According to the rational-comprehensive model of decision-making, an administrator will select the instrument or means which will most efficiently attain a given end. Implicit within the rationalist approach is the assumption that various instruments or techniques of policy implementation are, in most respects, substitutes for one another – hence, the sole criterion in the choice of instrument in any given case will be the maximization of technical efficiency in the attainment of that policy objective.

From a public choice perspective, Trebilcock *et al.* also view policy instruments as inherently interchangeable. However, they reject the technical efficiency thesis of the rational-comprehensive model,[78] arguing instead that political rationality, rather than technical rationality, is the major determinant of instrument choice – that governing parties will choose both policies and instruments that maximize their chances of re-election and, in particular, that they will select instruments that benefit marginal voters whose support the government seeks, while imposing costs on everyone else.[79] Although this approach to instrument choice is highly plausible at the intuitive level, it shares with many other propositions of the public choice model the disadvantage of being difficult to test empirically.

The third approach to instrument choice is based on the continuum of governing instruments mentioned earlier in this section. Doern and Wilson hypothesize that "politicians have a strong tendency to respond to policy issues (any issue) by moving successively from the *least coercive* governing instrument to the *most coercive.*"[80] Applied to the continuum in its latest form (as shown in Figure 13-3), this hypothesis suggests that governments will tend to respond first with symbolic outputs such as the establishment of a Royal Commission or some other study of the problem and with attempts to secure voluntary compliance with new policy goals through exhortation. Later, however, they may shift to expenditure instruments, and, if these incentives are insufficient to ensure compliance with policy objectives, they may subsequently deploy more coercive measures such as regulation or even public ownership. Thus, Tupper and Doern suggest that, in a majority of cases studied in their book on public corporations, "the direct ownership instrument was selected *after* extensive use of other instruments including regulation, spending and taxation."[81]

It is important to note that, unlike advocates of the other two approaches outlined above, Doern and his co-authors do not view policy instruments as direct substitutes for one another. When adopting new instruments as they move

---

[78]Trebilcock *et al.*, *The Choice of Governing Instrument*, pp. 23-27.

[79]*Ibid.*, p. 34.

[80]G. Bruce Doern and V. Seymour Wilson, "Conclusions and Observations," in Doern and Wilson, eds., *Issues in Canadian Public Policy*, p. 339. (Emphasis in original.)

[81]Tupper and Doern, "Public Corporations and Public Policy in Canada", p. 19. (Emphasis in original.)

along the continuum, policy-makers will rarely discontinue the use of less co-ercive means; hence, in more "mature" policy areas, in which government has been involved for some time, "all or most of the basic instruments could be uti-lized."[82] Instruments, differentiated from each other by the degrees of coercion attributed to them, are therefore additive or complementary in nature, rather than constituting alternatives. Thus, when public enterprises are established, rather than replacing other measures, "public ownership is more frequently *add-ed* to an array of existing instruments that have been tried and found wanting, or at least are *believed* to be found wanting."[83]

At first glance, the Doern-Wilson hypothesis of instrument choice also ap-pears plausible, although both it and the continuum from which it is derived are based upon a number of questionable assumptions which might not be accept-able to all public policy analysts.[84] It does have an advantage over the Trebilcock *et al.* model, for example, in that it can be empirically tested with relative ease. However, applications of the hypothesis to different fields of Canadian public yield mixed results. While the study of some policy areas such as energy policy lends support to the contention that governments progress along the continuum in developing policy responses, leaving regulation and especially public owner-ship as a last resort, examination of other sectors such as broadcasting and air transport indicates that public ownership was among the first instruments de-ployed by the federal government. Moreover, a number of authors have suggest-ed that, in recent years, federal governments have become increasingly "regulation-happy", resorting to this instrument first rather than (almost) last.[85]

A full explanation of the selection of policy instruments by governments has to take into account a multiplicity of economic, legal, political and external constraints on governmental freedom of choice. For example, within a federal system such as Canada, governments may be precluded from using the full range of instruments in some policy areas by the constitutional division of powers among jurisdictions. Thus, the federal government is effectively limited to ex-hortation and spending in many fields of Canadian social policy, including Medi-care. Economic constraints in a period of growing criticism of the expansion of public expenditures and budgetary deficits make both regulation and relatively hidden tax incentives more attractive than large, visible spending programs. In-ternational agreements such as the General Agreement on Tariffs and Trade (GATT) militate against raising tariffs (a form of taxation or regulation) and force

---

[82]Doern and Wilson, "Conclusions and Observations", p. 339.

[83]Tupper and Doern, "Public Corporations and Public Policy . . ." p. 19. (Emphasis in original.)

[84]See Nicolas Baxter-Moore, "Governing Instruments and Public Policy Analysis: A Critique of the Doern Continuum," unpublished paper, Department of Political Studies, Queen's University, Kingston, April 1985.

[85]See above and, for example, Douglas G. Hartle, *Public Policy Decision Making and Regulation* (Montréal: Institute for Research on Public Policy, 1979); William T. Stanbury, ed., *Government Regulation: Scope, Growth, Process* (Montréal: Institute for Research on Public Policy, 1980).

governments to resort to alternative methods (non-tariff barriers) to control the volume of imports flowing into the country. Even the nature of the policy-making process itself may have an effect. While routine, day-to-day or year-to-year policy-making may have a tendency towards the kind of incrementalist instrument selection hypothesized by Doern and Wilson, a study of policy-making in crisis management situations by Robert J. Jackson shows that, after initial symbolic responses, governments are most likely to resort to highly coercive instruments, including emergency regulations and the deployment of Armed Forces. Only after the crisis is over will they return to public spending in order to pre-empt the occurrence of further crises.[86]

Clearly, we need to learn far more about the dynamics of public policy-making in order to reach a more complete explanation of the choice of policy instruments by governments. But while the Doern-Wilson hypothesis and the concept of a continuum of governing instruments have weaknesses, they have proven to be useful heuristic (organizing) devices in promoting research and in sensitizing policy analysts to the multiplicity of means of policy implementation that governments have at their disposal. The application of policy instruments to various government objectives and some of the constraints which inhibit governments' freedom to manoeuvre in public policy-making form the subject of the next section of this chapter.

POLICY-MAKING IN A FEDERAL STATE

It is impossible to study public policy-making in Canada without reference to two major facets of Canadian political life which impose constraints on the activity of the federal government: the nature of the relationship between Canada and the United States; and the federal structure of Canadian politics.

The extent of foreign, largely American, investment in Canada has a profound effect on macro-economic policy-making. For example, the Bank of Canada defended the high interest rates of the early 1980s (which proved ruinous to many small businesses and farmers) by citing the need to remain competitive with the United States as a market for investment capital which might otherwise seek higher returns south of the 49th Parallel. Foreign ownership has also influenced economic development policies in a number of sectors. Critics of foreign investment allege that it has had adverse effects on industrial research and development, the extent of corporate concentration, exports and the balance of payments, investment opportunities for Canadians and the ability of Canadian governments to manage their own economy. A number of these perceived problems have prompted public policy responses; examples are the 1973 *Foreign Investment Review Act,* the creation of the Canada Development Corporation in 1971

---

[86]Robert J. Jackson, "Crisis Management and Policy-Making," in Richard Rose, ed., *The Dynamics of Public Policy,* p. 214.

and, perhaps most controversial, the Canadianization provisions of the 1980 National Energy Program (discussed below).

But Canadian/American relations have also affected what we have called "quality-of-life" policies. Many observers consider that the major environmental hazard of acid rain cannot be tackled successfully in Canada without cooperation from an American government which has hitherto shown remarkable reluctance to even admit that a problem exists. At the same time, the geographical proximity of the two nations, combined with a common dominant language and an imbalance in population and market size, has created a perceived threat to Canadian cultural and national identity which has engendered policies of cultural protectionism in broadcasting, publishing and other arts and communications fields.

If American economic and cultural penetration impose exogenous influences on Canadian policy-makers, the federal system is a source of internal constraints. The constitutional division of powers under the *BNA Act* and the *Constitution Act* places certain limitations on the ability of both levels of government to pursue their respective policy objectives. At the federal level, this constraint has been particularly marked in the field of social policy. The *BNA Act* gave exclusive responsibility for social welfare and most aspects of health policy to the provinces. Hence the story of the development of the modern Canadian welfare state has been one of a series of attempts by the federal government to use its spending power to break down resistance by the provinces to federal encroachment on their sphere of influence.[87] Indeed, the relatively late development of the welfare state in Canada compared with many West European nations may be partially attributed to the federal system, as well as to Canada's delayed industrialization.[88]

Similarly, the federal division of powers may have retarded progress toward equality of economic opportunity for women in Canadian society. Although recent federal administrations have adopted affirmative action programs in the public service and have made some moves toward "equal pay for work of equal value", the federal government can influence only about 10 percent of the total labour market – that portion which is covered by the *Canadian Labour Code* (mainly public sector workers) and, potentially, the private sector firms which have federal government contracts. The remainder of the labour force in Canada, including a large majority of women employees, is covered by provincial labour codes, but, at present, Québec is the only province to have enacted equal pay for work of equal value legislation.

In other policy areas, effective policy-making and policy coordination have been impeded by competition between federal and provincial governments using

---

[87]See, for example, Keith Banting, *The Welfare State and Canadian Federalism* (Kingston and Montréal: McGill-Queen's University Press, 1982); Kenneth Bryden, *Old Age Pensions and Policy-Making in Canada* (Montréal: McGill-Queen's University Press, 1974).

[88]On the influence of federalism on public sector growth, see David R. Cameron, "The Expansion of the Public Economy: A Comparative Analysis," *American Political Science Review*, vol. 72, no. 4 (December 1978), pp. 1243-1261. On industrialization and the welfare state, see Banting, *The Welfare State and Canadian Federalism*, pp. 32-34.

similar instruments to pursue contradictory objectives. The multiplicity of industrial assistance programs adopted by the federal government to foster national and regional economic development has been counterbalanced by a similar array of incentives offered by provincial governments intent on more particularistic goals of economic diversification and province-building.[89] Consequently, those who argue that Canada requires a national "industrial strategy" as a solution to the current economic malaise are now being forced to come to terms with the problems of building a federal/provincial consensus which would permit the required scale of economic planning to be undertaken.[90]

In the pages which follow, we present three short case studies of federal policy-making. We have selected one example from each of three main categories of domestic public policy (excluding macro-economic policy) identified in the classification of policy areas in Figure 13-1: energy policy as an example of sectoral economic development; Medicare as representative of social policy; and broadcasting/communications as a case of quality-of-life objectives. It must be emphasized that the purpose of these case studies is not to provide a comprehensive, documentary analysis of public policy-making in each area. Rather, they are intended primarily to illustrate the constraints imposed on federal policy-makers by the federalist structure of Canadian political life and/or by the nature of Canadian/American relations. In addition, they may serve to illustrate the variety of instruments that the federal government has deployed in pursuit of its public policy objectives.

Energy Policy

The field of energy policy demonstrates clearly the complex environment within which policy-makers operate in Canada. In the last decade particularly, the federal government has had to adjust to massive changes in international energy markets, while coping with political and economic pressures imposed by the American government and by multinational corporations which have dominated Canada's resource base. At the same time, the constitutional division of powers and the uneven distribution of both energy resources and economic development among the Canadian provinces have given rise to various dimensions of conflict within the federal system: between the federal government and the producing provinces over the authority to regulate, tax and manage natural resources; and between producing provinces and consuming provinces over the pricing of energy.

Although strictly speaking "energy policy" may denote government orientations and activities pertaining to a wide variety of energy sources, as well as to

[89]Michael Jenkin, *The Challenge of Diversity: Industrial Policy in the Canadian Federation,* Science Council of Canada Background Study #50 (Ottawa: Minister of Supply and Services, 1983); Allan Tupper, *Public Money in the Private Sector* (Kingston: Queen's University Institute of Intergovernmental Relations, 1982).

[90]See, for example, Hugh Thorburn, *Planning and the Economy: Building Federal-Provincial Consensus* (Toronto: Lorimer, 1984), especially Chapters 14 and 15.

energy conservation and consumption patterns, in practical terms energy politics in Canada has been primarily associated in recent years with the production, pricing, regulation and consumption of oil (or petroleum) and natural gas.[91] It is the oil and gas sector that has been at the heart of the most vehement political debates, especially those surrounding the National Energy Program of 1980, and its importance is amply demonstrated by the fact that oil and natural gas (and their subsidiary products) provide for approximately two-thirds of Canada's final energy consumption.

During the first quarter-century after oil was discovered at Leduc, Alberta in 1947, governments at both levels kept intervention to a minimum, leaving the development of Canada's fledgling oil and gas industry largely in the hands of a private sector that was increasingly dominated by American multinationals. Following the TransCanada pipeline debacle, which contributed to the downfall of the Liberal government in 1957, the new Diefenbaker administration established a Royal Commission on Energy (the Borden Commission). In keeping with the Commission proposals, the Conservatives created the National Energy Board as a regulatory and advisory agency in 1959.[92] In 1961, the government adopted a National Oil Policy which protected Western oil producers by dividing Canada into two consumer markets: areas east of the Ottawa Valley – Québec and the Atlantic provinces – imported cheaper oil from abroad, while Ontario and the West were supplied with more expensive Canadian oil and gas; surplus production was exported to the United States. This artificial division served to integrate the producing provinces further into the continental energy economy, a tendency which was heightened by increased foreign ownership of oil and gas resources.

In 1973, following the third Arab-Israeli War, world energy markets were seriously shaken by the quadrupling of world oil prices and a partial export embargo introduced by the Organization of Petroleum Exporting Countries (OPEC). Canada, like most other industrialized nations, was forced to re-evaluate its energy policy in the wake of these shocks to both prices and security of supply. To provide a window for the purpose of gathering information on an energy industry largely dominated by foreign multinationals, and to foster new exploration in the interest of energy security, the federal government established Canada's own state-owned oil company, Petro-Canada, in 1975.[93] In addition, to safeguard supplies, Ottawa first regulated, then imposed a tax upon, oil exports to the United States – and used the revenues generated by the export tax to compensate eastern Canada for the higher prices being paid for imported oil. The

---

[91]The most comprehensive coverage of Canadian energy policy is found in G. Bruce Doern and Glen Toner, *The Politics of Energy: The Development and Implementation of the NEP* (Toronto: Methuen, 1985). Other useful books on energy policy include James Laxer, *Oil and Gas: Ottawa, the Provinces and the Petroleum Industry* (Toronto: Methuen, 1983); and John N. McDougall, *Fuels and the National Policy* (Toronto: Butterworths, 1982).

[92]On the evolution and role of the NEB, see A.R. Lucas, "The National Energy Board," in G.B. Doern, ed., *The Regulatory Process in Canada* (Toronto: MacMillan, 1978), pp. 259-313.

[93]On the origins and evolution of Petro-Canada, see Larry Pratt, "Petro-Canada," in Tupper and Doern, eds., *Public Corporations and Public Policy in Canada*, pp. 94-148.

federal government also took steps to keep Canadian oil and gas prices below world market levels, largely to protect farming interests and Ontario's manufacturing industries.[94]

This flurry of federal government activity, much of it *ad hoc* reaction to the 1973 international oil crisis, coincided with increased provincial government intervention, especially in Alberta, where the Conservative government under Peter Lougheed had won the 1971 provincial election after promising to use an increased share of resource revenues to diversify the provincial economy.[95] By the end of 1973, Alberta and Saskatchewan had established mixed-enterprise or wholly-owned provincial oil companies and had each introduced legislation to enhance control over production, pricing and regulation of their energy resources. As well, they imposed new royalty schemes to allow their provincial treasuries to capitalize on rising energy prices. As both levels of government became increasingly interventionist, the oil and gas industry itself was squeezed, and federal/provincial conflict intensified between Ottawa (often supported by consumer provinces such as Ontario) and the producer provinces of Western Canada.

Even the energy conflicts of the 1970s were tame compared with the furor that blew up after the Liberal government announced the National Energy Program (NEP) as an appendage to its budget of October 1980. The Liberals had swept back to power the previous February in an election in which energy policy was a dominant issue – in particular, the Conservative proposals to raise domestic oil and gas prices closer to world market levels and to impose an 18¢ per gallon increase in the excise tax on transportation fuels, both of which had been part of the ill-fated Budget. An additional problem for the Conservatives in the election was the degree of public support for continued government ownership of Petro-Canada, which the Clark government had pledged to privatize.

The primary thrust of the NEP was oriented toward the achievement of three main goals: security, opportunity and fairness. Under the Program, the government sought to accomplish the following ends:

(a) to establish the basis for Canadians to seize control of the energy future through *security* of supply and ultimate independence from the world oil market;

(b) to offer Canadians, all Canadians, the real *opportunity* to participate in the energy industry in general and the petroleum industry in particular, and to share in the benefits of industry expansion;

(c) to establish a petroleum pricing and revenue-sharing regime that recognizes the requirement of *fairness* to all Canadians no matter where they live.[96]

---

[94] For a more detailed discussion of this period, see Doern and Toner, *The Politics of Energy*, pp. 88-99, 169-187.

[95] See John Richards and Larry Pratt, *Prairie Capitalism: Power and Influence in the New West* (Toronto: McClelland and Stewart, 1979), especially Chapter 9.

[96] Government of Canada, *National Energy Program* (Ottawa: Minister of Supply and Services, 1980), p. 2. (Emphasis added.)

To attain these objectives the government deployed a wide variety of policy instruments.[97] Among the more controversial was the Petroleum Incentive Program (PIP), which replaced the previous tax incentives for exploration with a system of direct grants weighted to benefit Canadian companies and to encourage exploration activity in areas under federal, rather than provincial, jurisdiction (*i.e.*, the Canada Lands and offshore). While the primary goal of the PIP was to foster the discovery of new resources in the interests of self-sufficiency and security of supply, the bias in favour of Canadian companies was part of a broader move towards increased Canadianization of the industry, with the aim of achieving 50 percent Canadian ownership of oil and gas production by 1990. However, it was perceived as discriminatory and nationalistic by both the multinational corporations and the American government, which vehemently denounced the NEP and the coincident Liberal proposals to strengthen FIRA.[98]

It has since been argued that, if nationalism was involved in the NEP, "it was far more anti-provincial nationalism than anti-US nationalism."[99] The emphasis on exploration in the Canada Lands; the enhanced role of Petro-Canada, whose subsequent purchase of Petrofina and the refining and distribution assets of British Petroleum was financed in part by a new tax, the Canadian Ownership Charge; a federally-imposed "made in Canada" pricing system; and an increased share of oil and gas revenues for the federal treasury – all these reflected a determination by the federal government to seize the initiative in energy priority-setting from the provinces, and incidentally to boost its own revenues in the process. There was an immediate and hostile response from the producing provinces. Alberta quickly announced a cutback in future oil production and a freeze on the proposed Alsands and Cold Lake mega-projects. Not until September 1981, after months of bitter confrontation, did Ottawa and Alberta reach an agreement on pricing and revenue-sharing that appeared to satisfy both levels of government.[100]

The National Energy Program has been subject to a number of different interpretations. From a viewpoint close to a public choice perspective, one author has described it as a plot by bureaucratic empire-builders to grab additional revenues for the federal government and to enhance the degree of public sector (hence also bureaucratic) control over the economy. [101] In a neo-Marxist analysis, the Canadianization provisions of the NEP may be seen as an attempt by the capi-

---

[97]For a detailed discussion of the implementation of the NEP, see Doern and Toner, *The Politics of Energy*, Part IV.

[98]See Stephen Clarkson, *Canada and the Reagan Challenge: Crisis in the Canadian-American Relationship* (Toronto: Lorimer, 1982), Chapter 3.

[99]Doern and Toner, *The Politics of Energy*, p. 34.

[100]*Ibid.*, pp. 260-275 and Appendix III, p. 507. See also John F. Helliwell and Robert N. McCrae, "The National Energy Conflict," and *Idem.*, "Resolving the National Energy Conflict: From the National Energy Program to the Energy Agreements," *Canadian Public Policy*, vol. 7, no. 1 (Winter 1981), pp. 15-23 and vol. 8, no. 1 (Winter 1982), pp. 14-23.

[101]See Peter Foster, *The Sorcerer's Apprentices: Canada's Super-Bureaucrats and the Energy Mess* (Toronto: Collins, 1982).

talist state to create profitable investment opportunities for the dominant finance capital fraction of the Canadian bourgeoisie and perhaps forge an alliance of interests between this fraction and Western resource capital as part of a new National Policy.[102] To the free-marketeers of Vancouver's Fraser Institute, the NEP represented a misguided and disastrous intervention that deliberately ignored market forces.[103] Doern and Toner, however, placed greater importance on the role of individual politicians. In part, they argued, the NEP could be seen as an attempt by Prime Minister Trudeau and Energy Minister Lalonde "to use what they both seemed to regard as their final – and unexpected – term of power to leave an indelible mark on Canadian history".[104] But, apart from the residual tension and suspicion left by the NEP experience, the "indelible mark" first became badly smudged and then all but erased. Taken together, the negative impact of the NEP on investment, the unforeseen collapse of world oil prices and the combined effects of recession and high interest rates in the early 1980s caused severe damage to the energy industry. Mega-projects were cancelled, as were many Arctic exploration ventures. Dome Petroleum, the flagship of the Canadian private sector, experienced serious financial difficulties. Federal government revenues from energy taxes fell below expected levels, while energy expenditures mushroomed alarmingly.[105] Increasingly, attention was diverted to offshore exploration; the discovery of Hibernia field embroiled the Liberal government in a new round of federal/provincial conflict, this time with Newfoundland.

Even before the Conservatives returned to power in September 1984, Brian Mulroney had reached an agreement with Newfoundland Premier Brian Peckford on the sharing of revenues and management of offshore resources. That agreement was quickly formalized by the new Conservative government. Then, in March 1985, Energy Minister Pat Carney announced the Western Accord, a settlement negotiated with the producer provinces which virtually killed the NEP, much to the approval of its critics in both Canada and the United States. Wellhead prices were to be deregulated, allowing Canadian oil prices to rise to world levels. Taxes and surcharges such as the Petroleum and Gas Revenue Tax and the Canadian Ownership Charge were to be abolished – as, in due course, were PIP grants. Thus, Canadian energy policy took another remarkable turn.

The National Energy Program, with its Canadianization provisions and a flagship role for public enterprise, might have provided the blueprint for a future sector-by-sector approach to industrial strategy in Canada. But both the NEP and energy policy in general demonstrate vividly the multiple constraints imposed on policy-makers by a complex series of relationships – between the federal government and the provinces; between the Canadian and American administrations;

---

[102]See Larry Pratt, "Energy: The Roots of National Policy," *Studies in Political Economy*, no. 7 (Winter 1982), pp. 27-59.

[103]G. Campbell Watkins and Michael A. Walker, eds., *Reaction: The National Energy Program* (Vancouver: The Fraser Institute, 1981).

[104]Doern and Toner, *The Politics of Energy*, p. 31.

[105]G. Bruce Doern, "Energy Expenditures and the NEP: Controlling the Energy Leviathan," in Maslove, ed., *How Ottawa Spends . . . 1984*, pp. 31-78.

between these three sets of government and the private sector companies that lobby for their support and protection; and between (largely American) multinational corporations and the Canadian economy. The remaining case studies are rather less complex, inasmuch as each is influenced only by one of the two major constraints on policy-making in Canada: the evolution of Medicare has been constrained by federal/provincial relations, while broadcasting and communications policies have been shaped mainly by Canada's proximity to the United States.

Medicare

Under the *BNA Act,* responsibility for health matters and most other areas of social policy was assigned to the provinces. But until the end of World War II the arrangement was of little consequence, since personal health care was viewed largely as a private concern.[106] Governments delegated powers of self-regulation to the health care professions and, to the extent that medical insurance schemes developed, they were privately operated and voluntary in nature. Although the British Columbia government proposed a highly selective health insurance scheme in 1935, to ease the burden of health costs on workers during the Depression, the legislation was never promulgated. The war-time federal government under Mackenzie King also drafted a health insurance scheme, but withdrew it in the face of opposition from the provinces at the Dominion-Provincial Conference of 1945.[107]

In the absence of federal/provincial agreement, then, the CCF government in the province of Saskatchewan, which had a long history of municipal involvement in health care, decided to go it alone, introducing compulsory hospital insurance for all residents in 1947.[108] By 1950, three more provinces, Alberta, British Columbia and Newfoundland, had health insurance plans, and Saskatchewan had gone a small step further with comprehensive medical insurance for the elderly. Also by this time, the federal government had become indirectly involved in health care, providing a range of grants under the National Health Program (1948) to contribute to the costs of hospital construction, health surveys, facilities for crippled children and other services.[109]

---

[106]Geoffrey R. Weller and Pranlal Manga, "The Development of Health Policy in Canada," in Atkinson and Chandler, eds., *The Politics of Canadian Public Policy,* p. 223. Apart from this source and others cited below, see also Chandler and Chandler, *Public Policy and Provincial Politics,* pp. 198-216; David Coburn *et al,* eds., *Health and Canadian Society: Sociological Perspectives* (Toronto: Fitzhenry and Whiteside, 1981); and Lee Soderstrom, *The Canadian Health System* (London: Croom Helm, 1978).

[107]Donald Swartz, "The politics of reform: conflict and accommodation in Canadian health policy," in Panitch, ed., *The Canadian State,* pp. 318-322.

[108]See Malcolm G. Taylor, *Health Insurance and Canadian Public Policy: The Seven Decisions that Created the Canadian Health Insurance System* (Montréal: McGill-Queen's University Press, 1979), Chapter 2.

[109]Weller and Manga, "The Development of Health Policy," p. 227.

Reproduced with permission – Pritchard, Star Phoenix, Saskatoon.

In 1955, the government of Ontario, which had been one of the most out-spoken critics of health insurance a decade earlier, began to urge the federal government to institute a national hospital insurance system – in part because it was under pressure from the labour movement in that province, but also because its hospital system was in dire financial straits, since less than 50 percent of the population had any insurance to pay their bills.[110] The federal response was the *Hospital Insurance and Diagnostic Services Act (HIDSA)* of 1957, which established a shared-cost program providing universal insurance coverage and access to hospital services to all residents of participating provinces. By January 1961, all provinces had joined the plan.

HIDSA proved to be extremely popular; it had a major redistributive effect in that hospital care was made available to all Canadians, who were now freed from the worry of the potential financial burden imposed by hospitalization. However, it too had the disadvantages of other shared-costs programs. From the point of view of the federal government, which was pledged to match provincial expenditures, it was difficult to predict future spending patterns. From the provincial point of view, the system was excessively rigid, since only certain services qualified for matching funds; in particular, the *Act* "distorted the allocation of health care resources by favouring acute care treatment", leading to a rapid escalation in health costs.[111]

While *HIDSA* was still attracting new provincial participants, Saskatchewan was already leading the way to more comprehensive medical insurance cover-

---

[110]Swartz, "The politics of reform," p. 323.
[111]Weller and Manga, "The Development of Health Policy," p. 229.

age.[112] Despite strong opposition from the provincial medical profession, which withdrew all but emergency services for 23 days, the *Saskatchewan Medical Care Insurance Act* came into effect in 1962. Around the same time, the Diefenbaker government set up a Royal Commission on Health Services (the Hall Commission), whose 1964 report recommended the establishment of a nation-wide, comprehensive, universal health insurance system. Despite further opposition from the medical profession and private insurance companies, as well as reservations on the part of some provincial governments, the *Medical Care Act* was passed in December 1966 and came into effect in July 1968, although it was not until 1972, when the Yukon Territory program was implemented, that coverage was extended to all Canadians.[113]

The *Medical Care Act* (Medicare) provided for federal cost-sharing in provincial health insurance schemes, on the understanding that each participating province would maintain a system that would be available to every resident, comprehensive in services, accessible to all insured persons, portable from province to province and administered on a non-profit basis.[114] In recent years, however, there has been mounting concern that some provinces are not living up to their end of the bargain, inasmuch as universal access to medical care is being eroded.[115] Three provinces, Alberta, British Columbia and Ontario, finance their insurance schemes partly through premiums, described as a "regressive form of taxation" by the Parliamentary Task Force on Federal-Provincial Fiscal Arrangements.[116] Alberta, British Columbia and Newfoundland permit hospitals to charge "user fees", while a growing number of doctors in Ontario and some other provinces have protested against low increases in fee schedules by "opting out" of provincial insurance schemes or by "extra-billing" patients over and above the scheduled fees against which they are insured. In each case, it is argued, since direct charges discriminate against low-income Canadians, they threaten to create a two-tier system of health care, one for the rich and organized (*i.e.,* those who can pay or have additional coverage under private insurance schemes) and one for the unorganized, the poor and the elderly.[117]

While the former Liberal government, especially Health Minister Monique Bégin, deplored the erosion of universal access, its powers to intervene were strictly limited, first by the constitutional assignment of health care to provincial jurisdiction and, second, by the federal government's reduced financial leverage under the Established Programs Financing scheme which replaced the old

---

[112]Taylor, *Health Insurance and Canadian Public Policy,* Chapter 5.

[113]*Ibid.,* Chapter 6.

[114]House of Commons, Parliamentary Task Force on Federal-Provincial Fiscal Arrangements, *Fiscal Federalism in Canada* (Ottawa: Minister of Supply and Services, 1981), p. 105.

[115]See, for example, William K. Carroll, *et al.,* "Medicare at Risk," in W. Magnusson *et al.,* eds., *The New Reality: The Politics of Restraint in British Columbia* (Vancouver: New Star Books, 1984), pp. 214-226.

[116]House of Commons, *Fiscal Federalism in Canada,* p. 106.

[117]Government of Canada, *Preserving Universal Medicare* (Ottawa: Minister of Supply and Services, 1983), pp. 21-22.

shared-cost arrangements in 1977. Although Bégin attempted to persuade her provincial counterparts to end extra-billing and user fees and to stimulate public support for Medicare, the government eventually resorted, in the 1984 *Canada Health Act,* to imposing financial penalties on provinces which continued to permit direct charges. But the fact that Ontario, for example, appeared willing to forego $50 million a year in funds withheld by the federal government from its EPF contribution suggests that, in this case at least, exhortation and expenditure instruments are insufficient as mechanisms whereby the federal government may ensure compliance with its national policy goals.

Broadcasting and Communications Policy

If the current crisis in Medicare demonstrates the problems faced by a government that is limited by constitutional arrangements to what Doern *et al.* call "less coercive" instruments, Canada's broadcasting policies show that the availability of "more coercive" instruments still gives no guarantee of success in achieving policy objectives. Despite the use of both regulation and public ownership, Canadian federal governments have at best been only partly successful in stemming the tide of American cultural penetration of the mass media.

Given technological developments since 1867, it is not surprising that jurisdictional responsibility for broadcasting and telecommunications was not assigned directly by the *BNA Act.* But, based on interpretation of sections 92(10)(a) and 91(29) of the *Act,* which provided for exclusive federal jurisdiction over telegraph systems and inter-provincial transportation, both the Judicial Committee of the Privy Council (JCPC) and the Supreme Court of Canada decided that radio broadcasting (and subsequently by extension, television) was to be a federal responsibility.[118] The same logic has been applied to give the federal government regulatory authority over all aspects of telecommunications – telephones, telegraphy, telex, cable and satellite systems *etc.* – with the exception of some provincial telephone companies whose services do not extend across provincial boundaries.[119] Thus, despite occasional provincial challenges to federal authority (especially with respect to regulation of Cable TV), the Constitution has, since 1932, imposed few constraints on federal policy-makers in this area.

Instead, telecommunications, and broadcasting policy in particular, have been influenced far more by Canada's proximity to the United States and by relations between the public and private broadcasting sectors. As early as 1928, in part because of "the threat posed to Canadian sovereignty by the burgeoning radio empires of the United States",[120] the federal government established a Royal Commission on Radio Broadcasting (the Aird Commission). The Aird Report

---

[118]Martha Fletcher and Frederick J. Fletcher, "Communications and Confederation: Jurisdiction and Beyond," in R.B. Byers and R.W. Reford, *Canada Challenged: The Viability of Confederation* (Toronto: Canadian Institute of International Affairs, 1979), pp. 161-162.

[119]*Ibid.,* pp. 167-170.

[120]David Ellis, *Evolution of the Canadian Broadcasting System: Objectives and Realities, 1928-1968* (Ottawa: Minister of Supply and Services, 1979), p. 1.

recommended the creation of a single, national, publicly-owned broadcasting corporation modelled on Britain's BBC. In the face of strong opposition from existing private stations and from the provinces, however, the Bennett government compromised by setting up the Canadian Radio Broadcasting Commission (CRBC), a strange hybrid agency empowered both to carry on public broadcasting and to regulate the entire broadcasting sector, public and private. The financial, political and administrative weaknesses of the CRBC were immediately apparent,[121] and in 1936 it was replaced by the current Canadian Broadcasting Corporation, which held similar powers but was awarded a greater degree of financial and operational autonomy. Though the broadcasting system remained under mixed ownership (with private stations competing with the public corporation), the CBC's regulatory powers were designed to ensure the dominance of the public sector, a status which it continued to enjoy until the 1950s.

In September 1952, the first Canadian television station, CFBT, went on the air in Montréal, and a new dimension was added to broadcasting policy. As had been the case with radio, the early years of TV broadcasting saw the emergence of a dual public sector/private sector service, with the CBC continuing to provide programming and serving as the regulatory and licensing agency. But the CBC was suffering from serious underfunding at this time and, unable to expand its TV facilities fast enough, it was encouraged by the federal government to grant licenses to private operations to pre-empt saturation of the Canadian market by American networks. Consequently, by 1958, of 44 licensed television stations, only eight were owned by the CBC.[122] From this point on, private commercial stations came to dominate the broadcasting scene, a trend which was further enhanced in 1958 when the new Diefenbaker government, more sympathetic than its predecessor to private interests, deprived the CBC of its licensing powers and turned them over to a new independent regulatory agency, the Board of Broadcast Governors (BBG).

Despite numerous Royal Commissions, committees of inquiry and legislative changes, the broadcasting system created in 1958 remains relatively unchanged today. In both radio and television, parallel public and private networks compete with each other as well as with American stations (now made more widely available by cable and satellite systems). The whole structure is regulated by a quasi-autonomous federal agency, the Canadian Radio-Television and Telecommunications Commission,[123] whose primary role was established by the 1958 *Broadcasting Act.* That legislation charged the CRTC's predecessor, the Board of Broadcast Governors, with

---

[121]*Ibid.*, Chapter 2.

[122]Paul Audley, *Canada's Cultural Industries: Broadcasting, Publishing, Records and Film* (Toronto: Lorimer, 1983), p. 255.

[123]The Canadian Radio-Television Commission replaced the Board of Broadcasting Governors under the 1968 *Broadcasting Act.* In 1976, its mandate was broadened, and its name lengthened, by the transfer of telecommunications regulation from the Canadian Transport Commission.

ensuring the continued existence and efficient operation of a national broadcasting system and the provision of a varied and comprehensive broadcasting service of a high standard *that is basically Canadian in content and character...*[124]

In 1959, the BBG announced the first Canadian content regulations, which required all television broadcasters to schedule at least 45 percent Canadian programming. Although "Canadian content" was loosely interpreted to include, for example, major sporting events like the World Series, the BBG was never successful in securing compliance from private broadcasters. The CRTC has been no more effective than the BBG in imposing Canadian content requirements, despite the fact that, as one author puts it, Canadian content is *the* major *raison d'être* of the CRTC.[125] Numerous studies have shown that, while the CBC/Radio Canada network has led the way in compliance with Canadian content quotas, private television stations have, at best, obeyed the letter but not the spirit of CRTC regulations.[126]

From the outset, two consistent themes have provided the central thrust of public policy toward broadcasting in Canada. The first is to create a nation-wide Canadian broadcasting system which would help inform and integrate all Canadians, no matter where they live, into a single national community; the second, to protect Canadian culture from penetration and/or domination by American media channels. The first objective has largely been achieved. The publicly owned CBC/Radio Canada has nation-wide networks serving both official language groups through radio and television; and, since 1961, CTV has emerged as a nation-wide private TV network. But several factors – the CRTC's failure to obtain effective compliance with Canadian content regulations; the budget cuts imposed on the CBC (the one network which does provide a genuine outlet for Canadian programming)[127] by the Conservative government in the fall of 1984; and the new problem of regulating cable and satellite systems – endanger the cultural objectives of broadcasting policy in Canada.[128] In the face of intransigence of profit-maximizing private sector operators, the increasing sophistication of com-

---

[124]Canada, *Broadcasting Act* (Ottawa: Queen's Printer, 1958), Section 10. (Emphasis added.)

[125]Robert E. Babe, *Canadian Television Broadcasting Structure, Performance and Regulation: A Study Prepared for the Economic Council of Canada* (Ottawa: Minister of Supply and Services, 1979), p. 141.

[126]See Chapter 4 above and, for example, Audley, *Canada's Cultural Industries,* pp. 256-261, especially Table 7-3, p. 260; Babe, *Canadian Television Broadcasting . . . ,* Chapter 7; R.E. Babe, "Regulation of Private Television by the Canadian Radio-Television Commission: A Critique of Ends and Means," *Canadian Public Administration,* vol. 19, no. 4 (Winter 1976), pp. 552-586; Colin G. Hoskins and Stuart McFadyen, "Market Structure and Television Programming Performance in Canada and the U.K.: A Comparative Study," *Canadian Public Policy,* vol. 8, no. 3 (Summer 1982), pp. 347-357.

[127]See Jeffrey Simpson, "The Missing Programs," *The Globe and Mail,* Toronto, February 5, 1985, p. 6.

[128]Even before the Conservative government came to power, former CBC head A.W. Johnson was calling upon the Liberal government to strengthen the CBC as the centrepiece of a "re-Canadianized" broadcasting system. See Al Johnson, "The Re-Canadianization of Broadcasting," *Policy Options,* vol. 4, no. 2 (March 1983), pp. 6-12.

munications technology and the overwhelming presence of American culture to the south, weak regulatory regimes and underfunded public enterprises are indeed inadequate instruments for the achievement of national cultural goals.

THE CHANGING CONTEXT OF CANADIAN PUBLIC POLICY

As the three case studies above indicate, public policy is dynamic. Policy objectives and priorities shift over time; mechanisms of policy implementation are refined; Crown corporations and regulatory agencies adjust their operations to meet new goals and conditions. All of this occurs because public policy-making is an integral part of the political process, and politics itself is a dynamic phenomenon. Changes in cultural values and expectations, in institutional structures and in political behaviour all impose both new demands and new constraints on federal policy-makers, as do the constantly shifting environments of international and federal/provincial relations. Last, but certainly not least, changes in the domestic and world economies are critical in determining the resources that policy-makers have at their disposal and the constraints within which they must operate.

In this last section of the chapter, therefore, we trace the dominant styles or patterns of federal policy-making since the Second World War and relate them to both the changing economic and political contexts in which they occurred and the theoretical approaches to public policy analysis outlined earlier.[129]

The Growth of the State Revisited

We have already shown in Chapter 2 that the Canadian state continued to expand its activities after 1945 at both the federal and provincial levels. Most of the major federal programs that comprise the modern Canadian welfare state were initiated or consolidated in the quarter-century after the Second World War, including hospital and medical insurance, the Canada and Québec pension plans, the Canada Assistance Plan and federal participation in other shared-cost programs such as post-secondary education. These were added to such war-time initiatives as unemployment insurance and family allowances to create a comprehensive package of social and welfare programs which, by 1968, paralleled those of the more established welfare states of Western Europe.

The expansion of state activities can be attributed to a number of factors. First, the period was marked by the emergence of Keynesian economics as the dominant paradigm of macro-economic management in most Western industrial societies. The Keynesian model legitimized large-scale government intervention, especially in social policy fields, as a means of manipulating the level of aggregate demand to control the kind of extreme cyclical fluctuations in the economy that had given rise to the Great Depression of the 1930s. It should be noted,

---

[129]For a brief outline of major policy priorities before 1945 and an extended discussion of the Trudeau era, see Doern and Phidd, *Canadian Public Policy,* pp. 229-231 and 234-252 respectively.

however, that Keynesian economics was never fully implemented in Canada since, although successive federal governments intervened to boost aggregate demand as an incentive to economic growth, they rarely followed Keynes' prescriptions of expenditure cutbacks and tax hikes to deflate the economy in times of expansion and inflation.

Second, the period from 1945 to 1970 was, by and large, an era of rapid and sustained economic growth fuelled by post-war reconstruction, the injection of foreign investment and the spread of mass affluence. This economic growth led to an expansion of government revenues through increasing tax returns and enhanced the fiscal capacity of the state to intervene. It also enabled the government to involve itself in major redistributive programs, since there were sufficient resources to distribute to the less privileged without depriving more affluent and politically influential groups of a share of the ever-expanding national pie.

From a pluralist perspective, therefore, the government as neutral arbiter became able to satisfy the demands of more societal groups, including an increasingly influential labour movement which had organized behind the trade unions and the growing electoral force of the CCF. In the public choice view, however, the growth of the state could be attributed to the competitive bidding practices of party politicians anxious to gain or hold onto governmental power and to the expansionist tendencies of bureaucrats seeking to build empires and enlarge their spheres of influence in the policy process.

The neo-Marxist approach would interpret the growth of the state in different terms again. The need to promote private capital accumulation after the war required the state to intervene on behalf of capital through incentives to investment, by boosting aggregate demand (*e.g.*, universal child allowances) and by helping to underwrite the costs of reproducing the labour force (*e.g.*, health and education policies). At the same time, the growing power of organized labour led the state, exercising its relative autonomy, to introduce programs which have helped to legitimate (or to mystify) its capital accumulation role and disguise the exploitative nature of capitalism. As capitalism becomes increasingly monopolistic and as the rate of profit falls (a central tenet of Marxian economics), the state will intervene more and more to maintain both capital accumulation and legitimation until it reaches what James O'Connor has called "fiscal crisis", a situation in which government revenues can no longer satisfy the simultaneous demands of the dual role of the state.[130] Thus, for some analysts, the current language of restraint and the social policy cutbacks undertaken by neo-conservative governments in Britain and the United States are natural consequences of fiscal crisis and the fundamental contradiction between the state's accumulation and legitimation functions. But before we look at the present era, some reference should be made to Prime Minister Trudeau's attempts to develop more "rational" policy-making in Canada in the late 1960s and early 1970s.

---

[130]James O'Connor, *The Fiscal Crisis of the State, passim.*

The Experiment with Rational Policy-Making

Of course, all policy-makers consider themselves to be rational, but the quest for "rational" policy-making in the federal government is most clearly associated with the early years of Pierre Trudeau's reign as Prime Minister. In contrast to his two most immediate predecessors, Prime Ministers Diefenbaker and Pearson, who tended toward incrementalist and *ad hoc* policy-making, Trudeau embraced a philosophy of policy-making that was very close to the rational-comprehensive model.[131]

Apparently believing in Weber's maxim that "knowledge is power" and mistrustful of entrenched interests in the federal bureaucracy, Trudeau presided over a fundamental reorganization of the structures of policy-making that was designed to enhance research and the flow of information to political decision-makers and to reduce the degree of uncertainty with which they had to contend. New coordinative ministries of state were established; the PCO and PMO were strengthened; and no government department or agency was complete without its full complement of policy-advisory, planning and research units.[132] The Planning, Programming, Budgeting System was implemented, and the government embarked on an ambitious series of priority-setting exercises to provide a framework of objectives against which all existing and future programs could be evaluated. But, while some of the reforms undoubtedly contributed to more informed decision-making in the federal government, it must be acknowledged that the hoped-for rationality in policy-making never fully materialized.

It may be argued that Trudeau's dream of rationality fell victim to bureaucratic, political and economic constraints. First, as Richard French has demonstrated, the quest for economic planning and a federal industrial strategy in the 1970s was frustrated by the conflicting diagnoses of and prescriptions for Canada's economic problems emanating from different government departments and advisory councils, each with its own agency ethos and entrenched interests to protect.[133] And, as we asserted in Chapter 9, government departments soon learned how to "work" the PPBS to their own advantage and to resist the coordinative efforts of central agencies and the new ministries of state.

Furthermore, critics of the rational-comprehensive approach argue that it is premised upon unrealistic expectations of the degree of value consensus in society. What may be rational for the federal government may not be so for the

---

[131]G. Bruce Doern, "Recent Changes in the Philosophy of Policy-Making in Canada," *Canadian Journal of Political Science*, vol. 4, no. 2 (June 1971), pp. 243-264.

[132]See Peter Aucoin and Richard French, *Knowledge, Power and Public Policy*, Science Council of Canada Background Study #31 (Ottawa: Information Canada, 1974); Michael J. Prince, "Policy-Advisory Groups in Government Departments," in Doern and Aucoin, eds., *Public Policy in Canada*, pp. 275-300.

[133]See Chapter 9 above, and Richard D. French, *How Ottawa Decides: Planning and Industrial Policy-Making 1968-1984*, 2nd ed. (Toronto: Lorimer, 1984), especially Chapters 2 and 5.

provinces, or at least for their governments. Thus, the values of provincial autonomy and economic diversification, which were rational for provincial politicians seeking re-election and for their bureaucrats, clashed sharply with the centralist vision of Canada and the national economic development goals espoused by the Trudeau government. In the absence of any mechanisms for forging consensus of values and goals between federal and provincial governments, rational policy-making was extremely difficult to implement in Canada's federal system.

Political constraints were also imposed by the Liberals' dependence upon NDP support during the minority government of 1972-74, a period in which long-term "rational" goals had to be sacrificed to the short-term expediency of staying in power. But even when the Liberals were returned with a clear majority in the 1974 general election, incrementalism and short-term "firefighting" still prevailed over long-term planning. The government's grand priorities exercise of 1974-75 collapsed in disarray as economic reality in the form of rising inflation and the effects of the international energy crisis imposed new public priorities on the privately-agreed objectives of the federal Liberals.[134] From the invocation of wage and price controls in 1975 onwards, federal policy priorities have been profoundly shaped by the new economic reality of stagflation, in which the sustained economic growth of the post-war years came to an end and, with it, the apparently inexhaustible fiscal capacity of the federal government. Since that turning-point, "restraint" has become the watchword of federal policy-making, as successive governments have attempted to cope with inflation, recession, declining tax revenues, growing deficits and the task of reviving a faltering Canadian economy.

Policy-Making in an Age of Restraint

One major consequence of the slowdown in economic growth has been the advent of what American economist Lester Thurow has labelled "the zero-sum society".[135] In earlier times, governments could redistribute resources to the underprivileged without eroding at least the money income, if not the relative position, of more affluent groups; that is, the growing national pie permitted "positive-sum" politics. However, once the pie stops growing, redistribution to some groups can be undertaken only at the expense of others. In the zero-sum society, then, distributional conflicts become more polarized, since somebody must "lose" for someone else to "win". Thus, new or expanded social programs must be financed either from savings, for instance, those realized by cutting incentives to business, or from increased revenues, obtained perhaps through higher personal and corporate income taxes. But, as the recession has lengthened unemployment lines and squeezed corporate profit margins, government revenues have been falling below expected levels – just when demand has been increasing for social expenditures such as unemployment insurance benefits and

---

[134]French, *ibid.*, Chapter 4.

[135]Lester C. Thurow, *The Zero-Sum Society: Distribution and the Possibilities for Economic Change* (New York: Basic Books, 1980).

welfare and pressure has mounted for the government to bail out failing businesses.

In the short term, of course, governments can try to escape from this dilemma by deficit financing – that is, by borrowing money to meet the shortfall between revenues and expenditures. But in recent years, the annual federal deficit has come to exceed $30 billion; the public debt envelope now consumes one-fifth of projected annual spending. Many politicians and external observers alike have argued that the limits of deficit financing, and perhaps even of the public sector, have been exceeded, causing a drain on private capital investment and on the economy in general.

It is under these conditions that restraint has become a recurring theme in federal political discourse. It was already evident in the late 1970s, both in the Liberals' sweeping expenditure cuts of 1978-79 and in John Crosbie's "short-term pain for long-term gain" Conservative Budget of December 1979. It resurfaced in the Liberals' "six and five" program of June 1982, which imposed limits on annual increases in public sector salaries and many social programs, and indirectly attempted to reduce public expectations of government. But the concept of restraint really came to the fore with the September 1984 election of a new Conservative government committed to trimming the federal deficit, cutting government expenditures, deregulating some areas of economic activity and privatizing a good proportion of the federal stable of Crown corporations.

In part, this commitment to unravelling government may be viewed as a response to what some observers consider to be the "overloading" of the political system in Canada. Alan Cairns, for example, has argued from an essentially pluralist perspective that competitive bidding by political parties, over-interpretation of public expectations and bureaucratic empire-building have contributed to the emergence in Canada of "big government" at both the federal and provincial levels, to the extent that representative political institutions can no longer make effective, accountable public policy. In this view, a federal system which resembles "eleven elephants in a maze" has added an extra dimension to the universal crisis of big government, in which policy-makers are no longer capable of doing everything they aspire to.[136]

From a neo-Marxist perspective, however, the ideology of restraint may be seen as a means of justifying cutbacks in "unproductive" social expenditures in favour of policies to foster capital accumulation, as part of the solution to the fiscal crisis of the state. According to neo-Marxists, the cuts in social spending introduced by President Ronald Reagan, combined with environmental deregulation and tax breaks, are quite consistent with the need to promote accumulation at the expense of traditional forms of legitimation through the provision of social programs.

---

[136]Alan C. Cairns, "The Other Crisis of Canadian Federalism," *Canadian Public Administration*, vol. 22, no. 2 (Summer 1979), pp. 175-195. See also the Symposium on "Can Government Govern?" *Canadian Public Policy* vol. 2, no. 4 (Fall, 1976); and, more generally, Anthony King, "Overload: Problems of Governing in the 1970s," *Political Studies*, vol. 23, nos. 2 and 3 (April-July 1975), pp. 284-296.

It is unlikely – and, in our view, undesirable – that the federal government will follow very far in the footsteps of the more radical neo-conservative administrations of Ronald Reagan and Margaret Thatcher, who have presided over savage cutbacks in social spending and either extensive deregulation or privatization of their respective economies. But the Mulroney government's vacillation over the "sacred trust" of universal social programs, the radical overhaul of the Social Security system advocated by the Macdonald Commission and the commitment of senior Cabinet Ministers such as Michael Wilson and Sinclair Stevens to a substantial reduction in the role of government have troubled many groups which benefit from the existing level of state intervention. The examples of Britain and the United States, together with the recent experience of British Columbia under Premier Bennett's policies, have demonstrated that the primary victims of restraint tend to be the poor, the sick, ethnic minorities and women.[137]

But it may be the case that the Conservatives' bark is worse than their bite. During their first months in office, just as they appeared to parallel the worst excesses of Liberal patronage despite all previous protestations to the contrary, they demonstrated that their economic policies could be equally incrementalist and responsive to political pressure from voters. By attempting to bail out the Canadian Commercial Bank and providing loan guarantees to the Domtar paper mill in Windsor, Québec, they added to federal spending commitments despite "the rhetoric of deficit cutting and gaining greater control over government expenditures".[138] The politics of restraint, like Prime Minister Trudeau's politics of rationality, must contend with the higher political rationality of ensuring re-election in a competitive party democracy, with the entrenched interests of bureaucrats and client interest groups, with the pressures of provincial governments in a federal system – in short, with the realities of politics in Canada.

OVERVIEW

Even in a chapter of this length it is not possible to explore all of the facets of federal policy-making. The primary objectives here have been to introduce the reader to some of the central concepts in policy-making and the most commonly used approaches to public policy analysis, as well as to illustrate some of the constraints within which federal policy-makers have to operate. Whichever macro-level perspective one takes on the role of the state in Canadian society, it is clear that certain fundamental realities of Canadian political life have a major influence on federal policy-making, and that their net effect at the micro-level is to

---

[137]See, for example, Stewart Hall and Martin Jacques, eds., *The Politics of Thatcherism* (London: Lawrence and Wishart, 1983); John L. Palmer and Isabel V. Sawhill, eds., *The Reagan Record: An Assessment of America's Changing Priorities* (Cambridge, Mass.: Ballinger, 1984); Magnusson *et al.*, eds., *The New Reality.*

[138]Christopher Waddell, "PC Bailout Policy Echoes the Grits," *The Globe and Mail*, Toronto, April 29, 1985, p. B1.

militate against rational-comprehensive decision-making in favour of a general tendency toward incremental policy-making or the fine art of "muddling through".

First, Canada is a liberal democracy in which political parties must compete for electoral support and governments must remain responsive to the promptings of key interest groups, both as lobbyists and as potential organizers of public opinion and votes. The need to win, and especially to maintain, electoral support from societal groups usually requires that governments refrain from making major policy changes which might alienate significant portions of the electorate.

Second, Canada enjoys, or suffers from, a federal system of government in which the constitutional division of powers imposes both legal and political constraints upon federal policy-makers. The legal constraints limit the instruments available to the federal government in pursuit of its objectives in many policy areas, while the values and goals of provincial governments and the policies these governments implement often contradict and reduce the effectiveness of federal policy outputs. As we showed in the case study on health insurance, the need to secure federal/provincial cooperation in many policy areas again dictates that policy-making must move in small, incrementalist steps rather than in giant strides.

Third, Canada is not a political system in isolation. Changes in the world economic and political environments create a climate of uncertainty for policy-makers of all nations. But the political and economic influence of the United States and of American-based multinational corporations impose extra demands and constraints on policy-makers in Canada. As our case studies of energy policy and communications demonstrate, federal policy-makers constantly have to adjust their priorities and instruments of policy implementation in response to events south of the 49th Parallel. The fate of the National Energy Program perhaps most clearly illustrates the limitations on radical policy changes which arise from Canada's unique international position.

None of this is intended to argue against policy-makers attempting to make more "rational" policy decisions. All Canadians would like to think that their federal government makes the most rational policy choices available to it, subject to the constraints under which it is working. However, the requirements of a democratic political process, a federal institutional structure and the constraints imposed by the domestic and international economies usually combine with short-term political expediency to ensure that policy-makers follow the path of least resistance by "muddling through". Canadians should, perhaps, demand of their governments that, if they are going to "muddle through", they at least do so in a more "rational" way.

CanaPress Photo Service

chapter 14

Foreign and Defence Policy
Canada in the World

SINCE THE LAST GREAT WAR the world has entered an era of rapid technological change, increasing economic interdependence and the threat of nuclear war. Canada is far from self-sufficient with regard to either economic prosperity or national security. Increasingly, the well-being and security of Canadian citizens depend on how they collectively respond to the constraints, opportunities and dangers which flow from the international environment.

What is Canada's place in the international order; how does it rank in terms of power, influence and prosperity? Measuring Canada's precise position in the world is difficult, if not impossible. Intuitive measures may be distorted by personal observations or national biases. Empirical measures based on indexes such as primary resources may fluctuate wildly because of changes in world supply and demand, and give an equally distorted view. However, some approximations of Canada's relative position are both necessary and instructive. Remaining cognizant of the problems involved in acquiring equivalent data from various countries, *The Book of World Rankings* placed Canada eighth in the world in terms of "National Power" as the 1980s approached.[1] It based its National Power index on a combination of several factors, including population, territory, economic capability and military capability.

At roughly the same time, Peyton Lyon and Brian Tomlin determined that Canada had an overall "capabilities index" of sixth among the 30 industrialized nations. According to them, Canada's economic capability was fifth highest, and the resources capability index – which measures people, energy and raw materials – showed Canada in fourth place in the world standings at that time. They concluded that Canada is "one of the clusters of powers immediately below the

---

[1]George Thomas Kurian, *The Book of World Rankings* (New York: Facts on File, Inc., 1979), pp. 50-55.

superpowers and China".[2] In view of the economic shifts of the past decade, a more realistic view might now place Canada in a third tier of nations, below not only the superpowers but also a second tier which would include the highly industrialized nation-states of West Germany, Britain, France and Japan. This placement would correspond with the view expressed by foreign elites in 1975 that Canada is "a sensible, responsible country, but not exceptionally influential in global affairs".[3] When asked to estimate Canada's weight in the world, 40 percent of the foreign elite interviewed by Lyon in 1975 replied that Canada ranked with the Scandinavian countries; 24 percent ranked it with the white Commonwealth. These opinions were repeated in 1983.[4]

Determining Canada's relative economic performance in terms of GNP is of course much easier than measuring power and influence. By this economic measure, Canada hovers on the border of the elite top ten. In the global perspective, Canadians are economically very well off. They have a high standard of living which furnishes them with many items which citizens of other countries would consider extreme luxuries, from automobiles to television sets. As John Holmes has put it, Canada is regarded as "filthy rich".[5]

Official relationships outside our borders are conducted by two basic methods. One involves maintaining active multilateral relations, particularly through international institutions. The other is accomplished by cultivating selective bilateral relations; Canada has official relations with 166 countries (see Table 14-1). Canada's foreign policy generally aims to build strong relationships with countries which are most important to Canada's economic development and which offer possibilities of long-term markets for Canadian exports. The parameters of these relationships are determined to a large degree by defence arrangements with Western Europe and the United States.

In this chapter we shall first examine the concept of foreign policy. We next turn to an examination of the sources and the history of foreign policy in Canada. The balance of the chapter discusses the four main components of Canadian foreign policy: trade policy, activity in international organizations, bilateral relations and defence policy. The last among these focuses on the international strategic environment, our role in the major defence organizations, peacekeeping, arms control and disarmament.

WHAT IS FOREIGN POLICY?

The domain of **foreign policy** includes all nation-state behaviour which has external ramifications. It includes government actions and objectives but not those

---

[2]Peyton V. Lyon and Brian Tomlin, *Canada as an International Actor* (Toronto: Macmillan, 1979), p. 70. For other ideas about Canada's international status see David B. Dewitt and John J. Kirton, *Canada as a Principal Power* (Toronto: Wiley, 1983); and John W. Holmes, *Canada: A Middle-Aged Power* (Toronto: McClelland and Stewart, 1976).

[3]Lyon and Tomlin, *op. cit.*, p. 79.

[4]The results of the 1983 survey are not published to date.

[5]John Holmes, cited in Lyon and Tomlin, *op. cit.*, p. 30.

of private actors in civil society.[6] As Kal Holsti aptly put it, students of foreign policy analyze "the actions of a state toward external environment and the conditions – usually domestic – under which those actions are formulated".[7] Therefore, the study of foreign policy can be distinguished from that of general international relations: while the former consists of an examination of government behaviour, the latter refers to the broader relations between nation-states and can even include non-governmental activity of citizens and corporations.

Foreign policy is not one-dimensional. Rather it has many components, including national security and economic and political interests. A Canadian government trade policy document in 1982 defined foreign policy as "the end product of an integration and balancing of the range of Canadian interests after the international environment in which these interests are pursued has been taken into account".[8] One of the most important aspects of that environment is, of course, the network of defence commitments. But in recent years the economic component of foreign policy has become increasingly important because of the growing interdependence of nations and the competitive search for economic growth.

The process of making foreign policy differs considerably from that of making domestic policy, and coordination is not always easy or even possible. The state is able to achieve domestic objectives because it has sovereign authority over its internal environment. Outside its borders, a government has no legal authority; as a result, foreign policy decisions must be set within the context of the opportunities and constraints of the international system. In concrete terms, foreign policy-making in Canada differs from domestic policy-making because the former sometimes amounts to little more than striking an image. Only rarely is legislation necessary; often Parliament and even the bureaucratic elite have little more than spectator status as the Prime Minister, the Secretary of State for External Affairs and the Departments of External Affairs and National Defence determine initiatives.

SOURCES OF CANADIAN FOREIGN POLICY

The traditional view of the relationship between politicians and civil servants depicts elected politicians as responsible for the determination of policy which bureaucrats administer. Politicans make decisions; bureaucrats merely implement

---

[6] For comprehensive discussions of the definitional problem involved see the following general texts in international affairs: K.J. Holsti, *International Politics*, 4th ed. (Englewood Cliffs: Prentice-Hall, 1983); Lloyd Jenson, *Explaining Foreign Policy* (Englewood Cliffs: Prentice-Hall, 1982); James Lee Ray, *Global Politics* (Boston: Houghton Mifflin, 1979); Bruce Russett and Harvey Starr, *World Politics* (San Francisco: Freeman, 1980); and Robert L. Wendzel, *International Politics* (New York: Wiley, 1981).

[7] K.J. Holsti, *op. cit.*, p. 19.

[8] *Canadian Trade Policy for the 1980s, A Discussion Paper* (Ottawa: Minister of Supply and Services, 1983), p. 40. For a discussion of the 1984 Conservative government's early approach to trade and foreign policy see *Competitiveness and Security* (Ottawa: Supply and Services, 1985).

them. However, as we have shown, the role of government bureaucracy has expanded into the realm of policy-making. This development is evident in the formulation of foreign policy, an area where Canada's political leadership depends heavily upon the bureaucracy's expertise and advice concerning the conduct of its international affairs. Nonetheless, the Prime Minister and the Ministers of External Affairs and National Defence remain at the apex of decision-making.

Prime Minister and Cabinet

At the level of political leadership, responsibility for foreign policy falls primarily on the Prime Minister and the Secretary of State for External Affairs. In fact, until 1946 the PM personally retained the External Affairs portfolio. It is only recently that foreign affairs have begun to involve the participation of other Cabinet members, as a result of efforts to strengthen the collective involvement of Cabinet in decision-making.[9] Today, greater use of committees and the insistence that the bureaucracy and ministers provide Cabinet with alternatives rather than allowing single-option recommendations and attempts to establish national priorities at the Cabinet level have helped to open the foreign policy process to other departments and ministers. Still, the PM remains the central political actor, able to provide leadership and place particular concerns high on the government's political agenda. Prime Minister Trudeau's promotion of a North/South dialogue and proposals for talks among the world's nuclear powers were examples from the early 1980s. In 1984, Brian Mulroney temporarily "institutionalized" the Prime Minister's authority in international affairs by disbanding the Cabinet committee on External Affairs and National Defence and assigning its responsibilities to Priorities and Planning, the committee which he chaired.

The role of the Secretary of State for External Affairs (commonly but incorrectly referred to as the Minister of External Affairs) is also extremely important. This Minister is not only the chief spokesman on international affairs and the top administrator for the Department of External Affairs, but often also the second most powerful person in the Cabinet. Louis St. Laurent and Lester Pearson both became Prime Ministers after being Secretary of State; Allan MacEachen held the dual position of Secretary of State and Deputy Prime Minister for several years.

---

[9]Kim Richard Nossal, *The Politics of Canadian Foreign Policy* (Scarborough: Prentice-Hall, 1985). For historical treatises see Kim Richard Nossal, ed., *An Acceptance of Paradox/Essays on Canadian Diplomacy in Honour of John W. Holmes* (Toronto: Canadian Institute of International Affairs, 1982). For a discussion of Trudeau's impact on foreign policy-making, see John J. Kirton, "Foreign Policy Decision-Making in the Trudeau Government: Promise and Performance," *International Journal*, vol. XXXIII, no. 2 (Spring 1978), pp. 287-311; Bruce Thordarson, *Trudeau and Foreign Policy: A Study in Decision-Making* (Toronto: Oxford University Press, 1972); Michael Tucker *Canadian Foreign Policy* (Toronto: McGraw-Hill Ryerson, 1980); and Harald von Riekhoff, "The Impact of Prime Minister Trudeau on Foreign Policy," *International Journal*, vol. XXXIII, no. 2, (Spring 1978), pp. 267-286.

Department of External Affairs

The Department of External Affairs (DEA) is at the centre of the bureaucratic complex responsible for Canada's foreign relations. The 1909 Act of Parliament which established it charged the Department with the conduct of foreign affairs, specifically "the conduct of all official communications between the Government of Canada and the government of any other country in connection with the external affairs of Canada".[10] These responsibilities have grown substantially since that time. Today, the Department performs three interrelated functions:[11] provision and integration of policy advice; coordination and integration of Canada's foreign relations; and the implementation of foreign operations.

TABLE 14.1 Distribution of Canadian Posts Abroad by Geographic Region, 1981

	Number of Canadian Posts		*Number of Countries with which Canada has Official Relations*	
Africa and the Middle East	26		64	
Anglophone Africa		8		25
Francophone Africa		11		22
Middle East		7		17
Asia and the Pacific	17		30*	
Northeast Asia		4		5*
Pacific		9		19
South Asia		4		6
Europe	34		34	
Eastern Europe		6		8
Western Europe		28		26
Latin America and Caribbean	18		37	
Caribbean		4		16
Latin America		14		21
United States	15		1	
International Organizations	9			
TOTAL	119		166	

*Totals include the colony of Hong Kong.

Source: Adapted from *Royal Commission on Conditions of Foreign Service,* (Ottawa: Supply and Services, 1981), p. 40.

---

[10]As cited in the *Royal Commission on Conditions of Foreign Service* (Ottawa: Supply and Services, 1981), p. 64. Note the use of the term "External" rather than "Foreign" affairs. This usage resulted from the fact that many of the relationships of countries with Canada involved other members of the British Empire and therefore were not regarded as foreign in the strict sense.

[11]Taken from the *Royal Commission on Conditions of Foreign Service.*

As policy advisor the Department conducts research and analysis, develops policy and policy options, contributes to domestic policy formulation and provides leadership in establishing policies in the international sphere. The coordination and integration of foreign policy involve providing a framework for the full range of governmental activities overseas, monitoring and influencing other departments and other Canadian governments' international activities and bringing coherence to a patchwork of priorities and programs. Foreign operations include representation of Canada's interests to other countries, analysis of information regarding developments abroad, negotiation and the management and supervision of programs overseas.[12] Tables 14-1 and 14-2 indicate the Department's size, activities and expenditures.

While the DEA retains primary responsibility for the conduct of Canada's foreign policy, other governmental and non-governmental bodies have become increasingly salient in the foreign-policy-making process. What were once considered purely domestic matters have increasingly taken on an international dimension. The foreign policy process has become more diffuse within government, and also more open in that non-governmental groups are increasingly involved. Domestically, interest groups, private citizens, business people, as well as regional interests and their provincial government spokesmen seek to influence foreign policy decisions. Internationally, a new layer of non-governmental organizations is active, including multinational firms pursuing commercial relations and private groups advocating protection of human rights. Traditional foreign-policy-makers have consequently had to accept increasing levels of participation of other actors in international affairs.

Changes in federal intragovernmental structures have also eroded the DEA's dominance in conducting Canada's foreign relations. The introduction of a new Cabinet committee system and a new expenditure management system subjected the Department's activities and policy proposals to scrutiny from other departments. Further, the Prime Minister's support agencies – the Prime Minister's Office and the Privy Council Office – have become more influential in foreign policy decisions. New or revamped departments have also eroded the former predominance of the DEA, to the point of duplicating some of the Department's functions. Many contemporary issues require expertise that External Affairs does not possess: the law of the sea, acid rain, energy policy,. nuclear exports and grain exports, to name only a few. The participation of such diverse departments and government bodies as Environment Canada, Energy, Mines and Resources, Petro-Canada, the National Energy Board, Atomic Energy of Canada, the Department of Agriculture and the National Wheat Board is therefore essential.

---

[12]Programs include promotion of trade, representation and protection of Canadian commercial interests, provision of technical and development assistance, admittance of refugees, processing of visa applications, monitoring of international criminal activities, enforcement of customs regulations, consular assistance to the public and reporting and liaison in specific policy areas including agriculture, finance, labour, health and energy.

TABLES 14.2 Department of External Affairs – Estimated Expenditures by Activity and Region, 1981-82

| | ACTIVITIES | | | | | | | | | |
| Regions | Relations with Foreign Governments and Intergovernmental Institutions | | Assistance to Canadians | | Information Activities and Cultural Relations | | Assistance to Other Programs | | Total | |
	$000	%	$000	%	$000	%	$000	%	$000	%
Asia and Pacific	12 301	27.8	1 682	3.8	2 869	6.5	27 333	61.9	44 185	100.0
Europe	23 835	27.3	4 753	5.4	9 273	10.6	49 556	56.7	87 417	100.0
Africa and Middle East	11 507	31.4	2 290	6.3	1 964	5.4	20 842	56.9	36 603	100.0
Western Hemisphere	19 063	24.9	4 327	5.7	7 461	9.7	45 740	59.7	76 591	100.0
Permanent Mission and Delegations	7 161*	40.6	82	0.5	6 183	35.1	4 192	23.8	17 618*	100.0
Headquarters Functional Support	18 403*	55.2	1 184	3.6	12 371	37.1	1 371	4.1	33 329	100.0
Total	92 270*	31.2	14 318	4.8	40 121	13.6	149 034	50.4	295 743*	100.0

*Does not include grants, contributions and assessments of $11 141 000.

Source: Main Estimates, 1980-81, quoted in *Royal Commission on Conditions of Foreign Service,* (Ottawa: Supply and Services, 1981), p. 131.

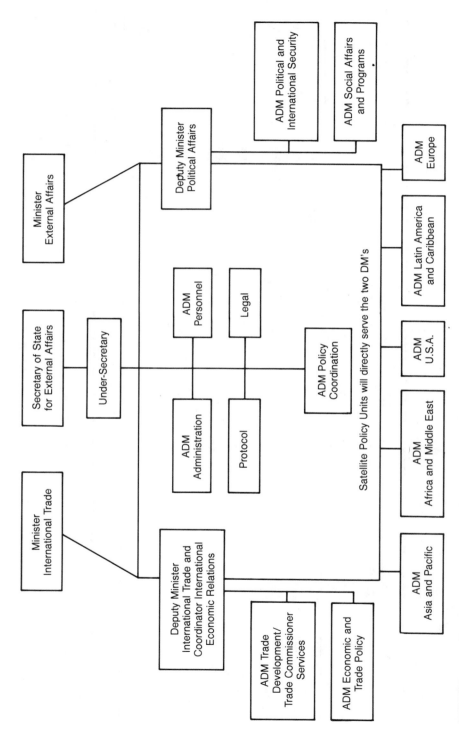

FIGURE 14.1   Department of External Affairs Reorganization

Source: Adapted from Memo, Under-Secretary, Department of External Affairs, "Department of External Affairs: Changes to Organizational Structure," July 8, 1983.

Provincial governments and their agencies and Crown corporations, too, have become important actors in the foreign policy process. While Québec's international activities tend to receive most publicity, nearly all the provinces are active on the international scene. Western provinces concern themselves with such matters as resource exports and tariffs, while Atlantic Canada has interests in fisheries, the law of the sea and offshore resources – all issues with important foreign policy implications. In addition, the provinces are all concerned with federal government policies which affect international trade.

As a response to the diffusion and openness of the contemporary foreign-policy-making process, attempts have been made to coordinate the various departments, groups and policies involved. In 1962 the Glassco Commission, in its review of the DEA, recommended structural changes and suggested periodic reviews and reforms of the department's internal structure. Further studies resulted in a 1970 federal white paper, *Foreign Policy for Canadians,* which led to the establishment of the Interdepartmental Committee on External Relations. It recommended that, to improve coordination, support services of all departments operating programs abroad be incorporated into the Department of External Affairs.

In March 1980, the federal government announced further consolidation of responsibilities. Foreign service officers at the senior executive level from the Department of Industry, Trade and Commerce and the Canadian Employment and Immigration Commission were integrated into the DEA, along with foreign service officers from Employment and Immigration at the operational level and the field staff from the Canadian International Development Agency. The stated purposes of the consolidation were to improve the economy and efficiency of foreign operations without affecting the policy and program development roles of the departments involved; to create a more cohesive and coherent foreign service; to strengthen the role of heads of post; and to improve the career prospects and experiences of foreign service personnel.[13]

Further restructuring of the Department of External Affairs was announced in January 1982. Its aims were to enhance Canada's ability to pursue international markets and to give greater priority to economic matters in the development of foreign policy, or, in the words of the then-Undersecretary of External Affairs, "to give greater weight to economic factors in the design of foreign policy, to ensure the conduct of foreign relations serves Canadian trade objectives,

---

[13]Gordon Osbaldeston, "Reorganizing Canada's External Affairs," *International Journal,* vol. XXXVII, no. 3 (Summer 1982), p. 461. The literature on the Department of External Affairs as an organization has been expanding rapidly. For samples, see W.M. Dobell, "Is External Affairs a Central Agency?" *International Perspectives,* May-July, 1979, pp. 8-11; Daniel Madar and Denis Stairs, "Alone on Killers' Row: The Policy Analysis Group and the Department of External Affairs," *International Journal,* vol. XXXII, no. 4, (August 1977), pp. 727-755; Kim Richard Nossal, "Allison through the (Ottawa) Looking Glass: Bureaucratic Politics and Foreign Policy in a Parliamentary System," *Canadian Public Administration,* vol. 22, no. 4 (Winter, 1979), pp. 610-626; G.A.H. Pearson "Order Out of Chaos? Some Reflections on Foreign Policy Planning in Canada," *International Journal,* vol. XXXII, no. 4 (August 1977), pp. 756-768.

to improve the service offered exporters in an increasingly competitive international marketplace and to ensure policy and program coherence in the conduct of Canada's range of relations with the outside world".[14] Trade policy and trade promotion functions of the Department of Industry, Trade and Commerce were therefore transferred to External Affairs, completing the consolidation.

The prominence of economic objectives was also reflected in the establishment of a three-minister team at External Affairs (see Figure 14-1). The Secretary of State for External Affairs is responsible for the management of the department, integrating its various parts as well as relating the department to the rest of the government. He or she is supported by two other Ministers in the External Affairs portfolio: the Minister of State for International Trade, who is responsible for the department's international trade and export development activities and the day-to-day responsibility for the Export Development Corporation and the Canadian Commercial Corporation; and the Minister of State for External Relations, who supports the Secretary of State in international, social, cultural and humanitarian affairs, relations with francophone Africa as well as other assignments and representational duties which may by required. This triad of Ministers is charged with providing a link between the concerns of government outside and within Canada. At least one member of the team attends every major Cabinet committee.

Concern for coordination is also evident at the senior bureaucratic level of the department (refer again to Figure 14-1). At the head of the department is the Undersecretary, who is supported by two Deputy Ministers. The Deputy Minister (Foreign Policy) is responsible for political geographic bureaus, international cultural matters, defence, arms control, multilateral institutions and security and intelligence. The Deputy Minister (International Trade) assists the Minister for International Trade and coordinates the entire range of interests of all the departments concerned with different aspects of Canada's international economic relations. Of special note is the fact that this DM is responsible for gathering and coordinating not only the ideas and proposals of other government departments, but also those of the private sector and the provinces in the formulation of international trade and economic policy. To ensure coherence within the Department of External Affairs and among the three ministers, the two Deputy Ministers report directly to one of the three Ministers, depending on the subject matter, simultaneously keeping the Undersecretary and each other informed.

The Department of External Affairs is now expected to be responsible for the delivery of all government programs abroad, through a single, unified foreign service. All positions are filled by career civil servants who are normally admitted into the service as junior officers on the basis of open competitive examination.[15] Officials change their postings every two or three years, with occasional intervals

---

[14]Marcel Massé, "Department of External Affairs: Changes to Organizational Structure," memo no. USS-241, Department of External Affairs, July 8, 1983: p. 1.

[15]There are exceptions. For example, the Canadian Ambassador in Paris and High Commissioner in London are often political appointees.

in Ottawa to broaden their experience. The most senior officials, for example, frequently alternate high-level positions in domestic government agencies with ambassadorships abroad.

Parliament and Political Parties

Legislatures and political parties provide an important link between citizens and their government in Western liberal democracies. In Canada, Parliament provides a forum for public debate, while parties mobilize public opinion, coordinate political activity and function as intermediate instruments of political activity for those not elected to office. Therefore, in the realm of foreign policy formulation, Parliament and political parties provide channels through which diverse pressures from the domestic community are brought to bear on the policy process.[16]

For example, Question Period in the House of Commons provides MPs the opportunity to raise foreign policy issues. The House of Commons Standing Committee on External Affairs and National Defence (SCEAND) and the Senate Committee on Foreign Affairs have conducted major reviews of various aspects of Canadian foreign and defence policy in addition to performing their routine function of examining the budgetary estimates of the foreign policy establishment. Special parliamentary task forces and subcommittees have been formed to report on important issues such as Canadian/American relations, North/South relations and others.

However, the role of Parliament and political parties in making foreign policy is constrained by the powers of the government. While Cabinet may take into consideration the anticipated reaction of Parliament in its policy deliberations, only a few cases exist in which formal parliamentary debate can be said to have had a decisive impact on government behaviour in the foreign policy field.[17] Because of the nature of diplomacy, governments have almost exclusive control over information in this area. Requirements of discretion over matters involving national security and relations with foreign countries therefore limit the impact of outside groups and individuals on the foreign policy process: the government's ability to assume policy and make treaties with foreign countries without ratification by Parliament constrains the impact of opposition parties and societal groups.

---

[16]The following discussion is derived from Denis Stairs, "The Foreign Policy of Canada," in James N. Rosenau, Kenneth W. Thompson and Gavin Boyd, eds., *World Politics: An Introduction* (New York: The Free Press, 1976), pp. 187-189.

[17]Important exceptions include the Suez Crisis of October 1956, in which the Liberal government supported American-sponsored efforts to force British, French and Israeli forces to withdraw from captured Egyptian territory; the issue of equipping Canadian fighter planes and missile system with nuclear warheads during Diefenbaker's prime ministership; and the TransCanada PipeLine debate. See D.B. Dewitt and J.J. Kirton, *Canada as a Principal Power*, pp. 171-177; Lawrence Martin, *The Presidents and the Prime Ministers* (Toronto: Doubleday, 1982), Chapter 12; and William Kilbourn, *PipeLine: TransCanada and the Great Debate – A History of Business and Politics* (Toronto: Clarke, Irwin, 1970).

Non-Governmental Actors: Interest Groups, the Media and Public Opinion

Other means of expression of domestic policy interests include representations from private interest groups, the media and popular opinion as measured by polling. How much influence each has varies from issue to issue, yet politicians cannot remain long in office without taking these views into consideration.

Interest groups attempt to reach those who have influence in the foreign-policy-making process, primarily members of the government and appropriate members of the public service.[18] Some groups possess sufficient expertise or political clout to be asked by government to participate in the process. For example, representatives of domestic interest groups are included among the advisors to Canadian delegations attending international conferences.[19] Most groups, however, must gain access to politicians and bureaucrats through meetings, presentation of position briefs, the media and/or mobilization of their constituents.

The number of associational interest groups concerned with foreign policy has grown substantially in recent years. New issues such as nuclear radiation and waste, acid rain, survival of whales and seals and the disruption of Arctic communities by resource development have joined traditional foreign policy matters, including global security and nuclear proliferation.

The media's impact on the foreign policy process is indirect. According to a prominent observer, the press "has little effect upon the substance of foreign policy *per se,* but . . . it exerts a very significant impact upon the day-to-day activities of the men who make it."[20] By providing coverage of external events, reports on specific issues and editorial positions, the media disseminates information and opinion and, at times, prescribes solutions, thereby articulating public and elite foreign policy concerns.

Professional diplomats' feelings toward the proper role of public opinion in foreign-policy-making are critical or ambivalent; many believe that it is not an ap-

---

[18]On the impact of interest groups and the media on foreign policy see Special Issue "Domestic Causes of Canada's Foreign Policy," *International Journal,* vol. XXXIX, no. 1 (Winter 1983-84); Elizabeth Riddell-Dixon, *The Domesic Mosaic: Domestic Groups and Canadian Foreign Policy,* (Toronto: CIIA, 1985); Donald Barry, "Interest Groups and the Foreign Policy Process: The Case of Biafra," in A. Paul Pross, ed., *Pressure Group Behaviour in Canadian Politics* (Toronto: McGraw-Hill Ryerson, 1975), pp. 115-147; and David R. Protheroe, *Imports and Politics: Trade Decision-Making in Canada, 1968-1979* (Montréal: Institute for Research on Public Policy, 1980), pp. 33-54.

[19]The Canadian delegation to the Stockholm Conference on the International Environment in June 1972, for instance, included advisors from the Canadian Labour Congress, the National Indian Brotherhood, the National Youth Conference, the Canadian Federation of Agriculture and the Mining Association of Canada. See Jack Davis, *Conference on the Human Environment: A Report of Canada's Preparation for and the Participation in the United Nations Conference on Human Environment, Stockholm, Sweden, June 1972* (Ottawa, 1972), cited in Denis Stairs, "Public Opinion and External Affairs: Reflections on the Domestication of Canadian Foreign Policy," *International Journal,* vol. XXXIII, no. 1 (Winter 1977-78), pp. 128-149.

[20]Denis Stairs, "The Press and Foreign Policy in Canada," *International Journal,* Vol. XXXI, No. 2 (Spring 1976), p. 238.

propiate guide for the conduct of foreign policy.[21] Because of the constraints diplomats face in the international arena, as well as the complexity of the issues, the impact of public opinion may at times be detrimental. According to Denis Stairs,

> From the professional's traditional perspective the international working environment is ... a world of nuance and subtlety and craft, and certainly no place for the amateur. But nuance, sublety, and craft are not the most obvious characteristics of the constituent public, or of their opinions. Public reactions to foreign policy issues, especially but not solely in political-security contexts, are often one sided, ill informed, transient, fickle, and given, at their worst, to emotional excess.[22]

While public opinion may not have an immediate impact on the determination of policy, it has the capacity to set limits on what policy-makers can do "politically". Policy-makers must take account of latent opinions and anticipate in advance the public's reactions to various policy alternatives. Thus, decision-makers consult public opinion polls not as a source of policy ideas but rather as an indicator of the public's potential response to various policy options. It is in this negative sense of ruling policy options out, that is, determining not so much what the public wants as what it does not want, that public opinion has its most significant influence.[23]

Provinces and Foreign Policy

Provincial governments have a keen interest in the conduct of Canadian foreign policy and have attempted to increase their capabilities to operate internationally.[24] Québec, for example, maintains 25 offices staffed by 300 men and women in fifteen countries on four continents. Such offices are important to provinces which depend heavily on external trade. Provincial governments sponsor trade and cultural missions, receive visiting foreign dignitaries, participate in ongoing multilateral conferences and become involved in joint federal/provincial foreign aid programs to Third World states.

Fields over which provinces have concurrent or exclusive jurisdiction have become increasingly important in the international arena. Such "localization" of international politics into the realm of domestic politics necessitates the inclusion of provincial concerns in the formation of Canada's foreign policy. Within the context of growing provincial power in Canadian federalism, provincial interests are important to the extent that, according to one author, "The range and fre-

---

[21]See Stairs, "Public Opinion and External Affairs," pp. 141-142.

[22]*Ibid.*, p. 142.

[23]*Ibid.*, pp. 133-134.

[24]For a discussion of the role of provinces in international affairs, see Ronald G. Atkey, "The Role of Provinces in International Affairs," *International Journal*, vol. XXVI, no. 1 (Winter 1970-71), pp. 249-273; P.R. Johannson, "Provincial International Activities," *International Journal*, vol. XXXIII, no. 2 (Spring 1978), pp. 357-378; and David B. Dewitt and John J. Kirton, *Canada as a Principal Power*, pp. 186-192.

quency of provincial international activity is now sufficient to complicate the design and conduct of Canadian foreign policy, indeed, to frustrate central control over foreign policy in some areas."[25]

Increased international activity on the part of provincial governments has not been without periods of confrontation and conflict. This is not surprising, given that matters of national interest in a country as large and disparate as Canada are in question. The federal government, presiding over a varied populace, is sometimes faced with incompatible demands.

Federal/provincial conflict in this field is exacerbated by the absence of a clear delineation of constitutional authority regarding treaties and international relations. Section 132 of the *Constitution Act,* for example, refers only to the implementation of treaties affecting the British Empire. Moreover, the range of powers vested in the provinces necessitates at least some measure of involvement in foreign policy. Consequently, there has been, and to some extent continues to be, both legal and political debate over the proper role of the provinces in foreign affairs.[26]

Those who argue for independent provincial international competence believe that the Constitution's silence on foreign relations implies that the provinces have a legal right to negotiate and sign treaties on provincial subjects. Support for this position is based on a number of factors.[27] First, the provinces were judicially conceded the exclusive right to implement treaties in the 1936 *Labour Convention* case. Since treaty-making and treaty implementation are virtually inseparable, it is argued that if provincial governments can legally implement provisions of treaties, they should also be able to negotiate them.

Second, international law, specifically the 1966 International Law Commission of the United Nations, adds support to the concept of provincial competence. According to Article 3(2): "States members of a federal union may possess a capacity to conclude treaties if such capacity is admitted by the federal constitution and within the limits laid down."[28] The silence of the Constitution is again assumed to be supportive of the provincial case.

Third, the experiences of other federal states where component units have been allowed to make treaties are noted as precedents. For example, treaty-making powers exist in the sub-units in Switzerland, the Federal Republic of Germany and the U.S.S.R..

Finally, efforts of various Québec governments to obtain recognition of their special linguistic and cultural status are claimed to have provided precedents strengthening the position of the provinces. For example, in 1964 Québec concluded an educational exchange agreement with France without the participation of or prior consultation with Ottawa. In November 1965 Canada

---

[25]P.R. Johannson, *op. cit.*, p. 357.

[26]See R. McGregor Dawson, *The Government of Canada*, 5th ed., rev. by N. Ward (Toronto: University of Toronto Press, 1970) *passim.*

[27]The various arguments are taken from Ronald G. Atkey, "The Role of Provinces . . .".

[28]*Ibid.*, p. 262.

and France signed a cultural agreement and arranged an exchange of letters recognizing possible *ententes* providing for educational and cultural exchanges between France and the provinces of Canada. However, that same month, Québec and France concluded an *entente* on cultural cooperation without reference to the Ottawa/France agreement. Although the federal government gave its consent to both the 1964 and 1965 exchanges, the agreements were initiated by Québec alone and implemented by Québec officials. Such actions are said to be creating a *de facto* provincial competence in international affairs.

Advocates of exclusive federal competence in all international matters view the situation differently.[29] The prerogative of treaty-making power for Canada, it is argued, was vested exclusively in the Queen in 1867, as stated in section 9 of the *BNA Act*. Through a process of evolution from 1871 to 1939, direct foreign affairs power devolved to Canada to be exercised by the Governor General. At no time during this period did the provinces acquire treaty-making power. Rather, as evidenced by the new letters patent issued to the Governor General by the Crown in 1947 and the *Seals Act* of 1939, the federal government was given all powers previously exercised by the British Crown.

Several Supreme Court judgements also support the federalist position. For example, the 1936 *Labour Convention* case, before it was appealed to the Judicial Committee of the Privy Council, drew comments from several Supreme Court justices, including Chief Justice Duff, that the authority to enter into international agreements resided exclusively in the federal government even on matters of provincial legislative competence. However, since the case concerned the power to implement and not negotiate treaties, the JCPC did not consider this issue relevant.

Finally, support for the exclusivity of federal treaty-making power is derived from the international law of recognition. Advocates of this position argue that, during Canada's evolution to independence, only the federal government, not the provincial governments, was recognized as having responsibility for foreign affairs.

Thus, both sides have recourse to legal precedents which make it difficult if not impossible to arrive at a legal solution by unilateral action. The dispute has necessitated a more functional approach that recognizes the concerns of both levels of government; it is this approach that has been adopted by the federal government. Reacting to the demands of Québec, the federal government issued what it perceived to be the proper international role for the provinces:

1. The provinces have no treaty-making powers, but they do have the right to enter into private commercial contracts with foreign governments, as

---

[29]For a discussion of the exclusive federal competence view, see the federal government's white paper, Canada, Department of External Affairs, *Federalism and International Relations* (Ottawa: Queen's Printer, February 1968) and its supplement, *Federalism and International Conferences on Education* (Ottawa: Queen's Printer, 1968). As well, see Ontario Advisory Committee on Confederation, *Confederation Challenged: Background Papers and Reports*, Vols. I and II (Toronto: 1967, 1970).

well as to make bureaucratic agreements of a non-binding nature with foreign governments.

2. The provinces may open offices in foreign countries in pursuit of their legitimate needs and interests in that country, so long as the office only engages in arrangements of a non-binding nature.

3. The provinces claim the right to be involved in the formulation stages of treaty-making activities when the subject matter of the treaty falls within provincial legislative competence.

4. The provinces may be included in Canadian delegations attending international gatherings as well as playing a role in formulating and enunciating the Canadian position, when the subject matter falls within provincial legislative competence.[30]

While the federal government's purpose was to prevent provincial government initiatives when possible, jurisdictional realities necessitated a framework which would accommodate provincial interests to some extent. Ottawa's policy of primacy in external affairs has therefore been tempered by accommodation, allowing provinces to participate within Canadian international delegations.

It is evident, then, that foreign-policy-making in Canada is becoming ever more diffuse. While the Department of External Affairs remains an important bureaucratic component, other departments, responding to demands from groups they represent and to the complexity of foreign issues which blurs the boundaries between domestic and foreign, have become more prominent. Increased activity of non-governmental actors continues the trend. The response of the federal government has been to initiate bureaucratic reorganization and to continue to seek accommodation of regional interests as expressed by provincial governments, in an attempt to provide a coherent and efficient foreign policy.

A BRIEF HISTORY OF CANADIAN FOREIGN POLICY

For historical and political reasons, Canadian foreign policy has always been directed predominantly towards Europe. Political relations, defence and economic policies have therefore all developed certain basic continuities. Long-standing defence ties, which are considered in detail later in the chapter, are with the United States and Western Europe through NATO and NORAD. Bilateral political and economic relations are strongest with the US, the Commonwealth, Western Europe and the French language community. Multilateral relations are primarily conducted through the United Nations and its related agencies. Before examining each of these continuities in more detail, we present an outline of Canadian foreign policy since Confederation.

Canada's economic lifeline is foreign trade. Economic relations are in turn inseparable from vital international political and security relations. Canada's im-

---

[30]P.R. Johannson, *op. cit.* pp. 361-362.

age and its relationships abroad on all these fronts have changed dramatically over the years. Three fairly distinct periods of dominant political tendencies are evident in Canadian foreign policy since Confederation: imperialism, isolationism and internationalism.[31]

The idea of imperialism dominated the early years of Canadian history. In concrete terms it consisted of overt sentimental and legal attachment to the British Empire and required dual loyalty to Canada and Empire. As part of that larger political organization, Canada was independent in domestic policy only. Until the 20th century Canadian negotiations with foreign countries were conducted by the British Foreign Office in London. General recognition of Canadian autonomy grew gradually as the country's interests and activities in the world expanded. The Canadian contribution to the war effort during World War I was a landmark in the evolution of an independent role in international affairs. Nearly one percent of the entire Canadian population was killed in that war. As a consequence, Canadians were no longer content to participate in wars in which their government had no voice. Nor were political leaders prepared to accept any longer the exacerbation of the schism between French and English Canadians arising from the demand for dual loyalty to Canada and the Empire. By the end of the war, Prime Minister Sir Robert Borden had demanded separate Canadian representation at the peace conference and separate membership in the newly formed League of Nations. The stage was set for the transformation of the Empire into the Commonwealth.

In 1926, at the culmination of a series of Imperial Conferences, the committee chairman, the Earl of Balfour, announced an agreement to award Canada sovereignty in international negotiations and affairs. The Balfour Declaration stated that the dominions were "autonomous communities within the British Empire, equal in status and in no way subordinate to one another in any aspect of their domestic or external affairs, though united by a common allegiance to the Crown, and freely associated as members of the British Commonwealth of Nations".[32] The intent of this declaration was enshrined in the 1931 Statute of Westminster, which formally ended the British Empire. Canadian diplomatic relations with the United States, the Commonwealth and other countries were established largely throughout the following decade and a half.

As imperialism faded as the primary concept in Canada's foreign policy it was replaced by isolationism, a view which reflected deep resentment of European politics and its high cost in terms of Canadian lives. Above all, isolationism implied non-involvement in European politics and entangling alliances. Canadian Prime Ministers regarded membership in the League of Nations as an important symbol of Canadian autonomy but sought to minimize Canadian obligations under its collective security provisions. They generally followed the British and French policies of appeasement toward the expansionary policies of

---

[31]See Kim Richard Nossal, *The Politics of Canadian Foreign Policy*, Chapter 2.

[32]G.P. de T. Glazebrook, *A History of Canadian External Relations*, rev. ed., Vol. 2, *In the Empire of the World 1914-1933* (Toronto: McClelland and Stewart, 1966), pp. 90-91.

Germany, Italy and Japan. This period of isolationism ended abruptly in September 1939 when Germany invaded Poland.

By the end of World War II, Canadian leaders had decided that isolationism was not the answer to avoiding war. Internationalism, with its emphasis on building strong international institutions as a forum for regulating or managing conflict between states, replaced isolationism as the dominant theme in Canadian foreign policy. An important feature of Canada's new internationalist stance was that the country became firmly aligned with the United States and Western Europe against the Soviet Union and the Communist Bloc. Since that time, internationalism within these parameters has provided a fundamental continuity in Canadian foreign policy.

The key Canadian political figures who pursued internationalism as a means of defusing the clash of interests that lead to war were Louis St. Laurent, Secretary of State for External Affairs in 1946 before becoming Prime Minister in 1948, and Lester Pearson, Undersecretary of State in 1946, Foreign Minister in 1948, and Prime Minister in 1963. The change of direction which they initiated was dramatic. The years immediately following the war saw strong Canadian commitment to and participation in the United Nations and its specialized agencies. At the same time, Pearson played an important role in structuring the modern Commonwealth and formulating the admission of republics like India. But the most decisive move to internationalism was the government's willingness in 1949 to join a peace-time military alliance, the North Atlantic Treaty Organization. International commitments mushroomed. Canadian troops were sent to Korea in the 1950-53 war. There followed a very active Canadian role in the United Nations peace-keeping operations – service in two truce supervisory commissions in Indochina and initiatives in the Suez Crisis of 1956 – for which Lester Pearson was awarded the Nobel Peace Prize.

In the 1960s, Canadian politicians debated the contentious issue of whether or not to accept nuclear weapons. John Diefenbaker, then Prime Minister, was reluctant to admit nuclear warheads onto Canadian soil. His minority government was defeated on a vote of confidence in the House of Commons, and in the ensuing 1963 election the nuclear issue was paramount. The Liberals, under Pearson, promised to accept nuclear warheads and were returned to power with a minority government.

The strongly internationalist brand of foreign policy was dampened somewhat when Pierre Trudeau became Prime Minister in 1968. He demanded "a severe reassessment" of Canadian foreign policy, which he felt had been too much determined by defence policy to the detriment of Canadian economic interests.[33] He believed that it had been designed for times of cold war and bipolarity between the two superpowers and questioned the relevance of NATO and NORAD

---

[33]The rising tensions in Canadian Foreign Policy in the early 1980s are well covered in Adam Bromke and Kim Richard Nossal, "Tensions in Canada's Foreign Policy," *Foreign Affairs*, vol. 62, no. 2, (Winter 1983-84), pp. 335-353. The short-lived Clark government changed very little in the continuities of Canadian foreign policy. See David Cox, "Leadership Change and Innovation in Canadian Foreign Policy: The 1979 Progressive Conservative Government," *International Journal*, vol. XXXVII, no. 4 (August 1982), pp. 555-583.

in a period of relaxation and multipolarity. Trudeau considered, too, that peace-keeping was overplayed, and that Canada should, in general, have a more modest role.

In 1970, the government white paper *Foreign Policy for Canadians,* the only comprehensive review of Canadian foreign policy during the Trudeau period, was published. It brought a so-called "fresh" approach. Not unexpectedly, it urged a reduction of commitments abroad, the adoption of a more modest role than that of a "middle power" and the placement of greater emphasis on the trade component of foreign policy.

Meanwhile, concrete measures were taken to reduce Canada's commitment abroad. Troop levels in Europe were cut, the defence budget was slashed and steps were taken to reduce Canada's nuclear role. In 1972, another document was tabled outlining the so-called "Three Options" that were possible for Canada, given the premises of the 1970 white paper. Canada, it said, could opt for the *status quo,* more economic integration with the US or a long-term strategy to reduce Canadian vulnerability to economic pressure from the United States.[34] The government chose the third option, and adopted measures to monitor and regulate foreign economic involvement in Canada through the Foreign Investment Review Agency. Initiatives were also taken to encourage diversification of trade from the United States to the European Community and Japan. Europe in particular was wooed, and a weak contractual link was formed. However, the European Community would not discriminate against the US and other non-Europeans by granting Canada special status. The oil crises and a general decline in European economies by the end of the 1970s dampened the idea of strengthening links between Europe and Canada. Efforts to diversify markets in Europe failed to mature, while trade with the United States continued to rise.

In spite of the stated intent of the 1970 foreign policy document to reduce commitments abroad, Canada did not abandon the fundamentals of post-war internationalism. After the 1980 election, foreign policy again appeared high on the political agenda. To give impetus to his Third Option policy, Trudeau introduced the National Energy Program, a scheme to make Canada self-sufficient in energy and to Canadianize the oil and gas industry. He also announced that FIRA would be strengthened. With a surge of international zeal he espoused a North/South dialogue to work toward a more equitable distribution of the world's resources among rich and poor nations. Although there was one international conference at Cancun, the idea progressed no further, partly because of the global recession and partly as a result of the difficulty of getting beyond discussion to concrete action.[35]

In the area of defence policy, one of the acts of the last Trudeau government was to agree to allow the United States to test an unarmed Cruise missile

---

[34]Don Munton and Dean Swanson, "Rise and Fall of the Third Option," in B. Tomlin, ed., *Canada's Foreign Policy* (Toronto: Methuen, 1978), pp. 175-213; and Harald von Riekhoff, "The Third Option in Canadian Foreign Policy," in *ibid,* pp. 87-109.

[35]For Canada's relations with the Third World generally see Peyton V. Lyon and Tareq Y. Ismael, eds., *Canada and the Third World* (Toronto: Macmillan, 1976). On North-South see, for example, Kim Richard Nossal, "Personal Diplomacy and National Behaviour: Trudeau's North-South Initiatives," *Dalhousie Review,* vol. 62 (Summer 1982), pp. 278-91.

over Canadian territory. The implications of this decision are discussed in the section on defence below. In 1982-83, as his departing gesture in foreign affairs, Trudeau took a more activist stance with a new peace initiative. Uneasy with President Ronald Reagan's confrontational rhetoric against the USSR, he hoped to bridge the chasm between the two superpowers with proposals to facilitate discussions. Trudeau visited several European capitals with his proposals, but nothing substantial came of the initiative.

When Brian Mulroney became Prime Minister in 1984, foreign policy issues were major political topics for the first time in nearly two decades. Not since Canadians had confronted the question of whether or not to accept nuclear weapons in the early 1960s had there been such widespread public debate over Canada's security role in NATO and what the Canadian contribution to North American defence should be.

The remainder of this chapter is devoted to outlining and assessing the four basic components of foreign policy: trade policy, activity in international organizations, bilateral relations and defence policy.

CANADIAN TRADE POLICY

Foreign trade is vital to Canadian interests. Canada possesses a low ratio of population to land and resources and is by necessity, therefore, one of the largest trading nations in the world. With a population of only 25 million, the domestic market is too small to sustain flourishing industries, with the result that nearly 31 percent of the GNP depends on exports.[36] Most of those exports come from primary industries based on natural resources, of which Canada has an abundance. Canada has three main kinds of natural resources. One is agricultural land, which climatic and soil conditions make amenable to cultivating crops and raising livestock. It is limited to the southernmost part of the country which, particularly in central Canada, is steadily being encroached upon by industrial development and urban sprawl. The second category of natural resources is comprised of those which are non-renewable, such as mineral deposits. Canada is one of the leading mineral exporting countries, particularly of crude petroleum, natural gas, iron ore, nickel and copper, in that order. The third type consists of renewable resources, of which wood, fish and fur are, or have been, particularly important to Canada's economic growth.

This brief outline serves to indicate that the Canadian economy is bizarre. Basically, Canada exports primary goods and imports secondary or manufactured goods. Most Canadians live and work in urban, industrialized areas, but it is agricultural products, lumber and mineral resources which continue to provide

---

[36]"Questions about Canadian trade policy assumed a new importance in the 1980s. For discussion of the topic see Rodney de C. Grey, *Trade Policy in the 1980s* (Montréal: C.D. Howe Institute, 1981); and Special Issue on "Trade Policy," *International Perspectives*, March/April 1984. The Canadian Government also assessed the trade environment in *A Review of Canadian Trade Policy: A Background Document to Canadian Trade Policy for the 1980s* (Ottawa: Minister of Supply and Services, 1983), p. 3.

the bulk of our exports and pay for imported manufactured goods. Yet only about 7 percent of the population is employed in primary industries.

During the 1970s, while defence issues were largely dormant in Canadian politics, the successive Trudeau governments concentrated on elevating other issues in foreign policy. The first step was the foreign policy white paper of 1970. In the ensuing years, the so-called Third Option was pursued, and the Department of External Affairs was restructured to provide better coordination and a higher profile for foreign trade policy. Then, in August 1983, for the first time, the Department issued two related documents dealing with Canadian trade policy. One, *Canadian Trade Policy in the 1980s,* was a discussion paper; the other, *A Review of Canadian Trade Policy,* a background paper.[37] Both attempted to link trade policy to other government concerns such as monetary policies, taxation, subsidies, transport and labour policies. Unlike the Third Option, which had called for building markets in countries other than the United States, these documents argued that Canada should promote both multilateral and regional or bilateral initiatives, stressing particularly the need to develop bilateral relations with the US.

Canadian trade is conducted on a bilateral basis, and requires careful day-to-day management of issues that arise between Canada and her main trading partners. However, the fact that the contractual framework for most of Canada's bilateral trade is provided by the General Agreement on Tariffs and Trade (GATT) illustrates the important multilateral dimension of international economic relations.

The GATT

After the Second World War, the US, Britain and Canada were the principal proponents of a new trading order. The end result in 1947 was the GATT, which continues to work toward establishing a new trading order based on reciprocity, non-discrimination and multilateralism.[38] It covers over 80 percent of world trade and includes most major industrialized countries, Canada among them. The USSR, China, East Germany, Venezuela, Mexico and most Middle East oil producing countries are not signatories. The GATT is both a treaty and an institution. As a treaty, it sets out a code of rules for the conduct of trade; as an institution, it oversees the application of the trade rules and provides a forum in

---

[37] *Canadian Trade Policy for the 1980s, A Discussion Paper op. cit.*; *A Review of Canadian Trade Policy op. cit..*

[38] For discussion about Canada and the world economy see A.F.W. Plumptre, *Three Decades of Decision: Canada and the World Monetary System, 1944-75* (Toronto: McClelland and Stewart, 1980); Robert Bothwell, Ian Drummond and John English, *Canada Since 1945: Power, Politics and Provincialism* (Toronto: University of Toronto Press, 1981); and Donald J. Daly, *Canada in an Uncertain World Economic Environment* (Montréal: Institute for Research on Public Policy, 1982). On general international economic organizations see Joan Edelman Spero, *The Politics of International Economic Relations* (New York: St. Martin's Press, 1977); and C. Fred Bergsten and Lawrence B. Krause, eds., *World Politics and International Economics* (Washington: Brookings Institution, 1975).

which countries can discuss trade problems and negotiate reductions in trade barriers.

The main benefit of the GATT for Canada is that it provides a contractual basis for Canada/US trade relations while facilitating the expansion of trade relations with other countries. As a signatory of the GATT, Canada can negotiate more easily with its powerful southern neighbour over basic resource needs. Between the formation of the GATT in 1947 and the time of writing, there have been seven multilateral trade negotiating conferences, the last of them in Tokyo in 1979.

Canada and the World Economy

World trade grew steadily after the GATT was founded and then slowed in the 1970s, with the OPEC countries showing most rapid growth during that decade. In 1981, for the first time since the GATT was established, there was no real growth in world trade. In recent years, the world economy has demonstrated three significant characteristics: slow international market growth, financial instability and increased international competitiveness. Financial markets have been volatile, with developing countries building enormous debt loads which threaten to disrupt the international economic system.

The changing structure of the world economy has seriously affected the Canadian economy. There has been a pronounced shift in industrial power towards Japan, Europe and the so-called "Newly Industrialized Countries" (NICs). Major oil exporting countries have retained their vastly increased purchasing power. New technologies are developing rapidly and forcing industries in developed countries to adapt to increasingly competitive conditions or be left behind as

TABLE 14.3   Production and Trade of Twelve Leading Developed Countries, 1980

	Production[1]	Exports of Goods and Services		Exports of Goods	
	(Billions of $US)	(Billions of $US)	(Percent of GDP)	(Billions of $US)	(Percent of GDP)
United States	2587.1	260.8	10.0	216.7	8.4
Japan	1040.0	145.1	14.0	129.2	12.4
West Germany	819.1	225.1	27.5	192.9	23.6
France	651.9	146.1	22.4	111.3	17.1
United Kingdom	522.9	148.5	28.4	115.1	22.0
Italy	394.0	99.5	25.2	77.7	19.7
Canada	253.3	74.3	29.3	65.0	25.6
Spain	211.1	32.9	15.6	20.7	9.8
Netherlands	167.6	89.0	53.1	74.0	44.1
Australia	140.0	25.4	18.1	22.0	15.7
Belgium/Luxembourg	121.1	77.2	63.8	64.6	53.4

[1]Gross Domestic Product

Source: As printed in *A Review of Canadian Trade Policy* (Ottawa: Supply and Services, 1983), p. 22.

standard technologies are taken over by developing countries with low labour costs.

There are some disturbing signs about the capability of Canada to adapt to this new world situation. While the volume of Canadian trade has continued to grow, its share of total world trade has steadily declined in the post-war years.[39] During the 1970s especially, Canada was unable to hold its own in world markets as an exporter of capital goods. During the same period the European Community became the world's largest trading bloc, its external trade equalling the combined shares of the United States and Japan.[40] While Germany and Japan in particular made spectacular gains in their share of world exports, other countries, including Canada, the US and the UK, saw their shares of world trade decline considerably. In relative terms, Canada's share of world trade underwent the largest decline among industrialized countries. Among the developed market economy countries, Canada ranked seventh in output and eighth in export of goods in 1980, as shown in Table 14-3.

INTERNATIONAL AND MULTILATERAL ORGANIZATIONS

Canada and the United Nations

Canada played a central role in creating the United Nations and in directing its evolution as an international organization. Sponsorship of the United Nations by the Canadian government demonstrated the radical change from the pre-war policy of isolationism to post-war internationalism as a means of avoiding war. Both Louis St. Laurent, who became Secretary of State for External Affairs in 1946 under Mackenzie King, and Lester Pearson, who followed in that position when St. Laurent became Prime Minister two years later, were avowed internationalists. Pearson wrote in his memoirs "Everything I learned during the war confirmed and strengthened my view as a Canadian that our foreign policy must not be timid or fearful of commitments but activist in accepting international responsibility."[41] The United Nations seemed the natural medium for bringing nations together to promote peace.

As president of the UN General Assembly, Lester Pearson was responsible for introducing one of the UN's most important innovations: the peace-keeping force. The UN Charter provided for a fighting army, but one was never created. The non-fighting army, to which Canada contributes troops, is designed to maintain a buffer zone in trouble spots. It continues to be of immense value in areas such as Cyprus.

Initially, the UN had 57 charter members, and in the decade of the 1950s Canada was a major participant. But the club was too restrictive. In 1955 Paul

---

[39]*Canadian Trade Policy for the 1980s*, p. 4.

[40]*A Review of Canadian Trade Policy*, p. 19.

[41]Lester B. Pearson, *Mike: The Memoirs of Lester Pearson, Vol. I: 1897-1948* (Toronto: University of Toronto Press, 1972), p. 283.

Martin, Chairman of the Canadian UN delegation, persuaded the UN Security Council to agree to a package deal for accepting new member states. New members flooded in, and today Canada is no longer a principal player, but merely one of 159 countries in an institution that is no longer dominated by Western democratic powers.

In recent years, the UN has been severely criticized, particularly by the United States, because the large membership with equal voting rights among very unequal nation-states restricts what the organization can accomplish. The General Assembly is too often used as a platform for public denunciations of nations by their enemies rather than as a forum for rational debate of the issues. One of Canada's former ambassadors to the UN, William Barton, described the situation as follows: "What we have is a UN where 125 weak powers pay two percent of the budget and a small percentage of the nations have the muscle, pay the bills and call the shots because they have the real power. So a dispute between small nations and big ones becomes a struggle against people with real power."[42]

However, no other organization has arisen to replace the UN as a forum for the discussion of world problems. Canada has been involved at the UN in several significant issue areas during recent years, including the Law of the Sea, the North/South dialogue between rich and poor nations, human rights and chemical warfare. Canada is also a strong supporter of the UN's many specialized multilateral agencies – the World Health Organization, the International Labour Organization, International Postal Union and the International Monetary Fund, among others – which have earned considerable respect throughout the world. Another agency, the International Civil Aviation Organization, has its headquarters in Montréal. These agencies are all working to improve the general quality of life, particularly in the large number of new nations represented at the UN, which look to it as a source of security and development assistance.

The rather tarnished contemporary image of the UN may be a result of exaggerated expectations of what it can accomplish. John Holmes, one of Canada's leading authorities on the UN, summarized the situation in this way, "When people worry whether the UN has lived up to the ideals of the Charter, in some ways it's the wrong question. Rather than see whether it has been able to carry out a mandate carved in stone it may be better to ask whether it has been able to grow and fit in with changing circumstances... To a great extent it has."[43]

The Commonwealth

As noted above, at Confederation Canada was part of the British Empire, exercising autonomy in domestic policy but dependent on Britain in foreign affairs. The First World War was the catalyst in the attainment of complete autonomy for Canada and in the transformation of the Empire into the Commonwealth. The transition was achieved at a succession of Imperial Conferences in the 1920s

---

[42]*The Toronto Star*, November 20, 1982.
[43]John Holmes, quoted in *The Toronto Star*, November 20, 1982.

which culminated with the Balfour declaration in 1926. The dominions within the British Empire were equal, autonomous communities "united by a common allegiance to the Crown, and freely associated as members of the British Commonwealth of Nations."[44] This sentiment was enshrined in the Statute of Westminster in 1931 which formally laid the old Empire to rest. The Commonwealth at that time consisted of Britain, Australia, Canada, Newfoundland, the Irish Free State, the Union of South Africa and New Zealand. Now, just over five decades later, it numbers 45 member states and embraces more than a billion people and about a quarter of the Earth's surface. Louis St. Laurent and Lester Pearson played an important role in the evolution of this radically new Commonwealth. Pearson particularly was a key figure in negotiating an acceptable formula for admission of new republics – a development which changed the essentially Anglocentric focus of the Commonwealth association.[45] Canada has consistently encouraged the advancement and strengthening of the association as a vehicle for practical cooperation between member nations.

At the practical level, Commonwealth heads of government meet regularly every two years and sponsor scholarships, various fields of technical cooperation and the Commonwealth games. There are no binding rules of membership, and decisions at these meetings are by consensus rather than votes. Perhaps the most valuable feature of Commonwealth meetings, however, is simply the opportunity for heads of state to meet relatively informally and discuss a variety of vital common issues such as human rights and intra-Commonwealth aid. For instance, at the meeting in Lusaka in 1979, in an atmosphere of civil war, the issue was how to end Rhodesia's illegal white supremacist regime. The Commonwealth meeting provided a forum for negotiations, and its result was an independent Zimbabwe. As Prime Minister Joe Clark put it at the time, the informality limited posturing and encouraged frankness; whereas the "economic summits allow leaders to appear to be addressing problems, to make statements...the Commonwealth meetings, I believe, allow leaders to try to resolve important issues."[46]

La Francophonie

In recent years the French language community of the world has been moving somewhat sporadically towards building its own organization similar to the British Commonwealth. Under Lester Pearson's leadership and especially under Pierre Trudeau, the Canadian federal government encouraged strengthening Canada's ties with francophone countries, mainly in the form of strengthening representation and development aid in these nations through multilateral programs and organizations such as the Agency for Cultural and Technical Corpora-

---

[44]G.P. de T. Glazebrook, *op. cit.*, pp. 90-91.

[45]See John Holmes, *Shaping of Peace*, Vol. 2 (Toronto: University of Toronto Press, 1982), Chapter 8.

[46]*The Globe and Mail*, Toronto, September 30, 1981.

tion. The Agency programs centre on three main areas: development, education and scientific and technical cooperation. The issue of Québec's participation as distinct from that of Canada has occasionally caused overt hostility between the respective governments when the federal government interpreted Québec's actions as a challenge to its primacy in foreign policy. However, since 1971 Québec has had "participating government" status in the Agency, a privilege that was also extended to New Brunswick in 1977.

Economic Summits

Canada belongs to many multilateral organizations concerned with the global economy and development. The best known and most prestigious of them are the Economic Summits, annual gatherings of the seven largest industrialized democracies and the Commission of the European Community. The Summits, which began in 1975 at Rambouillet in France, have taken on a semi-permanent character, although there is no permanent secretariat. They have become huge media events, but despite potential grandstanding they provide the opportunity for leaders to discuss trade issues and international economic topics.

The meetings are particularly important to Canada for several reasons. First of all, the Economic Summits provide recognition of status; political leaders want to be part of this elite group. But more importantly, Canada has a major stake in the economic relationships among the "Big Seven". Of the seven, Canada is the most affected by the economic policies of the United States. It is also the only country which does not have either a large domestic market or membership in a formal trading bloc.

Still, many observers believe that the Summits are meaningless exercises. A more balanced view is that they are significant, but that their importance is easy to exaggerate. As Prime Minister Margaret Thatcher remarked in her pre-summit briefing in 1984, "Blessed is he that expecteth nothing and he shall not be disappointed."[47]

Canada and the OECD

Another important international economic organization of which Canada is a member is the Organization for Economic Cooperation and Development (OECD). Established in Paris in 1961, the OECD replaced an organization of Western European countries which had been set up to coordinate and assist the efforts to reconstruct their war-shattered economies and administer the Marshall Plan. The OECD is a forum in which two dozen advanced industrialized nations

---

[17]Quoted in *The Globe and Mail*, Toronto, June 8, 1984. The global economy is described in David H. Blake and Robert S. Walters, *The Politics of Global Economic Relations*, 2nd ed., (Englewood Cliffs: Prentice-Hall, 1976). For a general description of international doctrines and decisions as they apply to Canada see Dewitt and Kirton, *op. cit.*

consult in major fields of economic activity, including agriculture, the environment, industry and multinational enterprises. Development assistance is also discussed.

An important feature of the OECD is that it brings together government officials and representatives from non-governmental bodies such as business and labour unions at the international level. The Canadian provincial governments send representatives to OECD meetings when subjects of particular interest to them are under discussion.

Canada and Foreign Aid: CIDA and the IDRC

Canada's official development assistance is channelled through the Canadian International Development Agency (CIDA), the International Development Research Centre (IDRC), Petro-Canada, which helps third world nations in energy planning and institutions such as the World Bank. CIDA operates two types of assistance programs, multilateral and bilateral, but Canada's major contribution is in the form of bilateral aid. Multilateral assistance programs are directed mainly toward the UN and its affiliated agencies and the World Bank.

The bilateral programs are controversial and have often drawn criticism because of their self-serving nature. The point of contention is that Canada's bilateral aid requirements are designed to tie aid to helping Canadian industries. There are various ways of doing so, but in this circumstance the implications of "tied" aid are that recipients of the aid are required to buy goods and services from Canada even if they are more expensive than those available from other countries. Beneficiaries of CIDA bilateral aid must spend 80 percent of the funds they receive in Canada, and their purchases must have at least two-thirds Canadian content. When all forms of development assistance are considered, 65 percent of Canada's aid in 1982 was tied. In that year, CIDA President Marcel Massé defended this type of bilateral aid, arguing that Canadian goods and services may be expensive but are of high quality. Moreover, procurement in Canada creates jobs and assists Canadian industry, thereby increasing support for foreign aid. "Development is just not charity any more,"[48] he asserted.

The sad truth about foreign aid is that most programs are undertaken for reasons which are not solely humanitarian; as a result, assistance often does not go to the countries that need it most. Generally, aid is designed to help the donor achieve certain political objectives: for example, to create political stability in the recipient country for strategic motives, to obtain or support allies or to influence the recipient's domestic or foreign policies.[49] However, by international standards, a very high percentage of Canadian aid money is reaching low-income countries; 37 percent in 1978, compared to 22 percent for the US, 26 percent for Japan and 23 percent for West Germany.

---

[48] *The Citizen*, Ottawa, May 14, 1982.

[49] See K.J. Holsti, *op. cit.*, pp. 231-239 for a discussion of this problem.

In 1983, the Canadian government spent 0.46 percent of the GNP, well over a billion dollars, on foreign aid. Asia was by far the largest recipient, followed by francophone Africa, Commonwealth Africa, Latin America and the Commonwealth Caribbean. The UN recommended in 1981 that in order to prevent large-scale global starvation and privation the rich nations should pledge 0.7 percent of their GNP to foreign aid by 1985. The Liberal government in its spring budget of 1984 reiterated its intention to meet that goal by 1990, but this date was changed to 1995 by the Mulroney government in late 1984. The Liberal government had also announced that half of the increase would be diverted to a new Aid/Trade Fund.[50] This proposal required CIDA to work in partnership with the Export Development Corporation and increase the ties attached to development loans. Inevitably, it raised questions about why CIDA does not switch more bilateral programs to lines of credit so that developing countries can buy what they want where they want.

Another perennial problem of Canada's foreign aid program is that Parliament has no effective way to scrutinize CIDA's budget. As the rules now stand, it can be examined only during the few days set aside to study the entire estimates for the Department of External Affairs; the result is that there is no thorough Parliamentary investigation of CIDA or its aid programs.

While CIDA administers development assistance, another small agency sponsors research. When it became evident in the 1960s that developing countries lacked the research capacities and facilities to identify and define their own problems and find solutions, the IDRC was set up in Canada to meet that need. Devoted to research, it is separate from CIDA, and more isolated from political pressures. About 3 percent of Canada's official development assistance goes to the IDRC.[51] Although it is financed by the Canadian government, an effort has been made to give the IDRC an international character. Half of the board of governors and one-third of its staff are non-Canadians. The IDRC does no research itself, but provides aid and scientific advice to help countries solve their own problems. Most of the IDRC's work is in rural areas, with an emphasis on such basic matters as agriculture, health, nutrition and hygiene.

Canada and the OAS

One further international organization to which Canada could belong, but does not, is the Organization of American States (OAS), the main institution which unites the nation-states of the western hemisphere. It was formed in 1948 from the Pan-American Union at a time when Canada was primarily concerned with seeking security through NATO and the UN and did not seriously consider joining the organization. The issue of Canadian membership first became significant in the early 1960s. Proponents argued that Canada should accept responsibility for being a member of the hemisphere and by so doing establish prestige in the region and increase trade opportunities. Antagonists warned that if Canada did join the OAS the country would soon become embroiled in disputes between the

---

[50]*The Globe and Mail*, Toronto, April 20, 1984.

[51]*The Citizen*, Ottawa, March 16, 1982.

United States and Latin America. The latter view was accepted by the government and the issue was not seriously raised again as a foreign policy option until the 1980s.[52]

Although Canada has never been a full member of the organization, it has had "permanent observer" status since 1972, a position which has provided a limited, but practical, forum for communication and cooperation with OAS members. Canada also participates actively in six principal agencies of the OAS, including the Pan-American Health Organization and the Inter-American Institute for Cooperation in Agriculture.

Over time, the arguments for joining the OAS have become stronger, although the political thrust to make that foreign policy initiative has not yet developed. Parliamentary advocates believe that membership would give Canada a stronger voice in planning development strategies for Latin America, as well as allow Canada to make a contribution in the field of human rights.[53] As countries like Mexico and Venezuela have become stronger, the strength of the argument that Canada would be caught in disputes between the United States and Latin America has diminished. Perhaps the most significant remaining barrier to membership is the Rio Treaty, which binds OAS members in a collective security network. It is unlikely that Canada would join the organization without first arranging exemption from this treaty.

CANADIAN RELATIONS WITH SELECTED COUNTRIES AND AREAS

Canada and the United States

Reproduced with permission – Pritchard, Star Phoenix, *Saskatoon.*

President John F. Kennedy once said on a visit to Ottawa that geography made us neighbours, history made us friends and economics made us partners. The simple fact is that there is no more important external relationship for Canada than

---

[52]Robert J. Jackson, "Canadian Foreign Policy in the Western Hemisphere," in Viron P. Vaky, ed., *Governance in the Western Hemisphere* (New York: Praeger, 1984), pp. 119-134.

[53]Minutes of Proceedings of the Standing Committee on External Affairs and National Defence on *Canada's Relations with Latin America and the Caribbean*, Issue no. 48, December 8, 1981, p. 8. Hereafter cited as *Interim Report*.

that with the United States. About 110 billion dollars in trade crossed the border in 1981 – by a large margin the world's leading trade relationship. The US accounted for 66 percent of Canadian exports and 69 percent of all imports, making it our most important trading partner by far (see Figure 14-2). On the other hand, Canada took only 17 percent of total American exports and provided 18 percent of its imports. Even at these significantly lower percentages of total trade, Canada is the United States' most important trading partner.[54] Leading Canadian exports to the US include passenger autos and chassis, natural gas, forest products, crude petroleum and petrochemicals. In turn, Canada imports motor vehicle parts, passenger autos and chassis, electronic computers, crude petroleum and aircraft. In spite of efforts to diversify Canadian trade, both import and export trade with the US has grown dramatically in recent years, as Table (14-4) shows.

Relations with the United States are clearly critical to Canada's economic well-being. The high degree of dependence is not, however, mutual. Though

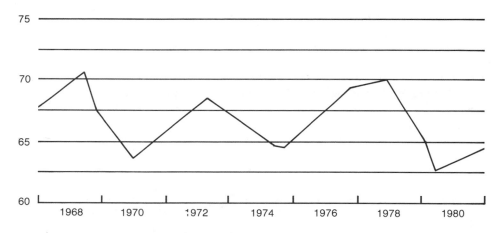

FIGURE 14.2   Canadian Exports to the United States (Percentage of total merchandise exports)

Source: Statistics Canada: The Conference Board of Canada, in *A Review of Canadian Trade Policy* (Ottawa: Supply and Services, 1983), p. 204.

---

[54]Literature on Canadian/U.S. relationships is voluminous. Some of the multiple perspectives are provided in two compendiums: Special Issue on "The Canada-United States Relationship," *International Journal*, vol. XXXVI, no. 1 (Winter 1980-81); H. Edward English, ed., *Canada-United States Relations* (New York: The Academy of Political Science, 1976). For a standard Canadian view see John W. Holmes, *Life with Uncle* (Toronto: University of Toronto Press, 1981). For an American view of Canada see Willis C. Armstrong and Francis O. Wilcox, eds., *Canada and the United States* (Cambridge, Mass.: Ballinger, 1982); and Charles F. Doran "The United States and Canada: Invulnerability and Interdependence," *International Journal*, vol. XXXVIII, no. 1 (Winter 1982-83), pp. 128-146. Data on Canada/U.S. trade is provided in *A Review of Canadian Trade Policy*, p. 204.

TABLE 14.4 Canada's Trade with the United States (billions of Canadian dollars)

	Exports	*Imports*
1976	25.2	25.8
1977	30.4	29.8
1978	36.7	35.4
1979	43.4	45.4
1980	46.7	48.2

Source: Cited in Jon M. Volpe, "Canadian-U.S. Trade Relations," in W.C. Armstrong, L.S. Armstrong and Francis O. Wilcox, eds., *Canada and the United States: Dependence and Divergence* Copyright 1982 by The Atlantic Council of the United States.
Reprinted with permission from Ballinger Publishing Company, Cambridge, Massachusetts.

both geography and history provided the backdrop for an early special relationship between Canada and the United States, inevitably it has often been one-sided. This fact was perhaps best illustrated in symbolic terms by the relative urgency assigned to initial political visitations at the highest level. The first Canadian Prime Ministerial visit to Washington was in 1871, only four years after Confederation; the first Presidential visit to Ottawa did not occur until over eight decades later, in 1943. The relationship between these unequal neighbours over the years has been friendly, but, on the part of Canadians, necessarily guarded, as the attitudes of American leaders were perceived to fluctuate from the extremes of annexation to complete indifference. Ulysses S. Grant, for example, aspired to absorb Canada in time for his 1872 election bid – in fact, he wanted the British to cede Canada in exchange for damage caused by a British ship![55]

With regard to defence, the long history of cooperation through NATO and NORAD belies the fact that much of Canada's history, including Confederation itself, was inspired by deliberate efforts to be independent from the United States and protected from American domination.

Because the Canadian economy is so closely entwined with that of the United States, a priority in foreign policy must be the solution of bilateral irritants. History has made Canada and the US friends, but in spite of obvious similarities in origins and aspirations there are also significant differences which affect every aspect of the relationship. Our governments are different in structure and functions, and subtle differences are not always understood or appreciated. In the early 1980s, for example, a bilateral fishing agreement was scuppered after long negotiations when the United States Senate refused to ratify it. This ratification procedure, which is foreign to the Canadian political system, brought howls of outrage. In Canada, ratification is part of the powers of the executive. There is no constitutional need for the government to seek parliamentary approval. This incident was particularly well-publicized, but not unusual. In fact, according to specialist Christian Wiktor there have been more than 200 treaties negotiated by American administrators with various countries over the

[55]Lawrence Martin, "The Presidents and the Prime Ministers" *op. cit.* p. 12.

past 200 years which were never ratified by the Senate, 18 of them concerning Canada directly.[56]

There are other important differences. The two governments have disparate approaches to the role of government in the economy. In Canada, both federal and provincial governments take an active role in the marketplace through such enterprises as Petro-Canada, the Canadian Development Corporation and Canadair to a degree unknown and unacceptable in the United States.

Perhaps the most obvious difference, however, is that Canada's population is only one-tenth that of the US. We discussed in Chapters 2 and 4 some of the inevitable repercussions of such a disparity; basically, it makes Canada vulnerable to pressures from the United States in the fields of culture, economy and defence. A few facts will serve to indicate the extent of the problem for Canadians: in 1982 citizens of the United States directly owned and controlled 54 percent of Canada's oil and gas industry; 58 percent of chemicals; 70 percent of petrochemicals; 41 percent of mining and smelting; 42 percent of all manufacturing; and 80 percent of all foreign investment in Canada.[57] This high level of foreign investment from one source is questioned because of the control restrictions it could place on Canadian economic independence.

Underlying economic and cultural differences between the two countries surface periodically as policy conflicts between Ottawa and Washington.[58] This was particularly evident in the 1970s, a decade of growing tensions between the two countries, both of which were caught in a deep economic recession. The poor economic climate exacerbated cleavages when each country acted to protect and strengthen its home industries. Management of bilateral irritants, which is an important part of the relationship between Canada and the United States, assumed major proportions. Disputes arose in many areas, fisheries, trucking regulations and advertising rights among them.

Most conflict, however, centred around the Canadian government's Foreign Investment Review Agency, set up to monitor and restrict foreign investment, and the National Energy Program, designed to increase Canadian ownership of natural resources. Both impinged on foreign interests, especially those of the United States. The conflict continued until the Canadian government declined to expand FIRA and the fall in the world price of oil made the NEP less offensive.

Measures such as the NEP and FIRA were adopted by the Canadian government to regulate escalating foreign ownership, which was seen as depriving Canadians of the ability to control and benefit from the country's industries, particularly resource industries. Canada's prosperity is linked to the rest of the world through not only trade, but also the importation of foreign capital. We have seen that the level of foreign investment is particularly high in manufac-

---

[56]Quoted in *The Globe and Mail*, May 7, 1981.

[57]Rowland C. Frazee in "Canada-U.S. Relations," paper delivered to the Economic Club of Detroit, Michigan, February 22, 1982.

[58]For an interesting view of Canada/U.S. tensions in the 1970s see Stephen Clarkson, *Canada and the Reagan Challenge* (Toronto: James Lorimer & Co., 1982).

turing and resource extraction. As one expert put it, "Canada cannot be compared with capital-rich economies such as the American and British. The combination of a small population and huge natural resources necessitate, even in the best of economic times, reliance on external financing to satisfy our economic expansions."[59] Individual Canadians save at double the rate of Americans, but the country does not come close to satisfying its own capital requirements.

In recent years, much foreign investment has not been "new" American capital but has come from within Canada itself. Foreign subsidiaries simply retain earnings and depreciation reserves and put them back into the economy as investments. Kari Levitt has estimated that during the years 1957-64 the funds generated from these investments and other Canadian interests accounted for 73 percent of American direct investments in manufacturing, mining and petroleum, and that only 15 percent involved "new funds".[60]

Most foreign capital comes in the form of direct investment, not interest or portfolio investment. This means that rather than involving bank loans or bonds, which can be paid off, investment in the Canadian economy brings a high degree of control and ownership by foreigners, especially in the manufacturing and resource sectors. There are over 8500 American controlled factories in Canada, 40 of them among the 100 largest firms. Such American branch plants allow the importing of American technology and market access as well as American values. They are subject not only to market forces and Canadian government regulation but also to American interests. John H. Redekop provides a classic instance: the incorporation of the Ford Motor Company of Canada gives "the Canadian firm market rights in all British Commonwealth countries (excluding the best, the U.K.), while the rest of the world is reserved for the U.S. parent firm or its other subsidiaries."[61]

There can be no doubt that foreign investment improves Canada's standard of living and has helped to transform Canada into an industrialized country. However, there is equally no doubt that it has greatly increased the dependence of the economy on that of the United States. Government concern over the economic relationship of Canada to the rest of the world, and particularly to the United States, was summed up best in the Gray report on Foreign Direct Investment in Canada:

> The high and growing degree of foreign, and particularly U.S. control of
> Canadian business activity has led to a Canadian industrial structure which
> largely reflects the growth priorities of foreign corporations ... these
> developments have made it more difficult for the government to control
> the domestic national economic environment. They have also influenced

---

[59]James R. Niniger, President, The Conference Board of Canada, quoted in *The Citizen*, Ottawa, May 14, 1984.

[60]Kari Levitt, *Silent Surrender: The Multi-National Corporation in Canada* (Toronto: Macmillan, 1970), pp. 63-64.

[61]John H. Redekop, "Continentalism: The Key to Canadian Politics" in Redekop, ed., *Approaches to Canadian Politics*, 2nd ed. (Scarborough: Prentice Hall, Canada, 1983) p. 45.

the development of the social, cultural and political environment in Canada.[62]

One of the most controversial trade issues of the 1980s is the question of free trade, a recurring theme in Canada's relationship with the United States. In the early years of nationhood, Sir John A. Macdonald won the hearts of Canadians when he espoused a National Policy of high tariffs to protect fledgling Canadian industries . Much later, in 1911, Sir Wilfrid Laurier failed to win re-election partly because he wanted to eliminate tariffs on less than one-quarter of cross-border trade. He could not compete with the opposition slogan of "No truck or trade with the Yankees". Following the GATT, after World War II, many tariff cuts were made. Today, three-quarters of Canada/US trade is duty free or will be by 1987. Some Canadian tariffs are still high, for example, those on petrochemicals and textiles. Other selected markets are protected by indirect means such as quotas, government "standards and specifications", health and safety regulations and even drawn-out customs inspections (such as those which delayed the 1983 delivery of Japanese cars by holding them in the port of Vancouver).

Today the controversy is over whether to move toward full free trade across the border or, as the Liberal government recommended in 1983, to build "sectoral free trade" in selected items, among them steel, agricultural equipment, urban mass transit equipment and "informatics" such as computer communications services. Free trade with the United States, even in specific sectors, would be a major political undertaking for any Canadian government. Advocates argue that it would raise productivity, lower inflation and create jobs, unlike protectionism, which hinders global trade. The sectoral free trade policy was dropped after the Conservatives came to office in 1984. Their position was buttressed by the 1985 report of the Royal Commission on the Economic Union and Development Prospects for Canada (the Donald Macdonald Commission), which argued strongly in favour of general free trade.[63] Opponents argue that free trade would destroy many Canadian companies (especially in textiles and footwear) and inevitably lead to the formation of common institutions which would be dominated by the US and would therefore erode Canada's political sovereignty. As captive neighbours on this continent, the only reasonable policy for both nations in this field, as in others, is one which will foster a mutually satisfactory relationship.

Canada and Western Europe

Canada's historical and cultural ties with Western Europe have always been close, and Canadian governments have counted on this region of the world to coun-

---

[62]*A Citizen's Guide to the Gray Report* (Toronto: New Press, 1971) p. 11, quoted in Redekop, *ibid.*, p. 44.

[63]*Report of the Royal Commission on the Economic Union and Development Prospects for Canada*, vol. 1, (Ottawa: Supply and Services, 1985). Also see Fred Harrison, "New Ways to Trade with U.S.," *International Perspectives* (March/April 1984), pp. 6-8.

terbalance American influence. In the 1970s in particular, fears were rife that Canada was too dependent on American markets. It was at this time that Trudeau initiated his Third Option to increase trade with Western Europe and Japan. As an extension of that philosophy, Trudeau achieved a weak contractual link with the European Community. However, little but platitudes came from this agreement, and trade with the United States continued to increase.

The Canadian/British link, the strongest tie Canada had in Western Europe, became weaker after Britain entered the European Common Market in 1973. At that time about 13 percent of Britain's exports came to Canada, compared to only about 3 percent by 1982. The Canadian share of the British market also decreased, although the trade balance has remained in Canada's favour. In 1982, Britain's exports to Canada totalled about $1900 million; its imports from Canada, $2664 million. Britain is the second-largest investor in Canada, and educational and travel links remain strong.

The twelve countries which make up the EEC constitute the world's largest trading entity. However, in recent years the European Community has been preoccupied with internal economic and political problems which have reduced its global competitiveness. The EEC is one of Canada's largest markets for agricultural products and several resource-based products, including forest products and fish. In 1981 the EEC imported 11 percent of Canada's total exports. Since this figure represented only 2 percent of total EEC imports, however, down from 3 percent in 1975, the relationship is much more important to Canada than the EEC.

Community members generally desire access to Canada's pulp, oil, uranium and other mineral resources, and in return would like to offer Canadians manufactured goods. The Canadian government is justifiably reluctant to accept these 19th century conditions of trade. On the other hand, access to the European Community markets is also difficult for Canadians to achieve, and despite traditional political ties the trade relationship is unlikely to improve much in the near future.

Canada and the Pacific Rim

As Canadian trade with Western Europe has gone stagnant or withered in recent years, it has increased rapidly in the Pacific Rim. In 1983, for the first time, Canada traded more with Asia than with Western Europe. At that time trade with Asia totalled $16.4 billion, compared to $15 billion with Western Europe.[64] It is increasingly evident that trans-Pacific trade is another opportunity for a counterbalance in the American-dominated Canadian economy: it is Canada's new Third Option.[65]

Countries of the Pacific Rim, Japan and Singapore in particular, are challenging world markets with outstanding management, technological and produc-

---

[64]Reported in *The Citizen*, Ottawa, May 7, 1984.

[65]See H.E. English, "National Policy and Canadian Trade", *International Perspectives* (March/April, 1984), pp. 3-6.

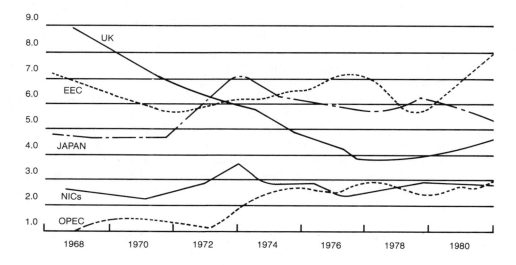

TABLE 14.5 Canada's Exports to Selected Areas, 1970-80 (Percentage of Total Canadian Exports)

Source: Statistics Canada: The Conference Board of Canada, cited in *A Review of Canadian Trade Policy* (Ottawa: Supply and Services, 1983), p. 214.

tion techniques. Their economies are growing more rapidly than those of Europe or any other major region. Since 1973, Japan has been Canada's second-largest national trading partner.[66] In 1981 two-way trade reached $8.6 billion. Japan is Canada's fastest growing export market among our major trading partners. Canada/Japanese trade relations are those of a resource-rich supplier and a resource-poor industrial nation: almost all of Japan's exports to Canada are fully manufactured, while 85 percent of Canada's exports are either raw materials or semi-processed products. Canada normally has a trade surplus with Japan, but is naturally concerned to secure better access for manufactured exports, not merely resources.

Canada, the Developing Countries and Others

Under the GATT, the developing countries of the world enjoy various types of differential and preferential treatment in the effort to nurture their nascent agriculture and manufacturing industries. Canadian trade with developing areas is relatively modest, although it has grown slightly in recent years. Most developing countries have economic situations similar to that of Canada and therefore compete in many of the same areas. They generally export tropical foodstuffs and raw materials. The more industrialized among them, including Brazil, Venezuela,

---

[66]*A Review of Canadian Trade Policy*, p. 218.

Mexico, China, Korea and Saudi Arabia, also produce labour-intensive standard technology goods and are considered by the Canadian government to be the best targets for expanded exports in the 1980s.[67] Over 68 percent of Canadian exports to these newly industrialized countries in 1980 were fabricated end products. On the whole, developing countries continue to be more important trade partners for Japan, the US and the EEC than for Canada, because these industrial giants need raw materials. Another serious problem inhibiting trade with these countries is their enormous debt burden.

Since Canada has no coherent foreign policy that embraces the entire hemisphere, Canadian relations with countries in South and Central America and the Caribbean consist mainly of bilateral trade, political, economic and humanitarian interests.[68] In 1979 (the latest year for which reliable statistics on imports and exports to the entire hemisphere are available), Canadian exports to these nations amounted to just over 3 percent of the total market of about $87 billion worth of goods and services. Over 33 percent of these exports were processed or manufactured goods – a considerably higher percentage of finished products than the 19 percent which Canada exports to the rest of the world.[69] Canadian imports from the area roughly equal the exports. They consisted primarily of petroleum products, particularly from Venezuela and Mexico, and tropical food products, as well as some manufactured products from Brazil and Mexico.

Canadian banks have been active in Latin America and the Caribbean since the 19th century, and about 75 percent of Canadian direct investment in developing countries is in this region.[70] In 1983, Canadian aid to Latin America and the Caribbean represented about 6 percent of official development assistance, with most going to the Caribbean countries for such reasons as historic ties, security and proximity.

Although economic and commercial matters are the most concrete evidence of Canadian relations south of the United States, political and humanitarian issues, too, concern Canadians.

Despite protest from the United States, Canada maintained political relations with Cuba after the 1959 revolution. As well, Canada continued trade relations in face of a US embargo. The Canadian government has disagreed with the ideological commitment and some of the policies and activities of the Cuban government, but, unlike some American administrations, it does not condemn Cuba and communism as the only sources of conflict in Central America and the Caribbean.

---

[67]*Ibid.*, p. 224.

[68]These are considered in detail in Robert J. Jackson, "Canadian Foreign Policy and the Western Hemisphere." For a historical summary, see D.R. Murray, "The Bilateral Road: Canada and Latin America in the 1980s," *International Journal*, vol. XXXVII, no. 1 (Winter 1981-82), pp. 108-131.

[69]Minutes of Proceedings of the Standing Committee on External Affairs and National Defence on *Canada's Relations with Latin America and the Caribbean*, October 1981, Issue No. 1, p. 14.

[70]*Interim Report*, p. 6.

Considerable media coverage has recently been devoted to Central America. With the exception of Costa Rica, the area has had an unsavoury history of coups, rigged elections and human rights violations. Against a tide of criticism, the Canadian government supported the 1982 and 1984 elections in El Salvador. The basic Canadian government position has been that a political solution, not a military one, is required to resolve the continued crisis in El Salvador.

Canada's best relations in the area are with Mexico, Brazil and Venezuela. All three have been given priority ratings by the Canadian government. Their large markets and relatively stable political systems, a contrast to those of many nations in the region, provide the foundation for increased, successful ties.

Canada naturally has links with other countries and areas, which, though important in other ways, are not very significant in an economic sense. Relations with Australia and New Zealand are long-standing and close because of the early Commonwealth connection. These countries are a small but important part of Canada's global trade relationship. Mention must also be made of the Soviet Union and the Eastern bloc countries. Canada's relations in this area are of course conditioned by East/West political and defence realities. These nations account for only a tiny percentage of Canada's total trade, but the USSR is a major grain importer and therefore important to Canada. The fact that Eastern bloc countries belong to a state-trading system in which government plays a major role in centrally planned economies, added to the difference in market rules, makes them relatively inaccessible, though not closed, to the West.

CANADIAN DEFENCE AND SECURITY POLICY

The objectives of defence and security policy are intertwined with foreign policy objectives and, more specifically, with deterring war. Over time, Canadian objectives in this field have varied according to changes in the international strategic environment and the political configuration of the country. But at all times there have been commitments to preserving the independence of Canada, its borders, institutions and values; to pursuing the peaceful settlement of disputes; and to preventing hostilities and warfare.

Such aspirations are accepted by almost all Canadians. However, the policies and programs required to fulfill these goals are constantly in dispute. Should Canada be a part of a collective security arrangement such as NATO, or, like Sweden, be more independent? Should Canada be part of the nuclear bomb club or keep these devices off native soil? Even if there were agreement on such general policies an analyst would still need to know what programs would be required to execute them. For example, should more government funds be spent on "arms than butter"? Should Canadians be deployed overseas in potential combat zones? Should Canadians participate in international peace-keeping missions?

These are deep and difficult questions which touch on the basic values of the nation. Given that Canadians are essentially a non-militaristic people, what visible security policies have been developed? Furthermore, what set of policies could be designed to protect 25 million citizens and to defend the second-largest land mass and the longest coastline in the world?

The ingredients of Canada's policy have remained essentially the same since the end of the Second World War. As the 1984 Defence Minister's statement explained it,

> For over thirty years, Canada's security policy has rested on three complementary foundations:
> – prevention of war and deterrence of aggression through collective defence arrangements of NATO and NORAD,
> – pursuit of verifiable arms control and disarmament agreements, and
> – commitment to the peaceful settlement of disputes and collective efforts to resolve the underlying causes of international tensions.[71]

Before turning to a description and assessment of these policies and their sources, as well as of contemporary defence issues, we shall examine the strategic environment in which Canada finds itself in the mid-1980s.

The International Strategic Environment

The basic pattern of the international environment is one of East/West and local/regional conflicts throughout the world, particularly in the developing Third World. Explanations for the continuation of hostile acts throughout the globe are beyond the scope of this book, but they would certainly include economic, cultural, religious and ideological frustrations and aggression.

The superpower struggle between the USA and the USSR is interwoven with most of these conflicts. The most direct impact of the situation on Canada is the division of Europe into NATO and the Warsaw Pact. There, the military power of the two blocs comes into direct contact and conflict. But, at the same time, Canada and her trading partners have economic interests in the countries of both blocs and throughout the globe.

The military balance between NATO and the Warsaw Pact is described in Figure 14-3. It shows that there is a rough parity at the strategic nuclear level which changes only marginally from year to year. At the beginning of 1984 the USSR retained a lead in numbers of strategic delivery vehicles, while the US held a slight advantage in strategic warheads.[72]

Below this level, the balance in nuclear weapons is unfavourable to NATO. The USSR has been augmenting the number of its intermediate-range ballistic missiles armed with nuclear weapons targeted on Western Europe for several years (see Figure 14-4). The Soviet introduction of SS-20 missiles in the late 1970s further increased the margin between the Warsaw Pact and NATO in the field of intermediate-range missiles. The Canadian Defence Minister's statement

---

[71]Minister's Statement, *Defence Estimates 1984-85*, p. 13. Hereafter cited as *Defence Estimates 1984-85*.

[72]*Ibid.*, p. 21.

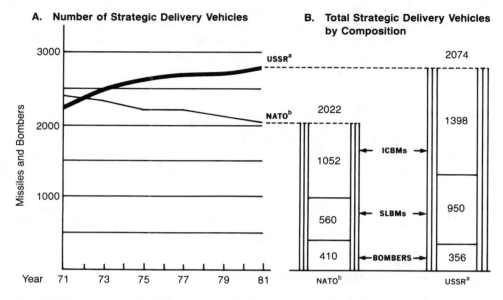

a) USSR figures include Soviet strategic missiles and BEAR, BISON and BACKFIRE bombers; the BACKFIRE bomber has been included in this figure because it has an inherent intercontinental capability although in its maritime and European land-attack roles it poses a serious threat to NATO Europe.

b) NATO figures include United States strategic missiles, 64 British strategic POLARIS SLBMS and United States B-52's and FB-11s. The United States-based FB-111 is included because it has a strategic mission.

FIGURE 14.3   Total Strategic Missiles and Bombers

Source: Minister's Statement, *Defence Estimates 1983-84*, p. 10.

of late 1983 reads, "Of a total of 378 SS-20s with their triple multiple independently-targetable re-entry vehicle (MIRV) warheads of a range of 5000 km deployed, 243 face Western Europe."[73] It was this move which led to the December 1979 NATO "two-track" decision to modernize NATO's weapons by the introduction of Pershing II and Ground Launched Cruise missiles (GLCMs) in Europe while continuing negotiations on arms control.

The main reason for the deployment of American missiles in Europe, however, has its basis in the same logic that keeps Canadian and US troops in Western Europe: the deployment serves to couple American nuclear policy planning with possible events in Western Europe. The doctrine is clear and precise. If the Warsaw Pact decided to attack the West, it would know that the US would retaliate with inter-continental ballistic missiles should it begin to lose the war. European leaders prefer this strategy of "forward basing", that is, the European-basing of American and Canadian troops and equipment. They worry that the basic military doctrine of nuclear reprisal would be meaningless without the presence of American forces because every American President would be too anx-

---

[73]*Ibid.*

ious about a Soviet attack on the United States to retaliate for Soviet aggression in Europe. In other words, for all its horrifying implications, the strategy is based on a doctrine of strategic nuclear reprisal in the face of the defeat of American and European forces.

Since neither side could win such a war, so goes the argument, mutual deterrence is achieved. This frightening doctrine is often called a "game of chicken" by individuals in the peace movement who fear the annihilation of humankind in a nuclear holocaust.

Canada's impact on the military strategy, and especially the nuclear doctrine and strategy, of the West is marginal. The government's decision to disallow nuclear weapons on Canadian soil is the primary expression of the desire to be a peaceful country. However, in 1984, despite divided public opinion, the gov-

NATO

None □

WARSAW PACT

(All missiles are located in the USSR with Soviet Forces)	SS-4	SS-5	SS-20
Warheads	1	1	3 MIRV
Range (km)	2000	4100	4400-5000
Operational Mode	Fixed	Fixed	Mobile
Global Number Deployed*	275	25	300
Year Operational	Late 1950s	Early 1960s	1977

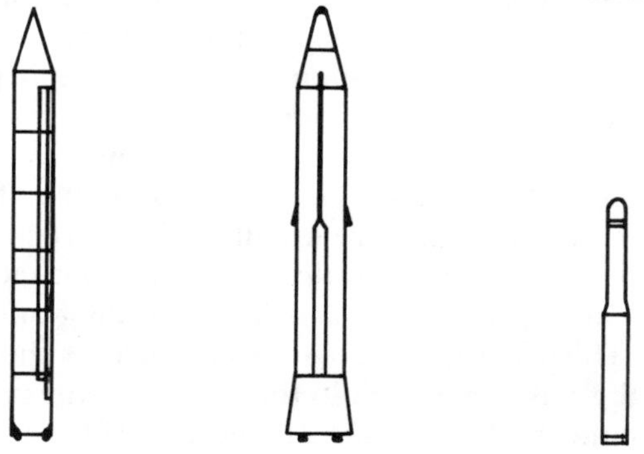

*Excludes refire missiles

□ In the absence of a concrete arms control agreement on longer-range INF missile systems, NATO plans to deploy in Western Europe up to 108 Pershing II missiles and up to 464 Ground Launched Cruise Missiles (GLCMS) commencing late 1983. The Pershing II is a mobile ballistic missile with one warhead with a range of 1800 km. The GLCM is a mobile missile with one warhead with a range of 2500 km.

FIGURE 14.4 Deployed INF Missile Systems Before NATO Response in 1983

Source: Minister's Statement, *Defence Estimates 1983-84, p. 11.*

ernment allowed the United States to test an unarmed Cruise missile over Canadian territory. This decision was justified as part of Canada's commitment to the 1979 NATO two-track policy mentioned above.

The tally in Western Europe shows that the Warsaw Pact leads by an even greater margin in conventional forces than in nuclear weapons. Figure 14-5 indicates that the Warsaw Pact has about double the number of divisions of NATO, and about three times as many tanks, anti-tank weapon launchers, artillery and armoured personnel carriers. In the air, the Warsaw Pact has a numerical advantage in most categories.

In Europe, therefore, NATO forces are barely adequate to defend Western territory. Since its conventional forces are weak, the basic military strategy of NATO since 1967 has been one of "flexible response" eventually leading to the use of nuclear weapons. The better conventional forces are able to withstand an aggressor, the higher is the "nuclear threshold", the level at which the West would have to resort to nuclear war in the event that conventional forces proved inadequate.

Outside the European theatre there is much less agreement on strategy and tactics. In the Pacific, Canada has no security arrangement as it does with NATO. However, the increase of Canadian trade in the Pacific – especially with Japan but also with China and the new industrializing countries – augurs for future Canadian discussion of commitment in the area. The USSR-Japan clashes, the Sino-Japanese competition and the Korean partition (where Canadian troops last fought) all call for vigilance.

In Africa, South East Asia and Latin and Central America, hostilities within and among nations have the possibility of affecting world stability. Canada's concerns, however, are usually only indirect. Canada has few concrete security interests and there is little it can do about most incidences of violence. As discussed earlier, however, Canada has trading and humanitarian interests in most of the Third World. Of most direct worry is the Middle East, where ideological and religious turmoil could threaten the energy supplies of Canada's friends in Europe and the Pacific and trigger a World War.

CANADIAN SECURITY POLICY

In the face of such vast and intractible conflicts around the globe it could be said that Canada's defence forces are insignificant. However, given the size of Canada's population and the few direct conflicts in which Canada is engaged, the military commitment is important. In 1983-84, 9 percent of the federal government's budget – $7840 million – was in the defence envelope.

Organization of National Defence

The Department of National Defence (DND) was created by the *National Defence Act* in 1922. Led by the Minister of National Defence, the DND is involved in

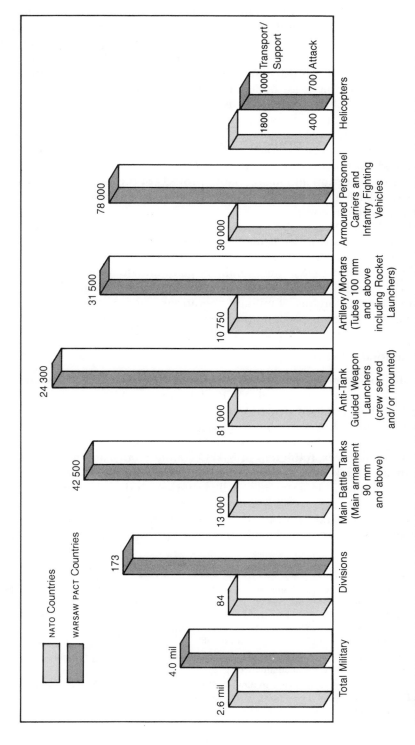

Notes: 1. WARSAW PACT divisions normally consist of fewer personnel than many NATO divisions but contain more tanks and artillery, thereby obtaining similar combat power.
2. Forces in place in NATO Europe, WARSAW PACT forces as far east as but excluding the Western Military Districts in Western Russia (Moscow, Volga and Ural Military Districts).

FIGURE 14.5   NATO – WARSAW PACT Land Force Comparison (In Place in Europe)

Source: Minister's Statement, *Defence Estimates 1984-85*, p. 24.

both the formulation and the implementation of Canadian defence policy. External affairs and defence policies are inextricably bound together, as the composition of the Cabinet committee, which handles these matters, would indicate: it includes both the Minister of External Affairs and the Minister of National Defence. The Defence Minister specifically, and the Cabinet generally, are accountable to Parliament for national defence matters.

The responsibilities of the Minister of National Defence include the control and management of the Department itself, the Canadian Armed Forces and all matters relating to works and establishments concerned with Canada's defence. The Minister is also responsible for Defence Construction Canada, a Crown corporation which functions as a contracting and construction supervisory agency for major construction and maintenance projects of the DND. It ensures that adequate standards of supervision and inspection are maintained throughout the life of construction contracts.

The Deputy Minister of the DND is the senior civilian advisor to the Minister. He or she heads a department which employs approximately 37 000 civilians.[74] The DM ensures that governmental policy direction is reflected in the administration of the DND and in military plans and operations. The senior military advisor to the Minister is the Chief of the Defence Staff (CDS), who is responsible for the conduct of military operations and for the preparedness of the Canadian Forces to meet commitments assigned by the government.

The Canadian Forces

The Canadian Forces are the military element of the Canadian Government and are part of the Department of National Defence.[75] Since 1968 the Canadian Forces have had a unified structure to carry out their tasks. They perform a number of roles, including surveillance of Canadian territory and coastlines, that is, protection of Canadian sovereignty; defence of North America in cooperation with American forces; fulfilment of NATO commitments; and performance of international peace-keeping roles.[76] The military also provides assistance to other federal government departments, civil authorities and civilian organizations; for example, air and ground transportation for royal visits, meetings of foreign government officials and sporting events; emergency and disaster relief; and a search and rescue program. Finally, the Forces provide training for allied military

---

[74]National Defence, Government of Canada, *Defence 83* (Ottawa: Supply and Services), p. 8. C.J. Marshal, "Canada's Defence Structure Review," *International Perspectives* (January/February 1976), pp. 26-29. Little has been written on the domestic sources of Canadian military policy. One exception is Kim Richard Nossal, "On the Periphery: Interest Groups and Canadian Defence Policy in the 1970s." unpublished paper, June 1982.

[75]Formally the Governor General of Canada, as the Sovereign's representative, is Commander-in-Chief of the Canadian Forces.

[76]Canadians have participated in almost all United Nations peace-keeping operations to date in Egypt, Israel, Syria, Lebanon, Cyprus, Korea, India, Pakistan, West New Guinea, the Congo, Yemen and Nigeria.

personnel in Canada and aid in the form of military training to developing countries.[77]

In 1983-84 the total personnel in the Canadian Forces reached almost 84 000 person-years. The importance of defence expenditures on the economy cannot be exaggerated – it has been estimated that in 1984-85 the defence expenditures would generate 240 000 person-years of employment.[78]

Defence expenditures are not, however, without their critics. The charges of opponents are often based on the belief that there is a so-called "military-industrial complex" which controls the government, especially in the United States. The basic argument is that there is collusion between powerful industrialists and military planners to keep international tension high in order to sell expensive weapons to the government. This assertion is usually coupled with a belief that such expenditures would be better used in other fields such as health, education and social welfare. Such a critique of defence expenditures is often based on assumptions about the nature of the international strategic environment which differ entirely from that set out in earlier sections of this book. Its exponents feel that the costs of Canadian defence could be reduced by a radical shift towards neutralism in international affairs. This argument will be further discussed below, but the issue is raised here merely to point to the fundamental debate over whether government funds should be spent on "guns or butter".

Perhaps the fear of a military-industrial establishment having too much power is best illustrated by the following exchange between President Eisenhower and Nikita Krushchev:

Eisenhower: "It's like this: My military leaders say, "Mr. President, we need such and such a sum for such and such a program." I say, "Sorry we don't have the funds." They say, "We have reliable information that the Soviet Union has already allocated funds for such a program." So I give in. That's how they wring money out of me. Now tell me, how is it with you?"

Krushchev: "They say, "Comrade Krushchev, look at this! The Americans are developing such and such a system." I tell them there's no money. So we discuss it more, and I end up giving them the money they asked for."[79]

What does Canada do with these expenditures on defence? Figure 14-6 shows the 1983-84 forecast for defence spending. Almost two-thirds of the funds are for the combined Maritime, Land and Air Forces in Canada, while Canadian combat forces in Europe consume about one-tenth of defence expenditures. This figure has been growing since 1978 when Canada, along with its NATO allies,

---

[77]Training teams have been sent to Ghana, Cameroon, Jamaica, Kenya, Tanzania, Malaysia, Nigeria, Zambia and other countries. Allied countries using training facilities in Canada include Great Britain, West Germany, Denmark, Norway, the Netherlands and the United States.

[78]*Defence Estimates 1984-85*, p. 54.

[79]Cited in James MacGregor Burns, J.W. Peltason and Thomas E. Cronin, *Government by the People*, 10th ed. (Englewood Cliffs: Prentice-Hall, 1978), p. 450.

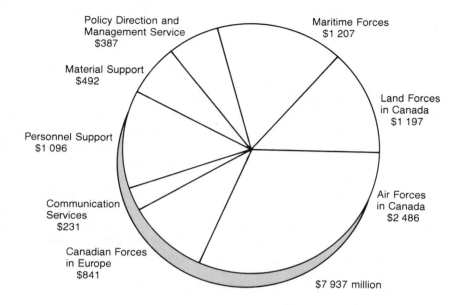

FIGURE 14.6 Defence Expenditure Forecast 1983-84 (in millions)

Source: *Defence 83* (Ottawa: Minister of Supply and Services, 1984), p. 10.

committed itself to a real 3 percent increase in defence spending until 1984. Canada also contributes to some common funded programs of NATO.

Canadian military expenditures basically cover protection of Canada's territory, a special partnership with the US in the North American Aerospace Defence Command and membership in the North Atlantic Treaty Organization. Although Canada is involved in strategic nuclear planning, the country's chief role in NATO involves stationing Canadian land and air forces in Europe as part of the forward defence strategy. The total peace-time strength of Canadian forces in Europe is approximately 6700, most of them stationed in Lahr and Baden-Soellingen in the Federal Republic of Germany. In case of war, the two European-based formations, four Canadian Mechanized Brigade Groups and one Canadian Air Group would be assigned to NATO's Supreme Commander. (Refer to Figure 14-7.)

Shortly after becoming Prime Minister in 1968, Pierre Trudeau reduced the number of troops stationed in Europe by half and slashed the defence budget. Although since that time there have been increases in Canada's commitment, as a percentage of GNP Canada still remains second-lowest among NATO partners as regards concrete support of defence measures.[80]

---

[80]Robert J. Jackson, ed., *Continuity of Discord: Crises and Response in the Atlantic Community* (New York: Praeger, 1985).

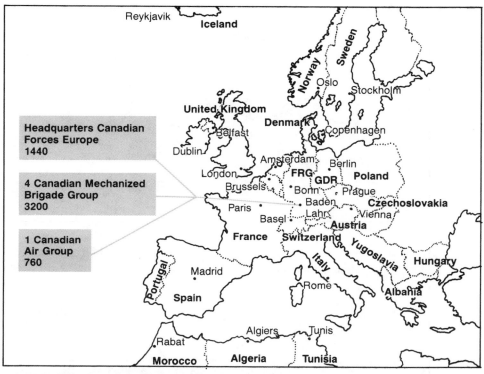

FIGURE 14.7 Canada's Forces in Europe

Source: Minister's Statement, *Defence Estimates 1984-85,* p. 41.

Peace-keeping

In keeping with the fundamentally non-military nature of Canadian security policy, the government's most visible activity has been in the field of international peace-keeping. The largest overseas force is with the United Nations troops in Cyprus (UNFICYP); approximately 515 persons serve in a multi-national contingent to prevent hostilities between Greek and Turkish Cypriots. In this force, established in 1964, the Canadian contingent is mainly responsible for patrolling the Nicosia area. Canada also participates to a lesser extent in two UN operations in the Middle East: the United Nations Truce Supervisory Organization (UNTSO) and the United Nations Disengagement Observer Force (UNDOF). UNTSO was formed in 1948 for the purpose of maintaining the cease-fire between Israel, Egypt, Lebanon, Jordan and Syria. UNDOF was established in 1974 and provides for observation of the Disengagement Agreement between Israel and Syria. (See Figure 14-8.)

The main political question concerning these peace-keeping operations involves their possibility of success. Canadian troops have been in Cyprus for twenty years and some critics now ask whether they are part of the solution or part of

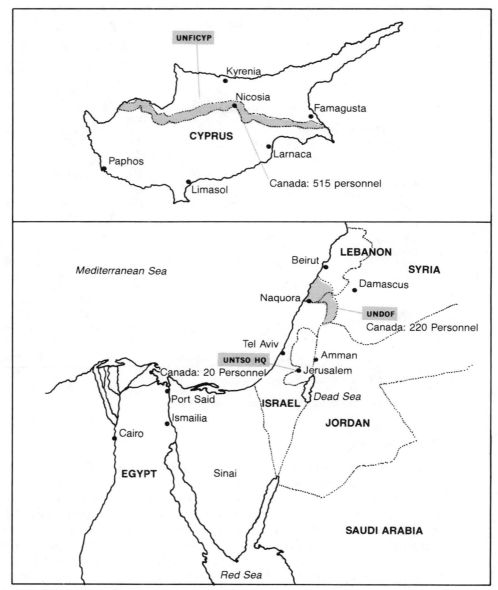

FIGURE 14.8   Canadian Forces Peace-Keeping

Source: Minister's Statement: *Defence Estimates 1984-85*, p. 37.

the problem. The 1983 declaration of independence by Turkish Cyprus has highlighted this intractable matter. Nonetheless, some arguments can be advanced for maintaining troops in Cyprus. Their presence has undoubtedly reduced the general level of hostility and the number of deaths on the island. Moreover, it has kept two of Canada's allies, Greece and Turkey, from outright warfare. Thus, NATO gains some cohesion on its Southern Mediterranean flank. Still, a question regarding this situation remains – how long should UN troops be kept in Cyprus?

Deterrence, Arms Control and Disarmament

The complexities of the issues surrounding the nuclear arms race are daunting.[81] Though peace and security have been dreamed about for centuries, the world continues producing ever-more sophisticated weapons. Over two decades ago President John F. Kennedy observed that the topic of world peace was so vital that he intended to devote a portion of every day to studying what could be done about it. The problems are even more pressing today.

The options facing world leaders today range from total disarmament to constant development of newer, more powerful weapons. Between these two extremes lies the rationale that has delivered Europe from global war for more than 35 years – the policy of deterrence. Deterrence rests on a strategic nuclear equilibrium between the US and the USSR. To work, it must provide security for both sides. But the paradox is that in order to attain this security both powers must remain insecure about their own defences. Neither side may achieve a perfect defence system, because the danger of war increases as soon as one side gains the advantage. In military parlance, this policy is explained in terms of "second-strike capability": deterrence is measured by the usable strength of the survivable second-strike force. Both sides must retain a sufficient amount of retaliatory power to withstand a first strike and remain capable of making an unacceptable second strike on the aggressor.

This type of deterrence policy is required because such basic conflicts in ideology, economics and politics exist between the United States and the USSR that one cannot realistically expect that either side will ever eliminate its nuclear arsenal. Deterrence is a two-sided affair; nothing can be achieved unilaterally.

Proponents of general disarmament hold a different view. They warn that armaments themselves are a fundamental cause of international hostility. Members of the peace movement expound the risks of deterrence, including the possibility of human error, the expansion of the number of countries with nuclear

---

[81]The literature on nuclear weapons is voluminous. On Canadian concerns in this field see Special Issue, "Arms Control", *International Journal*, Vol. XXXVI, no. 3 (Summer, 1981). For an introduction to the general topic see Spurgeon M. Keeny Jr. and Wolfgang K.H. Panofsky, "Nuclear Weapons in the 1980s," *Foreign Affairs*, Vol. 60. No. 2 (Winter 1981-82), pp. 287-346 and the Harvard Study Group, *Living with Nuclear Weapons*, (Cambridge, Mass.: Harvard University Press, 1983).

Reproduced with permission – The Globe and Mail, *Toronto.*

weapons, the threat of biological, chemical and neutron weapons, as well as the increasing sophistication of delivery systems and the possible stationing of nuclear weapons on satellites. They believe that the West should take a major first step in disarmament to prevent world destruction. However, there are those who fear that the Soviet Union would take advantage of the resultant vulnerability.

If general disarmament is discounted by Western governments, arms control or limited disarmament is not. Several agreements have been reached in recent years. In 1968 the nuclear powers signed a Nonproliferation Treaty pledging not to disseminate nuclear devices to non-nuclear countries. At the time of writing, six countries are known to be technically capable of detonating a nuclear bomb: the two superpowers, Britain, France, China and India. By 1992 the total number of countries capable of detonating a nuclear bomb could grow to 34, including South Korea, Iraq, Romania and Libya. It is difficult to predict whether any of these countries could develop an adequate delivery system or whether they would use the nuclear power for aggressive purposes, but the risks are clear.

In 1972 the United States and the USSR signed two agreements based on the Strategic Arms Limitation Talks (SALT I). These agreements limit the number and deployment of anti-ballistic missiles (ABMs). These modest achievements have not been improved to date, because the SALT II Treaty was never ratified by the US Senate. In 1982, new Strategic Arms Reduction Talks (START) began again between the two countries, but these were broken off by the Soviet Union because of American missile deployment in Western Europe. In the spring of 1985 these negotiations recommenced in Geneva.

At the strategic level, then, there is rough nuclear parity between the two superpowers. Both sides possess adequate retaliatory power to prevent aggression and the SALT agreements provide some measure of protection. This is not the case in the European theatre, where the balance with respect to nuclear weapons remains unfavourable to NATO. Efforts to limit the threat through talks on intermediate range missiles between the US and the USSR were broken off because of the 1983 deployment of American Cruise and Pershing missiles in Western Europe. Since these talks were between the superpowers only, Canadian participation was confined to discussions in NATO.

At the time of writing, East/West discussions on conventional weapons continue. These negotiations, called Mutual and Balanced Force Reduction (MBFR) talks have, however, been deadlocked for a decade. As well, in 1984 a new conference, the Stockholm Conference on Confidence and Security Building Measures and Disarmament, began, bringing together Warsaw Pact and NATO countries (including Canada) in the effort to reach an agreement on military and security questions.

Various other options for changing the nuclear death-game are proffered from time to time by concerned citizens and experts. They include declaring a freeze on the building of new nuclear weapons; setting up geographical zones where nuclear weapons will not be kept during peace-time (one of them being Canada); preventing the stationing of nuclear weapons in space; and declaring that the West will not employ nuclear weapons unless they are used first by an aggressor. All of these options, as well as more technical matters regarding the number, size and type of missiles and warheads still need to be negotiated between West and East.

In our view, arms control measures to reduce weaponry, without going as far as total disarmament, constitute the only possible solution, unless the differences over values and philosophies which separate people and nation-states are eliminated. The latter, utopian assumption is not accepted by responsible politicians anywhere in the developed world. A sound defence policy accompanied by arms control agreements is the best that can be expected in the near future. Unfortunately, this subject is much plagued by extreme rhetoric. As one astute observer put it, "The howls of the macho school for crude assertions of virility are matched by the wails of the utopians, paralyzed by the challenge of an international system devised by man rather than by God. The pragmatists are being shouted down."[82]

OVERVIEW

Canada's role in world affairs continues to develop. Among nation-states Canada is one of the most powerful both economically and politically. This relative position makes it mandatory that Canada participate fully in international organizations such as the United Nations and its specialized agencies. Canada's

---

[82]John W. Holmes, "The Way of the World," *International Journal*, vol. XXXV, no. 2 (Spring 1980), p. 211.

international importance has also increased because of economic necessity: Canada must trade in order to maintain its standard of living.

The importance of international relations to Canada is also illustrated by its defence policies. While Canada contributes to the security of the West by membership in NATO and NORAD, its overall military budget is small compared to that of most countries. Because of our essentially non-militaristic position we can be acceptable to many countries as an intermediary in troubled areas. The most concrete example is the Canadian contribution to peace-keeping in Cyprus and the Middle East.

The international strategic environment, however, is changing. Most conflicts take place outside the European theatre and Canada has little role to play in the superpower and religious conflicts of the Middle East. In the remainder of the world, essentially south of the Tropic of Cancer, Canada plays only a modest, usually a rhetorical, role. Efforts to make NATO into a world policeman have largely failed. The United States and the Soviet Union have been left to conduct these tasks on their own. Canada's efforts with four other nations to bring peace in Namibia, or to bring a political solution to troubled areas of Central America have generally landed on unfertile ground. In sum then the Canadian contribution to world politics outside North America, Europe and a few areas of old Commonwealth ties is quite marginal except at the symbolic and important humanitarian levels.

As shown above, decision-making in domestic and international policy spheres has been quite dissimilar. However the foreign policy process has been changing due to widespread concern for international peace and disarmament issues and a growing awareness of the importance of trade to the Canadian economy. Many new actors are now involved in foreign policy-making. The historic importance of the roles of the Prime Minister and the Ministers of External Affairs and National Defence remain but the relative significance of other departments and agencies has grown, as have interest group activities in this sphere.

As Canada evolved into a full-fledged nation-state it gradually adopted an internationalist posture and dropped its older style of isolationism. The fact that we exist in an interdependent world has become more vital to Canadians. Issues of peace, world trade and humanitarian interests actively concern many Canadians, and political leaders have forced the government towards a foreign policy which is in tune with Canada's domestic concerns and issues. By the mid-1980s the realization that no country can now be totally self-sufficient is an accepted maxim of international and domestic politics.

Selected Bibliography

Chapter 1

Alan C. Cairns, "Alternative Styles in the Study of Canadian Politics," *Canadian Journal of Political Science*, vol. 7, no. 1 (March 1974), pp. 101-128.

Bernard Crick, *In Defence of Politics*, 2nd. ed. (Harmondsworth: Penguin Books, 1972).

Robert J. Jackson and Michael B. Stein, *Issues in Comparative Politics* (New York: St. Martin's Press, 1971).

Joseph Lapalombara, *Politics Within Nations* (Englewood Cliffs: Prentice-Hall, 1974).

C.B. MacPherson, *The Real World of Democracy* (Toronto: CBC Publications, 1965).

Henry B. Mayo, *An Introduction to Democratic Theory* (New York: Oxford, 1960).

John H. Redekop, ed., *Approaches to the Study of Canadian Politics*, 2nd. ed. (Scarborough: Prentice-Hall Canada, 1983).

See also the periodical, *Canadian Journal of Political Science*.

Chapter 2

Richard M. Bird, *Financing Canadian Government: A Quantitative Overview* (Toronto: Canadian Tax Foundation, 1979).

J.B. Brebner, *North Atlantic Triangle: The Interplay of Canada, the United States and Great Britain* (Toronto: McClelland and Stewart, 1966).

Gurston Dacks, *A Choice of Futures: Politics in the Canadian North* (Toronto: Methuen, 1981).

W.T. Easterbrook and Melvyn H. Watkins, eds., *Approaches to Canadian Economic History: A Selection of Essays* (Toronto: McClelland and Stewart, 1967).

Daniel Glenday, Hubert Guindon and Allan Turowetz, eds., *Modernization and the Canadian State* (Toronto: Macmillan of Canada, 1978).

Ian Lumsden, ed., *Close the 49th Parallel etc: The Americanization of Canada* (Toronto: University of Toronto Press, 1971).

Kenneth D. McRae, "Empire, Language and Nation: The Canadian Case," S.M. Eisenstadt and S. Rokkan, eds., *Building States and Nations* (Beverly Hills and London: Sage Publications, 1973), vol. II, pp. 144-176.

Jon Pammett and Brian Tomlin, eds., *The Integration Question: Political Economy and Public Policy in Canada and North America* (Toronto: Addison-Wesley, 1984).

Chapter 3

Gabriel Almond and Sidney Verba, *The Civic Culture* (Boston: Little, Brown, 1965).

———————————————— , eds., *The Civic Culture Revisited* (Boston: Little, Brown, 1980).

David V.J. Bell and Lorne J. Tepperman, *The Roots of Disunity: A Look at Canadian Political Culture* (Toronto: McClelland and Stewart, 1979).

Stephen Brooks, ed., *Political Thought in Canada* (Toronto: Irwin, 1984).

William Christian and Colin Campbell, *Political Parties and Ideologies in Canada: Liberals, Conservatives, Socialists, Nationalists* 2nd. ed. (Toronto: McGraw-Hill Ryerson, 1983).

David Elkins and Richard Simeon, eds., *Small Worlds: Provinces and Parties in Canadian Political Life* (Toronto: Methuen, 1980).

Roger Gibbins, *Regionalism: Territorial Politics in Canada and the United States* (Toronto: Butterworth, 1983).

Louis Hartz, ed., *The Founding of New Societies* (New York: Harcourt Brace Jovanovich, 1964).

Gad Horowitz, "Conservatism, Liberalism and Socialism in Canada: An Interpretation," *Canadian Journal of Economics and Political Science*, vol. 32, no. 2 (May 1966), pp. 144-171.

M. Patricia Marchak, *Ideological Perspectives on Canada*, 2nd. ed. (Toronto: McGraw-Hill Ryerson, 1981).

William Mishler, *Political Participation in Canada: Prospects For Democratic Citizenship* (Toronto: MacMillan of Canada, 1979).

John Porter, *The Vertical Mosaic: An Analysis of Social Class and Power in Canada* (Toronto: University of Toronto Press, 1965).

Chapter 4

Paul Audley, *Canada's Cultural Industries: Broadcasting, Publishing, Records and Film* (Toronto: Lorimer, 1983).

Edwin R. Black, *Politics and the News: The Political Functions of the Mass Media* (Toronto: Butterworth, 1982).

Richard E. Dawson, Kenneth Prewitt and Karen S. Dawson, *Political Socialization*, 2nd ed. (Boston: Little, Brown, 1977).

John C. Johnstone, *Young People's Images of Canadian Society* (Ottawa: Queen's Printer, 1969).

Jon H. Pammett and Michael S. Whittington, eds., *Foundations of Political Culture: Political Socialization in Canada* (Toronto: MacMillan of Canada, 1976).

Arthur Siegel, *Politics and the Media in Canada* (Toronto: McGraw-Hill Ryerson, 1983).

Ted Tapper, *Political Education and Stability: Elite Responses to Political Conflict* (London: John Wiley and Sons, 1976).

Elia Zureik and Robert M. Pike, eds., *Socialization and Values in Canadian Society – Volume I: Political Socialization* (Toronto: McClelland and Stewart, 1975).

Chapter 5

Stanley M. Beck and Ivan Bernier, eds., *Canada and the New Constitution: The Unfinished Agenda*, 2 vols. (Montreal: Institute for Research on Public Policy, 1983).

Keith G. Banting and Richard Simeon, eds., *And No One Cheered: Federalism, Democracy and the Constitution Act* (Toronto: Methuen, 1983).

Ronald I. Cheffins and Ronald N. Tucker, *The Constitutional Process in Canada*, 2nd. ed. (Toronto: McGraw-Hill Ryerson, 1976).

Carl J. Friedrich, *Limited Government: A Comparison* (Englewood Cliffs: Prentice-Hall, 1974).

J. Stuart Langford, *The Law of Your Land: A Practical Guide to the New Constitution* (Toronto: CBC Publications, 1982).

J.R. Mallory, *Social Credit and the Federal Power in Canada* (Toronto: University of Toronto Press, 1954, 1977).

Charles M. McIlwain, *Constitutionalism: Ancient and Modern*, 2nd. ed. (Ithaca: Cornell University Press, 1947).

Edward McWhinney, *Canada and the Constitution 1979-1982: Patriation and the Charter of Rights* (Toronto: University of Toronto Press, 1982).

David Milne, *The New Canadian Constitution* (Toronto: Lorimer, 1982).

R.D. Olling and M.W. Westmacott, eds., *The Confederation Debate: The Constitution in Crisis* (Toronto: Kendall-Hunt, 1980).

Roy Romanow, John Whyte and Howard Leeson, *Canada Notwithstanding: The Making of the Constitution 1976-1982* (Toronto: Methuen, 1984).

Peter H. Russell, *Leading Constitutional Decisions: Cases on the British North America Act*, Rev. ed. (Toronto: McClelland and Stewart, 1973).

Chapter 6

Edwin R. Black, *Divided Loyalties: Canadian Concepts of Federalism* (Montreal: McGill-Queen's University Press, 1975).

Thomas J. Courchene, David W. Conklin and Gail C.A. Cook, eds., *Ottawa and the Provinces: The Distribution of Money and Power*, 2 volumes (Toronto: Ontario Economic Council, 1985).

Alain G. Gagnon, ed., *Québec: State and Society* (Toronto: Methuen, 1984).

Kenneth McRoberts and Dale Posgate, *Québec: Social Change and Political Crisis*, Rev. ed. (Toronto: McClelland and Stewart, 1980).

J. Peter Meekison, *Canadian Federalism: Myth or Reality*, 3rd. ed. (Toronto: Methuen, 1977).

Henry Milner, *Politics in the New Québec* (Toronto: McClelland and Stewart, 1977).

Larry Pratt and Garth Stevenson, eds., *Western Separatism: The Myths, Realities and Dangers* (Edmonton: Hurtig, 1981).

John Richards and Larry Pratt, *Prairie Capitalism: Power and Influence in the New West* (Toronto: McClelland and Stewart, 1979).

William H. Riker, *Federalism: Origin, Operation, Significance* (Boston: Little, Brown, 1964).

Donald V. Smiley, *Canada in Question: Federalism in the Eighties*, 3rd. ed. (Toronto: McGraw-Hill Ryerson, 1980).

Garth Stevenson, *Unfulfilled Union: Canadian Federalism and National Unity*, Rev. ed. (Toronto: Gage, 1982).

Chapter 7

Jean Blondel, *The Organization of Governments* (Beverly Hills and London: Sage Publications, 1982).

Colin Campbell, *Governments Under Stress: Executives and Key Bureaucrats in Washington, London and Ottawa* (Toronto: University of Toronto Press, 1983).

Colin Campbell and George Szablowski, *The Superbureaucrats: Structure and Behaviour in Central Agencies* (Toronto: MacMillan of Canada, 1979).

Walter Gordon, *A Political Memoir* (Toronto: McClelland and Stewart, 1977).

Thomas A. Hockin, ed., *of Power: The Prime Minister and Political Leadership in Canada*, 2nd. ed. (Scarborough: Prentice-Hall Canada, 1977).

Judy LaMarsh, *Memoirs of a Bird in a Gilded Cage* (Toronto: McClelland and Stewart, 1969).

William A. Matheson, *The Prime Minister and the Cabinet* (Toronto: Methuen, 1976).

R. Malcolm Punnett, *The Prime Minister in Canadian Government and Politics* (Toronto: Macmillan of Canada, 1977).

Richard Rose and Ezra N. Suleiman, eds., *Presidents and Prime Ministers* (Washington: American Enterprise Institute for Public Policy Research, 1980).

Patrick Weller, *First Among Equals: Prime Ministers in Westminster Systems (London: Allen and Unwin, 1985)*

Chapter 8

Gordon Aiken, *The Backbencher* (Toronto: McClelland and Stewart, 1974).

Colin Campbell, *The Canadian Senate: A Lobby from Within* (Toronto: Macmillan of Canada, 1978).

Harold D. Clarke, Colin Campbell, F.Q. Quo and Arthur Goddard, eds., *Parliament, Policy and Representation* (Toronto: Methuen, 1980).

Thomas d'Aquino, G. Bruce Doern and Cassandra Blair, *Parliamentary Democracy in Canada: Issues for Reform* (Toronto: Methuen, 1983).

William F. Dawson, *Procedure in the Canadian House of Commons* (Toronto: University of Toronto Press, 1962).

Robert J. Jackson and Michael M. Atkinson, *The Canadian Legislative System,* 2nd. rev. ed. (Toronto: Macmillan of Canada, 1980).

Michael M. Mezey, *Comparative Legislatures* (Durham: Duke University Press, 1979).

William A.W. Neilson and James C. MacPherson, eds., *The Legislative Process in Canada: The Need for Reform* (Montreal: Institute for Research on Public Policy, 1978).

David M. Olson *The Legislative Process: A Comparative Perspective* (New York: Harper and Row, 1980).

Special Issue on "Legislatures in Canada," *Legislative Studies Quarterly,* vol. 3, no. 4 (November 1978).

Special Issue on "Responsible Government Reconsidered," *Journal of Canadian Studies,* fol. 14, no. 2 (Summer 1979).

See also the periodicals, *Canadian Parliamentary Reviw* and *Parliamentary Government.*

Chapter 9

Robert F. Adie and Paul G. Thomas, *Canadian Public Administration: Problematical Perspectives* (Scarborough: Prentice-Hall Canada, 1982).

Peter M. Blau, *Bureaucracy in Modern Society* (New York: Random House, 1956).

Audrey D. Doerr, *The Machinery of Government in Canada* (Toronto: Methuen, 1981).

O. P. Dwivedi, ed., *The Administrative State in Canada: Essays for J.E. Hodgetts* (Toronto: University of Toronto Press, 1982).

J.E. Hodgetts *The Canadian Public Service 1867-1970: A Physiology of Government* (Toronto: University of Toronto Press, 1973).

Kenneth Kernaghan, ed., *Canadian Public Administration: Discipline and Profession* (Toronto: Butterworth/Institute of Public Administration of Canada, 1983).

———————————————— *Public Administration in Canada: Selected Readings,* 5th ed. (Toronto: Methuen, 1985).

Kenneth Kernaghan & David Siegel, *Public Administration in Canada: A Text* (Toronto: Methuen, forthcoming 1986)

Peter Self, *Administrative Theories and Politics*, 2nd ed., (Toronto: University of Toronto Press, 1977).

Sharon L. Sutherland and G. Bruce Doern, *Bureaucracy in Canada: Control and Reform*, Royal Commission on the Economic Union, Research Study No. 43 (Toronto: University of Toronto Press, 1985).

V. Seymour Wilson, *Canadian Public Policy and Administration: Theory and Environment* (Toronto: McGraw-Hill Ryerson, 1981).

See also the periodical, *Canadian Public Administration*.

Chapter 10

Sylvia B. Bashevkin, *Toeing the Lines: Women in Party Politics in English Canada* (Ottawa: Carleton University Press, 1985)

M. Janine Brodie and Jane Jensen, *Crisis, Challenge and Change: Party and Class in Canada* (Toronto: Methuen, 1980).

Maurice Duverger, *Political Parties: Their Organisation and Activity in the Modern State* (London: Methuen, 1954).

Frederick C. Engelmann and Mildred A. Schwartz, *Canadian Political Parties: Origin, Character, Impact* (Scarborough: Prentice-Hall Canada, 1975).

John Meisel, *Cleavages, Parties and Values in Canada* (Beverly Hills and London: Sage Publications, 1974).

George C. Perlin, *The Tory Syndrome: Leadership Politics in the Progressive Conservative Party* (Montreal: McGill-Queen's University Press, 1980).

Giovanni Sartori, *Parties and Party Systems: A Framework for Analysis* (London: Cambridge University Press, 1976).

Hugh G. Thorburn, ed., *Party Politics in Canada*, 5th. ed. (Scarborough: Prentice-Hall Canada, 1985).

Joseph Wearing, *The L-Shaped Party: The Liberal Party of Canada 1958-1980* (Toronto: McGraw-Hill Ryerson, 1981).

Reginald Whitaker *The Government Party: Organizing and Financing the Liberal Party of Canada 1930-1958* (Toronto: University of Toronto Press, 1977).

Conrad Winn and John McMenemy, eds., *Political Parties in Canada* (Toronto: McGraw-Hill Ryerson, 1976).

Chapter 11

David Butler and Austin Ranney, eds., *Referendums: A Comparative Study of Practice and Theory* (Washington: American Enterprise Institute for Public Policy Research, 1978).

Harold D. Clarke, Jane Jensen, Lawrence Leduc and Jon H. Pammett, *Absent Mandate: The Politics of Discontent in Canada* (Toronto: Gage, 1984).

——————————— *Political Choice in Canada* (Toronto: McGraw-Hill Ryerson, 1979),

Allan Frizzell and Anthony Westell, *The Canadian General Election of 1984: Politicians, Parties, Press and Polls* (Ottawa: Carleton University Press, 1985).

William P. Irvine, *Does Canada Need a New Electoral System?* (Kingston: Queen's University Institute of Intergovernmental Relations, 1979).

Enid Lakeman, *How Democracies Vote: A Study of Electoral Systems*, 4th rev. ed. (London: Faber and Faber, 1974).

John Meisel, *Working Papers On Canadian Politics,* 2nd. enlarged ed. (Montreal: McGill-Queen's University Press, 1975).

Howard R. Penniman, ed., *Canada at the Polls 1979 and 1980: A Study of the General Elections* (Washington: American Enterprise Institute for Public Policy Research, 1981). *Canada at the Polls 1984,* forthcoming.

Douglas W. Rae, *The Political Consequences of Electoral Laws* (New Haven: Yale University Press, 1967).

Mildred A. Schwartz, "Canadian Voting Behavior," Richard Rose, ed., *Electoral Behavior: A Comparative Handbook* (New York: The Free Press, 1974), pp. 543-617.

Walter C. Soderlund, Walter I. Romanow, E. Donald Briggs and Ronald H. Wagenburg, *Media and Elections in Canada* (Toronto: Holt, Rinehart and Winston of Canada, 1984).

Chapter 12

James Gillies, *Where Business Fails: Business-Government Relations at the Federal Level in Canada* (Montreal: Institute for Research on Public Policy, 1981).

David Kwavnik, *Organized Labour and Pressure Politics: The Canadian Labour Congress 1956-1968* (Montreal: McGill-Queen's University Press, 1972).

Robert Laxer, *Canada's Unions* (Toronto: Lorimer, 1976).

Leo Panitch, ed., *The Canadian State: Political Economy and Political Power* (Toronto: University of Toronto Press, 1971).

A. Paul Pross, ed., "Governing Under Pressure: The Special Interest Groups," *Canadian Public Administration,* vol. 25, no. 2 (Summer 1982).

——————————— *Pressure Group Behaviour in Canadian Politics* (Scarborough: McGraw-Hill Ryerson, 1975).

Richard J. Schultz, *Federalism, Bureaucracy and Public Policy: The Politics of Highway Transport Regulations,* (Montreal: McGill-Queen's University Press, 1980).

William T. Stanbury, ed., *Business Interests and the Reform of Canadian Competition Policy* (Toronto: Carswell/Methuen, 1977).

Fred Thompson and William T. Stanbury, *The Political Economy of Interest Groups in the Legislative Process in Canada* (Montreal: Institute for Research on Public Policy, 1979).

Hugh G. Thorburn, *Interest Groups in the Canadian Federal System,* Royal Commission on the Economic Union Research Study No. 69 (Toronto: University of Toronto Press, 1985).

Chapter 13

Michael M. Atkinson and Marsha A. Chandler, eds., *The Politics of Canadian Public Policy* (Toronto: University of Toronto Press, 1983).

Marsha A. Chandler and William M. Chandler, *Public Policy and Provincial Politics* (Toronto: McGraw-Hill Ryerson, 1979).

G. Bruce Doern, ed., *The Regulatory Process in Canada* (Toronto: MacMillan of Canada, 1978).

G. Bruce Doern and Richard W. Phidd, *Canadian Public Policy: Ideas, Structure, Process* (Toronto: Methuen, 1983).

Richard D. French (with Richard Van Loon), *How Ottawa Decides: Planning and Industrial Policy-Making 1968-1984,* 2nd. ed. (Toronto: Lorimer, 1984).

Anthony G. McGrew and M.J. Wilson, eds., *Decision-Making: Approaches and Analysis* (Manchester: Manchester University Press, 1982).

Richard Simeon, "Studying Public Policy," *Canadian Journal of Political Science*, vol. 9, no. 4 (December 1976), pp. 548-580.

Michael J. Trebilcock, Douglas G. Hartle, J. Robert, S. Prichard and Donald N. Dewees, *The Choice of Governing Instrument*, A Study prepared for the Economic Council of Canada (Ottawa: Minister of Supply and Services, 1982).

Allan Tupper and G. Bruce Doern, eds., *Public Corporations and Public Policy in Canada* (Montreal: Institute for Research on Public Policy, 1981).

See also the periodicals. *Canadian Public Policy, Policy Options,* and *How Ottawa Spends. . . ,* the annual review of federal spending priorities and policy developments, from 1980 to 1983, edited by G. Bruce Doern and published by Lorimer (Toronto), since 1984, edited by Allan M. Maslove and published by Methuen (Toronto).

Chapter 14

Stephen Clarkson, *Canada and the Reagan Challenge: Crisis and Adjustment 1981-1985*, 2nd. ed. (Toronto: Lorimer, 1985).

David B. Dewitt and John J. Kirton, *Canada as a Principal Power* (Toronto: John Wiley, 1983).

Kai J. Holsti, *International Politics: A Framework for Analysis*, 4th. ed. (Englewood Cliffs: Prentice-Hall, 1983).

John W. Holmes, *Life with Uncle* (Toronto: University of Toronto Press, 1981).

Robert J. Jackson, ed., *Continuity of Discord: Crises and Responses in the Atlantic Community* (New York: Praeger, 1985).

Peyton V. Lyon and Brian Tomlin, eds., *Canada as an International Actor* (Toronto: Macmillan of Canada, 1979).

Kim Richard Nossal, *The Politics of Canadian Foreign Policy* (Scarborough: Prentice-Hall Canada, 1985).

Brian W. Tomlin, ed., *Canada's Foreign Policy: Analysis and Trends* (Toronto: Methuen, 1977).

Brian W. Tomlin and Maureen Molot, eds., *Canada Among Nations 1984: A Time of Transition* (Toronto: Lorimer, 1985).

Michael Tucker, *Canadian Foreign Policy* (Toronto: McGraw-Hill Ryerson, 1980).

See also the periodicals, *International Journal* and *International Perspectives.*

CANADA

A Consolidation of

THE
CONSTITUTION
ACTS
1867 to 1982

DEPARTMENT OF JUSTICE
CANADA

Consolidated as of April 17, 1982

THE CONSTITUTION ACT, 1867

30 & 31 Victoria, c. 3.

(Consolidated with amendments)

An Act for the Union of Canada, Nova Scotia, and New Brunswick, and the Government thereof; and for Purposes connected therewith.

(29th March, 1867.)

WHEREAS the Provinces of Canada, Nova Scotia and New Brunswick have expressed their Desire to be federally united into One Dominion under the Crown of the United Kingdom of Great Britain and Ireland, with a Constitution similar in Principle to that of the United Kingdom:

And whereas such a Union would conduce to the Welfare of the Provinces and promote the Interests of the British Empire:

And whereas on the Establishment of the Union by Authority of Parliament it is expedient, not only that the Constitution of the Legislative Authority in the Dominion be provided for, but also that the Nature of the Executive Government therein be declared:

And whereas it is expedient that Provision be made for the eventual Admission into the Union of other Parts of British North America: (1)

I. - PRELIMINARY.

1. This Act may be cited as the *Constitution Act, 1867*.(2) Short title.

---

(1) The enacting clause was repealed by the *Statute Law Revision Act, 1893*, 56-57 Vict., c 14 (U.K.). It read as follows:

> Be it therefore enacted and declared by the Queen's Most Excellent Majesty, by and with the Advice and Consent of the Lords Spiritual and Temporal, and Commons, in this present Parliament assembled, and by the Authority of the same, as follows:

(2) As enacted by the *Constitution Act, 1982*, which came into force on April 17, 1982. The section, as originally enacted, read as follows:

> **1.** This Act may be cited as The British North America Act, 1867.

2. Repealed.(3)

II.—Union.

Declaration of
Union.

3. It shall be lawful for the Queen, by and with the Advice of Her Majesty's Most Honourable Privy Council, to declare by Proclamation that, on and after a Day therein appointed, not being more than Six Months after the passing of this Act, the Provinces of Canada, Nova Scotia, and New Brunswick shall form and be One Dominion under the Name of Canada; and on and after that Day those Three Provinces shall form and be One Dominion under that Name accordingly.(4)

Construction of
subsequent
Provisions of
Act.

4. Unless it is otherwise expressed or implied, the Name Canada shall be taken to mean Canada as constituted under this Act.(5)

Four Provinces.

5. Canada shall be divided into Four Provinces, named Ontario, Quebec, Nova Scotia, and New Brunswick.(6)

---

(3) Section 2, repealed by the *Statute Law Revision Act, 1893*, 56-57 Vict., c. 14 (U.K.), read as follows:

> **2.** The Provisions of this Act referring to Her Majesty the Queen extend also to the Heirs and Successors of Her Majesty, Kings and Queens of the United Kingdom of Great Britain and Ireland.

(4) The first day of July, 1867, was fixed by proclamation dated May 22, 1867.

(5) Partially repealed by the *Statute Law Revision Act, 1893*, 56-57 Vict., c. 14 (U.K.). As originally enacted the section read as follows:

> **4.** The subsequent Provisions of this Act, shall, unless it is otherwise expressed or implied, commence and have effect on and after the Union, that is to say, on and after the Day appointed for the Union taking effect in the Queen's Proclamation; and in the same Provisions, unless it is otherwise expressed or implied, the Name Canada shall be taken to mean Canada as constituted under this Act.

(6) Canada now consists of ten provinces (Ontario, Quebec, Nova Scotia, New Brunswick, Manitoba, British Columbia, Prince Edward Island, Alberta, Saskatchewan and Newfoundland) and two territories (the Yukon Territory and the Northwest Territories).

The first territories added to the Union were Rupert's Land and the North-Western Territory, (subsequently designated the Northwest Territories), which were admitted pursuant to section 146 of the *Constitution Act, 1867* and the *Rupert's Land Act*, 1868, 31-32 Vict., c. 105 (U.K.), by the *Rupert's Land and North-Western Territory Order* of June 23, 1870, effective July 15, 1870. Prior to the admission of those territories the Parliament of Canada enacted *An Act for the temporary Government of Rupert's Land and the North-Western Territory when united with Canada* (32-33 Vict., c. 3), and the *Manitoba Act, 1870*, (33 Vict., c. 3), which provided for the formation of the Province of Manitoba.

British Columbia was admitted into the Union pursuant to section 146 of the *Constitution Act, 1867*, by the *British Columbia Terms of Union*, being Order in Council of May 16, 1871, effective July 20, 1871.

Provinces of Ontario and Quebec.

6. The Parts of the Province of Canada (as it exists at the passing of this Act) which formerly constituted respectively the Provinces of Upper Canada and Lower Canada shall be deemed to be severed, and shall form Two separate Provinces. The Part which formerly constituted the Province of Upper Canada shall constitute the Province of Ontario; and the Part which formerly constituted the Province of Lower Canada shall constitute the Province of Quebec.

Provinces of Nova Scotia and New Brunswick.

7. The Provinces of Nova Scotia and New Brunswick shall have the same Limits as at the passing of this Act.

Decennial Census.

8. In the general Census of the Population of Canada which is hereby required to be taken in the Year One thousand eight hundred and seventy-one, and in every Tenth Year thereafter, the respective Populations of the Four Provinces shall be distinguished.

III.—EXECUTIVE POWER.

Declaration of Executive Power in the Queen.

9. The Executive Government and Authority of and over Canada is hereby declared to continue and be vested in the Queen.

Prince Edward Island was admitted pursuant to section 146 of the *Constitution Act, 1867*, by the *Prince Edward Island Terms of Union*, being Order in Council of June 26, 1873, effective July 1, 1873.

On June 29, 1871, the United Kingdom Parliament enacted the *Constitution Act, 1871* (34-35 Vict., c. 28) authorizing the creation of additional provinces out of territories not included in any province. Pursuant to this statute, the Parliament of Canada enacted the *Alberta Act*, (July 20, 1905, 4-5 Edw. VII, c. 3) and the *Saskatchewan Act*, (July 20, 1905, 4-5 Edw.VII, c. 42), providing for the creation of the provinces of Alberta and Saskatchewan, respectively. Both these Acts came into force on Sept. 1, 1905.

Meanwhile, all remaining British possessions and territories in North America and the islands adjacent thereto, except the colony of Newfoundland and its dependencies, were admitted into the Canadian Confederation by the *Adjacent Territories Order*, dated July 31, 1880.

The Parliament of Canada added portions of the Northwest Territories to the adjoining provinces in 1912 by *The Ontario Boundaries Extension Act*, 1912, 2 Geo. V, c. 40, *The Quebec Boundaries Extension Act*, 1912, 2 Geo. V, c. 45 and *The Manitoba Boundaries Extension Act*, 1912, 2 Geo. V, c. 32, and further additions were made to Manitoba by *The Manitoba Boundaries Extension Act*, 1930, 20-21 Geo. V., c. 28.

The Yukon Territory was created out of the Northwest Territories in 1898 by *The Yukon Territory Act*, 61 Vict., c. 6, (Canada).

Newfoundland was added on March 31, 1949, by the *Newfoundland Act*, (U.K.), 12-13 Geo. VI, c. 22, which ratified the Terms of Union between Canada and Newfoundland.

Application of Provisions referring to Governor General.

10. The Provisions of this Act referring to the Governor General extend and apply to the Governor General for the Time being of Canada, or other the Chief Executive Officer or Administrator for the Time being carrying on the Government of Canada on behalf and in the Name of the Queen, by whatever Title he is designated.

Constitution of Privy Council for Canada.

11. There shall be a Council to aid and advise in the Government of Canada, to be styled the Queen's Privy Council for Canada; and the Persons who are to be Members of that Council shall be from Time to Time chosen and summoned by the Governor General and sworn in as Privy Councillors, and Members thereof may be from Time to Time removed by the Governor General.

All Powers under Acts to be exercised by Governor General with Advice of Privy Council, or alone.

12. All Powers, Authorities, and Functions which under any Act of the Parliament of Great Britain, or of the Parliament of the United Kingdom of Great Britain and Ireland, or of the Legislature of Upper Canada, Lower Canada, Canada, Nova Scotia, or New Brunswick, are at the Union vested in or exerciseable by the respective Governors or Lieutenant Governors of those Provinces, with the Advice, or with the Advice and Consent, of the respective Executive Councils thereof, or in conjunction with those Councils, or with any Number of Members thereof, or by those Governors or Lieutenant Governors individually, shall, as far as the same continue in existence and capable of being exercised after the Union in relation to the Government of Canada, be vested in and exerciseable by the Governor General, with the Advice or with the Advice and Consent of or in conjunction with the Queen's Privy Council for Canada, or any Member thereof, or by the Governor General individually, as the Case requires, subject nevertheless (except with respect to such as exist under Acts of the Parliament of Great Britain or of the Parliament of the United Kingdom of Great Britain and Ireland) to be abolished or altered by the Parliament of Canada.(7)

Application of Provisions referring to Governor General in Council.

13. The Provisions of this Act referring to the Governor General in Council shall be construed as referring to the Governor General acting by and with the Advice of the Queen's Privy Council for Canada.

---

(7) See the notes to section 129, *infra*.

14. It shall be lawful for the Queen, if Her Majesty thinks fit, to authorize the Governor General from Time to Time to appoint any Person or any Persons jointly or several-ly to be his Deputy or Deputies within any Part or Parts of Canada, and in that Capacity to exercise during the Pleasure of the Governor General such of the Powers, Authorities, and Functions of the Governor General as the Governor General deems it necessary or expedient to assign to him or them, subject to any Limitations or Directions expressed or given by the Queen; but the Appointment of such a Deputy or Depu-ties shall not affect the Exercise by the Governor General himself of any Power, Authority or Function.

Power to Her Majesty to authorize Governor General to appoint Deputies.

15. The Command-in-Chief of the Land and Naval Militia, and of all Naval and Military Forces, of and in Canada, is hereby declared to continue and be vested in the Queen.

Command of armed Forces to continue to be vested in the Queen.

16. Until the Queen otherwise directs, the Seat of Gov-ernment of Canada shall be Ottawa.

Seat of Government of Canada.

IV.—LEGISLATIVE POWER.

17. There shall be One Parliament for Canada, consisting of the Queen, an Upper House styled the Senate, and the House of Commons.

Constitution of Parliament of Canada.

18. The privileges, immunities, and powers to be held, enjoyed, and exercised by the Senate and by the House of Commons, and by the Members thereof respectively, shall be such as are from time to time defined by Act of the Parlia-ment of Canada, but so that any Act of the Parliament of Canada defining such privileges, immunities, and powers shall not confer any privileges, immunities, or powers exceed-ing those at the passing of such Act held, enjoyed, and exercised by the Commons House of Parliament of the United Kingdom of Great Britain and Ireland, and by the Members thereof.(8)

Privileges, etc. of Houses.

---

(8) Repealed and re-enacted by the *Parliament of Canada Act, 1875*, 38-39 Vict., c. 38 (U.K.). The original section read as follows:

> **18.** The Privileges, Immunities, and Powers to be held, enjoyed, and exercised by the Senate and by the House of Commons and by the Members thereof respectively shall be such as are from Time to Time defined by Act of the Parliament of Canada, but so that the same shall never exceed those at the passing of this Act held, enjoyed, and exercised by the Commons House of Parliament of the United Kingdom of Great Britain and Ireland and by the Members thereof.

First Session of
the Parliament
of Canada.

19. The Parliament of Canada shall be called together not later than Six Months after the Union.(9)

20. Repealed.(10)

The Senate.

Number of
Senators.

21. The Senate shall, subject to the Provisions of this Act, consist of One Hundred and four Members, who shall be styled Senators.(11)

Representation
of Provinces in
Senate.

22. In relation to the Constitution of the Senate Canada shall be deemed to consist of Four Divisions:–

1. Ontario;
2. Quebec;
3. The Maritime Provinces, Nova Scotia and New Brunswick, and Prince Edward Island;
4. The Western Provinces of Manitoba, British Columbia, Saskatchewan, and Alberta;

which Four Divisions shall (subject to the Provisions of this Act) be equally represented in the Senate as follows: Ontario by twenty-four senators; Quebec by twenty-four senators; the Maritime Provinces and Prince Edward Island by twenty-four senators, ten thereof representing Nova Scotia, ten

---

(9) Spent. The first session of the first Parliament began on November 6, 1867.

(10) Section 20, repealed by the Schedule to the *Constitution Act, 1982*, read as follows:

> **20.** There shall be a Session of the Parliament of Canada once at least in every Year, so that Twelve Months shall not intervene between the last Sitting of the Parliament in one Session and its first Sitting in the next Session.

> Section 20 has been replaced by section 5 of the *Constitution Act, 1982*, which provides that there shall be a sitting of Parliament at least once every twelve months.

(11) As amended by the *Constitution Act, 1915*, 5-6 Geo. V, c. 45 (U.K.) and modified by the *Newfoundland Act*, 12-13 Geo. VI, c. 22 (U.K.), and the *Constitution Act (No. 2), 1975*, S.C. 1974-75-76, c. 53.

The original section read as follows:

> **21.** The Senate shall, subject to the Provisions of this Act, consist of Seventy-two Members, who shall be styled Senators.

The *Manitoba Act, 1870*, added two for Manitoba; the *British Columbia Terms of Union* added three; upon admission of Prince Edward Island four more were provided by section 147 of the *Constitution Act, 1867*; the *Alberta Act* and the *Saskatchewan Act* each added four. The Senate was reconstituted at 96 by the *Constitution Act, 1915*. Six more Senators were added upon union with Newfoundland, and one Senator each was added for the Yukon Territory and the Northwest Territories by the *Constitution Act (No. 2), 1975*.

thereof representing New Brunswick, and four thereof representing Prince Edward Island; the Western Provinces by twenty-four senators, six thereof representing Manitoba, six thereof representing British Columbia, six thereof representing Saskatchewan, and six thereof representing Alberta; Newfoundland shall be entitled to be represented in the Senate by six members; the Yukon Territory and the Northwest Territories shall be entitled to be represented in the Senate by one member each.

In the Case of Quebec each of the Twenty-four Senators representing that Province shall be appointed for One of the Twenty-four Electoral Divisions of Lower Canada specified in Schedule A. to Chapter One of the Consolidated statutes of Canada. (12)

23. The Qualification of a Senator shall be as follows: Qualifications of Senator.

(1) He shall be of the full age of Thirty Years:

(2) He shall be either a natural-born Subject of the Queen, or a Subject of the Queen naturalized by an Act of the Parliament of Great Britain, or of the Parliament of the United Kingdom of Great Britain and Ireland, or of the Legislature of One of the Provinces of Upper Canada, Lower Canada, Canada, Nova Scotia, or New Brunswick, before the Union, or of the Parliament of Canada, after the Union:

(3) He shall be legally or equitably seised as of Freehold for his own Use and Benefit of Lands or Tenements held in Free and Common Socage, or seised or possessed for his own Use and Benefit of Lands or Tenements held in Franc-alleu or in Roture, within

---

(12) As amended by the *Constitution Act, 1915*, the *Newfoundland Act*, 12-13 Geo. VI, c. 22 (U.K.), and the *Constitution Act (No. 2), 1975*, S.C. 1974-75-76, c. 53. The original section read as follows:

22. In relation to the Constitution of the Senate, Canada shall be deemed to consist of Three Divisions:

1. Ontario;

2. Quebec;

3. The Maritime Provinces, Nova Scotia and New Brunswick; which Three Divisions shall (subject to the Provisions of this Act) be equally represented in the Senate as follows: Ontario by Twenty-four Senators; Quebec by Twenty-four Senators; and the Maritime Provinces by Twenty-four Senators, Twelve thereof representing Nova Scotia, and Twelve thereof representing New Brunswick.

In the case of Quebec each of the Twenty-four Senators representing that Province shall be appointed for One of the Twenty-four Electoral Divisions of Lower Canada specified in Schedule A. to Chapter One of the Consolidated Statutes of Canada.

the Province for which he is appointed, of the Value of Four thousand Dollars, over and above all Rents, Dues, Debts, Charges, Mortgages, and Incumbrances due or payable out of or charged on or affecting the same:

(4) His Real and Personal Property shall be together worth Four thousand Dollars over and above his Debts and Liabilities:

(5) He shall be resident in the Province for which he is appointed:

(6) In the Case of Quebec he shall have his Real Property Qualification in the Electoral Division for which he is appointed, or shall be resident in that Division. (13)

Summons of Senator.

24. The Governor General shall from Time to Time, in the Queen's Name, by Instrument under the Great Seal of Canada, summon qualified Persons to the Senate; and, subject to the Provisions of this Act, every Person so summoned shall become and be a Member of the Senate and a Senator.

25. Repealed. (14)

Addition of Senators in certain cases.

26. If at any Time on the Recommendation of the Governor General the Queen thinks fit to direct that Four or Eight Members be added to the Senate, the Governor General may by Summons to Four or Eight qualified Persons (as the Case may be), representing equally the Four Divisions of Canada, add to the Senate accordingly.(15)

---

(13) Section 2 of the *Constitution Act (No. 2), 1975*, S.C. 1974-75-76, c. 53 provided that for the purposes of that Act (which added one Senator each for the Yukon Territory and the Northwest Territories) the term "Province" in section 23 of the *Constitution Act, 1867*, has the same meaning as is assigned to the term "province" by section 28 of the *Interpretation Act*, R.S.C. 1970, c. I-23, which provides that the term "province" means "a province of Canada, and includes the Yukon Territory and the Northwest Territories."

(14) Repealed by the *Statute Law Revision Act, 1893*, 56-57 Vict., 14 (U.K.). The section read as follows:

> **25.** Such Persons shall be first summoned to the Senate as the Queen by Warrant under Her Majesty's Royal Sign Manual thinks fit to approve, and their Names shall be inserted in the Queen's Proclamation of Union.

(15) As amended by the *Constitution Act, 1915*, 5-6 Geo. V, c. 45 (U.K.). The original section read as follows:

> **26.** If at any Time on the Recommendation of the Governor General the Queen thinks fit to direct that Three or Six Members be added to the Senate, the Governor General may by Summons to Three or Six qualified Persons (as the Case may be), representing equally the Three Divisions of Canada, add to the Senate accordingly.

27. In case of such Addition being at any Time made, the Governor General shall not summon any Person to the Senate, except upon a further like Direction by the Queen on the like Recommendation, to represent one of the Four Divisions until such Division is represented by Twenty-four Senators and no more.(16)

Reduction of Senate to normal Number.

28. The Number of Senators shall not at any Time exceed One Hundred and twelve. (17)

Maximum Number of Senators.

29. (1) Subject to subsection (2), a Senator shall, subject to the provisions of this Act, hold his place in the Senate for life.

Tenure of Place in Senate.

(2) A Senator who is summoned to the Senate after the coming into force of this subsection shall, subject to this Act, hold his place in the Senate until he attains the age of seventy-five years. (18)

Retirement upon attaining age of seventy-five years.

30. A Senator may by Writing under his Hand addressed to the Governor General resign his Place in the Senate, and thereupon the same shall be vacant.

Resignation of Place in Senate.

31. The Place of a Senator shall become vacant in any of the following Cases:

Disqualification of Senators.

(1) If for Two consecutive Sessions of the Parliament he fails to give his Attendance in the Senate:

(2) If he takes an Oath or makes a Declaration or Acknowledgement of Allegiance, Obedience, or Adherence to a Foreign Power, or does an Act whereby he becomes a Subject or Citizen, or entitled to the

---

(16) As amended by the *Constitution Act, 1915*, 5-6 Geo. V, c. 45 (U.K.). The original section read as follows:

> **27.** In case of such Addition being at any Time made the Governor General shall not summon any Person to the Senate except on a further like Direction by the Queen on the like Recommendation, until each of the Three Divisions of Canada is represented by Twenty-four Senators and no more.

(17) As amended by the *Constitution Act, 1915*, 5-6 Geo. V, c. 45 (U.K.), and the *Constitution Act (No. 2), 1975*, S.C. 1974-75-76, c. 53. The original section read as follows:

> **28.** The Number of Senators shall not at any Time exceed Seventy-eight.

(18) As enacted by the *Constitution Act, 1965*, Statutes of Canada, 1965, c. 4 which came into force on the 1st of June 1965. The original section read as follows:

> **29.** A Senator shall, subject to the Provisions of this Act, hold his Place in the Senate for Life.

Rights or Privileges of a Subject or Citizen, of a Foreign Power.

(3) If he is adjudged Bankrupt or Insolvent, or applies for the Benefit of any Law relating to Insolvent Debtors, or becomes a public Defaulter:

(4) If he is attainted of Treason or convicted of Felony or of any infamous Crime:

(5) If he ceases to be qualified in respect of Property or of Residence; provided, that a Senator shall not be deemed to have ceased to be qualified in respect of Residence by reason only of his residing at the Seat of the Government of Canada while holding an Office under that Government requiring his Presence there.

Summons on Vacancy in Senate.

32. When a Vacancy happens in the Senate by Resignation, Death or otherwise, the Governor General shall by Summons to a fit and qualified Person fill the Vacancy.

Questions as to Qualifications and Vacancies in Senate.

33. If any Question arises respecting the Qualification of a Senator or a Vacancy in the Senate the same shall be heard and determined by the Senate.

Appointment of Speaker of Senate.

34. The Governor General may from Time to Time, by Instrument under the Great Seal of Canada, appoint a Senator to be Speaker of the Senate, and may remove him and appoint another in his Stead. (19)

Quorum of Senate.

35. Until the Parliament of Canada otherwise provides, the Presence of at least Fifteen Senators, including the Speaker, shall be necessary to constitute a Meeting of the Senate for the Exercise of its Powers.

Voting in Senate.

36. Questions arising in the Senate shall be decided by a Majority of Voices, and the Speaker shall in all Cases have a Vote, and when the Voices are equal the Decision shall be deemed to be in the Negative.

---

(19) Provision for exercising the functions of Speaker during his absence is made by the *Speaker of the Senate Act,* R.S.C. 1970, c. S-14. Doubts as to the power of Parliament to enact such an Act were removed by the *Canadian Speaker (Appointment of Deputy) Act, 1895,* 59 Vict., c. 3 (U.K.) which was repealed by the *Constitution Act, 1982.*

The House of Commons.

37. The House of Commons shall, subject to the Provisions of this Act, consist of two hundred and eighty-two members of whom ninety-five shall be elected for Ontario, seventy-five for Quebec, eleven for Nova Scotia, ten for New Brunswick, fourteen for Manitoba, twenty-eight for British Columbia, four for Prince Edward Island, twenty-one for Alberta, fourteen for Saskatchewan, seven for Newfoundland, one for the Yukon Territory and two for the Northwest Territories.(20)

Constitution of House of Commons in Canada.

38. The Governor General shall from Time to Time, in the Queen's Name, by Instrument under the Great Seal of Canada, summon and call together the House of Commons.

Summoning of House of Commons.

39. A Senator shall not be capable of being elected or of sitting or voting as a Member of the House of Commons.

Senators not to sit in House of Commons.

40. Until the Parliament of Canada otherwise provides, Ontario, Quebec, Nova Scotia and New Brunswick shall, for the Purposes of the Election of Members to serve in the House of Commons, be divided into Electoral districts as follows:

Electoral districts of the four Provinces

1.—ONTARIO.

Ontario shall be divided into the Counties, Ridings of Counties, Cities, Parts of Cities, and Towns enumerated in the First Schedule to this Act, each whereof shall be an Electoral District, each such District as numbered in that Schedule being entitled to return One Member.

2.—QUEBEC.

Quebec shall be divided into Sixty-five Electoral Districts, composed of the Sixty-five Electoral Divisions into which Lower Canada is at the passing of this Act divided under

---

(20) The figures given here result from the application of section 51, as enacted by the *Constitution Act, 1974*, S.C. 1974-75-76, c. 13, amended by the *Constitution Act (No. 1), 1975*, S.C. 1974-75-76, c. 28 and readjusted pursuant to the *Electoral Boundaries Readjustment Act*, R.S.C., 1970, c. E-2. The original section (which was altered from time to time as the result of the addition of new provinces and changes in population) read as follows:

37. The House of Commons shall, subject to the Provisions of this Act, consist of one hundred and eighty-one members, of whom Eighty-two shall be elected for Ontario, Sixty-five for Quebec, Nineteen for Nova Scotia, and Fifteen for New Brunswick.

Chapter Two of the Consolidated Statutes of Canada, Chapter Seventy-five of the Consolidated Statutes for Lower Canada, and the Act of the Province of Canada of the Twenty-third Year of the Queen, Chapter One, or any other Act amending the same in force at the Union, so that each such Electoral Division shall be for the Purposes of this Act an Electoral District entitled to return One Member.

3.—NOVA SCOTIA.

Each of the Eighteen Counties of Nova Scotia shall be an Electoral District. The County of Halifax shall be entitled to return Two Members, and each of the other Counties One Member.

4.—NEW BRUNSWICK.

Each of the Fourteen Counties into which New Brunswick is divided, including the City and County of St. John, shall be an Electoral District. The City of St. John shall also be a separate Electoral District. Each of those Fifteen Electoral Districts shall be entitled to return One Member.(21)

41. Until the Parliament of Canada otherwise provides, all Laws in force in the several Provinces at the Union relative to the following Matters or any of them, namely,— the Qualifications and Disqualifications of Persons to be elected or to sit or vote as Members of the House of Assembly or Legislative Assembly in the several Provinces, the Voters at Elections of such Members, the Oaths to be taken by Voters, the Returning Officers, their Powers and Duties, the Proceedings at Elections, the Periods during which Elections may be continued, the Trial of controverted Elections, and Proceedings incident thereto, the vacating of Seats of Members, and the Execution of new Writs in case of Seats vacated otherwise than by Dissolution,—shall respectively apply to Elections of Members to serve in the House of Commons for the same several Provinces.

Continuance of existing Election Laws until Parliament of Canada otherwise provides

Provided that, until the Parliament of Canada otherwise provides, at any Election for a Member of the House of

---

(21) Spent. The electoral districts are now established by Proclamations issued from time to time under the *Electoral Boundaries Readjustment Act*, R.S.C., 1970, c. E-2, as amended for particular districts by Acts of Parliament, for which see the most recent Table of Public Statutes.

Commons for the District of Algoma, in addition to Persons qualified by the Law of the Province of Canada to vote, every Male British Subject, aged Twenty-one Years or upwards, being a Householder, shall have a Vote.(22)

42. Repealed.(23)

43. Repealed.(24)

44. The House of Commons on its first assembling after a General Election shall proceed with all practicable Speed to elect One of its Members to be Speaker. *As to Election of Speaker of House of Commons.*

45. In case of a Vacancy happening in the Office of Speaker by Death, Resignation, or otherwise, the House of Commons shall with all practicable Speed proceed to elect another of its Members to be Speaker. *As to filling up Vacancy in Office of Speaker.*

46. The Speaker shall preside at all Meetings of the House of Commons. *Speaker to preside.*

47. Until the Parliament of Canada otherwise provides, in case of the Absence for any Reason of the Speaker from the Chair of the House of Commons for a Period of Forty-eight consecutive Hours, the House may elect another of its Mem- *Provision in case of Absence of Speaker.*

---

(22) Spent. Elections are now provided for by the *Canada Elections Act*, R.S.C. 1970 (1st Supp.), c. 14; controverted elections by the *Dominion Controverted Elections Act*, R.S.C. 1970, c. C-28; qualifications and disqualifications of members by the *House of Commons Act*, R.S.C. 1970, c. H-9 and the *Senate and House of Commons Act*, R.S.C. 1970, c. S-8. The right of citizens to vote and hold office is provided for in section 3 of the *Constitution Act, 1982*.

(23) Repealed by the *Statute Law Revision Act, 1893*, 56-57 Vict., c. 14 (U.K.). The section read as follows:

> **42.** For the First Election of Members to serve in the House of Commons the Governor General shall cause Writs to be issued by such Person, in such Form, and addressed to such Returning Officers as he thinks fit.
>
> The Person issuing Writs under this Section shall have the like Powers as are possessed at the Union by the Officers charged with the issuing of Writs for the Election of Members to serve in the respective House of Assembly or Legislative Assembly of the Province of Canada, Nova Scotia, or New Brunswick; and the Returning Officers to whom Writs are directed under this Section shall have the like Powers as are possessed at the Union by the Officers charged with the returning of Writs for the Election of Members to serve in the same respective House of Assembly or Legislative Assembly.

(24) Repealed by the *Statute Law Revision Act, 1893*, 56-57 Vict., c. 14 (U.K.). The section read as follows:

> **43.** In case a Vacancy in the Representation in the House of Commons of any Electoral District happens before the Meeting of the Parliament, or after the Meeting of the Parliament before Provision is made by the Parliament in this Behalf, the Provisions of the last foregoing Section of this Act shall extend and apply to the issuing and returning of a Writ in respect of such vacant District.

bers to act as Speaker, and the Member so elected shall during the Continuance of such Absence of the Speaker have and execute all the Powers, Privileges, and Duties of Speaker.(25)

Quorum of
House of
Commons.

48. The Presence of at least Twenty Members of the House of Commons shall be necessary to constitute a Meeting of the House for the Exercise of its Powers, and for that Purpose the Speaker shall be reckoned as a Member.

Voting in
House of
Commons.

49. Questions arising in the House of Commons shall be decided by a Majority of Voices other than that of the Speaker, and when the Voices are equal, but not otherwise, the Speaker shall have a Vote.

Duration of
House of
Commons.

50. Every House of Commons shall continue for Five Years from the Day of the Return of the Writs for choosing the House (subject to be sooner dissolved by the Governor General), and no longer.(26)

Readjustment
of representa-
tion in
Commons.

51. (1) The number of members of the House of Commons and the representation of the provinces therein shall upon the coming into force of this subsection and thereafter on the completion of each decennial census be readjusted by such authority, in such manner, and from such time as the Parliament of Canada from time to time provides, subject and according to the following Rules:

Rules.

1. There shall be assigned to Quebec seventy-five members in the readjustment following the completion of the decennial census taken in the year 1971, and thereafter four additional members in each subsequent readjustment.

2. Subject to Rules 5(2) and (3), there shall be assigned to a large province a number of members equal to the number obtained by dividing the population of the large province by the electoral quotient of Quebec.

---

(25) Provision for exercising the functions of Speaker during his absence is now made by the *Speaker of the House of Commons Act*, R.S.C. 1970, c. S-13.

(26) The term of the twelfth Parliament was extended by the *British North America Act, 1916,* 6-7 Geo. V, c. 19 (U.K.), which Act was repealed by the *Statute Law Revision Act, 1927,* 17-18 Geo. V, c. 42 (U.K.). See also subsection 4(1) of the *Constitution Act, 1982,* which provides that no House of Commons shall continue for longer than five years from the date fixed for the return of the writs at a general election of its members, and subsecion 4(2) thereof, which provides for continuation of the House of Commons in special circumstances.

3. Subject to Rules 5(2) and (3), there shall be assigned to a small province a number of members equal to the number obtained by dividing

(*a*) the sum of the populations, determined according to the results of the penultimate decennial census, of the provinces (other than Quebec) having populations of less than one and a half million, determined according to the results of that census, by the sum of the numbers of members assigned to those provinces in the readjustment following the completion of that census; and

(*b*) the population of the small province by the quotient obtained under paragraph (*a*).

4. Subject to Rules 5(1)(*a*), (2) and (3), there shall be assigned to an intermediate province a number of members equal to the number obtained

(*a*) by dividing the sum of the populations of the provinces (other than Quebec) having populations of less than one and a half million by the sum of the number of members assigned to those provinces under any of Rules 3, 5(1)(*b*), (2) and (3);

(*b*) by dividing the population of the intermediate province by the quotient obtained under paragraph (*a*); and

(*c*) by adding to the number of members assigned to the intermediate province in the readjustment following the completion of the penultimate decennial census one-half of the difference resulting from the subtraction of that number from the quotient obtained under paragraph (*b*).

5. (1) On any readjustment,

(*a*) if no province (other than Quebec) has a population of less than one and a half million, Rule 4 shall not be applied and, subject to Rules 5(2) and (3), there shall be assigned to an intermediate province a number of members equal to the number obtained by dividing

(i) the sum of the populations, determined according to the results of the penultimate decennial census, of the provinces (other than Quebec) having populations of not less than one and a half million and not more than two and a half million, determined according to the results of that census, by the sum of the numbers of members assigned to those provinces in the readjustment following the completion of that census, and

(ii) the population of the intermediate province by the quotient obtained under subparagraph (i);

(*b*) if a province (other than Quebec) having a population of

(i) less than one and a half million, or

(ii) not less than one and a half million and not more than two and a half million

does not have a population greater than its population determined according to the results of the penultimate decennial census, it shall, subject to Rules 5(2) and (3), be assigned the number of members assigned to it in the readjustment following the completion of that census.

(2) On any readjustment,

(*a*) if, under any of Rules 2 to 5(1), the number of members to be assigned to a province (in this paragraph referred to as "the first province") is smaller than the number of members to be assigned to any other province not having a population greater than that of the first province, those Rules shall not be applied to the first province and it shall be assigned a number of members equal to the largest number of members to be assigned to any other province not having a population greater than that of the first province;

(*b*) if, under any of Rules 2 to 5(1)(*a*), the number of members to be assigned to a province is smaller than the number of members assigned to it in the readjustment following the completion of the penultimate decennial census, those Rules shall not be applied to it and it shall be assigned the latter number of members;

(*c*) if both paragraphs (*a*) and (*b*) apply to a province, it shall be assigned a number of members equal to the greater of the numbers produced under those paragraphs.

(3) On any readjustment,

(*a*) if the electoral quotient of a province (in this paragraph referred to as "the first province") obtained by dividing its population by the number of members to be assigned to it under any of Rules 2 to 5(2) is greater than the electoral quotient of Quebec, those Rules shall not be applied to the first province and it shall be assigned a number of members equal to the number obtained by dividing its population by the electoral quotient of Quebec;

(*b*) if, as a result of the application of Rule 6(2)(*a*), the number of members assigned to a province under paragraph (*a*) equals the number of members to be assigned to it under any of Rules 2 to 5(2), it shall be assigned that number of members and paragraph (*a*) shall cease to apply to that province.

6. (1) In these Rules,

"electoral quotient" means, in respect of a province, the quotient obtained by dividing its population, determined according to the results of the then most recent decennial census, by the number of members to be assigned to it under any of Rules 1 to 5(3) in the readjustment following the completion of that census;

"intermediate province" means a province (other than Quebec) having a population greater than its population determined according to the results of the penultimate decennial census but not more than two and a half million and not less than one and a half million;

"large province" means a province (other than Quebec) having a population greater than two and a half million;

"penultimate decennial census" means the decennial census that preceded the then most recent decennial census;

"population" means, except where otherwise specified, the population determined according to the results of the then most recent decennial census;

"small province" means a province (other than Quebec) having a population greater than its population determined according to the results of the penultimate decennial census and less than one and a half million.

(2) For the purposes of these Rules,

(*a*) if any fraction less than one remains upon completion of the final calculation that produces the number of members to be assigned to a province, that number of members shall equal the number so produced disregarding the fraction;

(*b*) if more than one readjustment follows the completion of a decennial census, the most recent of those readjustments shall, upon taking effect, be deemed to be the only readjustment following the completion of that census;

(*c*) a readjustment shall not take effect until the termination of the then existing Parliament.(27)

---

(27) As enacted by the *Constitution Act, 1974*, S.C. 1974-75-76, c. 13, which came into force on December 31, 1974. The section, as originally enacted, read as follows:

51. On the Completion of the Census in the Year One Thousand eight hundred and seventy-one, and of each subsequent decennial Census, the Representation of the Four Provinces shall be readjusted by such Authority, in such Manner, and from such Time, as the Parliament of Canada from Time to Time provides, subject and according to the following Rules:

(1) Quebec shall have the fixed Number of Sixty-five Members:

(2) There shall be assigned to each of the other Provinces such a Number of Members as will bear the same Proportion to the Number of its Population (ascertained at such Census) as the Number Sixty-five bears to the Number of the Population of Quebec (so ascertained):

(3) In the Computation of the Number of Members for a Province a fractional Part not exceeding One Half of the whole Number requisite for entitling the Province to a Member shall be disregarded; but a fractional Part exceeding One Half of that Number shall be equivalent to the whole Number:

(4) On any such Re-adjustment the Number of Members for a Province shall not be reduced unless the Proportion which the Number of the Population of the Province bore to the Number of the aggregate Population of Canada at the then last preceding Re-adjustment of the Number of Members for the Province is ascertained at the then latest Census to be diminished by One Twentieth Part or upwards:

(5) Such Re-adjustment shall not take effect until the Termination of the then existing Parliament.

The section was amended by the *Statute Law Revision Act, 1893*, 56-57 Vict., c. 14 (U.K.) by repealing the words from "of the census" to "seventy-one and" and the word "subsequent".

By the *British North America Act, 1943*, 6-7 Geo. VI, c. 30 (U.K.), which Act was repealed by the *Constitution Act, 1982*, redistribution of seats following the 1941 census was postponed until the first session of Parliament after the war. The section was re-enacted by the *British North America Act, 1946*, 9-10 Geo. VI, c. 63 (U.K.), which Act was also repealed by the *Constitution Act, 1982*, to read as follows:

51. (1) The number of members of the House of Commons shall be two hundred and fifty-five and the representation of the provinces therein shall forthwith upon the coming into force of this section and thereafter on the completion of each decennial census be readjusted by such authority, in such manner, and from such time as the

Parliament of Canada from time to time provides, subject and according to the following rules:

(1) Subject as hereinafter provided, there shall be assigned to each of the provinces a number of members computed by dividing the total population of the provinces by two hundred and fifty-four and by dividing the population of each province by the quotient so obtained, disregarding, except as hereinafter in this section provided, the remainder, if any, after the said process of division.

(2) If the total number of members assigned to all the provinces pursuant to rule one is less than two hundred and fifty-four, additional members shall be assigned to the provinces (one to a province) having remainders in the computation under rule one commencing with the province having the largest remainder and continuing with the other provinces in the order of the magnitude of their respective remainders until the total number of members assigned is two hundred and fifty-four.

(3) Notwithstanding anything in this section, if upon completion of a computation under rules one and two, the number of members to be assigned to a province is less than the number of senators representing the said province, rules one and two shall cease to apply in respect of the said province, and there shall be assigned to the said province a number of members equal to the said number of senators.

(4) In the event that rules one and two cease to apply in respect of a province then, for the purpose of computing the number of members to be assigned to the provinces in respect of which rules one and two continue to apply, the total population of the provinces shall be reduced by the number of the population of the province in respect of which rules one and two have ceased to apply and the number two hundred and fifty-four shall be reduced by the number of members assigned to such province pursuant to rule three.

(5) Such readjustment shall not take effect until the termination of the then existing Parliament.

(2) The Yukon Territory as constituted by Chapter forty-one of the Statutes of Canada, 1901, together with any Part of Canada not comprised within a province which may from time to time be included therein by the Parliament of Canada for the purposes of representation in Parliament, shall be entitled to one member.

The section was re-enacted by the *British North America Act, 1952,* S.C. 1952, c. 15, which Act was also repealed by the *Constitution Act, 1982,* as follows:

51. (1) Subject as hereinafter provided, the number of members of the House of Commons shall be two hundred and sixty-three and the representation of the provinces therein shall forthwith upon the coming into force of this section and thereafter on the completion of each decennial census be readjusted by such authority, in such manner, and from such time as the Parliament of Canada from time to time provides, subject and according to the following rules:

1. There shall be assigned to each of the provinces a number of members computed by dividing the total population of the provinces by two hundred and sixty-one and by dividing the population of each province by the quotient so obtained, disregarding, except as hereinafter in this section provided, the remainder, if any, after the said process of division.

2. If the total number of members assigned to all the provinces pursuant to rule one is less than two hundred and sixty-one, additional members shall be assigned to the provinces (one to a province) having remainders in the computation under rule one commencing with the province having the largest remainder and continuing with the other provinces in the order of the magnitude of their respective remainders until the total number of members assigned is two hundred and sixty-one.

3. Notwithstanding anything in this section, if upon completion of a computation under rules one and two the number of members to be assigned to a province is less than the number of senators representing the said province, rules one and two shall cease to apply in respect of the said province, and there shall be assigned to the said province a number of members equal to the said number of senators.

4. In the event that rules one and two cease to apply in respect of a province then, for the purposes of computing the number of members to be assigned to the provinces in respect of which rules one and two continue to apply, the total population of the provinces shall be reduced by the number of the population of the province in respect of which rules one and two have ceased

Yukon Territory and Northwest Territories.

(2) The Yukon Territory as bounded and described in the schedule to chapter Y-2 of the Revised Statutes of Canada, 1970, shall be entitled to one member, and the Northwest Territories as bounded and described in section 2 of chapter N-22 of the Revised Statutes of Canada, 1970, shall be entitled to two members.(28)

Constitution of House of Commons.

51A. Notwithstanding anything in this Act a province shall always be entitled to a number of members in the House of Commons not less than the number of senators representing such province.(29)

Increase of Number of House of Commons.

52. The Number of Members of the House of Commons may be from Time to Time increased by the Parliament of Canada, provided the proportionate Representation of the Provinces prescribed by this Act is not thereby disturbed.

Money Votes; Royal Assent

Appropriation and Tax Bills.

53. Bills for appropriating any Part of the Public Revenue, or for imposing any Tax or Impost, shall originate in the House of Commons.

Recommendation of Money Votes.

54. It shall not be lawful for the House of Commons to adopt or pass any Vote, Resolution, Address, or Bill for the

---

to apply and the number two hundred and sixty-one shall be reduced by the number of members assigned to such province pursuant to rule three.

5. On any such readjustment the number of members for any province shall not be reduced by more than fifteen per cent below the representation to which such province was entitled under rules one to four of this subsection at the last preceding readjustment of the representation of that province, and there shall be no reduction in the representation of any province as a result of which that province would have a smaller number of members than any other province that according to the results of the then last decennial census did not have a larger population; but for the purposes of any subsequent readjustment of representation under this section any increase in the number of members of the House of Commons resulting from the application of this rule shall not be included in the divisor mentioned in rules one to four of this subsection.

readjustment of representation under this section any increase in the number of members of the House of Commons resulting from the application of this rule shall not be included in the divisor mentioned in rules one to four of this subsection.

6. Such readjustment shall not take effect until the termination of the then existing Parliament.

(2) The Yukon Territory as constituted by chapter forty-one of the statutes of Canada, 1901, shall be entitled to one member, and such other part of Canada not comprised within a province as may from time to time be defined by the Parliament of Canada shall be entitled to one member.

(28) As enacted by the *Constitution Act (No. 1), 1975*, S.C. 1974-75-76, c. 28.

(29) As enacted by the *Constitution Act, 1915*, 5-6 Geo. V, c. 45 (U.K.).

Appropriation of any Part of the Public Revenue, or of any Tax or Impost, to any Purpose that has not been first recommended to that House by Message of the Governor General in the Session in which such Vote, Resolution, Address, or Bill is proposed.

55. Where a Bill passed by the Houses of the Parliament is presented to the Governor General for the Queen's Assent, he shall declare, according to his Discretion, but subject to the Provisions of this Act and to Her Majesty's Instructions, either that he assents thereto in the Queen's Name, or that he withholds the Queen's Assent, or that he reserves the Bill for the Signification of the Queen's Pleasure.

Royal Assent to Bills, etc.

56. Where the Governor General assents to a Bill in the Queen's Name, he shall by the first convenient Opportunity send an authentic Copy of the Act to one of Her Majesty's Principal Secretaries of State, and if the Queen in Council within Two Years after Receipt thereof by the Secretary of State thinks fit to disallow the Act, such Disallowance (with a Certificate of the Secretary of State of the Day on which the Act was received by him) being signified by the Governor General, by Speech or Message to each of the Houses of the Parliament or by Proclamation, shall annul the Act from and after the Day of such Signification.

Disallowance by Order in Council of Act assented to by Governor General.

57. A Bill reserved for the Signification of the Queen's Pleasure shall not have any Force unless and until, within Two Years from the Day on which it was presented to the Governor General for the Queen's Assent, the Governor General signifies, by Speech or Message to each of the Houses of the Parliament or by Proclamation, that it has received the Assent of the Queen in Council.

Signification of Queen's Pleasure on Bill reserved.

An Entry of every such Speech, Message, or Proclamation shall be made in the Journal of each House, and a Duplicate thereof duly attested shall be delivered to the proper Officer to be kept among the Records of Canada.

V.—Provincial Constitutions.

Executive Power.

58. For each Province there shall be an Officer, styled the Lieutenant Governor, appointed by the Governor General in Council by Instrument under the Great Seal of Canada.

Appointment of Lieutenant Governors of Provinces.

Tenure of Office of Lieutenant Governor.

59. A Lieutenant Governor shall hold Office during the Pleasure of the Governor General; but any Lieutenant Governor appointed after the Commencement of the First Session of the Parliament of Canada shall not be removeable within Five Years from his Appointment, except for Cause assigned, which shall be communicated to him in Writing within One Month after the Order for his Removal is made, and shall be communicated by Message to the Senate and to the House of Commons within One Week thereafter if the Parliament is then sitting, and if not then within One Week after the Commencement of the next Session of the Parliament.

Salaries of Lieutenant Governors.

60. The Salaries of the Lieutenant Governors shall be fixed and provided by the Parliament of Canada. (30)

Oaths, etc., of Lieutenant Governor.

61. Every Lieutenant Governor shall, before assuming the Duties of his Office, make and subscribe before the Governor General or some Person authorized by him Oaths of Allegiance and Office similar to those taken by the Governor General.

Application of provisions referring to Lieutenant Governor.

62. The Provisions of this Act referring to the Lieutenant Governor extend and apply to the Lieutenant Governor for the Time being of each Province, or other the Chief Executive Officer or Administrator for the Time being carrying on the Government of the Province, by whatever Title he is designated.

Appointment of Executive Officers for Ontario and Quebec.

63. The Executive Council of Ontario and of Quebec shall be composed of such Persons as the Lieutenant Governor from Time to Time thinks fit, and in the first instance of the following Officers, namely, — the Attorney General, the Secretary and Registrar of the Province, the Treasurer of the Province, the Commissioner of Crown Lands, and the Commissioner of Agriculture and Public Works, with in Quebec, the Speaker of the Legislative Council and the Solicitor General. (31)

Executive Government of Nova Scotia and New Brunswick.

64. The Constitution of the Executive Authority in each of the Provinces of Nova Scotia and New Brunswick shall,

---

(30) Provided for by the *Salaries Act*, R.S.C. 1970, c. S-2.

(31) Now provided for in Ontario by the *Executive Council Act*, R.S.O. 1980, c. 147, and in Quebec by the *Executive Power Act*, R.S.Q. 1977, c. E-18.

subject to the Provisions of this Act, continue as it exists at the Union until altered under the Authority of this Act. (32)

65. All Powers, Authorities, and Functions which under any Act of the Parliament of Great Britain, or of the Parliament of the United Kingdom of Great Britain and Ireland, or of the Legislature of Upper Canada, Lower Canada, or Canada, were or are before or at the Union vested in or exerciseable by the respective Governors or Lieutenant Governors of those Provinces, with the Advice or with the Advice and Consent of the respective Executive Councils thereof, or in conjunction with those Councils, or with any Number of Members thereof, or by those Governors or Lieutenant Governors individually, shall, as far as the same are capable of being exercised after the Union in relation to the Government of Ontario and Quebec respectively, be vested in and shall or may be exercised by the Lieutenant Governor of Ontario and Quebec respectively, with the Advice or with the Advice and consent of or in conjunction with the respective Executive Councils, or any Members thereof, or by the Lieutenant Governor individually, as the Case requires, subject nevertheless (except with respect to such as exist under Acts of the Parliament of Great Britain, or of the Parliament of the United Kingdom of Great Britain and Ireland,) to be abolished or altered by the respective Legislatures of Ontario and Quebec. (33)

Powers to be exercised by Lieutenant Governor of Ontario or Quebec with Advice, or alone.

66. The Provisions of this Act referring to the Lieutenant Governor in Council shall be construed as referring to the Lieutenant Governor of the Province acting by and with the Advice of the Executive Council thereof.

Application of Provisions referring to Lieutenant Governor in Council.

67. The Governor General in Council may from Time to Time appoint an Administrator to execute the office and Functions of Lieutenant Governor during his Absence, Illness, or other Inability.

Administration in Absence, etc., of Lieutenant Governor.

68. Unless and until the Executive Government of any Province otherwise directs with respect to that Province, the

Seats of Provincial Governments.

---

(32) A similar provision was included in each of the instruments admitting British Columbia, Prince Edward Island, and Newfoundland. The Executive Authorities for Manitoba, Alberta and Saskatchewan were established by the statutes creating those provinces. See the notes to section 5, *supra*.

(33) See the notes to section 129, *infra*.

Seats of Government of the Provinces shall be as follows, namely, — of Ontario, the City of Toronto; of Quebec, the City of Quebec; of Nova Scotia, the City of Halifax; and of New Brunswick, the City of Fredericton.

Legislative Power.

1.—ONTARIO.

Legislature for Ontario.

69. There shall be a Legislature for Ontario consisting of the Lieutenant Governor and of One House, styled the Legislative Assembly of Ontario.

Electoral districts.

70. The Legislative Assembly of Ontario shall be composed of Eighty-two Members, to be elected to represent the Eighty-two Electoral Districts set forth in the First Schedule to this Act. (34)

2.—QUEBEC

Legislature for Quebec.

71. There shall be a Legislature for Quebec consisting of the Lieutenant Governor and of Two Houses, styled the Legislative Council of Quebec and the Legislative Assembly of Quebec. (35)

Constitution of Legislative Council.

72. The Legislative Council of Quebec shall be composed of Twenty-four Members, to be appointed by the Lieutenant Governor, in the Queen's Name, by Instrument under the Great Seal of Quebec, One being appointed to represent each of the Twenty-four Electoral Divisions of Lower Canada in this Act referred to, and each holding Office for the Term of his Life, unless the Legislature of Quebec otherwise provides under the Provisions of this Act.

Qualification of Legislative Councillors.

73. The Qualifications of the Legislative Councillors of Quebec shall be the same as those of the Senators for Quebec.

Resignation, Disqualification etc.

74. The Place of a Legislative Councillor of Quebec shall become vacant in the Cases, *mutatis mutandis*, in which the Place of Senator becomes vacant.

---

(34) Spent. Now covered by the *Representation Act*, R.S.O. 1980, c. 450.

(35) The *Act respecting the Legislative Council of Quebec*, S.Q. 1968, c. 9, provided that the Legislature for Quebec shall consist of the Lieutenant Governor and the National Assembly of Quebec, and repealed the provisions of the *Legislature Act*, R.S.Q. 1964, c. 6, relating to the Legislative Council of Quebec. Sections 72 to 79 following are therefore completely spent.

75. When a Vacancy happens in the Legislative Council of Quebec by Resignation, Death, or otherwise, the Lieutenant Governor, in the Queen's Name, by Instrument under the Great Seal of Quebec, shall appoint a fit and qualified Person to fill the Vacancy.

Vacancies.

76. If any Question arises respecting the Qualification of a Legislative Councillor of Quebec, or a Vacancy in the Legislative Council of Quebec, the same shall be heard and determined by the Legislative Council.

Questions as to Vacancies, etc.

77. The Lieutenant Governor may from Time to Time, by Instrument under the Great Seal of Quebec, appoint a Member of the Legislative Council of Quebec to be Speaker thereof, and may remove him and appoint another in his Stead.

Speaker of Legislative Council.

78. Until the Legislature of Quebec otherwise provides, the Presence of at least Ten Members of the Legislative Council, including the Speaker, shall be necessary to constitute a Meeting for the Exercise of its Powers.

Quorum of Legislative Council.

79. Questions arising in the Legislative Council of Quebec shall be decided by a Majority of Voices, and the Speaker shall in all Cases have a Vote, and when the Voices are equal the Decision shall be deemed to be in the Negative.

Voting in Legislative Council.

80. The Legislative Assembly of Quebec shall be composed of Sixty-five Members, to be elected to represent the Sixty-five Electoral Divisions or Districts of Lower Canada in this Act referred to, subject to Alteration thereof by the Legislature of Quebec: Provided that it shall not be lawful to present to the Lieutenant Governor of Quebec for Assent any Bill for altering the Limits of any of the Electoral Divisions or Districts mentioned in the Second Schedule to this Act, unless the Second and Third Readings of such Bill have been passed in the Legislative Assembly with the Concurrence of the Majority of the Members representing all those Electoral Divisions or Districts, and the Assent shall not be given to such Bill unless an Address has been presented by the Legislative Assembly to the Lieutenant Governor stating that it has been so passed. (36)

Constitution of Legislative Assembly of Quebec.

---

(36) The Act respecting electoral districts, S.Q. 1970, c. 7, s. 1, provides that this section no longer has effect.

3.—ONTARIO AND QUEBEC

81. Repealed. (37)

Summoning of
Legislative
Assemblies.

82. The Lieutenant Governor of Ontario and of Quebec shall from Time to Time, in the Queen's Name, by Instrument under the Great Seal of the Province, summon and call together the Legislative Assembly of the Province.

Restriction on
election of
Holders of
offices.

83. Until the Legislature of Ontario or of Quebec otherwise provides, a Person accepting or holding in Ontario or in Quebec any Office, Commission, or Employment, permanent or temporary, at the Nomination of the Lieutenant Governor, to which an annual Salary, or any Fee, Allowance, Emolument, or Profit of any Kind or Amount whatever from the Province is attached, shall not be eligible as a Member of the Legislative Assembly of the respective Province, nor shall he sit or vote as such; but nothing in this Section shall make ineligible any Person being a member of the Executive Council of the respective Province, or holding any of the following Offices, that is to say, the Offices of Attorney General, Secretary and Registrar of the Province, Treasurer of the Province, Commissioner of Crown Lands, and Commissioner of Agriculture and Public Works, and in Quebec Solicitor General, or shall disqualify him to sit or vote in the House for which he is elected, provided he is elected while holding such Office. (38)

Continuance of
existing
Election Laws.

84. Until the legislatures of Ontario and Quebec respectively otherwise provide, all Laws which at the Union are in force in those Provinces respectively, relative to the following Matters, or any of them, namely, — the Qualifications and Disqualifications of Persons to be elected or to sit or vote as Members of the Assembly of Canada, the Qualifications or Disqualifications of Voters, the Oaths to be taken by Voters, the Returning Officers, their Powers and Duties, the Proceedings at Elections, the Periods during which such Elections may be continued, and the Trial of controverted Elections

---

(37) Repealed by the *Statute Law Revision Act, 1893*, 56-57 Vict., c. 14 (U.K.). The section read as follows:

> **81.** The Legislatures of Ontario and Quebec respectively shall be called together not later than Six Months after the Union.

(38) Probably spent. The subject-matter of this section is now covered in Ontario by the *Legislative Assembly Act*, R.S.O. 1980, c. 235, and in Quebec by the *Legislature Act*, R.S.Q. 1977, c. L-1.

and the Proceedings incident thereto, the vacating of the Seats of Members and the issuing and execution of new Writs in case of Seats vacated otherwise than by Dissolution, — shall respectively apply to Elections of Members to serve in the respective Legislative Assemblies of Ontario and Quebec.

Provided that, until the Legislature of Ontario otherwise provides, at any Election for a Member of the Legislative Assembly of Ontario for the District of Algoma, in addition to Persons qualified by the Law of the Province of Canada to vote, every male British Subject, aged Twenty-one Years or upwards, being a Householder, shall have a vote. (39)

85. Every Legislative Assembly of Ontario and every Legislative Assembly of Quebec shall continue for Four Years from the Day of the Return of the Writs for choosing the same (subject nevertheless to either the Legislative Assembly of Ontario or the Legislative Assembly of Quebec being sooner dissolved by the Lieutenant Governor of the Province), and no longer. (40)

Duration of Legislative Assemblies.

86. There shall be a Session of the Legislature of Ontario and of that of Quebec once at least in every Year, so that Twelve Months shall not intervene between the last Sitting of the Legislature in each Province in one Session and its first Sitting in the next Session. (41)

Yearly Session of Legislature.

87. The following Provisions of this Act respecting the House of Commons of Canada shall extend and apply to the Legislative Assemblies of Ontario and Quebec, that is to say, — the Provisions relating to the Election of a Speaker originally and on Vacancies, the Duties of the Speaker, the Absence of the Speaker, the Quorum, and the Mode of voting, as if those Provisions were here re-enacted and made applicable in Terms to each such Legislative Assembly.

Speaker, Quorum, etc.

---

(39) Probably spent. The subject-matter of this section is now covered in Ontario by the *Election Act*, R.S.O. 1980, c. 133, and the *Legislative Assembly Act*, R.S.O. 1980, c. 235, in Quebec by the *Elections Act*, R.S.Q. 1977, c. E-3, the *Provincial Controverted Elections Act*, R.S.Q. 1977, c. C-65, and the *Legislature Act*, R.S.Q. 1977, c. L-1.

(40) The maximum duration of the Legislative Assemblies of Ontario and Quebec has been changed to five years. See the *Legislative Assembly Act*, R.S.O. 1980, c. 235, and the *Legislature Act*, R.S.Q. 1977, c. L-1, respectively. See also section 4 of the *Constitution Act, 1982*, which provides a maximum duration for a legislative assembly of five years but also authorizes continuation in special circumstances.

(41) See also section 5 of the *Constitution Act, 1982*, which provides that there shall be a sitting of each legislature at least once every twelve months.

4.—NOVA SCOTIA AND NEW BRUNSWICK.

Constitutions of
Legislatures of
Nova Scotia
and New
Brunswick.

88. The Constitution of the Legislature of each of the Provinces of Nova Scotia and New Brunswick shall, subject to the Provisions of this Act, continue as it exists at the Union until altered under the Authority of this Act. (42)

89. Repealed. (43)

6.—THE FOUR PROVINCES.

Application to
Legislatures of
Provisions
respecting
Money Votes,
etc.

90. The following Provisions of this Act respecting the Parliament of Canada, namely,— the Provisions relating to Appropriation and Tax Bills, the Recommendation of Money Votes, the Assent to Bills, the Disallowance of Acts, and the Signification of Pleasure on Bills reserved, — shall extend and apply to the Legislatures of the several Provinces as if those Provisions were here re-enacted and made applicable in Terms to the respective Provinces and the Legislatures thereof, with the Substitution of the Lieutenant Governor of the Province for the Governor General, of the Governor General for the Queen and for a Secretary of State, of One Year for Two Years, and of the Province for Canada.

---

(42) Partially repealed by the *Statute Law Revision Act, 1893*, 56-57 Vict., c. 14 (U.K.), which deleted the following concluding words of the original enactment:

> and the House of Assembly of New Brunswick existing at the passing of this Act shall, unless sooner dissolved, continue for the Period for which it was elected.

A similar provision was included in each of the instruments admitting British Columbia, Prince Edward Island and Newfoundland. The Legislatures of Manitoba, Alberta and Saskatchewan were established by the statutes creating those provinces. See the footnotes to section 5, *supra*.

See also sections 3 to 5 of the *Constitution Act, 1982*, which prescribe democratic rights applicable to all provinces, and subitem 2(2) of the Schedule to that Act, which sets out the repeal of section 20 of the *Manitoba Act, 1870*. Section 20 of the *Manitoba Act, 1870*, has been replaced by section 5 of the *Constitution Act, 1982*.

Section 20 reads as follows:

> **20.** There shall be a Session of the Legislature once at least in every year, so that twelve months shall not intervene between the last sitting of the Legislature in one Session and its first sitting in the next Session.

(43) Repealed by the *Statute Law Revision Act, 1893*, 56-57 Vict., c. 14 (U.K.). The section read as follows:

> 5.—Ontario, Quebec, and Nova Scotia.

> **89.** Each of the Lieutenant Governors of Ontario, Quebec and Nova Scotia shall cause Writs to be issued for the First Election of Members of the Legislative Assembly thereof in such Form and by such Person as he thinks fit, and at such Time and addressed to such Returning Officer as the Governor General directs, and so that the First Election of Member of Assembly for any Electoral District or any Subdivision thereof shall be held at the same Time and at the same Places as the Election for a Member to serve in the House of Commons of Canada for the Electoral District.

VI.—DISTRIBUTION OF LEGISLATIVE POWERS.

Powers of the Parliament.

91. It shall be lawful for the Queen, by and with the Advice and Consent of the Senate and House of Commons, to make Laws for the Peace, Order, and good Government of Canada, in relation to all Matters not coming within the Classes of Subjects by this Act assigned exclusively to the Legislatures of the Provinces; and for greater Certainty, but not so as to restrict the Generality of the foregoing Terms of this Section, it is hereby declared that (notwithstanding anything in this Act) the exclusive Legislative Authority of the Parliament of Canada extends to all Matters coming within the Classes of Subjects next hereinafter enumerated; that is to say,—

Legislative Authority of Parliament of Canada.

1. Repealed. (44)

1A. The Public Debt and Property. (45)

2. The Regulation of Trade and Commerce.

2A. Unemployment insurance. (46)

3. The raising of Money by any Mode or System of Taxation.

4. The borrowing of Money on the Public Credit.

5. Postal Service.

6. The Census and Statistics.

7. Militia, Military and Naval Service, and Defence.

8. The fixing of and providing for the Salaries and Allowances of Civil and other Officers of the Government of Canada.

---

(44) Class 1 was added by the *British North America (No. 2) Act, 1949*, 13 Geo. VI, c. 8 (U.K.). That Act and class 1 were repealed by the *Constitution Act, 1982*. The matters referred to in class 1 are provided for in subsection 4(2) and Part V of the *Constitution Act, 1982*. As enacted, class 1 read as follows:

> 1. The amendment from time to time of the Constitution of Canada, except as regards matters coming within the classes of subjects by this Act assigned exclusively to the Legislatures of the provinces, or as regards rights or privileges by this or any other Constitutional Act granted or secured to the Legislature or the Government of a province, or to any class of persons with respect to schools or as regards the use of the English or the French language or as regards the requirements that there shall be a session of the Parliament of Canada at least once each year, and that no House of Commons shall continue for more than five years from the day of the return of the Writs for choosing the House: provided, however, that a House of Commons may in time of real or apprehended war, invasion or insurrection be continued by the Parliament of Canada if such continuation is not opposed by the votes of more than one-third of the members of such House.

(45) Re-numbered by the *British North America (No. 2) Act, 1949*.

(46) Added by the *Constitution Act, 1940*, 3-4 Geo. VI, c. 36 (U.K.).

9. Beacons, Buoys, Lighthouses, and Sable Island.

10. Navigation and Shipping.

11. Quarantine and the Establishment and Maintenance of Marine Hospitals.

12. Sea Coast and Inland Fisheries.

13. Ferries between a Province and any British or Foreign Country or between Two Provinces.

14. Currency and Coinage.

15. Banking, Incorporation of Banks, and the Issue of Paper Money.

16. Savings Banks.

17. Weights and Measures.

18. Bills of Exchange and Promissory Notes.

19. Interest.

20. Legal Tender.

21. Bankruptcy and Insolvency.

22. Patents of Invention and Discovery.

23. Copyrights.

24. Indians, and Lands reserved for the Indians.

25. Naturalization and Aliens.

26. Marriage and Divorce.

27. The Criminal Law, except the Constitution of Courts of Criminal Jurisdiction, but including the Procedure in Criminal Matters.

28. The Establishment, Maintenance, and Management of Penitentiaries.

29. Such Classes of Subjects as are expressly excepted in the Enumeration of the Classes of Subjects by this Act assigned exclusively to the Legislatures of the Provinces.

And any Matter coming within any of the Classes of Subjects enumerated in this Section shall not be deemed to come within the Class of Matters of a local or private Nature comprised in the Enumeration of the Classes of Subjects by this Act assigned exclusively to the Legislatures of the Provinces. (47)

---

(47) Legislative authority has been conferred on Parliament by other Acts as follows:

1. The *Constitution Act, 1871*, 34-35 Vict., c. 28 (U.K.).

Exclusive Powers of Provincial Legislatures.

92. In each Province the Legislature may exclusively make Laws in relation to Matters coming within the Classes of Subject next hereinafter enumerated; that is to say,— Subjects of exclusive Provincial Legislation.

    1. Repealed. (48)

---

    2. The Parliament of Canada, may from time to time establish new Provinces in any territories forming for the time being part of the Dominion of Canada, but not included in any Province thereof, and may, at the time of such establishment, make provision for the constitution and administration of any such Province, and for the passing of laws for the peace, order, and good government of such Province, and for its representation in the said Parliament.

    3. The Parliament of Canada may from time to time, with the consent of the Legislature of any province of the said Dominion, increase, diminish, or otherwise alter the limits of such Province, upon such terms and conditions as may be agreed to by the said Legislature, and may, with the like consent, make provision respecting the effect and operation of any such increase or diminution or alteration of territory in relation to any Province affected thereby.

    4. The Parliament of Canada may from time to time make provision for the administration, peace, order, and good government of any territory not for the time being included in any Province.

    5. The following Acts passed by the said Parliament of Canada, and intituled respectively, —"An Act for the temporary government of Rupert's Land and the North Western Territory when united with Canada"; and "An Act to amend and continue the Act thirty-two and thirty-three Victoria, chapter three, and to establish and provide for the government of "the Province of Manitoba", shall be and be deemed to have been valid and effectual for all purposes whatsoever from the date at which they respectively received the assent, in the Queen's name, of the Governor General of the said Dominion of Canada.

    6. Except as provided by the third section of this Act, it shall not be competent for the Parliament of Canada to alter the provisions of the last-mentioned Act of the said Parliament in so far as it relates to the Province of Manitoba, or of any other Act hereafter establishing new Provinces in the said Dominion, subject always to the right of the Legislature of the Province of Manitoba to alter from time to time the provisions of any law respecting the qualification of electors and members of the Legislative Assembly, and to make laws respecting elections in the said Province.

    The *Rupert's Land Act 1868*, 31-32 Vict., c. 105 (U.K.) (repealed by the *Statute Law Revision Act, 1893*, 56-57 Vict., c. 14 (U.K.)) had previously conferred similar authority in relation to Rupert's Land and the North Western Territory upon admission of those areas.

    2. The *Constitution Act, 1886*, 49-50 Vict., c. 35, (U.K.).

    1. The Parliament of Canada may from time to time make provision for the representation in the Senate and House of Commons of Canada, or in either of them, of any territories which for the time being form part of the Dominion of Canada, but are not included in any province thereof.

    3. The *Statute of Westminster, 1931*, 22 Geo. V, c. 4 (U.K.).

    3. It is hereby declared and enacted that the Parliament of a Dominion has full power to make laws having extra-territorial operation.

    4. Section 44 of the *Constitution Act, 1982*, authorizes Parliament to amend the Constitution of Canada in relation to the executive government of Canada or the Senate and House of Commons. Sections 38, 41, 42, and 43 of that Act authorize the Senate and House of Commons to give their approval to certain other constitutional amendments by resolution.

    (48) Class 1 was repealed by the *Constitution Act, 1982*. As enacted, it read as follows:

    1. The Amendment from Time to Time, notwithstanding anything in this Act, of the Constitution of the province, except as regards the Office of Lieutenant Governor.

2. Direct Taxation within the Province in order to the raising of a Revenue for Provincial Purposes.

3. The borrowing of Money on the sole Credit of the Province.

4. The Establishment and Tenure of Provincial Offices and the Appointment and Payment of Provincial Officers.

5. The Management and Sale of the Public Lands belonging to the Province and of the Timber and Wood thereon.

6. The Establishment, Maintenance, and Management of Public and Reformatory Prisons in and for the Province.

7. The Establishment, Maintenance, and Management of Hospitals, Asylums, Charities, and Eleemosynary Institutions in and for the Province, other than Marine Hospitals.

8. Municipal Institutions in the Province.

9. Shop, Saloon, Tavern, Auctioneer, and other Licences in order to the raising of a Revenue for Provincial, Local, or Municipal Purposes.

10. Local Works and Undertakings other than such as are of the following Classes:—

    (*a*) Lines of Steam or other Ships, Railways, Canals, Telegraphs, and other Works and Undertakings connecting the Province with any other or others of the Provinces, or extending beyond the Limits of the Province;

    (*b*) Lines of Steam Ships between the Province and any British or Foreign Country;

    (*c*) Such Works as, although wholly situate within the Province, are before or after their Execution declared by the Parliament of Canada to be for the general Advantage of Canada or for the Advantage of Two or more of the Provinces.

11. The Incorporation of Companies with Provincial Objects.

12. The Solemnization of Marriage in the Province.

13. Property and Civil Rights in the Province.

Section 45 of the *Constitution Act, 1982,* now authorizes legislatures to make laws amending the constitution of the province. Sections 38, 41, 42, and 43 of that Act authorize legislative assemblies to give their approval by resolution to certain other amendments to the Constitution of Canada.

14. The Administration of Justice in the Province, including the Constitution, Maintenance, and Organization of Provincial Courts, both of Civil and of Criminal Jurisdiction, and including Procedure in Civil Matters in those Courts.

15. The Imposition of Punishment by Fine, Penalty, or Imprisonment for enforcing any Law of the Province made in relation to any Matter coming within any of the Classes of Subjects enumerated in this Section.

16. Generally all Matters of a merely local or private Nature in the Province.

Non-Renewable Natural Resources, Forestry Resources and Electrical Energy

92A. (1) In each province, the legislature may exclusively make laws in relation to

    (*a*) exploration for non-renewable natural resources in the province;

    (*b*) development, conservation and management of non-renewable natural resources and forestry resources in the province, including laws in relation to the rate of primary production therefrom; and

    (*c*) development, conservation and management of sites and facilities in the province for the generation and production of electrical energy.

Laws respecting non-renewable natural resources, forestry resources and electrical energy

(2) In each province, the legislature may make laws in relation to the export from the province to another part of Canada of the primary production from non-renewable natural resources and forestry resources in the province and the production from facilities in the province for the generation of electrical energy, but such laws may not authorize or provide for discrimination in prices or in supplies exported to another part of Canada.

Export from provinces of resources

(3) Nothing in subsection (2) derogates from the authority of Parliament to enact laws in relation to the matters referred to in that subsection and, where such a law of Parliament and a law of a province conflict, the law of Parliament prevails to the extent of the conflict.

Authority of Parliament

(4) In each province, the legislature may make laws in relation to the raising of money by any mode or system of taxation in respect of

Taxation of resources

(*a*) non-renewable natural resources and forestry resources in the province and the primary production therefrom, and

(*b*) sites and facilities in the province for the generation of electrical energy and the production therefrom,

whether or not such production is exported in whole or in part from the province, but such laws may not authorize or provide for taxation that differentiates between production exported to another part of Canada and production not exported from the province.

"Primary production"

(5) The expression "primary production" has the meaning assigned by the Sixth Schedule.

Existing powers or rights

(6) Nothing in subsections (1) to (5) derogates from any powers or rights that a legislature or government of a province had immediately before the coming into force of this section. (49)

Education.

Legislation respecting Education.

93. In and for each Province the Legislature may exclusively make Laws in relation to Education, subject and according to the following Provisions:—

(1) Nothing in any such Law shall prejudicially affect any Right or Privilege with respect to Denominational Schools which any Class of Persons have by Law in the Province at the Union:

(2) All the Powers, Privileges, and Duties at the Union by Law conferred and imposed in Upper Canada on the Separate Schools and School Trustees of the Queen's Roman Catholic Subjects shall be and the same are hereby extended to the Dissentient Schools of the Queen's Protestant and Roman Catholic Subjects in Quebec:

(3) Where in any Province a System of Separate or Dissentient Schools exists by Law at the Union or is thereafter established by the Legislature of the Province, an Appeal shall lie to the Governor General in Council from any Act or Decision of any Provincial

(49) Added by the *Constitution Act, 1982.*

Authority affecting any Right or Privilege of the Protestant or Roman Catholic Minority of the Queen's Subjects in relation to Education:

(4) In case any such Provincial Law as from Time to Time seems to the Governor General in Council requisite for the due Execution of the Provisions of this Section is not made, or in case any Decision of the Governor General in Council on any Appeal under this Section is not duly executed by the proper Provincial Authority in that Behalf, then and in every such Case, and as far only as the Circumstances of each Case require, the Parliament of Canada may make remedial Laws for the due Execution of the Provisions of this Section and of any Decision of the Governor General in Council under this Section. (50)

---

(50) Altered for Manitoba by section 22 of the *Manitoba Act, 1870*, 33 Vict., c. 3 (Canada), (confirmed by the *Constitution Act, 1871*), which reads as follows:

22. In and for the Province, the said Legislature may exclusively make Laws in relation to Education, subject and according to the following provisions:—

(1) Nothing in any such Law shall prejudicially affect any right or privilege with respect to Denominational Schools which any class of persons have by Law or practice in the Province at the Union:

(2) An appeal shall lie to the Governor General in Council from any Act or decision of the Legislature of the Province, or of any Provincial Authority, affecting any right or privilege, of the Protestant or Roman Catholic minority of the Queen's subjects in relation to Education:

(3) In case any such Provincial Law, as from time to time seems to the Governor General in Council requisite for the due execution of the provisions of this section, is not made, or in case any decision of the Governor General in Council on any appeal under this section is not duly executed by the proper Provincial Authority in that behalf, then, and in every such case, and as far only as the circumstances of each case require, the Parliament of Canada may make remedial Laws for the due execution of the provisions of this section, and of any decision of the Governor General in Council under this section.

Altered for Alberta by section 17 of the *Alberta Act*, 4-5 Edw. VII, c. 3, 1905 (Canada), which reads as follows:

17. Section 93 of the *Constitution Act, 1867*, shall apply to the said province, with the substitution for paragraph (1) of the said section 93 of the following paragraph:—

(1) Nothing in any such law shall prejudicially affect any right or privilege with respect to separate schools which any class of persons have at the date of the passing of this Act, under the terms of chapters 29 and 30 of the Ordinances of the Northwest Territories, passed in the year 1901, or with respect to religious instruction in any public or separate school as provided for in the said ordinances.

2. In the appropriation by the Legislature or distribution by the Government of the province of any moneys for the support of schools organized and carried on in accordance with the said chapter 29 or any Act passed in amendment thereof, or in substitution therefor, there shall be no discrimination against schools of any class described in the said chapter 29.

Uniformity of Laws in Ontario, Nova Scotia and New Brunswick.

Legislation for Uniformity of Laws in Three Provinces.

94. Notwithstanding anything in this Act, the Parliament of Canada may make Provision for the Uniformity of all or any of the Laws relative to Property and Civil Rights in Ontario, Nova Scotia, and New Brunswick, and of the Proce-

---

3. Where the expression "by law" is employed in paragraph 3 of the said section 93, it shall be held to mean the law as set out in the said chapters 29 and 30, and where the expression "at the Union" is employed, in the said paragraph 3, it shall be held to mean the date at which this Act comes into force.

Altered for Saskatchewan by section 17 of the *Saskatchewan Act*, 4-5 Edw. VII, c. 42, 1905 (Canada), which reads as follows:

17. Section 93 of the *Constitution Act, 1867*, shall apply to the said province, with the substitution for paragraph (1) of the said section 93, of the following paragraph:—

(1) Nothing in any such law shall prejudicially affect any right or privilege with respect to separate schools which any class of persons have at the date of the passing of this Act, under the terms of chapters 29 and 30 of the Ordinances of the Northwest Territories, passed in the year 1901, or with respect to religious instruction in any public or separate school as provided for in the said ordinances.

2. In the appropriation by the Legislature or distribution by the Government of the province of any moneys for the support of schools organized and carried on in accordance with the said chapter 29, or any Act passed in amendment thereof or in substitution therefor, there shall be no discrimination against schools of any class described in the said chapter 29.

3. Where the expression "by law" is employed in paragraph (3) of the said section 93, it shall be held to mean the law as set out in the said chapters 29 and 30; and where the expression "at the Union" is employed in the said paragraph (3), it shall be held to mean the date at which this Act comes into force.

Altered by Term 17 of the Terms of Union of Newfoundland with Canada (confirmed by the *Newfoundland Act*, 12-13 Geo. VI, c. 22 (UK.)), which reads as follows:

17. In lieu of section ninety-three of the *Constitution Act, 1867*, the following term shall apply in respect of the Province of Newfoundland:

In and for the Province of Newfoundland the Legislature shall have exclusive authority to make laws in relation to education, but the Legislature will not have authority to make laws prejudicially affecting any right or privilege with respect to denominational schools, common (amalgamated) schools, or denominational colleges, that any class or classes of persons have by law in Newfoundland at the date of Union, and out of public funds of the Province of Newfoundland, provided for education,

(*a*) all such schools shall receive their share of such funds in accordance with scales determined on a non-discriminatory basis from time to time by the Legislature for all schools then being conducted under authority of the Legislature; and

(*b*) all such colleges shall receive their share of any grant from time to time voted for all colleges then being conducted under authority of the Legislature, such grant being distributed on a non-discriminatory basis.

See also sections 23, 29, and 59 of the *Constitution Act, 1982*. Section 23 provides for new minority language educational rights and section 59 permits a delay in respect of the coming into force in Quebec of one aspect of those rights. Section 29 provides that nothing in the *Canadian Charter of Rights and Freedoms* abrogates or derogates from any rights or privileges guaranteed by or under the Constitution of Canada in respect of denominational, separate or dissentient schools.

dure of all or any of the Courts in Those Three Provinces, and from and after the passing of any Act in that Behalf the Power of the Parliament of Canada to make Laws in relation to any Matter comprised in any such Act shall, notwithstanding anything in this Act, be unrestricted; but any Act of the Parliament of Canada making Provision for such Uniformity shall not have effect in any Province unless and until it is adopted and enacted as Law by the Legislature thereof.

Old Age Pensions.

94A. The Parliament of Canada may make laws in relation to old age pensions and supplementary benefits, including survivors, and disability benefits irrespective of age, but no such law shall affect the operation of any law present or future of a provincial legislature in relation to any such matter. (51)

Legislation respecting old age pensions and supplementary benefits.

Agriculture and Immigration.

95. In each Province the Legislature may make Laws in relation to Agriculture in the Province, and to Immigration into the Province; and it is hereby declared that the Parliament of Canada may from Time to Time make Laws in relation to Agriculture in all or any of the Provinces, and to Immigration into all or any of the Provinces; and any Law of the Legislature of a Province relative to Agriculture or to Immigration shall have effect in and for the Province as long and as far only as it is not repugnant to any Act of the Parliament of Canada.

Concurrent Powers of Legislation respecting Agriculture, etc.

VII.—JUDICATURE.

96. The Governor General shall appoint the Judges of the Superior, District, and County Courts in each Province, except those of the Courts of Probate in Nova Scotia and New Brunswick.

Appointment of Judges.

---

(51) Added by the *Constitution Act, 1964,* 12-13 Eliz. II, c. 73 (U.K.). As originally enacted by the *British North America Act, 1951,* 14-15 Geo. VI, c. 32 (U.K.), which was repealed by the *Constitution Act, 1982,* section 94A read as follows:

> **94A.** It is hereby declared that the Parliament of Canada may from time to time make laws in relation to old age pensions in Canada, but no law made by the Parliament of Canada in relation to old age pensions shall affect the operation of any law present or future of a Provincial Legislature in relation to old age pensions.

Selection of
Judges in
Ontario, etc.

97. Until the laws relative to Property and Civil Rights in Ontario, Nova Scotia, and New Brunswick, and the Procedure of the Courts in those Provinces, are made uniform, the Judges of the Courts of those Provinces appointed by the Governor General shall be selected from the respective Bars of those Provinces.

Selection of
Judges in
Quebec.

98. The Judges of the Courts of Quebec shall be selected from the Bar of that Province.

Tenure of office
of Judges.

99. (1) Subject to subsection two of this section, the Judges of the Superior Courts shall hold office during good behaviour, but shall be removable by the Governor General on Address of the Senate and House of Commons.

Termination at
age 75.

(2) A Judge of a Superior Court, whether appointed before or after the coming into force of this section, shall cease to hold office upon attaining the age of seventy-five years, or upon the coming into force of this section if at that time he has already attained that age. (52)

Salaries etc., of
Judges.

100. The Salaries, Allowances, and Pensions of the Judges of the Superior, District, and County Courts (except the Courts of Probate in Nova Scotia and New Brunswick), and of the Admiralty Courts in Cases where the Judges thereof are for the Time being paid by Salary, shall be fixed and provided by the Parliament of Canada. (53)

General Court
of Appeal, etc.

101. The Parliament of Canada may, notwithstanding anything in this Act, from Time to Time provide for the Constitution, Maintenance, and Organization of a General Court of Appeal for Canada, and for the Establishment of any additional Courts for the better Administration of the Laws of Canada. (54)

---

(52) Repealed and re-enacted by the *Constitution Act, 1960*, 9 Eliz. II, c. 2 (U.K.), which came into force on the 1st day of March, 1961. The original section read as follows:

> **99.** The Judges of the Superior Courts shall hold Office during good Behaviour, but shall be removable by the Governor General on Address of the Senate and House of Commons.

(53) Now provided for in the *Judges Act*, R.S.C. 1970, c. J-1.

(54) See the *Supreme Court Act*, R.S.C. 1970, c. S-19, and the *Federal Court Act*, R.S.C. 1970, (2nd Supp.) c. 10.

VIII.—Revenues; Debts; Assets; Taxation.

102. All Duties and Revenues over which the respective Legislatures of Canada, Nova Scotia, and New Brunswick before and at the Union had and have Power of Appropriation, except such Portions thereof as are by this Act reserved to the respective Legislatures of the Provinces, or are raised by them in accordance with the special Powers conferred on them by this Act, shall form One Consolidated Revenue Fund, to be appropriated for the Public Service of Canada in the Manner and subject to the Charges of this Act provided.

Creation of Consolidated Revenue Fund.

103. The Consolidated Revenue Fund of Canada shall be permanently charged with the Costs, Charges, and Expenses incident to the Collection, Management, and Receipt thereof, and the same shall form the First Charge thereon, subject to be reviewed and audited in such Manner as shall be ordered by the Governor General in Council until the Parliament otherwise provides.

Expenses of Collection, etc.

104. The annual Interest of the Public Debts of the several Provinces of Canada, Nova Scotia, and New Brunswick at the Union shall form the Second Charge on the Consolidated Revenue Fund of Canada.

Interest of Provincial Public Debts.

105. Unless altered by the Parliament of Canada, the Salary of the Governor General shall be Ten thousand Pounds Sterling Money of the United Kingdom of Great Britain and Ireland, payable out of the Consolidated Revenue Fund of Canada, and the same shall form the Third Charge thereon. (55)

Salary of Governor General.

106. Subject to the several Payments by this Act charged on the Consolidated Revenue Fund of Canada, the same shall be appropriated by the Parliament of Canada for the Public Service.

Appropriation from Time to Time.

107. All Stocks, Cash, Banker's Balances, and Securities for Money belonging to each Province at the Time of the Union, except as in this Act mentioned, shall be the Property of Canada, and shall be taken in Reduction of the Amount of the respective Debts of the Provinces at the Union.

Transfer of Stocks, etc.

---

(55) Now covered by the *Governor General's Act*, R.S.C. 1970, c. G-14.

Tansfer of
Property in
Schedule.

108. The Public Works and Property of each Province, enumerated in the Third Schedule to this Act, shall be the Property of Canada.

Property in
Lands, Mines,
etc.

109. All Lands, Mines, Minerals, and Royalties belonging to the several Provinces of Canada, Nova Scotia, and New Brunswick at the Union, and all Sums then due or payable for such Lands, Mines, Minerals, or Royalties, shall belong to the several Provinces of Ontario, Quebec, Nova Scotia, and New Brunswick in which the same are situate or arise, subject to any Trusts existing in respect thereof, and to any Interest other than that of the Province in the same. (56)

Assets
connected with
Provincial
Debts.

110. All Assets connected with such Portions of the Public Debt of each Province as are assumed by that Province shall belong to that Province.

Canada to be
liable for
Provincial
Debts.

111. Canada shall be liable for the Debts and Liabilities of each Province existing at the Union.

Debts of
Ontario and
Quebec.

112. Ontario and Quebec conjointly shall be liable to Canada for the Amount (if any) by which the Debt of the Province of Canada exceeds at the Union Sixty-two million five hundred thousand Dollars, and shall be charged with Interest at the Rate of Five Per Centum per Annum thereon.

Assets of
Ontario and
Quebec.

113. The Assets enumerated in the Fourth Schedule to this Act belonging at the Union to the Province of Canada shall be the Property of Ontario and Quebec conjointly.

Debt of Nova
Scotia.

114. Nova Scotia shall be liable to Canada for the Amount (if any) by which its Public Debt exceeds at the Union Eight million Dollars, and shall be charged with Interest at the Rate of Five per Centum per Annum thereon. (57)

Debt of New
Brunswick.

115. New Brunswick shall be liable to Canada for the Amount (if any) by which its Public Debt exceeds at the

---

(56) The three prairie provinces were placed in the same position as the original provinces by the *Constitution Act, 1930*, 21 Geo. V, c. 26 (U.K.).

(57) The obligations imposed by this section, sections 115 and 116, and similar obligations under the instruments creating or admitting other provinces, have been carried into legislation of the Parliament of Canada and are now to be found in the *Provincial Subsidies Act*, R.S.C. 1970, c. P-26.

Union Seven million Dollars, and shall be charged with Interest at the Rate of Five per Centum per Annum thereon.

116. In case the Public Debts of Nova Scotia and New Brunswick do not at the Union amount to Eight million and Seven million Dollars respectively, they shall respectively receive by half-yearly Payments in advance from the Government of Canada Interest at Five per Centum per Annum on the Difference between the actual Amounts of their respective Debts and such stipulated Amounts.

Payment of Interest to Nova Scotia and New Brunswick.

117. The several Provinces shall retain all their respective Public Property not otherwise disposed of in this Act, subject to the Right of Canada to assume any Lands or Public Property required for Fortifications or for the Defence of the Country.

Provincial Public Property.

118. Repealed. (58)

(58) Repealed by the *Statute Law Revision Act, 1950*, 14 Geo. VI, c. 6 (U.K.). As originally enacted the section read as follows:

118. The following Sums shall be paid yearly by Canada to the several Provinces for the Support of their Governments and Legislatures:

Dollars

Ontario	Eighty thousand.
Quebec	Seventy thousand.
Nova Scotia	Sixty thousand.
New Brunswick	Fifty thousand.

Two hundred and sixty thousand;

and an annual Grant in aid of each Province shall be made, equal to Eighty Cents per Head of the Population as ascertained by the Census of One thousand eight hundred and sixty-one, and in the Case of Nova Scotia and New Brunswick, by each subsequent Decennial Census until the Population of each of those two Provinces amounts to Four hundred thousand Souls, at which Rate such Grant shall thereafter remain. Such Grants shall be in full Settlement of all future Demands on Canada, and shall be paid half-yearly in advance to each Province; but the Government of Canada shall deduct from such Grants, as against any Province, all Sums chargeable as Interest on the Public Debt of that Province in excess of the several Amounts stipulated in this Act.

The section was made obsolete by the *Constitution Act, 1907*, 7 Edw. VII, c. 11 (U.K.) which provided:

1. (1) The following grants shall be made yearly by Canada to every province, which at the commencement of this Act is a province of the Dominion, for its local purposes and the support of its Government and Legislature: —

(*a*) A fixed grant —

where the population of the province is under one hundred and fifty thousand, of one hundred thousand dollars;

where the population of the province is one hundred and fifty thousand, but does not exceed two hundred thousand, of one hundred and fifty thousand dollars;

119. New Brunswick shall receive by half-yearly Payments in advance from Canada for the period of Ten years from the Union an additional Allowance of Sixty-three thou-

---

where the population of the province is two hundred thousand, but does not exceed four hundred thousand, of one hundred and eighty thousand dollars;

where the population of the province is four hundred thousand, but does not exceed eight hundred thousand, of one hundred and ninety thousand dollars;

where the population of the province is eight hundred thousand, but does not exceed one million five hundred thousand, of two hundred and twenty thousand dollars;

where the population of the province exceeds one million five hundred thousand, of two hundred and forty thousand dollars; and

(*b*) Subject to the special provisions of this Act as to the provinces of British Columbia and Prince Edward Island, a grant at the rate of eighty cents per head of the population of the province up to the number of two million five hundred thousand, and at the rate of sixty cents per head of so much of the population as exceeds that number.

(2) An additional grant of one hundred thousand dollars shall be made yearly to the province of British Columbia for a period of ten years from the commencement of this Act.

(3) The population of a province shall be ascertained from time to time in the case of the provinces of Manitoba, Saskatchewan, and Alberta respectively by the last quinquennial census or statutory estimate of population made under the Acts establishing those provinces or any other Act of the Parliament of Canada making provision for the purpose, and in the case of any other province by the last decennial census for the time being.

(4) The grants payable under this Act shall be paid half-yearly in advance to each province.

(5) The grants payable under this Act shall be substituted for the grants or subsidies (in this Act referred to as existing grants) payable for the like purposes at the commencement of this Act to the several provinces of the Dominion under the provisions of section one hundred and eighteen of the *Constitution Act, 1867*, or of any Order in Council establishing a province, or of any Act of the Parliament of Canada containing directions for the payment of any such grant or subsidy, and those provisions shall cease to have effect.

(6) The Government of Canada shall have the same power of deducting sums charged against a province on account of the interest on public debt in the case of the grant payable under this Act to the province as they have in the case of the existing grant.

(7) Nothing in this Act shall affect the obligation of the Government of Canada to pay to any province any grant which is payable to that province, other than the existing grant for which the grant under this Act is substituted.

(8) In the case of the provinces of British Columbia and Prince Edward Island, the amount paid on account of the grant payable per head of the population to the provinces under this Act shall not at any time be less than the amount of the corresponding grant payable at the commencement of this Act, and if it is found on any decennial census that the population of the province has decreased since the last decennial census, the amount paid on account of the grant shall not be decreased below the amount then payable, notwithstanding the decrease of the population.

See the *Provincial Subsidies Act*, R.S.C. 1970, c. P-26, *The Maritime Provinces Additional Subsidies Act*, 1942-43, c. 14, and the Terms of Union of Newfoundland with Canada, appended to the *Newfoundland Act*, and also to *An Act to approve the Terms of Union of Newfoundland with Canada*, chapter 1 of the Statutes of Canada, 1949.

See also Part III of the *Constitution Act, 1982*, which sets out commitments by Parliament and the provincial legislatures respecting equal opportunities, economic development and the provision of essential public services and a commitment by Parliament and the government of Canada to the principle of making equalization payments.

sand Dollars per Annum; but as long as the Public Debt of that Province remains under Seven million Dollars, a Deduction equal to the Interest at Five per Centum per Annum on such Deficiency shall be made from that Allowance of Sixty-three thousand Dollars. (59)

120. All Payments to be made under this Act, or in discharge of Liabilities created under any Act of the Provinces of Canada, Nova Scotia, and New Brunswick respectively, and assumed by Canada, shall, until the Parliament of Canada otherwise directs, be made in such Form and Manner as may from Time to Time be ordered by the Governor General in Council.

Form of Payments.

121. All Articles of the Growth, Produce, or Manufacture of any one of the Provinces shall, from and after the Union, be admitted free into each of the other Provinces.

Canadian Manufactures, etc.

122. The Customs and Excise Laws of each Province shall, subject to the Provisions of this Act, continue in force until altered by the Parliament of Canada. (60)

Continuance of Customs and Excise Laws.

123. Where Customs Duties are, at the Union, leviable on any Goods, Wares, or Merchandises in any Two Provinces, those Goods, Wares, and Merchandises may, from and after the Union, be imported from one of those Provinces into the other of them on Proof of Payment of the Customs Duty leviable thereon in the Province of Exportation, and on Payment of such further Amount (if any) of Customs Duty as is leviable thereon in the Province of Importation. (61)

Exportation and Importation as between Two Provinces.

124. Nothing in this Act shall affect the Right of New Brunswick to levy the Lumber Dues provided in Chapter Fifteen of Title Three of the Revised Statutes of New Brunswick, or in any Act amending that Act before or after the Union, and not increasing the Amount of such Dues; but the Lumber of any of the Provinces other than New Brunswick shall not be subject to such Dues. (62)

Lumber Dues in New Brunswick.

---

(59) Spent.

(60) Spent. Now covered by the *Customs Act*, R.S.C. 1970, c. C-40, the *Customs Tariff*, R.S.C. 1970, c. C-41, the *Excise Act*, R.S.C. 1970, c. E-12 and the *Excise Tax Act*, R.S.C. 1970, c. E-13.

(61) Spent.

(62) These dues were repealed in 1873 by 36 Vict., c. 16 (N.B.). And see *An Act respecting the Export Duties imposed on Lumber*, etc. (1873) 36 Vict., c. 41 (Canada), and section 2 of the *Provincial Subsidies Act*, R.S.C. 1970, c. P-26.

Exemption of Public Lands, etc.

125. No Lands or Property belonging to Canada or any Province shall be liable to Taxation.

Provincial Consolidated Revenue Fund.

126. Such Portions of the Duties and Revenues over which the respective Legislatures of Canada, Nova Scotia, and New Brunswick had before the Union Power of Appropriation as are by this Act reserved to the respective Governments or Legislatures of the Provinces, and all Duties and Revenues raised by them in accordance with the special Powers conferred upon them by this Act, shall in each Province form One Consolidated Revenue Fund to be appropriated for the Public Service of the Province.

IX. — MISCELLANEOUS PROVISIONS.

General.

127. Repealed. (63)

Oath of Allegiance, etc.

128. Every Member of the Senate or House of Commons of Canada shall before taking his Seat therein take and subscribe before the Governor General or some Person authorized by him, and every Member of a Legislative Council or Legislative Assembly of any Province shall before taking his Seat therein take and subscribe before the Lieutenant Governor of the Province or some Person authorized by him, the Oath of Allegiance contained in the Fifth Schedule to this Act; and every Member of the Senate of Canada and every Member of the Legislative Council of Quebec shall also, before taking his Seat therein, take and subscribe before the Governor General, or some Person authorized by him, the Declaration of Qualification contained in the same Schedule.

Continuance of existing Laws, Courts, Officers, etc.

129. Except as otherwise provided by this Act, all Laws in force in Canada, Nova Scotia, or New Brunswick at the Union, and all Courts of Civil and Criminal Jurisdiction, and

---

(63) Repealed by the *Statute Law Revision Act, 1893*, 56-57 Vict., c. 14 (U.K.). The section read as follows:

> **127.** If any Person being at the passing of this Act a Member of the Legislative Council of Canada, Nova Scotia, or New Brunswick to whom a Place in the Senate is offered, does not within Thirty Days thereafter, by Writing under his Hand addressed to the Governor General of the Province of Canada or to the Lieutenant Governor of Nova Scotia or New Brunswick (as the Case may be), accept the same, he shall be deemed to have declined the same; and any Person who, being at the passing of this Act a Member of the Legislative Council of Nova Scotia or New Brunswick, accepts a Place in the Senate, shall thereby vacate his Seat in such Legislative Council.

all legal Commissions, Powers, and Authorities, and all Officers, Judicial, Administrative, and Ministerial, existing therein at the Union, shall continue in Ontario, Quebec, Nova Scotia, and New Brunswick respectively, as if the Union had not been made; subject nevertheless (except with respect to such as are enacted by or exist under Acts of the Parliament of Great Britain or of the Parliament of the United Kingdom of Great Britain and Ireland), to be repealed, abolished, or altered by the Parliament of Canada, or by the Legislature of the respective Province, according to the Authority of the Parliament or of that Legislature under this Act. (64)

130. Until the Parliament of Canada otherwise provides, all Officers of the several Provinces having Duties to discharge in relation to Matters other than those coming within the Classes of Subjects by this Act assigned exclusively to the Legislatures of the Provinces shall be Officers of Canada, and shall continue to discharge the Duties of their respective Offices under the same Liabilities, Responsibilities, and Penalties as if the Union had not been made. (65)

Transfer of Officers to Canada.

131. Until the Parliament of Canada otherwise provides, the Governor General in Council may from Time to Time appoint such Officers as the Governor General in Council deems necessary or proper for the effectual Execution of this Act.

Appointment of new Officers.

132. The Parliament and Government of Canada shall have all Powers necessary or proper for performing the Obligations of Canada or of any Province thereof, as Part of the British Empire, towards Foreign Countries, arising under Treaties between the Empire and such Foreign Countries.

Treaty Obligations.

133. Either the English or the French Language may be used by any Person in the Debates of the Houses of the Parliament of Canada and of the Houses of the Legislature of Quebec; and both those Languages shall be used in the respective Records and Journals of those Houses; and either of those Languages may be used by any Person or in any

Use of English and French Languages.

---

(64) The restriction against altering or repealing laws enacted by or existing under statutes of the United Kingdom was removed by the *Statute of Westminster, 1931*, 22 Geo. V, c. 4 (U.K.) except in respect of certain constitutional documents. Comprehensive procedures for amending enactments forming part of the Constitution of Canada were provided by Part V of the *Constitution Act, 1982*, (U.K.) 1982, c. 11.

(65) Spent.

Pleading or Process in or issuing from any Court of Canada established under this Act, and in or from all or any of the Courts of Quebec.

The Acts of the Parliament of Canada and of the Legislature of Quebec shall be printed and published in both those Languages. (66)

Ontario and Quebec.

Appointment of
Executive
Officers for
Ontario and
Quebec.

134. Until the Legislature of Ontario or of Quebec otherwise provides, the Lieutenant Governors of Ontario and Quebec may each appoint under the Great Seal of the Province the following Officers, to hold Office during Pleasure, that is to say, — the Attorney General, the Secretary and Registrar of the Province, the Treasurer of the Province, the Commissioner of Crown Lands, and the Commissioner of Agriculture and Public Works, and in the Case of Quebec the Solicitor General, and may, by Order of the Lieutenant Governor in Council, from Time to Time prescribe the Duties of those Officers, and of the several Departments over which they shall preside or to which they shall belong, and of the Officers and Clerks thereof, and may also appoint other and additional Officers to hold Office during Pleasure, and may from Time to Time prescribe the Duties of those Officers, and of the several Departments over which they shall preside or to which they shall belong, and of the Officers and Clerks thereof. (67)

---

(66) A similar provision was enacted for Manitoba by Section 23 of the *Manitoba Act, 1870*, 33 Vict., c. 3 (Canada), (confirmed by the *Constitution Act, 1871.* Section 23 read as follows:

> **23.** Either the English or the French language may be used by any person in the debates of the Houses of the Legislature, and both those languages shall be used in the respective Records and Journals of those Houses; and either of those languages may be used by any person, or in any Pleading or Process, in or issuing from any Court of Canada established under the British North America Act, 1867, or in or from all or any of the Courts of the Province. The Acts of the Legislature shall be printed and published in both those languages.

Sections 17 to 19 of the *Constitution Act, 1982*, restate the language rights set out in section 133 in respect of Parliament and the courts established under the *Constitution Act, 1867*, and also guarantees those rights in respect of the legislature of New Brunswick and the courts of that province.

Section 16 and sections 20, 21 and 23 of the *Constitution Act, 1982*, recognize additional language rights in respect of the English and French languages. Section 22 preserves language rights and privileges of languages other than English and French.

(67) Spent. Now covered in Ontario by the *Executive Council Act*, R.S.O. 1980, c. 147 and in Quebec by the *Executive Power Act*, R.S.Q. 1977, c. E-18.

135. Until the Legislature of Ontario or Quebec otherwise provides, all Rights, Powers, Duties, Functions, Responsibilities, or Authorities at the passing of this Act vested in or imposed on the Attorney General, Solicitor General, Secretary and Registrar of the Province of Canada, Minister of Finance, Commissioner of Crown Lands, Commissioner of Public Works, and Minister of Agriculture and Receiver General, by any Law, Statute, or Ordinance of Upper Canada, Lower Canada, or Canada, and not repugnant to this Act, shall be vested in or imposed on any Officer to be appointed by the Lieutenant Governor for the discharge of the same or any of them; and the Commissioner of Agriculture and Public Works shall perform the Duties and Functions of the Office of Minister of Agriculture at the passing of this Act imposed by the Law of the Province of Canada, as well as those of the Commissioner of Public Works. (68)

Powers, Duties, etc. of Executive Officers.

136. Until altered by the Lieutenant Governor in Council, the Great Seals of Ontario and Quebec respectively shall be the same, or of the same Design, as those used in the Provinces of Upper Canada and Lower Canada respectively before their Union as the Province of Canada.

Great Seals.

137. The words "and from thence to the End of the then next ensuing Session of the Legislature," or Words to the same Effect, used in any temporary Act of the Province of Canada not expired before the Union, shall be construed to extend and apply to the next Session of the Parliament of Canada if the Subject Matter of the Act is within the Powers of the same as defined by this Act, or to the next Sessions of the Legislatures of Ontario and Quebec respectively if the Subject Matter of the Act is within the Powers of the same as defined by this Act.

Construction of temporary Acts.

138. From and after the Union the Use of the Words "Upper Canada", instead of "Ontario," or "Lower Canada" instead of "Quebec," in any Deed, Writ, Process, Pleading, Document, Matter, or Thing shall not invalidate the same.

As to Errors in Names.

139. Any Proclamation under the Great Seal of the Province of Canada issued before the Union to take effect at a Time which is subsequent to the Union, whether relating to

As to issue of Proclamations before Union, to commence after Union.

---

(68) Probably spent.

that Province, or to Upper Canada, or to Lower Canada, and the several Matters and Things therein proclaimed, shall be and continue of like Force and Effect as if the Union had not been made. (69)

As to issue of
Proclamations
after Union.

140. Any Proclamation which is authorized by any Act of the Legislature of the Province of Canada to be issued under the Great Seal of the Province of Canada, whether relating to that Province, or to Upper Canada, or to Lower Canada, and which is not issued before the Union, may be issued by the Lieutenant Governor of Ontario or Quebec, as its Subject Matter requires, under the Great Seal thereof; and from and after the Issue of such Proclamation the same and the several Matters and Things therein proclaimed shall be and continue of the like Force and Effect in Ontario or Quebec as if the Union had not been made. (70)

Penitentiary.

141. The Penitentiary of the Province of Canada shall, until the Parliament of Canada otherwise provides, be and continue the Penitentiary of Ontario and of Quebec. (71)

Arbitration
respecting
Debts, etc.

142. The Division and Adjustment of the Debts, Credits, Liabilities, Properties, and Assets of Upper Canada and Lower Canada shall be referred to the Arbitrament of Three Arbitrators, One chosen by the Government of Ontario, One by the Government of Quebec, and One by the Government of Canada; and the Selection of the Arbitrators shall not be made until the Parliament of Canada and the Legislatures of Ontario and Quebec have met; and the Arbitrator chosen by the Government of Canada shall not be a Resident either in Ontario or in Quebec. (72)

Division of
Records.

143. The Governor General in Council may from Time to Time order that such and so many of the Records, Books, and Documents of the Province of Canada as he thinks fit shall be appropriated and delivered either to Ontario or to Quebec, and the same shall thenceforth be the Property of that Province; and any Copy thereof or Extract therefrom, duly

---

(69) Probably spent.

(70) Probably spent.

(71) Spent. Penitentiaries are now provided for by the *Penitentiary Act*, R.S.C. 1970, c. P-6.

(72) Spent. See pages (xi) and (xii) of the Public Accounts, 1902-03.

certified by the Officer having charge of the Original thereof, shall be admitted as Evidence. (73)

144. The Lieutenant Governor of Quebec may from Time to Time, by Proclamation under the Great Seal of the Province, to take effect from a Day to be appointed therein, constitute Townships in those Parts of the Province of Quebec in which Townships are not then already constituted, and fix the Metes and Bounds thereof.

Constitution of Townships in Quebec.

145. Repealed. (74)

XI.—Admission of Other Colonies

146. It shall be lawful for the Queen, by and with the Advice of Her Majesty's Most Honourable Privy Council, on Addresses from the Houses of the Parliament of Canada, and from the Houses of the respective Legislatures of the Colonies or Provinces of Newfoundland, Prince Edward Island, and British Columbia, to admit those Colonies or Provinces, or any of them, into the Union, and on Address from the Houses of the Parliament of Canada to admit Rupert's Land and the North-western Territory, or either of them, into the Union, on such Terms and Conditions in each Case as are in the Addresses expressed and as the Queen thinks fit to approve, subject to the Provisions of this Act; and the Provisions of any Order in Council in that Behalf shall have effect as if they had been enacted by the Parliament of the United Kingdom of Great Britain and Ireland. (75)

Power to admit Newfoundland etc., into the Union.

---

(73) Probably spent. Two orders were made under this section on the 24th of January, 1868.

(74) Repealed by the *Statute Law Revision Act, 1893*, 56-57 Vict., c. 14, (U.K.). The section read as follows:

X.—Intercolonial Railway.

145. Inasmuch as the Provinces of Canada, Nova Scotia, and New Brunswick have joined in a Declaration that the Construction of the Intercolonial Railway is essential to the Consolidation of the Union of British North America, and to the Assent thereto of Nova Scotia and New Brunswick, and have consequently agreed that Provision should be made for its immediate Construction by the Government of Canada; Therefore, in order to give effect to that Agreement, it shall be the Duty of the Government and Parliment of Canada to provide for the Commencement, within Six Months after the Union, of a Railway connecting the River St. Lawrence with the City of Halifax in Nova Scotia, and for the Construction thereof without Intermission, and the Completion thereof with all practicable Speed.

(75) All territories mentioned in this section are now part of Canada. See the notes to section 5, *supra.*

As to Representation of Newfoundland and Prince Edward Island in Senate.

147. In case of the Admission of Newfoundland and Prince Edward Island, or either of them, each shall be entitled to a Representation in the Senate of Canada of Four Members, and (notwithstanding anything in this Act) in case of the Admission of Newfoundland the normal Number of Senators shall be Seventy-six and their maximum Number shall be Eighty-two; but Prince Edward Island when admitted shall be deemed to be comprised in the Third of Three Divisions into which Canada is, in relation to the Constitution of the Senate, divided by this Act, and accordingly, after the Admission of Prince Edward Island, whether Newfoundland is admitted or not, the Representation of Nova Scotia and New Brunswick in the Senate shall, as Vacancies occur, be reduced from Twelve to Ten Members respectively, and the Representation of each of those Provinces shall not be increased at any Time beyond Ten, except under the Provisions of this Act for the Appointment of Three or Six additional Senators under the Direction of the Queen. (76)

---

(76) Spent. See the notes to sections 21, 22, 26, 27 and 28, *supra*.

SCHEDULES

THE FIRST SCHEDULE. (77)

Electoral Districts of Ontario.

A.

EXISTING ELECTORAL DIVISIONS.

COUNTIES

1. Prescott.
2. Glengarry.
3. Stormont.
4. Dundas.
5. Russell.

6. Carleton.
7. Prince Edward.
8. Halton.
9. Essex.

RIDINGS OF COUNTIES.

10. North Riding of Lanark.
11. South Riding of Lanark.
12. North Riding of Leeds and North Riding of Grenville.
13. South Riding of Leeds.
14. South Riding of Grenville.
15. East Riding of Northumberland.
16. West Riding of Northumberland (excepting therefrom the Township of South Monaghan).
17. East Riding of Durham.
18. West Riding of Durham.
19. North Riding of Ontario.
20. South Riding of Ontario.
21. East Riding of York.
22. West Riding of York.
23. North Riding of York.
24. North Riding of Wentworth.
25. South Riding of Wentworth.
26. East Riding of Elgin.
27. West Riding of Elgin.
28. North Riding of Waterloo.

---

(77) Spent. *Representation Act*, R.S.O. 1970, c. 413.

29. South Riding of Waterloo.
30. North Riding of Brant.
31. South Riding of Brant.
32. North Riding of Oxford.
33. South Riding of Oxford. .
34. East Riding of Middlesex.

Cities, Parts of Cities, and Towns.

35. West Toronto.
36. East Toronto.
37. Hamilton.
38. Ottawa.
39. Kingston.
40. London.
41. Town of Brockville, with the Township of Elizabethtown thereto attached.
42. Town of Niagara, with the Township of Niagara, thereto attached.
43. Town of Cornwall, with the Township of Cornwall thereto attached.

B.

New Electoral Districts.

44. The Provisional Judicial District of Algoma.

The County of Bruce, divided into Two Ridings, to be called respectively the North and South Ridings: —

45. The North Riding of Bruce to consist of the Townships of Bury, Lindsay, Eastnor, Albermarle, Amable, Arran, Bruce, Elderslie, and Saugeen, and the Village of Southampton.

46. The South Riding of Bruce to consist of the Townships of Kincardine (including the Village of Kincardine), Greenock, Brant, Huron, Kinloss, Culross, and Carrick.

The County of Huron, divided into Two Ridings, to be called respectively the North and South Ridings: —

47. The North Riding to consist of the Townships of Ashfield, Wawanosh, Turnberry, Howick, Morris, Grey, Col-

borne, Hullett, including the Village of Clinton, and McKillop.

48. The South Riding to consist of the Town of Goderich and the Townships of Goderich, Tuckersmith, Stanley, Hay, Usborne, and Stephen.

The County of MIDDLESEX, divided into Three Ridings, to be called respectively the North, West, and East Ridings: —

49. The North Riding to consist of the Townships of McGillivray and Biddulph (taken from the County of Huron), and Williams East, Williams West, Adelaide, and Lobo.

50. The West Riding to consist of the Townships of Delaware, Carradoc, Metcalfe, Mosa and Ekfrid, and the Village of Strathroy.

[The East Riding to consist of the Townships now embraced therein, and be bounded as it is at present.]

51. The County of LAMBTON to consist of the Townships of Bosanquet, Warwick, Plympton, Sarnia, Moore, Enniskillen, and Brooke, and the Town of Sarnia.

52. The County of KENT to consist of the Townships of Chatham, Dover, East Tilbury, Romney, Raleigh, and Harwich, and the town of Chatham.

53. The County of BOTHWELL to consist of the Townships of Sombra, Dawn, and Euphemia (taken from the County of Lambton), and the Townships of Zone, Camden with the Gore thereof, Orford, and Howard (taken from the County of Kent).

The County of GREY divided into Two Ridings to be called respectively the South and North Ridings: —

54. The South Riding to consist of the Townships of Bentinck, Glenelg, Artemesia, Osprey, Normanby, Egremont, Proton, and Melancthon.

55. The North Riding to consist of the Townships of Collingwood, Euphrasia, Holland, Saint-Vincent, Sydenham, Sullivan, Derby, and Keppel, Sarawak and Brooke, and the Town of Owen Sound.

The County of PERTH divided into Two Ridings, to be called respectively the South and North Ridings: —

56. The North Riding to consist of the Townships of Wallace, Elma, Logan, Ellice, Mornington, and North Easthope, and the Town of Strathford.

57. The South Riding to consist of the Townships of Blanchard, Downie, South Easthope, Fullarton, Hibbert, and the Villages of Mitchell and Ste. Mary's.

The County of WELLINGTON divided into Three Ridings to be called respectively North, South and Centre Ridings: —

58. The North Riding to consist of the Townships of Amaranth, Arthur, Luther, Minto, Maryborough, Peel, and the Village of Mount Forest.

59. The Centre Riding to consist of the Townships of Garafraxa, Erin, Eramosa, Nichol, and Pilkington, and the Villages of Fergus and Elora.

60. The South Riding to consist of the Town of Guelph, and the Townships of Guelph and Puslinch.

The County of NORFOLK, divided into Two Ridings, to be called respectively the South and North Ridings:—

61. The South Riding to consist of the Townships of Charlotteville, Houghton, Walsingham, and Woodhouse, and with the Gore thereof.

62. The North Riding to consist of the Townships of Middleton, Townsend, and Windham, and the Town of Simcoe.

63. The County of HALDIMAND to consist of the Townships of Oneida, Seneca, Cayuga North, Cayuga South, Rainham, Walpole, and Dunn.

64. The County of MONCK to consist of the Townships of Canborough and Moulton, and Sherbrooke, and the Village of Dunnville (taken from the County of Haldimand), the Townships of Caister and Gainsborough (taken from the County of Lincoln), and the Townships of Pelham and Wainfleet (taken from the County of Welland).

65. The County of LINCOLN to consist of the Townships of Clinton, Grantham, Grimsby, and Louth, and the Town of St. Catherines.

66. The County of WELLAND to consist of the Townships of Bertie, Crowland, Humberstone, Stamford, Thorold, and Willoughby, and the Villages of Chippewa, Clifton, Fort Erie, Thorold, and Welland.

67. The County of PEEL to consist of the Townships of Chinguacousy, Toronto, and the Gore of Toronto, and the Villages of Brampton and Streetsville.

68. The County of CARDWELL to consist of the Townships of Albion and Caledon (taken from the County of Peel), and the Townships of Adjala and Mono (taken from the County of Simcoe).

The County of SIMCOE, divided into Two Ridings, to be called respectively the South and North Ridings:—

69. The South Riding to consist of the Townships of West Gwillimbury, Tecumseth, Innisfil, Essa, Tossorontio, Mulmur, and the Village of Bradford.

70. The North Riding to consist of the Townships of Nottawasaga, Sunnidale, Vespra, Flos, Oro, Medonte, Orillia and Matchedash, Tiny and Tay, Balaklava and Robinson, and the Towns of Barrie and Collingwood.

The County of VICTORIA, divided into Two Ridings, to be called respectively the South and North Ridings:—

71. The South Riding to consist of the Townships of Ops, Mariposa, Emily, Verulam, and the Town of Lindsay.

72. The North Riding to consist of the Townships of Anson, Bexley, Carden, Dalton, Digby, Eldon, Fenelon, Hindon, Laxton, Lutterworth, Macaulay and Draper, Sommerville, and Morrison, Muskoka, Monck and Watt (taken from the County of Simcoe), and any other surveyed Townships lying to the North of the said North Riding.

The County of PETERBOROUGH, divided into Two Ridings, to be called respectively the West and East Ridings:—

73. The West Riding to consist of the Townships of South Monaghan (taken from the County of Northumberland), North Monaghan, Smith, and Ennismore, and the Town of Peterborough.

74. The East Riding to consist of the Townships of Asphodel, Belmont and Methuen, Douro, Dummer, Galway, Harvey, Minden, Stanhope and Dysart, Otonabee, and Snowden, and the Village of Ashburnham, and any other surveyed Townships lying to the North of the said East Riding.

The County of HASTINGS, divided into Three Ridings, to be called respectively the West, East, and North Ridings:—

75. The West Riding to consist of the Town of Belleville, the Township of Sydney, and the Village of Trenton.

76. The East Riding to consist of the Townships of Thurlow, Tyendinaga, and Hungerford.

77. The North Riding to consist of the Townships of Rawdon, Huntingdon, Madoc, Elzevir, Tudor, Marmora, and Lake, and the Village of Stirling, and any other surveyed Townships lying to the North of the said North Riding.

78. The County of LENNOX, to consist of the Townships of Richmond, Adolphustown, North Fredericksburgh, South Fredericksburgh, Ernest Town, and Amherst Island, and the Village of Napanee.

79. The County of ADDINGTON to consist of the Townships of Camden, Portland, Sheffield, Hinchinbrooke, Kaladar, Kennebec, Olden, Oso, Anglesea, Barrie, Clarendon, Palmerston, Effingham, Abinger, Miller, Canonto, Denbigh, Loughborough, and Bedford.

80. The County of FRONTENAC to consist of the Townships of Kingston, Wolfe Island, Pittsburgh and Howe Island, and Storrington.

The County of RENFREW, divided into Two Ridings, to be called respectively the South and North Ridings:—

81. The South Riding to consist of the Townships of McNab, Bagot, Blithfield, Brougham, Horton, Admaston, Grattan, Matawatchan, Griffith, Lyndoch, Raglan, Radcliffe, Brudenell, Sebastopol, and the Villages of Arnprior and Renfrew.

82. The North Riding to consist of the Townships of Ross, Bromley, Westmeath, Stafford, Pembroke, Wilberforce, Alice, Petawawa, Buchanan, South Algoma, North Algoma, Fraser, McKay, Wylie, Rolph, Head, Maria, Clara, Haggerty, Sherwood, Burns, and Richards, and any other surveyed Townships lying Northwesterly of the said North Riding.

Every Town and incorporated Village existing at the Union, not specially mentioned in this Schedule, is to be taken as Part of the County or Riding within which it is locally situate.

THE SECOND SCHEDULE.

Electoral Districts of Quebec specially fixed.

COUNTIES OF-—

Pontiac.	Missisquoi.	Compton.
Ottawa.	Brome.	Wolfe and
Argenteuil.	Shefford.	Richmond.
Huntingdon.	Stanstead.	Megantic.

Town of Sherbrooke.

THE THIRD SCHEDULE.

Provincial Public Works and Property to be the Property of Canada.

1. Canals, with Lands and Water Power connected therewith.

2. Public Harbours.
3. Lighthouses and Piers, and Sable Island.
4. Steamboats, Dredges, and public Vessels.
5. Rivers and Lake Improvements.
6. Railways and Railway Stocks, Mortgages, and other Debts due by Railway Companies.
7. Military Roads.
8. Custom Houses, Post Offices, and all other Public Buildings, except such as the Government of Canada appropriate for the Use of the Provincial Legislature and Governments.
9. Property transferred by the Imperial Government, and known as Ordinance Property.
10. Armouries, Drill Sheds, Military Clothing, and Munitions of War, and Lands set apart for general Public Purposes.

═══════════

THE FOURTH SCHEDULE.

───────────

Assets to be the Property of Ontario and Quebec conjointly.

Upper Canada Building Fund.
Lunatic Asylums.
Normal School.
Court Houses,
    in
Aylmer.   } Lower Canada
Montreal.
Kamouraska.
Law Society, Upper Canada.
Montreal Turnpike Trust.
University Permanent Fund.
Royal Institution.
Consolidated Municipal Loan Fund, Upper Canada.
Consolidated Municipal Loan Fund, Lower Canada.
Agricultural Society, Upper Canada.
Lower Canada Legislative Grant.
Quebec Fire Loan.
Temiscouata Advance Account.
Quebec Turnpike Trust.
Education—East.
Building and Jury Fund, Lower Canada.

Municipalities Fund.

Lower Canada Superior Education Income Fund.

THE FIFTH SCHEDULE.

OATH OF ALLEGIANCE.

I, *A.B.* do swear, That I will be faithful and bear true Allegiance to Her Majesty Queen Victoria.

Note.—The Name of the King or Queen of the United Kingdom of Great Britain and Ireland for the Time being is to be substituted from Time to Time, with Proper Terms of Reference thereto.

DECLARATION OF QUALIFICATION.

I, *A.B.* do declare and testify, That I am by Law duly qualified to be appointed a Member of the Senate of Canada [*or as the Case may be*], and that I am legally or equitably seised as of Freehold for my own Use and Benefit of Lands or Tenements held in Free and Common Socage [*or* seised or possessed for my own Use and Benefit of Lands or Tenements held in Franc-alleu or in Roture (*as the Case may be*),] in the Province of Nova Scotia [*or as the Case may be*] of the Value of Four thousand Dollars over and above all Rents, Dues, Debts, Mortgages, Charges, and Incumbrances due or payable out of or charged on or affecting the same, and that I have not collusively or colourably obtained a Title to or become possessed of the said Lands and Tenements or any Part thereof for the Purpose of enabling me to become a Member of the Senate of Canada [*or as the Case may be*,] and that my Real and Personal Property are together worth Four thousand Dollars over and above my Debts and Liabilities.

THE SIXTH SCHEDULE. (78)

Primary Production from Non-Renewable Natural Resources and Forestry Resources

1. For the purposes of section 92A of this Act,

    (*a*) production from a non-renewable natural resource is primary production therefrom if

---

(78) As enacted by the *Constitution Act, 1982.*

(i) it is in the form in which it exists upon its recovery or severance from its natural state, or

(ii) it is a product resulting from processing or refining the resource, and is not a manufactured product or a product resulting from refining crude oil, refining upgraded heavy crude oil, refining gases or liquids derived from coal or refining a synthetic equivalent or crude oil; and

(*b*) production from a forestry resource is primary production therefrom if it consists of sawlogs, poles, lumber, wood chips, sawdust or any other primary wood product, or wood pulp, and is not a product manufactured from wood.

CONSTITUTION ACT, 1982 (79)

SCHEDULE B

CONSTITUTION ACT, 1982

PART I

CANADIAN CHARTER OF RIGHTS AND FREEDOMS

Whereas Canada is founded upon principles that recognize the supremacy of God and the rule of law:

Guarantee of Rights and Freedoms

1. The *Canadian Charter of Rights and Freedoms* guarantees the rights and freedoms set out in it subject only to such reasonable limits prescribed by law as can be demonstrably justified in a free and democratic society.

Rights and freedoms in Canada

Fundamental Freedoms

2. Everyone has the following fundamental freedoms:
(*a*) freedom of conscience and religion;
(*b*) freedom of thought, belief, opinion and expression, including freedom of the press and other media of communication;

Fundamental freedoms

---

(79) Enacted as Schedule B to the *Canada Act 1982*, (U.K.) 1982, c. 11, which came into force on April 17, 1982. The *Canada Act 1982*, other than Schedules A and B thereto, reads as follows:

An Act to give effect to a request by the Senate and House of Commons of Canada

Whereas Canada has requested and consented to the enactment of an Act of the Parliament of the United Kingdom to give effect to the provisions hereinafter set forth and the Senate and the House of Commons of Canada in Parliament assembled have submitted an address to Her Majesty requesting that Her Majesty may graciously be pleased to cause a Bill to be laid before the Parliament of the United Kingdom for that purpose.

Be it therefore enacted by the Queen's Most Excellent Majesty, by and with the advice and consent of the Lords Spiritual and Temporal, and Commons, in this present Parliament assembled, and by the authority of the same, as follows:

1. The *Constitution Act, 1982* set out in Schedule B to this Act is hereby enacted for and shall have the force of law in Canada and shall come into force as provided in that Act.

2. No Act of the Parliament of the United Kingdom passed after the *Constitution Act, 1982* comes into force shall extend to Canada as part of its law.

3. So far as it is not contained in Schedule B, the French version of this Act is set out in Schedule A to this Act and has the same authority in Canada as the English version thereof.

4. This Act may be cited as the *Canada Act 1982*.

(*c*) freedom of peaceful assembly; and

(*d*) freedom of association.

Democratic Rights

Democratic rights of citizens

3. Every citizen of Canada has the right to vote in an election of members of the House of Commons or of a legislative assembly and to be qualified for membership therein.

Maximum duration of legislative bodies

4. (1) No House of Commons and no legislative assembly shall continue for longer than five years from the date fixed for the return of the writs of a general election of its members.(80)

Continuation in special circumstances

(2) In time of real or apprehended war, invasion or insurrection, a House of Commons may be continued by Parliament and a legislative assembly may be continued by the legislature beyond five years if such continuation is not opposed by the votes of more than one-third of the members of the House of Commons or the legislative assembly, as the case may be.(81)

Annual sitting of legislative bodies

5. There shall be a sitting of Parliament and of each legislature at least once every twelve months.(82)

Mobility Rights

Mobility of citizens

6. (1) Every citizen of Canada has the right to enter, remain in and leave Canada.

Rights to move and gain livelihood

(2) Every citizen of Canada and every person who has the status of a permanent resident of Canada has the right
(*a*) to move to and take up residence in any province; and
(*b*) to pursue the gaining of a livelihood in any province.

Limitation

(3) The rights specified in subsection (2) are subject to
(*a*) any laws or practices of general application in force in a province other than those that discriminate among

---

(80) See section 50 and the footnotes to sections 85 and 88 of the *Constitution Act, 1867*.

(81) Replaces part of Class 1 of section 91 of the *Constitution Act, 1867*, which was repealed as set out in subitem 1(3) of the Schedule to this Act.

(82) See the footnotes to sections 20, 86 and 88 of the *Constitution Act, 1867*.

persons primarily on the basis of province of present or previous residence; and

(*b*) any laws providing for reasonable residency requirements as a qualification for the receipt of publicly provided social services.

(4) Subsections (2) and (3) do not preclude any law, program or activity that has as its object the amelioration in a province of conditions of individuals in that province who are socially or economically disadvantaged if the rate of employment in that province is below the rate of employment in Canada.

Affirmative action programs

Legal Rights

7. Everyone has the right to life, liberty and security of the person and the right not to be deprived thereof except in accordance with the principles of fundamental justice.

Life, liberty and security of person

8. Everyone has the right to be secure against unreasonable search or seizure.

Search or seizure

9. Everyone has the right not to be arbitrarily detained or imprisoned.

Detention or imprisonment

10. Everyone has the right on arrest or detention
(*a*) to be informed promptly of the reasons therefor;
(*b*) to retain and instruct counsel without delay and to be informed of that right; and
(*c*) to have the validity of the detention determined by way of *habeas corpus* and to be released if the detention is not lawful.

Arrest or detention

11. Any person charged with an offence has the right
(*a*) to be informed without unreasonable delay of the specific offence;
(*b*) to be tried within a reasonable time;
(*c*) not to be compelled to be a witness in proceedings against that person in respect of the offence;
(*d*) to be presumed innocent until proven guilty according to law in a fair and public hearing by an independent and impartial tribunal;

Proceedings in criminal and penal matters

(*e*) not to be denied reasonable bail without just cause;

(*f*) except in the case of an offence under military law tried before a military tribunal, to the benefit of trial by jury where the maximum punishment for the offence is imprisonment for five years or a more severe punishment;

(*g*) not to be found guilty on account of any act or omission unless, at the time of the act or omission, it constituted an offence under Canadian or international law or was criminal according to the general principles of law recognized by the community of nations;

(*h*) if finally acquitted of the offence, not to be tried for it again and, if finally found guilty and punished for the offence, not to be tried or punished for it again; and

(*i*) if found guilty of the offence and if the punishment for the offence has been varied between the time of commission and the time of sentencing, to the benefit of the lesser punishment.

Treatment or punishment

12. Everyone has the right not to be subjected to any cruel and unusual treatment or punishment.

Self-crimination

13. A witness who testifies in any proceedings has the right not to have any incriminating evidence so given used to incriminate that witness in any other proceedings, except in a prosecution for perjury or for the giving of contradictory evidence.

Interpreter

14. A party or witness in any proceedings who does not understand or speak the language in which the proceedings are conducted or who is deaf has the right to the assistance of an interpreter.

Equality Rights

Equality before and under law and equal protection and benefit of law

15. (1) Every individual is equal before and under the law and has the right to the equal protection and equal benefit of the law without discrimination and, in particular, without discrimination based on race, national or ethnic origin, colour, religion, sex, age or mental or physical disability.

Affirmative action programs

(2) Subsection (1) does not preclude any law, program or activity that has as its object the amelioration of conditions of disadvantaged individuals or groups including those that are

disadvantaged because of race, national or ethnic origin, colour, religion, sex, age or mental or physical disability.

Official Languages of Canada

16. (1) English and French are the official languages of Canada and have equality of status and equal rights and privileges as to their use in all institutions of the Parliament and government of Canada.

Official languages of Canada

(2) English and French are the official languages of New Brunswick and have equality of status and equal rights and privileges as to their use in all institutions of the legislature and government of New Brunswick.

Official languages of New Brunswick

(3) Nothing in this Charter limits the authority of Parliament or a legislature to advance the equality of status or use of English and French.

Advancement of status and use

17. (1) Everyone has the right to use English or French in any debates and other proceedings of Parliament.(83)

Proceedings of Parliament

(2) Everyone has the right to use English or French in any debates and other proceedings of the legislature of New Brunswick.(84)

Proceedings of New Brunswick legislature

18. (1) The statutes, records and journals of Parliament shall be printed and published in English and French and both language versions are equally authoritative.(85)

Parliamentary statutes and records

(2) The statutes, records and journals of the legislature of New Brunswick shall be printed and published in English and French and both language versions are equally authoritative.(86)

New Brunswick statutes and records

19. (1) Either English or French may be used by any person in, or in any pleading in or process issuing from, any court established by Parliament.(87)

Proceedings in courts established by Parliament

---

(83) See section 133 of the *Constitution Act, 1867*, and the footnote thereto.

(84) *Id.*

(85) *Id.*

(86) *Id.*

(87) *Id.*

Proceedings in
New Brunswick
courts

(2) Either English or French may be used by any person in, or in any pleading in or process issuing from, any court of New Brunswick.(88)

Communica-
tions by public
with federal
institutions

20. (1) Any member of the public in Canada has the right to communicate with, and to receive available services from, any head or central office of an institution of the Parliament or government of Canada in English or French, and has the same right with respect to any other office of any such institution where

(*a*) there is a significant demand for communications with and services from that office in such language; or

(*b*) due to the nature of the office, it is reasonable that communications with and services from that office be available in both English and French.

Communica-
tions by public
with New
Brunswick
institutions

(2) Any member of the public in New Brunswick has the right to communicate with, and to receive available services from, any office of an institution of the legislature or government of New Brunswick in English or French.

Continuation of
existing
constitutional
provisions

21. Nothing in sections 16 to 20 abrogates or derogates from any right, privilege or obligation with respect to the English and French languages, or either of them, that exists or is continued by virtue of any other provision of the Constitution of Canada.(89)

Rights and
privileges
preserved

22. Nothing in sections 16 to 20 abrogates or derogates from any legal or customary right or privilege acquired or enjoyed either before or after the coming into force of this Charter with respect to any language that is not English or French.

Minority Language Educational Rights

Language of
instruction

23. (1) Citizens of Canada

(*a*) whose first language learned and still understood is that of the English or French linguistic minority population of the province in which they reside, or

---

(88) *Id.*

(89) See, for example, section 133 of the *Constitution Act, 1867*, and the reference to the *Manitoba Act, 1870*, in the footnote thereto.

(*b*) who have received their primary school instruction in Canada in English or French and reside in a province where the language in which they received that instruction is the language of the English or French linguistic minority population of the province,

have the right to have their children receive primary and secondary school instruction in that language in that province.(90)

(2) Citizens of Canada of whom any child has received or is receiving primary or secondary school instruction in English or French in Canada, have the right to have all their children receive primary and secondary school instruction in the same language.

Continuity of language instruction

(3) The right of citizens of Canada under subsections (1) and (2) to have their children receive primary and secondary school instruction in the language of the English or French linguistic minority population of a province

Application where numbers warrant

(*a*) applies wherever in the province the number of children of citizens who have such a right is sufficient to warrant the provision to them out of public funds of minority language instruction; and

(*b*) includes, where the number of those children so warrants, the right to have them receive that instruction in minority language educational facilities provided out of public funds.

Enforcement

24. (1) Anyone whose rights or freedoms, as guaranteed by this Charter, have been infringed or denied may apply to a court of competent jurisdiction to obtain such remedy as the court considers appropriate and just in the circumstances.

Enforcement of guaranteed rights and freedoms

(2) Where, in proceedings under subsection (1), a court concludes that evidence was obtained in a manner that infringed or denied any rights or freedoms guaranteed by this Charter, the evidence shall be excluded if it is established that, having regard to all the circumstances, the admission of it in the proceedings would bring the administration of justice into disrepute.

Exclusion of evidence bringing administration of justice into disrepute

---

(90) Paragraph 23(1)(*a*) is not in force in respect of Quebec. See section 59 *infra*.

General

Aboriginal rights and freedoms not affected by Charter

25. The guarantee in this Charter of certain rights and freedoms shall not be construed so as to abrogate or derogate from any aboriginal, treaty or other rights or freedoms that pertain to the aboriginal peoples of Canada including

(*a*) any rights or freedoms that have been recognized by the Royal Proclamation of October 7, 1763; and

(*b*) any rights or freedoms that may be acquired by the aboriginal peoples of Canada by way of land claims settlement.

Other rights and freedoms not affected by Charter

26. The guarantee in this Charter of certain rights and freedoms shall not be construed as denying the existence of any other rights or freedoms that exist in Canada.

Multicultural heritage

27. This Charter shall be interpreted in a manner consistent with the preservation and enhancement of the multicultural heritage of Canadians.

Rights guaranteed equally to both sexes

28. Notwithstanding anything in this Charter, the rights and freedoms referred to in it are guaranteed equally to male and female persons.

Rights respecting certain schools preserved

29. Nothing in this Charter abrogates or derogates from any rights or privileges guaranteed by or under the Constitution of Canada in respect of denominational, separate or dissentient schools.(91)

Application to territories and territorial authorities

30. A reference in this Charter to a Province or to the legislative assembly or legislature of a province shall be deemed to include a reference to the Yukon Territory and the Northwest Territories, or to the appropriate legislative authority thereof, as the case may be.

Legislative powers not extended

31. Nothing in this Charter extends the legislative powers of any body or authority.

Application of Charter

Application of Charter

32. (1) This Charter applies

(*a*) to the Parliament and government of Canada in respect of all matters within the authority of Parliament

---

(91) See section 93 of the *Constitution Act, 1867*, and the footnote thereto.

including all matters relating to the Yukon Territory and Northwest Territories; and

(*b*) to the legislature and government of each province in respect of all matters within the authority of the legislature of each province.

(2) Notwithstanding subsection (1), section 15 shall not have effect until three years after this section comes into force.

Exception

33. (1) Parliament or the legislature of a province may expressly declare in an Act of Parliament or of the legislature, as the case may be, that the Act or a provision thereof shall operate notwithstanding a provision included in section 2 or sections 7 to 15 of this Charter.

Exception where express declaration

(2) An Act or a provision of an Act in respect of which a declaration made under this section is in effect shall have such operation as it would have but for the provision of this Charter referred to in the declaration.

Operation of exception

(3) A declaration made under subsection (1) shall cease to have effect five years after it comes into force or on such earlier date as may be specified in the declaration.

Five year limitation

(4) Parliament or the legislature of a province may re-enact a declaration made under subsection (1).

Re-enactment

(5) Subsection (3) applies in respect of a re-enactment made under subsection (4).

Five year limitation

Citation

34. This Part may be cited as the *Canadian Charter of Rights and Freedoms*.

Citation

PART II

RIGHTS OF THE ABORIGINAL PEOPLES OF CANADA

35. (1) The existing aboriginal and treaty rights of the aboriginal peoples of Canada are hereby recognized and affirmed.

Recognition of existing aboriginal and treaty rights

(2) In this Act, "aboriginal peoples of Canada" includes the Indian, Inuit and Métis peoples of Canada.

Definition of "aboriginal peoples of Canada"

PART III

EQUALIZATION AND REGIONAL DISPARITIES

Commitment to
promote equal
opportunities

36. (1) Without altering the legislative authority of Parliament or of the provincial legislatures, or the rights of any of them with respect to the exercise of their legislative authority, Parliament and the legislatures, together with the government of Canada and the provincial governments, are committed to

(*a*) promoting equal opportunities for the well-being of Canadians;

(*b*) furthering economic development to reduce disparity in opportunities; and

(*c*) providing essential public services of reasonable quality to all Canadians.

Commitment
respecting
public services

(2) Parliament and the government of Canada are committed to the principle of making equalization payments to ensure that provincial governments have sufficient revenues to provide reasonably comparable levels of public services at reasonably comparable levels of taxation. (92)

PART IV

CONSTITUTIONAL CONFERENCE

Constitutional
conference

37. (1) A constitutional conference composed of the Prime Minister of Canada and the first ministers of the provinces shall be convened by the Prime Minister of Canada within one year after this Part comes into force.

Participation of
aboriginal
peoples

(2) The conference convened under subsection (1) shall have included in its agenda an item respecting constitutional matters that directly affect the aboriginal peoples of Canada, including the identification and definition of the rights of those peoples to be included in the Constitution of Canada, and the Prime Minister of Canada shall invite representatives of those peoples to participate in the discussions on that item.

Participation of
territories

(3) The Prime Minister of Canada shall invite elected representatives of the governments of the Yukon Territory and the Northwest Territories to participate in the discus-

---

(92) See the footnotes to sections 114 and 118 of the *Constitution Act, 1867.*

sions on any item on the agenda of the conference convened under subsection (1) that, in the opinion of the Prime Minister, directly affects the Yukon Territory and the Northwest Territories.

PART V

PROCEDURE FOR AMENDING CONSTITUTION OF CANADA
(93)

38. (1) An amendment to the Constitution of Canada may be made by proclamation issued by the Governor General under the Great Seal of Canada where so authorized by

General procedure for amending Constitution of Canada

    (*a*) resolutions of the Senate and House of Commons; and
    (*b*) resolutions of the legislative assemblies of at least two-thirds of the provinces that have, in the aggregate, according to the then latest general census, at least fifty per cent of the population of all the provinces.

(2) An amendment made under subsection (1) that derogates from the legislative powers, the proprietary rights or any other rights or privileges of the legislature or government of a province shall require a resolution supported by a majority of the members of each of the Senate, the House of Commons and the legislative assemblies required under subsection (1).

Majority of members

(3) An amendment referred to in subsection (2) shall not have effect in a province the legislative assembly of which has expressed its dissent thereto by resolution supported by a majority of its members prior to the issue of the proclamation to which the amendment relates unless that legislative assembly, subsequently, by resolution supported by a majority of its members, revokes its dissent and authorizes the amendment.

Expression of dissent

(4) A resolution of dissent made for the purposes of subsection (3) may be revoked at any time before or after the issue of the proclamation to which it relates.

Revocation of dissent

39. (1) A proclamation shall not be issued under subsection 38(1) before the expiration of one year from the adoption

Restriction on proclamation

---

(93) Prior to the enactment of Part V certain provisions of the Constitution of Canada and the provincial constitutions could be amended pursuant to the *Constitution Act, 1867*. See the footnotes to section 91, Class 1 and section 92, Class 1 thereof, *supra*. Other amendments to the Constitution could only be made by enactment of the Parliament of the United Kingdom.

of the resolution initiating the amendment procedure there-
under, unless the legislative assembly of each province has
previously adopted a resolution of assent or dissent.

Idem

(2) A proclamation shall not be issued under subsection
38(1) after the expiration of three years from the adoption of
the resolution initiating the amendment procedure there-
under.

Compensation

40. Where an amendment is made under subsection 38(1)
that transfers provincial legislative powers relating to education or other cultural matters from provincial legislatures to
Parliament, Canada shall provide reasonable compensation to
any province to which the amendment does not apply.

Amendment by
unanimous
consent

41. An amendment to the Constitution of Canada in
relation to the following matters may be made by proclamation issued by the Governor General under the Great Seal of
Canada only where authorized by resolutions of the Senate
and House of Commons and of the legislative assembly of
each province:

(*a*) the office of the Queen, the Governor General and the
Lieutenant Governor of a province;

(*b*) the right of a province to a number of members in the
House of Commons not less than the number of Senators
by which the province is entitled to be represented at the
time this Part comes into force;

(*c*) subject to section 43, the use of the English or the
French language;

(*d*) the composition of the Supreme Court of Canada; and

(*e*) an amendment to this Part.

Amendment by
general
procedure

42. (1) An amendment to the Constitution of Canada in
relation to the following matters may be made only in
accordance with subsection 38(1):

(*a*) the principle of proportionate representation of the
provinces in the House of Commons prescribed by the
Constitution of Canada;

(*b*) the powers of the Senate and the method of selecting
Senators;

(*c*) the number of members by which a province is entitled to be represented in the Senate and the residence qualifications of Senators;

(*d*) subject to paragraph 41(*d*), the Supreme Court of Canada;

(*e*) the extension of existing provinces into the territories; and

(*f*) notwithstanding any other law or practice, the establishment of new provinces.

(2) Subsections 38(2) to (4) do not apply in respect of amendments in relation to matters referred to in subsection (1).

Exception

43. An amendment to the Constitution of Canada in relation to any provision that applies to one or more, but not all, provinces, including

Amendment of provisions relating to some but not all provinces

(*a*) any alteration to boundaries between provinces, and

(*b*) any amendment to any provision that relates to the use of the English or the French language within a province,

may be made by proclamation issued by the Governor General under the Great Seal of Canada only where so authorized by resolutions of the Senate and House of Commons and of the legislative assembly of each province to which the amendment applies.

44. Subject to sections 41 and 42, Parliament may exclusively make laws amending the Constitution of Canada in relation to the executive government of Canada or the Senate and House of Commons.

Amendments by Parliament

45. Subject to section 41, the legislature of each province may exclusively make laws amending the constitution of the province.

Amendments by provincial legislatures

46. (1) The procedures for amendment under sections 38, 41, 42 and 43 may be initiated either by the Senate or the House of Commons or by the legislative assembly of a province.

Initiation of amendment procedures

(2) A resolution of assent made for the purposes of this Part may be revoked at any time before the issue of a proclamation authorized by it.

Revocation of authorization

Amendments
without Senate
resolution

47. (1) An amendment to the Constitution of Canada made by proclamation under section 38, 41, 42 or 43 may be made without a resolution of the Senate authorizing the issue of the proclamation if, within one hundred and eighty days after the adoption by the House of Commons of a resolution authorizing its issue, the Senate has not adopted such a resolution and if, at any time after the expiration of that period, the House of Commons again adopts the resolution.

Computation of
period

(2) Any period when Parliament is prorogued or dissolved shall not be counted in computing the one hundred and eighty day period referred to in subsection (1).

Advice to issue
proclamation

48. The Queen's Privy Council for Canada shall advise the Governor General to issue a proclamation under this Part forthwith on the adoption of the resolutions required for an amendment made by proclamation under this Part.

Constitutional
conference

49. A constitutional conference composed of the Prime Minister of Canada and the first ministers of the provinces shall be convened by the Prime Minister of Canada within fifteen years after this Part comes into force to review the provisions of this Part.

PART VI

AMENDMENT TO THE CONSTITUTION ACT, 1867

50. (94)

51. (95)

PART VII

GENERAL

Primacy of
Constitution of
Canada

52. (1) The Constitution of Canada is the supreme law of Canada, and any law that is inconsistent with the provisions of the Constitution is, to the extent of the inconsistency, of no force or effect.

Constitution of
Canada

(2) The Constitution of Canada includes

---

(94) The amendment is set out in the Consolidation of the *Constitution Act, 1867*, as section 92A thereof.

(95) The amendment is set out in the Consolidation of the *Constitution Act, 1867*, as the Sixth Schedule thereof.

(*a*) the *Canada Act 1982*, including this Act;

(*b*) the Acts and orders referred to in the schedule; and

(*c*) any amendment to any Act or order referred to in paragraph (*a*) or (*b*).

(3) Amendments to the Constitution of Canada shall be made only in accordance with the authority contained in the Constitution of Canada.

Amendments to Constitution of Canada

53. (1) The enactments referred to in Column I of the schedule are hereby repealed or amended to the extent indicated in Column II thereof and, unless repealed, shall continue as law in Canada under the names set out in Column III thereof.

Repeals and new names

(2) Every enactment, except the *Canada Act 1982*, that refers to an enactment referred to in the schedule by the name in Column I thereof is hereby amended by substituting for that name the corresponding name in Column III thereof, and any British North America Act not referred to in the schedule may be cited as the *Constitution Act* followed by the year and number, if any, of its enactment.

Consequential amendments

54. Part IV is repealed on the day that is one year after this Part comes into force and this section may be repealed and this Act renumbered, consequentially upon the repeal of Part IV and this section, by proclamation issued by the Governor General under the Great Seal of Canada. (96)

Repeal and consequential amendments

55. A French version of the portions of the Constitution of Canada referred to in the schedule shall be prepared by the Minister of Justice of Canada as expeditiously as possible and, when any portion thereof sufficient to warrant action being taken has been so prepared, it shall be put forward for enactment by proclamation issued by the Governor General under the Great Seal of Canada pursuant to the procedure then applicable to an amendment of the same provisions of the Constitution of Canada.

French version of Constitution of Canada

56. Where any portion of the Constitution of Canada has been or is enacted in English and French or where a French version of any portion of the Constitution is enacted pursuant

English and French versions of certain constitutional texts

(96) Part VII came into force on April 17, 1982. *See* SI/82-97.

to section 55, the English and French versions of that portion of the Constitution are equally authoritative.

English and
French versions
of this Act

57. The English and French versions of this Act are equally authoritative.

Commence-
ment

58. Subject to section 59, this Act shall come into force on a day to be fixed by proclamation issued by the Queen or the Governor General under the Great Seal of Canada. (97)

Commence-
ment of
paragraph
23(1)(*a*) in
respect of
Quebec

59. (1) Paragraph 23(1)(*a*) shall come into force in respect of Quebec on a day to be fixed by proclamation issued by the Queen or the Governor General under the Great Seal of Canada.

Authorization
of Quebec

(2) A proclamation under subsection (1) shall be issued only where authorized by the legislative assembly or government of Quebec. (98)

Repeal of this
section

(3) This section may be repealed on the day paragraph 23(1)(*a*) comes into force in respect of Quebec and this Act amended and renumbered, consequentially upon the repeal of this section, by proclamation issued by the Queen or the Governor General under the Great Seal of Canada.

Short title and
citations

60. This Act may be cited as the *Constitution Act, 1982*, and the Constitution Acts 1867 to 1975 (No. 2) and this Act may be cited together as the *Constitution Acts, 1867 to 1982.*

---

(97) The Act, with the exception of paragraph 23(1)(*a*) in respect of Quebec, came into force on April 17, 1982 by proclamation issued by the Queen. *See* SI/82-97.

(98) No proclamation has been issued under section 59.

SCHEDULE

to the

CONSTITUTION ACT, 1982

MODERNIZATION OF THE CONSTITUTION

Item	Column I Act Affected	Column II Amendment	Column III New Name
1.	British North America Act, 1867, 30-31 Vict., c. 3 (U.K.)	(1) Section 1 is repealed and the following substituted therefor: "1. This Act may be cited as the *Constitution Act, 1867*." (2) Section 20 is repealed. (3) Class 1 of section 91 is repealed. (4) Class 1 of section 92 is repealed.	Constitution Act, 1867
2.	An Act to amend and continue the Act 32-33 Victoria chapter 3; and to establish and provide for the Government of the Province of Manitoba, 1870, 33 Vict., c. 3 (Can.)	(1) The long title is repealed and the following substituted therefor: "*Manitoba Act, 1870*." (2) Section 20 is repealed.	Manitoba Act, 1870
3.	Order of Her Majesty in Council admitting Rupert's Land and the North-Western Territory into the union, dated the 23rd day of June, 1870		Rupert's Land and North-Western Territory Order

SCHEDULE

to the

CONSTITUTION ACT, 1982—*Continued*

Item	Column I Act Affected	Column II Amendment	Column III New Name
4.	Order of Her Majesty in Council admitting British Columbia into the Union, dated the 16th day of May, 1871.		British Columbia Terms of Union
5.	British North America Act, 1871, 34-35 Vict., c. 28 (U.K.).	Section 1 is repealed and the following substituted therefor: "1. This Act may be cited as the *Constitution Act, 1871*."	Constitution Act, 1871
6.	Order of Her Majesty in Council admitting Prince Edward Island into the Union, dated the 26th day of June, 1873.		Prince Edward Island Terms of Union
7.	Parliament of Canada Act, 1875, 38-39 Vict., c. 38 (U.K.).		Parliament of Canada Act, 1875
8.	Order of Her Majesty in Council admitting all British possessions and Territories in North America and islands adjacent thereto into the Union, dated the 31st day of July, 1880.		Adjacent Territories Order

SCHEDULE

to the

CONSTITUTION ACT, 1982—*Continued*

Item	Column I Act Affected	Column II Amendment	Column III New Name
9.	British North America Act, 1886, 49-50 Vict., c. 35 (U.K.)	Section 3 is repealed and the following substituted therefor: "3. This Act may be cited as the *Constitution Act, 1886*."	Constitution Act, 1886
10.	Canada (Ontario Boundary) Act, 1889, 52-53 Vict., c. 28 (U.K.)		Canada (Ontario Boundary) Act, 1889
11.	Canadian Speaker (Appointment of Deputy) Act, 1895, 2nd Sess., 59 Vict., c. 3 (U.K.)	The Act is repealed.	
12.	The Alberta Act, 1905, 4-5 Edw. VII, c. 3 (Can.)		Alberta Act
13.	The Saskatchewan Act, 1905, 4-5 Edw. VII, c. 42 (Can.)		Saskatchewan Act
14.	British North America Act, 1907, 7 Edw. VII, c. 11 (U.K.)	Section 2 is repealed and the following substituted therefor: "2. This Act may be cited as the *Constitution Act, 1907*."	Constitution Act, 1907

SCHEDULE

to the

CONSTITUTION ACT, 1982—*Continued*

Item	Column I Act Affected	Column II Amendment	Column III New Name
15.	British North America Act, 1915, 5-6 Geo. V, c. 45 (U.K.)	Section 3 is repealed and the following substituted therefor: "3. This Act may be cited as the *Constitution Act, 1915*."	Constitution Act, 1915
16.	British North America Act, 1930, 20-21 Geo. V, c. 26 (U.K.)	Section 3 is repealed and the following substituted therefor: "3. This Act may be cited as the *Constitution Act, 1930*."	Constitution Act, 1930
17.	Statute of Westminster, 1931, 22 Geo. V, c. 4 (U.K.)	In so far as they apply to Canada, (*a*) section 4 is repealed; and (*b*) subsection 7(1) is repealed.	Statute of Westminster, 1931
18.	British North America Act, 1940, 3-4 Geo. VI, c. 36 (U.K.)	Section 2 is repealed and the following substituted therefor: "2. This Act may be cited as the *Constitution Act, 1940*."	Constitution Act, 1940
19.	British North America Act, 1943, 6-7 Geo. VI, c. 30 (U.K.)	The Act is repealed.	

SCHEDULE

to the

CONSTITUTION ACT, 1982—*Continued*

Item	Column I Act Affected	Column II Amendment	Column III New Name
20.	British North America Act, 1946, 9-10 Geo. VI, c. 63 (U.K.)	The Act is repealed.	
21.	British North America Act, 1949, 12-13 Geo. VI, c. 22 (U.K.)	Section 3 is repealed and the following substituted therefor: "3. This Act may be cited as the *Newfoundland Act*."	Newfoundland Act
22.	British North America (No. 2) Act, 1949, 13 Geo. VI, c. 81 (U.K.)	The Act is repealed.	
23.	British North America Act, 1951, 14-15 Geo. VI, c. 32 (U.K.)	The Act is repealed.	
24.	British North America Act, 1952, 1 Eliz. II, c. 15 (Can.)	The Act is repealed.	
25.	British North America Act, 1960, 9 Eliz. II, c. 2 (U.K.)	Section 2 is repealed and the following substituted therefor: "2. This Act may be cited as the *Constitution Act, 1960*."	Constitution Act, 1960

SCHEDULE

to the

CONSTITUTION ACT, 1982—*Continued*

Item	Column I Act Affected	Column II Amendment	Column III New Name
26.	British North America Act, 1964, 12-13 Eliz. II, c. 73 (U.K.)	Section 2 is repealed and the following substituted therefor: "2. This Act may be cited as the *Constitution Act, 1964.*"	Constitution Act, 1964
27.	British North America Act, 1965, 14 Eliz. II, c. 4, Part I (Can.)	Section 2 is repealed and the following substituted therefor: "2. This Part may be cited as the *Constitution Act, 1965.*"	Constitution Act, 1965
28.	British North America Act, 1974, 23 Eliz. II, c. 13, Part I (Can.)	Section 3, as amended by 25-26 Eliz. II, c. 28, s. 38(1) (Can.), is repealed and the following substituted therefor: "3. This Part may be cited as the *Constitution Act, 1974.*"	Constitution Act, 1974
29.	British North America Act, 1975, 23-24 Eliz. II, c. 28, Part I (Can.)	Section 3, as amended by 25-26 Eliz. II, c. 28, s. 31 (Can.), is repealed and the following substituted therefor: "3. This Part may be cited as the *Constitution Act (No. 1), 1975.*"	Constitution Act (No. 1), 1975

SCHEDULE

to the

CONSTITUTION ACT, 1982—*Concluded*

Item	Column I Act Affected	Column II Amendment	Column III New Name
30.	British North America Act (No. 2), 1975, 23-24 Eliz. II, c. 53 (Can.)	Section 3 is repealed and the following substituted therefor: "3. This Act may be cited as the *Constitution Act (No. 2), 1975*."	Constitution Act (No. 2), 1975

Index

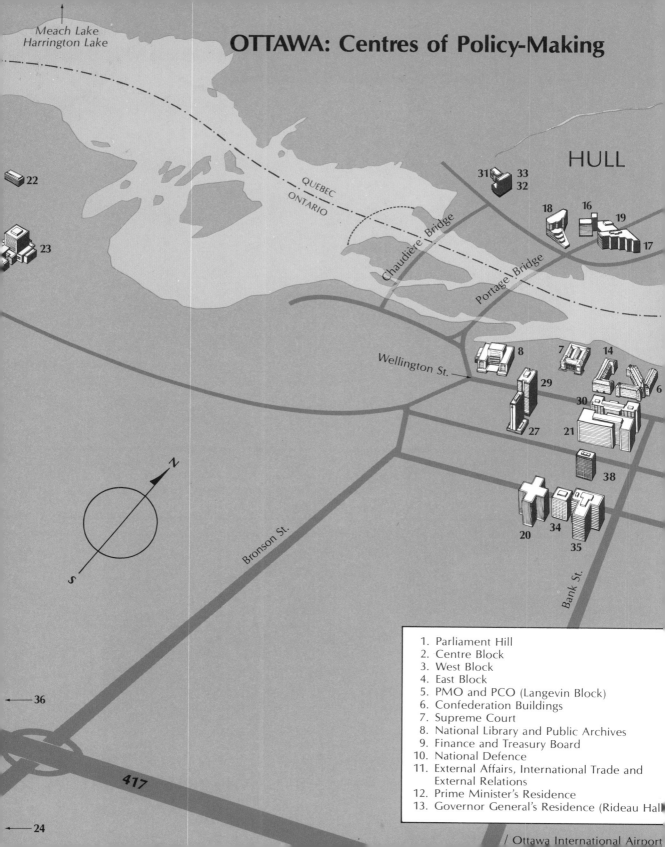

OTTAWA: Centres of Policy-Making

Meach Lake
Harrington Lake

QUEBEC
ONTARIO

Chaudière Bridge

Portage Bridge

HULL

Wellington St.

Bronson St.

Bank St.

417

1. Parliament Hill
2. Centre Block
3. West Block
4. East Block
5. PMO and PCO (Langevin Block)
6. Confederation Buildings
7. Supreme Court
8. National Library and Public Archives
9. Finance and Treasury Board
10. National Defence
11. External Affairs, International Trade and
    External Relations
12. Prime Minister's Residence
13. Governor General's Residence (Rideau Hall

/ Ottawa International Airport